Handbook of
North American Indians

Handbook of North American Indians

WILLIAM C. STURTEVANT

General Editor

VOLUME 8

California

ROBERT F. HEIZER
Volume Editor

SMITHSONIAN INSTITUTION

WASHINGTON

1978

For sale by the Superintendent of Documents,
U.S. Government Printing Office, Washington, D.C. 20402.
Stock Number: 047-000-00347-4

Library of Congress Cataloging in Publication Data

Handbook of North American Indians.
    Bibliography: pp. 721–768
    Includes index.
    CONTENTS:
                v. 8. California.
    1. Indians of North America. 2. Eskimos.
I. Sturtevant, William C.

E77.H25   970′.004′97   77-17162

Contents

This map is a diagrammatic guide to the coverage of this volume rather than an authoritative depiction of tribal ranges. Sharp boundaries have been drawn and no territory is unassigned. Tribal units are sometimes arbitrarily defined, subdivisions are not mapped, no joint or disputed occupations are shown, and different kinds of land use are not distinguished. Since the map depicts the situation at the earliest periods for which evidence is available, the ranges mapped for different tribes often refer to quite different periods, and there may have been many intervening movements, extinctions, and changes in range. Not shown are groups that came into separate political existence later than the map period for their areas. For more specific information see the maps and texts in the accompanying chapters.

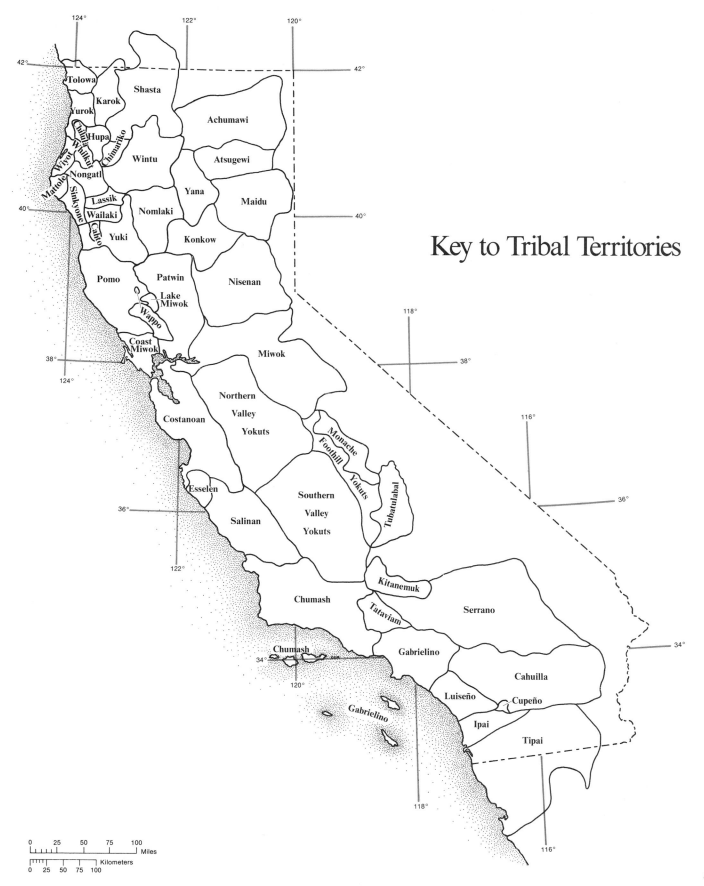

Key to Tribal Territories

Tolowa

Karok

Shasta

Yurok

Achumawi

Chilula

Hupa

Chimariko

Whilkut

Wintu

Atsugewi

Wiyot

Nongatl

Yana

Mattole

Lassik

Maidu

Sinkyone

Wailaki

Nomlaki

Cahto

Yuki

Konkow

Pomo

Patwin

Nisenan

Lake Miwok

Wappo

Coast Miwok

Miwok

Costanoan

Northern Valley Yokuts

Monache

Foothill Yokuts

Esselen

Tubatulabal

Salinan

Southern Valley Yokuts

Kitanemuk

Chumash

Tataviam

Serrano

Chumash

Gabrielino

Cahuilla

Luiseño

Cupeño

Gabrielino

Ipai

Tipai

0 25 50 75 100
Miles

0 25 50 75 100
Kilometers

Technical Alphabet

Consonants

		bilabial	labiodental	dental	alveolar	alveopalatal	velar	back velar	glottal
stop	vl	p		t	t		k	q	ʔ
	vd	b		d	d		g	ġ	
affricate	vl			θ̂	c	č			
	vd			δ̂	ȝ	ǯ			
fricative	vl	φ	f	θ	s	š	x	x̣	h
	vd	β	v	δ	z	ž	γ	γ̇	
nasal	vl	M		N			N		
	vd	m		n			ŋ	ŋ̇	
lateral	vl				ł				
	vd				l				
semivowel	vl	W				Y			
	vd	w				y			

vl = voiceless; vd = voiced

Other symbols include: λ (voiced lateral affricate), ƛ̸ (voiceless lateral affricate), ʕ (voiced pharyngeal fricative), ḥ (voiceless pharyngeal fricative), r (medial flap, trill, or retroflex approximant). Where in contrast, r is a flap and R is a continuant.

Vowels

	front	central	back
high	i (ü)	ɨ	u (ɨ)
	ɪ		ᴜ
mid	e (ö)	ə	o
	ε		ɔ
		ʌ	
low	æ	a	a

Unparenthesized vowels are unrounded if front or central, and rounded if back; *ü* and *ö* are rounded; *ɨ* is unrounded. The special symbols for lax vowels (ɪ, ᴜ, ε, ɔ) are generally used only where it is necessary to differentiate between tense and lax high or mid vowels. *ɨ* and *a* are used for both central and back vowels, as the two values seldom contrast in a given language.

Modifications indicated for consonants are: glottalization (*i̓, ƙ,* etc.), retroflexion *(ṭ),* palatalization (*t^y, k^y, n^y, l^y*), labialization (*k^w*), aspiration (*t^h*), length (*t·*). For vowels: length (*a·*), three-mora length (*a:*), nasalization (*ą*), voicelessness (*A*). The commonest prosodic markings are, for stress: *á* (primary) and *à* (secondary), and for pitch: *á* (high), *à* (low), *â* (falling), and *ǎ* (rising); however, the details of prosodic systems and the uses of accents differ widely from language to language.

Words in Indian languages cited in italics are written in phonemic transcription. That is, the letters and symbols are used in specific values defined for them by the structure of the sound system of the particular language. However, as far as possible, these phonemic transcriptions use letters and symbols in generally consistent values, as specified by the standard technical alphabet of the Handbook. Deviations from these standard values as well as the specific details of the phonology of each language (or references to where they may be found) are given in an orthographic footnote in each tribal chapter. This footnote also specifies those few languages whose italic transcriptions are standard practical orthographies, used by native speakers, or are standard but nonphonemic.

Square brackets set off symbols which have their standard technical values but not necessarily the specific phonemic values of a particular language.

No italicized Indian word is broken at a line end except when a hyphen would be present anyway as part of the word. In Indian words written in italics or in phonetic symbols capital letters are not used for proper names or at the beginning of a sentence. The glosses, or conventionalized translations, of Indian words are enclosed in single quotation marks.

Indian words recorded by nonspecialists or before the phonemic system of the relevant language had been analyzed are often not written accurately enough to allow respelling in phonemic transcription. Where phonemic retranscription has been possible the citation of source has been modified by the label "phonemicized" or "from." Words that could not be phonemicized are not printed in italics, but they have been normalized, where so labeled, by being rewritten in the standard technical alphabet. Words that have not been normalized sometimes contain letters used in values appropriate to various other transcriptional alphabets. The most common of these are ä for the Handbook's æ, â for ɔ, c for š, ç for θ, ¢ for δ, j for ž, ǯ, or y, L for ƛ̸, ñ for ŋ, tc for č, and ' for ʔ (or glottalization of preceding consonant).

Nontechnical Equivalents

Correct pronunciation, as with any foreign language, requires extensive training and practice, but simplified (incorrect) pronunciations may be obtained by ignoring the diacritics and reading the vowels as in Italian or Spanish and the consonants as in English. For a closer approximation to the pronunciation or in rewriting into a nontechnical transcription the substitutions indicated in the following table may be made.

technical	nontechnical	technical	nontechnical	technical	nontechnical
æ	ae	M	mh	Y	yh
β	bh	N	nh	$\check{z}$	zh
c	ts	η	ng	$\mathfrak{z}$	dz
$\check{c}$	ch	$\mathcal{N}$	ngh	$\check{\mathfrak{z}}$	j
δ	dh	$\mathfrak{o}$	o	$\mathfrak{?}$	'
$\hat{\delta}$	ddh	θ	th	$\dot{k}, \dot{p}, \dot{t}$, etc.	k', p', t', etc.
ε	e	$\hat{\theta}$	tth	$a\cdot, e\cdot, k\cdot, s\cdot$, etc.	aa, ee, kk, ss, etc.
γ	gh	ϕ	ph	q, ϱ, etc.	an, en, etc.
$\dagger$	lh	$\check{s}$	sh	k^y, t^y, etc.	ky, ty, etc.
λ	dl	W	wh	k^w	kw
$\mathcal{X}$	tlh	x	kh		

English Pronunciations

The English pronunciations of the names of tribes and a few other words are indicated parenthetically in a dictionary-style orthography in which most letters have their usual English pronunciation. Special symbols are listed below, with sample words to be pronounced as in non-regional United States English. Approximate phonetic values are given in parentheses in the standard technical alphabet.

ŋ: thing (η) ä: father (a) ə: about, gallop (∂) ō: boat (ow)

θ: thin (θ) ā: bait (ey) ĭ: bit (ι) oŏ: book (υ)

ð: this (δ) e: bet (ε) ī: bite (ay) ōō: boot (uw)

zh: vision ($\check{z}$) ē: beat (iy) ô: bought ($\mathfrak{o}$) u: but (Λ)

ă: bat (æ)

ˈ (primary stress), ˌ (secondary stress): elevator (ˈeləˌvātər) (éləvèytər)

Conventions for Illustrations

Map Symbols

- • Indian settlement
- ▪ Non-Indian town
- Mountain range, peak
- – – – – – National boundary
- – — – — – State boundary
- - - - - - - - County boundary
- River or stream
- Intermittent or dry stream
- **Yokuts** Tribe
- **Bay Miwok** Tribal subdivision
- Sacramento Settlement, site, reservation
- *San Joaquin R.* Geographical feature

Toned areas on tribal maps represent estimated territory.

Credits and Captions

Credit lines give the source of the illustrations (often the copyright holder), or the collections where the artifacts shown are located. The numbers that follow are the catalog or inventory numbers of that repository. When the photographer mentioned in the caption is the source of the print reproduced, no credit line appears. "After" means that the *Handbook* illustrators have redrawn, rearranged, or abstracted the illustration from the one in the cited source. All maps and drawings not otherwise credited are by the *Handbook* illustrators. Measurements in captions are to the nearest millimeter if available; "about" indicates an estimate or a measurement converted from inches to centimeters. The following abbreviations are used in credit lines:

Amer.	American	Ind.	Indian
Anthr.	Anthropology, Anthropological	Inst.	Institute
		Instn.	Institution
Arch.	Archives	Lib.	Library
Arch(a)eol.	Arch(a)eology, Arch(a)eological	Mus.	Museum
		NAA	National Anthropological Archives
Assoc.	Association		
Co.	County	NCFA	National Collection of Fine Arts
Coll.	Collection(s)		
Dept.	Department	Nat.	Natural
Div.	Division	Natl.	National
Ethnol.	Ethnology, Ethnological	opp.	opposite
fol.	folio	pl(s).	plate(s)
Ft.	Fort	Soc.	Society
Hist.	History	U.	University
Histl.	Historical		

Metric Equivalents

10 mm = 1 cm	10 cm = 3.937 in.	1 in. = 2.54 cm
100 cm = 1 m	1 m = 39.37 in.	1 ft. = 30.48 cm
1,000 m = 1 km	10 m = 32.81 ft.	1 yd. = 91.44 cm

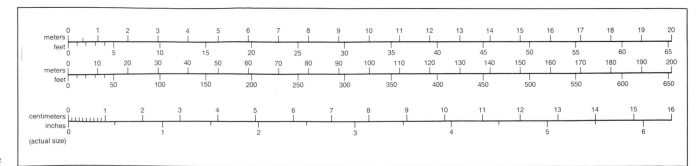

Preface

This is the first to be published of a 20-volume set planned to give an encyclopedic summary of what is known about the prehistory, history, and cultures of the aboriginal peoples of North America who lived to the north of the urban civilizations of central Mexico. Volumes 5-7 and 9-15 treat the other major culture areas of the continent.

Certain topics relevant to the California area are excluded from this volume because they are more appropriately discussed on a continent-wide basis. Readers should refer to volume 1, Introduction, for general descriptions of anthropological and historical methods and sources and for summaries for the whole continent of certain topics regarding social and political organization, religion, and the performing arts. Volume 2 contains detailed accounts of the different kinds of Indian and Eskimo communities in the twentieth century, especially during its third quarter, and describes their relations with one another and with the surrounding non-Indian societies and nations. Volume 3 gives the environmental and biological backgrounds within which Native societies developed, summarizes the early and late human biology or physical anthropology of Indians and Eskimos, and surveys the earliest prehistoric cultures. (Therefore the Paleo-Indian or Early Man period in California is treated in volume 3 rather than in this volume.) Volume 4 contains details on the history of Indian-White relations. Volume 16 is a continent-wide survey of technology and the visual arts—of material cultures broadly defined. Volume 17 surveys the native languages of North America, their characteristics and historical relationships. Volumes 18 and 19 are a biographical dictionary; included in the listing are many California Indians. Volume 20 contains an index to the whole, which will serve to locate materials on California Indians in other volumes as well as in this one.

Preliminary discussions on the feasibility of this *Handbook* and alternatives for producing it began in 1965 in what was then the Smithsonian's Office of Anthropology. A history of the early development of the *Handbook* will be found in volume 1. Detailed planning for the California volume began during a meeting of the General Editor and the Volume Editor with a specially selected Planning Committee (listed on p. v) in Berkeley, California, March 5-6, 1971. At that time a tentative table of contents was drawn up, and qualified specialists

on each topic were listed as potential authors. The chapter headings in the final volume reproduce almost exactly the list decided upon at that meeting, and most of the authors were those first invited. Inevitably, some replacements had to be made as people were unable to accept invitations or later found that they could not meet their commitment to write. Albert B. Elsasser and William J. Wallace deserve special thanks for writing several chapters, in addition to those originally assigned them, when the authors first chosen were unable to submit them.

At the time they were invited, contributors were sent brief indications of the topics to be covered, and a "Guide for Contributors" describing the general aims and methods of the *Handbook* and the editorial conventions. As they were received the manuscripts were reviewed by the General Editor, the Volume Editor, and usually one or more referees (frequently including a member of the Planning Committee). Suggestions for changes and additions often resulted. The final published versions frequently reflect more editorial intervention than is customary for academic writings, for the encyclopedic aims and format of this publication made it necessary to attempt to eliminate duplication, avoid gaps in coverage, impose some standardization of organization and terminology, and keep within strict constraints on length.

One convention has been to avoid the present tense, where possible, in historical and cultural descriptions. Thus a statement in the past tense, with a recent date or approximate date, may also hold true for the time of writing.

The first manuscript submitted was received on February 14, 1972, and the last on April 2, 1976; the first final acceptance of an author's manuscript was on January 3, 1973, and the last on April 4, 1976. Edited manuscripts were sent from the Washington office to authors for their final approval between August 27, 1974, and June 21, 1976. These dates for all chapters are given in the list of Contributors. Late dates may reflect late invitations as well as late submissions.

Linguistic Editing

All words in Indian languages submitted by authors have been referred to consultants with expert knowledge of the languages involved (except in cases where the authors themselves are linguists). Each consultant rewrote all recognizable words in that language (wherever they appear in the *Handbook,* unless otherwise credited) in the appropriate technical orthography; such words are printed in *italics.* The consultants and the spelling systems are identified in an orthographic footnote to each tribal chapter; these footnotes were drafted by the editors. Words from Indian languages that are printed in roman type are in spellings that give only imprecise approximations of the correct pronunciation.

Statements about the genetic relationships of Indian languages have also been checked with linguist consultants, to ensure conformity to recent findings and terminology in comparative linguistics and to avoid conflicting statements within this *Handbook.* In general, only the less remote genetic relationships are mentioned in the individual tribal chapters. The chapter "Native Languages of California" treats more remote relationships, and further information will be found in volume 17.

Ives Goddard, editor of volume 17, Languages, has also served as coordinator and editor of these efforts by linguist consultants. A special debt is owed to these consultants, for all provided advice and assistance without compensation. Victor Golla, William Bright, and Geoffrey Gamble were particularly helpful on these and other matters.

Synonymies

Toward the end of each tribal chapter (or, sometimes, in the introductory chapter covering several tribal chapters) is a section called "Synonymy." This describes the various names that have been applied to the groups and subgroups treated in that chapter, giving the principal variant spellings used in English and, sometimes, in Spanish, and often the names applied to the groups in neighboring Indian languages. This material has been coordinated by the editors, who have often added names from the literature or from other manuscripts submitted for the *Handbook* (from which they have then been deleted) and names and analyses provided by linguist consultants. These sections should assist in the identification of groups mentioned in the earlier historical and anthropological literature. They should also be examined for evidence on changes in the identifications and affiliations of groups, as seen by their own members as well as by neighbors and by outside observers.

Radiocarbon Dates

Authors were instructed to convert radiocarbon dates to dates in the Christian calendar. Such conversions have normally been made from the dates as originally published, without taking account of changes that may be required by developing research on revisions of the half-life of carbon 14, long-term changes in the amount of carbon 14 in the atmosphere, and other factors that may require modifications of absolute dates based on radiocarbon determinations.

Binomials

The scientific names of plant and animal genera and species, printed in italics, have been checked by the General Editor to ensure that they reflect modern usage by biological taxonomists. Scientific plant names have been brought into agreement with those accepted by Munz and Keck (1973), while zoological nomenclature has been revised in consultation with Smithsonian staff in the appropriate departments.

Bibliography

All references cited by contributors have been unified in a single list at the end of this volume. Citations within the text, by author, date, and often page, identify the works in this unified list. Wherever possible the *Handbook* Bibliographer has resolved conflicts between citations of different editions, corrected inaccuracies and omissions, and checked direct quotations against the originals. The bibliographic information has been verified by examination of the original work or from standard reliable library catalogs (especially the National Union Catalog and the published catalog of the Harvard Peabody Museum Library). The unified bibliography lists only sources cited in the text of the volume, omiting personal communications. The sections headed "Sources" at the ends of most chapters provide general guidance to the most important sources of information on the topics covered.

Illustrations

Authors were requested to submit suggestions for illustrations: photographs, maps, drawings, and lists and locations of objects that might be illustrated. To varying degrees most complied with this request. However, considerations of space, balance, reproducibility, and availability required modifications in what was submitted. In addition the *Handbook* Illustrations Researchers and Scientific Illustrators provided much original material from research they conducted in museums and other repositories and in the published literature. All maps were prepared by the *Handbook* Cartographer or Scientific Illustrators, who redrew some submitted by authors and compiled many new ones using information from the chapter manuscripts and from other sources. The base maps for all are authoritative standard ones, especially U.S. Geological Survey sheets. Layout and design of the illustrations has been the responsibility of the Chief Scientific Illustrator, who has worked in consultation with the Illustrations Researcher. Captions for illustrations and maps were usually composed by the Illustrations Researcher and Scientific Illustrators. However, all illustrations, including maps and drawings, and all captions have been approved by the authors of the chapters in which they appear, and authors have frequently participated actively in the selection process and in the improvement of captions.

We are indebted to Donnelly Cartographic Services (especially Sidney P. Marland III, resident manager) for their meticulous care in converting the map art work into final film.

Acknowledgements

The *Handbook* editorial staff at the Smithsonian in Washington has consisted of the following persons:

General Editor: William C. Sturtevant (1966-)
Linguistic Editor: Ives Goddard (1970-)
Editorial Assistants: Betty T. Arens (1972-); Carol H. Blew (1969-1972)
Coordinator: Diane Della-Loggia (1976-)
Manuscript and Copy Editor: Diane Della-Loggia (1972-)
Bibliographer: Lorraine H. Jacoby (1972-)
Bibliographic Assistants: Caroline Ladeira (1976-); Mark Passen (1974-1976)
Chief Scientific Illustrator: Jo Ann Moore (1972-)
Scientific Illustrator: Brigid Melton Sullivan (1975-1976)
Cartographer: Judith C. Wojcik (1975-)
Illustrations Researcher: Joanna Cohan Scherer (1970-)
Assistant Illustrations Researcher: Nancy Henderson (1973-1975)
One-year Research Assistants: Paula Rabkin (1975-1976); Laura Conkey (1974-1975); Nancy Stasulis (1973-1974); Susan Golla (1973-1974); William L. Merrill (1972-1973)
Summer Research Assistant: Ira Jacknis (1973-1975)
Secretaries: Alice N. Boarman (1975-); Filomena Chau (1975); Gloria Harman (1974-1975); Rosemary De Rosa (1973-1974); Marianna Koskouras (1969-1973).

In the Center for the Study of Man, Smithsonian Institution, administrative support for the *Handbook* has been provided by: the Director, Sol Tax (1968-1976); the Program Coordinator, Samuel L. Stanley (1968-1976); the Administrative Officer, Sherrill Berger (1975-); the Administrative Assistant, Jennifer Burdick Stephen (1968-1975); and Secretaries Lydia Ratliff (1972-), Melvina Jackson (1974-), and Rebecca Noah (1973-1974). Other Smithsonian staff who have provided crucial support and assistance include S. Dillon Ripley (1965-), Secretary; David Challinor (1971-) and Sidney R. Galler (1965-1970), Assistant Secretaries for Science; Charles Blitzer (1968-), Assistant Secretary for History and Art; Porter Kier (1976-), Director, National Museum of Natural History and Director, Center for the Study of Man; James F. Mello (1976-), Assistant Director, National Museum of Natural History; Catherine J. Kerby (1976-), Assistant to the Director, National Museum of Natural History; Stephen Kraft (1971-), Managing Designer, Smithsonian Institution Press; Victor E. Krantz (1972-) of the Smithsonian Photographic Laboratory (especially for photographing objects); and Jack F. Marquardt (1972-) and Carolyn S. Hahn (1972-), both of the Smithsonian Libraries. The Department of Anthropology, National Museum of Natural History, Smithsonian Institution, released the General Editor from part of his curatorial and research time.

Preparation and publication of this volume have been supported by federal appropriations made to the Smithsonian Institution, in part through its Bicentennial Programs.

The Volume Editor, Robert F. Heizer, acknowledges the assistance of the following at the University of California, Berkeley: Karen Nissen (especially for locating manuscripts of C. Hart Merriam used by various authors), the Lowie Museum of Anthropology (especially Albert B. Elsasser and Frank A. Norick for locating photographs and artifacts for illustrations), Sean Swezey (for bibliographical research), and the Archaeological Research Facility (especially Suzanne Sundholm) for secretarial assistance.

July 18, 1977

William C. Sturtevant
Robert F. Heizer

Introduction

ROBERT F. HEIZER

The aim of this volume is to provide a summary of what is presently known of the aboriginal culture forms and practices of about 60 California tribes. The background for these syntheses is provided in the form of a series of articles that describe the environment, prehistoric archeology, historical archeology, language classification, culture, population numbers since the time of European discovery, and the history of exploration and settlement by Whites. Certain topics of general interest, about which only brief mention is made in the ethnological summaries, have been treated separately at the end.

This volume provides an account of the aboriginal culture of each tribe and a sketch of its history from the time each came under the domination of Whites, whether this was in the 1770s in one of the Franciscan missions along the coast or as late as 1849 or 1850 in the far northern and Sierra Nevada regions. Entire tribal populations were drawn into the 21 missions extending from San Diego in the south to Sonoma in the north, and their native ways of life were changed to one imposed on them by the missionaries (Cook 1943). In 1834, some dozen years after Mexico had secured her independence from Spain and gained control of Alta California, the missions were secularized, and the resident populations numbering about 15,000 persons were released from their physical and religious bondage. The American seizure of California occurred in 1846 as an event early in the Mexican War. Despite the wealth of documentary records collected at the various missions between 1769 and 1834, and an even greater amount of information existing in newspapers and personal records from the American period beginning in 1846, there is not available a single history of a tribe. A beginning at the collection of references to significant record material has been made by Wuertele (1975), Heizer, Nissen, and Castillo (1975), and Beroza (1974). Some small groups in remote areas were so hard hit in the early gold rush period that they disappeared with scarcely a word said about them, but for others a great deal would be known if the information were only searched out and written as ethnohistorical narrative. Now that the aboriginal cultures are gone, the opportunity exists for more research on tribal histories that lead up to the present day. The massive immigration of Native Americans from other states into California beginning in World War II has been little studied (Heizer, Nissen, and Castillo 1975:48-56), and before the

trail becomes too cold, it and its effects should be followed.

Although California Indian cultures were treated on a tribal basis by Alfred L. Kroeber (1925) in his monumental *Handbook of the Indians of California,* much has been learned in the ensuing half-century, and this knowledge has been consulted and referred to for this volume. Each author has attempted to utilize and cite all the important sources available in order that the volume may be thoroughly up to date.

By the California culture area we do not mean an area congruent with the geographical borders of the present state. The state boundaries were established in 1850 when California was admitted to the Union, and the area then selected was a portion of the territory ceded to the United States following the Mexican War of 1846-1848. With reference to Native American populations and the occurrence of types of aboriginal culture, the California culture area is somewhat more restricted. If anthropologists in the past (for example, Powers 1877 and Kroeber 1925) treated the native cultures of the political state, that was because they were only trying to provide information on the people and cultures that had existed within the state boundaries (fig. 1). Any anthropologist employed by the state of California in the university might have been criticized if some taxpayer at Cedarville, Truckee, Needles, or Lone Pine had bought a book on the Indians of California and found that the native peoples in the area where he was living were ignored as being outside the California culture area as anthropologists envisaged this. Perhaps for this reason it became customary to write about the Indians of California in terms of the political state. Even though Holmes (1919:114-117, fig. 41) set aside a California "culture characterization" area and correctly saw that northwestern California had cultural ties with the Northwest Coast area and that southern California was culturally linked with the Southwest (which he called the Arid area), he mapped the California area as comprising the entire state with a southeastern salient running across the Colorado River to include a portion of western Arizona. Wissler (1938:fig. 58) is not very specific in either mapping or defining the California culture area, but he does point to Central California tribes as the most "typical" and recognizes that in the north, east, and southeast influences from other culture

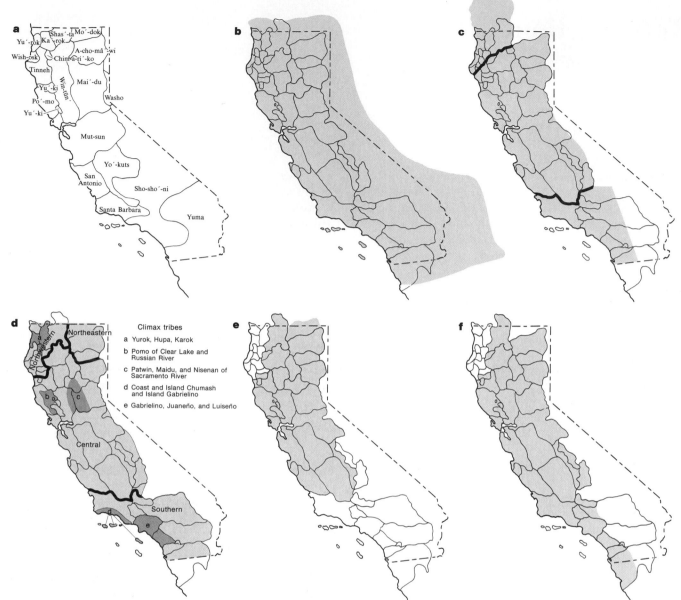

Fig. 1. Anthropologists' interpretations of the California culture area. a, linguistic stocks according to Powers 1877, culture areas according to Holmes 1919; b, Holmes 1919; c, Kroeber 1925; d, Kroeber 1936; e, Murdock 1960; f, Driver 1961.

areas are apparent. Driver (1961:map 2) outlines the California culture area much as we do in this volume.

Kroeber (1925:fig. 73) divided the state into subculture areas—Northwestern, Lutuami, Central, Southern, and Great Basin. He examined in some detail the relations of the Northwestern subculture area with the North Pacific Coast culture centering in British Columbia. The Lutuami subculture area comprised the territory of the Modoc, whose affiliations lay mainly to the north with the people of Klamath Lake. The Great Basin, constituting the eastern border of the state beyond the Sierra Nevadas, included the larger portion of the desert area of the southern part of the state. This area is, of course, the western fringe of the larger Great Basin area of interior drainage covering most of Utah and Nevada. Southern

California was seen as having received strong cultural influences from the Southwest proper lying east of the Colorado River. Kroeber (1936:map 1) returned to this culture classification problem and suggested modifications of his earlier scheme. The Lutuami area was slightly expanded to include the territory of the Pit River tribes (Achumawi and Atsugewi) and renamed Northeastern. The narrow zone of the western border of the Colorado River was separated from the former Southern California area and named Colorado River culture area. In addition to his final estimation of culture areas lying within the present boundaries of California, Kroeber (1936) gave his judgment as to which tribe or tribes represented the climax development of the particular subset of the whole—that is, "hearth tribes" of the subculture areas to

2

the extent that there are distinctive developments enabling the ethnographer to identify them (see fig. 1).

The coverage in this volume includes the Northwestern, Central, and Southern culture areas in their entirety. The Great Basin tribes of modern California are reported in volume 11 of this series, and the Colorado River culture area in California is treated as a part of the Southwest in volume 9. Only a portion of the Northeastern culture area in California is incorporated here, the southern half occupied by the Achumawi and Atsugewi. The northern half, held by the Modoc, is considered as part of the Plateau in volume 12.

Because the Northwestern California and Southern California subareas are seen as adumbrations of the larger Northwest Coast and Southwestern culture areas, the Central subculture stands as the most distinctively Californian. Kroeber (1936:105) characterizes this region as follows:

> The Central Californian area . . . leans to no serious degree on anything. To the west was an unnavigated ocean, to the east the Great Basin with scattered tribes eking out a bare subsistence. To the north and south lay the two contrasting areas [Northwestern, Southern], from which some cultural material was no doubt derived, but in so trickling and perhaps so ancient a stream, that, simply patterned as the Central culture was, it was able to mould this material over into its own patterns as fast as it came in. This is shown by the fact that the Northwestern and Southern elements in the Central area are, after all, few in comparison with those specific to it: 14 and 21, respectively, as against 160. The Central culture thus is definitely not a mere transition or blend between those of the Northwest and the South. It is a culture of lower potency, of less rich characterization, and, hand in hand with this, of less sharply definable climax. But in another sense, it is more independent than its Californian neighbors which, after all, are essentially local workings-over of distant greater culture impulses.

In the larger perspective, therefore, Northwestern California—with its industrial emphasis on woodworking, twined basketry, stone-handled adz, rod armor, elkhorn wedge, bell-shaped stone maul; salmon fishing with nets, weirs, traps, and harpoons; dentalium currency; dugout canoes; plank houses with double-pitch roof; sea mammal hunting with heavy harpoons with attached retrieving lines; and emphasis on wealth as a means of acquiring power and status—is seen as a kind of pale reflection of the more brilliant Northwest Coast culture development of the British Columbia shore. In a descriptive sense the culture of the California Yurok, Tolowa, and Wiyot represent what Kroeber suggested as formative Northwest Coast culture that was "originally a river or rivermouth culture, later a beach culture, and only finally and in part a seagoing one." He viewed Northwest Coast culture, of which Northwestern California is a part, as "least affected by influences from Middle (Nuclear)

America" and having been "reached to an unusual degree by influences from Asia" (Kroeber 1939a:28).

The Southern California culture area, heavily influenced by the Southwest, can trace many of its constituent elements to an origin among the Pueblos or the ancestors or cultural kinsmen of the Pueblos. However, the province is not a mere extension of the Southwest, for it has generated indigenous focuses (Kroeber 1925:913). But, since the Southwest or Pueblo area has clearly been partly shaped in its development from influences radiating north from the Mesoamerican heartland, so also does Southern California share, even though one more step removed, in having been stimulated from the civilizational hearth of Nuclear America.

Thus, Central California, into which diffused some traits from Northwestern California and some also from Southern California, at the same time was so distant from the main diffusion centers of British Columbia and the Southwest that these impulses could be absorbed and reworked into the Central California pattern, which presumably retained the basic features of the undifferentiated American Indian culture. Central California, in this sense, can be seen as representing a buffer zone lying between the dynamic Asiatic-stimulated Northwest Coast culture and the equally dynamic, though different, Mesoamerican-stimulated Southwest. Although anthropologists no longer discuss culture areas much, and may even tend to think of this concept as outmoded, regional types of native culture surely did exist, and this understanding of the placement of the California area is important.

The archeological record of man in the California area has become reasonably well known for the period of about the last 4,000 years. Beyond that in time the record is much less full and is therefore difficult to piece together to gain a coherent picture of what areas were occupied and the nature of the environmental adjustment. There are clear hints of the presence of Paleo-Indian hunters who were making Clovis-type weapon tips, but thus far no occupation site producing evidence of how these people lived has come to light. Humans were surely present in California by 10,000 or 11,000 years ago, but how much earlier than that is obscured by a surprisingly large number of unsupported claims that propose that stone tools or human bones ranging in age from 26,000 to 48,000 years have been found (Bada, Schroeder, and Carter 1974). While such proposals are made by competent laboratory scientists and cannot be ignored, most archeologists prefer to take the "wait and see" attitude until such time as the dating methods and their results are proved beyond all doubt to be accurate. Reserving acceptance of such datings is encouraged by a regrettable history of claims of extreme age for man in California made earlier at such "sites" as the Death Valley terraces, Texas Street roadcut near San Diego, Santa Rosa Island fossil elephant localities, and Calico Hills gravel fan.

3

None of these has in the end proved to be acceptable to archeologists as an archeological site; hence, archeologists are reluctant to give approval to more recent claims for the oldest direct dates yet secured for man in the New World. California has been the scene of a considerable number of such propositions. At the same time there are no final and absolute answers, and we may expect the claim and counter-claim game to continue. For a wider perspective than afforded in this volume of Paleo-Indian cultural materials and the earliest skeletal remains from North America, consult volume 3 of this series.

Some effort, but not nearly so much as would be desired, has been made in attempting to trace back the ethnographic cultures into the prehistoric period. The "direct historical approach" in archeology has not been much employed in California as a means of tracing back into prehistoric times the identifiable historic cultures, though some initial efforts have been made in this direction in Central California (Heizer 1941b) and Northwestern California (Elsasser and Heizer 1966:1-6). Efforts to chronologize the history of the Achumawi and Atsugewi (Baumhoff and Olmsted 1963, 1964) by comparing glottochronological and archeological time-depths were reasonably successful, but thus far no similar studies have been attempted. Kroeber (1909a:4) pointed out the interesting fact that "even the geographical limits of subordinate types of culture, and the distribution of specialized forms of implements, coincide almost absolutely so far as archaeology and ethnology have been able to determine." It does seem to be true that regional culture specializations in California have deep localized roots in the past, but where Kroeber could find no clear evidence of culture succession in the archeological data available at the time he wrote, we now know that there has occurred a succession of cultures, and presumably populations, in nearly all areas of the state. Where these have not come to light the reason is more likely to be that they have not yet been uncovered rather than that they are lacking.

The first systematic ethnographic work in California was done in 1871 and 1872 by Stephen Powers, who in 1875 was appointed to collect objects of Indian manufacture for display in the Centennial Exhibition in Philadelphia. Powers (1877) collected and printed his ethnographic observations under the title *Tribes of California.* Before Powers there are only incidental records that might be generally characterized as ethnohistorical data. About 1900 under Kroeber's guidance the systematic recording of detailed tribal ethnographies was begun; it was essentially completed 40 years later. In the first decades of the twentieth century California's White population was not very large, and native Californians survived in some numbers in out-of-the-way places. Many of these people who served as informants for ethnologists had been born before the gold rush (cf. Heizer and Nissen 1973) and were able to provide, from actually remembered experience, accounts of what native life was like before the Whites appeared. But not all ethnographic informants were persons who were alive in or before 1850, and as ethnologists continued to record data for tribal ethnographies not only did it become more and more difficult to find informants, but also most of these were determined as having been born in the 1860s, 1870s, 1880s, and 1890s. Therefore, the supposed record of precontact, aboriginal culture was increasingly being supplied by individuals born in California under the United States flag among more and more acculturated native groups. How much culture change occurred among the survivors of the native Californians after 1850 is not known because this problem has never been examined. We can suppose, however, that a considerable amount of change did occur and that to some degree the accounts of aboriginal cultures presented in ethnographies published after 1900 are, in fact, a record of changed and acculturated societies. These societies may have been rather different in detail in the early sixteenth century before the European discovery of California or before the catastrophic effect of the gold rush. This situation was specifically noted by Powers in 1872, but its consideration does not enter into the reports of ethnographers such as Kroeber, Barrett, Dixon, and other students of California Indian culture who published their monographs in the University of California scientific series (cf. Heizer 1975). Voegelin's (1956:4) recommendation that ethnographers admit "the fact that North American Indian ethnographies be taken as relating in general to a period coincident with the early years of the informants who supplied the data upon which such ethnographies are based" seems a sound one, but it has thus far not led to any major reassessment of the California ethnographic record through ethnohistorical data. However, this examination and reevaluation of the assumed aboriginal ethnographic cultures will almost inevitably come, if for no other reason than that it offers such rich results. This promise will make such inquiries attractive to students of Native American cultures that no longer exist even in the memories of living people. Not only social and cultural anthropologists will turn to this subject, I predict, but so also will archeologists who depend so heavily upon the ethnographic accounts for hints and leads in their effort to interpret the facts of prehistory. The "new anthropology" in California is likely to have a strong ethnohistorical orientation rather than remain concerned with the systems approach or "processual" interpretation, which in the mid-1970s seems to have caught the interest of some students. Much of this last-mentioned work seems to be unduly hypothetical and to extrapolate from solid data into quite unproved, and perhaps unprovable, projections. But the course of any science, both social and natural, is continually examining such innovations, and in the end they are accepted if sound and rejected if they are untenable.

By the time ethnographers began to systematically record the names and territories of individual tribes, a procedure instituted by Powers in the 1870s, a certain amount of territorial readjustment, through expansion or retraction of tribal lands engendered by severe population diminishments among some groups, may have occurred. And, despite the relative plethora of tribes in California, by the time the ethnographers got around to asking survivors of decimated groups the names of all their neighbors, it is perfectly possible that some small independent tribes had become extinct some generations earlier and that even the memory of their existence had been lost. Kroeber (1925:610) discusses the supposed tribe named the Giamina, who may have spoken a Uto-Aztecan language and who were neighbors of the Bankalachi and Palewyami; nothing is known of them, not even the proof that they actually existed. Equally mysterious are the Watiru and Kammatwa, two groups that spoke both Karok and Shasta, and whose identity as either Shasta or Karok has never been satisfactorily established (Heizer and Hester 1970b:134). What has been accepted as firmly established as regards speech affiliation or territorial holdings of some groups is still being modified. Examples are the Saclan, who were doubtfully classed as Costanoan by Kroeber but who prove on the basis of Arroyo de la Cuesta's (1821) word list to be Miwok, and the Alliklik, who were recently identified as at least in part a Chumashan- rather than a Uto-Aztecan-speaking tribe. The long-accepted view that the Marin Peninsula was occupied by Coast Miwok is now questioned on the basis of a dozen and a half words, recorded in 1775 from villagers living on the shore of San Francisco Bay near Angel Island, that prove to be Costanoan. Coast Miwok informants in the early 1900s affirmed their ownership of this territory and supported that allegation by naming village spots and features of the terrain. Perhaps what happened was the early removal of the Costanoans living north of the Golden Gate to the mission in San Francisco and the occupation of their abandoned territory by the Coast Miwok whose lands lay just to the north. By the time ethnographers recorded ethnogeographic details for the Marin Peninsula area, the Costanoans were all gone and the Coast Miwok had forgotten in the course of the preceding century that their occupation was recent, a result of events that came about through missionization. One wonders how many such territorial readjustments may have occurred of which there is no hint in the documentary record. There will no doubt be other such corrections as scholars continue to sift the recorded information.

Kroeber's (1925) monumental work is a most authoritative treatment of California Indians in one volume, although it is obviously "dated" since it reflects only what was known when it went to press in 1923. This volume covers fewer tribes and a smaller area than Kroeber's, and the two differ in approach and aim. By first defining regional patterns of various aspects of native culture, Kroeber did not need to repeat them for every tribal group. The saving in space thus allowed him, when writing about the tribes of northwestern or central or southern California, to expand on some particular tribal development without undue sacrifice of general coverage. The core of this volume, on the other hand, is 44 chapters by 33 authors, each being a self-contained synthesis of the culture of a tribe or group of closely related tribes that can be considered as a unit. While there is some unavoidable duplication of information between this volume and Kroeber's, at the same time the two volumes can be taken as complementing each other. Most students who have access to both volumes, and to whom library resources are available, should have little difficulty in becoming informed about or guided to the great bulk of information available on particular tribes or topics.

This volume employs, in a few instances, language classifications and tribal names that differ from those used by Kroeber. Shoshonean has disappeared as a distinct subgroup of Uto-Aztecan; Konkow is now the accepted designation for the Northwestern Maidu; Ipai has come into vogue as the name for the Northern Diegueño and Tipai for the Southern Diegueño and Kamia. Less abrupt in being more easily identified is the current usage of Cahto for the people reported in the earlier literature under the name Kato.

One matter concerning social and political organization of California Indians should be mentioned here in order to make clear what is meant by the word *tribelet*. The word was coined by Kroeber to indicate the basic, autonomous, self-governing, and independent sociopolitical group found all over the state. The term *village community* has also been used in the same sense. The tribelet consisted of the aggregation of people living in two or more (often up to a dozen) separate villages, acknowledging the leadership of a chief who usually resided in the largest and most important of the several settlements. The data on number and nature of the tribelets of some larger tribes (that is, linguistic units) is known with fair completeness. The Pomo, for example, were divided into 34 tribelets living on 3,370 square miles of land and numbering altogether about 8,000 persons (Stewart 1943). The Achumawi were divided into 11 tribelets and their total numbers are calculated at 3,000 persons, their territory comprising about 6,000 square miles of plateau land (Kniffen 1928). Kroeber (1962) discusses the nature of California tribelets in detail and summarizes much of what is recorded about them.

History of Research

ROBERT F. HEIZER

A complete and detailed history of anthropological research in California would take the form of a narrative that identified each investigator, specified the native group or topic he was concerned with, analyzed his theoretical biases, method of approach and results achieved, and included a complete documentary bibliography to all published and unpublished records. A large volume would be required to encompass all this.

A considerably more modest summary is attempted here to introduce the reader to the events in the main course of the accumulation of knowledge on the archeology, ethnography, folklore, and linguistics of the Indians of California. No attempt is made to mention the names or cite the published reports of all the persons who have worked in the field of California anthropology. Those persons listed are mentioned mainly because they did particular pieces of research that at the time were important.

The history of California ethnography strictly speaking is part of the documentary record of exploration and settlement by Euro-Americans ("The Impact of Euro-American Exploration and Settlement," this vol.; Heizer, Nissen, and Castillo 1975). California was first seen by Europeans just 50 years after the discovery of America by the Juan Rodríguez Cabrillo expedition of 1542-1543 (Wagner 1928; Kroeber 1925:552-556; Heizer 1972a). The garbled copy of the original log of the Cabrillo expedition contains the first description and place-names of California Indians—mainly the Chumash. The people seen along the southern California coast and at Monterey were friendly, but they had no gold or silver to encourage conquest or colonization, and, because until about 1700 the Pacific Ocean was exclusively a Spanish sea, little was done in the way of further exploration. The second recorded California visit of Europeans was by the Francis Drake expedition in 1579. A valuable description of the Indians visited with—identifiable as the Coast Miwok ("Coast Miwok," fig. 2, this vol.)—together with a few words and phrases has survived (Heizer 1974a). By the late 1700s other European nations were becoming active in the Pacific and the Spanish Crown realized that their claim to all the lands north of Mexico must be affirmed by the act of settlement. As a result, the Franciscan Order was granted the privilege of establishing missions in Alta California. The Jesuit Order, which had missionized Baja California, was expelled in 1767. The first Franciscan mission of Alta California was established in 1769 at San Diego, and in all some 21 missions were founded between 1769 and 1823 along the coastal zone (the "Mission Strip") as far north as Sonoma.

The Franciscan missionaries were not concerned with recording the "heathenish customs" of their "gentile" (that is, unbaptized) wards, whom they generally classed as ignorant and stupid savages. The few exceptions to the rule that priests wrote nothing about the Indians under their direction includes the attempt by Fr. Geronimo Boscana to describe the religion of the Juaneño in a work titled "Chinigchinich" written between 1814 and 1825 (see Reichlen and Reichlen 1971; Kroeber 1959:282-293). There were some important linguistic recordings by Fr. Felipe Arroyo de la Cuesta in the early nineteenth century, some of which are published (Arroyo de la Cuesta 1861, 1862; J.A. Mason 1916); the copies of the replies from 18 missions to the official questionnaire sent in 1812 by the Spanish government (Heizer 1975a); Bonaventure Sitjar's (1861) vocabulary recorded at San Antonio Mission; and an account of life in Mission San Luis Rey written by a neophyte, Pablo Tac (1930, 1952) about 1834. Because there is so little fact recorded during the Spanish-Mexican period (1542-1846) on Native Californians in either their "wild" or "domesticated" (missionized) situations, the journals of Spanish, French, German, Russian, and English voyagers who visited the California coast to reprovision their vessels are ethnohistorically important (Weber 1968). There are also observations by pre-Mexican-War-period visitors or settlers such as Alfred Robinson, J.J. Warner, J.A. Sutter, J.C. Frémont, Z. Leonard, G. Yount, and G. Nidever. The ethnological gleanings from these sources are usually slim and often in error; nevertheless, when taken as a total body they are important because they are all that is available for the period. A survey of these sources has been written by Barbara Beroza (1974).

The year 1850 marks entry into the Union by California, and one by-product of the activities of the flood of humanity that came to California in search of gold was the publication in newspapers and journals of some descriptive accounts of the cultural practices of those native peoples the Argonauts encountered who had survived missionization (for example, Gibbs 1853, 1973; Meyer 1855; von Loeffelholz 1893), peonage under the Mexicans from 1821 to 1846, and the side-effects of introduced diseases, which spread far beyond the limited zones of European settlement. This historical preamble is important in the present context since there must have been an incalculable loss of ethnographic fact between 1769 and 1850 due to the population decrease from about 300,000 in 1769 to about 100,000 in 1850. The 1850 population was at least halved in the ensuing 20 years, so that by 1871, when Stephen Powers began to collect the data that appeared in his *Tribes of California* (1877), there were living only about 16 percent of the Native Californians who were present a century earlier.

Some historians of California anthropology would probably credit Alexander S. Taylor with the honor of being the first anthropologist (Cowan 1933). Taylor was interested but untrained, and he found an outlet for his prolific but unorganized outpourings on California-Northern Mexican history, Native Californian cultures, and Franciscan missions in *The California Farmer and Journal of Useful Arts,* San Francisco, which was owned and published by his father-in-law, J.L.L. Warren. Taylor's rambling "Indianology of California" appeared in the *Farmer* from February 22, 1860, to October 30, 1863. Kroeber (1925:963) felt, when he completed the writing of his *Handbook* in 1917, that the "Indianology" was worth republication. Although that is no longer true, the series may continue to be mined for bits and pieces of original information (cf. Heizer 1973a). It may be of interest to record that Taylor, probably in 1856, had published on legal-size paper a three-page vocabulary schedule in English and Spanish, completed copies of which (presumably used as printer's copy for the "Indianology" series) are preserved in the J.L.L. Warren Papers in the Bancroft Library, University of California, Berkeley. Taylor's schedule, titled "California Indian Languages," is obviously adapted from the one by Henry R. Schoolcraft dated March 28, 1848, captioned "Comparative Vocabulary of the Indian Languages of the United States." Taylor in 1864 drew up a map purporting to show the location of Indian tribes in California. Although it is replete with errors, it is of historical interest in being the first such effort (Heizer 1941d).

Hugo Reid (b.1811, d.1853), an early settler in southern California who married a Gabrielino woman, wrote a series of letters about the Indians of Los Angeles County, which were published in 1852 in the Los Angeles *Star.* These have been reprinted several times, most recently by Heizer (1968). The 1852 report of Benjamin D. Wilson (1952), Indian agent for southern California, was published in the *Star* in 1868. Beyond the Reid and Wilson documents there is nothing else for the 1850s of real substance (see Wuertele 1975). The famous hoax of the "Calaveras skull" found in 1866, which was believed by some to be of Pliocene age, attracted a good deal of written comment and opinion (for listing see Heizer 1948:3-7). The final exposé of the skull resulted from the investigations into the matter by William H. Holmes

(1901:454-469) and Aleš Hrdlička (1907:21-28). There were numerous prehistoric artifacts uncovered during the extensive diggings that accompanied the gold rush, and to many of these finds were attributed great antiquity. Holmes (1901) reviewed the evidence and provided a reasoned evaluation of this question.

In the 1870s, regrettably after the severe native population decline attributable to the Spaniards and Americans with consequent loss of information, there was instituted the beginnings of the accumulation of a reliable body of anthropological fact. Foremost in this effort are the data recorded by a journalist, Stephen Powers, who spent the summers of 1871 and 1872 visiting Indians in the northern two-thirds of California. Powers first published his observations in 18 articles appearing in the *Overland Monthly, Proceedings* of the California Academy of Science, and *Atlantic Monthly,* 1872-1875; these have been reprinted (Powers 1975). A few years later, after some rearrangement and additions effected by the author, this corpus of data appeared under the title *Tribes of California* (Powers 1877). That real anthropology was then being written is indicated by J.W. Powell's efforts to control the overfree speculations of Powers regarding the inflated estimate of aboriginal population and the Chinese origin of California Indians. A century ago Powell had enough knowledge and insight to recognize these for what they were, namely, amateurish and unsupported theories. Not only is Powers's work the first effective attempt at presenting an organized description of the variety of native California cultures, but also there is in it the first map showing the geographical boundaries of what he called linguistic stocks. See "Introduction," figure 1, this volume for simplified version of this map.

Also in the 1870s the Alphonse Pinart-Leon de Cessac expedition from France made archeological and linguistic investigations in California (Heizer 1952; Reichlen and Heizer 1963); Paul Schumacher, working for the U.S. Coast Survey, made extensive archeological investigations on the Santa Barbara coast and offshore islands (for a list of his publications see E.N. Anderson 1964:49-50); members of the U.S. Geographical Survey West of the One Hundredth Meridian, Lt. G.M. Wheeler in charge, did extensive excavation in mainland sites near Santa Barbara (Putnam et al. 1879). The situation anthropology was in at that time is illustrated by Putnam's statement (Putnam et al. 1879:17-18) that the California Indians were in a "lower status of barbarism" and by Carr's evaluation that the crania he had measured "cannot be said to be a high order of skull" (ibid.:286), going on to argue that dolichocephals are inferior to brachycephals and that therefore the long-headed prehistoric people of San Clemente and Santa Catalina Islands were remnant survivors (ibid.:292).

In the 1870s the first effective efforts at linguistic classification were made, and while they were at times in error, these nevertheless were essential first steps. Albert

S. Gatschet contributed a number of linguistic analyses (see citations in Bright 1964:222) as well as a large comparative set of vocabularies that was published as an appendix to the Wheeler survey (Putnam et al. 1879:403-485). John W. Powell's (1877) appendix on linguistics in Powers's *Tribes of California* contains 80 word lists, which are identified as belonging to 13 families. Fourteen years later Powell and his aides had increased the number of language families of California to 22 (Powell 1891). For a history of early attempts at classification see Heizer (1966), Sturtevant (1959), and Kroeber (1961). Shipley (1973) provides a documented survey of language research and classification since the Dixon and Kroeber (1912, 1913, 1919) basic revisions, recombinations, and reductions. Bright (1964:217-235) has compiled a complete bibliography of published works on California linguistics and thus provides a useful potential guide to historical development if it is rearranged chronologically. Earlier linguistic work in southern California is summarized by Barrows (1900:9-25).

About 1900 Alphonse Pinart, a Frenchman with some pretensions of being a linguist (and once married to the famous Zelia Nuttall), compiled a manuscript of 870 pages entitled "Vocabularios de las Lenguas Indigenas de la Alta California" in the apparent hope of publishing it in France. However, this imposing work was never printed, and the original resides in the Beinecke Library, Yale University. The contents consist of already published word lists, or ones presently in the National Anthropological Archives, Smithsonian Institution. Curiously, the important word lists recorded by Pinart himself in California some 30 years earlier, and now in the Bancroft Library archives (cf. Heizer 1952), do not occur in this manuscript. Pinart worked as a copyist for Hubert H. Bancroft, and in view of the irascible temperament of both individuals it seems probable that a rift developed and Pinart was thus unable to secure copies of the word lists he had compiled in the late 1870s. Another perceptive review of the development of linguistic knowledge can be found in Dell H. Hymes's (1962) annotations to the reprinting of Kroeber (1908e).

Bancroft, a historian, together with a staff of writers, compiled five volumes on Native Americans in the West. Volume 1 (Wild Tribes) contains a lengthy chapter that incorporates, with references, nearly everything ever written about the California Indians up to 1874. As a handy, albeit inchoate, reference it is invaluable (Bancroft 1874-1876, 1:322-470). Volume 3 summarizes what was reported to the date of publication on languages and folklore, and volume 4 lists all known archeological finds. Bancroft's volumes are a valuable historical datum. He was the first writer to recognize formally and to treat the broad culture types of the state, labeling these Northern, Central, and Southern (cf. Elsasser 1960a).

Otis T. Mason (1889) wrote a still-valuable treatise on the material culture of the Hupa, which was based on materials accumulated by the Smithsonian Institution from about 1840 to 1885.

In 1901 the joint Department and Museum of Anthropology was established in the University of California, Berkeley. Frederic Ward Putnam (fig. 1) was the chairman, Alfred L. Kroeber was instructor, and Pliny Earle Goddard was the assistant in anthropology. The story of the founding and early years of the Berkeley department and museum have been presented by Thoresen (1975), Gifford and McCown (1951), Anonymous (1968a), and Kroeber (1946). Although the research program was formally titled "Ethnological and Archaeological Survey of California" (Wheeler and Putnam 1903; Kroeber 1906a; Putnam 1905), the greatest emphasis in research was on ethnography. The series University of California Publications in American Archaeology and Ethnology (UCPAAE) was launched in September 1903 with the appearance of Goddard's *Life and Culture of the Hupa*, which contained 88 pages of text and 30 plates and sold for $1.25. There then followed a steady production of monographs dealing with tribal ethnographies, linguistics, special topics (for example, religion, basketry, social organization, archery), folklore, physical anthropology, and archeology. Seven years later Kroeber (1908e), in an address delivered as the retiring vice-president of Section H of the American Association for the Advancement of Science, was in possession of enough knowledge to block out the cultural and linguistic divisions of California. Gradually, as the field of anthropology developed and more practitioners came within the orbit of the Berkeley department, the range of coverage in the UCPAAE series expanded to include monographs on Peruvian archeology, Philippine ethnography, and the like. Through the 45 years of Kroeber's service at the University of California his was the steady guiding hand that raised funds for fieldwork and saw to it that the results were written up and published in journals or in University of California publication series. Kroeber's overall aim, though never explicitly stated by him, was to procure and publish as complete a record of the anthropology of California as was possible (fig. 2). A really extraordinary amount of data was recovered in the half-century or so by the stimulus of this remarkable man, and for that devotion to the commitment to see that the ethnographic record would be as complete as humanly possible, American anthropology is the richer. Beginning in 1901 with little more than Powers (1877) as a source of data, Kroeber by 1917 had completed the writing of his monumental *Handbook of the Indians of California* (Kroeber 1925), whose coverage was remarkably thorough. The UCPAAE series, published from 1903 to 1964, runs to 50 volumes that contain 241 separately authored contributions. A continuing series, University of California Anthropological Records (UCAR) (vol. 1, 1937 to vol. 28, 1975) maintains the tradition of student and faculty

Fig. 1. Left to right, unidentified woman, Mrs. Putnam, Frederick Ward Putnam, and Alfred L. Kroeber. Photographed at Catalina Island, 1904.

research publication under the university's imprint, though the pace has slowed considerably.

Over the years the University of California expanded to comprise a statewide system of nine campuses, each offering a full range of academic courses. On each campus there was established a department of anthropology within which the faculty taught and carried out research. From the late 1930s on these new university anthropology departments helped swell the body of monographs in the UCPAAE and UCAR series. The beginning of World War II marks the end, generally speaking, of the attempt to complete the ethnographic record for native California. Kroeber's retirement in 1946

and the realization that 180 years of acculturation had almost completely erased even the memory of precontact cultures seem to have been the principal causes for abandoning the effort. But in the mid-1930s Kroeber himself realized that there was very little time remaining to make even a last-moment attempt to fill out the gaps in the ethnographic record. He conceived of the intensive program of investigation that came to be known as the "Culture Element Survey of Native Western North America" (Kroeber 1935, 1939b). The culture element surveys entailed locating the most reliable informants possible, sitting down with them, one at a time, and entering on a written list of traits a plus for presence and

Dept. of Anthr., Archaeol. Research Facility, U. of Calif., Berkeley.
Fig. 2. Alfred L. Kroeber and Ishi, a Yahi Yana. Photographed 1912–1915.

a minus for its absence. Between May 1934 and July 1938, 13 field investigators made 20 trips and returned with 279 filled-in lists representing 254 separate tribes or groups ranging from the Chilkat Tlingit in the north to the Yaqui in the south and extending as far east as the Ute of eastern Colorado. The mass of data was analyzed statistically to secure intertribal correlations and cultural groupings. As much care as could reasonably be taken was made to secure an accurate and unambiguous record. All in all, despite the mechanical, atomistic nature of the data and the nonassessable amount of error present, the 20 published culture element distribution monographs do

constitute an invaluable systematic record of the native cultures of western North America as it was remembered in the 1930s.

Due acknowledgement for important research must be accorded C. Hart Merriam (fig. 3) (b.1855, d.1942) and John P. Harrington (fig. 4) (b.1884, d.1961). These men were friends and cooperated with each other. They also shared an antipathy to Kroeber, which possibly drew them together. Both lived in Washington, D.C., Harrington working on the staff of the Bureau of American Ethnology and Merriam being privately supported by a bequest established by Mary W. Harriman (Osgood 1947; Kroeber 1955a). Additional shared traits of Harrington and Merriam were a devotion to fieldwork that was little short of superhuman and a reluctance to publish their data. The C. Hart Merriam Collection, maintained as part of the archives of the Archaeological Research Facility, Department of Anthropology, University of California, Berkeley, is a veritable gold mine of ethnogeographic data, ethnoscience, and linguistics. Merriam, regrettably, had no training in linguistics, but for languages that are now extinct his word lists are important. Some of Merriam's data have been published posthumously under his name. Harrington's records are deposited in the National Anthropological Archives and the Department of Linguistics, University of California, Berkeley. Harrington had remarkable talents as a linguist and ethnographer and was imbued with a passion to record as much Indian knowledge as possible before it was lost. How much detail he could wring out of informants is illustrated by his cultural-linguistic monograph on Karok tobacco (Harrington 1932a). Harrington was not problem-oriented, and he was almost pathologi-

Dept. of Anthr., Archeol. Research Facility, U. of Calif., Berkeley.
Fig. 3. C. Hart Merriam, center, and the Mitchell brothers, Patwins from the Colusa region. Photographed in Sept. 1936.

HEIZER

Fig. 4. Left to right, John P. Harrington, F. Echeverria (Cahuilla), Angel Quilpe (Cahuilla), and Juan Chutnikat (Cupeño), at the mouth of Palm Canyon, Colorado Desert. Photographed in 1920s (Callaghan 1975).

cally secretive (Laird 1975)—a trait that made him reluctant to share information, even in publication. His massive accumulation of data is still not completely explored or organized, and his records will for long continue to be an important lode to be mined by linguists and ethnologists. A rich body of Chumash folklore collected by Harrington was edited by Blackburn (1975).

Mention is also appropriate of Roland B. Dixon, attached to the American Museum of Natural History, New York, who wrote ethnographies of the Northern Maidu (1905) and the Shasta (1907), which are still among the fullest and most accurate tribal sketches available. Dixon was also much involved with linguistics and folklore, as may be seen by the listing of his published works in Kroeber (1925:947).

A great deal of research has never gone further than being recorded in notebooks. Much has been written up

in some form or other and copies deposited in archival collections. The latter situation applies more to archeology than ethnography, perhaps for the reason that it is more difficult to get publication of the former subject. These collections will doubtless be exploited by students in the future. There has been, up to the launching of the *Journal of California Anthropology* in 1974, no serious subscription journal in California with the exception of the Southwest Museum *Masterkey* (vol. 1, 1936), which contains a large number of important articles that are, usually, very brief. There have been launched various local archeological society journals or newsletters, but since these usually depend on the work of one or two devoted persons, they have had brief floruits. The California Academy of Sciences gave promise in the nineteenth century of including in its purview the "science of man," but after the 1906 earthquake this organization abandoned what little interest it ever had in the subject. The result of the absence of continuing California journals available generally to anthropologists has been either lack of publication of material or its confinement to the dozen or so in-house publication series of museums and academic institutions.

Mythology or folklore was a research subject of much interest up to about 1940. Early attempts to organize the considerable body of tales are those of Gifford and Block (1930) and Gayton (1935). Despite the rich body of data that exists, folklorists have not made much use of it (see "Comparative Literature" and "Mythology," this vol.).

Archeological research began in the 1870s with sporadic digging for museum materials. What had been learned up to 1900 is summarized by Meredith (1900), Thomas (1898:187-202), and Yates (1900). In 1901, through the interest and financial support of Phoebe A. Hearst, the Department and Museum of Anthropology were established at the University of California, Berkeley. With the stimulation of F.W. Putnam, who was the absentee chairman (Thoresen 1975), and J.C. Merriam, both with a strong interest in archeology (and especially Early Man), some systematic work was done in shellmounds and caves. This search for ancient man is reported by J.C. Merriam (1906), Putnam (1906), and Sinclair (1904, 1908); fuller documentation is in Heizer (1948). Max Uhle (1907) excavated the Emeryville shellmound on the east shore of San Francisco Bay; Nels C. Nelson conducted a walking survey of sites of San Francisco Bay (1909) and excavated the Ellis Landing shellmound some 6 miles north of Emeryville (1910); and Philip M. Jones (1922, 1956, 1969), employed as a collector by Hearst, excavated near Stockton and on San Nicolas and Santa Rosa islands. While a bit of archeology continued to be done by the Department of Anthropology at Berkeley, mainly by Llewellyn L. Loud who was occasionally given a few dollars and a few weeks off from his museum duties (Loud 1918; Heizer 1970a), by W. Egbert Schenck who held a nonsalaried research appointment in the Museum of Anthropology (Gifford and Schenck 1926; Schenck and Dawson 1929), or by Ronald L. Olson (1930) who was a regular faculty member, it is surely true that the main research interest lay in ethnography.

As "full culture" ethnographic descriptions were abandoned the long-deferred investigation of California prehistory began in the late 1920s. After Putnam's retirement in 1909 from the Department of Anthropology at Berkeley, Kroeber decided that the archeology could safely wait in the ground and that the task of recording the ethnology before the last survivors died was more urgent. Some such choice obviously had to be made because there were too few workers and too little funds to do both. To acknowledge Putnam's special interest in archeology and perhaps to signal the end of primary concern with the subject, Kroeber summarized what was

known of archeology in the anniversary volume assembled in honor of Putnam (Kroeber 1909a). Unfortunately for the archeology of California the prehistoric sites were nearly as vulnerable as the living Indian survivors, and by the time work began to be done in earnest in the mid-1940s a great deal of it had already been destroyed. There remain large sections of the state about which nothing is known because all the archeological sites have been erased. Some progress on chronology had been made in witness of which can be cited M.J. Rogers's (1929) important paper on the San Diego area in which he proposed a cultural sequence, those of David B. Rogers (1929) and Ronald L. Olson (1930) on mainland and offshore Santa Barbara Channel island sites where two somewhat different or at least incongruent culture sequences were proposed, and the expectable three-period system (Early, Middle, and Late) that was proposed for the Sacramento delta region (Lillard and Purves 1936; Lillard, Heizer, and Fenenga 1939; cf. Ragir 1972:6-12; Schenck and Dawson 1929; Beardsley 1954). Although it has been said that Uhle (1907) first demonstrated the practicality of stratigraphic analysis in his report on the Emeryville shellmound, it is also true that his interpretation is incorrect. Dixon (1913:550), who surely knew of Uhle's report, did not think it worthy of mention but used Nelson's (1910) Ellis Landing shellmound data on shore subsidence as indicating "a very considerable age for the lower layers of these mounds." Apparently with such a limited amount of artifact material to analyze, and that usually of a simple nature, it was very difficult to distinguish cultural differences within the earthmounds and shellmounds of California. Kroeber (1909a) found this so in writing his contribution to the Putnam anniversary volume, and it was still true in 1917 (Kroeber 1925:919-939). Kroeber (1936b:115) subsequently saw some real hope for developing prehistoric culture sequences, noting that "the prehistory of the eastern United States had been dealt with for a hundred years, or twice as long as that of California, and we do not yet understand it. In both areas we may be on the very brink of organization of the foundations of permanent interpretation." Those were prophetic words: by 1939 a clear-cut culture sequence was demonstrable in the lower Sacramento Valley area of California (Lillard, Heizer, and Fenenga 1939), and two years later the Brownian agitation of the prehistory of the Eastern United States quite suddenly precipitated into a stratified sediment of time-ordered cultures (Ford and Willey 1941).

The Southwest Museum in Los Angeles has made important contributions since its founding in 1907 to the accumulation and publication of knowledge of Native Californians. Associated with this institution have been C.F. Lummis, F.W. Hodge, M.R. Harrington, and B. Bryan. In 1948 there was instituted in the Department of Anthropology at Berkeley the University of California Archaeological Survey (UCAS) (Heizer 1948a, 1949a). In

1960 the UCAS was transformed into the Archaeological Research Facility. The Archeological Survey established in 1958 at the University of California at Los Angeles has made steady progress in excavating, training students, and publishing results in its annual reports. In 1948 there was founded the Archaeological Survey Association of Southern California (ASASC) aimed at coordinating the activities of a number of museums, historical societies, and academic institutions. The ASASC *Newsletter* contains reports on the activities of the member organizations. A bibliography of published works on California archeology up to 1970 (Heizer, Elsasser, and Clewlow 1970) provides a guide to the subject. No adequate summary or survey of California prehistory has ever been written, but the broad development of the subject can be followed in Kroeber (1909a, 1936b), Heizer (1964, 1964a), Willey (1966:361–379), Meighan (1959a, 1965), and Warren (1973), which, taken as a whole, will bring the reader up to 1970. Useful bibliographical summaries of published archeological site excavations and surveys can be found in Baumhoff and Elsasser (1956) and Eberhart (1970). A notable lack of cooperation among California archeologists, the blandishments of "conservation archeology" engendered by the federal and state environmental protection laws, and the absence of responsible leadership are suggested as the principal reasons for the condition of confusion in the study of California prehistory in 1975 (cf. Heizer 1966a).

No attempt is made here to trace the course of federally supported (Federal Emergency Relief Administration, Works Progress Administration, River Basin Surveys) or federally mandated (Environmental Policy Act of 1969) archeological salvage surveys and excavation. There has, since the 1930s, been continuous activity in this kind of work, but on the whole the published record is quite minimal if assessed in amount of time and money devoted to it (cf. Heizer 1964a, 1966a). This is not to say that the various reasons why such rescue archeology was done in California at the time were wrong, but merely that the effort was relatively unproductive in terms of making generally available the results of the endeavor.

A further deficiency that should be mentioned is the failure of the state legislature to establish the kind of archeological program that a number of other states have long since done. Perhaps it was assumed that the colleges and universities would do this, and they would have been glad to do so if their requests for funds had been approved. Or, possibly, the citizen taxpayers and legislators merely thought that California's prehistory was of no particular interest. The only state agency that has attempted to accomplish anything is the Department of Parks and Recreation (formerly Beaches and Parks) in the State Resources Agency. Even though hampered by inadequate funds, understaffed and overworked, a good deal has been accomplished by this state agency in regard to both excavation and publication.

Physical anthropological studies of the living and the dead have suffered from neglect. Aside from Gifford's (1926) basic compilation of data upon which most later work rests, there has been little serious effort to try to unravel the complicated sequence of prehistoric populations in California. A good many skulls have been measured (see Heizer, Elsasser, and Clewlow 1970:74–78), but beyond contributing to the descriptive data all of this seems to have been quite pointless. There have been some important studies of paleopathology (Brabender 1965; McHenry 1968; Hoffman 1976; Roney 1959). It would seem that physical anthropology has not been a truly productive area of research, or alternatively, that its star has not yet risen. In 1975 there is an increasingly strong protest being voiced by Native Americans against the despoliation of the cemeteries of their people, and demands have been made for the giving over for reburial of the skeletal remains collected by archeologists and housed in museums. It is possible that scholars are now in possession of nearly all the facts they will ever have about the anthropometry of the Native Californians. If this forecast eventuates to reality, anthropological knowledge will be the poorer, but the possibility is a real one.

Research in Californian linguistics has a long history. Stephen Powers and John W. Powell developed what may be called the first significant ordering of the available California data. Dixon and Kroeber (1919) pointed out, on the basis of careful comparative work, various relationships that allowed reduction of the number of language families to seven. Further refinements were made, on the basis of field studies, but a new era dawned in 1953 with the establishment on the Berkeley campus of the University of California of the Survey of California Indian Languages. This research program, carried out under the direction and indefatigable zeal of Mary Haas, has resulted in the accumulation of a considerable reference archive, and many volumes in the University of California Publications in Linguistics of texts, dictionaries, and grammars. This rebirth of linguistics is a little reminiscent of the final effort that Kroeber generated in "salvage ethnography" by way of the Culture Element Survey.

In an abbreviated historical assessment such as this a few salient points in the development of anthropological study can be pointed out. Alexander S. Taylor in the 1860s was making an attempt to systematically collect vocabularies recorded on printed schedules; Stephen Powers in the 1870s did likewise. Powers (1877:206) anticipated the concept of glottochronology, made the first real ethnobotanical study of a California tribe (ibid. 1875), pioneered in the methods of calculating aboriginal population by extrapolating numbers of persons per bank mile of salmon streams (Powers 1875a; cf. Baumhoff 1963) and prehistoric village populations by counting house pits and multiplying by numbers of persons in a family (Powers 1877; cf. Cook and Heizer 1965, 1968), first detected the linguistic relationship between Wappo and Yuki, and drew up the first map of California tribal territories and linguistic stocks (Powers 1877:map in end pocket). The fullest ethnobotany is that of Chesnut (1902), which mainly concerns the Yuki of Round Valley and the Pomoans of Ukiah. Not far behind is Barrows's (1900) ethnobotany of the Cahuilla. Yates (1887) anticipated settlement pattern studies of a half-century later in a discussion of Alameda County shellmounds. Jones (1900) was fully aware of the vulnerability of the San Francisco Bay shellmounds since he worked in the area from February 1900 to September 1901 and carried out what might be termed the first archeological site salvage excavation in California. He refers to a large site at San Bruno that was "in no danger of being disturbed" and therefore decided to "expend my time and money at my disposal in sections which were in danger of soon being completely excavated by the 'curio hunter' and commercial collectors." In archeology a few innovations occurred in the California field. Among these may be mentioned Gifford's (1916) "midden analysis" and J.H. Steward's (1929) study of petroglyphs, which for the first time placed these prehistoric materials in anthropological perspective with analysis performed by anthropological methods. A unique attempt at presenting ethnographic detail is Kroeber's device of writing a Yurok ethnography as a parallel to that of the Twana (Kroeber 1960). An important proposal by W.S. Robinson (1951) on a technique for seriating archeological objects helped archeol-

ogy in general along its present path of utilizing mathematics as an analytical tool. The reawakened interest in ecology was not lost on California anthropologists, as the important papers of Beals and Hester (1960) and Meighan (1959) show.

California has produced its share, perhaps even more than its quota, of hoaxes like the Calaveras skull, wholly unsupportable claims of "Third Interglacial Man" (for instance, at Texas Street in San Diego County and Calico Hills in San Bernardino County), and the ordinary variety of crazy theories such as Powers's (1874c) on the Chinese origin of California Indians.

In 1976 the anthropological study of California Indian cultures is still a field with some activity with reference to native languages and prehistory. The old-style ethnographic work has ended because the aboriginal cultures are extinct. Many languages are no longer spoken, and the number of surviving tongues is steadily decreasing as the last speakers die. Folklore has shifted to interests other than recording myths, but a large and essentially unstudied body of tales exists for examination by scholars. A strong reaction to archeology by Native Americans may, it seems likely, lead in future to a severe reduction of this kind of investigation. Interest in Native Californian cultures is high among the public, and college courses in the subject are well attended. If this interest is sustained, and there seems no reason to believe it will not be, coming generations of scholars, both Whites and descendants of Native Californians, will be mining and remilling the vast body of published direct-testimony

Dept. of Anthr., Archaeol. Research Facility, U. of Calif., Berkeley.

Fig. 5. Herman James, a Kashaya Pomo consultant, and Edward W. Gifford visiting the West Berkeley shellmound site during its excavation. Photograph by Robert F. Heizer, 1951.

State Ind. Mus., Sacramento, Calif.

Fig. 6. Samuel A. Barrett filming Lizzie Enos, a Nisenan, while she is grinding acorns. Photograph by Norman Wilson, Oct. 1958.

14

ethnographies, ethnohistoric accounts, unpublished archival material, and museum collections. Contemporary Indian subcultures may also be the scene for research, but acculturation and social anthropological investigations are almost lacking for reasons that are unclear. This may be due in part to a disinterest in such studies by anthropologists and in part due to objections to being so studied by Native Americans themselves. Therefore, the future of anthropological studies of Native Californians is uncertain, but it is likely to become for the most part an academic subdiscipline that will appear to be ethnosociology (cf. Kroeber and Parsons 1958) and ethnohistory.

Environmental Background

MARTIN A. BAUMHOFF

The northern three-fourths of California is a long narrow valley (the Great Central Valley) surrounded on all sides by mountains, which are high on the east (the Sierra Nevadas and the Cascade Range) and rather lower on the west (Coast Ranges and Klamath Mountains). Southern California has low mountains on the Coast (Transverse and Peninsular ranges) and semimountainous desert inland (the Mojave Desert) (fig. 1). Most of the state has Mediterranean climate with precipitation from 15 inches a year in the south to 40 inches in the north and up to 70 inches in the extreme northwest and at high elevations. The climatic exceptions are the west side of the San Joaquin Valley and the Mojave Desert, which have desert climate and less than seven inches of rainfall annually (R.J. Russell 1926). This is the inorganic environment.

Food Resources

The major part of the biological environment to be considered is the elements that produce the staple foods

Fig. 1. Geomorphic provinces.

and what may be termed secondary or substitute staples. The staple foods are acorns, fish and other sea foods, and large mammals. Acorns are clearly the most important and most characteristic California staple. Even in areas where they were secondary, such as the Northwest Coast, and in areas where not many were available—Northeast California—they were still of very great importance and were so considered by the people. The principal oaks are listed below and their desirability rating as taken from Baumhoff (1963:163) is given. A rating of 1 indicates a preferred species and the rating goes up to 3 for an undesirable species.

Species	Average Rating
Tan oak (*Lithocarpus densiflora*)	1.0
Black oak (*Quercus kelloggii*)	1.5
Blue oak (*Quercus douglasii*)	1.5
Valley oak (*Quercus lobata*)	1.9
Coast live oak (*Quercus agrifolia*)	2.0
Oregon oak (*Quercus garryana*)	2.0
Engelmann oak (*Quercus engelmannii*)	2.2
Maul oak (*Quercus chrysolepis*)	2.2
Interior live oak (*Quercus wislizenii*)	2.3
Scrub oak (*Quercus dumosa*)	2.5

These ratings are of some importance because in many areas people would travel a long way to a single tree of a preferred species while ignoring nearby groves of an undesirable species. The less desirable species should be classed as secondary staples.

Among the sea foods of California the most important were probably the salmon or anadromous fishes. These were the king or chinook salmon (*Oncorhynchus tshawytscha*), silver or coho salmon (*O. kisutch*), and steelhead trout (*Salmo gairdnerii*). Their importance may be judged by their occurrence as shown in figure 2. Salmon were paramount on the Smith River, the Klamath and its tributaries, and in Eel River drainage. It was of major importance but perhaps not quite paramount on the Sacramento and its tributaries.

Marine life (pelagic fish, mollusks, and sea mammals) were also of great importance as attested by the large shell mounds along most of the coastline. These were especially large and numerous south of Point Conception, in Monterey Bay, San Francisco Bay, and coast north of San Francisco. The principal component of these mounds is shells from edible mollusks, but in some areas, especially the extreme north and on the channel coast, the bones of sea mammals are also important. The main shellfish in the south are sea mussel (*Mytilus californianus* and *M. edulis*), abalone (*Haliotis* sp.), Pismo clam (*Tivela stultorum*), oyster (*Ostrea lurida*), scallop *Pecten circularis*), and California venus clam (*Chione* sp.). For the northern coast they are sea mussel, bent nose macoma (*Macoma nasuta*), Washington clam (*Saxidomus nuttalli*), and oyster. Some of these shellfish may have been of paramount importance in some areas.

The sea mammals, usually taken by clubbing them on the beaches, were the sea lion (*Eumetopias jubata* or

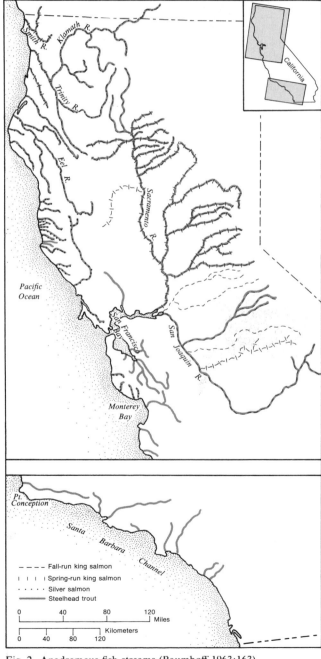

Fig. 2. Anadromous fish streams (Baumhoff 1963:163).

Zalophus californianus), the sea otter (*Enhydra lutris*), and the harbor seal (*Phoca vitulina richardii*). These were especially important on the northwest coast and the Santa Barbara Channel coast.

The third category of staple food comprises the large game mammals: deer (*Odocoileus hemionus*), Roosevelt elk (*Cervus canadensis roosevelti*), tule elk (*Cervus nannodes*), and pronghorn antelope (*Antilocapra americana*). Deer were found throughout the state except in dense redwood and in the central valley (they were present on the fringes of the latter during winter and spring). They grazed when the new grass came up but mostly were browsers. They were hunted mostly by ambushing and stalking. Roosevelt elk occupied the North Coast Range, especially on the edge of the redwood forest; their feeding habits were like those of deer. The tule elk or dwarf elk was found around the marshes of the Sacramento-San Joaquin Valley and fed off the plants that grew there. The pronghorn antelope was found in great numbers in the grasslands of the central valley. Their food was nearly all gotten through grazing so they were more or less confined to that region.

Besides these principal staples there are three secondary or emergency staples that should be mentioned. These three are the buckeye, sage seed or chia, and epos root. The buckeye (*Aesculus californica*) was the true emergency staple throughout the California areas. This apparently was never eaten except in times of starvation, but it was quite nourishing and there was plenty available. The fact that it is now often found near Indian sites indicates that the seeds were carried there by people, since they are too heavy for wind transport and, because they are poisonous, they are not carried by animals. For human use the poison is leached out by pouring water over them.

Another secondary food is chia or the seed of sage (*Salvia* sp.). The sage is plentiful in the South Coast Range and along the coast from Point Conception to San Diego. This food was evidently well liked but did not become a primary staple because it is difficult to harvest enough seed to last over a long period of time. In times of acorn failure this could be combined with whatever else was available to tide the group over until the next harvest.

The final plant food to consider here is the root of the epos or yampa. This is a plant of the genus *Perideridia* (Umbelliferae), usually *P. gairdneri* in California. Across much of Northern California and the Pacific Northwest, *P. gairdneri*, *P. oregana*, *P. bolanderi*, *P. parishii*, and *P. kellogii* were used as food (Chuang and Constance 1969:23–24). The tuberous roots were eaten raw or cooked, and when boiled, assumed a nonbitter flavor similar to that of a carrot. The raw tuber had an aromatic nutty taste (Palmer 1878:600–601; Havard 1895: 108–109).

Aboriginal Environment

The two basic questions one asks with respect to aboriginal California ecology are: what effect did environment have on the peoples and their cultures? and what effect did the people have on their environment? This does not differ from other ecological studies, particularly human ecology. In addition one hopes to be able to show the interaction between these two factors, to show the extent they are mutually supportive or destructive or, to use a currently fashionable phase, to specify an ecological system.

In dealing with extra-human environment it would have been possible to consider any number of elements in addition to vegetation, for example soils, climate, or faunal areas. However, these are either otiose or irrelevant for the following reasons. Factors such as climate and soils are important only insofar as they effect vegetation. It is not the case, as in the arctic, that temperatures impose of themselves certain modes of living; nor is there any place, outside a few parts of the desert, where water is unobtainable. The fauna, on the other hand, are nearly completely determinate once the vegetation is specified, since the animals are dependent on the vegetation. Predators are similarly dependent at one remove. The categories used here make up a classification much simplified from that of Wieslander and Jensen's (1946:6–7) soil-vegetation map and comprise the following types: Desert Shrub, Grassland, Woodland-Grass (or Parkland), Chaparral, Pine-Fir Forest, and Redwood Forest (fig. 3).

The Desert Shrub type of environment consists of sagebrush and creosote bush together with various grasses that appear only in years of good rainfull. While falling within the state boundaries of California, desert ecology belongs to the culture area of the Great Basin, volume 11.

Grassland in aboriginal times, before the introduction of the now dominant wild oat, was stocked "with various bunch grasses such as *Stipa pulchra, S. cernua, Poa scabrella,* and *Aristida divaricata*" (Munz and Keck 1959:17). It provided seed crops for the Indians in addition to grazing grounds for pronghorn antelope and for deer during parts of the year. This vegetation was found mainly in the central valley and was dominant there everywhere except on the banks of rivers and streams where there were gallery forests of oak, cottonwood, and willow. The gallery forests, not shown on figure 3 because of limitations of scale, were of great importance to the inhabitants of these areas.

The Oak Woodland-Grass area largely consists of a zone bordering grassland and at a higher elevation, about 1,000 to 4,000 feet. It is basically grassland with grasses the same as those lower down but with trees and brush scattered at varying intervals over the landscape. This was probably the most important California floral zone

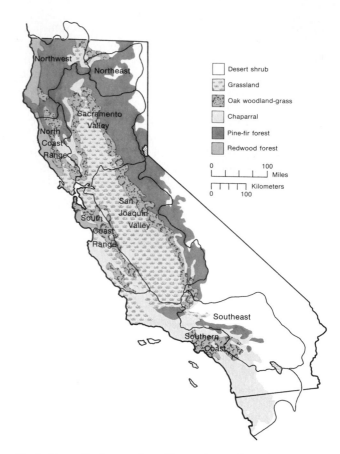

Fig. 3. Generalized vegetation with superimposed tribal culture areas.

for the Indians because it produced large quantities of acorns and grass seed and also because it provided both forage and browse for deer.

Woodlands differ in various parts of California. Some of the principal components as given by Munz and Keck (1959:16) are, for Northern Oak Woodland: Oregon oak, black oak, maul oak, interior live oak, and buckeye. This component is found from Napa County northward in the North Coast Range. Southern Oak Woodland contains: coast live oak, Engelmann oak, and black walnut (*Juglans californica*); it occurs in interior valleys from Los Angeles to the Mexican border. Foothill Woodland, consisting of blue oak, maul oak, coast live oak, interior live oak, valley oak, digger pine (*Pinus sabiniana*), and buckeye, occurs in the Sierra Nevada foothills and on the interior side of the Coast Range. These differences are important because the dominant oaks in the southern areas were ones whose acorns were not used or used only with great reluctance. This means that the foothills and northern areas were considerably richer in this all-important crop than was the south.

Chaparral in the Sierra Nevada is a thin strip of dense brush between the Woodland-Grass and the Pine-Fir Forest. For reasons of scale it is not shown on figure 3. In the Coast Ranges and south to the Mexican border it occurs in quite large areas. On north slopes, it is mixed chaparral with manzanita (*Arctostaphylos* sp.), scrub oaks, and ceanothus in addition to chamise (*Adenostoma* sp.). On south slopes it is dominated by chamise. Chaparral, when it is mature, is useless to man and to the animals on which he preys. The bushes become heavy and inedible to deer and in any case the growth gets so thick that it is impenetrable, hence only useful on the fringes. This zone is useful only when suitably managed by fire.

The Pine-Fir Forests are quite variable depending mainly on elevation, but in any case they seem to be uniform for the purposes of the Indians since they were not interested in timber quality. In the Sierra Nevada at about 3,000 to 6,000 feet is a zone dominated by ponderosa pine (*Pinus ponderosa*), incense cedar (*Calocedrus decurrens*), sugar pine (*P. lambertiana*), and black oak. Above 6,000 feet this gives way to a forest of red fir (*Abies magnifica*), white pine (*P. monticola*), and jeffrey pine (*P. jeffreyi*). On the inland side of the redwood belt from Cape Mendacino north up to an elevation of 4,500 feet the forest is dominated by douglas fir (*Pseudotsuga menziesii*), tanbark oak, and sugar pine. Other variations exist but for the most part they serve the Indians in similar ways. One exception is that where the sugar pine is present, pine nuts are available, sometimes in considerable quantities.

The Redwood Forest is of course dominated by the redwood but also has some douglas fir and tanbark oak. This differs from the pine-fir category in that it was much less open and therefore less accessible to humans and game animals.

Culture Areas

Northwest California

The peoples and culture of the northwest were the least Californian of any under consideration, being an extension of the Northwest Coast culture area (vol. 7). Environmentally the area differs from the remainder of the state in: having greater rainfall (up to 100 inches annually), being given over almost entirely to timberland (redwood or pine-fir) and consequently having relatively small acorn and game production, and having the best fish resources in California. The last two factors combined with their cultural heritage make these folk primarily fishermen rather than hunters or gatherers and concentrate their population almost exclusively along the major salmon streams. While their total population and overall density was rather low (4.25 people a square mile as against 6.02 for the North Coast Range), they cannot be said to be sparse in a normal sense, since they were very dense indeed along the streams. The effect of their ecology on technology is obvious, with high development of things such as fish spears, fish dams (see "Hupa, Chilula, Whilkut," fig. 2, this vol.), and the like. The

environmental effect on their population size seems rather less. The tribal or linguistic groups seem to top out at about 3,000 people, for reasons not entirely clear. Possibly the superabundance of some areas was more apparent than real. For example, the Yurok at the mouth of the Klamath had almost unlimited fish resources but failed to exploit them. If these had been fully exploited then the people upstream would have been deprived and probably would have initiated some action. This fact then effectively limited their fish resources.

So far as the social system of Northwest California it is difficult to discern any effect of the environment either directly or mediated through the demography as it evidently was in Central California. Society here may be characterized as individualistic, prudish, and given to litigation. The extreme crowding of the rivers may have had something to do with the last feature; for example, one was entitled to use any boat beached on the river bank in order to cross a stream but one was liable for the value of the boat if anything happened to it while in use. Incidents such as this must have had greater frequency where population was thicker. Beyond this, it is difficult to see any meaningful relation between environment and society or demography and society.

Northeast California

The northeast area also is not typical of California in general. Physiographically it is in the Cascade Mountains and in the Modoc Plateau, both areas being more typical of Oregon and Washington than of California. Second, it is all moderate to high elevation; no part of it was at or near sea level as is the case for all other areas of California. Finally, almost all territory was timberland, either pine and douglas fir or juniper. The exception is the one rather extensive patch shown on figure 3 as desert shrub. Actually this was part grassland and part sagebrush and was of great importance as a producer of the epos root and as habitat favorable to pronghorn antelope.

Open areas are important in the production of epos, which is heavy in carbohydrates but has up to 15 percent protein at certain times of the year (Yanovsky and Kingsbury 1938:661). Since this food is storable and comes in large quantities it is a genuine staple. Whether it surpasses the acorn in total caloric value per square mile is not known, but certainly oaks are scarce over most of this country and therefore this was relied on heavily.

This reliance on root crop as a staple by the people of Northeast California indicates their relationship with Plateau people to the north. Among the Klamath in particular the wokas (*Nuphar polysepalum*), a water lily harvested for its bulb, occupies a position analogous to the epos among the Achumawi and Atsugewi. Throughout the entire area the camass (*Camassia quamash*) is used for its root and among some groups was a staple food. It is at this point not possible to determine whether this root crop emphasis was more heavily influenced by culture or environment. It seems to be a fact, though, that there were no very good tree crops available, either acorns or pine nuts. Therefore one must conclude that environment was a major if not governing factor.

Animal food in this area must also have been important. Both deer and antelope were abundant and the Fall River valley was an intersection or confluence of two of the major north-south flyways of migratory waterfowl.

The population of this area is not known so it is difficult to speculate about the environmental effects on society as mediated by population size and density. It is clear from the archeology that the population was heavy along Pit River and possibly even more so in Fall River valley, where the large number of waterfowl gathered, but it is impossible to be specific about numbers. There seems to have been no lineage or other form of formally organized corporate kin group beyond the immediate family. For what it is worth this indicates a population level like that of the Northwest California Coast and also a comparable resource level.

North Coast Range

The North Coast Range is probably California's richest area environmentally for a non- or preagricultural population. One of the reasons for this is variety. Figure 3 shows that there are no large areas of any one vegetation type. In particular there are no large areas of timberland (redwood or pine-fir), grassland, or desert. The variegated pattern is even more marked than is shown on this simplified version of Weislander and Jensen (cf. Baumhoff 1963:map 4). The original shows innumerable tiny patches of woodland, grassland, and chaparral, some not more than a mile in diameter, scattered over the area. Therefore, in addition to large acreage of land highly productive of mammal and vegetable food the area also approaches a maximum of border mileage, that is, boundary mileage between two vegetation types. Modern range management indicates that a maximum of "edge," particularly in chaparral, is most productive for deer (cf. Biswell 1967), and it seems also to be the case for edible plants.

The second reason for the richness of the North Coast Range is abundance of rainfall. The South Coast Range shows a pattern of variable floral zones similar to that of the North Coast, but whereas the latter has rainfall of 30 to 50 inches per year the former has only 10 to 25 inches.

These factors combine, then, to make the North Coast Range extremely rich. These riches in turn produced what seems to be the most densely populated area of California. The population of the coast from Santa Barbara south is not known in any detail but evidently was also dense, although it was probably less dense than that of the North Coast.

The result of the heavy population was the formation of corporate unilineal kin groups. The argument on this point is that of Goldschmidt (1948) and runs along the

following lines. When the population is sparse and in particular when the population of the functioning socio-political group (in this case Kroeber's 1932a tribelet) is small then any given adult will know each of his fellow members as an individual and can deal with them on the basis of achieved status. At some point, when local population becomes dense and the tribelet population large, there will simply be too many people for this; then, status is ascribed at birth and the total population is categorized with respect to any given individual. Since ascription happens at birth, the categories are based on kinship and in this the most convenient initial division is between mother's kin and father's kin, which in turn forms the basis of corporate unilineal kin groups or lineages. These lineages existed for some groups but it is not known for all whether or not they were organized in this fashion. However, it is possible to test this question by looking at the kinship terminology as recorded by Gifford (1922). The most convenient thing to look at in this respect is the cross-cousin terminology and in particular for Crow and Omaha terms. That is, for Crow the mother's brother's child is merged down with one's own children while the father's sister's child is merged up with father's sister and just the reverse for Omaha. Crow terminology indicates strong matrilineality while Omaha indicates patrilineality (Gifford 1922:map 15). In the first place, all North Coast Range groups south of the Yuki (except the Kashaya Pomo) exhibit one or the other of these types. Outside the North Coast Range Omaha terms are found in both the San Joaquin and the Sacramento valleys. In the San Joaquin this may be explained by the fact that the bulk of the population was concentrated on the river or in the foothills. In the Sacramento these terms were used among the Wintuan speakers on the west side but not by the Maiduans on the east side. Data in the Sacramento Valley are insufficient to go further at this time.

Here in Central California is found the most far reaching effect of environment on native society. This effect on society is quite comparable to that of full-scale agriculture and should be treated as such.

Baumhoff (1963) has shown that the population of the North Coast Range may be expressed with considerable precision by the equation: population = 3.5 (acorn index) + 1.8 (game index) − 250, where the indices are basically functions of area. This means that the societal phenomena mentioned are in fact indirect results of environment. To put it another way, the particular social organization was essential in achieving an equilibrium given the interaction between the techno-environmental status and the demography.

Sacramento Valley

The Sacramento Valley territory has vast areas of both grassland and timberland in addition to fair quantities of variable woodland and chaparral in the foothills of the

Sierra and in the Coast Range. The variable land was most important in production of vegetable food and as deer habitat. The valley grassland was important for antelope, and along the Sacramento River and its principal tributaries there was a large gallery forest with many valley oaks, which were important acorn producers. The river and its tributaries also produced large quantities of salmon, apparently greater amounts than the Klamath. Thus this area, and also the San Joaquin, relied on the full range of staple foods available to any Californians.

Also to be considered for this area is the formation of unilineal kin groups. Gifford (1922:map 15) shows that Omaha cousin terminology is found among Wintuan speakers only, that is, it is confined to the west side of the valley. This does some damage to the notion that this terminology is associated with unilineal kin organization, in turn dependent on high population density and therefore rich and varied environment. The difficulty is that the west side of the valley seems much poorer than the east side. The only explanation is that the Wintuans lay partially in the North Coast Range, an area having an optimum environment. In addition, of Gifford's (1922:13) 10 informants, 9 lived in or near the foothills or high-producing part of their area, although where they came from originally is not known. In spite of these explanations and in spite of the fact that the aboriginal population of the Sacramento Valley is not known, this example is anomalous in terms of the hypothesis advanced above.

San Joaquin Valley

The San Joaquin Valley is environmentally very similar to the Sacramento except in two particulars. One of these is the relative dryness. The entire valley floor averages less than 10 inches of rain per year. The west side of the valley is particularly dry and therefore the vegetation extremely sparse. The other peculiarity is definitional, by including the Plains Miwok, who live in the delta of the Sacramento and San Joaquin rivers and could just as easily have been included in the Sacramento as the San Joaquin area. In any case it is clear that this delta was an enormously rich area. There were great quantities of oaks on the high ground within the delta and on its fringes, both antelope and tule elk were plentiful, and the amount of waterbirds and fish was probably as great as anywhere in California. These factors are evident in the territory itself and further reveal themselves in the archeology of the area (Cook and Heizer 1951).

A notable feature of the San Joaquin is the relationship between the environment and the population. Whereas the population on the Northwest California Coast is a function of fish resources, and that in the North Coast Range, of acorns and game, it seems clear that in the San Joaquin the equation: population $= 3$ (acorn index) $+ 2$ (game index) $+ 3$ (fish index) $- 210$ achieves a fair degree of accuracy (Baumhoff 1963:221). Although the

same is no doubt true of the Sacramento, there are no figures to demonstrate it. It will be seen that this is nearly the same equation used for the North Coast Range but with a fish component added. The richness of the fish resources in the area combined with a social or cultural decision produced this demographic result. The same equation or one very much like it could be applied to the Sacramento Valley. Baumhoff (1963:map 7) has calculated population densities on this basis.

South Coast Range

If one simply maps the South Coast Range then one might believe that the situation there is similar to that of the North Coast Range because the vegetation shows a similar pattern of variation. Unfortunately for the Costanoans and Salinans this is not the case, for at least two reasons. One reason is that rainfall there is much less than it is in the north. This means that woodland there for the most part and at lower elevation is what Munz and Keck (1959:16) call Southern Oak Woodland—areas dominated by coast live oak and Engelmann oak. The nuts of these trees are much inferior to those of the North Coast and Foothill zones, particularly those of the black oak, the blue oak, and the valley oak. They were inferior both in native preference and in terms of production. Therefore the acorn resource is poor; to some extent this is probably also true of subsidiary seed products. Also related to lack of rainfall is a scarcity of good live streams that in other places provide both anadromous and freshwater fishing.

The second reason for their poverty was that the sea was not readily accessible. On most of the coast here there are extremely high bluffs rising immediately from the sea; therefore, most shellfish-gathering spots are difficult and time consuming to get to. This contrasts sharply with the coast north of San Francisco where many streams flowing into the sea provide coves and inlets ideal for marine life. It also contrasts with the coast from Point Conception south where there are again excellent fishing grounds off wide beaches in shallow water. These contrasts are shown archeologically by the scarcity of shellmounds on the South Coast Range whereas they are (or were) large and abundant in the other two areas.

For these reasons, if not others as well, the population of the South Coast Range must have been much smaller than that of the North Coast Range. Early travelers such as Gaspar de Portolá and Francisco Palóu comment on this, although since they are comparing the area to Santa Barbara they may have taken a somewhat pessimistic view. Compare the relative density estimates made by Kroeber (1939a:map 19) with those made by Baumhoff (1963:map 7). Kroeber puts the Salinan at third on a scale of five or less than one person per square mile and the Costanoan second on that scale of five at four persons per square mile (Baumhoff 1963:map 7). Both Kroeber and Baumhoff have probably overestimated the relative densities. Except for San Francisco Bay and Monterey Bay, the population must have been extremely sparse, say one per square mile over the entire area if Kroeber's absolute figures are right and 2.5 per square mile if Cook's (1957) and Baumhoff's are right.

In these demographic circumstances then one would expect to find minimal societal accommodation of the form E-P-S, or Environment affects Population with consequent effect upon Society. On the other hand, there is no negative effect due to excessively scarce goods as in the desert (cf. J.H. Steward 1938). In fact, this minimal societal accommodation is a point of pure inference since information on societal forms or even kinship terminology is either very poor or totally lacking.

Southern Coast

In the Southern Coast area are included all coastal groups from the Chumash south to the Tipai. This makes sense from an environmental standpoint but is rather more ambiguous culturally. Kroeber (1939a) included the entire area as a part of the greater Southwest. From a subsistence standpoint the people here were strictly Californian, particularly in having a fundamental reliance on acorns. Another contradiction is that Kroeber puts the Diegueño (Ipai-Tipai) in the Peninsular California subarea and the groups north of that in the Southern California subarea where Baumhoff kept them all together. From the point of view of ecology they probably should be split into two or three groups with the Takic speakers distinguished from Chumash and Ipai-Tipai. This should be done because the two Hokan groups had villages immediately on the beach wherever possible while the Takic-speaking villages were about 10 miles back from the water, thus placing themselves in quite different environmental circumstances. This distinction has not been shown because the map scale used here does not reveal such fine divisions.

The reduced rainfall noted for the South Coast Range becomes, if anything, even more marked from Santa Barbara south to the Mexican border. The woodland here is of the Southern Oak Woodland type with coast live oak and Engelmann oak dominant over most areas. These were considered quite undesirable, and great effort was expanded to harvest the black oak, which grew at 3,000 or 4,000 feet and above. Thus the acorn supply was somewhat smaller than in many parts of California, perhaps comparable to that of the South Coast Range. However, this feature of the environment was offset by the comparative riches of the marine environment, which consisted of sea mammals (mostly sea otters and seals), fish (tunas, bonito, and yellowtail), and shellfish (abalone, Pismo clam, and oysters). The sea mammals and pelagic fish were most common offshore from the Chumash and Gabrielino while the shellfish, as evidenced by the archeological sites, were abundant all along this coast. The

volume of sea creatures available during aboriginal times seems to have been of the same order of magnitude of that of the Northwest California Coast.

The extreme richness of marine resources was evidently responsible for the large coastal population reported in early accounts both as to number and size of villages. This meant there was a very dense population along the coast, but to judge from the archeology it was much thinner inland (see Brown 1967:map 1). Kroeber (1939a) averaged this out to suggest a density second from highest on his scale (about 1.5 per square mile). Translating this by the factor that Cook (1955, 1956) and Baumhoff (1963) found yields about five persons per square mile or a total of almost 78,000 (as against Kroeber's 23,000). To judge from the archeological sites the larger figure is entirely possible. Cook and Heizer (1965:21) suggest a figure of 18,000 to 22,000 for mainland Chumash alone, and Brown (1967:80) suggests that this may be very reasonable. Both these studies were done with considerable data and sophistication so they are probably accurate.

If the figure of five persons per square mile is correct, then the demographic effects upon society might be expected to be less than in the North Coast Range. The fundamental organization seems to have been in local autonomous groups, like Kroeber's tribelets (Strong 1929:324). Among the Takic speakers the governing group was apparently the patrilineage. Unfortunately the Chumash and Ipai-Tipai are not sufficiently known to make a judgment of this kind, but probably there was something similar in those cases as well. To judge by what is known from the kinship terminology the lineage organization was not so well developed as in the north; for example, cross-cousins were either called by a single term or simply distinguished according to sex. This may be an indication of a density of population lower than that of the Central California groups mentioned previously.

Aboriginal Effect on Environment

What was the effect of aboriginal Californians upon their surroundings? In California the aboriginal population had considerable effect on the landscape, almost entirely by means of fire, as explained by the insightful analysis of H.T. Lewis (1973). The following summary of the fire ecology of grassland, woodland, chaparral, and coniferous forest relies heavily on his work.

Fire was used in the grasslands of the central valley but it is difficult to determine the extent of its use. The reasons for its use were apparently both to control the growth of brush and promote the growth of seed-producing grasses and also to facilitate hunting.

What evidence there is indicates that woodland areas of the various groups were burned (annually?) to control brush and promote growth of seed-producing plants valuable from a subsistence standpoint. Whether fire driving of game was also important is not clear, but the practice is said to have been almost universal in California (Driver and Massey 1957:188). The usual time for burning was "after the seed harvest," which may have been any time from July to October depending on the crop of particular interest.

In this respect it is interesting to note that prior to 1900 the woodland areas were relatively open. This was due to Indian burning in aboriginal times and to burning by White settlers in the nineteenth century. After 1900, when burning was prohibited, brush became much thicker in these areas until after World War II, when controlled burning was used to bring back the open conditions known previously. If climatic conditions were the same prior to the occupation of these areas by the Indians (or before the advent of their customary burning), then a quite different set of circumstances would obtain. It is the case that natural fire is quite rare in this sort of vegetation since most lightning occurs higher in the mountains. Under those conditions the brush would have gotten very thick and when fires did start it would have been devastating to the oaks. The Indian practice then, whenever it started, would have contributed to a dynamic equilibrium with respect to trees, grasses, and shrubs that resulted in open parkland productive of acorns, grass seeds, and winter feed for deer and other grazers.

In the chaparral belt there is a situation in which problems of fire ecology are most complex. According to Sweeney (1956:143):

In the Chaparral regions of California, fires are frequent and periodically reburn the same areas. Many species of plants and numerous individuals not previously evident "suddenly" appear following fire. . . . Many such herbaceous plants are so characteristic of burned areas in the chaparral that they are often referred to as "burn" species. Some species occur in abundance only the first season following fires and are rarely encountered in abundance on open sites adjacent to the burns. Other species have been observed to persist in varying numbers and for varying periods of time on older burns.

The result of regular fires in chaparral is to increase the production of both shrubs and herbaceous plants. When chaparral is mature (that is, when there is no fire over long periods) it does little more than maintain the shrub growth and is little benefit to either man or the animals he hunts. In an experiment, "an area of prescribed-burned chamise chaparral was compared with a similar unburned area as a control. Counts of deer in the burned area showed a summer population density of about 98 per square mile after the initial burning treatment. This rose to 131 in the second year and dropped to 84 in the fifth and sixth years. In the dense, untreated brush the summer density was only 30 per square mile" (Biswell 1967:81).

H.T. Lewis (1973) points out that a balance in the chaparral is achieved by means of fire. If it is allowed to become "mature" it becomes unbalanced and dangerously unstable because when a fire does finally occur it is catastrophic rather than helpful. Thus chaparral is more than simply adapted to fire; it is part of the adaptation of California's brushlands.

From the standpoint of range management, the evidence indicates that the aboriginal practices were near optimum. The two elements of such management are burning in open areas (spot burning) within brush stands and burning both fall and spring. The first element, spot burning, is desirable because it maximizes the amount of edge vegetation (producing superior browse for deer) and also provides many areas of grass and herbaceous plants useful to both humans and game animals. Burning both fall and spring is also desirable. As Biswell (1967:81) explains:

After spring new sprouts [on bushes] appear in three or four weeks and supply highly protein-rich browse for deer during dry summer months. However, after burns made in April, new seedlings do not appear until the next year, and by that time seedbed conditions are not favorable to them. The greatest number of new seedlings come in the spring after fall burning. Apparently spring burning favors sprouting shrubs over nonsprouting species. Since some of the better shrubs are nonsprouting species, perhaps a combination of spring and fall burning is preferable to burning only in the spring.

On both points H.T. Lewis (1973) documents very convincingly, considering the amount of ethnographic information available, that both these practices were followed in aboriginal California. With respect to seasonality there is more evidence for fall burning than spring burning. This is easy to understand, because the growth promoted by fall burning would largely be of plants important directly to the Indians as food, rather than those important indirectly as deer fodder. It is important to note that the Indians knew why they were burning and not simply doing it blindly or superstitiously. A Karok informant stated that "the wild rice [grass] plants also they burn, so that the wild rice will grow up good" (Harrington 1932a:64). This sort of statement is found repeatedly concerning grassland, woodland, and chaparral.

The fire ecology in the pine-fir forest of the Sierra Nevada is to be distinguished from that of the North Coast Range, the latter bordering for the most part on redwood forest. The redwood forest is not much subject to natural fires. For one thing redwood itself does not burn easily; second, redwood is found in areas of high rainfall and generally damp climate. Finally, the North Coast Range, where most redwood forest is found, is not much subject to lightning. For these reasons the heavy forest was burned rarely if at all. On the other hand, there existed within the forest clearings of various sizes called prairies or bald hills that were burned regularly in order to prevent encroachment by the forest and to promote growth valuable to man and his game animals. So far as it is possible to judge from the ethnographic literature the same pattern prevailed in the pine-fir forest on the inland side of the redwoods. It is interesting to note two motives for burning these clearings that were perhaps stronger than the range management effects—to clear and fertilize patches for the sowing of tobacco and to promote the growth of materials used in making baskets.

For the pine-fir forest in the eastern part of the state the situation was different. The timber burned more easily, the summer was drier and longer, and more frequent lightning must have made fire moderately frequent even before man came there. The effect of the Indians was simply to make these fires even more frequent and at times of the year other than summer when lightning fires were most common. The motives for aboriginal burning are as a device for hunting animals and to promote the growth of wild seed crops. A major effect of the burning was to keep the brush, litter, and seedlings cleared from the undergrowth with the result that the forest was much more open than it otherwise would have been. In the first part of the twentieth century where man-made fire was forbidden and lightning fires were contained the undergrowth became extremely dense so that when a fire got a good start it generated enough heat to go to the top of the timber resulting in a crown fire with devastating effects. Hence the result of the natural and Indian management of this area was the preservation of what has turned out to be economically valuable timber in spite of the fact that there was no motivation in this direction.

Post-Pleistocene Archeology, 9000 to 2000 B.C.

WILLIAM J. WALLACE

In the long interval between 9000 and 2000 B.C. the pre-historic societies of California underwent slow but fundamental changes in their food-getting habits. An initial hunting-based mode of existence was replaced by one emphasizing seed collecting, and this in turn gave way to a variety of subsistence specializations, reflecting improved adjustment to local environments. Modifications in technical culture, settlement patterns, and general life-styles accompanied the economic shifts. Certain ramifications of these alterations and the factors that touched them off remain obscure, for the archeological data are still quite scanty and by no means unequivocal.

Period I: Hunting

The widespread scattered presence of hunting communities in California is attested by the finding of projectile points and other stone implements adapted to the chase at ancient campsites in the northern, central, and southern sections of the state and near its eastern edge. The nature of the hunters' quarry remains conjectural, for animal bones of any kind are scarce. Most probably they stalked and killed large mammals of species still alive. Fossilized bones of extinct animals have been recovered, but they cannot be firmly associated with the artifacts. The size and weight of the missile tips suggest that the weapon was the dart, propelled by a throwing stick. Big-game hunting probably did not constitute the sole economic pursuit. The region's ancient inhabitants must have combined this activity with the taking of lesser mammals and waterfowl as well as with some fishing and collecting of shellfish and vegetal foods. Grinding implements for processing plant foods were, if not unknown, extremely uncommon, strongly suggesting that the rich wild-plant resources were not heavily exploited.

Since very little has been found other than the equipment used in the hunt and for the preparation of the meat and hides of the slain animals, few details concerning the life of these early people are known. Apparently their dwellings were such as to leave few traces in the ground. Only open-air settlements have been recognized though they may occasionally have resorted to shelter beneath rock overhangs or in caves. The absence of deep refuse deposits at the dwelling places points to temporary or brief recurrent occupancy. Sociopolitical inferences are hazardous, but the economics of a simple

hunting life must have demanded groups of limited size. Perhaps a few families related by kinship hunted and traveled together. As yet no skeletal remains of the hunters themselves have been certainly identified; therefore, nothing can be said regarding their physical type or mortuary practices.

Two separate hunting traditions, distinguishable primarily on the basis of their typical projectile points, seem to have existed at least in part concurrently and to have overlapped in space. The first is characterized by fluted points that closely resemble the Clovis-Folsom category; leaf-shaped and shouldered forms without longitudinal grooves on their faces mark the second.

Fluted missile tips have been found at two major sites—Borax Lake at the eastern edge of Clear Lake in the coastal ranges of north-central California and Tulare Lake in the southern San Joaquin valley (fig. 1). The Borax Lake settlement lies in a shallow basin that contains the remnant of a lake formed during a time of heavier rainfall. Fifteen fluted points, which seem more in the style of the older Clovis form rather than Folsom (fig. 2), were recovered from its surface and five others were obtained through digging (M.R. Harrington 1948:63-81). Borax Lake also produced a wide array of different projectile types and various other stone articles. The original excavator concluded that the locality had been camped upon by successive parties of hunter-gatherers, attracted by nearby obsidian quarries (M.R. Harrington 1948:117).

The proper cultural and temporal position of Borax Lake has never been agreed upon. A restudy, undertaken in an effort to accurately determine the ancientness of the site, led to the conclusion that neither the geological nor the typological evidence is inconsistent with an antiquity up to 12,000 years for the original occupation (Meighan and Haynes 1970). Obsidian hydration datings give added support to the reasonableness of such an age. The only classes of artifacts regarded as typical of the first period of habitation comprise fluted points and chipped-stone crescents. The crescents, similar to specimens found in early contexts in several parts of western North America, may have functioned as transverse projectile points for stunning waterfowl.

Thirteen complete and 17 fragmentary Clovislike specimens (fig. 3) were collected from the surface of the south shore of Tulare Lake in an area measuring one

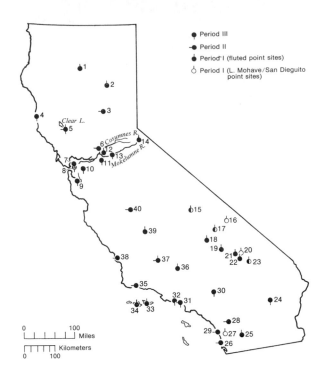

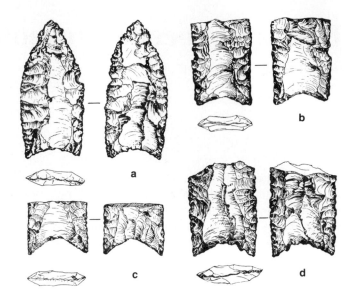

Harrington 1948: a, fig. 21; b, fig. 23; c, pl. XIVc; d, pl. XVa.

Fig. 2. Borax Lake Fluted points of obsidian. Length of a, about 6.8 cm.

Fig. 1. Archeological sites. 1, Samuel Cave; 2, Big Meadow; 3, Mesilla; 4, Mendocino; 5, Borax Lake; 6, Arcade Cr.; 7, Ellis Landing Shellmound; 8, West Berkeley Shellmound; 9, University Village; 10, Stone Valley; 11, Bear Cr.; 12, Tracy Lake; 13, Camanche Res.; 14, Ebbetts Pass; 15, Owens Valley; 16, Death Valley; 17, Panamint Valley; 18, China Lake; 19, Pilot Knob Valley; 20, North Central San Bernardino Co.; 21, Tiefort Basin; 22, Fossil Spring; 23, Lake Mohave; 24, Pinto Basin; 25, Cuyamaca Mts.; 26, San Diego Co. Coast (La Jolla); 27, San Dieguito R.; 28, Pauma Valley; 29, Agua Hedionda Lagoon; 30, Cajon Pass; 31, Topanga Canyon; 32, Zuma Cr.; 33, Christy's Beach; 34, Arlington Canyon (Early Dune Dweller); 35, Santa Barbara Co. Coast (Oak Grove); 36, Tehachapi Mts.; 37, Buena Vista Lake; 38, Diablo Canyon; 39, Tulare Lake; 40, Tranquillity.

The close resemblance of the specimens to Clovis-Folsom probably means that California formed a peripheral outpost of the Great Plains Fluted Point tradition. Apparently, makers of the distinctive dart or spear points established themselves in the Great Basin with a few parties pushing farther west in search of new hunting grounds. A real problem hinges upon the age of the California examples: whether they extend as far back in time as Clovis (11,000–11,500 years ago) or Folsom (10,000–11,000) is not known. None has been found in direct association with remains of extinct fauna or in a stratigraphic-geologic context permitting precise dating.

and one-half miles long and one-half mile wide (Riddell and Olsen 1969). A wide range of other kinds of stone implements was also present, with crescents of several forms making up a sizable percentage of the surface materials. Like Borax Lake, the locality appears to contain several distinct artifact assemblages mixed together. Evidently it was occupied at various times over a long span of years. Mineralized bones of several extinct species of large mammals (horse, bison, sloth, and possibly elephant) were picked up along the Tulare lakeshore.

Stray projectile points with channels formed on one or both faces have turned up at a number of places in California (Davis and Shutler 1969; Glennan 1971). The majority come from the state's eastern fringe with a few additional examples from the southern, central, and northern sections (fig. 1). A good deal of size and shape diversity characterizes these sporadic surface finds.

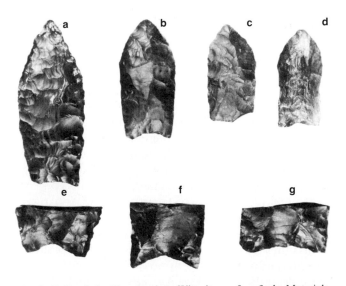

Fig. 3. Tulare Lake Fluted points, Witt site, surface finds. Materials are: a–c, f–g, chert; d, translucent silicate; e, obsidian. Length of a, 5.3 cm. Photograph by Edith Wallace, 1952.

26

Quite possibly they represent poorer and later derivatives of the Plains fluting technique.

Leaf-shaped and shouldered points of several kinds have been found at other sites once occupied by ancient hunters. Two localities—Lake Mohave near the center of the Majave Desert in San Bernardino County and the San Dieguito River in western San Diego County—are of principal interest in connection with these materials.

Lake Mohave was an immense body of fresh water that formed during the Pleistocene and maintained a high level in early Postglacial times when streams continued to empty into it. Conditions around the lake must have been ideal for aboriginal habitation and small groups made their home on its margins. Several thousand stone tools, almost all fashioned by chipping, have been recovered from the deserted encampments (Campbell et al. 1937). Typical are projectile points with long tapering stems, weak shoulders, and short blades. Less distinctive are more definitely shouldered and leaf-shaped forms. Other stonework includes knife blades, crescents (fig. 4), flake scrapers, rude perforators, chop-

Southwest Mus., Los Angeles.
Fig. 4. Lake Mohave chipped stone crescents (Campbell et al. 1937:pl. 38).

pers, and scraper planes. Seed-grinding implements are noticeably scarce with two pecked cobbles, presumably employed as mullers, and a possible milling stone making up the total.

Two fragments of fossilized bone, too small for certain identification, constitute the only potential vestiges of food. In addition to hunting, the Lake Mohave people may have done some fishing, but no devices attributable to this pursuit have been found. The near absence of implements suited for processing plant foods suggests that this source of nutriment was neglected.

The age of the lake and the correlations between its stands and the cultural remains have long been in dispute. Present opinion seems to favor human occupation of the lakeshore at the time when the ancient body of water had reached its maximum size and stood at its highest level. This must, of course, have been during a cycle of much moister climate, such as prevailed during the closing phase of the last deglaciation. Freshwater mussel shells, possibly deposited when the lake was slowly falling, have been radiocarbon-dated 7690 ± 240

B.C. and 8050 ± 300 B.C. Some of the artifacts may be of comparable age.

A very similar assemblage has been unearthed in the banks of the San Dieguito River in western San Diego County (Warren and True 1960-1961; Warren 1966). Projectile points, present in small number, are leaf-shaped or short-bladed with weak shoulders. Among the other chipped-stone objects occur knives, crescents, flake scrapers, and engraving tools. Along with these come the usual rough-and-ready choppers and hammers. Seed-grinding devices are absent. Carbon-14 analyses of charcoal and carbonaceous earth demonstrate that the San Dieguito occupation began before 7080 ± 350 B.C. and persisted until some time between 6540 ± 400 B.C. and 5670 ± 380 B.C. (Warren 1968:2).

Close correspondences between the Lake Mohave and San Dieguito assemblages betray their common ancestry. In all probability they represent regional variants of an early hunting tradition that prevailed over a wide area in southern California, with a known distribution from coastal San Diego County north and east into the Mojave Desert and northward as far as Death, Panamint, and Owens valleys (fig. 1). The tradition may have had its origin in an old cultural stratum present over a large part of western North America (Warren and True 1960-1961:278). If so, it came to California from the north via the Great Basin.

Clues to early hunting populations that cannot be definitely linked to either the Fluted Point or Lake Mohave-San Dieguito tradition have come to light at two sites, both in the San Joaquin valley. Excavation into a deeply buried occupational layer at the southern shoreline of Buena Vista Lake, located near the upper end of the valley, resulted in the recovery of 14 recognizable artifacts (Fredrickson and Grossman 1966; Grossman 1968). Noteworthy are three crescents and a ground-stone engaging hook for a dart-thrower. Two pieces of crudely made missile tips appear to be from leaf-shaped specimens. That the ancient inhabitants of Buena Vista Lake followed an unspecialized hunting-collecting mode of subsistence is shown by the miscellaneous food remains, consisting of deer, bird, fish, and turtle bones, and freshwater clam shells. Three carbon-14 determinations yielded dates falling between 6250 and 5650 B.C.

Farther north near Tranquillity in Fresno County, highly mineralized human skeletons and artifacts were discovered in seeming association with remains of extinct camel, bison, and horse (Hewes 1946). The Tranquillity locality, clearly inhabited for a long time, yielded a variety of stone articles as well as a few made of bone and shell. A diverse series of heavy missile tips is included. The human skeletons show a degree of fossilization equal to that of the Pleistocene animals (Angel 1966:16); and close similarity in fluorine, carbon, nitrogen, and water content between the two argues for their contemporaneity (Heizer and Cook 1952). A second test for nitrogen and fluorine agrees with the earlier one but a radiocarbon age of 2550 ± 60 years on bone collagen throws doubt on the connection of man and extinct fauna (Berger et al. 1971:47–48).

Period II: Food Collecting

A changeover from hunting to the collection of seed foods is clearly reflected in the archeological record for the period between 6000 and 3000 B.C. The importance of seeds in the diet of the prehistoric peoples can be seen in the numbers of food-grinding implements present at their settlements.

Food-collecting cultures, grouped together in a Milling Stone Horizon (Wallace 1954), flourished in the southern California coastal strip from San Luis Obispo County at the north to San Diego County on the south. Several geographical variants can be recognized: Oak Grove in the Santa Barbara area; Topanga in the Los Angeles-Santa Monica Mountains region; and La Jolla in San Diego County (Kowta 1969:36). Many Milling Stone sites have been discovered and a fair number excavated. The earliest radiocarbon dates for the Santa Barbara and San Diego districts range around 5500 B.C. A much older determination (about 7300 B.C.) has been made for an Oak Grove occupation at Diablo Canyon in San Luis Obispo County (Greenwood 1972).

That much, if not most, of the Milling Stone Horizon peoples' food came from the harvesting of wild seeds and other edible plant parts is demonstrated by the plentiful milling stones and mullers. Some hunting was always carried on, for a few projectile points and animal bones occur in the occupational debris. The virtual absence of marine shell and fish and sea-mammal bones in the refuse of certain village sites suggests that the earlier coast dwellers had not yet realized the full possibilities of ocean resources. They soon acquired a taste for sea foods, however.

A lack of variety characterizes the artifact assemblages. Heavy, deep-basined mills and handstones predominate (figs. 5, 6). The rare projectile points are typically heavy, indicating continued employment of darts and throwing sticks. Crude service tools fashioned from cores or thick flakes commonly occur. Bone and shell items are scarce. Polished stone disks, some with notched edges ("cogstones"), and simple charmstones are occasionally found.

An increased size and stability of settlement is evident, for the dwelling places consist of middens of considerable extent and depth. Disposal of the dead was accomplished in several ways with some communities following more than one practice. Flexed burials, extended burials, and reburials have been unearthed. Often rocks or milling stones lie heaped up over the bodies (fig. 7). Grave goods are never elaborate or abundant. Shell beads and mills represent the most common accompaniments.

Fig. 5. Milling stone, Little Sycamore site, Ventura Co. Photograph by Edith Wallace, 1952.

The closely comparable makeup of the Milling Stone manifestations points to a common cultural ancestry. As to their origin, there are two possibilities: (1) they developed locally from a preceding hunting tradition; or (2) they resulted from the spread seaward of interior food-collecting communities. Actually both explanations may prove useful, according to the particular geographic area involved. A transition from the San Dieguito hunting tradition to the food-gathering La Jolla has been detected in materials from an Agua Hedionda Lagoon site in western San Diego County (Moriarty 1967), and the Pauma complex distributed throughout the northeastern part of the county (True 1958) seems to combine elements of both. Migrations of inland food-collectors may well have occurred. Seed gathering has a long history in the Great Basin although no such subsistence pattern on an early time level has yet been discovered in the now-arid interior of southern California. Correspondence between the earliest Oak Grove and La Jolla radiocarbon dates and the estimated beginning of the Altithermal, an epoch marked by gradual warming and drying of the climate and the disappearance of inland lakes, may prove more than a coincidence. As climatic conditions worsened and the interior became less habitable, its inhabitants may have moved westward. A thinning of the inland population evidently did take place at about this time for no cultural remains have been found that clearly demonstrate that human habitation continued during the prolonged drought.

Outside southern California seed collecting is less well documented. This mode of subsistence has not manifested itself on the seacoast north of San Luis Obispo County but its apparent absence may be due to deficiencies in the archeological record. Very few investigations have been carried on in the coastal district from San Luis Obispo County to San Francisco Bay and the distribution may be pushed farther north as more fieldwork is done in the area.

A simple seed-gathering pattern is represented in the southern San Joaquin valley. The remains disclosed in

Fig. 6. Handstones, Little Sycamore site, Ventura Co. Length of stone on left, 12.6 cm. Photograph by Edith Wallace, 1952.

the lowest level at two Buena Vista Lake sites seem to be those of food-collecting communities (Wedel 1941: 103-104, 136, 153-154). Virtually no artifacts save mullers and mealing slabs were present. The nature of the lakeshore dwellers' weapons, utensils, and ornaments remains conjectural. They buried their dead in a fully extended position in shallow graves. At a neighboring locality, handstones, mills, and flake scrapers occurred in a stratum separated by 40 centimeters of sterile soil from an overlying one containing later cultural materials (Fredrickson 1965). Collections from Tranquillity include numerous mullers but only two fragmentary milling stones (Hewes 1946:214).

Fig. 7. Cairn of milling stones, Little Sycamore Site, Ventura Co. Photograph by Edith Wallace, 1952.

To date, evidences of food collectors have been encountered at only one site in the Sacramento valley. Erosion of the banks of Arcade Creek, a small stream just north of Sacramento, revealed an artifact-bearing layer under nine feet of soil (Curtice 1961:20-25). Of the 75 artifacts collected (excluding cores and flakes), 35 percent are handstones. Mills are represented by one whole and three broken specimens. Other food-processing devices consist of a fragmentary mortar and two pestles.

The two projectile points are large and stemmed. Flaked cobble choppers and hammerstones make up most of the remainder of the implements. It can be reasoned that additional settlements of this kind lie deeply buried beneath river-deposited alluvium, for the Sacramento valley has been subjected to periodic flooding and consequent sedimentation over the centuries.

Traces of food gatherers have been noted in the western foothills of the Sierra Nevada near Oroville in the Feather River country. Handstones and mills number among the diagnostics of the Mesilla complex, which represents the earliest and least-known habitation in the area (Olsen and Riddell 1963:52; Ritter 1970:172). Heavy stemmed and side-notched missile tips occur, and use of the dart-thrower is proved by the finding of a stone engaging hook and two fragmentary weights (Olsen and Riddell 1963:32). Bone pins and spatulae, olivella shell beads, and shaped pestles and bowl mortars are also present. Burials attributed to the Mesilla complex lay flexed on their sides, occasionally covered with milling stone or rock cairns. The subsistence pattern is judged to have been seasonal exploitation of local food resources, particularly hard seeds (Ritter 1970:180). A scarcity of animal bones in the village refuse indicates only limited hunting. Utilization of the river resources seems likely. Mesilla's temporal span is not known but a reasonable inference is that its beginnings go back beyond 3000 B.C.

To the west, cultural remains of peoples who foraged for a living have been discovered in the northern Coast Range. The second assemblage at Borax Lake, which encompasses the major part of the site occupation, includes handstones and mills, as well as square-stemmed points, and coarse single-face blades (Meighan and Haynes 1970:1220). This assemblage, which probably follows a break in habitation, has an apparent age of 6,000 to 8,000 years. Similar materials extend through the north Coast Range (Meighan 1955) and adjoining region to the northeast (Frederickson 1974:42-44).

Sufficient evidence has been accumulated to demonstrate that food collectors had established themselves over a wide area in central and northern California. The artifacts from their campsites are scanty and unspectacular with mullers and mills dominating. Dating these materials is difficult and inconclusive. Further, it is not clear whether a relationship exists between these food-gathering and seed-grinding manifestations and those of the southern coast. The major uniting criteria—the possession of milling stones and handstones and an economy relying upon plant foods—are generalized traits. It will be necessary to detect additional common elements of a more specific nature before a convincing case can be made for historical linkage. A few do exist. Charmstones from Borax Lake closely resemble those from several Milling Stone Horizon sites and the custom of placing the dead in the grave under cairns of mills or rocks is shared by the Mesilla complex with the south. The recovery of analogous materials in the intervening districts would, naturally, strengthen the argument for a connection.

Period III: Diversified Subsistence

After about 3000 B.C. broad changes begin to become evident in the prehistoric cultures, with a definite trend toward adjustment to the region's various natural environments. Everywhere increased subsistence efficiency in the form of wider exploitation of available food resources can be seen.

The transition toward a more diversified economy came slowly to the southern California coast. In the San Diego region the La Jolla variant of the Milling Stone Horizon persisted with few alterations. Technological changes are barely perceptible. Projectile points occur more regularly but are still quite rare; mortars and pestles appear but are few in number (Warren 1968:3). A short-lived intrusive culture may have been assimilated.

Conservatism also marked the Los Angeles-Santa Monica Mountain district. Here too the native peoples adhered to the older Milling Stone pattern. The Zuma Creek site at Point Dume (Peck 1955), dated at 3000 ± 200 B.C., is fairly representative. The disproportionate number of handstones and milling stones leaves little doubt that Zuma Creek inhabitants gathered and processed large amounts of plant foods. But they also collected quantities of mussels, abalones, and other shellfish. Hunting and fishing formed only a minor part of their food-getting activities. The artifact assemblage looks, detail for detail, much like that of earlier times. Of comparable age are Phase 2 materials of the Topanga culture, confined to the upper 18 inches of the archeological deposit at the Tank site, located four miles inland from the ocean. They disclose no major shift in subsistence, wild plant foods evidently remaining the primary source of nutriment. A few changes are noticeable in the implements employed. The mortar and pestle come into use but are not abundant, and missile tips become smaller and increase in frequency (Treganza and Bierman 1958:72; K.L. Johnson 1966:19).

On the Santa Barbara coast, a new, apparently intrusive, Hunting culture makes its appearance (Rogers 1929:356-366; Harrison and Harrison 1966). It exhibits a subsistence emphasis distinct from that of the preceding Oak Grove. Faunal collections reveal that the Hunting people gained their food from both land and sea. Shellfish, fish, sea mammals, and large and small land mammals were procured. Vegetable foods must have added an important element to the diet because implements for processing them are plentiful. Typical artifacts comprise large notched, stemmed, and leaf-shaped projectile points (fig. 8) and several kinds of knife blades.

Santa Barbara Mus. of Nat. Hist., Calif.
Fig. 8. Santa Barbara Hunting culture projectile points. Variations in notch placement, form of blade, and the characteristics of the basal edge can be observed. Point on right is black obsidian, about 3 cm in length (Harrison and Harrison 1966:fig. 3).

Mortars and pestles (figs. 9, 10) match milling stones and mullers in frequency. The dead were interred in a flexed posture, not uncommonly under cairns.

Three radiocarbon determinations demonstrate that the Hunting culture became established in the Santa Barbara region by 3000 B.C. Two occupational phases, the second more sea-oriented, have been recognized with contemporaneity between the earliest of the two and terminal Oak Grove assumed (Harrison and Harrison 1966:64). The appearance of the Hunting culture on the Santa Barbara coast is attributed to migration. Since the artifacts closely parallel those found farther east in Pinto Basin and elsewhere, movement of an inland hunting-gathering population to the Pacific shore seems a logical conclusion. Ecological adaptation would not have proved too difficult for a people with well-developed hunting and collecting techniques and technology. An alternative view of a migration southward from Alaska by means of coastal navigation (Harrison and Harrison 1966:68) finds no support in the archeological record.

Humans had made their way to several of the Channel Islands off southern California by at least 3000 B.C., and there are some radiocarbon dates in excess of 10,000 years. Serviceable boats and some seafaring ability would, of course, have been needed to colonize the islands, 10 to 70 miles offshore. The ocean waters had to furnish practically all the islanders' sustenance, for the

Fig. 9. Santa Barbara Hunting culture mortars. The hole in the bottom specimen was punched through from the inside. Interior horizontal diameter of top specimen, 15.3 cm (Harrison and Harrison 1966:fig. 8).

Fig. 10. Santa Barbara Hunting culture pestles, site SBa-53. The long pestles generally exhibit use on both ends. On the short pestle second from right, the two broad surfaces are ground in the same manner as a muller and may have served this purpose. The far right short pestle is more rectangular; all sides are ground nearly flat. Both short pestles show usage on both ends. Length of pestle at far left, 17.5 cm (Harrison and Harrison 1966: fig. 9).

windswept, dry, and rocky terrain supports only a sparse vegetation and land fauna.

The archeological remains bear witness to a maritime economy from the beginning. On Santa Rosa, Early Dune Dweller middens, dated by the radiocarbon method between 5500 and 4800 B.C., contain a limited amount of fish and sea-mammal bones but quantities of waste shell, preeminently red abalone (Orr 1968:96-99, 114-130). No mortars or pestles or grinding implements of any kind are so far known. Very few stone artifacts occur; and bone articles, though well made, are scarce. Shell ornaments, the majority fashioned from olivella, are few in number. The dead were interred among the

sand dunes in a sitting-up posture. Red pigment was liberally sprinkled over the heads of the deceased but relatively few objects were placed in the grave. The lowermost levels of three dwelling sites on Santa Cruz produced cultural materials (Christy's Beach Phase) that match Early Dune Dweller fairly well (Hoover 1971: 249-251). Mortars and pestles are present but rare. Bone gorges, bone pendants, olivella beads of several kinds, abalone ornaments, twined and wicker basketry were manufactured. Most of the burials lay in prone position, but six were sitting. Powdered red ocher and shell beads were present in the graves.

A cycle of increased rainfall that began about 3000 B.C. once again made the desert province suitable for human settlement. As the vegetation and animal life became reestablished, aboriginal bands commenced moving in to take advantage of them. It is clear that the country supported a reasonable population, for many campsites, some of considerable size with signs of protracted or recurrent residence, have been discovered.

The best known are those at Pinto Basin in northeastern Riverside County (Campbell and Campbell 1935). Here a series of prehistoric encampments has been found along the banks of a dry water course, through which a sluggish river once flowed. Artifacts collected from their surfaces are limited to those made of stone. Missile tips marked by weak, narrow shoulders and concave bases are characteristic (fig. 11). Other chipped-

Fig. 11. Pinto Basin projectile points. Materials are: a, obsidian; b, jasper; c, rock crystal; d, rhyolite. Length of a, about 3.6 cm (Campbell and Campbell 1935:pl. 13).

stone articles consist of leaf-shaped knife blades, drills, and scrapers. A substantial quantity of rough service tools—hammers, choppers, and scraper planes—is present. Seed-grinding implements, handstones, and milling stones occur in small numbers. The camping spots produced no clear-cut evidences of shelters, hearths, or foodstuffs. Obviously the sustenance of Pinto Basin inhabitants came from a combination of hunting and gathering. The main reliance must have been on hunting, for artifacts associated with the chase outnumber those devised for preparing plant foods.

Assemblages of tools exhibiting a typological affinity to those from Pinto Basin occur over practically the entire desert country of southern California (Wallace 1962:175-176), but their makeup is not everywhere identical. Even the main unifying feature, the weak-shouldered, concave-based point, shows diversity in details. In the vicinity of Cajon Pass, San Bernardino County, the Pinto Basin complex interdigitated with the coastal Milling Stone culture (Kowta 1969:39-40).

Very little knowledge has been accumulated concerning happenings in the San Joaquin valley during the 3000-2000 B.C. period. The same holds true for the Pacific coast between San Luis Obispo County and San Francisco Bay. It seems entirely reasonable to assume that a broader-based pattern of food acquisition was adopted in these two regions as elsewhere but there are yet no archeological data to support such an inference.

Much more information is available for the Sacramento River valley. It is in this time span that the Windmiller (Early Horizon) culture flourished in the lower valley (Heizer 1949; Ragir 1972). Most knowledge of the Windmiller people and their way of life comes from graveyards. Of the seven known sites, two represent cemeteries with little sign of having been lived upon. The other five contain both habitation debris and burials. Evidently the dead were interred on low rises, above flood level. In the course of time the surrounding lowlands filled up gradually with river sediments that almost completely covered the burial knolls, so that they now barely protrude above the valley floor. Much of the village areas must have been located on lower ground and now lie hidden beneath a thick accumulation of silt.

A greater wealth and variety of artifacts distinguishes Windmiller sites from those of earlier peoples. The cultural materials show a more advanced technology in that greater attention was paid to finished products and to artistic elaboration. Large heavy projectile tips, evidently designed for use on darts or spears, take several shapes (fig. 12). Employment of the throwing stick is confirmed by the finding of a hook for engaging the cupped butt end of the dart shaft (Olsen and Wilson 1964:17-18). Stone mortars, pestles, milling stones and mullers are present, though not abundant. Bone implements, not particularly numerous, consist of fishhooks, gorges, awls, pins, daggers, flat spatulate objects, and bird-bone tubes. Trident fish-spear points are made of antler. The Windmiller people manufactured several kinds of beads and pendants from marine shells, acquired apparently through trade from coastal tribes. Most typical are small rectangular abalone and olivella beads, drilled at the center for stringing or attachment to garments (fig. 13). A few hand-molded, baked-clay objects may have functioned as cooking stones. Twined basketry is evidenced by impressions in clay.

Easily the most conspicuous artifacts are the superbly fashioned and highly polished charmstones (fig. 14). Plummet-shaped and phallic forms occur (Heizer 1949:18-19; Ragir 1972:166-177). Almost invariably the stones have a biconically drilled hole at one end. Traces of asphaltum on a few specimens bear marks of fine twisted string. The perforations and the cord impressions suggest that the objects were suspended in some

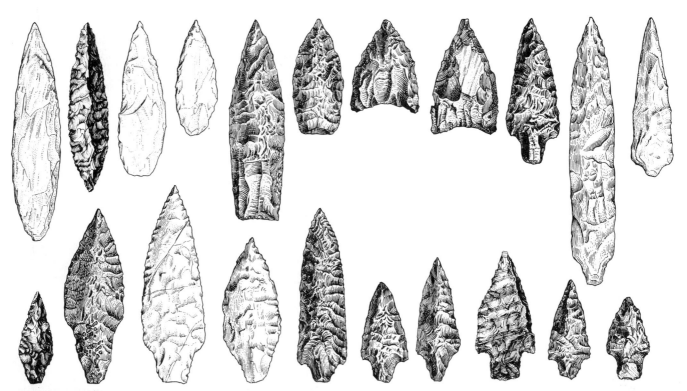

Heizer 1949:figs. 11, 12, 13.

Fig. 12. Windmiller culture projectile points. Length of upper left point, about 10.7 cm.

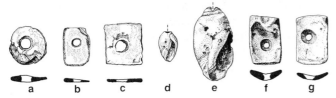

Lowie Mus., U. of Calif., Berkeley: a, 1-48782; b, 1-46321; c, 1-48849; d, 1-46405;
e, 1-46323; f, 1-48860; g, 1-48889.

Fig. 13. Windmiller culture shell beads. Materials are: a-c, haliotis;
d-g, olivella. Diameter of a, 1.0 cm.

fashion. Special discussion has been given more than once to the purpose of the charmstones. Perhaps they served as luck charms in hunting or fishing or had some other magical function. The stones must have been carefully guarded against damage for they usually exhibit no battering, chipping, or signs of wear.

An extraordinary interest attached to burial of the dead. Corpses were placed on the ground outstretched and face down, oriented with the head to the west. The Windmiller people were fond of decking out their dead

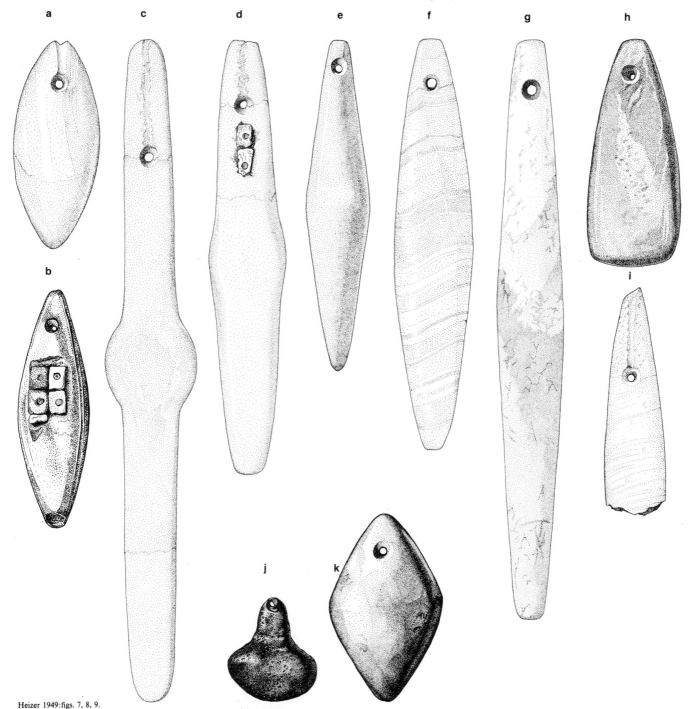

Heizer 1949:figs. 7, 8, 9.

Fig. 14. Windmiller culture charmstones. Materials are: a, f-g, i, alabaster; b-d, h, amphibolite schist; e, diorite; j, steatite; k, serpentine. Length of a, 9.1 cm.

POST-PLEISTOCENE ARCHEOLOGY, 9000 TO 2000 B.C.

with shell necklaces and pendants. Most graves contain additional articles such as clear quartz crystals, charmstones, and projectile points. Inhumation took place in special cemeteries on knolls or in graves dug within the village area.

Windmiller economy probably rested primarily upon hunting (Heizer 1949:30; Ragir 1972:99). Faunal remains are present in the accumulated living debris in sufficient numbers to show that a wide range of animals, large and small, was killed and eaten. That fish secured from the rivers constituted a significant source of food is attested to not only by the occurrence of salmon vertebrae, ribs, and jaws of smaller species, and sturgeon plates, but also by the finding of fishing gear. Seeds and nuts may have been fairly important items in the daily food supply (Ragir 1972:98).

The Windmiller culture probably had its beginnings somewhat prior to 2500 B.C. The earliest radiocarbon date based on charcoal obtained from one of the sites is 2400 ± 250 B.C. Antecedents remain obscure. The implement assemblage includes a few items (for example, milling stones and handstones) that may be carryovers from the previous food-collecting stage. Conceivably Windmiller represents nothing more than a later, highly evolved and specialized version of the earlier complex that featured seed-grinding implements (Baumhoff and Olmsted 1963:280); but a world of economic and technical change lies between the two. Quite possibly Windmiller did not derive its inspiration solely from the local scene, but was the product of a blending of ideas contributed by more than one cultural tradition. Cultural influences and even whole populations, impelled by the extreme desiccation of the Altithermal, may have entered Central California from the Great Basin at this time (Ragir 1972:158).

Most of the recorded Windmiller sites cluster around the lower Cosumnes and Mokelumne rivers, tributaries of the Sacramento. One is situated farther south on the bank of a small stream, Bear Creek, near Stockton. Traces of the presence of this culture have also been noted in the Sierra foothills bordering the valley. Ten extended burials unearthed at a settlement in the Camanche Reservoir locality on the Mokelumne River have been ascribed to the Windmiller phase (Johnson 1967:204, 216). A few distinctive rectangular shell beads accompanied three of the interments. Additional Windmiller-type specimens turned up in the midden.

Cultural materials conforming to those obtained at Windmiller sites have been uncovered at several San Francisco Bay locations. The lowest stratum at the West Berkeley Shellmound contained an artifact inventory similar in many respects to that of the lower Sacramento River valley (Wallace and Lathrap 1952). Besides shared elements such as rectangular shell beads, the West Berkeley weapon tips and knives possess the same general characteristics as Windmiller specimens. Correspon-

dences can be seen too in perforated charmstones from the two regions. Certain rare West Berkeley items (bone fishhooks, bipointed bone objects, asbestos rods), significant because of their uniqueness, have Windmiller analogues.

There are also dissimilarities: the Sacramento valley culture is much richer. One of its diagnostic traits, extended burial accompanied by elaborate grave goods, is wanting on the bay shore, where flexed interment with few, if any, mortuary offerings is customary. Turned-about, grooved, and notched net sinkers plentiful at West Berkeley have no inland counterparts; and the abundance of mortars, pestles, and bone implements in the bay region is not repeated at Windmiller sites.

Also the basic subsistence pattern differs in the two areas. The mass of discarded molluscan shells embedded in the West Berkeley midden clearly shows that the bay inhabitants supported themselves principally by collecting mussels and oysters. Fish must have formed another dietary mainstay, for their bones are plentiful as are net sinkers. In contrast to Windmiller, hunting seems to have been a minor method of procuring food. Proof that the West Berkeleyans depended fairly heavily upon plant foods comes from the substantial number of mortars and pestles.

Carbon-14 age determinations indicate that the West Berkeley occupation must have begun by 2000 B.C., if not earlier. Three radiocarbon dates fall near 1800 B.C. Two or three centuries must be added to this figure to allow for the build-up of the lower 12 inches of the refuse deposit, which did not produce a sufficient amount of charcoal for dating purposes.

A second bay-shore settlement, University Village near Palo Alto in San Mateo County, has yielded materials comparable to those from West Berkeley (Gerow 1968). The projectile points, mortars, and pestles are much alike. Added shared forms include perforated charmstones, notched sinkers, and asbestos rods. The University Village bone industry appears less developed because, although most of the West Berkeley types are present, they appear in reduced numbers. Essential uniformity can be seen in shell beads and ornaments. As at West Berkeley, the University Village people inhumed their dead in a flexed posture, with few grave goods. Little doubt exists that the two assemblages are closely related and overlap in time, although radiocarbon datings demonstrate that habitation began more recently at the Palo Alto location.

Scanty evidence in the form of a generous supply of net sinkers and a few large missile tips raises the possibility that the deepest stratum in the Ellis Landing Shellmound, located only a few miles north of West Berkeley near Richmond, contained an analogous complex. Unfortunately the most ancient layer lay below water level and could not be thoroughly explored when the midden was excavated (Nelson 1910). Back from the bay shore, stemmed projectile points and other articles compatible with those from West Berkeley turned up in the lowest occupational zone of the Stone Valley settlement at Alamo in Contra Costa County (Fredrickson 1965a:20). A virtual absence of shell beads and a limited repertory of bone articles hinders comparisons with West Berkeley materials. The Stone Valley burial position was exclusively flexed. A radiocarbon determination places the age of the earliest habitation at 2500 ± 500 B.C.

Cultural assemblages that agree closely with West Berkeley or Windmiller have not been certainly identified beyond San Francisco Bay. The coast and bay shores of Marin County northward combine land and sea food resources that may well have attracted settlement by an early population. But despite the fact that considerable archeological research has been carried on in this region, no comparable remains have yet been discovered. In the North Coast Ranges the long-established food-collecting lifeway persisted. The third, and terminal, habitational phase at Borax Lake is typified by concave-based points without fluting, by stemmed points, and by the persisting use of milling stones and handstones (Meighan and Haynes 1970:1220). This complex is believed to have an age of about 3,000 to 5,000 years. Out of it, there developed in other locations the Mendocino complex (Meighan 1955:5, 27–28).

Summary and Perspective

As far as they can be traced in the archeological record, the main trends in California's aboriginal history during the 9000–2000 B.C. period involved expanding utilization of the rich and varied native food resources, technological improvement and elaboration, overall growth in population, enlargement and increased stability of individual communities, and, finally, as time passed, the gradual emergence of regional cultures (see table 1).

The most ancient remains pertain to small, presumably roving, bands whose life revolved around the pursuit and killing of game animals. Their campsites are distinguished by projectile points and other items consistent with a hunting economy. It is certain that these early Californians did not follow a specialized type of big-game hunting comparable to Folsom bison hunting or the pattern shown by the Clovis finds in association with the mammoth. Lesser game animals received greater attention as did other foodstuffs. Whether they availed themselves of the abundant and diversified edible plants remains unknown. The discoveries suggest infiltration of the region by groups with two separate hunting traditions. Both have substantial antiquity, extending back as far as 8000 or 9000 B.C., with overlapping in time and space.

After 6000 B.C. the balance of subsistence shifted from animal to plant foods. Once established, this form of livelihood endured for several millenniums. It is best

seen in prehistoric settlements on the south coast. Their sets of implements, still quite rudimentary and remaining notably constant, strongly feature handstones and mills, underscoring the importance of seed gathering and grinding. Food remains and other categories of artifacts show that the food quest also embraced hunting, fishing, and shellfish collecting. The village sites, giving signs of considerable permanency, appear to have housed fair-sized populations.

Specialized and selective exploitations of particular environments began to evolve around 3000 B.C. In general, dependence was upon a combination of hunting, fishing, and collecting, with one of the activities receiving somewhat greater emphasis. The artifact assemblages, each with a local flavor, exhibit enriched content. Mortars and pestles are added to milling stones and mullers for processing plant foods. Chipped-stone objects are more skillfully made and varied. Bone implements and shell ornaments tend to increase in number. Most of the complexes seem to have developed out of those belonging to the previous food-collecting stage. Only the Santa Barbara Hunting culture is clearly intrusive, though Windmiller may be. By the end of the millennium the new ways and techniques had become firmly established and formed the basis for succeeding cultural traditions.

Sources

The published material for these crucial years in California prehistory is uneven and often sadly inadequate. There is a lack of precise data on the early hunting cultures. The California fluted point tradition is documented by reports on the Borax Lake (M.R. Harrington 1948) and Tulare Lake (Riddell and Olsen 1969) cultures and by brief descriptions of scattered finds. A degree of obscurity in regard to Borax Lake has led to its restudy and reevaluation (Meighan and Haynes 1970). The Lake Mohave culture is detailed in Campbell et al. (1973). Lack of a consensus has led to considerable discussion in print on the age and significance of the Lake Mohave finds. New excavations at the San Dieguito site have greatly increased the understanding of this closely related culture (M.J. Rogers 1929; Warren and True 1960–1961; Warren 1967).

The collecting stage is well documented only for southern California, with a dozen or more detailed site reports (for example, Wallace et al. 1956; Shumway, Hubbs, and Moriarty 1961; Owen, Curtis, and Miller 1963–1964; Greenwood 1969). Present studies provide only sketchy information for the remainder of the state and this dearth of data complicates any attempt to trace the distribution of this mode of subsistence during the 6000–3000 B.C. period.

Knowledge of the series of cultures occupying the mil-

Table 1. Prehistoric Cultures

		Southern Coast	Southern Desert	San Joaquin Valley	Sacramento Valley	Sierra Foothills	San Francisco Bay	Coast Range
PERIOD III Hunting, fishing, and collecting	3000–2000 B.C.	Modified Milling Stone (San Diego, Los Angeles cos.)	Pinto Basin	?	Windmiller	Windmiller	West Berkeley	Modified Milling Stone Mendocino
Hunting		(Santa Barbara, San Luis Obispo cos.)						
PERIOD II Collecting	6000–3001 B.C.	Milling Stone (Oak Grove, Topanga, La Jolla)	(drought)	Milling Stone	Milling Stone	Milling Stone, Mesilla	?	Milling Stone
PERIOD I Hunting	9000–6001 B.C.	San Dieguito	Lake Mohave, Fluted Point	Fluted Point	Fluted Point	Fluted Point	?	Fluted Point

lennium between 3000 and 2000 B.C. is spotty. Late manifestations of a Milling Stone assemblage have been described for the Los Angeles area (Peck 1955; K.L. Johnson 1966) and for an extensive site near Cajon Pass in San Bernardino County (Kowta 1969). For Santa Barbara, the formulation of the Hunting culture, originally defined by Rogers (1929), has been elaborated upon (Harrison and Harrison 1966). In the desert, the widespread Pinto Basin complex (Campbell and Campbell 1935) is relatively well documented. Best known is the Windmiller (Early Horizon) culture of the lower Sacramento valley (Heizer 1949; Ragir 1972).

Additional sources are listed in Heizer, Elsasser, and Clewlow (1970).

Development of Regional Prehistoric Cultures

ALBERT B. ELSASSER

By 1916 there was considerable agreement that 2000 B.C. was probably the beginning date for the prehistoric Indian occupation of Northern California, at least in the San Francisco Bay region (Nelson 1909; Gifford 1916). In 1930 results of excavations in the Santa Barbara area (Rogers 1929; Olson 1930) presented ample evidence for development or change through time even in the comparatively simple cultural remains of nonagricultural coastal populations.

A cultural sequence for the lower Sacramento Valley and in part for the San Francisco Bay area was later established (Lillard, Heizer, and Fenenga 1939), with the estimated 2000 B.C. still playing an important role as an archeological marker. These earlier estimates, based upon geological or climatological principles as well as intuition, were all approximately confirmed by carbon-14 dating after 1950.

This chapter is directed toward relating the various archeological regions of California to one another wherever possible with concrete evidence, during a span of about 3,500 years. The necessarily telescoped delineations can conveniently begin with Central California, the largest area considered, which includes all of the Great Central Valley, the San Francisco Bay region, and part of the Pacific Coast north and south of the bay.

Central California

Alameda, Diablo, and Cosumnes Districts

Beardsley (1948, 1954) in expanding earlier work on the Sacramento–San Joaquin Delta region to San Francisco Bay area, adopted the designations Early, Middle, and Late Horizons as a chronological framework. He subdivided the entire region into *zones* and *provinces,* which contained *facies,* defined as a group of intimately related *components.* Components are defined as an archeological record of human occupation at a single locality at a specific time. Beardsley's Horizon sequence and his term facies are used here, but for his zones and provinces the expression *district* has been substituted. Significant facies for Alameda, Diablo, and Cosumnes Districts are summarized graphically in figures 2-6, with sites giving names to the facies located in fig. 1.

Heizer (1949:39) estimated 1500 B.C. as the termination date of the Early Horizon in the Delta; there was not sufficient evidence at this time firmly to indicate an

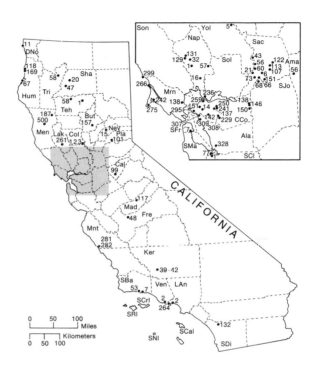

Fig. 1. Some archeological sites and locations. Designations for sites follow system of abbreviation for present county names.

Early Horizon expression on San Francisco Bay. However, Middle Horizon peoples were then thought to have appeared on the bay at some time between 1500 B.C. and 1000 B.C. Later, 2000 B.C. was suggested as the time when the Early Horizon in the Delta either began to develop into, or was replaced by, the Middle Horizon culture (Heizer 1958:7).

Since 1958 additional excavations and carbon-14 dates from the bay region have given substance to the idea of the existence of an Early Bay culture (Gerow and Force 1968:12). This is proposed as the Berkeley facies herein (fig. 2) and linked with the Windmiller facies (Early Horizon-Lower Sacramento Valley) on the basis of resemblances in olivella bead types; haliotis ornaments; perforated charmstones; stone projectile points; bone fishhooks of a rare, specific type; and comparatively little use of obsidian as an implement material.

Correspondences between coast and interior (Delta)

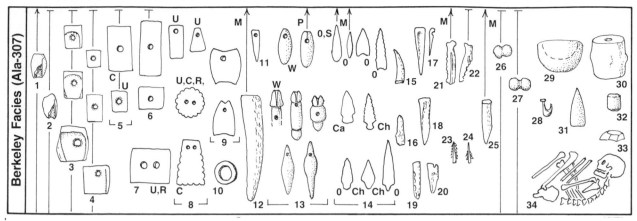

Chart by J. A. Bennyhoff, 1972.

Fig. 2. Early Horizon, Berkeley Facies, Alameda District: Significant artifact types. Shell beads approximately actual size; relative scale attempted for remainder within related groups but not among different classes of artifacts. Position on chart of specimens within facies has no chronological significance. Bead typology from Lillard, Heizer, and Fenenga 1939. C, *Haliotis cracherodii;* Ca, chalcedony; Ch, chert; M, trait carries over into Middle Horizon; O, obsidian; P, trait survives into Patterson facies (Early-Middle Horizon Transition); R, *Haliotis rufescens;* S, slate; U, haliotis, unidentified sp.; W, cf. charmstone types of blue schist from Early Horizon, Interior, Types B2, E2.

1-4, olivella beads: 1. Small, spire-lopped, Type 1a; 2. Small, diagonal ground, Type 1c; 3. Thick rectangle, shelved, Type 2b; 4. Thick rectangle, simple, Type 2b. 5. *Mytilus* rectangular, square beads. 6-8, haliotis beads and ornaments: 6. Rectangular, square, Type 1a; 7. Rectangular, with double perforation, also incised, Type 2; 8. ornament. 9. Steatite pendants (may represent Patterson facies, Early-Middle Horizon Transition). 10. Steatite ring. 11. Mammal-bone pendant. 12. Antler spatula. 13. Perforated charmstones. 14. Chipped-stone projectile points and/or knives. 15. Antler-tine flaker. 16. Mammal-bone (ulna) flaker. 17. Mammal-bone awls. 18. Mammal cannon bone gouge. 19. Chipped mammal-bone tool. 20. Mammal-bone fiber stripper (?). 21. Serrated mammal scapula (Bay region form). 22. Serrated mammal scapula (Napa region form). 23. Unmodified sting ray spine. 24. Ground sting ray spine. 25. Antler wedge. 26. Notched stone net sinker. 27. Grooved stone net sinker. 28. Bone curved fishhook. 29. Stone mortar. 30. Whale vertebra container (?). 31. Stone pestle, conically shaped. 32. Stone pestle, "stubby." 33. Chert scraper-plane. 34. Flexed burial with no set orientation characteristic.

Chart by J. A. Bennyhoff, 1972.

Fig. 3. Middle Horizon, Alameda District: Significant artifact types and temporal changes, from Patterson (Early-Middle Horizon Transition) facies to Sobrante facies (Late Middle Horizon), taken from representative sites. Olivella beads shown approximately actual size; relative scale attempted for remainder within related groups but not among different classes. Position of specimens shown within facies has no chronological significance. Bead typology from Lillard, Heizer, and Fenenga 1939. A, appliqué in asphalt decoration; C, *Haliotis cracherodii;* Ch, chert; E, trait persists from Early Horizon; F, "fishtail" charmstone; I, double-line facial incision; L, trait persists into Late Horizon; MA, Meganos Aspect (hybrid expression of Early and Middle Horizon cultures) trait; O, obsidian; Q, quartzite; R, *Haliotis rufescens;* U, haliotis unidentified. References to oyster, mussel, and clam indicate frequency of these mollusks in midden deposits through time.

1-12, olivella beads: 1,2. Split-drilled, Type 3b1; 3. Small spire-lopped, Type 1a; 4. Spire-lopped, Types 1a, 1b; 5. Modified "saddle," Type 3b2; 6. Small "saddle," Type 3b2; 7. Round "saddle," Type 3b; 8. Full "saddle," Type 3b; 9,10. "saucer," Type 3c; 11. Ring, Type 3c; 12. Tiny disk, Type 3d. 13. *Mytilus* disk bead. 14-16, haliotis beads: 14. Large amorphous beads, Type H4b; 15. Nacreous disk, Type H3a; 16. Large disk, Type H3b2. 17-21, haliotis ornaments. 22. Earspool with haliotis appliqué at one end. 23. Mica ornament. 24. Slate pendant. 25. Slate ring with olivella appliqué. 26. Slate pendant. 27. Steatite "constricted" beads. 28. Bone tubes, beads (often with olivella appliqué). 29. Antler pendant. 30. Perforated bone hairpin. 31. Flat bone pin. 32,33. Bone pendants. 34. Incised bone (pendant). 35. Long bipointed pin. 36. Bear tooth pendant. 37. Canid tooth pendant. 38-41. Bone, antler spatulae. 42. Perforated head scratcher (bone). 43. Forked head scratcher (bone). 44. Split rib strigil. 45. Long bird-bone whistle, central stop. 46. Short bird-bone whistle, central stop. 47. Human (?) tibia whistle. 48. Bird-bone whistle, end stop. 49. Slate bar with olivella appliqué. 50. Whole, fractured, quartz crystals. 51. Steatite or marble "cloud blower" (?), often with olivella appliqué. 52-56. Charmstones (52-54 with asphalted ends). 57-60. Chipped stone spear, dart points. 61. Obsidian knife. 62. Bone (ulna) flaker. 63. Antler tine flaker. 64-67. Bone atlatl spurs. 68. Antler wedge. 69. Sting ray spine. 70. Barbed bone fish spears. 71,72. Unbarbed bone fish spears (?). 73. Ground beaver incisor. 74. Bone (ulna) awl. 75. Cannonbone awl or punch. 76. Ground bone awl. 77. Serrated rib. 78. Serrated fish bone. 79. Serrated mammal scapula. 80. Bone fiber-stripper. 81. Shaped stone mortar. 82. Incised (decorated) stone mortar. 83. Boulder mortar. 84. Cobble pestle. 85-93, Mortuary complex (available data not precise—emphasis is on variable flexed and semiflexed positions, with presumed local or no fixed orientation): 85. Flexed, with orientation to NW and NE quadrants; 86. Ventral extension, a marker for Meganos Aspect, significant at site CCo-151, orientation to SW, NW, and NE quadrants; 87. Dorsal extension, of rare and scattered occurrence; 88. Orientation to SW and NW quadrants; 89. Orientation to all points except NE quadrant; 90. Orientation to all quadrants, varying site to site within facies; 91. Dorsal extension, rare; 92. Orientation to NW quadrant; 93. Cremation, confined to Patterson (Early-Middle Horizon Transition) facies.

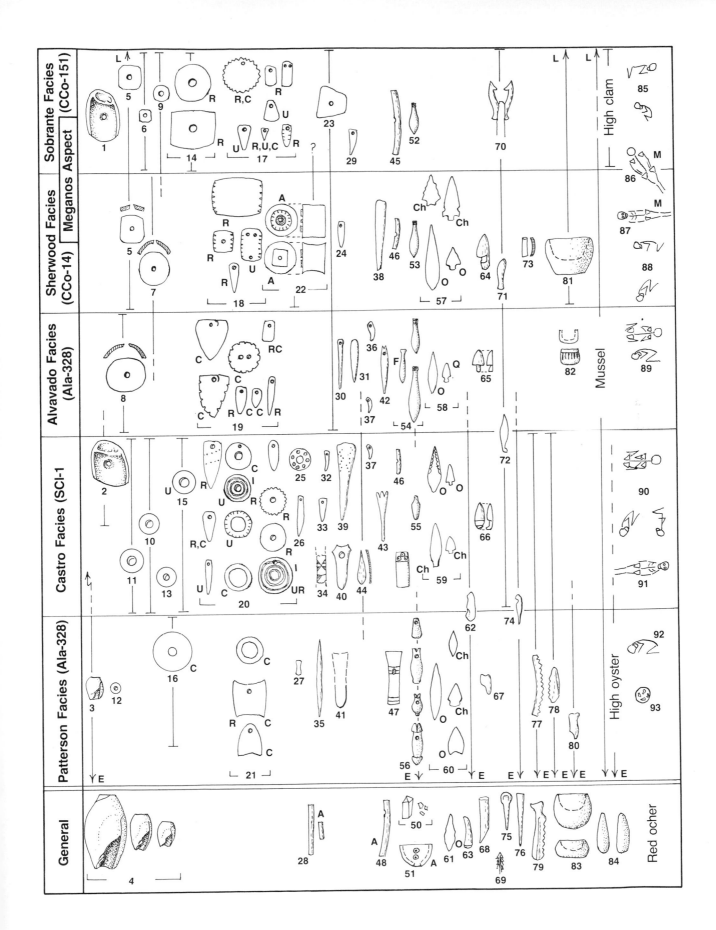

DEVELOPMENT OF REGIONAL PREHISTORIC CULTURES

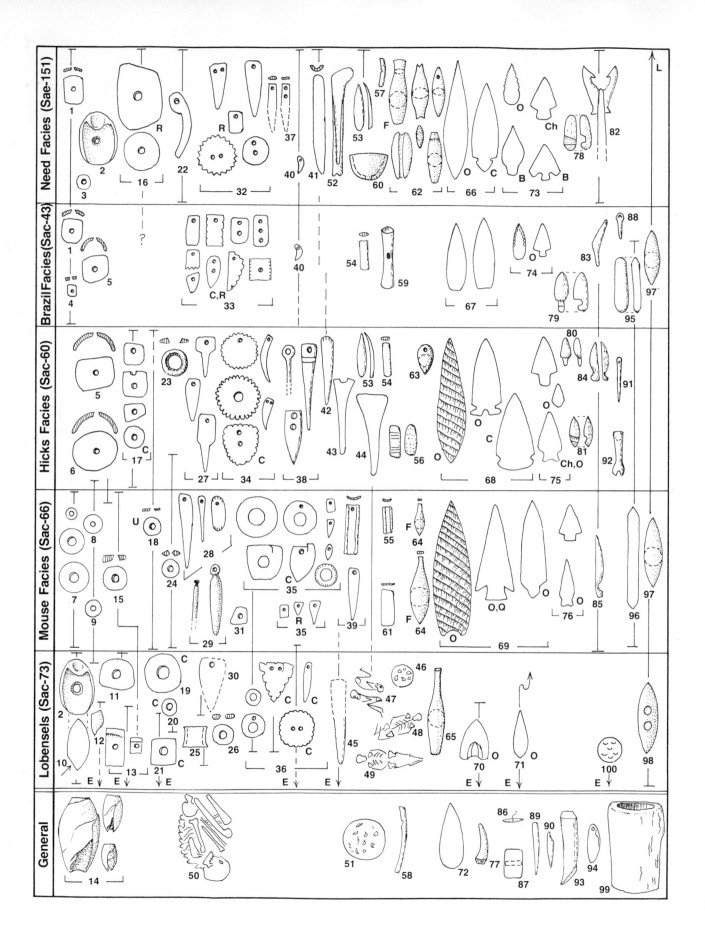

Early sites are by no means one-to-one. There are several traits, such as burial postures (flexed in Bay region, ventrally extended in lower Sacramento Valley) and a comparative abundance of stone mortars and pestles as well as bone artifacts in the Bay sites, that tend to set the two districts apart.

The earliest carbon-14 date of Early Bay culture (M-125) is from site Ala-307 (Berkeley facies)—about 1900 B.C. The oldest date (L-187B) from University Village site (SMa-77), probably in part contemporaneous or included in the Berkeley facies, is about 1200 B.C. Three additional finds from the coastal region, all predating 2000 B.C. (carbon-14 samples W-185, UCLA-259, UCLA-1425 A, B) may be indicators of man's early presence in the Bay region, but none of them can be connected precisely with any of the early facies here discussed. Thus, the Windmiller facies (Delta) sites are, on present evidence, older than those of the Berkeley facies. The times of earliest occupation in Interior and Coast regions are uncertain, but it is here suggested that the Early Horizon as a whole (Coast and Interior) terminated at around 1000 B.C.

While considerable developmental change is recognized in deposits assigned to the Early and Middle Horizon sites, there has not been unanimity of opinion on the causes of these changes. One explanation rests on linguistic categories. The Great Central Valley was occupied almost totally by groups identified as speakers of Penutian languages. The Hokan speakers are spread, with some intervals, around the periphery of the valley, and this distributional peculiarity has given rise to the supposition that the Hokans were early occupants of the region, later to be displaced by migrating Penutians coming from some area (Great Basin?) outside of California in response to marked climatic change.

Whatever the case, the Transition facies (Patterson and Lobensels facies, figs. 3 and 4) falling between Early and Middle Horizons imply a steady development, unmarred by sudden increments of foreign peoples. Thus it seems possible that Penutians may have entered the Central Valley in a gradual way, in a number of comparatively minor "waves," slowly replacing the original (Hokan?) peoples.

The rationale for distinguishing between Middle and Late Horizon facies, apart from the differing contents of site components, may ultimately rest on the proposal that by the time of the transition (about A.D. 300–500) the Penutian settlement in Central California was virtually complete. Observations that the Middle Horizon peoples left behind an abundance of bone objects, while those of the Late Horizon seemed to elaborate shell artifacts such as beads and ornaments, certainly do not lead to the impression of great peaks of technological achievement at any time during a span of about 2,500 years.

Nevertheless, figures 2-6 do show evidence of steady, detailed changes in several classes of artifacts. Variations in form or design of objects in all categories—stone, bone, and shell—are sufficient to confirm deep roots for the pattern of California ethnography enunciated by Kroeber (1925) and here paraphrased: general sameness, but with many minute regional differences.

In summarizing the identifying features of the Middle Horizon, primary dependence has been placed on Beardsley (1954), but figures 3 and 4 place the various traits in a more precise framework than Beardsley was able to offer. It is obvious that the major diagnostic and most sensitive indicators of change through time in the various facies of both Middle and Late Horizons are shell beads and ornaments, which are almost as useful to

Chart by J. A. Bennyhoff, 1972.
Fig. 4. Middle Horizon, Cosumnes District: Significant artifact types and temporal changes, from Lobensels (Early-Middle Horizon Transition) facies to Need (Late-Middle Horizon) facies. Olivella beads shown approximately actual size; relative scale attempted for remainder within related groups but not among different classes. Position of specimens shown within facies has no chronological significance. Bead typology from Lillard, Heizer, and Fenenga 1939. B, basalt; C, *Haliotis cracherodii;* Ch, chert; E, trait persists from Early Horizon; F, "fishtail" charmstone; L, trait persists into Late Horizon; R, *Haliotis rufescens;* U, haliotis unidentified. 1-14, Olivella beads: 1. Modified "saddle," Type 3b2; 2. Split-drilled, Type 3b1. 3. Small "saucer," Type 3c; 4. Small modified "saddle," Type 3b2; 5. Full "saddle," Type 3b; 6. Round "saddle," Type 3b; 7. Ring, Type 3c2; 8. Large "saucer," Type 3c; 9. Small "saucer," Type 3c; 10. "Bevelled" bead (arrow points to bevel), Type 3b1; 11. Oval "saddle," Type 3b; 12. Diagonal spire-lopped, Type 1c; 13. Thick shelved rectangle, Type 2b; 14. Spire-lopped, Types 1a, 1b. 15. *Macoma* disk bead. 16-21, Haliotis beads: 16. Large, amorphous, Type H4; 17. Small, amorphous, Type H4; 18. Nacreous disk, Type H3; 19. Large disk, Type H3; 20. Small disk, Type H3; 21. Square, Type H1a. 22. Steatite "claw" pendant. 23. Steatite ring. 24. Steatite lenticular disk bead. 25. Steatite "hourglass" earspool. 26. Steatite flat disk bead. 27,28. Flat slate pendants. 29. Cylindrical slate pendants. 30. Flat slate pendant. 31. Biotite ornament. 32-36. Haliotis pendants. 37-39. Bone pendants. 40. Canid tooth pendants. 41-45. Deer tibia and antler spatulae. 46. Cremation. 47. Flexed burial, all orientations. 48. Burial, ventral, semiextended, all orientations. 49. Burial, ventral, extended, all orientations. 50. Burial, tight flexure (most distinctive of Middle Horizon, though other positions, including rare extension, also occur), all orientations. 51. Cremation (rare, none for Brazil facies). 52. Mammal tibia "wand." 53. Split rib strigil (Type 1). 54. Whole rib strigil (Type 2). 55. Flat bone strigil (Type 3). 56. Bone dice. 57. Bird-bone whistle, central stop. 58. Bird-bone whistle, end stop. 59. Mammal-bone whistle, central stop. 60. Steatite perforated cup ("cloud blower"?). 61. Flat stone bars. 62-65. Charmstones. 66-76, Chipped-stone artifacts: 66-69. Probably spear points (note careful diagonal flaking, on 68, 69, to left); 70. Knife designed for hafting; 71. Bipointed knife (occurs in all facies but most common in Lobensels); 72. Leaf-shaped knife; 73-76. Dart points. 77. Antler-tine flaker. 78-81. Atlatl spurs (?) of bone. 82. Barbed bone fish spear. 83-85. Unbarbed bone fish spears (?). 86. Bone gorge hook. 87. Bone mesh gauge. 88. Cannon bone awl, pointed distally. 89. Ground bone awl. 90. Bone splinter awl. 91. Bone needle. 92. Socketed antler handle. 93. Antler wedge (rare). 94. *Margaritifera* spoon, perforated. 95,96. Flat slab pestle for use with wooden mortar. 97. Cylindrical bipointed pestle for use with wooden mortars. 98. Pitted bipointed pestle. 99. Wooden mortar.

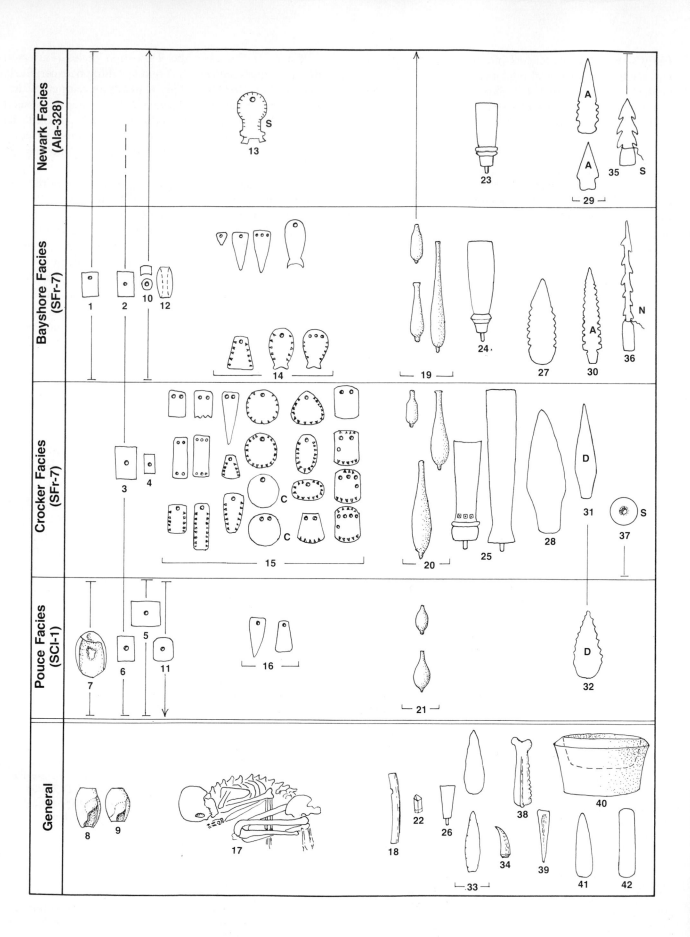

California archeology as are potsherds in other parts of North America for analyzing culture processes.

During the Late Horizon, Phase 1, population was probably greater; consequently, there was a larger number of sites than in Middle Horizon. Interior earth middens show a similar wide distribution, as before, but the soil is darker and not so compacted as in the average Middle Horizon site. Late Horizon components succeeded those of Middle at numbers of sites.

Some Late Horizon characteristics not recorded in figures 5 and 6 all refer to contrasts with Middle Horizon, that is, a lesser use of red ocher in the burial complex but greater use of baked clay objects than before, and more importance in acorn gathering and preparation than in Middle Horizon (Delta region). Preinterment grave-pit burning (fig. 6, XX), described as burning of basketry and other offerings in graves before the body itself was deposited, became a common practice in Late Horizon, Phase 1. The small, side-notched projectile points, often of obsidian, suggest appearance of bow and arrow, probably supplanting use of heavier dart points with atlatl.

The traits enumerated for the Diablo District in Late Horizon, Phase 1 (fig. 6) can serve as well to describe the Cosumnes District in the lower Sacramento Valley during the same period of time. However, differing environments in the two regions, Bay and Delta, account for several persistent distinctions among the several districts involved, such as the use of wooden mortars and baked clay objects in the interior and the virtual absence of these in the coastal lands, where more stone was available for artifacts.

Beyond these easily explainable differences there were other circumstances for which no ready accounting can be offered. One of these may be seen in the Alameda District in the latter part or Newark facies of Phase 1 (fig. 5). Here and at other sites of the same time level on parts of San Francisco Bay some unknown factors seem to have brought about a desertion of settlements or relatively sudden movement of population. It has been assumed that a migration of some sort probably took place from large village sites, such as Ala-328, to smaller ones in the surrounding area.

Marin District

No Early Horizon sites such as those proposed for San Francisco Bay's Berkeley facies have yet come to light in the Marin District, which is defined here as comprising practically the entire Marin County littoral, including a substantial portion of shore on northern San Francisco Bay. One site on the bay, Mrn-138, probably of McClure facies (equated temporally with Castro facies in Alameda District, fig. 3), has a carbon-14 date of about 700 B.C. (I-5797).

Notable similarities of McClure facies with Middle Horizon facies on San Francisco Bay or the Delta region are seen in (1) bone ornaments and implements such as hairpins, whistles, bipointed gorge hooks, forked "head scratchers," mesh gauges (for fish nets?), triangular shaped antler or bone spatulae, ringed or "eyed" daggers or pendants; (2) mica ornaments; (3) abundance of red ocher with burials; (4) olivella beads, Type 3c ("saucer"); (5) haliotis ornaments, rectangular, with end perforation; (6) flexed burial position, although loose flexure rather than tight was more characteristic of Marin District than either Alameda or Cosumnes; (7) heavy, nonstemmed chipped points, with greater ratio of nonobsidian to obsidian used for these points than in subsequent (Late Horizon) facies; (8) grooved or notched stone sinkers—frequent in Berkeley facies.

Distinctions of Marin District, specifically noted for McClure facies, are (1) basin-shaped structures of baked earth in midden deposits; (2) markedly curved, chipped obsidian objects—"eccentrics"; (3) human figurines of baked clay (fig. 7).

Cauley facies, assigned to later Middle Horizon, shares a number of traits with its predecessor, McClure, but is distinguished by several characteristics. First, the olivella beads are Type 3b2, the modified "saddle" shape. Second, there is evidence of head taking in the form of detached skulls in burial; this trait is present in Early Horizon and again in ethnographic times in Central California. Cauley facies also shows the earlier McClure characteristic of baked clay human figurines. Both McClure and Cauley are remarkable for their scarcity or total lack of shell beads and haliotis ornaments. The ex-

Chart by J. A. Bennyhoff, 1972.
Fig. 5. Late Horizon, Phase 1, Alameda District: Significant artifact types and temporal changes, from Ponce facies (Middle-Late Horizon Transition) to Newark facies (Late Phase 1). Olivella beads shown approximately actual size; relative scale attempted for remainder within related groups but not between different classes. Position of specimens shown within facies has no chronological significance. Bead typology from Lillard, Heizer, and Fenenga 1939. C, *Haliotis cracherodii;* N, known only in northern (e.g., Carquinez Straits) region; S, known only in south (San Francisco) Bay region.

1-11, Olivella beads: 1. Rectangular, end-perforated, Type 2a2; 2,3. Rectangular, centrally perforated, Type 2a1; 4. Same as 2,3, "narrow variant"; 5. Same as 2,3, "wide variant"; 6. Same as 2,3; 7. Split-punched, Type 3a2; 8. Spire-lopped; 9. End-ground; 10. Cupped, Type 3e; 11. Modified "saddle," Type 3b2. 12. Steatite bead. 13-16. Haliotis ornaments, normally *H. rufescens*. 17. Simple flexed burial. 18. Bird-bone whistle, with end stop. 19-21. "Piled" charmstones. 22. Quartz crystal. 23-26. Tubular smoking pipes, usually steatite (note bead appliqué on collared pipe, No. 25). 27,28. Obsidian spear points. 29,30. Obsidian arrow points. 31,32. Obsidian dart points. 33. Obsidian knives. 34. Antler flaker. 35,36. Bone harpoons. 37. Perforated discoidal. 38. Serrated mammal scapula. 39. Cannon bone awl. 40. Shaped stone mortar. 41,42. Stone pestles.

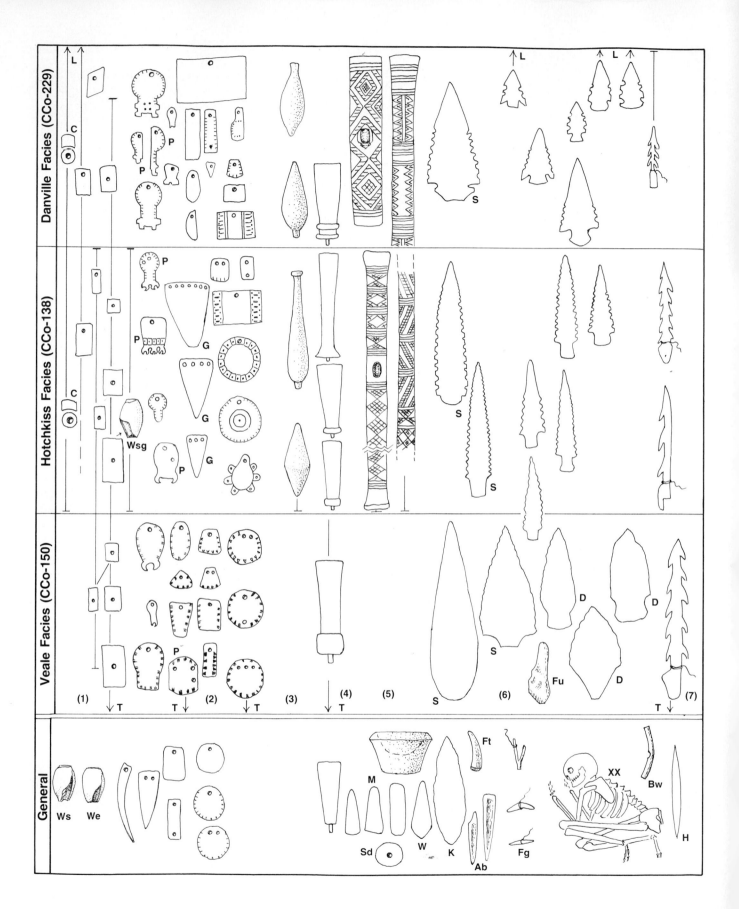

Danville Facies (CCo-229)

Hotchkiss Facies (CCo-138)

Veale Facies (CCo-150)

General

(1)   (2)   (3)   (4)   (5)   (6)   (7)

Ws   We

Ws   We

Sd

M

W   K

Ab

Fg

Ft

XX

Bw

H

planation for this seems to be that these coastal peoples, in whose living sites many species of mollusks, including haliotis, are found in abundance, were simply not so much interested in fashioning ornaments as were the inland people who had to import the shell from the coast.

The Mendoza facies, the Late Horizon, Phase 1 representative of Marin District, presents certain enigmas as far as association with any specific facies of the Bay or Delta regions is concerned, especially since olivella shell beads, which serve as definite time markers for the Bay-Delta facies, are lacking.

Cremations in Mendoza facies are complete (in contrast to "partial," which may be a variant of preinterment burning already described for Delta region) but, as in many Late Horizon sites, more often include grave goods than do primary burials. Unexpectedly, cremations also contain perforated phallic charmstones, usually considered an Early or early Middle Horizon trait in Central California. Light, stemmed, chipped obsidian points; diminished numbers of notched or grooved stone sinkers; shaped flat-bottomed mortars; biconically drilled, tubular, flanged stone pipes; "killing" of grave artifacts—all these elements correspond with Late Horizon, Phase 1 facies elsewhere. Apparent impoverishments in the Mendoza facies suggest phenomena in Marin District similar to those already mentioned for Alameda District toward the end of Phase 1, Late Horizon.

Colusa District

Judging from the number of sites and the richness of artifactual remains found in them, the Sacramento-San Joaquin Delta region must have been an innovative center of cultural development. Thus the Colusa District to the north, mainly along the Sacramento River, seemed to be chiefly on the receiving end of influences exchanged back and forth between it and the Cosumnes District. In Sandhill facies (for example, site Col-3, equated in time with Diablo District, Veale facies—see fig. 6), Late Horizon Phase 1 links with the south are seen in the presence of rectangular and split-punched olivella beads, Types 2a1 and 3a2 (fig. 5), haliotis ornaments of the modified "banjo" type, dorsally extended

burial position, tubular stone pipes with flanges, and small side-notched obsidian points.

Several traits from Cosumnes District such as flat-bottomed, shaped mortars and complete cremations did not penetrate to the north. Use of shaped baked clay objects from Cosumnes entered Colusa District but seemingly never achieved much importance. Moreover, a number of practices common to the Delta during Phase 1, such as preinterment grave-pit burning, deep angular serration of obsidian points, and incising of bird-bone tubes, did not appear in Colusa District until Phase 2. This has given rise to the supposition that there was a migration at some time from the south to the comparatively poor region of the north.

People of the Sandhill facies seemingly were subjected to influences probably from the north, and Olsen and Riddell (1962) have recorded there probably the earliest appearance in California of a type of projectile point called Gunther-barbed after similar specimens found in quantity in Northwestern California around Humboldt Bay.

Napa District

It is evident that the prehistoric populations of the Napa Valley and environs had close ties with both San Francisco Bay and Sacramento-San Joaquin Delta regions (Heizer 1953).

At least two sites (Nap-129 and Nap-131, fig. 1) have been suggested, on the basis of artifacts like manos, basalt core tools, and concave-based, fluted points like those from Borax Lake, as equatable with Early Horizon in Central California.

Investigations at several stratified sites (for example, Nap-1, Nap-32—see fig. 1) have indicated that Middle Horizon is represented in the lower levels, principally by: flexed burials; "saucer" and "saddle" olivella beads, Types 3c and 3b1; probably nonserrated, nonstemmed obsidian points, of which the sequential picture of the specimens is not altogether clear, since they do not have burial association data; circular ear plugs (?) of stone, of a type found in Middle Horizon contexts in San Francisco Bay sites (but in both Middle and Late in Sacramento Valley as well); reworked obsidian prisms—"ban-

Chart by J. A. Bennyhoff, 1972.

Fig. 6. Late Horizon, Phase 1, Diablo District: Significant artifact types and temporal changes. Olivella beads shown approximately actual size; relative scale shown for projectile points; other classes of artifacts not to scale. Position of specimens within subphases has no significance except for projectile points. Approximate order of artifacts represented, from left to right: 1. Olivella beads; 2. Haliotis ornaments (note that first appearance of heavy incision on many ornaments is in Middle-Late Horizon Transition); 3. Charmstones; 4. Stone pipes; 5. Decorated bone ear tubes and whistles; 6. Stone projectile points; 7. Bone harpoons. Legend: Ab, bone awls; Bw, bone whistles; C, "cupped" olivella beads; D, dart point (undesignated points are presumed arrow points); Fg, Fishhook or gorges of wood (top), shell, and bone (bottom); Ft, antler tine flaker; Fu, bone (ulna) flaker; G, ornaments worn as girdle; H, bone hairpin; K, stone knife; L, trait carries over to Phase 2, Late Horizon; M, stone mortar and pestles; P, ornaments usually found paired in mirror image; S, spear point; Sd, stone discoidal, perforated; T, trait appears for first time in Transition phase, between Middle and Late Horizons; W, stone pestle for use in wooden mortars; We, whole end-ground olivella bead; Ws, whole spire-ground olivella bead; Wsg, whole side-ground olivella bead; XX, flexed burial position (27% grave pit burning; 32% have northwest orientation).

gles" or "tinklers"—also found in some frequency in McClure facies, Marin District; large obsidian points with unique scalloped edges along blade and tip (cf. fig. 3, no. 59, Castro facies); grass cutters (?)—deer scapulae despined and with serrated edges (contrasted with a San Francisco Bay region form that is not despined—fig. 2).

Burial complex data suggest an equation of primary inhumation at Napa with Middle Horizon culture, while cremations are essentially identified with Late Horizon, Phase 2. The schema thus intimates that evidence for Phase 1 Late Horizon as already noted for Alameda and Marin Districts is virtually nonexistent in the region.

The Napa area is unusual in that it appears to have served as a waypoint in the marine mollusk trade from the coast to the Sacramento Valley. Furthermore, it was definitely a source of obsidian for San Francisco Bay, Marin County, and the Sacramento-San Joaquin Delta regions. Like those of Marin District, Napa County peoples evidently did not produce numbers of elaborate shell ornaments even though the mollusks were certainly available to them. In almost all the Napa region sites so far investigated, however, there is evidence that, besides

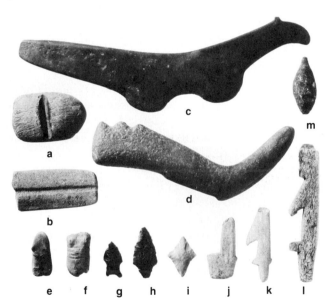

Lowie Mus., U. of Calif., Berkeley: a, 1-24338; b, 1-90096; c, 1-18093; d, 1-97825; e, 1-22479; f, 1-148136; g-i, 1-124797, 124823, 124824; j, 1-97842; k, 1-115766; l, 1-98508; m, 1-125016.

Fig. 7. Artifacts of stone and bone. a, Steatite arrow shaft straightener. From site in Owens Valley, Calif. b, Sandstone arrow shaft smoother (one of pair?). Site Hum-169. c, Slate animal-form club (?), "slave-killer." Site Hum-167. d, Stone adze handle, without blade. Site Hum-169. e, Baked clay female figurine, attributed to Yuki. From unnumbered site in Mendocino Co., Calif. f, Baked clay female figurine, Middle Horizon. Site Mrn-365. g-i, Obsidian (left) and chert projectile points (cf. Intermediate period). Site Mnt-281. j, Antler harpoon head fragment, with line shoulder. Site Hum-118. k, Bone harpoon head fragment, with bilateral line guard. Site Hum-169. l, Antler harpoon head fragment, with unilateral line guard; remains of groove at tip for placement of hollow-base stone point. Site Hum-169. m, Sandstone plummet-shaped object with polished shoulder, probably used as reamer in manufacture of C-shaped shell fishhooks. Site Mnt-281.

exporting obsidian from quarries, the residents made ample use of it in manufacturing their own implements.

Monterey County—Coastal Region

For the southern Monterey County coast, usually considered as part of the South Coast Ranges, Central California links are weak.

Two sites at Willow Creek, near the southern border of Monterey County (Mnt-281, Mnt-282), have been analyzed. The sites, which lie one on top of the other, literally, separated by a sterile gravel deposit, seem to show successive occupation by the same or closely related peoples. Carbon-14 dates from the lower and unquestionably older of these sites, Mnt-282, are A.D. 50 and 100 (C-628, C-695). At this time, apparently, a developed marine-adapted economy consisting of line-fishing, mollusk taking, and sea-mammal hunting was thriving. On fairly sketchy evidence from such artifacts as can be compared with those from facies in San Francisco Bay, for example, it appears that the Willow Creek sites were occupied during the late Middle Horizon. The carbon-14 dates cited are thus in accord with the cultural evidence.

Mnt-281 and Mnt-282 produced material representing numbers of practices that could ultimately have been derived from either north or south (Pohorecky 1964): flexed burials, cremation (rare), grooved or notched stone sinkers, red ocher in burials, pitted stones or small cobble mortars, gorge fish hooks, matting needles of bone, bone awls, bird-bone beads, stone cairns over graves, perforated stone discoidals, abalone ring ornaments, and incised slate tablets (fig. 8j).

Elements derived from the south—coastal San Luis Obispo or Santa Barbara County—are found, such as hopper mortars, curved shell fishhooks, bone "abalone pries," heavy use of asphaltum with abalone shell, chert and obsidian projectile points (fig. 7g-i), probable asphaltum adhesive around bases of projectile points, stones covered with asphaltum—perhaps "tarring pebbles" for rendering baskets waterproof.

Cultural features that could be derived from the north are olivella beads, Type 3c; bone "fiber strippers" (cf. fig. 3, no. 80). On balance, it appears that the Willow Creek sites may have been at or near an early cultural boundary line (perhaps Costanoan-Salinan) that survived into the historic period.

Southern San Joaquin Valley

At Buena Vista Lake, Wedel (1941) excavated several sites (Ker-39-42) that indicated a long sequence of occupation corresponding in several key details to all the archeological horizons known in the Delta region to the north. In addition, a number of direct chronological links with the Santa Barbara Coast cultures were recorded.

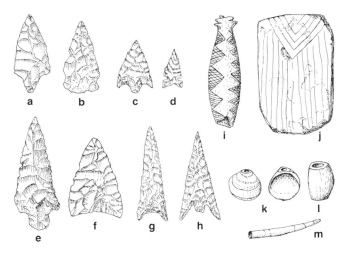

a-d, after Elsasser 1960; e-h,j, Lowie Mus., U. of Calif., Berkeley; e, 1-159154; f, 1-158597; g, 1-158753; h, 1-158820; i, after Elsasser and Heizer 1966; j, 1-125176; k-m, idealized.
Fig. 8. Artifacts of stone, bone, and shell. a-d, Projectile points from Nev-15: a-c, Martis complex points of basalt, contracting stemmed, side-notched, and barbed types; d, Desert side-notched point of chert. e-h, Chert projectile points from site DNo-11: e, stemmed; f, concave-based, for use on bone or antler simple harpoon tips; g, lighter concave-based arrow point; h, "Gunther-barbed" point (original in fragmentary condition). i, Decorated bone "head scratcher" from Site Hum-118. j, Incised slate tablet from Site Mnt-281. k, *Glycymeris* shell bead, northern Calif. l, Pine-nut bead, northern Calif. m, Dentalium shell bead, northern Calif.

Similarities to the Delta region in the Middle Horizon are seen in the presence of Buena Vista Lake of bone sweat scrapers and decorated bone spatulae; olivella beads, for example, split-punched, Type 3a2 (cf. fig. 5, Ponce facies) and possibly disks, Type 3d (cf. fig. 3), and haliotis disk beads, Type H3 or H4 (cf. fig. 4).

Flexed burials at this time were common to both Delta region and Santa Barbara Coast as well as to Buena Vista Lake. Hopper mortars, not a characteristic of the Delta region during Middle Horizon, apparently occur at Santa Barbara and at Buena Vista Lake during the same time period.

In concurrence with Late Phase 1 in the Delta region, there were present at Buena Vista Lake small triangular projectile points, perforated steatite discoidals, haliotis ornaments with multiple perforations and split-punched and disk types of olivella beads.

Limpet shell ornaments, ring-shaped and platter-shaped, similar to those from Santa Barbara Coast are found at Buena Vista Lake, suggesting continuing relationships with the Coast through Late Horizon. A highly developed steatite industry, including numbers of unique reel-shaped objects at Buena Vista Lake may have begun in Late Horizon, Phase 1, but along with other Santa Barbara Coast traits such as wooden grave markers, abalone shell receptacles, and use of perforated fish vertebrae, may have reached the highest peak of emphasis in the protohistoric period (Phase 2 Central California sequence).

To the north of Buena Vista Lake, near the present town of Tranquillity is a site (Fre-48) that from the time of its first excavation has been a source of controversy (Hewes 1946). Discussion centered around the discovery in 1943 of highly mineralized human skeletons in possible association with an extinct Pleistocene fauna. With the human remains were artifacts then thought to be of Middle Horizon Central California affiliations. Olivella beads, obliquely spire-ground, Type 1c (fig. 9, no. 1—Southern Coast, about 500 B.C.) and mullers and milling stones at Fre-48 point to relations with southern California. However, the 1c beads (also reported from Berkeley facies, Early Horizon—fig. 2, no. 2), large stemmed points of chert, obsidian, and other materials, as well as large obsidian concave-based forms also suggest links with San Francisco Bay or the lower San Joaquin Delta region. Berger et al. (1971:48) have determined a carbon-14 date of about 600 B.C. on human bone collagen from the site. This dating agrees chronologically with the evidence from the artifacts, but does nothing to clarify the meaning of the human bone–extinct faunal bone association (Angel 1966).

Redding District

"Redding District" includes complexes in what were formerly designated (Meighan 1955) parts of the North Coast Ranges. As a blanket term the one used here is also possibly misleading, inasmuch as it subsumes several distinct localities on two or three different river drainage systems. Representative sites from each of these subareas are shown on fig. 1: Men-187, Round Valley (Eel River); Tri-58 (Trinity River); Sha-20, Sha-47, Teh-58 (McCloud, Sacramento rivers). Added to this is the observation that separate ethnographic groups (the Yuki in Mendocino County and the Wintu in Shasta and Tehama counties) occupied the territory in question. Nevertheless, the archeological evidence points to common sources for the prehistoric cultures disclosed in these subareas—the Central Valley in Late Horizon, Phases 1 and 2, and less precisely, either Northwestern California or the Columbia River region. No radiocarbon dates are available from sites excavated in the Redding area, and the earliest estimates of time of any considerable occupation, at least, are about A.D. 900 (Treganza 1959a:26).

The common presence in the subareas of the Redding District so far investigated of late prehistoric and historic materials indicates a continuous development from Late Horizon, Phase 1, to about A.D. 1850. However, it appears in Round Valley that clamshell beads may have been introduced to the Yuki, not from the Sacramento Valley, but by the ethnographic Pomo in postcontact times (Meighan 1955:33). Also, Treganza and Heicksen (1960:23) reported from a site near Redding clamshell disk beads in upper levels, in association with historic European material, but not present in burials from the

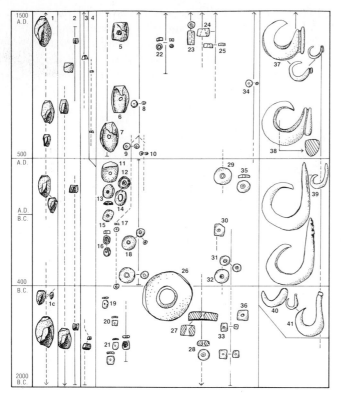

Chart by Chester King, 1972.

Fig. 9. Southern California Coast shell beads and single-piece fishhooks. Dashed lines show possible temporal range; solid lines indicate more confident estimates of range or relationship of types. Arrows denote survival from or extension to earlier and later time period. Bead typology from Lillard, Heizer, and Fenenga 1939.

1-22, Olivella beads: 1. Whole spire-looped, Types 1a, 1b (small and large), and 1c (diagonally ground); 2. "Barrel-shaped," spire and base ground, Gifford's (1947) Type G1a; 3. Gifford's Type G1b, more of base ground off than in Type G1a; 4. Gifford's Type G1c, cuplike bead made from spire; 5. Rectangular, split-punched, Type 3a3; 6. Split, but with perforation made by grinding convex surface of wall, Type 3a variant; 7. Split-punched, Type 3a2; 8-10. Variants of small disk, Type 3d; 11. Split, drilled, Type 3b1; 12. Round "saddle," Type 3b variant; 13. Oval "saddle," Type 3b variant; 14. Rare type, shaped like small contemporary limpet ornaments; 15. Modified "saddle," Type 3b2; 16. Unique, with convex surface ground and drilled perforation; 17. Small disk, Type 3e variant, with some examples ground flat; 18. "Saucer," Type 3c; 19. Rectangular, with rounded edges and lenticular cross-sections, Type 2b (?); 20. Rectangular, Type 2b; 21. Rectangular, sometimes ground on concave surface, Type 2b; 22. Cupped, Type 3e. 23-28, *Tivela* sp. beads and ornament: 23. Small cylinder; 24. Thick disk; 25. Thinner disk; 26. Large ring bead or ornament; 27,28. Disks. 29-33, *Haliotis* sp. disk beads: 29. Circular, Type 3; 30. Rough rectangular (amorphous) Type 4; 31,32. Circular, Type 3, note size range; 33. Small rectangular, Type 1a. 34-36. *Mytilus* disk beads, circular and rectangular. 37-41, Shell and bone fishhooks: 37. *Mytilus*—haliotis hooks (not shown) of this type usually have shorter shanks than most *Mytilus* specimens; 38. Rare bone type, with grooved shank; 39. *Mytilus,* with plain and notched shanks—hooks of these types are also made of haliotis and bone; 40. Haliotis with undefined shank; 41. Bone, with knobbed shank—some hooks of this type also occur in shell.

protohistoric levels. Glycymeris shell beads or ornaments found in Redding District (fig. 8k) do not appear characteristically in archeological deposits in coastal Northwestern California, although they were used there in ethnographic times. These point to another possible postcontact diffusion into the Redding District.

The hopper slab acorn mortar is widely distributed among ethnographic groups of northern California. It is characteristically present in many prehistoric sites of Redding District, but its ultimate place of derivation remains indefinite. Examples on the Columbia River (Strong, Schenck, and Steward 1930:pls. 22e, 26a) are not definitely dated, and the Southern California distribution does not extend through Central California in Phases 1 or 2, Late Horizon.

One exaggeratedly large ceremonial obsidian blade was found in a burial associated with clamshell beads at site Teh-58 in Redding District. The specimen is similar to blades known among the ethnographic Yurok and is probably the largest such blade ever found archeologically in California. The obsidian itself probably came from Modoc County, near the present California-Oregon border, and the trait is suggested as indigenous to Northern California, perhaps first developing among the prehistoric Yurok.

Pine-nut beads (fig. 8l) are so common in both Northwestern California and Redding District that independent indigenous development in each region may easily be inferred, although such beads are known elsewhere, even as far distant as the Humboldt Valley in western Nevada (Heizer and Krieger 1956:26) where they are classed as trade items.

Incised mammal-bone pendants (fig. 8i) from Redding District have their counterparts in specimens from Northwestern California, where they have been referred to as head scratchers, louse killers, and the like (Loud 1918:pl. 20). In view of the apparently advanced development of bone working on the Coast, it seems likely that the Redding specimens ultimately were derived therefrom.

So-called charmstones in most of the Redding District are of the type recorded for the ethnographic Wintu by Du Bois (1935). They are curiously shaped stones, fossilized bones, or at most undeveloped spindle-shaped objects. Although such odd stones may be found in almost any archeological site in Central California, it is noteworthy that with one exception these Redding examples do not seem to cooccur there with the finely shaped charmstones found in Late Horizon in the Sacramento River Delta region. The exception is seen in Round Valley, where phallic-shaped stones reminiscent of, but by no means identical with, lower Sacramento Valley types have been found. In both Marin District and the Napa region phallic charmstones were found in Late Horizon contexts.

Delicately chipped, side-notched, concave-based projectile points (fig. 8d), commonly referred to as "Desert side-notched" (Baumhoff and Byrne 1959) have a widespread distribution in California, including the lower Sacramento Valley, in Phase 2, Late Horizon, and in historic times. In the Redding District occurs a distinctive subtype that Baumhoff and Byrne appropriately call the "Redding subtype," characterized by deep diagonal notching, a bell-shaped base, slightly concave sides, and often a delicate, "extended" tip, which has also been noted on several types of points from the Columbia River region (Cressman 1960:fig. 41c).

The custom of placing corpses in graves in flexed position could have come from either north or south. Cremations rarely occur at several sites, but are believed to have been introduced in historical times in Redding District.

Relatively definite links with cultures from the lower Sacramento Valley, Central California Late Horizon, are olivella beads (rectangular, and split-punched), preinterment grave-pit burning (rare), and haliotis ornaments (rectangular and circle-shaped) with single or double perforations.

With the region to the north, either Northwestern California or the Columbia River valley, the Redding District sites share dentalium beads (fig. 8m); arrow-shaft smoothers (fig. 7b) of some abrasive stone, presumably used in pairs; possibly flanged pestles; salmon harpoon points of bone (in McCloud River area—cf. Collier, Hudson, and Ford 1942:pl. VIII); and the distinctive type of stone projectile point with short stem and long barbs, the Gunther-barbed point.

North Coast Ranges

Having already eliminated several of the archeological cultures suggested by Meighan (1955) from the penumbra of the North Coast Ranges, outlining of what may be considered the core complex of that region remains. Excavations in the 1960s at a site in Lake County (Lak-261) to the east of Mendocino County (fig. 1) together with some carbon-14 dates (1740 B.C. at I-2754), have given some confirmation for Meighan's proposed sequence for the region. The 1740 B.C. date was reportedly taken from a level that included nonfluted, concave-based points as its chief marker. Following this early period (which may relate to the later Borax Lake culture), there developed a culture characterized by distinctive, slightly shouldered or rounded-base points. In an upper level of Lak-261 are shown some cultural relationships to Meighan's Mendocino complex (1955), to the northern extension of the McClure complex in Marin District (Son-299), and to sites in Napa County that have certain Middle Horizon affiliations. A carbon-14 date of 150 B.C. (I-2791) has been assigned to this level.

The Mendocino complex, named from analysis of one key site, Men-500, includes nonfluted, concave-based points, mostly made of chert (not of obsidian, as are the larger points of the same general style from earlier cultures in the region), stratigraphically the oldest points in the complex. Little shell was recovered; hence it is impossible to relate the complex to any particular facies of the Middle Horizon in Central California. Burial position, where this could be determined from the few graves encountered, was loosely flexed. Grinding stones were bowl mortars of two types, one simple, like bowl mortars found in other parts of California, and one unique, with a pointed bottom. The latter type may be diagnostic of the complex. Manos and milling stones (metates) were also used. Milling stones were also found in several places in the Redding District to the north: Round Valley (Treganza, Smith, and Weymouth 1950:117) and near Redding itself (Treganza and Heicksen 1960:37). Such occurrences possibly were connected with the Mendocino complex.

Even if Men-500 is truly representative of North Coast Ranges cultures approximately contemporaneous with those of Middle Horizon in Central California, its relationship with the Middle Horizon cultures in terms of artifact inventory is distant. However, at Men-500 also appeared a later culture, which Meighan designated as the Clear Lake complex. This was named on the basis of upper-level Men-500 artifacts recovered, on certain inferences drawn from ethnographic Pomo and Yuki materials, and from comparisons with other late (protohistoric) cultures known in Mendocino, Lake, and Sonoma counties. This complex obviously has numbers of parallels with Phase 2 of the Central California developmental sequence and emphasizes again what has been observed in varying degrees for several of the archeological areas so far covered—that parts of assemblages from Phase 1 of the sequence turn out to be missing or poorly represented.

At Men-500, Clear Lake complex is denoted by tightly flexed burial position; large chert blades of the kind also found in Redding District; slab mortars; magnesite and glass trade beads; small triangular side-notched points; Desert side-notched; and carefully made stone-lined earth ovens, such as those described ethnographically for the Yuki. Added to these (but not found at Men-500) should be cremation, with ashes or bones buried in baskets; haliotis pendants; charmstones; baked clay slingstones; clamshell disk beads; olivella disk and whole-shell beads; bone whistles and awls; stone bead-grinding slabs; and small clay figurines used as dolls (fig. 7e).

This complex almost certainly represents, in different sections of the North Coast Ranges, the ancestral Pomo, Yuki, and perhaps parts of the Wappo and Miwok. Separation of the later (Clear Lake complex) peoples from those who lived in Redding District at about the same time is tenuous, according to this interpretation, but groups near Redding were nevertheless different in that they were more heavily subject to influences from the north that presumably never reached the people of the Clear Lake complex.

Northwestern California

Along the Pacific coast from just south of Humboldt Bay north to the present California-Oregon border and perhaps 100 miles beyond along the Oregon shore are found evidences of a fairly uniform archeological area designated here simply as Northwestern California.

The ethnographic groups of the area are usually treated as an outlying or marginal expression of the more spectacular maritime cultures to the north—the Northwest Coast between Puget Sound and southern Alaska. However, indications of remarkable maritime adaptations are by no means continuous from the Columbia River mouth, for example, south to the Klamath River, and there is also to be considered a strong riverine adaptation associated with the so-called coastal cultures of the region. This adaptation is clearly based upon salmon fishing, but unfortunately archeological investigation along rivers like the Klamath or Trinity does little to elucidate the ultimate interior source or course of diffusion of many aspects of culture into this mixed coastal environment.

It has long been assumed that the Wiyot and the neighboring Yurok, both Algonquian-speaking groups, came into the region about 1,000 years ago (Kroeber 1917a). Judging from their comparatively remote linguistic relationship even though within the same stock, they must have split off from some parent group either to the north or northeast long before 1,000 years ago. In any event, ancestors of either tribe could have originally come independently, most likely from along the coast or from the northeast, for example, from the upper Columbia River region.

Excavations at less than 10 important sites during the past 50 years have, with one exception, disclosed the presence on the coast of stable groups depending heavily for subsistence upon fish, mollusks, and sea mammals. The culture has changed in several details, but not in its basic tenor, since the time of its supposed entry into the region. Radiocarbon dates from two sites, Hum-67 and Hum-118, of about A.D. 900 and A.D. 1300, respectively (I-2352, GX-0182), serve to support the idea of the beginning date first suggested by Kroeber and do not conflict with postulations concerning the subsequent course of cultural development in the region. The one exception to this pattern is found to the north, at Point St. George, in the territory of the ethnographic Tolowa, an Athapaskan-speaking group (DNo-11, fig. 1). Here Gould (1966a) has identified a lower level in the site: sandy soil deposit without thick lenses of shell or bone and lacking in bone tools, stone woodworking tools, or fishing equip-

ment. These lower deposits contain crudely chipped stone tools, markedly different from those found in the upper levels of the site. Carbon-14 dating of about 300 B.C. (I-4006) for this level thus points to a group preceding, and quite possibly not connected in any way with, the later prehistoric groups represented in the upper levels. In short, the only deposit for which an early carbon-14 date is at hand has practically no information about the basic economy of the people who were responsible for it. From lexicostatistical data on the Athapaskan languages, it seems most unlikely that the ancestral Tolowa could have left these meager remains. The Athapaskan penetration of Northern California and Southern Oregon probably did not take place much before A.D. 900 (cf. Hoijer 1956:232) at the earliest and perhaps was even several hundreds of years later.

In the later deposits of site DNo-11 and in deposits from other excavated sites in Northwestern California are found artifact assemblages (presumably after A.D. 900) that tend to link them together in a common maritime-adapted culture.

• BURIAL COMPLEX   Simple interments with the dorsally extended position evidently were the preferred mode; flexed burial positions also were not unknown. On Gunther Island in Humboldt Bay, a burial practice that seems closely related to the preinterment grave-pit burning of Central California was observed. Conceivably this may in some cases be confused with cremation, but the kind of "complete" cremation common in Phase 2 Late Horizon in Central California assuredly was not the custom.

• SUBSISTENCE ACTIVITIES   Evidence for fishing is found notably in bone netting shuttles and notched or grooved stone sinkers. On these rests the idea that net fishing was even more important in Northwestern California than in Late Horizon, Marin District, to the south. Several types of bone fishhooks, including composite specimens with bipointed pins used as barbs and similar pins that probably were used as gorges, have been found. The most frequently occurring type of definite fishhook was a curved (C-shaped) specimen with pointed, unbarbed tips; this type resembles fishhooks from the Santa Barbara Coast far to the south.

Numerous types of harpoons and spears were used for both fishing and sea-mammal hunting. Simple bone harpoons with or without slotted tips for the reception of stone points, for use against sea mammals, are of interest here, for they are among the few classes of specimens that demonstrate a chronological sequence of forms, from the earliest one called a bilateral line (attachment) shoulder to one with a unilateral line guard (fig. 7k-l). This last one is the type in use ethnographically among the Yurok and Tolowa (Bennyhoff 1950:321).

Mention has already been made of the crude, pointed-stemmed, chipped stone points from the early levels of site DNo-11. Gould (1966a:52) has suggested a developmental series of projectile points beginning with these pointed-stemmed forms and proceeding through concave-based to finely chipped, tanged (barbed) points. However, the barbed ones, usually called the Gunther-barbed variety of points, have a widespread distribution in Oregon and northern California and may not have developed on the coast at all. Examples of points just discussed are shown in figure 8e-h.

Arrowshaft smoothers or grooved abrasive stones (fig. 7b) seem to have a distribution about equally widespread as that of the Gunther-barbed points. Likewise, they are assumed to have a northern derivation, as specimens almost identical to Northwestern California and Redding District examples have been found on the Columbia River (cf. Collier, Hudson, and Ford 1942:161). Unfortunately, the sites from which those specimens were recovered have not been placed in a definite time sequence; hence, the direction of diffusion is not known.

Steatite dishes or "grease catchers," as used in the salmon smoking process by ethnographic Yurok, are found in several of the coastal sites. This trait is known to the north, but in an attenuated form compared to the Northwestern California development.

There is no clear evidence that the use of stone bowl mortars precedes that of hopper slab mortars in Northwestern California sites, although the former have been reported from several localities in the region. Whatever its derivation, the hopper slab mortar was here the dominant type of grinding stone, just as in the probably coeval Redding District. Pestles of several forms were used, but the most distinctive are those showing a flange near the distal (impact) end.

• WOODWORKING TOOLS   Chief among woodworking tools are the curved stone adze handles (fig. 7d), which appear to be unique to the region and not to have diffused to other parts of California. These were probably used prehistorically with shell blades, continuing in use in ethnographic times with iron blades. Antler wedges and the bell- or pear-shaped stone mauls used to pound them, in the splitting of wood probably intended for house planks, are apparently derived from a northern source (cf. Olson 1927).

• CEREMONY, WEALTH, AND DECORATIVE ART   In Northwestern California certain artifacts recovered from archeological deposits, like dentalium beads and large obsidian blades, are known ethnographically to have been used primarily as wealth items, although they may only appear at prescribed ceremonies. Others, like clay figurines and slate animal-form clubs, do not appear in the ethnographic record, and it is therefore speculative in which of the categories they should properly be placed.

The obsidian for the large blades (which may be more than two feet long) probably came from the upper Klamath River region, not from near the coast. Despite this, and the fact that the largest of the blades of this kind yet recovered was from Redding District, it seems safe to say that the blades were an indigenous Northwestern California trait. This is based upon the frequency of these objects in archeological deposits, and upon their elaboration by the ethnographic Yurok.

Animal-form clubs (also called "slave killers," fig. 7c) possibly were intended only as grave accompaniments, presumably for the wealthy. Although inspiration for designs of these objects seemingly comes from the Northwest Coast, their specific form permits the suggestion that they also are a local indigenous trait.

Decorated tabular mammal bone pendants (head scratchers or "louse killers"?)—perforated, plain ended, or provided with end constrictions—occur frequently in Northwestern California, and again one may suggest an original center for elaboration there, at least of geometrically designed pieces. Some geometrically designed specimens (fig. 8i) resembling the coast examples have been recovered at one site in the Redding District (Treganza and Heicksen 1960:26). Elsewhere, for instance on the Santa Barbara Coast, similar objects have also been found (cf. Gifford 1940a:220).

Pine-nut beads may represent late prehistoric diffusion to the coast, though their very simplicity may also point to local independent origin. Spire-lopped olivella beads are in this same category; that is, while ideas of their use may have come from elsewhere, the bead itself could stem from original impromptu use by the local people who in this case found naturally "prepared" beads on their beaches.

The occurrence of clamshell disk beads is practically negligible. However, small olivella disk beads, probably Type 3d, also a common Central California type, have been reported from one site in the northwest (Hum-67) and from sites on the Columbia River as well (Strong, Schenck, and Steward 1930:72; Collier, Hudson, and Ford 1942:94).

There is little doubt that dentalium beads were the most important form of shell artifact in Northwestern California, prehistorically and ethnographically, and that they were derived predominantly from the north along the coast. However, whether or not the northern California (for example, Redding) occurrences were related by diffusion from the lower Klamath River peoples is not quite clear. Dentalium beads are known also from late prehistoric and historic sites on the Columbia River (Strong, Schenck, and Steward 1930:72), and Kroeber (1925:320) has recorded "some dentalia" going down the Klamath River in trade from the ethnographic Modoc. This implies a route established at some undetermined time for dentalia from the traditional source on the north coast of Vancouver Island, south on the coast and up the Columbia, perhaps then up the Deschutes River and finally to Northeastern California, where live the Modocs.

Finally, fired clay artifacts (figurines, pipes, and small balls) must be noted in Northwestern California. Normally, all these kinds of specimens would be thought to have been derived from Central California; however, their counterparts have not been reported from the Redding District, astride the most likely line of diffusion from the Sacramento Valley. The pipes and clay balls could be merely simple local variants of ideas of what to do with baked clay in a culture familiar with girdled, grooved stone sinkers (balls?) and stone (sucking or smoking) pipes. This does not hold for the figurines, most of which so far found in Northwestern California follow the specific pattern of such objects from Marin District, Middle Horizon Central California. These are headless, usually provided with female mammae representations, and bearing punctate or incised decoration on the body (fig. 7f).

Clay figurines for use as toys have been noted among the ethnographic Pomo in the North Coast Ranges. Illustrated here (fig. 7e) is one such clay figure without exact provenience, from the Coast Yuki territory. It may be an archeological piece, related to the Northwestern California figurines.

In a brief overview of prehistoric Northwestern California, there is evidence first of a relatively ancient stratum (DNo-11) that, although unidentifiable as to origin, can be interpreted at least as a nonmarine adapted culture. Following this are abundant remains of people who seemed originally to have come to the coast fully equipped to deal with this environment, possibly the ancestors of some of the ethnographic peoples like the Yurok, Tolowa, or Wiyot. Some aspects of this culture, so far as is known without excavation in pertinent cemeteries, did not survive into historic times: animal-form clubs and other ground slate artifacts; baked clay objects, such as female (fertility?) figurines; and a type of olivella disk bead. For the rest, there is no mistaking a continuity, dating probably from about A.D. 900.

This culture, though owing its significant cast to the north (Northwest Coast or Columbia River region), experienced a local flowering of its own in California. Evidence of its relations with Central California, for example, in Redding District, also seems to bear out the notion that, whatever its beginning, the lower Klamath River culture at the start of the historic period was radiating to north, south, and east rather than receiving strong influences from any of these directions.

Sierra Nevada

Of all the archeological regions treated so far in this chapter, the Sierra Nevada is the most diverse, and the very idea of considering it as a single distinct region presents some difficulties. Prehistoric cultural influences from the Great Basin, from the little-known southern

Cascade region, from Central (Valley) and even Southern California have been felt there in varying degrees, yet it would be misleading to regard the Sierra as a marginal area where outliers of several different cultures impinged on each other.

Southern Cascade Mountains

In surveying the relationships that existed between Sierra Nevadan cultures and those from outside the province, it will be best to begin with a summary of what is known archeologically of the southern Cascade Mountains region, which adjoins the Sierra Nevada on the north. The Cascades in California, except for two high peaks, Mount Shasta and Mount Lassen, are lower and show more broken terrain than the Sierra Nevada. They are characterized by rough basaltic formations in contrast to the dominantly granitic morphology of the Sierra Nevada. Otherwise there is at least a superficial continuity between the northern reaches of the Sierra Nevada and the Cascades. River drainage patterns for some distance north and south of the "break" between the ranges are similar in that both have several permanent streams forming tributaries to the upper Sacramento River.

Cultural affinities with the Redding District are seen in late prehistoric sites in the (Cascade) upper Pit River area, in the form of clamshell disk beads; pine-nut beads; spire-lopped olivella beads; dentalium shell beads; flexed burial position; and a variety of small, stemmed, serrated points, including Desert side-notched specimens, of which none of the Redding subtype is found.

Unlike the Redding District (Central Valley and North Coast Ranges) later deposits in the upper Pit River are underlain by more than a mere suggestion of older cultures, perhaps extending back to more than 3000 B.C. This estimate is made on the basis of chipped stone points that resemble putatively ancient specimens found in the Great Basin and in the Klamath Lake area of Oregon. In the Klamath Lake region Cressman (1956:415) has recorded a sequence including leaf-shaped, large side-notched, and stemmed points, to which the Pit River series can significantly be compared. A carbon-14 date of about 1350 B.C. (UCLA-127) from a site on a Pit River tributary is associated with artifacts that may point to some time during the Early-Middle Horizon transition in Central California (Baumhoff and Olmsted 1963).

Some basalt points in the Pit River series also resemble stemmed specimens of the Martis complex (or tradition) of the northern Sierra Nevada.

In the foothills of the southern Cascades, in ethnographic Yana territory, a cultural sequence with a time range somewhat later than that of the upper Pit River has been worked out. Site Teh-1 (fig. 1) is one of several rockshelters or open sites in this region that is thought to equate in its beginnings with Middle Horizon Central California and the Martis complex of the Sierra Nevada (Baumhoff 1955; Johnson 1972). Manos and metates and flat-ended pestles and hopper mortars here suggest simultaneous utilization of a variety of small seeds besides acorns, but the virtual cooccurrence in all midden levels affords no information on temporal precedence of either set of grinding implements. Burials were in flexed position, as is common in Middle Horizon Central California. Chipped stone points of basalt resemble certain forms from that horizon as well as from Martis complex sites, for example, large triangular stemmed and corner-notched specimens. No reports of objects called "boat-stones" or atlatl weights, such as might be inferred by the presence of large basalt projectile points, have so far been made for this region. At least one type of singly perforated rectanguloid haliotis pendant, resembling Middle Horizon forms of the lower Sacramento Valley (cf. fig. 4, no. 33), was recovered.

In the later levels of sites in Yana territory (corresponding to Late Horizon, Central California, especially Phase 2) have been reported clamshell disk beads; magnesite beads; haliotis ornaments with single perforations of circular and small triangular forms (fig. 5, nos. 14-15); olivella beads, spire-lopped and single-perforation squarish (Type 2a) examples; and a few Desert side-notched points. Pine-nut beads and points of the Gunther-barbed series are links with the Redding District.

In the southern Cascade region only a relatively minute number of sites recorded have bedrock mortars in association. Such mortars are known throughout the Sierra Nevada, but are most frequent in the central or southern Sierra, where they occur even at elevations as great as 9,000 feet, which is beyond the range of the oak (Bennyhoff 1953), usually in late prehistoric or protohistoric sites.

Northern Sierra Nevada

The first putatively ancient Sierra Nevadan archeological complex described was called Martis, after the name of a valley near Truckee, California, in which Pla-5 (fig. 1) is located (Heizer and Elsasser 1953). The Martis complex was thought to represent a high-elevation seasonal hunting and seed-gathering culture east of the main crest of the range, and later work has disclosed manifestations of this complex in the western part of the Great Basin and in the foothills of the western slope of the Sierra Nevada.

On the basis of equation in time of Martis series points, principally with some Nevada forms with which they also cooccurred (such as Elko-eared and corner-notched—O'Connell 1967) and carbon-14 dating (I-1999), Elston (1971) has suggested a beginning of the Martis complex at 1000 B.C.

Excavations at site Nev-15 in the western foothills of the Sierra Nevada (fig. 1) disclose that Martis people were present there, perhaps as early as 1000 B.C. No conclusive cultural stratification was noted at the site, suggesting a transition from the Martis culture to that of the ethnographic Maidu, whose ancestors presumably held part of the territory during or after the time of the Martis occupation. However, there were found a few Desert side-notched points in middle and upper levels of the deposit. Such points are not likely to date before A.D. 1000, and even A.D. 1400 would seem to be a more suitable date for their entry into California (Baumhoff and Byrne 1959).

Another site, Pla-101 (see Ritter 1972) near Auburn, California, shows strong Martis affiliation and has a carbon-14 date of about 1400 B.C. (Gak-2246). Ritter has suggested a chronological seriation of certain Martis forms (contracting stemmed, side-notched, and barbed projectile points), roughly in the order given, and this sequence could be fitted into the picture at Nev-15 without serious contradictions (cf. fig. 8a-c). The upper level of Pla-101 contains Desert side-notched points, and the next lower level, without such points, has a radiocarbon date of about A.D. 1000 (Gak-2244, 2245).

Also, from the western Sierran foothills near Oroville, about 35 miles northwest of Nev-15, a local cultural sequence beginning about 1000 B.C. and continuing through to the ethnographic period of the Maidu has been recognized (Olsen and Riddell 1963). A carbon-14 date of about 950 B.C. (I-3170) refers to site components that show affiliations with both Middle Horizon Central California and the Martis complex.

Succeeding cultures, from perhaps A.D. 1 (Ritter 1970:174) retain some of the Martis traits, including emphasis on manos and metates as grinding implements, large basalt drills, and large leaf-shaped, corner- and side-notched as well as wide-stemmed points, mostly of basalt. Around A.D. 800 the Martis complex elements in the Oroville region seem to have been almost entirely supplanted, except for leaf-shaped basalt knives, which continue in use. For other traits, a Phase 1 Late Horizon affiliation can be suggested: dorsally extended or semi-flexed burial position; tubular stone pipes; a banjo-type haliotis ornament; olivella beads, split-punched and rectangular, center-perforated.

The final phase in the region, definitely corresponding with Phase 2, Late Horizon in the Sacramento Valley, contains items such as clamshell disk beads and olivella beads (thin lipped—Type 3a1), incised bird-bone tubes, Desert side-notched points, and other small stemmed, barbed points.

The dilemma of the northern Sierra Nevada, in sum, is not concerned with the derivation of the Martis people: their roots seem to lie in the Great Basin. If they crossed the Sierra Nevada about 1000 B.C., they could have represented another wave of migrants from the Great Basin to Central California, possibly Penutian speakers.

There is no distinct border between the Martis region and the Sierra Nevadan terrain to the south, which also shows evidence of occupation from around 1000 B.C. However, it can be suggested that Great Basin influence here was secondary compared to that deriving from the Central Valley of California. Investigations in two localities on the eastern margin of the valley floor (Johnson 1967, 1970) have disclosed sites ranging from early Middle Horizon to the historic period. The earlier levels contain remnants, probably peripheral survivals, of Early Horizon customs such as use of manos and metates and several Early types of shell beads and ornaments. With these is a large inventory of characteristic Middle Horizon traits, including large slate and basalt projectile points, some of which, such as leaf-shaped and stemmed triangular specimens, resemble Martis forms. In addition to these are haliotis pendants, rectangular and circular, serrated types; "saddle" and "saucer" olivella beads; and a variety of slate rings and pendants like those recovered in the Delta region.

These marginal valley floor sites provide a definite Middle Horizon link between the Delta people and those residing near the limestone caverns of the Sierran foothills. In such caverns, apparently used exclusively as burial places (Wallace 1951), have been found numerous skeletons together with conventional mortuary offerings, prominent among which are the diagnostic olivella beads, saddle- and saucer-shaped and a thick, shelved rectangular type (2b); haliotis pendants of circular form with serrated and unserrated edges, along with some of triangular and rectangular shape (fig. 4, nos. 32-33); and bone atlatl hooks.

Late Horizon cultural manifestations in this foothill and valley region are virtually indistinguishable from those of the Delta region. The limestone burial caverns evidently were not used in Late Horizon times (Merriam 1909), although numbers of small rockshelters in the area seem to have been utilized as occupation spots. Bedrock mortars probably also came into use at this time in the western Sierra Nevada.

In the foothills south of the Stanislaus River, Middle Horizon Delta influences were still strongly felt, although no definitely dated sites older than about 200 B.C. have yet been reported there (cf. Moratto 1971:143). Yosemite Valley is a special case, representing a heavy prehistoric settlement, with a chronological sequence based upon a wide variety of projectile points (Bennyhoff 1956; Fitzwater 1968). Some of these points—the larger and earlier ones of obsidian—resemble Great Basin and Martis examples, which were predominantly of basalt. The Yosemite sequence again suggests, on the basis of point size and weight, the transition from early use of the atlatl to later use of bow and arrow. A carbon-14 date of about 100 B.C. (UCLA-278) has been suggested as representing the earlier occupation in Yosemite, while the later sites are equated with the protohistoric Miwok. The later culture is characterized by frequent use of bedrock mortars, even at high altitudes (Bennyhoff 1953); steatite and clamshell disk beads; and small concave-based, tanged, and side-notched (including Desert side-notched) points.

The area south of Yosemite to the Fresno River also was included in ethnographic Miwok territory. Intensive excavations in this region, especially along the Chowchilla River (T. F. King 1969; Moratto 1970b), have produced evidence of a series of foothill cultures that in many ways resemble those of the Yosemite region, but which show in addition great numbers of chronologically diagnostic shell artifacts not present there. These are, for example, olivella beads, "saddle," split-drilled, and "saucer" types; and haliotis disk beads in the earlier sites; and olivella thin-lipped and cupped for the later ones. Some shell artifacts probably came from the Santa Barbara Coast, but those just enumerated, and other classes of artifacts as well, represent positive links with Middle and Late Horizons in the Delta region to the north.

A carbon-14 date of about A.D. 100 (I-5362) for the Buchanan Reservoir sites supports the idea of a developmental sequence there approximately parallel to that of Yosemite. For both regions, postulated earlier beginning dates have not been confirmed by radiocarbon dating.

South of the Fresno River only a few sites show some slight evidence of dating before about A.D. 1000. The southern Sierra Nevada, from Yosemite to the southern part of Owens Valley, thus shows a remarkable cultural uniformity in the late prehistoric period.

A crude kind of pottery, usually called Owens Valley brownware, seems to have diffused west across the range, possibly in connection with the Western Mono separation from the linguistically related Owens Valley Paiute about 500 years ago (Kroeber 1925:580). Sherds of this pottery are found in territory of the ethnographic Western Mono and some neighboring Yokuts groups in the foothills and San Joaquin Valley, and it was still in use in historic times among the three groups named on either side of the range (Gayton 1929; J. H. Steward 1933).

Unlike the pottery, which remained restricted in distribution, several similar kinds of small projectile points have been found in sites of the indicated time period in the western Sierra Nevada foothills and higher ranges. Bedrock mortars are often associated with these sites, although manos and metates may still turn up in the site deposits. Steatite disk beads and vessel sherds are often found, and occasionally clamshell disk beads are discovered.

Southern California Coast

Despite the enormous amount of excavation and survey on the Southern California coast from not far north of Santa Barbara to San Diego, general agreement among archeologists about culture sequences and datings there has not yet been achieved. Early syntheses by Rogers (1929) and Olson (1930) concerning the Santa Barbara region (mainland and Channel Islands) have since been expanded and modified to fit the Santa Barbara data into a wider context. In subsequent reinterpretations fortified with radiocarbon dating, it has become apparent that about 3,000 or 4,000 years ago essentially plant-food-gathering societies in which hunting and fishing played a secondary role probably dominated the entire coast. The characteristic implements of these groups were the muller and milling stone (mano and metate), and indeed the term Milling Stone Horizon (Wallace 1955) has been coined to represent this long period, which may have begun as early as 5000 B.C.

While the designation Milling Stone Horizon, with its functional implications, is acceptable in reference to the earlier culture, some such connotative term could not justifiably apply to the succeeding period, which corresponds roughly to the time of the Hunting People already named by Rogers (1929). Accordingly, Wallace (1955) chose the term Intermediate for this period, and this will be used herein to refer to the culture, as yet only broadly outlined, that prevailed on the coast from about 2000 B.C. to A.D. 500. In the present state of knowledge and with a paucity of stratified sites from which conclusions may be drawn, these dates cannot be presented as rigid marking points. If the Southern California coast is arbitrarily divided into four subregions from north to south—the Santa Barbara mainland, the Channel Islands, Los Angeles (Santa Monica Mountains), and San Diego—a different date for the beginning of the Intermediate period must be postulated for each of them. Furthermore, it appears that in the San Diego region there was only slight representation of the Intermediate culture at most. This was perhaps a segment of the La Jolla culture, which may have persisted there until late prehistoric times, possibly until about A.D. 1300 or 1400 (cf. K. L. Johnson 1966:19; Kowta 1969:90).

In summarizing the characteristics of the Intermediate cultures, it can be said that basket hopper mortars and bowl mortars and pestles appear at this time, although use of mullers and milling stones was not given up. Broad leaf-shaped blades and relatively heavy side-notched, leaf-shaped, and stemmed projectile points, suggesting use on atlatl darts, were present in many sites. A relatively limited number of kinds of beads of bone and shell was found. Bone and antler implements as well as use of asphalt and steatite for ornaments were much less plentiful than in the succeeding phase (Late Horizon) of Southern California prehistory. Burials were in flexed position, face down, and red ocher was in common use, along with the custom of heaping stones over burials.

Radiocarbon dates for the end of the Milling Stone Horizon or the beginning of the Intermediate period in the Los Angeles (Santa Monica Mountains) region seem to indicate a time from about 1000 B.C. to 600 B.C. for the transition: Parker Mesa site, Late Milling Stone, 1050 B.C. (UCLA-275); Malibu, LAn-264, Early Intermediate, 654 B.C. (UCLA-218E); Topanga, LAn-2, Late Milling Stone, 600 B.C. (A-94, A-97).

On the Channel Islands, mullers and milling stones, the hallmarks of the pre-Intermediate archeological horizon, were, for good reason (lack of sufficient quantities of usuable seeds) not present. However, carbon-14 dates from Santa Rosa Island have demonstrated human presence there long before 2000 B.C. Meighan (1959) reported on a complex at Little Harbor on Catalina Island with a carbon-14 date of about 1925 B.C. (M-434), which can be equated with the Intermediate period. He pointed out that because of the nature of his collections, no precise cultural affiliation with other island or mainland sites could be worked out for the Little Harbor site. Nevertheless, it is suggested that this site is representative of the time in Southern California prehistory when the distinctive maritime adaptations, including the use of seaworthy canoes, probably began to develop. These characteristic traits were certainly well displayed in later cultures, both on the mainland and the islands. Fish, mollusks, and sea mammals were the staples at Little Harbor, although, unexpectedly, no bone harpoons for hunting the mammals were recovered in the site deposit.

On San Nicholas Island radiocarbon dates of about 2000 B.C. and 1300 B.C. (UCLA-147, UCLA-165, UCLA-196) suggest an early Intermediate culture, not nearly so rich as and only vaguely comparable to that disclosed at Little Harbor. Reinman (1963-1964) has postulated an early, relatively unspecialized San Nicolas Island phase of a maritime culture, on the basis of absence of circular shell hooks (not definitely associated with Little Harbor site either), a near absence of mortars and pestles, and a high percentage of molluscan species compared to other animal remains in deposits. Later deposits have many circular shell fishhooks, some mortars and pestles, and a lesser number of molluscan genera represented in the deposits. These later deposits (cf. Rozaire 1959) are correlated with the Canalino culture, which had its greatest expression along the Santa Barbara coast and islands to the north. If Reinman is correct, again the status of the Intermediate cultures as a developmental stage in a maritime adaptation is indicated.

Linkages of the Little Harbor site with presumably Intermediate island and mainland cultures in the Santa Barbara Channel region are also tenuous. However, the Late Dune Dweller culture (Orr 1968) on Santa Rosa

Island, with a carbon-14 date of about 2300 B.C. (UCLA-140), has in common with the Catalina Island site barrel-shaped and spire-lopped olivella beads and stone bowl mortars.

Hoover (1971) has reexamined Olson's (1930) material from Santa Cruz Island sites and has come to the conclusion that one of the newly designated phases, called Frazer's Point, also corresponds in certain typological details with the Late Dune Dweller phase of Santa Rosa Island. Frazer's Point and Little Harbor share all three of the traits just mentioned, and to these are added "doughnut" stones (perforated digging-stick weights?) leaf-shaped, stemmed and side-notched stone points, bird-bone awls and tubular beads. With the Santa Barbara mainland phase of the Intermediate (Hunting) culture designated as the Extraños phase (Harrison and Harrison 1966), Frazer's Point shares flexed burials, doughnut stones, stemmed, leaf-shaped and side-notched points, and globular mortars.

Hoover (1971) has suggested that Frazer's Point sites show affiliations with Middle Horizon Central California. The presence of spire-ground and thick rectangular olivella beads (Types 1a and 2b) and rectangular haliotis beads (Type 4), plus a variety of circular and rectangular haliotis ornaments, bone beads, stone mortars, flexed burials, stemmed, leaf-shaped and side-notched projectile points, and evidence of both twined and coiled basketry bear out this supposed relationship.

The beginning date proposed for Middle Horizon Central California—about 1000 B.C.—obviously does not mesh well with the Intermediate (Island) dates of Meighan and Orr. Explanation for this apparent discrepancy may lie in the simple postulation of earlier beginnings in the south, or it may be that the somewhat labored series of connections between complexes or phases just made lacks sufficient precision to support conclusions of close cultural relationships between them. Thus it is possible that both the Little Harbor and Late Dune Dweller complexes correspond with Early Horizon in Central California. Meighan (1959:403) in fact points out, in a comparison with other California sites, that the greatest number of similarities, in 19 out of 34 categories of artifacts from Little Harbor, are shared with Early Horizon Central California. At the same time he proposes a time depth even earlier than 2000 B.C. for the Intermediate period's inception.

Questions about time of beginnings of the Intermediate cultures in Southern California are only part of the problem surrounding this relatively indefinite archeological period. An equally elusive quality applies to ideas of its ending date, or dates, in different subregions. These uncertainties are probably grounded in another basic question about the development of culture in the Southern California coastal region. Originally, Rogers (1929) had posited separate groups of people as responsible for the significant cultural variances that he saw at

different time levels in the Santa Barbara area. Subsequently many investigators preferred to interpret these differences as expressions of distinctive environmental adaptations through time (Meighan 1959). Thus it is conceivable that an ancient group, most likely a Hokan-speaking group, first entered the region and subsequently filled the different ecological zones, without any major disruptions, at least in the Milling Stone and Intermediate period.

In the case of the cultures following the Intermediate Period, which are best referred to as Late Horizon, the diagnostic traits are: increased use of bow and arrow, as inferred from finely chipped projectile points, usually stemless and with either concave or convex bases; circular shell fishhooks; steatite containers and arrow straighteners; increased use of asphalt as adhesive; bone tools many and varied; many shell, bone, and stone ornaments; elaborate mortuary customs, with abundant grave goods; increased evidence of land and sea-mammal hunting (cf. Wallace 1955).

Unfortunately, widely separated beginning dates have been proposed for the several so-called Late cultures of Southern California. Of these the most difficult to reconcile with dates from other coastal Late sequences refer to the Early Canalino Period, the beginning of which Orr (1968:101) places at about 1000 B.C. This date would seem to fit more comfortably with the Intermediate period and is the one suggested by both K.L. Johnson (1966) and N.N. Leonard (1966) for the beginning of Intermediate in the Santa Monica Mountains areas.

Figure 9 shows sequential development of certain key shell and bone artifacts on the Southern California Coast. The chart is based upon seriation of samples from midden and burial lots, and no notations beyond approximate date markers are given, although it is understood that the Intermediate and part of the Late periods are expressly involved.

It has already been indicated that the San Diego area is little known, especially in the matter of nonlithic artifacts in the time range covered by the chart. The San Luis Rey I site of Meighan (1954) is estimated to have been occupied after about A.D. 1400, and the only artifact types represented on the chart that might apply to this late complex are the olivella spire-lopped and disk beads. The disk beads are fairly large examples, and probably offshoots, of the small disk, Type 3d (fig. 9, no. 17).

There are other correspondences, such as the dominance of small, stemless, concave-based points, which link the late San Diego complex with sites of the Late Period from farther north along the coast. There are also some marked differences, including bedrock mortar and milling stone use in the south rather than globular or hopper mortars. The appearance of pottery vessels in the San Diego region at about A.D. 1700 (Meighan 1954:223) points to another significant difference. Wallace (1955:226) suggested that the dating of the San Luis Rey sites after A.D. 1400 may be too late to allow for certain subsequent cultural developments in the region.

Not surprisingly, figure 9 shows, in its olivella and haliotis bead sequence, a marked similarity to that demonstrated for Central California at levels of the later part of Early Horizon and the following Middle and Late (Phase 1) Horizons.

Summary

Suggestions have been made about the varying directions from which prehistoric cultures in California may have been derived—the Great Basin, the North Coast, or the Columbia River region. Nevertheless, the main conclusion is not that new groups were constantly entering the region and either replacing or absorbing earlier populations. Rather it is proposed that, with few exceptions, the various original groups remained essentially in their first-settled regions until protohistoric times. It has been assumed that after 2000 B.C. there were no large-scale climatic disruptions and that the chief reasons for cultural variance in the several regions, besides "normal" change through time, were based upon the necessarily differing cultural adaptations to the regional environments.

Common elements for all occupants of prehistoric California are found in hunting implements, with the early groups apparently equipped with the throwing stick—atlatl—of which there are a few examples (Payen 1970) and darts with heavy stone points. Use of milling stones for small seed grinding probably accompanied the kind of hunting carried out with atlatls. The bow and its lighter tipped arrows probably were introduced around 1,500 or 2,000 years ago. Whatever the implement, hunting of land or sea mammals or both remained important throughout the range of time covered by this chapter.

Presumably the rich acorn resources in all parts of California considered here were sufficient to bring about a change in grinding implements, with stone-bowl mortars, hopper-slab mortars, or bedrock mortars ultimately gaining predominance in different areas. Both before and after the time of effective transition in plant food resources, probably between 2000 and 1000 B.C., marine resources were being exploited. In the San Francisco Bay region mollusks seem to have been most important, while in the Santa Barbara area the entire range of marine adaptation developed, including pelagic fishing, mollusk gathering, and sea-mammal hunting.

With concomitant exploitation of acorn and marine resources, cultural climax regions, characterized by elaborations in technology and art, developed along the Santa Barbara coast and the San Francisco Bay-Sacramento-San Joaquin Delta regions. Later, it appears that essentially riverine-coastal cultures, exemplified by the ethnographic Yurok, also experienced a climax; again marine exploitation seems to have played a contributing part.

Each culture in the climax regions had distinguishing material-culture features, and from these may be inferred numbers of other differences—social and ceremonial—that cannot be precisely delineated in the archeological record. However, in many cases the record of continuous development in the nonperishable material sphere permits close identification of the prehistoric cultures with those in the subsequent ethnographic period.

Carbon-14 dating and comparisons of artifacts of certain categories, especially shell beads, indicate that even though there may have existed much separatism among groups living at a given time, trade and other influencing contacts were by no means absent throughout the entire period.

DEVELOPMENT OF REGIONAL PREHISTORIC CULTURES

Protohistoric and Historic Archeology

CHESTER KING

The state of knowledge of protohistoric and historic California archeology is limited due to a general lack of intensive archeological investigations and failure of archeologists to distinguish protohistoric archeological components from earlier components. The documentation of a sample of different ethnic groups larger than in most areas of equal size in North America is in contrast to a virtual absence of data on the archeology of some groups such as the Salinan and Esselen and extremely meager data on other groups (see fig. 1, table 1).

Archeological data show that California Indian cultures were more complex in the protohistoric period than they were after populations had been reduced by disease and their economic resources had been preempted by nonnative settlers in the historic period. The cultures present in the protohistoric period were evolved from local traditions that date back to at least as early as A.D. 1000 (in most areas much earlier). Although the boundaries of the major California Indian nationalities changed relatively little prior to historic contact, there were changes in the distributions of local populations. Changes in food processing, hunting, fishing, or gathering will not be discussed here, but rather changes in social behavior. In general, the major food-procurement techniques used were developed before the protohistoric period.

The protohistoric period is equivalent to Phase 2 of the Late Horizon in the terminology used in Central California (Bennyhoff 1961; Beardsley 1948; Bennyhoff and Heizer 1958). This identification is based on: (1) the cooccurrence of Phase 2 materials with objects associated with European trade (iron spikes and sixteenth-century Chinese porcelain) at Drakes Bay on the Marin Coast, indicating that Phase 2 began prior to 1595 (King and Upson 1973); (2) the record of names of villages that were being abandoned during the beginning of Phase 2 and the absence of names of large, early historic-period villages that archeologically date early in Phase 2 in the exploration accounts of the Santa Barbara Channel area in 1542 by Juan Rodríguez Cabrillo; and (3) radiocarbon dates associated with materials both antedating and contemporary with Phase 2, which indicate a beginning date for Phase 2 of about A.D. 1500. Phase 2 is followed by the historic period and Spanish missionization, beginning about A.D. 1770 and ending around 1834, when the final secularization decree was promulgated by Mexico and the Franciscan missions were ceasing to recruit neo-

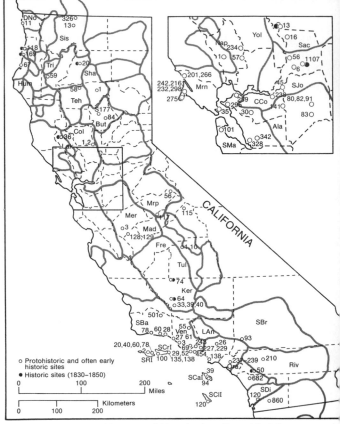

Fig. 1. Selected protohistoric and historic sites. See table 1 for explanation of site numbers.

phytes. The use of shell-bead types diagnostic of the mission period actually starts around 1785.

Shell Beads

The most sensitive indicators of change over time regularly found in late archeological contexts in California are the beads and ornaments that were used in the organization of social behavior. Beads varying in materials—shell, stone, magnesite, and bone—can be further categorized by shape—disk, cylinder, tube, globular, and pendant—on the basis of the relationship among their diameters and thicknesses, rounded or squared edges, and placement of perforations. Certain types of shell beads were used over large areas of California, and regularities of changes in their form enable archeologists to identify

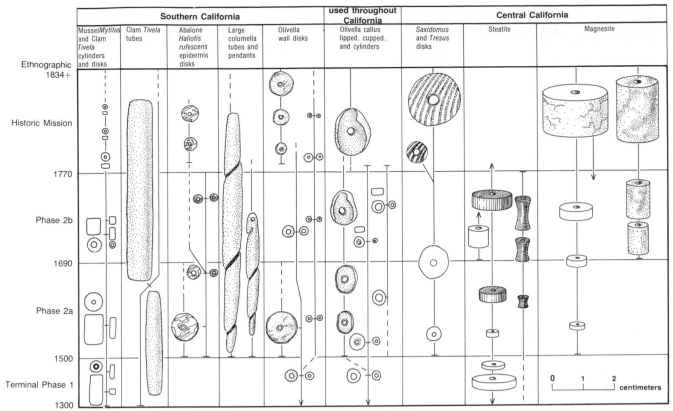

	Southern California				used throughout California	Central California			
	Mussel *Mytitus* and Clam *Tivela* cylinders and disks	Clam *Tivela* tubes	Abalone *Haliotis rufescens* epidermis disks	Large columella tubes and pendants	Olivella wall disks	Olivella callus lipped, cupped, and cylinders	*Saxidomus* and *Tresus* disks	Steatite	Magnesite

Fig. 2. Common California protohistoric and historic beads.

archeological components that are probably contemporary.

The ethnographic literature is relatively complete in specifying the precise form of beads and ornaments used about 1834 (fig. 2) and after. The ways beads were worn (fig. 3) are essentially analogous to those described a century later for the Central Sierra Miwok by Barrett and Gifford (1933). For southern California, Harrington (1912–1923) and Strong (1929) described beads used. Ethnographic and historic data concerning the uses of these beads have been tested against the associations of bead types in mortuary contexts and partially confirmed. For example, different types were associated with burials of different statuses (see L.B. King 1969:56–60).

The callus (or columella) of the *Olivella biplicata* is composed of a high proportion of enamel and is very hard. Only one callus bead could be made from each shell (fig. 4), and the size of the bead was determined to a large degree by the amount of work spent in grinding it down. The beads produced from the callus are rather inconspicuous in comparison with the amount of work expended in their manufacture. Lipped olivella callus beads are found in the Chumash area either singly or in low numbers in lots or occasionally in high frequencies sewed on bags or in long strands. Used over a large area of California (fig. 5), these were evidently one of the less valuable "money" beads.

The columellae of univalves larger than *Olivella* sp. were shaped into pendants or longitudinally drilled tubes

NAA, Smithsonian.
Fig. 3. Costanoan man wearing shell necklace and shell beads attached to headdress. Lithograph (Choris 1822) based on lost watercolor by Louis Choris, 1816.

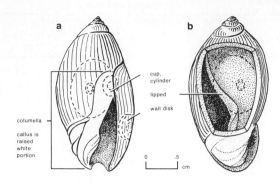

Fig. 4. Areas (a, obverse; b, reverse with cutaway) of *Olivella biplicata* used to make shell beads.

(fig. 2) to represent money forms of high value. According to Maria Solares, Harrington's main informant for the Ynezeño Chumash area, *šowow** (olivella wall disks or cups) were worth less than *ʔiɬɨmɨš* (*Tivela* sp., *Mytilus* sp., and serpentine cylinders), *ʔape* (*Hinnites* sp. beads), *čipʰɨʔ* (*Kelletia kelleti* tubes), and *čǧilwoy* (Harrington 1912–1923).

In the Medea Creek cemetery (LAn-243), located inland in the southeastern Chumash area, three major social groups can be deduced from differences in burial behavior. It has been suggested and partly substantiated (L.B. King 1969) that the areas of burials of the different social groups represent plots used by associations (perhaps kin groups) whose members had differential access to resources and power. Major cemetery areas at LAn-243 have been designated as eastern, central, and western. Each area contained different relative frequencies of shell beads. The eastern area of the cemetery contained the remains of people who apparently had low ascribed status. In this area the most common shell beads were those made from the columellae of univalve shells. Olivella lipped beads, olivella cylinders, olivella spoons and tubes, and small columella pendants and tubes were found almost exclusively in the eastern and western areas; and olivella cups and *Kelletia kelleti* tubes were found in all areas. These "money" beads could evidently be used by individuals of all statuses: both the highest, who were buried in the western area, and the lowest, in the eastern area. The more decorative "money" beads were frequently found in the east, but not in the central area, where other beads were used.

At the Menjoulet site (Mer-3) in the western part of the Central Yokuts area, there are also regularities in the association of beads with burials of individuals of different social statuses. Olivella lipped beads seem to have been used by individuals of low ascribed status who were buried in an outdoor plot, often as partially extended

* Madison Beeler has provided the spellings for all Chumash words in this chapter.

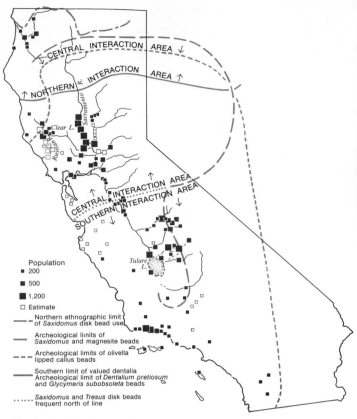

Fig. 5. Distribution of villages of over 200 people at European contact, and distribution of common Phase 2 historic beads.

inhumations, while higher-status individuals were usually buried as cremations in the floor of a community structure (dance house), with the highest-status burials clustered at the south edge of the structure (Pritchard 1970). The different proportions of lipped to steatite disk beads found in different areas of the Schwabacher site (Mad-117) (T.F. King 1968), across the valley from Mer-3 in the area held in ethnographic times by the Southern Sierra Miwok, also suggest use of different beads by individuals of different ascribed social statuses.

Olivella callus beads were evidently accessible to everyone regardless of ascribed status in most areas of California (fig. 5). These "money" beads apparently could be used by anyone in trade, in exchange for goods.

Disk beads made from stones and the walls of shells, and cylinder beads, were used differently from beads already discussed, which included or were made from the columellae of univalves. Like the olivella "money" beads, these beads had value resulting from costs of manufacture; however, they were not considered as "money" beads but rather as "decorative" beads. They were used to validate high social statuses and were involved in interactions in which there were lags between the giving of beads and return flow of goods or services rather than no lags as was the case of "money" beads.

Beads found in both the western and central areas at Medea Creek in some frequency were small *Haliotis rufescens* epidermis disks, *Olivella* sp. disks (medium range), *Mytilus* sp. disks, cylinders of *Mytilus* sp. and *Tivela* sp., and tube beads of *Tivela* sp. and *Mytilus* sp. Burials in the central area of the LAn-243 cemetery have been interpreted as those of individuals who were allowed to attain positions of high social status by birth rather than by obtaining wealth in the commercial economy. These positions were probably often associated with religious control functions. It was evidently in the interest of members of this group to invest in beads that validated status. Centering in the western area of the cemetery and infrequent in the other areas were medium-sized *Haliotis rufescens* epidermis disks strung with medium-sized *Olivella* sp. wall disks, medium-sized *Olivella* sp. wall disks with oblique incisions interspersed with plain disks, small *Olivella* sp. wall disks, *Hinnites* sp. beads, and globular *Tivela* sp. beads. These items were probably mainly reserved for those of high birth or the extremely wealthy.

At the Menjoulet site *Tivela* sp. cylinders and tubes were associated with cremations in the "dance house," and other "decorative" and "money" beads were found mainly with the burials at the south edge of the structure. *Tivela* sp. and *Mytilus* sp. cylindrical beads were called *ʔiẖimiš* by Maria Solares and other Chumash informants. They were said to be more valuable than *mučučuʔ* (small olivella wall disks). Informants also said *ʔiẖimiš* were used only as ornaments. *mučučuʔ* were described as being used to decorate the carrying strap of a cradle and to decorate a band that passed over one shoulder and under the opposite arm. One of these broad bands is said to have been worn by chiefs at fiestas. Both *ʔiẖimiš* and *mučučuʔ* were said to have been used for bracelets (Harrington 1912-1923). There is a historic reference to the use of what were probably cylindrical beads in a ceremony recognizing leadership. At the mouth of Sespe Creek in the area of the eastern interior Chumash, the first Spanish land expedition in 1769 was met by seven chiefs who came with a retinue of men with unstrung bows, all together 500 Indians. In addition to a generous present of food, the Spaniards received other gifts: "The chiefs, having learned who was in charge, offered to the commander, to us [the priests], and to the officers, several necklaces of little stones [shells and possibly stone], white [*Tivela* sp. cylinders], black [serpentine or *Mytilus* sp. cylinders], and red [*Haliotis rufescens* epidermis?], whose texture was similar to coral" (Palóu 1926, 2:143).

In summary, it is possible to differentiate two categories of shell beads according to use. One type consists of "money" beads, which could be obtained by selling goods (food or manufactured products), and which could be used by anyone regardless of the status position they were born into. The other category of shell beads was used either by those who were allowed to obtain, or by those who inherited, positions of rank. Both categories were composed of beads that differed in value according to the amount of labor required for their manufacture. In areas where regular olivella currency was less used than among the Chumash of the Santa Barbara Channel region, beads that for the Chumash served decorative or status functions evidently often took on moneylike functions. For example, the clamshell disks and cylinders of *Tivela stultorum* that occur in some frequency north of the Chumash up to the Costanoan area were most commonly used as currency south of Monterey, especially by Southern Yokuts groups. In California north of Monterey (except in the Tolowa region) currency functions were served by disk beads of *Saxidomus* sp. and *Tresus* sp. (According to James A. Bennyhoff, personal communication 1972, Gifford 1947:32 misidentified *Tresus* sp. as *Saxidomus gigantea*, Washington clam.) Next to those of olivella callus, these clam beads were the hardest, most durable form of shell bead that was commonly used in California.

In Northern California, there was a decline in the proportion of use of olivella callus money in relation to clam disk beads, especially in comparison with the Santa Barbara Channel area. This relationship follows from a hypothesized relationship between degree of environmental diversity and the degree of efficiency of a monetized economy in contrast to a politically controlled economy (King 1971). That is, monetized economies are more efficient in decreasing the influence of fluctuations in available food supplies where there are many variable resources (both geographically and seasonally). Political regulation is more efficient for decreasing the influence of fluctuations when there are relatively few important variable resources.

It is probably because of this relationship that farther north along the Pacific coast societies used beads that require less labor in manufacture and that control of exchange was mainly through political manipulations. In comparison with the Northwest Coast and the Southern California coast, Central California can be viewed as having an economic system that was in a sense both political and monetized, with neither aspect so developed as in the case of groups to the north and south. The ethnographic economies of Central California have been described by Chagnon (1970) and Vayda (1966). Ethnographic and historical description of the economic system of the Chumash has been presented by King (1971).

Bead forms changed during the historic and protohistoric periods. Phase 2 of the late time period begins with the development of new bead types in all areas of California. Olivella callus cupped beads differentiated into large, lipped and small, cupped or cylinder beads. In Southern California, there was a development of numerous other types of olivella callus as well as columella beads made from other species of shell. In general, it can be postulated that the potential for successful participation in the money economy was made more open to people of all social groups (kin groups, villages, and nationalities) and that the California money economy reached its heights of development. The changes in the olivella lipped beads following their development from round (Phase 2a) to oval thin-lipped (terminal Phase 2a) to oval full-lipped (Phase 2b) and large, lipped with frequent unlipped variants (historic) seems to represent an increasing differentiation from cupped beads with an accompanying decrease in their value. These changes are significant in establishing the chronology of Phase 2 throughout California.

In Southern California, some shell materials were first used for tube (columellae and *Hinnites multirugosus* hinges) and cylinder (*Mytilus californianus*) beads. There was also an expansion of the diameter ranges of all disk beads in early Phase 2a, followed by a reduction by Phase 2b to diameters similar to disk beads of late Phase 1. Phase 2b was followed by an increase in diameters again in the mission period. It is tempting to hypothesize that at the beginning of Phase 2a, there was a period of rapid human population growth with increased potential for the members of at least some sectors of the society to attain higher status.

It is mainly the costs of drilling holes and rounding the circumferences that determine the value of beads. Numerous small-diameter beads woven into beadwork patterns or strung in parallel strands are no more visible than relatively few large bulky beads. Accordingly, periods of increases in diameter of "decorative" beads can be interpreted as having been times in which there was a greater potential to attain particular social statuses than periods when the cost of obtaining sufficient beads to validate or show status would be prohibitive.

It is interesting to observe the changing pattern of types and uses of Central California shell beads in the light of the above discussion. Phase 2 began here with the development of a number of new types of beads using new materials. *Saxidomus* sp. shells, *Tresus* sp. shells, and magnesite (a stone quarried near the boundary between Lake Miwoks and Pomoans and baked in the process of manufacture) were first used in Phase 2; and the clam disk beads were the most common type used over most of California north of the San Francisco Bay area. Early use of *Saxidomus* sp. and *Tresus* sp. beads was accompanied by the phasing out of earlier rectangular olivella wall beads used in the Central California area and by an increase in cylindrical or tubular steatite beads. In general, throughout Phase 2 and into the historic period, Central California "decorative" bead diameters increased. Using the hypothesized relationship between bead diameters and attained social status suggested for Southern California, it would appear that in Central California there was an increase in potential for status attainment throughout the protohistoric and historic periods. With European contact the population was significantly reduced by disease, increasing the potential to obtain some status positions. If this postulated devel-opment for Central California also explains the similar development in Southern California and the Yokuts area in the mission period, then ethnographic data collected in the early part of the twentieth century and later part of the nineteenth reflect much less clearly stratified societies than typified the protohistoric period.

Protohistoric Bead Use Areas

The population and village location data for figure 5 are derived from written accounts by early Spanish expeditions and by early European settlers and military personnel, but this information is in many areas partially substantiated by archeological data (for example, Cook and Heizer 1968). The inhabitants of large villages and towns in at least parts of the state north of the Tulare Lake area were often living together only seasonally. Most of the large villages and towns south of there, except possibly those in the Ipai area, were occupied virtually throughout the year during the protohistoric period. All the large villages and towns were important as interaction centers and probably dominated the control of intervillage trade in their particular areas. The cluster of large settlements in the Sacramento River, Russian River, and Clear Lake areas can be viewed as the centers of an interaction network in which *Saxidomus* sp. and magnesite beads were frequently used in the protohistoric and historic periods.

The clusters of large village communities in the Tulare Lake drainage and the Santa Barbara Channel were involved in a Southern California area in which olivella wall disks and clam tubes and cylinders were exchanged and shown. All the more common types of Southern California (fig. 2) were used as well throughout the San Joaquin Valley.

The limits of these large interaction networks occurred in areas of lower population density and smaller villages. In these boundary zones, only the most common and low-valued forms of beads were usually owned. In the area where *Saxidomus* sp. beads were frequently used, *Tresus* sp. beads, which are thinner and smooth surfaced, were evidently less valued; they are found in the San Francisco Bay and San Joaquin delta areas in high proportions, along with olivella lipped beads. Olivella lipped beads always increase in proportion to other bead types outside the larger population centers, except in the northern part of California where their use was relatively infrequent.

Archeological evidence indicates that the common beads used in the large interaction areas of Southern and Central California were manufactured from traded or local shells or stone in coastal, Coast Range, Central Valley, and Sierra Nevada foothill areas. The amount of residue from manufacturing at different villages varies widely from the extremes in the bead-manufacturing villages of the Santa Barbara Channel Islands to occasional bead blanks found in some Central Valley villages.

Table 1. Sites and Sources

Site Number	Site Name	Source
Ala-328	Coyote Hills (Newark)	Davis and Treganza 1959
Ala-342	Warm Springs	King 1968
But-84	Tie-Wiah	Ritter 1968
But-S177	Porter Rockshelter	Pritchard et al. 1966
CCo-30	Alamo	Fredrickson 1968
CCo-141	Palm Tract (Orwood Mound 2)	Lillard, Heizer, and Fenenga 1939
CCo-238	Hotchkiss	Lillard, Heizer, and Fenenga 1939
CCo-259	Fernandez	Davis 1960
CCo-295	Ellis Landing	Nelson 1910
Col-1	Miller Mound	Lillard, Heizer, and Fenenga 1939
Col-2	Howell's Point Mound	Lillard, Heizer, and Fenenga 1939
DNo-11	Point Saint George	Gould 1966a
Fre-115	Vermillion Valley	Lathrap and Shutler 1955
Fre-128	Little Panoche Reservoir	Olsen and Payen 1968
Fre-129	Little Panoche Reservoir	Olsen and Payen 1968
Hum-67	Gunther Island	Heizer and Elsasser 1964
Hum-118	Patrick's Point	Elsasser and Heizer 1966
Hum-169	Tsurai	Elsasser and Heizer 1966
Ker-33, 39, 40	Buena Vista Hills	Wedel 1941
Ker-64	Elk Hills	Walker 1947
Ker-74		Riddell 1951
Lak-36	Rattlesnake Island (Elem)	M.R. Harrington 1948
LAn-26	Sheldon Reservoir	Walker 1952a
LAn-52	Arroyo Sequit	Burnett 1944
LAn-454	Point Dume	Burnett 1944
LAn-29	Lechuza Canyon	Burnett 1944
LAn-138	Malaga Cove	Walker 1952a
LAn-227, 229	Century Ranch	King, Blackburn, and Chandonet 1968
LAn-243	Medea Creek	L.B. King 1969
Mad-117	Schwabacher	T.F. King 1968
Mer-3	Menjoulet	Pritchard 1970
Mrn-35	Tiburon	Gifford 1947
Mrn-201, 266	Tom's Point, McClure Mound	Beardsley 1954
Mrn-232	Estero Mound	Beardsley 1954
Mrn-242	Cauley Mound	Beardsley 1954
Mrn-275	Mendoza Mound	Beardsley 1954
Mrn-216, 298	Limantour Sandspit	King and Upson 1973
Mrp-56	Yosemite Village	Rasson 1966
Nap-1	Goddard Mound	Heizer 1953
Nap-57	Wooden Valley	Heizer 1953
Nap-234	Capell Valley	E. Robinson 1964
Ora-237–239	Santiago Canyon	Hudson 1969
Riv-50	Temecula and Vail	McCown 1955
Riv-210	Snow Creek	Michels 1963–1964
Sac-1	Cantrell Mound	Schenck and Dawson 1929
Sac-6	Johnson Mound	Schenck and Dawson 1929
Sac-16	Bennett Mound	Gifford 1947
Sac-56	Mosher Mound	Gifford 1947
Sac-107	Windmiller Mound	Lillard, Heizer, and Fenenga 1939

Table 1. Sites and Sources *(Continued)*

Site Number	Site Name	Source
SBa-28	Burton Mound	Harrington 1928
SBa-60	Goleta	McKusick 1960–1961
SBa-78	Dos Pueblos	Harrison 1965
SBa-501	Salisbury Potrero	Grant 1964
SBr-93	Las Flores Ranch	Smith and Moseley 1962
SCaI-39	Isthmus Cove	Finnerty, Decker, and Leonard 1970
SCaI-94	Miner's Camp	Meighan and Rootenberg 1957
SClI-120	Big Dog Cave	McKusick and Warren 1958–1959
SCrI-100	Posa Landing	Gifford 1947
SCrI-135, 138	Smuggler's Cove	Gifford 1947
SDi-120	San Vicente	McCown 1945
SDi-682	Rancho San Luis Rey	True 1966
SDi-860	Dripping Springs	True 1970
Sha-20	McCloud River	Smith and Weymouth 1952
Sis-13		Wallace and Taylor 1952
Sis-326	Iron Gate	Leonhardy 1967
SJo-80	Stockton Channel Mound	Schenck and Dawson 1929
SJo-82	Walker Slough Mound	Schenck and Dawson 1929
SJo-83	Ott Mound	Schenck and Dawson 1929
SJo-91	Walker Slough Island Mound	Schenck and Dawson 1929
SMa-101		Oliphant 1971
SRI-2	Skull Gulch	Orr 1968
SRI-40	Canada Verde Flats	Jones 1956; Gifford 1947
SRI-60	Ranch House Jones 1, 2	Jones 1956; Gifford 1947
SRI-20	Ranch House Jones 11	Jones 1956; Gifford 1947
SRI-78	Ranch House Jones 3	Jones 1956; Gifford 1947
Teh-1	Kingsley Cave	Baumhoff 1955
Teh-58	Red Bluff	Treganza 1954b
Tri-59	Trinity Reservoir	Treganza 1958a, 1959a
Tul-1	Greasey Creek	Pendergast and Meighan 1958–1959
Tul-10	Slick Rock	Fenenga 1952
Ven-3	Ventura (*šišolop*)	Greenwood and Browne 1969
Ven-27	Pitas Point	King et al. 1970
Ven-55	Mutah Flat	Eberhart and Babcock 1963
Ven-61	Soule Ranch	Susia 1961–1962
Ven-69	Conejo Rockshelter	Glassow 1965
Yol-13	Mustang Mound	Gifford 1947

Ethnographic Areas

The large interaction areas can be divided into a number of subareas based on different relative frequencies of beads, the presence of local types of beads, differences in *Haliotis* sp. ornaments, and differences in other traded objects. The definition of these areas and their correlation with ethnographic groups has been one of the most clearly defined problems guiding much of the research done with material from the protohistoric period.

The California Indian groups in this volume are identified and named on the basis of language. Linguistic relationships have been used as the most objective criteria for defining social groups variously described as tribes, nationalities, and cultures. Forbes (1966), Brown (1967), and Bennyhoff (1961:64) have shown that there is a correlation of types of personal names, for instance, by suffix, in mission registers with tribal groups. Bennyhoff (1961) and True (1966) have noted that certain aspects of archeological data, especially those related to mortuary practices, can be used to define the boundaries of historic and ethnographic groups.

Historic Village Abandonment

Although the protohistoric period has been arbitrarily considered to end around 1770 when the Spanish first migrated into the southern littoral area, it actually ended at different times in different areas of the state, ranging from 1769 to about 1850.

The abandonment of most protohistoric sites along the littoral area between San Diego and San Francisco was caused by the introduction of pastoral-agricultural technologies and often the presence of imposed Spanish religious and political institutions. In most of the areas where there were Roman Catholic (Franciscan) missions, many of the native villages were abandoned as their occupants died or were incorporated into new villages associated with the missions. The dates of last recorded baptisms from Indian villages located in the littoral zone correspond with the sequence of historic-period artifacts found among the remains of villages that were missionized. For instance, villages from which Indians were last baptized in 1804 have no artifacts made only after 1804, and those abandoned in 1834 have no artifacts unique to the succeeding period. Archeological data therefore help confirm the detailed picture of village abandonment that can be interpreted from baptismal registers.

In some cases, Indians left villages that had been occupied at the end of the protohistoric period in order to work on ranches or to practice agriculture. Indians were often later baptized from these ranches, villages, and autonomous semiagricultural villages. A description of the association of an Indian village with ranching was made by Father Vincente de Maria in 1795. At the location later used for San Fernando Mission he described a village.

> In this place we came to a rancheria near the dwelling of said Reyes (alcade of the pueblo of Los Angeles)—with enough Indians. They take care of the field of corn, beans, and melons, belonging to said Reyes, which with that of the Indians could be covered with two fanegas of wheat. These Indians are the cowherds, cattlemen, irrigators, bird-catchers, foremen, horsemen etc. To this locality belong, and they acknowledge it the gentiles of other rancherias, such as the Taapa [eastern Chumash], Tacuyama [San Francisquito Tataviam?], Tucuenga [Tujunga or Cabuenga, San Fernando Valley Indians], Juyunga [Huam-El Escorpion: half Chumash, half San Fernando Valley Indians], Mapipinga [San Fernando Valley?] and others, who have not affiliated with Mission San Gabriel (Engelhardt 1927:5).

Prior to their secularization, the missions had baptized all the Indians in the littoral zone between San Diego and Bodega Bay as well as from a number of villages in the western half of the San Joaquin Valley. After secularization, some Indians were given small land grants; others moved to villages associated with large ranches, where they worked as laborers; and others moved on to unclaimed land. On the upper half of the San Luis Rey River, Indians were living in their native villages, although baptized at the Pala chapel associated with San Luis Rey Mission. These are Indians who did not abandon their native sites.

In 1833 a major malaria epidemic caused the abandonment of many large villages. Archeological data from the Plains Miwok area (Bennyhoff 1961) substantiates the abandonment of many villages, probably partly caused by the epidemic. From secularization in 1834 until the gold rush of 1849, boundaries between autonomous Indian villages and Mexican-controlled areas of California remained fairly stable except on the northern frontier—in the Pomoan, Wappo, Lake Miwok, Patwin, Nisenan, and Plains Maidu areas. In these areas Indians were incorporated into large ranching operations by men such as John Sutter, Mariano Guadalupe Vallejo, and John Bidwell. These Indians often maintained themselves in their native villages, although some moved in order to take better advantage of new opportunities or were moved because it was in the interests of ranchers. In a few cases semimilitary expeditions are said to have destroyed whole villages and massacred their inhabitants.

It was not until after 1849 that the area north of Clear Lake, north of the town of Chico, the Sierra Nevada Mountains, and the Cahuilla and Tipai areas could be said to become historic. The initial effects of the gold rush on the Indian populations in gold-bearing areas often resulted in changes of village locations and village extinction. The first was usually the result of the exploitation of Indians and the second was the result of homicide.

After the United States government claimed possession of California, Indians were often relocated so that land could be made available for nonnative settlers. Where Indians were living on land of little interest to American citizens in the last half of the nineteenth century, they were often able to maintain their communities as measured by continuity in cemetery use, and in some cases they retained land rights.

Protohistoric Village Changes

The narrative of the Cabrillo expedition of 1542 lists the names of certain villages in the Santa Barbara Channel and on Santa Catalina Island. Many of these villages are named in the baptismal records of missions. The names of a number of the largest villages present in the historic period do not occur in the Cabrillo narrative lists; conversely, the names of other villages on the Cabrillo lists do not represent historic-period villages. Moreover, ethnohistoric information collected by Harrington (1912-1923) from Fernando Librado (b. 1805, interviewed around 1913, Indian name Kitsepawit), a highly accurate and learned informant, shows that villages were moved and new ones were founded in the historic period. The largest missionized coastal villages, especially those not included in the 1542 lists, were described by Librado as having been composed of subpopulations who spoke different major Chumash dialects, particularly inland and island dialects.

Archeological data support the hypothesis of population movement. Large sites such as SBa-78 (*mikiw*, larger of the two villages at Dos Pueblos), SBa-60 (*šaxpilil*, largest of the historic Goleta Slough area towns), and Ven-3 (*šišolop* 'port', at Ventura) all have artifacts characteristic of Phase 2. SBa-60 and Ven-3 were evidently first founded during Phase 2. Artifacts from Ven-3 indicate the village was probably founded in the middle or earlier part of Phase 2a, about 1500-1600. The protohistoric (1542) village of Misnagua (Ven-27, fig. 6), at Pitas Point six miles north of Ven-3 on the coast, was abandoned in early Phase 2a at the time of the establishment of Ven-3. Historically and ethnographically Pitas Point was the location of a fish camp used by Indians from Ven-3 as well as a landing place for traders from the islands. The Pitas Point village contained 6 to 10 circular houses ranging between 30 and 40 feet in diameter; it was much smaller than Ven-3, which included 30 houses of the same size in 1769 (Palóu 1926, 2). Inland from Ven-27 and Ven-3 are a number of village sites in the Ojai Valley region. The Soule Ranch site (Ven-61) and sites in the Las Casitas Reservoir area all seem to have been virtually abandoned during Phase 2a.

It appears that prior to the beginning of Phase 2 numerous small villages were dispersed to relate to local food resources. During Phase 2a these villages were depopulated as large multiethnic, that is, multitribal, coastal villages were founded at locations determined more by trade networks than by local resources. Excavations at some of the most impressive "late" time period sites on the Channel Islands support this supposition. SCri-100 (Posa Landing) was, according to burial-lot data, probably abandoned during about the middle of Phase 2a (1500-1600). At SRI-2 (Skull Gulch) two burial plots, probably family plots, were last used at the very beginning of Phase 2a. One other plot was used through-out Phase 2. This village was recorded by Cabrillo as "Nicalque" (which he also named Santa Rosa Island) and appears in mission records as a moderate-size island village called Nia-cila. Cabrillo in 1542 recorded fewer island villages than those known to have contributed mission converts after 1770, whereas he recorded as many or more villages for sections of the mainland coast; thus, it appears that as mainland populations formed larger villages by grouping together, island populations were dispersing to found new island villages as well as migrating to large mainland villages. This contention is also supported by the burial lots recovered from SRI-40 and SRI-60 (Jones 1956), which all date from about 1600 to the historic period, that is, not earlier than the middle of Phase 2.

In the San Francisco Bay region there is also archeological evidence for redistribution of populations. The large bay-shore shellmounds on the east bay in Alameda and Contra Costa counties, which were village locations during Phase 1, were apparently abandoned during Phase 2a. Little excavation has been done in sites other than the large shellmounds. One site (Ala-342), located away from the bay shore at the foot of the hills on the east side of the bay, produced materials diagnostic of the missing time segment. Early Spanish diaries record a number of small villages along the foothills of the east bay area, and mission records contain baptisms from the area of redwoods behind Oakland. The Ala-342 site differed from the large bay shellmounds by the presence of large quantities of burned rock and baked clay associated with large earth ovens used for the preparation of soaproot bulbs (*Chlorogalum pomeridianum*) as food and by large storage pits. It is tempting to hypothesize that it was the development of improved methods of processing soaproot, historically reported by Font (1933) in 1776 to be the staple food of east San Francisco Bay Indians, that resulted in relocation of populations with availability of firewood determining new village locations. The continual growth of population due to increased food supply during early Phase 2 would explain the reoccupation of bay shore shellmounds in Phase 2b.

In the Chowchilla River area in the Sierra Nevada foothills (Mad-117) at the beginning of Phase 2 there appears to be an increase in population that was reflected by the occupation of many new sites by small groups of people as well as by an increase in the size and complexity of large central villages. Similar changes occurred in many areas of the Sierran foothills (Moratto 1971:24-38).

The quantity of archeological data produced in almost every area of the state during the protohistoric period certainly indicates a marked population increase. It appears that as populations increased, the cultures increased in complexity as measured by (1) large specialized structures—dance houses and sweathouses, (2) complexity and quantity of artifacts that were used in the organization of social behavior, and (3) degree of hierar-

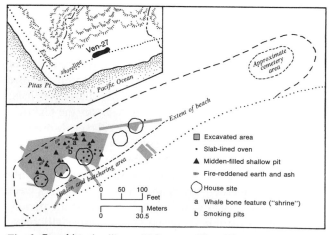

Fig. 6. Protohistoric village of Misnagua (Ven-27).

66

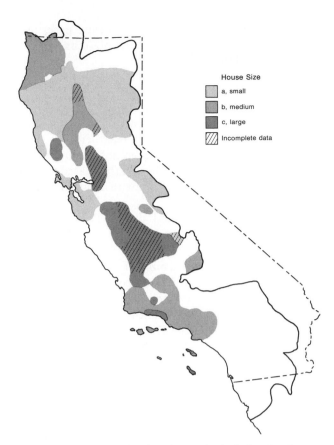

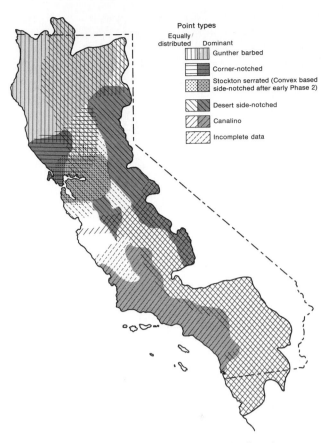

Fig. 7. Protohistoric house sizes based on archeological and early historic data. a, most houses in village less than 15 feet diameter; one or more large houses up to 30 feet diameter; b, most houses in village 15-20 feet diameter, in Northwest area 15 by 20 foot rectangle; one or more large houses up to 60 feet diameter; c, most houses in village 25-50 feet diameter; one or more large houses up to 150 feet diameter.

Fig. 8. Distribution of common protohistoric projectile points.

chical ordering of sites by size as compared with earlier periods, that is, an increase in the range of site size, both smaller and larger.

House Size

During the protohistoric period, California Indian communities varied in their organization in a number of ways. Differences in house sizes (fig. 7) reflect differences in the size of households and in the kinds of activities performed together or separately inside residential houses rather than in community structures such as dance houses, sweathouses, or outdoor work areas. Small residential houses were mainly used in areas where there were relatively few resources; however, large houses have been occasionally found in such areas. The causes of variation in house size are as yet poorly understood.

Projectile Points

Stone arrow points were described historically and ethnographically as being used in all areas of California (fig. 8).

These chipped-stone points can be divided into types on the basis of (1) configuration of base, (2) the presence and location of notches, and (3) treatment of blade edges. Differences in the forms of California projectile points have often been assumed to be the result of differences in ideological traditions, but the evidence on figure 8 does not substantiate this assumption. Microscopic analysis of Stockton serrated points has resulted in the suggestion that this type of point was at least occasionally used for purposes besides tipping arrows (Nance 1970:81–82). Edge wear was interpreted as indicating use in both light slicing and whittling motions. Projectile base forms may be related to hafting requirements (fig. 9) for points that have multiple uses—for example, piercing, cutting, whittling, warfare, game hunting. However, other types of protohistoric projectile points have not been systematically examined for wear or patterns of breaking due to use.

The most common points used in the protohistoric period can be classified into the following types (fig. 10).

(1) Gunther barbed, basally notched so as to make the lower corners into barbs. The edges of the stem are usually parallel-sided or contracting.
(2) Desert side-notched, concave-based side-notched points. These were evidently used in California

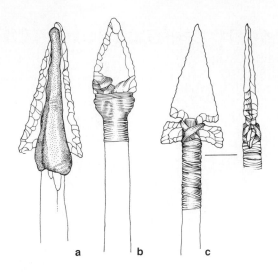

Dept. of Anthr., Smithsonian: a, 19709; b, 2807; c, 15699.
Fig. 9. Hafting techniques. a, split wooden shaft, sinew wrapping covered with asphaltum; b, split wooden shaft, sinew wrapping; c, split wooden shaft, sinew wrapping.

only during Phase 2 (see Baumhoff and Byrne 1959).
   (a) general subtype, side-notched with concave base.
   (b) Sierra subtype, concave-based with notch in center of base.

   (c) Delta subtype, deeply concave base, usually made of stone other than obsidian.
   (d) Redding subtype.
   (e) Panoche side-notched (Olsen and Payen 1968).
(3) Unnotched Canalino points.
   (a) concave-based (Cottonwood triangular), common from the later part of Phase 2a through 2b; found as a rare type earlier.
   (b) convex-based, precedes in the southern California coast area the concave-based type; most common type of point in Phase 1 and early Phase 2a.
(4) corner-notched, found during Phase 1 in many areas where side-notched points were common in Phase 2.
(5) Stockton serrated, a number of notches along both edges; common in Phase 1 contexts as well as early Phase 2, but rare thereafter.
(6) convex-based side-notched, followed the Stockton serrated type in the Delta area.
(7) straight-based side-notched.

The distributions of point types across territory and through time are correlated with changes in population distribution. These changes were the result of shifts in activity and consequent differing needs for demographic organization. This suggests that different frequencies of projectile point types reflect differences in the way arrow points were most commonly used.

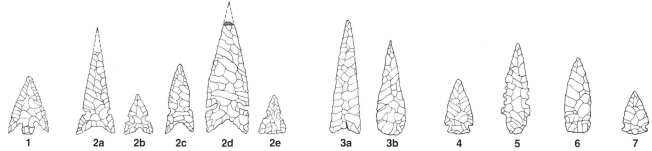

Lowie Mus., U. of Calif., Berkeley: 1, 1-151797; 2a, 1-57847; 2b, 1-134698; 2c, L1528; 2d, 1-151796; 2e, 1-169000; 3a, 1-4503; 4, 1-58066; 5, 1-134180; 6, 1-134159; 7, 1-58070.
Fig. 10. Arrow point types. 1, Gunther barbed; 2a, Desert side-notched, general subtype; 2b, Desert side-notched, Sierra subtype; 2c, Desert side-notched, Delta subtype; 2d, Desert side-notched, Redding subtype; 2e, Panoche side-notched; 3a, unnotched Canalino, concave-based; 3b, unnotched Canalino, convex-based, idealized; 4, corner-notched; 5, Stockton serrated; 6, convex-based side-notched; 7, straight-based side-notched.

Indian–Euro-American Interaction: Archeological Evidence from Non-Indian Sites

ROBERT L. SCHUYLER

Spanish Period, 1769–1822

Since 1769, when the Spanish founded San Diego, the nature of archeological remains on the West Coast—hence archeological research—was radically altered. Historic-sites archeology is a new discipline and in California has developed as a major theme only since the 1950s. For this reason the archeological perspective of Euro-American settlement of California and its direct impact on the native peoples of the state are just beginning to emerge.

Spain as an imperial power had been entrenched in the New World for over 250 years before California was added to her holdings. Ironically, this settlement occurred only 50 years before the dissolution of that empire. California was always a peripheral and frontier area, with Spanish settlement occupying a thin strip along the coast. This coastal margin of European culture, or more accurately Iberian-Indian culture, was unique in several aspects when compared to either Spain or more developed areas like Mexico or Peru. Over five decades a settlement pattern evolved that involved three major types of sites: towns, some with associated presidios, a chain of 21 Franciscan missions, and cattle ranches separate from those of the missions.

Although the creation of the Franciscan chain of missions spans the entire Spanish period, major geographical expansion was limited to the eighteenth century. Within the first decade of Spanish colonization, exploration knowledge of the California shoreline was used to extend settlement from San Diego to San Francisco. Eight missions were founded, at least on paper, before 1780, although not all of these have as yet been subjected to archeological investigation.

Mission San Diego de Alcalá

The San Diego mission was not constructed at its present site until 1774. One of the attractions of southern California in 1769, besides the excellent harbor at San Diego, was the many local groups of Yuman- and Takic-speaking peoples. As Mission Indians a number of these groups are still designated by their former associations, for example, Gabrielino. It was to Nipaguay, the new village of the Yuman Ipai-Tipai (once called Diegueño), that Father Junipero Serra moved his mission from San Diego (Moriarty and Weyland 1971:124–126). After its almost immediate destruction by the Indians, it was reestablished in 1775 substantially in the form in which the reconstructed ruins still exist.

Starting from 1774 there are numerous documentary references to the adjacent Indian village, or rancheria, and these continue intermittently until the American period (Brandes 1966:15–22). Originally consisting of 14 huts of poles and tules, the village was enlarged and rebuilt with "palisades" and tule in 1779. Archeological verification of documentary allusions to this and other occupation areas still awaits excavation, but rich samples of historic Ipai-Tipai as well as European artifacts have already been recovered (Brandes 1967). One area has produced Ipai-Tipai pottery and surface indications of several small, rectangular rooms that may be Indian quarters (Brandes 1966:8).

More specific evidence of acculturation includes a growing bead collection and Indian "graffiti" found on floor tiles (Moriarty 1971:22), all of which will eventually form part of a culture-historical reconstruction of a key ecclesiastical site and its impact on native Californians from 1774 to the mid-nineteenth century.

Mission San Luis Obispo de Tolosa

Founded north of present Santa Barbara in 1772 by Father Serra, San Luis Obispo was thrice attacked before 1774, although by 1804 almost 1,000 Indian neophytes had been gathered around it from neighboring villages.

Scattered references exist to early archeological work (Pilling 1952:1) at the site of this small mission, but it was not until 1971 that serious excavation commenced. Test pits in the area by Jay Von Werlhof have produced both prehistoric and historic Chumash materials, including trade beads (P.J.F. Schumacher 1971:13). Also discovered was the first pottery to be reported from San Luis Obispo County. Because it was of two types (one showing an Ipai-Tipai maze design, the other an import from western Yokuts—Tachi—of Owens Valley brownware) the question is raised of the emergence of a historic pan-California Indian culture. To what degree did the mission system facilitate contact between different Indian groups both within the area of Spanish settlement and into the interior (Heizer 1954:85)? When the irrigation system at the Ventura mission, for example, was constructed, labor was supplied by Christian Indians from San Gabriel brought in by Serra (Greenwood and Gessler 1968:64). By the end of the Spanish period was there a pan-Indian culture both in the sense of a sharing of common European traits and of what were formerly localized aboriginal traits spread throughout the settled zone by the mission system?

Mission San Antonio de Padua

It was Serra who founded San Antonio de Padua in 1771. It flourished as a center for the Salinan Indians and as a prosperous cattle and sheep ranch until the Mexican period.

In an area adjacent to the mission that may be the former Salinan Indian rancheria, three midden areas were opened, producing a wide range of Indian and Spanish-Mexican artifacts as well as Cantonese trade pottery (Howard 1970). More significant than the rich assortment of European artifacts is the evidence of alterations in Salinan culture at the mission. Faunal and floral remains show a retention of use of some native wild plants, but also a marked dependence on European introductions such as pigs, cattle, and sheep. On the ideological level this shift is seen in crude clay figurines of a dog, Christ, and as yet unidentified fire-clay pieces decorated with crosses and radial designs.

Within the first decade of Spanish colonial efforts in California the southern and northern ends of the settled region were firmly based. Between 1780 and 1790 the geographical expansion of the mission system slackened. Because of the considerable distance separating the northern and southern groups, three new missions were built. All were located in the intermediate area occupied by the Chumash Indians, whose many villages and dense population (Brown 1967) offered fertile ground for proselytism. Two of these missions have been explored archeologically.

Mission San Buenaventura

In an area across from San Buenaventura Mission in present-day downtown Ventura, cobble foundations of a large adobe structure were discovered along with artifacts stratified into prehistoric Chumash, mission and postmission periods (Greenwood and Browne 1966, 1968:18-19, 38). Glass trade beads and other introduced items were reported, but of equal interest is a wooden structural post under which an Indian laborer had placed, possibly as a votive offering, a cut abalone shell.

One of the finest examples of historic-sites archeology that has reached a completed state is also within the sphere of the Ventura mission. Sometime between 1792 and 1809 an outlying chapel, named for Saint Gertrude the Great, was placed inland to serve the Indians of the Ventura River valley. The Santa Gertrudis Chapel was soon the focus for Indian settlements, and their thatch houses gave rise to the name of Casitas, which still designates the area.

Evidence of Indian occupation was not abundant enough to indicate that the excavators had encountered a satellite village coeval with the chapel. On the other hand, enough artifacts and midden deposits were uncovered to demonstrate possible trends in the historic period. Except for a few trade beads and one Franciscan crucifix similar to others found on sites in California, Mexico, and the American Southwest, the only other historic Indian object was a projectile point chipped from amber or olive glass. Within the midden deposits a break that probably reflects pre- and post-chapel periods was statistically discernible. A continuation of dependence on faunal resources, while shifting to domesticated forms (67 percent), is evident, while a sharp decrease in utilization of shellfish is also clear (Greenwood and Browne 1968:35-40). Associated with shellfish usage was a sample of eight large, crude shell beads, similar to finds at the main Ventura mission. When compared to the large numbers found at local Chumash protohistoric sites these seem to indicate a degeneration in aboriginal bead manufacture in the mission period. In this example, Spanish influence on Chumash culture is seen, but the process of acculturation is frequently a two-way affair when direct contact is present. At Santa Gertrudis (fig. 1), evidence of Chumash material culture

Fig. 1. Excavated foundations of the Chapel of Santa Gertrudis. Located at the entrance to Casitas Pass near the Ventura River. Photograph by Roberta Greenwood, 1966.

influencing the Franciscans is seen in the use of asphaltum. Used aboriginally as an adhesive and a waterproofing agent for baskets, there is an increase of this material between the pre- and post-chapel periods, from 11.9 to 88.1 percent, respectively. This change probably represents a continuation of the original uses and also an expansion into new areas such as roofing material (Greenwood and Browne 1968:17-18, 40) for mission buildings like the chapel.

Mission La Purísima Concepción

North of Santa Barbara but still within Chumash territory is the site of La Purísima Mission, the third to be founded (1787) between 1780 and 1790. Unlike Santa

70

Barbara, this mission has been the scene of extensive and original archeological work since the 1930s.

La Purísima is actually composed of two archeological sites. The first, La Purísima Vieja (1787–1812), is today located in downtown Lompoc. After its total destruction by the great earthquake of 1812, the mission was moved four miles inland to the present site (1812–1840s) of the restored church.

In 1933 Santa Barbara County acquired part of the ruins at the second location and a Civilian Conservation Corps camp was erected at the site. When in 1935 title to an even larger tract, including much of the original mission complex, was transferred to the state of California, the framework was created for the earliest major project in historic-sites archeology on the West Coast. Archeological investigation of the site began in 1934 and continued intermittently until the early 1940s. Minor excavations in 1934 unearthed ceramic pipes and reservoirs—parts of the original water system. Starting in 1935 a series of new excavations was opened that eventually outlined mission residences, tallow vats, workshops, a series of outbuildings, the cemetery, and the primary church. These extensive excavations, of quite high standards for the 1930s, amassed a wealth of architectural and artifactual remains that were fully exploited in the exceptional restoration of La Purísima.

More germane to the subject of Spanish-Chumash interaction is a scatter of Indian and introduced items as they were found in three specific areas.

•NEOPHYTE OCCUPATION AREAS On a hillslope west of the major mission buildings were found two small structures: a probable mill and another utility building (Harwood 1937:1–3). Between them was a midden stratum of faunal remains, pottery, and other artifacts, which, along with several nearby cooking pits, indicate a Chumash living area. Surface collecting of the area by local residents added a string of beads (both native shell and glass trade beads), a bronze crucifix, pestles, mortars, manos, and an arrow straightener. Assuming this assemblage and the structures are contemporary, and they seem to be, it represents Indian labor running an introduced industry but with a strong carry-over of native material culture. If cooking was a female activity this evidence may also reinforce an acculturation differential based on sexual division of labor.

Excavations south of the former Civilian Conservation Corps camp exposed two other structures, one 19 feet by 113 feet and the other 19 feet by 60 feet. A series of postmolds indicated crude, wattle-daub buildings that were later directly altered into adobe huts with tile roofs (Harwood 1936:3–5). Fire hearths, metates, pottery, and shells further implied Indian neophyte quarters, perhaps including an infirmary. A similar "palisade" structure was later discovered in the same area by M.R. Harrington (1939:1–2). Three rows of posts about nine feet apart supported the walls and ridgepole of a simple brush

house that was probably roofed with tiles. What is seen in these buildings is the evolution of neophyte dwellings. After the earthquake of 1812 it was necessary that temporary units be rapidly constructed at the new La Purísima site (M.R. Harrington 1940:3). There is supporting evidence from documents that on occasion neophytes were housed in native-type villages at the missions (Gabel 1952:10). In any case, a square or rectangular structure with a pole framework covered by willows or bark and topped with tiles may indeed reflect a combination of Spanish and Chumash architectural elements. Even if the wattle-daub construction was already in the Franciscan background in Europe or Latin America, certainly it would easily fit the aboriginal Chumash house pattern. Buildings such as those discovered at La Purísima probably recapitulate under extreme and ephemeral conditions the slower evolution of Indian architecture under Hispanic influence throughout California. Round or oval pole-bush huts were replaced by square or rectangular adobe-walled, tile-roofed, houses.

•CEMETERY This Indian cemetery, according to mission records, contained close to 1,500 burials. M.R. Harrington (1940a) exhumed 17 burials of adults and children, all interred in Christian fashion. Unless disturbed most were extended on their backs, heads to the east, and accompanied by almost no grave goods. One exception to this pattern was an infant burial enclosed in a small vault made of three floor tiles and possibly associated with a blue trade bead.

Humphrey (1965) continued Harrington's work by opening a large test area that contained over 50 burials. The uniform pattern of extended, supine burials oriented in the same direction was repeated. The aboriginal pattern of flexed burials, numerous grave goods, and extensive disturbance by new burials is almost totally lacking. Two exceptional burials, differently oriented and with grave goods, are probably later in time.

La Purísima's Indian cemetery clearly shows the tremendous ideological impact of Christianity on native Chumash beliefs and practices.

•INDIAN BARRACKS The two-building Indian barracks has proved to be the most significant discovery at La Purísima as far as Hispanic-Indian interaction is concerned. Certain documentary clues implied that Building 102 was the Indian infirmary, but M.R. Harrington (1939) later disposed of this hypothesis with a few test pits. His suggestion that it was an Indian barracks has proved correct. An oblong building (554 feet by 25 feet) subdivided into small rooms, 12 of which were totally or partially dug out, was revealed along with a wealth of in-situ artifacts (fig. 2) that established its general domestic nature. After the restoration of the mission, the barracks once again was the subject of archeological work, which uncovered 20 rooms, some with crude fire-hearths. One of these was built of fragments of mission tiles as well as rock and adobe. Over 2,000 recovered

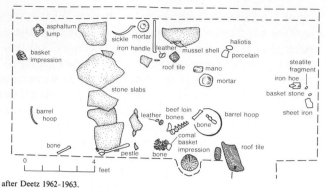

after Deetz 1962-1963.

Fig. 2. Artifacts on floor of room at La Purísima Indian Barracks, reflecting differential continuity of Chumash material culture.

artifacts reflect a mixed domestic European-Chumash pattern. Introduced objects, such as trade beads and iron tools, were found with some metates and comals as well as combined categories such as a projectile point chipped from glass (Gabel 1952:17-22). This work was supplemented by artifact analysis, including Meighan's (1951) trade bead typology for Purísima specimens, and by more surveys (Harrison and Lyon 1960) of the Indian areas at the mission.

Deetz (1962-1963) reexcavated the blacksmith shop uncovered earlier by the CCC and also worked on: the tanning vats, part of the subterranean pipe system, a midden area, and a previously unexcavated section of the Indian barracks. The base of the blacksmith shop had been leveled by native builders with the addition of a Chumash basket hopper mortar to the foundations. More generally the associated food refuse and artifacts repeat a pattern noted earlier from the CCC work at the mill site. A mass of green abalone shells, pestles, comals, and basket impressions, and steatite bowl fragments, added to Spanish domestic items, found in two rooms in contradistinction to forge hardware in the third show a clear relationship (Deetz 1962-1963:175-177). Chumash males were working iron with introduced tools while their families resident at the site of this industrial activity continued the use of basic aboriginal material culture. Similar patterns appeared at the tanning vats and at the newly excavated section of the barracks. The vats, which are European in form and function, produced a combined Hispanic-Chumash assemblage. Tools for removing the hair and working the hides, which would normally be iron, were bone beamers and chert flakes. In sum, this situation reflects "an aboriginal practice (beaming), being done as part of an introduced technology (tanning) with a tool made from material known and used aboriginally (bone) obtained from an animal introduced by the Europeans (cow)" (Deetz 1962-1963:172). When discoveries at the Indian barracks are added to these findings, the result is the best-reported archeological record of acculturation at a Euro-American site in California.

Deetz (1962-1963:180-181, 186-188) conclusively demonstrated that two separate buildings were involved and exposed seven rooms that contained an extremely rich, and mainly undisturbed, artifact inventory directly on floors or sealed between double stratified floors. Comparisons among this material, that from a slightly earlier adjacent dump, and a nonmission Chumash site highlighted significant differences. In the earlier dump, shell beads were three times more numerous than glass beads compared to the proportions recovered from the rooms (Deetz 1962-1963:190). This expected difference, resulting from increasing Spanish acculturation, is not so informative as the marked variation between the barracks material and that from Alamo Pintado.

Located inland near Los Olivos, this historic Chumash site was occupied just before the founding of the second La Purísima. After applying a series of measures to make the Alamo Pintado collection comparable with that from the barracks, variations noted between them are informative. Although acculturation under the mission system was rapid and pervasive, it was quite uneven. Male-oriented activities, for example, in hunting (lithic technology), degenerated rapidly and were replaced totally, or at least formally, by Hispanic behavior patterns. This change is emphasized by the high number of projectile points and related tools and flakes at Alamo Pintado compared to their almost total absence at the mission. Both the tanning-vat artifacts and the dearth of male aboriginal items in the barracks compared to their abundance at the contact site highlight this substitution. On the other hand, female-oriented activity as seen in the cooking and food preparation assemblages of ground-stone artifacts, baskets, and related utensils, such as comals, is high at the aboriginal site and carries over strongly at the barracks. In fact, introduced items, such as ceramic vessels or Mexican metates, supplemented rather than replaced this aboriginal pattern.

Thus La Purísima as a historic site has produced, after almost 40 years of excavation, one of the clearest archeological pictures of Franciscan influence on California native peoples.

Mission San Luís Rey de Francia

Between 1790 and 1800 there was another major period of mission growth with two new additions to the Franciscan chain in the south and five in the north. When expansion at already existing sites is added, it is clear why this decade is designated the "golden age" of California missions.

Closing the gap between San Diego and San Juan Capistrano Mission, San Luís Rey was established in 1798. By the early nineteenth century this was California's most affluent mission and perhaps the most prosperous in Spain's New World empire. As the center for a large Takic-speaking Luiseño Indian population, remnants of which still live on the Pala Reservation and use its historic chapel, this mission offers an ideal situation for an anthropological study combining archeology, history, and contemporary ethnography.

Between 1956 and 1960 Father Anthony Soto extensively excavated the mission's *lavandaría* (wash area), lime kiln, and soldiers' barracks (M.R. Harrington 1958). His excavations were productive both in exposing the elaborate Indian-built washing areas and in recovering many artifacts (Soto 1961). Bone gambling sticks, pottery, shell beads, arrow straighteners, and trade beads (Soto 1960) were unearthed.

In 1955 and 1956 Maida Borel Boyle surveyed the mission grounds and in 1966 began an extensive survey and testing program with students from Los Angeles City College. The results of the survey and limited excavation (Boyle 1968) located Indian occupation areas and covered a temporal range spanning a contact (premission) period, a mission period, a postsecularization period, an Anglo period, and a recent era. Realization of the obvious potential of San Luís Rey will depend on a prolonged study.

An outlying site that was within the orbit of the main mission at San Luís Rey was Temeku, an *asistencia* or chapel, and rancho subsidiary community north of Pala chapel. Besides serving the religious needs of the local Indians, the chapel was a center for the control of mission herds and agriculture. In 1951 McCown (1955) excavated a number of mounds in the area, exposing ramada and adobe structures and many historic and prehistoric artifacts. One adobe building with a tile roof is clearly Spanish in origin, as was a smaller storeroom and kiln. Ramadas with crude fire hearths, and one pit house, are in turn Indian. Two separate locations at the site produced abundant remains—754 whole or fragmentary projectile points, for example—but since there was intensive prehistoric as well as historic habitation in the area the temporal integrity of any assemblage is blurred. Specific European-Indian artifacts include a crucifix, four glass trade beads (McCown 1955:32), a painted clay bead, a projectile point chipped from a wine bottle fragment (ibid:15), and mission tiles incised with motifs similar to Luiseño pottery designs.

Levels one and two, equaling one foot of deposit, contained the mass of European items and probably represent about a century, although Temeku was inhabited by Indians for hundreds of years before this period and even later, after the collapse of the chapel, into fairly recent years.

Mission Nuestra Señora de la Soledad

In the vicinity of Monterey, Soledad Mission was founded in 1791 to the south of the already existing San Carlos mission.

Soledad was a small mission and its Cholon Costanoan population never exceeded 700. Both the Franciscans and their converts suffered from severe weather conditions and other adverse health factors, including a serious epidemic in 1802. After 1805 the Indian population started a steady decline and it was the mortality rate as much as secularization that destroyed the mission in 1835.

Restoration began in a concerted fashion in 1954 and archeological exploration commenced in 1967 (Howard 1970a). Fifteen exploratory trenches showed the Indian cemetery to be badly disturbed, but a substratum produced Mexican earthenware and majolica sherds, as well as Cantonese porcelain trade wares and glass trade beads. Other exploratory trenches yielded both Hispanic and Indian implements, including several projectile points. More successful was the excavation that located two coffins in the original church floor. Evidence of tooth wear and traces of a rosary may indicate an Indian mayordomo or alcalde and his spouse.

Mission San Juan Bautista

The ring of missions around Monterey was completed with the construction inland of San Juan Bautista in 1797. Its unique church with three naves was the largest in California and consecutively served a Costanoan Indian congregation and the Anglo town in which it stands today.

Early archeological activity at the site has created some artifact collections (Pilling 1952:1, 18), and more recent work (Clemmer 1961) has concentrated on the neophyte Indian village near the church. Archeological data combined with mission records suggest an interesting comparative picture of the tempo of house construction and demographic fluctuations. While records usually speak of "houses" the archeology shows the actuality of long dormitory structures, which thus makes intelligible the 80 dwellings for over 1,000 neophytes (Clemmer 1961:iv-vi). Using these findings the excavator compiled a chart (fig. 3) that clearly shows the impact of the Mexican revolution and then an unexpected resurgence of Indian population between 1819 and 1823 with the temporary return of more stable conditions.

Although much of the activity reviewed extended well into the nineteenth century at various missions founded in the previous century, after 1800 the expansion of the mission chain virtually halted. With the 1810 Mexican

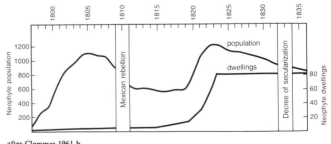

after Clemmer 1961 b.

Fig. 3. Demographic and construction fluctuations at the neophyte village of San Juan Bautista Mission.

revolution events were set off that within two decades would doom the entire system. Only three missions were founded between 1800 and 1823 and two of these, Santa Ynez and San Rafael Arcángel, still await the archeologist's spade. The third, San Francisco de Solano, is the subject of a classic study in historic-sites archeology by Bennyhoff and Elsasser (1954). However, evidence of Indian-Spanish interaction was not a major goal of their study and the later search by Treganza (1954a:19-20) for local neophyte villages was also totally negative. Some clues to the former Indian cemetery, including amateur collections of ceramics and trade beads, were noted.

San Diego Royal Presidio

California's symbol for the Spanish period is, especially as far as native populations are concerned, the mission; however, the Franciscan effort was a means to an end. Alta California was settled by Spain primarily for reasons of international politics and mercantilistic economics. Even the initial exploration of the area in the sixteenth century was a move to secure the region for the eastbound manila galleon on its transit from the Philippines to Mexico.

When the first colonization group arrived, one of their first acts, prompted in part by English and Russian expansion, was to start construction on a presidio at San Diego in 1769 and a year later another in Monterey, at the other end of a 400-mile frontier. By 1800 there was a defensive line of four presidios—San Diego, Santa Barbara, Monterey, and San Francisco—and other fortifications. By that date the European population numbered only about 1,000, mainly concentrated in three pueblos (Fehrenbacher 1964:17-18).

As the first permanent Spanish enclave on the California coast, San Diego Royal Presidio holds a unique position in the history of the state. By 1770 it consisted of a crude, wooden stockade with its two bronze cannons symbolically arranged; one pointed out to sea, the source of other European forces, and the other pointed at an adjacent Indian village. Eventually the fort protected four major missions and three *asistencias* covering a distance of 125 miles to the north (Anonymous 1968:7-9). Yet by the end of the Spanish period this presidio and San Diego had been eclipsed by other settlements, and it was not long before the bypassed site was deteriorating. With the American period a ruin occupied what had once been a key link in the California defense system.

In 1965 a long-term archeological project was initiated at the presidio. Data on secular Spanish-Indian interaction have been recovered, as was expected, since when the Spanish arrived in 1769 there was a large native village, Cosoy, at the base of what was to become Presidio Hill. Discoveries include worked shell, an abalone fishhook, and Tipai-Ipai pottery (Anonymous

1968:20). Acculturation is seen in certain Tizon brownware vessels with ring bases, a European ceramic trait, added to their bottoms.

Santa Barbara Royal Presidio

Professional archeological excavations started at the Santa Barbara presidio site in 1962. Further excavations unearthed the poorly preserved foundations of the presidio chapel, erected in 1786 (fig. 4), and a number of

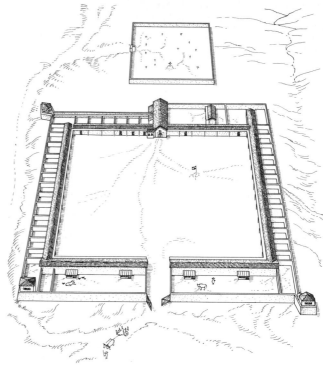

after Ruiz 1967:4.

Fig. 4. View of the Santa Barbara Royal Presidio in the late 1780s, according to a modern reconstruction.

associated burials (Hillebrand 1967; Glassow 1971:2-9). Since the few Hispanic-period artifacts have not been analyzed there is little to indicate Chumash involvement with the site. Historical records do, on the other hand, emphasize such contact. The first three Chumash to be converted were baptized within the fort with Felipe de Goycoechea, commandant of the presidio, acting as godfather, while the first neophyte Christian marriage, on March 21, 1787, was in the chapel (Ruiz 1969:20). At its founding the fort was placed halfway between the Santa Barbara mission site and a large coastal Chumash village, Yuctu (Ruiz 1967:1-5). Indians from the mission as well as those from Yuctu, the "Presidio Indians," spent the daytime working inside the presidio, resulting in constant contact with Spanish secular culture.

Fort Ross

Fort Ross was the only permanent non-Hispanic settlement in early California.

In 1809 and 1811 tentative attempts at settlement at Bodega Bay—where earlier Spanish attempts had failed—were made by the Russian-American Fur Company. Then in 1812 a new location 90 miles north of San Francisco Bay was selected as an agricultural base as well as a center for the fur trade for the erection of Fort Ross (1812-1841). A tricultural community evolved of Russian administrators, Aleut fur hunters from Alaska, and local Pomo Indians as laborers and agriculturalists. For 29 years this relationship continued, until by the 1840s the depletion of the local sea otter population, the failure of the agriculture venture, and the state of international politics provoked a Russian withdrawal from California.

In 1953 Treganza (1954) opened the first extensive archeological program at the fort, gaining a great deal of information basic to reconstruction. In 1970 and 1971 his work inside the stockade was expanded by new excavations first under Donald Wood and then William Pritchard (P.J.F. Schumacher 1971, 1972). In reference to the unique three-way culture contact situation at Fort Ross, Treganza (1954:18) located five sizable village sites within one-half mile of the stockade, at least one of which seems contemporary with the Russian occupation. Around its still-discernible house pits were historic artifacts. Another of the sites, on the basis of architectural stratigraphy, was built after the Russian withdrawal; however, native-made pendants fashioned from Russian porcelain reflect an impact on Pomo material culture. Treganza did not attempt to locate the site of the Aleut settlement. White (1970) continued this research with an extensive site survey of the fort park specifically designed to seek out evidence of Russian-Pomo-Aleut contact. His survey and test excavations at Madshui-nui, the large Pomo village adjacent to the fort, have in turn been continued by Donald Wood (P.J.F. Schumacher 1971). Proof of the intense impact on the Pomo is observed not only in introduced items but also in the reworking of Russian glass and porcelain artifacts into a Pomo context. A similar Russian-Pomo-Aleut (Kodiak Islander?) mixture of artifacts has been recovered on the Farallon Islands (Riddell 1955; Pilling 1955) off San Francisco Bay, where a Russian outpost once operated.

Mexican Period, 1822-1847

Padre Miguel Hidalgo's revolution of 1810 did not immediately disrupt California society but merely led to its greater isolation from Spain. Archeological sequences from California historic sites between 1800 and 1830 in many cases show a continuation of older patterns. As California ties to Mexico were always tenuous, a mother country-colony dependency did not reemerge. Rather an internal socioeconomic development commenced. If local, secular California institutions were to expand on an indigenous economic base it was inevitable that it would be at the expense of the Franciscan missions that held most of the country's wealth in land and livestock. The florescence of the rancho system, carved out of mission lands, accelerated after the legal secularization of the missions in 1834. By the end of the decade the entire system was a shambles, with some missions losing even their religious structures as well as their land. The coastal Indian population, so closely tied to the mission as their basic social unit, was scattered and decimated by secularization as well as an old problem that had finally caught up with new additions from proselytism—European-introduced disease. Within the Mexican area many Indians were absorbed into the new ranchos as vaqueros or servants, while others reverted, or attempted to revert, to old patterns. For example, at La Purísima cemetery the monotonous Christian burial pattern is broken by one burial, probably interred after secularization, with grave goods and an arrangement similar to aboriginal Chumash patterns (Humphrey 1965:190).

Most archeological research on the Mexican period has concentrated on ranchos. Adobes, many of which were the *casa campo* of such great ranchos, have long been examined from the architect's and historian's perspective. Archeological investigation, however, has been confined to 10 such adobe structures or related features, and in only four of these was excavation extensive enough to reveal basic cultural patterns including local Indian elements.

Sepulveda Rancho

José Andrés Sepulveda perhaps more than any other individual symbolizes the rancho era in southern California. After carving a huge private estate out of the San Capistrano mission holdings in 1837, he settled down to the life of a caballero (Sleeper 1969:1-20).

While he held the ranch he constructed or took over several houses, including his "first hacienda" near modern Newport Bay. Ironically this structure had been built at the start of the Mexican period by the mission as a local headquarters for its Indian vaqueros (Chace 1969:39). He took possession in 1837 and the building was inhabited until 1864. In 1968 exploratory trenches at the sites, headquarters of what was officially designated the Rancho Cerrito de Las Ranas, failed to encounter any foundations. Evidence in the form of floor tiles, roof asphalt, and possible adobe borrow pits did indicate the presence of a crude structure (Chace 1969:40-43). Both Indian and Euro-American artifacts were numerous, reflecting the type of social unit that according to an 1850 census consisted of 10 members of the Sepulveda family and five California Indian laborers. An inventory of recovered pottery gives an informative range of identifiable sherds: English, 50 percent; local Indian, 7 percent; Mexican, 4 percent; Chinese, 3 percent; American, 2 percent; French, 2 percent; and Scottish, 1 percent (Chace 1969:52). On one hand, the lack of industrial production in California is shown in its clear dependence on international, especially English, trade for its ceramics; at the same time, a continuing presence and contribution of aboriginal culture in the Mexican period is underscored.

Los Cerritos Ranch House

Built in 1844 by an American immigrant, John Temple of Massachusetts, Los Cerritos is today in Long Beach. In the 1850 census its residents, or associated persons, numbered 36 people, 22 of them Indians, five of whom were women (Evans 1969:74-75). There is some evidence of earlier Spanish remains (Evans 1964) but intermittent archeological work between 1957 and 1965 has basically produced a rich Mexican-Anglo collection. Grinding-stone fragments, awls, scrapers, and other artifacts demonstrate a strong continuity in aboriginal forms (Evans 1961:3), which is highlighted even more by the ceramics. Enough sherds were uncovered to reconstruct nine whole or partial vessels and to defend a new type, Cerritos brown, of the Tizon brownware, with a temporal range of at least 1800 to 1850 (Evans 1969:71-76). Geographically, similar material has been found at a number of historic sites extending as far north as the Los Angeles area. The occurrence of lumps of clay and crude figurines added to the known historic presence of Indian women argues for a local production; it may indicate that although fine wares were Euro-American imports, domestic kitchen pottery continued to be native in origin. Thus Los Cerritos has revealed a significant Indian contribution to California Mexican rancho society.

Hugo Reid Adobe

In the latter part of the Mexican period the presence of foreigners in California became commonplace. By 1845 there were about 600 Americans in the state, half of which had entered by overland routes (Fehrenbacher 1964:27). Such individuals frequently married into Hispanic families and lived in town or rancho houses.

Don Perfecto Hugo Reid was such a man, an educated Scotsman who settled in California in 1834 and obtained the Santa Anita Rancho, once part of the San Gabriel mission lands, in 1839. His marriage to Bartolomea (Victoria) Comicrabit, a Gabrielino mission Indian, led him to write later on a series of letters that is one of the finest ethnohistorical sources on southern California Indians in the historic period (Heizer 1968). On his rancho holdings he constructed, probably in 1840, an adobe that still stands in the Los Angeles County Arboretum in Arcadia. Between 1956 and 1958 William Wallace and his colleagues carried out extensive work inside and outside of the adobe. As a result the various archeological reports on the Hugo Reid adobe make up one of the finest examples of historic-sites archeology in California.

From historical (Wallace 1959) and archeological data (Wallace, Desautels, and Kritzman 1958; Wallace and Wallace 1959) emerges a firm picture of a simple,

three-room structure, with clay-dirt floor and brea roof—a much more realistic view of most nineteenth-century California rancho houses than what many romantics propose (fig. 5). A wealth of historic, mostly

Fig. 5. Exploratory trench outside the south wall of a wing (a later addition) of the Hugo Reid Adobe. The adobe foundations and the packed dirt floor of the house are visible. Photograph by Edith Wallace, 1957.

American-period (Wallace and Taylor 1961) artifacts and a smaller Indian sample (Wallace and Wallace 1958:74-81) were obtained from the excavations, especially those inside the house.

Reid and his Gabrielino wife only occasionally lived at the adobe, having a better house near San Gabriel Mission as well as other residences. However, there was probably a contemporary Gabrielino village, Aleupkigna, near the ranch house, and Indian vaqueros also may have used the building. Discounting earlier materials, a range of items postdating construction of the house includes projectile points, scrapers, blade fragments, hand- and hammerstones, shell beads, potsherds, and miscellaneous objects. One of the points and one scraper are chipped from green bottle glass. The Wallaces propose that such lithic materials may have been dropped by interior Indians who are known to have raided the area in the mid-nineteenth century. Deetz's (1962-1963) discovery of rapid atrophy of lithic technology at La Purísima would support this thesis, but the fact that artifacts chipped from glass or ceramics have been found on a number of sites within the settled zone opens this conclusion to question. Similarly, an inference by them that native pottery was not made in the 1840s seems to have been disproved by more recent data on the distribution of Cerritos Tizon brownware (Evans 1969:74).

Hugo Reid has left a record, both in his writings and in the ground, of a continuing and integral Indian involvement in Mexican California society.

Petaluma Adobe

North of San Francisco Bay, in Sonoma County, on the edge of the Spanish-Mexican settled zone are several archeological sites related to one of California's great rancheros—Gen. Mariano Guadalupe Vallejo. Miwok, Wintun (Patwin), and Wappo laborers and Kanaka (Hawaiian) craftsmen built for Vallejo, starting in 1834, the largest ranch house in the state. Built around a plaza, this two-story structure with outbuildings for specific industrial functions was similar to a mission in the sense that it was a centralized economic and social focus for a huge area. Indians not only built the structure but also served as some of the vaqueros and laborers at the house.

Although there has been extensive archeological work at the site, there has been no attempt to analyze recovered artifacts, which were badly mixed in most areas. Indian artifacts might be from a previous aboriginal site or deposited by Indians associated with the ranch house (Treganza 1959:5). Along the small stream east of the house a thin veneer of midden was attributed by Treganza (1959:22) to the Vallejo and post-Vallejo periods. Gebhardt (1962:16-19) recovered historic articles, for example, a red glass trade bead; but as most artifacts came from the upper six inches, they were badly disturbed by farming. A structure 150 feet by 22 feet found on the other side of the creek may well be a Vallejo-constructed Indian dwelling.

American Period, 1847–1972

Initially the pattern of the American period had its roots in the Mexican period, as is seen in the examples of Hugo Reid or that of a Swiss immigrant who in 1839 constructed, on a huge estate granted him by the Mexican authorities, a fortified communal unit in the lower Sacramento River valley. John Sutter's "New Helvetia" was directly within the tradition of Euro-Indian enclosed communities at missions and ranchos as well as an example of a trading center. With local Indian labor he built, using adobe construction, a fort that was garrisoned in part by Indians. Many individual buildings with specific functions (for example: a kitchen, perhaps tended by an Indian, a shoemaker shop, carpenter shop, brewery-distillery, and a trading post area) made up what has been called by some historians a feudal barony. One of the overall functions of Sutter's Fort was to trade with the interior Indians.

Excavations in the 1950s and the discovery in 1958 of an 1848 map (fig. 6) (Künzel 1848) solved many structural problems involved in restoration and helped to direct further explorations. Olsen (1961) and Payen (1961) uncovered areas extensive enough so that some cultural as well as architectural inferences may be drawn.

Sutter's claim that the site on which he built was un-

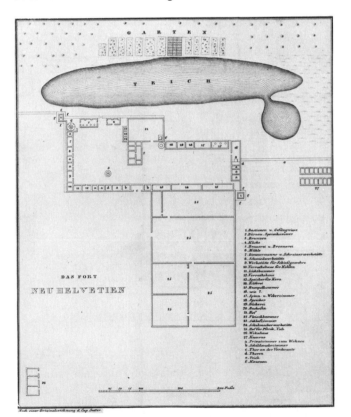

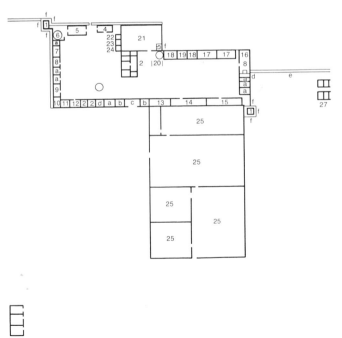

Fig. 6. Ground plan of Sutter's Fort (Künzel 1848 after an original map by Sutter). Detail on right. Key: 1, bastion and jails; 2, office, pantry; 3, well; 4, kitchen; 5, brewery, distillery; 6, mill; 7, carpenter and cabinet-maker workshop; 8, smithy; 9, gunsmithery; 10, coal storage; 11, candlemaker's workshop; 12, storage room; 13, granary; 14, cooperage; 15, lumber-room; 16, see 7; 17, spinning and weaving room; 18, warehouse; 19, bakery; 20, baker's oven; 21, yard; 22, meat storage; 23, sleeping quarters; 24, shoemaker's workshop; 25, horse and cattle pens; 26, house; 27, barracks: a, private living quarters; b, sentry's room; c, front gate; d, gates; e, pond; f, cannons.

77

occupied in 1839 is supported by archeology; however, Indian villages in the vicinity of the fort were contemporary with it. Two glass beads from the floor of the shoemaker shop were probably part of Sutter's trade goods or dropped by Indian employees (Olsen 1961:45, 52). In a small courtyard within the fort, the *Hof* (21) on the Künzel map, a hard packed floor containing midden materials was located. Associated postmolds may be the remains of a crude building, which a cache of fire-cracked cobbles, gun flints, an incised bone tube, and two obsidian points indicate may have been an Indian dwelling. Further analysis of the recovered artifacts and more excavations are needed to expand these hints of a key early acculturation focal point for interior Indians.

Close Indian contact with Anglo historic sites that represented the same earlier pattern as did Sutter's Fort are seen in a few cases as with the Wintu and the William B. Ide Adobe (Treganza 1958). When sites unique to American culture are reviewed in contrast, a very different relationship emerges. By 1850 California had been so populated by gold miners, farmers, and town dwellers that it entered the Union as a state. Between 1847 and the turn of the century, when California began to fully industrialize, a settlement pattern consisting of urban sites, ranch/farm sites, and specialized sites, such as military forts and mining camps, literally sprung up throughout the state.

Urban sites, such as Old Sacramento, and the numerous mining camps that have been surveyed or tested reveal, at least in what has been published, no evidence of Indian involvement. Even in the case of a site like Fort Humboldt (Jewell and Clemmer 1959; Jewell 1966), established in 1852 in Wiyot territory to protect the inhabitants of the new Anglo community of Eureka from local Indians, evidence is scanty. Twenty years of occupation left a great amount of refuse and remains. No analysis of these collections has appeared, but in all reports issued there is no indication of an Indian presence at the site. When viewed in the light of rather extensive documentation in the National Archives on the fort's relationship to Indians, the archeological situation seems to indicate a unidirectional, White to Indian relationship, with no countering influence.

Several Anglo ranches or farm sites have been located in recent archeological surveys in central and eastern California. One of these in the Buchanan Reservoir region, Madera County, was purposely excavated to check for Anglo-Indian acculturation (Mannion 1969:248-258). When the White Ranch was settled in 1852 local Indians still lived only 2.5 miles to the northwest; nevertheless, Chinese labor was used to build the ranch house. The results of the excavations have been totally negative as far as Indian remains are concerned.

Although the variety and quantity of sites from the early Anglo period are far greater than those from ear-

lier eras, evidence of Indian contact at such sites is inversely less than at those of the Spanish or Mexican periods.

Conclusion

Examination of historic sites that date from 1769 to the end of the nineteenth century reveals a brief and radical pattern in reference to California Indians. The emerging picture depends as much on the vicissitudes of historic-sites archeology on the West Coast (Heizer 1950; Schuyler and Sneed 1968) as on the historical sequence of the events and patterns being studied. Such data, combined with work at contemporary Indian contact sites and ethnohistoric sources, may be viewed from either a historical or anthropological perspective. By viewing the Pacific coast of America in the eighteenth and nineteenth centuries as only an example of general anthropological cultural processes (Fontana 1965; Schuyler 1970), the contribution of historical archeology is greatly enhanced.

Ignoring the intriguing situation of a Hispanic culture intruded into a geographical area spanning over 400 miles and encompassing numerous ecological zones and also ignoring as primary questions the internal evolution of Hispanic society as well as contact with other Europeans, California may be viewed as an example of highly successful and demographically dense but primitive cultures brought into contact successively with preindustrial and industrializing Euro-American societies. This development, which covered only a little over a century, may be seen in an evolutionary typology:

Native Cultures
Assimilation
Transition
Cultural Fusion
Preindustrial Society
Remnant Assimiliation
Extinction
Isolation
Culture Conflict
Industrial Society

Preindustrial Contact

Some scholars have seen the fate of California Indians in terms of a sequence involving a successful missionization attempt, its destruction by the Mexican revolution and secularization, a resulting exploitation and scattering of Mission Indians, and then a final eclipse under a totally hostile Anglo invasion. However, by concentrating on economic and ecological variables rather than questions of ethics and morals, the specific interplay of events is seen as a shortcircuiting of a gradual evolution to a higher stage. Hispanic culture was clearly technologically and organizationally more complex than California Indian bands, but this cultural gap was lessened by frontier conditions, including an ecclesiastical ethos, and dense native populations. External factors concerned with the Spanish empire and navigational technology influenced Spanish settlement, but so did indigenous settlement patterns. One of the patent recurrences at most Hispanic archeological sites is their location on or in areas of contact (and prehistoric) Indian sites. The Spanish settled, in part, where there was a ready-made population of potential Christian converts that would also supply labor for running the mission system that was their economic underpinning. Such a situation led to the planned acculturation of Indians, and less so Spaniards, and the creation of a Hispanic-Indian culture along the coast.

Independence, with its anticlerical perspective, and the rise of the rancho system destroyed the missions. Historically it is known that men like Vallejo planned on Mission Indians' becoming townsmen and the missions local parishes. This, of course, did not work out. What transpired was the collapse of controlled acculturation, replaced by an informal but open structure. Lack of control led many Indians to move into the interior (Heizer 1954:85–86) or attempt to revert to old patterns, but this review has shown that there is indeed a strong Indian element in the rancho system.

In sum, archeological data indicate an intensive and encapsulated acculturation, not uniform in all aspects of culture, within a special (Franciscan) framework. The removal of this structure opened the way for an introduction into a more general Hispanic structure via the ranchos, then the final result of absorption.

Industrial Contact

Contrasts between an industrial, or industrializing, civilization and a band society are so marked that planned or gradual acculturation on a massive level is unlikely. Usually culture shock and destruction, or at best isolation by geographical withdrawal or legal withdrawal (reserves), is the result. It was not Anglo ethics or hate for Indians that predetermined the course of events, for as archeology and written history demonstrate, the first Anglos to enter California had contact with Indians within the rancho framework. Or they came as specialized, frontier offshoots of a distant society, such as Sutter and his trading post, that had already resulted in much of North America in the adaptation of native peoples to the fringes of Euro-American culture. When the gold rush and farming potential of the state drew in literally tens of thousands of immigrants in a year's time, a total society was transported into California overnight. In this situation, with few exceptions, the Indian had no economic function. In 1850 the relationship between the Anglo and Indian was closer to that between a man and a natural feature that happened to exist, and happened to be in the way, than between one culture and another.

Archeologically a preindustrial contact situation is reflected in the close ties between Spaniard and Indian and between Mexican and Indian as seen at both contact sites and at Hispanic sites themselves. An industrial contact situation is seen in overwhelming acculturation at Indian sites and an almost total lack of Indian materials at post-1850 Anglo sites and finally in reserves and reservations. There was a place for the Indian in Spanish California; in fact, he was an integral part of its economic underpinning. There was a continuing place, albeit much less important, in Mexican California; but the nature of Anglo culture excluded him and forced him close to extermination.

Native Languages of California

WILLIAM F. SHIPLEY

Presumably, at one time it was common for a great many highly divergent languages to be spoken within a modest geographical area. Such a situation still obtains in various parts of the world—in the Caucasus, in West Africa, in New Guinea, in the mountains and gorges at the convergence of Upper Burma, Thailand, and southwestern China. Another such tangle of languages, perhaps in some ways the most complex of all, was found in the California culture area until the European conquest, which began just two centuries ago. Over the mountains, valleys, and deserts of the area were spread no fewer than 64—and perhaps as many as 80—mutually unintelligible tongues, further differentiated into an unknowably large number of dialects. Miraculously, something more than two dozen of these languages have survived through the middle of the twentieth century—as terminal cases, it is true, and spoken only by a few elderly persons. These languages have provided the modern researcher with a glimpse, however faded, of a marvelous linguistic diversity with its origins lying millennia in the past.

The orderliness of Darwinian theorists inspired nineteenth-century linguists to reach certain conclusions about the mechanisms of diachronic or historical change in languages. Thus a detailed study of the historical development of the Indo-European family of languages, the principal pastime of nineteenth-century linguists, led to the formulation of clear-cut tenets with regard to the dynamisms of linguistic change. The maturation of this understanding about language was much abetted by the nature of the data from which such understanding was derived. Not only are there dozens of modern Indo-European languages to which anyone may have massive access, but also there are extensive records of older languages—Sanskrit, Greek, Hittite, Latin—sometimes going back as far as 3,500 years. The analysis of this ocean of material provided insights of vast importance to the study of language: that, for example, sound-change in language is regular, recurrent, and predictable and that apparent exceptions are always due to special circumstances about which individual statements may be made, given sufficient information. One of the most important types of special circumstance is that in which words have been borrowed by one language from another. Such words, of course, do not reflect the historical development of the borrowing language prior to the time of their adoption.

It is only in the light of these principles that the situation with regard to the languages of California can really be understood. A basic system of recurrent sound correspondences is the only known certain diagnostic for validating a genetic relationship among any group of languages. Such a validation is possible in California for small families of languages; in fact, it has been done for Miwokan (Broadbent and Callaghan 1960), Yokutsan (Golla 1964), Palaihnihan (Olmsted 1964), Pomoan (McLendon 1973; Moshinsky 1974), Maiduan (Ultan 1964), and Yuman (Langdon 1968, 1975; Wares 1968). Those California languages belonging to the three relevant exterior stocks—Algic (Algonquian-Wiyot-Yurok), Na-Dene, and Uto-Aztecan—have been genetically identified in the very process of discovering their exterior relationships, a simple and obvious task in the case of the Uto-Aztecan and Athapaskan languages but much more difficult in the case of Wiyot and Yurok (Sapir 1913, 1915, 1915a; Michelson 1914, 1915; Haas 1958).

An example from the Miwokan languages will make the nature of this validation clear (Broadbent and Callaghan 1960; Callaghan 1970).

	'heart'	'swim'	'fly' (verb)	'eye'
Southern Sierra Miwok	wɨhki	ʔipɨh	hileˑt	hintɨ
Central Sierra Miwok	wɨ̣ski	ʔipɨ̣ṣ	ṩileˑt	ṩintɨ
Plains Miwok	wáski	ʔəpə́h	sɨlέˑt	——
Bodega Miwok	wúṣki	ʔupúh	——	ṣút

It will be noted that wherever Southern Sierra Miwok has an h, Central Sierra Miwok has an ṣ. This recurrent correspondence, along with the various obvious identities (ɨ to ɨ, for instance), validates the genetic relationship between the Southern and Central Sierra languages. Matching this h : ṣ correspondence, Plains Miwok has s in the words for 'fly' and 'heart' but h in the word for 'swim'. A parallel pattern with ṣ and h obtains in Bodega Miwok. These h variants in Plains and Bodega Miwok are due to the occurrence of the sound in final position. The correspondence, then, is h in Southern Sierra Miwok, ṣ in Central Sierra Miwok, h finally and otherwise s in

Plains Miwok, and *h* finally and otherwise *ṣ* in Bodega Miwok. The genetic relationship of these four languages is certified by the marshaling of such evidence in as much detail as possible.

For the two great language stocks—Hokan and Penutian—that have been proposed as subsuming a majority of the California languages, there is as yet no demonstrable evidence of the type presented for Miwokan. There are many provocative resemblant forms among the languages, particularly among the Penutian ones, as well as certain general grammatical features that may be labeled Penutian or Hokan. In short, the terms Penutian stock and Hokan stock are names for unverified hypotheses. It is likely that both theories will eventually be validated, probably with minor, possibly with major alterations and rearrangements.

Various factors complicate the situation. One of the major difficulties has to do with linguistic diffusion, the borrowing of language material—speech sounds, words, grammatical constructions—by one language from another. The freedom and ease with which most of the California languages borrowed terms from Spanish is a case in point (Shipley 1962). Hundreds of Spanish words, linked with diffused elements of Spanish culture, invaded the aboriginal tongues in the nineteenth century, very probably representing an old continuing tradition of linguistic borrowing. Bilingualism and multilingualism were common among the California Indians, undoubtedly accompanied, over the centuries, by a steady process of acculturation and exchange of linguistic material in all directions. Many animal, bird, and plant names are widespread, crisscrossing all known boundaries between linguistic families. Some of these, like words for 'goose', 'crane', and 'frog' are scattered over the whole continent. Indeed, the word for 'bluejay'—Karok *ka·y* 'sound of a bluejay', Maidu *k̓áy*, Nisenan *čayit*, Wappo *čay*, Chukchansi Yokuts *čaičay*, Barbareño Chumash *cay*—is reflected even by Latin *gaius* and English *jay*. To say that these words are onomatopoetic is simply to name the phenomenon without explaining it. The fact that some linguistic diffusion is global, some continental, and some areal is directly involved with the problem of elucidating prehistory in California as well as elsewhere.

Quite apart from the correspondence of sounds as an attestation of genetic connections among languages, there is the equally important but much more complex matter of grammatical evidence for the historical relationship of one language to another. Such evidence may be inflectional or derivational (such as the noun cases in Latin, Greek, Sanskrit, German, and Russian, which reflect the common Indo-European origin of these languages) or syntactic, (that is, having to do with the structures of sentences). Inflexional and derivational elements have been explored to some extent for the California languages. The validating criteria involved in syntactic comparisons are, as yet, very poorly character-

ized. The difficulties come in separating the genetic similarities between two grammars from those that are due to chance or sporadic diffusion. For example, English is, in some ways, grammatically closer to Chinese (by chance) than it is to German (to which it is closely related genetically).

In order to make a realistic assessment of what can be known about interrelationships among the languages of California, the complications and difficulties described above must be kept clearly in view. All sorts of things are very possible: that Esselen, for example, is not Hokan but Penutian, or that it is neither Hokan nor Penutian but the single remnant of a language family that has long since vanished.

With all these caveats in mind, what deductions can be made from the distribution of the California languages, based on the current views regarding their provenience?

The oldest language group still more or less in situ in California would seem to be Hokan. Perhaps these languages were spoken over most of the area, very likely along with speech families of which no trace remains. They were then disrupted by the incursion of Penutian, which, spreading through the great central valley, forced Hokan to the periphery. A later Uto-Aztecan thrust in

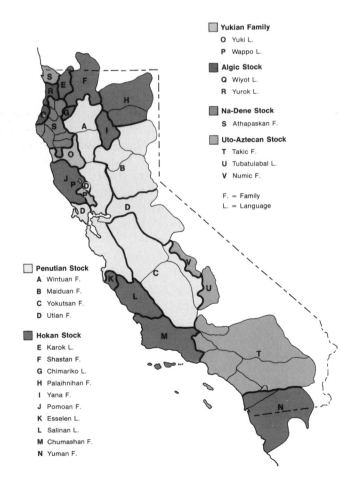

Fig. 1. Language stocks and families of the California culture area.

southern California may have pushed the Yuman languages still farther away from their Hokan congeners.

Somewhat earlier than this, the ancient forms of Yurok and Wiyot speech were brought into the northwest, though not necessarily at the same time. The common ancestral form from which Wiyot, Yurok, and Proto-Algonquian sprang was certainly never spoken in California, so that ancient Yurok and ancient Wiyot must have been separate languages while they were still somewhere to the east or north.

The latest arrivals were probably the Athapaskans, whose ancestors may have drifted down the rivers and coast from Oregon.

The Yukians present the greatest uncertainty. If, as Elmendorf (1963, 1964) suggests, they are related to Siouan, then the circumstance of their presence in California parallels that of Wiyot and Yurok. This is based on the assumption that Wappo is Yukian, for Wappo and Northern Yukian are very remotely related. Such speculation is very tenuous without further research. It is even conceivable that Yukian speech is older in California than Hokan.

In the delineation that follows, languages, language families, and language stocks are organized provisionally, based on the current consensus of researchers. Estimates of numbers of speakers in the various groups are based largely on Kroeber (1925; see also "Historical Demography," this vol.).

Penutian Stock

The Penutian stock was first identified and named by Dixon and Kroeber (1913, 1919). Further attempts to elucidate and define Penutian have been made by many scholars over the years (Sapir 1921–1923, 1921b, 1929; Shafer 1947, 1952; Hymes 1957a, 1964, 1964a; Pitkin and Shipley 1958; Shipley 1957, 1966; Broadbent and Pitkin 1964; Callaghan 1967). The name is a compound of the word for 'two' in Maiduan (Proto-Maiduan *pé·ne) and Costanoan (Proto-Costanoan *uṭxi).

The relationship among the Penutian languages is a very old one. Validation of the group as a "true" linguistic stock has been difficult to achieve, though evidence adduced by Hymes (1964) and Shipley (1966) would seem to be conservative and reliable enough to carry conviction. The situation has been complicated by the efforts of various scholars to add languages and language groups outside California to the inventory of Penutian tongues (Sapir 1929a; Freeland 1931; J.A. Mason 1940; F. Johnson 1940; Sapir and Swadesh 1953; Swadesh 1954, 1956; Hymes 1957a, 1964, 1964a; Newman 1964, Shipley 1966, 1969, 1970). It would be irresponsible to say that California Penutian has been established as a genetic group in the sense that Indo-European is so established. However, there seems to be little doubt that further research will eventually certify the relationship. Reviews of the history of Penutian research have been published by Callaghan (1958) and Shipley (1973).

The characteristics of the protolanguage from which the Penutian languages are descended may be adumbrated to some extent. The sound system was of moderate complexity with two series of voiceless stops (plain and aspirated), probably a labiovelar *k^w*, perhaps no more than the two spirants *s* and *h*, and very likely the sonorants *m, n, r, l, w* and *y*. Most of the languages are not so simple as this (though the Utian group is actually simpler), but the evidence points to a diffused origin for the glottalized consonants so commonly found, while the proliferation of spirants and affricates in Wintuan, Yokutsan, and Costanoan may be due to defunct systems of consonantal symbolism. There were five vowels: *i, u, e, o, a*. The typical stem-morpheme shape proposed long ago by Sapir (1921–1923) has been borne out by subsequent research. In its modern version, the formula may be stated as a disyllabic stem with a single initial and single medial consonant, with or without a final consonant: CVCV(C). As Sapir pointed out, the vowels in the two syllables are often the same.

Certain aspects of the grammar of Proto-Penutian are fairly clear. There was probably a rather complex system of postfixed case markers on nouns and pronouns. The pronoun system was particularly elaborate, with markers not only for case but also for singular, dual, and plural numbers. In addition to subject, object, and possessive cases, the nouns and pronouns were almost certainly marked for the locative and instrumental.

Verbs were marked with suffixes denoting various aspects, modes, and tenses but probably not for person. It is possible that there were instrumental prefixes, though the evidence for this is unreliable. Prefixing in general was minimal or lacking.

There were four families in the Penutian stock: Wintuan, Maiduan, Yokutsan, and Utian. All these names are derived from terms meaning 'person' or 'human being' except Utian, which is based on the Miwok-Costanoan word for 'two'.

Wintuan Family

The three languages in the Wintuan family are Wintu, Nomlaki, and Patwin. Wintu and Nomlaki are quite similar; Patwin is clearly more remote. Harvey Pitkin (personal communication 1962) has suggested that many of the resemblances between Patwin and Wintu may be the result of diffusion and that the genetic relationship is, perhaps, more distant than a superficial inspection of the data would indicate. Kroeber (1925:883) estimated the number of Wintuan speakers at 12,000 in preinvasion times, of which probably at least half were speakers of Patwin.

These Wintuan languages, particularly Wintu, are much more complex phonologically than Proto-Penutian. There were four series of stops: plain, aspirated, glottalized, and voiced; in addition, Wintu had several extra spirants as well as a two-way velar contrast between fronted and backed stops and spirants (*k* and *q* as well as *x* and *x̣*). This last feature may very well have been in Proto-Penutian though no other California Penutian language retains it.

Wintu was the northernmost language of the family, with nine known dialects (Pitkin 1963): McCloud River, Trinity County, Shasta County, Upper Sacramento, Bald Hill, Hayfork, Keswick, Stillwater, and French Gulch.

Closely related to Wintu is Nomlaki (*nom* 'west', *laki* 'speech'?), spoken just to the south in the upper end of the Sacramento Valley. Nomlaki is the least known of the Wintuan languages and probably had no more than 1,000 or so speakers, with at least two dialects and perhaps as many as six.

The area of Patwin speech extended southward to the delta of the Sacramento-San Joaquin river system. There were perhaps 6,000 speakers of Patwin, with many dialects, some of which are known: Hill, River, Cache Creek, Lake, Tebti, Dahcinci, and Suisun. The Patwin (*patwin* 'person') played a dominant cultural role in Central California. Many Patwin words were diffused into the neighboring languages.

Maiduan Family

The Maiduan languages exhibit three phonological innovations of particular interest when compared with the postulated system for Proto-Penutian: there is a glottalized stop series; there are two voiced imploded stops, *b* and *d;* and there is a sixth vowel, the high central unrounded *ɨ*. Konkow and Nisenan have yet a seventh vowel, a mid-central unrounded *ə*. The origins of these two extra vowels are obscure. The high vowel is found in some Miwokan and Yokutsan languages as well as in Maiduan, specifically in those languages that are contiguous to or near the Uto-Aztecan languages to the east and south of the Sierra Nevada, all of which have such a vowel. Silverstein (1970) has shown that *ɨ* may very well have developed from *u* under the influence of a neighboring *y*.

Maiduan stems tend to be monosyllabic. The Proto-Penutian stem type CVCV(C) has often been reduced by the loss of the medial consonant or of the second syllable.

There are three languages in the family: Maidu (Northeastern Maidu, Mountain Maidu), Konkow (Concow, Northwestern Maidu), and Nisenan (Southern Maidu). Although they share a large inventory of near-identical stem morphemes, they are quite different from one another grammatically and are not mutually intelligible. Phonological and lexical reconstructions have been made (Shipley 1961; Ultan 1964). According to Kroeber (1925:883) there were some 9,000 speakers in aboriginal times, Nisenan being probably the largest group.

Maidu was spoken entirely in the high mountains to the east and south of Mount Lassen. There is little reliable evidence for dialect differentiation though it seems reasonable to assume that there were different dialects originally in the four major areas of Maidu settlement: Susanville, Big Meadows, Indian Valley, and American Valley. Grammars, texts, and a dictionary of the language are available (Dixon 1911, 1912; Shipley 1963, 1964).

Southwest of the Maidu, along the Feather River and its tributaries and in the adjacent Sacramento Valley, were the Konkows, who spoke a large number of dialects: Otaki, Metsupda, Nemsu, and Eskewi near Chico; Pulga, Feather Falls, Challenge, and others near Oroville and in the Feather River Canyon; and doubtless other dialects in the region around the Marysville Buttes.

Nisenan was also spoken in various dialects. Those that can be identified are: Valley Nisenan, Oregon House, Auburn, Clipper Gap, Nevada City, Colfax, and Placerville. Although no Nisenan grammar has been written there is a partial description in manuscript of the Auburn (Uldall 1940) and Clipper Gap (R. Smith 1964) dialects. A dictionary and collection of texts are available for Auburn Nisenan (Uldall and Shipley 1966).

Yokutsan Family

The Yokutsan-speaking people, some 18,000 in number (Kroeber 1925:883), occupied the San Joaquin valley from the delta to Tehachapi, including the contiguous foothills of the Sierra and the Coast Range. There were 40 to 50 small tribes in this area, each with a distinctive dialect (Kroeber 1925:474), a state of affairs unlike any other in California. Kroeber (1963) classified these dialects into 12 groups belonging to two divisions; his arrangement was based on lexical material collected for 21 of the dialects.

These facts make it very difficult to say how many Yokutsan languages there were—indeed, the very notion of language becomes blurred in such a context. Linguists have called two forms of speech two languages if they are mutually unintelligible. This is an extremely unreliable practice if only for the reason that the term "mutually unintelligible" cannot be defined. Probably any Yokutsan dialect was intelligible to the speakers of immediately neighboring dialects with only some minor adjustments; on the other hand, speakers of two widely divergent dialects were almost certainly incapable of understanding each other. Perhaps there were two Yokutsan languages (corresponding to the two divisions) or 12 (corresponding to the 12 groups). It is not possible to decide nor is it important to attempt to do so, given the circumstances.

Yokutsan is much more complex phonologically than Proto-Penutian. No only is there a series of glottalized voiceless stops as in Maiduan and Wintuan, but there is also a set of glottalized continuants: *m̓, n̓, ŋ̓, w̓, y̓,* and *l̓.* There are extra stops and spirants in the palatal area, perhaps, as elsewhere, the result of old consonant symbolism.

Yokutsan has a very involved system of alternating verb and noun stem shapes, specifically with regard to vowel changes and vowel loss in certain grammatically definable situations. This has been described by Newman (1944, 1946) within the framework of his general description of the Yokutsan languages and has been partially restated by Kuroda (1967) and others (see references in Hockett 1973 and Pullum 1973).

There are three extensive treatments of Yokuts dialects. Yawdanchi and Yawelmani were described by Kroeber (1907). Several dialects, principally Yawelmani, were described by Newman (1944), who also did a later sketch of Yawelmani alone (1946). Of special interest is an annotated reconstitution of a grammatical sketch of the long-extinct Nopchinchi dialect, written in the early nineteenth century by Father Arroyo de la Cuesta (Beeler 1971).

Utian Family

The Utian languages fall into two clearly defined subgroups: Miwokan and Costanoan. Though there is considerable grammatical diversity among these languages, they share certain clear-cut phonological characteristics that set them off sharply from the other Penutian languages. All of them (except Lake Miwok) have but a single series of stops—a situation even simpler than that postulated for Proto-Penutian. Functional distinctions based on glottalization and aspiration are entirely absent. There is some proliferation of palatal stops and spirants as in Yokutsan. There is an underlying basic five-vowel system, though the eastern Miwok languages have a functional sixth high-mid vowel (Plains Miwok had a seventh, like Maiduan Nisenan), undoubtedly due to the innovation discussed in connection with Maiduan. Some of the Costanoan languages have a stem-morpheme structure that invariably matches Šapir's (1921-1923) formulation: CVCV(C) with the two vowels frequently identical.

There are 15 languages in Utian, seven Miwokan and eight Costanoan. Significant lexical and phonological reconstructions have been done for Miwokan (Broadbent and Callaghan 1960; Callaghan 1972), for Proto-Miwok and Mutsun (Callaghan 1962), and for Costanoan (Levy 1970a).

The Miwokan languages were spoken in a (probably) continuous belt across central California, from Marin County on the west to the southern Sierra Nevada on the southeast.

Lake Miwok territory, just to the southeast of Clear Lake, was geographically separated from the other Miwokan languages; Lake Miwok was also unique in the possession of a complex phonological system with four stop series—plain, aspirated, glottalized, and voiced—

presumably borrowed either from Pomo or, more likely, from Patwin (Callaghan 1964, 1965).

Closely related to Lake Miwok, but with a regular, simple, Miwokan-type sound system, was Coast Miwok, probably with two dialects: Bodega and Marin (Callaghan 1970).

Across the Carquinez Strait the long-extinct Saclan was spoken. This language, about which very little is known, was only recently identified as Miwokan (Beeler 1955, 1959).

Farther to the east, in the valley area around Stockton, was Plains Miwok.

Still farther east, from north to south in the Sierra, were three closely related languages: Northern, Central, and Southern Sierra Miwok. The southernmost of these is the most fully described (Broadbent 1964), though some material is also available on the central language (Freeland 1951; Freeland and Broadbent 1960).

The Costanoan languages were spoken around most of San Francisco Bay and southward along the coast to Point Sur, south of Carmel. From what is known of them, they appear to have been much more like one another than were their Miwokan congeners, though a good deal of variability is found in some details of their grammars. Levy (1970a) identified and named the eight languages for which there is evidence: Karkin, Chochenyo (East Bay), Tamyen (Santa Clara), Ramaytush (San Francisco), Awaswas (Santa Cruz), Mutsun (San Juan Bautista and the Pajaro River drainage), Rumsen (Carmel and the lower Salinas River), and Chalon (Soledad, farther up the Salinas River). The classification of the Northern Costanoan languages was carried out by Beeler (1961).

Although the most important nineteenth-century word lists for Costanoan were assembled and published by Heizer (1952, 1955), none of the material collected by Harrington (1921-1938) has appeared in print. Harrington's data on Chochenyo, Mutsun, and Rumsen are extensive and phonetically accurate.

Relations outside California

Within two years of the full-scale display of the evidence for California Penutian (Dixon and Kroeber 1919), Sapir (1921b) proposed a much-expanded inventory of Penutian languages. In its later "classical" form (Sapir 1929), this expansion became the Penutian superstock, an amalgam containing many Oregon languages, Tsimshian on the British Columbia coast, and Mixe-Zoque and Huave in southern Mexico. Although Sapir's proposal was couched in conservative and tentative terms, his Penutian theory has dominated the thoughts and researches of interested scholars ever since, in spite of the fact that no conclusive or definitive evidence for most of the proposed linguistic relationships outside California has ever been brought forward. This is not to say that the Penutian hypothesis of Sapir is wrong; careful research will probably eventually bear it out in the main. The point is that it is a hypothesis.

Various other candidates have been proposed for membership in the Penutian stock over the years. The two that remain viable are Mayan (F. Johnson 1940; J.A. Mason 1940; Swadesh 1956) and Zuni (Swadesh 1956; Newman 1964).

In this connection Klamath-Modoc deserves special mention. Some of the speakers of Klamath-Modoc lived in what is now northern California. Strong lexical evidence has been adduced to show that Klamath-Modoc is related to Nez Perce and other Sahaptian languages of northern Oregon, Idaho, and southern Washington (Aoki 1963). It has also been shown with reasonable certainty, again on the basis of lexical evidence, that Klamath-Modoc is genetically related to the California Penutian languages (Shipley 1966). Thus, it seems safe to infer that the Sahaptian languages are also Penutian.

Hokan Stock

The Hokan stock was identified and named by Dixon and Kroeber (1913); however, the classical characterization of the stock was made by Sapir (1917). The word Hokan is based, as is Penutian, on the word for 'two', presumably from Atsugewi *hoqi*.

Cross-family studies within Hokan have been made for Northern Hokan (Bright 1954), Eastern Pomo and Yana (McLendon 1964), Palaihnihan and Shasta (Olmsted 1956–1959), Shasta and Karok (Silver 1964), and Washo and Karok (Jacobsen 1958). Haas (1964), though ostensibly concerned with Yana-Karok cognates, presents a large amount of data on the other Hokan languages as well as on other California languages outside the Hokan stock as it is presently defined.

A comparison of the Hokan situation with the Penutian one brings to light a dramatic contrast. The interrelationships of the Hokan languages lie much deeper in time, a fact paralleled by their geographical discontinuity. They are dispersed like a broken chain around the margins of the compact California Penutian heartland.

Langdon (1974:87) has outlined the consensus as to the probable nature of the Hokan protolanguage:

> Proto-Hokan probably had a rather simple sound system, with very little trace of the more marked categories exhibited by many of the attested languages. Contrasts involving plain *versus* aspirated and perhaps even glottalized consonants may well turn out to be accountable as independent developments; voiceless sonorants are already accounted for as innovations in Pomo and Yuman, and Washo. Vowels may not have been more than three with a probable length contrast—Proto Yuman has such a system. In the few available good cognate sets, the persisting elements appear to be essentially conservative. The great diversity of the daughter languages, it seems, must be accounted for by repeated processes of loss of vowels leading to subsequent loss and

change of consonants (particularly in the laryngeal area), with resulting lexical items where little remains that is truly comparable. Typical Hokan morphemes must have been short (monosyllabic).

Many of the morphemes found in the attested Hokan languages would seem to be the result of what Silver (1975) has called "morphemization," that is, a historical process whereby old compounds blend into single morphemes with the passing of time. English has a few morphemes of this type: boatswain, knowledge, blackguard, forecastle. Only the archaic spelling reveals the fact that these words were not always single morphemes. Haas (1954, 1963) has marshaled evidence for a general shortening of various words in the modern Hokan languages by comparison with longer ancient forms that themselves may have been strings of two or more morphemes. Even more provocative is her postulation of possible lexical intersections between Hokan and Penutian, specifically with the terms for 'ear' and 'navel' (Haas 1964).

The California Hokan languages and language families are: Karok, Shastan, Chimariko, Palaihnihan, Yana, Pomoan, Esselen, Salinan, Chumashan, and Yuman. Sapir (1925) placed Karok, Shastan, Chimariko, Palaihnihan, Yana, and Pomoan in a separate Northern Hokan subgroup. Subsequent investigations have not validated this subgrouping on the basis of the linguistic evidence.

Karok Language

The Karok language (*káruk* 'a considerable way upriver') was described by Bright (1957). The speakers of Karok, estimated at between 1,500 and 2,000 in aboriginal times, lived along a stretch of the Klamath River in northwestern California. The language is not closely or obviously related to any other; its presumed Hokan affiliations are distant. There was no known dialect differentiation.

Shastan Family

Shastan, a family of four languages, originally had some 2,500 speakers. The languages were: Shasta, New River Shasta, Okwanuchu, and Konomihu. Shasta proper was spoken in at least four dialects: Oregon Shasta, extending up to the Rogue River in southern Oregon, Scott Valley Shasta, Shasta Valley Shasta, and Klamath River Shasta. The dialect situation with the other Shastan languages is not known; they occupied small territories to the south and are all extinct. Shasta has been described by Silver (1966).

Chimariko Language

Chimariko was spoken by only a few hundred people along a 20-mile stretch of the Trinity River, just south of the New River Shasta. Although the language has long been extinct, there is some published material in Dixon (1910a) as well as various manuscript resources including an extensive collection of linguistic data by Harrington (1921-1928).

Palaihnihan Family

Southeast of the Shasta in northeastern California were the speakers of Palaihnihan (from a Klamath word for the Achumawi). There were two languages in the family: Achumawi, spoken in several closely related dialects by the nine bands along the Pit River, and Atsugewi or Hat Creek, with two dialects, Atsuge (also called Hat Creek) and Apwaruge (Dixie Valley). These two languages were very distantly related, though they were apparently closer to each other than to any other Hokan language (Olmsted 1964). There were probably about 3,000 speakers in aboriginal times, the majority being Achumawi. There are descriptive materials available on both Achumawi (Angulo 1926a; Angulo and Freeland 1931; Olmsted 1966; Uldall 1935) and Atsugewi (Garth 1944; Kroeber 1958a; Olmsted 1958, 1961; Talmy 1972, 1975).

Yana Family

East of the Wintu and west of the Atsugewi and the Maidu were the Yana (*yaana* 'person') numbering altogether some 1,500 speakers. There were two languages, Yana with three dialects (Northern, Central, and Southern) and a separate language, Yahi (*yaaxi* 'person') (Sapir and Swadesh 1960). Yana has long been extinct; the famous Ishi was the last speaker of Yahi (T. Kroeber 1961). Although no full-scale grammar of Yana has been written, there is considerable descriptive material (Sapir 1909, 1910, 1918, 1922, 1923, 1929a; Sapir and Swadesh 1960; Nevin 1975).

Pomoan Family

There were seven languages in the Pomoan family (*pomo* 'person, people'), with a total of some 8,000 aboriginal speakers. The Pomoans lived between the Sacramento Valley and the ocean, largely in what is now Sonoma County. Since there were no aboriginal names for the languages, they have been given directional designations: Northeastern, Eastern, Southeastern, Northern, Central, Southern, and Southwestern. Southwestern Pomo has come to be called Kashaya, a name that is probably derived from a stem meaning 'agile, nimble' (Oswalt 1961, 1964).

The Pomoan languages are phonologically among the most complex of the Hokan stock. A great deal of comparative work has been done on the relationships among them. Among early classifications are those of Barrett (1908) and Kroeber (1925). Halpern (1964) improved the grouping on the basis of a survey made in 1939-1940; Oswalt (1964a) made a careful count of shared cognates and proposed some revisions (see "Pomo: Introduction," fig. 1, this vol.). By far the most imposing document on Proto-Pomo is McLendon's (1973) monograph in which she carried out an extensive phonological and lexical reconstruction. Note must be taken of Oswalt's (1964b) binary comparison of Kashaya and Central Pomo as a forerunner of McLendon's work.

There are descriptive materials, some of them extensive, on four of the languages: Eastern (Angulo 1927; Kroeber 1911; McLendon 1975, 1969), Southeastern (Moshinsky 1975), Kashaya (Oswalt 1958, 1961, 1964; Worth 1960), and Northern (Vihman 1975).

Esselen Language

Esselen is very little known. The language was spoken by a few hundred people on the upper reaches of the Carmel River and on the coast around Big Sur. It was classified as Hokan on the basis of a few lexical resemblances. Only word lists are available (Heizer 1952; Kroeber 1904a).

Salinan Language

The Salinan language was spoken by some 2,000 persons in at least two dialects: Migueleño and Antoniaño, named for the two Spanish missions that were established in their territory. There may have been a third dialect along the coast, which Kroeber (1925:546) refers to as Playano; of this form of Salinan speech there are no records whatever. The language is extinct. Aside from some word lists (Heizer 1952), there are two descriptive documents (Kroeber 1904a; J.A. Mason 1918). The Salinans occupied the middle and upper Salinas Valley and the Coast Ranges to the west almost as far south as the town of San Luis Obispo.

Chumashan Family

According to Beeler (1975), the Chumashan family consisted of at least six languages, which may be subgrouped into three dialect areas: a central group consisting of the languages once used around the missions at Ventura (including Emigdiano), Santa Barbara (including Castac, formerly thought to be Uto-Aztecan but shown by Beeler (1972; Beeler and Klar 1974) to have been Barbareño as spoken by certain Indians displaced in mission times), Santa Ynez, and La Purísima; the speech on the islands of San Miguel, Santa Rosa, and Santa Cruz; and the language of San Luis Obispo. These languages are all extinct. There were possibly 10,000 speakers of Chumashan in aboriginal times. In addition to nineteenth-century word lists assembled by Heizer (1952, 1955), further descriptive information is available (Beeler 1975; Applegate 1975; Harrington 1974).

Yuman Family

The Yuman family of languages is the most peripheral geographically. Most of the Yuman languages are or were spoken outside California, in Arizona and Baja California. Although the relationship among these languages is clear and has been extensively studied by many workers, an authoritative classification has not yet been determined. Two classifications are to be noted: that of Kroeber (1943) and the much later one of Joel (1964). The latter study is based on a much larger and more accurate body of data than the former. The only Yuman language in the California culture was Diegueño (Langdon 1970), of which there are at least three dialects, all still spoken, Ipai ('Iipay), Kumeyaay, and Tipai (Tiipay).

Relations outside California

Early versions of the Hokan hypothesis (Kroeber 1915; Sapir 1917) proposed the inclusion of groups partly or entirely outside the California area: Washo, in the Great Basin; Yuman; Seri, in Sonora; and Chontal (Tequistlatec), in southern Oaxaca. Then the languages of northeastern Mexico and southern Texas that Swanton (1915) had classed together as Coahuiltecan were added to the Hokan roster (Sapir 1920). Sapir's (1921b, 1929:140-141) even more inclusive Hokan-Siouan superstock has been abandoned, and other, even more incredible, proposals, including the postulation of Hokan congeners in South America, have largely been considered unsubstantiated. Even Hokan-Coahuiltecan remains far from being established as a genetic reality.

Yukian Family

The small, isolated Yukian family of languages had four members: Yuki, Coast Yuki, and Huchnom in Mendocino County and Wappo, a considerable distance to the south in Lake and Napa counties. The three northern languages were very similar; indeed, they may have been little more than dialects of a single language. In 1975 there was one known surviving speaker of the northern group, which may have had about 2,000 speakers aboriginally. Wappo (from Spanish *guapo* 'handsome') is very different in grammar and lexicon from the northern languages. Either the genetic connection is a remote one or it may be that Wappo is not a Yukian language at all but owes what Yuki-like features it has to the effects of ancient contact and diffusion. There were some 1,000 Wappos originally, with four dialects, one of which was spoken by a small group on the southern end of Clear Lake, geographically separated from the other Wappos. Descriptive material is available on Yuki (Kroeber 1911), Wappo (Radin 1929; Sawyer 1965), and on Yukian generally (Barrett 1908).

Various proposals have been made suggesting links between Yukian and other language groups: Penutian (Radin 1919; Shipley 1957), Hokan (Sapir 1921b, 1929; Swadesh 1954; Gursky 1965), Siouan (Sapir 1921b, 1929; Elmendorf 1963), and Yuchi (Sapir 1921b, 1929; Elmendorf 1964). Of all these, Elmendorf's evidence for a distant Yukian-Siouan-Yuchi affiliation seems the most credible.

Peripheral Stocks

All the other languages that were spoken in aboriginal California have been clearly identified as belonging to larger linguistic stocks with most of their member languages in other parts of North America. These exterior stocks are Algic, Na-Dene, and Uto-Aztecan.

Algic

Algic is represented by two languages, Wiyot and Yurok, both of which were spoken in Northwestern California. These two languages are very distantly (though certainly) related to each other; they are about equally distantly related to the Algonquian languages in the eastern and central parts of the continent (Teeter 1964a; Haas 1966; Hamp 1970). Thus Algonquian, Yurok, and Wiyot are the three equally remote members of a very old family of languages that has been called Algonquian-Wiyot-Yurok, Algon-Ritwan (Haas 1967), or simply Algic (I. Goddard 1963; Teeter 1965:225).

Wiyot was spoken by no more than 1,000 people who lived around Humboldt Bay and the mouth of the Eel River and in the immediate hinterland. The language was described by Kroeber (1911:384-431), by Reichard (1925), and by Teeter (1964a). The language is now extinct.

Yurok was spoken on the coast to the north of the Wiyot by a much larger group, perhaps 2,500 persons, around the mouth of the Klamath River, with territory extending upriver as far as the confluence of the Klamath and the Trinity, some 30 miles. The name Yurok is from the Karok word *yúruk* 'a considerable distance down the river'. There is a brief grammatical description by Kroeber (1911:414-426) and a much fuller one by Robins (1958).

Na-Dene

The Na-Dene languages of California all belong to the Athapaskan family, which contains most of the languages in the Na-Dene stock. The four California Athapaskan languages were Tolowa, Hupa-Chilula-Whilkut, Mattole, and Wailaki-Nongatl-Lassik-Sinkyone-Cahto (Hoijer 1960).

Tolowa (from Yurok *toloweł*) was spoken by perhaps 1,000 people in the extreme northwestern corner of California, with some territory in Oregon. No descriptive material is available on Tolowa except for a study of the phonology (J.O. Bright 1964).

The other Athapaskan languages, separated from Tolowa by Yurok territory, were spoken over a continuous area from Hupa in the north to Cahto in the south, the latter being just to the north of Yukian. There were three languages involved; two of these had varying dialects associated with distinctive political groups.

There may have been some 2,000 speakers of Hupa-Chilula-Whilkut. The Hupa dialect was described by Goddard (1905) and by Golla (1964, 1970; "Sketch of Hupa, an Athapaskan Language," vol. 17). The Chilula and the Whilkut have long been extinct.

Mattole, spoken by a few hundred people on the coast south of the Wiyot, is also extinct. There is a description by Li (1930). The Bear River dialect differed slightly.

There are no remaining speakers of any of the dialects of the third language. There were an estimated 1,000 speakers of the Nongatl-Lassik-Sinkyone group, perhaps 1,000 speakers of Wailaki, and no more than 500 speakers of Cahto. There are a grammar of Cahto (Goddard 1912) and a collection of Wailaki texts (Goddard 1921–1923).

Uto-Aztecan

The third exterior stock, Uto-Aztecan, is represented in the California culture area by a number of languages, mainly in the south. These are grouped into three branches: Takic, Tubatulabal, and Numic. The first two branches are entirely within California, while Numic is an extensive family spreading over most of the Great Basin and even including Comanche on the southern Plains (Lamb 1964; Langacker 1970; Seiler 1965, 1967).

There were six Takic languages, two along the coast—Gabrielino-Fernandeño in Los Angeles County and Luiseño-Juaneño to the south—and four in the interior desert—Serrano, Kitanemuk, Cahuilla, and Cupeño. In addition, there was a language spoken on San Nicolas Island (Kroeber 1907b:153) and the Tataviam language of the upper Santa Clara valley, which are so poorly known as to be impossible to classify.

Virtually nothing is known of the Gabrielino-Fernandeño language. There may have been as many as 5,000 speakers, with several dialects, in the San Fernando Valley and the great Los Angeles basin to the south as well as on Catalina Island. The names come from the missions of San Gabriel and San Fernando.

Luiseño-Juaneño, also with some 5,000 speakers in precontact times, has been studied by several workers. Descriptive materials (Kroeber and Grace 1960; Malécot 1963–1964), and a dictionary (Bright 1968) are available. A teaching grammar of Luiseño by Hyde (1971) has also been written. The names are from the missions of San Luis Rey and San Juan Capistrano.

The largest of the inland language groups was Serran (K.C. Hill 1967; Bright 1975) with more than 3,000 speakers including the Serrano and Kitanemuk languages, plus the Vanyume, who undoubtedly spoke at least a distinctive dialect. The language name Serrano has often been applied to the entire Serran group.

Between the Serrano and the Ipai-Tipai were the Cahuilla with more than 2,000 speakers. There were three dialects: Desert, Mountain, and Pass (Seiler 1970). Some

information on the phonology (Seiler 1957; Bright 1965) is available, as well as a small amount of grammatical material (Seiler 1958).

The Cupeño lived inland from the Luiseño and north of the Kumeyaay. They were among the smallest distinct groups in California with about 500 people living in two villages, *kúpa,* from which they get their name, and *wilákalpa.* There is a grammar of the language (Hill and Nolasquez 1973) and a historical study (Bright and Hill 1967).

Tubatulabal is classified as an isolated language within Uto-Aztecan. There were possibly some 1,000 speakers, living in the upper Kern River valley at the southern end of the Sierra Nevada. A description of the language (C.F. Voegelin 1935, 1935a) and a short dictionary (C.F. Voegelin 1958) have been published. The distinctiveness of Tubatulabal speech points to its being an older idiom in California than the other Uto-Aztecan languages. The term Tubatulabal is from one of the Numic languages, meaning 'pine-nut eaters'.

The Numic languages were spoken over a vast fan-shaped area of the intermountain west. The name for this family is adapted from *nimi, niimmi, niwi,* the words for 'person' in the various languages (Lamb 1958). Only one of these languages was spoken within the California culture area: Mono, of which there were two main groups, speaking several dialects. The Eastern Mono along the eastern side of the Sierra Nevada, notably in the Owens Valley, were culturally in the Great Basin, while the Western Mono or Monache on the western side of the Sierra crest were in the California culture area. All together, there may have been as many as 4,000 speakers, with the larger number in the eastern group. There is a description of Monache by Lamb (1958a).

Summary

The following classification is somewhat informally arranged in that different orderings and subgroupings are used in explicating different language families. The real situation, even as postulated, was more complex than any systematic presentation can characterize without distortion and simplism. The details as given here are based on the most reliable sources available; nevertheless, there are unavoidable shortcomings. The dialect listings are highly variable in reliability. In many cases the omission of dialect information is simply the result of ignorance; in other cases, such as Chimariko and Esselen, there probably really was no dialect differentiation. The designation of languages is probably more reliable, though there are problems. Most important, the various classifications themselves are subject to revision or rejection as future research may dictate. Only those portions of a family or stock that were spoken in the California culture area (fig. 1) are included in this outline.

1. Penutian Stock.
   Wintuan family.
      Wintu language. Dialects: McCloud River,
         Trinity County, Shasta County, Upper
         Sacramento, Bald Hill, Hayfork, Keswick,
         Stillwater, French Gulch.
      Nomlaki language. Dialects: Hill, Valley.
      Patwin language. Dialects: Hill, River, Cache
         Creek, Lake, Tebti, Dahcinci, Napa, Suisun.
   Maiduan family.
      Maidu language. Dialects: Susanville,
         Big Meadows, Indian Valley, American
         Valley.
      Konkow language. Dialects: Otaki,
         Metsupda, Nemsu, Eskewi, Pulga,
         Cherokee, Feather Falls, Challenge,
         Bidwell Bar.
      Nisenan language. Dialects: Valley,
         Oregon House, Auburn, Clipper Gap,
         Nevada City, Colfax, Placerville.
   Yokutsan family (Kroeber 1963:237).
      Foothill division.
         Buena Vista group: Tulamni, Hometwoli,
            Chuxoxi.
         Poso Creek group: Palewyami, Kumachisi.
         Tule-Kaweah group: Yawdanchi, Wikchamni,
            Gawia, Bokninwad, Yokod.
         Kings River group: Chukaymina,
            Ayticha, Choynimni, Entimbich(?)
            Toyhicha.
         Intermediate between Northern Valley Group
            D and Kings River Foothill group;
            living in hills: Gashowu.
      Valley division.
         Northern Valley groups.
            Group A, far north on lowest San
               Joaquin: Chulamni, Lakisamni.
            Group B, on San Joaquin below Fresno
               River: Chawchila, Hewchi,
               Nopchinchi.
            Group C, on upstream plains along
               San Joaquin: Pitkachi, Wakichi,
               Hoyima.
            Group D, actually living in San
               Joaquin foothills: Chukchansi,
               Kechayi, Dumna, Dalinchi,
               Toltichi (?).
         Southern Valley groups.
            Group A, on Kings River and Tulare
               Lake: Wechihit, Nutúnutu, Chunut,
               Wowol, Apyachi, Tachi.
            Group B, on lower Kaweah to Kern
               rivers: Wo'lasi, Choynok, Yawelmani,
               Wimilchi, Telamni, Koyeti.

   Utian family.
      Miwokan subfamily.
         Western division.
            Lake Miwok language.
            Coast Miwok language. Dialects:
               Bodega, Marin.
         Eastern division.
            Saclan language.
            Plains Miwok language.
            Sierra Miwok group.
               Northern Sierra Miwok language.
               Central Sierra Miwok language.
                  Dialects: West Central, East Central.
               Southern Sierra Miwok language.
                  Dialects: Merced-Yosemite,
                  Mariposa-Chowchilla.
      Costanoan subfamily.
         Northern division.
            Karkin language (a separate division
               according to Beeler 1961).
            Chochenyo language.
            Tamyen language.
            Ramaytush language.
            Awaswas language.
            Chalon language.
         Southern division.
            Mutsun language.
            Rumsen language.
2. Hokan Stock.
   Karok language.
   Shastan family.
      Shasta language. Dialects: Oregon, Scott
         Valley, Shasta Valley, Klamath River.
      New River Shasta language.
      Okwanuchu language.
      Konomihu language.
   Chimariko language.
   Palaihnihan family.
      Achumawi language. Dialects: Hammawi,
         Qosalektawi, Hewisedawi, Astariwawi,
         Atwamsini, Ajumawi, Ilmawi, Itsatawi,
         Madesiwi.
      Atsugewi language. Dialects: Atsuge,
         Apwaruge.
   Yana family.
      Yana language. Dialects: Northern,
         Central, Southern.
      Yahi language.
   Pomoan family.
      Northeastern Pomo language.
      Eastern Pomo language.
      Southeastern Pomo language.
      Western branch.
         Northern Pomo language.
         Southern group.
            Central Pomo language.

Southern Pomo language.
Kashaya language.
Esselen language.
Salinan language. Dialects: Migueleño,
Antoniaño.
Chumashan family.
Central group.
Ventureño-Emigdiano language.
Barbareño language.
Ynezeño language.
Purisimeño language.
Island Chumash language.
Obispeño language.
Yuman family.
Diegueño language. Dialects: Ipai (Northern),
Kumeyaay (Southern), Tipai (Mexican).
3. Yukian family.
Yuki language. Dialects: Yuki proper, Coast Yuki,
Huchnom.
Wappo language. Dialects: Clear Lake, Western,
Northern, Central, Southern.
4. Algic Stock.
Wiyot language.
Yurok language.
5. Na-Dene Stock.
Athapaskan family.

Tolowa language.
Hupa language. Dialects: Hupa, Chilula,
Whilkut.
Mattole language. Dialects: Mattole, Bear
River.
Wailaki language. Dialects: Nongatl, Lassik,
Sinkyone, Wailaki, Cahto.
6. Uto-Aztecan Stock.
Takic family.
Cupan group.
Gabrielino-Fernandeño language. Dialects:
Gabrielino, Fernandeño, and others.
Luiseño-Juaneño language. Dialects: Luiseño,
Juaneño.
Cahuilla language. Dialects: Desert,
Mountain, Pass.
Cupeño language.
Serran group.
Serrano language. Dialects: Serrano,
Vanyume.
Kitanemuk language.
Tubatulabal language.
Numic family.
Western group.
Mono (Monache).

Historical Demography

SHERBURNE F. COOK

Aboriginal Population

The first serious attempt to reach a reliable estimate of the population of California before Hispanic contact was that of Merriam (1905). His point of departure was the number of Indians baptized in the missions, a number which he badly miscalculated. His final estimate for the state was 260,000. Twenty years later Kroeber (1925: 883) drastically reduced this number, putting the total at 133,000. Subsequently Cook (1943) reviewed Kroeber's analysis and made a moderate revision to 133,550, after having excluded several peripheral tribes.

Later Cook reassessed the entire situation and studied a few important regions in detail by the use of one or more of several sources. The first of these is the vast array of village and other sites, several thousand in all, that, in certain areas and under restricted circumstances, can be used as an index to intensity of habitation. Second is the body of information obtained by ethnographers from living informants. Third are the written reports and letters of pioneer explorers, soldiers, and settlers, together with those of civil officials and clerical organizations. Fourth, for California in part, is the mass of documents relating to the missions. Here are included correspondence, annual reports, censuses, baptism and burial books. Fifth is the ecological approach, developed by Baumhoff (1963) for California, which utilizes subsistence levels and the carrying capacity of land surfaces, stream courses, and sea coasts.

Since all these methods are not equally applicable to every portion of the state, and since, indeed, the demographic history varies widely from one region to another, it has been found convenient to establish a series of subdivisions and to estimate the aboriginal population of each separately (fig. 1).

Population Decline, 1770–1900

Like all other native people in the Western Hemisphere, the Indians of California underwent a very severe decline in numbers following the entrance of White civilization. From the beginning to the end of the process, the native population experienced a fall from 310,000 to approximately 20,000, a decline of over 90 percent of the original number. This collapse was due to the operation of factors inherent in the physical and social conflict between the White and the Red races.

The destruction of the Indians in California occurred in a series of steps, separated geographically as well as temporally. The first of these stages accompanied the settlement of the coastal strip from San Diego to San Francisco, and was associated distinctly with the development of the Catholic missions. This phase may be considered as beginning with the expedition of Gaspar de Portolá and Junipero Serra in 1769 and as lasting until secularization in or near 1834. During this period the indigenous population was being drawn off into the

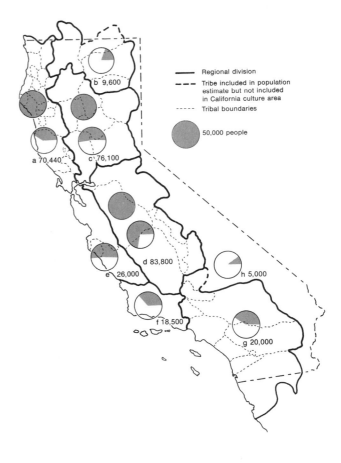

a, Cook 1956; d, Cook 1955; b,c,e,f,g, Cook 1974a; h, author's estimate.
Fig. 1. Estimated aboriginal population by regional subdivision; total is 310,000 ± 30,000.

missions and there converted to Christianity. In the missions the depletion in number of converts was very rapid in spite of replacement by many thousand births. Cook (1974a) has estimated the number of souls who inhabited the entire mission area south of San Francisco Bay as 64,500. To these must be added at least 7,500 Coast Miwok, Southern Pomo, Wappo, and Patwin who supplied converts to San Rafael and Solano. The total would be 72,000.

In 1830 there were approximately 18,000 neophytes enrolled at the missions, and few, if any, unconverted heathen were left in the territory. Some of those at the missions had been brought in from the San Joaquin valley, but these were more or less balanced by the numerous fugitives who had absconded to their former homes. The net reduction over a span of 60 years was therefore not far from 54,000.

The most powerful force depressing the local populations was disease. Particularly within the mission communities, introduced European pathogens were responsible for crude death rates reaching nearly 100 per 1,000 adults and 150 per 1,000 children. Children especially were susceptible to febrile infections of all kinds. It is noteworthy, however, that both adult and child death rates had undergone significant reversal by the time of secularization (see Cook 1940). Secondary factors also contributed to a high death rate and to a probably lower birth rate. Among these were concentration in large aggregates at the missions, a change in dietary habits, and the imposition of a new society with discipline and regimentation.

The unconverted residue of the aboriginal population who remained within the sphere of mission influence, although not subject to the demographic disadvantages of internal mission life, were nevertheless, by virtue of propinquity and frequent intercourse, exposed to the attack of disease. To this was added complete disruption of native family and community organization through withdrawal of many persons to the missions and constant harassment by the civil and military authority.

During the first 30 years of the mission period, the friars were occupied with the conversion of those heathen within relatively easy reach. After the year 1800, they began to draw upon the tribes of the interior. It is probable that roughly 10,500 were introduced from the central valley and the delta region, together with 3,500 from the tribes in the counties north of San Francisco Bay, a total of 14,000. Many of these converts died in the missions, many remained after secularization, but undoubtedly the majority returned to their native country. The introduction of disease and of social disturbance was accentuated by the presence of these fugitives. Without concrete evidence bearing on the problem, a likely supposition is that the population reduction among these groups was very appreciable. To the influence of fugitives must be added the effect of the

numerous military expeditions that entered the interior between 1805 and 1830, some of which resulted in pitched battles and heavy Indian casualties. The attrition of population referable to all these causes cannot be calculated with precision, but it must have amounted to fully 10,000. Therefore, the native inhabitants, in the state as a whole between 1770 and 1830 must have diminished from 310,000 to the vicinity of 245,000.

The second stage in the destruction of the native extended from the end of the mission period until the Mexican War in 1845. Two damaging processes were localized in and more or less restricted to the densely populated central valley and bordering foothills. One was disease, the other the opening up of the land to White settlement. In the early 1830s occurred a pair of devastating epidemics. The first was probably malaria (Cook 1955a), the greatest severity of which was felt along the lower Sacramento and San Joaquin rivers. The second was smallpox, which was most lethal in the coast ranges north of San Francisco. To these and to minor outbreaks was added the effect of syphilis, a malady known to have been communicated to the natives in the earliest years of Spanish domination.

The precise extent of mortality in these epidemics has never been assessed in numerical terms; however, the testimony of eyewitnesses is unanimous and emphatic that the losses should be computed in thousands. Repeated mention is made of entire villages of several hundred people being exterminated, of masses of skeletons found for years thereafter (Cook 1943a, 1955a). The focus of the 1833 epidemic was the series of settlements on the river system from Tulare Lake in the south to Red Bluff and Oroville in the north. According to population estimates (Cook 1955, 1974a) there must have been close to 100,000 Indians living in this area in the early nineteenth century. Of these fully one-half must have perished, if the contemporary accounts can be credited. The smallpox outbreak was less extensive and was confined to the Pomo and adjacent tribes. The mortality may have reached 10,000. Thus the total deaths from acute epidemics in the 1830s may be reckoned at 60,000.

In the meantime settlement by Whites was building up. There may have been 4,000 Spaniards and Mexicans in California just prior to the gold rush, together with an increasing number of Americans. In the mission area, both north and south, much of the land was preempted for stock raising and agriculture, and the natives were reduced to the lowest social and economic level. In the interior, large land grants were made to enterprising citizens such as John Sutter, John Bidwell, James D. Savage, and George C. Yount, who destroyed much of the native subsistence and relegated the former inhabitants to the status of peonage. If roughly 60,000 were victims of widespread epidemics, another 40,000 would have perished, throughout the occupied portion of the state, as the result of endemic disease, armed conflict, and destruction of food supply. The residual population in 1845 may be set at no more than 125,000–150,000.

The third and final stage of population decline accompanied the discovery of gold in 1848 and the rapid filling of the state with a new wave of White immigrants. The Indian territory that until this point had escaped direct contact with European influence now succumbed, for it was exactly the remote valleys of the Sierra Nevada, Cascades, and Siskiyous that attracted miners, while commerce and agriculture took possession of the central valley and coast ranges. The overwhelming assault upon the subsistence, life, and culture of all California natives during the short period from 1848 to 1865 has seldom been duplicated in modern times by an invading race. The story has been set forth in extensive detail by Cook (1943, 1943a, 1943b), Heizer and Almquist (1971), and W.W. Robinson (1952). Reference should also be made to the file of testimony in the Indian Claims Cases Docket Nos. 31 and 37. Also there have been numerous articles in *The Indian Historian*, published by the American Indian Historical Society, San Francisco.

After 1848 the Indian population was estimated by numerous persons—principally officials of various persuasions—and the results are to be found scattered widely through the documents of the time (Cook 1943a:table 1 and notes). It is evident that by 1850 the Indian population of the entire state had been reduced to about 100,000. The decline during the worst decade, 1845 to 1855, was incredible—from approximately 150,000 to 50,000. This desolation was accomplished by a ruthless flood of miners and farmers who annihilated the natives without mercy or compensation. The direct causes of death were disease, the bullet, exposure, and acute starvation. The more remote causes were insane passion for gold, abiding hatred for the Red man, and complete lack of any legal control.

By 1865 many of the surviving natives had discovered remote niches where they might exist undisturbed or had been resettled on reservations; nevertheless, the great upheaval of the 1850s was still felt, and the population continued to decline. Agents of the Bureau of Indian Affairs began to make annual reports of numbers that probably included those Indians under direct government supervision plus some others. The United States census reported 20,385 in 1880, 16,624 in 1890, and 15,377 in 1900. Merriam (1905:599) accepted these figures in principle but thought that they should be increased slightly. Kroeber (1925:891) agreed with Merriam's estimate of 15,500 in 1900 and considered a value of 16,000 appropriate for 1910. Although it is very probable that these figures are all too low, there is little room for doubt that the minimum level in the population of the California Indians was reached in the decades between 1880 and 1900.

Population Increase, 1900–1970

There are now available data pertaining to the period of 1900 to 1910 that were not employed by Merriam or Kroeber. These start with the Census of Non-Reservation Indians in California, which was compiled by C.E. Kelsey in 1905–1906 (1971). This special Indian agent made a personal examination of 36 counties north of the Tehachapi Mountains. He found a total of 12,961 persons. For nine of the remaining counties he used the figures from the census of 1900—a very small value—only 340 individuals. For San Francisco, Santa Clara, and Solano counties no Indian settlements were reported and were omitted by Kelsey, although it has since been ascertained that numerous Indians live there.

Apart from Kelsey's count the local census at Hoopa Reservation in 1910 showed 705 persons and at least 1,500 must have been at Round Valley, Tule River, and in scattered rancherias. Kelsey's total of 12,961 must therefore be increased by 2,500, making close to 15,500 in 36 northern counties. In the southern part of the state the census taken by the Mission Agency in 1902 showed 2,547 persons enrolled. Hence, if 500 are allowed for the Paiute and Washo under the jurisdiction of the Carson City Agency but living in California, and 2,550 for those under the Mission Agency, the total becomes 18,500. This is a subminimal figure, for it takes no account of the many Indians in the 12 counties that Kelsey did not visit nor of those in the south who were not dependent upon the Mission Agency. Hence the population of 1900 to 1910 must have exceeded 20,000 and may have reached 25,000. Kroeber's estimate of 16,000 in 1910 is far too low.

In the 1920s began the compilation of a series of Great Rolls, each of which was intended to include the name of every California Indian who applied for and who qualified for a special financial subvention by the United States government. These rolls were assembled by the Bureau of Indian Affairs rather than the Bureau of the Census. The first roll was formed in 1928 but received additions and was revised until 1933. In its final version it contains the names of 21,977 persons.

The second roll was established between 1950 and 1955. The last date of birth allowed for inscription was May 24, 1950, although the list did not reach final form until 1955. It contains 36,094 entries. As a result of the favorable settlement of the claims cases in the 1960s, a new roll was constructed in 1970. In the alphabetical list there are 69,911 names. Meanwhile the national censuses have become more complete and show a steadily increasing Indian population. The census of 1960 gave 39,014 as the total of all Indians living in California, but in 1970 the census of that year showed this figure to have more than doubled to 91,018.

The truly phenomenal rise in the recorded number of Indians from perhaps 25,000 in 1910 to the order of

90,000 in 1970 deserves comment. At the same time the difference between the national census reports and the Indian Bureau rolls is noteworthy, for this difference in 1970 amounted to nearly 20,000 persons.

The first factor involved is of a technical and legal nature. The national censuses report all persons of Indian descent, regardless of tribal or geographic origin. The agency rolls admit only Indians who can prove descent from aboriginal Californians, for these alone can qualify for a federal stipend. Specifically, the ancestor must have been a resident of California in 1848, the year when the Treaty of Guadalupe Hidalgo was signed. Consequently all those who have entered from other states, although they appear in the national censuses, are excluded from the lists of the Bureau of Indian Affairs. To determine their exact number would require a detailed examination of the original census sheets, a task of formidable proportions. It is recognized, however, that the influx to California in recent years has been massive, particularly from those states of the Middle West that contain large Indian populations. Perhaps most of the differential in favor of the 1970 census over the 1970 enrollment is due to this migration.

A second factor, which is psychological and emotional, affects both census and enrollment, although not necessarily in the same manner. Historically, since the 1840s, the California Indian has been subject to oppression by the dominant White race. Any kind of normal life in the American community, rural or urban, was substantially impossible. Moreover, in the early years of the reservations conditions there were atrocious. As a result many natives fled to the most remote refuges and almost all of them sought in every possible way to avoid White society. One manifestation of this widespread tendency was a strong disinclination to be counted in a census or to have any relations whatever with government officials. In the early 1900s this feeling was still widely pervasive, and it may be observed even today among the older generation. The effect has been, of course, to reduce drastically the reported number of Indians in the state. In a more general reaction, thousands of them simply renounced their race for public purposes and allowed themselves to be considered as of non-Indian origin. This mode of behavior was especially characteristic of those mixed-bloods who merged imperceptibly into the segment of the population that was of Mexican derivation. More recently, these restrictions have been loosened and many individuals who had withdrawn themselves from the category of Indian for census purposes have allowed their names to be restored to both the rolls of the census and those of the Bureau of Indian Affairs.

It is also true that since the First World War the effort to submerge the Indian element has run counter to certain opposing influences. Of these one is the rapidly evolving drive for minority racial groups to assert their legal and economic rights and to emphasize rather than deprecate their racial affiliation. Thus the Indians of California have been very active in promoting their cultural interests and have lost much of their fear of being known as Indian. The other primary motive from rejecting concealment is perhaps less laudable. Beginning in the 1920s, when a substantial federal fund was made available to the Indians whose ancestors had been dispossessed in the nineteenth century, it became necessary for each person who wished to receive this support to prove his descent from an aboriginal inhabitant of the state. This requirement meant that a formal public statement should accompany the application, and that there could be no attempt at concealment or secrecy. The result was that hundreds of persons who had always been regarded as non-Indian now added their names to the list.

The third factor is biological, the undoubted natural increase that the Indian population has displayed during the past century. The precise magnitude of this increase is unknown because there are no statistics available relative to Indian birth and death rates. On the other hand it is possible to make indirect use of the age data in the recent enrollment records. Thus in the 1950 list there are the names and ages of approximately 36,000 individuals. When these are tabulated the age distribution shows a very youthful population. There is 16.63% under the age of five years and 4.98% over the age of 65 years. The median age is approximately 19.6 years. The degree of Indian blood was not specified, but the heavy representation of conservative and remote tribal elements in the 1950 roll indicates that the proliferation of the entire Indian race was in full progress at that time. The data from the 1970 roll show a continuation and perhaps intensification of the natural increase.

Consideration of these factors and of the apparently tremendous increase in population of the California Indians throughout the twentieth century leads one to hypothesize that all the estimates, counts, and censuses from 1865 to 1930 yield values that are much too low. Natural increase plus immigration from the east, although both have been heavy, cannot account for a rise from 25,000 in 1930 to an enrollment figure of 70,000 in 1970 or a doubling of the census count in the single decade 1960 to 1970. The only reasonable explanation must be that both the Bureau of Indian Affairs and the Bureau of the Census failed to notice thousands of Indians who had withdrawn physically and emotionally from American civilization after the debacle of the 1850s and whose descendants have only recently been emerging under the influence of a new social climate and of possible material benefits.

Age Composition

One of the major characteristics of a population is its age distribution. This parameter may be expressed either

94

by means of the proportion of total population that falls within specified age brackets or by means of the prevailing age-specific mortality rates. The latter values are usually derived from appropriate life tables, but unfortunately the necessary mortality records are lacking for the Indians of California, restricting the study of age composition to the relative sizes of rather arbitrary categories. In order to establish them it is convenient to segregate the population into consecutive age groups (at 1, 5, or 10 years), which may then be combined to form three major entities: youthful (0-14 years), adult (15-64 years), and aged (over 64 years). Of the three the most useful for the purpose of comparing the population at different times and places are the first and the third, the very young and the very old.

In order to examine the age structure of the precontact population of California, recourse may be had to the extensive series of skeletons that is stored in the Lowie Museum of Anthropology at Berkeley. Although an exact analysis of this material is not feasible, it is clear that in the sample there were relatively many young persons and few older ones, a respect in which the California natives resembled those that have been investigated in the Middle West and the East. T.D. McCown personally reported to me many years ago that of the several hundred individuals whose skeletons had been excavated in northern California, approximately 22 percent had died prior to the age of 20 years, and only 3 percent had lived to reach that of 50 years. The analogous values for living Indians found in the 1950 roll of the Bureau of Indian Affairs are close to 40 percent and 14 percent respectively. The small number of child skeletons in the Lowie Museum sample is referable in part to the rapidity with which infant bone decomposes after burial, and in part to the disinclination of investigators to preserve those that cannot be recovered. In the original state, therefore, the native race was characterized by a high birth rate and a high death rate, particularly among children and young adults.

The first record of Indian age composition, compiled by Whites, was the list of gentile baptisms formulated by the Franciscan missionaries. The friars noted carefully the baptism of each heathen who was converted to Christianity and included his stated or estimated age. The baptism book of every mission consequently reflects the age pattern of the local Indian population as it was progressively recruited for life in the mission, a process that usually was spread over a period of from 20 to 40 years. Examination of the baptism books for nine missions, all but one in the north, shows that roughly 47 percent of the converts were in the age group 0-14 years, and 3.5% were over 64 years of age. The median age was only 16.10 years. The number of old persons was very small, although greater than might be inferred from the skeletons excavated at prehistoric habitation sites.

There is no doubt that the recorded gentile baptisms constitute a selected, biased sample. The missionaries initially baptized infants and small children and only later converted the adult and elderly component of the population. In the course of several years the oldest group would be diminished by death and the final number of their baptisms would be spuriously low. However, the distribution is so overwhelmingly in favor of the younger age range that the distortion due to differential baptism cannot entirely account for the preponderance of the young. In a very general way, therefore, the mission statistics confirm the archeological findings and support the thesis that there existed a high birth rate-high death rate regime in the pre-Hispanic population.

No further data concerning age composition emerged until well after the establishment of the Bureau of Indian Affairs, and in the meantime the native population had undergone a profound transformation. In the late nineteenth and early twentieth centuries some of the agencies of the Bureau carried out counts of the Indians who were under their administrative care. Among these were the Hoopa and the Mission Agencies, the former operating at the Hoopa Reservation and in the Klamath River basin, the latter supervising the small reservations and rancherias in the southern counties. Each agency census embraced several hundred Indians, although the number varied from time to time, as did the number of individual settlements included. In all cases the ages of the persons counted were given. The proportions found in the three principal age brackets are shown in table 1, as is the median age of each census population.

It is apparent that among these restricted populations the persons under 15 years old amounted to roughly 30 percent, whereas those under 64 years in age reached 7 or 8 percent. Thus there had been considerable aging of the population since aboriginal times. This feature is also emphasized by the relatively high median ages of 22 to 28 years. Nevertheless, these are small, highly selected samples. They were aggregates of Indians who were closely associated with federal agencies and who may have been living under better social and economic circumstances than the majority scattered over the state at large.

A much more representative enumeration was made for the Roll of 1928. This list contained the age of nearly every Indian who filed an application for the federal subsidy that was distributed a few years later. Not all, but the great majority of qualified Indians filed an application, a total of 21,977, of whom 20,379 have been used to determine the proportions shown in table 1. There was 37.16% from 0 to 15 years old and 6.50% 65 years or over. The median age was relatively low at 20.77 years.

The younger group is therefore larger and the aged group smaller than would be expected from consideration of the local agency censuses. The reason lies in the fact that the 1928 roll embraced a different population, one that included thousands of nonreservation Indians who were living as part of the general society of the state, rather than in association with the federal government. Thus the 1928 roll reflects more truly than any other document up to that time the actual age status of the California Indians. It is quite evident that the native population, despite the continuous demographic disturbance to which it had been subjected, had moved strongly from the aboriginal high birth rate–high death rate pattern to one that more closely approached that of American society as a whole. On the other hand, the Indian pattern departed clearly from that of the American White population in showing a higher proportion of younger and a lower proportion of older members. Indeed, the Indian gave evidence of being in the state of demographic transition that is characterized by a residual high birth rate in conjunction with a reduced mortality. In this respect the Indian population of California in 1928 resembled the related peoples in many parts of Latin America.

Subsequent to 1928 a new list was constructed that cut off enrollment in 1950. It was based upon revision of the 1928 roll plus addition of many new applicants. The total reached slightly above 36,000. The excess over the 1928 roll was assignable not only to the natural increase of population but also to the inclusion of many persons who missed the earlier enrollment. The relative number of young individuals rose, while that of persons over 65 years fell; meanwhile the median age declined. This change during two decades is a clear indication that the Indian population was reproducing at a very rapid rate whereas the losses due to death were being reduced. It is of interest to discover that a continuation of this trend is manifested by the new roll terminating in 1970. At any

event it is evident from the study of age distribution that the California Indian has effectively recovered from the traumatic demographic experience of the nineteenth century.

Degree of Blood

The term "degree of blood," however inaccurate it may be genetically, and however distasteful to the demographic purist, nevertheless enjoys almost universal popular acceptance. Thus "pure-blooded" denotes a racially integral condition, "half-blooded" refers to the person whose parents were pure-bloods of different races. In the case of the California Indians it has become customary to describe the racial state in sixteenths. Thus the pure strain is represented by $^{16}/_{16}$, a half blood by $^{8}/_{16}$ a quarter blood by $^{4}/_{16}$. Fractions smaller than $^{1}/_{16}$ are frequently employed, such as $^{1}/_{32}$, $^{1}/_{64}$, or even less, but there is room for serious question whether, at such an extreme dilution, consideration of the Indian component is warranted scientifically, even though its existence may at times be convenient socially. For purposes of calculation it is a simple device to omit the denominator and treat degree of blood as a whole number, where 16, representing full-blood, can be progressively diminished to 1, or actually $^{1}/_{16}$, Indian in the genetic sense.

Racial mixing began immediately upon the arrival of the Spaniards in 1769, although on a very minor scale. The male immigrants, mostly soldiers, married native women and indeed were encouraged to do so by both clerical and military authorities. In the course of time to these were added the male progeny of all types of union, for very few unattached females were introduced from Spain or Mexico. Nevertheless the number of mixed bloods prior to 1849 must have remained small. There is no concrete information concerning the real number, although some estimate might be derived from Bancroft (1886) and similar lists of colonial inhabitants.

Under Spanish and Mexican rule the progeny of mixed marriages were accepted economically and socially by the Whites, for according to the ancient Mexican tradition the mestizo was an integral and respected component of the multi-racial civilization. With the advent of the Americans, and particularly under the conditions of the gold rush and settlement by pioneers, certain fundamental changes took place. First, the number of Whites vastly increased at the same time that the Indians were declining in population. Hence the frequency of contact and the statistical probability of union of the sexes increased markedly. Second, many White males now used Indian women for pleasure, not for matrimony, and thereby created a scandalous moral situation. Another result was the production of numerous half- and quarter-breed children. Third, these children, unlike those in the Spanish period, were rejected by the dominant society and were forced to affiliate themselves closely with the Red rather than the White race. This

Table 1. Age Distribution

Source		Percent of population in age group			Median age in years
		0-14	15-64	Over 65	
Nine missions gentiles baptized		46.90	49.62	3.48	16.10
Agency censuses					
Hoopa	1887	32.82	59.79	7.39	22.57
	1897	33.47	58.98	7.55	23.74
	1910	36.00	57.46	6.54	23.37
	1920	36.85	56.08	7.07	22.05
	1930	28.44	62.32	9.24	25.18
	1940	21.85	68.93	9.22	27.83
Mission	1902	31.12	60.98	7.90	25.17
	1922	28.46	63.66	7.88	26.89
	1940	30.39	62.96	6.65	25.47
1928 Roll		37.16	56.34	6.50	20.77
1950 Roll		40.11	54.91	4.98	19.59
1970 Roll		44.65	51.49	3.86	16.84

status of racial subordination was maintained for decades after 1850 and was extended to persons with any visible admixture of Indian blood.

With the exception of a few local agency censuses there has been no comprehensive survey of the ethnic character of the California Indians except the Roll of 1928. In that year each applicant for a federal subvention was asked to state the degree of his Indian blood. The list of nearly 22,000 names therefore constitutes a very valuable clue to the genetic constitution of the Indian population at that time. Neither of the two rolls compiled since 1930—in 1950 and in 1970—shows degree of blood. Hence even the Indian Service is compelled to rely upon the 1928 roll as the basic source of information. For a discussion of this and other documents bearing upon racial fusion, reference may be made to Cook (1943e).

In order to study racial mixture it is useful to segregate the mission from the nonmission population. This step can be taken because the 1928 roll indicates mission origin in its characterization of tribal affiliation. Initially, however, three categories of individuals are removed from consideration: the Quechan, on the ground that they were Colorado River rather than California natives; those born during the few months between January 1, 1928, and the closing of the roll; and those reporting less than $\frac{1}{16}$ Indian blood, nearly all of whom traced their ancestry from Mission Carmel. After making these adjustments there are left 20,197 persons. Of these, 1,612 stated their tribal affiliation to have been some mission, for example, Mission San Juan Bautista or Mission San Luis Rey. The remainder, 18,585, reported themselves as members of the numerous tribes of the center and north or as associated with one of the small reservations in the south.

The descendants of the mission Indians, whose forbears had been exposed to racial mixture of 150 years prior to 1928, were drawn from most of the former 21 missions, although the majority were derived from those of the south. Of the 1,612 whose records are on file, only 309, or approximately 19.2% were of pure Indian origin; 20.8% were half-Indian; and 4.8% reported $\frac{1}{16}$ Indian blood. Among the descendants of nonmission Indians, 18,585 in all, 7,306 were full-bloods, or roughly 36.2%; 21.0% were half-Indian; and only 139, or 0.7% were $\frac{1}{16}$ Indian.

The distinction between the two categories—mission and nonmission—is also brought out clearly by consideration of age or date of birth. For each calendar decade previous to 1928 or for each 10-year age interval the mean degree of blood may be calculated. The geometric rather than the arithmetic mean is employed because the scale from $\frac{1}{16}$ to $\frac{16}{16}$ degrees of blood moves in geometric, not arithmetic progression. With the mission descendants the mean degree of blood of those 0–9 years old in 1928, that is, those born 1918–1927, is 24.8% of full

blood, whereas for the nonmission descendants the corresponding value is 43.8%. Those 40–49 years of age (born 1878–1887) give respectively for the two groups 50.7 and 67.1%, whereas those 80–89 years old (born 1838–1847) show 58.3 and 99.6% pure Indian origin.

Whether or not these figures are precisely accurate, they demonstrate unequivocally that at or near the point of American settlement, 1845–1855, those mission Indians who had survived and who were still living in the coastal mission area had received a heavy infusion of non-Indian blood. With this group the process of mixing continued without apparent interruption up to 1928. Meanwhile, the unconverted natives both north and south retained essentially unaltered their aboriginal genetic character until they were overwhelmed by the White invasion of the 1850s.

There is no reason to believe that the progress of racial consolidation has significantly diminished since 1928, although there are no comprehensive data to support a hypothesis in either direction. If the trends demonstrated during the century preceeding 1928 can be extrapolated, it may be predicted that some elements of the native stock will be fully amalgamated with other ethnic components within no more than one or two generations. Other units will require a much longer time. However, such extrapolations may be nullified at any time by changing social conditions.

Continuity

A problem that has perplexed both ethnographers and lawyers is whether the aboriginal tribal units persisted into modern times. During the confusion attending the destruction of native California society in the mid-nineteenth century, not merely individuals but whole aggregates were removed from one place to another, and tribal names were lost, distorted, or even coined de novo by White men without reference to ethnic or geographic accuracy. As a result many of the smaller units disappeared from contemporary knowledge or became, as Kroeber and Heizer express it, "ethnographically extinct." Utilizing the 1928 roll at Sacramento to recover information concerning several of the smaller aboriginal groups, Kroeber and Heizer (1970) compiled a report and submitted it in evidence at the Berkeley hearings of Dockets 31 and 37 in 1955.

Kroeber and Heizer (1970) were able to show that many of the groups that had apparently vanished as racial and physical entities were indeed still in existence and that the present members had descended in an unbroken line from the former ethnic divisions. The descendants of mission Indians, to whom they devote much attention, have already been discussed. In addition, especially noteworthy are the Athapaskans of Humboldt and Mendocino counties, of whom Kroeber and Heizer found 83 persons living in 1928 who were derived from 8 divisions of that stock: Chilula, Whilkut,

Mattole, Nongatl, Sinkyone, Lassik, Wailaki, and Cahto. However, this is a minimal figure. The true number of Athapaskans alive in 1972 is probably much greater than is indicated by the 1928 roll. Also of interest are the Yokuts. Although Kroeber and Heizer do not list them, the 1928 roll contains the names of approximately 200 Yokuts, whose affiliation is attested by mention of some 15 tribelets, all from the southern San Joaquin valley and adjacent foothills.

The larger tribal units, such as the Yurok, Hupa, Pomo, Achumawi (Pit River Indians), Paiute, and many others are well represented in the roll. There can be no doubt concerning their persistence as recognized Indian entities, many with tribal councils and other forms of local government. It is Kroeber and Heizer's achievement that they demonstrated similar continuity in the existence of the smaller, almost invisible ethnic elements.

Redistribution of Population

Aboriginally in California the Indians were hunter-gatherers who lived uniformly distributed through the food-producing regions and who formed no larger aggregates than the village of at most several hundred inhabitants. After the invasion by the Whites they tended to adhere as far as possible to the old pattern and gravitated to small settlements located in relatively isolated rural areas. Then, in the late nineteenth century, there began a migration, at first slow, of the younger generation from their remote enclaves to the centers of White population. This movement toward urbanization has accelerated during the twentieth century. It has been favored by the demand for labor during two world wars and has been notably facilitated by the ready availability of the automobile as a source of transportation.

The magnitude of the migration toward the cities can be evaluated quantitatively in several ways. One approach is to follow the distribution of residence according to county. The rural portions of northern California were well covered by Kelsey (1971) for his census of the nonreservation Indians in 1905-1906. A block of 14 counties in the northeastern part of the state, which contains no reservations, and which extends from Siskiyou to Calaveras, showed a count of 3,787 persons. The 1970 census (U.S. Bureau of the Census 1971) gives for these same counties 5,882 Indians. Meanwhile, according to Kelsey, the seven counties bordering San Francisco Bay held only 83 Indians. For Marin and San Mateo counties he used the figures from the 1900 census; there were 43 in Alameda County and none whatever in the others. The 1970 census gives a total of 17,107 for the seven counties, most of whom were born in California. Even if some immigrants from others states are included, the increase in 65 years is prodigious. It is unfortunate that Kelsey could give no estimate for Los Angeles County.

Another device is to examine the addresses given by the applicants whose names are on the 1928 and the 1950 rolls at the office of the Bureau of Indian Affairs at Sacramento. In many instances only the post office is mentioned, but even so a judgment can be made concerning the size of the locality. In other instances a street address is given, a sure indication of removal to an urban environment. This method, applied to the 1928 roll, formed the basis of a study (Cook 1943d:40-41) in which it was concluded that "whenever the native race, in California, has entered upon a period of intensified contact with the whites, there has been a response in the form of emigration . . ." and that "the direction of migration has been uniformly toward the centers of white population with the result that an Indian urban class has come into existence." In this study it was found that in the 1928 roll 11 percent of the names recorded had street addresses. Furthermore, of the migrants within the state, 40 percent were living in cities, whereas this condition was true for only 7.4% of the nonmigrants.

A random sample consisting of 20,023 names was taken from the 1950 roll. Of these, 18.1% were living in homes with street addresses. It was also observed that 9.3% lived outside the state of California, mostly in Oregon and Nevada; 6.1% were within the San Francisco Bay area; and 6.0% inhabited Los Angeles County. These percentages were significantly increased by 1970. It is highly probable, therefore, that urbanization continued unabated between the dates of the three enumerations, from 1928 to 1970.

A third method is offered by the United States censuses, in particular the volume on California of the 1970 census. The number of Indians counted in the state was 91,018. Concerning this figure it must be emphasized that *all* Indians, not merely descendants of California inhabitants of 1848, are included. The migration from elsewhere accounts for most of the discrepancy between the census report and the 1970 roll compiled by the Bureau of Indian Affairs, which shows only about 70,000 names.

With the census reporting 17,107 Indians in the San Francisco Bay area and 24,509 in Los Angeles County (of whom half are probably immigrants), it is clear that close to 45 percent of all Indians in the state are concentrated in the two great metropolitan areas. The 1970 volume on California (U.S. Bureau of the Census 1971:66, table 17) designates 69,802 persons, or 76.7%, as "urban" and 21,216, or 23.3%, as "rural." Of the rural component 1,671 live in places of 1,000 to 2,500 inhabitants, and the remaining 19,545, or approximately 21.5%, still adhere to the type of settlement that was common to their ancestors.

The broad conclusion from all these pieces of evidence must be that the California Indian in the 1970s is moving as rapidly into the urban, industrial environment as are the Californians of other ethnic origins and that the redistribution of the aboriginal native population is substantially complete.

The Impact of Euro-American Exploration and Settlement

EDWARD D. CASTILLO

Traditionally California Indians have been portrayed in history as a docile primitive people who openly embraced the invading Spaniards and were rapidly subdued. This simplistic contention adds little to a realistic understanding of native history in California and undoubtedly is derived from crude feelings of racial superiority on the part of its advocates. As a part of a larger reevaluation of Indian-White relations in history, the story of California Indians must be reassessed incorporating as much native documentation as possible. The extent of primary resource data written or dictated by Indians in the past is surprisingly broad and will be used here to complement more traditional sources of information.

The cultural legacy of the Spanish-speaking persons who invaded California in 1769 was far different from that of the nearly 300,000 unconquered natives living there. In contrast to the Indians, these Hispanos (of African, American Indian, and Spanish descent) were members of an authoritarian empire whose society was populous, complex, and widespread. Further, they were steeped in a legacy of religious intolerance and conformity featuring a messianic fanaticism accentuating both Spanish culture in general and Catholicism in particular. Hispanos invading Alta California also possessed a political philosophy that condoned large-scale duplicity in order to gain goals not revealed to the peoples being dealt with. Perhaps most important, these Iberians were heirs to a culture with a history of almost constant warfare stressing conquest.

The tribal Americans in California lived in societies whose major concepts and institutions present striking differences. For instance, California Indians lived in relatively small political units usually made up of 50 to 500 persons (Kroeber 1962). Anthropologists have confirmed that over 300 different dialects were spoken in aboriginal California. Organization for war was difficult since tribes were generally democracies and the majority decided most issues facing the tribe. Concepts of conquest by invasion and exploitation were foreign to them. Closely related to their lack of conquering and exploiting other peoples is the almost total lack of experience in organizing and carrying out wars. This fact becomes even more amazing considering California had a higher preconquest population density per square mile than any other region in North America (Kroeber 1939a:153). The significance of this high population, multiplicity of tribes, and lack of warfare seems to have gone unrecognized by sociologists who generally agree that linguistic and cultural differences together with high population density afford many opportunities for friction and war among different groups. Yet this does not seem to have occurred in preconquest California. This aspect of California Indian society deserves more than the passing reference given here but unfortunately is outside the scope of this article.

The major factors that contributed to the changing social environment to which native peoples were forced to accommodate themselves were: hostile military campaigns, introduced labor systems, disease and epidemics, changing nutrition patterns, and colonial government relations. All these factors in one form or another contributed to the destruction of native life, property, culture, and society. Finally by considering the philosophy and laws and practices of colonial societies as background to the Indian history, a deeper and more sophisticated understanding of the tragedy that befell California's native people may be elicited.

The Spanish Period

Early sixteenth-century Spanish exploration north of New Spain was prompted by persistent rumors of a rich northern Indian civilization. These rumors consisted of a number of tales, the most famous of which became known as the "Seven Cities of Cíbola." These stories along with others became the core of a collection of legends known as the "Northern Mystery." In a series of northern explorations the Spanish Crown unsuccessfully attempted to discover "another Mexico." In conjunction with Francisco Coronado's expedition, both Hernando de Alarcón and Melchor Díaz commanded explorations that might have set foot in Alta California during 1540. However, most historians agree that Juan Rodríguez Cabrillo in 1542 was the first European to visit California. Sent out under the orders of Viceroy Antonio de Mendoza, the purpose of his expedition was to discover the long-rumored, though mythical, Straight of Anian (Northwest Passage). Sailing up the coast of California, Cabrillo visited the bay of San Diego, Catalina Island, San Pedro, and the Channel Islands area (Wagner 1929:73-93).

The next European visitor to the California coast was the English adventurer Francis Drake in 1579, who landed along the coast of Miwok territory, probably the Bodega Bay or Drake's Bay area. Staying among the friendly Miwok for five weeks, Drake mistook their ceremonies and hospitality as conferring some kind of religious veneration upon himself and his crew (Heizer 1947:264-269). The Englishmen then, like Cabrillo, declared this whole territory for the Imperial Crown by "right of discovery" and promptly departed.

Thereafter, California was looked upon by the Spanish authorities in Mexico primarily as a possible port of call for the annual Manila galleons on their way to Mexico. To establish ports, the Crown sponsored various expeditions to explore the coast of California. Sebastian Rodriguez Cermeño made a disastrous exploration in 1595, which ended in the destruction of his ship by storms at Drake's Bay (Wagner 1929:154-168). The merchant-adventurer Sebastián Vizcaíno made another exploration of the coast in 1602 in which he exaggeratedly reported a splendid harbor at Monterey (Wagner 1929:180-273). This myth of a harbor of Monterey played a central part in later plans for colonization of Alta California.

A lapse of 167 years intervened between Vizcaíno's expedition and the first permanent European colony established in California. This long period of isolation after first contacts with the Spanish emphasized the low value placed on this territory. Unfortunately these were the last years of peace and contentment that California natives were to enjoy. For the next two centuries the Indians were locked in a violent struggle, first with the Spanish, then the Mexicans, and finally the Anglo invaders, in order to preserve their homes and way of life.

The consolidation of New Spain's northwestern frontier and its extension to Alta California seems to have been the result of the personal ambitions of the mentally unstable Visitor-General Jose de Gálvez. As a part of Spanish imperial reform under Charles III, Gálvez proposed the consolidation and development of Chihuahua, Sinaloa, Sonora, and California into a governmental unit called commandancy-general. Gálvez's justification for this reform was the perennial Spanish fear that the British or Russians might establish themselves on the Pacific Coast and menace Mexico from the north. He also believed that Alta California might ultimately provide a lucrative source of royal revenue (W. Bean 1973:31).

The visitor-general's plans for the colonization of Alta California were realized with the organization of the "sacred expedition" in 1769. This group of adventurers was divided between soldiers under the command of Capt. Gaspar de Portolá and missionary personnel under the leadership of Father President Junipero Serra (Crespí 1927: 20-50). There was a third contingent bringing by sea some supplies and church furniture. The objective of the expedition was the founding of a presidio (military fort) and a mission at San Diego as a way station for the journey to establish a colony at Monterey. These contingents arrived in San Diego between April and July 1769. On July 16, 1769, they founded the first of 21 California missions (fig. 1), and the occupation of Alta California by imperial forces of Spain became a reality.

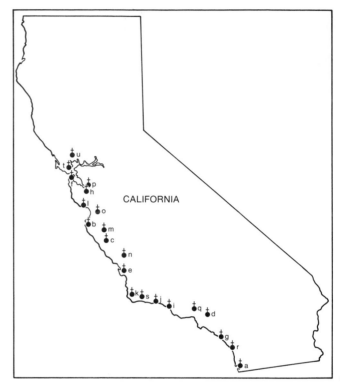

Fig. 1. Missions established in Alta California: a, San Diego de Alcalá, 1769; b, San Carlos Borromeo (Carmel), 1770; c, San Antonio de Padua, d, San Gabriel, 1771; e, San Luis Obispo de Tolosa, 1772; f, San Francisco de Asís (Dolores), g, San Juan Capistrano, 1776; h, Santa Clara, 1777; i, San Buenaventura (Ventura), 1782; j, Santa Bárbara, 1786; k, de la Purísima Concepción, 1787; l, Santa Cruz, m, de la Soledad, 1791; n, San Miguel, 1796; o, San Juan Bautista, p, San José, q, San Fernando Rey de España, 1797; r, San Luis Rey de Francia, 1798; s, Santa Inés (Ynez), 1804; t, San Rafael, 1817; u, San Francisco Solano (Sonoma), 1823 (Bowman 1965).

Spain's Indian policies at the time of the invasion of California were a mixture of economic, military, political, and religious motives. Indians were regarded by the Spanish government as subjects of the Crown and human beings capable of receiving the sacraments of Christianity (Hanke 1959:74). Other motives of the colonial system set up to regulate Spain's interests in the natives could be realized by the encomienda system, which called for the "giving of Indians" to—that is, requiring Indians to labor for—various Spanish citizens for the public good. In reality this institution was a variation of the feudal-manorial labor system. This encomienda system along with Christianization would ultimately absorb the Indian into the Spanish colonial society—at its lowest levels—and consolidate Spanish control over more territory.

When early explorers had encountered California natives they universally characterized Indians as shy and friendly people providing travelers with water, food, and hospitality whenever asked. However, permanent colonization almost from the beginning raised native suspicions and ultimately led to violence. The Ipai-Tipai among whom the San Diego mission and presidio were established proved to be reluctant hosts. Within a month they attacked the Spanish camp attempting to drive the invaders from their territory, but the Spanish soldiers using their guns defended their settlement and an uneasy peace ensued. Yet it would be another two years before Mission San Diego could record its first baptism (Bancroft 1886-1890, 1:138-139).

Over the ensuing half-century the Spanish soldiers, padres, and colonists established authority along the narrow coastal region stretching from San Diego north to Sonoma. In this territory the Spanish invaders established their institutions of conquest and colonization: the mission, the presidio, and later the civil pueblo.

The mission was the most important institution used by the Spanish in the Americas to establish control of Indian territory and peoples. The type established in California was the *reducción*. This type of mission was established to gather natives living their free way of life in small scattered villages into one central mission site. Despite romantic interpretations found in literature and history, the California missions were coercive authoritarian institutions. It is impossible to understand the effect missionization had upon native Californians without realizing that once inside the mission system the neophytes, as converts were called, were not free to leave. Constantly under the absolute control of the Franciscans and soldiers, the Indians were forced to observe a rigid discipline (fig. 2). In order to enforce Catholic moral codes, at night unmarried men and women were separately incarcerated in unhealthy and crowded mission barracks. Whipping with a barbed lash, solitary confinement, mutilation, use of stocks and hobbles, branding, and even execution for both men and women characterized the "gentle yoke of Catholicism" introduced to the

Museo Naval, Madrid: ms. 1723-1.

Fig. 2. Indians of Mission San Carlos Borromeo at Carmel, lined up with military precision to greet the French exploring expedition under Jean François de Galaup de la Pérouse. Watercolor attributed to Tomás de Suría or José Cardero, 1791, after a lost original painted at the occasion by Gaspard Duché de Vancy, 1786.

THE IMPACT OF EURO-AMERICAN EXPLORATION AND SETTLEMENT

neophytes (Cook 1943:91-135). An exneophyte from Mission San Luis Rey commented about cruelty in the missions: "When I was a boy the treatment of the Indians was not any good—they did not pay us anything—they only gave us food, a loin cloth and a blanket every year, and many beatings for any mistake even if it [the mistake] was slight, it was more or less at the mercy of the administrator who ordered the beatings whenever and how many he felt like" (Cesar 1878:4). Lorenzo Asisara, a neophyte born at Santa Cruz Mission in 1819, reported that "the Spanish padres were very cruel to the Indians: they treated them very badly . . . and they made them work like slaves" (Asisara 1877:90-113). Father President Fermín Francisco de Lasuen rationalized such cruelties this way: "It is evident that a nation which is barbarous, ferocious and ignorant requires more frequent punishment than a nation which is cultured, educated and of gentle and moderate customs" (Cook 1943:124). However, not all of Lasuen's friars were in agreement with such practices. In 1799 Padre Antonio de la Concepción Horra of Mission San Miguel enraged his contemporaries by reporting to the viceroy in Mexico that the Franciscan Order in California was guilty of cruelty and mismanagement of Indians in their jurisdiction. Horra charged: "The treatment shown to the Indians is the most cruel I have ever read in history. For the slightest things they receive heavy floggings, are shackled, and put in the stocks, and treated with so much cruelty that they are kept whole days without a drink of water" (Bancroft 1886-1890, 1:593). The unfortunate padre was quickly isolated, declared insane, and taken under armed guard out of California. Tales of this clerical "reign of terror" within the missions rapidly spread to unconverted tribes. As a result it is not surprising that as early as 1787 the missionaries began to use the military to "recruit" reluctant tribes for conversion (Cook 1943:73-80).

The ultimate purpose of the mission institution can be described best as Indian control. Lesser motives included economic support for military establishments, forced assimilation of the Indian into Hispanic society (see "Basketry," fig. 7d, this vol.), and conversion to Spanish Catholicism (fig. 3). Finally, let there be no doubt that the mission was much more than a merely religious institution. On the contrary, it served as a primary instrument of conquest for the sole benefit of the Spanish Crown (Ricard 1966:15-38).

The other major institution of Spanish colonization was the presidio. These military forts had been established at San Diego, Santa Barbara, Monterey, and San Francisco by 1800. In addition there were lesser numbers of soldiers stationed at other missions. However, military control was not the sole purpose of the presidio. These places also served as areas where native labor was exploited and Indian women were forced to entertain Spanish soldiers. The presidios, like the missions and

British Mus.: Van. 196.
Fig. 3. Catholic padre's hat made by Chumash Indians with native basketry technique. Collected by George Vancouver at Santa Barbara, 1792-1793. Diameter about 40 cm.

most other buildings in colonial California, were built with free native labor provided by the neophytes and prisoners. As soldiers' families began to acquire Indian servants this ultimately fostered the development of a *gente de razón* ruling class of Hispanos served by a mass of native laborers.

From the native viewpoint the Spanish invasion and occupation was a catastrophe of indescribable proportions. The coastal native population was rapidly reduced due to disease and sickness introduced by concentration in unhealthy mission environments (Cook 1940:35-48). Missionization imposed on neophytes a physical and social environment far different from their aboriginal village life. The mission housing aggregated many people in a relatively small area with bad sanitation and minimal ventilation and heat, providing a favorable environment for the spread of contagious diseases. Christianization meant for many inland tribes relocation from warm interior weather to the cool damp coastal region. Indians in California, like Indians throughout the Americas, were highly susceptible to most European diseases; and contact between the two races almost inevitably resulted in a high native death rate. Hispanos first infected the neophytes with venereal disease, which quickly spread to nonmission tribes as early as 1800 and thereafter increased steadily. Although it has not been proved conclusively that venereal disease decreases fertility, it certainly weakened individuals and made them more susceptible to all diseases. Three major epidemics occurred during the Spanish occupation. The first was reported at Mission Santa Clara in 1777 and was said to have been respiratory in nature. In 1802 a pneumonia and diphtheria epidemic, almost entirely confined to the young, ravaged the natives from Mission San Carlos to San Luis Obispo. The most devastating malady of this era occurred in 1806 when a measles epidemic decimated native peoples from San Francisco to Santa Barbara. In this catastrophe at least 1,600 natives died and in some missions it was reported that children under 10 years of age were almost completely wiped out. In all, modern research has determined that about 45 percent of the population decline during Spanish occupation was the direct result of introduced diseases and sickness (Cook 1943:13-22).

In addition to disease the rapid decline of Indian population under mission influence can be attributed to changes in diet and inadequate nutrition. It is doubtful that food provided in the missions was adequate. Accustomed to a rich and varied aboriginal diet of acorn, wild seeds, small game, and fish, the neophytes' diet was confined to a daily ration of a highly starchy cereal soup called atole, sometimes with a little meat. The monotonous diet had the overall effect of lowering resistance to other diseases, causing deficiency conditions such as avitaminosis, and finally causing partial or complete starvation.

In response to the invasion of the territory, California Indians almost at once began to offer all forms of resistance to the new order. Due to their various tribal social orders and political independence native resistance usually occurred in a haphazard and piecemeal fashion. Nevertheless, two types of native resistance resulted from this situation: the first was active or violent resistance and the second was passive.

One of the earliest and most successful demonstrations of native resistance to colonization was the destruction of Mission San Diego on November 4, 1775. Under the leadership of the neophyte Francisco of the Cuiamac Rancheria, the Ipai-Tipai organized nine villages into a force of about 800 men who not only completely destroyed the mission but also killed three Hispanos including Padre Jaume. That these normally independent villages could unite in common rebellion bears testimony to the recognition of the threat the invaders presented. Questioned after the rebellion, one Indian leader declared that he wanted to kill the priests and soldiers "in order to live as they did before" (Cook 1943:66). These Indians were not pacified until late 1776.

Other less spectacular resistance occurred in the San Francisco Bay area beginning about 1793. In February of that year a runaway neophyte named Charquin began a struggle against the Spanish. The Saklan and Chuchillones (Costanoan tribelets) of the northeast bay area soon began to resist parties recruiting converts and looking for runaway neophytes. After some three years of sporadic warfare, they were finally subdued by the Spanish military (Bancroft 1886-1890, 1:547-549). Some resistance was also noted among the Costanoan Indians against Mission San Jose in 1800.

There were many unsuccessful revolts. The Gabrielino under the leadership of a medicine woman named Toypurina were thwarted in an attempt to destroy Mission San Gabriel in 1785-1786. The Indians from Missions La Purísima and San Luis Obispo together plotted a revolt that was discovered by the missionaries and resulted in several arrests. Sporadic resistance also occurred between 1790 and 1800 at Missions Santa Clara and San Juan Bautista (Bancroft 1886-1890, 1:547).

In addition to violent group resistance, individual neophytes occasionally attempted to murder the Franciscan priests. In 1801 a number of priests were reportedly poisoned at Missions San Miguel and San Antonio. Eleven years later neophytes from Santa Cruz killed Father Quintana so cleverly that the murder was not discovered for two years (Asisara 1877:1-15).

Perhaps the most spectacular Indian rebellion in California during this era was the 1824 revolt at Missions La Purísima and Santa Barbara (Bancroft 1886-1890, 2:527-537). The reason for the revolt was ill treatment and forced labor imposed by the soldiers and priests upon neophytes in the area, but the immediate cause was a fight that broke out at the flogging of a La Purísima neophyte at Santa Ynez in February. Apparently no one was killed but a large part of the mission buildings was destroyed by fire. That same afternoon as many as 2,000 Indians attacked and captured Mission La Purísima. Soon they were bolstered by reinforcements from Santa Ynez and San Fernando. They immediately began preparations for defense by erecting palisades, mounting cannons and swivel guns, and cutting gun ports in the walls of the church and other buildings. Meanwhile the news of the uprising at La Purísima and Santa Ynez reached Santa Barbara. Upon its receipt the neophytes armed themselves and began to remind themselves of the ill treatment they had received from the soldiers. After some futile negotiation with the priests, the neophytes were attacked by the soldiers. A battle of several hours ensued throughout the mission; finally the soldiers withdrew to the presidio. The neophytes then sacked the mission and retreated to the back country. Indian losses were reported at two killed and three wounded, while the soldiers suffered four wounded. A month passed during which the Spanish authorities were able neither to persuade the Santa Barbara Indians to return nor to recapture La Purísima Mission. It was not until March 16 that the Spanish soldiers attacked the 400 defenders at La Purísima with hundreds of armed and mounted men and four-pounder guns. The neophytes answered with a volley of musket and cannon fire and a shower of arrows. The battle raged all morning until a ceasefire was negotiated with the aid of the padres. The Spanish suffered five killed and numerous wounded, while the Indians reported 16 killed and a large number wounded. During the early part of April Spanish soldiers pursued the Santa Barbara neophytes to the plain of the Tulares where after two skirmishes the soldiers retreated to Santa Barbara. Reports then began to reach Santa Barbara that many neophytes from San Fernando had run away to join the Indians from Santa Barbara and that neophytes at San Buenaventura and San Gabriel were showing alarming signs of revolt. At the end of May Spanish soldiers marched to the Tulares, negotiated a truce with the rebel neophytes, and allowed them to return to the mission with their arms. Despite these concessions as many as 400 refused to return. In the latter part of July a criminal prosecution was carried out against the La Purísima rebels that resulted in the execution of seven neophytes. Four leaders of the revolt—Mariano, Pacomio, Benito, and Bernarde—were sentenced to 10 years of chain-gang labor; Benito and Bernarde eventually escaped (Stickel and Cooper 1969).

Although violent opposition occurred sporadically throughout this period nonviolent or passive resistance was by far the most significant and widespread form of native resistance. The most obvious form of nonviolent resistance was escape from the missions into the interior. Reports of fugitivism from the missions occurred in each mission for every year until secularization. Usually Indians ran away from the missions in small groups or individually; however, in 1795 over 200 Costanoan Indians abandoned Mission Dolores in a mass escape to freedom. In most cases the escaped neophytes later turned to active resistance to insure their freedom. One observer noted:

Indians of course deserted. Who would not have deserted? Still, those who did had hard times of it. If they proceeded to other missions, they were picked up immediately, flogged and put in irons until an opportunity presented of returning them to undergo other flaggellations. . . . the only alternative left them was to take to the mountains, where they lived as they best could, making occasional inroads on the Mission property to maintain themselves (Heizer 1968:80).

The runaway neophytes also introduced Spanish horses, weapons, and military tactics to the unconverted interior tribes and convinced them to stiffen their own efforts at resistance to missionization (Holterman 1970:43–45).

Another devastating result of missionization was the state of psychological depression that inevitably seized long-term neophytes. It is indeed depressing to find repeated reports of this phenomenon throughout the mission system. One sympathetic observer noted, "At first, surprise and astonishment filled their minds; a strange lethargy and inaction predominated afterwards" (Heizer 1968:76).

Another widespread form of nonviolent resistance was the practice of abortion to prevent births in the missions. In addition, infanticide was practiced upon children born out of the forced concubinage of Indian women by priests and soldiers. A contemporary at mission San Gabriel wrote that "they necessarily became accustomed to these things, but their disgust and abhorrence never left them till many years after. In fact every white child born among them for a long period was secretly strangled and buried" (Heizer 1968:70).

Although the padres had attempted to eliminate all persons having any native spiritual authority, nearly all neophytes continued to practice some form of their traditional native religion within the missions (Cook 1943:145–153). This form of resistance is known to have occurred on a large scale in the Santa Barbara area around 1801 (Heizer 1941a). After a very destructive epidemic in the area a neophyte received a vision telling him that all the converts must recommit themselves to their own god if they hoped to survive. It appears that all the Chumash of the area were involved without the knowledge of the local Hispanos. In fact the movement was still reported as active 10 years later. During the latter years of the mission era a priest who compared California tribesmen to a species of monkeys corroborated the persistence of native faith at Mission San Juan Capistrano: "Superstitions of a ridiculous and most extravagant nature were found associated with these Indians, and even now in almost every town or hamlet the child is first taught to believe in their authenticity" (Boscana 1933:61). After a careful examination of all mission reports on this subject Cook (1943:147) concluded that "no competent contemporary authority . . . vouchsafed the unqualified assertion that the neophytes had to a significant degree given up their primitive customs and superstitions." This situation remained the same until the end of the mission system in California.

The Mexican Period

The years 1821 through 1823 marked the transition of California from a distant outpost of a dying empire to a marginal province of a much-troubled Mexican republic (Hutchinson 1965). Mexico inherited from Spain a vast and overextended colonial empire embracing much of the southwestern portion of the North American continent. Alta California at this time, as it was throughout the Mexican period, remained at the far fringes of the empire, isolated and sparsely populated by Hispanos. As in the Spanish period, Mexicans could claim control over only a narrow coastal strip of territory, occupied by its inherited institutions of colonialism—the missions, the military presidio, and the civilian pueblos. Although nearly all the interior continued under the control of its native people throughout the Mexican period, the impact of the coastal occupation was phenomenal.

The status of the Indian in the eyes of the Hispanos was that of a minor. The Mexican attitude toward the Indians was essentially the same as that of the Spanish. Neither Spain nor Mexico acknowledged Indian ownership of the land, but simply a right of occupancy. Indeed the entire policy and practice in regard to the natives was fraught with inconsistencies. Despite the adoption of the Plan of Iguala by the Mexican government in 1821, an act that guaranteed citizenship to Indians and protection of their person and property, Indian neophytes and gentiles alike were seized for forced labor and their property confiscated. Indeed, up to 1836 the mission fathers continued to "recruit" Indian converts with military campaigns to bolster the diminishing labor force in the missions. These later military campaigns tended to concentrate on territories east of the coastal missions on lands recently "acquired" by Mexican colonists in land grants from the Mexican government (Cook 1962).

Lacking the cultural and religious fanaticism of the Spanish occupation, the Mexican government soon bowed to the ascending middle-class interests throughout Mexico and in a series of acts brought about formal secularization of the missions from 1834 to 1836. However, instead of dividing the land and property between the surviving mission Indians and clerical authorities, as was originally intended, secular authorities appropriated most of the mission wealth for themselves and their relatives. The price of missionization had indeed been high: only 15,000 neophytes survived conversion of a total of 53,600 baptized between 1769 and 1836 (Bowman 1958). The sacking of the mission resources, including livestock, tools, and building materials, signaled a turning point in California Indian history.

The entire economy of the Mexican colony now shifted from the missions to the large landed estates of wealthy Mexicans. At the end of the mission period, the Indians formerly under mission influence scattered. Some went into the civilian pueblo areas to seek work, others became laborers on the private ranchos, and many returned to the mountains to seek refuge in their aboriginal homeland.

Those who went to the pueblos to seek work found only a life of poverty and debauchery. Sad indeed was the plight of the former missionized Indians who had nowhere else to turn since their original homeland had begun to fill with foreigners. An exneophyte from Mission Dolores made these observations:

I am very old . . . my people were once around me like the sands of the shore . . . many . . . many. They have all passed away. They have died like the grass . . . they have gone to the mountains. I do not complain, the antelope falls with the arrow. I had a son. I loved him. When the palefaces came he went away. I do not know where he is. I am a Christian Indian, I am all that is left of my people. I am alone (Johnston 1958).

Those who remained at or near the White settlements could find subsistence only as domestics and were ruthlessly exploited by their employers. In fact many who employed Indians would pay them only with alcohol, thus further contributing to their destruction. Life in the settlements led to an almost immediate breakdown of tribal organization and loss of cultural identity for the individual.

Indians who came under the influence of wealthy Mexican land barons found little improvement in their lot over earlier mission labor systems. The hacienda-peon society was transplanted intact from Mexico to California. This peonage system was rapidly developed by the rancheros and maintained by methods ranging from economic persuasion to outright slavery. By 1840 there were some dozen of these feudal establishments, each with 20 to several hundred Indians, in all perhaps as many as 4,000. In northern California many Pomo, Wappo, Patwin, Maidu, Plains Miwok, and Central Valley Yokuts came up against this type of economic exploitation. In the southern part of the state the Luiseño, Cupeño, and Serrano experienced dislocations and exploitation from Mexican colonists while the Gabrielino and Chumash began to experience the last stages of extinction.

In the interior of California, the situation was characterized by widespread intermittent warfare between non-Christianized tribes and Mexican colonists. During the years 1830 to 1846 the interior native population suffered more extensively from brutality and violence than might perhaps be anticipated. Violence was a critical factor among tribes that resisted more stubbornly, especially the Sierra Miwok and Wappo. The Mexican military responded to the demands of the expanding rancho economy for new laborers by initiating a new style of warfare. There was a change from the Spanish tactic of large, organized campaigns to frequent small private actions for the purpose of wreaking reprisal or seizing slaves (Cook 1943a:5). One such filibustering expedition led by Jose Maria Amador in 1837 was characteristic of the barbarity and inhuman treatment accorded central valley Indians by Mexican colonists during this period. According to Amador his party

invited the wild Indians and their Christian companions to come and have a feast of pinole and dried meat. They all came over to our side of the river. As soon as they reached our shore the troops, the civilians and the auxiliaries surrounded them and tied them all up . . . we separated 100 Christians. At every half mile or mile we put six of them on their knees to say their prayers, making them understand that they were about to die. Each one was shot with four arrows, two in front and two in the back. Those who refused to die immediately were killed with spears. . . . On the road were killed in this manner the 100 Christians. . . . The Ensign told me to do what ever I thought best (with the others). I answered that I thought all the prisoners should be shot, having previously made Christians of them. They should be told they were going to die and they should be asked if they wanted to be made Christians. I ordered Nazario Galindo to take a bottle of water and I took another. He began at one part of the crowd of captives and I at another. We baptized all the Indians and afterwards they were shot in the back. At the first volley 70 fell dead. I doubled the charge for the 30 who remained and they all fell (Cook 1962:197–198).

Moreover, native resisters could no longer look to the church for pardons such as the earlier resistance leaders Francisco and Toypurina had received.

In response to the expansion of settlement into the Sacramento valley and these new military excursions, native resistance began to stiffen. Adopting guerilla warfare tactics perfected earlier by native resistance leaders like Estanislao, tribesmen underwent considerable physical and military adaptation. With the acquisition of horses from the colonists, these Indians changed from peaceful, sedentary, localized groups to semiwarlike, seminomadic groups. They began to take the offensive, making widespread cattle raids to supplement their diminishing native food supply. Typical of this new resistance were the exploits of Yozcolo, a former Laquisamne (Plains Miwok) neophyte at Mission Santa Clara. Credited with many stock raids throughout the 1830s he and his followers eluded Mexican officials for many years. Then, after a raid on the Rancho del Encino Coposo in 1839, which resulted in the death of two Hispanos, he and about 100 of his followers were captured near Los Gatos after an all-day battle. Wounded, Yozcolo was forced to fight a hand-to-hand battle with a soldier who killed him, cut off his head and rode triumphantly back to Santa Clara (Holterman 1970a).

Well-known colonists such as Gen. Mariano Guadalupe Vallejo became wealthy and powerful after military campaigns against native people. In 1834 Vallejo attacked and killed over 200 Satiyomi (Wappo) tribesmen and captured 300 others (Cook 1943a:9). Instead of declining, the violence and brutality increased. In fact as the later years of the Mexican occupation progressed, the colonial government's ability to cope with stock raiding deteriorated. Evidence of this situation is reflected in the Mexican assembly's resolutions of 1846 to devote surplus revenues to "active efforts" against Indians. If the surplus did not suffice, civil employees were to be called upon for part of their salaries. In addition, it was resolved that a military border police be established and a fortification be built at Pacheco Pass to prevent further raids (Bancroft 1886-1890, 5:566-567). In the central valley the Indian offensive reached a peak in 1845 and then rapidly decreased due to rear attacks suffered from American colonists filling the valley. In the south from 1841 to 1848 warfare became much more intensified. Due to internal power struggles after 1841, the situation became so confused and the power of the Mexican administration so weak that even nominal control over the military activity of its citizens was lost. Although no estimates are available for the southern part of the state, it has been estimated that military casualties accounted for about 6 percent of the population decline, a critical demographic element in the cases of specific tribes.

Even more devastating than military incursion were the White man's diseases. Venereal disease continued to be reported widespread, as the general health conditions among natives continued to deteriorate. Other maladies followed: measles, pneumonia, diphtheria, and other respiratory diseases ravaged missionized tribes in a series of major epidemics until 1827. In 1833 smallpox first appeared to an alarming extent, along with scarlet fever, cholera, and tuberculosis. In the same year the Wintun, Maidu, Miwok, and Yokuts suffered an unknown disease called the "Pandemic of 1833" in which as many as 4,500 Indians died—a total loss of about 10 percent for all tribes involved. A smallpox epidemic struck the Pomo, Wappo, and Wintun five years later, killing more than 2,000 before it was spent. In 1844 smallpox attacked the Miwok. A new epidemic of "fever" ravaged the Wintun two years later. Finally a more virulent strain of smallpox devastated the Pomos of Clear Lake in 1850. Overall losses for northern California are estimated at 11,500 between 1830 and 1848. Disease accounted for a net population decrease of up to 60 percent—five times greater than homicide. By the end of the Mexican occupation the total native population had been reduced to about 100,000 persons (Cook 1943a:16-20).

When the Mexican War came to California, some well-known Indians were recruited by the Mexicans for defense purposes. Bancroft (1886-1890, 5) reports the organization of a company of California Indians (probably Gabrielino) in Los Angeles and another to serve New Helvetia, under John A. Sutter. In John C. Frémont's battalion, Company H consisted of 40 Tulare Indians whose duty it was to raid Mexican ranchos of cattle and horses for the Americans. Generally known as the "40 thieves," these Indians proved to be very accomplished at their task; for years after the war they continued their raids on horses and cattle for their own people. There seems to be no evidence that any of these Indian groups participated in any battles of the war to a significant degree.

There was one incident during the Mexican War that illustrated the tragic consequences of the loss of racial unity suffered by native people. In this incident a group of Luiseño under Manuelito Cota and Pablo Apis was suspected of killing 11 Hispanos at Agua Caliente on J.J. Warner's rancho. It appears that this occurred a few days after the battle of San Pascual in December 1845. The Mexicans regarded the incident as an Indian rebellion, since the Luiseño at Mission San Luis Rey had abandoned the mission en masse at about the same time. Gen. Jose Maria Flores ordered Jose del Carmen Lugo to punish the Indians. Lugo recruited the aid of the Cahuilla Chief Juan Antonio and his followers, and joined by forces from Mission San Luis Rey he marched on the Luiseño rancheria at Temecula in February 1847. Drawn into an ambush, the poorly armed Luiseños were slaughtered in a crossfire. Although Cota escaped, his losses are reported at 33 to 100 killed. This tragic episode had the dubious distinction of being the bloodiest battle of the Mexican War in California (Parker 1971:7). Indeed, more lives were lost in this one engagement than the total of all casualties of the Mexican War in the entire state. Indians in California committed the tragic error of all Indians, in allying themselves against their own people.

The American Period

In February 1848 the Treaty of Guadalupe Hidalgo ceded sovereignty over Alta California, New Mexico, and Arizona to the United States. A new colonial order soon seized power in California, with disastrous results for the native people. Until 1845 the Hispano population in California numbered only a few thousand persons, mostly concentrated along the coast. In contrast, Anglo hegemony was characterized by the introduction of colonists seeking land and intense exploitation of natural resources. Spanish and Mexican colonial government had attempted to incorporate the Indian into its economic and social order, but the Anglo-American system had no place for the Indian except to the extent that he performed as a White man (Cook 1943b). Thus Indian life, which was more valuable to the Mexicans because they institutionalized Indian labor for wealth, was seen as worthless to the Americans. Further, Mexican custom sanctioned miscegenation for lower classes, while Anglos were appalled by it.

Given the attitude of the new invaders, it is not surprising that war between native people and the Anglos commenced almost at once. Anglo invaders began to seize land in the interior valley and along the northern coast. Yuki, Cahto, Yurok, and Tolowa tribesmen suffered greatly from these incursions. The number of Whites soon increased rapidly with the arrival of hordes of lawless adventurers seeking quick wealth in 1849. During these early years action against the native consisted of widespread and small personal combats between individuals and little groups. In a letter to the commissioner of Indian affairs, Agent Adam Johnson reported on the character of "Indian wars" in California:

The majority of tribes are kept in constant fear on account of the indiscriminate and inhuman massacre of their people for real or supposed injuries. They have become alarmed of the increased flood of immigration much spread over their country. . . . it was just incomprehensible to them. . . . I have seldom heard of a single difficulty between the whites and the Indians in which the original cause could not readily be traced to some rash or reckless act of the former. In some instances it has happened that innocent Indians have been shot down for imaginary offenses which did not in fact exist. . . . when cattle were missing it was quickly supposed that they had been stolen by the Indians and the lives of several were paid. Again where a man was absent a few days longer than expected his death was imagined and the lives of several paid the penalty for the supposed murder (Johnston 1958a).

Lib. of Congress: Browne 1864:305.
Fig. 4. "Protecting the Settlers." This sarcastically titled 1864 engraving depicts the fate of the Indians of Nome Cult Valley during the winter of 1858–1859. Considered "only Diggers" (Heizer 1974), California Indians could be attacked without fear of government justice.

The Clear Lake Massacre illustrates the character of some larger military operations against natives at this time. The trouble began over the killing of two White men by the Pomos in 1849. These two men had brutally exploited the Indians at Clear Lake by enslaving and abusing them, and many died as a result. The military answered the killing of the White men with a campaign in 1850 under Capt. Nathanial Lyon. Equipped with boats, the soldiers

went across [the lake] in their long dug-outs, the indians said they would meet them in peace. So when the whites landed the indians went to wellcom them but the white man was determined to kill them. Ge-Wi-Lih said he threw up his hands and said no harm me good man but the white man fired and shoot him in the arm . . . many women and children were killed around this island. One old lady . . . saw two white men coming with their guns up in the air and on their guns hung a little girl, they brought it to the creek and threw it in the water . . . two more men came . . . this time they had a little boy on the end of their guns and also threw it in the water. alittle ways from her . . . two white men stabbed the woman and the baby . . . all the little ones were killed by being stabbed, and many of the women were also. This old lady also told about the whites hung aman on Emerson's Island . . . . The Indian was hung and alarge fire built under [him] another . . . was tied to atree and burnt to death (Benson 1932:271–272).

The army reported 60 out of 400 Indians were killed on the island, while another 75 were murdered on the Russian River nearby. That this was without a doubt a massacre is substantiated by the reports of only 2 wounded Whites and over 135 natives killed.

Many expeditions against the Indians were the result of local conspiracies to gain Indian property and political capital for ambitious office seekers. Special Government Investigator J. Ross Browne provides this description of a typical militia expedition against Humboldt Indians:

During the winter of last year a number of them [Indians] were gathered at Humboldt. The whites thought it was a favorable opportunity to get rid of them altogether. So they went in a body to the Indian camp, during the night when the poor wretches were asleep, shot all the men, women, and children at the first onslaught, and cut the throats of the remainder. Very few escaped. Next morning 60 bodies lay weltering in their blood—the old and the young, male and female—with every wound gaping a tale of horror to the civilized world. Children climbed upon their mothers' breasts and sought nourishment from the fountains that death had drained; girls and boys lay here and there with their throats cut from ear to ear; men and women, clinging to each other in their terror, were found perforated with bullets or cut to pieces with knives—all were cruelly murdered (Browne 1944:62).

The state and federal government subsidized these conspiracies by reimbursing these "private military forays" for expenses incurred. Almost any White man could raise a volunteer company, outfit it with guns, ammunition, horses, and supplies, and be reasonably sure that the state government would honor its vouchers. The state legislature passed acts in 1851 and 1852 authorizing payment of over $1,100,000 for suppression of Indian hostilities. Again in 1857 the legislature issued bonds amounting to $410,000 for the same purpose. Congress eventually reimbursed the state for nearly all the bonds issued, indeed a dreary story of subsidized murder (12 Stat. 199-200).

Up to 1860 overall loss of life due to military homicide accounted for at least 4,267 deaths, or about a 12 percent reduction of population (Cook 1943b:5-9). Military casualties reached their peak from 1854 to 1857. None of these so-called Indian wars in the California valley was more than an attempt at wholesale slaughter of native people (Bancroft 1886-1890, 7:477).

After 1848 Indians in California began to experience the threatened destruction of their native economy for the first time. The Indians had a precisely balanced relationship with their food supply. Soon after the arrival of the Americans serious depletions of that supply began to occur: mining operations adversely affected salmon fishing and destroyed fish dams (Cook 1943b:27-46). The Anglos' total disregard for the destruction of the natural environment in their frenzy to exploit the land struck a mortal blow to the Indians' sacred relationship with nature. Extensive agriculture prevented communal hunts for rabbit and deer. The Whites' fences prevented women from gaining access to oak groves for acorn gathering. At the same time, cattle and hogs ate huge supplies of grasses and acorns, seriously depleting the seed supply. Another factor that helped destroy native food supplies was the destruction of stored foods during the "Indian wars." The overall impact of this destruction of the food supply can be characterized by a lowering of resistance to disease, especially among the young and older people. Prolonged undernutrition contributed to mental lassitude and infant mortality because of mothers' inability to withstand childbirth and decreases in milk. This depletion of the aboriginal food supply in part also explains the increase in stock raiding among California tribes.

Shortly after the Mexican War, Anglos introduced new labor conditions upon the Indians that proved even more disastrous than during the Mexican era. As the native economy began to break down, more and more Indians were forced to attempt to accommodate themselves to new modes of making a living. However, Indians had a difficult time understanding the work ethic of the new order. They were at a disadvantage because of their unfamiliarity with the economy and because of differing cultural values, which, for example, stressed conflicting time concepts. There was also a general decline in the demand for labor as the huge ranchos began to break up, ending forever the pastoral peonage society and its economy. The end of the gold rush soon flooded the labor market with Whites, leaving only domestic work and subsistence labor available to the Indian.

In 1850 the legislature passed a law that seriously affected the Indians' labor position. This law declared that any Indian, on the word of a White man, could be declared a vagrant, thrown in jail, and have his labor sold at auction for up to four months with no pay. This indenture law further said any Indian adult or child with the consent of his parents could be legally bound over to a White citizen for a period of years, laboring for subsistence only. These laws marked the transition of the Indian from peonage to virtual slavery; they gave free vent to the exploitative ethos of Americans who soon took advantage of the situation (Heizer and Almquist 1971:39-58). Nearby Indians were rounded up, made to labor, and turned out to starve and die when the work season was over. Correspondence to the superintendent of Indian affairs in January 1853 described one such incident:

I went over to the San Pablo rancho, in Contra Costa county, to investigate the matter of alleged cruel treatment of Indians there. I found seventy-eight on this rancho, and twelve back of Martinez, and they were there most of them sick, all without clothes, or any food but the fruit of the buckeye. Up to the time of my coming, eighteen had died of starvation at one camp: how many at the other I could not learn. These present Indians are the survivors of a band who were worked all last summer and fall, and as the winter set in, when broken down by hunger and labor, without food or clothes, they were turned adrift to shift for themselves (U.S. Congress. Senate 1853:9).

The labor laws in California also fostered the institutionalization of kidnapping of Indian children. Evidence indicates that this practice was widespread throughout California. An editorial in the Marysville *Appeal* of December 6, 1861, revealed:

But it is from these mountain tribes that white settlers draw their supplies of kidnapped children, educated as servants, and women for purposes of labor and lust. . . . It is notorious that there are parties in the northern counties of this state, whose sole occupation has been to steal young children and squaws from the poor Diggers . . . and dispose of them at handsome prices to the settlers, who, being in the majority of cases unmarried but . . . willingly pay 50 or 60 dollars for a young digger to cook and wait upon them, or 100 dollars for a likely young girl (Cook 1943b:58).

These crimes against humanity so enraged the Indians in that area that they began to retaliate by killing the Whites' livestock. At once an order from the army headquarters was issued to chastise the "guilty." Under this indefinite order a company of U.S. troops, accompanied by a large volunteer force, pursued the Indians persistently. The kidnappers followed at the heels of the soldiers to seize the children after their parents had been murdered.

The practice of legalized kidnapping and seizure of Indian children and young girls lasted for 15 years until 1867, when in compliance with the Fourteenth Amendment of the U.S. Constitution, it was stricken from state law. Well over 4,000 Indians had been victims of this most cruel form of slavery.

During the American period, diseases and epidemics did not occur in large outbreaks among the Indians; however, disease attacked the Indians in chronic form or by small local outbreaks. This had the effect of exacting a steady toll of lives over a long period of time. The most common diseases remained tuberculosis, smallpox, pneumonia, measles, and venereal diseases. In fact intensification of infections nearly increased with the coming of the Anglos. There was at this time a general syphilis infection of approximately 20 percent, while gonorrhea was reported to be 100 percent. Such an onslaught of infection seriously damaged the physical stamina and moral fiber of the native people. Some tribes suffered up to 90 percent population decrease due to infection of these diseases. Similar to the earlier Mexican period, disease constituted the greatest single factor in the population decrease. Cook (1943b:24) estimates for this period a 65 percent decrease in population due solely to diseases.

Administration by Agents

Official relations between the Indians of California and the United States government were initiated by the military governor, Gen. S.W. Kearney, in April 1847. He appointed three Indian agents for northern, southern, and central California. Their duties were to deal chiefly in "good advice," explain changes in colonial governments, and make promises or threats to keep the Indians pacified. During these early years the agents did little and no official policy was established. Between 1851 and 1852 three treaty commissioners negotiated 18 treaties with random groups of California natives, promising over 7 million acres of reservation land in exchange for the entire state (Heizer 1972). These treaties enraged Whites, who bombarded Congress with an abusive campaign that resulted in their rejection.

The creation of the state government at this time introduced yet another unfavorable factor into the situation that confronted the Indians. This government inevitably reflected the frontiersman's contempt for and impatience with any policy that looked toward the solution of the Indian problem on a basis of fairness toward the Indian or any idea that the Indian could have any rights that a White man was bound to respect. In his 1851 message to the legislature Gov. John McDougall outlined the state's genocidal aim with "Jacksonian logic": "That a war of extermination will continue to be waged between the races until the Indian race becomes extinct, must be expected. . . . the inevitable destiny of the race is beyond the power or wisdom of man to avert" (California. Legislature. Senate and Assembly 1851:1). Further, the rejection of the 18 treaties and the adoption of the state's labor laws seem to have put the status of the Indian outside of federal control and quickly led to conflicts between state and federal authorities. This conflict allowed the development of the state militia's punitive expeditions, which proved to be so devastating to native people. In fact throughout this period many times U.S. troops were not even contacted for aid. The militia hoped to make financial and political capital by handling the situation themselves. The so-called Mariposa War of 1851 is a good example of this situation (Bunnell 1911). The Mariposa tribes, reacting to dispossession and exploitation by White miners and squatters, began stock raiding, which resulted in the organization of a local militia. When the militia failed to defeat the tribesmen, Indian Subagent Adam Johnson and trader James D. Savage went not to the United States military commander of the Pacific stationed at Benicia but to the governor at San Jose to seek aid. Both Johnson and Savage claimed to the governor that little help could be expected from the federal government, although it was later shown that they did not even try to contact the U.S. military headquarters authorities at Benicia until after their journey to San Jose. Naturally Savage was bound to profit heavily by a state campaign there since he owned the only trading post in the area.

Indeed one unnecessary and tragic consequence of the confusion of authority among federal, state, and local governments in regard to Indian policy resulted in the Garra uprising of 1851. The revolt occurred among the Cahuilla, Quechan, and Cocopa tribes and centered in the Cupeño village of Agua Caliente in a mountainous region of central San Diego County. The immediate cause of the outbreak was a state tax imposed upon the property of these Indians in 1850. The next year Antonio Garra, Sr., an exneophyte from Mission San Luis Rey, organized several Indian villages near Thermal Springs to refuse to pay the tax after the head of the state militia advised Garra that Indians could not be taxed. In response to the continued insistence on the part of the local authorities for the tax, Garra attempted to bring together a broad confederacy of southern California Indians to expel the Whites from their territory. The Cocopa and Quechan Indians first responded by attacking and killing two Anglos and two Mexicans and confiscating their stock. Shortly thereafter the Cupeño village at Agua Caliente rose up and attacked nearby Warner's ranch, destroying the house and store and killing four White men at Thermal Springs. The state militia with the regular army organized several attacks on Garra's Cupeño and Cahuilla strongholds, which resulted in the destruction of the Agua Caliente rancheria. Several prisoners were taken, and during the course of the outbreak five Indians and one White man were all tried by militia courts and executed. Garra was eventually captured by a rival Cahuilla captain and turned over to the Whites. He was tried by a paramilitary court, found guilty of murder, and shot January 10, 1852. Once Garra and his closest followers were captured and executed, the confederacy dissolved leaving the tax issue unresolved for some years (Loomis 1971:3-26).

In order to see that the Indian Trade and Intercourse Act was complied with in California, Congress appointed Edward F. Beale as new superintendent of Indian affairs. Beale arrived in California in the fall of 1852. One of his first acts as superintendent was to dismiss Treaty Commissioners Redick McKee and O. M. Wozencraft, who had not visited the Indians for over six months. He soon developed plans for the establishment of reservations in the state in conjunction with military posts. Early in 1853 Congress responded by authorizing the establishment of not more than five military reservations in California for $250,000. The following September, Beale gathered together some 2,000 Indians to establish the Tejon Reservation of 50,000 acres of land near the extreme southern end in the San Joaquin valley. Here the Indians were given instructions in agriculture and provided with seeds and provisions until the first harvest. In concentrating all his efforts and energies here, Beale seriously neglected the other 61,000 hungry

and pursued natives throughout the state. In defense of his one-reservation policy, Beale declared that "humanity must yield to necessity, they are not dangerous, therefore they must be neglected" (U.S. Congress. Senate. Documents 1853). In the summer of 1854 he was removed from office. He was charged with failure to keep proper financial records and insinuations were made that he had been guilty of peculations.

It would appear that the dismissal of Beale was a small indication of massive corruption. In 1853 Treaty Commissioner Wozencraft was charged with "irregularities" in his purchase and delivery of beef to starving Indians. Savage, a licensed trader to the Indians, was also charged with fraud. One of his employees testified: "My instructions from Savage were that . . . I was to take receipts for double the number actually delivered, and make no second delivery and to deliver one-third less than were receipted for. I also had orders to sell all beef I could to miners, which I did to the amount of about $120.00 or $130.00, and to deliver cattle to his clerks, to be sold to the Indians" (U.S. Congress. Senate 1853: 4-5). Many other irregularities resulted from corrupt management and neglect of the state's Indians by Beale.

In 1854 Beale was replaced by Col. T.J. Henley. The new superintendent authorized by Congress set about establishing reservations at Klamath River near the Oregon border, Nome Lackee on Stony Creek in Colusa, Nome Cult, Mendocino, Fresno Indian Farm, and Kings River Indian Farm. Despite Henley's establishment of these reservations it quickly became apparent that his administration of the Indian Service was even more corrupt than that of Beale. The large reservations established by Henley—Nome Lackee, Nome Cult, and Mendocino—suffered a lack of water and a scarcity of game. Many problems resulted from the fact that only Nome Lackee had been surveyed. In consequence an influx of White squatters began. Their cattle destroyed fenceless Indian fields and seriously depleted the acorn harvest. Most of these squatters were business partners or relatives of Henley and therefore impossible to remove. At Mendocino two White men owned a logging operation and a steam sawmill on the reservation, which seriously effected the salmon fishing. There was an unauthorized White-owned store there as well (ARCIA 1861:104).

Further evidence of Henley's incompetence and corruption derived from his employment of more persons than his instructions allowed and retention of employees who were confessed accomplices in various frauds. Henley and his agents kept few books or accounts of various purchases, and where kept they were incomplete or incomprehensible. He was also unable to account for the vast herds of cattle provided to the Indian Service for starving Indians. Henley's total disregard for Indian life can be illustrated by his failure to provide aid to beleaguered Yokuts tribesmen who were victims of the "Tulare War of 1856" and also by charges by federal investigators that Indians on the reservations had been slaughtered in consequence of alleged depredations upon private property belonging to officers of the Indian Service. Finally the army charged Henley with turning reservations into almshouses where periodically goods were distributed to native people. Henley's policies destroyed the intention that the reservations should be permanent homes for the Indians. The army also charged Henley with providing only 2,000 or so Indians with homes while thousands of natives remained "trespassers on the public domain."

In April 1858 Special Treasury Agent J. Ross Browne forwarded charges of fraud and malfeasance against Henley. Yet he continued to act in his capacity as superintendent up to June 3, 1859, 14 months after the original charges were preferred and nearly a year after they were proved. In his reports Browne observed: "In the history of Indian races I have seen nothing so cruel and relentless as the treatment of these unhappy people by the authorities constituted by law for their protection. Instead of receiving aid and succor, they have been starved and driven away from the reservations, and then followed into their remote hiding places, where they sought to die in peace, and cruelly slaughtered, till but few are left, and that few without hope" (U.S. Congress. Senate 1860:13).

In response to the blatant corruption and mismanagement of Henley's administration, Congress passed the General Appropriation Act of February 1859, which in part called for a reorganization of Indian administration in California and a reduction of the Indian Services budget for California from $162,000 a year to $50,000. Obviously this did little to feed the starving Indians. It would not be unjust to say that the history of the government's relation with California Indians in these first 10 years of management was entirely corrupt. Subagents gerrymandered reservation boundaries to buy developed land, beef was seldom delivered to the Indians for whom it was intended, private businesses were allowed to operate on the reservation, books were incomplete and vouchers irregular. It is little wonder that few Indians ever stayed on the reservations. Native people found themselves again used as forced labor to enrich their overseers.

The beginning of the next decade witnessed the gradual disintegration of the colonial system first established by the United States upon the natives of California. This situation was the result of several factors. On the national level the Civil War created severe fiscal problems for the administration of the Indian Service in California. Within the state, disease continued to take a terrific toll of native life. The dwindling Indian population surrounded by a hostile frontier society with its indenture laws and the continued profiteering in the Indian Service all contributed to a wholesale abandonment

of several reservations and the ultimate failure of the entire reservation system in the state (Dale 1949:42).

Government documents indicated a continuous decline in the Indian population throughout this period. There were several reasons for this situation. To be sure, disease and sickness continued to take a steady toll of lives. This problem was further complicated by the persistent reports of starvation and destitution among California tribes; however, the steady decrease was not due solely to starvation and illness. Hostilities continued to be a factor in the decrease of Indian residence on government reserves. The Konkow and Hat Creek (Atsugewi) tribes living with other tribes at Round Valley in 1862 were confronted by squatters encroaching on the reservation and told that since there was no food on the reservation they would be forced to steal or starve and that if they did not abandon the reservation the Whites would kill them all. The Indian agent apparently did little to aid the harassed natives. In August of that year 25 armed Whites came on the reservation and surrounded these Indians' camp and massacred about 45 of them. From Round Valley the 461 survivors of the Hat Creek and Konkow tribes fled to Chico. The next August those Indians were accused of killing two White boys. In response the Whites tied two Indians to a tree and scalped them and demanded that the Indians be either removed or exterminated. Meanwhile back at Round Valley, marshall law was declared because of trouble when the squatters on the reservation massacred more than 20 Wailaki men, women, and children there. Apparently the squatters then blamed the Indians for burning a barn containing 30 tons of hay. In retribution the army executed five Indians and in turn two-thirds of the Indian crop was destroyed by the squatters. The presence of the army, instead of providing security for the reservation, simply further agitated the natives by the soldiers' seizing Indian women and introducing an epidemic of venereal diseases. Finally in 1863 the Hat Creek and Konkow tribes were returned to Round Valley. In a letter to the Indian Service, Army Capt. C.D. Douglas reported on the condition of these unfortunate natives: "I found all the Indians that were sent or brought on the reservation from Chico, about 10 days ago in an almost dying condition, through sickness and the *gross* neglect of duty of the present supervisor. I was also informed that nearly 200 sick Indians are scattered along all the way for forty miles, and that they are dying by *tens* for want of care and medical treatment and from lack of food" (ARCIA 1864:414).

Although records are incomplete, there can be no doubt that the total number of Indians under federal supervision decreased from approximately 3,000 to slightly over 1,000 for this time period. Eventually it became apparent that the California reservation system as envisioned by Beale and established by Henley was becoming a monumental failure. The state's indenture law was used by nearby Whites to get the most able-bodied Indians from the reservation indentured to them for terms of 10 or 15 years. The problem of employees and former employees of the Indian Service contributing to the failure of the reservations continued, as can be traced in the annual reports of the Commissioner of Indian Affairs. It was not uncommon to find a superintendent of Indian affairs leaving his post with debts up to $35,000 unaccounted for, as Superintendent Charles Maltby did in 1867. The most serious problem was the ability of former high-placed officials of the Indian Service to gain control of lands surrounding and including portions of various reservations and Indian farms. By 1863 Beale had managed to acquire a 12,000-acre ranch adjacent to the Tejon Reserve. Now as a private rancher Beale openly expressed his desire to abolish the reservation. It is not difficult to imagine the demoralizing effect this had upon the Indians there. The man who claimed to be their friend a few years earlier was now demanding the dispossession of his former wards. At the Tule River Indian Farm established in 1861 near Visalia, the former agent, John P.H. Wentworth, managed to lease the entire farm to his enormous profit in 1863. Colonel Henley, the former superintendent, was the ruling spirit among the squatters encroaching upon the Round Valley Reservation (ARCIA 1864:129). In 1867 Special Government Agent Robert J. Stevens confirmed that Henley was originally responsible for inviting squatters into Round Valley Reservation and at the same time notifying Washington that the *entire* valley should be reserved for the Indians. Thus Henley set up the government by backing squatters' claims that the government should pay for their improvements and urging the government to buy out these interlopers. Henley also stood to profit heavily from this deal since he held extensive claims in the valley himself (ARCIA 1867:120). A further obstacle to the success of the early reservation system in California was the rapid and widespread turnover in the Indian Service personnel.

Perhaps the most persistent and decisive element contributing to the failure of the reservation system was the hostile frontier society that bordered on the government reserves. At Nome Lackee squatters held portions of the reservation including a mill and seized upon teams and farming implements belonging to the government. Claiming they acted under the sanction of Colonel Henley, they refused to surrender the government property. A sawmill at the mouth of the Noyo River reportedly destroyed salmon fishing upon which the Indians at the Mendocino Reserve relied as their staple food. Round Valley Reservation was literally overrun with White squatters who occupied about four-fifths of the reservation.

In addition to problems caused by the seizure of reservation land and property, the mere presence of Whites on the reservation disrupted the Indian community. At

Round Valley the agent reported that "a large majority of the Whites were unmarried men who constantly excite the Indians to jealously and revenge by taking their squaws from them" (ARCIA 1861:148). Here also a government investigation revealed that corners of the Indian fences had been raised by chunks of wood to allow the squatters' hogs to feed on Indian fields. Cattle from the squatters' herds destroyed considerable portions of unfenced Indian fields at Nome Lackee and Tejon. In 1867 the government reported on the character and impact of White influence on the Indians.

[Squatters] evidently think an Indian has no rights that a white man is bound to respect; that all should be killed off except such as the settlers covet as men servants or maid servants. This class of settlers are continually creating disturbances amongst the Indians by selling or giving away liquor among them; by enticing women and children away from the reservation, and not unfrequently by boasting of the number of "buck" [Indians] they have killed, as if it were an achievement to be proud of. . . . No man, however guilty, can be convicted of a misdemeanor for selling liquor to Indians . . . (ARCIA 1868:104).

Although the government apparently was aware of the many problems caused by the presence of Whites on the reservation no action was taken.

Given the adverse environment the Indians and reservations were forced to cope with, it is not surprising that the Indian Service bowed to the state's citizen pressures and began to abandon the reservations. As early as 1861 the government abandoned Fresno and Kings River Indian Farms, transferring the few remaining families to the new Tule River Indian Farm. In December of that year the Klamath River Reservation was abandoned after a destructive flood. In early 1863 the new superintendent in California found that at Nome Lackee the former agent had not paid the man in charge there who consequently sold all the movable property for back wages. The few remaining Indians scattered and the reservation was abandoned. Yielding to private interests Tejon Reserve was abandoned in 1864. Finally after eight years as a promising potential reservation Smith River Indian Farm north of Mendocino was abandoned in 1869 (Dale 1949).

Despite the vast expenditure of money and energy by the government to remove Indians to reservations the majority of California natives struggled to survive without any government aid whatsoever. This was the case of the Hupa tribe who persistently resisted White encroachment and efforts by the government to remove them. So successful was their resistance that in 1864, after five years of constant warfare, the Hupa tribe was guaranteed a reservation in the Hoopa Valley. In southern California the Indians were almost totally neglected. In May 1865 the Indian Service convened a meeting with southern tribal delegates at Temecula. Here the government doled out a few agricultural implements and seed while hearing complaints from the Cahuilla who had been dispossessed of San Timoteo Canyon after fleeing from a smallpox epidemic there. Southern California tribesmen began to learn a difficult lesson about co-optation of native leadership when in 1865 the Indian Service reappointed Manuelito Cota over Chief Francisco to govern the Temecula Rancheria. The demoralizing effect of this official neglect of the nonreservation Indians was outlined by a federal report of 1866.

The Indians other than those before mentioned reside in various sections of the State, in small communities; in some localities their presence is obnoxious to the citizens; in others they are tolerated on account of the labor they perform for the whites; their condition is deplorable and pitiful in the extreme; they are demoralized both physically and morally. This condition, lamentable as it is, is the result of their intercourse and contact with the lowest class of the white population . . . The Indians in this superintendency are placed, by circumstances over which they had no control, under peculiar hardships . . . with no lands, no treaties, no annuities, no power or means of extricating themselves from the influences with which they are surrounded . . . (ARCIA 1866:94).

This situation was particularly true in southern California where no reservations or regular government aid were to be established for some years.

The "Quaker Policy"

A significant change in the administration of Indian affairs occurred shortly after President Grant took office. In an attempt to correct the national scandal of dishonest and incompetent Indian agents, the President initiated a new policy whose major aspect was the use of army officers and nominees of various religious denominations to govern Indian affairs throughout the country. Known as the "Quaker policy" for the denomination to which Grant first turned, Congress quickly terminated the use of army officers and thereafter relied on the churches (Tatum 1970). Under this system various territories and state superintendencies were distributed among different denominations. In California by far the majority of Indians who considered themselves Christians were Roman Catholic. Therefore with the typical forethought and sensitivity of a bureaucracy the California superintendency was "given" to the Episcopalians. Apparently the scandal civil-service employees had brought to the Indian Service was so embarassing that no one bothered to realize this new system constituted a union of church and state functions, which federal law prohibits. Ironically this policy enraged Catholic Church officials who had made no consistent effort to assist Christian Indians since the mission days. Archbishop José Sadoc Alemany of San Francisco testified to Indian Service officials that the Church could not do anything for the Indians while they remained under political con-

trol and might be reassigned to the administration of another denomination at any time. The Catholic Church would accept only a "permanent control" (Wetmore 1875:25). By 1871 the Episcopalians had established a regular ministry on Round Valley and Tule River reservations. Secular authorities were willing to allow California natives to practice many of their traditional religious ceremonies; the churches were not. Church administrators initiated a vigorous campaign to prohibit these practices and suppress the influence of anyone having native religious authority. This policy had the overall effect of creating and intensifying social and religious disorientation among California tribesmen. Details of this process can be found in the Annual Reports of the Commissioner of Indian Affairs (1869-1881).

About this same time a renaissance of native cultism resulted from the influence of the 1870 Ghost Dance originating from the Walker Lake Paiutes. The most consistent manifestation of this resurgence of native religion was the belief that the end of the world was near and that the dead would return with the disappearance of the Whites. By 1871 this cult had spread westward to the Washo, Modoc, Klamath, Shasta, and Karok tribes. Shortly thereafter it spread to the Yurok, then Achumawi, Northern Yana, Wintun, Hill Patwin, and finally Pomo peoples. Eventually the Ghost Dance spread as far south as the Southern San Joaquin valley (Gayton 1930a; Du Bois 1939). Although this religious revival developed into many forms, it was principally instrumental in reshaping native shamanism and probably helped native Californians withstand pressures to adopt Christianity. However, the overall impact of this movement had little significance on the history of the Indian in California. This period also witnessed the last outbreak of organized violent resistance among Indians of the state in the Modoc War of 1872-1873 (Dillon 1973).

The general condition of the Indians from 1850 to 1870 continued to deteriorate. Disease and chronic illness complicated by severe social, moral, and political disintegration created considerable hardships on the surviving natives. The upheaval and turmoil to which natives were constantly subjected loosened and tore asunder their social framework. Thousands of minor incidents and pressures contributed to the overall demoralizing effect. Indian people were seriously pauperized by repeated hostile incursions into their territory, almost always featuring the destruction of their stored foods and property. These incursions usually led to the abandonment of their villages, disruption of the native economy, and excessive hardships for the sick and starving. Captivity and removal of over 10,000 natives for labor and slavery through the California indenture act of 1850 also took a frightful toll. Forcibly uprooting more than one-fifth of the native population was bound to result in serious social upheaval—the disintegration of both family and community life (Cook 1943a:28).

The Indian population in the state continued to decline. Because of the establishment of the new southern California reservations, reservation Indian populations as a whole increased. However, at older reservations such as Hoopa, Round Valley, and Tule River, populations decreased from 30 to 50 percent due primarily to disenchantment with reservation management and continued sicknesses. Despite these disadvantages and hardships the majority of natives within the state struggled to survive by farming small subsistence gardens in addition to laboring off-reservation. Unfortunately, due to their unfamiliarity with the White economy and the controversy surrounding their legal status most Indians were not able to make subsistence farming and outside labor provide a steady economic base.

Although outside labor was generally available settlers universally took advantage of Indians in every way possible. Heavy manual farm labor constituted employment opportunities for both men and women. Gross fraud in the payment of wages was the most common form of labor exploitation. In many instances goods of one kind or another, generally of no account to them, were given in lieu of money so as to make the price of a day's labor to the employers not to exceed 10¢. It was not uncommon to dock laborers for imaginary neglect or fail to pay them altogether. Still other employers insisted on doling out Indian wages in cheap liquor, which further contributed to a lack of steady work habits that developed due to this rampant labor exploitation (Cook 1943b:46-75).

Outside labor, despite its disadvantages, became imperative as foreigners rapidly overran former native landholdings. While Indian agents and tribes on government reserves struggled to turn back encroaching squatters, nonreservation natives found their villages preempted by homesteaders or part of newly confirmed Spanish and Mexican land grants. Government agents in southern California reported in 1877 that Indians had already been driven from the best land and that their villages were threatened by White settlers who set up claims of a more or less valid character on almost every village site. Although most Indian tribes and individuals claimed their villages and surrounding territory by right of "immemorial possession," a few Indians even attempted to confirm their various claims through the court system. In 1879 two Luiseño Indians, Jose and Pablo Apis, attempted to have the District Court of California confirm their claim to a two-league grant to the La Jolla Rancheria. Because this grant had other antecedent claims on it, the court decided the Apis brothers could not prove they had continued possession and the confirmation was denied (Gates 1971:416). Even where Indians were relatively secure in their landholdings, neighboring Whites frequently interfered with their water supply and imposed exhorbitant fines for damages done by Indian livestock, sometimes confiscating their stock altogether.

Although President Grant's "Quaker policy" was supposed to have introduced reform into the Bureau of Indian Affairs, few innovations were inaugurated. Controversy and mismanagement continued to characterize the government's efforts for California Indians. Native peoples in the southern part of the state were finally given a reservation under an executive order in January 1870 that established the San Pasqual Pala Reservation. Immediately, local citizens enraged at the thought of giving land to the Indians carried on an abusive crusade in San Diego newspapers against the establishment of the reservation. Indians were afraid to locate on the proposed reservation after hostile settlers threatened to kill any Indians who might do so. A deluge of protest regarding the reservation from local squatters persuaded the government to have the reservation returned to the public domain (ARCIA 1870:92). In the San Joaquin Valley a new Tule River reservation was set aside by executive order in 1873, but removal to the proposed reserve of Indians and government property was prevented when government inspectors condemned it as unsuitable for reservation purposes. In 1877 another reservation was established on the waters of the Tule River embracing 91,837 acres. This site was approved and natives were removed to their new home. Southern Indians gained relief between 1875 and 1877 when a series of executive orders created 13 separate reservations for the so-called Mission Indians (Ipai and Tipai, Luiseño, Serrano, Cupeño, and Cahuilla although some of these peoples were never really missionized). These reservations, which together reserved over 203 square miles or 130,000 acres of land to southern California Indians, were usually located on or near native villages. Over the next 30 years they sometimes had various parts returned to the public domain or enlarged by acts of Congress. Unlike larger reservations to the north, the Mission Indian reservations were administered from one central agency located in San Bernardino. This made contact with the Indians difficult since some of the reservations were over 100 miles away. These reservations served as the first of many moderate-sized reservations to be established for the homeless "Mission Indians" (Dale 1949:80-94).

Church influences in the Indian Service prompted the inauguration of the first government efforts at providing elementary education for California Indians. In 1871 government day schools were established on the reservations at Hoopa Valley and Round Valley. About 100 students were enrolled at Round Valley with an average attendance of 45, while at Hoopa attendance was considerably lower. Many traditionalists among the Indians opposed education and missionary work on the reservations, believing that these institutions were contributing to the undermining and disintegration of native culture. At Hoopa the traditionalist influence prevailed and ultimately caused the school to be closed in 1876 due to lack of attendance (ARCIA 1876:12–14).

Despite the progress made in establishing new reservations and schools for native people, the Indian Service continued to suffer from mismanagement and incompetence. The Indian agent at Hoopa Valley without government authorization allowed White sharecroppers to harvest grain on the reservation in 1876 in return for a percentage of the total harvest. Apparently this situation proved so scandalous that the agent was removed and the administration of the reservations was turned over to the army. The military authorities were shocked to discover that the former agent had allowed the gristmill, houses, barns, and sawmill to fall into a dilapidated and useless condition. Even more shocking was the realization that the former agent had sold wagons, thrashing machines, reapers, mowers, and other farm tools to neighboring Whites at mere nominal costs. This caused considerable discontent among the Indians who wanted to farm their land but were unable to because their tools had been sold. It was also discovered that the agent had sold Indian Service hay to the army for $44.00 a ton while offering it to local Whites for $1.50 per ton. Unfortunately fraud and misconduct were not confined to Hoopa. The Tule River agent reported in 1879 that a large grove of valuable timber on the reservation could not be used by the Indians:

I would therefore recommend the restoration to the public domain a strip four miles wide along the entire eastern boundary of the reservation. This would enable the people living in the plain country to open up roads to this timber and supply themselves with lumber . . . The government would also realize a profit, if not directly in the sale of this timber, indirectly in the improvement of large tracts of lands contiguous to it. Justice would then be meted out to all parties, and every pretext for complaint of the Indian service removed. Citizens would have their just rights and the timber be taken where Providence evidently designed it should (ARCIA 1879:12).

By the end of the decade, it was painfully apparent that President Grant's "Quaker policy" had failed to bring about reform of the Indian Service and had in fact merely introduced the church as yet another hostile factor to the situation confronting California natives. Final admission by the government of its failure to bring about reform of the Indian Service was evident when the government stopped assigning Indian agents from the Episcopalian orders after 1881.

Land Status and Legal Status

Over the next two decades the federal government became increasingly concerned with providing education to Indian people throughout the country. At this time sentiment within the federal government strongly favored the detribalization of Indian people and their gradual integration into the economy of the nation.

Since tribes could no longer support themselves due to the destruction of their traditional economy, the government proposed to train the Indians in the ways of Whites so that they might survive. In order to achieve this, the government set out upon a course of self-righteous suppression and destruction of all vestiges of tribalism and Indian culture. The philosophy, methods, and objectives of Indian education were originated at Carlisle, the first federal boarding school. With acculturation as a rationale, the method of enforcement was coercion. Indian youths were abducted from their homes, to be taught basic English and vocational trades. Native languages were forbidden and all aspects of Indian culture and values were suppressed. The government also hoped to benefit from this policy because they reasoned that a detribalization policy would result in assimilated Indians willing to sell the millions of acres of valuable land still held by tribes nationwide. It was within this framework of national policy that the educational programs for California Indians were established.

In California three types of educational programs were established for native peoples. The first was the federal government reservation day school. The second type was the boarding school fashioned after Carlisle. And finally, the nearby public school that allowed Indians to attend began a slow though steady increase in popularity among policymakers.

Although the Indian Service reservation day school was introduced in California a decade earlier, the real effort to establish widespread elementary education for native peoples began in 1881. This action was primarily taken to establish day schools for the thousands of Indians under the newly established Mission Agency reservations in southern California. The number of day schools throughout the state increased until 1888, when the Indian Service ruled that schools with fewer than 20 students be closed. After this time a steady decrease in the number of day schools occurred as it became more difficult to fill the classroom from a steadily decreasing Indian population. The day school had many obstacles to success. In drought years large decreases in school attendance were noted as parents took their children from their arid reservations in search of work. Another serious problem resulted from the gathering of Indian children in small ill-ventilated school rooms, which inevitably spread communicable disease. Sickness resulting in absenteeism closed many day schools throughout this period. Perhaps the greatest obstacle to the success of the day school was opposition from parents who "objected to the school because they wish their children to grow up as Indians" (ARCIA 1891:220).

Older Indians quickly recognized the threat the schools offered to Indian culture and values. As a result considerable resistance to the schools developed. Native peoples destroyed the day school at Potrero in 1888 and burned the school at Tule River in 1890. At Pachanga a

Luiseño named Venturo Molido burned the school and assassinated the school teacher in 1895 (ARCIA 1895:131). Despite widespread opposition to the day school, native people were to learn they were far less destructive of Indian communities than boarding schools.

According to the Carlisle government school philosophy, the best way to make an Indian assimilate into the White world was to remove him from the "corrupting and backward" influences of his parents. To carry out this philosophy, which the Indian Service made mandate, the government introduced the boarding school to California in 1881 at Tule River Reservation. Boarding schools were established at Round Valley in 1883, Middletown in Lake County in 1885, Hoopa Valley Reservation and Perris in 1893, and Fort Bidwell in 1898.

The Indian Service made school attendance compulsory in 1891. Typical recruitment methods practiced by Indian agents were included in this agency report from Hoopa: "to compel the children to attend school he [the agent] has decided that no issue of clothing will be made to the children unless they go to the agency school" (ARCIA 1883:15). Boarding school attendance had an even greater effect upon the lives of Indians than the day school. For instance, severe mental anguish resulted from the forced separation of children from their families. Similar to earlier indenture laws and slavery, boarding schools practiced what they called an "outing system" (Pratt 1964). This was a system in which Indian children were used as domestics in nearby White homes, which served the dual purpose of preventing children from visiting their families during vacations while exploiting their labor with only token remuneration.

Like the day schools, boarding schools were plagued with infectious diseases and encountered stiff opposition from students and parents alike. When the Mission Agency boarding school at Perris, California, first opened, an epidemic of influenza attacked 80 percent of the children and nearly caused the school to close. Student opposition to conditions within these institutions was forcibly expressed when five boys at the Round Valley School burned it to the ground in 1883. Yet despite their unpopularity among California natives the boarding school enjoyed the enthusiastic support of the Indian Service and continued to replace and supplant the day school system.

Together with the education program the Indian Service's "Civilization Division" helped create a mechanism for the extension of health services to California Indians. This was prompted by the realization that the Indian population was continuing to decrease due primarily to sickness, poor living conditions, and extreme poverty. There is no evidence that a system of health care was established in the state before 1890. That year it was reported that a few doctors were contracted to periodically administer health care to Indians within the various agencies of the state. Another feature of this program was the introduction of field matrons who acted as practical nurses and provided sanitary advice to native households. Yet little good resulted from these early efforts at health care. Because of long distances between reservations and agency headquarters, doctors could not effectively reach those in most need. Further illnesses were universally complicated by the undernutrition and lack of adequate shelter. Finally this program intensified the persecution of native medicine men already hounded by Christian missionaries and school officials.

Between 1880 and 1900 two diametrically opposed forces within the government shaped the land situation in California. The first was the Dawes Severalty Act of 1887. This law was aimed primarily at large eastern tribes and called for the breaking up of communal tribal landholdings and the allotment of 160 acres of reservation land to family heads. The philosophy behind this law was forced assimilation of the Indian into the White landholding system of private property. On the other hand the acquisition of numerous reservations was authorized by an Act of Congress dated January 12, 1891 (26 Stat. 712-714) and amended in 1898. These acts were responsible for the purchase of nearly all the 17 reservations established during this period. These opposing tendencies—breaking up tribal landholdings while establishing tribal landholdings—confused the Indians, created suspicion and distrust, and finally added to problems already facing various reservations throughout the state.

Fourteen of the 17 reservations established were in the Mission Agency of southern California. Although the amount of land granted the "Mission Indians" under this and earlier acts was large, nine-tenths of it was practically worthless. Most southern California reservations were barren and unable to support their populations. Lack of adequate water supply was the major reason for this situation, which was "brought about by the White settlers diverting the waters of streams . . . from which the Indians obtain their supply of water" (ARCIA 1897:117).

Other complications occurred when the railroads were granted alternate sections of land along their right of way. Many reservations became chopped up in checkerboard fashion. Oftentimes Indians found their villages or fields belonged to the railroads. A lack of clearly identifiable boundary markers for many reservations created problems as squatters began to encroach upon Indian lands. In 1888 the government got tough with these interlopers and successfully removed them from Morongo and Capitan Grande reservations. However, when it attempted to do the same in the long-troubled Round Valley Reservation, the squatters got an injunction against the army and succeeded in preventing the government from consolidating the reservation.

While the government was attempting to establish reservations for the state's native peoples it was at the same time trying to comply with the Dawes Act. Native people understood full well the implications of allotment and offered considerable resistance. Nevertheless the Bureau of Indian Affairs began ordering allotments of various sizes at Rincon, Morongo, and Pala reservations in 1893. The next year allotments were begun at Round Valley Reservation. By the turn of the century 1,615 individual allotments were made among eight reservations in the state. Although most tribes were coerced into agreeing to the dividing up of their reservation landholdings the Ipai-Tipai at Mesa Grande refused to be intimidated and threatened to kill any allotment agents on the reservation.

Surprisingly, the government, prompted by concerned liberals in the East, began to fight legal battles to assist Indians threatened by ejection from confirmed Mexican land grants. In 1885 the Bureau of Indian Affairs employed an attorney to defend tribes in such cases. The Indian Rights Association paid all legal costs and received a favorable decision in the State Supreme Court case *Byrne* v. *Alas et al.* in 1888. The court ruled that Indians could not be legally ejected from Mexican land grants. At this time the Cupeños from Warner's Ranch began a suit to stop their eviction (fig. 5) that ultimately reached the Supreme Court.

The two decades before the turn of the century might be characterized as an era of acculturation under duress;

however, the deliberate undermining of native culture by government education, health programs, and allotment did not go unanswered. Although resistance was haphazard it was continous. In 1886 the Indians at Tule River burned the agency headquarters. The steady destruction of schools might also be characterized as a form of resistance. Native people successfully harassed and destroyed private property of Indians who collaborated too readily with the Indian Service. Field matrons were evicted from reservations when they attempted to lay claim to reservation property. Finally, the outright refusal by some natives to comply with allotment policies points out native determination to resist total submission.

While widespread attention by the government was called to instances of resistance, little recognition was given native-initiated adaptation to their rapidly changing world. When the Luiseño at Temecula were evicted by White squatters in 1882 they relocated from the valleys to the foothills where they dug wells with great labor to develop domestic waters. Even more significant was the adaptation and initiative shown by the small band of Yokayo Pomos who successfully purchased their own home site in 1881. At this time no reservation or government assistance was provided for these people. Recognizing that their entire tribe and culture might disintegrate if they could not stay together, their headmen decided to purchase a tract of good land for their people. After collecting nearly $1,000 from their people the

Fig. 5. Cupeño Indians' camp on Pauma Ranch after their eviction from their traditional home at the hot springs of Warner's Ranch (Agua Caliente). Photograph by Sawyer of the *Los Angeles Herald*, May 1903.

117

THE IMPACT OF EURO-AMERICAN EXPLORATION AND SETTLEMENT

headmen selected a 120-acre site near the Russian River and made the down payment. The Yokayo group prospered; they paid the entire balance owed on their land and even saved enough to purchase farm machinery shortly thereafter (Kasch 1947).

By 1900, after 131 years of foreign colonization and domination, there were approximately 16,000 to 17,000 native Californians (Kroeber 1957a). Yet the Indian Service reported in 1900 that only 5,497 had received government aid of any kind and of that number 1,317 received only education and medical services (ARCIA 1900:638). The Indian Service through administrative fiat alone denied welfare aid and health services to nonreservation Indians, which through a confusion of authority resulted in state and county aid being withheld to these unfortunate bands and individuals as well. There can be no doubt that the impact of this drastic demographic change and hardships had reduced these once-proud owners of this land to a severely demoralized and hopeless condition. Government reports and Indian testimony constantly called attention to the widespread hunger and destitution Indians suffered during the years after the turn of the century. This testimony by an Ipai-Tipai woman serves to illustrate not only the hunger that haunted her people but also the cultural breakdown that accompanied it: "Some Indians made necklaces of shells, but we didn't. We always needed more food; we were poor and never had time for necklaces. I don't know how to make those things now, only how to find food" (Cuero 1968: 57).

Indeed conditions did seem to be worse than ever; however, the humanitarianism in which White Americans take such an inordinate pride did manage to stir a few reformers to take an active interest in the welfare of California Indians.

Although Indian Service response to Indian welfare organizations varied from cooperation to federal indictments for conspiracy against the government, the Bureau of Indian Affairs was embarrassed into action. In 1906 Congress authorized an investigation into the conditions among homeless Indians in California and the development of some plan for their improvement. This resulted in the appropriation of $100,000 for purchase of land and water development for the state's native people (34 Stat. 333).

Indian interest groups brought pressure on the government to provide better health services as well as more land. State health authorities argued that since Indians lived on nontaxpaying reservations, they must look to federal authorities for health care. In response to this and some progressive public concern the Indian Service gradually began to expand its services. In 1912 Congress initiated a survey of Indian health conditions that reported that Indian people suffered a 15 percent overall infection of tuberculosis as well as trachoma, an infectious eye disease that eventually causes blindness. At

federal boarding schools these rates were considerably higher due to inadequate sanitary conditions.

The first permanent Indian hospital established in California was located at the new nonreservation boarding school Sherman Institute at Riverside in 1901. By 1930 six others were in operation throughout the state. In 1924 public health nurses were allowed to assist in the Indian Service health work.

Despite the Indian Service's establishment of a separate administrative division for health in 1924, the effectiveness of its program must be regarded with severe doubt. Serious problems for the state's native people developed when by administrative fiat alone the Bureau of Indian Affairs decided to limit health care to reservation residents, thus leaving perhaps as many as one-third of the state's Indians in a legal limbo. These unfortunate bands and individuals were denied state health care because they were Indians and unable to get help from the federal government because they had no land. Substandard or incompetent care in tuberculosis institutions probably accounted for the fact that these early hospitals had a reputation for being places where people went to suffer and die. Charges of criminal neglect and incompetence were often leveled against the health service personnel. A severe smallpox epidemic among Pit River tribes in the winter of 1921-1922, complicated by starvation and a lack of medical care, prompted the government to launch an investigation into charges of willful neglect against the health service in 1929 (U.S. Congress. Senate. Subcommittee on Indian Affairs 1929-1939: 579). Perhaps sensing the severe shortcomings of the health program the government later admitted that "even if they [government doctors] provided minimally satisfactory medical treatment they took too little interest in related aspects of Indian community life" (Raup 1959:12). By ignoring the impact of poverty and starvation and its relation to general health conditions, the government shifted attention from its failings by stepping up attacks on shamans and blaming their influences for poor sanitary conditions.

Land problems continued to be a paramount issue to the survival of Indians as a people. Responding to pressure groups and Indian demands Congress initiated a series of acts beginning in 1906 to provide land for homeless Indians in California. By 1930, 36 reservations were set aside for native Californians. These reservations were scattered throughout 16 northern counties and were mostly home sites or rancherias between five and a few hundred acres each. In southern California none of the many landless bands or individuals were provided with home sites as a result of these appropriations. For the most part these federal funds were used to enlarge existing reservations and improve water systems. Although the establishment of these reservations and rancherias was of immense importance, still there were millions of acres of land excellent for agriculture, grazing, and timber held by the government at this time, so little of it was made available to native people.

An important part of native land problems was the almost complete lack of domestic water and irrigation systems on reservations throughout the state, particularly in the south. The federal government began to develop water projects for California Indians with funds provided by Congress in 1906. Shortly the Bureau of Indian Affairs began digging wells on several Mission Agency reservations. These projects brought temporary relief; however, not all government water systems were satisfactory. For instance the Sequoya League reported in 1906 that an extraordinarily expensive ($18,000) water system was built at Pala Reservation by the Bureau of Indian Affairs. This expensive project was a dozen times larger than there was land or water to irrigate. Furthermore, this engineering disaster was built on the side of a hill and incapable of delivering any water whatsoever! Despite the tribes' desperate need for water, irrigation projects caused intertribal controversies because the Indian Service conceived and carried out these programs with little or no consultation with reservation residents. During the 1920s tribesmen complained that irrigation projects were often constructed by the Indian Service with liens on allotted reservation lands. The right of Indians to water and the duty of the Indian Service to protect that right gradually became an issue as the government began to construct water projects. Unfortunately, the Indian Service seriously neglected its duty over the years. The Indian Service seemed very reluctant to bring those persons who impinged upon native water rights to court, as in the case of a White man near Palm Springs, who had diverted Indian water by building an irrigation project across the reservation. Instead of prosecuting him, the BIA simply bought his water project. In another case, 17 Indians from the Campo Reservation were convicted of tearing up an irrigation pipeline belonging to White ranchers. Apparently these Whites had diverted water upstream and laid a water pipe across a section of the reservation. The Bureau of Indian Affairs offered no legal advice or assistance to these people.

After the turn of the century the government's allotment program continued to force native people to accept the White system of private ownership of property by dividing native communal property into individual parcels of various size. By 1930 approximately 2,300 allotments had been made throughout the state. Yet a considerable number of these were surrendered or canceled because Congress failed to appropriate the necessary money. Nevertheless, a general opposition by more traditional native people continued against the detribalizing aims of the Allotment Act. Confidence in the Indian Service suffered as Congress failed to provide support. Failure of the Bureau of Indian Affairs to confirm tentative allotments created an atmosphere of suspicion and distrust, even among Indians who cooperated with the government. At Palm Springs a team of surveyors entered the reservation in 1924 despite protests that the tribe had not been consulted as to their feelings about allotment. In response the headmen wired twice to the secretary of the interior:

We protest and ask that action be stopped at once and the Indians consulted.
We were not notified and don't want allotments, we have patent to our lands and want to hold them always together. Please stop surveyors . . .

Pedro Chino,
Capt. Francisca Patencio,
Lee Arenas (Anonymous 1923)

There can be no doubt that the Bureau of Indian Affairs used allotment in an attempt to divide Indian communities and keep them politically impotent. The 1920s witnessed a series of court suits and countersuits among native communities over the distribution of allotments. These actions had the general effect of planting the seeds of family feuds among various tribes, the destructive and divisive influences of which still plague native communities today. At the head of organized opposition to allotment was the Mission Indian Federation. In a newspaper interview, Federation President Adam Castillo outlined the Indian Service's methods of securing allotments at the cost of disrupting native community life:

Non-Federation Indians, some from out of the county, were prevailed upon by H. E. Wadsworth, Special Indian Agent, sent to fix the claims to file for lands already cultivated. None of the allotees could point out as to where their land was located nor prove the lands were selected by them. Only those that were in good graces of the Indian agent and the government farmer had chosen land occupied by old Indians. Those living off the reservations never applied for nor selected any allotments. Mr. Wadsworth came to them as solicitor and persuaded them to fill out applications for five acre allotments (Castillo 1931).

Widespread opposition to the Dawes Act along with the realization by the government that allotted Indians were unable to compete economically in the American capitalistic-corporate society and that society was reluctant to accept Indians as equals, all prompted the Indian Services to begin to extend trusteeship over allotted lands for periods upward of 10 years. The result of this step was the total disruption of goals of the Dawes Severalty Act.

Years of effort by Indians and their White allies to secure title to Indian villages on confirmed Mexican land grants came to a tragic climax in 1901. Despite earlier favorable court decisions in 1888 (*Byrne* v. *Alas*) the United States Supreme Court decided in 1901 against the right of the Cupeño Indians to retain their homes at Warner's Hot Springs in *Barker* v. *Harvey* (181 U.S. 481). The Indians argued that Mexican law and Article 8 of the Treaty of Guadalupe Hidalgo recognized Indian right to villages on land grants, but the Court decided that: the Indians had failed to present their case to the Land Commission in the allotted time, the BIA had failed to bring about legislation to reaffirm title to these Indians, and the land actually belonged to Mission San Diego, which reported the land abandoned. This decision affected over 250 Indians scattered throughout several villages on confirmed land grants. At several villages native families locked themselves in their homes as sheriff's deputies broke down their doors with axes to evict them. With considerable pressure Indian interest groups forced Congress to appoint a commission to provide new homes for these evicted natives. Soon a ranch in the Pala Valley was purchased and the dispossessed Cupeños removed to it in 1902 (ARCIA 1903:79).

Other bizarre land problems developed. In 1904 the Tule River Indian agent reported that several White men were making large claims on portions of timberland within the eastern border of the reservation. These White men claimed to have had patent to this land and had begun to cut timber. A survey indicated that extensive fraud had been perpetrated to gain possession of this most valuable asset of the reservation. Twenty-nine years later the Bureau of Indian Affairs reported that the city of San Diego condemned the El Capitan Reservation to establish a municipal water system. The Indian Service did not fight the condemnation proceedings, and the Indians were displaced. These problems and others like them made most responsible Indian leaders extremely cynical about the government's role as protector of Indian interests.

Like the Allotment Act, the government education system was aimed primarily at detribalizing California Indians. After 1900 the Indian Service began to realize that the best method of reaching this goal would be the widespread enrollment of native children in public schools. After 1917 the Bureau of Indian Affairs began making contractual agreements with the State Department of Education for paying cost in lieu of taxes for the admission of Indian students to public schools where available (a few native children were admitted to public schools under similar circumstances as early as 1881). However, racial and cultural intolerance against native children was widespread and prevalent. Segregated public schools for Indian children were established in some areas. It was also common for Indian children to be refused admittance to public schools because they lacked shoes and clothing. After 1917 a relative decline in federal Indian school construction and attendance occurred and the public school Indian enrollments soared.

Despite the increased enrollment in public schools, as many as one-third of all Indian students continued to attend federal Indian schools until 1948. Unlike the public schools, the Bureau of Indian Affairs schools always included vocational training. This training was built upon the concept of the Indian girl as an ultimate house servant and the Indian boy as a farm hand. These schools were habitually plagued by institutional problems. For example, before the Depression a special investigating committee complained that the 20¢ a day subsistence allowance for each student was not enough to provide the minimum protein requirements. School officials argued inadequate funding forced them to rely too heavily upon students for purely institutional upkeep. In 1929 Congressional hearings revealed that at some schools Indian children were continually exhausted from this type of work while many White employees held outside jobs. In 1931 the commissioner of Indian affairs reported that several cases of brutality to Indian children resulted in the dismissal of several employees from the service. At Hoopa, the government school made Christian church services and Sunday school mandatory. By far the greatest institutional obstacle to successful federal schooling was the enormous annual turnover in teachers, sometimes as high as 48 percent. These problems were obvious to students who in response reacted negatively to the oppressive atmosphere surrounding them. At Round Valley Boarding School students burned down the girls' dormitory in 1911. The next year the temporary dormitory was set fire twice. Finally in 1914 the boys attempted to burn their dormitory twice and succeeded in destorying the main school building. However, the most common form of resistance offered (like resistance to the mission system) was simply to withdraw. In 1926 the government could not report one student in any grade above 10. They simply quit. Noted educator Georganna Caroline Carden commented upon the overall education of California Indian children in 1926: "Their education has been perfunctory characterized at best by condescending kindliness and at worst by well-nigh criminal neglect" (Carden 1944).

In general, the whole atmosphere of forced assimilation of the Indian into White ways was the result of undemocratic decision-making within the Bureau of Indian Affairs. The years between the turn of the century and depression were characterized by greater and greater interference by the Indian Service in every aspect of native life. Reservation leaders found it impossible to secure tribal funds for urgent reservation needs, because the Bureau of Indian Affairs controlled all funds. The Indian Service continued to appoint reservation leaders over traditional or popularly elected leaders. One of the most damaging aspects of the government's interference in native community life was its increased persecution of native customs and religious practices. In 1902 the Bureau of Indian Affairs advised reservation agents:

You are therefore directed to induce your male Indians to cut their hair, and both sexes to stop painting. . . . Noncompliance with this order may be made a reason for discharge or for withholding rations and supplies . . . Indian dances and so-called Indian feasts should be prohibited. . . . Feasts are simply subterfuges to cover degrading acts and to disguise immoral purposes. . . . The government has a right to expect a proper observance of rules established for their good. . . . There was no idea of interfering with the Indian's personal liberty . . . (ARCIA 1903:14-15).

To resist these laws and the great psychological pressure to conform to White society's standards required a great tenacity of spirit that seemed to sustain native resistance throughout their history. Through the Indian Service's failure to adequately protect native water rights and a lack of suitable land, reservations continued to be non-self-supporting, forcing the Indians to seek employment in the White community.

This control and manipulation of Indians undoubtedly contributed to the mutual distrust and contempt between natives and Indian Service personnel. Reacting to the stifling paternalism of the Indian Bureau, a number of Indians at the Cahuilla Reservation killed the resident agent in 1913. As in earlier periods, reservation agents continued to bring scandal to the Bureau of Indian Affairs. The Indian agent at Morongo Reservation stole $40,000 from his jurisdiction in 1929. Two years earlier, Indian Agent George J. Robinson and two sheriff's deputies were charged with murdering two Indians on the Campo Reservation.

By 1917 the legal status of the California Indian became a puzzling and confused issue. Without a doubt some Indians had for many years been regarded by the state and federal governments as citizens, paying taxes and voting. This became apparent when the federal government began to draft some Indians for the First World War. Although many were drafted many more noncitizen Indians enlisted and served with distinction in Europe. Partially in gratitude for their service in the First World War and partially to further assimilation goals of the government, in 1924 Congress conferred citizenship upon all Indians born in the United States. However, the BIA interpreted the granting of citizenship as not affecting its authority over the tribal and individual property of Indians and therefore insured its continual control over Indian lives, property, and resources by extraconstitutional means.

In 1930 the native population in the state numbered about 19,212 persons, of which approximately one-half lived on reservations, while the remainder generally lived in nearby rural communities. The conditions of native communities for the years during and after the Depression were characterized by complicated and often contradictory Bureau of Indian Affairs policies, which continued to hamper native community and economic adaptation. Under the New Deal, Commissioner of Indian Affairs John Collier commented upon effects of its earlier policies:

As this [native] leadership was destroyed, it became more and more necessary for the government to deal with Indians as individuals, which, of course, served still further to destroy leadership, and thus set up a vicious circle of bureaucratic paternalism and resulted in disorganization among the Indians. This knifing of Indian leadership and emasculation of tribal organization, further aided by the separation of the Indian from his land and the destruction of his land estate through forced allotments, did work havoc with Indian culture, Indian energy, Indian group capacity, and Indian citizenship, but they were not effective in totally destroying the local democracy of the Indians (ARCIA 1941:13).

Government Indian policy after 1930 largely revolved around two opposing philosophies. The first of these called for a reconstitution of Indian tribes while the other simply demanded the withdrawal of all governmental services to Indians.

The earliest of these philosophies crystallized under Indian Commissioner Collier. Briefly Indian policy took a different direction as a result of the Wheeler-Howard Act (Indian Reorganization Act) of 1934. This legislation did three important things: it offered tribes an opportunity to reestablish corporate governments under certain regulation (previously outlawed by the Dawes Act of 1887 and the Curtis Act of 1898), it repealed the Dawes Act and stopped allotment, and finally it provided a revolving loan fund to stimulate tribal economic development. In support of the Indian Reorganization Act, Collier explained what had been obvious to native people all along, that the allotment law was a disaster. It was "principally an instrument to deprive Indians of their lands . . . of the lands owned by Indians in 1887 the year of the allotment law two-thirds have been lost by various processes of dissipation" (U.S. Department of the Interior 1933:108). It is significant that this legislation came in the middle of the nation's worst depression; perhaps the government found it absurd to preach rugged individualism to Indians while the entire economic order of America was collapsing. Ten California reservations and rancherias reconstituted themselves under Reorganization Act laws, while many others adopted other forms of governing councils to avoid the paternalistic overtones of Reorganization Act governments. Unfortunately, due to bureaucratic inertia, especially in the middle and upper echelons of the Indian Service, neither the tribes nor Collier could bring about overall reform in Indian policy. Reform depended upon the goodwill of Congress while power ultimately rested at the national and regional level and not at the democratically oriented tribal level. When the war came, budget cuts occurred as the nation turned to other concerns.

During the Second World War thousands of California Indians served in the armed forces. While many men were away, reservation economy underwent something of a boom. The Department of the Interior reported that although in the war year of 1944 individual income was approximately two and one-half times that of the 1938 level, one-third of the Indian families resident on the reservation still had annual incomes of less than $500 and nearly two-thirds received less than $1,000 (U.S. Department of the Interior 1946:351). Even Indian groups with potentially multimillion-dollar land assets, like the Palm Springs Cahuilla, were unable to gain control of their land. These Indians were forced by the courts to grant security liens on their lands for questionable attorneys' fees and lived in abject poverty for many years.

The end of allotment brought a halt to the division of Indian trust lands and inaugurated attempts by the government to supplement existing reservations with grants of additional lands. Between 1933 and 1941 the Congress purchased approximately 6,492 acres of land adjacent to four southern California reservations.

While the native population slowly increased, health problems continued to plague Indian communities. Poor living conditions and poverty remained the root causes behind chronic infections of tuberculosis, trachoma, pneumonia, and other respiratory diseases. In response the government built and staffed six Indian hospitals in the state before the war, with a total capacity of only 164 beds. In 1938 the discovery of sulfanilamide made possible the treatment and cure of the painful and blinding trachoma eye disease.

Yet, despite this hopeful improvement in health service, the government at the same time expressed its intention to transfer its health responsibility to local, county, and state facilities as recommended in both the Meriam Survey of 1928 (Brookings Institution, Washington, Institute for Government Research) and the Hoover Commission survey of 1948. As a result of the 1948 recommendations, which included the government's termination policy, all BIA health services to California Indians were ended in 1955. As usual this policy was adopted without legislative authorization and despite protests by Indian people. There can be no doubt that the ending of health care and the closing of the Indian hospitals created unnecessary suffering and a confusion over county, state, and federal responsibility for Indian health needs. In April 1956 hundreds of Southern California Indians protested government policy: "We Indians urgently request Congress to re-open the Soboba Indian Hospital located at the Soboba Indian Reservation, Riverside, California, for the Indians that need medical care. At present, many Indians report that they have been turned down, when they try to enter the county hospital, and finally being accepted only when it is too late, in many cases death being the result"

(California Legislature. Senate Interim Committee on California Indian Affairs 1957:55). Unfortunately, this confused situation continued for California Indians until 1969.

In the late 1920s and early 1930s the Indian Service continued to abandon the federal day schools throughout the state and began to limit enrollment of California Indian students at Sherman Institute. As a result, native children were admitted to public schools in ever-increasing numbers.

Termination

After the war, as the United States spent millions of dollars rebuilding Germany and Japan, the government hoped to rid itself of its embarassing failure to "rebuild" Indian nations by simply withdrawing government aid to Indian people. This philosophy was expressed in the Hoover Commission survey of 1948. Indeed that year the Bureau of Indian Affairs declared its intention to "terminate" all government services to all Indians and divide their tribal assets (land and resources) among individuals. This so-called new policy was little more than a warmed-over version of the Allotment Act. Its implementation would detribalize native groups and put their property on tax rolls as well as repudiate the federal government's moral commitment and responsibility to aid the people whose poverty and powerlessness it had created.

California Indian tribes were to be among the first targets for termination. The commissioner of Indian affairs who inaugurated this policy, Dillon Meyer, was principally known as the man responsible for administering Japanese-American concentration camps during World War II. In 1952 the Bureau of Indian Affairs began to energetically push termination: the Indian Service introduced to Congress several termination bills specifically for California, and in anticipation of that policy the government ended all Indian Service welfare payments to pauper Indians in the state. In addition, the Indian Service began an accounting and inventory survey of all government property buildings and equipment, while the BIA sold 129 allotments and closed the accounts of hundreds of Indians having money in trust. In 1953 Congress passed Public Law 280, which brought California Indian reservations under the criminal and civil jurisdiction of the state. This was significant because before this time some tribes were able to exercise police powers in their own community. In 1953 also the California State Senate created the Senate Interim Committee on Indian Affairs, composed entirely of non-Indians, to aid the federal government in making the transition of Indian Services and property to state jurisdiction. This committee made inquiries and wrote recommendations, most of which were ignored.

It soon became apparent to the government that the Indians did not want termination. In fact, all the government's preliminary actions for termination caused considerable suffering and confusion among Indians whose many services had already been abruptly cut off, while county and state agencies were expected to fill the void. In 1953 the county of San Diego refused to provide welfare for a reservation Indian on grounds that reservation residence made her ineligible. In *Acosta* v. *County of San Diego* the court ruled that residence on an Indian reservation does not disqualify an Indian otherwise eligible for general assistance. Other problems with the termination policy arose. In 1956 Indians complained to the governor that Section 2B of Public Law 280 was being violated by the state as welfare and old-age pensions were cut off because Indians refused to sell their land. At a large and representative meeting of southern California Indians during that year, a petition was sent to the state:

We Indians request the repeal of Public Law 280. This has not worked out because the sheriffs are called and do not come. In cases they have been known to arrive three or four days later, when emergencies were reported. Indians are afraid to sign complaints since the sheriffs do not come when called and they are afraid they will be beaten, for without the law to turn to what can they do? One evening the sheriffs were called and did not come out. That same evening a murder took place. No sheriff came out until they were called again the following day (California. Legislature. Senate Interim Committee on California Indian Affairs 1957:55).

Overall the undemocratic policymakers who literally attempted to stampede Indians into termination were generally opposed by a majority of tribes and rancherias who knew better than anyone that it would destroy their culture and rob them of their lands.

The longer the controversy over termination raged the more arbitrary and scandalous the BIA's coercion of disorganized and powerless rancherias became. Hoping to gain quick legislative authorization for its questionable policies ending nearly all federal services for the state's native people Congress acted in 1958 by passing the Rancheria Act (27 Stat. 619 as amended by 78 Stat. 390). This act authorized the method by which Indian groups could vote to terminate themselves. Considerable pressure and persuasion were used to encourage Indians, especially small and powerless rancherias, to agree to terminate. Surely few of the people who came under those pressures knew or understood their rights on trust property or the consequences of losing the trust status of their land. Eventually 36 rancherias voted to terminate for financial reasons, which resulted in the loss of 5,000 acres of trust property.

The decade of the 1960s witnessed the long and drawn-out battles between Indian leadership and the government to gain compensation for nineteenth-century land losses through the Land Claims cases (see "Litigation and Its Effects," this vol.). Government pol-

icy throughout this period continued to attempt the gradual withdrawal of the remaining government services to the state's Indians. Although the state legislature opposed termination in 1954, the state government created the successor to the Senate Interim Committee on Indian Affairs in 1961, called the State Advisory Commission on Indian Affairs. This commission was to investigate and make recommendations regarding termination and other aspects of Indian policy. All Commission members were non-Indian. This paternalistic approach toward Indian problems caused native people to react when a bill that would have made the commission a powerful state agency was introduced to the legislature in 1968. Indians managed to amend the bill so it would establish an all-Indian commission. However, the state's elitist posture was obvious when the commission chairman, Sen. William Coombs, killed the bill in committee. The commission ran into further problems the next year when the California Indian Education Association brought two lawsuits against it dealing with the "open meetings and public record laws" and immunity of legislators from civil process.

Yet another Bureau of Indian Affairs program that seriously affected the California Indians' political position in the state was the government's relocation program (employment assistance). This program was part of the government's nationwide attempt to depopulate reservations by bringing Indians into urban areas for vocational training and job assistance. The Bureau of Indian Affairs hoped that the Indians would remain in the city and gradually disappear into the melting pot of the urban proletariat. The government estimates that since the beginning of the relocation program as many as 60,000 to 70,000 out-of-state Indians have settled in the Los Angeles or San Francisco bay area. This accounts for more than one-half the relocated Indians in the United States. Unfortunately many of these relocated Indians, who had permanently abandoned their tribes and economically and politically socialized into the dominant society, were able to gain considerable political power by getting leadership positions in California Indian affairs. This situation had the dual effect of stunting the growth of a native California leadership in statewide affairs, while placing urban Indians in positions of power in some cases over the affairs of rural and reservation native people.

With the withdrawal of health services for California Indians the already poor health conditions of native people deteriorated further. Leading causes of death were reported to be tuberculosis, cirrhosis of the liver, accidents, influenza, pneumonia, congenital malformation, and diseases of early infancy. Death from these conditions occurs at rates from 1.7 (for congenital malformations) to 6 times (for tuberculosis) rates of death from the same causes among non-Indians. These problems are aggravated by conditions of poor housing and sanitation, lack of employment, and poor nutrition. A lack of medical facilities near the reservation, transportation problems, and sometimes delays by local health officials all prevented prompt care and contributed to the decline in the general health of California Indians. This history of inadequate health care was responsible for a lowering of the life expectancy for Indians to 42 years, compared to the average of 62 years for the general population. This tragedy is not confined to the adults alone. The infant death rate is 41.8 deaths in 1,000 live births, which is 70 percent higher than the rate for infants in the population as a whole (California State Advisory Commission on Indian Affairs 1966:40).

Perhaps one of the most significant events in recent Indian history has been the establishment of the California Indian Demonstration Health Project. This program originated in the State Department of Public Health Bureau of Maternal and Child Health in 1967. Nine projects were set up among reservation communities throughout the state. Funded by state and federal health departments these pilot projects stressed Indian participation and control and have acted as a catalyst for community cooperation in bringing medical and dental health services to rural and reservation Indians. These projects were at first staffed by volunteer doctors and dentists, but eventually funding increased to allow payment for their services. By 1973, 16 projects had been set up on reservations and rural areas throughout the state. Each project is governed by a local all-Indian committee and is almost completely autonomous. Statewide coordination is supplied by the California Rural Indian Health Board, made up of project representatives. Although hard data are lacking, the impact of this new approach to Indian health has been extremely encouraging. Not only has this program provided desperately needed health care, but it has allowed policies of self-determination to grow under its structure. After decades of stifling paternalism by various government projects this is indeed a healthy change.

While termination battles occupied Indian leadership, attention was diverted from critical issues of education, which became shockingly apparent to the state in 1965. It was at this time that the Division of Labor Statistics and Research published a review of statistics that discredited the entire history of Indian education in the state. The report stated that 5 percent of all rural or reservation Indians had received no schooling at all, while 43 percent had not gone beyond the eighth grade, and as many as 57 percent had completed less than one year of high school. The dropout rate for Indians was reported three times higher than among non-Indians; some schools reported a 30 percent to 75 percent rate of Indian student withdrawal (California Department of Industrial Relations. Division of Labor Statistics and Research 1965:10). At the same time a national test reported that Indian students in the twelfth grade had the poorest self-image of all minority groups examined. The California State Advisory Commission on Indian Affairs (1966:39) attributed the failure of education for the Indian to "the lack of teacher concern or the failure of the school system to devise compensatory teaching techniques to cope with students of differing cultural backgrounds."

Three years later a senate investigating committee made a scathing denunciation of both federal and public education for American Indian youth. Senate investigators visiting Sherman Institute reported finding an inadequate staff both administratively and academically. Other deficiencies there included inadequately identified goals, outdated vocational training, a severe shortage of counselors, and little vigor on the part of the administration in defending the interest of the students. That year newly readmitted California Indians could find little improvement over public schools in what an unnamed investigator termed the "rigid uncompromising, bureaucratic, authoritarian, non-innovative feudal barony" that controlled Sherman (U.S. Congress. Senate. Special Subcommittee on Indian Education 1969:75). The committee found conditions in public schools almost as deplorable. Public schools reflecting the values and judgments of White middle-class communities exhibited a self-righteous racial and cultural bigotry. These attitudes, the lack of accurate library material on Indians, and the distorted and biased American history texts all contribute to the alienation of Indian youth.

Organized efforts on the part of California Indian people to deal specifically with the problems of false and inaccurate textbooks were begun by the American Indian Historical Society in 1964. This all-Indian organization of scholars and native historians testified before the California State Curriculum Commission: "We have studied many textbooks now in use, as well as those being submitted today. Our examination discloses that not one book is free from error as to the role of the Indian in state and national history. We Indians believe everyone has the right to his opinion. A person also has the right to be wrong. But a textbook has no right to be wrong, or to lie, hide the truth, or falsify history, or insult and malign a whole race of people" (Henry 1970:7). The Historical Society then presented criteria for the adoption of statewide history and social-science books that deal with American Indians; however, despite hard work and initiative taken by Indian people the commission has so far ignored these recommendations. In addition, the American Indian Historical Society founded one of the first all-Indian scholarly journals, *The Indian Historian.* Long-time tribal chairman of the Cahuilla Reservation, Indian activist Rupert Costo was the founder and first president of the American Indian Historical Society. Since its establishment the Society has founded a publishing house and inaugurated in 1973 an Indian monthly newspaper, *Wassaja.*

Another significant development contributing to increased reservation and rural Indian involvement in education was the founding of the California Indian Education Association in 1967. This organization conducted the first all-Indian, Indian-controlled conference on education in the United States. The large and representative Indian membership has held several statewide conferences to discuss the problems of Indian youth in both federal and public schools. Briefly, the Association has recommended more involvement by Indian people at all levels of the educational process. In the public schools it has called for: Headstart programs for preschool children, teacher-training programs to help instructors cope with special Indian learning problems, Indian counselors at the junior high and high schools, and more emphasis on the positive aspects of native heritage expressed in the entire curriculum. The Association has also recommended that Sherman Indian High School be governed by an all-Indian board of education. An increase in California Indian enrollment, curriculum changes to express Indian concepts, a lower student-teacher ratio, and accommodations for visiting parents are among the many projects this organization has pursued.

The Owens Valley Paiutes in 1968 acquired an Education Center on their reservation that has been successful in encouraging native students to complete high school and even go to college. The project has through community cooperation elected Indians to the local school board and has provided a good opportunity for Indian and White parents to discuss some racial problems in the community. The result has been favorable not only for students but also for employment opportunities for adults as well.

In order to give Indian students an even chance at gaining an education changes must be made in both federal and public schools in California. What shocks many people concerned with public education is the fact that since 1958 federal funds were supplied to various public school districts with high Indian student enrollment for such changes. Indian students have qualified at least 25 counties for federal monies through the Impact Aid (Public Laws 874 and 815) and Title I of the Elementary and Secondary Education Act programs. Earlier California Indians attended public schools under provisions of the Johnson-O'Malley Act of 1934, which provided federal funding to local school districts to pay costs for reservation residents in lieu of local taxes. California Indians were told Impact Aid funds would replace Johnson-O'Malley monies, yet the statewide Impact Aid total never came near the annual $318,000, supplied in 1953 under Johnson-O'Malley. The Bureau of Indian Affairs proposed that Impact Aid be used for public schools' general operating funds in lieu of taxes while Johnson-O'Malley funds could be used for special compensatory programs for Indian students. Yet Johnson-O'Malley

funds were terminated in 1953. Thus Impact Aid money went into general operating budgets for public school districts, no special Indian programs were inaugurated, and local White landowners were given a tax break at the expense of Indians. In addition, Title I funds are difficult to locate and account for. Virtually all Indian students qualify to receive compensatory education services that this act is supposed to support. Yet only a handful of projects for Indians were undertaken throughout the entire state. Nationally, widespread abuse of Title I monies has been reported. A much closer accountability of these federal funds is necessary in order to insure that they are used for the benefit of Indian students for which they were intended.

The past years of federal and state Indian education programs in California have indeed been dismal failures. The problems began when the government attempted to change the Indian into the shadow of the White. This coercive assimilation policy by both the state and federal school systems has resulted in the school's becoming a kind of battleground where the Indian child attempts to protect his integrity and identity as an individual by defeating the purposes of the school. As a result a record of absenteeism, dropouts, negative self-image, low achievement, and ultimately academic failure has followed the great social engineering policies of the White race. Ultimate failure in education has insured the desperately severe and self-perpetuating cycle of poverty for the rural and reservation Indians.

California Indians can be justly proud that they have risen to the occasion and organized groups like the American Indian Historical Society and California Indian Education Association to insure a representative and scholarly Indian involvement at all levels of education. One example of this type of effective input from the state's Indians resulted in the reestablishment of Johnson-O'Malley funds in 1969-1970. However, obstacles continue to exist. Racist attitudes of the White community and its institutions continue to harass, sometimes by threatening job loss, those Indians who have become outspoken in demanding Indian rights. Long distances of many reservations and Indian communities from school board meetings and the lack of easily obtainable information on the use of Title I and Impact Aid funds both contribute to the lack of their effective involvement.

Another important development since the 1960s was the creation of Native American Studies departments at major universities in California. In the fall of 1969 Indian students at the University of California at Berkeley, Los Angeles, and Davis and at Sacramento State University demanded that these institutions begin programs and offer courses on Indian culture and history. As a result, considerable academic research has been done in areas generally totally neglected by the academic community. Indian law programs and the graduate Public

Health programs at Berkeley also offer advanced study programs for Indian students. These programs offer good opportunities for Indian students to train themselves in various professions that could be important to the future of Indian tribes and communities.

The 1970s

Despite advances made by these and other programs, the condition of the California Indian today remains a monument of disgrace to both the federal and state governments. A state report summarized the most outstanding problems of the reservation communities:

Housing is grossly inadequate: living conditions are crowded, existing houses are structurally poor, foundations are lacking, electrical wiring is faulty, houses generally do not furnish the minimum necessary protection from extreme climatic conditions, from 30 to 50 percent of the homes need replacement, and 40 to 60 percent need improvements or repairs. Sewage disposal facilities are unsatisfactory in 60 to 70 percent of cases; two county health departments report highs of 71 percent and 97 percent unsatisfactory conditions. Water from contaminated sources is used in 38 to 42 percent of the homes on California reservations; and water must be hauled, presumably under unsanitary conditions, in from 40 to 50 percent of all reservation homes (California State Advisory Commission on Indian Affairs 1966:32).

Of course all these problems have their origin in the poverty suffered by almost the entire Indian race.

Besides the government's bureaucratic bungling, the major reason for the vicious cycle of poverty among rural and reservation Indians remains lack of jobs. Indians have the highest rate of unemployment of any group in the state. The California State Advisory Commission (1966) reported that the median annual income for the reservation population was $2,268 for each family. Incomes among California Indians in rural and urban areas are comparable. Lack of job opportunities can be traced to various sources. In rural California most work is seasonal and when jobs are found, commuting is expensive and inconvenient because of a lack of transportation or poor roads. Working away from the reservation usually consumes all earnings because of low wages and high cost of living. Indian education has done little to prepare Indians for jobs since most lack employment skills. Local prejudices also made it difficult for Indians to compete against Whites for jobs. Finally, poor quality land and a scandalous lack of water made economic development on the reservations all but impossible.

Even more disturbing than these accounts is the aftermath of the government's termination policy. Since 1958 several terminated rancheria populations have brought court action against the Bureau of Indian Affairs over responsibility of the Indian Service in carrying out provisions of the Rancheria Act. Specifically, they have charged the government with allowing both substandard domestic water systems and housing to exist at the time of termination knowing full well that neither could meet county or state standards. They have also charged the Bureau of Indian Affairs with failure to: provide access roads to Indian land, prevent Whites from encroaching on rancheria lands, and make known opportunities for education and training under Section 9 of the Rancheria Act. The BIA task force reported that the loss of some rancheria land was due to sale to meet tax payments (Anonymous 1972:5).

By 1974, 10 of the original terminated rancherias have passed completely out of Indian ownership because of taxes and other forms of dissipation. As a result of these court actions the BIA surveyed terminated rancherias and concluded in 1972 that it would cost the government $3,876,000 to correct deficiencies in the water systems and provide new housing. Unfortunately, the BIA did not make recommendations on the steady loss of land to taxes. Nearly four million dollars of improvements will simply hasten the loss of land because of higher tax-assessed land values. Therefore, whether the government provides the money for improvements or not, these communities will continue to lose their land either slowly or quickly unless the termination process is reversed.

The cultural survival of the Indians of California depends largely on two factors. First is the ability of Indian groups to maintain a tax-free land base on which to build a viable economy. The second is an awareness by Indian groups of not only their rights but also the value of their own cultural and social patterns. There have been encouraging signs in both of these areas.

The most significant issue facing California tribes in the 1970s is self-determination. "ONLY the Indians can solve their situation; only the INDIAN, with his own leadership and in his own way, can make headway" (Costo 1968:8). Driven to the depths of poverty from which they have yet to recover, the sovereignty of Indian communities has been steadily eroded by the government in its constant bungling attempts to force Indians into the melting pot. The Bureau of Indian Affairs keeps a stranglehold on native sovereignty by virtue of its administrative control over Indian land, resources, water, tribal funds, and a host of social services. With the BIA under the Department of Interior, conflicts continually arise from other agencies whose interests often adversely affect Indians, for example, the Department of Reclamation or the National Parks.

Closely related to the issues of sovereignty and self-determination is the powerless position Indians hold in the body politic of the state and nation. Because of their small and scattered numbers, there is no direct representation for Indians in the state legislature. Here Indians are dependent on goodwill rather than any reliable source of influence to affect legislation.

Immediate self-determination is the only answer. The tedious reports of government task forces on Indian problems, which without exception are filed away and promptly forgotten, do not solve problems. Indian communities must be allowed to control all federal monies earmarked for the state's Indians. Until Indians cease to be the poorest and least powerful group of people in the state and regain much of their sovereignty the dreadful moral responsibility for their present pitiful condition will continue to weigh on the conscience of those individuals and institutions that practice a neocolonial policy toward Indians.

The future for the approximately 40,000 Indians of California is not certain; however, after 204 years of constant struggle the Indians have not accepted forced acculturation or proletarianization as an acceptable alternative to their native culture and values. They have chosen instead to retain their Indianness at all costs. It is this tenacious spirit that has never totally accepted the White system and that has given strength and comfort throughout the California Indians' incredible struggles against forces that at times they could resist only with their hearts. Indians must be accepted by the dominant society on their own terms and allowed to develop their societies along their own lines. Francisco Patencio, longtime traditional leader of the Palm Springs Cahuilla, once put it very simply: "The way of the Indian was very hard. First they learned the way of the Spanish Fathers. Then they learned the way of the Mexicans. Then they had to learn again, very different, the way of the white man. So they could not please everyone" (Patencio 1943:68).

Tolowa

RICHARD A. GOULD

Language, Territory, and Environment

The Tolowa ($^{\prime}$tōləwu) Indians of northwestern California are one of the few groups of Athapaskan-speaking people whose territory includes a substantial stretch of seacoast. Sometimes referred to as Smith River Athapaskan (J. O. Bright 1964:101) the Tolowa language is more closely allied to Athapaskan dialects spoken by groups like the Tututni immediately to the north, along the Oregon coast, than to the Athapaskan language of the Hupa Indians of the interior of northwest California (Bright and Bright 1965:249). Despite the common possession of several place-names, Hupa and Tolowa Athapaskan are not mutually intelligible languages.*

At the time they were first contacted directly by Whites in 1828 the Tolowa resided for most of the year in eight villages along or close to the coast (fig. 1). Seven of these were large in area and may have contained as many as 300 persons each. The village was the principal social unit, though much visiting and movement among villages occurred. Each village claimed a tract of shore frontage that, in nearly every case, included both a segment of rocky headland and some stretches of sandy beach. The boundaries to each village-owned shore tract were well defined and were defended if necessary against encroachment by neighboring villages. Whales and sea lions that washed ashore were claimed by the villagers on whose beach they landed. These villages were occupied between 9 and 10 months of every year by the entire population and were never completely abandoned even during seasons of the year when the bulk of the population was residing elsewhere.

The Tolowa differed from their more riverine neighbors, the Yurok, Karok, and Hupa, in the predominantly coastal orientation of their large villages. The Smith River (the principal river of this region) and its tributaries could not match the abundance of salmon, eels, and other resources of the much larger Klamath River to the south and east. Tolowa speakers occupied a territory that extended from the mouth of the Winchuck River on the north (immediately to the north to the present Oregon-California state line) to the mouth of Wil-

*The best orthography for Tolowa is that of J. O. Bright (1964). Tolowa words in this article have been respelled in that orthography by Victor Golla, who located all but one (təłme?, which Golla suggests might also be dəłme?) in J. O. Bright (1962–1963).

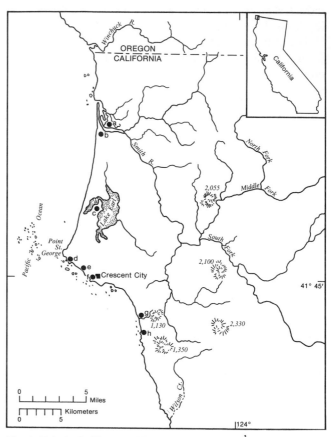

Fig. 1. Principal villages and landmarks. a, xaawank^{w}əd; b, yā?daagəd; c, ?eetšuuled; d, da?tiĩdən; e, me?słtełdən; f, taa?aadən; g, təłme?; h, šinyəłšii.

son Creek (about 17 miles south of Crescent City, California). Territorial boundaries in the interior were less clearly marked, but families from particular villages had claims on acorn groves and salmon-fishing areas up to about 15 miles inland from the coast, and trading parties traveled regularly to localities that, like Big Flat, lie 25 to 30 miles inland. Intervillage cooperation seems to have been limited to an annual first sea-lion hunt, and it applied only when the canoes from each village sailed together on the outbound part of this offshore hunt.

Geographically, the Tolowa occupied an area of approximately 640 square miles, which enclosed four main habitats of varying economic importance. First, there was a *coastal strip,* consisting of rocky headlands and offshore islets that were rich in rock-clinging shellfish like mussels, barnacles, and limpets as well as providing rookeries for shorebirds like cormorants and for sea mammals like the northern sea lion (*Eumetopias jubata*). Sandy beaches furnished smelt in late summer fishing. The treeless, grassy area along the shore, varying from a few hundred yards to as much as a half-mile in width, was generally poor in staple food resources but rich in supplemental plant foods like wild berries and in fibrous plants like wild iris, used in making fishnets. The general marine habitat supplied important coastal and offshore fishing and large amounts of edible seaweed.

The second region, a narrow but dense belt of *redwood forest* situated in an area of low hills immediately inland from the coastal strip, was generally poor in food resources, but it contained some solitary game like deer and elk and provided redwood for making plank houses and canoes as well as ferns for basketry. Third, a *Douglas fir-oak flat habitat* lay inland from the redwood belt

in an area of steep mountains ranging from 1,000 to 3,000 feet in elevation and culminating in the 7,000-feet elevations of the Siskiyou Mountains to the east. Oak-covered flats of varying sizes occurred between these mountains and furnished an abundant supply of acorns of at least three edible species. Fourth, the Tolowa possessed a *riverine habitat,* consisting mainly of the Smith River and its tributaries, which cut across the three other habitats and provided an abundant seasonal supply of salmon and eels. Included within this habitat were areas of both fresh- and brackish-water marshes that harbored waterfowl and furnished important raw materials like tule reeds.

Subsistence

The Tolowa followed a cyclical pattern in exploiting natural resources that were available on a seasonal basis.

NAA, Smithsonian.

Fig. 2. Woman making a basket. The baskets around her were used mainly for holding acorn gruel. To the left, against the house, is a smooth rock used for pounding acorns. Photographed near Crescent City, Calif., about 1900.

They resided throughout the rainy winter season at their permanent villages along the coast, leaving them only in late summer (usually August) to visit the sandy beaches to catch smelt. From there, families went inland to catch salmon and collect acorns. Throughout this time women constantly carried baskets of dried fish and acorns back to their villages for storage and later processing, so the villages were never entirely abandoned. Acorn collecting generally continued through October, and by mid- to late November most people had returned to their villages. The Tolowas depended entirely upon hunting and gathering wild foods for their subsistence, although there is some evidence to suggest that they cultivated tobacco. Most hunting and gathering activities took place within a 10- to 15-mile radius of the village, with men doing most of the strenuous activities like sea-lion hunting, boat building, and salmon fishing and related activities like stone chipping and net weaving. Women concentrated on collecting and transporting plant foods, particularly acorns, and on preparing foods for storage and consumption (fig. 2).

Population

Estimates of the pre-White contact population of the Tolowa differ widely, ranging from an extreme low by Cook (1943a:4) of 450 individuals to extreme highs by Cook (1956:101) and Baumhoff (1963:231) of 2,400 individuals. Kroeber (1925:883) estimated the precontact Tolowa population at 1,000. By 1910 a government census of northwestern California and southwestern Oregon revealed that only 383 Tututni and 121 Tolowa Indians remained in this region (Curtis 1907–1930, 13:96), so accurate estimates by direct enumeration of population are no longer possible. The estimate of 450 individuals at the time of contact is certainly too low, and considering the extent of protohistoric and early historic village sites in the area, the estimate of 1,000 also seems too low. In terms of the somewhat subjective grounds of abundant natural resources of this region and wide extent of archeological and historic remains, the highest estimates appear to be the best offered so far. The drastic decline in the Indian population of northwestern California after 1850 can be attributed mainly to introduced diseases, and in the case of the Tolowa, mainly to measles and cholera.

Kroeber (1925:5) and Sapir (1921:214) both noted that despite the wide diversity in language among the Indians of northwestern California, the nonlinguistic culture of the area was virtually homogeneous. Recent studies by Bright and Bright (1965) have suggested that the linguistic structures of this region may be less diverse than had been previously thought. Intermarriage between Tolowa Indians and their neighbors was common, and ceremonial interaction with Yurok, Karok, Hupa, and Tututni also occurred regularly. Trading networks extended throughout the region and beyond into the interior of Oregon and northern California and up the Pacific coast at least as far as Puget Sound.

Material Culture

The cultural homogeneity of this region was perhaps most pronounced in the realm of material culture. In their basketry the Tolowa shared styles of design and shape with the Yurok and Karok, although the quality of their work in this craft was generally regarded as inferior to baskets produced along the Klamath River. River and seagoing canoes of redwood (fig. 3) essentially like those of the Yurok were made by the Tolowa, and the wide array of tools used for hunting, fishing, woodworking, and other crafts was virtually identical among these groups. These tools included bow and arrows (with finely pressure-flaked stone points), harpoons and harpoontoggles, fishing nets and netsinkers, woodworking wedges made of antler; stone pounders and adze handles for woodworking, groundstone pestles for grinding acorns, and bone needles for weaving mats of tule reeds.

Fig. 3. Sam Lopez refinishing a traditional river canoe of redwood, at his home near Crescent City, Calif. The stern peak has been leveled off to provide a mounting for an outboard motor. Photograph by Richard Gould, 1964.

Like their neighbors, the Tolowas built substantial houses of redwood planks, although in style these differed slightly from those of the Yurok, Karok, and Hupa. Tolowa dwelling houses (the so-called family house) were square structures with an outer wall of upright redwood planks extending about 15 feet on each side and a square interior pit about two to three feet deep and about 10 feet on each side (fig. 4). Tolowa "family houses" had simple two-pitched plank roofs instead of the three-pitched roofs favored by the Yurok, Karok, and Hupa. The sweathouse (fig. 5) was a subter-

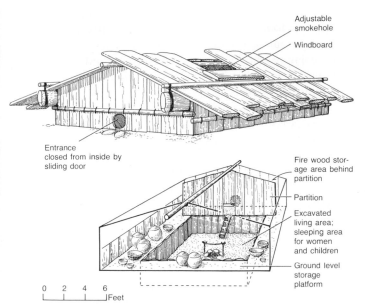

Fig. 4. Reconstruction of dwelling house. Exterior viewed from front, interior viewed from rear.

Labels on figure: Adjustable smokehole; Windboard; Entrance closed from inside by sliding door; Fire wood storage area behind partition; Partition; Excavated living area; sleeping area for women and children; Ground level storage platform

0 2 4 6 Feet

Fig. 5. Sweathouse at village of *taɬme ʔ*. Photograph by Fred Endert, Crescent City, Calif., about 1910.

Social Culture

Tolowa society lacked any definite stratification, and Tolowa villages were without formal chiefs or councils. But within each village there were headmen, called *mīīxašxe,* whose prestige was based upon the possession and display of wealth (fig. 6). Wealth in the case of the Tolowa consisted of specific items or "treasures" (Du Bois 1936:50), namely, large bipointed blades of chipped obsidian, redheaded woodpecker scalps (often sewed

NAA, Smithsonian.

Fig. 6. Transvestite male shaman, a headman from the village of *meʔstteɬdən.* In his nose he wears a horizontal bone noseplug and vertical dentalium shell beads; both denote his wealth. Hat, collar-necklace of trade beads and coins, and dance apron are all women's apparel. The apron is fringed with thimble tinklers, which replaced obsidian pendants used earlier. The collar-necklace is made of perforated coins, which were substituted for shells used before European contact. Photograph by Fred Endert, Crescent City, Calif., about 1910.

ranean structure with a single-pitch, shedlike roof instead of the two-pitched roof style of the Klamath River people. Unlike the Klamath River people, the Tolowa preferred to bury their dead in cemeteries at a distance from the villages rather than close to or alongside their dwellings. Despite these minor differences in style, the principles of Tolowa architecture and material culture were essentially like those of their neighbors.

The Tolowa "family house" was a place where a man's wives, unmarried daughters, and infant sons resided. In each village, the adult men and boys from the age of puberty onward lived together in the so-called sweathouse (where sweatbaths were only one of a series of male-oriented activities—gambling, net making, bow making—carried out in this building). Each coastal village also had a separate detached area devoted to activities like making stone tools, splitting wood, heavy butchering of sea lions, and fish cleaning.

onto deerskin strips or headdresses), and dentalium shell beads (tied on strings to make necklaces and stored in carved elkhorn purses) (fig. 7). All anthropologists who have worked with the Tolowa agree that the principle of acquiring wealth to gain prestige was essential to the whole operation of Tolowa society, but there are differing views concerning the way this principle operated. Du Bois (1936:50) distinguished between "prestige" and "subsistence" economies within Tolowa society. The prestige economy was based on transactions involving the "treasures" mentioned above, while subsistence was on a barter basis, with no exchanges being carried out

NAA, Smithsonian.

Fig. 7. Sam Lopez wearing a redheaded woodpecker scalp headdress and strings of dentalium shell beads. He is holding an obsidian blade, a sign of wealth, and a traditional painted bow. Photograph by Edward S. Curtis, in 1923 or before.

between the two economies. Thus, Du Bois concluded, the "treasures" acquired and manipulated by the Tolowa were not true money, since they were not all-purpose currency, to be subdivided and exchanged for goods of any kind. Drucker (1937a:241) accepted Du Bois's basic distinction between prestige and subsistence goods but nevertheless argued that "treasures" were true money. He pointed out on the one hand that kin-based exchanges of food could not be called a special economy, and on the other hand that "treasures" could be used by the Tolowa to buy everything that was for sale and therefore were true money. While Du Bois (1936:55–56) emphasized the importance of manipulation and haggling on the part of Tolowa men to achieve wealth, Drucker (1937a:242) stressed the role of direct, patrilineal inheritance as the principal means of becoming a wealthy man.

Although the Tolowa did not ordinarily purchase food with "treasures," recent evidence indicates that in times of stress such transactions did occur (Gould 1966:78), particularly in the case of people who lacked close kin ties to wealthy individuals. More important was the fact that Tolowa men used "treasures" as bride price, to purchase wives. Women were important economically in at least two ways: they performed the hard and tedious labor connected with preparing a wide variety of staple foods for consumption and storage (most notably acorns, smelt, salmon, and sea-lion meat); and they could produce daughters who would attract a bride price later on. The Tolowa were polygynous, and wealthy men tended to have several wives. A man with several fertile and productive wives might be able to increase his wealth through direct sale of his stored sur-

pluses of food in times of shortage (a relatively rare occurrence but nevertheless known to have happened) and, more important, he could attract a substantial amount of bridewealth if he were lucky enough to have more daughters than sons.

Manipulation and haggling were at least as important in acquiring wealth as was direct inheritance (Gould 1966:84), and a variety of approaches was open to ambitious men.

• HAGGLING OVER BRIDE PRICE This was carried out by wealthy men who acted as intermediaries in the negotiation. If a man wanted to marry but lacked the full amount of a bride price he could enter into a "half-marriage," similar to the institution described among the Yurok by Waterman and Kroeber (1934:1), in which he made an initial part payment of the bride price to his wife's parents. Postmarital residence among the Tolowa was patrilocal, but in the case of a "half-marriage" the wife continued to reside with her own kin until the remainder of the bride price was paid. Thus the bride's parents, by driving a hard bargain over the bride price, might get some (and eventually all) of the payment due to them while at the same time retaining rights to their daughter's productive labor and the labor and bridewealth of any daughters she might produce while still living with them.

• OBTAINING A BRIDE FROM A DISTANT VILLAGE By this strategy, a wealthy man avoided paying bridewealth to affinal kin within his own village. Since there were few wealthy men in any one village, such a man would almost certainly have to marry a woman from a family poorer than his own, thus narrowing the economic gulf between himself and his in-laws (which could undermine his prestige as a wealthy man in his own village).

• SISTER EXCHANGE A poor man, with no living older brothers or father in his family, could avoid the disadvantages of a "half-marriage" by exchanging an unmarried sister for the woman he intended to marry. This arrangement provided the in-laws with a replacement daughter. Opportunities like this were not common, but when they occurred they were quickly put to use.

• SORORAL POLYGYNY The levirate was present but was used less often than the sororate. Having sisters as cowives not only helped to maintain amicable relations between women in the household but also confined the bridewealth to the same block of kin to whom it had been paid before. In such cases the brideprice was usually less than it had been for the first wife. If the first wife died before a man had time to acquire additional wives or had any children he either received his bridewealth back from his in-laws or else obtained an unmarried sister of the deceased wife in lieu of this returned bridewealth.

• TRADE All the items classed as "treasures" were unavailable locally and had to be traded into the coastal

132

Smith River region. Certain individuals became wealthy men largely by their ability to manage the trade in these items.

• FINES AND INDEMNITIES   Tolowa men watched for opportunities to claim compensation in the form of "treasure" items for a wide range of transgressions. These included payment for homicide or physical injuries, utterance of the name of a dead relative, violations of mourner's rights (such as the right of a wealthy man who had just suffered the loss of a close relative to engage in killing the first sea lion of the season), and adultery. This last would more correctly be termed "incipient adultery," since men watched their wives so closely in the hopes of finding any would-be transgressors that actual adultery was difficult. The Tolowa did not engage in organized warfare, but fighting between Tolowa villages and with Yurok villages occurred often enough for heavy indemnities to develop between certain kin groups. These claims were settled through intense haggling with wealthy men acting as intermediaries in much the same way as in marriages.

• DEBT SLAVERY   This practice was more commonly associated with the Yurok but also occurred in the southernmost Tolowa villages where the incidence of intermarriage with Yurok Indians was higher. A poor man might incur a large debt through a homicide or some other transgression. He could repay his debt by laboring for the man to whom he owed it. Any injury to the slave was deemed worthy of compensation to the owner rather than to the slave or his kin. Du Bois correctly observed that this practice among the Tolowa was more like a form of adoption than penal servitude (Du Bois 1936:55).

• INFANT BETROTHAL   A poor man faced with a heavy debt could promise one of his infant daughters in payment of the debt. The girl lived at her father's house until she was old enough to work, at which time she moved to her husband's house. This often resulted in young girls becoming married to old men, but it was a more common practice among the Tolowa than debt slavery.

• GAMBLING   The stick game was popular among the Tolowa as well as among other Indian groups in northwestern California. Although it was a game of chance, an aggressive player sometimes could manipulate the situation to his advantage and thereby add to his collection of "treasures." Women also gambled, using mussel-shell gaming buttons, but they played for lower stakes which did not involve "treasure" items.

Success in the quest for wealth gave a man high prestige, which was marked by his role as an intermediary in marriage and blood-feud negotiations, in his ability (thanks largely to the labor of his wives) to sponsor festivities like the 10-Night Dance and Flower Dance and generally to be liberal with respect to food, and in his role in giving advice on matters like initiating the annual taking of the first sea lion, salmon, smelt, and eels. The status of men with high prestige was further marked by the fact they alone were entitled to wear a small and often decorated bone noseplug (fig. 6). Dances sponsored by a wealthy man also served as opportunities for him to display his wealth by means of allowing some of his poorer relatives to wear his woodpecker-scalp headdresses and dentalium shell necklaces and to brandish his obsidian blades in their hands.

• WOMEN   Although women were an important part of the Tolowa wealth-quest, their role was essentially passive. Women tended to show a greater interest than men in folktales, and a number of these stories, involving stock characters of American Indian mythology such as Coyote, Dog, Seagull, Founder, Mosquito, Sandhill Crane, Owl, Crow, Sea Otter, Bear, Raven, and Pigeon, as well as special stories about wealth-questing (at times involving a character called ʔeenaaɣaa who would wrestle with people and sometimes kidnap them or steal their food) have been recorded (Curtis 1907–1930, 13:199–201; Du Bois 1932:261–262; Valory 1967:2–3; Goddard 1902–1911). Women also made baskets, which constituted the only important form of decorative art among the Tolowa. Tolowa basketry was all made by twining but included many shapes for a wide variety of functions: soup bowls, women's hats, large storage baskets, open-twined work baskets and baby-carrying baskets, burden baskets (used with a tumpline), storage baskets for valuables, trays, sifters and hoppers for processing acorns, and several other types (fig. 2).

• TRANSPORTATION   The Tolowa, along with the coastal Yurok, were unusual among California Indians in their use of large seagoing dugout canoes made of redwood (fig. 3). These were 30 to 40 feet long and 5 to 10 feet in beam. In historic times these canoes were used primarily by the Yurok for coastal trading and by the Tolowa for sea-lion hunting expeditions at a series of sea-lion rookeries about eight miles offshore. There is archeological evidence that in prehistoric times the Tolowa were using seagoing canoes for deepwater fishing and sea-lion hunting (Gould 1968:37) as well as historic evidence to indicate that similar canoes were in use by the coastal Yurok of Trinidad Bay when they were first contacted by Juan Francisco de la Bodega y Quadra in 1775 (in Loud 1918:243).

• LIFE CYCLE   There was no ceremony accompanying the birth of a child, but naming of a child before puberty received ritual elaboration. As with so many other aspects of Tolowa social life, much of the importance of the naming ritual depended upon its role in the wealth-quest. Names of deceased relatives were reactivated by assigning them to children, thus avoiding the risk of having to pay fines later on for inadvertently uttering them. These naming rituals were convened by wealthy men to name their own children, but other people brought their children in for naming on these occasions, too. The naming ritual was accompanied by a feast supplied by the wealthy man who convened it. For boys there were no initiatory ordeals at puberty, but girls were usually tattooed before puberty (three parallel, vertical lines on the chin) and kept in seclusion for 10 days along with fasting and ritual bathing. Wealthy men sponsored a dance for their daughters at puberty that was characterized by a strong element of ritual. Marriages lacked ceremonial elaboration, but burials were accompanied by complicated rituals and formulae. Bodies were wrapped in tule mats and taken out through a loose board in the side of the house. Later the body was unwrapped and washed along with the grave goods, which included dentalium shell beads. The body was rewrapped in tule mats, placed in the grave, and covered with a plank directly over it and earth on top. Between the time of death and burial, people passing through the village were subject to a fine paid to the mourners; and any dances or gambling that may have been in progress were stopped.

Ritual and Shamanism

Much of Tolowa ritual activity was focused on ceremonies connected with the taking of the first salmon, eels, smelt, and sea lion. The annual first sea-lion hunt was the most elaborate of these, involving a joint expedition of large canoes from each village to the rookeries offshore. The canoes rendezvoused and sailed out together but split up as soon as they reached the rookeries. From then on each canoe proceeded to hunt and transport its catch independently, with each returning to its own village's beach.

The Tolowa practiced shamanism based upon possession by a spiritual power, or, as Drucker (1937a:257) terms it, a "pain," rather than by a guardian spirit. Tolowa shamans were mainly women or transvestite males (fig. 6), and they could charge heavy fees for their services in curing. Often Tolowa patients sought cures from powerful Yurok or Karok shamans (like Fanny Flounder and others in historic times), while Indians from other areas hired Tolowa shamans. In working a cure the shaman went into a trance and danced violently until she vomited up an object (often a lizard, produced by sleight of hand) that was said to be the "pain." Sometimes the "pain" was sucked out of the patient by the shaman, who claimed to see it while in her trance. Shamans sometimes were also feared for their abilities as sorcerers, and Drucker has noted that the ʔeenaaɣaa (so-called Indian devils) appearing in many Tolowa oral traditions were regarded by his informants as sorcerers (Drucker 1937a:259).

History

The first direct contact between Tolowa Indians and Whites occurred on June 9-24, 1828, during the over-

Calif. State U., Humboldt.

Fig. 8. Woman wearing a native dance apron and skirt over a non-Indian bodice. The apron is made of buckskin with *Glycymeris* shell decorations and fringed with obsidian tinklers. The beaded skirt is fringed with abalone shell tinklers. On her cloth-wrapped braids are thimble tinklers. Photograph by A.W. Ericson, about 1890.

134

land explorations of Jedediah Smith. This encounter was brief, and few anthropologically useful observations were made. Nevertheless, on their first day of contact, at a point along the coast halfway between the mouth of the Klamath River and the present site of Crescent City, Smith noted of the Indians: "They were great speculators and never sold their things without dividing them into several small parcels asking more for each than the whole was worth" (J.S. Smith 1828:103). Thus from the first the Tolowa tried to apply the same haggling approach to their interactions with Whites as they had used among themselves and with other Indians. Actually, indirect contact with Whites came earlier than Smith's visit, for there is evidence in the form of archeological remains and oral traditions that a large Tolowa village on the westernmost tip of Point Saint George (a few miles north of Crescent City) was abandoned prior to direct contact due to an epidemic disease—probably cholera (Gould 1966a:96-97)—which may have been introduced to the region by the crews of European explorers like Bodega and George Vancouver, who visited Trinidad Bay in 1775 and 1793, respectively. Evidence suggests that the survivors of this epidemic moved to another village, called daʼīīdən, located on the south side of Point Saint George, where they and their offspring continued to live in historic times.

Introduced diseases and, to a lesser extent, attacks (of a pseudomilitary nature) by Whites on Indian settlements and individuals led to further decline in Tolowa population during the historic period. The U.S. Government Indian Census Map for 1960 records between 100 and 500 Indians living in Del Norte County, California, a political entity that approximates the traditional area of Tolowa occupation. However, not all the Indians recorded in this census were Tolowa, and in 1963-1965 only 10 traditionally oriented Tolowa Indians could be found living in Del Norte County with whom useful interviews could be held.

Intensive White settlement of this region came around 1850, with the founding of Crescent City and some abortive attempts at gold mining near the mouth of the Klamath River. In or around 1908 a tract of land near the mouth of the Smith River was purchased by the Indian Office for displaced California Indians (Baumhoff 1958:227), and this tract became the basis for the Smith River Rancheria, which was in the process of final termination in 1963-1965 along with another small rancheria near Crescent City. Although there were attempts at one time to develop Crescent City into an important commercial center, the area still lacks a good harbor or railroads, and thus it has remained essentially rural in character. Many younger, educated Indians work in the local lumbering industry, and some have clerical and other jobs in Crescent City or else have sought employment as far away as San Francisco.

During the historic, rancheria period the Tolowa, like other groups of California and Oregon indigenes, found themselves reduced in numbers and relocated onto small reservations where they came in close contact with other diverse groups of Indians. Two major religious movements entered northwestern California and strongly influenced the Tolowa during this period—the Ghost Dance of 1870 and the Indian Shakers. Both these movements reached the Tolowa from the north, by way of the Siletz reservation in Oregon (Du Bois 1939:18; Valory 1966:102). The Ghost Dance reached the Tolowa around 1872 and led to the development of a local dream-dance cult, led by three principal shamans, which persisted there for about 10 years (Du Bois 1939:20). The Yurok received the Ghost Dance from the Tolowa but accepted it less wholeheartedly. The Indian Shaker movement started at Puget Sound in 1881 but was not introduced into northwestern California until 1926, when it took hold among the Yurok. Shakerism spread to the Tolowa in 1929-1930 and to the Hupa in 1932 (Barnett 1957:78-79). The Indian Shaker movement went through its peak of popularity in this area during the 1930s and 1940s and then began a steady decline. In 1966 the church at Smith River served as the focus for the only active Shaker congregation in California and the southernmost one in the entire movement.

Archeology

Archeological excavations in 1964 at the site of DNo-11 Point Saint George led to the establishment of a stratigraphic sequence for this region. Two natural units containing cultural material were distinguished. The upper one consisted of shell-midden deposits with some projectile points, bone needles, stone netsinkers, and other artifacts typical of a material culture like that of the historic Indians of northwestern California (including the Tolowa and Yurok). This protohistoric culture was called the Point Saint George II occupation. Underlying this midden deposit in part of the site was a layer of smooth, dark brown sand containing chipped-stone projectile points and other artifacts that differed in style from those occurring in the midden levels. This earlier occupation was designated as Point Saint George I. A radiocarbon date of 2260 ± 210 B.P. or 310 B.C. was obtained for the Point Saint George I occupation, making this the earliest dated human occupation so far identified from the northwestern California coast. Structural remains from the Point Saint George site included a stone-chipping "workshop" from the Point Saint George I occupation and a dwelling of the "family house" type from the Point Saint George II occupation. No radiocarbon dates have been analyzed from the Point Saint George II levels of the site, but stratigraphy and cultural materials indicated that this occupation probably dates to sometime within the last 500 years and ended before the time of direct contact with Whites. A comparison of artifact assemblages shows that there are close resemblances between the materials from the Point Saint George II occupation and those excavated from Gunther Island (Loud 1918; Heizer and Elsasser 1964), Patrick's Point (Elsasser and Heizer 1966), and Tsurai (Heizer and Mills 1952)—all sites dated to within the last 1,050 years.

Synonymy

The Tolowa lacked a sense of tribal identity and did not possess a tribal name. They referred to themselves as *xaš* 'person, people'. The word Tolowa was not their own but was applied to them by their Algonquian-speaking neighbors, the Yurok and Wiyot. Kroeber noted that the Yurok distinguished between Athapaskan speech of the Tolowa variety (ni-tolowo) and Athapaskan speech of the Hupa-Chilula-Whilkut variety (no-mimohsigo), and he further pointed out that the word Tolowa was probably derived from a village near Lake Earl named Tolokwe (Kroeber 1925:124-125), whose exact status and location are obscure. Waterman (1925:531) placed the village of Tola´kʷ in the vicinity of *yáʔdaagəd* 'Burnt Ranch', suggesting the possibility that these Indians had more than one name for this important village. Sometimes Whites would refer to these Indians in terms of the names of their villages, the most common of these references being to the "Etchulets." This name, derived from *ʔeetšuuled,* an important village near Lake Earl, is of Tolowa origin and was not, as indicated in Hodge (1907-1910, 2:773), a Yurok name. This term, along with references to the "Lagoons"—another reference to Lake Earl—appeared frequently in early newspaper articles in Crescent City. According to Loud (1918:292), the Wiyot referred to the Indians of Crescent City and Smith River as Dalawa. Other names sometimes used include Tollowa, Tol´-lo-wah, Tolewahs, Tahlewahs, Talawas, Yantuckets, Tahluwah, and Tolana.

Sources

Ethnographic sources on the Tolowa are numerous but scattered, and they include a large body of archival material. Among the published anthropological sources, those most often consulted are Drucker (1937a), Du Bois (1936), and Gould (1966). The most comprehensive discussion of Tolowa prehistory to date is Gould (1966a). All these are available in most university libraries, but there are additional publications that are useful but harder to find. Among these are Curtis (1907-1930, 13, including folios), which contains some of the finest photographs available of these Indians; Bledsoe (1881), which is a local history that discusses early Indian-White relations from a strongly pro-White point of view; and Hubbard's (1861) notes on the Tututni in "The Indianology of California," which is the first systematic published description of the Athapaskan-speaking Indians of this region.

Unpublished, archival sources on the Tolowa include: the journals of Jedediah S. Smith (1828) and Harrison G. Rogers (1918), P.E. Goddard's corpus of unpublished field notes (1902-1911, 311 pages consisting mainly of tales and texts), T.T. Waterman's notes on Tolowa culture and geography (1921-1922, 148 pages, with four maps), and C.H. Merriam's field notes and vocabulary collected at Smith River and Crescent City (1910-1938). These unpublished sources as well as such miscellaneous but useful items as back issues of the *Crescent City Courier* and *Crescent City Herald* (particularly for 1854-1855, 1872, and 1874) and the *Crescent City News* (especially for 1893-1894) and the B.I. Hayes scrapbooks of newspaper clippings from Del Norte County can be most easily obtained by consulting the University Archivist, University of California, Berkeley. Finally, there are extensive ethnographic collections of Tolowa material culture at the Peabody Museum of Anthropology, Harvard University, and at the Lowie Museum of Anthropology, University of California, Berkeley (along with the archeological collections from the Point Saint George site), with smaller collections also at the American Museum of Natural History, New York.

Yurok

ARNOLD R. PILLING

Language and Territory

Before 1850, the Yurok ('yŏŏ₁räk) lived in ancestral homes situated in permanent villages along the Pacific coast between modern Trinidad and Crescent City and on the lower 45 miles of the Klamath River. A wealth of shellfish, salmon, sturgeon, eel, candlefish, surf fish, deer, elk, sea lion, and acorns allowed sedentary living.

In the 1870s Powers (1877:44) and Powell (1877:460) introduced Yú-rok from Karok *yúruk* 'downriver' as a linguistic label; later Powell's classification of Indian languages (1891:131–132) referred to it as Weitspekan.

Sapir (1913) was the first to classify Yurok and Wiyot as Algonquian languages, although his suggestion was immediately questioned by Michelson (1914, 1915). A later reassertion by Sapir (1929) and Haas's ultimate proof (1958) of the Algonquian affiliation of Yurok have become accepted by most scholars, in contrast to the statement by the author of the only lengthy analysis of Yurok speech available in 1971, who writes that "the question of the Algonquian affiliation of Yurok must be left undecided" (Robins 1958:xiv).*

In the early 1970s Yuroks claimed that there were minor dialect variations between males and females, between aristocratic and nonaristocratic families, and among villages; however, a Yurok speaker in her eighties in the late 1960s stated that the only difference between Requa and Weitchpec speech was that the most commonly employed label for one or two introduced European concepts was not shared. Kroeber (1925:15), writing in 1917 when the Yurok speech was still regularly used in public, says:

On the coast a difference of dialect became perceptible, according to some accounts, at Espau [ʔespew] a more marked one at Orekw [ʔorekʷ], and a third, most divergent variety, at Tsurau [čurey]. Actually these differences must have been very slight, since recorded vocabularies and texts show an appreciable difference only for the region of Big Lagoon and Trinidad; and even this dialect was intelligible on the river.

* Italicized Yurok words are written in Robins's (1958:1–10) orthography, but with γ in place of his g, and č, č̓ for c, c̓. The spelling of Yurok words in this chapter has been corrected by Howard Berman; doubtful instances are marked with question marks, and cases that could not be interpreted are left unitalicized.

• INTERTRIBAL TIES In northwestern California, inhabitants of villages near tribal boundaries commonly spoke both their own language as well as that of the adjacent tribe. At Yurok *wečpus*, persons also spoke Karok; at *reʀʷoy*, both Yurok and Tolowa were used.

The Yurok shared with the Hoopa Valley Hupa and the Karok of Somes Bar and Orleans one group of northwestern California Indian life-styles (see Goldschmidt 1951). Beyond this core area of Yurok-centered life-styles, there was a peripheral zone where at least a few persons, occasionally, shared in some Yurok patterns. The individuals involved were from the linguistically related Wiyot of the lower Mad River; the Athapaskan Hupa-speaking Chilula of lower Redwood Creek; Hokan-speaking Chimariko, Clear Creek and Happy Camp Karok, Scott Valley and Bear Creek (Oregon) Shasta; and the Athapaskan-speaking Applegate Creek (Oregon), Tututni, Chetco, and Tolowa of Smith River and Crescent City.

Those narratives and records concerning Yuroks before 1860 that survive suggest that personal kin and economic ties across tribal lines were extensive. For instance, in the late 1960s, Tolowa oral tradition indicated that, in 1828, during the transit of Yurok territory by Jedediah Smith, Tututni males were visiting near Yurok *wečpus* (Mattz 1968). Another account from the late 1960s lists the wives of the major polygynist of *reʀʷoy* who died about 1859, noting spouses from the Tututni, Chetco, Smith River Tolowa, Crescent City Tolowa, Somes Bar Karok, *wečpus* Yurok, Hoopa Post Office Village Hupa, and Wiyot (probably Indian Island, that is, Gunther Island). Comparable intertribalism is noted in the late nineteenth century. For example, a Chilula family living near the falls of Redwood Creek served as host to many Yuroks when the salmon were running. In 1880 its head, Tom Hill, spoke Yurok as well as Hupa in his home; apparently owned certain whale rights on the coast between Trinidad and the mouth of Redwood Creek; owned ceremonial regalia that he loaned to established partners at Trinidad, *wohtekʷ*, and Hoopa; and had several doctors in his family, including one who received a wife for his son, Dan, from a *wohtekʷ* Yurok as a doctor's fee. Tom himself had a sister who had married a *wohtekʷ* Yurok and another who had married a *wečpus* Yurok. In the 1890s a major Hupa leader from the Hoopa Valley, Captain John (Wallace 1947a:323;

Kroeber and Heizer 1968:99), at times acted as a mediator in cases between Yuroks, while "a high man from the Tolowa" may have had a recognized function in a ceremony at weɬkʷew (Kroeber and Gifford 1949:97).

Between about 1895 and 1933, intertribal social relations were considerably increased, for in those years able-bodied, adult males from many of the northwestern California and adjacent Oregon Indian communities worked during the summer in the salmon industry at Requa. In 1970 the traditional ceremonialism as it survived at Hoopa and the newer Indian Shaker religion with its own church building in Smith River acted to perpetuate intertribal, as well as intercommunal, ties among northwestern California Indians.

BOUNDARIES   The solid lines of traditional tribal maps (for example, Kroeber 1925:pl. 1) give a somewhat inaccurate impression of Yurok boundaries. Review of Yurok Robert Spott's comments suggests that Yurok tribal limits should be defined as the recognized geographical limits of the area in which only Yurok (as opposed to Karok, for example) customary law was considered to be applicable.

In 1970, a Requa informant commanded data, probably attributable to his teacher and sponsor, Robert Spott, concerning the nature of two boundaries of Yurok law: the Tolowa-Yurok and the Hupa-Yurok boundary. The Tolowa-Yurok boundary was conceptualized as a line drawn across the sand and into the sea from a point of land about a half-mile south of Wilson Creek (see Waterman 1920:229). One-quarter mile south of this line there existed the Yurok village of Omen—sometimes called ʔoteworeyet (?) 'where the division comes' (Spott and Kroeber 1942:183). A dispute occurring south of this line was settled according to Yurok law; one to the north was settled according to Tolowa guidelines.

The Yurok-Hupa boundary, unlike the Tolowa-Yurok boundary, involved a transitional area between the full Yurok and the full Hupa legal jurisdictions. According to Robert Spott's protégé, the end of full Yurok legal jurisdiction was the Klamath River at Weitchpec; full Hupa legal jurisdiction started about two or three miles up the Trinity River in one of its uninhabited stretches (see also Daggett 1965:57; Waterman 1920:255–256). The Yurok village of pekʷtuɬ was in the transitional zone of the first few miles of the lower Trinity. If a Hupa warrior returning from a raid on a Yurok village had been killed in retaliation on Yurok territory, for example at wečpus or further down the Klamath River, only half his normal worth had to be paid in compensation; whereas if a Yurok retaliator had followed the Hupa to pekʷtuɬ or beyond, he would have had to pay the full value of any Hupa killed.

Well-defined boundaries probably existed between the Wiyot and Yurok to the south of Trinidad, between the Yurok and Chilula on Redwood Creek, and between the Yurok and Karok on the Klamath River, but details of these shifts in jurisdiction are not known beyond the statement that ʔočepor was the last Yurok village upstream (Gibbs 1852; Waterman 1920:225; Spott and Kroeber 1942:200; Daggett 1965:57) and that the "Little river . . . was the frontier between two tribes, the Yurok and the Wiyot" (Waterman 1920:221).

The geographical limits of Yurok law, as opposed to Karok or Chilula law, for instance, are difficult to define once one is away from the coast, rivers, and towns. On the rugged, rocky peaks and ridges to the north of the Klamath River villages, the Yurok boundary was at most nominal, for the area was thought by Yuroks to be a sacred and neutral zone.

Data on the Yurok-Chilula boundaries on the south side of the Klamath and east of the Coast Yurok suggest that these are possibly best considered in the context of oak groves in which Yuroks commonly camped during fall acorn gathering. But even with owned snaring places for deer and oak groves occupied every fall, the areas away from the rivers and between the Yurok villages and Chilula villages were conceptualized as areas not owned exclusively by any one group (see fig. 1).

Prehistory

Archeology in Yurok territory has not been extensive, and what has been carried out reveals approximately the same way of life as has been described by the early historic travelers and traditional Yuroks.

Historic čurey (site Hum-169 in the records of the University of California Archaeological Research Facility) was excavated during August and September 1949 by a group from the University of California at Berkeley. Heizer and Mills (1952:7–13), Mills (1950:23), and Elsasser and Heizer (1966:58–102) analyzed the recovered material and established that čurey was not settled until 1620. Prehistoric Hum-118, at Patrick's Point State Park, dug in the summer of 1948, was occupied as early as A.D. 1310 according to radiocarbon dating; and apparently it was not abandoned until after the White settlement of nearby Trinidad in 1850. Study of artifacts from Hum-118 revealed a three-stage prehistoric harpoon chronology as well as a loss of interest in both zoomorphic clubs and miniature obsidian ceremonial blades by the time of White settlement (Mills 1950:23; Bennyhoff 1950:310; Heizer and Mills 1952:9; Elsasser and Heizer 1966:23–24, 33–35, 40–44, 53–55, 57, 103). Cone Rock, off the coast near Patrick's Point, was also investigated in 1948, revealing a "ceremonial depository for the ritual disposal of sea lion crania" (Heizer 1951). Briefly in both November 1969 and June 1970, archeological investigations were undertaken at historic Ca·pekw, on Stone Lagoon, by a group from San Francisco State College (Moratto 1970, 1970a; Anonymous 1970).

History

Although from the start of the regular Manila galleon run in 1565 (Hoopes 1966:3–5), many Spanish ships must have sailed or been driven by storms along the Yurok coast and have been seen by Yuroks from the shore, no proved contact between Yuroks and Europeans predates 1775 (see table 1). Accounts of the 1775

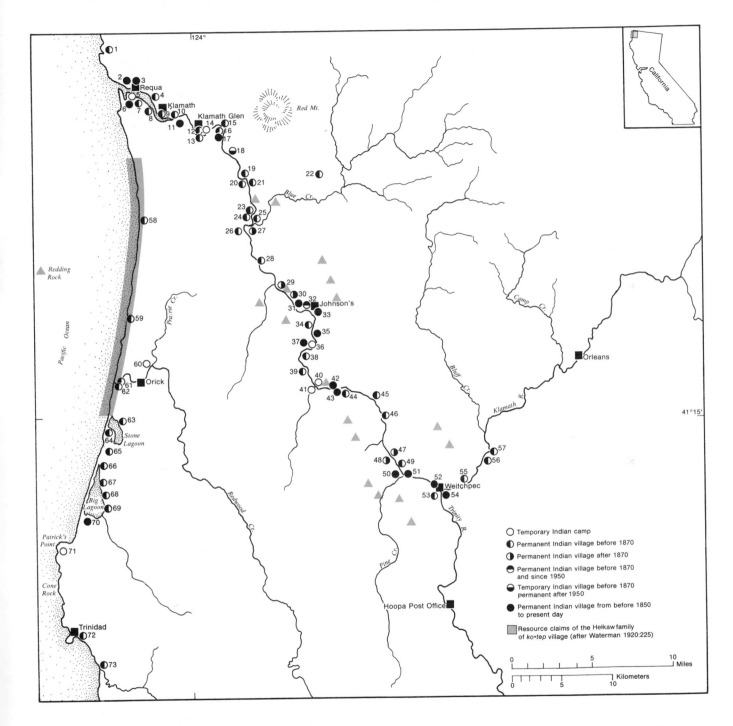

Fig. 1. Tribal villages and camps: 1. Omen; 2. *rek̄ʷoy;* 3. *tmɹy;* 4. A·menok; 5. Otwego; 6. *weɬkʷew;* 7. Tsekweɬ; 8. Kere; 9. O·menok; 10. *hopew;* 11. Wo·kel; 12. A·lo·ɬ; 13. Yo·ktɹ; 14. Tɹwɹ; 15. *saʔaɬ;* 16. *kohpey;* 17. *turip;* 18. Sta·wen; 19. Rliʔkenpets; 20. Howego; 21. To·ctɹ; 22. O·luʔuk; 23. Tora·; 24. Nageɬ; 25. Rnɹ; 26. Oʔpo·; 27. Oyoɬ; 28. *sɹpɹh;* 29. Tekta; 30. *wohkeroh;* 31. *wohtekʷ;* 32. *ko·tep;* 33. *pekʷon;* 34. Yoktɹ; 35. *sreyon;* 36. Keikem; 37. *metah;* 38. Wɹʔɹgɹ; 39. Nacko·; 40. Himet; 41. Weikem; 42. *murekʷ;* 43. *kepel;* 44. *saʔaɬ;* 45. *waʔaey;* 46. *meri·p;* 47. Okweya; 48. Kenekpul; 49. Tsetskwi; 50. *kenek;* 51. *wahsekʷ;* 52. *wečpus;* 53. *ʔɹɹ̣yɹʔ;* 54. *pekʷtuɬ;* 55. Loʔolego; 56. *ʔekoʔoh(?);* 57. *ʔočepor;* 58. Osegon; 59. *ʔespew;* 60. Oraw; 61. Sikwets; 62. *ʔorekʷ;* 63. Hɹkwɹ; 64. Ca·pekw; 65. Tsotskwi; 66. Paʔar; 67. Oɬokw; 68. Keikem; 69. Maʔac; 70. *ʔoketey;* 71. Olem; 72. *čurey;* 73. Metskwo.

Table 1. European visitors before 1850

Date	Locations	Persons	Sources
June 9–19, 1775	*čurey*; village at mouth of Little River	Bodega,	Heizer and Mills 1952:21–28
		Hezeta,	Heizer and Mills 1952:29–37
		de la Campa,	Heizer and Mills 1952:38–44
		Mourelle,	Heizer and Mills 1952:45–52
		Perez	Heizer and Mills 1952:53–56
May 1793	*čurey*	Menzies	Heizer and Mills 1952:61–62; Eastwood 1924:296–297
		Vancouver	Heizer and Mills 1952:63–67; Vancouver 1798, 2:240–248
		Hewett	Hewett 1792; Dalton 1897; Franks 1891; Hewett 1793; Read 1892; Pilling 1969b
Aug. 1793	*čurey*	Eliza	Heizer and Mills 1952:68–69; Wagner 1931:335–336
May 1804	*čurey*	William Shaler	Heizer and Mills 1952:75–78; Murray 1943:7–16
June 11–24, 1806	*čurey*, Humboldt Bay	Capt. Jonathan Winship, Jr.	Heizer and Mills 1952:82–83; Murray 1943:flyleaf
Oct. 1808	Trinidad	Alexander Rezanof	Genzoli and Martin 1961:1
1809	Humboldt Bay	Capt. Jonathan Winship, Jr.	Hoopes 1966:12; Genzoli and Martin 1965:4
July 24, 1817	*čurey*	Capt. John Jennings	Heizer and Mills 1952:84, 101–102
Feb. 1827	Martin's Ferry, *pekʷon*	Peter Skene Ogden's men	Murray 1943:21–24
May–June 1828	Hoopa Valley, *metah, sreɣon,* near *reꝁʷoy*	Jedediah Strong Smith	Chase 1958; R.K. Roberts 1934:3
		Harrison G. Rogers	Chase 1958:13–29; Murray 1943:25–74
1836	*reꝁʷoy*	Captain Brotchie of the Hudson's Bay Company	McBeth 1950:3
Sept. 1841	Happy Camp	Lt. George Foster Emmons	Murray 1943:91; Wilkes 1845, 5
Dec. 1849	Trinidad, Big Lagoon, Humboldt Bay	Lewis Keysor Wood, under Josiah Gregg	Murray 1943:111–175

visit to *čurey* note the presence of iron among the Yuroks and the Spanish success at trading for pelts (Heizer and Mills 1952:24–26, 45).

The first known direct interaction between interior river Yuroks and Europeans apparently took place in 1827 when fur traders from the Hudson's Bay Company penetrated into Yurok territory and reported seeing "various trading articles from American ships" (Murray 1943:22). A year later, in May and June 1828, Jedediah Smith, after traveling down the Trinity River, contacted Yuroks and found them in possession of beads, knives (Chase 1958:15), and "arrow points of iron", as well as having a desire to purchase more knives. The Smith party bought a few beaver pelts, paying for them in beads and awls (Murray 1943:35–36, 43–44). In summary, even the 1775 Yuroks already knew and occasionally used iron when contacted by the first Whites whose observations have survived. Data on perishable features of earlier Yurok culture are lacking.

The long and costly inland transportation route to the Trinity gold fields stimulated the search for an adequate seaport. In 1850 a series of real estate development schemes—each supporting its own candidate for a port—suddenly brought intensive and extensive White contact to Yuroks and Wiyots: Warnersville, the antecedent to Trinidad, was named on April 10 (Murray 1943:160; Bledsoe 1885:64), while Klamath City, near 1970 Klamath, was laid out on April 19 (McBeth 1950:15; Bledsoe 1885:65).

Soon the local gold resources were being searched out. In June 1850 prospectors sampled the sand bars from the mouth of the Klamath River all the way to Happy Camp (Anonymous 1882:104). In January 1851 a minor gold rush exploded over the beach sands at Gold Bluffs, in present-day Redwood National Park (Bruff 1949:471–483; Bledsoe 1881:137–140; Crook 1946:11–12).

Within a year of first local White settlement, Yuroks became wage laborers for Whites at Trinidad, Gold Bluffs, Klamath City, Kepel, and Weitchpec.

Some estimate of the violence of early contact with gold-seeking Whites is provided by Gibbs (1853:145), who notes at *wečpus,* about October 1, 1851, that "the chief, with great formality, displayed a bone, marked on one edge with twenty-six notches, being the number of White men admitted to have been killed upon the Klamath; while the other side of it contained twenty-seven, as the number of Indians killed by the Whites." From the context, this comment appears to include the deaths from all the early massacres of Yuroks except an additional "seven or eight" (Bruff 1949:474–475; McBeth 1950:27) who were killed at Maʔac, on Big Lagoon, in April 1850 and such Yuroks as may have been killed at the Karok village of Red Cap in early 1855 (although reports of Yurok deaths at Red Cap seem absent, Bledsoe 1885:88–89; A.J. Rosborough 1947).

During the first century and a quarter of intensive contacts between Yuroks and Whites at least some of the formal or informal White leaders were well-known allies of local Yuroks. For instance, the letters of A. M. Rosborough (A.J. Rosborough 1947:203) document how William M. Young acted to protect the Indians at Red Cap in early 1855. Young was one of the most important White men living between *wohtek*ʷ and *wečpus* from the early 1850s until his death about 1893. His first wife was the Chilula widow of a Yurok at *wohtek*ʷ; his second wife was Yurok from *waʔsey*. Young was the captain of the local militialike volunteers—the Big Bar Rifle Rangers (Pilling and Pilling 1970:113–114). His third-in-command, Samuel P. Tuley, Sr., lived on the same part of the Klamath River with a spouse from *pek*ʷ*on*, whom he had purchased in traditional Yurok fashion. From 1851 until 1875, when former Klamath County, California, was divided, it included nearly all Yurok territory (McBeth 1950:34). The Klamath County sheriff from 1862 until 1875 was Thomas M. Brown, a well-known friend of Karoks and upriver Yuroks. From 1877 until shortly after 1900, Brown served as the Humboldt County sheriff (Anonymous 1882:149, 178, 184), the county into which nearly all of Yurok territory was placed in 1875. The pro-Indian attitudes of Judge John L. Childs of Del Norte County, which includes Yurok *reₖ*ʷ*oy* and adjacent villages at the mouth of the Klamath from Blue Creek downward, are famous; he was Del Norte County district attorney from 1897 until 1903, and county judge from 1903 until 1920 (E. R. Smith 1953:123; Nixon 1966:200, 206). Childs was well known for having secured the franchise for full-blood Yurok males in the first decade of this century, more than 20 years before California Indians, generally, became voters.

Traditional Social Categories

Yurok language apparently contained relatively few terms for social statuses. To understand the modern operation of the social structure, the traditional local system of social stratification must be considered. This class system operated concurrently with, but in part independently of, the group of social features that were the conspicuous social units of the Yuroks: the district, the village, the house, and the individual. Yuroks also formerly had trading partnerships, work-exchange partnerships, debt "slavery," some part-time occupational specialities, as well as social patterns relating to kinship, marriage, and social disharmony.

Social Stratification

The Yurok were one of the southernmost of the sedentary hunters and gatherers of the Northwest Coast, deriving a large part of their livelihood from fishing and having social forms which recognized social stratification.

Comparison between the aristocracies of Europe's recent past and the former patterns of the Yuroks shows striking similarities. The Yurok aristocrats owned heirlooms classifiable as treasure; they lived at named house sites that were built at high elevations, labeled by terms that designated their locality; from their ranks were recruited those who performed the religious functions; they wore clothing that marked them as followers of high style; occasionally, they used attendants to aid them in their activities; their households enjoyed imported foods as part of a pattern of epicureanism; they had special eating etiquette; they acted as hosts at ceremonial gatherings where they fed the guests; they relished any ability to speak a language other than Yurok; and they traveled widely to gain knowledge and such experiences served as a symbol of their prestige.

Aristocrats had a high-flown, carefully enunciated speech, rich in its expressiveness. There was an aristocratic version, as opposed to a contracted "commoner" version, of many words. The verbal style of the aristocratic raconteur was elaborate and brought in details of vision quest and other esoterica. Interestingly, these features of aristocratic Yurok speech patterns carried over after 1850 to English usage by aristocrats.

Most famous of aristocratic patterns was the ownership of treasure: the holding of heirlooms such as paired 15-inch obsidian blades or an albino deerskin, to be displayed at one of the Yurok ceremonies. Even more impressive was the ability "to put up a whole dance," that is, to provide most of the necessary regalia for a whole team of 9, 11, or 13 dancers, as the custodians of the Spott family Brush Dance headdresses did in 1969. Eyewitnesses to the taking of A. W. Ericson's oft-reproduced photo (Nixon 1966:167) of the 1893 Jumping Dance at *pek*ʷ*on* noted that the short man wearing no feather headdress pictured to the left of the dancers was the rich man *ko·tepiš* who had "put up" the *ko·tep* regalia being worn.

Ownership of other types of heirlooms was also considered symbolic of aristocracy by Yuroks. For instance, in the early 1920s an old woman of the Spott family used an ancient pestle recovered from a prehistoric site for her routine acorn grinding. By the late 1960s, in contrast to former times, shell- and seed-decorated dresses (fig. 2) worn by adolescent females on ceremonial occasions had come to be famous heirlooms (Gould 1966:74–75), one being given an estimated value of several thousand dollars, while others were allegedly being stored in bank vaults for their protection (Robbins 1967).

Only hints of the fundamental elements of Yurok aristocracy are presently available in the literature. An aristocrat was called *peᵧerk* and referred to in English as "a man" or "a real man" (Kroeber 1925:40, 1960:322). A knowledgeable informant of the late 1960s suggested

Fig. 2. Young girls dressed to participate in a Jumping Dance at *pekʷon*. They are wearing dance aprons and skirts decorated with *Glycymeris* shells, abalone pendants, and juniper berry beads. They are also wearing dentalium necklaces. Photograph by Ruth K. Roberts, 1926.

into training, carrying sweathouse firewood, and praying and crying for success in his future. At the age of 16, when his sponsor felt the student's physical strength adequate, the student went through the "test," in which he survived a lengthly isolation in the high mountains or his swimming feat and returned with a vision. Shortly thereafter, he might act as an assistant in a ceremony. Remaining in a ceremonially pure state required sweating and sexual abstinence. Many *peɣerk* were not active in ceremonial affairs between their teens and middle age. Regular sweating and actively being a *peɣerk* formerly were synonymous (cf. Spott and Kroeber 1942:168–170).

The training pattern for those whom the Yurok called "'real' women" was comparable (Spott and Kroeber 1942:159), although for women the pattern of selection most commonly started when a young girl was asked to assist a middle-aged female curer in the Brush Dance.

In the late 1960s there were a few teenage Yurok males who were spoken of as being "in training"; however, possibly the only adequately trained male aristocrat from *rekʷoy* had not found it possible to gain a protégé. The traditional system for the production of Yurok aristocrats was almost a thing of the past by 1970. Most Yurok *peɣerk* were over 70.

Analysis of population data as far as they are available suggests that such *peɣerk* represented about 5 percent of the population, that is, 10 percent of the males. They and their spouses, in most instances, practiced family limitation by abstinence—and, possibly, in rare cases, as in other California groups, by abortion and infanticide. It appears that as much as 40 percent of Yurok households may have been headed by *peɣerk*, who sweated regularly; possibly one-third of the population lived in households headed by aristocrats.

Out of proportion to their numbers, the majority of Yurok data has been recorded from aristocrats. Erikson's (1943) three informants were all aristocrats; and, interestingly, this work, which many consider to be a discussion of Yurok child-rearing, seems to have been derived from only these three informants, only one of whom, a male, had ever been a parent. Spott and Kroeber (1942) has a similar bias. Likewise, Driver's (1939) informant from the upriver Yurok was apparently a *peɣerk* married to a female doctor. Possibly Driver's Requa informant, Billy Brooks, provided the only well-labeled body of Yurok data from a nonaristocrat; but his home had been an aristocratic one, for his wife was a woman of wealth (Spott and Kroeber 1942:182).

There is little documentation concerning "commoners" in the nineteenth century. Apparently, such couples bore more children than aristocrats. They lived at the lower elevations in villages, possibly in part because they owned few if any heirlooms that might be washed away by floods. "Poor men" are not reported to have been hired to work the food-producing resources controlled by the wealthy (Posinsky 1957:4).

that all such *peɣerk* had undergone "training" and had ultimately, under sponsorship, gone through a vision experience. For some, this experience occurred in the mountains (Spott and Kroeber 1942:168; Kroeber 1957:205); for others, the vision came while swimming, either in a lake or in whirlpools in the river or ocean (Spott and Kroeber 1942:158–159). Data on these aspects of Yurok aristocracy are frustratingly meager. It seems that an elderly male aristocrat chose for his trainee an intelligent, earnest, and responsible boy of about six. He first taught him how to make a bow, then how to make an arrow, and how to chip stone arrowheads. By the age of about eight, the novice had begun joining his sponsor in his sweathouse. He was taught by his sponsor the details of Yurok law and case precedent over the next decade. His sponsor urged him to learn, not only from him, but also from other *peɣerk* and women who had undergone special training. The young man went

142

What has been called slavery among the Yurok is inadequately known. The persons referred to in the Yurok literature as slaves were not enemy Indians captured in war or raiding. They do not seem to have related to the kidnapping of Indian children as carried out by Whites in the Fort Bragg area or to Indians indentured according to acts of the California legislature in 1850 and 1860, as documented for southern Humboldt County (Heizer and Almquist 1971:42, 51-58). A Yurok "slave" was a debtor working for the man to whom he owed a debt, or a girl whose father had given her to pay a debt, or a starving person who had given himself over to a wealthy man as "a slave" for his keep and protection (Driver 1939:357).

Only the richest Yurok males are reported to have held "slaves," and these, at most, had two at one time. Most "slaves" were male and seem to have represented only about one in 500 to one in 1,000 of the population, meaning that probably only two to five "slaves" were extant at any one time among the Yurok. Kroeber (1960:319) suggests that "slaves" were "at most one percent of the total population." Still, the importance of Yurok-style slavery should not be underestimated; interview of aged Yuroks in the late 1960s established that several had been reproached as children when they had acted improperly toward children from other families or had damaged the property of someone else. They had been asked: "Do you want to be a slave?" that is, the child was threatened with becoming a "slave" for lack of items owned by his family to be given in compensation for injury to property or person.

The District

The *peγerk* of a district seem formerly to have occasionally sat as a panel of mediators in disputes as well as sitting in the same grouping to arrange details of ceremonies (Kroeber and Gifford 1949:43). Presumably it was a "jury" of *peγerk* from a district that settled disputes before ceremonies, as Yurok writer Lucy Thompson (Kroeber and Gifford 1949:88) stated was done before the *pekʷon* Jumping Dance, and as George Crook (1946:70) noted was done before the *keρel* Fish Dam ceremony. Curtin (1898:xxi) suggested that as late as the 1880s *peγerk* would come together at one time to "yearly, hold converse, put questions, [to an immense tree, and] receive answers."

A *peγerk* had strong sanctions at his disposal. *peγerk* and female doctors were famous for their ability to make "good prayers" and "bad prayers." At least some *peγerk* knew karatelike techniques or other death-producing methods, which they had learned as part of their "training."

The following were districts before 1850: *wečpus*, *keρel-wohtekʷ*, *reƙʷoy-turip*, *ʔorekʷ*, and Lagoon, possibly including *čurey* (Kroeber and Gifford 1949:2). Additionally, the Blue Creek area was possibly once a separate district, before being severely disrupted in the great floods of 1861-1862 (Waterman and Kroeber 1934:7). Douglas (1971:28), in his review of Yurok geography, stated that *saʔaɬ* formerly had "lots of dances and sweathouses." Until about 1860, there existed on upper Blue Creek at least one permanent village, having a sweathouse; Crook described a Blue Creek village about 1858 (1946:73-75); and a journal from the Jedediah Smith expedition mentions a fish weir on Blue Creek in 1828 (Murray 1943:48).

The *peγerk* of the *reƙʷoy* district were last known to have met in the mid-1930s. Ceremonies lasted at *pekʷon* until 1939, meaning that at that date *peγerk* of the *keρel-wohtekʷ* district were meeting on ceremonial, if not social control, matters. By 1916 almost all other districts had stopped functioning as social units (Kroeber and Gifford 1949:88). Yet in the early 1970s Yurok *peγerk* and regalia owners were still meeting around the campfires of the Brush Dance, Jumping Dance, and Deerskin Dance of the "Downriver Side" in the Hoopa Valley.

The elementary school districts of 1970 coincided almost exactly with the late nineteenth-century ceremonial districts—Trinidad, Orick, Requa, Pecwan, and Weitchpec.

In 1970 teams for playing shinny—a version of field hockey, known locally in English as the "stick game" (fig. 3)—bore the names of districts: Weitchpec, Hoopa, and Requa (K. Martin 1969; Anonymous 1969). *wohtekʷ* (under its non-Yurok name of Johnson's) had a team in the 1920s.

Calif. State U., Humboldt.

Fig. 3. Men playing the game of shinny or field hockey on the river far below *pekʷon*. Shinny was played on certain days during the 10-day Jumping Dance cycle. Photograph by Ruth K. Roberts, probably fall 1926.

The Village Cluster

rek̄ʷoy (fig. 4), ancient Omen, and *tmɹy* formed a village cluster about 1800; by 1900, this cluster was made up of *rek̄ʷoy, tmɹy,* and modern Requa. The Weitchpec area has another cluster.

These village clusters unified to act as rivals against other village clusters within the same district, allegedly due to common descent from one or another important "house" with many descendants. The Weitchpec cluster formerly competed against Martin's Ferry in shinny (Pilling 1969:11). The rivalry between Requa, on the north side of the Klamath River, and "Dad's Camp" (the old Yurok village of *weɫkʷew*), on the south side, was obvious in the late 1960s.

The Village

Kroeber (1925:16) has made available an 1852 census and house count for the river Yurok villages from *keṗel*

downriver, by a "trader" named York (Cook 1956:83). Other Yurok village lists are available in Gibbs (1853:138), Curtis (1907-1930, 13:221), and Cook (1956:85-92). An 1852 house count by village made by Gibbs is presented in table 2; in it, spellings of village names have been modernized by use of Robins's orthography. A corresponding map of Yurok villages survives (Gibbs 1853a).

In 1882 there was no significant settlement by upriver Yuroks away from the named traditional villages (M. V. Roberts 1894); however, by 1920 the settlement pattern had become less concentrated because of the wide dispersion of land allotted to Yuroks in the upriver area in 1892 and 1893 (Anonymous 1893a). In the late 1960s the only concentrated settlements were *tmɹy* (then "Requa"), *wohtekʷ* and *wohkeroh* (then combined as "Johnson's"), *wečpus* (by 1970 surviving in two concentrated

Coll. of William Schoenrock, Wayne State U., Detroit.

Fig. 4. The village of *rek̄ʷoy* showing both the traditional plank house and Euro-American wooden houses and giving an indication of how traditional house sites were situated. Note the lack of grass in the village area. It was removed from the site by controlled burning, in order to decrease the risk of grass fires that might ignite the plank houses. Photographed in the 1890s.

144

Table 2. House count for Klamath River Yurok, 1852

Village name	House estimate	Comments
ʔočepor	5	
ʔekoʔoh (?)	6	
heyomu (?)	4	
wečpus	16	32 burnt
pekʷtuɬ	6	7 burnt
ʔɹɬɹɹʔ	5	9 burnt
ʔokeɣey (?)	5	
wahsekʷ	11	
kenek	4	
waʔsey	2	9 burnt; at Young's ferry
kepel	4	12 burnt; old Tompkins' ferry
murekʷ	5	20 burnt
metah	6 or 7	
sreɣon	6	
pekʷon	a	
ko·tep	30	
wohtekʷ	4	
sɹpɹh	2	
turip	4	
kohpey	4	
hopew	a	
reʀʷoy	8	
weɬkʷew	7	

SOURCE: Gibbs 1853a.
a Omission probably unintentional.

segments as Weitchpec and "New Village"), and *pekʷtuɬ* (in 1970 known as "Pearson's"); persons claiming to live in "Martin's Ferry" were spread along the north side of the Klamath for about four miles.

Traditionally, a Yurok village occasionally acted as a unit in a feud or similar action, although Goldschmidt (1951:511) and possibly Kroeber (1960) deny this: Kroeber (1925:52) mentions a feud between *weɬkʷew* and *hopew;* Crook reports that *saʔaɬ* was threatened with attack by "upriver Indians," for practicing famine sorcery (Crook 1946:77). Villages owned communal property (Kroeber 1960:309 denies this, too), like the acorn grove and camp which *meri·p* (or *merip*) continued to use until the late 1890s or the whale rights owned by *čurey* (Waterman 1920:221; see table 3). Waterman refers twice to precise boundaries between adjacent villages, for example, a *čurey-ʔokeɪey* boundary (1920:268).

A village name might be a part of the status term for a person: *sraʔmew* designated 'widower of *sraʔ*.' In the 1960s this usage survived in terms for some Whites: one heard of "Crescent City doctor," "Weitchpec teacher," and "*wohtekʷ* preacher."

Formerly, specific villages were spoken of as being a "side" in a major ceremony. A village with its own major regalia owner would provide "the things" for a dance, as Requa was spoken of as having done during the 1969 "Fourth of July Brush Dance," when the rega-

lia for the Downriver side was provided by Requa (that is, the Spott family side of Requa).

Such a village (actually, its rich man) customarily was the host during religious ceremonies at what was once called in Yurok—and later in English—"a fire," where visitors were given free food. As early as 1910, the term "fire" seems to have been replaced by the word "table" at the Weitchpec Deerskin Dance, probably reflecting that by that early date Yurok "rich men" were feeding their guests at tables. In Hoopa, in the late 1930s, the term "fire" was still in use (Goldschmidt and Driver 1940:106), although by the 1960s it had been replaced by "table" there too. Villages once competed against each other in the hand guessing and gambling game (Warburton and Endert 1966:79-80, 85).

The Descent Group

By the 1960s only a few vestiges of the traditional descent group survived.

A descent group was traditionally referred to by the name of its house site; Waterman (1920) wrote of such a group as "a house." By the late 1960s a descent group was spoken of as a "family" and was designated by the last name presently associated with the family leader who had an English name about 1900; for example, the descendants of Lame Billy of *wečpus* bear the surname of Williams (P.L. Pilling 1972).

Formerly, an individual's personal designation was commonly based upon the label for his house, as in *čeʔɣiʔ ʔukeɣey* 'doctor [from the descent group] of *čeʔɣiʔ*' (a house in *wohkeroh*) (Spott and Kroeber 1942:166).

A "house" owned the use-right to certain land (Waterman 1920:218), houses, and regalia, any of which might be sold or paid as a doctor's fee; however, housesites were only very occasionally sold. Oral tradition tells of one at *pekʷon* being "bought" by a new family about 1835.

Some families had traditions, such as the *ʔespew* family famous for its female doctors and the *sreɣon* family whose members traditionally went to a specific location on their vision quest (Spott and Kroeber 1942:159, 168).

On the death of a powerful family head, the house and its site passed to that descendant who cared for the elderly person in his last illness, usually his eldest son and wife. The property away from the house site and the regalia sometimes passed with the house site or it came to be jointly held by the surviving members of the family, no matter where they lived. In such cases, permission of all inheritors would have had to be gained for any use of the property or regalia. In such cases of joint ownership of regalia, there was a tendency for any coinheritor who could afford to host a "table" or regularly to care for the regalia (a very time-consuming task) and store it to become ultimately its exclusive owner.

Descent of membership in a "house" has traditionally been neither firmly patrilineal nor matrilineal but arranged in each marriage separately. Before 1850 about 75 percent of marriages were ones where the young couple lived with the husband's family and the children at birth gained primary affiliation with their father's "house," this being termed a "full marriage" by Yuroks. About 25 percent of marriages were arranged to have initial and permanent residence with the wife's family and as children were born they became members of their mother's descent group, what Yuroks called a "half marriage" (Waterman and Kroeber 1934:5). By the 1960s postmarital residence was usually either with the wife's family or away from the parental home of either newlywed.

As was the case in some Polynesian descent groups, Yurok marriage arrangements not only produced active membership in a specific family but also provided the participants in, and descendants of, a marriage with latent membership in a series of descent groups. Among the Yurok, landslides, floods, tsunamis, even massive winter storms, as well as the founding of trading posts, were relevant factors in stimulating reaffiliation. The ecology of a locality could be suddenly massively altered. Family-owned or personally owned property—like house sites, major fishing sites, even shellfish-producing offshore rocks—could be rendered worthless either permanently or for a long time, thereby making useful both the geographical dispersal of family or individual ownership and also the option of realignment of descent-group membership through activation of latent ties. However, even with such ecological basis for reaffiliations, the alleged cause of recorded realignments was most commonly a personal conflict.

The Individual

A controversy between Harold Hickerson and Harold Driver in 1967 centered around the presence and importance of individual versus descent-group ownership among traditional—indeed, pre-1850—Yuroks. The best evidence presently available suggests that Yuroks probably observed descent-group, as well as individual, ownership of nearly all varieties of goods.

Instances of individual ownership included partly felled redwood trees, fishing sites, houses, regalia, songs, Brush Dance steps, whale flipper rights, and sea-lion flipper rights. All but the last two types of property mentioned required an expenditure of labor by an individual. Once produced, such an item could be claimed by its producer, sold to or inherited by another person or descent group, passed into general use in the culture, or placed permanently under taboo at the death of the creator. Many women had their own personal song that they sang when traveling or lonely; such songs became permanently taboo on the death of their owner, unless given to another person. In contrast, "everybody" owned—that is, the passage of the item into the general culture—was the fate of Old Domingo's modification in the Brush Dance steps during the 1880s.

For at least 60 years White California inheritance laws have been sufficiently significant to Yurok to block some marriages of coresident sexual mates. Yuroks of wealth commonly have preferred nonmarriage cohabitation and retention of property in the descent group. Traditional Yuroks, at least as early as the 1890s, sometimes participated in marriages in which both the husband and wife retained all their own property individually.

The extent to which an individual Yurok could hold power in traditional society had limits. The rich man's regalia was displayed in the name of his village; his generosity provided the food for guests of the village "fire" or "camp" at big ceremonies. The "rich man" of a small village controlled that unit. Some "rich men" ruled their descent group with an iron hand; for instance, in 1969 a descendant reported that, during the 1860s, her great-grandfather had killed with impunity a member of the household that he then headed. But even if a "rich man" dominated his village, there is no indication that an individual could control a whole district, or even a large village.

Ownership of Natural Resources

Much has been written about ownership of natural resources among traditional Yuroks (Kroeber 1962; Goldschmidt 1951: 507-508). The extent to which the land claims of a family could be dispersed is shown in figure 1, which plots the Heɫkaw family claims as stated by one of its members, Amic, an aristocrat and the 1906 *keɵel* ceremonial assistant formulist (Waterman 1920:225; Kroeber and Gifford 1949:81, 155). Temporary use-rights to an oak grove (Waterman 1922:291) or a fishing site (Kroeber 1925:34) could traditionally be acquired on a share basis.

Other Social Forms

Kroeber (1917:374-376, 1934) and Gifford (1922:27-29) have described Yurok kinship terminology; Waterman and Kroeber (1934) and Spott and Kroeber (1942:148) have discussed marriage.

Nonmarital partnerships for economic and other purposes and partnerships for the temporary loaning of ceremonial goods were traditional patterns (Pilling 1969:10; Kroeber 1905b:691). Analysis of northwestern California ethnographic data (Goldschmidt 1951:510) suggests that formerly the clique of men who came together regularly for sweating composed a meaningful social unit for other purposes as well; however, this unit may have been no more than another manifestation of the descent group.

The bastard, 'a child whom no man would recognize as his', had an especially unfavorable status (T. Kroeber 1959:163; Spott and Kroeber 1942:148, 224-225; Wa-

Table 3. Traditional ownership of natural resources

Variety of rights	"Everybody" ownership	Several villages jointly (?)	Village ownership	Groups of houses	"House" or "Family"	Individual ownership	Fractional individual ownership shares
Acorn-collecting groves	x		x	x	x	x	x
Snaring places for deer and/or elk			x		x	x	
Eddies for fish-netting salmon	x		x		x	x	x
Eddies for taking eels						x	
Stranded whales on specific beaches	x		x				
Specific whale cuts					x	x	
Whale flippers						x	
Sea-lion hunting grounds use	x				x		
Sea-lion flipper					x	x	
Standing uncut redwoods	x		x				
Partly cut redwoods						x	
Driftwood logs in flood waters						x	
Driftwood stranded on specific beaches	x				x		
Shed elk horn					x		
Shellfish-producing rocks	x		x		x	x	
Wild tuber beds			x		x	x	
Grass seed fields		x	x				
Surf fish netting	x						
Water lily seed collecting					x		
Tobacco-growing plots						x	
Houses					x	x	
House sites					x	x	
Sweat houses					x	x	
Cemeteries			x		x		
Mountain altar use					x	x	

SOURCES: Waterman 1920; Spott and Kroeber 1942; Pilling 1967–1969.

terman 1922:292–293). The status term *kimolin* 'dirty' (Waterman 1922:289) was applied to an unmarried woman who bore a child.

Traditional Yurok law was entwined with a complex system of compensating for deaths, injuries, even insults and destruction of another's property (Kroeber 1925:20–22, 28, 35–37, 1928a, 2). Even feuds elaborate enough to be called wars were ended by compensation (Kroeber 1945). Basic Yurok legal principles specified that the host was liable for the injury of his guest; the person initiating any request was liable for any injury resulting therefrom (Spott and Kroeber 1942:202, 206; Crook 1887:22). However, the threat of force was there;

in feuds, if a counter-killing occurred, it was likely to be of a member of the "house" of the initial culprit; if feuds between villages remained unsettled, any person from the offending village was in danger (Spott and Kroeber 1942:184, 192; Powers 1872:538–539).

The amount of compensation for injuries or deaths was worked out by go-betweens who moved back and forth between the parties. Yuroks also recognized what they called "judges" (Spott and Kroeber 1942:152, 186). Until compensation was agreed upon, persons on opposite sides in a dispute were in a special reciprocal status of avoidance and perpetual distrust (Waterman 1922:289, 295); in the late 1960s such negative relationships were still extant between some persons over the age of 50; the status was termed in English "enemy."

A few actions may have been recognized as crimes against the common good, rather than torts; the acts apparently formerly treated as crimes consisted exclusively of abnormal sexual behavior (Spott and Kroeber 1942:234). It was the "judges" who decided guilt in such rare cases, who sentenced the criminal to death, and who specified which "house" was to perform the execution.

Traditional Yurok society had few occupational specialties other than formulist and "doctor." There may traditionally have been a few men who specialized in canoe manufacture; by 1900 there certainly were such specialists. Formerly, a few rich men manufactured regalia as a part-time specialty, although it may have been primarily for display of their own wealth (Spott and Kroeber 1942:206); in 1972, very few traditional Yurok regalia technologists survived. In the early 1900s, fiddlers were significant Yurok labor specialists (Genzoli 1970:cover, 7). By 1970 Yuroks were found in a wide diversity of occupations, including an aide to the California governor, a college administrator, school teachers, army and navy officers, an architect, accountants, nurses, several motel owners and store operators, as well as skilled workers in the fishing and lumber industries.

Culture

Ceremonies

By 1970 none of the traditional major ceremonies was being performed on Yurok territory, nor had any been held at a traditional Yurok site since 1939. Even in 1950, before the death of the *kepel* formulist George Meldon, sufficient knowledge may have remained to have revived any of the river Yurok ceremonies; but in 1972 only the *pekʷon* Jumping Dance could possibly be held again.

The major Yurok ceremonies included the great Deerskin Dance, at which deerskins and obsidian blades were displayed (Sutton and Sutton 1969:290, upper right), and the Jumping Dance, where headdresses containing about 70 redheaded woodpecker scalps were worn (Seiter and Williams 1959:unn.6, upper; Warburton and Endert 1966:114–116, 143; Graves 1929:12–13; Drucker 1965:pl.25; Lavrova 1928; Posinsky 1954). Table 4 lists details of each Yurok ceremony.

Revivals of Yurok ceremonialism brought about a September 1972 Brush Dance at Weitchpec, with a new middle-aged female Yurok formulist and a Labor Day Brush Dance at Requa in both 1971 and 1972. The last Brush Dance at *čurey* was held in 1907 and 1908 (Heizer and Mills 1952:182). It has been many years since there was a Brush Dance at any other Yurok locality.

The actual routine choreography of the Brush Dance was vigorous. Yuroks delight in telling how the Brush

Dance step was performed as a warming exercise during World War II in the Battle of the Bulge, when a Yurok taught it to his non-Indian unit mates. In 1969 the step was in use at Yurok male drinking parties, where it accompanied the resinging of songs from past Brush Dances. Some of these songs were humorous, including a few which originated as attempts to ridicule specific persons.

Three other types of ceremonialism have not been practiced for so long that, by 1969, no living person had seen any of them: the doctor-making ceremony, or Kick Dance (Spott and Kroeber 1942:154), although at least one Yurok living in 1972 knew the accompanying song; the Ghost Dance of 1872 (Kroeber 1925:62; 1905); and the War Dance. The Peace, or Settlement, Dance was performed as late as 1890. There was also a Death Purification Dance, again possibly performed as late as 1890.

In 1927 Indian Shakerism was introduced into Yurok culture and became popular among the Yuroks at the villages of Requa and Johnson's. Its importance waned in the 1940s and 1950s; but by 1970 it again had a considerable following, including some among the age group below 50 (Valory 1966; Gould and Furukawa 1964; H. M. Williams 1969). During the 1950s and 1960s many Yuroks were attracted to the Assembly of God, for which church structures were present at *wohtekʷ*, *murekʷ*, and *pekʷtuɬ*, in the late 1960s; but in 1970 a Shaker revival left these Assembly of God services sparsely attended, even when held.

There was formerly ritual treatment of deer bones (Spott and Kroeber 1942:170), sea-lion skulls (Heizer 1951), and salmon caught at certain places near Blue Creek (Waterman 1920:236–237), as well as rites performed by a young man when he killed his first deer.

Curing

As late as 1970, a child was present all night during Brush Dance performances in Hoopa, although her presence was only symbolic of its former curing function.

Yuroks who remember the period between 1885 and 1930 tell of doctors, especially the famous Fanny Flounder of Requa (see Kroeber and Heizer 1968:150), making house calls to ill patients as well as curing at their own home (Warburton and Endert 1966:76–78; Spott and Kroeber 1942:164). Traditional curing techniques included the confession of wrongs done by a person or his living or deceased ancestors; anything that had been done wrong could cause illness in a person or his descendant. Positive prayer by the curer was part of postconfession procedure. Babies who had been subject to sorcery were formerly prayed over by curers who "blew off" former "bad prayers."

Long before 1900 special performances of the Jumping Dance were held on top of Red Mountain to end a

Table 4. Major Yurok ceremonies

Location	Ceremony	Year last performed	Villages participating	Sources
wečpus	Deerskin and Boat Dances	ca. 1915	wečpus, wahsekʷ, pekʷtuł, formerly Loʔolego	Power 1907; Spott and Kroeber 1942: 253; Weitchpec Grammar School 1907–1909; Waterman 1920: 257–258
wečpus	Jumping Dance	ca. 1915	Same as above (?)	Waterman 1920:258
keþel	Fish Dam	1913		Cody 1942; Catanich 1968; Crook 1946:70; J. McKee 1853:158–160; McKee 1853:193
pekʷon	Jumping and Boat Dances	1939	sreɣon, murekʷ, pekʷon, wohtekʷ, formerly ko·tep	Baker 1967:9, 11; Nicholson 1935; Nixon 1966:167; Graves 1929:24–25, 1934:42–43, 49
wohtekʷ	Deerskin Dance	ca. 1918	keþel; possibly no hosting	Waterman 1920:240
reɣʷoy	Jumping and Boat Dances	1904	reɣʷoy, wełkʷew	Spott and Kroeber 1942:253
wełkʷew	First Salmon rite	ca. 1865		Spott and Kroeber 1942:171–179
ʔokełey	Jumping and Boat Dances	ca. 1880	5 villages	
ʔorekʷ	Jumping Dance	ca. 1880	ʔorekʷ, possibly ʔespew	

disaster, especially an epidemic, by *peɣerk* who came to dance as a sort of prayer.

In 1970 the curing techniques of Indian Shakerism and White medical doctors tended to be preferred by the young adults; Yuroks lacked any surviving and active traditional curer and, if one was called for, resort was to one of two non-Yurok, Indian female curers. The most favored in 1972 lived in Anderson, near Redding.

Sorcery

Assertions of witchcraft were not things of the past among Yuroks in 1972. In 1970 sorcerers, known locally as "Indian devils," were still considered able to command such events as a tree falling on a person or an auto accident. Persons accused of sorcery in the 1960s were often elderly aristocrats, in some instances regalia owners, probably in part because *peɣerk* were thought to be taught how to make "bad prayers" effectively in their "training." An account of an early (about 1875) accusation of sorcery, likewise, specified a major regalia owner as the sorcerer (Pilling 1969a).

Traditionally, sorcerers were thought to own special costumes for use when they went out at night on their nefarious trips. Flint projectile points with concave bases were described as hanging from a taut sinew network on the inside of a sorcerer's headdress and jangling, emitting blue sparks. Yellow was a color traditionally associated by Yuroks with sorcery; in 1967, on at least one occasion yellow was seen being worn as an indication of power as a sorcerer.

Aside from charges that a sorcerer had caused the illness or death of a single person, there formerly were times when general famine sorcery was charged. Robert Spott describes an accusation of starvation sorcery in the 1830s (Spott and Kroeber 1942:202); George Crook found himself involved in such an event in the late 1850s (Crook 1946:77).

Death and Mourning

Several sources discuss traditional Yurok funeral, mourning, and burial patterns, primarily as observed in the early 1850s at *čurey* (Bruff 1949:473, 528, 529, 560–561; Gibbs 1853:140; Meyer, in Heizer and Mills 1952:129–130; K. von Loeffelholz 1893:110; Curtin 1889a; Cody 1942–1943:162).

One of the most persistent of Yurok death practices was the offering of a reward for recovery of the body of a drowning victim. Robert Spott mentions the traditional pattern (Spott and Kroeber 1942:228); a report from the early 1890s (Anonymous 1893) tells of it; and rewards were still being offered in the local newspapers and on posted placards in the late 1960s, not only by Yuroks but also by Hupas and Karoks.

Traditionally, a body was taken out of the split redwood plank house by removal of roof boards; ashes were sprinkled around the opening after the body was handed out. As late as 1969 the body of an old traditionalist was removed from her home out of the window.

In 1851, at *čurey*, each grave of an aristocrat was fenced and the top of each split redwood picket was decorated with feathers; storage baskets with their bottoms broken out were placed upside down around the grave (Bruff 1949:528-529, 560-561). Informants indicate that elderly Yuroks formerly prepared the boards for their own graves. Photographs of graves at *wohtek^w* about 1923 show individually fenced graves and clothing and dishes on the grave (R.K. Roberts 1918-1934). In 1970 family house-site graveyards were still maintained and used at *rek^woy, hopew, pek^won,* and above *wahsek^w* and *pek^wtuł* (Anonymous 1969a); some had graves individually fenced.

Traditionally, a widow or widower sat at the grave for several nights following burial of the spouse, after which time the soul of the deceased was believed to have moved on elsewhere. Guarding of the fresh grave also served to keep any alleged sorcerer from returning to dig up the deceased in an attempt to recover the death-causing "medicine."

After a death in the family, Yurok men, women, and children wore plaited grass necklaces until they fell off some months later (Spott and Kroeber 1942:228); a person might wear three or four at once, if many close to him had died recently. The practice seems to have lasted until at least 1895.

Technology

• WOODWORKING Yuroks depended heavily on wood as an industrial material, using redwood especially for the split-plank house (figs. 5, 6) (Mason 1889:201-209; Baker 1967:17; Bruff 1949:527, 558-559, 561; Crook

Wayne State U., Detroit.

Fig. 5. Vacant plank family house at *wohtek^w* with single-pitched roof. The sealed entranceway at the left shows that the house is not in use. Photographed about 1925.

1887:21; Drucker 1963:pl. 8; Josephy 1961:321; Warburton and Endert 1966:72-75), the dugout canoe (fig. 7) and paddle (Mason 1889:230-231; Drucker 1963:pl. 10; Gould 1968; Warburton and Endert 1966:67-71; Andrews 1960:164), the sweathouse pillow, the stool, and, rarely, for storage boxes (Kelly 1930:355, pl.118). Temporary shelters at acorn-gathering, fish-drying, and Jumping Dance camps were built of boughs. Bows were produced from wood, as were arrows and many fishing devices. Several larger-than-life-sized, redwood-slab human effigies were reported in the 1870s as having been raised by a Yurok warrior in triumph for having killed the distant enemy portrayed in the effigy (Powers 1877:57; A. W. Chase 1877).

As late as 1970, several elderly Yurok woodworkers survived. The technological knowledge for the construction of a traditional house, dugout, stool, bow, and some fishing items was still present and such items were occasionally made. Although most of these woodworkers were born before 1910, a few men younger than 30 commanded the skills for house construction, mush-paddle carving (fig. 8) (Drucker 1965:pl. 12; Kelly 1930: 350-353, pls. 109-112), and possibly those for dugout construction.

• BASKET WEAVING Since the 1920s, when O'Neale (1932) studied Yurok basket making, conspicuous changes have occurred. By the late 1960s few weavers made "work hats" (see Kroeber and Heizer 1968:112 for an example) or other brown and buff utilitarian pieces; the fine weaving still being produced (Wiglama 1971:56; New 1971:132) was of the "fancy" type (Kroeber and Heizer 1968:12; Gifford 1926:pl. 7), that is, with extensive use of black and white, and of red and/or yellow. By 1970 many traditional forms were not commonly made, including the mush bowl, the acorn hopper-basket, the large mush pot, the large lidded storage basket for regalia, and the Jumping Dance basket. Some new forms have come in, including the fruit basket, the place mat, and miniature baskets to be worn as earrings or as pins. Some long-established forms showing White influence were only rarely being made, such as the basketry-covered glass bottle.

Coarse work, that is, openwork twining, was still being made in the early 1970s in the form of baby-carrying baskets (Warburton and Endert 1966:141; Stellmon 1967:26, right), occasionally copies of White dinner plates, as well as miniature eel baskets. The large eel baskets and large burden baskets (fig. 10) (Stellmon 1967:16, lower; Andrews 1960:160, 161) were only rarely made.

In the early 1970s, a major revival of basketmaking—especially of fine weave—was reported, allegedly considerably increasing the number of weavers over a nadir of about 15; however, few of the new weavers knew how or where to gather basketry material.

Fig. 6. View of Indian village at Trinidad Bay, Calif., which was stated by the artist to have been made "of drift slabs of pine." Traditional plank houses are shown with double-pitched roofs. Drawn by J. Goldsborough Bruff, 1851.

Knowledge

There are reports of a traditional Yurok technique for calculating the fertile periods of a female and birth date of an unborn child (Marshack 1972:337) and assertions of two systems for higher mathematics, a decimal and a duodecimal pattern. A list of the Yurok months is in Warburton and Endert (1966:65-67). Yurok music has been commented upon briefly in the literature (Robins and MacLeod 1957; Kroeber 1925:96-97).

Erikson (1943) and even more Robert Spott (Spott and Kroeber 1942; Spott 1960) provide an introduction to Yurok philosophy. Kroeber (1957) discusses a few Yurok dreams.

One Yurok oral literature style is well represented by Waterman's (1922) recording of an elderly Yurok female. Spott and Kroeber (1942:222) give a brief discussion of the Yurok classification of types of oral literature.

Publications attributed to Yurok are restricted to those by Lucy Thompson (1916), Robert Spott (in Spott and Kroeber 1942), and Fay G. Aldrich and Ida McBride (1939), although several Yurok have served as newspaper reporters. Harry D. ("Timm") Williams helped prepare one pamphlet (Seiter and Williams 1959); Frank Douglas aided extensively with another (Parsons 1971); while several fine pieces of Yurok fiction have been written by H. K. Roberts (1969).

Mythology and Folklore

The main figure of Yurok belief was *wohpekumew*, a Yurok human creator (Warburton and Endert 1966:14-17, 50-58; Rosborough 1875:6, 8). There is a series of folk stories devoted to *pulekuk*ʷ*erʔ* (or *pulekuk*ʷ*erek*), a minor hero who ridded the world of bad things, and another series concerned with *seɣep* 'coyote', a trickster and the main character of many minor origin stories (Curtis

Fig. 7. Man and woman in a traditional blunt-ended dugout canoe. The woman is holding a small infant in a baby basket. Photograph by Grace Nicholson, about 1910-1920s.

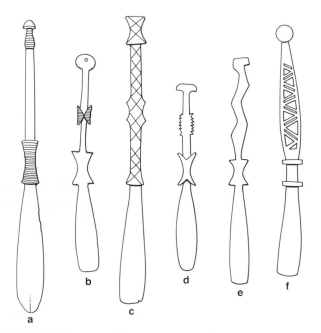

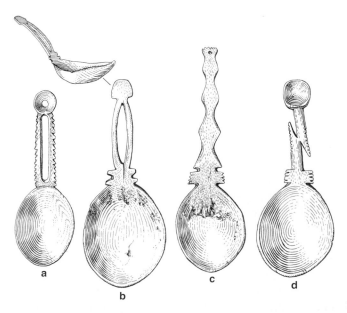

a, Dept. of Anthr., Smithsonian: 411709; b-f, after Kelly 1930:pls. 110, 111.

Fig. 8. Wooden mush paddles. a, height 94.5 cm; collected about 1929; b-f, same scale.

Dept. of Anthr., Smithsonian: a, 411714; b, 411716; c, 411715; d, 328097.

Fig. 9. Men's spoons. a, manzanita wood, length 15.2 cm; b-d, elkhorn, same scale; collected 1920s.

Calif. State U., Humboldt.

Fig. 10. An older woman of the Spott family carrying driftwood used for firewood in an openwork twined burden basket by a forehead tumpline. She is wearing a "fancy" basketry hat while carrying out this everyday duty; such use of fancy items was a means of displaying wealth. Photograph by Harry K. Roberts at the beach below *rekʷoy*, early 1920s.

1907–1930, 13:185–191; Cody 1941; Warburton and Endert 1966:28–32; Aldrich and McBride 1939:8). A typical Coyote story—Coyote and Panther—tells how Coyote tried to acquire dentalium money in the Vancouver Island area.

Population

Although George Gibbs's house count for the River Yurok (table 2) and a crude population estimate of 1,500 for the River Yurok (McKee 1851–1857, 3:634 but see McKee 1853:194) survive from the early 1850s and there is a 1905–1906 census for the non-Klamath River Yurok (Kelsey 1971:17, 30, 31, 32–33), apparently no reliable head count for all Yurok is available for any data from 1850 onward. Cook's (1956:84) assertion of 3,100 tribal members probably is slightly higher than the actual population prior to 1850. James (1909:53) stated concerning Yuroks that "the Indians and White settlers have intermarried so that there is little pure blood among them." Certainly by 1970 there were few, if any, full-blood Yuroks below the age of 20. Persons considering themselves Yurok in a few cases claimed as little as one-eighth Indian genetic ancestry. In 1970 persons recognizing some Yurok ancestry probably numbered between 3,000 and 4,500.

Synonymy

This list of synonyms is prepared to allow readers of other sources to recognize references to Yuroks. What follows is not an exhaustive list: Al-agnas (Crook 1946:69); Al-i-kwa (Powell 1877:460–461); Alioquis (Heizer and Mills 1952:113, citing Bruff); Aliquois (Bruff 1949:481); Aliquor (C. A. Murdock 1921:49); Allequa (Meyer in Heizer and Mills 1952:128–129); Alth (Joyce Sundberg 1972); Cuthacs (Dougherty 1894:206); Down River, Hoopa Valley usage in 1969 and Graves (1929:99); Down-stream People, Karok English usage from Curtis (1907–1930, 13:225); Eurocs (Powers 1872; Carter 1971:v); Eurok (Gatschet 1877:163); Eurooks (Bruff 1949:529, 560); Eurucks (Graves 1929:13; J. R. Jones 1971:4); Hiktin-taretahihl, Wiyot usage in Curtis (1907–1930, 13:228); Kanuck, Kenuck (P. H. Ray 1886); Kenuk, Hupa language usage in Hostler and Hostler (1967:13); Kiruhikwak, Shasta of Salmon River usage, 1904 (Kroeber 1910:1013); Klamath (Azpell 1877; Salem Indian School 1935; Crescent City English usage in 1967; Reynolds 1971:20); Klamath River (Wells 1881:127); Kyinnáa, Hupa usage from Curtis (1907–1930, 13:220); Lower Indians (Bledsoe 1885:74); Lower Klamath (J. McKee 1853:161; Dunn 1886:168); Palegawonáp (Gatschet 1877:163); Palik-Ai-li-qua (Bledsoe 1885:74); Poh-lik (Gibbs 1853:151; J. McKee 1853:161); Polikla, C. Hart Merriam in Heizer (1966:37, Heizer et al. 1969); Poliklan, C. Hart Merriam in U.S. Congress. House Committee on Indian Affairs (1926); Puliklan (Curtin 1889); Tlamath (Bruff 1949:477); To-lick Si-liqua (Anonymous 1882:152); Tútlmús, Tolowa usage in Curtis (1907–1930, 13:230); Ulrucks (Bruff 1949:483); Wait'spek (Powers 1877:44); Weithspek (Kroeber 1910:1014); Weits-pek (Powell 1891:131–132); Weitspekan (Curtin 1898:xxi); Wish-pooke (Kroeber 1910:1014); Witsch-piks (Meyer 1855:282); Youruk (Gibbs 1853:151); Yurock (James 1909:100); Yurúsárar, Karok usage in Curtis (1907–1930, 13:225).

Sources

Yurok life-styles are extensively documented by Bruff (1949); Cody (1941, 1942, 1942–1943); Crook (1887, 1946); Curtis (1907–1930, 13:37–54, 185–191, 220–221); Driver (1939); Endert (Warburton and Endert 1966);

Erikson (1943); Gibbs (1851, 1852, 1853, 1853a); Gifford (1922, 1926); Goldschmidt (1951); Graves (1929, 1934); Heizer and Mills (1952); Kroeber (1910, 1917, 1925:1-97, 1928a, 2, 1934, 1945, 1960); Spott and Kroeber (1942); Kroeber and Gifford (1949); Theodora Kroeber (1959); Kroeber and Heizer (1968); J. McKee (1853); O'Neale (1932); Posinsky (1954, 1957); Powers (1872, 1877); L. Thompson (1916); Valory (1970); Waterman (1920, 1922); and Waterman and Kroeber (1934). A standard ethnographic bibliography of the Yurok prepared by Riddell (1962:6-9) is available. Hedrick (1941) has based a historical novel on the Yurok. An ethnohistorical bibliography has never been prepared; and there are hundreds of obscure sources on the Yuroks in manuscripts and the local press of northwestern California.

Major collections of Yurok ethnographic specimens are held at Del Norte County Historical Society Museum, Crescent City; the Clarke Memorial Museum, Eureka; Field Museum of Natural History, Chicago (John W. Hudson Collection); The Trees of Mystery tourist attraction, Klamath, California; American Museum of Natural History, New York; Lowie Museum and Merriam Collection (Heizer et al. 1969:65), University of California, Berkeley; the British Museum, London (Vancouver Collection); Southwest Museum, Los Angeles; and in various family collections including, in 1970, that of Frank Colegrove, Josephine Peters, and Vivian Hailstone of I-Yee Quee Gift Shop, all of Hoopa.

Significant collections of Yurok photographs are held at the Smithsonian Institution; the Lowie Museum of Anthropology, University of California, Berkeley; the Henry E. Huntington Library and Art Gallery of San Marino (Grace Nicholson Collection); the Humboldt County Collection at California State University, Humboldt (Ruth and Harry K. Roberts Collection and William Schoenrock Collection); and Wayne State University, Detroit.

Wiyot

ALBERT B. ELSASSER

Language

The first significant contacts by Europeans with the Indians of Northwestern California by Juan Francisco de la Bodega y Quadra in 1775 and George Vancouver in 1793 undoubtedly were with the Yurok Indians, the northern coastal neighbors of the Wiyot ('wē₁yät). Not until 1806 was Humboldt Bay, the approximate center of Wiyot territory, entered by White explorers, whose descriptions of the Indians who then lived around the bay were very sketchy. It was not until 1851 that deliberate observations and written reports on the Wiyot were made, in this instance by Redick McKee and George Gibbs, both representing the United States government. It was then asserted that the coastal tribes from about Cape Mendocino to Mad River, as far up the Eel River as the mouth of Van Duzen River (fig. 1) spoke essentially the same language.

Certainly more has been written about the language of the Wiyot than about any other aspect of their culture.* The language was early (and erroneously?) referred to as Wishosk, and this name remained until about 1913, after which it is usually seen in publication as Wiyot. In 1854 Wiyot and Yurok were suggested, without adequate supporting data, as being related to each other. Ideas about this connection were fortified by Dixon and Kroeber (1913), who formalized the concept by including Yurok and Wiyot in a provisional group called Ritwan. Sapir (1913) contributed further support to the concept of an Algonquian Ritwan affiliation; finally, Haas (1958) conclusively demonstrated this relationship in terms acceptable to modern linguists.

The paradox of neighboring peoples with obviously related cultures like the Wiyot and Yurok, speaking languages in some respects distantly related but within the same stock (Kroeber 1911:414) is offered only scant promise of resolution. It has been crudely estimated (Swadesh 1959:23) that between 51 and 61 centuries at least have elapsed since both Wiyot and Yurok diverged from a common parent Algonquian language but that

these two California languages diverged from each other about 23 centuries ago. This estimate does not correspond with the earliest carbon-14 date in the Wiyot region, about A.D. 900 (M-938: I-2352), which may represent the date of entry of either Yurok or Wiyot into northwestern California. At present, then, language studies cannot be utilized to determine either the route or the time of arrival in California from some presumed eastern or northern location of either of these far western Algonquian groups.

Sapir (1929) has posited a relationship between the Wakashan languages (for example, Nootka) and Salish, of the Northwest Coast, and Algonquian. If this has validity, then an ultimate northern cultural affiliation for Wiyot and Yurok seems feasible. Kroeber (1934:18, 1941:287) has shown that the Yurok-Wiyot kinship system is in certain respects like that of the Salish-Nootka

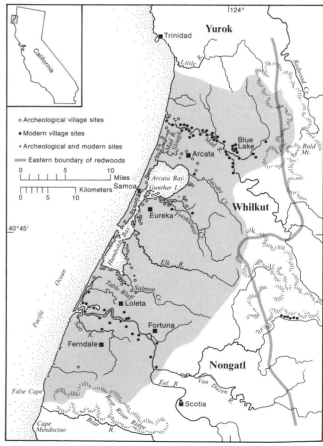

Fig. 1. Tribal territory.

---

*Wiyot words are spelled in the phonemic system of Teeter (1964), with the following substitutions: *a* is here written for Teeter's o, ə is written for his a, *r* for d, *R* for r, *β* for b, and *γ* for g. The acute accent ´ indicates a maximum-stressed syllable with high pitch, and the grave ` indicates a maximum-stressed syllable with falling pitch. The correct forms of the Wiyot words cited in this article were provided by Karl V. Teeter.

rather than like that of any of their immediate Athapaskan or Hokan-speaking neighbors, such as the Hupa or Karok.

Territory and Population

Figure 1, adapted from Loud (1918) and Nomland and Kroeber (1936) shows what are probably the best estimates of the north and south borders of the Wiyot, that is, Little River and the Bear River Mountains. The eastern border has been variously drawn, with deviations from Loud's map (see Nomland and Kroeber 1936:47) mainly concerning the Eel River Wiyot occupancy south and east of the mouth of the Van Duzen River. In general, the Wiyot eastern boundary follows the crest of the first mountain range behind the coastal plain or forest that represented most of the their land.

A significant feature of this territory is that it is almost entirely within the redwood belt. Predictably, this feature would have a strong effect on material culture, but it also means that acorns probably were not readily available to the Wiyot. While the so-called redwood forest region does not totally exclude oak trees (see table 1) it can be assumed that Wiyot acorns were either imported from Athapaskan neighbors or, most likely, acquired by special expeditions to the hinterland (cf. Gould 1966a:89 for a discussion of a similar problem among the Tolowa, who lived north of the Yurok along the coast).

Comparison of Wiyot and Yurok Populations

	Aboriginal estimates		1910 Census	Reservation population	
	Kroeber 1925	*Cook 1956*	*Kroeber 1925*	*Weybret et al. 1955*	*Levine and Lurie 1968*
Wiyot	1,000	3,300	150	62	131
Yurok	2,500	3,100	688	383	959

Note: In Weybret et al. (1955) residents of two small reservations, at Blue Lake and Loleta (Table Bluff), are referred to, respectively, as Blue Lake and Miami Indians. Levine and Lurie (1968) list these reservations as Blue Lake (Wiyot) and Miami (Wiyot). Both these reservations were terminated, i.e., released from federal government jurisdiction, in 1958 (T.W. Taylor 1972:238).

The Wiyot, with many miles of ocean front, bay, and lower courses of rivers in their territory, by most standards have to be designated as a coastal population; however, Nomland and Kroeber (1936:45) have pointed out that they used the ocean very little for either subsistence or travel. Rather, they were inclined to live near "still water," such as the protected shores of Humboldt Bay and near the mouths of rivers like the Eel and Mad. Fish, principally salmon, must have been the main source of animal protein (table 1), although mollusks, deer, and other game animals were evidently of some significance in the diet as well.

Long stretches of coastal plain are almost entirely lacking in California. North of San Francisco Bay, the 100-feet contour line is virtually the coastline itself, unbroken except by small streams until the Humboldt Bay region. Here there are lowlands, sand dunes, and marshes also broken by streams, the largest of which is the Eel River. Considering that the Wiyot region is also, in effect, contained on its eastern border by a practically continuous mountain range, this kind of land could support a considerable aboriginal population. This potential may explain the rapid near-demise of the Wiyot, as the land was also highly desirable for White settlers in the nineteenth century.

In the early 1850s, both McKee and R.C. Buchanan, employing without doubt a good measure of sheer guesswork, assessed Indian population numbers in northern California. McKee did not specify the number of Wiyot proper in his report, but probably he was thinking about figures around 500 or 600. Buchanan (1857) submitted a figure of 800 for the Wiyot in 1853. In attempting to estimate the numbers in precontact times, Loud (1918) arrived at a total of 1,000, with the statement that calculations of more than 1,500 at the outside would be "pure folly."

Finally, Cook (1956:93), utilizing mostly information gathered by Loud, Nomland and Kroeber, and C.H. Merriam, came up with a total of 3,300 for the Wiyot population. This figure was based primarily upon counting the number of village houses or remains of those used within memory, observed or reported by ethnographers and Wiyot informants. These counts were multiplied by the (conservatively) estimated figure of 7.5, that is, the number of original residents in each house.

It may be seen in table 1 that the Yurok probably controlled slightly fewer "fish miles" (104 compared to 125 for the Wiyot) but had a much greater area of land (ca. 750 square miles to 297 for the Wiyot) and a greater total of resource indices, 2496 to 1282. Nevertheless, the Yurok population was smaller than that of the Wiyot, according to Cook's (1956) reckoning: 3,100 persons in precontact times. The apparent lack of correlation between population and food resources may be based upon certain possibly dubious assumptions by demographers, for example, that all the house sites reported were actually occupied during approximately the same period in precontact times. On the other hand, Baumhoff (1963:185) has shown that acorn or game resources in Northwestern California, statistically diagrammed against population, result in random scatters, while in similar plotting of fish resources a fairly neat curve is described. In this light the inconsistencies in the Yurok and Wiyot data, while still not inconsiderable, are not so glaring as when all resources are lumped together.

Table 1. Food Resource Index for Wiyot

Type of Resource	Extent	Coefficients			Indices		
		Fish	Acorn	Game	Fish	Acorn	Game
Fishery	(fish miles)[a]						
Ocean	80	.5 × 10			400		
River (primary)	12	2 × 10			240		
River (secondary)	12	1 × 10			120		
River (tertiary)	21	.5 × 10			105		
Total	125 (104)[b]						
Vegetation	(sq. mi.)						
Redwood forest	254.5		.5	.75		127.3	190.9
Pine-fir forest	7.6		.5	1		3.8	7.6
Chaparral	12.6		.5	2		6.3	25.2
Grassland	22.7		.5	2		11.3	45.4
Total	297.4 (750)[b]						
Total Wiyot resource indices					865	148.7	269.1
Expressed as single index (total) 1,282.8							
Comparative resource indices for Yurok					1,265	581.5	649.6
Expressed as single index (total) 2,496.1							

SOURCE: Baumhoff (1963).

Note: Coefficients derived from evaluation of relative productivity or resource areas. Thus Eel River (primary) has twice the fish productivity of Mad River (secondary), which in turn has twice that of such streams as Little River (tertiary), and of the ocean shore (including Humboldt Bay). Fish resource index is taken as 10 times the product of extent and coefficient in order to approximate the same order of magnitude as the acorn and game indices. Similar ratings apply to vegetation source coefficients.

[a] Fish miles are linear miles of coast or course of salmon streams.

[b] Figures in parentheses are comparative Yurok totals.

Baumhoff further suggested that the Yurok environmental situation may have encouraged a form of population control that was not necessarily operative among the Wiyot.

Prehistory

Results of archeological excavations in Northwestern California all suggest that the ethnographic peoples were continuous, in situ, from the prehistoric occupants. One of the vexing problems here has been that evidence of prehistoric cultures is not sufficiently differentiated from one subregion to another to allow identification, for example, of a distinctive substratum referring to any group as specific as the Wiyot. Thus the large shell mound on Gunther Island (site Hum-167), though in Wiyot territory and assuredly known to have been occupied by Wiyot in the nineteenth century, may well have represented a Yurok site in its earlier levels, which have been dated at about A.D. 900.

Bone netting shuttles, hopper slab mortars, antler wedges and pear-shaped stone mauls, curved stone adze handles, and dentalium beads are among the kinds of artifacts found in archeological sites that continued in use among the ethnographic peoples. These all point to a relatively long-term development of local cultures like Wiyot or Yurok.

Culture

When Klimek (1935) attempted to define Northwestern California as a distinctive culture area he utilized about 100 specific characteristics, referring to both material and social aspects of culture, for this purpose. Of these the Yurok and Wiyot are shown to share more than 90. Driver (1939) listed presence or absence of about 2,500 culture items in a comparative set of tables for Northwestern California tribes. At the same time Kroeber (1939:426), in evaluating Driver's data and considering statistical "coefficients of similarity," concluded that the Yurok, Hupa, and Karok tribes formed the closest interrelated groups. The Wiyot, sharing with the Yurok the specialized Northwestern California culture, were yet barely within the type.

Assigning values of different weights to Driver's 2,500 culture traits in efforts to give a firmer statistical foundation to the idea that the Wiyot truly differed in their form or ethos from the Yurok, for example, has so far not been attempted. Also it is not possible to give reasons for the cultural differences between Wiyot and groups such as the Yurok, although some of them might be conditioned by different environmental demands. After all, many Wiyot were littoral or "tidewater" peoples, while the Yurok, although coastal in part, had a more strongly riverine cultural emphasis, centered upon the Klamath River.

157

The following outline (mostly based upon Driver 1939), may tend to repeat certain Yurok data, but in a subsequent section (see also table 2) are presented some contrasts between the Wiyot and their closest neighbors that may support the idea that the Wiyot, in Kroeber's (1939) words, were "barely within the type" of Northwestern California culture.

Subsistence

Mollusks, especially clams, were exploited, along with sea mammals, for example, sea lions and stranded whales. Among land mammals, deer and elk were most important. The flesh of wolf, fox, bear, and skunk was not eaten. Surf and other saltwater fishing was practiced, but probably most heavy emphasis was placed upon the anadromous salmon, the main source of animal protein for the Wiyot.

Kroeber and Barrett (1960) have recorded 72 cultural items concerned with fishing (for example, traps, nets, weirs, platforms, and practices surrounding their use) that were characteristically used in Northwestern California. The Wiyot shared 61 of these traits with their closest neighbors, the Yurok, with whom they also shared the large redwood dugout boat with blunt (shovel-shaped) bow and stern. Since the Wiyot had much still water in their territory, they could employ fish poisons, not usual for most of Northwestern California.

Although Loud (1918:232) does not even include the oak as a plant of importance to the Wiyot, others (see Driver 1939:315) indicate that the Wiyot were not at all unfamiliar with the gathering and preparation of acorns, with the hopper slab mortar as the basic grinding implement. Moreover, the frequency of shaped stone pestles in the archeological site on Gunther Island suggests that the prehistoric Wiyot utilized acorns as a regular food resource. According to Loud (1918) berries (especially huckleberries) were an important plant food, and this resource may have been more immediately at hand than acorns.

Structures

Dwellings were rectangular in plan, made from split redwood planks, with two- or three-pitch roof, a smoke hole at the top, and usually with flush side entrances provided with sliding wood doors. Two or more families usually occupied such houses, and both men and women slept in them, that is, the men did not regularly sleep in the sweathouse. In addition, sexual intercourse was permitted inside of permanent dwellings.

The Wiyot did not make or use separate birth or menstrual huts; women were not required to move from the permanent dwellings during these critical periods.

There was usually only one sweathouse in a Wiyot village. It was not unlike the dwelling house in form except that it was usually smaller and had the two-pitched roof planks often extending to the ground on either side of the house. Inside, the sweathouse was provided with a stone-lined fire pit and a wooden foot drum. The structure was used for sleeping, gambling, and ceremony, although it was seemingly invested with less spiritual importance than was the sweathouse among the Klamath River Indians.

Clothing, Textiles

For the upper part of the body, robes of deerhide and of woven rabbitskin were worn. Men wore breechclouts of buckskin, although one-piece shirts or aprons, of deer fur for men and inner bark for women, are also reported, mostly for adornment or dancing. Double aprons of buckskin falling to between knee and ankle, fringed, strung with nuts or other seeds and having animal-shell embroidery, were women's dress. Moccasins with seams at instep and heel, and sometimes decorated with shells, were worn by both sexes.

In Klimek's (1935) listing of "matrix" traits of Northwestern California, 14 elements (out of a total of around 100) pertain to twining (the basic technique), decoration,

Lowie Mus., U. of Calif., Berkeley: 1-164128; 1-67265.

Fig. 2. Twined basketry hats with domed peaks (attributed to the Wiyot). Warp elements probably hazelnut (*Corylus cornuta*) shoots; weft materials *Xerophyllum tenax* (light-colored) and leaf midrib fibers of *Woodwardia fimbriata* chain fern (dark), both overlying conifer root strands except as "starters" at peaks of hats. Darker dyeing of *Woodwardia* on specimen (top) is probably achieved through burying in mud, while lighter (bottom) is from reddish alder-bark dye. Both hats about 19.2 cm width. Specimen 1-67265 collected about 1851-1861.

Lowie Mus., U. of Calif., Berkeley: 1-9407.

Fig. 3. Small twined cooking basket. Warp elements probably of hazelnut (*Corylus cornuta*), wefts of willow root (*Salix* sp.) and unidentified conifer root. "Speckled" overlay decoration of *Xerophyllum tenax*. Reinforcement consists of lattice-twined conifer root over multi-element rod. Width of basket at top about 22.7 cm. Collected about 1903.

and types of basketry. Although the Wiyot shared 12 of these characteristics with the other groups in the region, their basketry is nevertheless distinctive. In twined (dress) hats, for example, the dome-shaped peaked form, rather than one with a flat top, was preferred (fig. 2). Figure 3 shows an example of a container, probably a cooking basket, that incorporates several features peculiar to Wiyot baskets of this type. Such baskets are flared from the bottom, but then incurving above the reinforcing rows. The design, often a "speckled" effect, is not centered on the reinforcing rows.

Rabbitskin blankets, an item common to Central California and elsewhere to the east, were made by the Wiyot but not by their neighbors to the north. This difference probably reflects the environmental distinctiveness of the Humboldt Bay region compared to the northern forested lands.

Social Organization

Like all the people of Northwestern California, the Wiyot had neither formal tribal organization nor clans. Descent was patrilineal, and only blood relatives were prevented from marrying (Curtis 1907–1930, 13:80). Driver (1939) records no kinship avoidances in ordinary intercourse among the Wiyot.

Postnuptial residence was ordinarily patrilocal. "Half-marriages," executed for example when the man did not have the full bride price or perhaps no home of his own, resulted in matrilocal residence. Although wealth was the chief basis of stratification among the Wiyot, according to Driver (1939:357) they held no slaves, even debt slaves. In any case, as in all of Northwestern California, "commoners" were related to "nobles."

While Wiyot women did not have equality with men, it seems that regulations governing their conduct were more casual among them than with any of their northern neighbors. It may be questioned whether separate huts for menstruation or childbirth (neither used by the Wiyot) represent a sort of banishment or a privilege. In any case, a whole series of menstrual taboos observed in other parts of Northwestern California also seems not to have been operative among the Wiyot. Thus regulations against menstruating women's cooking meat, for example, or pounding acorns, did not apply among the Wiyot. Also, Yurok taboos against husbands of menstruating women hunting, fishing, or gambling were not in effect.

Another possible indication of a female status different from that of any of their neighbors stems from the information that female berdaches, who dressed like men and hunted, were to be found among the Wiyot. This report, however, came from a Mattole or Bear River informant. Male berdaches were present in Wiyot society and in others in Northwestern California.

Boys' adolescence ceremonies were nowhere important in Northwestern California, but it should be noted that the usually ritual-poor Wiyot celebrated girls' adolescence with comparatively more elaboration than did their northern neighbors, the Yurok (Kroeber 1925:864).

Ceremonialism, Shamanism

Probably the most elaborate of Northwestern California rituals, called "World Renewal" or "Big Time," involved recitations, displays (such as of fine, large chipped obsidian blades), and a whole series of complex dances with an array of showy costumes, plus dentalium bead decoration, mink-fur ribbons, woodpecker-scalp and other bird-feather headbands. The Wiyot carried out these ceremonies, but they did so irregularly and certainly without the élan given to them elsewhere. Two important named dances, directly or indirectly related to World Renewal, were the White Deerskin and Jumping Dances; only the latter was performed by the Wiyot, and this was reported to have occurred in the northern part of their territory, with Yurok sometimes said to have been in attendance. Another characteristic dance of Northwestern California, the Brush Dance, ostensibly given for curing a sick child, also was not performed by the Wiyot.

Victory dances were carried out when an enemy was killed. The Wiyot were perhaps unusual in the region in permitting women to participate in such dances.

The Wiyot paralleled many California Indian groups in their theories relating to disease: they held beliefs in causes by intrusion of poison objects, by soul loss, or by certain breaches of taboo. Herb doctors gave medicine, recited curative formulas, but were known to be able only to weaken or check disease objects. Sucking doctors, expert at removing the poison objects, were both

159

men and women. Fees were paid to doctors before the cure.

Wiyot shamans were not financially liable for declining a (perhaps hopeless) curing case; this is unusual for Northwestern California but is in a way in keeping with the Wiyots' apparently reduced emphasis on property and wealth when compared with Klamath River groups.

One unusual Wiyot shaman's costume accessory has been preserved, a suspended feather headband (figs. 4, 5) virtually unique in Northwestern California.

Mythology and Religion

Analysis of a series of Wiyot stories discloses certain creation myths that are without parallel in Northwestern California. Moreover, the Wiyot seemed to have lacked the conception of the prehuman race, which is typical of tribes of the northwestern region. On ideas of the origin of death there is resemblance to other northwest tribes but also to the tribes of Central California. In culture-hero stories, on the other hand, are found quite exact parallels between Wiyot and other northwestern groups.

Lowie Mus., U. of Calif., Berkeley: 1-9416.
Fig. 4. Shaman's feather head ornament, worn in front of shoulders, hung from forehead. Hide strips wound or plaited over with bear grass (*Xerophyllum tenax*). Feathers are mainly from turkey, Guinea fowl, red-shafted flicker, and blue jay; attached are glass trade beads, *Glycymeris* shells, abalone ornaments, modern buttons, and brass cartridge-shell cases. Length of feathers about 43.4 cm. Collected 1906 (see also Kroeber 1925:117-118).
Fig. 5. Type of plaiting of bear grass (*Xerophyllum tenax*) used for pendants as in fig. 4. It is woven about a sinew or hide strip that may be looped at end to attach abalone or other pendant. With minor variations in the plaiting, such strips are common decorations on skirts and other kinds of costume in the entire lower Klamath River region. Length shown 12.0 cm.

160

Loud (1918:282) reported a unique Wiyot "Noah myth," in which a boy and his sister were set afloat in a basket before a great flood. When the flood receded the boy built a hut, married his sister, and the world became created again.

Although the Wiyot creator (*ku ratəri kakwił* 'that old man above') is specific to them, there is little question that the creator concept, and certain animal tales as well, were derived from Central California. Possibly the derivation was through the Athapaskan neighbors of the Wiyot, but this cannot conclusively be demonstrated.

DEATH Corpses were left in the house until time of burial, when they were carried out through the door on a plank or a pole stretcher. The stretcher was not used by northern neighbors, and the Wiyot probably used it because corpses were too heavy to be carried any long distances, and Wiyot cemeteries characteristically were located away from the village. Bodies were placed, in extended position in plank-lined graves, along with the deceased's money and valuables. Buried property was usually not broken (see Gibbs 1973). Wives were buried in the same cemetery as husbands.

Homes of the dead were purified with tobacco or other aromatic vegetation. After-death taboos on hunting, travel, gambling, and sexual activity were observed for about five days by undertakers. Widows and blood relatives also observed a number of taboos, for example, against eating meat or making baskets, for a period of around five days.

Wars and Feuds

Usual causes for physical conflict were murder, insult, or poaching. Surprise attack was most common, as with other Northwestern California groups, but the Wiyot also engaged in prearranged battles with enemies. Men wore combat costumes, including elkhide armor and rectangular rawhide shields. Bows and arrows were the usual weapons. Women and children were not killed in wars, and compensation by both sides in the fighting for all property destroyed was customary.

Formal purification of killers was observed, and a victory dance, as already noted, was performed by the nominal winners. According to Loud (1918:323) the Wiyot were evidently considered by the Whites to possess much less physical vigor and prowess than the neighboring mountain Indians of Athapaskan stock. Judging from comparative population figures of Northwestern California (Kroeber 1925:883) the neighboring Athapaskans (except the Hupa) could not have put up a much stouter resistance than the Wiyot against the White encroachment. On this score the Klamath River peoples (Yurok, Karok, and Hupa) could, however, seem more aggressive than the Wiyot, although it should be reiterated that the desirability of the Wiyot land to Whites may have been a crucial factor in the reduction of Wiyot population.

Comparison with Yurok

The clues to understanding Wiyot culture as presented here are partly flawed by the fact that their population was already drastically reduced at the time of ethnographic research, while that of the Yurok remained comparatively intact. This is almost certainly one of the reasons why Yurok data, especially on material culture, are often cited as applicable directly to the Wiyot. Despite the relatively few characteristics examined in this chapter, it is clear that the Wiyot were qualitatively, at least, much different from their closest neighbors in culture. This again brings into focus what seems to have been true over great parts of native California: linguistic or geographical barriers are not always critical elements in conditioning cultural differences between any two groups. Certain significant differences may arise whether or not each of these is present.

It is true that in most aspects of material culture, excepting some that were dependent upon different environmental situations, the Yurok and Wiyot were virtually identical; however, in remaining features there were what could be called striking discrepancies between them (table 2). Thus the Wiyot appear not to have been poor relatives of the Yurok, but rather a people with a style entirely different from the Yurok. They were more pragmatic—much less surrounded with taboos, ceremonialism, strongly developed ideas of social and sexual status, as well as with notions of physical and spiritual purity—than the Yurok. All of this deviance arose despite the reality of each group's making its everyday living in much the same way.

It is inconceivable that the penetrating psychological study of the Yurok by Erikson (1943) could ever be made to include the Wiyot. Erikson and others have emphasized the extraordinary importance of the Klamath River in the Yurok world. Apparently neither the Eel River, not at all an inconsequential stream, nor Humboldt Bay, nor any other feature of the Wiyot land or seascape seems to represent for them (at least in Erikson's psychological terms) what the Klamath was to their northern neighbors. Perhaps it is significant that the lower Eel River Wiyot seemed to have much less in common with their upriver Athapaskan neighbors than the Yurok did with theirs.

History

Of all the native groups of Northwestern California, the Wiyot have suffered most in terms of dispossession and displacement during the past 100 years. It is certainly no accident that the largest White population in this region is concentrated on land formerly belonging to the Wiyot: it is the most favorable coastal area for modern commerce in California north of San Francisco.

In contrast to what happened to the Indians along the

Table 2. Some Wiyot Differences from Yurok Customs

Subsistence

First salmon ritual not observed
Sexual continence not practiced before fishing

Housing

Houses not named
Sexual intercourse not taboo in permanent dwelling
Women did not have separate huts for birth or menstrual periods, i.e., these events could take place in dwelling house
Only one sweathouse in each village
Men did not sleep regularly in sweathouse
Men used sweathouse sometimes for curing disease
No fuel-gathering ritual in sweathouse

Social Customs

No debt slavery
Female berdaches
No taboos against menstruating women cooking or pounding acorns
No taboos for husbands of menstruating women against hunting, fishing, or gambling
Girls' adolescence ceremony comparatively elaborate (Kroeber 1925:864)
Barrenness not grounds for husband's divorcing wife
Women could perform in victory dance

Ceremonialism, Shamanism

Woodpecker scalps also worn by women
World Renewal rites performed at irregular times
World Renewal: Women dancers wore basket hat, haliotis spangles, and mink-fur hair ribbons
No Deerskin Dance, no Brush Dance
Shamans not financially liable for declining a hopeless case

Mythology and Religion

Creator concept (*kuratəri kakwił*) (Kroeber 1905a:91)
Particular fondness for animal characters in mythology (Kroeber 1905a:91)
No concept of prehuman race (Kroeber 1905a:91)

Death Observances

Corpse not taken out of house through wall
Ashes not thrown out after corpse
Corpse not painted, nose and ears not pierced, dentalium not placed in nose and ears
No horizontal plank on grave, not in private family plot close to dwellings
Tracks not covered or obliterated around graves
No well-defined contamination scapegoat (gravedigger)

Wars and Feuds

Witchcraft or rape not a cause
Deceased wife's blood money given to wife's family
No manufactured wooden war clubs

SOURCE: Driver 1939, except as noted.

southern coast of California, that is, in the sphere of the Franciscan missions, the displacement of the Wiyot occurred much later and as a comparatively piecemeal affair. Effective reductions of Wiyot began around 1852, with individual shooting sometimes in retaliation for killings of Whites, but also for relatively minor transgressions of the White settlers' "law." Occasionally there was reported the slaughter of a small Wiyot group, for these "reasons." A near culmination came about with the so-called massacre at Gunther Island and perhaps elsewhere in their territory, in 1860 (Loud 1918:329; Heizer and Almquist 1971:30–31). Here, an estimated 50 or 60 or up to 250 were killed, and subsequently many of the survivors were taken to reservations on Klamath River or Smith River to the north. The events of 1860–1862 appear to have resulted in a serious blow to the entire Wiyot population.

While both Loud (1918) and Merriam (1925) listed a whole series of atrocities against the Wiyot in the nineteenth century, mostly reported in newspapers, a summary of what is known about their later population statistics is likewise revealing about their fate. Again the standard for comparison is the neighboring Yurok group, and again the caution about use of population estimates by different persons must be made. Even though the latest figures shown in the population chart refer to Indians using the reservations as mailing addresses and moreover do not take into consideration the amount of genetic mixture that has taken place in the last 100 years, they give a fair idea of the decimation of Wiyot population as compared with Yurok.

The Wiyot are perhaps not actually extinct, although what constitutes "extinction" is not easy to define. Nevertheless, their gene pool, such as it is, is heavily diluted with increments from Whites and other Indians. As-suredly they are not in a favorable position to interact as a specific minority with the dominant White society, as are, for example, the Yurok and Hupa. On the other hand, the recent attention given to movements like pan-Indianism and influences such as those of the Shaker religion among the Indians of Northwestern California (see Gould and Furukawa 1964; chapter on Yurok in this volume) may make irrelevant the whole question of Wiyot survival as an effective modern social unit.

Synonymy

The Wiyot at the time of contact with Euro-Americans were evidently divided into three principal groups, not markedly differentiated dialectically. From north to south these were the *patəwát* on lower Mad River, the *wikí* on Humboldt Bay, and the *wíyat* along the Eel River. *wíyat* is the native name of the Eel River delta, and "Wiyot" is the name first applied to the Eel River people by Gibbs (1853). The term *sulátələk* appears as a name for the language, although it is sometimes employed as well for a general tribal designation. Buchanan (1857) for example, referred to the groups on lower Eel and Mad rivers and Humboldt Bay as So-lot-luck and Merriam (1966–1967, 2:178–180) was still using Soo-lah-te-luk interchangeably as a cultural and linguistic designation in the 1920s. Validity of usage of this term is somewhat diminished by Kroeber's reference to da-sulatelu as "the Wiyot name of a non-Athapascan people of upper Mad River" (Loud 1918:301). Whatever the case, the name for the Eel River division (Wiyot) now has almost exclusive preference in descriptive accounts pertaining to the entire group.

Powers (1877:100) recognized the lower Humboldt Bay and Eel River peoples as Viard (obviously a variant of Wiyot), contrasting them with the Batawat of Mad River region. However, he quotes Gibbs (Powers 1877:478) as designating the Humboldt Bay and Mad River peoples Wishosk, the name allegedly used by the Eel River people for the northern subgroups. Unfortunately Gibbs applied this term as a linguistic family name that included the Eel River Wiyot as one of its members. Another usage of Wishosk has been described as a misapplication of the Wiyot name for their Athapaskan neighbors (Curtis 1907–1930, 13:67–87).

Sources

Ethnographic specimens from the Wiyot are comparatively rare, and for the most part are not listed specifically among the collections of the large museums of the United States or Canada (Hunter 1967). Those in the R.H. Lowie Museum of Anthropology, University of California, Berkeley, collected mostly by A.L. Kroeber

Dept. of Anthr., U. of Calif., Berkeley.
Fig. 6. Jerre James and wife. Although this woman has vertical-line tattooing on her chin, solid tattooing was more characteristic among Wiyot women. The men were not tattooed on the chin at all.
Photograph by C. Hart Merriam, Sept. 1910.

162

around 1900, are limited, compared with those recorded or collected from the groups of the lower Klamath River area such as the Yurok or Hupa.

Archeological material from Gunther Island in Humboldt Bay, at least that from the upper levels of a large occupation site on the island, is probably representative of the prehistoric and early historic Wiyot. Much of this collection, which is housed at the Lowie Museum of Anthropology, has been described in publications (e.g. Loud 1918). Another collection of Gunther Island artifacts and other Wiyot specimens is in the Clarke Memorial Museum, Eureka, California.

While most known ethnographic information on the Wiyot has been published, there are some unpublished specialized notes, for example, on geography, linguistics, and numerals, in the archives of the University of California, Berkeley. Authors of these notes are E.W. Gifford, C.E. Kelsey, A.L. Kroeber, L.L. Loud, and P. Radin (see Valory 1971). Freeman (1966) lists several references to manuscripts pertaining to the Wiyot language in the Library of the American Philosophical Society, Philadelphia.

Hupa, Chilula, and Whilkut

WILLIAM J. WALLACE

HUPA

Language, Environment, and Territory

Along the lower course of the Trinity River in northwestern California lived the Hupa (ˈhoōopu), a small ethnic group numbering about 1,000 when first reached by White Americans in 1850. They shared a distinctive way of life with the adjoining and more populous Yurok and Karok of the Klamath River with whom they had frequent contacts and close relations. Similar customs and institutions were shared by the Wiyot and Tolowa but the Hupa had little direct intercourse with them.

Nothing is known of the Hupa past, for no systematic archeology has been carried out in their territory. Their speech, one of several Athapaskan languages in northern California, indicates that they originally came from the north; but how and when they arrived remain matters of speculation. Application of the glotto-chronological method to the speech stock demonstrates a surprisingly low time depth for the arrival of Athapaskan speakers on the Pacific Coast. Lexicostatistical dating suggests that the Pacific Coast languages broke off from the common Athapaskan body in the north only about 1,300 years ago, and that their movement south began almost at once and was essentially completed within three centuries (Hoijer 1956:232). The Hupa divergences from the northern idioms fall within a time span of roughly 900–1,200 years ago—or, by other estimates, about 1,300 to 1,700 years ago (Hymes 1957). If the movement into their historic seat took place so recently, acculturation of the Hupa to the specialized northwestern California culture must have proceeded at a rapid pace.*

Six-mile-long Hoopa Valley, sheltered and picturesque, formed the center of the Hupa homeland (fig. 1). Through it winds the swift-flowing Trinity River, the main tributary of the Klamath. Except for the level valley floor, one to two miles wide, the country is mountainous and difficult of access. A moderate climate without lengthy periods of cold or heat prevails. Rain, totaling more than 40 inches annually, falls mainly between November and March. Ordinarily the remaining months are quite dry. Snow rarely reaches the valley floor though it often clothes the surrounding mountains during the winter months.

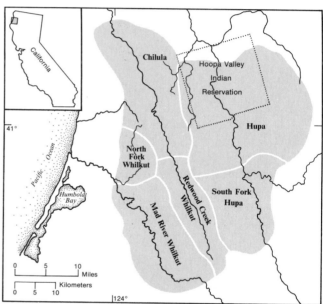

Fig. 1. Hupa, Chilula, and Whilkut territories.

Dense vegetation covers most of the region. Evergreen forests of pines, cedars, and Douglas firs overspread the mountain ridges and chaparral grows thickly on the lower slopes and in the less fertile sections of the valley. A varied and plentiful animal and bird life inhabits the region and the Trinity abounds with fish seasonally.

Subsistence

Many natural foods were available to the Hupa. Of these, two—salmon and acorns—provided the bulk of the native diet.

Salmon thronged the Trinity each spring and fall to spawn in its upper reaches. At these times the year's supply was taken by a variety of efficient devices (Kroe-

---

* Italicized Hupa words have been respelled by Victor Golla in the orthography described for the Hupa language in vol. 17. He has also provided translations of most of the village names. The names of all the Hupa villages occurred in his collection of linguistic data; however, the transcriptions of most of the Chilula and Whilkut village names are only educated guesses (the more doubtful ones being indicated by parenthetical question marks). Those names for which no respelling could be suggested are given in roman type.

ber and Barrett 1960). During the spring run fishermen, standing on platforms erected over suitable pools and eddies, dipped out the salmon with long-handled nets. When the river was low in the fall, a weir of poles and withes was built across it (fig. 2). Fish swarming against the obstruction were scooped up by men strategically positioned on small platforms along its top. The weir was constructed communally and placed in alternate years near one of two principal settlements. Other methods of capturing salmon included gill nets set in still pools and long dragnets hauled by groups of fishermen. Where water conditions permitted, salmon were impaled with bone-pointed harpoons (fig. 3).

Fig. 2. Hupa salmon weir below Mill Creek. Photograph by Pliny E. Goddard, 1906.

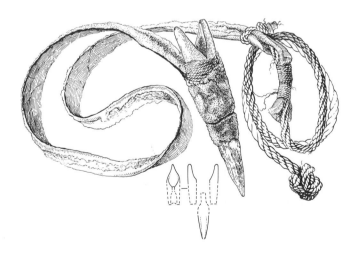

Fig. 3. Toggle-head for salmon harpoon, Hupa. Made from deer horn, wound with fiber thread and sealed with pitch, attached with elk hide leather strap to Indian-made rope. In use it is attached to a sapling. Inset shows construction of toggle-head. Length of head 9.0 cm, collected before 1928.

Quantities of salmon flesh, sliced thin and smoke-dried, were preserved for winter use. In this state it lasted for a considerable time. The commonest method of cooking fresh salmon was broiling on pointed sticks propped up before the fire.

Another fish of importance consisted of the steelhead, a sea-running trout that returned to the river to spawn. Sturgeon, valued not only for their mass of flesh but also for the glue obtained from their heads, were caught in fewer numbers. Lamprey eels, migrating upstream in the spring, were much relished. Surplus stocks of all three were preserved for future consumption by drying in the smoke of fires. Trout and other varieties of small fish present in the Trinity and its tributaries throughout the year were sometimes taken with hook and line. The river's swift current ruled out drugging.

Women harvested acorns when they began to drop from the trees in the fall of the year. Most esteemed were those of the tan oak, but in the event of a short crop, those of other species were collected. Gathered in conical baskets, each large enough to hold a bushel or two, the nuts were prepared for storage and eating (fig. 4) in the regular California Indian manner (Goddard 1903-1904:27-28). Acorn meal, cooked by heated stones and stirred about with a carved wooden paddle two to four feet long, was customarily served as a thin mush. Less often, dampened flour was baked into a cake on a hot stone. A wide range of other plant foods—nuts, seeds, berries, fruits, roots, and greens—gave variety to the diet.

Although their land was rich in game, the Hupa did not exploit this source of food extensively. Deer and elk were stalked in the forests, driven by trained dogs to waiting huntsmen, or forced into the river by shouting men and barking dogs, and then pursued in canoes. At times, a hunter disguised with deerhead and skin simulated movements of the animal in order to get within bowshot. A short, sinew-lined bow (fig. 5) with stone-tipped arrows was the standard weapon of the chase (Mason 1889:227-229). Nooses of strong iris-fiber rope were frequently placed along trails followed by deer or elk. Little attention was paid to lesser game. Rabbits, squirrels, and birds were shot with a simple bow and arrows lacking stone heads, or captured in snares or traps. Meat was roasted on coals, broiled on skewers, or stone-boiled. That not needed for immediate consumption was cut in strips and cured over a fire.

Not all potential food resources were exploited. The flesh of several species of birds and animals was not eaten because of religious taboos. All reptiles and amphibians except the turtle were shunned. The Hupa showed much repugnance to the idea of eating insects and larvae, delicacies to many native Californians.

Normally the Indians had plenty to eat; and sizable stores of dried salmon, acorns, and other foodstuffs guaranteed against want. But there were occasional lean

Fig. 4. Mrs. Freddie, Hupa, pouring water from a basket cup into acorn meal being leached in a hollow in the sand. To her right is an acorn-collecting basket. Photograph by Pliny E. Goddard, 1902.

years when the yield of salmon and acorns was not up to expectations. At such times the people knew hunger, though probably never famine.

Material Culture

As with most aboriginal groups who were above all fishermen, the Hupa occupied permanent houses for a large part of the year. They lived in substantial rectangular structures built wholly of cedar planks. Overlapping boards covered the three-pitched roof. The interior contained an excavated pit, its sides retained by planks set on edge, with an elevated earthen shelf left between it and the house walls. Near the center of the pit lay a shallow depression bordered with stones for the fire. The doorway, at one corner, consisted of a circular hole just large enough to squeeze through; a notched plank served as a stairway down into the dug-out portion. Of-

ten a neat cobble pavement covered the ground in front of the residence.

Customarily a dwelling housed a single family. Here its members assembled for meals and here the women and children slept. Space on the earthen shelf next to the walls was utilized for storing stocks of food, firewood, and family possessions. Only briefly during the autumn acorn-gathering season did the family residence stand empty. When in the countryside for the harvest the families took to roofless brush shelters or camped in the open.

In addition to the family houses, every Hupa village contained several sweathouses. Smaller than the dwellings, these structures were built around a rectangular pit about four feet deep and lined with planks to prevent a cave-in. Only the pitched roof and the surrounding stone pavement were visible above ground. Entrance was through an opening in the roof with descent into the pit

Fig. 5. Big Willis, Hupa, with hunting equipment. He wears a breechclout of cloth instead of the traditional deerskin and a waistband of dentalium shells and perforated coins. Photograph by A.W. Ericson, 1890s.

by means of a plank with cut footholds. Generally a sudatory was built and used by a group of men related to one another through the male line. It served not only for daily sweating but also as workshop, clubhouse, and sleeping quarters for men and older boys.

The generally mild climate made heavy clothing unnecessary. A breechclout of deerskin or of several smaller animal skins sewed together formed the only article of dress worn daily by males (fig. 5), and elderly men lounging about the sweathouse or wandering around the village commonly dispensed with even this. Female garb was more elaborate, comprising a two-piece buckskin skirt, extending from the waist to below the knees. The larger section, its border fringed, covered the back and hips, whereas a narrow piece, consisting of many strips attached to a belt, concealed the front of the body. For added warmth, men and women alike threw robes of deer or other animal skins over their shoulders or wrapped them around the body. Footgear was rarely worn, buckskin moccasins being put on only when departing on a long journey. Hunters and travelers passing through brushy country covered their thighs with knee-length leggings of the same material. Close-fitting, bowl-shaped basketry caps (fig. 4), designed to afford protection from the carrying strap of burden baskets and baby cradles, were worn almost constantly by women.

Both sexes wore the hair long. Males tied theirs in two bunches, which hung in front of the shoulders, or in a single one behind. Females arranged the hair in two rolls, each held together with a thong. Women had three broad vertical bands tattooed on their chins (fig. 4) and sometimes marks were added to the corner of the mouth (Sapir 1936). The earlobes of all individuals were punctured for the insertion of shell ornaments.

Woodworking and basketweaving constituted the most important industries. Hupa men manufactured house planks, chests for the storage of ceremonial regalia, platters and bowls, low stools, and sweathouse headrests from cedar, a soft and easily worked material. Other articles, such as bows and tobacco pipes (fig. 6), were fashioned from harder varieties. The woodworkers achieved excellent results with a limited stock of tools.

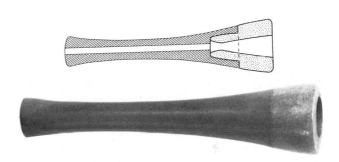

Fig. 6. Hupa wooden pipe with steatite bowl. Inset shows construction. Length 11.0 cm, collected before 1913.

Basketweaving, carried on exclusively by females, provided most household utensils as well as storage containers, cradles, caps, and special dance appurtenances. The baskets were fashioned by one technique—twining. They were either closely woven so that the warps did not appear at all, or open, the twigs of the foundation being merely held in place by chains of wefts. Hazel shoots provided the warps for nearly all baskets; strong filaments from tree roots served as wefts. Ornamentation was achieved by overlaying with white bear grass and introducing geometric patterns in black maidenhair fern stems and giant fern stems, colored red with alder bark.

Men showed considerable proficiency in working horn, particularly elk. Large spoons were steamed and cut into shape. The spoons were used for eating solely by males; ordinary mussel shells sufficed for women. Additional horn and bone articles included money boxes (fig. 7), net-mesh measures, wedges, and stone-flaking tools. The men also manufactured arrowpoints and other weapons and tools of stone, braided rope and twine, wove nets (fig. 8), and tanned animal hides.

For water transport the Hupa employed canoes hollowed out of one-half of a redwood log. These were not made locally but obtained in trade from the Yurok. Such craft were capable of carrying five or six adults or sev-

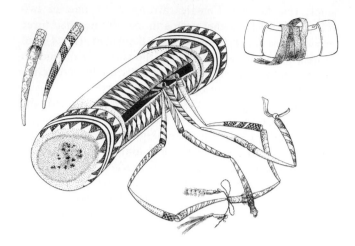

Dept. of Anthr., Smithsonian: Purse, 126521; Dentalium money, 21322.

Fig. 7. Hupa elk-horn purse (money box) with contents of strung dentalium. Purse is decorated with incised triangles rubbed with black pigment and grooved lines painted red. The exposed porous end of the elk horn is also red. Length 16.1 cm, collected 1883. Upper right shows manner in which purse opening was covered by splint and secured by its buckskin wrapping. The splint is made from an ivory scale for a centigrade thermometer, manufactured on the East Coast. Left inset shows detail of decoration on two of the dentalia. The left one is incised, and both are wrapped in reptile skin. Length of each 5.2 cm, collected 1875.

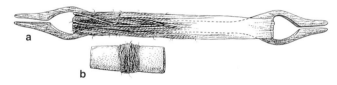

Dept. of Anthr., Smithsonian: a, 131151; b, 341287.

Fig. 8. a, Hupa netting shuttle made of wood wrapped with length of two-ply fiber twine. Length of shuttle (needle) 39.7 cm, collected 1889. b, Hupa net winder, used for winding fish-net twine; made from section of rib bone wrapped with length of two-ply fiber twine. Same scale, collected before 1928.

the coastal dwellers with acorns and additional inland foods. Considerably less trade was carried on with the riverine Yurok and Karok, because the products of these people were too much like those of the Hupa to allow for extensive bartering. Sporadic commerce was also conducted with other Indian groups.

Instead of bartering for them, products were sometimes purchased with dentalium shell money (fig. 7). Each of the thin, tubelike shells, which came from the waters off Vancouver Island, was evaluated according to its length, with examples less than an inch and one-half long not considered as currency. Standardized ways of measuring the dentalia included matching five strung shells of equal size with one of a series of marks tattooed on the inside of a man's left forearm (fig. 9).

Lowie Mus., U. of Calif., Berkeley.

Fig. 9. Mr. McCann, Hupa, measuring dentalium shell money against tattoo marks on his forearm. Photograph by Pliny E. Goddard, 1901.

eral thousand pounds of cargo. They were propelled with narrow-bladed, square-ended paddles.

Though water travel was the preferred form of transport, there was considerable foot traffic. Well-worn pathways linked the villages, and trading trails led across the mountains to the coast and elsewhere. Along the trails were traditional stopping places where passersby removed their packs and rested. Special trees into which arrows were shot for good luck and votive spots where a traveler dropped a stick or stone and offered a prayer for safety on his journey lay along the routes (Goddard 1913).

Exchanges of commodities took place chiefly with the Yurok inhabiting the coast near the mouth of the Klamath. In return for dried seaweed, which yielded salt, surf fish, and other marine products, the Hupa supplied

Social and Political Organization

A minimum of conventional organization characterized Hupa society. The family formed the fundamental unit. Typically this numbered six to seven persons and was composed of a man, his wife, their children, and an unattached relative or two; however, social ties extended beyond the immediate family and linked several patrilineally related households together into a larger informal grouping. The families resided near one another and cooperated in many activities. The men built and occupied a common sweathouse.

Generally several such groups of near kin shared a village site though the inhabitants of a smaller community were sometimes all blood relatives or nearly so. The village had no real solidarity and its members were likely to act together only if they were kindred. Regular village chiefs and councils were wanting.

The 12 main Hupa settlements were strung out along the banks of the Trinity, each separated from its neighbor by less than a mile (fig. 10). Almost without exception, they lay near a spring or tributary stream from which drinking water could be obtained. Near at hand too was a sandy stretch of river bank, suitable for beaching canoes. The villages had no discernible planned layout.

Above Hoopa Valley is the "Sugar Bowl" whose bottom harbored Haslinding, the southernmost of the principal settlements. A few miles farther upriver in little patches of valley were two additional permanent settlements, both quite small. Others were mentioned in early sources as being in this region.

Communities differed considerably in population, having from 50 to 200 inhabitants. The number of houses varied from 6 to 28 (table 1). Each village had its own name, taken from a landmark ('deep-water place'), peculiarity ('place of canoes'), or mythical incident ('place where he was dug up').

Table 1. Hupa Villages

Village	Number of Houses			
	1851	1852	1903	1956
xonsahdiŋ	9	9	11	
dahk'isxa·nǫid[a]			7	
k'inč̓ʷiWǫid			8	
če·ʔindigoidiŋ			12	
misǫid	6	6	9	
taʔk'imiłdiŋ	20	20	14	
ce·wina·ldiŋ	10	10	6	
tołča ʔčdiŋ[b]				8
miʔdildiŋ	28	28	22	
xowaŋǫid			14	
diyšta·ŋʔa·diŋ		9	13	
xahslindiŋ		6	9	

Source: Cook 1956:100.

[a] Inhabited until about time of military occupancy of Hoopa Valley.
[b] Deserted in 1850; estimated figure.

A loose arrangement of settlements into upriver and downriver divisions existed for the purpose of holding important religious ceremonies and for constructing the communal fishweir. Certain regional loyalties may also have been involved since the two supplied the opposing forces in the valley's only major internecine war (Goldschmidt and Driver 1940:104). There was no unit above these geographical divisions. Like peoples everywhere, the Hupa were conscious of their identity as a separate division of mankind, sharing the same language and customs. But they did not see themselves as a political entity and felt no obligations or allegiances toward their fellows.

The complete absence of tribal-wide political authority and leadership did not mean that there was no law and order, for a precise code of rules that regulated individual conduct had been worked out. Its key principle was that every wrong, intentional or not, had to be compensated for, preferably in money, though the threat of force and blood revenge was always present. Offenses were against the individual and initiative to bring action rested with the injured party or his family. An impartial go-between, employed to settle a dispute, negotiated with the principals until satisfactory redress was agreed upon. Prolonged haggling was customary because the aggrieved had to show tenacity in insisting upon his rights or he lost face. The law did not have everywhere the same force, since the numbers, wealth, and power of the kin groups involved, as well as their resolution, figured heavily in the settlement.

Many person-to-person quarrels arose, but it was usually possible to settle them by mediation so as to avoid any exercise of force and resultant bloodshed; however, violence occasionally flared up, most often in reprisal for an unatoned killing or to avenge an illness or death believed to have been caused by witchcraft. Normally hostilities concerned only a few individuals and took the form of blood feuds between Hupa kin groups or with corresponding divisions among a neighboring people (Wallace 1949). Rarely, an entire village community became involved but never the Hupa as a whole.

Fighting weapons included bows and arrows, short stabbing spears, stone knives, and ordinary rocks. For protection a few warriors wore corselets of vertical wooden rods or heavy elkhide shirts. Shields were unknown. Generally the conflicts were short-lived and the casualties few, but a rather protracted war with the Yurok, which took place sometime between 1830 and 1840, resulted in a heavy loss of life on both sides (Kroeber 1925:50-51; Spott and Kroeber 1942:202-209; Sapir 1927). Ambushes and surprise raids were the preferred tactics. Hostilities ended with a formal peace-making ceremony arranged by an intermediary. Each death and injury suffered was paid for separately and recompense was made for all property taken or destroyed.

The Hupa and their immediate neighbors were unique among California Indians in their extraordinary preoccupation with wealth and social position. Wealth meant, in addition to shell currency, skins of albino or unusually colored deerskins, large chipped blades of imported black or red obsidian, scarlet-feathered woodpecker scalps glued to wide buckskin bands (figs. 11-12), and a number of lesser valuables. These rare and precious things, proudly displayed at group festivals, formed the basis of a person's fortune and consequent social position. They exchanged hands only in important transactions such as payment of a bride price, a shaman's fee, or an indemnity for a killing. Certain other forms of private

169

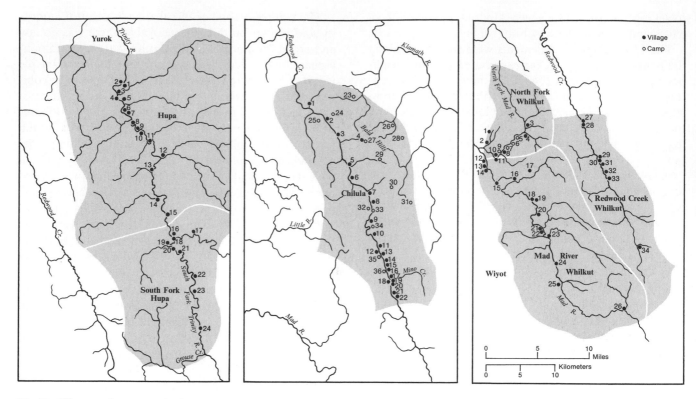

Fig. 10. Villages and camps of the Hupa, Chilula, and Whilkut.

Hupa villages. 1. *xonsahdiŋ* '(water) is deep-place'. 2. *dahKʸisxa·nqid* 'a tree grows above-on'. 3. *KʸinčʷiWqid* 'its nose-on'. 4. *če·ʔindigoidiŋ* 'it wiggled out of the ground-place'. 5. *misqid* 'cliff-on'. 6. *taʔKʸimiłdiŋ* 'one prepares acorn mush-place'. 7. *ce·wina·ldiŋ* (not translatable). 8. *tołčaʔčdiŋ* 'seepage-place'. 9. *miʔdildiŋ* 'boat-place'. 10. *xowaŋqid* (not translatable). 11. *diʸšta·ŋʔa·diŋ* (or *ʒiʸšta·ŋʔa·diŋ*) 'diʸš-promontory-place'. 12. *xahslindiŋ* 'eddy-place'. 13.–15. Hupa names uncertain. 16. *ta·Kʸiwe·lcilqid* 'it squats into the river-on'. 17. *miyimiʔ* 'taboo place-in it'. 18. *łe·ldiŋ* 'confluence-place'. 19. *dilčʷihsʒidiŋ* 'little pine tree-place'. 20. *čiłte·ldiŋ* 'bed mat-place'. 21. *qosta·ndiŋ* 'basket hat-place'. 22. *łčiWdiŋ* 'sand-place'. 23. *ło·qmiʔ* 'salmon-in it'. 24. *da·čʷanʔdiŋ* (or perhaps *dahčʷinʔdiŋ* 'gooseberry-place').

Chilula villages and camps. 1. *xowana·qid*. 2. *nolihdiŋ* 'falls-place'. 3. *Xoʔʒimiʔ* 'small glade-in it'. 4. *kʸiŋkʸohlayʔ* 'big timber-point, summit'. 5. *kʸiŋyikʸa·wmiŋwah* 'timber which is big-near it'. 6. *yisiʔniŋʔayqid* 'downhill ridge-on'. 7. *činʔsila·diŋ* 'bones lie there-place'. 8. *to·ndinandiŋ*. 9. *yinaginomice·diŋ* 'upstream door-place'. 10. *xontihłmiʔ* 'flat-in it'. 11. *Xoʔʒiqid* (?) 'little glade-on' (cf. 3.). 12. *łčiWina·Wdiŋ* 'dust, sand flies-place'. 13. *qayliWtahdiŋ* 'among the willows-place'. 14. *qayliWce·ŋʔe·Xdiŋ* 'willows stick out-place'. 15. *sikʸiŋčʷiŋmitahdiŋ*. 16. *Kʸinaʔxontahdiŋ* 'Yurok house-place'. 17. *Kʸidina·tahdiŋ* (?). 18. *xowaŋqid* (not translatable). 19. *dahčina·ldiŋ* (?). 20. *dahsaŋʒiqid* (?). 21. *mismiʔ* 'cliff-in it'. 22. *qa·xistahdiŋ* 'arrow-wood among-place'. 23. *čidilye·diŋ* 'ceremonial dance place'. 24. *Xoʔʒxoda·wilindiŋ* 'little glade-water flows down hill-place'. 25. *yici·ʔne·qidčiŋʔ* 'toward downhill'. 26. *tihsʔayqid* 'sticks into the water-on'. 27. *ce·na·lma·čdiŋ* 'stones in a circle-place'. 28. *Kʸidiłwisqid* 'fire drill-on'. 29. *niʔwilcowmiyih* 'ground bent-under it'. 30. *Kʸiʒiwʔna·me·diŋ* 'its ear swims around-place'. 31. *čʷaŋʔxa·lʔa·diŋ* 'dung sticks up-place'. 32. *miŋqidigʸe·yima·nčinʔčiŋʔ* 'lake to the West'. 33. *xodahdiniʔ* (?). 34. *Xohdayʔxa·lʔa·diŋ* 'wild oats-stick up-place'. 35. *gaWkʸohmiʔ* 'redwoods-in them'. 36. *xosdaʒimiʔ* (?).

Whilkut villages and camps. 1. *Xo·qiʒ* (?) 'little prairie'. 2. Kawchosishtintang. 3. *xayahmiʔ* 'fishing claim-in it'. 4. *če·yKʸina·diwilwoʔdiŋ* (?) 'brush (?)-place'. 5. *nolihmiʔ* 'waterfall-in it'. 6. *Kʸisdayʔqid* (?). 7. *qayliWdiŋ* 'willows-place'. 8. Hootsoechookah. 9. Katsiatoo. 10. *mikʸiʔdimiʔ* 'its tail (mouth of creek)-place'. 11. *ta·kʸiWčinʔdiŋ* 'sweathouse-toward-place'. 12. Djinakhoeten. 13. *dilgaydiŋ* 'whitish-place'. 14. *če·nče·diŋ* 'it blows out from somewhere-place'. 15. *mikʸohdiŋ* 'its bigness (grizzly bear)-place' (?). 16. *ʔa·diʒła·n·ce·wilindiŋ* 'many grasshoppers-pour out-place'. 17. *yidaŋnolihdiŋ* 'uphill waterfall-place'. 18. *kʸaʔ·dahsila·diŋ* 'skirts-they lie on top-place'. 19. Whotsdjotachetin. 20. *ce·ditisdiŋ* (?) 'stones on top of one another-place'. 21. *dilčʷihyiwqid* 'underneath the pine tree-place'. 22. *xodinte·lmiʔ* (?). 23. Yinalinowhot. 24. *miyimiʔ* 'taboo place-in it'. 25. Whilkut name unknown. 26. *ce·na·niŋʔa·diŋ* 'rock stretches across the river-place'. 27. *čiłqanʔdiŋ* 'one roasts it-place'. 28. *yinahčiŋʔdiyšdiŋ* 'upstream toward-(?)-place'. 29. Estishchemmeh. 30. *cinʔdiłgaymiʔ* 'white bones-in it' (?). 31. Mestatimteng. 32. *ta·na·na·qid* (?). 33. *čime·no·ŋʔa·qid* 'fir tree lies extended to there-on'. 34. *na·yisWa·łqid* 'it hooks (fish)-on'. The following five villages cannot be mapped, although they probably belong in this order between nos. 33 and 34: *ce·na·daʔayqid* 'rock stands up-place' (on the east side of Redwood Creek, far up, near Chaparral Mt.), *łiʒma·qid* 'clay-on' (formerly on the ridge on the east side of Redwood Creek), *me·me·qid* 'fern-on' (former big village on Mamakut Creek), *XiwWto·miʔdiŋ* (?) 'snake-water in-place' (formerly on the east side of Redwood Creek), and *na·sqa·na·qid* (?) (formerly high up on Redwood Creek).

170

Fig. 11. Hupa participants in the White Deerskin Dance displaying paraphernalia indicating wealth. Photograph by A.W. Ericson, before 1897.

property—house sites, the choicest and most productive fishing spots, hunting and gathering places—also possessed great economic value. In contrast, little monetary value attached to ordinary utilitarian objects.

Individuals were ranked according to the amount of wealth they possessed. This led to a series of intergrading social positions. Theoretically it was possible to better one's station in life by industry, extraordinary ability, or luck. Actually, because property was difficult to accumulate and was passed on in family lines, a man poor in worldly goods was likely to remain so. Rank distinctions were evident in the deference paid to a rich man, in the valuation placed upon a person involved in a legal suit, and in dozens of other ways. Clustered about a wealthy man was a group of kinsmen, close and remote, and various hangers-on, who were willing to follow his advice and do his bidding out of respect for his riches and personal prestige and for his support in time of need or when embroiled in a dispute. Such a man's influence did not extend beyond his immediate followers and he was in no sense a village chief or headman.

A form of slavery was recognized, though it was scarcely important. Enslavement came solely through debt. The usual cause was failure or inability to pay a fine levied in a legal case. A man held in bondage performed work similar to his master's and did not suffer maltreatment. If an owner liked and respected his slave,

he might buy him a wife (Driver 1939:414). The bondsman and his family retained the privilege of purchasing his liberty.

Life Cycle

Certain critical periods in the cycle of life—birth, girls' puberty, and death—were accompanied by traditional magical and religious observances. Marriage was treated in a more matter-of-fact manner, in many ways like a business transaction.

As soon as she knew a baby was coming, a woman fell subject to many regulations to keep it from harm (E.S. Taylor 1947). She had to be careful of her diet, avoiding meat and fish and eating sparingly of other foods. Magical formulas were recited over her to insure an easy birth and the well-being of her unborn child (Goddard 1904:275-277). Aside from being obliged to refrain from sexual intercourse, the husband was immune from restraints.

With the first labor pains, the mother-to-be retired to the seclusion of the dwelling, attended by an older kinswoman. During parturition she assumed a sitting position and held fast to a leather strap attached to a roof beam. If the delivery proved difficult, a special formula was said. Immediately following the birth, the midwife cut and tied the navel cord. Next she bathed the infant

Fig. 12. Hupa participants in the Jumping Dance at the Yurok town of *pekʷon* on the Klamath River. By A.W. Ericson, 1893.

and steamed it over a cooking basket containing a decoction of boiling water and herbs.

For 10 days the mother lay in a pit lined with heated stones covered with damp wormwood or sand to hasten her recovery from the effects of childbirth. Meat, fresh fish, and cold water were excluded from her diet. The father too ate no meat and for 10 days did no hunting or gambling. When the remaining stub of the infant's umbilical cord dropped off, he deposited it in a gash cut into a young pine. It was believed that as the tree grew, so grew the child.

The newborn was not nursed for the first few days of life. Instead it received a thin gruel of mashed pine nuts or hazelnut meats. Thereafter it was given the breast whenever it manifested signs of hunger. Nursing continued for two to three years. On the tenth day following its birth, the baby, wrapped in a soft deerskin, was strapped into a basketry cradle of the sitting type, and here it remained, except for bathing and exercising periods, until it learned to walk. No personal name was bestowed until the child reached the age of five years or more. Up until that time it was addressed as "baby," "little girl," or by an affectionate term.

Children were left pretty much to their own devices and most of their time passed in play; however, they were carefully instructed in etiquette and morality with particular attention devoted to correct eating habits (Wallace 1947). Necessary technical and economic skills were acquired gradually, largely through seeing and doing. Disciplinary methods were mild, the usual punishment being a reprimand. At the age of eight or thereabouts a boy joined his father and male kinsmen in the sweathouse.

A pubescent girl was considered unclean and her glance contaminating, so she remained secluded for 10 days. Precautionary measures to protect others included covering her head with a deerskin when it became necessary for her to go outdoors. The menstruant was put

172

under the usual food taboos and was permitted to drink only warm water. Scratching with the fingernails was prohibited, a nicely carved piece of bone (fig. 13) being provided for this purpose. As the girl's actions at this time supposedly influenced her future behavior, her mother and other female relatives, who visited her daily, urged her to keep clean and be good-tempered and industrious. In families of high station a girl's coming of age was celebrated with a public ceremony. No observances marked a boy's arrival at adulthood.

Marriage took place at 15 or 16 for a girl, a year or two later for a boy. The choice of a mate was limited by blood relationship. Near kin, whether on the father's or the mother's side, could not marry. Unions between young people from families of corresponding social status were preferred. Negotiations were initiated by the boy's relatives through an intermediary and a bride price in shell money and other valuables agreed upon. Even though closely bargained, the sum finally settled upon was generous because the social standing of the couple and their offspring depended upon it. A bride brought a dowry of essential household goods to the marriage. No wedding ceremony was held, merely a feast and an exchange of gifts between the two families. As a rule the young married couple settled in the husband's village.

For a youth whose kindred were too poor to afford the bride price or unwilling to raise it, there was the less prestigious "half-marriage." Under this arrangement part of the purchase price was paid and the groom went to live in his father-in-law's house. Various other situations, such as a family having no sons or a parent being unwilling to permit a daughter to leave home, also led to this alternative form. Children of half-marriages belonged to the wife's family.

Polygyny was permissible but only a few rich and prominent men could afford more than one spouse. Relatively few conventional regulations governed relationships between relatives acquired by marriage. A man could talk freely to his wife's mother and his bride to his father.

Sexual relations between husband and wife were severely limited by the many occasions, including the pursuit of wealth, that required continence, and the practice of maintaining separate sleeping quarters for males and females. Cohabitation was confined largely to the late summer and fall when the family camped out together. Understandably it was during this period that practically all conceptions occurred.

If a matrimonial alliance failed, it was usually quickly dissolved. The male partner who sent his wife back to her people for legitimate reasons (laziness, ill temper, barrenness, or infidelity) demanded refund of the full purchase money if the union had been childless. A woman could leave her husband for just causes, such as maltreatment or unfaithfulness. Again, if there were no offspring, the entire bride price was returned.

Hard, steady labor on the part of both males and females characterized adult life; however, time was set aside for visiting, games, story telling, and other diversions. The hand game, played with a bundle of sticks, one marked with a black band, was a favorite of the men. Women wagered on the toss of four mussel-shell disks. Athletic contests included wrestling and a rough type of shinny. Story telling helped pass many a long winter night. Smoking furnished a bedtime relaxation for males. Tobacco grown in small gardens near the village was smoked in a short tubular pipe fashioned from hardwood, with a soapstone inset (fig. 6).

When someone died the body was disposed of as soon as burial arrangements could be completed. The corpse, wrapped in deerskin and tied to a board, was carried out through a hole in the house wall and lowered into a shallow plank-lined grave. A board placed on top made a complete box, which was then covered with earth. No large amount of personal belongings was placed in the grave, but utensils, implements, and clothes, broken or torn to render them useless, were deposited on top of it. Bereaved relatives in attendance at the burial expressed their grief in loud wailing.

The funeral over, grave diggers, corpse handlers, and the deceased's family underwent ritual purification to remove the polluting effects of death. Close relatives, men and women alike, cropped their hair as a sign of mourning. In addition, members of the household wore twisted grass necklaces to ward off dreaming of the dead. To utter the departed person's name in the hearing of a kinsman constituted a serious offense. It often happened that the name contained a word for some common animal or object and a new designation had to be invented at least for use in the presence of the bereaved (Goddard 1901). A widow was expected to marry one of her dead husband's brothers, though this was not strictly enforced. Similarly, if a wife died without bearing children, her family substituted a sister or other kinswoman.

Before journeying to the land of the dead, an individual's soul was believed to haunt the village for four days, endeavoring to reenter its former residence. On the fifth

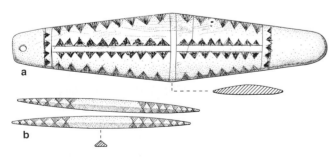

Dept. of Anthr., Smithsonian: a, 77198; b, 77199.
Fig. 13. a, Hupa scraper for crushing hair lice; elk bone with design incised and filled with dark pigment; length 19.0 cm, collected 1885. b, Hupa bone hairpins, also incised, collected 1885, same scale.

day it descended to a damp, dark underworld. Only the spirits of shamans and singers in the major ceremonies followed a trail to a more pleasant abode in the sky. Disembodied souls were thought to reappear at times to plague the living, particularly relatives.

Religion

Religious beliefs and practices played an important part in everyday life. An almost endless series of taboos had to be scrupulously observed, daily supplications made for health and wealth, and preventive acts performed to bring luck. Too, each person was supposed to maintain a devout frame of mind throughout the day, particularly during important group rituals when reverent thoughts by participants and onlookers were considered essential for its successful accomplishment.

The most colorful part of Hupa religion centered around two group ceremonials designed to revitalize the world for the coming year and to ward off famine, disease, and other disasters (Woodruff 1892; Kroeber and Gifford 1949). Enacted by men, they were held annually in the late summer or fall and each lasted 10 days. Providing regalia for the occasions was the privilege of certain influential families or kin groups, thus affording them an opportunity to exhibit their major treasures, for much of the paraphernalia consisted of objects of high value. The traditional procedures for the two public spectacles were precisely prescribed and inseparably linked to particular hallowed spots or localities. Recital of a long narrative formed the most sacred part of both. This told how the ritual had been established by an ancient race of supernaturals. Recounting the actions of these beings and their ensuing effects supposedly produced like results.

Although the two world-renewal and wealth-display ceremonies—the White Deerskin and Jumping Dances—conformed in many of their essential features, each had its own dance steps, songs, and finery. Performers in the White Deerskin Dance held albino or other oddly colored deerskins aloft on long poles (fig. 11) or carried obsidian blades wrapped around with a piece of buckskin (Goldschmidt and Driver 1940). The distinctive Jumping Dance appurtenances consisted of woodpecker-scalp headbands (fig. 12) and tubular baskets containing straw to preserve their shape (Barrett 1963).

Less elaborate observances were held each year to sanctify the first eating of acorns and salmon, and thus to insure a continuing supply of the two foods upon which Hupa livelihood rested. The Acorn Feast was celebrated in the autumn when the nuts began to fall from tan oaks; the First Salmon ceremony took place when the spring run of fish began (Goddard 1903–1904:78–81; Kroeber and Gifford 1949:57–60). The acorns or salmon were obtained and ritually cooked by a regular officiant who also repeated a lengthy for-

mula, said prayers, and executed various sacred acts. Until these procedures were completed, no one ate the food. The first eel taken in the spring received similar treatment.

When pestilence threatened, a 10-day dance was performed to keep it away. Another class of rites comprised those conducted for the benefit of an individual, a sick child, a pubescent girl, or a novice shaman. Regalia were not elaborate but singing and dancing were featured.

The Hupa believed in the existence of a myriad of supernatural beings but by and large they received little ritual attention. A divinity born of the union of sun and earth was invoked by young men seeking wealth. The vegetable world was controlled by a bearded dwarf and the people were careful not to offend him by wasting food. Spiritual beings tended the deer, and hunters prayed and sang at the time of embarking on an expedition to keep them content. Numerous local spirits had their abodes in mountains, rocks, riffles, and other features of the landscape. Passersby offered prayers to these supernaturals to ensure safe passage or success in the task at hand.

Diseases and Cures

Illnesses were ascribed mostly to supernatural causes and there were professional shamans to diagnose and treat them. Shamanism took on a unique aspect among the Hupa and their nearer neighbors in that the practitioners were predominantly females. Men could become healers, but few males followed the calling. A medicine woman received her extraordinary power from swallowing a "pain," a semianimate object described as being an inch or two long. Normally this was placed in her mouth by the ghost of her mother or other close female relative, formerly engaged in the profession. Usually this occurred unexpectedly in a dream but a few women deliberately sought power through nightly vigils in lonesome places. After acquiring a pain, the novice learned to control it during an arduous period of instruction under the direction of an experienced medicine woman. A public dance terminated her training and announced her readiness to minister to the sick.

A pain, caught out of the air or shot into the body by an evilly disposed person, produced illness in an ordinary individual and had to be removed by a shaman. Called to treat a patient, the doctor smoked a special pipe before applying her lips. She sucked with great force until the harmful object became dislodged.

Medicine women charged high fees, payable in advance, for their services. If a patient failed to show improvement or died within the year, the charge was refunded. An unsuccessful shaman was not killed unless she refused to make restitution. Medical practitioners were people of consequence and exceptionally powerful ones were known far and wide.

Lesser disorders like an upset stomach or headache were treated with spoken formulas, almost always accompanied by herbal medicines. The medications were administered in such minute quantity or in such a way as to have little or no effect. Relief was supposed to stem from the words uttered rather than from the plant substances. Medicine formulas, handed down in family lines, represented a valuable form of property since a stiff charge was made for their recital.

Certain formulas, sometimes repeated over and over again, could be used to destroy an enemy or to cause him to fall ill. Sorcery could also be worked by burying a person's nail parings, a lock of his hair, or a piece of his clothing near a grave or in a damp spot, or by introducing "poisons" into his food or tobacco (Wallace and Taylor 1950). The most terrifying doers of black magic were those who, under cover of darkness, struck down their fellows with invisible missiles loosed from a miniature bow shaped from a human rib and strung with sinew taken from the wrist of a recently interred corpse. Evil could be worked by anyone who knew the correct procedures but was believed to have been employed most often by males.

Literature, Art, and Music

Hupa mythology recognized an ancient era definitely set apart from the recent period. At this time the earth looked much as it does today. On it lived the Kixunai (*kʸixinay*), human in form and nature, but endowed with supernatural powers. It was in this early epoch that Hupa customs, industries, and arts were founded, many by the Kixunai leader, Lost-across-the-ocean (Goddard 1904:123–134). Through trickery he liberated deer and salmon from their owners. Lost-across-the-ocean also instituted the modern method of childbirth, women having previously been cut open at the time of delivery. Among his other exploits was the destruction of several cannibals. This culture hero was not wholly good and altruistic. He constantly sought sexual gratification and his actions were frequently governed by his elation or chagrin as he succeeded or failed with a woman.

When smoke on the mountainsides signaled the coming of mortals, the Kixunai, fearing contamination, fled in canoes downriver and across the ocean to dwell forever in a land beyond the bounds of the known world. The appearance of humans was not attributed to a special creation: they merely sprang into existence. Lost-across-the-ocean remained behind briefly to teach the people how to live. Since their ancestors were believed to have come into existence within their own territory, the Hupa had no legend of migration from another land.

Besides the myths a great many stories of a less serious nature were told. Adults and children alike showed a fondness for adventures of the mischievous trickster, Coyote. Coyote tales, not particularly numerous, tended to be short and simple. Of a different order were narratives which referred to the Indian world. Some told of recent happenings; others, into which mythical or supernatural elements had crept, dealt with the more distant past (Wallace 1948).

The Hupa shared a purely geometric art with the Yurok and Karok. Designs were carved into the handles of wooden mush paddles and horn spoons and incised upon dentalium money purses (fig. 7) and minor articles of bone (fig. 13) and horn (Kelly 1930). Art also found expression in basketry decoration. Combinations of triangles and other figures in black and red were woven against a white background (fig. 4). Basketry patterns were more varied and complex than those seen in carving or incising. Although named from supposed likenesses to living and nonliving things, they had no symbolic meaning. Painted designs embellished a few utilitarian and ceremonial objects.

Music was primarily vocal. A distinctive and peculiar singing style was held in common with the Yurok and Karok. This showed a more rhythmical pattern and a wider range of intonation and richness than that of other Californians. Instruments used to accompany singing included a wooden clapper, a bone whistle, and a deerhoof rattle. Young men played on a wooden flute for amusement or to serenade a lady love. In aboriginal times the Hupa knew no drum. A plank, stamped upon or kicked, served as a substitute. A drum made from a box and with a cover of hide came into use during the historic period. It was beaten in time with gambling songs.

History

The Hupa remained secluded in their remote valley until near the middle of the nineteenth century. Fur trappers, passing through to other destinations, were the first outsiders to enter their country. More sustained contacts came in 1850, following the discovery of gold on the upper Trinity River. White and Chinese miners prospected in Hoopa Valley and several gold-bearing gravel bars were discovered, but these were soon worked out.

A few miners took up land and homesteaders slowly drifted in. Troubled conditions and fearful rumors led to the stationing of federal troops at Fort Gaston, established in Hoopa Valley in 1858. It was not until 1892, long after the need for it had passed, that the little military post was abandoned. The idle soldiers constituted a continuing menace to the Indians' well-being and their presence resulted in a large infusion of Caucasian blood into the native population.

In 1864 Congress authorized the setting aside of almost the entire Hupa territory for a reservation (E. Anderson 1956). White settlers were reimbursed for their land and improvements and forced to move out. Uninterrupted occupancy of their homeland greatly benefited the Hupa. It helped to make the proportion of survivors one of the highest in California (table 2); and, in combination with the remoteness of their country and the absence of White settlers, it slowed down the disruption of native life. Old customs dropped out and were replaced so slowly that the people were able to adjust to changing conditions. Pressures from American civilization did not lead to messianic movements as they did elsewhere in California. Though they knew the 1870 Ghost Dance, accepted by their Yurok and Karok neighbors, the Hupa took no part in it, presumably because their traditional religion still had so powerful a hold (Du Bois 1939:24).

Gradually the Indians settled into a rural American type of life and became self-supporting. They began to till small plots of valley land and to keep livestock. Some found employment at the fort or on the reservation, in seasonal work on nearby ranches, in logging, and in other occupations. A boarding school and government-run hospital were set up on the reservation. Organized missionary activity commenced and some Hupa became converted to Christianity.

Today the Hoopa Reservation is the largest (87,000 acres) and most populous in California and has the greatest accumulation of tribal funds (California State Advisory Commission on Indian Affairs 1966:91-92). The reservation is very rich in timber. When trees are felled by private lumbermen, the Indians are compensated. Tribal revenue exceeds $1,000,000 a year. A portion of this income is distributed semiannually to the more than 1,100 persons on the tribal rolls (in 1970) with a $1,000,000 reserve maintained.

Prosperity and modernization followed World War II. The postwar lumber boom created an abundance of well-paid jobs in the woods and in the four mills. New businesses added to the number of goods and services available to the community. Most of the businesses are owned and operated by Whites, several hundred of whom moved into the valley. The shift to a wage economy and dependence upon tribal timber funds brought an end to virtually all farming and stock raising. The standard of living, though not high, is far superior to that of most California Indians. Increasingly the Hupa are managing their own affairs through the tribal council. Their offspring attend public schools with White children.

Notwithstanding the overwhelming preponderance of alien content in their contemporary culture, the Hupa retain a strong sense of ethnic identity (Bushnell 1968). The native language is still spoken, though many of the younger Indians know only a few words and phrases; and even most older people who speak it well feel more at ease in English. Efforts are being made to perpetuate or revive some of the cherished aspects of the aboriginal life. This growing concern for the fate of their legacy has little, if any, reference to the generalized pan-Indian movement. The Hupa insist that the traditions be kept just as they were given to their ancestors by the Kixunai

and Lost-across-the-ocean and not mixed with imports from other tribes.

Table 2. Hupa Population 1851-1962

Date	Total	Source
1851	1,000	Based on 7.5 persons in a household (Kroeber 1925:130)
	2,000[a]	Based on 10 persons in a household (Cook 1956:99-100)
1870	641	U.S. Indian Bureau reservation census (Kroeber 1925:131)
1906	420	C.E. Kelsey reservation census (Kroeber 1957a:220)
1910	639	U.S. census (Kroeber 1957a:222)
1962	992	Estimate (California State Advisory Commission on Indian Affairs Progress Report 1966:56)

[a] This figure, based on a higher house count and average occupancy, can be rated as much too high.

Synonymy

The term Hupa is not a native word but a rendering of the Yurok designation for their territory (Kroeber 1925:130). Like so many other tribal peoples, the Hupa had no name for themselves as a group. They have also been called Nabiltse, Natano, and Trinity Indians.

SOUTH FORK HUPA

Directly south of the Hupa lived a group of Indians closely affiliated with them culturally and linguistically. These people have been so generally classed with the better-known Hupa as to have no accepted name. They have been treated as a separate unit under the designation Kelta (Powers 1877:89) and have also been referred to as the Tsaningwha (Baumhoff 1958:210). It is said that the Hupa called them the *łe·lxʷe·*, from *łe·l* 'the convergence of two streams', and *xʷe·*, the usual termination signifying 'people'. Locally they were known as the South Fork Indians.

Their territory embraced the South Fork of the Trinity River, from the junction of the South Fork with the main Trinity to Grouse Creek, a distance of about 15 miles. The land is mountainous and forested and the streams flow in deep canyons; nevertheless it seems to have been rather well populated. There were at least nine villages, all situated on high benches overlooking the canyons (fig. 10). At South Fork, where the river branches, stood the principal settlement, the town of Tlelding, which figured prominently in Hupa myths.

South Fork culture was substantially like that of the Hupa, although of less complexity and intensity. The important differences lay in religious matters (Goddard 1903-1904:7). The language diverged only slightly from that spoken in Hoopa Valley.

The South Fork inhabitants maintained close contacts with the Hupa, whom they regularly visited, and the Chilula. They were almost out of touch with the Yurok and Karok. Trading and social relationships existed with the Wintu and Chimariko.

Those South Fork Hupas remaining were taken to the Hoopa Reservation shortly after its founding in 1876. Here they merged with their compatriots.

CHILULA

Language, Environment, and Territory

Flanking the Hupa on the west were the Chilula (chĭ'lōōlu), who were almost indistinguishable from their eastern neighbors in speech and differed from them in customs mainly in such matters as resulted from variations in their respective habitats. In a few particulars the Chilula shared the culture of groups farther south rather than that of the Trinity River.

The Chilula occupied most of the lower portion of Redwood Creek to a few miles above Minor Creek and the Bald Hills district. They were shut off from the seacoast by a Yurok group, known to them and the Hupa as "Teswan," who occupied villages at the mouth of the stream. Redwood Creek is confined on either side by steep hills. The western valley wall is heavily forested with redwoods, among which stand many tan oaks. On the eastern side the slope is broken by the valleys of numerous small tributaries, separated from each other by short transverse ridges. The higher portions of these ridges and much of the main range are devoid of timber and for this reason are called the Bald Hills. South of Bald Hills the stream is bordered by a series of flats on which many of the important native villages were situated.

Subsistence

Chilula economy was based primarily on the resources of Redwood Creek; but because this stream was less bountifully endowed with fish than the Klamath or the Trinity, greater emphasis was placed upon the exploitation of other products. Salmon were generally taken in the small branches by spears or at the base of natural waterfalls by means of dip nets (Goddard 1914:270). Large dragnets and gill nets appear not to have been employed (Driver 1939:312). A temporary brush fence was thrown across the creek to catch steelhead as they came back downstream after spawning (Kroeber and Barrett 1960:21). The fish were too emaciated for drying though still suitable for eating fresh. A more elaborate weir was erected for taking lamprey eels. Fishermen manipulated dip nets from two small platforms built near the center of the barrier. When the water was low, wad-ers threw stones to drive fish toward waiting men and women who scooped them up in baskets. Other methods included angling with hook and line and catching with the bare hands. In the dry season when there were pools with little flow between them, suckers and trout were drugged with soaproot.

Great dependence was placed upon vegetable foods. Various bulbs and seeds of grasses were sought during the summer and acorns were gathered in the fall.

The Chilula are reputed to have surpassed the Hupa as hunters. Meadows in the redwood forests were frequented by herds of elk and the half-open and half-timbered hills on the east attracted deer. The hunting techniques duplicated those of other northwestern tribes.

Material Culture

Typical northwest California rectangular wooden houses and small square sweathouses were built by the Chilula in their permanent villages. Two settlements contained large circular dance houses, evidently like those common in the central part of the state. Structures shaped like the regular dwellings, but without a pit and enclosed with bark instead of split lumber, were set up at acorn-gathering camps.

No basic differences separated the Chilula from the Hupa in dress and technology; however, minor dissimilarities in a few of the industrial arts did exist. For example, the Chilula knew and sometimes prepared headbands of yellowhammer quills, such as were worn ceremonially by central Californians. They did not make or use the dugout canoe; Redwood Creek is too small a stream to be navigable except in times of torrential floods.

Social and Political Organization

Social and political practices very closely paralleled those of the Hupa. Wealth received emphasis and rich men exerted considerable influence. One striking difference in property ideas apparently prevailed: fishing places do not seem to have been individually owned (Driver 1939:316). Hunting land, advantageous spots for snaring game, and seed-gathering tracts were privately held.

Communities were quite small, the average strength being 30 persons. Names and locations of 22 villages have been recorded (Goddard 1914:272–275; Baumhoff 1958:203–207). All but two lay on the eastern side of Redwood Creek (fig. 10), where the hillsides receive more sun and the timber is lighter. A few were situated as much as a mile from the stream.

Temporary camps were established annually at certain localities. In the summer the people dwelt chiefly in the grassy Bald Hills, where seeds as well as bulbs abounded and game was plentiful. In autumn they continued to reside in the Bald Hills or crossed Redwood Creek to harvest acorns on the shadier hillsides that slope down to the stream from the west. Sites of 14 camps are known (Goddard 1914:276-278; Baumhoff 1958:203-207).

Religion

Chilula religion seems to have been much less complex than that of the Hupa, at least in its public aspect. No certainty exists that these Indians followed the ceremonial pattern of their more affluent neighbors. They are said to have once performed the White Deerskin Dance, but neither the form of the ritual nor the spot at which it took place is remembered. In more recent times the Chilula participated as guests and contributors to the Hupa world-renewal dances; possibly, but not certainly, they did so in the past.

No special acts were carried out when salmon entered Redwood Creek each year. Likewise, no ceremony celebrated the ripening of the acorn crop. Specific rites were not held over the first catch of eels, except that lampreys had to be cooked and eaten on the adjacent stream bank during the initial five days of the life of the weir. Conversely, drying had to be done at home or at least away from the dam.

Ritual observances designed to promote the welfare of a pubescent girl were much like those of the Hupa. The menstruant remained confined to the dwelling, but only for five days, avoided meat, salt, and cold water, and employed a bone scratcher (Driver 1939:351-353). A public dance ended her seclusion. No special ceremony seems to have been performed over a sick child but a doctor-making dance was held.

In broad outline, magico-religious practices concerned with death and burial conformed to those of the area. The body awaiting burial was addressed as follows: "You are going away from me. You must not think of me" (Goddard 1914a:378). Evidently the purpose of this brief supplication was to discourage the deceased's spirit from lingering about the village or returning from the land of the dead. After a funeral, the principal mourners, pallbearers, and grave diggers had to be ceremonially cleansed from defilement. Formulas were recited, but the ritual bath in the river, an important part of Hupa purification, was not permitted.

Diseases and Cures

Concepts regarding illness and its cure varied little, if at all, from those of the Trinity and Klamath River Indians. Again most shamans were women. They acquired their curing ability in the same manner, through swallowing and learning to control a semianimate object of the kind that caused sickness.

Herbalists handled minor complaints. Their treatment included the reciting of a formula and giving medicine internally.

Literature

Chilula myths and tales show only small differences from those of the Hupa (Goddard 1914a). Exploits of the culture hero figure prominently in the stories.

History

The population when Whites appeared numbered 500-600, but the Chilula were decimated in the first five years of California statehood. Soon after mining opened on the Klamath and Salmon rivers in 1850 gold seekers and pack trains carrying their supplies began to pass through the Bald Hills, which were crossed by trails from both Trinidad and Humboldt Bay. Trouble soon arose and the Indians began waylaying miners and robbing pack trains (Gibbs 1853:124). Whites in turn shot them on sight.

Settlers organized a volunteer company and entered on a campaign of extermination and deportation. A large party of Chilulas, peacefully assembled for a council with the volunteers, were rounded up and removed to Humboldt Bay. Following a long delay, the captives were put on board ship and taken to Fort Bragg on the Mendocino coast, where they were placed on a reservation. While attempting to return home, all but one or two were massacred on the way by Lassik Indians. Chilulas who had not been taken prisoners, joined by several Hupas and Whilkuts, avenged their fellows by making several successful raids into Lassik territory (Goddard 1914a:351-352).

As hostilities continued, all travelers avoided Bald Hills and pack trains went to the mines over alternative routes. After some years the Indian agent at Hoopa successfully sought peace. The remaining families, with the exception of one or two, moved to Hoopa Valley. On the reservation they gradually lost the distinctiveness of their language and fell into the ways of the Hupa. As a separate people the Chilula no longer exist.

Synonymy

Chilula comes from the American rendering of the Yurok *čulula?* and *čulula·?* 'they frequent Bald Hills, they pass through Bald Hills' (*čulu* 'Bald Hills') (Kroeber 1925:137; Howard Berman, personal communication 1973). Local settlers always called them Bald Hills Indians.

WHILKUT

In the eyes of their Chilula and Hupa neighbors, the Whilkut (ʼhwĭlkut) represented a poor, backward, and less-settled hill people, to be treated with condescension. Their speech formed a fairly well-marked dialect as compared with Hupa in both pronunciation and vocabulary (Goddard 1903–1904:7).

The Whilkut lived along the upper course of Redwood Creek, above the Chilula. They also occupied the middle stretch of the Mad River, 10 miles or so from the mouth, and the North Fork as well. Apparently they had a settlement or two across the divide to the east in the Trinity drainage. The country is broken, rugged, and forested.

Very little can be said about the customs of these Indians for there is next to nothing in the way of ethnographic information. While they may have been influenced somewhat by their Wintu and Nongatl neighbors on the east and south, they maintained a manner of life quite like that of the Chilula. In spite of holding a considerable extent of territory, they cannot have been very numerous, perhaps totaling 500.

Subsistence

The placement of their villages in proximity to the banks of Redwood Creek and Mad River reflects dependence on the produce of these streams. Salmon, steelhead, and lamprey eels must have supplied a large proportion of the Whilkut food supply. It can be safely assumed that like the Chilula they too drew heavily upon the plant and animal resources of the land. Acorns and venison must have been staple articles of native diet.

Material Culture

Whilkut houses were rectangular in groundplan. But they were constructed of bark slabs instead of planks and were without a pit. Board-covered sweathouses like those of their northern neighbors were not built. A round structure, presumably dirt-covered, was erected for holding indoor ceremonies. This structure is the central California earth lodge or dance house.

Basketmaking formed one of the more, if not the most, important handicraft. The baskets were primarily twined, though a few coiled containers were used. The coiled ware was probably acquired through barter.

Social and Political Organization

The names and locations of 16 Mad River villages and an additional six on the North Fork (fig. 10) have been recorded (Baumhoff 1958:203–209). On upper Redwood Creek sites of eight settlements are known. The designations for five more have been reported but their precise locations remain uncertain. The size of the individual communities is problematical; each must have been quite small.

Hostilities with the Wiyot, who lived to the west, occurred with some frequency. Wiyot women caught harvesting acorns in groves that the Whilkut considered as their own property were often killed (Curtis 1907–1930, 13:68). Their kinsmen retaliated and petty feuds ensued.

Religion

Marked differences in religious practices are said to have set the Whilkut off from the Chilula and Hupa (Goddard 1903–1904:7); however, no details of their supernaturalism have been reported.

History

The Whilkut suffered heavily in the same strife with the Whites that destroyed a large part of the Chilula. The routes of pack trains lay through their territory; and conflicts, which took a large toll in Indian lives, repeatedly happened. The survivors were taken to the reservation at Hoopa soon after its establishment. After 1870 they drifted back to their traditional homes where they continued to live. In 1972 only a remnant is left, perhaps only 20 to 25 individuals.

Synonymy

The name Whilkut is derived from the Hupa designation (*xʷiɬqidxʷeˑ*) for the group (Kroeber 1925:141), the meaning of which is obscure. The Whilkut are also called Redwood Indians, the popular local name for them.

SOURCES

The Hupa rank among the best studied of California Indian groups and there has been a steady flow of literature on their language and culture. The best general work remains Goddard (1903–1904). Goddard (1904) supplements this monograph with a good sampling of myths and formulas. Powers (1877), Kroeber (1925), and Curtis (1907–1930, 13) contain chapters on the Hupa as does Wallace (1963). Driver (1939) includes two Hupa culture trait lists.

A series of articles dealing with particular aspects of the native life has also appeared (Murdock 1960:77–78). As for manuscript material, field notes include Sapir's (1927) linguistic texts, O'Neale (1930) on basketry, Gifford (1940–1942) on ceremonialism, and Wallace (1945–1949) on the life cycle.

By contrast, the cultures of the Chilula and Whilkut are very poorly documented. Goddard (1914) is the standard source for the Chilula, and Goddard (1914a) gives some myths and medicine formulas. Driver (1939) has one list of traits for the Chilula but none for the Whilkut. Only brief notes on Whilkut life and customs have been published (for example, Kroeber 1925:141). Information on Chilula and Whilkut settlements collected between 1910 and 1920 by C. Hart Merriam has been organized and published (Baumhoff 1958).

Karok

WILLIAM BRIGHT

Language and Territory

Karok is usually pronounced in English as ˈkǎˌräk, though the pronunciation ˈkǎˌro͞ok is sometimes heard. The Karok language has no close relatives, and thus was classified by Powell (1891) as constituting the isolated Quoratean family; however, Dixon and Kroeber (1913) were able to discover distant relationships with other languages in California, which they grouped into the Hokan family. The recognition of a still more distant relationship to languages of Mexico led Sapir (1929) to classify Karok in a subgroup of the Hokan-Coahuiltecan division of his Hokan-Siouan phylum. These wider relationships have not been fully established. Sapir's "Northern Hokan (a)" subgroup, including Chimariko, Shasta, Atsugewi, and Achumawi, has been renamed Kahi by Bright (1954).*

The Karok are defined, by themselves and by anthropologists, mainly in terms of their distinctive language. This is especially true because their culture differed little from that of the neighboring Yurok and Hupa, and no unifying tribal organization, definable politically or socially, existed.

There is little evidence of cultural or dialectal subdivisions within the Karok, except for a marginal group at the northernmost end of the territory, along the Klamath River between Seiad and Happy Camp, in an area of Shasta bilingualism (Curtis 1907-1930, 13:58; Kroeber 1936a:35-37).

The Karoks occupied the middle course of the Klamath River, where it flows mostly north to south; the northernmost village was just downriver from Seiad, and the southernmost was at Bluff Creek, north of Weitchpec. There were also villages on Indian Creek, west from Happy Camp, and up the Salmon River, east from Somes Bar (cf. Kroeber 1936a; Bright 1957:453-457). Villages were located on the river or on tributary streams; the mountain country on each side was visited for hunting, gathering, and ceremonial activities (Kroeber 1925:100). Those elements of the natural environment that were most important to the Karok were the

river, up which the salmon swam each year; the fir forests on the mountain slopes, in which game could be hunted; and the oak groves, visited annually for the acorn harvest.

Though linguistically separate from all their neighbors, the Karok share most features of their distinctively northwestern California culture with the neighboring Yurok and Hupa; ceremonial and marital ties existed with the Yurok in particular. The more distant Tolowa and Wiyot, though in the same culture area, were known less well. Upriver, trade was carried on with the Shasta, but cultural differences were relatively greater.

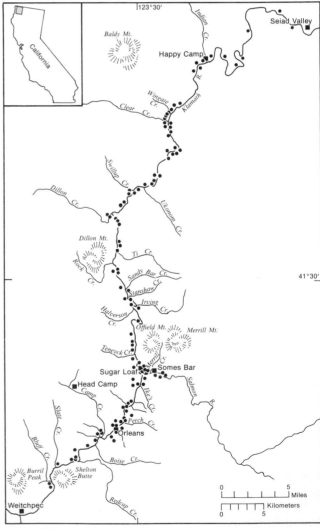

Fig. 1. Tribal area and village sites.

*The transcription of Karok words follows the system of Bright (1957) except that β is here written in place of the earlier v, an unrounded voiced bilabial spirant. r is a single alveolar flap. For the complex details of pronunciation indicated by the accents, see Bright (1957:11-14).

Aboriginally the only significant groupings of Karok population were villages or clusters of neighboring villages (fig. 1). Population was densest in three principal clusters of towns: around *panámni·k,* Orleans, above Camp Creek; at *kaʔimʔí·n* 'upper falls' and *yuʔimʔí·n* 'lower falls', above and below the mouth of the Salmon River; and at *ʔinna·m,* Clear Creek.

After the arrival of the Whites, no reservation was set up in Karok territory; but in the nineteenth century some Indians moved to reservation lands in Scott Valley, aboriginally part of Shasta territory. Many Karoks subsequently moved into White settlements in their old territory, such as Orleans and Happy Camp, or remained living near former village sites.

Culture

In spite of the fact that Powers (1877:19) spoke of them as "probably the finest tribe in California," no systematic ethnographic sketch of the Karok has been published up to now. The most comprehensive collection of data on native California describes Yurok culture in detail but devotes only a few pages to the Karok, saying that "the two peoples are indistinguishable in appearance and customs, except for certain minutiae" (Kroeber 1925:98). The following description of Karok culture refers to the period of time immediately preceding the White invasion.

Values

Many details of Karok custom can only be understood in terms of the outlook of the Karoks toward their universe. The system is clearly similar to that described by Kroeber (1959:236-240) for the Yurok, though the Karok are perhaps somewhat less compulsive than their downriver neighbors. Kennedy (1949) summarized the most important values, with their interrelations, as follows:

(1) Great emphasis was placed on the acquisition and possession of property, in the form of dentalium shells or other wealth objects such as woodpecker scalps and obsidian blades. Such "money" was only occasionally used to purchase necessities such as food, which was abundant; rather the importance of wealth was as a mark of high social position.

(2) The highest respect and prestige was accorded to the wealthy person; Karoks speaking English sometimes use the term "good people."

(3) Abstemiousness and thrift were valued. As one of Kennedy's informants said: "Good people didn't have many children. Some people never married, so they had lots of acorns. Lizzie's mother told her it was a good thing not to marry, because then you can think about money, how to get things."

(4) Another road to wealth was to be industrious; the first lesson taught children was not to be lazy.

(5) As another means to become wealthy, magic was highly regarded; thus men performed songs and prayers for success in hunting or in gambling. Some people, called "Indian devils," supposedly employed witchcraft to enrich themselves; such sorcerers were feared but not necessarily condemned.

(6) For all their wealth, rich people were not supposed to show off or be stingy, lest poor people make bad luck for them. "You should treat poor people just the same as good people."

(9) For success in life, it was important to observe many magical practices and taboos. Many of these related to sex, which was regarded as the enemy of wealth. Puritanical attitudes toward sex were the result.

All the above attitudes resulted in a typical Karok personality type that is not unfamiliar in Anglo-American culture: anxious about property, status, and the neighbor's opinion; suspicious of the unknown; and yet, as Powers wrote (1877:21), "brave when need is . . . extremely curious, inquisitive, and quick to imitate . . . talkative and merry with his peers."

Subsistence

Like most tribes in California, the Karoks lived by fishing, by hunting wild animals, and by gathering wild plant foods. The only cultivated crop was tobacco (Harrington 1932a).

The important fish was the salmon, whose run upriver in the spring was celebrated with a ceremony. Fishing practices have been described in detail by Kroeber and Barrett (1960). Several methods were used for catching fish. Most commonly, a fishing platform was built on the edge of a stream; salmon were caught with a "lifting net" lowered on an A-frame (fig. 2) and then killed with a club. Sites for fishing platforms were privately owned but could be rented for a share of the catch. Less often, a smaller "plunge net" on an oval frame was used to scoop fish, including steelhead and trout, out of rapids (fig. 2). Nets were made of fiber extracted from wild iris leaves. Fisherman also used harpoons with detachable points, and eels were caught with dip nets or with gaffs.

The most prized game was deer. The hunter prepared himself by sweating, bathing, scarification and bleeding for luck, by smoking his weapons with herbs, and by fasting and sexual continence. Deer-head masks were used as decoys, and dogs were used to run deer into noose snares set on their trails. After the kill, deer were butchered in the woods and carried home in a bundle; offal was hidden in the woods. After being eaten, the deer were believed to "go back uphill" and be reborn.

Elk were sometimes herded with dogs into ravines where they could be killed. Bears were hunted in the winter, when they were hibernating in caves; the hunter first shouted to the bear to come out, then dragged him out of the den to be killed. Rodents were caught for food by smoking them out of their holes or by poking them out with a stick. Traps made of twigs and netting were used for small mammals and birds. Animals never eaten included the dog, coyote, wolf, fox, wildcat, gopher, mole, bat, eagle, hawk, vulture, crow, raven, owl, meadowlark, bluejay, snake, lizard, frog, grasshopper, and caterpillar. There was a taboo against eating bear meat and fresh salmon together.

Fresh fish and meat were normally cooked by roasting over a fire or hot coals. Meat and edible plant bulbs were sometimes cooked in an earth oven of hot stones,

with a fire built on top. Both salmon and deer meat could be dried on a scaffold and preserved for later use.

The major plant food was acorns, those of the tanbark oak being preferred. Families camped out each fall, living in temporary houses of fir bark while gathering the acorns from the ground. To become edible, the acorns needed to have the bitter tannic acid removed from them; the most common method was to crack and dry them, rub them to remove the skins, then grind them to flour with a stone pestle on a flat slab, sift the flour, then

NAA, Smithsonian.

182   Fig. 2. Little Ike fishing for salmon, with a plunge net at *pame·kyá·ra·m,* Klamath River, Calif. Photographed before 1898.

leach it in a sand pit. The resulting acorn dough was mixed with water and boiled in a large basket with heated rocks in order to make acorn soup or mush. The dough could also be cooked on hot stones to make bread. Less often, whole acorns were buried in wet ground to soak for a year or more, then boiled with the hull still on, and cracked with the teeth for eating.

Wild grass seeds gathered for food were parched with coals in a basket. Other plant foods included a wide variety of edible nuts, bulbs, and greens (Schenck and Gifford 1952). Salt was obtained from certain natural deposits in the area as well as from seaweed imported from the coastal Yurok.

An important group of plant resources was that used in basketry, mainly hazel twigs and pine roots for warp and weft respectively. Regular burning off of brushy areas produced good second-growth hazel twigs, which after two years were picked, peeled, and dried in the sun. Pine roots were dug up, roasted under a fire, then split, dried, soaked, and scraped. Bear lily, Woodwardia fern, and maidenhair fern were also gathered for overlays in basketry decoration.

Technology

The materials used by the Karok for their artifacts were primarily wood, stone, and plant fiber; tools used in producing these articles were made of wood, stone, bone, and horn.

Wooden planks were obtained from logs split with horn wedges and stone mauls, and then worked with stone adzes; these were used for housing. Finer carving of wood with stone tools produced storage boxes, cooking paddles, and wooden spoons (see Kelly 1930). Wooden seats and headrests were also used by men. Boats made of hollowed-out redwood logs were purchased from the Yurok, in whose territory the redwood grew.

In addition to the pestle, grinding slab, and other stone implements mentioned above, oval steatite dishes were produced to catch the grease from roasting salmon. Small obsidian knives, chipped out with a piece of deerhorn, were attached to wooden handles and used for cutting up game; large obsidian blades, on the other hand, were prized wealth objects, displayed only at ceremonies.

The principal weapon was the bow made of yew wood, with sinew backing and a sinew bowstring. Arrows were of syringa wood, with obsidian heads for use in warfare. The quiver was made of animal skin (fig. 3). For defense, armor of elkhide or of wooden rods was worn.

Other tools included carved elkhorn spoons for men, mussel-shell spoons for women, bone awls for sewing hides, wooden or bone arrow straighteners, and wooden hand drills for making fire. The pipe for smoking to-

NAA, Smithsonian.

Fig. 3. Jim Pepper with bow, arrow, quiver, and a headband of redheaded woodpecker scalps. Photographed in 1894.

bacco generally consisted of a straight wooden tube with a steatite bowl.

The principal use of plant fibers was in making twined basketry (figs. 4, 5). Materials, techniques, designs, and uses are discussed in detail by O'Neale (1932).

Structures

The major types of structure were the living house, one for a family, and the sweathouse (fig. 6), several in a village. The living house was mainly the dwelling of women and children, visited by the men for meals. Otherwise men slept, sweated themselves, gambled, and conversed in their sweathouses, which were taboo to women except for the initiation of a female shaman.

Both types of house were rectangular, of roughhewn planks (preferably of cedar), and semisubterranean, with a stone-paved porch outside, and a stone-lined firepit inside. The living house normally had two ridgepoles, the sweathouse only one. Doors were small and low, so that people had to crawl in, then descend a plank ladder on the inside; sweathouses had separate doors for entry and exit. The gathering by men of firewood for the sweathouse had important religious implications; limbs were supposed to be cut from the uphill and downhill sides of tall fir trees, accompanied by ritual weeping and prayer for success in hunting and gambling, which were the main means of acquiring wealth.

Fig. 4. A young woman, probably Phoebe Maddux, making a twined basket. She is wearing dentalium necklaces and a deerskin apron decorated with braid fringes. The finished basket on the left is a carrying basket. Photographed in 1896.

In addition to the above, small wooden huts were built for menstruating women.

Clothing and ornament

The usual material for clothing was animal hide, especially buckskin, processed with deer brains and moss. A woman's everyday costume consisted of a deerskin with the hair on, worn over the back, covering the upper body, and a double apron of fringed buckskin around the waist (fig. 4); for ceremonial occasions, these garments were decorated with strings of digger-pine nuts, abalone and olivella shells, bear-lily braids (fig. 7), and, after the Whites arrived, silver coins. Maple-bark skirts were worn only when performing ceremonial or curing functions. A fur cape might be worn in cold weather. Men wore a piece of buckskin (breechclout) between their legs or went nude. A basketry cap was used by both sexes; women wore it habitually, with elaborate patterns, while men wore a plain cap only when there was need to protect the head. Buckskin moccasins with elkhide soles were worn for rough traveling, and men might also wear buckskin leggings. Snowshoes were made of hazelwood with iris-cord netting and buckskin ties for the feet.

For ceremonial occasions, women wore shell necklaces; men wore headbands and "bandoliers" decorated with woodpecker scalps and other feathers (fig. 3). Face paint was made of soot and of red or white minerals mixed with grease. The pierced earlobes and nasal septum could also carry ornaments; the Karok are said to have differed from the Yurok and Hupa in the wearing of nose pins (Barnett 1940:32). Women's hair was worn long, parted in the middle, and tied with strips of buckskin or fur so as to hang in front of the shoulders. Men's hair was also long, worn in a single roll down the back, or tied up at the nape.

At adolescence, all girls' chins were tattooed with three vertical stripes, using a sharp stone, soot, and grease (fig. 7). Indians sometimes explain that this was done to women "so they wouldn't look like men."

Social control

Northwestern California had the loosest kind of political and social organization, approximating ideal anarchy. "The village was the only political, and the family the only social, division" (Curtis 1907–1930, 13:60). Within the village, rich men were the leaders due to the prestige of their wealth; but there were no "chiefs" in the ordinary sense. Rather, the community was regulated by the set of values shared by its members. Family life was organized on similar principles, within the framework of the kinship system.

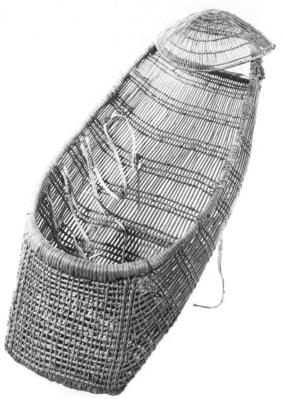

Fig. 5. Openwork baby carrier or cradle. In use it was either hung from its top or propped up vertically. The infant, bound in with leather thongs, sat on strands closing off the toe, with its feet hanging free (see also fig. 4). The separate round hood may be added to shade the face. Length 68.0 cm, collected about 1929.

Fig. 6. A sweathouse at *pame·kyá·ra·m*. Photograph by John P. Harrington, about 1928-1929.

Karok thought recognized no crimes against the tribe or community. Instead, undesirable behavior was interpreted in two ways: transgression against the supernatural by the breaking of taboos, which would bring retribution to the wrongdoer in the form of bad luck, or transgressions against private persons or property, which would then have to be paid for in the form of indemnities to the offended individuals or families. Thus, individualism was encouraged; a person could commit trespass or murder without being stigmatized as a crimi-

Fig. 7. Young girl from the Salmon River region wearing deerskin skirt and basket cap. She has tattoo marks on her chin and arms. Drawn by George Gibbs, Nov. 12, 1851.

nal, but he could expect to be "called to account" in quite a literal sense—being required to "pay for his misdeeds," not by undergoing punishment, but by paying indemnity in the form of shell money or other valuables. If anyone refused to pay, he was likely to be killed by the people he had offended; and this killing could in turn result either in indemnification, or in further violence between the families concerned. As Powers described it (1877:21): "If the money is paid without higgling, the slayer and the avenger at once become boon companions. If not, the avenger must have the murderer's blood, and a system of retaliation is initiated which would be without end were it not that it may be arrested at any moment by the payment of money."

What is sometimes referred to as "war" in northwest California was simply this type of retaliatory activity, expanded to involve fellow villagers of the aggrieved parties. Such feuds could be settled with the aid of a go-between, who was paid for his services. When a settlement was arranged, the opposing parties would face each other, the men doing an armed "war dance" in front of the settlement money while singing songs to insult the other side. If the women were successful in restraining the men from further violence, the settlement would conclude with an exchange and breaking of weapons.

Thus the basic principle of Karok law was that everything had its price, including the human person. Another example is the case of the "slave": a poor person could sell himself into slavery to a rich man, in order to be fed; but such a slave might subsequently be redeemed and freed if his relatives could repay the price.

Life Cycle

It is said that most children were born in the spring, since it was taboo for men and women to sleep in the dwelling house together, and intercourse was most likely to occur while camping out to gather wild foods in the summer. Mothers gave birth to babies in the living house, reclining backward and holding a strap from the roof. After the birth, the mother avoided cooking, traveling, or attending funerals for about a month; she ate alone, taking no mammal flesh or cold water during this time. The child was named, sometimes after a deceased relative, when he was weaned, between ages one and three. From around three years, boys slept in the sweathouse, where the adult men indoctrinated them in the virtues of thrift and industry.

There was no special observance connected with boys' adolescence; but a so-called flower dance was held in the summer for girls who had begun to menstruate. At this nocturnal ceremony, the girl had her face painted and carried a deerhoof rattle; men and women sang and danced together. Girls were told that they would behave the rest of their life in the same way they behaved during the puberty rite.

Many taboos applied to menstruating women throughout life: for example, they were forbidden to eat or cook meat, to pound acorns, or to have sexual intercourse. During her period, a woman stayed in the menstrual hut; new mothers and women who had miscarried were similarly isolated.

There was no particular prohibition against premarital sex; but if a woman became pregnant and a child was born, the father was expected to pay indemnity in order to legitimize the child. If this was not done, the child was considered a bastard; it was said that he was "not paid for," and he remained a pariah throughout life, disallowed from attending the deerskin dance.

Marriage itself was essentially a financial transaction; the bridegroom struck a bargain with the bride's father, and "that family is most aristocratic in which the most money was paid for the wife" (Powers 1877:22). Sometimes two men would exchange sisters in marriage; but even then, payments had to be made for both brides. The new couple went to the husband's parents' home, where an exchange of gifts completed the wedding. Later a husband might acquire his own house, but it would normally be adjacent to that of his parents. On the other hand, if a man could not pay part of the bride price, he could become "half-married"—that is, go to live with and work for his father-in-law.

The Karok practiced both the levirate and the sororate, that is, a widow was expected to marry her husband's brother or her sister's husband. A token bride price would be paid in such cases. A man could thus have two wives, or might take a second wife from outside the family, such as a girl whom he had impregnated—"she was going to have a baby, so he had to pay money." Polyandry was not practiced.

When a wife was unfaithful, her husband could demand indemnity from the other man or assault and kill him. In the latter case, the husband would of course be expected to pay indemnity to the family of the man he had killed. Alternatively, divorces could be sought by either partner on the grounds of unfaithfulness or incompatibility; such a divorce would consist in a repayment of money, negotiation of the amount depending on the number of children. Here as elsewhere, this important principle operated: the money paid in connection with sexual matters was not so much a price for a woman as it was a way of legitimizing potential offspring.

A dead person's body was removed from the house through a partially dismantled wall; the house was subsequently purified with incense. For burial, the corpse was taken to a family-owned grave plot near the dwelling site. There it was washed and dentalium shells were inserted in the nose and ears. The body was then extended supine, head in an upstream direction, and lowered into the grave with ropes. Money and valuables were broken and then buried with the corpse. A fence was built around the grave by lashing pickets to a horizontal pole; clothes and utensils were hung on this and left to rot. The male kinsman who acted as gravedigger slept by the grave for five successive nights. He and the other mourners were considered contaminated during this period; they had to sweat themselves, scarify their bodies, and avoid hunting, gathering, basketmaking, travel, sex, gambling, and the eating of fresh meat. After the five days, the ghost of the deceased was believed to go to the sky, where an especially happy place was reserved for rich people and ceremonial leaders. If anyone in the community wished to sponsor a dance within a year after someone's death, the mourners had to be paid an indemnity. Widows wore their hair singed short until they planned remarriage.

Uttering the name of a dead person was a serious offense; whether done either as a deliberate insult or by accident, it had to be compensated by payments to the survivors. However, the name was no longer taboo when formally regiven to a new baby in the family (see Bright 1958).

Kinship

The kinship system of the Karok was described, in its main outlines, by Gifford (1922:31-33); a comparison with other northwestern Californian systems was subsequently published by Kroeber (1934). The data as reelicited appear with some corrections in the lexicon of Bright (1957).

The basic terms for blood relatives are as follows:

ʔákka 'father'.

tá·t 'mother'.

kač 'son'.

yá·čkan 'daughter'.

ʔáttiš 'grandrelative through a man', i.e., father's parent or son's child.

kú·t 'male grandrelative through a woman', i.e., mother's father or daughter's son.

kí·t 'female grandrelative through a woman', i.e., mother's mother or daughter's daughter. These terms for grandrelatives also include granduncles, grandaunts and grandchildren.

típpa 'brother', further distinguishable as ʔári 'older brother' and čá·s 'younger brother'.

kústa·n 'sister', further distinguishable as nánnač 'older sister' and či·š 'younger sister'. These terms for siblings are also extended to cousins.

pára 'paternal uncle'.

mí·θ 'paternal aunt'.

xúkkam 'maternal uncle'.

θúxxaθ 'maternal aunt'.

ʔaxxi·č 'man's brother's child' (either sex).

yí·š 'woman's sister's child' (either sex).

ná·θ 'man's sister's son'.

ʔúffiθ 'woman's brother's son'.

fúriθ 'daughter of one's opposite-sexed sibling', i.e., man's sister's daughter, woman's brother's daughter.

A number of secondary terms can be derived from the above. The affixes -ya·n, -píya·n, and ʔip- . . . -píya·n, when joined to grandrelative terms, add a generation, as in ʔatišpíya·n 'paternal great-grandfather, son's grandchild'. With other terms, these affixes designate step-relatives, for example (from tá·t 'mother') ʔiptatpíya·n 'stepmother'. The suffix -βa·s indicates that a linking relative is dead, e.g. ʔatíšβa·s 'parent of one's dead father, child of one's dead son'. For deceased kin, terms are substituted for the basic ones, e.g., ʔihku·s 'deceased mother' instead of ta·t.

The basic terms for relatives by marriage (ná·m, ná·miš) are as follows:

ʔáβan 'husband'.

ʔirô·ha 'wife'.

ʔí·ni 'cowife', used between two women married to the same man.

fíkβa·n 'father-in-law'.

faratíppiš 'mother-in-law'.

ʔíkkam 'son-in-law'.

ʔíram 'daughter-in-law'.

ʔê·r 'man's brother-in-law', i.e., his sister's husband or wife's brother. The term also includes his aunt's husband or wife's nephew.

ʔú·t 'woman's sister-in-law', i.e., her brother's wife or husband's sister. The term also includes her uncle's wife or husband's niece.

ʔimna·s 'opposite-sexed sibling-in-law', i.e., a man's brother's wife or wife's sister, or a woman's sister's husband or husband's brother. The term also includes a man's uncle's wife or wife's nephew, and a woman's aunt's husband or husband's nephew.

xakanifmá·r 'sister-in-law's husband'.

xakanyárar 'brother-in-law's wife'.

Games

The most popular recreation for Karok men was gambling with so-called Indian cards—a group of small sticks, one marked with a ring around the middle, which were held in two hands and shuffled behind the back; then an opponent attempted to guess which hand held the marked stick. Play was accompanied with drumming and singing, intended to bring luck to the players.

Men also played a form of shinny known locally as the "stick game." In this game, three-man teams, equipped with heavy sticks, competed to throw a "tossel" (two wood blocks attached by a buckskin cord) across opposing goal lines. Players attempted to hinder their opponents by grappling, wrestling, and cudgeling with their playing sticks.

Minor games included cat's cradle, archery, dart throwing, and a type of dice game played with mussel shells by women.

Oral literature

Also classifiable as recreation, perhaps, was story telling, which served simultaneously as a form of education. The most important type of narrative is the myth, often with interpolated songs, told mainly in the winter; this was an account of events prior to the creation of mankind, when the earth was populated by a type of being known as ʔikxaré·yaβ. A myth typically climaxed and ended with the coming of mankind and the simultaneous transformation of the protagonists into species of animals, or sometimes into disembodied spirits, which exist on the earth today. The largest published collection of such myths, in Karok and English, is in Bright (1957: 162-261); also useful are Angulo and Freeland (1931) and Harrington (1931, 1932). An especially large and popular class of myths has Coyote as its trickster-hero (see Bright 1954a, 1957:162-205).

Some myths are also magical formulas (ʔánnaβ 'medicine'), transmitted by individuals as their personal property and used to acquire love, luck, or wealth. Such a myth tells, for instance, how a female ʔikxaré·yaβ, Evening Star, lost her lover and sang to bring him back again; the story, concluding in the singing of Evening Star's love song, was supposed to bring a wandering sweetheart back to a woman who recited it (cf. Bright 1957:250).

Cosmology

Little has been recorded concerning Karok views of the physical universe; the fact that no creation myth has been collected strongly suggests that none ever existed. However, many myths describe how the ways and features of the world were ordained by ʔikxaré·yaßs before their transformation—for example, the use of salmon and acorns. In fact the Karoks seem mainly interested in their immediate surroundings. The Klamath River, running between Klamath Lakes and the sea, is the basis for their terms of spatial orientation: *káruk* 'upriver', *yúruk* 'downriver', *máruk* 'away from the river, uphill', and *sáruk* 'toward the river, downhill' are the four cardinal points.

The land of the dead was thought to be in the sky, and the Milky Way was called the road of the dead; the only other terms known for stars refer to the morning star, the evening star, and the Pleiades. A 13-month lunar calendar was observed, beginning with the winter solstice (cf. Harrington 1932a:81-83). The ritual numbers were 5 and 10, which also formed the basis for the counting system.

Ceremonies

The principal rites of the Karok were those concerned with "renewing the world" and assuring its stability between annual observances. These are correlated with the seasonal availability of major food resources: in spring, when the salmon started running, the Jumping Dance was held at ʔame·kyá·ra·m, where salmon were mythically created. In the fall, at the time of the acorn harvest and the second great run of salmon, Deerskin Dances were held at Orleans, *kaʔtimʔí·n,* and Clear Creek. These ceremonies involved ritual activity by priests and priestesses, as well as feasting, display of wealth, and dancing. These dances, like all others, were accompanied by singing; unfortunately, little description of either dance style or song style has ever been carried out for the northwestern California tribes. Details of the rites were published by Kroeber and Gifford (1949).

A less important ceremony was the Brush Dance, held to cure a sick child. Such dances are still performed with some regularity, with the added functions of recreation and the attraction of tourist spending.

Curing

Most cases of disease were treated by two classes of curers, the "herb doctor" and the "sucking doctor." The herb doctor, who might be a man or a woman, treated patients by administering herbal medicine internally or externally and by fumigating them with tobacco and plant incense, along with recitation of magical formulae; such a practitioner was qualified simply by learning the appropriate procedures. The sucking doctor, who was usually a woman, had to have a "vocation." When a girl continually dreamed and mourned over dead relatives, neglecting her food and acting strangely, she could be considered a novice doctor, and a "doctor dance" or "kick dance" could be held in a sweathouse for 10 consecutive nights. Within a year's time the novice was expected to go to a remote place in the mountains to sing and pray for the supernatural power of curing. If her quest was successful, she acquired a disease object or "pain" which she kept within her body and learned to control—vomiting it up, displaying it, and absorbing it into her body again. With the aid of her own "pain," the sucking doctor then cured by sucking on her patients' bodies and magically withdrawing (without breaking the skin) the "pains" that were causing illness. The curing procedure involved singing, dancing, smoking (doctors were the only women who smoked), and display of the offending pain before its magical dispersal.

Sometimes a sucking doctor was also clairvoyant, able to indicate where to find lost objects. Such a doctor could examine a sick baby and determine that the illness was caused by some wrongdoing on the part of a family member. The doctor then elicited a confession before the entire community, whereupon the baby would recover (cf. Gifford 1958, 1:245-255).

A curer's fee was paid before treatment but had to be refunded if the treatment were unsuccessful. If the patient died within a year, the fee again had to be refunded. But a curer could not readily refuse a case: if he did, and the patient died, the curer would have to indemnify the survivors in the amount of the normal curing fee.

History

The first Whites seen by the Karoks were probably traders from the Hudson's Bay Company in the early nineteenth century, but this contact seems to have had little effect. Then suddenly, in 1850-1851, the Karok territory was invaded by gold miners. The impact of this invasion was greater on the Karok than on their neighbors since Yurok territory offered less rewarding prospects for mining. Karok land was "overrun by unscrupulous individuals who had no intention of settling or establishing cordial relations with the natives" (Barnett 1940:23). In 1852, after clashes between Whites and Indians around *panámni·k,* the Whites burned most of the Indian towns as far north as the Salmon River, and the Indians fled to the hills; the White town of Orleans was then founded. When the Indians returned, they found Whites' houses and farms on their village sites. Military operations in that year claimed 15 Karok lives, and 75 more in 1855. But subsequently, "some of the refugees were given permission to build houses in unoccupied places near the farms, and thus began their unattached existence, which in most cases has continued to the present day" (Curtis 1907-1930, 13:58).

After the mines had given out in the late nineteenth century, the Karoks were left more or less to their own devices. Sexual liaisons between White men and Indian women had resulted in children who, classified as bastards in the native social system, "aped their white fathers in contempt and skepticism of the sanctions and taboos, and did not suffer thereby . . . . This disaffected group presented a continuing and finally disruptive attack on the elders and their prescriptions" (Kennedy 1949:15). By 1948 it was reported that scarcely two dozen elderly full-bloods remained with an orientation to the old culture (Kennedy 1949:1–2). But by 1972, when being an Indian was at last coming to be once more a matter of pride in America, the world renewal ceremony had been revived at both Clear Creek and ka⁊imⁿíꞏn, and there were once more prospects for the preservation of Karok identity.

The Ghost Dance religion of 1870, spreading from Nevada and promising the return of dead Indians and traditional life, reached the Karok through the Shasta in 1871 (Kroeber 1904). Dances were held at Happy Camp, at ka⁊imⁿíꞏn, and at ⁊ameꞏkyáꞏraꞏm but seem to have made no lasting impression.

The aboriginal Karok population, as of 1848, has been estimated by Cook (1956:98) at 2,700. Military operations, "social homicide," privation and disease (especially syphilis, introduced by the Whites) caused the population to drop rapidly in the early years. There was some recovery in the more peaceful years of the late nineteenth century, followed by a drop in the twentieth century, as assimilation to White culture resulted in decreasing numbers of ethnically identifiable Indians. The following population estimates are from Cook (1943b:98, 105), except where otherwise stated:

1851	1,050	
1866	1,800	
1876	1,300	
1880	1,000	
1905	994	(Kroeber 1957a:224)
1910	775	
1915	870	

In the U.S. census of 1930, a total of 755 people were identified as Karoks, of which 16.4% were said to be full-bloods and 6.2% were monolingual. Such figures undoubtedly exclude many persons of part-Karok blood. By contrast, the Sacramento office of the Bureau of Indian Affairs reported (personal communication 1972) that 3,781 individuals were identified as having at least some Karok ancestry.

Synonymy

The label Karok has been in general use since Powers (1877); the variant spellings Cahroc or Cahrok were used earlier. The term is from Karok káruk 'upstream', contrasting with yúruk 'downstream', adopted by Whites to refer to the Yurok tribe. J.P. Harrington in his various publications used the English form Karuk. The Karok, like most California tribes, originally called themselves simply ⁊áraꞏr 'person, Indian'; some nineteenth-century writers used this as a tribal name, in the English spelling Arra-Arra.

Other terms applied by Whites in the nineteenth century were Quoratem, derived from the Yurok name for a Karok site, ⁊asapípmaꞏm, at the mouth of the Salmon River; Eh-nek or Ehnik, derived from the Yurok name for the Karok village of ⁊ameꞏkyáꞏraꞏm; and Peh-tsik, derived from the Yurok word for 'upriver'. Powell (1891:176) coined the adjective Quoratean to refer to the linguistic family constituted by the Karok language, but the term found little use subsequently.

Sources

Other than publications already cited, the most important collections of data on the Karok are the tabulations of cultural traits ("element lists") published for northwestern California as a whole by Driver (1939), the unpublished ethnographic MSS of Harrington and of Gifford (1939, 1939a, 1940), the modern Karok autobiographies contained in Kennedy (1949), and the lexicon and ethnographic texts of Bright (1957).

Mattole, Nongatl, Sinkyone, Lassik, and Wailaki

ALBERT B. ELSASSER

Language

In northern California and adjacent Oregon there were a number of groups speaking closely related Athapaskan languages but differing in culture. Thus the Tolowa, near the present California-Oregon border, who shared a language with the Tututni and other Rogue River groups, were a marine-oriented people culturally quite distinct from their southern neighbors, the speakers of the Hupa-Chilula-Whilkut language on or near the lower Klamath River. Even more distinct are the people who comprise the five groups referred to collectively as the southern Athapaskans. Of these, the Nongatl ('näng₁gätəl), Sinkyone (sing'kyōnē), Lassik ('lăsĭk), and Wailaki ('wī₁läkē, 'wī₁läkē) spoke dialects of a single language; Mattole (mə'tōl) may also have been a dialect of this language, or it may have differed enough to qualify as a separate language. Although the Cahto of the upper South Fork Eel River region, south of the Sinkyone and Wailaki, spoke another dialect of the Nongatl-Sinkyone-Lassik-Wailaki language, culturally they were not typical of the southern Athapaskan enclave but were more closely allied to Central California (specifically the Pomo) than to Northwestern California, with which the five components of the enclave are usually associated (cf. Driver 1939).*

* No phonemic analysis of the languages spoken by these groups has been worked out. The tentative phonemicizations of native terms used in italicized words here have been supplied by Victor Golla on the basis of the work of Li (1930) and Goddard (1921-1923); the information on language and dialect relationships is also from Golla (personal communications 1974, 1975).

Table 1. Coefficients of Intertribal Relationships or Similarities

		Hupa	Mattole	Nongatl	Sinkyone	Cahto	Yuki[a]	Wintu	Wailaki
Hupa	[b]Q_6		.80	.62	.69	.22	.12	.47	.46
	[c]Q_2		.17	.63	.47	−.21	(−.36)		
Mattole	Q_6	.80		.92	.96	.57	(.53) .39	.77	.84
	Q_2	.17		.61	.64	.43	(.42)		
Nongatl	Q_6	.62	.92		.95	.68	.64 (.59)	.80	.91
	Q_2	.63	.61		.79	.41	(.21)		
Sinkyone	Q_6	.69	.96	.95		.71	(.69) .66	.46	.92
	Q_2	.47	.64	.79		.45	(.32)		
Cahto	Q_6	.22	.57	.68	.71		.99 (.97)	.69	.89
	Q_2	−.21	.43	.41	.45		(.86)		
Yuki[a]	Q_6	.12 (.12)	(.53) .39	.64 (.59)	(.69) .66	.99 (.97)		.58	.84
Wintu	Q_6	.47	.77	.80	.46	.69	.58		.80
Wailaki	Q_6	.46	.84	.91	.92	.89	.84	.80	

[a] Figures in parentheses refer to Coast Yuki.

[b] Q_6 Klimek 1935 formula, based upon 232 selected material culture elements applying to all of California.

[c] Q_2 Driver 1939 formula, based upon approximately 2,400 culture elements designated primarily for Northwestern California; see also Kroeber 1939.

Two of the five southern Athapaskan tribes, the Lassik and Wailaki, though also showing certain marked cultural relationships with non-Athapaskan-speaking groups like the Pomo, Yuki, and Wintu to the south and east, probably were more closely allied culturally to one or another of their three close linguistic relatives than to any other group.

Ethnographic and linguistic studies concerning the five groups point to their major cultural affiliations to the north rather than to the east or south, even though their position is marginal and in some sense midway between the "climax" groups (Kroeber 1936:102) of the Klamath River region (Yurok-Hupa) and Central California (Pomo-Patwin). In the course of these studies, it has also been noted that the southern Athapaskans differ both linguistically (within their stock) and in culture content from one another. This is in consonance with observations of many native groups in California who may be neighbors separated geographically by a single mountain ridge, for example, but yet find themselves behaving like so many small, separate nations.

The degree of cultural relationship among the five groups has been determined quantitatively by Driver (1939), Kroeber (1939), and Klimek (1935). There are unsatisfactory aspects to the statistical processes employed by these scholars, such as the choice of cultural element lists and questioned reliability of certain statistical formulas used in connection with the lists. Yet table 1 suggests a general similarity of results, even though the data stems from two widely differing methodologies.

If the five southern Athapaskan groups treated here are regarded as separate tribes on the basis of their having separate speech dialects, it should be noted that the case of the Mattole and their neighbors to the north, the Bear River people, presents a quandary. The dialects of these two peoples were recognizably distinct and they were slightly different in culture. Because they at least shared a continuous section of coastline and because they are not separated in the earlier literature, being called simply Mattole (Loud 1918; Kroeber 1925), they will be considered here as a single unit.

Territory

Little is known of political subdivisions among the Mattole and Bear River beyond what Kroeber (1932a:258) has called "tribelets," units that can be easily distinguished among all southern Athapaskan groups. The tribelet is defined as a single group with a small territory, usually a single drainage area, and a principal town or settlement; often a chief is recognized by the whole group, and the tribelet may have a specific name, perhaps based on the name of its principal town. Each tribelet acted as a homogeneous unit in matters of land ownership, reaction to trespass, war, and major ceremonies.

Bear River territory comprised almost the entire drainage of Bear River proper and the coast near its mouth (fig.1). In the north, it included the western side of the Eel River from near the mouth of the Van Duzen River to the present town of Scotia. No tribelet names are recorded, but seven village names have been cited (Baumhoff 1958), taken from several authors.

The Mattole controlled a good part of the Mattole River drainage from the Pacific coast to near the mouth of the Upper North Fork River. On the coast they held the shore from Davis Creek south to Spanish Flat. Probably the Mattole had two tribelets, but their names are unknown. Sixty village sites have been identified (Baumhoff 1958).

On linguistic evidence, the Sinkyone have been subdivided into a northern group, the Lolangkok, after the name for Bull Creek, and the Shelter Cove, with the name derived from a preferred spot on the coast near Point Delgada. The entire land includes a portion of the "main" Eel River and a long stretch of the south fork of the Eel River, especially the western side of the drainage, from present Scotia to Hollow Tree Creek on the south. They also held the upper reaches of the Mattole River and a strip of the coast from Spanish Flat south to about the mouth of Usal Creek (fig. 2). Of the two Sinkyone subdivisions, the Lolangkok had two tribelets, while the Shelter Cove had four. The named Lolangkok villages recorded along the main Eel River and the South Fork

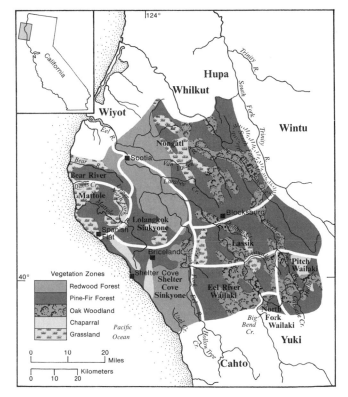

after Baumhoff 1958, 1963.

Fig. 1. Tribal territories with zones of vegetation.

Fig. 2. Shelter Cove Sinkyone village of Usal. Photograph by Pliny E. Goddard, 1902.

numbered about 50, while for the Shelter Cove people about 18 villages were known by name.

In virtually every description of southern Athapaskans, the Nongatl are associated with all or most of the Van Duzen River drainage, including its main affluent, Yager Creek. Besides these areas, they also held a considerable stretch of the Upper Mad River and a small section of the Eel River and practically all of its tributary, the Larabee Creek drainage. The Nongatl evidently were subdivided into six tribelets or dialect groups, and 35 named or otherwise identified village sites have been recorded for them.

The Lassik occupied the drainage of the main Eel River between the mouths of Dobbyn and Kekawaka creeks and the headwaters of the North Fork Eel and Mad rivers. The crest of the South Fork Mountains on the east served as a boundary between them and the Wintu of Upper Trinity River. The Lassik probably comprised three tribelets and about 20 named villages.

Of all the southern Athapaskans, the Wailaki present the most confusion as far as names are concerned. First of all, according to Baumhoff (1958:167, 176), following Merriam, there are three major subdivisions of the group: Tsennahkennes (Eel River Wailaki), Bahneko (North Fork Wailaki), and Pitch Indians, farther up the North Fork Eel River (ǯehtaγə 'those among the pitch', Goddard 1924:217, phonemicized, appearing with various suffixes as Che-teg-ge-kah, Che-teg-ge-kay, and Che-teg-gah-ahng). Goddard also notes the name Salt Indians for the Pitch Indians.

Taken as a whole, the Wailaki occupied most of the Eel River drainage from Kekawaka Creek south to Big Bend Creek and most of the North Fork Eel River, including Hull's Creek and Casoose Creek, affluents to the North Fork Eel. Altogether there were 19 known tribelets among the Wailaki and a total of 95 named villages.

Environment and Subsistence

The southern Athapaskans occupied the extreme northern part of the North Coast Range geomorphic province. This is a system of longitudinal mountain ranges usually from 2,000 to 4,000 feet elevation, with occasional peaks reaching altitudes of 6,000 feet or so (Jenkins 1938). A large portion of the entire Eel River drainage was held by the five groups, with the South Fork Mountains on the east separating the Athapaskans from the Wintu of the Trinity River region. To the west, the Mendocino Range formed the watershed between the Eel River drainage and the coastal strip held by the Mattole and Sinkyone. Baumhoff (1963:179, 193) shows all groups but the Lassik and Wailaki with redwood forests in parts of their territory. Pine-fir forests are represented in each tribal region. Grassland, especially near the coast, occasional stretches of chaparral, and tracts of oak-woodland forests complete the vegetation cover for this part of the province (fig. 1).

Tanbark oak (*Lithocarpus densiflora*) and Oregon oak (*Quercus garryana*), both of which may be found in or around the coastal redwood belt, were the species probably most important as edible seed producers. All five groups utilized acorns, even though the Mattole, for example, had no notable oak resources in their territory. Species of buckeye (*Aesculus californica*), manzanita (*Arctostaphylos columbiana*), pine, several varieties of berries, and many other minor food plants occur in the North Coast ranges; they were used in varying degrees by all southern Athapaskans.

Along the Pacific Coast, sea lions, mollusks, and fish were exploited by the Mattole and Sinkyone, but it seems that neither of these groups depended heavily upon products from the sea (Kroeber 1925:116). Throughout the inland region, large and small game was abundant, with the Columbian black-tailed deer (*Odocoileus hemionus columbianus*) and Roosevelt elk (*Cervus canadensis roosevelti*) most important.

There is no doubt of the tremendous importance of fish, particularly salmon, as a food resource in Northwestern California as a whole. Among the southern Athapaskans, however, only the Mattole and Sinkyone appear to follow the pattern of the lower Klamath River peoples like the Yurok and Karok in exploiting fish as a primary resource, more than game and acorns. Baumhoff (1963:173) presents data on the anadromous fish streams of California in which he distinguishes primary salmon streams as lower courses of rivers having one or both of the following: (1) spawning runs of all three species—king salmon, silver salmon, and steelhead trout, and (2) both a spring and fall spawning run of the king salmon. Secondary streams are the higher courses of the primary streams and the entire courses of lesser streams. Among the southern Athapaskans, only the Sinkyone and the Nongatl have a "primary" part of the Eel River in their territory. The Mattole River is a "secondary" stream but evidently carried a large volume of fish. Tobin (1858:403) called it "perhaps the best fishing station on the north coast."

The relative importance of fish may be represented in another way. In fishing techniques, of 71 traits referred to as characteristic of Northwestern California by Kroeber and Barrett (1960) only 13 are not employed by any of the southern Athapaskans. The Mattole-Bear River groups are known to have shared 49 of the 71 traits (68%); the Sinkyone, 46 (65%); the Nongatl, 36 (51%); the Lassik, 23 (32%); and the Wailaki, 10 (14%).

Table 2 summarizes the total food resources of the Mattole and Wailaki, evidently the extremes among the southern Athapaskans so far as dependence upon fish is concerned. The Lassik and possibly the Nongatl were closer to the Wailaki than to either the Mattole or Sinkyone in the proportions of food resources, possibly because there were more and larger acorn tracts in their territories.

Table 2. Food Resources of the Mattole and Wailaki

Type of Resource	Extent		Fish				Acorns				Game			
	Mattole	Wailaki	Mattole		Wailaki		Mattole		Wailaki		Mattole		Wailaki	
			C[a]	I[b]	C	I	C	I	C	I	C	I	C	I
Fishery	(fish mi.)	(fish mi.)												
River	25	38	10	250	10	380								
Ocean	17		5	85										
Vegetation	(sq. mi.)	(sq. mi.)												
Pine-fir forest	124	186					1	124	1	186	1	124	1	186
Chaparral	8	15					½	4	½	8	2	15	2	30
Grassland	88	8					½	44	½	4	2	176	½	4
Oak woodland		207							2	413			2	413
Total			335		380		172		611		315		633	

Source: adapted from Baumhoff 1958, 1963.

[a] Coefficients (C) represent gross evaluations, on a scale from ½ to 2, of importance of resources. All rivers in both Mattole and Wailaki territories are classified as secondary, and their coefficients are increased tenfold in order to bring them into scale of comparison with calculations involving square miles.

[b] Indices (I) are fish miles or square miles multiplied by coefficient.

Settlement Patterns and Population

Standard methods of calculating aboriginal populations in California—such as utilizing actual head counts or determining number of villages and house sites within them and estimating the number of occupants of each house—have all been applied among the southern Athapaskans (cf. Cook 1956). The head counts, mostly in the nineteenth century by government officials or other observers, obviously were not very reliable both because of their late date and because of the relatively marginal or isolated situation of the southern Athapaskans. Kroeber's (1925) total for these five groups amounted to only 3,500, but this figure was arrived at in the face of a comparatively small amount of official government or ethnographic data. Later investigations by Cook (1956) more than trebled that estimate. Baumhoff (1958), by using all ecological and other demographic data available at the time, has produced an estimate slightly exceeding Cook's final figure. Baumhoff's total for the five southern Athapaskan tribes in aboriginal times is 13,193.

Judging from the distribution of village sites—usually along streams for the southern Athapaskans (Baumhoff 1958)—it appears that Kroeber's (1939) concept of the "natural area" in North America applies almost ideally for this territory. Each tribe, subtribe, or tribelet may occupy a drainage region, with its borders therefore represented most commonly by ridges of mountains separating valleys. In cases where two groups occupy different stretches of the same stream, a narrowing of the valley or canyon would serve as an approximate demarcating line (Goddard 1923:95). A possible exception to this idea appears in the Lassik territory, which Kroeber (1939:427) noted as "not looking like a natural one," that is, its north and south boundaries were probably not well defined by a canyon narrowing along this section of the Eel River. In such cases the boundaries might be marked simply by location of certain tributary streams.

A given population group did not spend all its time along the streams but repaired to the slopes of the hills and even into the cool forests during the summer, at which time plant food availability was at an optimum

(Baumhoff 1958:158). Since summer living had a mobile quality, characterized by temporary settlements, camp-sites in the hill regions are not nearly so well marked as those used at other times of the year along streams. Most of the known village sites represented by Baumhoff (1958) thus are shown in his various maps as occurring along streams. It is rarely possible in any case to assume that all living sites in an area are known or to determine accurately the time level at which they were occupied.

Nevertheless, Baumhoff (1963:185) has demonstrated that intimate knowledge of primary food resources of a group will help to provide a reasonably sound basis for estimating population densities of areas like those of the southern Athapaskans. Table 3 summarizes the final population estimates for all the southern Athapaskans. Several methods were employed in arriving at these estimates, the most valid of which seems to derive from population figures pertaining to fishing miles.

Table 3. Southern Athapaskan Population Data

Group	Area (sq. mi.)	Fishing miles	Aboriginal population (Baumhoff 1958)	Area density	Fishing mile density	1910 Population (Kroeber 1925)	Reservation population (Levine and Lurie 1968)
Bear River	121	21	1,276	10.55	60.8		31[a]
Mattole	219	42	1,200	5.48	28.6		—
Sinkyone							
Shelter Cove	350	67	2,145	6.13	32.0	100	—
Lolangkok	254	43	2,076	8.17	48.3	100	—
Nongatl	855	85	2,325	2.72	27.4	100	—
Lassik	389	25	1,411	3.63	56.4	100	—
Wailaki	416	38	2,760	6.63	72.6	200	—

Source: adapted from Baumhoff 1958, 1963.
[a] Rohnerville, terminated 1958.

Prehistory

There is little doubt that aboriginal occupation of the North Coast Ranges dates back to at least 4,000 years ago, and probably much earlier. Fredrickson (1974:43) has reported a date of about 1700 B.C. (I 2754) for a site in Lake County, part of an early complex called Borax Lake, which Meighan (1955) located in the central part of the North Coast Ranges. Two later complexes, Mendoci-no (ca. A.D. 500–1000) and Shasta (post-1600) according to Meighan both included as their locale parts of north-ern Mendocino and southern Humboldt counties, the homeland of the southern Athapaskans.

It is not possible to associate either of the later archeological complexes specifically with the historic Athapaskans because no extensive excavations have been made in the pertinent territory. On the other hand, linguistic evidence suggests that the Athapaskans came to northern California probably around A.D. 900. In glotto-chronology—dating by means of comparing retention of cognate words among several languages within a given stock—results from comparative studies of Athapaskan languages show a fair degree of reliability, insofar as dates of divergence of languages such as Navajo and Apache from a northern parent language can be partly confirmed by inferences drawn from archeological data. According to several methods and considerations by

Hoijer (1956:226), Hymes (1957:292), and Kroeber (1959:258), the date of separation of Hupa and Mattole speakers lies somewhere between 1,000 and 1,300 years ago. Even though these two peoples recently have been close to each other geographically but distant culturally, it is suggested that at one time they were a single people, perhaps coming from the northeast but separating before or after arrival in California. The Mattole took up residence in Bear River and Mattole River valleys and the Hupa on the lower Trinity River valley, and their linguistic separation seems in a way parallel to the cultural separation, each indicating only token or indirect intercourse between the two groups during the past 900 or so years.

History

Whatever the time of their arrival in the North Coast Ranges, the southern Athapaskans seem not to have been known to Euro-Americans until about 1853, at which time the U.S. government began to record their existence officially. This was in connection with federal assignment to reservations such as those in Round Valley, on the Upper Eel River, and on the Smith River near the Oregon border. It is obvious from the Commissioners' Reports of the U.S. Office of Indian Affairs up till about 1870 that each of the five Athapaskan subgroups considered itself a separate people, although they spoke dialects or at least closely related languages of the same stock.

In works on local history, for example, on Humboldt and Mendocino counties (Carpenter and Millberry 1914; Irvine 1915), there occur repeatedly allusions to local Indians, but almost invariably the southern Athapaskans were slighted in print in favor of better-known groups like the Wiyot and Hupa to the north and the Pomo to the south. When Athapaskans are named, it evidently was not so much for ethnographic description, but rather for identification as transgressors or outlaws and recounting of actions taken by Whites against them. Thus Carpenter and Millberry (1914:95) record the 1861 affair in which "500 Wylackies drove off [from Round Valley] thirty-seven horses, and were overtaken at Horse Canyon by ten whites and 40 Indians; one hundred and twenty of the raiding party were killed. Of the pursuing party only two were wounded." This and similar reports, though almost certainly exaggerated, suggest that the Wailaki were practically exterminated during the summers of 1861 and 1862. Menefee (1873:336) states that in the occupation of Round Valley by the federal government in 1856, many persons were induced to accompany the government train "from fear of wild tribes surrounding the valley"; the tribes are unnamed.

Another history (Bledsoe 1885) mentions a punitive local White committee resolution against the Mattole that requires, among other things, that they no longer set fire to the grass; the resolution applies to the Mattole only, and not to their neighbors on Bear River or the Eel River. The Indian Affairs Reports portray removal of Indians from their native land to reservations, conditions at reservations, some subsequent transfers to other reservations, and finally return by some to the native lands, titles of which were no longer officially clear or existent for the Indians. Under these conditions it would be most difficult to take proper account either of the number or of original tribal affiliations of the returnees. By 1930, subtribal identity was nonetheless retained, although ethnographers after that date have noted the scarcity of native informants in each of the five groups.

As indicated in table 3, the only reservation that contained any specifically identifiable southern Athapaskans was at Rohnerville, where in 1956, 30 "Bear River Indians" were listed as in residence (Levine and Lurie 1968:end chart). There is no further breakdown of the composition of this group, but in any case T.W. Taylor (1972:238) lists this reservation as terminated in 1958.

While there may be a considerable number of southern Athapaskans alive in the 1970s, these are almost unquestionably mixed with other Athapaskans such as the Hupa or Cahto or with non-Athapaskans. The Round Valley Reservation in Mendocino County has had a mixed Indian population of around 800 (Levine and Lurie 1968), which may include some individuals of southern Athapaskan derivation; however, identity as Nongatl or

Mattole may be effectively submerged because there are probably too few persons alive who could converse with each other specifically in any of the old dialects. Therefore, in the following sections it will be necessary to speak of the southern Athapaskans as if they have become extinct, even though this may not actually be the case.

Culture

In the following discussion the five southern Athapaskan groups will be treated as a single unit, even though it has already been emphasized that the tribes sometimes varied considerably from one another in certain usages. In most instances the variations depended upon the relative isolation or the particular outside influences to which a group was subjected. In others, noted differences may have been based upon the specific situational responses of the comparatively few informants available to ethnographers such as A.L. Kroeber, H.E. Driver, G.A. Nomland, F.J. Essene, or E.M. Loeb. Thus a single Sinkyone informant who lived along the coast, for example, might present a markedly different view of life from a Lolangkok Sinkyone whose home was on the Eel River.

Social Organization

The largest corporate social group among the southern Athapaskans was the tribelet. Although wealth certainly must have played a part in the choice of headmen, the title of tribelet chief, evidently reserved for males, was not lifelong except possibly among the Lassik and Wailaki, where it was also reported to be on a patrilineal basis (Essene 1942:38). For the other groups it was not even necessarily hereditary. Privileges and duties of headmen included the possession of several wives (rare among ordinary southern Athapaskans), the providing of the largest share of food and property at ceremonies, and the settling of disputes.

The simple family (including husband, wife, and their children) was the primary social unit. Emphasis on wealth was present but was less strongly developed than among the Klamath River peoples to the north and therefore did not lead to the fragmented villages and tight family organization of people such as the Yurok and Hupa. Social stratification under these circumstances was probably less rigid than to the north, and none of the southern Athapaskans seems to have held slaves of any description.

Life Cycle

• BIRTH Childbirth took place in the dwellings of most southern Athapaskans, although a separate hut has been reported as sometimes used by the Lassik. Midwives assisted in all groups; a rare feature of birth procedures, found among the Mattole and Lassik, is that a male shaman could also assist at the birth. The Lassik shaman was reportedly merely a sucking doctor who was present more for moral support than as assistant obstetrician (Essene 1942:32).

Among all southern Athapaskans the navel cord was cut with flint. Other practices, including food and behavioral taboos on both mother and father, varied from tribe to tribe, although for mothers most groups observed meat and cold-water taboos (including bathing in streams) for varying periods after birth. For fathers, there were commonly restrictions against gambling and hunting, usually for four or five days. Among the Sinkyone and Lassik, fathers were required to remain indoors for three or four days; the Sinkyone fathers reportedly also had to lie down for a like period after the birth of a child.

Names were given soon after birth or up to six months or a year later. Commonly among southern Athapaskans namesakes were not relatives. Only among the Sinkyone were the child's ears pierced soon after birth (Driver 1939:350).

The idea of abortion was known to most of the groups, with the eating or drinking of medicine probably the most usual means employed. Infanticide (for instance, of bastards) was known, at least by the Sinkyone and Lassik. All groups except the Wailaki seem to have treated twins the same as other children. The Wailaki, according to Loeb (1932:92), considered twins ill-omened and killed one, for otherwise both would die.

Means of preventing conception, consisting of the drinking of a mixture of burnt sea shells and water, or of some plant infusion, were known to the Lassik (Essene 1942:33).

• PUBERTY   Usages connected with the coming of age of puberty by girls were much more abundant and complex than those having to do with boys. Taboos for girls against meat eating or use of cold water, requirement of eating alone and confinement (or, as among the Nongatl and Lassik, in a menstrual hut), restrictions on sleep and touching oneself (with associated use of special head scratchers of wood, bone, or horn), covering of the eyes or head in public (among the Sinkyone "in order not to blast the world with her disastrously potent glance" according to Kroeber 1925:149)—all were common to the southern Athapaskans and some of their neighbors to the north in the Klamath River region as well.

The practice of tattooing girls at puberty was found among the Lassik; in other groups such tattooing took place shortly thereafter, from ages 15 to 17 (fig. 3). Another peculiarity reported from the Lassik was that the girl's suitor was marginally connected with the puberty rite in that he could not hunt, fish, or gamble at the time.

Puberty "schools" were present among the southern Athapaskans, probably relating them in this respect to groups to the south rather than to the north. Among the Mattole and Sinkyone both boys and girls attended. Essene (1942:91) reports for the Lassik a "preaching" by the chief to boys and girls, which took the place of a school.

Lowie Mus., U. of Calif., Berkeley.

Fig. 3. Jenny Young, a Shelter Cove Sinkyone, with face tattoos. Photograph by Pliny E. Goddard, Briceland, 1903.

Girls' puberty dancing rites were common in all of northern California, but among the southern Athapaskans, where large cult dances such as those of the Hupa and Yurok were lacking, the girls' dances may be said to have had a relatively greater social importance. Kroeber (1925:149) noted that the Sinkyone, for example, lacked all the dance paraphernalia of the northwest, but they did use the yellowhammer quill headbands and other objects characteristic of Central California for the girls' ceremony.

• MARRIAGE   Among the Sinkyone and Lassik, girls could be betrothed before puberty, although such betrothal might be looked upon merely as a goodwill pledge. The practice cf negotiating the bride's "purchase" price was widespread. In some cases (for instance, Sinkyone) the suitor might propose personally; the usual first approaches were made through an intermediary.

Among each of the five tribes, during the time of the wedding itself, gifts were exchanged. Weddings were at the bride's house in some groups and at the groom's in others. First and final residence for the newly married was also not the same among all groups. Either in the beginning or later, residence was matrilocal, patrilocal, or variable; and in some instances, as among the Nongatl,

196

the couple started life at the husband's parents' house but later had their own. Sexual intercourse does not seem to have been taboo (as among the Hupa and Yurok) inside permanent dwellings.

Both the simultaneous (polygynous) and successive (postmortem) sororate were known to most groups, as was the levirate (postmortem only).

Kinship avoidances (for example, mother-in-law, son-in-law) were not well developed either among the Klamath River peoples or the southern Athapaskans, except for the Sinkyone, Lassik, and Wailaki (cf. Loeb 1932:94; Essene 1942:31). Probably the Wailaki derived their practices from the south—from the Pomo or Yuki.

Divorces took place in all groups, with the usual reasons given as incompatibility (either spouse); unfaithfulness, barrenness, or laziness on the part of the wife; and unfaithfulness or maltreatment on the husband's part. The bride price was commonly returned to the husband's family following divorce. Children were either divided or all sent to husband's or wife's family, often depending upon the acceptance or refusal of the repayment of the bride price. Return of the bride price, conversely, was frequently dependent upon the number of children the husband's family kept. Among the Lassik, all children still nursing and the girls would go to the wife's family, while boys over seven years old would go to the husband's family.

• DEATH All groups left the corpse in the house until buried, usually a day or so after death. Cemeteries were located at varying distances from the village, not among dwellings as with some lower Klamath River peoples. Wives were usually buried at the husband's plot or locality, although the Nongatl, who had family-owned grave plots, followed the practice of allowing wives to be buried there.

Undertakers were usually, except among the Lassik and probably the Wailaki, blood relatives. They were subject to numbers of taboos (such as hunting, gambling, sexual relations) as well as a variety of purificatory devices, such as recitations of formulas or rubbing of plants on the body.

Interment in extended position in redwood plank-lined graves was common to all except the Wailaki and the Lassik. Lassiks buried their dead in a flexed position, sitting up, wrapped in a blanket (Essene 1942:36). Curtis (1907–1930, 14:30) states that the Wailaki buried their dead extended, head to east, in deep graves later piled with stones. Other groups oriented heads southeast, east, or south, or "upstream."

Cremation was rare but has been reported for both Mattole and Sinkyone, probably referring to persons who died away from home (Kroeber 1925:142, 146). Among the Lassik, affinal relatives or those married-in from another village were sometimes cremated, with their ashes brought home in a basket (Essene 1942:66).

Usual procedures concerning belongings of the dead were to burn or tear down their houses and to dispose of their valuables in a number of ways. Probably the most common practice was to bury the goods (broken or unbroken) with the body, but they could be burned as well, and among the Nongatl any personal property might be willed (Driver 1939:411). Dogs were often sacrificed with owners.

Names of deceased were taboo among most groups for an indefinite period. Widows, besides observing numbers of other taboos, cut or burned off hair, and often female blood relatives of the dead man cut off hair as well. Lassik widows are reported not to have been able to marry again until their hair grew out, that is, about one or two years (Essene 1942:66).

Religion

General beliefs in the importance of spirits for living creatures and ideas about their presence in inanimate objects as well seem to have been held by all southern Athapaskans. Origin myths probably were not uniform among all groups; however, Coyote seems not far removed from the role of creator, even though he is not always specifically designated as such. The Wailaki creator Ketanagai (*kəiəʼʼ nagay* 'night traveler') had, according to Loeb (1932:73), some of the attributes of Coyote, such as a proneness to deceive women, and this has given rise to the suggestion that Coyote was the older creator from whom Ketanagai usurped some evil as well as beneficent characteristics.

Among the Lassik, and in conjunction with a belief that the "first people" were animals, Coyote was looked upon as "the" creator (Essene 1942:48). His role of trickster, benefactor, and dupe here and elsewhere presents a dualistic motif that must have seemed consistent with the apparent contradictions in the state of man's welfare.

For the Sinkyone, in contrast, Nagaicho (*nagayčo* 'great traveler') was the creator who was never depicted as tricky or erotic, yet there are myths among the Sinkyone about Coyote himself stealing the sun in order to give him daylight. Kroeber (1925:150) emphasizes this dualism among the Sinkyone by stating that "Coyote . . . assisted in the establishment of the world, but is also responsible for death and much that is wrong in the scheme of things. These are all standard central Californian beliefs."

• SHAMANISM The principal connection between religion and shamanism is to be found in spirit beliefs. Of the three types of shamans among the southern Athapaskans—sucking doctors, soul-loss doctors, and herb doctors—only the herb doctors seem to have depended upon empirical knowledge for curing ills rather than upon the basic power acquired from a particular personal spirit. Both men and women could become doctors of any kind. Before sucking doctors or soul-loss doctors could properly qualify, a spirit vision, either sought or unsought, was necessary. Usually the spirit was represented as a human being; for example, among the Sinkyone the guardian spirit could be that of a dead relative (Driver 1939:418). Wailaki doctors alone were said to be able to see and communicate with Ketanagai, whom they called 'father' (Loeb 1932:73). All three types of doctors might receive instruction by older doctors, although among the Mattole, Lassik, and Wailaki there were schools for sucking or soul-loss doctors in which novices could receive visions and be allowed to practice on patients (Loeb 1932:76). In addition, public "doctor-making" dances were held by most groups, at which novices also could practice some of the professional techniques of sucking or soul-loss doctors.

The herb doctor usually treated diseases through recitation of a formula or by administering medicine internally. These methods of treatment probably were of less importance to any given group than were the more esoteric devices of the other two kinds of doctor. The main causes of disease were thought to be intrusion of poison objects, soul loss, and breach of taboo (that is, offense against a spirit or ghost). Curing took the form of identifying, often with the help of the shaman's spirit, the poison and withdrawing it by sucking. A lost or strayed soul was recovered by the doctor himself or through him by his guardian spirit. The curing itself usually took place with the accompaniment of singing, dancing, and the smoking of tobacco. If the treatment were not successful, fees were either not taken, not offered, or returned.

Although both sucking and soul-loss doctors were primarily curers, they had numbers of special functions in some groups, such as the finding of lost or stolen articles, or of foretelling the future.

Another form of curing shaman, usually called a bear doctor, allegedly derived his particular power from the bear. Such doctors were known only by the Lassik and Wailaki among the southern Athapaskans, although the idea of bear shamanism occurs widely in central California. Ultimately, and despite the gap represented by the northern California and Oregon coasts, the California form almost certainly was derived from the Pacific Northwest Coast (Loeb 1932:85). Other southern Athapaskans had many beliefs connected with bears, for example certain malicious persons, not doctors, were known to impersonate bears, thus supernaturally acquiring invulnerability and the power of rapid travel (Driver 1939:364).

• CEREMONIES Kroeber (1925:861) noted that "poor and rude tribes make much more of the [girls'] adolescence ceremony in California than those possessed of considerable substance and specialized institutions." This applies quite specifically to the southern Athapaskans, who had a large number of dances, such as those dedicated to salmon, dogs, coyotes, acorns, or clover; however, with a few exceptions, none of these seems to have exceeded the girls' ceremony in importance. Certainly none of their dances reached the peak of elaboration seen among northwestern or central Californians in their cult ceremonies.

One exception may have been found among the Lassik, for their camas (edible bulbs of the lily family) ceremony was said to be the most important ceremony of the year (Essene 1942:72). This does not say that the bulbs were the most valuable plant food to the Lassik, for acorns must have been of much greater concern to them. It does suggest a marked deviation from the "world renewal" or "big time," which was so significant among the lower Klamath River peoples.

For southern Athapaskans, the "big time" has not been specifically reported for the Nongatl, Lassik, and Wailaki; and the Sinkyone and Mattole apparently observed it in slightly diluted form. It was held irregularly by the Mattole, with no ritual specialists associated with it; and only the Mattole carried obsidian blades, one of the key features of the dance among the Hupa and Yurok. Performing within a brush enclosure, the dancers wore yellowhammer headbands and feather cloaks on net foundations and employed single split-stick rattles. All these features were not found in the north and were probably derived from Central California (cf. Kroeber 1925:149).

The Sinkyone observed an annual ancestor-impersonation dance, "to appease the spirits of the chiefs and wealthy tribesmen's dead relatives" (Nomland 1935:167). No other impersonation dances have been reported among the southern Athapaskans, although it may be significant that the Wailaki god Ketanagai, though not impersonated, yet corresponded in certain ways to the Eastern Pomo god who was impersonated in the Kuksu ceremony (Loeb 1932:73).

Warfare

The usual cause for wars or for feuds between tribelets or families was revenge or retaliation for murder, witchcraft, insult, jealousy over women, and, to a lesser extent, abduction and rape. Essene (1942:68) states that among the Lassik rape and abduction became an issue only if the woman were an important person. In general, the southern Athapaskans were not particularly warlike; they seem to have fought among themselves but not much with outsiders. The Bear River and Mattole fights with the Wiyot are an exception to this.

In some groups, battles were characteristically prearranged, often following breakdown of negotiations over payment for an offense; however, surprise attacks probably were more frequent. Ceremonial dances, or "dances of incitement" took place before battles among all groups. Except among the Mattole, chiefs did not lead the people in war, although they might advise them when to conduct a war; in most groups they also acted as peace envoys.

The usual weapons of war were the sinew-backed bow and arrow, with knives, clubs, sticks, slings, spears, and rocks used in varying degrees by different groups. For all groups but the Mattole, elkhide armor has been reported. The Wailaki alone apparently used elkhide shields (Powers 1877:129). No prisoners were taken, but some groups killed children and women, particularly if they had taken part in the conflicts. Scalps were taken by all groups but the Mattole and Nongatl.

Victory dances were common. Paradoxically, compensation for the dead, the injured, and destroyed property was also observed; and dances of settlement were held, after or before the payment of compensation.

Structures

The permanent or winter dwelling houses among the southern Athapaskans stood in fair contrast to the comparatively elaborate rectangular plank houses of the lower Klamath River peoples, in that they were usually circular in ground plan, conically shaped or with hip roof, and containing a single ridgepole. The Sinkyone, for illustration, had both conically shaped lean-tos and a wedge-shaped house of pieces of bark leaned against a pole resting in two upright poles, the front nearly vertical, the combined back and roof gently sloping (Kroeber 1925:147).

The Mattole showed the only notable exception to the circular ground plan, for they had in addition (for the wealthy) a rectangular ground plan house, a double lean-to with side walls (Driver 1939:384). All these houses were covered with redwood or fir slabs or bark (fig. 4); doors consisted of swinging or lifting mats, bark, or boughs. Floors were excavated about two feet among the Mattole, Sinkyone, and Wailaki; other groups built houses over an unexcavated place. Fireplaces were either

Fig. 5. Interior of Nongatl slab house with baskets and metal utensils near hearth. Photograph by Pliny E. Goddard, 1903.

in a shallow depression or on the floor surface, in about the center of the house. Entrances were mostly flush with the front wall of the house, although the Lassik and probably the Nongatl had houses with projecting entrances, in which firewood could be stored.

Usually two or more families occupied a single house, although most probably had but one fireplace (fig. 5), which was regularly equipped with a drying scaffold above it. Bedding of hides with fur left on was probably most common; woven rabbitskin blankets and tule, rush, or innerbark mats were also used in some places.

The characteristic sweathouse also was circular in ground plan, conically shaped or with hip roof. It was used as a ceremonial house in the winter by the Nongatl and Lassik. Earth covering of the lower part of the sweathouse was seemingly known only to the Lassik and probably the Wailaki, although the excavated sweathouse with center pole of the Sinkyone had a smoke-hole entrance, hence also was probably at least in part earth-covered. Sweathouses in this part of California were all of the direct fire heat type. Only among the Mattole were there any considerable parallels in usages of sweathouses to those of the lower Klamath River peoples. Mattole women, for instance, were not allowed in sweathouses except for ceremonies.

In summer the brush shelter or flat shades were used for camping, or people simply slept in the open.

Houses, like most other property except land, was personally owned. Communally owned land was probably most common among the southern Athapaskans, including fishing and hunting spots, seed-gathering spots, and trees. There were some exceptions to this, with the Nongatl observing private ownership of some hunting lands and tobacco plots, much like the lower Klamath River groups (Driver 1939:317).

Fig. 4. Nongatl slab house. Photograph by Pliny E. Goddard, Blocksburg, 1906.

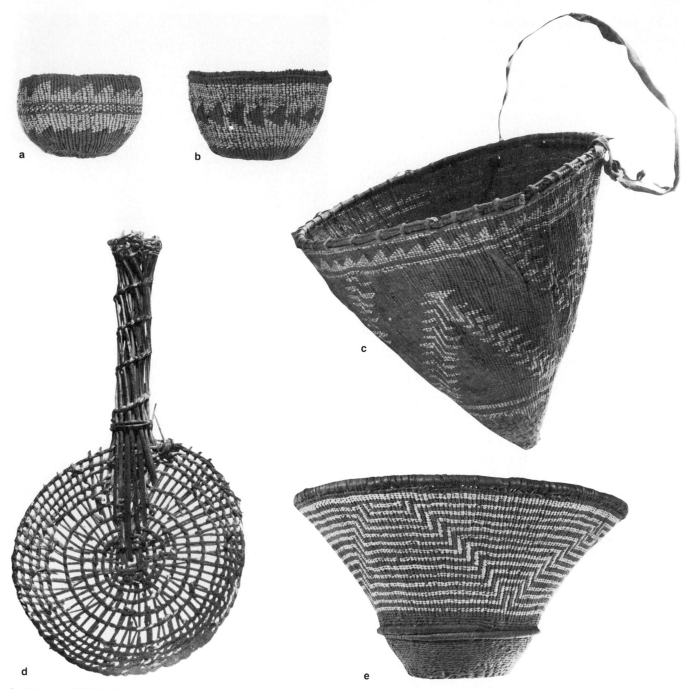

Lowie Mus., U. of Calif., Berkeley: a, 1-9578; b, 1-9577; c, 1-2534; d, 1-2530; e, 1-2541.

Fig. 6. Twined baskets. Sinkyone: a, mush server with 2 3-strand twining courses within central decorative band, resembling Nongatl technique; b, mush server with lattice-twined reinforcing rod near selvage, resembling Wailaki technique. Lassik: c, burden basket; d, seed beater; e, hopper for stone mortar. Diameter of a, 13 cm, b-e, same scale. a-b collected in 1903; c-e, collected about 1906.

Technology

• TEXTILES   All the southern Athapaskans used cordage netting for various purposes, such as dip nets in fishing. Woven mats or rabbitskin strip blankets were used by some groups for bedding. The textile arts, as for most California Indians, were predominantly represented by basketry (fig. 6).

All basketry followed fairly closely the techniques of the lower Klamath River peoples; that is, it was plain-twined, made mostly of hazel shoots and conifer root fibers, and decorated by overlay patterns in bear grass (*Xerophyllum tenax*), maidenhair fern (*Adiantum*), and giant fern (*Woodwardia fimbriata*). Dye for decoration was almost exclusively from alder bark.

200

Coiled basketry was found rarely among the Sinkyone and Wailaki. Kroeber (1925:153) asserts that the Wailaki derived their sporadic coiling practices from the Yuki and that such baskets served as valuables and gifts rather than as utensils.

Certain twined baskets, like the hoppers for shallow-depression slab mortars used in practically all of northern California for grinding acorns, were not easily distinguishable from any one subarea to another. However, despite the generic similarity of all southern Athapaskan basketry to that of the northwestern area, many subtle differences have been noted. Kroeber (1925:147) emphasizes the persistence of the northwestern California twining complex (including as a key feature the women's cap) to its southern limit among the Wailaki. He nevertheless points out that Sinkyone basketry, for example, "is much less finished than among the Yurok, and the ornamentation simpler. Minor distinctions, such as a somewhat greater depth of flat baskets, the occurrence of four vertical dyed stripes on conical burden baskets, and some tendency toward a zigzag pattern arrangement, do not obscure the complete adhesion to the fundamental type. . . ."

In aspects of form and function of basketry, the five groups were all approximately alike, although even here have been noted some unique occurrences among them, such as the Mattole possession of a cylindrical basketry fish creel (Driver 1939:379) and the Wailaki use of a long woven basket like a fish trap for catching quail (Loeb 1932:89).

Included as textiles are the Wailaki "charms" (fig. 7) of grass or rush wound diagonally around two crossed sticks (Kroeber 1925:154). The specific purpose of this is not known, but it seems to be a unique occurrence in northern California and is perhaps another illustration of the unpredictability of cultural diffusion, even among the so-called marginal tribes of native California.

• BOATS Four sorts of water transportation were used by southern Athapaskans: the shovel-nose-and-stern dugout characteristic of the lower Klamath peoples, a smaller dugout canoe probably not so well made as those on the Klamath, log rafts, and large baskets.

The shovel-nosed canoe has been reported definitely for the Sinkyone, for use on the Eel River up to the entrance of the South Fork Eel. Driver (1939:322) reported that this kind of canoe among the Mattole was purchased from the Wiyot. Nomland (1938:114) states that the Bear River people had a small dugout canoe, probably crude and unstable; this type seems also to have been used by the Lassik. For both kinds of dugouts, single-bladed paddles were used and, occasionally, plain poling rods.

Log rafts were commonly used, poled in shallow water but also simply towed by swimmers, as among the Lassik. The Wailaki had no dugout canoe (Loeb 1932:88), hence rafts must have been of some importance to them.

Lowie Mus., U. of Calif., Berkeley: 1-12192.
Fig. 7. Wailaki tule-woven "charm" with cocoon (*Antheraea polyphemus*) rattles. Height 28 cm, collected 1903.

Evidently large baskets were used by the Lassik and their southern neighbors, probably including the Wailaki, mostly for ferrying goods and children, towed by swimmers.

Games and Music

Probably all southern Athapaskan children played the usual games of jumping rope, swinging, and running races, with boys playing with small bows and arrows and girls with some kind of doll. From all or most groups have been reported tops, and acorn or other buzzer or hummer toys operated by cordage strung between fingers on opposite hands.

Games for adult men and women were shinny, played with a curved stick and a puck of oak gall or pepperwood nut. Sinkyone men played two games not recorded elsewhere among the five groups but known, respectively, to the north and south: spear or dart throwing contests, and the hoop and pole game. Men had archery contests in all groups.

In gambling, both men and women played one form or another of the hand (guessing) game, either with grass or with many sticks. In most groups only women played the dice game, with dice consisting of seashell disks or marked flat wooden sticks.

Lesser diversions for men and women were represented by the ring and pin game (fig. 8), with fish or deer bones

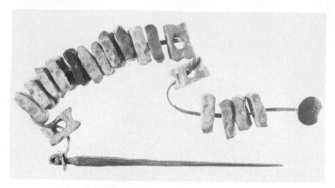

Lowie Mus., U. of Calif., Berkeley: 1-725.
Fig. 8. Wailaki ring and pin game. Rings are bored deer astragali. Length 21.5 cm, collected 1901.

for rings, and cat's cradles, where mostly static figures were produced, although moving ones were known by the Sinkyone.

Musical instruments consisted of drums, rattles or clappers, whistles, and flutes. The wooden drum, a regular feature in central California ceremonialism, was absent among all groups except the Wailaki (Loeb 1932:87), who probably derived the custom from the Pomo. The Mattole and Sinkyone had a hide drum, one form of which was used by Sinkyone men when gambling (Driver 1939:398). All groups had split-stick clappers used in several different kinds of ceremonies for keeping time in dancing. Flutes, mostly of elderberry, with from three to six holes and mouth-blown at the end, were played by all groups.

In contrast to the flute and its melodic potentialities, the bull-roarer was not really a musical instrument. Among the southern Athapaskans, it was only vaguely affirmed for the Wailaki. It also was known by the Sinkyone, who allegedly used it to stop or start the wind's blowing (Driver 1939:398).

Clothing and Grooming

Clothing obviously was dependent on the weather, as scanty or no clothing in the summer has been reported for men and women of several groups. Basketry hats for women, standard for lower Klamath River peoples, were habitually worn only by Nongatl women, although known by others. Sinkyone and Nongatl men and women used them, for example, when carrying with pack strap. Mostly, men wore fur caps or headbands.

Both men and women wore hair at shoulder length or longer, while children, especially boys, had hair cropped. Soaproot brushes were the usual means of combing hair, but bone head scratchers were also used, and the Mattole are said to have used whale (gray whale?) whiskers held between flat sticks as combs (Driver 1939:393). Cutting of hair was done with a stone knife. Some men allowed beards to grow, while others plucked their hair, either with fingernails or a stone flake opposed to the fingernail.

For the upper part of the body, usual covering was deer hide with hair on. The Sinkyone and Mattole also wore rabbitskin blankets. Lower body clothing was an apron-style buckskin breechclout, mostly for men; a one-piece skirt or apron, of deer fur for men and inner bark (sometimes maple) for women; and a double apron of buckskin for women. Moccasins were worn by all but the Wailaki (Loeb 1932:87) by men and women. Made of buckskin wrapped around the ankles and calf, they were worn at least among the Lassik in summer as a protection against rattlesnakes; in winter they were not worn because water and mud would make them soggy and useless.

Ceremonial dress included, in most groups, yellowhammer quill headbands and half-length feather garments on net foundations.

Bear grease was rubbed on the body by the Sinkyone and Lassik as a protection against cold and wet.

Implements

The sinew-backed bow of yew wood, strung with sinew and with recurved ends, was most frequently used in combat and probably hunting, while the self-bow was used for other minor purposes. Arrows were of wood or cane, equipped with foreshafts when cane, and untipped or tipped with pressure-flaked barbed stone points. In manufacture, arrows were smoothed with a two-piece grooved abrading device.

Elkhorn and wooden wedges were used with ground-stone, pear-shaped mauls for splitting wood, especially for houses. The fine composite adzes of the lower Klamath River peoples were generally lacking among the southern Athapaskans.

In preparation of acorns, the hopper slab mortar with ground stone pestle was commonly used. Carved, undecorated wooden paddles were employed as acorn mush stirrers, in boiling baskets; two sticks were used as tongs for the hot stones in the boiling process. Elkhorn or deer-skull spoons were used by most groups in eating acorn gruel.

Hand drills of buckeye or willow together with hearths of willow or alder were used in making fire; dry moss served as tinder.

Bone awls were used for sewing buckskin, although the Sinkyone also had eyed bone needles for this purpose.

Summary

The five groups here designated as southern Athapaskans are by most standards rightly called marginal to the climax or elaborate cultures of northwestern or central California; however, except in the matter of ceremonialism, they were not mere pale reflections of the surrounding peoples. Together they represent a specific and successful adaptation to a huge territory, almost the entire Eel River drainage region. While each group

202

certainly took on customs of its nearest non-Athapaskan neighbors, each nevertheless seems to have retained its separate identity, and this separateness often extended to the level of the so-called tribelets within each of the major tribes.

Inclusion of the Wailaki and exclusion of the Cahto from the southern Athapaskan enclave are probably arbitrary procedures but are based upon statistical grounds (table 1) and upon other less measurable factors, such as frequent mentions by native informants of interaction with neighboring groups.

Because of their isolated geographical situation, these five tribes have been among the least known to California ethnography. It is only by combining data from several different and limited sources that these Athapaskans can be placed in the well-known cultural patterns of northern California. This is characterized by local independence and relatively peaceful sovereignty, flourishing in a sort of loose confederation conditioned by similar linguistic or physiographic environments.

Synonymy

No distinct name has been preserved for the Bear River people, though Níˑekení is what they called both themselves and the Mattole (Nomland 1938:92, normalized; cf. Nek'-an-ni' of Merriam, cited by Baumhoff 1958:200).

Mattole is probably from the Wiyot river name βétul, métul (Goddard 1907b:822; Curtis 1907–1930, 14:188), though Kroeber (1925:142) suggests that this may have been borrowed from English; compare Mattoal (Powers 1877:105), Bettōl', Pet'-tōl', or Mattol' (Merriam in Baumhoff 1958:196). Another name, Tul'bush, is Wailaki dəlbaš 'babblers, foreigners' (Powers in Goddard 1970b:822).

The designation Sinkyone is derived from Sinkyo or Sinkyoko, the name of the south fork of the Eel River (Swanton 1952:514; Kroeber 1925:145); the suffixes are -ni 'tribe of' and -ko or -kok(?) 'at, group at'. The word Sinkyone is not always used to include both branches of the group, although Nomland (1935:149) refers to all Sinkyone as Kaikomas, and again the name Tulbush has been noted as applying to both Mattole and Sinkyone by the Wailaki (Powers 1877:124). The names for the northern Sinkyone, such as Lo'langko or Lolonko, are variants of names for Bull Creek or a settlement at its mouth (Kroeber 1925:145): Flonho (typographical error); Flonk'-o, Flonko (English corruption of Lo-lon'-kūk, according to Powers); Lo-lahn'-kok; Loloncook; Loloncooks; Lolonkuh; Lolonkuk; Lo-lon-kuk; Loolanko (Merriam 1966–1967, 2:193). For the Shelter Cove subdivision are found the names Mankya or Bankya, said to have been given by the native inlanders to the coastal Sinkyone (cf. baŋ 'shore, coast'), and Usal, given by the coastal dwellers by the Whites (Kroeber 1925). Also probably applied to coastal peoples were the terms Bay-ma-pomas and Kush-Kish (Tobin 1858:405).

The name Nongatl is Hupa noŋgahł 'Athapaskan to the south', perhaps from a verb 'to go to a distance', or an equivalent form in a dialect of the Wailaki type (Victor Golla, personal communication 1975); cf. Wailaki nóŋkał 'Nongatl' (Curtis 1907–1930, 14:186, normalized). Goddard's (1910a:410) restricted use of Nongatl followed Powers's (1877:124) usage of Noan'-kakhl, but Merriam (1923:276), who rendered the term Nung-kah[HL], claimed that it was a general term for "all the southern Athapaskan tribes . . . including the . . . Wilakke." However, Merriam also applied the name Kit-tel' to the Nongatl (Baumhoff 1958:181). Powers (1877:124) stated that Noan'-kakhl was a Wailaki name for the Sai-az (Nongatl) while Merriam (1923:276) asserts that the Wiyot gave him the word Si'-az as the name "for a Wilakke tribe in the Middle Eel River region." The Hupa used the term Saia (saˑyaˑ) for the Nongatl when speaking to Whites (Goddard 1910a:410); alternative spellings from nineteenth-century sources are Siaws, S-yars, Siahs, and Sians.

Goddard (1907c:761) suggests that the name Lassik was that of a chief, though he was probably a chief of the Nongatl (Powers's Lassik) rather than the group now called Lassik, who speak a subdialect of Wailaki (Victor Golla, personal communication 1975). The name has not suffered many alterations, although Keane (1878:519) lists Lassics or Lessics for those of "Tinney [i.e., Athapaskan] stock . . . a Hoopah tribe on Mad River."

The name Wailaki is a Wintu word meaning 'north language' but was applied to all groups, Wintu and foreign, to the west (Swanton 1952:517). Eventually its reference in English was narrowed to the dominant group of Athapaskan speakers on the Round Valley Reservation. Powers (1877:114) gives the terms Ken'-es-ti (Wailaki kənəsʼieʔ 'person, Indian', Li 1930:130, phonemicized), Kastel Pomos, and Kak-wits. Kakwits is said to mean 'north people' among the Yuki, "but the more general Yuki appellation was Ko'il, 'Athabascan'" (Kroeber 1925:151), also given as kóidl (Curtis 1907–1930, 14:188). Alternative spellings or other renditions of Wailaki extracted from nineteenth-century U.S. government records and other sources (Goddard 1910b:894; Merriam 1966–1967, 1:48) are: Tlachee, Tlackes, Uye-Laches, Uye-Lackes, Wi-Lackees, Wilacki, Wi-Lak-ke, Wy-Tackees, Wi-Tackee-Yukas, Wry Lackers, Wye-Lackees, Wylacker, Wylachies, Wylackies, Wy-laskies, Wylaks, Ylackas.

Sources

Kroeber (1925) provides basic sketches on all the southern Athapaskan groups. Baumhoff's two monographs (1958, 1963) provide a wealth of ecological data on the

California Athapaskans collected from various sources. There are ethnographies on the Bear River people (Nomland 1935) and the Sinkyone (Nomland 1938) and a summary of Wailaki culture included in a study of the Kuksu cult (Loeb 1932). Culture element distribution lists for the Lassik (Essene 1942) contain supplementary material.

At the University of California, Berkeley, there are unpublished notes of A.L. Kroeber, P.E. Goddard (Kroeber and Valory 1967; Valory 1971), and C.H. Merriam (Heizer et al. 1969) on the southern Athapaskans. Copies of some of Goddard's filed notes, especially on Athapaskan linguistics, are also in the Library of the American Philosophical Society, Philadelphia (Freeman 1966).

It was evidently not possible to collect extensive lots of ethnographic specimens from any of the five groups; the small collection in the Lowie Museum of Anthropology, University of California, Berkeley, consists mostly of basketry and is by no means representative. No museum in the United States has listings specifically indicating collections from any of the southern Athapaskan tribes (cf. Hunter 1967).

Chimariko

SHIRLEY SILVER

Language and Territory

The language and the culture of the Chimariko nation are extinct. This tiny group, numbering only a few hundred people before White contact, was located in a narrow canyon that extends roughly 20 miles along the Trinity River in the western part of Trinity County in northern California. Kroeber (1907c) says in 1903 there were nine survivors. In 1849 they may have numbered 250 (Kroeber 1925:109).

Earliest White contact was with trappers, in the 1820s or 1830s. In the 1850s Chimariko territory, abundant in gold placers, attracted Whites whose mining activities threatened the supply of salmon, a primary food source. In the 1860s bitter conflict developed. Aroused by Púyelyalli, of Big Flat, the Chimariko for a short while got the upper hand. However, the Whites ultimately

> taught [them] that they must not presume to discuss with American miners the question of the proper color for the water in the Trinity River. [The Chimariko] were hunted to the death, shot down one by one, massacred in groups, driven over precipices. . . . In the summer of 1871 . . . there was not an Indian left. The gold was gone too, and the miners for the greater part, and amid the stupendous ripping-up and wreck of the earth which miners leave behind them, in this grim and rock-bound cañon. . . . one finds himself indulging in this reflection: 'The gold is gone, to return no more; the white man wanted nothing else; the Trinity now has nothing but its salmon to offer; the Indian wanted nothing else' (Powers 1877:94-95).

What remnants there were of the Chimariko nation took refuge chiefly with Shastan peoples on the upper Salmon River or in Scott Valley. After years of exile, the survivors returned to their home country. By 1906 all but a few were dead.

Information about the Chimariko is scant. Unless otherwise indicated, the ethnographic source for this chapter is Driver (1939).

The Chimariko language is considered a member of the Hokan stock, a linguistic grouping spread geographically from southern Oregon to Mexico and Nicaragua.* The

---

* The italicized Chimariko words cited here are from J.P. Harrington's unpublished field notes (1921-1928), in a broad phonetic orthography with ṭ, č, q, x, and š in their standard Handbook values substituted for Harrington's equivalent symbols, length indicated by a raised dot rather than a macron, and aspirated obstruents marked with ʰ.

neighbors of the Chimariko to the west and northwest were the Redwood Creek Indians (Whilkut) and the Hupa, who were Athapaskan speakers. To the south and east were the Wintu, whose language belongs to the Penutian stock.

Although the Chimariko were friendly with the Wintu when the Whites arrived, it is possible that in a previous time they had been pushed down the Trinity by the Wintu; and, although the Chimariko feared the Hupa and fought against them, there was some friendly interaction, such as intermarriage.

To the north on the lower New River, a tributary of the Trinity, were the Chimalakwe; on the upper New River, the New River Shasta; on the Salmon River, the Kono-mihu. The Konomihu and the New River Shasta spoke Shastan languages.

It is not known if the Chimalakwe were part of the Chimariko nation or identical with it. When the Whites arrived, the Chimalakwe were being absorbed and conquered by the Hupa; only 2 families (about 25 persons) still spoke Chimalakwe, and all the rest used Hupa. By 1872 the Chimalakwe were extinct (Powers 1877).

The Chimariko homeland stretched along the Trinity River from approximately the mouth of the South Fork of the Trinity to about as far as Big Bar, some five or six miles above the mouth of French Creek. Statements indicate that Chimariko territory may once have extended along the South Fork to some 15 or 20 miles south of Hyampom (Dixon 1910a:296; Harrington and Merriam 1967:227-228).

Chimariko country was mountainous and forest-covered. The rivers and creeks flowed through deep ravines (fig. 1). čʰiti (Trinity River) and čáltasom ʔaqʰa (New River) flowed near ʔawu ṭeˑta, a 5,200-foot mountain (Ironsides Mountain) to whose top the first people made pilgrimages when they got old and where they would pray and descend young again. Ironsides Mountain is also called čaliˑta ʔawu as well as wáywóli, which is said to be the "old Chimariko language name" (Harrington 1921-1928).

Six villages are known (fig. 2). In addition, the Chimariko had temporary hunting camps on the New River and in other foreign territory.

Fig. 1. Rope and plank bridge on New River trail, Trinity River Canyon. Photograph by C. Hart Merriam, Aug. 1936.

Culture

Structures

Each Chimariko village had a sweathouse, heated by direct fire, which accommodated 8 or 10 men. There the men sweated daily, gambled, and slept when they felt like it. Women were excluded except for ceremonial sweating together with the men.

Sweathouses and dwellings were constructed on a circular ground plan, had single ridge poles, and were covered with earth over madrone bark. Rectangular ground-level entrances faced east and were placed in the middle of the side of the house. The fireplace was in the center or between the center and the door.

Dwellings, 10 to 14 feet in diameter and accommodating two or more families, were furnished with wood or stone stools and furred-hide and rabbitskin blankets.

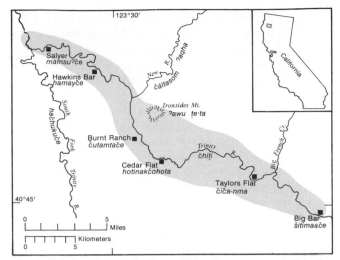

Fig. 2. Tribal territory and villages. Chimariko names are italicized. The location of *mamsuʔče* is uncertain.

Social Organization

The largest Chimariko social unit was the village community. There was one headman for each village group. His position was lifelong and hereditary through the male line. He settled disputes, declared war, and led his people in war. He also directed communal food quests, provided the largest share of food and property for ceremonies, and fed impoverished visitors. He was given food free; his son or another relative hunted for him.

Chimariko social status was determined by wealth or a combination of wealth and birth. The neighboring Hupa had a similar status system, but the Chimariko do not seem to have practiced the Hupa form of debt slavery. However, Harrington (1921–1928) records a term for 'slave', *šičela exaʔidew,* and a comment that "if one Indian farts in [a] house where high-up Indians are eating, they make him a dog and he has to assent."

Items of wealth and prestige included dentalia (imported, feather-tipped, sometimes wrapped with snakeskin, kept in cylindrical horn purses), clamshell cylinder beads, woodpecker scalps, red obsidian blades, and silver fox-skin blankets. The Chimariko imported red and black obsidian from the Wintu. Knives of red obsidian, *tʰikiṭi,* in value equivalent to 10 dollars for a short one, 50 dollars for a long one (two feet or more in length), were thought to have been made by *tiʔrámta čimára* 'long-ago people' when the world was created (Harrington 1921–1928). These objects were rarities and were displayed in dances.

Indications of status are found in statements that compensation for injury or death in war or a dispute was paid according to wealth; the richer a person, the more compensation was paid. Such indications also occur in comments about receptacles, utensils, and dress. Men of high status used trays made of elkhorn into which they put glue and dipped moss when applying sinew to the backs of bows, rich men used horn spoons with carved handles, and others used plain-handled spoons. Women of high status wore shell-decorated aprons; others did not. Woven, shell-decorated belts were considered handsome and valuable. A headman's daughter wore one four or more inches wide; others wore narrow ones.

Clothing and Adornment

Men and women wore their hair past shoulder length. A man's hairdo consisted of one full-length roll down the back with a tie at the back of the neck, ends loose. A woman parted her hair in the middle, wore two full-length rolls in front of the shoulders, two shoulder-length "clubs" at the sides of the head, and a three-strand braid. Women used ribbons of buckskin or mink to tie the hair. Boys and girls wore their hair close-cropped. Girls had temple locks and bangs; boys had a scalp lock down the back. Hair was trimmed by singeing. Fishbone combs and soaproot brushes were used in grooming; soaproot was used to wash hair, and hair was greased with animal fat.

Men grew beards and plucked them with fingernails. Women started tattooing early in life; it was done with a stone knife on the chin, cheeks, arm, or hand. A child's ears were pierced at two years.

On ceremonial occasions men wore round haliotis ear ornaments or dentalium pendants. Women wore rectangular haliotis pendants. Also on ceremonial occasions, body and face paint was used; men wore head plumes of condor and eagle tail feathers, beartooth necklaces, and yellowhammer quill headbands; both men and women wore bear-claw and dentalium necklaces; women wore haliotis shells on clothing.

The headbands of men and women from prominent families were of buckskin or fur and were decorated with woodpecker scalps. For ordinary dress, women wore buckskin-fringed double aprons strung with nuts and seeds; men wore buckskin trousers; deerskin robes or woven rabbitskin blankets were worn on the upper body.

Women habitually wore undecorated twined basket caps. Both men and women used these caps for carrying, and men also used them when fishing.

Technology

Closework and openwork twining were the only techniques used in basketmaking. (In Chimariko mythology, the spider's web is considered the origin of openwork twining.) Basket decoration involved banded woven ornamentation, ornamentation in three colors besides the background, and overlay twining. Willow bark was one source of color. The Chimariko wove a variety of baskets including hoppers, used in grinding. Before introduction of the hopper basket and slab in the mythical period, all grinding was done with portable stone bowl mortars, thought to be made by a myth character.

Receptacles of steatite and unburned clay were also made. Shallow steatite vessels were used for eating and as water containers; deeper ones, for boiling. Small clay bowls were used for catching grease drippings.

Clay was also used to make play objects such as miniature canoes and images of men and women. One such object was of a woman carrying a nine-inch-high packbasket (Harrington 1921–1928).

Wood was used to make meat platters, carved cylindrical chests for feathers and valuables, and mush stirrers with carved blades inlaid with red obsidian. Dugout canoes made of pine were worked with horn wedges.

Spoons were made either of horn or of mussel shells. Women used mussel-shell spoons; men used horn spoons.

To make hafted stone axes, used for war and hewing, a large flake of stone retouched by percussion was inserted into the split of a certain tree limb; when the tree grew fast around the blade the limb was cut off and a complete ax was thus produced.

Bows were of yew, sinew-backed, painted on the back and with sinew bowstrings. Feathering on arrows consisted of three radial feathers. Singleshaft arrows had no head or had a stone head; foreshaft arrows were headless. War arrows were stone-headed. The liver of a deer struck by a rattlesnake, gall, or rattlesnake venom were used as arrow poisons.

Subsistence

The food supply was so abundant that a number of potential resources were not exploited. The Trinity River provided an ample supply of salmon; acorns were the main vegetable food; deer, elk, and bear made up the larger part of the game supply. Eels, pine nuts, several varieties of wild seed, berries, several kinds of roots, and various fowl and small mammals were also eaten.

Fishing, gathering, and hunting places were communally owned. Tobacco plots were fenced and privately or jointly owned for a season only.

Chimariko men fished, using nets and traps. A flat net like a tennis net was either set or used in seining. A sacklike net made of iris, about eight feet wide at the mouth, was set. This kind of net was said to have been used before dip nets were known. Various other fishing methods included harpooning, scooping with baskets, the use of bare hands, shooting with bow and arrow, and clubbing.

Both men and women gathered acorns and pine nuts. Seed gathering included burning for a better wild-seed crop. Digging sticks were used in gathering roots.

Men were responsible for hunting, using methods such as smoking out (bear, rodents), spring-pole traps (deer, wildcat, small mammals, and birds), and driving and trailing (deer, rabbit, quail). In addition, two converging fires were used in hunting both large and small game.

Certain hunting observances were followed by men: maintaining sexual continence, bathing, and smoking (two puffs of tobacco) before the hunt and rubbing aromatic plants on the body.

The soul of the deer was considered immortal. Deer were butchered lying in the woods; the nose was cut. The slayer offered the meat to every visitor. It was brought into the house through an opening in the back of the house and was kept and prepared in the back of the house.

Certain taboos were observed when eating certain animal food: sex was taboo when eating bear meat; deer meat and fresh salmon were not eaten together; the deer tongue, eyes, ears, and other parts of the head were taboo food for females; the deer fetus was taboo food for persons under 50 years of age.

The highlights of Chimariko cuisine were boiled meat; broiled or whole-roasted fish and small mammals; smoke-dried fish and mammal meat; acorn bread baked on stone, coals, or in earth ovens or ashes; seeds parched with coals or hot stones in a basket; vegetable products baked in earth ovens; and manzanita cider.

No one ate breakfast until after bathing. Each person had his or her own eating basket, and, in general, men were served first. After eating deer meat, both men and women washed their hands in baskets. After meals, a pipe was passed around; tobacco was also smoked at social gatherings.

Men sat on stools or Turkish style while eating or visiting; they also sat Turkish style when playing the many-stick game. While eating (or visiting), women sat with one leg crossed over the other above the knee, with both legs to the side.

Life Cycle

• MARRIAGE   Before marriage, the bridegroom hunted and fished for his future wife's family so that everyone would know the marriage was to take place, and the girl's father bought clothes for his prospective son-in-law. The wedding took place at the bride's home.

A newly married couple could live with her family, his family, or in their own home. Marriage usually took place within a local group and was contracted through the negotiation of a bride price by an intermediary.

If a dying wife told her husband and sister to marry, they were obliged to; otherwise, the sororate was not obligatory, but if it occurred there was no additional payment for the second wife. The levirate was infrequent and nonobligatory; when it did happen, there was no additional payment. If two men exchanged sisters in marriage, simultaneous payment was made for both brides. Successive exchange was also possible; for example, a man might marry his sister's husband's sister. When nonaffinal remarriage of a widow or widower occurred, the widow's family paid the former husband's family.

Only prominent men practiced polygyny with unrelated wives. The maximum number of wives paid for was five; the maximum number of wives in each house was two.

Adulterers were socially ostracized by being denied

access to the sweathouse for three or four months. If a wife was unfaithful, she was beaten, or at times killed, by her husband. A seducer had to pay a fine to the husband; if the husband killed him, the husband paid a fine to the adulterer's family.

Men divorced women for unfaithfulness or laziness; women divorced men for unfaithfulness or maltreatment. Incompatibility was also grounds for divorce. Divorce was effected by repayment of the bride price by the wife's family to the husband's family. The amount repaid depended on the number and status of the children. The wife's family took the girls and the husband's family took the boys.

• BIRTH   A Chimariko child was born in the dwelling house or in a separate hut. A midwife, who was recompensed, assisted in the birth. If the baby's feet came first, she would push them back in and work the baby around until the head came first.

For 20 to 30 days after the birth the mother could not make baskets. For 10 days after parturition, she could not eat fresh or dried mammal meat, could not cook for her family, ate alone from separate dishes, and slept in the childbirth hut. At the end of the 10-day period she bathed, dressed in fine clothes, held the child in a cradle, and prayed and sang for it and herself.

The infant was placed in a cradle one day after birth. Before nursing, it was fed hazelnut or acorn broth. The child was weaned at one and one-half years.

There were no restrictions on the father, and the sex restriction on the parents consisted of continence starting six months after pregnancy. If a husband knew his wife had attempted abortion, he would kill her.

There was no particular time to name a child. Its name, that of a living paternal relative, was given at a certain rock in the river by a paternal or maternal relative.

Children were instructed according to their sex roles; for example, a child was taught to swim in ways appropriate to its sex.

• PUBERTY   For all Chimariko girls there was public recognition of puberty. A 10-day puberty rite was held inside the dwelling house two years after the onset of menses. Both men and women danced and sang, the girl dancing with her mother in the center of the house. The entire assemblage was fed publicly, and at the end the girl was ceremonially bathed.

For the two years after the onset of menses the girl was confined to a separate hut and had to observe a number of restrictions. She lived in the hut alone or with a female relative of the same age; lay most of the time on straw; wore the double apron; and was taught songs, moral conduct, and mythology by older female relatives. At the end of the two years medicine was made from an aromatic root roasted in ashes. Then the girl was purified by bathing, "dipping" five times; after bathing her betrothed embraced her publicly, each rubbed the other's body all over with the medicine, and then both dressed in fine clothes. The marriage was consummated a month or so later.

Like a girl at puberty, a menstruating mature woman also was confined and observed a number of more or less the same restrictions. Here, the period of time was for five days after the onset of menses, with a purification bath at the end of the period.

• DEATH   The Chimariko buried their dead. Cemeteries were off away from the village. A corpse was left in the dwelling until burial time when it was carried out on one person's back to the family-owned grave plot where it was washed with medicated water. The body was extended supine and wrapped in a blanket with the head pointing east. A wife was buried at her husband's plot or locality.

A deceased's money and valuables were buried with him. Worthless personal articles were placed on top of the grave. Most of the deceased's property was kept a year by the spouse or a close blood relative and then distributed among all relatives. If there were no relatives, the property was burned. If the surviving spouse and family wished, the deceased's house was burned.

Blood relatives acted as undertakers and, when doing so, observed hunting, gambling, travel, and sexual continence taboos. All mourners participated in purification bathing.

A widow's hair was cut or burned off and the ends were burned. The widow wore a mourning necklace made of plants. Blood relatives also wore such necklaces, and a separate one was worn for each relative deceased within the past year.

The Chimariko believed that the ghost of the deceased left the grave one day after death and went up to the sky.

Illness and Curing

There were two kinds of doctors, sucking and herb, and both men and women could be doctors. For the Chimariko, disease was caused by the intrusion of an inanimate poison object. The sucking doctor cured by sucking out the object, exhibiting it, and then making it disappear by sleight-of-hand. The herb doctor recited formulas and gave medicine internally.

Doctoring power tended to run in families. A sucking doctor acquired his powers through the observance of taboos lasting two years, the smoking of two puffs of tobacco, and the burning of angelica root. A public doctor-making dance was held in a dwelling for two days or nights, during which period the novice was forced to dance and was assisted in the ritual by older doctors. Herb doctors received instruction about formulas from older herb doctors, who were paid a fee.

After a cure, doctors were paid a fee. If the cure was unsuccessful, the fee was not offered, or not taken, or was returned.

A sucking doctor also had special functions other than curing. He or she could find lost or stolen articles, money or persons, could foretell whether a patient would live or die, and could "see" at distance.

Ceremonies

Other than the doctor-making ceremony and the girl's puberty rite, the Chimariko seem to have had only the sweat dance and an annual summer dance. Although salmon and acorns were among the most important foods, the Chimariko, unlike the Hupa and other northwestern California groups, did not have any first-salmon or first-acorn rites.

The annual dance, in which both men and women took part, seems to have had little ceremonial importance. It was of 10 days duration. Open house was held for all visitors. Free food was provided by the headman, with his wives and daughters assuming responsibility for the abundance of food. The dancing took place either outdoors or inside a dwelling. Men, unmarried girls, and young boys took part in an abreast formation in which all dancers sang. Men, unmarried girls, and matrons participated in a circle formation.

They did not practice the Deerskin Dance of the neighboring Hupa and Yurok (Kroeber 1907c).

Music and Games

A painted split-stick clapper was used in the puberty rite dancing. Other musical instruments were the hide drum and the flute. Flutes were made of elderwood and were used mainly in courting.

Chimariko games consisted of archery, a kind of quoits, and two varieties of gambling: the many-stick game and the grass game. It seems that only men played the gambling games.

Mythology

According to Dixon (1910a), little is known of Chimariko mythology. Dog was the most powerful being. He knew everything beforehand and foretold a flood. To escape it, he and Coyote built a stone house with an underground room. When the flood came, all other people were destroyed except Frog, Mink, Otter, and one man. After the flood subsided, the man found a bone fragment in a canoe in which Frog had taken refuge. This fragment later came to life as a girl child. The man married her, and it was from this union that the Chimariko, one of the smallest nations in pre-White America, were descended.

Synonymy

The Chimariko called themselves čimaríǩo (cf. čimar, čimal 'person'). The name Chimalakwe, given to that group by Powers (1877:91–93), is derived from the same stem as Chimariko.

The Hupa called the Chimariko yinahč̓in 'people from upstream' and probably called the Chimalakwe q̓alcahsn (Victor Golla, personal communication 1973).

Swanton (1952:483) cites kwoshonipu as the name

probably given the Chimariko by the Salmon River Shasta; however, it is unclear whether the term Salmon River Shasta refers to the New River Shasta or to the Konomihu, as both these Shastan groups occupied territory on the Salmon River.

Sources

Other than Driver (1939), the principal sources of information about the Chimariko consist of historical and ethnographic accounts by Powers (1877), Dixon (1910a), Harrington and Merriam (1967), and Kroeber (1925). Dixon's work also contains a sketch of the Chimariko language.

Unpublished linguistic sources include Harrington (1921–1928) and Grekoff (1967–1968). The Harrington material also contains fragments of ethnographic information.

Native scholar sources include Mrs. Dyer (Dixon 1910a), Sally Noble and Abe Bush (fig. 3) (Harrington 1921–1928), and Lucy Montgomery (Harrington 1921–1928; Driver 1939).

Discussion of the state of archeological knowledge of the Chimariko is found in Leonard and Toney (1968) and Chartkoff et al. (1968).

Dept. of Anthr., U. of Calif., Berkeley.
Fig. 3. Abe Bush. Photograph by C. Hart Merriam, Aug. 1921.

Shastan Peoples

SHIRLEY SILVER

Dixon (1910c) and Kroeber (1925) include in the term Shastan six northern California groups—Shasta, Konomihu, Okwanuchu, New River Shasta, Achumawi, and Atsugewi, whose languages comprised a family in the Hokan phylum (cf. Dixon and Kroeber 1913). Subsequent comparative linguistic studies (Bright 1954; Olmsted 1956-1959) suggest that the Achumawi and Atsugewi are not to be included in the Shastan grouping; therefore, the term Shastan is redefined here to include only the Shasta ('shăstə), Konomihu (ˌkōnə'mēhōo), Okwanuchu (ˌōkwə'nōochōo), and New River Shasta. Although the relationship of the languages spoken by these four groups has been established (Dixon 1905b, 1907a), the specific nature of that relationship is yet to be demonstrated.*

The Shastan peoples held territories in an area now shared by California and Oregon: the Shasta in northern California and southern Oregon, the Konomihu and New River Shasta to the southwest, and the Okwanuchu to the southeast of the California Shasta (fig. 1).

Shasta settlements, all speaking the same language, grouped loosely into divisions, one occupying parts of Oregon's Jackson and Klamath counties, the others occupying most of California's Siskiyou County. The three main California divisions were in Shasta Valley, Scott Valley, and in the Klamath River area from the Scott River to the present-day town of Hornbrook. Shasta territory along the Klamath extended up as far as the headwaters of Jenny Creek in Oregon; however, it is unclear whether the dialectally divergent Shasta living northeast of Hornbrook were affiliated with the Klamath River division. (Although dialect variation exists within the Shasta language, what correlation this variation may have with sociopolitical groupings is unclear.)

A minority group called the Kammatwa lived on the fringes of Shasta territory. To the Shasta the word Ṛ̌a·máĭwa· signified an inability to speak Shasta properly; in other words, the Kammatwa spoke "half-language." Curtis (1907-1930, 13:232) says the Kammatwa spoke

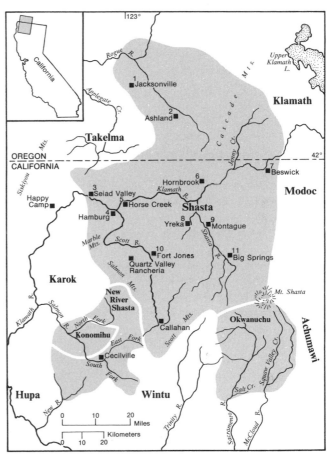

Fig. 1. Tribal territories with a few Shasta place-names: 1, *ikwahawa;* 2, *Ṛ̌wa·xa·xa* 'where the crow lights'; 3, *sam·ay?;* 4, *ayṚ̌a·* or *ahúʔay* 'down inside'; 5, *itiwákha;* 6, *u·kwa·yíˑk;* 7, *če·čutúk;* 8, *Ṛ̌usta;* 9, *čaráywa;* 10, *čunčastúk* or Kwah-pä́-sah-se-rah (Heizer and Hester 1970b).

---

* Italicized Shasta words are from Silver's dictionary file derived from linguistic field notes (Silver 1957-1963), written in the orthography she developed (Silver 1964). The Shasta and Konomihu words cited with Harrington (1928-1933) as source are in his phonetic notation except that č, q, x, and š (in their usual Handbook values) are substituted for Harrington's special symbols and a raised dot replaces his macron to mark length.

---

both Shasta and another language. Another such minority, the Watiru, lived west of the Kammatwa on the fringes of Karok territory in the area from Seiad Valley to present-day Happy Camp. Curtis (1907-1930, 13:232) gives two Shasta Valley Shasta forms, Katíru and Watíru, identifying Watíru as Shasta Valley dialect. The Watiru (affiliated with the Karok) and the Kammatwa (affiliated with the Shasta) provided a communication link between the Karok and the Shasta. According to Sargent Sambo (fig. 2), a Klamath River Shasta, "the Watiru talked to the Karok and the Kammatwa, the Kammatwa talked to

211

the Watiru and the Shasta, but the Karok and the Shasta could not talk to each other" (Silver 1957–1963).

In pre-White times the total population of the Shastan groups approximated 3,000 (Cook 1964), with the Shasta comprising the major portion.

At the time of first contact there were about 2,000 Shastas (Dixon 1907:390). In 1906 approximately 121 Shastas lived in Siskiyou County (Kelsey 1971). As of 1962, it was estimated that there were 36 Shastas living on the Quartz Valley (Scott Valley) rancheria (U.S. Bureau of Indian Affairs 1963); there are also a handful of Shastas elsewhere, including a few persons at the Siletz and Grande Ronde reservations in Oregon.

The Konomihu population must have been very small when the Whites came (Kroeber 1925:283). In 1955 it was estimated that there were at least 5 persons alive who could trace some degree of Konomihu descent (Kroeber and Heizer 1970:6).

The population of the New River Shasta probably consisted of less than 300 persons in 1850 (Kroeber 1925:282). In 1955 there appear to have been only two survivors with any New River Shasta ancestry (Kroeber and Heizer 1970:6).

It is estimated that the Okwanuchu population consisted of no more than 200–300 persons in the late nineteenth century; by 1918 there were no survivors (Kroeber 1925:284).

SHASTA

Among the Shastas living in the mid-1970s actual knowledge of the aboriginal culture was practically nonexistent, and the language was on the verge of extinction. The gold rush and the Rogue River Indian wars of 1850–1857 contributed to the disintegration of Shasta culture. "The great influx of miners had crowded [the Shasta] from their fisheries and hunting-grounds, and the commencement of permanent settlements threatened to abridge their movements still more. Many of their villages had been burned and their people shot. . . . [The Whites] had determined to wage a war of extermination against the Indians on the upper Klamath and its tributaries . . ." (Gibbs 1853:162).

History

The Shasta word for 'White' is *pa·stin* (from Chinook Jargon based on the name Boston). The first Whites they came in contact with were fur trappers in the 1820s and 1830s (cf. Elliott 1910). In 1851 a treaty (never ratified) made with the headmen of the California Shasta divisions established a reservation in Scott Valley (Heizer 1972:97–99). The Shasta played a major role in the Rogue River wars, with Scott Valley and Shasta Valley groups going to the aid of the Oregon Shasta; in 1856 Oregon and California Shasta survivors were taken first to Grande Ronde and then to Siletz.

By the 1870s the Shasta way of life had been badly shattered, and the Shasta adapted themselves to continuing disappointments by embracing versions of the 1870 Ghost Dance religion (DuBois 1939). They first heard of the Ghost Dance prophecy from Modocs who brought word to Shastas in the northeastern part of California Shasta territory. From there Shastas spread the word south and west and converted Karoks to the new religion. In 1871 the Shasta learned of the Earth Lodge cult from the McCloud River Wintu who lived south and east and in 1872 carried that doctrine north to Shastas at Grande Ronde and Siletz. The third, and last, version of the new religion to reach the Shasta was the Big Head cult (the localized northern offshoot of the 1870 Ghost Dance discussed by DuBois 1939:117–127, 148, pl. 2d), which was diffused to them from the Trinity River (Western) Wintu. The spread of this cult ended with the California Shasta, who made an unsuccessful attempt to introduce it into Oregon.

The following cultural summary is derived primarily from studies by Dixon (1907), Voegelin (1942), and Holt

Shirley Silver.
Fig. 2. Sargent Sambo, Klamath River Shasta, wearing headdress of feathers and bead work, buckskin shirt decorated with dentalium shells and beads, feather collar, and shell necklaces. Photographed about 1881.

(1946), which present a relatively homogeneous picture of Shasta culture.

Environment and Settlement

The Rogue River flowed along the northern edge of Oregon Shasta territory, and there were three major streams in the California area—Shasta, Scott, and Klamath rivers. The Shasta homeland, with elevations almost everywhere above 2,500 feet, was mountainous and forested (except for Shasta and Scott valleys). The Cascade range bordered the east side of the territory, with Mount Shasta in the southeastern corner of Shasta Valley; the Marble, Salmon, and Scott mountains formed western and southern boundaries; and the Siskiyous formed a west-to-east barrier between the Oregon and California Shasta.

Along the Klamath River, the favored Shasta village site was at the mouth of a creek into the main river; a few villages, situated near oaks, were located away from the river in the high hills. In the Shasta and Scott valleys, villages were usually located at the edge of the valley where a stream came down out of the mountains. Heizer and Hester (1970b) provide a map and list of approximately 150 Shasta settlements.

Internal and External Relations

The Shasta Valley and Scott Valley peoples had bitter feuds, and the Kammatwa made raids against the Klamath River Shasta; however, there was also much friendly intragroup interaction. When visiting a different district, people took food typical of their own area to their host and brought home food typical of the host's area. For example, Klamath River people took pine nuts and salmon to the Scott and Shasta valleys and to Oregon; they brought back antelope meat from Shasta Valley and varieties of bulbs from Oregon and Scott Valley. When people from neighboring divisions met to gamble, one group came to the other's village, but two nonneighboring groups met at the village of an intervening district.

Revenge was the primary Shasta reason for intertribal conflict. They occasionally fought the Achumawi and had a number of battles with the Wintu. One battle, which the Shasta won, was fought with the Wintu near Callahan in the southeastern part of Scott Valley; another noteworthy battle, which the Shasta lost, took place at Castle Crags in Wintu territory (Merriam 1955:15–16). The last great battle between the two groups occurred in Wintu territory at Antler on the Sacramento River; the Shasta were defeated.

Retaliatory forays against the Modoc, who conducted annual summer raids into California Shasta territory, were the closest the Shasta came to organized warfare; the Shasta Valley and Klamath River groups banded together to retaliate, and when someone from another Shasta group was killed during a Modoc raid into Klamath River or Shasta Valley country, the deceased's people would join in the retaliation (Holt 1946:313).

Although the Oregon Shasta and their neighbors in the Rogue River area were longtime enemies and in frequent conflict for territory, they shared attempts to resist invasion by White miners and settlers.

The Shasta were friendly with their western neighbors; however, they were apprehensive of the Hupa and Yurok who came into their territory. Wicks (1971:61) comments: "Indians down the coast and those down the Klamath—they were . . . devil-possessed . . . [the Shasta] were scared of them and . . . had to be so careful when they . . . came, to see that they didn't get insulted. . . ."

Trade

The Shasta obtained obsidian from the Achumawi. They imported pine nut necklaces from the Wintu (Voegelin 1942:198) and traded buckskin, obsidian, and dentalia for acorns. Although they traded relatively little with the Klamath or Modoc, there was trade with Oregon peoples. The California Shasta traded dried acorn paste with the Rogue River Athapaskans for dentalia. The Shasta Valley Shasta imported buckskin clothing from the Warm Springs Indians, using dentalia for exchange, and also went north to trade clamshell disk beads for otterskins (Voegelin 1942:199). The Shasta were also a trade medium through which the Achumawi received dentalia from the Columbia River country (Curtis 1907–1930, 13:131).

The trade emphasis in California was with the Karok, Hupa, and Yurok from whom the Shasta received acorns, baskets, dentalia, haliotis and other shells in exchange for pine nuts, obsidian blades, juniper beads, and Wintu beads. Dixon (1907:427) asserts that salt was obtained chiefly from the tribes of the lower Klamath; however, Holt (1946:309) says there were two large salt deposits in Shasta territory from which all Shasta groups got salt in the summer. The Shasta Valley people made obsidian blades used by western neighbors of the Shasta. The Klamath River Shasta acted as middlemen for the Karok and the Shasta Valley Shasta, taking goods downriver to trade when the Karok held the White Deerskin Dance. At other times of the year, trading between the Klamath River Shasta and the Karok was carried on through the Kammatwa. The Klamath River Shasta also sent wolfskins, woodpecker scalps, and white deerskins to the Karok and, in turn, imported pepperwood gourds (Voegelin 1942:197, 201).

The Karok, Hupa, and Yurok often came into Shasta territory to trade. Wicks (1971:61) reports that Indians from down the Klamath and the coast "came out and traded for buckskin. . . . Sometimes they would bring out food and acorns and dried fish they had smoked, or shell that they get from the coast. . . . They had a trail that went back and forth. They went clear through Hupa and down through there. They had trails everywhere."

Culture

Political Organization

The Shasta family, bilateral with patrilineal bias, was the basic social unit; many villages consisted of only one family.

Each large village, and each of the Shasta divisions, had a headman who preserved peace, advising his people and settling intra- and intergroup disputes. The headmen of the four divisions were considered equal; however, when there was "big trouble," the Oregon Shasta chief mediated. The Oregon chieftainship appears to have been hereditary, passing to the next oldest brother, or if there was none, to the oldest son; however, there was probably loose hereditary succession in all four groups.

When offenses were committed, the headman negotiated appropriate payment of property in settlement. If the offender could not pay, the headman paid for him; consequently, wealth was a necessary qualification for chieftainship. The headman acted as mediator in minor affairs (like theft); more serious crimes (like murder) required not only the headman as mediator but also hired go-betweens. Although a chief did not take part in war, he and the enemy headman, aided by old men from each side, agreed on peace terms.

It was also the headman's responsibility to exhort the people to live in peace, do good, have kind hearts, and be industrious. His wife would occasionally talk for him if she had a good voice. (She occupied the same position in relation to the women as her husband did to the men.)

Property payment was usually simple to arrange because every person had a fixed value, determined by the price paid for his or her mother in marriage. The standard value was based on clamshell disks and dentalia. Additional wealth items included olivella, haliotis, deerskins, and woodpecker scalps. The average bride price was one or two deerskins, 15-20 long dentalia, 10-15 strings of disk beads, and 20-30 woodpecker scalps.

Everyone except those within the immediate family settled difficulties among themselves by means of payment. Acceptance of payment was obligatory, but compensation could be complicated. For example, if a man committed murder, revenge on him or his relatives might be taken before a payment offer was made; if revenge was taken on anyone other than the murderer, regular payment for such a person must be made to relatives, thus offsetting in part or in whole the sum required to pay for the original crime.

There were traces of personal ownership of land among the Shasta, and each village had a well-recognized territory within which the areas of the various families lay. Fishing places were privately owned only along the

Klamath from Hamburg downriver. A few wealthy families had fishweir rights, whose owners depended on communal assistance in building the weirs; therefore, they had to give salmon to those who asked for them, and they sometimes let others fish for a limited time.

Hunting and fishing places were inherited in the male line. Upon the death of a family member, restrictions were imposed on their use. However, during a man's lifetime, anyone belonging to the same local group could hunt his territory.

Tobacco plots were privately owned for a single season only. At the seasonal camping place for gathering acorns, the oak tree immediately next to a family abode was considered to belong to the family. Among the Shasta Valley Shasta, although tobacco plots and fishing places were not privately owned, hunting places were.

Structures

In winter one or more Shasta families occupied a rectangular dwelling house; in spring families moved into brush shelters and lived there through the summer; during acorn season single-family bark houses were used; and, when in the mountains for the fall hunt, people camped out. The Shasta Valley Shasta are said to have also used multi-family conical dwelling houses throughout the year (Voegelin 1942:66, 185).

The dwelling house was about 16 by 20 feet and excavated to a three-foot depth, with a steeply sloping roof, dirt sidewalls and board end walls. Houses were built facing the water. Building took place in early summer and neighbors helped; men did the construction and women packed the dirt walls and floor and built the fireplace pit, which was in the center of the house.

Furnishings consisted of tule pillows and wooden stools. Bedding included elkhide or deerskin blankets or imported buffalo hides. The Shasta Valley Shasta also used tule coverings, and the Klamath River Shasta, raccoonskin blankets. Cooking utensils were kept beside the door in two nooks, where acorns were pounded.

Large villages had an assembly house, located in the center of the village. If a villager had more visitors than he could accommodate, the headman would invite them to sleep there. Novice doctors also danced there alone. In the Shasta Valley the assembly house was used not only for general gatherings but also for multi-family living and as a sweathouse.

The headman (or two or three prominent men) proposed and planned the construction of the assembly house; other men helped build it and old women kept it swept clean. If the headman died, it became the property of his male heir; if there were only female heirs it was burned; if there were no heirs, it was abandoned.

The assembly house was similar in construction to the dwelling house, but larger (about 20 by 27 feet) and excavated to about 6 ½ feet. Its sides and almost flat roof were dirt-covered. It had split-board sidewalls, one ridgepole, a centerpost (painted red and black in the Shasta Valley) and a fireplace on the far side of the centerpost.

All the Shasta divisions had an assembly house, but only large villages along the Klamath River and in the lower Scott and lower Shasta valleys had the men's sweathouse, also used by men from neighboring villages. Built like the assembly house, it was smaller and had somewhat different door and interior arrangements (Holt 1946:307). Always built near a stream and heated by direct fire, the men's sweathouse was large enough to accommodate 15-20 men, who sweated there almost daily. Women were not allowed in, but, if there was no assembly house, a novice doctor could dance there. The headman regulated its use; men lounged or worked there during the day, and boys after the age of 10 to 12, unmarried men, and visiting men slept there at night. In villages with no men's sweathouse, men as well as women and children slept in the dwelling house.

The Shasta had another type of sweathouse (dome-shaped, made of willow poles, pinebark slabs and skins, with an opening facing east) in which sweating was induced by steam from water thrown on hot rocks. This sweathouse was family property and used by both sexes. It was used chiefly by women after menstruating, childbirth, or during mourning; if a woman's husband was under taboos, he sweated there with her. In the Shasta Valley men sweated in the steam sweathouse for luck in hunting and gambling; among the Klamath River Shasta such sweating took place in the men's sweathouse.

A menstrual hut, built by women, was located on the west side of a village, some 8 to 10 feet from the dwelling house. Among the Klamath River Shasta it was built on the same general plan as the dwelling house, although smaller; in the Shasta Valley it was a bark-covered double lean-to with a dirt-covered roof.

Life Cycle

• BIRTH   Childbirth took place in the menstrual hut, with an elderly female maternal relative assisting in the delivery. From the beginning of the pregnancy, both parents-to-be observed food taboos and other restrictions on their activities. After the birth there were requirements and restrictions incumbent upon both parents, but observation of all these regulations was not uniform among the Shasta divisions (Voegelin 1942:117-118). Release from regulations required sweating and swimming by both parents. There were also differences among divisions as to specifics of delivery practices, disposal of afterbirth, and care and disposal of the umbilical cord.

Children were named about a year after birth. There were divisional differences as to who did the naming. A boy was named for a deed or major occupation of his father or grandfather; a girl for a deed or major occupation of her mother, grandmother, or father's sisters. Everyone had a different name. In the Shasta Valley, a

person could give his name to someone else and take a new name; if he did so, he was paid for his old name.

Relatives adopted a child if the parents were impoverished. An orphan was adopted by either maternal or paternal kin (Klamath River) or only by maternal relatives (Shasta Valley). The mother's mother took an illegitimate child (Klamath River), or the mother kept it (Shasta Valley); in both cases the father provided for it.

• PUBERTY   When a boy reached puberty, he made an optional "trip for luck" into the mountains. This vision quest, a purely male activity, was to secure success in, for instance, hunting, fishing, gambling, and racing, and it could be repeated throughout adulthood. A one-day quest was undertaken yearly in the winter (Klamath River) or a four- to six-day quest in the spring or summer (Shasta Valley). During a quest there were ritual observances to be followed. Power came to the seeker in a trance or dream, though some seekers never obtained a vision. The successful seeker smoked tobacco, observed particular taboos, and gave his first kill to an old man.

The most important Shasta ceremony involved public recognition of puberty for girls. It began the night of the onset of menses, lasted 8 to 10 nights, and was repeated during one or two subsequent menses. Lack of ritual obligations on the part of any participant except the menstruant made it the most popular and well-attended of all the dances.

At puberty a girl was confined to the menstrual hut and was subject to a number of restrictions. Periods of seclusion lasted 8 to 10 days for the first one and one or two days subsequently. After puberty, menstrual customs included, among others, seclusion for five days and nights.

• MARRIAGE   Marriage of blood relatives (permitted among the Kammatwa and Watiru) did not occur among the Shasta, who counted relationship in both maternal and paternal lines. People usually married out of the local group (the Shasta Valley Shasta often married outside the tribe). A dignified, industrious girl of good parentage was eminently marriageable, as was an industrious young man who could pay the bride price. Marriage negotiations usually took place through an intermediary. It was dangerous to refuse an adequate bride price offer since the rejected suitor had methods of revenge, including the use of magic.

At the time of marriage, the girl was taken to the boy's village and all the relatives assembled for a feast. After a visit to the bride's family, the young couple resided in the husband's father's home, soon building a house for themselves. If the wife's father was old and had no son and if the husband's father was younger, or had another son to help him, the couple resided in the wife's village.

Marriage without benefit of bride price payment was strongly disapproved of. A poor man sometimes sold his services to his father-in-law and lived at his bride's house, hunting and fishing for the family until the purchase price had been worked off. If a widow had a daughter she might give her to a good hunter in order to have a man to do the hunting; if there was a child, the man's father paid a bride price in order to establish the child's status. (Among the Kammatwa, in such a situation, a man hunted, fished, cooked, and gathered vegetable food; among the Shasta such behavior was not considered proper for a man.)

An ordinary man seldom had more than one wife; if he did they were usually acquired through the practice of marrying one's brother's widow. If a wife died, she must be replaced by a sister or other female relative. A wealthy man might have more than one wife. Among the Klamath River and Oregon Shasta the maximum number he paid for was five; in Shasta Valley the maximum number was three. The first wife outranked the others.

Maltreatment by husband, adultery, jealousy, fighting, and laziness were grounds for divorce, which was rare. In Shasta Valley barrenness was also cause; among the Klamath River and Oregon people, a barren woman's family had to supply a second wife free to her husband. When a wife was at fault, repayment of the bride price was expected, unless there were children, since repayment would ruin the children's status. If a wife left an unfaithful husband there was no repayment of bride price. In cases of divorce the boys usually stayed with the father and the girls with the mother or grandmother; a wife kept a nursing baby.

Child betrothal was sometimes practiced among wealthy families; among the Klamath River Shasta bride price payment was made at the time of betrothal; in the Shasta Valley payment was made at the time of marriage.

• DEATH The Shasta buried their dead; only those who died far from home were cremated, the ashes being carried home for burial (Powers 1877:249-250). Each family had a burial plot. The deceased's personal property was burned or buried with the corpse (Shasta Valley). The deceased's dwelling house was abandoned or torn down and rebuilt (Klamath River) or deserted temporarily (Shasta Valley). Among the Klamath River Shasta a headman's house was burned.

The deceased's widow cut her hair immediately after the funeral; a widower burned his hair slightly. A widow also coated her head and face with a mixture of pitch and charcoal (among the Shasta Valley Shasta so did the widower) and removed it only upon remarriage. Use of such a mixture is explained in the myth of the introduction of death into the world; when Black Cricket's child died, Coyote vetoed its being brought back to life, so the child was buried; consequently mourners pitched themselves black like Cricket (Voegelin 1942:232).

A widow observed food taboos and a widower observed food, hunting, and fishing taboos. Other regulations included seclusion for the widow and sweating for both the widow and widower; among the Shasta Valley Shasta a widower also spent 10 nights on a vision quest.

Parents observed taboos for a dead child; in the Shasta Valley children observed taboos for a dead parent. After the funeral, mourners and undertakers were subject to taboos. There were also community taboos, such as a taboo against utterance of the deceased's name extended indefinitely (Klamath River) or until the name was formally regiven (Shasta Valley). If someone violated the taboo in the presence of the deceased's kin, compensation was paid.

Subsistence

Shasta territory was rich in food resources. Significant nonvegetal foods included deer meat (a staple), bear, small mammals and fowl, salmon, trout, suckers, eels, crawfish, turtles, mussels, grasshoppers (Shasta Valley and Oregon), and crickets (Shasta Valley). According to Dixon (1907:424), mountain lion and wildcat were also eaten; however, Holt (1946:311) says these animals were used only for their fur. If people from other divisions were visiting in Shasta Valley at the right time, they also gathered and ate crickets (Voegelin 1942:177). Among important vegetal foods were acorns (a staple) and other nuts, seeds, bulbs, roots, greens, and berries and other fruits. Milkweed supplied a chewing gum and manzanita berries were the source of a cider drink.

Men hunted and fished; women gathered seeds, bulbs, roots, insects, and grubs and caught fish in baskets. Men and women shared in the acorn and pine nut gathering. Women carried water and men made fires. In the Klamath River area women did the wood gathering; in the Shasta Valley both men and women gathered wood.

Hunting methods were various—tracking game, driving it into enclosures, smoking out (bear, rodents), and using pitfalls, deadfalls, and basket traps (birds).

Offerings of paint and tobacco, accompanied by the recitation of formulas, were made to ensure hunting success. When hunting deer or bear, a hunter followed a number of ritual observances. For group hunts there was a ceremony involving singing, dancing, and praying. A youth and his parents could not eat the youth's first kill. When, for the first time, a youth ate game he had killed, he was whipped with his bowstring.

Fishing methods included the use of set, dip, and long flat seine nets; basket traps; weirs; hook and line; and spears (fig. 3). Along the Klamath River, in the spring, women and children dived for mussels.

In the Shasta Valley the first salmon of a run was caught with a line; after that the salmon could be speared. The Shasta had no special first-salmon observance; however, the Klamath River people did not begin to fish until the first salmon of the summer run was caught downriver by a Kammatwa who performed a ritual (Holt 1946:310). After the rite was completed, the Klamath River people could catch, dry, and store salmon and trout; however, they could not eat them until the Karok had performed the White Deerskin Dance. A

Fig. 3. Fish harpoon point, one of a pair. Bone with an iron tip cemented with gum, cotton cord. Length of point 8.6 cm, collected 1902.

fisherman who disregarded this rule could be killed. In the Shasta Valley the first fish of a run was taboo to youths; among the Klamath River Shasta the first run of fish was taboo to adolescent girls.

Vegetal food gathering techniques included use of forked-stick grapples or straight poles for acorns and pinecones and digging sticks for roots.

Shasta land management involved burning for better wild seed and tobacco crops; the Shasta Valley Shasta also scattered wild seed to produce a better crop.

Tobacco crops, either wild or sowed, were gathered when green. Tobacco plants were thinned (Shasta Valley) or pruned (Klamath River). In dry weather the Klamath River Shasta watered the plants by hand, using a basket.

Shasta cuisine was varied. Meat was boiled, baked (earth oven), broiled, or dried; salmon, when eaten fresh, was roasted, and small mammals were roasted whole. Dried meat, fish, and fishbones were ground into meal and flour. Insects were parched or baked. Vegetal foods were baked or pounded in a mortar; acorn meal was leached, and white oak and live oak acorns were buried in mud and then boiled whole. Bread or mush was made from prepared acorns and seeds. Vegetal foods, dried meat and fish, and salmon flour were stored outside in pits or indoors in baskets or twined tule sacks.

Berries and fruits were eaten fresh, cooked, and dried. Dried blackberries, elderberries, wild grapes, and choke-cherries were boiled and eaten with parched and powdered grass seed. Manzanita meal was used to sweeten cooked elderberries and plums, and manzanita cider was drunk with deertail or dry, powdered epos. Wild parsley, steamed, dried, and molded into a block, was pounded and eaten with acorns or deerhoof soup, or dissolved in hot water and eaten with fish.

Everyone had his own eating basket. At meals men were served before women, if there was a crowd. There were two main meals daily and, whenever a visitor arrived, a meal was made for him.

Clothing and Adornment

Hair styles differed among the Shasta divisions, and, in general, coiffures varied according to a person's sex and age (Voegelin 1942:82–83). Cranial deformation, ear and nose piercing, and tattooing were practiced. Women wore chin tattoos consisting of three wide stripes. Face and body paint was made of a mixture of grease or marrow and red, white, yellow, or black pigment. The Klamath River people used a body powder of chalk; the Shasta Valley people, a powder from puffballs.

Everyday wear included basketry caps (women), buckskin caps (men), buckskin clothing, deer-and-bearskin robes, and buckskin leggings (men); in winter men wore fur caps and leggings. Kammatwa and Watiru women wore shredded willowbark skirts; "they were too poor to afford buckskin . . . " (Voegelin 1942:199).

Footwear consisted of buckskin ankle-length moccasins (the Shasta Valley Shasta also wore boot-length moccasins and, in winter, used twined tule slippers); in winter, kite-shaped snowshoes were used (Voegelin 1942:200).

On ceremonial occasions shamans wore yellowhammer feather bands; women wore feathers at the sides of the hair and men wore headbands set with woodpecker scalps, complete with the bills. Woodpecker scalps used for women's ornaments had the bills removed.

Both males and females wore ornaments of beads, shells, and feathers (fig. 2), including ear and nose pendants of shell or long dentalia. Necklaces were made of clamshell disk beads, haliotis pieces, pine nuts, bear claws, or elk teeth. The Klamath River Shasta also wore bear-tooth or bird-claw necklaces, and Klamath River children wore deerhoof necklaces.

Belts and expensive dresses were decorated with dentalia, and strings of dentalia were worn as ornaments. Women's belts, of hair intertwined with buckskin, or of buckskin, were often elaborately decorated with beads or porcupine quillwork, which was done primarily by the Shasta women of the upper Rogue River valley, upper Klamath River, and Shasta Valley.

Technology

Although the Shasta relied heavily on imported baskets, they also made a variety of their own. Closework and openwork twining were the only techniques used. (fig. 4).

Pipes, carved and plain mush paddles, digging sticks, and spoons were made of wood; scrapers, awls, wedges, arrow flakers, and salmon-gigs were made of bone or horn.

Fish glue, pine pitch, or chokecherry pitch were used as adhesives.

Work in stone included cylindrical pestles, serpentine

217

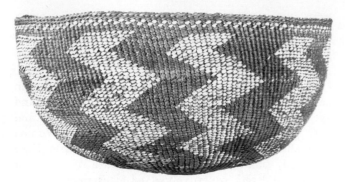

Fig. 4. Twined cooking basket with overlay of *Xerophyllum*. Diameter 30 cm, collected 1902.

pipe tips, obsidian knives and scrapers, and shallow and deep soapstone receptacles.

Spoons were also made of elk kneecaps and deer skulls. Mussel-shell spoons, valued in Oregon Shasta territory for their rarity, were used in the menstrual hut (Holt 1946:303).

Work in hide included deerskins of excellent quality and rawhide containers, modeled on the Wintu carrying basket, for carrying seed and small roots (Holt 1946:303). Rawhide, stretched over a basketry framework, was also used in the manufacture of seed beaters.

Cordage and netting were made from wild hemp, and deersnares, from iris. Grapevine and willow withes were also used.

Few canoes were used or made; along the Klamath nearly all canoes were purchased from the Karok or Yurok. Shasta-made dugouts, from sugar pine logs hollowed by burning, were used in the Shasta Valley and along the Klamath up as far as Gottville; above Gottville, and in Shasta Valley, tule rafts were used.

The Shasta made painted sinew-backed wooden bows. Arrows were painted to match the bows. Foreshaft arrows with obsidian points were used for war and hunting large game; headless singleshaft arrows or arrows with heads of wooden or bone points were used for small game and birds. A rich man's quiver was of gray fox or otter hide; an ordinary man's of raccoon, wildcat, fawn or kit fox hide (fig. 5).

For use in war the Shasta made both elkhide and stick armor (fig. 6).

Warfare

War involved raiding hostile villages to avenge murder, rape, witchcraft, or an insult to a headman; the war leader was selected by his fellow fighters. Before the departure of a war party, a dance of incitement was held; on return of the party, the warriors, still in battle regalia, held a victory dance.

The meeting between warring groups to negotiate a peace settlement took place in the daytime. Both groups

Fig. 5. Shasta chief and his wife. The woman is wearing an apron made of pine nuts and shells, and the man has an animal-skin quiver. Photograph by C. Hart Merriam, Sept. 1919.

Fig. 6. Rod armor vest. Rods of split branches woven with hemp cord, edges bound with leather, shoulder straps of fur, decorated with 4 horizontal bands of red paint. Black checkered portion on back is woven with cord of human hair. Height 76.2 cm, collected 1841.

danced, dressed for war; after payment was made in settlement, the dancers disarmed.

Occasionally young women accompanied the war parties, armed with knives with which they cut and slashed enemy bowstrings and quivers. Fighting consisted of surprise attacks and hand-to-hand combat. In intertribal wars women were taken prisoner for later ransom; in addition, the Shasta Valley Shasta took children prisoners for use as slaves. The Shasta Valley Shasta also took scalps.

Ritual

Aside from the puberty ceremony, war dances and doctor-making ceremonies were the extent of important Shasta ritual. A Circle Dance, sometimes performed in the summer for pleasure, was also incorporated into the puberty ceremony. The Big Head Dance was introduced in association with a wave of the 1870 Ghost Dance movement into Shasta Valley via the Wintu. In addition to these ceremonies, the Shasta sometimes attended Karok and Yurok dances.

Simple, personal rituals for acquiring luck included songs for protection against grizzly bears, a sun ritual, songs to bring luck in hunting deer, a ritual for luck in fishing, a rainmaking ritual, love "medicine," and songs (known only to a few women) for protection from rattlesnakes.

Music and Games

The Shasta had few musical instruments: deerhoof rattles, bone flutes, elder flutes, hide drums.

Klamath River children played with acorn tops and buzzers of deer carpal; in Shasta Valley bark or wood buzzers were used by both adults and children. In the spring young people made string figures during the first quarter of the moon to encourage it to grow.

In December and January, during the waning of the moon, adults played a ring-and-pin game (fig. 7) related to a myth concerning 10 moons, of which 5 were killed. Mostly women played shinny; men played target games. The grass (hand) game, played by men, and the many-stick game, played by women, were gambling games.

Curing

Shasta territory abounded in *axé·kiʔ* 'pains', spiritual forces that were the cause of all disease, death, and trouble but from which doctors also received curing powers. *axé·kiʔ* existed in rocks and mountains, in the sun, moon, stars, and rainbow, and in a large number of animals. (They lived in houses like those of humans and argued among themselves about their respective powers.) Always trying to shoot their pains (in the form of iciclelike objects) into people, *axé·kiʔ* varied in power, the most powerful being in the Rogue River area. The more powerful the *axé·kiʔ*, the greater the feats the doctor could perform. However, doctors were not effec-

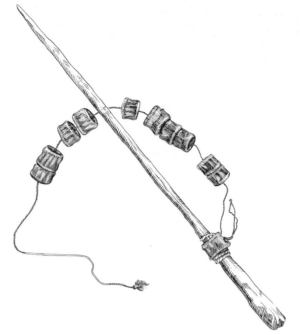

Lowie Mus., U. of Calif., Berkeley: 1-14532.
Fig. 7. Ring and pin game. Salmon vertebrae on an iris fiber cord, wood pin. Length of pin 8 cm, collected 1902.

tive in treating colds because *axé·kiʔ* were prone to catching them.

With the possible exception of colds, there was no such thing as an accidental sickness or injury. All disease and injury were caused by *axé·kiʔ* or by some person's hatred or ill will. All *axé·kiʔ* could be seen by any doctor; however, a particular *axé·kiʔ* was the guardian of only one doctor and was hereditary within a family.

Doctors were nearly always women. There could be no more than one woman doctor in the same family at the same time; only one male doctor per family was permitted, and only if he had no doctor sister alive. The oldest doctor in a family was the most powerful. Doctors could not gamble or take part in any general dance except the puberty ceremony; only relatives attended a doctor's funeral, and she attended only family funerals.

Nightmares were the first indication of potential doctoring ability, and dreaming of swarms of yellowjackets (that is, *axé·kiʔ*) was positive proof. During the dreaming phase the prospective doctor observed particular food taboos and other regulations.

Doctoring power came to the dreamer during a trance in which the *axé·kiʔ* taught her his song, which revealed his name and where he lived. Refusal of the power was dangerous as it might involve sickness or death. After coming out of the trance, the novice underwent a training period involving two winter rituals: the first, a dance that she performed alone; the second, a public dance. Both rituals were held for five nights (two or three nights in Shasta Valley). On the third night of the second dance the novice became a qualified doctor. The public dance was repeated yearly for five years (eight years in Shasta Valley); after the second repetition it was held for only two or three nights.

The doctor's power, in the form of 'pains', was located in her head, heel, and shoulder. A doctor who no longer wanted to practice could have her power removed by another doctor; *axé·ki⁷* thus removed then belonged to the officiating doctor.

It often took many years to collect the doctoring paraphernalia, and the collection had to be complete before a doctor could practice. The paraphernalia included 10 each of buckskins, silver-gray fox, wolf, coyote, fisher, and otter skins, eagle tail and wing feathers, and yellowhammer and woodpecker tails. Doctor's equipment also included a pipe; red, blue, and yellow paint; and a special buckskin. Paint and dance ornaments worn while a doctor officiated varied according to which *axé·ki⁷* was the power source.

The chief times for doctoring were at sunrise, just before dark, and after dark until midnight. The ceremonies were public and lasted two or three nights (one or two in Shasta Valley). The doctor had two assistants (one in Shasta Valley) who called the *axé·ki⁷* and interpreted for onlookers.

The doctor diagnosed by singing and dancing, blowing tobacco smoke over the patient. After her *axé·ki⁷* told her the location of the disease object, she sucked at the seat of the 'pain' and then pulled it out in her hand. She then danced again while disposing of it.

Both the doctor and her *axé·ki⁷* were paid a curing fee. If the patient died, the doctor had to return the whole fee. If too many patients failed to recover, the doctor was killed. If there was much illness in a village, a powerful doctor was hired by the wealthy men of the village (Holt 1946:332–333). Special doctors treated rattlesnake and grizzly bear bites. Doctors also had functions other than curing; they were hired to kill a person's enemy by shooting a 'pain' into him, to find lost or stolen articles, to find persons lost or killed and persons responsible for a killing.

There was also nonshamanistic care of sickness and accident. Women knew about the use of herbs and how to nurse and care for the sick and injured. Some were especially skilled and continually in demand. No charge was made for such services (Holt 1946:340).

There were many therapeutic beliefs, some related to myths; for example, the Klamath River people believed that a person who choked on a fishbone would recover if he called on Rattlesnake (who swallows food without chewing it) and drank water with river foam in it.

Knowledge and Myth

Five was the Shasta sacred number; in the numeral system the numbers one to five are primary, and there are basic form changes at 6, 10, and 20. The count is quinary to 10, decimal from 10 to 20, and vigesimal beyond 20.

The Shasta recognized only two cardinal directions, "daylight side" (east) and "dark side" (west). They believed that after death a soul first traveled east up into the sky and then east to west along the Milky Way, finally arriving at the home of Mockingbird, who migrated up the Klamath in the spring and down in the autumn (Dixon 1907:469; Voegelin 1942:236).

The Shasta year was counted by moons from the two solstices. The beginning of autumn was marked by the first appearance of the Pleiades at daylight, and their disappearance marked the beginning of summer; in general, seasons were marked by the appearance of such natural phenomena. Various periods of the day were marked by the progress of the sun (the most powerful of the *axé·ki⁷*), which the Shasta believed was the ultimate and unfailing source of information.

The power of evil thought was important in Shasta belief. In the myth about the introduction of death into the world there is a typical expression of it: "They thought, 'Would that Coyote's child might die!' So it died and Coyote cried" (Holt 1942:24). Coyote, a major figure in Shasta myths, was not only trickster but also hero and benefactor.

Myth telling was mainly for the benefit of children; however, adults used story fragments to illustrate points in conversation. The Shasta believed in the direct magical effect of myth telling; for example, a magic formula consisted of narration of an event in the life of a prehuman character while performing an appropriate act. The magic effect of storytelling is also implied by the closing formality of an evening of narration (Holt 1946:338). The narrator (an old woman) takes each of the children in the audience in turn and, pressing on successive vertebrae (starting with the neck), mentions various animal characteristics the listener should have, for instance, "This is the grizzly bear and you must be strong and brave like the grizzly bear."

In storytelling sessions the children repeated after the narrator sentence by sentence, each word being repeated until the story was learned. If children did not learn the stories it was believed they would grow up humpbacked (Dixon 1907:471).

It was believed that Rattlesnake took offense at storytelling (a winter evening activity) taking place in the summer, in the same way that a person resented mention of the name of a deceased relative. Such resentment provided a recurring theme in Shasta myths.

Many Shasta myths reflect a cultural preoccupation with social interrelations and personal prestige; the Shasta were more concerned with the ordering of the world and human life than they were with cosmological or philosophical speculation. They had no true creation myth. "In the beginning," explained Sargent Sambo, "it was just a plain world, and everything, people and trees, grew afterward" (Holt 1942:8).

Little is known of the Konomihu. The major source for this overview is Merriam (1966-1967, 2:230-249), with supplementary information taken from Dixon (1907:495-498), Kroeber (1925:283-284), and Harrington (1928-1933). The Konomihu homeland, approximately 20 square miles of mountainous territory, was located up from the forks of the Salmon River seven miles along the South Fork, five miles along the North Fork, and four miles down the main river. The mining over of the Salmon River area in the early 1850s contributed to the decimation of the Konomihu population. There is ethnographic knowledge of 21 Konomihu villages (cf. Merriam 1966-1967, 2:239-240).

Although the Konomihu feuded with the Scott Valley Shasta (Harrington 1928-1933:294), they traded leggings and robes to them and intermarried with them (Dixon 1907:496). They imported shell disk beads from the Shasta and dentalia from the Karok. The nature of the contact with other tribes is unknown.

Culture

Structures

When drying salmon in the summer, the Konomihu lived in brush huts; when hunting deer they lived in bark houses. Permanent structures included dwelling houses, dance houses, sweathouses, and menstrual huts. A dwelling house, made of planks, was circular (15-18 feet in diameter) and had a fireplace in the middle. The smoke hole, in the roof, was directly over the fire. The house entrance was closed by a skin or a door. The dance house, circular and partly underground, had wood-slab walls and a sloped, plank roof. For a dance, the top plank was removed so people could look in. The fireplace was in the center and there was an entrance from which steps led down to the floor from ground level. (Besides dance houses there were outdoor dancing places; the man who owned the ground a dance was held on was usually the master of ceremonies.) The sweathouse, also partly underground, had a roof covered with wood slabs and earth. The roof rafters radiated from a centerpost and there was no smoke hole; direct heat was provided by a fire in the center.

Life Cycle

A parturient, accompanied by one to three old women, delivered in the menstrual hut. For one month after the birth she remained there where she and the baby sweated daily. Her husband was not allowed in.

There is no direct information about puberty observances; however, a place-name, wapxé·ʔtúk (cp. Shasta wa·pxí· 'girl at puberty') has this comment associated with it (Harrington 1928-1933:26): "Three rocks are

sitting . . . like people with blankets over them. [A] girl, her sister and her grandmother turned to rock there. People walk around these 3 rocks all night every night for 10 days. The 8th night . . . you feel something. The 9th night you hear talking; it is these 3 rocks talking to each other. When you hear this . . . you should quit for if you keep on [you too will turn into rock]. The girl is the rock in the middle."

The Konomihu buried their dead six feet deep in coffins. Before burial, a mourning ritual was observed. The body, washed, dressed in the deceased's finest clothing, and decorated with beads and Indian money, was laid on a plank in the deceased's house. A line of people, outdoors, sang and cried while they walked around the corpse, throwing in strings of beads. A male attendant raised the corpse each time a string was thrown in and put it on the body. Alternate chains were placed on alternate sides, each string passing over one shoulder and under the other arm, crossing the middle of the breast. As the mourners' procession passed by, a line on each side, the attendant kept lifting the body and putting on more and more strings of beads. The corpse was then carried out of the house, covered with a blanket of skins that had ashes sprinkled on it.

The Konomihu believed that a body contained a spirit that, after death, remained in its vicinity for five days and then went away forever.

Social Organization

The Konomihu practiced bride purchase; a woman's value in shell money was equivalent to about 200 dollars. Illegitimate births were not allowed. If an unmarried girl became pregnant, she was dressed in her best clothing with all her beads and ornaments and told to run a race; as she ran she was pushed into a big fire in which she was cremated.

All that is known of Konomihu sociopolitical organization is that there were no headmen. All that is known about religious practices is that there were both men and women doctors; in addition, there is fragmentary information about the existence of shrines (Harrington 1928-1933:102-108).

Clothing

Men and women wore buckskin clothing; robes, leggings, and skirts were fringed and decorated with shell, beads, and painted designs in black, white, and red. Combs were made of fish ribs braided in twigs.

Subsistence

Fish (including salmon, which was speared), game, and acorns were important foods. There were large underground caches for acorns; dried deer, elk, and bear meat; and dried fish. The place-name hú·kwàk̓tù·k 'grouse place', may be evidence that the Konomihu also ate grouse. There is also place-name evidence that the

Konomihu ate serviceberries and hazelnuts (Harrington 1928–1933:241, 230).

Acorns (pounded in wooden mortars) were treated in several ways; some were buried in springs and allowed to remain with water running over them all winter. The main acorn supply was kept in huge storage baskets.

Deer, elk, and bear meat was roasted on coals or cooked in a ground oven.

Tobacco was cultivated; every spring after burning logs and brush, wild tobacco was planted. There was a tobacco garden at Butler Flat and others elsewhere.

Technology

The Konomihu used elkhorn wedges and a type of iron ax (origin unknown) that had a very broad blade and a long pointed pick on the back. There is also evidence that black obsidian was used (Merriam 1966–1967, 2:231), and Harrington (1928–1933:236–238) records a place-name indicating the Konomihu knew of red obsidian. Spear points were of hard wood painted with carbonized salmon-head glue; quivers were of wildcat skin.

Stone platters and trough-shaped vessels were used for various purposes. Spoons were made of deer skulls (Harrington 1928–1933:916) or elkhorn with wood. A place-name, háxtàwíꝁtú·k 'paddle-for-stirring-acorn-soup place' (Harrington 1928–1933:293), suggests the use of mush paddles.

Dixon (1907:496) comments that the Konomihu made no baskets, obtaining them all in trade; however, Merriam (1966–1967, 2:234) discusses briefly the preparation and use of basketmaking materials. Large, watertight buckets made of deerhide, with a wooden rim, were also used (Harrington 1928–1933:1122–1123; Dixon 1907:496).

A Shasta term for a place on the north fork of the Salmon River (Harrington 1928–1933:286) may be evidence that the Konomihu used fishtraps. The term refers either to where the trap was made or to the material gathered to make it.

Music and Mythology

The Konomihu rattle differed from those of most groups in that it consisted of the dried skin of a squirrel fastened on a stick that, when shaken, made a crackling sound. Bone whistles, elder split-stick clappers, and hide drums were also used.

The only hint of Konomihu mythology is Dixon's (1907:496) statement that there was no migration tradition and that they believed Coyote created the world.

NEW RIVER SHASTA

What is known of the New River Shasta comes from Kroeber (1925:282–283) and Merriam (1930b). New River Shasta territory, an area of approximately 45 square miles, was located on the east and south forks of the Salmon River to just above the present-day town of Cecilville, and extended to the southwest over the Salmon Mountains to the forks of the New River in Trinity County. The east fork of the New River was probably a territorial boundary. Merriam (1930b:289) considers the Chimalakwe, who may have been part of the Chimariko nation (Dixon 1910a:296), and the New River branch of the New River Shasta to form a group (Tlo'-hōm-tah'-hoi) distinct from the Salmon River branch of the New River Shasta (Hah-to-ke'-he-wuk). Dixon (1931:264) says that Merriam's linguistic evidence does not support "setting up a 'new language' to be called Tlo'-hōm-tah'-hoi" and presents evidence that supports the unity of the New River Shasta area presented here.

New River Shasta territory was extremely rugged, heavily forested, and characterized by a number of high ridges, snow-covered most of the year and separated by deep precipitous canyons. Three villages are attested, all from Hupa sources (Merriam 1930b:288) and with Hupa names (Victor Golla, personal communication 1973).

Only conjectures can be made about the New River Shasta way of life. (During the 1850s and 1860s these people, in attempting to resist encroachments on their territory, were nearly exterminated by the activities of gold seekers and United States Army troops.) There must have been a fair abundance of game (deer, elk, black and grizzly bears, raccoons), grouse, quail, salmon, and acorns. It is thought that they had no salt in their country. It is possible that there were no ceremonial or dance houses, that their dwellings were of bark with the smoke hole left as an opening between two sticks at the top, that they raised tobacco by planting the seeds under burnt logs, and that their pipes were straight.

OKWANUCHU

Knowledge of the Okwanuchu must be gleaned from a few hundred words recorded by Merriam (1925a), a single comment by Voegelin (1942:209) that they intermarried with the Achumawi Pit River band, and a few short remarks by Kroeber (1925:284). Okwanuchu country, a heavily forested mountainous region, covered an area of roughly 60 square miles from the junction of the north fork of Salt Creek and the upper Sacramento River to the headwaters of the Sacramento and up the McCloud River from its junction with Squaw Valley Creek.

SYNONYMY

Shasta

The name Shasta is of obscure source and meaning but may have originated with neighbors of the Oregon Shasta (Heizer and Hester 1970b; cf. also Curtis 1907–1930,

13:232; Dixon 1907; Merriam 1926c). In the older literature Rogue River Indian and Klamath River Indian are also used, and the term Shasta has the variants Shaste, Shastie, Shasti, Sasti, Shastl, Shasty, Chastays, Tcheste, Tchasta, Chasta, Shasto, Shastika, and Shasteeca.

The Shasta word for their language was k̄ahús·arí· (k̄- 'deverbative', -ahus·a- 'talk', -rí· 'right'), and they referred to their homeland as k̄ahús·ariyé·ki (-e·ki 'among').

When identifying individuals or groups within Shasta territory, the Shasta often used terms referring to specific locations, like a village; however, there are cover terms for some of the divisions. The California Shasta knew the Oregon Shasta as ikirakác·u is 'from-back-behind-people'. The Shasta Valley Shasta were known as ahútire?é·cu 'from the open place'. The Scott Valley Shasta were called iru·?áycu 'from lengthwise along the river'; ?wik·wehé·waka? (?wik·wa 'corner', -ehé·w- 'downstream', -aka? 'progressive aspect') was used in identifying the people living at the lower end of Scott Valley and ?wik·wikwayá·ka? 'corner toward the daylight' in referring to people from the upper end. The Klamath River Shasta sometimes referred to both the Scott Valley and the Shasta Valley Shasta as uwá·tuhúc·u 'from the other side'.

There is no convenient cover term for the Klamath River division. The Oregon people identified these Shasta as ?wa·su·rukwác·u 'from down the canyon'. The Shasta Valley people referred to them as ?wiruhi·kwá·cu 'from along the river upstream'.

Dixon (1907:388) cites two Shasta names for the Klamath River Shasta, Wirūhikwai'iruk!a and Kamma'twa. Curtis (1907-1930, 13:232), however, places the Kammatwa, an extinct group, on the Klamath River below the Scott River as far as Thompson Creek (just below Seiad Valley) and in the Scott River canyon up as far as Scott Bar. The Klamath River Shasta spoke of the Scott River canyon Kammatwa as ukwa·hu·rúc·u 'from up the creek'. There were also Kammatwa living among the Klamath River Shasta in the area from Scott River to Horse Creek (Holt 1946:301). The Kammatwa called the Shasta k̄ika·č (or k̄ika·čik, cp. Shasta -ika- 'sound') (cf. Curtis 1907-1930, 13:232; Holt 1946:301).

The Takelma (an Oregon Penutian group) called the Shasta wùlx 'enemy' (Sapir 1907:252). A Tututni (Oregon Athapaskan) name for them is cited as sásti (Curtis 1907-1930, 13:230), while the Klamath form is sesti (Barker 1963). The Achumawi name is sástí·či (Bruce Nevin, personal communication 1973); Merriam (1926:49-50) says that this term, also used by the Madesiwi, was additionally applied to the Okwanuchu and, further, that the name was given to the Shasta by the Pit River Old Man Coyote diety. The Ilmawi called the Shasta ekpīmi (Swanton 1952:814; Olmsted 1966).

Bright (1957) lists two Karok designations for the Shasta: tišrávara 'Scott Valley Shasta' (cf. tíšra·m 'valley',

-ara 'characterized by') and kah?árah 'upriver person' (Klamath River Shasta?).

tax·a·?áycu is possibly a Shasta term for the New River Shasta; according to Sargent Sambo it was "the name of a tribe living to the southwest down near the Yurok" (cf. tax?á?ay 'Cecilville' in Harrington 1928-1933:1504). Merriam 1966-1967, 2:242) records another term as Hohah'-pah-soo'-ish. xáttùk̄ihivu?, that is, the Cecilville Indians (Harrington 1928-1933:1498), is another possible Shasta name for the New River Shasta (cf. Hah'-to'-ke'-he-wuk, Merriam 1930b:283); however, compare also Shasta xatukwi·wa 'Wintu'.

The Hupa term x̄oh-mitah-xʷe· 'grass-in amongst it-people of that place' was applied to the Shasta, the Karok, and the New River Shasta (Victor Golla, personal communication 1973); this is Merriam's (1930b) Tlo'-hōm-tah'-hoi. Kroeber (1925:130) cites Kiintah as a Hupa name for the Shasta.

The Wintu referred to the Shasta as way yuke 'north enemy' or sa·?e (Harvey Pitkin, personal communication 1973; see also Merriam 1955:9-10). The Yana designated the Shasta as iiloomxȝiyaa 'up in the mountain to the west people' (Sapir and Swadesh 1960).

Konomihu

The Konomihu name for themselves was k̄unummíhiwu? (Harrington 1928-1933:804-807). The Chimariko called the Konomihu hunomníčxu (Harrington 1921-1928). The Konomihu term for the New River Shasta is Kah-hoo'-tin-e'-ruk (Merriam 1966-1967, 2:242). The Shasta may have called the Konomihu ?iwáppi (Harrington 1928-1933:202; cf. iwa·pi? 'Karok'). masuh?árah 'Salmon River person' (Bright 1957) is the Karok term for the Konomihu (and the New River Shasta according to Kroeber 1925:99); the Konomihu called the Karok ki·sappuhí·wu? (Harrington 1928-1933:998).

New River Shasta

The name New River Shasta is confusing in that the major part of New River Shasta territory was not on the New River but on the upper, north and south forks of the Salmon River. What the New River Shasta called themselves is unknown. Hupa terms may have been yidahčin 'those from upcountry (away from the stream)' and yidaġnilinġih k̄ʸiwinya?nya·n 'up-country-stream(s)-along people' (Victor Golla, personal communication 1973); see also Merriam's (1930b:280) forms E-tah'-chin, E'-tahk-na-lin'-nuk-kah, and Kewn-yahn'-ne-ahn and Kroeber's (1925:283) form Amutahwe.

A Karok name for the New River Shasta may have been kasah?ára·ra 'person of kà·sah' (Bright 1957:358; see also Curtis 1907-1930, 13:225). Kroeber (1925:99) cites this term as a name for the Wintu and Chimariko of the Trinity River.

Hoo-num'-ne-choo (Merriam 1966-1967, 2:242) is possibly a Chimariko designation for the New River Shasta; however, compare Chimariko *hunomnícxu* 'Konomihu'.

Okwanuchu

The origin of the name Okwanuchu is unknown. The terms ye·tatwa (Voegelin 1942:209) and Ikusadewi (Kroeber 1925:284) are cited as Pit River band names for the Okwanuchu. Merriam (1926:48) cites Ā-te' as a Madesiwi term; compare *yēt* 'Mount Shasta' (Olmsted 1966). The northern Wintu referred to the Okwanuchu as *waybo·s* 'north people' (Harvey Pitkin, personal communication 1973); cp. wi-bos (Merriam 1955:10). Pitkin suggests that *waybo·s* was probably not specific to any one tribe but was used for any group in the north; compare also wi'-in (Merriam 1955:10), which Pitkin reads as *wayin* 'north place'.

SOURCES

Very little is known about the histories, cultures, and languages of the Konomihu, New River Shasta, and Okwanuchu. Published ethnographic treatments of the Konomihu include Dixon's (1907:495-498) appendix to his Shasta ethnography, Merriam's (1966-1967, 2) ethnographic notes, and Kroeber's (1925:283-284) fragmentary sketch. Dixon's and Merriam's studies also include short vocabularies. Published works containing ethnographic information on the New River Shasta include Kroeber (1925:282-283), Merriam (1930a, 1930b), and Dixon (1931). For the Okwanuchu see Kroeber (1925:254) and Voegelin (1942:209).

Unpublished ethnographic and linguistic materials on these Shastan peoples are found in the C. Hart Merriam Collection, University of California, Berkeley (Merriam 1969). There is also material on the New River Shasta in the Kroeber Collection in the Bancroft Library, University of California, Berkeley. An unpublished Konomihu word list was collected by Angulo (1928a). The Konomihu linguistic material collected by Harrington (1928-1933) is a mixture of Konomihu and Shasta data primarily dealing with place-names in Konomihu territory; it also contains fragments in English of myths, but whether these fragments are Konomihu or Shasta in origin is unclear.

Unpublished Shasta ethnographic and linguistic materials are found in the Merriam and Kroeber Collections. Except for a vocabulary (Bright and Olmsted 1959), Shasta linguistic material exists in unpublished form: field notes (Harrington 1928-1933), field notes and tapes (Silver 1957-1963), grammatical descriptions (Angulo and Freeland 1928-1930; Silver 1966), texts (Dixon 1908-1910; Freeland 1927; Silver 1957-1963), and a dictionary (Gatschet 1877b).

Published ethnographic material concerning the Shasta includes that of Dixon (1907), Curtis (1907-1930, 13), Kroeber (1925), Voegelin (1942), and Holt (1946). A sketch by P. Martin (1971) is mostly drawn from the studies by Dixon, Kroeber, and Holt. Much of what is known of subcultural variation is found in Voegelin's study, in which the labels SW (Western Shasta: Klamath River and Oregon) and SE (Eastern Shasta: Shasta Valley) do not include the Scott Valley Shasta; also, Voegelin's SW discussion does not always make clear how much of the detail actually concerns the Oregon Shasta.

There are published accounts by Shastas (Wicks 1971; W. Nelson 1971: 62-63, 66).

What is known of Shasta archeology is primarily derived from the Iron Gate, California, site, which cannot conclusively be shown as representative of the Shasta (Leonhardy 1961).

Shasta artifacts have been collected by the American Museum of Natural History, New York; Robert H. Lowie Museum of Anthropology, University of California, Berkeley; Merriam Basketry Collection, University of California, Davis; Siskiyou County Museum, Yreka, California; and Fort Jones Museum, Fort Jones, California.

Collections of Shasta myths include those of Burns (1901), Dixon (1910), Farrand (1915), and Holt (1942).

Material of historical interest pertaining to the Shasta includes that of Armstrong (1857), Bancroft (1874-1876, 1886-1888, 2, 1886-1890, 3 and 7, 1888), E.S. Carter (1896), Duflot de Mofras (1844), Edwards (1890), Elliott (1910), Emmons (in Wilkes 1845, 5), Gibbs (1853), Hale (1846), Lockley (1930), Metlar (1856), J. Miller (1873), Powers (1877), Schoolcraft (1851-1857), Victor (1894), Wells (1881, 1889), Wool (1853). Unpublished accounts include those of Anthony (1869), Cardwell (1878), and Ross (1878).

Achumawi

D. L. OLMSTED AND OMER C. STEWART

Language

Achumawi (ˌächōō'mäwē or ˌajōō'mäwē) forms, together with Atsugewi, the Palaihnihan branch of the Hokan family of languages (Olmsted 1964, 1965, 1966).* Hokan, in turn, has been linked by various investigators with other languages into a Hokan-Coahuiltecan stock, and connections have been suggested with Siouan and other languages widely distributed in North and Middle America.

Geography and Material Culture

The Achumawi or Pit River Indians had a varied material culture in response to the great variation in elevation, climate, and vegetation of their homeland (fig. 1). In the west Mount Shasta, 14,162 feet, and Lassen Peak, 10,466 feet, served as the northwest and southwest corners of Pit River Indian territory. The eastern boundary separating the Achumawi from the Northern Paiute was marked by the Warner Range with a half-dozen peaks ranging from 7,843 to 9,934 feet above sea level. Twenty peaks over 6,000 feet elevation were scattered over the Pit River interior area, breaking it into many distinct valley and stream systems. From the high of over 14,000 feet, Achumawi territory descended to sections of Pit River canyon below 2,000 feet elevation. Most of the valleys and plains vary in elevation between 3,500 and 5,500 feet. The zoologists Grinnel, Dixon, and Linsdale (1930) defined six life-zones in the territory: Lower Sonoran, Upper Sonoran, Transitional, Canadian, Hudsonian, and Barren. The U.S. Forest Service distinguished 12 vegetation types including "Barren," on Mount Shasta and Lassen Peak, and "Cultivated, Urban, and Industrial." By use of early travelers' accounts and government surveyors' notes an approximation of vegetation types under aboriginal conditions has been reconstructed by Stewart.

Usually lost sight of in generalized life-zone maps or vegetation maps are swamps and wet meadows, some lakes and streams that are of great importance in the lives of the Indians, and several barren flows of lava.

The edges of the geologically recent lava flows were important as hunting places for large ground hogs, or marmots, an important food in spring; and they also served as fortifications or refuges for the local population, whether invaded by ancient Indian enemies, such as the Modoc, or by the United States Army under Gen. George Crook (1946).

The uplands were covered with fir and pine, kept open by frequent fires set by the Pit River Indians. Meadows and grasslands were also burned over. The Indians burned fields and forests to drive game, stimulate growth of seed and berry plants, collect insects, and, at times, as an aid in warfare (Kniffen 1928; Garth 1953; Longhurst, Leopold, and Dasmann 1952; Stewart 1941).

Although it is recognized that each type of vegetation provided some unique products to the Achumawi, the various vegetation areas have been combined into categories of vegetation in figure 1.

Less easily revealed on an ordinary map is the extent of fishing streams and lakes. Streams, lakes, meadows, and swamps were especially important to the Pit River Indians because they provided such a large proportion of their food and shelter. There were in Achumawi territory about 50 miles of salmon streams (fig. 2) and 150 miles of streams from which bass, catfish, lamprey, pike, suckers, trout, and a number of species of minnows were taken. Both crawfish and mussels were also taken from the streams for food.

"Five kinds of nets were made by the Achumawi, three of them being dip-nets, one a gill-net, and one a seine. . . . Large quantities of minnows were caught for drying by means of a basketry trap made of willow rods and pine-root weft" (Curtis 1907–1930, 13:136–137). Goose Lake, in the extreme northeast corner of Achumawi territory, and Eagle Lake, near the southeastern border of Pit River territory (in the far eastern section of the Atsugewi area), were both used for fishing. Eagle Lake and its feeder streams were famous for producing great abundance of trout (Garth 1953:135–136).

Sometimes associated with fish streams but frequently isolated away from permanently running water were scores of swamps scattered throughout the land of the Achumawi and Atsugewi. The two largest swamps were near the geographical center of the territory. Near the great falls of Pit River, at the upper limit of the salmon run, occurs the Fall River swamp of about 36 square

*The orthography used here for Achumawi words is that of Olmsted (1966:9), except that, to conform to the standard Handbook transcription, ӡ is here written for j and x for ḥ; also, the three accents indicating pitch phonemes are omitted.

miles. About twice as large is the one 20 miles up the Pit River where Ash and Willow creeks enter. Another important swamp filled the valley of the South Fork of the Pit River extending about 15 miles from Alturas to Likely. These and dozens of smaller swamps attracted large numbers of waterfowl, some on a permanent basis and some to come to rest during migrations. Leopold (1951) estimated that between 3,000 and 10,000 pairs of

waterfowl used the swamps of Pit River as annual breeding grounds. A number of species of ducks and geese as well as one swan species were taken by Achumawi for food and feathers. Eggs of waterfowl were collected and added an important variation to the diet (Dixon 1908:212). Coot or mudhen, cranes, grebe, and pelicans were also eaten and a skin of the coot was "used for a glove or mitten" (ibid.:210).

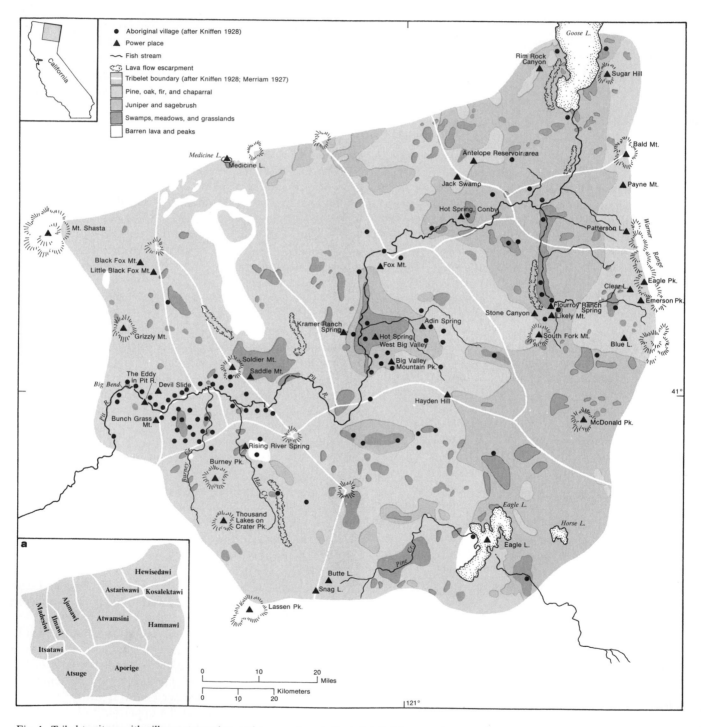

226 Fig. 1. Tribal territory with villages, vegetation, and power places indicated; tribelet names shown on lower inset.

Fig. 2. Green fir bough hut overhanging Big Bend, Pit River, where salmon were speared. Photograph by C. Hart Merriam, 1907.

Waterfowl were caught by stretching nets across flyways in tule swamps and across rivers. Young and mature birds during molting were clubbed to death.

Swamps provided more than food. Tules, although eaten when first sprouted in the spring, were of major importance as floor and house covering. "Tule stalks were strung together on cords to form mats, which were used for seat pads and mattresses, and for covers of anything that required protection from sun or rain. . . . In the caps, tule fibers are the only material. . . . The summer habitation was a conical or hemispherical, rarely an oval, tipi covered with tule mats. In such huts as these, menstruating women isolated themselves in all weather" (Curtis 1907–1930, 13:137–139). Tule fibers were used for twine and woven into shoes (Kniffen 1928:301) and were shredded and made into a cloak (Voegelin 1942:87). They were also employed in balsa rafts, used in hunting and fishing, and for crossing streams and lakes (Curtis 1907–1930, 13; Stewart 1941; Voegelin 1942).

The grasslands were important as the source of vegetable foods, vegetable fibers, and insects.

Epos, the local name for squawroot or yampah (*Perideridia* spp.), is a wild member of the parsley family that provided bushels of carrotlike roots dug from Pit River meadows, dried, and stored for winter. Camas and brodiaea bulbs were also collected in sufficient quantity to be an important part of the diet. Tiger-lily bulbs, wild onions, and other bulbs of the lily and parsley families were dug and consumed as a summer special condiment or dried for winter (Schulz 1954; Voegelin 1942; Kniffen 1928). From dogbane or milkweed (*Apocynum*) the Indians procured long fibers, which they twisted into string for the manufacture of all kinds of nets and for use generally as cordage (figs. 3, 4). Sunflowers furnished edible seeds. Both clover and thistle were eaten in early spring

Fig. 3. Dance cap of fiber netting with abalone pendants and white glass beads; chin strap is red flannel. Width of cap about 35.0 cm, collected 1875.

Fig. 4. Woman's rope skirt of milkweed fiber. Length 68.0 cm, collected 1875.

when the plants were very young. There were numerous wild grasses that furnished small seeds that were collected in the fall by means of baskets and seed beaters. Some of the grasses were tough enough to be successfully woven into flexible baskets and could serve as a thatch for winter houses, which were also covered with earth (Curtis 1907–1930, 13:139). Mustard seed was collected for seasoning and soaproot was dug to use in hair washing. Wild tobacco was collected, dried, and smoked for pleasure and as a part of a curing ritual.

When the grasslands, with their weeds and herbs, dried in the late fall they were set on fire nearly every year, because the Achumawi recognized that burned-over plots produced tobacco and wild seeds more abundantly than the areas not burned (Stewart 1941:376).

One ancient practice that continues (observed 1956 by Omer C. Stewart) among the Pit River Indians is the collection of epos, other wild root plants, and wild tobacco to be used in rituals. Tules are also cut and woven into mats for home use, whereas basketry is carried on as a folk art that has a ready market. All baskets are made by the twine method, whether they are finely woven and flexible or large fish traps and carrying baskets.

Digging for roots, bulbs, and tubers exposed angleworms that were collected and added to the soup pot. The underground nests of the yellowjacket wasp were sought and exposed so that the larvae could be procured for eating. The larvae of ants, bees, and hornets were also eaten. Crickets, grasshoppers, caterpillars, and salmonflies were also used as food. The periodic plagues of Mormon crickets were remembered as times of plenty, for the crickets were roasted and formed into cakes for storage. Fields might be encircled with fire to drive grasshoppers together and be roasted in the process of capture. They were then ready for winter when placed in sacks of vegetable fiber.

Pine forests surrounded Achumawi country and were scattered throughout the interior. The pine forests and the very extensive juniper and sagebrush areas were most important as hunting areas, yet throughout were patches of swamp and meadow, and fish streams were usually nearby.

Kniffen (1928:301) characterized the Madeline Plains, the drier southeastern extension of Pit River Indian territory, as a "great, treeless, dry bolson. . . . a sort of no-man's land, only the moister margins being visited in summer for the gathering of roots." Achumawi informants in 1956 explained that the sagebrush-covered Madeline Plain (as with the other very extensive sagebrush areas of Pit River Indian territory) had a limited, but important, place in Achumawi economy. First were the great number of eggs of the sage hen that were collected in the spring. Males of the sage grouse perform a mating dance in the spring and become more vulnerable to the hunter during such dances. In the fall the sagebrush regions were attractive for hunting antelope and

jack rabbits as well as sage grouse. Sage hens were shot with arrows, snared, and driven into nets (Kniffen 1928:302).

Sagebrush and juniper frequently occur together in vast areas that might be considered transitional between the juniper forest and the extensive plots of pure sage. Most of the birds could be found in several zones, although some species favor particular habitats. Meadowlarks and blackbirds favor swamps, like the waterfowl, yet might be found in the bushes and trees near their favorite places. Besides sage hens, several other grouses were taken by Achumawi for food. Ruffed grouse, short-tailed grouse and pine hens were captured in various forest zones. Crows, hawks, magpies, and eagles could be found in either juniper woodlands or pine forest, although the eagles preferred nesting on the tops of mountains.

Most birds were eaten but some, like the humming bird, which gave luck in gambling, were captured to get feathers rather than food.

A few game animals, like the mountain sheep, occurred only on the tops of the highest mountains. The elk was said to be found only on Mount Shasta, yet elk-hide armor was used throughout Pit River country. Elk-hide shields were popular and elk were hunted for food and robes as well (Voegelin 1942:59, 87). Antelope were sought for food, for hides to make into quivers, caps, blankets, and shirts. Their hoofs were made into rattles and their antlers became wrenches for straightening arrows.

Badgers furnished skin quivers, caps, capes, moccasins, and food (Stewart 1941). Bears were hunted for their meat and hides but also for the supernatural power they conveyed (Garth 1953:133). Beaver furnished good luck in gambling as well as furs and food.

Coyotes, although a source of supernatural power, were hunted for food, clothing, quivers, and blankets.

Deer were numerous. One method for trapping deer, digging large pitfalls along animal trails, was so common that early settlers named the river Pit River and called the people Pit River Indians. Deer were driven with fire in the fall. Deer occurred in all vegetation but were caught most in the forests surrounding the grasslands and swamps. Venison was a staple and deerskin was tanned with deer brains and manufactured into many articles: quivers, caps, capes and robes, skirts, belts (fig. 5), shirts and leggings, moccasins, and dresses. Dried deer meat was an important winter food.

In addition to the major food animals listed above, there were many others utilized whenever found; the entire Achumawi territory was exploited for the general or special products available. Other animals hunted were: beaver, chipmunk, fisher, fox, gopher, ground hog, marten, mink, mole, mountain lion, otter, porcupine, raccoon, rats, skunk, squirrel, turtles, wildcat, weasel, and

Fig. 5. Deerskin belt decorated with olivella and other shells, glass trade beads, and buttons. Length not including thongs 69.0 cm, collected 1875.

wolf. Rattlesnake venom was procured as an arrow poison (Stewart 1941:385) and other reptiles were sought for the supernatural power they conveyed.

Forest and sagebrush lands provided important vegetable and mineral products to the Achumawi. First was fuel, needed in great quantities during the long winters. The elevation of the valleys at 3,000 to 4,000 feet above sea level made deep snow a regular winter occurrence. Sagebrush, dried juniper branches, and wind-toppled pine trees furnished most of the fuel. Lacking stone axes and adzes, the Achumawi were dependent on trees naturally felled, which might be divided into various lengths by fire for the center poles and large cross beams of their large semisubterranean winter houses, usually about 15 feet square (Curtis 1907-1930, 13:138). "Poles, and slabs split from logs with aid of antler chisels and stone hammers" (ibid.: 139) served as base for grass, tule, and bark on which a heavy coat of earth was placed.

The central smoke hole with a ladder, having cross pieces tied on with vegetable fiber, served for usual entry and exit, although children might come and go by means of a tunneled draft hole in the side.

Besides fuel and foundation material for house construction the Pit River forests supplied the Indians with many vegetable foods and material for implements. Forest foods included bear berries, buckthorn berries, chokecherries, currants, elderberries, gooseberries, Oregon grape, huckleberries, manzanita berries, plum, skunk berries, salmonberries, and serviceberries. Various nuts were collected: piñon pine nuts in limited sections of the eastern Achumawi country and nuts from the digger and sugar pines scattered throughout the territory. The sap of pines was used as "sugar," which gave the sugar pine its name; and pine sap was used as a medicine.

In the extreme west-central region, on both sides of Pit River, oaks grew, and there (as well as in other parts of Achumawi country due to trade and transportation) acorns were a staple of the diet. Dried, pounded, and leached with warm water, acorn meal became freed of its tannic acid and could be cooked into a nutritious soup. It is in the oak-growing area, which is also the region of least elevation and includes the stretch of Pit

River reached by salmon, that the Achumawi aboriginal population was most dense (see fig. 1).

Another important product of the western lower and moister section is the yew tree. Although it is of limited distribution in Achumawi country, yew wood was considered the best wood for manufacture of bows by all Achumawi. Most bows were sinew-backed whether of yew, mahagony, or juniper. Arrowshafts were made of several materials—wild rosewood, cane, serviceberry, and willow. When a foreshaft was added in arrow making, greasewood was used. Arrow points were most frequently made of obsidian or volcanic glass. The mountain peaks on the north, west, and south of Pit River Indian territory, and some of the peaks within the tribal borders were of volcanic origin. (Lassen Peak remained, as of 1972, an active volcano). Crude implements are also made of cherts and chalcedony, occurring in the area and designated flint (Schulz 1954:73). Because of great quantities and excellent quality of pure obsidian at Little Glass Mountain and Glass Mountain near Medicine Lake on the north-central border of Achumawi land to which the Pit River Indians frequently traveled, obsidian for arrow points, spear points, knives, and scrapers was abundant throughout the Pit River Indian territory. Smaller deposits of obsidian might occur in many places. Volcanic action also supplied the region with pumice stone, which was used for working arrow shafts. Colored minerals were also abundant in the area; designated paint by the Indians, pigments of black, blue, white, red, and yellow were collected and employed in decorating arrows, bows, skin clothing, gaming pieces, as well as people. Some pigments of vegetable origin were also known, such as black from charcoal and soot. Ashes of different colors come from burning different woods: a white-fir burl produced a red ash when burned (Garth 1953:147), the same color also being obtained from a fungus (Voegelin 1942:83).

Juniper, locally called cedar, provided more for the Achumawi than already mentioned. Cedar bark helped insulate winter homes, but it was also shredded and hung as a kilt or skirt. A tightly wrapped "rope" of cedar bark was ignited at one end and carried by hunters and travelers as a "slow match," so that a fire could be started without using the fire drill. The fire drills were often made of juniper wood twirlled into a depression on a piece of sagebrush wood as hearth. Snowshoes used in winter hunting were often made of juniper, and juniper berries were considered a medicine. Both juniper and pine were used in the manufacture of simple dugout canoes.

Basketry, although using the willows and grasses of the wet meadows as primary materials, used maidenhair fern, pine roots, and redbud bark in the decorative elements (figs. 6, 7).

Salt as a mineral was not known to the Achumawi,

Fig. 6. Twined carrying basket. Rim diameter 53.5 cm, collected 1902.

but a substitute was found in saltbush (*Atriplex*) leaves and seeds (Stewart 1941: 429).

Medicines were obtained from plants from all vegetation zones and from such diverse plants as trees, herbs, and moss. In 1956 a dozen Achumawi informants were asked the use of various plants and where they might be found. Twenty-one plants were designated as having medicinal value. A number, such as sagebrush and manzanita, were named by almost all informants. The list follows: angelica root; balsam (*Balsamorhiza sagittata* and *Lomatium dissectum*); bear berries (*Arctostaphylos nevadensis*); chokecherry bark; white fir (*Abies concolor*); greasewood (*Sarcobatus vermiculatus*); Oregon grape (*Berberis aquifolium*); hazel bark; juniper berries; tiger lily; water lily; manzanita berries (*Arctostaphylos patula*); milkweed; black moss (*Alectoria fremontii*); mountain balm (*Eriodictyon californicum*); mullein (*Verbascum thapsus*); oak bark; wild parsley (*Ligusticum grayi*); pine pitch; sagebrush (*Artemisia tridentata*); sunflowers (*Wyethia mollis*).

Sociopolitical Organization

Achumawi sociopolitical organization was in terms of what Kroeber called tribelets, which he defined (Kroeber 1932a:258) as "groups of small size, definitely owning a restricted territory, nameless except for their tract or its best-known spot, speaking usually a dialect identical with that of several of their neighbors, but wholly autonomous." Such units have been variously named in connection with the Achumawi; Merriam (1926) called them "tribes," and they have also been referred to as "bands" (Olmsted 1966). The tribelets, Anglicized here from their Ajumawi (that is, Fall River dialect) names,

Fig. 7. Lily Chip holding unfinished twined baskets. Photograph by Omer C. Stewart, August 1936.

are listed in order from farthest downriver to farthest upriver: Madesiwi, Itsatawi, Ilmawi, Ajumawi (used here for the Fall River tribelet only, reserving Achumawi for the Pit River people as a whole), Atwamsini, Astariwawi, Hammawi, Qosalektawi, Hewisedawi. (See fig. 1).

Each of these tribelets functioned as an autonomous political unit, though socially they were connected by intermarriage and by the consciousness that they spoke a common language not shared by their neighbors. Though there were some dialect differences (C. F. Voegelin 1946), they did not impede intelligibility among members of different Achumawi tribelets. The relationship to the Atsugewi was a special one, characterized by intermarriage and by fairly easy communication resulting from Atsugewi bilingualism: Atsugewi people frequently learned Achumawi, but not, apparently, vice versa (cf. Olmsted 1954). With their other neighbors, Achumawi relations were more distant: the Shasta, Yana, and Paiute were all rather far away for frequent interaction, and what evidence there is seems to suggest that communication with them was limited to encounters while hunting along the ill-defined borders of each other's territory or to occasional trading sessions. With the Modoc, the situation was again different, being marked by hostility on the part of the Modoc, who raided the Achumawi country for slaves. The Achumawi reaction was usually not to respond in kind but to hide out until the raiders had given up and left for home.

Social and Mental Culture

Kinship

Achumawi personal names, while not secret or sacred in any respect, were not ordinarily terms of address. Rather they were used for reference when not in the presence of the person named. Terms of address were kin terms like aunt or brother for the appropriate relatives and nicknames for covillagers not nameable by kin terms; strangers were addressed by the names of their tribelets or villages. Calling a man by his personal name was, as Angulo (1930) put it, "considered rude, insolent and provocative."

The kin terms that served as terms of address for most people on most occasions also functioned to bind people together by reminding them of their mutual obligations and responsibilities. The Achumawi system of naming kin, though formally reciprocal, is also curiously nonsymmetrical. For example, terms are to some extent reciprocal between alternating generations, that is, between grandparents and grandchildren but not completely so. Each child called his/her paternal grandfather *apun* and he used the same term in return, regardless of the sex of the child; similarly, the maternal grandfather was called *akun* and he returned the term to either sex of grandchild. The paternal grandmother, *amun*, used that same term to grandchildren of both sexes and the maternal grandmother, *ažun*, spoke likewise to both boy and girl grandchildren. Thus, for a grandparent, both his/her sex and that of the intervening parent is crucial in determining the term used, whereas in addressing a grandchild sex is irrelevant, the term chosen being simply the same as that used by the child to the elder person. Another way of stating the asymmetry of the system is to note that a girl, for example, is called by any of the four terms in childhood but only by *amun* and *ažun* when she is a grandmother. The terminological fate of the boy is similar, since he receives all four terms in childhood and only *apun* and *akun* as a grandparent. A parallel situation holds for aunt and uncle terms, which are partially reciprocal with niece and nephew terms as follows:

	Paternal	Maternal
Uncle	se?aw	ažini
Aunt	hamut	žeman

Thus, both boys and girls use *se?aw* to paternal uncles and receive the same from them; the term also means niece (brother's daughter) and nephew (brother's son). The other terms are used in parallel fashion.

Terms for the parental generation are not reciprocal, even in part. Father *wa?i*, mother *tati* (reference), *neh* (address), son *pola·ži*, and daughter *ata* are all used in familiar fashion. Sibling terms are extended to cousins on both sides, being distinguished by date of birth only, as follows:

	Older	Younger
Brother	apaw	atun
Sister	apis	e·nun

From this it seems clear that the system was essentially bilateral, with incest taboos extended to cousins on both sides, since they were classed with siblings. In practice, the system was limited in scope by the fact that people remembered the relationships only of persons living in the same village or nearby villages, so that place of residence played a role in keeping down the number of "siblings," which, in theory, would rapidly come to include most of the tribe if all the children of ego's cousins were called brother and sister by his own children. Were such to result, the number of potential spouses would soon be severely limited for any given ego. One may never marry a relative, provided the relationship is remembered. When a couple married, presents were exchanged between the families, which were regarded as buying a husband for the wife and a wife for the husband. If one spouse died, the other was still regarded as being "owned" by the deceased's family, so that he/she could be obligated to marry some other suitable partner from that family. Of exceptional importance, therefore, were terms for in-laws: father-in-law *ahak*, mother-in-law *mallu*, daughter-in-law *awta*, son-in-law *wimma*. As a mark of respect, parents-in-law were always addressed with dual forms of the verb, even when only one was being spoken to.

Spouses called each other *yawi* 'husband' and *lumme* 'wife' or *tat* 'wife'. Cowives called each other *mallista*, a term said by Gifford (1922) to mean 'widow', but identified by our informants as 'cowife'. Cowives were either *wanužži* 'first wife' or *wanumži* 'later wife'.

Although stepsiblings were called by sibling terms, they could be identified by reference terms peculiar to their status: *tilliela maži* 'stepchild', *tunula mati* 'stepfather', *tunula maži* 'stepmother'. Although a number of more complicated versions of Achumawi kinship have been offered, the above sketch is thought to be essentially accurate since it is based on the work of Angulo (1930), who had excellent opportunities to observe the system in action because he lived among the Pit River people for prolonged periods at a time when the culture was still very much alive. Alternate terms presented by other students of this culture are collected in Olmsted (1966).

Life Cycle

Puberty ceremonies are minimal for the boy, who simply has the nose and ears pierced, but without ceremony, though he is encouraged to seek a tinihowi. Girls at first menses sing and dance all night for 10 days. Hoof rattles are used. When the girl tires, she is supported at each arm by a man (who may be young or old, so long as he is not a blood relative); the men change when tired, but the girl must continue until dawn, always facing east. She eats little, and sleeps out the day. The next time she menstruates, the same ritual is performed for nine days, followed in succeeding months by eight-day sessions, seven-day ones, and so on until, after the tenth month, she is an adult woman. The occasions are social festivals, with members of neighboring villages invited, much singing of ribald songs, and, on one day of each session, sexual intercourse "back in the bushes" (Angulo 1928). Sexual shame was unknown aboriginally but was rapidly learned from the Whites.

There were no rites of the chase, though sometimes wives remained quietly in the village while their husbands hunted far away. There were no songs of the hunt.

When death came to an Achumawi, there were no rites of purification and no ceremony. The corpse was taken to a spot where wood was available and cremated. Close relatives shaved their hair and covered their heads with pitch, while everything belonging to the deceased was burned. Then the survivors forgot as soon as possible. The name of the dead one was taboo; his soul had gone to the western mountains and no one wanted to give it an excuse to return, since the soul does not want to travel alone and might return to get a traveling companion from among those most dear to it. This would involve the death of such a person and thus the dead are feared. One did not know—or ask—what happened to the souls of the dead in the western mountains. There was no belief in reincarnation. At the death of a great chief, an attractive young woman stayed the night with the corpse in the communal earthlodge, while the others in the village, together with members of neighboring tribelets, lamented and howled outside. In theory anyone could enter and make love to her, but there were few takers, such was the power of fear of the corpse. This curious approach-avoidance situation is not explained. On such an occasion, two or three other members of the band were killed to add to the dignity of the chief's departure and to provide him with traveling companions in his journey to the western mountains. Those selected were the least popular—an old scold, an idiot, or a shaman suspected of evil practices. They were surprised from the rear and killed quietly.

Religion and Medicine

Achumawi religion was closely connected with folk medicine. Indeed, the principal concept of each was the *tīnihō·wi* (Anglicized hereafter), which is variously translated as 'guardian spirit' and as 'medicine'. It was usually sought in a lonely mountain quest by the adolescent boy at the time when he had his nose and ears pierced. Not all who sought the tinihowi found one. It could be put off by unsatisfying odors, particularly those resulting from contact with women at the time of the search. Thus continence was a requisite. However, the tinihowi could appear at any time, not necessarily when sought. Compared to the visions of Plains Indians, those of the Achumawi when on quest were less stereotyped, less ritualized, more improvised, according to Angulo (1928), the expert on the subject, whose work seems about as definitive as possible at this late date in the study of the culture. Possession of a tinihowi rendered a young man special; however, sometimes it could leave him without warning and without reason. The tinihowi represents the acquisition of supernatural power. He makes good hunters, invincible warriors, lucky gamblers, and powerful shamans ("doctors"). The Achumawi had no desire or respect for riches. What counted with them was the popularity of chiefs, which was derived from ability to carry out the duties of the chief, and the acquisition of supernatural power through the tinihowi.

The one functionary of Achumawi religion and medicine was the shaman, always referred to in English as "doctor"; the Achumawi term is *ʒikiʔwā·lu*. The shaman derived his (or her, since about half of Achumawi shamans were women) power from his tamakomi, which was like a tinihowi, except much more powerful. The tamakomi is referred to in English by the alternate translations 'power', 'medicine', and 'poison', which gives a good idea of his potentialities and functions. No distinction was made between material poison and spiritual poison.

The shaman's activity typically begins with a call to a sick person. The patient lies down with his head toward the east (whence comes the light). The seance is not formal, mysterious, or symbolic, but it is an ordinary social occasion with smoking and joking between chants. The songs are for the purpose of calling the shaman's tamakomi. Each song is no more than a line or two long, with two or three musical changes, repeated continuously, while beating time with hands. The songs have no symbolic or magical significance, according to Angulo (1928), but are designed to attract the tamakomi by their aesthetic value alone.

Once the tamakomi is within range, the shaman begins talking to him in a loud, high voice, as if to someone deaf. He speaks ordinary language that everyone can understand, but rapidly and monotonously. All is repeated, virtually word for word, by the shaman's assistant or "interpreter," who lets the audience hear what the shaman is saying. Angulo believed that the interpreter was a vital anchor for the doctor, preventing his becoming schizoid during the frenzies of the trance by providing a link to physical reality. Our own view supports Angulo's and emphasizes, in addition, the link to social reality offered by the shaman's unavoidable listening to his own words repeated to an audience that will judge him, pay his fees, and remember any suggestion of chicanery or malpractice. The shaman keeps moving toward an autistic state of ecstasy; but the "interpreter," with his accompanying obbligato, served up in ordinary tones, tends to damp the doctor's mental oscillation and keeps him/her in touch with the group, as well as with the tamakomi. At first, the shaman and the tamakomi carry on a lively dialogue about their experiences during the interval since they last got together and the patient's troubles. The shaman then requests the tamakomi's assistance in locating the source of the trouble and dealing with it.

Angulo (1928), who was a physician, noted that during his day the most prevalent diseases among the Pit River people were respiratory, with tuberculosis the main scourge, followed by influenza and measles. He noted little incidence of alimentary difficulties and called them virtually immune to venereal disease. There was high infant mortality, but those who survived infancy seemed to him very resistant to disease. Angulo described "Indian disease" (so-called by the people in local English): a person is consumed by sadness and ennui, has no taste for any of his usual pursuits, is in constant bad temper, finally takes to his bed, and complains of a vague general sickness. Some die of this, though usually a shaman is called and gives successful treatment, often by discovering and removing a source of "poison" (either spiritual or physical).

The shaman's diagnoses were divided by Angulo into four main categories: (1) visible accidents, (2) "bad blood," (3) poisoning by another shaman, and (4) soul-loss.

Visible accidents are most often, along the Pit River, broken bones, wounds from logging accidents or from shootings or stabbings. For these the Achumawi would, even in Angulo's time, have been happy to have had the services of White physicians but usually could not because of inability to afford it; even in the 1970s such physicians are inaccessible to the rural population, whether Anglo or Achumawi. Thus the aboriginal population turned to the shaman, even though they knew that he had no particular power in such cases. The patient knows the shaman cannot do much for such a wound but asks for his help, via his tamakomi; Angulo likened the process to praying for better health by Christians. In addition, the shaman is asked to divine whether the patient will live or die, so that he can order his affairs for the indicated event. Even if the patient is fortunate enough to get a White physican to treat the wound, he may still consult the shaman for any added help he may be able to give, probably in part because of the social nature of the shaman's intervention, in contrast to the remoteness and impersonality of the physician's method of treatment.

As for "bad blood," the Achumawi had, aboriginally, no idea of the circulation of the blood but believed it suffused the entire body and was susceptible to "humors" of the old-fashioned Western medical sort. This category is usually used by the shaman for internal non-psychogenic organic illness. The treatment involves sucking at the patient, usually in the region of the appearance of the disease; and after prolonged sucking and extended travail by the tamakomi, the shaman expectorates a bloody fluid, which Angulo assumes comes from his own stomach. Although this treatment does no good for organic disease, it may ease the patient's mind and does not, apparently, diminish confidence in the "doctor's" powers, any more than ineffective treatment does among patients in Western medical practice.

Poisoning by another shaman: here the true nature of Achumawi shamanism is displayed. The shaman calls his tamakomis one after another and sends them to look for the cause, the means employed by the poisoner shaman. The experience does not yield to logic but is like poetic comparison (Angulo 1928). They believe firmly in transubstantiation, for example, a tamakomi in a bit of hair. The shaman's feather hat contains a little box with his equipment in it, including whatever he "extracts." Sometimes the poisoner is in the audience; particularly if he lives in the same village, he cannot afford to be absent. Sometimes the "curer" introduces poison of his own to make the disease worse, so that he will be payed again. A husband-wife team of shamans known to Angulo differed on this point: the husband introduced extra poison when curing, whereas the wife was "honest." If a shaman recovers a poison stronger than his own, it is prudent to bury it, or place it in a vase of water, where it will be recovered later by its owner, who in the circumstances can hold no grudge.

The Achumawi word *telamʒi* 'soul-shadow' is related to the word *telalamʒi* 'aurora, dawn'. The *telamʒi* goes west at the moment of death or at some time up to a week or so before death. When the person's death rattle ends, the lamentations begin. There is then great danger that the departing soul will induce another's to follow. One man who lost his soul because it wanted to follow that of his dead father-in-law got it back when the father-in-law appeared to him in a dream and announced that he had sent it back. Usually the shaman is called upon and he enlists the help of his tamakomi in recovering the lost soul before the patient dies. One shaman who lost his soul was unable to get the help of another and so operated on himself with the aid of his "interpreter." The soul is not contrasted to the body in native belief; *I* is used of both soul and self.

One of the checks on the shaman's activities is the capriciousness of the tamakomi. He can be used only sparingly for unethical endeavors. For example, it is dangerous to send him to kill someone, since he is likely to become drunk with bloodletting and refuse to return. Elaborate precautions then have to be taken to get him back.

The shaman's office is not hereditary. Young people who seem fitted by temperament for the shaman's life and practice are chosen as apprentices by their elders. No one is anxious to become a shaman, since it is too dangerous a calling. In Angulo's opinion (and in view of his psychiatric training and great experience with Achumawi medicine, no one is likely to be better informed on the subject) shamans are generally neurotics, suffering from anxiety neurosis for the most part. Somewhere between the onset of puberty and the age of 25 or 30 years, the future shaman undergoes his first crisis, a genuine nervous episode lasting sometimes weeks. He appears mad, wanders around the mountains, sleeps out in all weathers, and causes great worry to his friends and relations. They deplore his state but do not interfere. His visions continue and his general conduct suggests to some veteran shaman that he is a good prospect as an apprentice shaman.

Achumawi mythology has no religious significance: that is, the narratives are stories, not true myths (fig. 8). These *tilasini ʔi* 'old time stories' are told, primarily by old people, when all are lying down in the earth lodge. Much time was consumed in this way, especially on cold winter days, when all huddled together for warmth, amidst the smoke, while outside, the grim lava-bed landscape was swept by snowy winds from off Mount Shasta. Story telling was an activity like novel reading or theater going, as opposed to the practice of the Pomo, where it was an activity comparable to Bible reading. The Pomo

Dept. of Anthr., U. of Calif., Berkeley.
Fig. 8. Place of origin of the Achumawi, known as the jumping rock of the first people. Photograph by C. Hart Merriam, Big Bend; date not recorded.

234

possess orthodox versions of creation myths, while Achumawi have a wide latitude of versions, some of which may be improvised on the spot, their places in the repertoire being gained as a result of aesthetic success rather than logical consistency or canonical fidelity. There was a great variety of Coyote stories, mostly extremely sexually explicit. As opposed to the dignified Coyote found among the creations of the Pomo or Miwok, the Achumawi character is cruder, more secular, more lascivious, and frankly designed for entertainment.

Angulo (1928) concluded: "The life of (stone-age peoples) is shot through with religious feeling, but it is vague, diffuse, without formulas, dogmas or precise form. It is, *par excellence,* the mystic spirit."

Games

The principal game of the Achumawi, as of many other peoples of western North America, was the hand game, a gambling game played in several versions. Among the Achumawi, it was permeated by religio-mystic feeling, since winning involved, in their view, something more than pure chance. One's tinihowi might be particularly efficacious for assisting the gambler. Success displayed the winner's powerful life-force, which was not attainable without a good tinihowi. There was no ritual connected with the game, as there was elsewhere in California. During the game there was singing, which reached almost to the point of ecstasy. In addition, they played a version of shinny (a kind of lacrosse), wrestled, and engaged in foot races.

Twentieth-Century History

In 1956, the Achumawi Indians appeared to take pride in their knowledge of and use of aboriginal medicines and foods. Several informants provided samples of their medicinal herbs and displayed supplies of dried vegetable foods they had collected. Pride in the knowledge of the extent and resources of their aboriginal home territory is matched only by Achumawi self-esteem for successful survival in their homeland in spite of the arrival and settlement by a much larger White population.

The Pit River Indians keep faith in the powers of their own medicine men to the extent of calling on them when visits to modern hospitals are not successful in bringing about cures. In 1956, 40 "power places," isolated spots difficult to reach where Indian seekers after supernatural power would go, were named and located (see fig. 1).

From an aboriginal population of 3,000 Pit River Indians, as calculated by Kniffen (1928:299) and accepted by Macgregor (1936:1), Kroeber (1955:308), and Cook (1943b:105), the number had diminished to about 1,000 in the 1910 U.S. Census.

In 1936 Macgregor estimated the population at 500. For a mail ballot in 1963 on whether to accept a compromise settlement of the California Claim Case, 750 notices were mailed to eligible Pit River Indian voters according to U.S. Indian Service officials. The above figures indicate that the Achumawi and Atsugewi together form one of the largest Indian groups in California.

The strong and ancient subdivisions within the Pit River Indians (fig. 1 insert) were still evident in 1936, so that Macgregor could identify nine communities within the nine different aboriginal triblet areas. Similar subdivisions persisted into the 1970s. The group at the village of Likely are mostly Hammawi people under the direction of Ike Leaf. Leaf assumed the leadership to file and prosecute case number 347 under the Indian Claims Commission Act of 1946. Allowed to speak for the Pit River Indians as a whole, Ike Leaf hired an attorney who filed the case at the last possible moment in 1951.

The Pit River Indians filed as a separate group entirely within California; they were allowed to present their case in 1957 and received a favorable preliminary judgment distinct from most other California Indians, who had a combined case. Following a ruling in favor of the Pit River Indians in July 1959, the attorneys for the Pit River group were convinced that the Pit River Indians must join the overall Indians of California group in order for a favorable ruling to be made for the general case for Indians of California.

In 1963 all the attorneys for the Indians of California and the attorneys for the U.S. Department of Justice agreed to a compromise settlement under which the Indians of California would share $29,100,000. In a vote of Pit River Indians at Alturas, Ike Leaf led 105 voters to reject the compromise, while 75 accepted it. Later a mail ballot brought the votes to 408; 212 voted "yes," 188 voted "no," and 8 spoiled their ballots. Ike Leaf and his followers from Likely continued to 1972 to oppose the settlement.

Even though Leaf actively and outspokenly assumed leadership of all the Pit River Indians, there has never been legally established an organization of Pit River Indians. A large group (identified by Macgregor 1936) who moved onto the 8,760-acre XL Ranch purchased by the government in 1939 as a rancheria for all Pit River Indians said little about the claims case. The ranch, situated in the territory of the ancient Hewisedawi about the same distance north of Alturas as the village of Likely is south, has been managed by the Forrest family, for many years led by Erin Forrest.

In 1936, Macgregor named the Wrights, remnants of the ancient Madesiwi triblet, as leaders of the western section of Pit River territory. Macgregor mentioned that the Pacific Gas and Electric Company was buying up as many Pit River Indian allotments as possible. In 1972, James Wright and members of the Montgomery family were leading the sit-ins and going to court to try to regain some of the lost forest land acquired by that company.

The Pit River Indians, although they have suffered a large reduction in population from aboriginal times, have enough people in their ancient homeland to constitute an active independent force in American Indian affairs notwithstanding the fact that in local situations former subdivisions and regional competition appears to influence behavior.

Synonymy

Another traditional spelling is Achomawi, which does not reflect so closely the Achumawi word from which the tribal designation is drawn: *aǯuma·wi* 'river people', from *aǯuma* 'river (it flows)' from the verb *-aǯum-* 'to flow'. It should be emphasized that *aǯuma·wi* was not the people's general name for themselves but indicated, aboriginally, only the Fall River tribelet. It was extended by anthropologists and historians to apply to all who speak closely related dialects of the same language, but it is not so used by the people themselves when speaking English. Then they, together with the surrounding Anglos, refer to the group as Pit River Indians, a term which sometimes includes also the Atsugewi, although that group is sometimes distinguished by the name Hat Creeks (Olmsted 1966). The label Pit River Indians derives from the practice, along this river, of trapping deer in pits dug for the purpose. The variant spelling in Pitt River Indians is a hyperurbanism.

Designations derived from the languages of neighboring peoples have also been applied to this group. For example, Shawash, from the Yuki name for the Achumawi taken to the Round Valley reservation (Kroeber 1925:308), and Palaiks or Palaihni (whence the name for the linguistic branch) from Klamath *blaykni·* 'uplanders; Achumawi' (Barker 1963:64, 544; Powell 1891:97; Gatschet 1890:269). Another Klamath name for Achumawi is *mo·watwa·s* 'home in the south' (Barker 1963:242), while in Maidu the Achumawi are *ʔodókpepē* 'clam eaters' (Shipley 1963:203).

Sources

There are collections of Achumawi artifacts, mostly baskets, in the museums of the Departments of Anthropology at the University of California, Berkeley, and the University of California, Davis. There are also some surface-collected artifacts in the Fort Crook Museum near Fall River Mills, California.

The account of the Pit River peoples in Kroeber (1925:305–317) is, though incomplete, not inaccurate in major details. The language is described in the grammar of Angulo and Freeland (1931) and the dictionary of Olmsted (1966). The most valuable accounts of Achumawi geography and material culture are Merriam (1926) and Kniffen (1928). For Achumawi creation myths, see Merriam (1928); for social anthropology and religion, see Angulo (1926, 1928, 1930).

Atsugewi

T.R. GARTH

Language and Territory

The Atsugewi (ˌătsōō'gāwē or ˌätsōō'gāwē) of north-eastern California differed markedly from the Achuma-wi, their neighbors to the north, although the languages of these two groups formed the Palaihnihan branch of the Hokan linguistic stock (Olmstead 1964, 1965).* Proximity and a common language united the two Atsu-gewi subgroups. The Atsuge or "pine-tree people" occu-pied the rugged lava-strewn valleys north of Mount Las-sen and the Apwaruge (nicknamed *mahuopani* 'juniper tree people') a large and more barren plain (elevation ca. 5,000 feet) to the east (fig. 1). Heavy snows forced a six-month residence in winter villages, so that stored food

*Atsugewi words are given in the orthography presented by Olmsted (1958), who has himself respelled those cited in this chapter. To conform to Handbook standards, however, Olmsted's j has been replaced by ž.

was crucial to survival. Abundant water made summers fairly productive in fish, game, and plant edibles (Garth 1953).

Although peaks, lakes, and other geographic features helped define territorial limits, border areas (especially those with the Maidu to the south and Paiute to the east) were disputed and may have been used in common. At-sugewi holdings included an area from the western edge of Burney Valley to the tableland east of Hat Creek and fringed the Pit River valley to the north, including Snag Lake and the northern half of Mount Lassen (Kniffen 1928; Merriam 1926). Apwaruge territory extended east of a line drawn from Bald Mountain through Blacks Mountain to Poison Lake, including Hayden Hill, part of the Madeline Plains, Horse Lake, and Eagle Lake to about half of Willow Creek. The heavy forest cover to the west dwindles rapidly to junipers and grasslands to the east.

Established at lower elevations along streams, winter

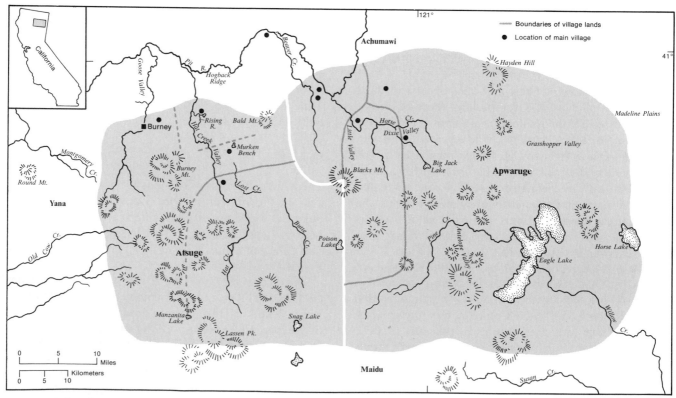

Fig. 1. Tribal territory.

Fig. 2. Bark house, Dixie Valley, Lassen County. Photograph by Eugene Golomshtok, July 1922.

villages consisted of from 3 to 25 earth lodges or bark houses (fig. 2). Because each chief, or rich man, had his own special followers living close by, the larger villages were characterized by several widely separated house clusters. The village chief controlled considerable surrounding territory (see fig. 1 for the Atsuge). A similar situation probably existed for the Apwaruge, though details are lacking. The five main Atsuge villages probably had under 350 people in 1850. The Apwaruge, with a possible population of 500, had a correspondingly larger territory. Settlements concentrated in the more favorable lowlands in Dixie and Little valleys and along a portion of the Pit River from Horse Creek to Beaver Creek. Outlying villages were near Eagle Lake, on Willow Creek, and in the Grasshopper Valley.

Political Organization

The village was the basic autonomous political unit. No overall tribal authority existed, though popular chiefs were influential far outside their own areas and could make decisions overriding those of lesser chiefs. Chiefs adumbrated the "rich man" concept of northwestern California. More important, they guided day-to-day economic pursuits, a feature of adjacent Numic and some central California tribes. Although he had no power to punish or impose fines, as did the Shasta (Dixon 1907), an Atsugewi chief could withdraw his support so that a miscreant became a social outcast. Chiefs were far from autocratic and acceded to popular will or sought to mold it by eloquence. The title *ǯúswaheǯar* 'life saver' indicates their paternalistic concern for their people. Chiefs intervened in disputes and made certain weregild was paid, contributing themselves if need be. At early dawn a chief awakened his settlement by loudly shouting: "Get up and do something for your living. Be on your guard. Be on the lookout for Paiute. You have to work

hard for your living. There may be a long winter so put away all the food you can." Chiefs likewise set an example by working hard at activities like hunting, fishing, and net making (Garth 1945). Though a chief received small gifts of produce for the use of his lands, large contributions were made only when a feast was in prospect. Possibly because of excessive feast giving, chiefs were not always the wealthiest men in the village. In theory the eldest son became chief, but actually the most capable son or even a cousin was so chosen. Sons were specially trained for the office.

A village might also contain several wealthy 'headmen' *pawi*, who spoke for and led the group of friends and relatives who lived with them or in adjacent houses. It was advantageous to live near such a man, for his property and special hunting or gathering sites could be used and his abundant supplies might tide the less fortunate over a hard winter.

Culture

The Wealth Concept

The Atsugewi work-wealth scheme permeated all phases of their social and economic life and gave it a distinct patterning. At every turn hard work was inculcated as the means to success. The northwest California wealth concept was modified to fit their much less generous environment. With beads the only nonutilitarian form of wealth, ordinary utensils and tools took on the surrogate status of wealth goods and were said to be "owned" only by the rich. Such things as canoes, basketry sifters, nets, or pestles would be borrowed from a rich man when needed and the loan perhaps paid for by small gifts of produce. The industrious rich personified the cultural ideal. *nohalal* ('going all the time'), a prominent rich man at Rising River, was famed for staying up most of the night making string or doing other work. Occasionally he called his group to a midnight feast of fish caught in the late hours. In a myth Daylight Woman arises at the first faint signs of dawn to gather wild foods and is soon able to marry a rich man's son. Children were continually counseled to shun laziness, to work and be lively, and to throw their covers aside at earliest dawn and jump out of bed. A woman who had difficulty in childbirth was said to be suffering from *ǯenéhwu pwenewok* 'the sun she met' due to her having lain in bed past sunrise. Her baby would then be lazy and reluctant to be born. Women were chided not to gossip or eat when digging roots, but to work apart from others from dawn till late evening. Men would watch the older girls returning and select as wives those carrying the most roots and seeds.

Men, too, were expected to be at the hunt whenever possible, even in the dead of winter. The paucity of ceremonials may well be due to their single-minded concern with the food quest. In contrast, the nearby Maidu and the Wintun, for instance, had elaborate dances and ceremonials. At times visiting Atsugewis participated in Maidu dances but they never adopted them or even used the woodpecker headbands. The only Atsugewi ceremonial of any note was the puberty dance and this, for both sexes, was oriented at achieving industrious productivity.

Yet the pressure of the work motif was not completely unrelieved. Every six days or so the chief called a day of rest (yemiwəka) when everyone stayed in camp, the women to prepare foods and the men to work on their equipment or to gamble. In winter the rest day often preceded a communal hunt. There was little feeling that gambling violated the work ethic. Men who returned early from hunting might spend most of the afternoon gambling, even wagering the roots their wives were to bring home that evening (Garth 1945:554–566). The puberty dances and feasts were also occasions for relaxation and socializing.

The social hierarchy held sasyawahéӡar 'wealthy man' at one extreme and the prumui 'poor lazy person' at the other. Rich families tended to intermarry, and close relatives of a rich man basked in reflected prestige. Utter contempt was shown the rag-clothed prumui, whose laziness or incompetence rendered him dependent on the largess of others to survive. Probably few actual prumui existed; such a person was a pariah whom no one would marry. An easy social mobility is suggested by the frequently repeated story of the poor orphan boy raised by an only grandmother to become industrious and rich and so able to marry a rich man's daughter.

Frequently mentioned forms of wealth were beads, furs, and buckskins. The skins might be displayed ostentatiously by the lodge to denote wealth and hunting prowess. In contrast to northwestern California, white deerskins had no extraordinary value, nor did long stone knives occur. Valuables were hidden in the rocks or trees when away from the winter lodge. Old men often gave property to friends and relatives—especially sons—before death. Personal items like clothing, bow, pipe, and knife were likely to be buried with the owner. Other property, such as canoes, quivers, snares, and nets, were commonly used until worn out and then burned. Inheritance, especially of land and some goods, was important in keeping property in one family line. Yet the utilitarian nature of wealth plus the fact that beads were often buried with rich men or distributed to various relatives militated against the accumulation of wealth goods in one family. In this rather democratic wealth system almost anyone could become rich if willing to exert himself sufficiently. There was even the heretical belief that rich men were not entirely smart in working so hard and allowing the indolent to live off the extra food they provided.

External Relations

The Atsugewi were normally on the best of terms with immediate neighbors and shared hunting and gathering resources, thus insuring that when a wild crop failed in one area its inhabitants could always use a neighbor's land where crops were better. Groups of Atsugewi, Achumawi, Yana, and Maidu congregated for salmon on the Pit River or for acorns or roots in other areas. Such fraternization led to frequent intertribal marriages, an important factor in cementing intertribal bonds. At times the connections were strong enough to cause people to move permanently to join relatives in another tribe. Nonetheless, intertribal frictions and warfare might arise when shamans in one tribe were suspected of poisoning people in another.

Though one retaliatory war excursion to the Sacramento River is recorded, rarely did Atsugewi war parties visit distant areas. There was no memory of an expedition into Modoc or Paiute territory in spite of almost endless provocation. Horse-riding Paiute and Modoc-Klamath slave raiders coming from the unprotected north and east created severe population attrition, beginning possibly as early as 1725 (Garth 1965:148–151). The unmounted Atsugewi could offer little resistance. Pit River slaves became important in trade at the great Dalles mart on the Columbia River. Informants cited the Spanish as their earliest contact with Whites, suggesting that the Paiute-Shoshoni may have carried Pit River slaves as far as the Southwest (Garth 1965). To protect themselves the Apwaruge built at least two stone forts. One had a bluff on one side, with a number of interconnected roundish enclosures 8 or 10 feet across, behind which families could hide while the men fought off the enemy. These raids may well be why the Atsugewi thought of themselves as cowards and natural peacekeepers, a contention hardly supported by facts. They, along with the Achumawi, were notorious for repeatedly attacking Whites who attempted the Pit River route to the Sacramento Valley from Oregon (Neasham 1957: 7–28).

An approaching enemy might be signaled by deer running past camp, birds suddenly flying, tracks called womuni 'war trail' or a shaman's dream of blood or impending disaster. Retreat to a fort or to a place of hiding ensued. Retaliation took the form of a surprise dawn raid or a formal battle. In a battle the two sides stood in opposing lines while a poʔӡasi 'peacemaker' sought to arrange a settlement. If unsuccessful, he stood aside and the battle began. Arrows were exchanged with much dodging until one side or the other was defeated. Good warriors, possibly wearing hide armor, stood at intervals along the battle line and at the ends. A chief might or might not fight. If he did not, his person was inviolate. He could halt the battle and arrange a settlement whenever he wished. The actual battle was directed by a warrior of special renown: it was he the enemy was most anxious to kill.

At home the women performed a war dance once in the morning and again in the evening in simulated battle formation and facing the direction the men had gone. They shouted encouragements to the men while throwing water into the air from baskets. Before leaving, the men might pantomime a successful raid—menacing the women with drawn bows, yelling, and snatching up baskets or other property. Returning warriors were purified by the women's pouring pounded epos roots over them and rubbing them with wild tea or pine branches. After a feast that evening a war dance was held around a large fire with the men forming the inner of two circles, shouting and brandishing their weapons as they danced. Enemy scalps mounted on four-feet poles were carried by dancers who had lost relatives in the battle. Captive women and children might also be forced to dance. Warfare was a crisis situation similar to those at puberty and birth and was liable to bring spirit visitation. An Apwaruge slayer underwent a month-long isolation during which he ate alone, remained continent, used special utensils (including a head scratcher), avoided meat and hunting and fishing—even discarded his bow and arrows. He also went on frequent power quests.

Social Activities and Trade

Feasting was a concomitant of most social gatherings. In summer members of several tribes working an area were often invited to large suppers. The grand occasion, however, was the *pakapi* 'big time' called by a chief when he felt sufficient food had been accumulated. Knotted strings were sent to other villages and tribes, a knot to be untied for each day before feast day. The host chief then stood on his lodge roof and welcomed visitors. Toward evening the visitors might perform a dance, after which the host would allot large baskets of acorn mush, meat, sunflower seeds, and other food to each visiting chief, who distributed them to his people. For the next several days there were contests and games of chance—wrestling, foot races, weight lifting, archery, stick games—with large bets made. Relatives tended to combine wagers and losers were often left destitute. Surplus food was divided among departing guests.

Sweat dances were confined to the winter season and often occurred in the large earth lodge before communal hunts. Only occasionally did young women or children participate. The ventilator door was closed and the fire built high with a smokeless type of wood. While a singer beat time with a split-stick rattle, men danced separately, vying to see who could stand the intense heat longest, and emerging finally to roll in the snow or dive in icy water. About 1880 the Plains-type domed skin-covered sweat lodge was introduced.

Trading was important in strengthening intertribal ties. Prominent men had special trading partners (often relatives) in each neighboring tribe with whom gifts were exchanged. 'Big times' were also occasions for direct trading. Dentalia were less valued than clamshell beads, the common medium of exchange.

Crimes and Torts

Welfare of the kin group was the prime factor in Atsugewi law. Loss of a member by murder or by stealing a wife or widow necessitated a payment. Otherwise the aggrieved family tried to kill a member of the offending kin group. Weregild varied according to the nearness of kin. A murderer might have to support the family of a murdered kinsman. Members of a foreign village had to pay a much higher weregild and a go-between arranged the settlement, preferably a woman, which then made the two groups kin. A powerful family might frighten the other into accepting only a token payment. Accidental injuries usually required no payment, but an accidental death required full redress. Often shamans were hired to locate a thief. The chief could only request, not force, return of stolen property.

Marriage and Kinship

In theory brides were purchased as in northwestern California, but actually there was merely an exchange, initiated by the groom, of gifts almost equal in value. The closest to true purchase was the payment demanded if a wife deserted her husband for another man or if a widow failed to marry a husband's brother or cousin. In one case an old man claimed his dead son's wife (Garth 1953:165). A woman was worth more than a man because of her food-gathering abilities. Rights to a widow might be bought with two or three strings of beads. Gifts were exchanged with in-laws throughout the marriage, cementing bonds of friendliness and cooperation. The sororate and levirate were favored, with siblings and cousins preferably finding marriage partners in the same affinal kin group.

Foremost requisites in a mate were wealth and the ability to make a living. Divorce was easy for men, who might return a lazy unproductive wife to her family. Wealthy men were hard to please and might try four or five women until they found one who was suitably industrious. When a girl neared puberty, a betrothal marriage might be arranged by parents by sending the proposed groom with a gift of meat, for which roots were returned. Gifts were then exchanged periodically until the marriage took place a year or two later. At this time the boy merely stayed overnight with the girl, remaining late in bed so that the chief could announce their new status.

In regular marriage called *lay ʔoksi* 'both families love each other' the suitor visited the girl and attempted to sleep with her. Should she reject him she hit him with her elbow; hitting with an open palm meant the possibility of future acceptance. A groom lived with and worked for his father-in-law for up to a year, when the couple returned permanently to the man's settlement. Polygyny was practiced, five being the maximum wives noted, but bickering and dissension made such marriages unstable. Women particularly were under a strict moral code. Extramarital affairs were said to be rare and an immoral woman was ostracized. An adulterous wife might be beaten or even killed. Frequently she was divorced. The lover might also be killed, but could go unscathed as the woman was thought to be mainly responsible.

Life Cycle

Since children were much desired, a barren woman felt disgraced and might drink bead scrapings or hire a shaman to diagnose her trouble. Deformed children were allowed to live and an unwed mother would not destroy her child. A mysterious bond was thought to unite parents and child, especially before birth. Parental industriousness was particularly necessary; also, fighting was to be avoided or the baby would be mean and cause a difficult birth. After 1900 a husband's drunkenness was considered the cause of a slow painful birth—that is, "the baby was drunk and would not cooperate." A woman returned to her parents as her time approached, staying in an old winter cook house or in a special brush enclosure in summer. Here her mother built a fire, covering it with dirt and grass when labor began. The woman sat on this hot bed wrapped in blankets, with a hot grass-wrapped rock on her stomach until parturition occurred. For the next few days procedures were almost identical to those in the puberty ceremony, with similar restrictions and dancing (Garth 1953:157–160).

Lowie Mus., U. of Calif., Berkeley.

240 Fig. 3. Cradle basket. Photograph by Thomas Garth, 1938-1939.

The maternal grandmother made the first cradle, a small oval basketlike affair with a shade (fig. 3). Later there was a large, flat, ovoid cradle with a pointed base which could be stuck in the ground while the mother worked. Moral training was considered important. Modesty and bashfulness in the presence of the other sex was desirable. Lying and fighting were strongly discouraged and disobedient children were switched with a coyote tail. For exceptional mischief a child might have his ears pierced and be ducked in water. Too, there were stories of giants, spirits, and ghosts who were said to attack children who did not behave.

• PUBERTY CEREMONIES The Atsugewi share with the Shasta an almost complete lack of ceremonial dances other than the puberty dance. At her first menses a girl ran to the mountains for luck and commenced dancing that night in an old buckskin dress and moccasins, woven wristlets, and a headband of buckbrush. Apwaruge girls added a belt and anklets as well as a cloak extending to the ankles, all of buckbrush. Up to 200 people might attend a dance, held in a winter lodge or in a semicircular brush enclosure 7 feet high and 30 feet across. Three different dances were performed. In the first, women danced in a circle taking long gliding steps to the side, while a woman singer beat time on a stick. The second was the round dance, *paninápone*, which lasted from dusk to midnight. This was primarily a social dance and might occur at times other than the puberty ceremony. Men and women alternated in a large circle about the fire, dancing with short steps to the side followed by short jumps with feet together. Finally the *yokálpone* 'girl's dance' began. The initiate danced back and forth by the fire carrying a cane and facing east. Her betrothed or two girl friends danced by her side, supporting her as she tired. Everyone was expected to sing, led by a man facing east wielding a deerhoof rattle. Restrictions on sexual conduct were relaxed and couples disappeared from time to time into the brush. The initiate was required to be lively; to tire and be sleepy was a sure sign of becoming a *prumui* 'poor lazy person'. At dawn a capable industrious woman lifted the girl, handed her a deerhoof rattle, and sent her running toward the east where she assiduously gathered pine cones to insure success in future food gathering. In summer the girl worked hard all day digging roots; in winter she stayed in the cook house going occasionally for wood. The ceremony ended four to six days later, but it could be repeated on each of several subsequent menstrual periods, lasting only three days or so each time. Ceremonies ended by her sponsor's piercing the girl's earlobes with a sharp twig.

Boys, too, underwent a ceremony at puberty (when their voices changed). They were said to be having *aitše ʔiki* 'monthlies' and wore skunk-brush belts. The father or another industrious man lectured the boy, pierced his ears, whipped him with a bow string or coyote tail, and sent him on a power quest. The sponsor acted and worked energetically so that the novice would magically acquire abilities similar to his own. The novice built small fires near mountain springs, traveling from one to another and piling rocks. At each he took a sip of water, gargling first with sand. Near midnight he napped on a bark pillow, but jumped up immediately on waking. He then threw rocks in all directions. If he heard a fawn bawl, he knew he now had a hunting power. The groan of an old man meant he was to be a doctor. Three days later he returned to camp and ended his quest with a final swim.

• DEATH Soon after death the body was dressed in its best buckskins, drawn up tightly in a flexed position with thongs, and then wrapped in a skin blanket. Burials of commoners, which only a few relatives attended, took place in the lava rocks some distance from the village. A chief or rich man was often buried in the floor of his earth lodge, which was then burned. Close personal possessions might be put in the grave. Afterward the surviving spouse and parents, especially the women, underwent a long period of mourning, cropping their hair and covering their heads with pitch, soot, and chalk.

Religion and Shamanism

Countless nature spirits peopled the Atsugewi world and intimately affected daily life. These often took human form and exhibited human personalities. Most ill fortune was attributed to offended spirits or vagaries in their behavior. Spirits enabled success in all manner of endeavor and everyone needed at least a minor spirit or two to keep him healthy and bring reasonable luck in economic pursuits. Men were prone to undertake a power quest whenever their luck was poor. A woman might do so to develop industrious traits necessary to acquire a husband. Spirit guardians were also acquired or lost during times of life crises. If a spirit liked a person it sang to him. The human then repeated the song and used it to call the spirit for help. Anyone hearing his spirit's song began to sing and dance violently, imitating his guardian. Songs were practiced either alone in the hills or with others in the winter lodge. The group singing is a practice reminiscent of the guardian-spirit dancing of tribes in Oregon and Washington.

Shamans merely had more numerous and powerful spirits than others. These resided as "pains" in a unique feather headdress called a *qaqu* (fig. 4). There was a blending of the "pain" concept of northwestern California with the guardian-spirit idea so common in North America. The pain might be a whisker of a guardian animal; it might be a little man; or it might be the guardian animal itself when it possessed the shaman and talked and sucked for him in curing. Doctors could shoot other objects into people besides the hairlike

Lowie Mus., U. of Calif., Berkeley.
Fig. 4. Sam Williams wearing a *qaqu*. Photograph by Eugene Golomshtok, 1924.

pains, according to the nature of their guardians—small snakes, glass, flint, bear claws, deer sinew, splinters of wood, or flies. A woman's pain was said to make its victim vomit. A shaman underwent a particularly rigorous program of singing and fasting. Mastering perfectly the song of each of the 15 or 20 pains in his *qaqu* might take up to five years. When a novice thought he had sufficient mastery of a song, he prepared to capture its spirit owner. As he sang with the help of others in the winter lodge, the pain approached and entered, whereupon the novice began shouting and dancing in a frenzy, pursuing the pain with outstretched hands. On seizing it, he fell unconscious, bleeding at the mouth. Assistants caught him and put his closed fist in a basket of water, blew smoke over him, and sprinkled him with water to pacify the pain so that it would not kill him. On reviving, the novice exhibited the pain to the assembly. This was followed by more singing till daylight, when the pain was put away in a section of feather or elder twig. Each pain was similarly pacified or "controlled" and transferred to the *qaqu*, which was uprooted from its place in the mountains and exhibited in the lodge as the final token of full doctorhood. People were curious to know how powerful the new doctor was, and he was soon called to cure someone or to demonstrate his power by killing a dog with a pain, making rain or lightning, or sucking blood from a cane. An older doctor might challenge him to a duel, the one able to cough up his adversary's pain being judged the more powerful.

Although most sickness was thought to be caused by pains, soul loss and having bad blood were also causatives. Bad blood was thought to be semigaseous and able to flow through an unbroken skin into objects handled by the sufferer. Shamans would suck on baskets before women dug their first roots in the spring to determine which owners had bad blood and required treatment (Angulo 1928:572-573). A person suffering from soul loss was listless and would die unless a shaman could send his guardian spirit to recapture the soul from the evil spirit that had taken it.

If the local shaman were unsuccessful in a cure, a shaman from another village or tribe might be called in, necessitating a much larger fee. Doctors dressed appropriately to a chosen guardian and might wear a feather cloak, a mink collar, or carry a cocoon rattle. For difficult cases he wore his *qaqu* attached to a hair net on his head. With his interpreter, the shaman left the lodge and began singing nearby, calling his spirits one by one. He then returned and continued singing with the help of spectators. A pain soon entered his body causing bleeding at nose and mouth, and spoke through him using Achumawi, Atsugewi, or the Maidu language. The pain spoke only if it knew the cause of illness; if it did not, another pain was called. Diagnosis was often difficult and might not occur until the third night or perhaps not at all. To extract a foreign pain, the doctor sucked with his own pain, which might appear as a small black spot on his tongue. The extraction caused the doctor to stiffen and fall senseless. Attendants caught him and poured water on his head till he revived and coughed up the foreign pain in a small sack of blood or mucus. He then either killed the pain or returned it to the sender with instructions to kill, changing it slightly so the sender would not recognize it.

Subsistence

Although most edibles were utilized, some animals were avoided for reasons of religion or flavor; these included martin, mink, gray fox, coyote, frog, eagle, buzzard, magpie, and crow. Over 100 plants were said to have been used, including tree moss in early spring when starvation threatened. As in most of California, fish and acorns were the staples, although salmon were obtained only by invitation of the western Achumawi on Pit River. In the spring, trout and other fish swarmed out of the larger lakes to spawn in the smaller streams and were taken in quantity with loosely woven baskets, dip nets, or spears. Baskets were suspended from limbs jutting out over a waterfall (weirs were unknown). Long gill nets were used in lakes and streams, as were trot lines bearing small bone hooks. Fish spearing from canoes (fig. 5) by torchlight was and still is practiced.

Fig. 5. Canoe on Rising River. Photograph by Eugene Golomshtok, 1924.

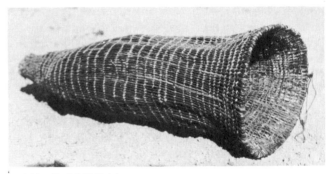

Fig. 6. Fish trap. Photograph by Eugene Golomshtok, 1924.

Open-twined basketry traps about five feet long were also in common use; a conelike entrance discouraged fish from escaping (fig. 6). In quiet pools, fish might be stunned with pounded wild parsley. After being split and dried, the catch was stored in small bales or baskets. All these fishing methods were employed by men; on rare occasions when women fished, they used only hook and line.

Though fish were probably far more important as a food resource, venison was the prestige food associated with wealth. Men spent much of their time hunting, usually alone, but occasionally in a group effort guided by a chief. After a night of singing power songs and planning in the big earth lodge, the men joined in drives of various kinds. They might set fires at intervals around a mountain or form a long line to drive game past waiting marksmen. By singing special songs they could charm deer or antelope so that they could be surrounded and easily killed. The Apwaruge used a long tule rope with streamers in surrounding charmed antelope. Up to 15 deer might be killed in a big hunt. Each participating chief divided his share of the meat among his villagers. Even a lone hunter turned his deer over to the chief for general distribution. Surplus meat was smoked and dried on long poles strung between trees and stored in pits or in baskets hung in trees.

Individual hunting methods included pursuing a deer until it was exhausted, shooting deer from a brush blind near a deer trail, stalking deer with a deerhead disguise, calling a doe by imitating with a grass stem the bawling of her fawn, and using rope snares or pits along a deer trail. The last method was apparently common enough to inconvenience early travelers and to give the Pit River its name.

Other game was either snared or shot with the bow and arrow. Especially virulent arrow poison was used in killing grizzlies and the killer was held in high esteem. Groups of hunters sometimes drove rabbits into nets or in widespread formation moved over an area shooting game as it was flushed. In the numerous lakes abundant ducks and mud hens were taken. Some were run down just before they were ready to fly or when too fat to fly. Special arrows and nets were also used for birds.

Even the eastern Apwaruge, who had no oak trees, valued acorns as a staple, making long trips to Atsuge, Yana, or Achumawi areas to get them. Men climbed the trees and knocked down the acorns, which were gathered into baskets and taken home by stages. Storage was in special bark bins or in pits. Other primary foods included epos and camass roots and sunflower seeds, of which there were five varieties. These foods were usually dried for storage and then pulverized in a basketry hopper before being made into cakes and cooked in the earth oven or made into mush cooked in the mush basket.

Dept. of Anthr., Smithsonian: 360497.
Fig. 7. Twined basket. Rim is wrapped with maidenhair fern. Diameter 32.7 cm, collected before 1931.

History

Their mountain habitat spared the Atsugewi direct contact with White civilization until relatively late. Peter Skene Ogden in 1827-1828 may have been the first

White in the area (Elliott 1909). The Hudson's Bay Company men trapped the region through the 1830s, establishing a trail from near Klamath Lake down the Pit River to Hat Creek, where they cut across the mountains to the Sacramento Valley. Prospectors who entered the area in 1851 were soon followed by settlers. In 1856 (Neasham 1957:29-112) the Indians attacked a stage and murdered ferry operators at Fall River, precipitating a punitive war by White volunteers. Fort Crook was built at Fall River in 1857 and the Indians, who suffered severely, soon sued for peace. Renewed friction developed in 1859 with a massacre of Whites at the Hat Creek station, probably by Atsuge under chief Shavehead. White volunteers mistakenly annihilated a friendly Apwaruge village on Beaver Creek and shortly afterward all Indians to be found were removed to the Round Valley Reservation near the coast. The few remaining natives continued depredations, and soon those at the reservation filtered back. Many of the early settlers took Indian wives and so came to have a measure of influence on the tribes. Eventually many of the Indians settled on small allotments in Dixie Valley or along Hat Creek, continuing to gather the native foods and to practice shamanism. Some worked for White ranchers or in the saw mills. One of their large earth-covered dance houses used in the Ghost Dance revival of 1890 was partly standing in 1940. In 1972 there were five or six Atsuge families living on allotments along Hat Creek and in Burney. There is also a block of Indian land in Susanville, California. Except for a recent revival of basket- and cradle making on Hat Creek, few remnants of the old culture survive.

Synonymy

The name Atsugewi derives from *atsuke,* the native name for a spot on Hat Creek in the middle of Atsuge territory. Synonyms listed in Hodge (1907-1910, 1:114) include Adwanuqdji, an Ilmawi name; Atsugei; Chenoya, Chenoyana, and Chunoiyana (Yana names); and Hat Creek Indians. Powers (1874:418) calls them Pacamallies, from Pacamala, an Achumawi designation.

Sources

Garth (1938-1939) gathered information from five Atsuge and eight Apwaruge informants. Dave Brown from Hat Creek and Ida Peconom from Dixie Valley were fluent in English and able to relate details of their youth in the native culture. Neasham's (1957) history of Fall River valley contains invaluable pertinent material on the Indians.

Cahto

JAMES E. MYERS

Language and Territory

The Cahto (ˈkäˌtō), along with the Nongatl, Lassik, Wailaki, and Sinkyone, spoke a language of the Athapaskan linguistic family. The Cahto were the southernmost Athapaskan-speaking tribe on the Pacific coast.

Cahto is the spelling preferred by the people themselves today; the other common spelling is Kato. The word is derived from a Northern Pomo word for 'lake', their name for an important Cahto village site. The same lake was called to·ʒiɫbiʔ by the Cahto, whence their own name for themselves at time of contact: to·ʒiɫbiʔkiyahəŋ 'the people of to·ʒiɫbiʔ'.*

The Cahto occupied the Cahto and Long valleys of Mendocino County and generally the upper drainage of the South Fork of Eel River (fig. 1). They were enclosed on three sides by Yukian speakers—the Coast Yuki to the west, the Yuki proper to the east, and the Huchnom to the south. To the south were the Northern Pomo, to the north were the Sinkyone, and to the northeast the Wailaki.

Although geographically separated by a narrow strip of land occupied by Yuki, the Cahto were considerably influenced by friendly contact with the Northern Pomo. This connection is evidenced by the similarity of their cultures, by the fact that some Cahto spoke Pomo in addition to their own language, and by frequent ethnographic reference to the Cahto as Kaipomo. The resemblance to the Pomo culture was apparently responsible for the Cahtos' being erroneously classified by Powers (1877:150–155) as Pomo. Kroeber (1925:154) placed the Cahto, along with the Huchnom, in the role of transmitter of religious cults and various other cultural features from the Pomo to the Yuki and Wailaki.

The Cahto were also influenced by the Yuki. Cahto baskets were almost indistinguishable from Yuki baskets (fig. 2). Yuki and Cahto gambling games, men's hair

nets, bulb cooking in the ground, the large dance house with a roof door, and the victory ceremony with a display of enemy scalps were also similar.

The Cahtos traveled to Blue Rock, about 20 miles to the north, where they exchanged arrows, baskets, and clothing with the Wailaki. They also traveled to Coast Yuki territory on the coast, where they gathered shellfish and seaweed.

The Cahto lacked a true tribal organization. During precontact time there are estimated to have been 50 villages, with the permanent settlements situated in the three valleys where the town of Cahto once stood, and the towns of Branscomb and Laytonville now stand. Each village had a headman who was generally succeeded by his son. The six villages in Long Valley were unique in that they had a collective name for themselves, "Tlo-kyahan" 'Grass Tribe' (Curtis 1907–1930, 14:4). By the 1920s the Cahto population had been reduced from approximately 500 to about 50 persons, residing either on the Round Valley Reservation or on the rancheria set aside for them by the government near Laytonville.

---

*The Cahto language is extinct. The orthography used by Goddard (1912) has been reinterpreted by Victor Golla (who has also suggested the above spellings for the Cahto self-designation). Goddard's b d g represent voiceless unaspirated stops, but his "fully sonant" final -g is probably an allophone of γ (which Goddard elsewhere writes G). His dj is ʒ or ǰ, the voiceless unaspirated equivalent of č and č̣. Myers provides other equivalents: ʔ for Goddard's ɛ; ƛ̣ for L; š for c; ɫ for ʟ; h for h, ᶜ; č for tc; ŋ for ñ; i for ī, i; ə for û; o for ō,ū; e for e, ę; a for a, ą.

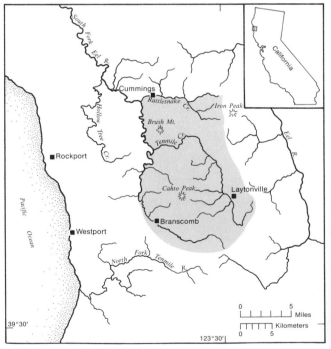

Fig. 1. Tribal territory.

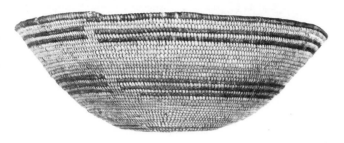

Fig. 2. Coiled Cahto basket identical in design, materials, and technique to Yuki baskets. Diameter 34 cm, height 11 cm. Collected 1910.

Each village had a headman or chief; some had two. There was generally patrilineal succession to the office. The headman's duties and powers were mainly advisory. When important decisions were to be made the headman consulted the elders and yielded if the elders' consensus were unfavorable to his plans.

Culture

Marriage was arranged between the two persons concerned. Most girls married before the menarche. Mother-in-law avoidance, levirate, and sororate were observed. Polygyny was practiced. The newly wedded couple lived with or near the bride's parents until the husband was able to build a new house, at which time they resided with or near his family. Divorce was easy to obtain, as either spouse could leave the other for any reason. Generally, the father retained the male children and the mother the female children.

Men owned their bows and arrows, knives, deer hides, hair nets; women owned their clothing, baskets, and rocks used for the boiling of mush. The village owned the dance house and doctors' paraphernalia. The family owned their living house. There was no private ownership of songs and stories.

Pregnancy was known by cessation of menses. There were no food taboos for pregnant women. Old women served as midwives. The umbilical cord was cut with a flint knife, and the cord and the placenta were buried in the ground. The mother stayed in bed one month after childbirth and did not sleep with her husband until the child was weaned. Deformed children and twins were killed at birth.

Girls underwent a six-day menstruation ceremony during which they observed a fish and meat taboo. They then lived a quiet life for five months. Boys, at about age 12, were put in the dance house where they remained all winter, receiving warnings about dangers and admonitions to be good. Men impersonating ghosts and clowns sang songs. No ordeals other than confinement and a meager diet were observed during this period.

After a Cahto died, his corpse was washed, clothed in good garments, and buried with valuable possessions. If death occurred away from home the body was burned and the ashes brought home for burial. Women in mourning smeared pitch over their bodies and cut their hair. Men cut their hair only as a sign of mourning. A widow could remarry after two winters. Names of the dead were never mentioned.

Although warfare on a large scale was rare, murder or trespassing frequently led to brief conflicts among the Cahto and Sinkyone, Yuki, Huchnom, Wailaki, or Northern Pomo, with loyalties often shifting from war to war depending upon the state of relationships at the time and the matter under dispute. At the end of the war, payment was made for those killed on both sides. Kroeber (1928) reports that the war chief and peace chief were the same man for any given battle. Loeb (1932:16) contradicts this, stating that the peace chief, "Nunkatinen," and war chief, "Klanantin kut nunkatinen," were two different individuals, except in a time of peace when the war chief could substitute for the peace chief and admonish his people to be good. War dances were held before each battle. Close combat was avoided. The bow and arrow, deerhide sling, and spear were the only weapons. Mortalities were usually low. Scalping was practiced.

In trade, the Cahto supplied clam disk beads to the Lassik; hazelwood bows to the Coast Yuki; and baskets, arrows, and clothing to the Wailaki. The Cahto received salt, mussels, seaweed, abalone, surf fish, clamshells, and dry kelp (for salt) from the Coast Yuki; dentalia from the Wailaki; salt from the Northern Wintun; hazelwood self bows from unspecified tribes; and dogs from the "north."

The grass game, shinny, forked-stick game, bark-spinning game, stone throwing, running and swimming races, and wrestling were played. Children played camping games, skipped rope, and spun acorn tops.

Cahto religion centered around two original beings, "Nagaicho" 'Great Traveler', and "Tcenes" 'Thunder'. Tcenes was regarded as the more powerful of the two and the actual creator of man, the other animals, and inanimate objects. The origin of trickery and rivalry among people was traced to the competition between the two original beings. The Cahto were also practitioners of the western Kuksu cult, a religious system that involved the acquisition of spiritual powers by direct contact with supernatural personalities (Loeb 1932).

The Cahto had three types of shamans, or doctors—sucking doctors, singing and dancing doctors, and Bear doctors. The sucking doctors served as diagnosticians and curers of "inside" sickness, while the singing and dancing doctors attended to "outside" (fright) sickness. The Bear doctors enjoyed great prestige for their presumed ability to kill enemies of the Cahtos. They wore a bear skin which they believed imparted superhuman speed and invulnerability to the wearer.

Some Cahtos dressed up as ghosts and frightened victims by "shooting" pain into them. Various forms of magic were practiced before war, hunting and fishing, funeral ceremonies, and births.

The Cahto prayed frequently: before rising, while eating, going to bed, after sneezing, when sick.

Children were not allowed to see live or dead raccoons; the names of dead persons were never mentioned; numerous taboos were involved with burial and the dead; a meat taboo was observed for elders in a house where doctoring was in process; there were meat and fish taboos for girls undergoing the puberty ceremony; and there was a taboo on conversation between a menstruating woman and her husband.

Musical instruments included whistles, bull-roarers, the foot drum, split-stick rattle, cocoon rattle, acorn string, musical bow, and flute made of elderberry with six holes. Women enjoyed singing in chorus around a fire in the evening. Infants were sung to while in the cradle. There was group and individual singing at initiation ceremonies.

A tribal and intertribal ceremony was held in winter and summer. Neighboring villages were invited when a host determined he could feed a large number of guests. Men and women danced for a week. The creation story was told and the headman gave admonitory speeches.

The Acorn Dance was held in winter. Men, women, and children all participated to insure a plentiful acorn harvest for the coming season. The Feather Dance, a pleasure dance, was performed by six men, women, and children. The "Necum" Dance was a pleasure dance with six women on one side of the fire and six men on the other side.

The dwelling house was built over a two-feet-deep circular excavation with four forked main posts set in a square to support the rafters, which were covered with layers of pine or spruce slabs and which in turn were covered with bark and sometimes earth. The roof had a slight slope to the rear. The doorway was a narrow opening from ground to roof. Such a house could hold up to three families. Houses were rebuilt after two winters. Large villages had a dance house with a diameter of about 20 feet for ceremonies, dances, and sweating.

Stone was used as material for arrow points, cylindrical beads, knives, hopper mortar bases, and pestles. Bone was used for awls and fish spear points. Beads and scrapers were made from shell and bows and arrow and spear shafts from wood. Skin was used for clothing. Wedges for splitting wood were made of elk antler. Cordage and nets were made from iris fiber. Basketry—the most conspicuous handicraft of the Cahto—was of two types: usually twined (fig. 3), sometimes coiled.

Canoes were not used as streams were too small for navigation; however, transportation over water was possible by a raft the Cahtos made of five or six logs lashed together.

Lowie Mus., U. of Calif., Berkeley: 1-7396.
Fig. 3. Openwork twined seed beater. Length 53 cm. Collected before 1900.

Money was in the form of disk beads, clamshell, flint, and magnesite beads. Dentalium beads were not used.

Men and women wore a tanned deerhide apron. Summer clothing was made of dehaired skins; winter clothing was made of hides with the hair left on. Men and women wore the hair long (fig. 4) and used iris hairnets. Deerhide bracelets were worn by both men and women, as were nose and ear ornaments. Tattooing in perpendicular lines was optional on the forehead, cheeks, chin, chest, wrists, or legs of both sexes.

Tobacco grew wild by the rivers and was smoked in pipes only by elderly men.

The dog was the only domesticated animal. It was used in deer, raccoon, and bear hunting. Birds, rabbits, and coyotes were sometimes kept as pets.

The staple foods were dried salmon, acorns made into soup and bread, and natural products of the soil, especially tarweed seeds and other plants. Deer was the chief meat source, supplemented with fish, black and cinnamon bears, minks, raccoons, skunks, moles, squirrels, gophers, and birds. Caterpillars, grasshoppers, bees, and hornets were also eaten.

Meat was broiled over coals or on a spit. Fish were broiled between hot rocks or in hot ashes. Acorn soup was stone-boiled in baskets. Meat and fish were also dried or roasted for storage.

Hunting instruments included traps, snares, bows and arrows, slings, nets for taking fish and birds, and harpoons. Fish were sometimes poisoned with angelica roots and soaproot thrown in streams. Clubbing small animals after smoking them out of trees and hollow logs was another hunting method.

The Cahto obtained impure salt at Westport on the coast, and dried and burned kelp to secure its salty residue.

In the sexual division of labor, men hunted, fished, and were generally responsible for obtaining game, while women collected seeds, pinole, clover, and various tubers. Men, women, and children all gathered acorns.

The Cahto recognized seasons and gave them the following names: winter (root time), spring (fire gone gone time), summer (hot day time), and fall (leaf on top time). The month was divided according to phases of the moon.

NAA, Smithsonian.
Fig. 4. A young woman. Photographed by Edward S. Curtis, 1915-1924.

There was some specialization in surgery, midwifery, and medicine. Generally doctors were not called in to treat minor sickness as most persons knew these cures. Illnesses commonly treated by individuals were headaches, toothaches, earaches, stomachaches, rattlesnake bites, arrow wounds, diarrhea, and rheumatism.

In addition to numerous myths of origins that involved the two original beings, Thunder and Great Traveler, Cahto myths typically recounted events between human beings and various forest animals, including the mischievous coyote.

History

The Cahto were first mentioned by Col. Redick McKee, a federal treaty commissioner, in 1851. McKee was on an overland journey from San Francisco to Humboldt Bay charged with making as many treaties with Indians as possible.

In 1856 the now extinct town of Cahto came into existence with the settling of two pioneers. In the same year Indian reservations were established in Mendocino County at Fort Bragg and Round Valley. During these early years there were frequent altercations between Whites and Indians in the Cahto and Long valleys, the most serious reportedly occurring in 1859, when 32 Long

Valley Indians were killed by Whites in retaliation for alleged stealing of livestock. In 1880 the town of Laytonville was established.

In January 1972 the Cahto tribal roll consisted of 95 persons. The tribal name, Cahto, appears to be used as a convenience term to account collectively for the Indians who have been designated by the tribal council as eligible for the Cahto roll. The Cahto roll in fact includes persons who individually recognize themselves as being Pomo, Nomlaki, Cahto, Maidu, and Cherokee.

The Cahto Tribal Council consists of three persons who serve a one-year term of office. The council is elected by tribal-roll Indians who are 21 years of age or older. There is considerable disagreement among the Laytonville Indians over the question of who is a "real" Cahto Indian.

The 264-acre Laytonville rancheria is located approximately two miles southwest of Laytonville, a town of 897 people. Most of the Indians in the Laytonville area live on the rancheria. The majority of dwelling units on the rancheria are mobile homes and prefabricated houses. Unemployment is low because most of the Indians are employed at a lumber mill in Branscomb, a small town 10 miles west of the rancheria. However, the income of the Indians is low; most families earn between $4,000-$5,000 annually.

Intermarriage between Indians and Whites has long been accepted and is a common practice.

Population

Date	Population Estimate	Source
Precontact	1,100	Cook 1956:103
1770	1,000 maximum, 500 probably	Kroeber 1925:155
1851	500	Goddard 1907a:665
1910	51	Curtis 1907-1930, 14:183 (cites federal census of 1910)
1915	50	Kroeber 1925:155
1963	50	California State Advisory Commission on Indian Affairs 1966:56
1972	95	Cahto Tribal Council

Education continued to be a problem in the 1970s. In the 20 years before 1972 fewer than 10 Indians graduated from the local high school and no Cahto Indian graduated from college. Yet high school administration and Indian leaders believed the situation to be steadily improving.

The traditional Cahto culture is gone. There are no speakers of the Cahto language and all knowledge of ancient Cahto arts and crafts is lost. The Cahto religion, ceremonies, and dances are no longer practiced; however, one Indian woman expressed hope of reviving some traditional games and dances.

Synonymy

Batem-da-kai-ee (Gibbs 1853b:434); Kai Po-mo (Powers 1877:148-150); Kaipomo (Kroeber 1925:154); Ka-to-Po-mo (Powers 1877:148-150); Kato Pomo (Goddard 1903:375-376); Cahto Pomo (Powers 1872a:500); Kato (Goddard 1907a:665; Merriam 1851-1939; Kroeber 1925:154; Loeb 1932:14-54); Kahto (Merriam 1851-1939); Cahto (Goddard 1903:375-376; Merriam 1851-1939); To-chil-pe ke-ah-hahng (Merriam 1851-1939).

Sources

There is a paucity of ethnographic data on the Cahto. A good general ethnography is Curtis (1907-1930,14), which is the principal source for the cultural summary here. It is also available in the Library of American Civilization Microbook, card number 22416. Goddard (1907) is the best source of Cahto myths; he also wrote on language (1912). Kroeber (1925) and Goddard (1907a) contain notes on the Cahto. Kroeber has a good account of Cahto warfare (1928). Loeb's (1932) treatment of the Cahto is good, although most of his data may also be found in Curtis. An important discussion of Cahto precontact population is in Cook (1956). The University of California Archives, Berkeley, contains 107 typed pages of unpublished Cahto folklore recorded by F.J. Essene in 1935. The Department of Anthropology at Berkeley has 35 pages of unpublished Cahto data collected by C. Hart Merriam (1851-1939).

Yuki, Huchnom, and Coast Yuki

VIRGINIA P. MILLER

The Yuki, ('yōōkē), Huchnom ('hōōch,nom), and Coast Yuki speak three dialects of a language usually known simply as Yuki, which has been grouped with Wappo in the Yukian family. This small group has no known linguistic relatives (Powell 1891:136; Kroeber 1925:159), though various tentative hypotheses of relationship have been made (Radin 1919; Sapir 1929; Swadesh 1954; Shipley 1957; Elmendorf 1963).*

YUKI

Yuki territory in 1850 included most of the drainage of the upper Eel River in the rugged Coast Range Mountains of Northwest California, although ethnographers disagree on exact boundaries (Heizer 1966:15–25; Foster

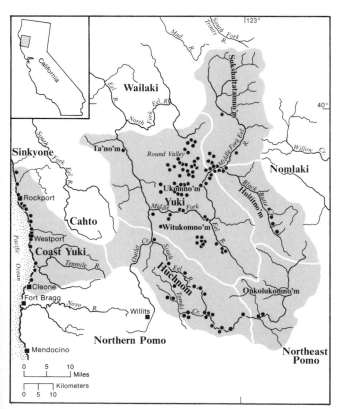

Fig. 1. Territories and villages of the Coast Yuki, Huchnom, and Yuki with Yuki tribal subdivisions.

* In the absence of a phonemic orthography, Yuki forms have been cited in the spelling of the available sources.

1944:157). There were six major Yuki tribal subdivisions—Ta'no'm, Ukomno'm, Huititno'm, Witukomno'm, Onkolukomno'm, and Sukshaltatamno'm (fig. 1). In addition, two minor ones, the Lalkutno'm and the Ontitno'm, lay immediately south of the Ukomno'm, who, occupying the Round Valley area, were the most favorably situated in this mountainous region and probably the most numerous. Curtis (1907–1930, 14:186–187) lists Eden Valley Yuki as separate and gives nine named divisions of Round Valley Yuki.

History and Prehistory

The Yukis' first intensive contact with Europeans came in 1856, when the Nome Cult Indian Farm was established in Round Valley. In 1858 the farm officially became a reservation, and other Indians—including Wailaki, Maidu, Nomlaki, Achumawi, Atsugewi, Pomoans, Lassik, Modoc, and Yana—were brought to live there. White settlers also arrived in the valley, appropriating much of it for stock raising. Their cattle destroyed the Yukis' natural food sources, forcing the Indians to poach. The settlers then proceeded to exterminate the Yuki. Federal troops and the declaration of martial law did not deter their genocide, and the results may be seen in table 1, which shows the spectacular drop in the Yuki population between 1850 and 1864 (Miller 1970).

After 1865 the story of the Yuki merged with that of other tribes on Round Valley Reservation. During the early 1870s, two waves of the Ghost Dance reached Round Valley and attracted some Yuki followers but had no lasting effect (Du Bois 1939:105–108). The Yukis eked out an existence by hunting and gathering, along with some farming. Following the Dawes Severalty Act of 1887, individual farm plots were allotted to some Indians, but in the 1930s Foster (1944:219) found the Yukis generally economically deprived, with the Pentecostal church working to discourage the practice of the native religion. Following the Indian Reorganization Act of 1934, the different tribes in Round Valley jointly elected a "tribal council," which still functioned in 1972 to manage tribal business.

In 1963 Molohon (1969) found all the Round Valley Indians leading a rural life and, while not actually

Table 1. Population

Year	Yuki	Huchnom	Coast Yuki
1850	6,880[a]	2,100[a]	750[b]
1864	300[c]	——[d]	50[c]
1870	238[e]	79[e]	——[d]
1880	168[f]	50[f]	——[d]
1910	95[g]	15[h]	15[i]
1926	——[d]	——[d]	4[j]
1937	50[k]	8[l]	——[d]
1973	32[m]	1[n]	——[o]

[a] Cook 1956:108.
[b] Ibid:106.
[c] ARCIA 1865:119.
[d] No data.
[e] ARCIA 1871:75.
[f] U.S. Census Office 1880, 4.
[g] Kroeber 1925:168. In 1905-1906 an additional 84 Indians of Yukian stock were not living on reservations (Kelsey 1971:27, 65, 71); 44 of these were undoubtedly Huchnom.
[h] Kroeber 1925:203.
[i] Ibid:213.
[j] Gifford 1939b:292-293.
[k] Estimated from Foster (1944:155), "ten full bloods and several dozen mixed bloods."
[l] Estimated from Foster (1944:225), "few remaining Indians of at least part Huchnom blood."
[m] California Judgment Roll 1973. Bureau of Indian Affairs, Sacramento, Calif. Only two Yuki in 1973 were full bloods.
[n] California Judgment Roll 1973. Bureau of Indian Affairs, Sacramento, Calif.
[o] Ethnographically extinct. No one remains who speaks the Indian language or is culturally Indian. There may well be numbers of genetic survivors mixed with other native and Caucasian elements (Kroeber and Heizer 1970:3).

assimilated into the White culture, sharing more cultural characteristics with the Whites around them than with their ancestors. They still hunted and gathered some wild foodstuffs, supplementing these with garden produce and ranch products. Tribal identities had given way to a sense of primary affiliation with a matriarchal, extended family kin group. The Indian languages had been all but forgotten; in 1972, only a few Yukis spoke even a few phrases of the Yuki language.

In the late 1960s the Indians of Round Valley Reservation shared with other rural California Indians the problems of obtaining adequate health care and water and sanitation systems (California State Advisory Commission on Indian Affairs 1969:11, 48). Ownership of much of the allotted land was complicated by multiple heirship, and some White-owned land was interspersed with the Indian land. These problems continued in 1972 for the approximately 350 Yuki, Wailaki, Nomlaki, and Pomoan Indians who lived on the reservation and in the nearby town of Covelo. A threat to dam the Eel River

and flood Round Valley was especially prominent in the mid-1960s and loomed large in 1972.

Archeological work in the Yuki area has consisted primarily of site surveys, and the results testify to the remarkably dense population for the area (Treganza, Smith, and Weymouth 1950; R.L. Edwards 1966). Almost 500 sites are recorded in Yuki territory, of which 225 are in Round Valley alone, including 32 historic sites. Treganza et al. excavated one prehistoric and historic Yuki site in the valley and uncovered nine skeletons, all displaying the distinctive Yuki physical type of short-statured, long-headed individuals with deep chests. This discovery affirms continuous occupation of the area by the Yuki at least into the immediate prehistoric period.

Culture

Aboriginal Yuki culture (about 1850) combined a simple material culture with an elaborate ceremonial life. Their lush environment easily supported the Yuki during times of leisure required by ceremonies. Neighboring tribes feared the fierce and warlike Yukis, who in later reservation days recalled this reputation with pride.

Sociopolitical Organization

The basic unit of Yuki life was the village or rancheria, which ranged in size from a single family to 150 individuals and was presided over by a local chief. Rancherias were grouped into tribelets around one large rancheria containing a dance house and the tribelet chief's residence. Varying numbers of tribelets then composed each of the tribal subdivisions, whose members felt a sense of affinity through dialect similarity. Specific information on rancheria and tribelet names and territories can be found in Barrett (1908), Kroeber (1925, 1958), Foster (1944), and Merriam (1910-1929). The elected tribelet chief's main duties were to encourage his people to lead a good life and to settle disputes. There was a separate war chief. The land and its products were communally owned; of portable property, women generally owned the household goods while men owned the fishing, hunting, and ceremonial equipment.

The Yuki kinship system was of the Central California type. Yukis differentiated between relatives of the maternal and paternal lines but treated all cousins as siblings (Gifford 1922:119-120; Kroeber 1917:372-373). Marriage was initiated by either the couple or their families and was marked by an exchange of gifts. Blood relatives were forbidden to marry and although polygyny was permissible, it was rare. The levirate was practiced. There was no postmarital residence rule, although a mild in-law avoidance was observed (Foster 1944:184).

Life Cycle

Women gave birth in a dwelling house attended by midwives. The mother observed postpartum taboos, while the father observed a mild couvade with hunting and fishing restrictions. A relative or friend named the child. Names had no special significance and were not secret.

There were no special adolescence ceremonies for boys, but girls strictly observed the hamnam-wok 'menstrual dance' to ensure good fortune for both the girl and the tribe. This ritual included seclusion for a month following first menses and concluded with a general feast.

The dead were flexed and tied, wrapped in a skin, and buried facing east. Property of the deceased was buried with the corpse or burned. Mourning lasted about a year. Female relatives cut their hair short and smeared pitch over their heads and faces. There was a taboo against mentioning the dead by name (Foster 1944:178-188).

War and Trade

The Yuki fought in both prearranged battles and surprise attacks. Before fighting, they danced a war dance; they celebrated victory with a scalp dance. Generally allied with the Wailaki, their particular enemies included the Nomlaki, Pomo, and intermittently, the Cahto. Kroeber (1928) and Goldschmidt, Foster, and Essene (1939) provide detailed accounts of some Yuki wars.

Trade was principally with the Huchnom and Pomoans to the south. Primary exports were food products, which were exchanged for clamshell beads, magnesite, dentalia, and seafood. Salt was obtained from the Northeastern Pomo.

Religion

Taikomol 'he who walks alone' was the Yukis' anthropomorphic creator and supreme being, although they also recognized lesser spirits dwelling in the mountains and streams (Schmidt 1926-1949, 5:37-86 provides additional information; for a comparison of Taikomol with the creators of neighboring tribes, see Dangel 1927, 1934.) The Yuki believed a hereafter existed for those who led good lives on earth. They held two principal religious ceremonies for the young men in the tribe. These died out soon after the Whites arrived and so are incompletely known (Kroeber 1925:183-191; Loeb 1932:64-68; Foster 1944:209-211). The taikomol-woknam 'lying dance' was a wintertime period of confinement in the dance house for all young men. There old men taught them tribal mythology, and some of the boys trained there became doctors. The hulk'ilal-woknam 'eye-striped initiation' or 'ghost dance' was the second principal ceremony. Boys who underwent it learned poisoning techniques and some became doctors. The Ta'no'm Yuki had neither of these ceremonies. Like their Wailaki neighbors, they held a kičil-woknam 'obsidian school', a sort of tribal puberty rite for both boys and girls (Foster 1944:211-212; Loeb 1932:71-72; Kroeber 1925:191-195).

Fig. 2. Yuki double-reed whistle bound with sinew and caulked with asphaltum. Length 11.0 cm, collected in 1889.

There were two principal types of doctors. True shamans were usually men who received their power as a result of a supernatural encounter and then were further trained in the taikomol-woknam. They treated illness by sucking, singing, and dancing. A few were limited to curing rattlesnake bites. Nonshaman doctors, always men, included sorcerers for poisoning and curing, and singing doctors. These doctors were not divinely inspired but learned their trade from an older doctor in the hulk'ilal-woknam. Bear shamans, dangerous individuals who reportedly could transform themselves into bear form, and "Indian bears," men who dressed up in a bearskin, were also reported for the Yuki (Foster 1944:212-219).

Ceremonial regalia and apparatus included feather headdresses and capes, bull-roarers, split-stick and cocoon rattles, and bone and reed whistles (fig. 2).

Music and Games

Both men and women participated in social dances, wearing feather headdresses, feather capes, and dance skirts (fig. 3), and dancing to the accompaniment of a log drum, split-stick rattles, and singing. The Acorn Sing, held in January and May, was a happy time of singing and dancing to please Taikomol so that he would send abundant acorns and other wild crops (Foster 1944:190-192). Gambling games were adult favorites. Shinny, string figures, and contests of skill and endurance were also popular.

Structures

Yuki dwelling houses were circular, conical structures of bark and poles about 10 feet in diameter, excavated and banked with earth. A fire pit occupied the center. In summer the Yukis lived in brush huts. Similar to the dwelling house, the dance house was larger and used also for sweating.

Technology

Tools and utensils included the slab mortar with basketry hopper, stone pestle, and knives and mauls of stone. Mush paddles, skin scrapers, fish spears, and fire drills were of wood. String and nets were of hemp. The Yuki also used mussel-shell spoons, bone awls, and elkhorn wedges. They made sinew-backed wooden bows and feather-decorated arrows with flint or bone points. Other

Fig. 3. Ralph Moore, a Yuki man in dance costume consisting of a flicker quill headband, head net filled with eagle down and a forked feather plume, a netted feather cape, and a deerskin skirt. Photograph by T.D. Jones in 1900.

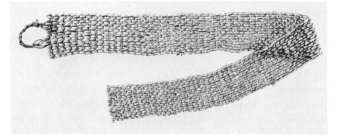

Fig. 4. Clamshell beads on hemp string used as Huchnom dancer's belt. Width about 8.5 cm, collected in 1875.

but moccasins were apparently unknown. Personal adornment for both men and women included tattooing and a small bone inserted in the nasal septum and each earlobe (Foster 1944:167–172).

Knowledge and Mythology

Most Yuki "knowledge" has been lost forever. Apparently, their new year began in winter and calendrical terms described the seasonal round. The Yuki also recognized and named phases of the moon and stellar constellations. Their numeral system was octonary, rare in California. They named and exploited most if not all the plants in their surroundings, using them for medicinal purposes as well as food (L.S.M. Curtin 1957).

Kroeber (1932) has recorded several versions of the Yuki creation myth involving Taikomol and his assistant, Coyote, and some other Yuki myths taught in the taikomol-woknam.

Subsistence

The Yukis pursued a hunting, fishing, and gathering life, with deer, salmon, and acorns their dietary mainstays. In general, men hunted and fished while women gathered; whole families gathered acorns. The Yuki had a "phoenix concept" regarding game, in that they thought for every animal killed, another took its place. A boy's first kill was taboo to him, a common observance in aboriginal California.

Men often hunted alone, shooting deer with bow and arrow or snaring them. Hunters used a deerhead disguise. Before hunting a man avoided his wife, sweated, and fasted. Several men might band together to rouse and kill a hibernating bear for its skin. Small game and birds were taken with bow and arrow, snares, slings, and clubs. Salmon, trout, and steelhead, caught seasonally in the Eel River with spears, nets, traps, weirs, or poison, provided a year-round supply of fresh fish. Most game and fish were roasted and eaten, although deer meat and salmon might be dried and stored in baskets for later use. The Yukis did not eat grizzly bear, panther, fox, wolf, coyote, gopher, weasel, snakes, lizards, or beaver.

weapons included spears, flint daggers, clubs, and slings. No poison was used on weapons (Foster 1944:168–171).

Yuki basketry contained design elements like those of other Northern California tribes. Coiled baskets (see "Cahto," fig. 1) were usually decorated and served for cooking and storing food. Undecorated twined ware included seed beaters, hoppers, and sifters (Kelly 1930a:443).

Strings of clamshell beads served for money (fig. 4). Old people smoked strong, wild tobacco in tubular wooden pipes. The Yuki had no watercraft.

Clothing and Adornment

Dress was minimal. Men went naked or wore a deerskin cover around their hips (fig. 3). Women wore a fringed leather apron. Deerskin capes were worn in cold weather,

Merriam Coll., Dept. of Anthr., U. of Calif., Berkeley.
Fig. 5. Yuki woman gathering clover. Photographed in 1890s, possibly by Carpenter of Ukiah City, Calif.

The most important vegetable food was the acorn. Women cracked and dried acorns for storage. Later these were ground into meal, which was then leached in a shallow sand basin before being stone-boiled into soup or baked into bread in an earth oven (Chesnut 1902). Other vegetable foods were clover (fig. 5), seeds and nuts, tubers, and berries. Miscellaneous foods included grasshoppers, mushrooms, bird eggs, honey, larvae, and "army worms," the last regarded as a periodic gift from Taikomol (Foster 1944:161–167).

Synonymy

The name Yuki is from Wintu *yuke* 'enemy'. Spelling variants are Eukas (ARCIA 1865:119), Uca (ARCIA 1863:359); Uka (Taylor 1860–1863, 13(3)); Uki (ARCIA 1874:325); Ukies (ARCIA 1866:112); Ulkies (ARCIA 1871:75), undoubtedly a printer's error; Yucas (E. Russell 1875:74); Yukas (ARCIA 1859:300); Yukeh (Gibbs 1863:123); Yuke (Powers 1877:483); Yukiah (Anonymous 1860:50); Yuques (Gibbs 1863:123). The Yuki

have also been called Yuki proper and Round Valley Yuki (Curtis 1907–1930, 14:187).

Another Wintu designation, meaning 'western tribe', is recorded as Noam-kekhl (Powers 1877:230), Noam-kult (Powers 1877:230), Nome-Cults (ARCIA 1857:251), Nomee Cult (Taylor 1860–1863, 13(3)), Numculty (Merriam 1910–1929:12).

Variants of a Pomo word for 'stranger' or 'enemy' used for Yuki south of Round Valley (Merriam alone uses it for the Huchnom) include: Choo-mi′-ah (Merriam 1910–1929), Chu-mai′-a (Powers 1877:136), Chumaya (Powell 1891:136), Shumairs (Anonymous 1860:50), Shumaya (Anonymous 1860:49), Shumeias (Powers 1872b:312), Tcimaia (Barrett 1908:247).

Sources

Knowledge of Yuki culture and history is incomplete. Principal ethnographic sources are Powers (1877), Kroeber (1925), and Foster (1944), the last being the most comprehensive and the primary source for this chapter. Miller (1970) deals with the early history of Round Valley, while Molohon (1969) considers the valley in 1963. Robert H. Lowie Museum of Anthropology, University of California, Berkeley, has a collection of Yuki ethnographic specimens, including over 100 baskets.

HUCHNOM

The Huchnom spoke a dialect of the Yukian language, undoubtedly partially intelligible to Yuki speakers (Kroeber 1925:211). Their territory lay along the drainage of the South Eel River (fig. 1).

History and Prehistory

It is likely that Huchnom history of European contact parallels Yuki history, except that the Huchnom probably knew of the Whites earlier, through their Pomoan neighbors. Unlike the Yuki, the Huchnom were "timid" Indians, but they also suffered harassment and attack from Whites. Some were removed to Round Valley Reservation around 1869, where they were known as Redwoods. On the reservation, their lot was the same as that of the other tribes confined there, and table 1 reflects their decline in number. By the early 1900s only a few remained, and in 1972 they were considered ethnographically extinct (see Kroeber and Heizer 1970).

Over 30 Huchnom living sites are recorded, all on the banks of the South Eel River and its tributaries, thus testifying to the inhospitable ruggedness of the mountainous terrain (Barrett 1908:258–260; Kroeber 1925:203; Childress and Chartkoff 1966). No excavation has been carried out in any of these sites.

Culture

Huchnom culture was a mixture of Yuki and Pomoan traits, the former predominating, although it should be noted that Yuki, Huchnom, Pomoan, and Cahto cultures all had much in common (Foster 1944:225). Only significant divergences from the Yuki are mentioned here.

Village organization was apparently like that of the Yuki; however, there is no evidence for political units corresponding to the six principal Yuki subdivisions. The Huchnom were generally friendly with Pomoans, sometimes allying with them in fights against the Yuki. The Huchnom, Pomo, and Cahto commonly held the taikomol-woknam and the hulk'ilal-woknam ceremonies jointly. In peacetime, the Huchnom served as intermediaries in the Yuki-Pomoan exchange of trade goods.

Death practices definitely followed those of Pomoans. The Huchnom cremated their dead, adding personal property of the deceased and gifts to the pyre (Foster 1944:232). Huchnom basketry also shows Pomoan influence, with lattice twined ware (Kelly 1930a:441) and intricately decorated coiled ware (ibid.:433).

Unlike the Yuki, the Huchnom did observe a brief "first acorn" and "first salmon" ceremony in which a shaman made small offerings of the food to the four cardinal directions. They held an Acorn Sing only once a year, in January, to ensure a good crop (Foster 1944:226).

Synonymy

The name Huchnom, given to this group by the Yuki of Round Valley, means 'tribe outside (the valley)'; various spellings are Hūchnom (Powers 1877:139), Hoochnom (Mason 1904:368), and Húch-no 'm for húčnoʔm (Curtis 1907-1930, 14:186). Merriam (1910-1929) used the name Choo-mí-ah for the Huchnom; see the Yuki synonymy. Other names are Nár-ko Pomah (Merriam 1910-1929); Red Woods (ARCIA 1870:188) and Redwoods (Powers 1877:139), after the valley in which some of them lived; Taco (Mason 1904:328), given as a Pomoan name for them; and Táh-do (Merriam 1910-1929), Tahtoo (Bancroft 1874-1876, 1:448), Tatu (Powers 1877:136).

Sources

Knowledge of Huchnom culture and history is sketchy. Ethnographic sources are Powers (1877), Kroeber (1925), and Foster (1944:Appendix I), the last two the most reliable. The Robert H. Lowie Museum of Anthropology at University of California, Berkeley, contains a small collection of artifacts.

COAST YUKI

The Coast Yuki spoke a dialect of the Yukian language that was partially intelligible to the Yuki. Probably Coast Yuki and Huchnom were equally distant from Yuki (Kroeber 1925:211).

The 11 groups that comprised the Coast Yuki occupied a 50-mile strip along the rugged Mendocino Coast. Group names from north to south were: Onch'ilka-ontilka, Oluntehem-ontilka, Melemisimok-ontilka, Hisimelak-ontilka, Alwasa-ontilka, Mishbul-ontilka, Mishkei-ontilka, Mishkeun-ontilka, Metkuyak-ontilka, Lilhuyak-ontilka, and Lalim-ontilka. Some village sites are noted in figure 1.

History and Prehistory

White ranchers and lumbermen first came to the Coast Yuki area in the early 1850s. Their activities quickly deprived the Indians of natural food resources. In 1856 Mendocino Reservation was founded, subsuming the southern end of Coast Yuki territory, and soldiers rounded up nearby Indians for the reservation. Most Indians ran away; in 1867 the reservation was abandoned and the remaining Indians returned to their former homes, where they settled and worked on the Whites' ranches. A few Coast Yuki joined the Pomo Earth Lodge cult, a derivative of the 1870 Ghost Dance. The population dropped drastically after the Whites arrived (table 1), and in 1972 the Coast Yuki were considered ethnographically extinct.

There has been no systematic archeological work in Coast Yuki territory. Roughly 50 village and camp sites are known, probably only a fraction of all sites occupied (Gifford 1939b:296). The archeological potential of the Coast Yuki has been assessed by Thomsen and Heizer (1964).

Culture

The Coast Yuki were a small group of shellmound dwellers who made beach camps during the summer, then moved inland for the winter. Their culture was a simplified version of Central California type, overlaid with a number of Northwest California cultural traits (Gifford 1928:113). Only significant divergences from the Yuki culture will be considered here.

Each Coast Yuki group had its own elected headman, dance house, and communally owned territory extending from the ocean eastward to the eastern boundary of Coast Yuki territory. The kinship system resembled an abridged Yuki system, with less elaborate bifurcation between the maternal and paternal lines (Gifford 1922:121).

Birth practices and girls' puberty rites resembled those of the Yuki. After death, an individual was decorated with beads and wrapped in skins, then buried at full length with the head to the north. Property was buried with the body or burned, and the deceased's house was moved to a new location. The corpse-handler and gravedigger observed a scratching taboo. Other mourning practices resembled those of the Yuki.

The Coast Yuki were generally friendly with their Cahto, Pomoan, and Sinkyone neighbors. But wars between them did occur, usually beginning with a killing or suspected witchcraft. Coast Yuki groups sometimes fought each other with sticks, but it is said that no one was killed in these encounters.

Coast Yuki groups visited one another's territory to gather a particular food plentiful in that area, for instance mussels at Westport. Groups also reciprocated annual trade visits with the Cahto and Pomoans. In this manner they received acorns and wild grasses and seeds, giving mussels, fish, and ocean products in return. From interior tribes, they obtained flint, obsidian, and tobacco, which old men smoked in tubular wooden pipes. From the south, they obtained clamshell disks and beads, which they used as money (Gifford 1939:304-306).

Koyimke 'walker' not the Yuki Taikomol, was the Coast Yuki creator. There were two sessions of telnik 'school' for adolescent boys. All boys attended the first school, when they were confined in the assembly house and old men taught them tribal lore. A few years later, prospective shamans attended a second school involving three winter months of confinement, when shamans taught them curing practices and witchcraft. At the end of this seclusion, those selected to be shamans would become sucking doctors, receiving additional power through dreams and visions. They could then kill by witchcraft as well as cure. Bear shamans were reported, but not documented, by informants (Gifford 1939:369-371).

The Coast Yuki lived in conical, redwood bark-covered structures erected on the ground surface. For summer shelter they built brush huts. Assembly houses were larger, more elaborate structures with a center post; they also served as sweathouses (Kroeber 1925:213).

In addition to the tools listed for the Yuki, the Coast Yuki tool inventory included wooden spatulas for prying abalone off the rocks and an "artificial thumb nail" of mussel shell to separate iris fibers for rope and twine, the latter device probably derived from Northwest California. The Coast Yuki bow was sinew-wrapped, not sinew-backed. Although an ocean-dwelling people, they used no boats.

Coast Yuki men did the hunting and fishing, while women gathered vegetable foods. Everyone collected mussels. The diet consisted principally of salmon, mussels, acorns, and grass seeds, although many other foods—including deer and elk—were also eaten.

Salmon were taken from the South Fork of the Eel River. Sea lions and seals were killed with clubs, harpoons, or bow and arrow. Food was prepared, preserved, and stored as among the Yuki, except that the Coast Yuki did not use earth ovens. Salt was collected from pockets of evaporated ocean spray in the rocks. Dogs were kept, but not eaten, perhaps a reflection of the attitudes toward dogs of the Northwest California tribes (Gifford 1939b:312-330). An extensive list of native ethnoscience terms is given by Gifford (1939b:306-311).

Gifford (1937) has collected many Coast Yuki myths. These contain a good number of maritime characters, reflecting the littoral environment and implying long residence in the area.

Synonymy

The Yuki names for the Coast Yuki are formed from ʔúʔuk̲hoṭʰ 'ocean' (literally 'big water'; "Wappo," this vol.) and mean 'those on the ocean' or 'ocean people'. Spellings of the Yuki proper name are Ùk-hoat-nom (Powers 1877:126) and Ukhót-no‘m (Curtis 1907-1930, 14:186), and of the Coast Yuki equivalent Oo-ko-ton-tel-ka, Oo-kōt-ón-til-kah (Merriam 1910-1929), and Ukoht-ontilka (Kroeber 1925:212). A Pomoan name, supposed to mean this same thing (Kroeber 1925:212), has been rendered Camebell-Poma (Anonymous 1860:15), Camel-el-pomas (Tobin 1858:405), Kam-a-lel Pomo (Powers 1877:155), and Kam-ah-lel po-mah (Merriam 1910-1929). Other names are Bedatoe, after a Pomoan name for Ten Mile River (ARCIA 1859:301; Kroeber 1925:212), and Bayma-pomas (Tobin 1858:405).

Sources

Knowledge of Coast Yuki life is adequate but not complete. The principal ethnographic source is Gifford (1939b). Kroeber (1925) contains a brief account. Some historical information may be found in L. Palmer (1880). A list of specimens attributed to the Coast Yuki in the Robert H. Lowie Museum of Anthropology, University of California, Berkeley, is contained in Thomsen and Heizer (1964).

Wappo

JESSE O. SAWYER

Language

Wappo (ˈwäpō) belongs to a small family of four languages including Yuki, Coast Yuki, and Huchnom. Wappo has always been considered the most different of the four; Elmendorf (1968) argues that the other three are mutually intelligible dialects while Wappo stands as a separate language. The fact that Wappo has lost the Proto-Yukian system of tones is sound evidence for assuming that Wappo has innovated more freely than have the three dialects that constitute the other branch of Yukian. This must be true because Wappo sometimes confuses lexical items that differ only in tone in Yuki. Looking for cognate words between Yuki and Wappo does not produce a particularly impressive array. Mostly one finds very short sequences, root syllables presumably, in which either the initial and a medial vowel or an initial consonant, the medial vowel, and a final consonant match rather well. An example would be Yuki k̇ismik̇ 'bathing, swimming' as compared with Wappo čése? 'swimming'.*

Fieldwork in both Yuki and Wappo uncovered some of the reasons for the assurance on the part of earlier investigators of genetic relationship (Kroeber 1925: 159-160; Radin 1929:7; Elmendorf 1968:2-6). The systems of sounds found in Yuki and Wappo are much alike, differing largely in the fact that Yuki has tones, nasalized vowels, and a set of back velar consonants that do not exist in Wappo; and Wappo has a series of affricates, c, ċ, cʰ, that do not appear in Yuki. Moreover, a three-dimensional pronominal system, the alienable-inalienable contrast, and certain kinship terms in common in both languages (although the individual terms may

not be alike in sound) point to a close relationship. The verb morphology is also similar in many details. In addition there are noun compounds that are identical translations though none of the morphemes is cognate. For instance Yuki ?ú?uk̇hoṭʰ 'water big, ocean' is exactly reflected in Wappo laYméy 'big water, ocean'. The word order difference is unimportant in that neither language places great weight on word order.

Wappo has been considerably influenced by the languages with which it has had contact. There are borrowings from all the languages that surround the Wappo island—the Lake and Coast Miwok; the Southern, Eastern, and Southeastern Pomo; and various Wintun dialects. The exact nature of these influences is not now fully known but the data necessary for determining the influences will be available eventually.

The effect of Spanish on Wappo has been quite great in the realm of vocabulary. The Wappo borrowed the Spanish terms for most of the things they were to borrow from Western culture. These borrowings occur in two or three identifiable strata: (1) terms preceding the physical presence of Spanish speakers, words for trade items and words sifted from one Indian language to another moving wavelike in advance of the approach of the Spanish themselves, (2) words that can be associated with the missions and with direct contact with Spanish speakers (r first appears as a Wappo consonant during this period; in the earlier period Spanish r was Wappo l), and (3) the few items that appear to have been adopted after the mission period.

The fact that Radin (1929:7) found small Spanish influence on the Wappo vocabulary arises out of the fact that there is little Spanish in the vocabulary of the texts he collected. Since his texts were mostly traditional and did not include obvious situations drawing on western culture, it is apparent why no Spanish vocabulary appeared. The vocabulary of daily life was, of course, that part of the language in which Spanish influence appeared.

A rarer evidence of the effect of western culture occurs in a few translation descriptions. To cross oneself was to 'count one's own head'. Reading was 'counting paper'. And butter may still be referred to as mánte·ka? or alternatively as ?èyk̇a čéyu 'baby feces'. Rarer still was the influence of English, which left practically no mark on the language at all.

---

*Italicized Wappo words are written by the author in a phonemic orthography with the following symbols: p, t, ṭ, s, š, c, ċ, čʰ, k, l, m, n, w, W, y, Y, h, ? and the vowels

    i   u

   a e o.

t and ṭ are fronted and backed sounds, respectively, the fronted not too unlike English th in thin; ṭ is close to the English t in loot but with the tongue a bit farther back. c is a sequence like ts. ? is the glottal stop found medially in English "Huhuh!" The vowels occur either long or short. Length is marked with a raised dot. Three degrees of stress occur, the heaviest two marked with an acute accent and a grave accent. Aspiration is marked with ʰ and glottalization with '.

Wappo is said to have been spoken in five dialects—Clear Lake, western or Russian River, northern, central, and southern. Although it is agreed that these were all mutually intelligible differing mostly in a small number of vocabulary items, there is no clear record of such differences. The Berton vocabulary (1880) from Clear Lake does not vary greatly from the contemporary Russian River dialect and the short comparative list of the three northern dialects in Barrett's (1908:112) ethnogeography provides no real differences if one allows for the fact the items identically glossed are not usually comparable. For instance, western and northern *kata* and Clear Lake *katiše* are glossed as 'laugh'; but *kata* undoubtedly was the noun, 'laughter', and *katiše* was not a different dialect form but simply the verb form 'laughs'. There are forms, but very few, suggesting a closer relation between the Northern Wappo and the Clear Lake Wappo but the evidence is so slight as to be questionable. The conclusion seems to be that the Wappo dialect areas were not significant.

Territory

The territory in which the Wappo dialects were spoken consisted of two divisions, one large and the other small. The small division held a patch of little more than five square miles on the south edge of Clear Lake. The larger area including the Western, Northern, Central, and Southern subdivisions extended from just above Napa and Sonoma in the south to Cloverdale and Middletown in the north (fig. 1).

The salient feature of Wappo geography has always been its physical separation from the territory of the groups with which its language is most closely related, its existence as an isolate surrounded by the lands of Indians with genetically different language backgrounds. It has always been assumed that this isolation would generate differences in language and in culture that would reflect the separation. In fact, Yuki has preserved a major feature of the protolanguage, the system of tones, that has been lost in Wappo.

A further feature of Wappo territory is the fact that some of the Wappo probably made annual summer excursions to Clear Lake and to the Pacific Ocean. The existence of the permanent Wappo enclave at the south end of Clear Lake must, at least in part, have been the result of this annual trek.

Within these territories and in various directions outside of them there were places with Wappo names. Of the about 100 names that can be found, only *cʰo·nóma*, a probable Wappo place name for the town of Sonoma, remains in use outside the original boundaries. Its etymology is not clear, but Laura Somersal, the last speaker of Wappo, felt that *cʰo·nóma* might have been its origin. The only meaning the word seems to have is 'abandoned camp'. Its likelihood rests in the fact that it appears in

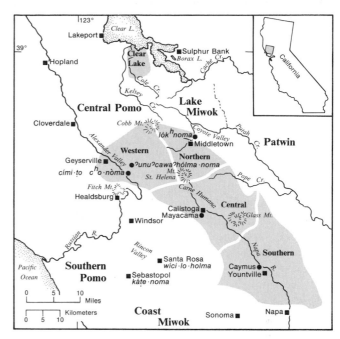

Fig. 1. Tribal territory.

other names, as for instance in *cími·ṭo cʰo·nòma* 'humming bird campsite', a former village site south of the Geyserville rancheria, or *holo·ị́éẁ cʰo·nòma* 'ant campsite', a name for an abandoned campsite between the Russian River and Fitch Mountain. 'Ant campsite' is interesting in being a literal translation of a Southern Pomo name for the place.

Some of the most common morphemes in Wappo place-names are: *nóma* 'camp, place'; *cʰo·nóma* 'abandoned camp'; *nókʰ* 'friend'; *núẏ* 'sand'; *lél* 'stone'; *ʔéyču* 'creek'; *méy* 'water'; *meynán* 'spring'; *hóča* 'sweathouse, dancehouse, cave, hole'; *ịúl* 'field'; *móṭa* 'mountain'; *hól* 'tree, stick, wood'; *hólma* 'woods'; *péṭi* 'barbecue pit'.

Other words occurring in place-names include a variety of trees, bushes, snakes, and birds, mostly appearing in one place-name only. Animal names are curiously absent except for *húị* 'coyote'.

The fact that the Wappo traveled outside their own territories is evidenced by literal translations of Pomo names (Sebastopol is called *káṭe·noma* 'elderberry camp' after its Southern Pomo name) and by names for places that would not possibly have been part of their lands, such as *wíci·lo·holma* 'meadow-lark woods' for Santa Rosa and *meyhínawela* 'water other side' for San Francisco.

History

The archeology of the Napa valley shows occupation from about 2,000 or at most 4,000 years ago (Heizer and

Squier 1953:324). Elmendorf's (1968:8) suggestion of 1000 B.C. for the separation of Wappo from the other Yukian languages matches well with Heizer's 2000 B.C. for the earliest use of the Napa valley Glass Mountain area and suggests that the Wappo may have been the first settlers after the people of the Borax Lake complex (David Fredrickson, personal communication 1973). The physical differences between the Wappo and the Yuki remain a problem. There is no physical evidence to link the Wappo with the shorter, more long-headed Yuki. A possible conclusion is that a Yukian language came to be spoken in the Napa and Russian river areas by a group of Indians not related in blood to Yukian people and that Wappo is the language and people resulting. Again, the example of the tones is suggestive. The fact that the Wappo appear to have confused vocabulary items that differed in Yuki only in tone implies that the language movement was from the Yukian source to the Wappo and not the reverse, at least in that feature.

There remains the problem of the separation of the Wappo language by Pomo land from the other languages to which it is related. Did the Pomo intrude and separate the Wappo or did a group of Yukian speakers migrate? The evidence is tenuous but seems to lean toward migration.

In their later history the Wappo were considerably influenced by the languages and cultures surrounding them. They were probably always a minority and by and large they seemed to get along well with the people around them.

One of the few known exceptions to their generally peaceful reputation among other Indians was the Wappo-Pomo war. The Wappo apparently attacked the Alexander Valley Pomo who had carried off some Wappo supplies of acorns. In the two attacks made a number of Pomo were killed. The Pomo sought peace, which was granted at once, but they never returned to their Alexander Valley villages. The abandonment of the Alexander Valley to the Wappo is the only documented account of any change in the boundaries between the Wappo and the surrounding tribes.

The Napa valley Wappo must have fought bitterly and unsuccessfully against the Spanish. The remainder were drafted for labor from time to time but seem not to have actually gone to war. Some were held at the mission at Sonoma between 1823 and 1834; these must have included Wappo from all parts of the territory. Among the names of villages represented in the mission at Sonoma appear many that were probably Wappo: Conoma, Canijolmano, Caymus, Locnoma, Mayacama, Utinomanoc. Russian River villages seem not to be included, but the Spanish loanwords in Western Wappo leave no doubt that the mission was a powerful influence. This influence can only be interpreted as due to primary contact with Spanish—for western as well as southern dialects. In 1842 there were still 70 Indians at Sonoma Mission. Of course, only a fraction of these were Wappo. Whether the Franciscan mission Saint Turibius founded in 1870 on the south shores of Clear Lake ever had any influence on the Wappo is unknown but appears unlikely.

In 1856 the ill-starred reservation at Mendocino was established, and 240 Wappo were moved there from the Russian River valley. Two years later, although about 1,500 Indians had been moved there, only 722 remained. In 1867 the reservation was closed. The Mendocino reservation was remembered by the Indians—and it is still remembered—as a place of fear and uncertainty or worse.

The settlement of Wappo at Clear Lake has always been little known. Even the name, lileʔek, is untranslatable although it may be the Wappo word for 'lake' in one of the less-known dialects, lile 'flat', ʔek 'water'. Compare meyléle 'water flat, lake' in the Russian River dialect and ʔukšiʔ 'drink', the root ʔuk of which may be the source of ʔek in lileʔek. Certainly Wappo came to Clear Lake to fish, even up to very recent times, particularly during the spawning season. Perhaps some simply stayed year-round. A probably true story tells of a disagreement over the Cole and Kelsey creeks fishing rights that ended in the Wappos' using their digging sticks to effect a juncture of the creeks near their mouth. This story is important in that it places a permanent settlement of Wappo on Clear Lake perhaps as early as 1810 and weakens other arguments for a later settlement there (Barrett 1908:192–193). Now and then the settlement was augmented unexpectedly. Laura Somersal told of a gathering of Indians in the Russian River area who had abandoned their permanent homes and supplies in preparation for some ultimate religious cataclysm. When their numbers became too great the army was called in and the Indians were driven or fled to Clear Lake. Among this group was the grandmother of Laura Somersal (who also figured in Laura's knowledge of the Mendocino reservation).

In 1851 Francis Berton, the Swiss consul at San Francisco, visited the Clear Lake settlement and wrote down a small vocabulary of Clear Lake Wappo words. In 1879 he informed his editor that the group had entirely disappeared.

Sometime before 1877 J.R. Bartlett took down a wordlist from "a tribe living near Knight's farm, at the head of the valley toward Clear Lake" (Powers 1877:483). A sufficient number of the words recorded share differences found in Berton's list to suggest that these may have been part of the group at Clear Lake or at least closely related to them. It is unfortunate that the lists are not really complete enough to be useful.

After Clear Lake little remains to be chronicled except the final disappearance of the Wappo as a viable group. Population estimates are difficult to interpret. In 1836,

258

8,000 Indians were reported in the Napa valley (Yount 1966:154–155), including one group of Miwok and four of Wappo. By 1855 Yount thought no more than 500 Wappo remained in the valley. Of 3,000 Indians in the Napa valley in 1843, including Wappo and Wintun, 400 were said to live in the Wappo village Caymus. Kroeber (1925:221) estimated 500 to 1,000 for the total Wappo "former number." In 1860, 240 Wappo moved from the Russian River area above Healdsburg to the Mendocino reservation. By 1908 the estimated population of Wappo, Huchnom, and Yuki combined was only 40, excluding the mixed but largely Yuki population of Round Valley. Yet in the 1910 census, 73 persons reported themselves as Wappo, three-fifths of them full-blood (Kroeber 1925:221). Although Radin (1929:7) estimated that in 1917, 20 Wappo had some knowledge of the language, only one had any extensive knowledge of the mythology. By 1960 perhaps five Wappos had some knowledge of the language. From a partial survey of the California Roll of 1970, there were an estimated 50 persons of Wappo parentage then living (Cook, personal communication 1973).

Nonmaterial Culture

The Wappo were found by Driver to have a very simple culture, perhaps one of the least complex to have been reported in the Americas. It is conceivable that this simplicity is the result of some upheaval in the not too remote past of the Wappo or it could represent the effects of repeated and conflicting contacts with the diverse groups surrounding the Wappo. Of course, estimates of ethnographic complexity largely ignore the life of the mind, which may have loomed large among them: the language encourages that kind of complexity.

Village Organization

The sociopolitical unit was the village, which was usually located on a creek or near other sources of water and included one or two sweathouses. The last native village reported, ʔunuʔcawaʔhólma·noma 'Toyon Woods Camp' (Driver 1936:201–207), consisted in 1870 of 11 grass houses serving 21 families totaling 92 persons. Occupants in each house ranged from 21 to 4, averaging 9 with an average of 4.5 persons in each family. The Wappo claimed at least seven villages in the Geyserville area of the Russian River, at least four with as many as 40 houses. If this claim is realistic, then Kroeber's guess that the original total Wappo population never exceeded 1,000 would be incorrect, since the Geyserville area of the western group would alone have totaled more than 1,500.

The office of chief reflected a tendency of the group to reject any kind of imposition of authority. The chief could be elected, appointed, or chosen by virtue of functioning in one or more of the roles for which a need was felt. He might train his own successor or his successor might assert himself in a similar role or in a different one. The interest of the tribe in one activity or another might result in the existence of more than one chief at one time. When a woman was chief—and there have been several—her function was somewhat curtailed in that she would not ordinarily direct the male activities in the same way they might be directed by a male. The four functions served by the chiefs included (1) relations with other villages, including warfare, (2) internal functioning of the village, (3) dances, ceremonies, and medicine, and (4) transmission of news and information. The position was held until death. A successor would simply be any other chief in the village whose following was larger than that of others.

Life Cycle

Birth was marked by the most complex couvade to be found in North America. For four days or more both the mother and father were confined under rigid taboos intended to guarantee the welfare of the child. An unwanted child could be killed by the mother immediately after birth.

No ceremonies accompanied the adolescence of the male child, but a girl's first menstruation began with four days of confinement in the menstrual room during which the girl could have no animal food and drank from a special basket. When necessary she could leave the room by a private exit, but with her head covered in deerskin. She dared not see the sun, the moon, or any snake. At the end of four days, bathed and sung over, she was allowed the freedom of the house but could not move freely out of doors until after her second menstruation. Subsequent menstruation was marked by the food taboos and the four-day confinement but the deerskin was not required when leaving the house. The husband's activities were also curtailed during each four-day menstrual confinement of the wife.

Marriage was relatively informal. Only one wife was allowed although in recent times it was not uncommon for a man to have two wives in different places. Even such arrangements may have been effectively monogamous. Relatives could not marry, and intervillage marriages were frequent. A marriage ceremony consisted of an exchange of equal gifts between the two families and a day of feasting and celebration. A marriage was difficult to achieve if either family disapproved. Divorce was equally informal. One partner simply went away. However, there are accounts of wives who went after an errant husband, collared him, and brought him more or less forcibly home.

Death brought no more panoply than marriage or divorce. The day after a death the body, washed and dressed in its best, was carried by six men on three sticks to a pyre prepared a mile or more from the village. Most of the dead person's personal effects would be burned with the body. The women related to the dead person would cut off their hair and put clay on their heads. They scored their flesh with their nails and with pieces of flint. All wailed in a rhythm reminiscent of the dances. Occasionally a wife or mother of a dead man would attempt to throw herself upon the pyre. She would inevitably be held back. In the twentieth century burial replaced cremation.

External Relations

To speak of war in the context of Wappo culture is somewhat incongruous. Life was not easy and at times some token of serious protest was required in order to maintain one's territory and to protect one's own life. The raids and avenging expeditions which took place stemmed for the most part from stealing, murder, and poisoning. None of these except conceivably stealing was likely to involve more than one or two persons in opposition to the group. The skirmishes with the Spanish or Spanish and Indians in the Napa valley were different in that large numbers fought or were killed; even there, however, the scale and intensity of war was not great. In most engagements, an attack terminated when one important person was killed or the sun went down. At most a full-scale "war" might end with the death of 6 or 10 people. Women and children were usually spared. Weapons, clothing, and eagle wings were the trophies usually taken. The dead were burned on the battlefield; enemy dead were abandoned, sometimes with their eyes gouged out. Victory was normally followed by a celebration of dancing and feasting to which one's neighbors were invited.

If war did not loom large, trade did not loom large either. In early times bows and yellowhammer headbands were imported from the north. After this trade ceased other minor importations continued. A small fish caught in the creeks emptying into Clear Lake continued to be sought after until the end of the nineteenth century. Magnesite cylinders were also imported from Lake County. In 1960 only the abalone and clamshells and seaweed that came from the coast recalled the ancient ways. The last items to survive as trade items were the foods that had to be imported from distant places. A minor exchange of basketmaking materials and clamshell beads also existed as trade activity in the 1960s.

Closely connected with trade and the food economy was travel. The Wappo were seasonal and inveterate travelers, particularly in the Russian River area. A minor kind of travel involved moving one's domicile each year from the permanent villages on the high ground to the summer camps along the river. This seasonal movement may have been more usual along the Russian River than elsewhere because that river regularly flooded vast expanses of the lowlands along its banks and a permanent camp could easily be a mile or two away from the path taken by the river in summer. Even

in the 1970s a week of camping on the river or a trip to the coast are prime sources of pleasure.

Originally trips to the coast allowed the Wappo to secure firsthand their favorite shells: clam, abalone, and the mussels that were once used as spoons. They also brought back various fish, shellfish, and seaweed, which has always been popular. The Pomo and Miwok through whose lands they passed seem not to have objected. The Wappo name for Sebastopol is probably evidence of one stop along the two-day annual trip to the ocean. A similar but much shorter trip to Clear Lake was made several times each spring and summer for fish and probably for magnesite. The fish were dried at the lake, a process requiring at least one or two days, bringing each trip to a minimum of four days or more.

Other travel included Glass Mountain near Calistoga from which obsidian was available. By far the most important travel may have been to dances and celebrations at Nicasio, Yountville, Hopland, Sulphur Bank, Lakeport, and Coyote Valley near Middletown among, probably, a variety of places near and far. Record of travel is available only for the Russian River area. Intermarriages going back a century have led to including the Wappo among the Kashaya Pomo at Stewart's Point in the dances and celebrations held there. In spite of extensive travel, Wappos have remained faithful to their original lands and return there regardless of the attractions of other places.

Activities

Visits to neighboring groups may have occurred most commonly on feast days, occasions of celebration usually marked by dancing. It is difficult now to know what Wappo dancing might have been like. A half-dozen songs survive that are called Wappo, but no analysis of them has been done. They may be borrowed from the Pomo as are all the instruments: plank drum, cocoon rattle, split-stick clapper, double-boned whistle, and flute.

There is no doubt that the Wappo were devoted dance enthusiasts, as they were of all their amusements. The fact that they borrowed from their neighbors seems to mean that the songs, dances, and games were shared over large areas comprising people completely unrelated. A singer leading a dance might know the songs and dances of many tribes. His success and fame rested in part on the wideness of his repertory. The dance leader seems to have been a doctor, and the dances were not just a pleasant amusement but part of a shamanistic ritual the details of which are for the Wappo largely unrecoverable.

Games too were essentially those of the Pomo: the grass game, shinny, dice, and various guessing games, as well as a variety of games involving tests of strength and physical prowess. Card games were introduced by the Spanish together with all the terminology needed for play. The terms were applied later to card games introduced by American settlers. The use by the Wappo of the tarotlike names of the Spanish card deck for the French deck brought by the American settlers is surprising and in part anachronistic: hearts, *kó·pa?*, Spanish 'cups'; diamonds *?ó·ro?*, 'coins'; clubs *wástu?*, Spanish *basto;* and spades *?áspa·ẟa?*, Spanish *espada* 'swords'.

Religion

Whatever the religion of the Wappo may have been, its unique aspects have certainly been lost. What remains is essentially identical with some Pomo tradition. Connections with the Kuksu cult are also probable. The only clues lie in the language, and one fact stands out: there may have been some sort of taboo on animal names. Animal names other than coyote do not appear in place-names, although they do appear freely in personal names. Moreover, the word for deer is borrowed from Pomo, and no clear single word exists for bird or rabbit. Both are *číča,* which seems to mean 'a bird or rabbit prepared for cooking'. Such mild taboos may only have reflected the hunter's unwillingness to name his object or may have been accidental.

The individual family certainly observed a variety of vague superstitions designed to make life safe and comfortable. Four was the magic number. A four-day celebration ending on the fourth of July was a latter-day epitome of a "big time." Four cents each was the price of clamshell beads in the 1960s.

Relatives by marriage did not use one another's personal names. The names of relatives by marriage are still avoided. The names of the dead were also avoided.

Material Culture

The last traditional village for which descriptions survive (Driver 1936:201–210) consisted of 11 oval houses oriented north and south on the east side of a creek and east-west on the other, near Geyserville. Made of grass thatch over a framework of bent poles, each house had a door and a smoke hole for each family occupying the structure. In the twentieth century, houses were of lumber (figs. 2, 3). Tools consisted for the most part of stones and sticks and shells (figs. 4, 5). Wedges, axes, and fire drills were used. Animal skins were scraped. Shells and baskets served for dishes. Only the baskets were decorated, and the art of basketmaking, probably strongly influenced by the Pomo, was the Wappos' one great art. Upon baskets they lavished their greatest efforts. The proportions are satisfying and the various decorations were executed with care and great attention to detail. Certainly their basketwork ranks with the best of the world's basketwork. Again, however, it is difficult to determine which elements were uniquely Wappo. More likely than not, few were.

Fig. 2. Mishewal rancheria, with houses of late type and sunshade on left. Photograph by C. Hart Merriam, July 1927.

Money existed in the form of clamshell beads and magnesite cylinders, both of which were worn as decorations. Food included a variety of saltwater and freshwater creatures among which were abalone, clams, mussels, crabs, eels, turtles, bullheads, chub, salmon. Ducks, geese, and quail were eaten as well as deer and rabbit. The most important plant foods were acorns, buckeye, a variety of roots, and a wide range of "clovers." Seaweed was dried and brought back from the coast as a flavoring. Salt came from a lake near Valley Ford, and sweet pitch and honey were secured locally. Breakfast was at eight or nine in the morning; dinner, at sundown.

An interesting aspect of Wappo cooking was the existence of a variety of Mexican dishes, some of which may have been learned and preserved from the period of first Spanish contact. The early vocabulary, that dating from the period before the founding of the missions at San Rafael and Sonoma in 1817 or 1823, includes the following items (Sawyer 1964:173):

Wappo	Spanish	English
čí·čalo?	*chícharo*	pea
tíli·ku?	*trigo*	wheat
híwhoł	*frijol*	bean
?áli·na?	*harina*	flour
toltí·ya?	*tortilla*	tortilla
číčlo?	*chicharrón*	crackling
wése·lu?	*becerro*	calf
wóle·ka?	*borrego*	sheep
?isáł	*asar, guisado*	fried
?isáłsa?	*asar, guisado*	fry
saltéň	*sartén*	frying pan
kúča·la?	*cuchara*	spoon
déne·do?	*tenedor*	fork
tíhe·la?	*tijera*	scissors

Probably to these should be added the various combinations of *šáwo,* originally a Nahuatl word that came to mean 'bread' and for a variety of which a Wappo recipe

Dept. of Anthr., U. of Calif., Berkeley.

Fig. 3. House at Mishewal rancheria on west side of Russian River, south of Jimtown Bridge. Photograph by C. Hart Merriam, July 1927.

still survives, *húmiš šàwo* 'fried bread', which may have been original. In 1960 it was still possible to find a Wappo breakfasting on a tortilla folded around fried seaweed.

The unique qualities of the Wappo were their kindness and their self-effacing qualities. They spoiled their children. Children were normally raised by any senior female relative who was no longer producing children of her own. They held firmly to their lands and families; however, property was essentially a disfavored concept.

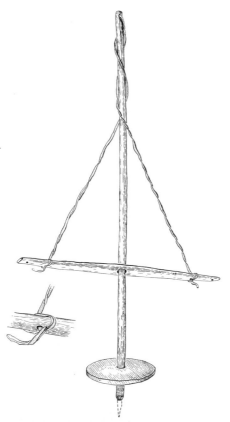

Lowie Mus., U. of Calif., Berkeley: 1-233750.

Fig. 4. Pump drill for beads. Wood with leather thongs; flint point is missing. Length 62.8 cm, made and used by Jack Woho about 1900.

Lowie Mus., U. of Calif., Berkeley: 1-14513.

Fig. 5. Wooden mush paddle. Length 66.0 cm, collected 1908.

Private ownership almost implied piracy or seizure. One owned something only at the expense of someone else. Life moved in a leisurely way with few excitements. If you met a friend and you had two pieces of news, you would tell him the first when his visit was half over and the second about halfway between the first announcement and his departure. A death would be announced as an example of bad luck. Although a quite usual causative meaning occurs in the Wappo verb, one won't hear or see it very often. In most situations to force anyone to do anything is immoral. In part, of course, these are attributes found widely in California, but the Wappo were endowed with more of these qualities than most.

Synonymy

The name Wappo is believed to be a borrowing of the Spanish word *guapo* 'harsh, severe; daring, brave; handsome, showy'. Almost any of these meanings may justify the name, but tradition has it that the Wappo got their name because they were harsh, severe, and brave in opposing the Spanish-American invasion of their lands and destruction of their culture, particularly in the Napa valley. This etymology seems slightly questionable, but no better one has been offered. In any case, the name was probably not used by the Indians themselves, a fact sig-

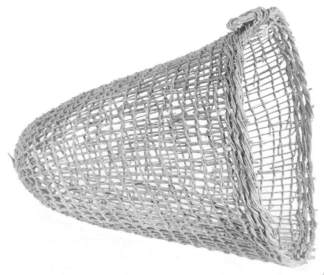

Lowie Mus., U. of Calif., Berkeley: 1-14505.

Fig. 6. Openwork carrying basket. Rim diameter 42 cm, collected 1908.

SAWYER

Fig. 7. Twined meal sieve. Rim diameter 29.7 cm, collected 1901.

naled by the absence of the final glottal stop that marks all but one or two of the Spanish loanwords used by the Wappo. They called themselves the ʔonaʞátis 'the people who speak plainly and truthfully, the outspoken ones'. This name may not have been used outside the Russian River villages and does not appear in any of the older writings in which the Wappo are mentioned.

Other names derived from *guapo* are Guapos, Wapo, Wappa, Wattos.

Ashochemies or Ash-o-chi-mi was a Pomo, probably Southern Pomo, name for the Wappo. Etymologically, it must refer to a specific village, as the -chi-mi exactly translates the Wappo place-name suffix *-nóma*, which was said to mean 'place where we used to live, abandoned campsite'.

Mishewal was a Lake Miwok name for the Alexander Valley. The *-wal* apparently meant 'place'. The 'Santa Rosa Language, Wappo' was *míṣṣowal ʞáataw* in Lake Miwok (Callaghan 1965:153, 94). In the 1960s surviving Wappo thought that the Mishewal were a group of Wappo who had lived somewhere around Geyserville. Obviously this is again a foreign word for part of the territory they occupied.

Carne humana given as a Spanish name for lands around Calistoga is a folk etymology of a name that has appeared as kolijolmanok and as Conahomanas (Yount 1966:153). This is Wappo *ʞáni-* or *kolihólmanokʰ*, literally 'person/back[?] woods people'. The phrase referred to the people living at a specific wooded place in the Napa valley south of Calistoga.

Mayacama, perhaps one of the most frequent names for the Napa valley Wappo, appears as Miyahkmah, Maiyakma, Mayacomos, Myacomas, and so on. It is probably a Miwok name, but its origins and relations are unknown.

In their earlier contacts with western culture, Wappo were also known as Rincon, Caymus, Indiens de la Vallée de Napa et du Clear Lake and Lili'ek. The multiplicity of names reflects the fact that there was no unitary Wappo tribe as such, assuming that all were Wappo who spoke Wappo. The only tribal name was ʔonaʞátis, and this name seems to have been unknown and unused by the groups surrounding the Wappo.

Sources

Information about the Wappo is scant and generally incomplete. Driver's (1936) account is the best ethnography. Archeological studies (Greengo and Shutler 1953; McClellan 1953) give some idea of earlier history but for that area only. For later history read Yount (1966). Merriam (1955:43–48) is useful in explaining the relations between the Miwok and the Wappo, relations that have resulted in an exchange of loanwords between the two languages.

For information about Wappo language and literature the texts and grammar by Radin (1924, 1929) are not so useful as one might hope. Sawyer (1964, 1965) and fieldwork (1958–1968) provide linguistic studies. For language history Elmendorf (1968) contains the largest collection available. For discussions of remote relations of Yukian consult Gursky (1965), Elmendorf (1963), and particularly Shipley (1957).

Lake Miwok

CATHERINE A. CALLAGHAN

Language and Territory

Linguistically, the Lake Miwok ('mē₁wäk) are Penutian speakers and represent the northermost extension of the Mewan or Moquelumnan linguistic stock. The Lake Miwok were linguistically isolated from other Miwok peoples to the south but were in frequent contact with peoples of other linguistic stocks, such as the Pomo and to a lesser extent, Wappo. Neighboring groups included the Eastern Pomo *xa·bé-na·pʰò* on the northwest, the Southeastern Pomo *qámdot* on the north, bands of foothills Patwin to the east, and the Wappo (Miyahk'-mah) on the west (Merriam 1955:48).

The Lake Miwok language* is closely related to Coast Miwok, spoken from the Marin Peninsula north to Bodega Bay, and more distantly related to the Eastern Miwok languages, formerly occupying the western slopes of the Sierra Nevadas and stretching inland from Ione to Stockton. There was also an Eastern Miwok speech area (Saclan) somewhere around the Walnut Creek-Lafayette area.

The Miwok family is in turn related to Costanoan, extending from San Francisco south to Monterey, with a probable pocket on the southern end of the Marin Peninsula. Miwok-Costanoan may be more distantly related to other Penutian languages.

The Lake Miwok were hunters and gatherers who had permanent dwelling areas along the drainages of several small creeks and stream valleys south of Clear Lake. Apparently no settlements were situated on the lake itself; rather the upper affluents of Cache Creek (the outlet of Lower Lake) and the tributary headwaters of Putah Creek comprised the territory in which major village sites were located (fig. 1).

The oldest Lake Miwok settlement was *tú·leyomi* 'deep place' located three or four miles south of Lower Lake. This is Old Man Coyote's home and the site of many myths. *tú·leyomi* was a general designation for a larger area, apparently analagous to the entire Lake Miwok

* The orthography used for italicized words in Lake Miwok is the phonemic one developed by the author, in which a few substitutions of symbols have been made to conform to standard Handbook usage. The inventory is: (voiceless unaspirated stops) *p, t, ṭ* (retroflex), *k, ʔ;* all the former except *ʔ* also occur aspirated, for example, *pʰ,* and glottalized, like *p̓;* (voiced stops) *b, d;* (voiceless unaspirated affricates) *c, č;* (voiceless glottalized affricates) *c̓, č̓, ƛ̓;* (spirants *s, ṣ, ł, h;* (nasals) *m, n;* (sonants) *w, l, r, y;* (vowels—all occur both short and long, marked by a raised dot) *i, e, u, o, a.*

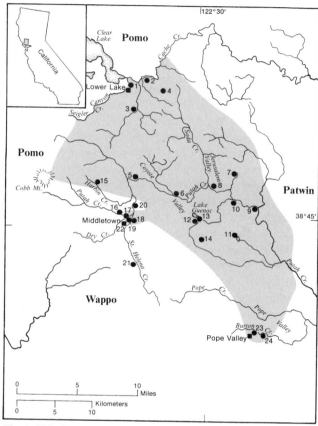

Fig. 1. Tribal territory and villages. 1, *cíccapukut;* 2, *ká·wiyomi;* 3, *tú·leyomi;* 4, *ʔaló·ko pó·ye* (?); 5, *kílli yó·kepukut* (?); 6, *ʔolé·yomi;* 7, *tumístumis;* 8, Wo-de'-di-teṗpe po'goot; 9, *ṣó·yomi;* 10, *hukúhyomi;* 11, Kebū'lpūkūt; 12, Haw'-hawl-po-goot; 13, *ṣálṣalpukut;* 14, *ṣáttiyomipukut;* 15, Kū-pē'tcū; 16, Pe'tīnōma; 17, Kah-dah'-yo-me; 18, *lálmukpukut* (?); 19, *lakíhyomipukut;* 20, Ūyū'hanōma; 21, Mēhwale'lenoma; 22, *wí·lokyomi;* 23, *có·kyomi púkut;* 24, *ʔalókyomi púkut.*

All names from Barrett 1908 and Merriam 1955; those italicized have been respelled by Catherine Callaghan (with doubtful spellings queried). The names of 16, 20, and 21 are Wappo.

territory (Merriam 1955:43-48). Merriam (1907) notes that the designation Tu'-le-am'-me for the Lake Miwok derives from an ancient settlement with this name situated a few miles south of Lower Lake and was perhaps the ruling village of the northern division (Merriam 1955:43). O'-lā-am'me (*ʔolé·yomi* 'coyote place') is the name of a more recent, southerly settlement in Coyote Valley along Putah Creek, which may have been the principal village of the southern division.

History

Early contact with Whites was highly traumatic. On November 6, 1821, Luis Arguello, in command of a military escort of 67 men, entered Lake Miwok territory and passed through several villages, one of which he identified as "Oleyomi" (Arguello 1821). Several Lake Miwok guides whom he had pressed into service "escaped" on November 8, apparently when the contingent entered Wappo territory.

Mission records from San Rafael, Sonoma, and San José indicate that neophytes were obtained from Lake Miwok villages during the period of forced conversion in the early 1800s (Merriam 1955:175-187).

Ranchers to the south often kidnapped Indians from the Lake Miwok area to use as a work force. One rancher, Salvador Vallejo, set out in March 1843 with a large party of citizens to attack Lake Miwok settlements, purportedly in retribution for the theft of a cow near Sonoma and also to secure a labor force for the harvesting of his wheat crop. He massacred numerous Indians during a raid in the Clear Lake area in which he took several hundred Indians prisoners (Bancroft 1886-1890, 4:362-363; Heizer 1973:66-74). In June 1848 Salvador Vallejo's brother, Mariano G. Vallejo, signed a treaty of nonaggression with a number of Lake Miwok chiefs, ostensibly to keep the peace between Indians and Whites "in and about the Big Lakes on the Sonoma Frontier of Upper California" (Heizer and Hester 1970a:108-109).

The first Americans in the area were Andrew Kelsey and Charles Stone, who bought out Salvador Vallejo's grazing operation in Sonoma. Their brutal treatment of the Indians triggered a number of incidents that culminated in the murder of Kelsey and Stone in 1849. Regular United States troops from Sonoma proceeded, in 1850, to slaughter a large number of Indians who had retreated to an island on Clear Lake (Heizer 1973).

Kroeber (1925:275, 883) estimated that the aboriginal Lake Miwok population did not number in excess of 500 persons. Barrett (1908:316) noted the existence of one inhabited Lake Miwok village in 1903, Hukuhyume, on Putah Creek. The village consisted of six houses, a small dance house, and about 25 inhabitants who had established the settlement about 30 years before by coming several miles downstream from the old village of ʔolé·yomi.

In the 1905 census of California Indians undertaken by Kelsey (1906), 41 Lake Miwoks were represented. Barrett (1908:42-43) closely approximated this figure, giving 35 individuals as the 1908 "Moquelumnan" population. A federal census in 1910 counted only seven individuals, which may be assumed to reflect only a fraction of the total population at that time (Kroeber 1957a:224). The only remaining Lake Miwok settlement in 1975 is wí·lokyomi 'dusty place', the Middletown rancheria. In 1972 a few older speakers of Lake Miwok lived there.

Formerly, the inhabitants lived in kilá·yomi 'old place' on Richard's Ranch.

Environment and Subsistence

Hunting, gathering, and trading expeditions took Lake Miwoks from the top of the Coast Range to Bodega Bay, giving them intimate familiarity and use of a wide ecological range. Settlements were usually located along stream courses in fertile valleys, and the surrounding inner Coast Range environment included chaparral and live oak woodlands in the canyons and lower foothills. At high elevations, coniferous vegetation was composed of Douglas fir (Pseudotsuga menziesii), sugar pine (Pinus lambertiana), and yellow pine (Pinus ponderosa).

The oak woodlands, which formed the prevalent vegetation in the inhabited valleys, supplied many important economic plants. Several species of oak (notably the valley oak, Quercus lobata), madrone (Arbutus menziesii), and buckeye (Aesculus californica), were common. Along the stream bottoms, pepperwood or California laurel (Umbellularia californica) and willow (Salix spp.) were abundant. Common shrubs included manzanita (Arctostaphylos spp.) and poison oak (Rhus diversiloba); and a variety of flowering plants and grasses provided greens, seeds, and bulbs.

Important mammals included deer, elk, grizzly bear, rabbits, and squirrels, while numerous species of birds including quail, woodpeckers, and waterfowl were common. Trout and other small freshwater fish were found in the larger streams.

The acorn was the starch staple. Several species of acorn were gathered in the fall and later pounded into flour and leached with cold water in a sand basin, to be made into soup or bread. Acorn mush was cooked in watertight baskets by stone-boiling; acorn cakes were made by mixing valley oak acorn flour with a red soil called "Indian baking powder," which counteracted the tannic acid. Half acorn kernels were added, the cakes were put in a nest of black oak leaves and placed between layers of hot rocks, then the pile was covered with dirt and left overnight. The cakes emerged black all the way through and sweet.

The Lake Miwok ate the nuts of both the yellow and sugar pines and sometimes roasted green cones and ate the seeds. They also chewed the pitch of the yellow pine. Buckeye nuts were made edible by boiling them in hot water until the shells came off and then mashing and leaching the fruit in cold running water. Manzanita berries were dried and pounded into a flour that was later dampened, rolled into balls, and eaten as candy. Pepperwood berries were also roasted and eaten. Pinole was made from wild grains that were toasted with coals in a basket.

Seawood was dried, baked, and later eaten. Mineral salt came from mountain and creek deposits.

A variety of plant sources was utilized for natural dye. Green oak galls were squeezed to produce permanent blue-black ink for tattooing. Burned pepperwood berries were employed to mark the skin for dance ceremonies. Boiled tan oak bark was used to dye fish nets.

Deer (ṣúkki) was the most important game animal and was hunted all year long; ṣúkki was also the generic term for meat. Only men hunted ducks and flushed deer with baked clay pellets cast with slings. Deer were often snared along game trails or pursued until worn out. Small animals such as rabbits, quail, and woodpeckers were taken in snares and nets.

Deer meat was eaten fresh or salted and dried into jerky. Deer bones were saved, warmed, and cracked open for the marrow. Ground rabbit bones and deer blood were collected in watertight baskets, allowed to clot, and baked between leaves in the coals. The product had the consistency of cottage cheese but was crumbly.

The Lake Miwok considered roasted yellow jacket grubs a delicacy, and grasshoppers were roasted and eaten.

Both men and women might fish. Some men learned to catch fish with their bare hands. Otherwise, fish were taken in weirs, basketry traps, gigs, and dip nets; they were speared or poisoned in a slow-moving stream with powdered dove weed (*Marah* sp.). When a fish was landed, its spine was broken either by clubbing or biting. Fish were preserved by drying, often on wooden frames outdoors, or were baked in a fashion similar to acorn bread.

Culture

Technology

Basketry was very highly developed, from both an artistic and a utilitarian standpoint (fig. 2). Baskets provided practically all cooking, carrying, and storage containers. Willow sticks were used for the warp, three- and four-stick baskets being watertight. Grass roots gathered in the fall or fresh pine roots usually formed the weft. Bulrush roots, perhaps *Carex* sp. (Gifford and Kroeber 1939:214), were blackened in the ashes and used for the dark part of the design; redbud sprouts (*Cercis occidentalis*) introduced the red ornamentation.

Large baskets provided transport and storage. Men in particular often made and used net sacks and bell-shaped carrying baskets. Loosely woven baskets to serve as strainers, twined winnowing trays, seed beaters, large burden baskets, and tule mats were also manufactured. Infants were carried in cradle baskets (fig. 3) decorated with red-shafted flicker feathers. When the bottom of a basket wore through, it was still useful as a hopper to set over a mortar hole to keep acorn particles from flying off as they were being pounded with a stone pestle.

Ceremonial baskets were decorated with abalone pendants, and bird feathers were woven into beautiful designs (fig. 4). The feathers were taken from birds killed in the spring. Such baskets were stored in dry pepperwood leaves as a protection against moths. These baskets were probably once burned on funeral pyres. After

Lowie Mus., U. of Calif., Berkeley: 1-224810.
Fig. 3. Sitting-type cradle of willow shoots. Length 35 cm, collected about 1910.

Lowie Mus., U. of Calif., Berkeley: 1-230649.
Fig. 2. Lattice twined basket. Diameter 32.8 cm, collected 1908–1912.

Fig. 4. Sun basket with shell beads and abalone pendants and geometrical design of colored feathers. Diameter 29.8 cm, collected 1885-1910.

contact with the Spanish, it became fashionable to weave glass beads into tiny ornamental baskets.

Two-ply string and rope made from milkweed fiber (*Asclepias* sp.) as well as wild grapevine withes served a variety of cordage functions. Bowstrings were made from Indian hemp cordage (*Apocynum* sp.). Dip nets were woven from this same string and tied to a branch. String was strengthened by rubbing it with beeswax.

Blankets were made by intertwining dried strips of rabbit fur with string weft. Woodrat fur strips were added for designs. Deer skins were made into blankets, men's breechclouts, and women's skirts.

Obsidian and flint were used for axes, lance tips, and arrowheads; flaking tools were fashioned from deer antler. Bows were fashioned from hazel, oak, or dogwood, and sinew-backed bows were imported from the Pomo to the north. Elder or willow supplied material for arrows, which were carried in a quiver of wildcat or bear cub fur. Arrows were often poisoned with a powder made by drying and pounding the red sacs of black widow spiders.

Canes were manufactured from manzanita wood. Holes were drilled in ashwood (*Fraxinus* sp.) to make tubular pipes. Wild tobacco (*Nicotiana* sp.) was kept in a fawnskin pouch. Informant John Knight reported that canoes were made by hollowing cottonwood or pine logs, but he never saw one.

Clamshell disk beads formed the medium of exchange. Clamshell and magnesite cylinders were manufactured by the Lake Miwok and were also highly valued. Olivella shell beads were not of monetary value; rather they were worn as ornaments.

Adornment

The hair was cut with a piece of burning wood or an obsidian flake and combed with a frond from a sharp-stalked plant. Both men's and women's hair was braided, and men often wore a woven hair net. A sharped stick or bone was used to make a hole in children's ears. Haliotis pendants and ornaments were commonly worn as adornments.

Structures

Permanent, multifamily dwellings were round houses constructed over an excavation. Poles were used for the framework with a large center pole as support, leaving a hole in the roof to let out smoke and a side opening for a door. Brush, leaves, or tule were piled on the poles and the house covered with dirt. A basket was placed against the door hole at night. Large ceremonial houses (*lámma*) with tunnel entrances were constructed in the same way on a larger scale.

In the summer, willow sticks were set in a square or circle, with brush over them, and tied together with wild grapevines to make a ramada. Small earth-covered sweathouses were also constructed, and sweating by direct heat from a fire was practiced.

Life Cycle

Women gave birth in a special small grass hut. After birth, mother and child were confined to the childbirth hut until the child's umbilical cord fell off. The mother or father carefully disposed of the cord, throwing it away in a certain direction but not watching where it landed. During childbirth and for a period afterward, women were forbidden to eat meat, engage in strenuous work, or travel any great distance. When a baby was named, a string of beads was placed around his neck. He was taken to the sweathouse keeper (*mállele*), who sucked the side of the baby's head and called upon his familiar spirit to make the baby strong. Babies were often named for a person on either side of the family or long-deceased relatives. If a mother died before her baby was weaned, the child was buried with her.

Adoption could occur at any age as the result of instructions during a dream. A family would put beads around a person's neck, and he would be considered a relative.

There is little information on puberty rites. When boys reached adolescence, they went on their first hunt, and both boys and girls fasted for the first time. They abstained from meat other than turtle and fish. One could eat pinole, bread, acorn mush and, more recently, vegetables, potatoes, and rice. Girls fasted to ensure the health of their children. A girl's first menstrual period (*há·ya*) marked the beginning of a complex set of taboos that would also involve her husband once she married. She was confined to the house for eight days during her first menstrual period. She was not allowed to eat flesh or to wash herself, and she had to use a wooden scratching stick. At the end of the eight-day period, she was bathed and given new clothes. Thereafter, a four-day period of seclusion was observed during subsequent menstruations.

A woman could not eat woodpecker for fear her baby would cry a lot. Eating salmon might cause sores on her child's head or eyes, and eating canteloupe could result in a general rash, pimples, or sores on the body. Spleen was avoided at all times for fear of difficult childbirth. Young children of both sexes and pregnant women refrained from eating the woodrat because they believed the sharp nest would appear on the baby's head. A menstruating girl did not walk in the mountains or go down to the creek to bathe. In the latter case, she might get cramps from seeing snakes. She was not allowed to touch other people's food, to drink water after sundown, or to eat with others. To become pregnant, a woman visited *há·yapawih* 'puberty mountain'. Girls did not play with poppies because their breasts might go dry when they had children. A man did not hunt when his wife was menstruating for fear of personal misadventure.

Marriage seems to have been arranged between children by their parents through an exchange of gifts, usually consisting of shell beads and baskets. Upon the death of a husband or wife, levirate or sororate marriage was practiced. Intermarriage with neighboring, non-Miwok-speaking groups was common.

Funerals were times of mourning for all close relatives. According to John Knight, it was the only time adult Indians cried. The dead were cremated or interred, but cremated remains were not immediately buried. Clamshell beads, baskets, and other offerings were thrown into the cremation fire by mourners, and personal possessions were destroyed or interred with the deceased. Later, a grave robber might dig up the treasures. Such a ghoul wore a coyote skin and made coyote noises in the process. It was said he had to be a person with no close relatives because he would die a hard death.

Men and women cut their hair short when in mourning and men refrained from sweating for several days after the funeral. A widow singed her hair and placed a mixture of white clay and pitch on the stubble.

The second burning of the dead was held a year after the death of a prominent person, and the cremated remains were reburned with material offerings. Gifford and Kroeber (1939:221) consider the following ceremony (described by Loeb 1932:119–120) a postcontact phenomenon and possibly of Coast Miwok origin:

> Certain of the doctors dreamed that the dead people wanted food and clothing. They told the yomta [shaman] and the yomta informed the entire village....
>
> A long pole was erected. The image of a man was made

from a deerskin blanket. Beads were put inside this image and it was attached to the top of the pole. The pole was called luma and the image halu (man). In more recent times a banner was also put on top of the pole. The people danced around the pole and piled gifts at its base. Food, consisting of acorns, pinole, meat and fish, was also included in the sacrifice. A yomta stood there and talked and prayed.... The people did not cry at the time, but probably did later when the pole and all the gifts were consumed in flame.

Games

Anyone could participate in a game called *hapómṭi* 'handball'. The ball was a bunch of angelica leaves tied together. Contestants gathered in a circle and batted the ball back and forth with their hands. A player might send the ball to any other player and if he missed, he was out. The game continued until only one person was left.

Women played a dice game called *múlli*. The dice were made by cutting branches in half and then in sections and burning designs into the smooth sides. Each die was about four inches across and eight or nine inches long, and several were used in a game. If they all came burnt side up, the player won. If three marked sides fell face up or face down, the person got a point. There were two teams composed of as many as wanted to play. The side that bid first cast first, each player tossing once until someone failed to make a point. Then the dice passed to the opposing team, and so on until one side had 20 points. The women gambled for clothes and beads.

The grass game (*kóṣi*) also involved gambling and was usually played by two men on a side. A player would take two willow sticks wrapped in grass, one smooth and the other with a strip of bark around the middle, and shift them from hand to hand while singing and dancing. One might also use two rabbit bones, about three inches long, one of which was tied around with string. The object in either case was to guess which hand held the wrapped stick. From time to time the player taunted his opponent, shouting "Guess me! Guess me!" If his opponent guessed wrong, he had to give him a stick from a pile of counters. The one who suggested the game was first guesser. After he missed, his partner guessed until he made a mistake. Then the turn passed to the opponents. The game continued until one side had all the sticks or an agreed number of sticks.

Hoop and pole, shinny, and cat's cradle were also played.

Political Organization

Tribal leadership loosely resided in a hereditary male chief, the *hóypu*, who delivered orations to the people in the dance house, detailing proper behavior and tasks to be performed. An assistant chief (*málle*) helped the *hóypu* in enforcing these administrative harangues. There also existed a female leader known as *má·yen*, and she was often the chief's wife. Political organization was probably no higher than the village level, or on rare occasions, a community of two adjacent villages (Barrett 1908:17). Dance ceremonies were not presided over by the *hóypu*, but by special ceremonial officials.

Religion

• SHAMANISM Shamans (*yómta*) were the ceremonial and religious leaders of the community as well as the doctors. Shamans were of two different types. The sucking doctor (*łú·bak yómta*) sucked or brushed the sick area during a ritual dance to extract the foreign bodies (feathers, stones, obsidian flakes, or charmstones) causing the disease. Sometimes the doctor made two or three incisions and sucked blood from the affected area, spitting it into a little can of ashes. Originally, flint was used for incision, but glass later became common. The "power" or "singing" doctor neither sucked nor lanced but doctored by magical power alone. He diagnosed and cured illness by singing and dancing. He usually possessed a fetish sack in which he kept tobacco (which he smoked before singing), obsidian, and other power objects. During a curing performance, a shaman prayed to his familiar spirit, Noble Person (*yomúnnaka kó·ca*) or Morning Star (*ʔáwwe tóʔle*). An interpreter might make explanatory remarks to those unfamiliar with the language spoken by the doctor.

A shaman fasted four days and nights when doctoring and slept very little. If he became sick, his wife or assistant took an elderberry stick with white feathers on it and rubbed his body with the feathers while asking his familiar spirit to return the disease he had drawn out of the sick person to its original source. If the shaman became tired, the assistant might take over. Male shamans could not practice when their wives were menstruating, and the same restriction applied to poisoners.

A novice acquired his or her power individually or was taught curing techniques and given training by older shamans. Medicines and songs were often acquired by a singing doctor from his father or grandfather. A shaman sometimes learned to control intrusive spirit "pains" for curing purposes. Animal guardian spirits were often the sources of a shaman's power, telling him the methods by which he could cure a particular illness.

Dreaming of a doctor's song was regarded as a call to shamanism. Failure to answer the call would result in death or some other form of disability. In particular, a person was punished if he dreamed a song that would cure another but refused to sing it. A shaman dreamed what feathers should be used on his rattle. His songs usually remained his exclusive property, but if he chose to transmit them, both he and his apprentice must fast during instruction. Indian doctors did not charge. A person paid what he thought the treatment was worth.

Bear shamanism was also practiced in the area by members of a secret society. A novice proved his worthiness by stopping a large rock that was rolling downhill.

Initiates donned bear skins with appropriate ceremony and breastplates of armor. They achieved invulnerability and were able to travel long distances at superhuman speed. According to a Bodega Bay informant, female bear shamans used their powers to gather food and sea shells from distant places, but the males were dangerous and might kill anyone they encountered.

Specific information concerning poisoners is hard to come by for obvious reasons, and information on record pertains to the Lake County area generally. Certain people knew the techniques of producing illness in others and would do so for a price. They might operate directly by placing natural poisons such as ground poison oak berries in a person's food. More recently, battery acid was used for this purpose. Another method consisted of placing a snake skin near a person's home. There were also poisoners who relied solely on incantation. Like the shamans, they fasted four days. Lake Miwoks were suspicious of strangers that inquired after people's names and they were careful not to spit in public, since they believed both personal names and saliva could be used in black witchcraft. When a poisoner traveled at night, he carried beads to bribe potential captors into letting him go.

Poisoners that operated for hire were sometimes grudgingly tolerated, since they were often the only recourse for people with serious grievances. However, if a person had been unjustly bewitched, a powerful shaman might, upon the victim's request, return the magic to strike down the poisoner.

Another type of poisoner, the *wállipo*, was totally dysfunctional. He dressed in owl feathers and ran at high speeds, hooting as he went. Anyone in his path risked sickness or death, and the Indians sometimes ambushed such men and killed them.

• CEREMONIES Ceremonies took place in a large dance house specially constructed for the purpose (fig. 5). Men sometimes stuffed the smoke hole and danced around the center fire, fanning the hot air onto one another as an endurance test. They then jumped into the cold waters of a creek. Women did not normally enter the dance house for fear of some misfortune. This rule was relaxed on special occasions.

The Big Head (Bole-Maru) Dance extended from the Sacramento Valley to Stewarts Point and was known to the Lake Miwok when they were still living at the Old Rancheria (*kilá·yomi*). *tú·leyomi* village was apparently the site of major performances in aboriginal times. Loeb (1932:123) notes that in more recent times, the Lake Miwok sent their boys to Sulphur Bank to be initiated into the cult by the Pomo. Only men danced, except during periods of audience participation when women and children might join in.

Before the festival, a flagpole was erected in front of the sweathouse during a special ceremony. The dreamer's flag was on top with one flag for each head, usually

Fig. 5. Dance house at St. Helena Creek near Middletown. Photograph by C. Hart Merriam, Nov. 1928.

totaling four. The dreamer dreamed the design for his flag.

The dancers prepared in a roofless dressing room outside the sweathouse. (The rear of the sweathouse could be partitioned off for this purpose if it was raining.) The dreamer held the Big Head feather upright and circled it around the dancer's head four times while chanting a song that had come to him in a dream. He then raised and lowered the feather four times and placed it on the dancer's head the fifth time. The leader put on the headband, flicker stick, and hair shaft.

The dance ceremony was highly structured. It lasted four days and nights. Order was kept by the caretaker (*mállele*), who had people thrown into the fire if they misbehaved. If a singer was called upon to sing, he must do so or pay the caretaker. The caretaker, the dreamer, and the dancers must all fast. The caretaker gave each a stick with beads to give to the cook. He did not dance but provided rhythm by means of a foot drum and a rattle. The rattle was a split-stick rattle made from an elderberry branch, a cocoon rattle, or a hollowed-out fir cone with pebbles. The rattles were decorated with hawk, bluejay, or robin feathers.

A person who dreamed a dance song must release it with his rattle before it could be used in another sweathouse.

The timekeeper (*helá·ma*) cued the performers as to when to dance, slow down, and stop. Dancers must go into the sweathouse at least four times. While drumming, the caretaker prayed to his familiar spirit to protect the dancers on their way home after the festival. The singers also shook the rattle.

The dance started at sundown. The leader shouted four times like a cougar, as a signal to the spectators to enter, and made a speech in front of the flagpole. Then the dancers came in pairs. They sometimes entered differently, but once inside, they followed the same rules. The dancers announced themselves by whistling and shaking rattles at the front door. The timekeeper signaled them to come in by crying ʔóˑw.

A leader and the dancer wearing the Big Head, not necessarily from the same tribe, entered and circled the fire once. The leader went clockwise and the Big Head counterclockwise. They danced four times on the right side from the entrance, directed by signals from the timekeeper. Sometimes two pairs danced at once. The Big

270

Head returned to the door after each dance. Relatives threw beads and money on the dancers, which were collected by the director (*méce*), who also watched the fire.

After the dancers had danced four times to the right, they danced four times to the left. Then the chief said *ṣaltu wer*, and the dancer turned 90° counterclockwise and made a second circle. He did this four times and then backed out through the door. He went to the preparation room, where his assistants took his feathers. Then the leader danced on the far side of the fire, turned clockwise 180°, and danced near the fire. Afterward, the audience, male and female, could dance also.

The dreamer gave his rattle to an old man or old woman of the tribe who sang once sitting with his back to the fire, very slowly, then sang louder while standing up. The singer usually sang twice, once on each side of the fire.

People were not supposed to wander around once the dance started. It was dangerous to touch the feathers on the dancers' heads. The director picked up any that had fallen and handed them to the leader, who took them out to the dressing room. The dance lasted till dawn and began again the following night, for a total of four nights.

Several other Lake Miwok ceremonials are named and briefly described by Loeb (1932:124) and Gifford and Kroeber (1939:221-222).

The Big Head Dance might be followed by a Ball Dance (*poló·lo*), which was held other times as well. The dancers wore printed shirts and dresses. The women danced on one side of the fire and the men on the other.

The ghost initiation, also performed at *tú·leyomi*, was a four-day impersonation ritual in which "ghosts" and secret-society shamans put young boys through ordeals and instructed them in proper ritual behavior and dance steps (Loeb 1932:121-123; Gifford and Kroeber 1939:160, 221). During initiation a young boy was tossed back and forth over the fire and treated roughly, had burning coals placed on his hands or neck, and finally was thrown out the smoke hole. He lay belly down over the hole and a small arrow was shot into his navel. He was then rolled down and his parents bathed him in cold water. At the end of the initiation period, a general feast was held in the dance house.

Both men and women took part in the Old Time Dance. The women danced in place in a circle around the fire, and the men danced counterclockwise in a larger circle. The women wore headpieces and both men and women wore feather coats. This dance was often performed at the end of a festival.

Everyone smoked from the same pipe during the Tobacco Song, also taking a puff for each absent relative. Then the one who passed the pipe around smoked by himself or gave it to a friend to help smoke it up.

The Indian Song or Direction Song was very powerful and could give invulnerability if chanted on a hill for 10 days while fasting. However, if sung improperly it could bring death or sickness to one's relatives.

The Coyote Dance celebrated the recovery of a sick person. His family would invite the chief, who in turn contacted dancers and singers. His relatives paid expenses, put up beads outside the house, and donated food for the feast table. Dances were also given to celebrate departures or returns.

The First Fruits ceremony was held in the spring when the flowers blossomed. Under the supervision of the *yómta*, men, women, and children danced with flowers in their hands and hair. Dancers handled rattlesnakes as part of the performance. First-time participants in this ritual abstained from eating meat or fish for the following year and in subsequent years observed a four-day taboo after the rite (Loeb 1932:123-124; Gifford and Kroeber 1939:221).

For the Dance of the Dead (*ʔú·lup*), held at Sulphur Bank every other year, people from all around were invited to attend. The dance lasted four days. According to John Knight, only doctors who had fasted and singers went into the sweathouse. They summoned specific dead people, and the chief announced them by name and tribe. The dead man's adult relatives came out of their houses to see him. Children were kept in the house. They often became emotional and grabbed at the spirit but only touched air. The dead person walked around and then went behind the sweathouse and disappeared. It was thought that they all came from a local cemetery, even those who had been buried elsewhere. The dead relatives of the chief were summoned first. After that, the order was immaterial. Since Henry Knight reported seeing a dead dreamer with his flagpole, there apparently was impersonation of ghosts by certain of the dancers.

Informant James Knight gave a somewhat different account. People waited in the sweathouse for their dead relatives, who entered from the outside after they were announced.

The *yómta* was often employed to conjure up ghosts of the deceased in the dance house for bereaved relatives, who paid shell money to the chief for the performance (Gifford and Kroeber 1939:220). There was also a Rabbit Dance but no details are recorded about it.

Beliefs

The elderberry tree was thought to afford protection against lightning because of its hollow trunk and limbs.

One might suffer sore feet or some other misfortune from imitating the meadowlark, who was thought to speak some Lake Miwok. Bothering porcupines could cause rheumatism, a nose bleed, or a headache.

The eagle was considered capable of carrying off small children or fawns and eating them. It was bad luck to keep a quail as a pet.

Strange or deformed things were taboo, and touching them might produce convulsions. Yet lizards with forked tails were supposed to bring good luck in gambling if one knew the proper ceremonial procedure. Warts or skin diseases could result from handling sea shells other than those that were part of the ceremony. Dogs and snakes were never eaten, and a snakeskin belt might cause rheumatism and liver or kidney disorders. It was considered bad luck to keep the rattles from rattlesnakes. Lake Miwoks also thought illness would result from handling a certain shiny black rock (menú· lúppu).

Red and white bats were stuffed while singing a special song and kept for good luck.

Certain women were able to stop the wind by prying a lizard's mouth open, pointing it into the wind, and talking to it, according to Henry Knight.

A name-of-the-dead taboo was observed. Spirits of the dead underwent tests. They went first to the ocean, then to other places. Ghosts were thought to travel in whirlwinds.

Game animals were believed to be immortal and under spirit control, and it was believed that animals sometimes transformed themselves into other species. Rattlesnakes, lizards, and several types of birds turned into fish. Mountain sliders became four-legged trout. John Knight knew two people who had seen such creatures. Mudhens became blackfish during the winter. Lizards turned into small fish, and rattlesnakes changed into perch. John Knight thought that lizards and rattlesnakes would assume their original shape once they had become tired of the water.

Lunar eclipses occurred because a bear had swallowed Old Man Moon and was going to kill him. The Indians shouted at the bear to let him go, and a few minutes later, the moon would brighten up. Falling stars were considered omens of good or bad luck. Lake Miwoks waited for a bright southern star (Sirius?) to rise, and they referred to the stars in making weather predictions. The moon was also thought to contain a large spreading oak tree. Adults prayed to the new moon for good health, babies were held up toward the first new moon in winter, and children were made to jump toward the moon so they would grow fast.

There is a good luck rock one and one-half feet long that travels like a snake. But a person might get sick from handling it unless he knew the right songs.

One was not supposed to call a woodrat by its right name (yúllu), so they called him túmay kó·k 'wood tail'. Old people used to say children's hearts were growing when they hiccoughed.

Coyote's Knee Rock is a pair of rocks located a few miles south of Lower Lake. A man would embrace one of them if he wanted a son and the other if he wanted a daughter; then he would have sexual intercourse with his wife. Water spiders were allowed to bite expectant mothers so that their breasts would not grow too large. The water spider sting on a child's Adam's apple was supposed to help him become a good singer.

Curing

Some ailments were treated with herbs and natural remedies. A poultice from the shaved bark of a tree and crushed angelica (hutú·li) was applied to a sore spot, but not an open sore. Victims of bee stings drank a gruel made from a medicinal plant called končalá·wa and rubbed tobacco powder onto the swollen places; končalá·wa brew was drunk for any fever. Splints for broken bones were made from the interior of elderberry trees and rags. Large leaves from cuppuni?ala 'stinging bush' were placed over the broken areas. Pepperwood-leaf poultices were applied to the cheek to prevent toothache.

Sugar from the sugar pine was administered to treat colds. Bear meat was thought to be good for people with tuberculosis. Milk was used by the elderly for sore eyes, but it is not clear if this custom is precontact, since only human milk was available aboriginally. There was an interesting belief concerning how to avoid getting poison oak—spit on it! Poison oak rash was treated by bathing in Borax Lake or applying moss from the lake to the sores. Certain springs were believed to have curative powers. One of these was čiṣkuwe, north of Middletown.

Mythology

Lake Miwok mythology is exceedingly rich and centers around the exploits of members of a prehuman race that combined animal and human characteristics (Merriam 1910). The culture hero was Old Man Coyote, a projection of man at his best and worst. In his sublime aspect, he gave form to the world and peopled it, manufacturing men and women out of wood. He was affectionate toward his grandson, Bullet Hawk, but in one of his ludicrous moments, he tried to seduce the Bullet Hawk's wife. He commanded magical powers but suffered the weaknesses of old age. Throughout everything, he was still Coyote, the trickster and scavenger. Apparently there was also a higher entity with whom Coyote communed.

The sun and moon are often featured in Lake Miwok mythology, but the stars seldom are, although several constellations had specific names. The Milky Way was called utel'muk 'spirit road'; the Pleiades, mutsuyuk; big evening star (Venus?), uyuhayat; and Orion's belt, yotopugel (Gifford and Kroeber 1939:221).

Synonymy

The Lake Miwok call themselves Pomo when speaking English. Aboriginally they apparently called themselves kó·ca 'people'. Kroeber (1911:292) used the terms Lake Miwok or Northern Coast Miwok, while Barrett (1908) labeled them Northern Moquelumnan. Spellings of the village name tú·leyomi include Tulivoni (Bancroft 1886-1890, 4:363 quoting Vallejo), Tu'-le-am'-me, and Tu'-le-yo'-me (Merriam 1907). The ?olé·yomi settlement appears as Oleyomi (Bancroft 1886–1890, 4:448 quoting Ordaz diary of 1821), O′-lā-am′-me, O′-lā-yo′-me (Merriam 1907), and ōlē′yōme (Barrett 1908:317).

Sources

There is a paucity of early ethnographic data on the Lake Miwok Indians. Callaghan's (1956–1960) field notes recorded from informants Alma Grace, James Knight, and John Knight must be regarded as dating from a time when the culture was already much disintegrated and the distinctive characteristics of local groups were being lost. Museum specimens of Lake Miwok culture are few and indistinguishable in form from those of the neighboring Pomo. The earliest ethnographic survey work done among the Lake Miwok was carried out by Barrett (1908) and subsequent data of importance were collected by

Loeb (1932) and Gifford and Kroeber (1939). Historical materials pertaining to the Lake Miwok are scarce and fragmentary; however, references to contact-period villages and groups identifiable as Lake Miwok may be found in Arguello (1821), Bancroft (1886–1890, 4), Hittell (1885–1897, 2), Heizer and Hester (1970a), and Heizer (1973). Information concerning village locations, territorial boundaries, population, and linguistic affiliation was collected by Merriam (1907, 1955), and supplemental information may be found in Kroeber (1911, 1925, 1957a). Examples of Lake Miwok oral tradition have been published by Merriam (1910), Angulo and Freeland (1928), and Freeland (1947). Some unpublished ethnographic data and photographs are in the Merriam Collection (see Tuleyome, Oleyome in Heizer et al. 1969).

Sean L. Swezey assisted in collecting and organizing scattered ethnographic data for this chapter.

Pomo: Introduction

SALLY McLENDON AND ROBERT L. OSWALT*

From the second half of the nineteenth century on, speakers of seven distinct and mutually unintelligible languages in northern California have been referred to in the anthropological literature as a single group, primarily under the rubric Pomo (^{ı}pō$_{\text{ı}}$mō). It is common in this literature to speak of Pomo baskets or Pomo houses or Pomo mythology analogous to the way in which one refers to Navajo blankets or Navajo mythology; however, the social and linguistic groups referred to under the rubric Pomo differ in a number of important respects from the social and linguistic group referred to as Navajo.

Linguistically no two of the Pomoan languages spoken by people referred to as Pomo are as closely related as Navajo is to any of the varieties of Apache. The most divergent Pomoan languages are about as distantly related as the Athapaskan language Navajo in Arizona is to Tanaina in Alaska. In fact, the most divergent of the Pomoan languages differ from one another more than do the Germanic languages: German, English, Danish, Dutch, Norwegian, and Icelandic. Thus one cannot talk about the Pomo language, but only about the Pomoan family of languages.

Pomoan Languages

The earliest linguistic materials on these languages were word lists collected in 1851 by George Gibbs (1853). Powell (1891), in his classification of North American Indian languages, took the title of one of these lists, Hulanapo, to create Kulanapan to designate the family. The ultimate source is the name of one of the two large Eastern Pomo communities on Clear Lake: *quˑłá-naˑpʰò* 'water lily people/place'.

Barrett (1908) firmly established that there were seven distinct speech forms, delineated their geographic boundaries, and assigned them names according to their position relative to one another: Southwestern Pomo, South-

ern Pomo, Central Pomo, Northern Pomo, Northeastern Pomo, Eastern Pomo, and Southeastern Pomo. Unfortunately, Barrett persistently called these seven languages dialects, although he realized (1908:54) that "the differences between dialects are sufficient to warrant their separation into distinct languages according to customary usage in regard to European languages" but not, it seems, according to the usage prevalent then among those studying native American languages. Barrett's geographic designations are unambiguous enough but have had the effect of continuing the misconception that there is one language, Pomo, consisting of seven slightly varying dialects.

Of the seven language groups, one has a name for themselves as opposed to speakers of other languages, namely *Ɍahšáˑya;* consequently the anglicization of that native term, Kashaya (kə^{ı}shäyə), is preferred here to Barrett's Southwestern Pomo.

Classifications of the interrelationships of these languages have been advanced by Barrett (1908:100), Kroeber (1925:227), Halpern (1964:90), and Oswalt (1964a:416). Halpern, the first phonetically competent linguist to collect extensive materials on all seven languages, proposed a classification based on phonetic shifts, although no evidence was given: Southeastern Pomo, Eastern Pomo, and the other five as a group, which he calls the Russian River group. Although he could not state the relationships within the Russian River group with complete assurance, Halpern (1964:90) did state that "Northeastern Pomo is the most individualized member and that Southern Pomo appears to preserve the largest number of archaic features." His conclusions are summarized in figure 1.

Oswalt (1964a:413-427) has proposed the classification shown in figure 1c based on a statistical analysis of 100 lexical items. On this basis three languages—Kashaya, Southern Pomo, Central Pomo—are the most closely related of the seven languages, about as similar as the Western Romance languages Italian, Spanish, and French. These three are next most closely related to Northern Pomo in a subgroup called the Western Branch, to about the extent that Western Romance is related to Rumanian. This lexical subgrouping is supported by morphological evidence (Oswalt 1975). Oswalt's classification differs from Halpern's in not including Northeastern Pomo in a subgroup at a higher level

---

* The first section of this chapter is by McLendon and Oswalt jointly. The subdivisions of the Synonymies and Ethnogeography section are separate contributions, by Oswalt on Western Pomo (Kashaya, Southern Pomo, Central Pomo, Northern Pomo) and Northeastern Pomo, and by McLendon on Eastern Pomo and Southeastern Pomo. Oswalt is responsible for the maps, which are considerably corrected and revised, often on the basis of new field data, from those of Barrett (1908). McLendon has contributed the sites on the maps of the Eastern Pomo and Southeastern Pomo areas.

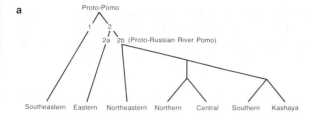

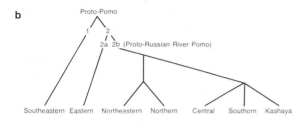

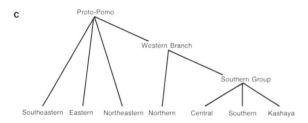

Fig. 1. Interrelationships of the Pomoan languages. a, b, Two alternate possibilities suggested by Halpern 1964; c, Classification of Oswalt 1964a.

Cultures

Culturally, although there were many similarities there were also important differences among the speakers of these seven distinct languages. According to one of the best observers of several of the Pomoan groups, E.W. Gifford, they were

> divided into a number of small groups, which at one time or another have been called tribes, villages, village-communities, or tribelets. Each of these was completely autonomous and owned a tract of land which might or might not be exactly defined but was substantially recognized by all neighboring communities. According to most informants, nearly every community also spoke a slightly but perceptibly distinct subdialect [dialect of one of the seven languages]. Each normally possessed a main settlement or central village, which in many of the groups appears to have remained fixed for generations (Gifford and Kroeber 1939:117).

The extent and nature of the tract of land claimed by each village-community seems to have been determined largely by the nature of the terrain, its ecology, and the nature of the group's adaptation to that ecology. The absolute square footage controlled was not particularly

but both agree on the great divergence of Eastern Pomo and especially Southeastern Pomo. At a much deeper time depth, it has been proposed that Pomoan is a member of the scattered, widespread linguistic stock called Hokan (see Langdon 1974).

Along with their many differences, the Pomoan languages have many lexical, phonological, and grammatical features in common. All have a simple system of five vowels coupled with a very complex array of consonants. Morphologically, the verb is by far the most intricate part of speech. It may include an element denoting direction of movement (a suffix in some languages, a preverb in others); a prefix indicating an instrument, body part, or natural force (fire, wind, gravity) involved in the action; a suffix showing how the speaker learned what he is talking about (by hearsay, by seeing the action, by hearing the sound of the action but not seeing it, by inference); and various cognate subordinating, aspectual, and modal suffixes.†

---

† The sound systems of the seven Pomoan languages are fairly similar (see McLendon 1973, and as revised below). The orthographies used in the Handbook for italicized Pomoan words can be described by reference to the phonemic inventory of Kashaya and Central Pomo. In these two languages the stops *p, t, ṭ, k,* and *q* occur in three series: voiceless unaspirated (written with plain letters), voiceless aspirated (written *pʰ* etc.), and glottalized (written *p̓* etc.). In addition there is a glottal stop (*ˀ*); a bilabial and an alveolar voiced stop (*b, d*); the affricates *c, č, č̣, čʰ, č̓;* three spirants (*s, š, h*); two nasals (*m, n*); two

semivowels (*w, y*); and the alveolar lateral *l*. There are five vowels, *i, e, a, u, o,* which may occur short (unmarked) or long (with following raised dot). The above symbols have the usual Handbook values; subscript dots indicate voiceless alveolar stops. An acute accent indicates raised pitch.

Southern Pomo differs in lacking the *q* series, in having consonant length (indicated by a following raised dot), and in lacking phonemic accent (the penultimate syllable in a phrase predictably having a raised pitch).

Northern Pomo lacks the *q* series and has no *čʰ* (it having merged into *š*). Northern Pomo syllables marked with an acute accent have higher pitch; Central and Northern Pomo may have a secondary accent, which perhaps involves stress, but it is not well understood and is not distinguished herein.

Northeastern Pomo lacks the *q* series and *c, č, pʰ,* and *s.* It adds an *f.* Halpern's recordings also contain *r, ł,* and an accent, but their phonemic status is uncertain. Whether a lateral spirant *ł* would have existed in a "pure" Northeastern Pomo is unknowable; the last speakers were fluent in Patwin, in which it is common.

Eastern Pomo lacks *qʰ,* but adds *cʰ, x, r,* and the voiceless series *M, N,* and *ł.* The acute accent indicates primary stress, while a grave accent marks the reduced stress found in compounds. For a detailed description see McLendon (1975:9–30).

Southeastern Pomo lacks the aspirated series but adds *f, x,* and *x̣.* Stress is marked, although it always falls on the first syllable.

The italicized words from Pomoan languages have been written in the above phonemic orthographies. Oswalt has provided these forms for the Western Pomo languages; unless otherwise indicated they are taken for Kashaya from Oswalt (1957–1975); for Southern Pomo from Oswalt (1963–1968); for Central Pomo from Oswalt (1958–1968); and for Northern Pomo from Halpern (1939–1940). Northeastern Pomo forms have been provided by Oswalt (1976a). McLendon has provided the Eastern Pomo forms from McLendon (1959–1976), and the Southeastern Pomo forms from Moshinsky (1974) and Halpern (1936, 1939). Eero Vihman provided McLendon and Oswalt with an inventory of Northern Pomo place-names, and his etymology of the word Pomo.

275

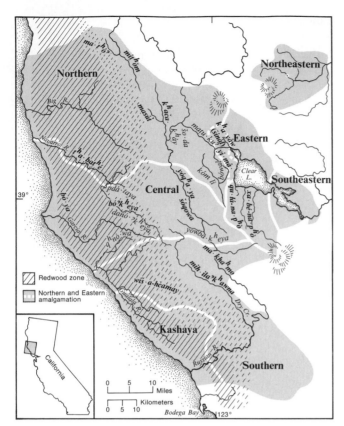

Fig. 2. Territorial extent of the 7 Pomoan languages and their constituent tribelets or village-communities, with probable boundaries at the time of first White contact. The redwood zone is approximated.

important. Rather, the size of the tract of land claimed seems to have been determined by the need to assure access to a sufficient supply of food (which is why the absolute limits of a group's territory are sometimes not clear). Differences in the carrying capacity of the environment resulted in several village-communities sometimes being in close proximity, as along the Russian River, and others being rather distant (fig. 2).

Apparently the size of the population of these village-communities varied considerably (only estimates of precontact population size are available). Thus, in Redwood Valley, Kniffen (1939:375) estimates that the single Northern Pomo village-community of Kacha had a population of approximately 125. The Central Pomo village-community of Yokaya on the Russian River was said by Stewart (1943:43) to have a population of 500–1,000 persons, while the Central Pomo village-community of Shokowa who inhabited the precontact village of Shanel south of the Yokaya had a population of 1,500 according to a Central Pomo, Jeff Joaquin, who was born about 1859 and whose father had been a member of this group (Stewart 1943:45). These estimates are supported by what is known of village size. Kniffen (1939) says the permanent village of Kacha consisted of 12 communal dwellings. When Powers (1877:168, fig. 19) mapped the ruins of Shanel in the 1870s he found 104

dwelling-house pits and foundations of five assembly houses. It is not clear that all these houses were occupied simultaneously, but if they were, multiplying by 14, the average number of inhabitants per house elsewhere, would give a population of 1,456 (Cook 1956:116). However, Powers (1877:168) specifically says that "in each one" of their large lodges lived "several families, sometimes twenty or thirty persons," which would mean that not all the houses needed to be simultaneously occupied for the population to be near 1,500.

In some of these village-communities important sources of food such as large manzanita trees, acorn trees, and good fishing sites were privately owned by individual families (as among the Kacha, Yokaya, Shokowa and the three Southeastern-Pomo-speaking island village-communities at Clear Lake). In other village-communities all lands and sources of food were held communally (as among all the Eastern Pomo and the Northern Pomo of Sherwood Valley).

The social and political organization of these groups seems to have varied considerably too. For example, the kinship systems of a number of these groups were remarkably different. The Northern Pomo village-community of Kacha had a single chief who was elected (Kniffen 1939:375). The Central Pomo village-community of Yokaya had a head chief and three subchiefs (Stewart 1943:43). The right to the chieftainship passed from a man to his sister's son. The Central Pomo village-community of Shokowa seems to have had the most complex political organization of all, for according to Stewart (1943:45) before the arrival of Europeans they were governed by 20 chiefs. There were two main chiefs, a war captain, seven speaking assembly house chiefs, and one or more ordinary assembly house chiefs (or assistant chiefs) for each ceremonial assembly house. Only the war captain was elected. All the others were chief by virtue of inheritance, the incumbent chief picking his successor from among his kinsmen.

Gifford summarized the ethnographic reality rather well:

> what we call Pomo—the Indian had no word for it—refers to no definable cultural entity, but only to a sort of nationality expressed in speech varying around a basic type. . . . There was therefore no Pomo culture except as an abstraction made by ethnographers and other white men. There was a series of highly similar but never quite identical Pomo cultures, each carried by one of the independent communities or tribelets (Gifford and Kroeber 1939:119).

Although it has been claimed that the "Pomo" are among the best-known groups in California (Kroeber 1925; Cook 1956), knowledge about them leaves much to be desired. There are three main problems with the data available. First, almost none of the extant published ethnographic material on the social, cultural, and religious organization of these groups is based on actual observations. Only Powers (1877) and Gibbs (1853)

276

involve reports of actual observations. There is actually disappointingly little information in Gibbs, while many details of social organization, ritual practice, and material culture provided by Powers come not in fact from direct observation but from White settlers in the area claiming to have expert knowledge of the group in question.

Second, scholars since Powers (for example, Barrett, Freeland, Gifford, Kroeber, Kniffen, and Stewart), have necessarily depended virtually exclusively on descriptions of precontact society elicited in the form of prescriptive statements. This information was provided by the oldest member(s) of a given Pomoan group willing to talk to the researcher about the old ways. These individuals were always knowledgeable and usually were exceedingly careful to attempt to describe accurately whatever features of the society they grew up in that the researcher wanted to know about. These investigations were invariably carried out in English, rather than the particular Pomoan language of the individual providing the information, and usually during a remarkably short period of fieldwork, frequently a matter of weeks with any given community. Normally only a few members of the group were consulted. No attempt seems ever to have been made to talk systematically to all the surviving members of a group (both men and women) above a certain age.

Third, except in the area of material culture, researchers have unfortunately tended to collect data from speakers of two or three of the seven language groups, usually Northern Pomo, Central Pomo, and Eastern Pomo, on the basis of which claims are made about all seven groups. Thus Loeb's (1926) valuable monograph is entitled *Pomo Folkways,* yet in his introduction Loeb says that only five individuals, all men, were chiefly made use of, all from Eastern Pomo, Central Pomo, and Northern Pomo communities. Representatives of communities speaking Kashaya, Southern Pomo, Southeastern Pomo, and Northeastern Pomo do not seem to have been consulted (although one Kashaya ceremony is described). According to Kunkel (1962:235), Barrett told him that his data on political organization in his reports on Pomo ethnogeography (1908) and ceremonies (1917) were "based on either Yokaia [Yokaya] or Cokoa [Shokowa] informants or both," that is, on information provided by members of Central-Pomo-speaking communities.

Synonymies and Ethnogeography

Pomo

The word Pomo originated in two Northern Pomo forms that are quite distinct in the native language but that became confused in early writings. The earliest known recordings were by Col. Redick McKee (1851-1857, 3) on an 1851 reconnaissance of the area and by Gibbs (1853) in a report on the same expedition. Both give Pomo as the name of an Indian group on the east fork of the Russian River. For a village in southern Potter Valley, on the east

fork of that river, Vihman (1966-1969) provides the full phonemic form: $pʰoˑmoˑ$ 'at red earth hole'. $pʰoˑ$ can refer to magnesite, a mineral from which valued red beads were made, or to a red earth or clay, possibly hematite, which was mined in the area and mixed with acorn flour to give the resulting bread a desired flavor and color (Merriam 1955:38). *mo* is 'hole' and the final vowel length of $pʰoˑmoˑ$ is 'at'.

A second source, frequently written Poma, is based on Northern Pomo $pʰóʔmaʔ$ (Halpern 1939-1940), which is added to place-names to designate those that live at that place. It is a derivative of the verb $pʰó-$ 'reside, live in a group'. Thus $pʰoˑmoˑ$ $pʰóʔmaʔ$ would mean 'those who live at red earth hole'.

In English, these two forms, Pomo and Poma, came to be used interchangeably, until a trend was started, possibly by Powers (1877), toward using Pomo for those who spoke the same language as those of the village of Pomo (that is, the Northern Pomo language). On the basis of linguistic similarity, Powers (1877:146) suggested including under this rubric other groups to the south (Central Pomo) who did not call themselves Pomo (that is, $pʰóʔmaʔ$). Barrett (1908:118ff.) solidified the use of Pomo for the whole linguistic family, although in his etymology of the term he merged the two sources $pʰoˑmoˑ$ and $pʰóʔmaʔ$. In the anthropological literature Poma survives in compound terms to designate particular groups of Northern Pomo.

Kashaya

The history of the Kashaya differs from that of other Pomo groups in that their first direct contact with Caucasians was not with Spaniards or Anglo-Americans, but with Russians at the Fort Ross colony 1811-1842. Partly as a result of their unique history, with slower acculturation and relative freedom from forced removal to missions and reservations, they are now the best preserved of the Pomo groups. Of the 200 or so who identify themselves as Kashaya in 1976, about half can speak their language in some fashion. There is evidence of former dialectal variation in the language, but this has largely been leveled out in favor of a single standard. There is more variation by age, with younger speakers showing progressive loss of vocabulary and replacement of some of the complex morphology by constructions adapted from English.

The Kashaya are the only Pomo linguistic group with a name for themselves as a whole. Kashaya is the closest English adaptation of that native term, *ƙahšáˑya*, probably derived from *ƙahša* 'agile, nimble'. The Southern Pomo call them *ƙahšaˑya*, containing *ƙahša* 'light (weight)'; the Central Pomo *qášaˑya*, containing *qá* 'gambling' and *ša* 'expert'; the Northern Pomo *kašaˑya*, with no recognized meaning for the first two syllables. In several of the Pomo languages the final syllable is a suffix forming names of groups. The Wappo call them *ƙášaˑya*, with no analyzable meaning. In governmental records, the spelling Kashia is used. Other variations have been Kacia (Stewart 1943:49), Kacaya (Loeb 1926:194), Kah-chí-ah (Merriam 1955:144), Kashaiya, and Ka-shiah.

In anthropological literature, the term Southwestern Pomo is common.

Erio, for the Kashaya at the mouth of the Russian River, and Erusi or Erussi, for those at Fort Ross, are probably from Spanish *el rio* and *el ruso*. Venaambakaiia (Powers 1877) seems to be the native phrase *wina·má· bakʰe yaʔ* 'person from on the land', which is opposable to *ʔahqʰa yów ʔbakʰe yaʔ* 'person from in the water', a term for those at Fort Ross from across the seas—Russians, Eskimos, and Aleuts. The Russian designations Severnovskiya 'northerners' (that is, north of the Indians at their other, more southern establishment at Bodega Bay) and Chwachamaju or Khwakhamaiu are completely unrecognizable to the present-day Kashaya.

Another name for them has been Gualala, although this term has also been applied to the Southern and Central Pomo at the mouth, or along the lower course, of the Gualala River. The initial G is not pronounced and crept into the official spelling of the town and river Gualala through a mistaken hispanicization. The name is an old one: in a letter dated October 7, 1813, from Kuskov to Baranov (cited in Davidson 1889:264), Indians north of Fort Ross are called Wallálakh. The Russian must have acquired the term from the Alaskan sea hunters at the Ross colony because the final -kh appears to be the Eskimo or Aleut absolutive case suffix. The sea hunters, in turn, had probably adapted one of the native names for the site of the town Gualala (figs. 3-4): Kashaya *qʰawála· li* 'water coming down place', often shortened to *walá·li* 'coming down place'; Southern Pomo *hiw·ala· li* 'flowing down place'; Central Pomo *qʰáhwala· li* 'water coming down place'.

In English, particular groups of the Kashaya are often

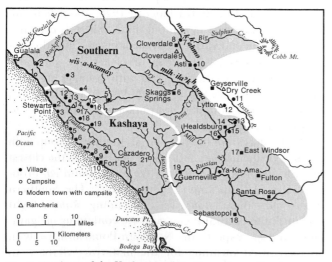

Fig. 3. Territory of the Kashaya and Southern Pomo. For the names corresponding to the numbers, see text.

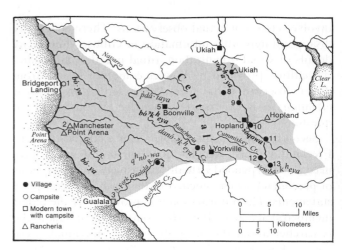

Fig. 4. Territory of the Central Pomo. For the names corresponding to the numbers, see text.

referred to by their place of residence: Fort Ross Indians, Stewarts Point Indians, Haupt Ranch Indians. The Kashaya refer to subdivisions of themselves by adding to the place of residence *bakʰe* 'from' and *yaʔ* 'person' or *yacʰma* 'people'; for example, *láʔlahqʰa bakʰe yacʰma* 'people from wild goose spring'.

Aboriginally, the Kashaya occupied about 30 miles of the coast of northwest Sonoma County and extended inland for 5 to 13 miles. In 1976, some of the Kashaya live on the small 40-acre reservation within this territory, but more are scattered elsewhere in the county nearer schools and places of work.

The southern and northern boundaries have been contracted from those given by Barrett (1908:map) because almost all the later evidence is that the Kashaya ranged no farther south than Duncans Point, about five miles south of the mouth of the Russian River, and that, in the north, the Southern Pomo occupied a section of the coast, separating the Kashaya from the Central Pomo.

The lower two-thirds of the inland boundary is reproduced substantially as given by Barrett (1908:map) because nothing is known to contradict it; but there is also little evidence for it. The Kashaya used parts of Austin Creek; therefore, its entire watershed is included. However, the principle that the drainage divides were boundaries does not fit with the Kashaya settlement patterns in the more permanently occupied redwood zone. They held no rich valleys; the more desirable living sites, especially in winter, were near springs in the relatively open land atop the ridge divides, above the dark densely forested canyons and riverbanks, and inland from the coastal wind and fog.

The exact placement of the northern third of the inland border has been made by taking a consensus of all ethnographers and Kashaya who have expressed an opinion on the subject; no Southern Pomo have been in the area for many years. If there is rather balanced disagreement, or no opinion on a particular spot, a decision has been made by the language of the name for that or a neighboring site. For example, there is disagreement on whether *hibu· wi* 'potato place' is Kashaya or Southern; the name is slightly irregular for either language. However, immediately to the south, a minor campsite (not on the map) has a name that is Southern Pomo in form, even when said by Kashaya: *cay ƙohsa ʔdoča·ni* 'where a man's elbow is placed'. The Kashaya equivalent would be *ʔacaʔ q̓ohsa ʔdočal li*. The next spot south has a Kashaya name and the boundary is set between the last two.

Over 200 place-names are still known; some of the more prominent sites are listed below in Kashaya followed by a translation and the English name of the site, if there is one. The numbers refer to locations on figure 3. More names are in Oswalt (1964:map).

On the coast, north to south:

1. *q̓owíšal* 'mussel upslope', Black Point area.
2. *danaka*, no meaning, Stewarts Point area.
3. *duwi máʔča ʔel li* 'where Coyote's sweathouse is', by a conical knoll south of Stewarts Point.
4. *húmčiwaʔ* 'húm(?) crawling out', Horseshoe Point area.
5. *tʰa·batʰé· wi* 'at much gravel', Fisk Mill Cove area.
6. *qʰaʔbe síhla wina·* 'on flat rocks', Salt Point area.
7. *čihtó·naw* 'bereaved', Walsh Landing. A woman is said to have been killed here from a fall over a bluff while trying to escape from some Mexicans.
8. *čʰiṭíbida·qal li* 'where alder creek flows out', Stillwater Cove area. The same name is also applied to a different site three miles northwest.
9. *súlme·wey*, containing *súl* 'condor', the rest has no meaning; Timber Cove area.
10. *mé·ṭiʔni*, no meaning, Fort Ross and surrounding area. The antiquity of the name is attested by an early Russian recording as med-zhi-ny (cited in Gibson 1975). Other English citations, such as mad-shui-nui (Barrett 1908:231), probably stem from a misinterpretation of the Cyrillic alphabet.
11. *šóhqʰa wi* 'at the south water', area at the mouth of the Russian River.

In the interior, north to south:

12. *muča· wi* 'grain place'.
13. *ʔačaʔ šiná· čawal li* 'where a human head is sitting'.
14. *čuʔnúʔnu šinal* 'huckleberry heights', Stewarts Point Rancheria.
15. *duʔƙašal* 'abaloneville'.
16. *pʰo·tol* 'on red earth'.
17. *súlkʰeya· wi* 'at condor's crest'.
18. *láʔlahqʰa* 'wild goose spring'.
19. *qʰale čúma·yal* 'tree sitting'.
20. *seʔe pí ʔna ma·čey* 'brush stunted going in (?)', the last two syllables are dialectally divergent; Seaview.
21. *ƙolómmal li* 'hollowed out place', Cazadero.

Southern Pomo

The aboriginal territory of the Southern Pomo lay in Sonoma County and extended from about five miles south of Santa Rosa northward for 40 miles, nearly to the county border, and from the eastern drainage of the Russian River westward to Kashaya and Boya (Central Pomo) territory, with a narrow extension to the coast between those two. This coastal extension is the only major boundary revision from Barrett (1908:map). The Southern Pomo held the lower half of the Russian River except for the mouth (Kashaya) and a section between the towns of Geyserville and Healdsburg (Wappo). For an account of the precontact, early-nineteenth-century conquest by the Wappo of part of this section see Barrett (1908:265-266). Communication between the Southern Pomo north and south of the ceded territory was not interrupted because it was an easy walk from the Russian River valley over a low ridge to *mih·ilaʔkʰawna*, the valley of Dry Creek, which runs parallel to, and only about four miles from, the Russian River.

The Southern Pomo population was decimated early, especially in the southern part of their territory, by missionization, Mexican slave raids, disease, and denser settlement by immigrants. Ethnic identity was lost in the region of Santa Rosa and Sebastopol several generations ago; the dozen or so speakers remaining in 1976 originate from north of Healdsburg.

Southern Pomo is now the dominant term for this linguistic group, but variations of Gallinomero have been applied to the same people, especially those south of Healdsburg. The huge number of variants include Cainameros, Cainemeros, Calajomanes, Calle-namares, Calle-Nameras, Canaumanos, Canimares, Gallinomeros, Gallonimero, Gallynomeros, Kainamares, Kanimares, Kanimarres, Kianamares, and Kyanamara. When the Russian Kostromitonov (1839:80) wrote of some "Steppe Indians" as the Kainama, he was probably giving a form of this name. Kai-mé, which Powers (1877:174) gives as a tribe separate from the Gallinomero, could be merely another in the series of distortions of that term; it is otherwise unidentifiable. Kalme (Kroeber 1925:233), for an unlocatable Southern Pomo division, has probably arisen as a miscopying of Kaime. None of the above appears to be based on a native term. Powers (1877:174) says that the early Spaniards derived Gallinomero from Gallina, a name they had given to one of the native chiefs.

A separate set of appellations for the Southern Pomo north of Healdsburg originates in the native *mus·a·lahkon* 'long snake', said to have been the name of a former chief; it is also the name of a supernatural snake that guards water from the approach of menstruating women. The native term is well represented by the spelling Musalakon and by Musalacon, the version on an 1846 Mexican land grant that included the present town of Cloverdale. Other variants have been Masalla Magoons,

Misálamagūn, Mi-sál-la Ma-gún, Musalakan, Musalakun, Mu-sal-la-kűn, Muscalcon, and Musulacon.

The speakers of Southern Pomo did not have a word for themselves opposed to speakers of neighboring languages. Names of local groups were formed freely with the element -hčamay 'people' added to any term for a geographical location or direction, for example, ʔam·ak·o-hčamay 'dirt field people' and ʔaš·o-hčamay 'easterners, the Wappo', the latter being the Ashochími of Powers (1877:196-203). In anthropological literature, -hčamay has been incorporated into some tribelet names as -chemie, -chimi, -chum-mi, -ctemi, -tcamai, -tcemei, -tcemi, and -tum'-mi. A native-based term for all the Southern Pomo could be derived by an adaptation of this element, something like Chamay (ˈchä₁mī).

The small number of remaining speakers represent two slightly different dialects: the speech of the ma·kʰahmo-hčamay 'salmon hole people' at the northern end of the territory and that of the mih·ilaʔkʰawna-hčamay 'west creek people' along Dry Creek. A rarer dialectal variant of mih·ilaʔkʰawna is mihinkʰawna. These names have been represented as Mahilkaune, Ma-hin-kow. The speakers of the above two dialects remember that a more different, now extinct, dialect was spoken by the Healdsburg Indians, the kʰal·e-hčamay 'water-midst people' and the kʰa·towi-hčamay 'people at the lake'. The last term is probably what is intended by "Kataictemi of Healdsburg" (Stewart 1943:53) and Káh-tah-we chúm-mi (Merriam 1955:144).

Those farther south were called ʔiy·oko-hčamay 'southerners'. Bitakomtara and Konhomtara, names given by Stewart (1943:53-54) for tribelets near Santa Rosa and Sebastopol respectively, are unrecognizable to the present-day speakers, but they probably contain the ending -mtaṭa, known in only two words, one given in the next paragraph, the other a well-known name for Bodega Bay (and people?) in Coast Miwok territory: ʔahkʰamtaṭa 'water-mtaṭa'. One of Stewart's terms contains konho 'mountain mahogany'; the other perhaps bidʔakʰa 'river'.

Those who lived in the hills between the Russian River and the coast were known collectively as the wiš·a-hčamay 'ridge people'. Merriam (1955:144) represented this name as Wé-shah-chúm-mi; he also gave We-shúm-tat-tah as a separate division, although they could be the same group with a different suffix: wiš·amtaṭa. Yotiya (Stewart 1943:47) and Yutaya (Loeb 1926:194) are the Boya word yó·taya 'southerners' for the same people.

References by Russians (Kostromitonov 1839:80) to large settlements Japiam (that is, Yapiam) and Kajatschim are quite unrecognizable.

A selection of the more prominent place-names is cited below from west to east and then southward (fig. 3). The phonemic form is followed by a translation and the English name of the place, if there is one, then by some of the representations in earlier writings.

1. seʔe ton 'on a bush'; four miles south of Gualala on the coast; seéton.
2. kubʔahmo wi 'at ball hole'; south side of the confluence of Rockpile Creek and the Gualala River; kūbahmóī.
3. ma·kʰawša 'salmon ridge'; a mile northeast of Annapolis; Mákawica, Makauca.
4. hibu· wi 'potato place'; four miles southeast of Annapolis near the Kashaya border; hībűwī, Hí-po-wi.
5. hi·walhmuy 'flowing down together'; referring to the confluence of House Creek, Wolf Creek, and the Gualala River. The Kashaya name hi·wálhmuʔ is a partial adaptation of the Southern Pomo and is probably the source of citations as Hiwalhmu. It was formerly a meeting place for Kashaya and wiš·a-hčamay work parties gathering to go to the agricultural fields eastward.
6. ʔahkʰaho ʔwa·ni or kʰaho ʔwa·ni 'where the hot water is'; Skaggs (Hot) Springs; kahówanī.
7. ma·kʰahmo 'salmon hole'; on Big Sulphur Creek near its confluence with the Russian River. The early importance of this community is attested by Kostromitonov's (1839:80, 90) mention of a large valley settlement called Makoma and Makomow'schen (Makomo). The name has been closely represented by transcriptions like Mah-kah-mo, Makahmo, and Makamo.
8. ʔiy·o·tok·o wi 'at the lower field'; Cloverdale, town and valley.
9. kʰa·lanhko 'tall willow'; Cloverdale Rancheria; Kah-lung-ko, Kalanako, Kalaňko.
10. ʔam·ak·o 'dirt field'; on the east bank of the Russian River across from Asti; Ah-mah-ko, Amákō, Amako.
11. ʔohsok·o wi 'at clover field'; in Alexander Valley, ceded to the Wappo in the early nineteenth century (Barrett 1908:265-266); ōssōkō'wi.
12. ʔahšaben 'fish + ben (?)'; north side of Lytton, ceded to the Wappo; acában.
13. wo·ṭohkʰa ton 'on muddy water'; northeast of Healdsburg. The name is not now known but was reconstituted from Barrett's (1908:218) wotokkátōn 'dirty lake'.
14. kʰal·e 'water midst'; Healdsburg at the town square; kále.
15. kʰa·ṭo wi 'at the lake'; by a former lake and marsh on the southeast side of Healdsburg; Kah-tah-we, Katai, Ka'tōwī.
16. ʔam·aṭ·a yow 'under red dirt'; north side of the confluence of Mill Creek and Dry Creek; reconstituted from Barrett's amatī'ō.
17. čol·ik·o wi 'at redwing (blackbird) field'; East Windsor; tsōlīka'wī.
18. baṭʰ·inkʰlehča wi 'at elderberry house'; Sebastopol;

batíklētcawī, batinklētcawī, Batiklechawi, Bah-tin-kah-le.

19. *moʔq̓óš pewlo* 'stump town'; not an aboriginal site but a nineteenth-century lumbering town. The form is a Kashaya translation of the former English name Stumptown (now called Guerneville); *pewlo* 'town' is from Spanish *pueblo*.

Central Pomo

The territory of the linguistic group known as the Central Pomo lies in southern Mendocino County in an irregular band from the coast to about 40 miles inland and a border with the Eastern Pomo at the crest of the range east of the Russian River. Along the coast it extended from the boundary with the Northern Pomo just north of the Navarro River southward about 35 miles to the border with the Southern Pomo in the vicinity of the mouth of the Gualala River. Inland, along the Russian River, the northern boundary lay either north of the town of Ukiah or south of it (Barrett 1908:125ff.) and from there the territory extended southward for 20 miles slightly beyond the southern border of the county.

The Central Pomo were beyond the range of missionization and were thus free from at least one factor that destroyed so many Southern Pomo. The Central Pomo language has about twice as many surviving speakers as Southern Pomo and is spoken in 1976 in two quite divergent dialects: the coastal, or Boya, dialect and the interior dialect of the Yokaya and Shanel. There probably was some variation within each of these two main divisions but the differences were relatively slight.

The Central Pomo had no name for themselves as a whole opposed to speakers of other languages, but they did have names for various subdivisions. A restricted set of names for groups is formed directly with the suffix *-ya* 'people'. More generally, *-ya* is preceded by *-ʔkʰe* 'of, from' or by a plural suffix *-ta-*, forming terminations *-ʔkʰeya* (especially common in Yokaya) and *-taya* (more common in Boya).

Boya (ˈbōyä). The coastal Central Pomo are called *bóˑya* 'westerners' by themselves and by all the surrounding Indians—other Central Pomo, Northern Pomo, Southern Pomo, and Kashaya—even though in the languages of the last two peoples *bóˑ* does not mean 'west'. The logical anglicization Boya would seem to be the preferred native-based designation, but it is not much used in anthropological literature, although it does appear in Merriam (1955:144) as Bó-yah and in Heintzelman (1855) as Bo-i-os. Probably the Moi-ya of Gibbs (1853:112), an otherwise unidentifiable form, is meant to be this name.

A principal village was *p̓dáhaw* 'at the stream mouth', on the Garcia River, formerly near the ocean. The name is now transferred four miles upstream to the present-day Manchester Rancheria (2, fig. 4), where a few Boya and former Bokeya live; more are at the nearby Point Arena

Rancheria. Two campsites are *cʰdó batʰé* 'big flower', at Bridgeport to the north (1), and *qʰáhwalaˑli* 'where water comes down', at the mouth of the Gualala River (3). An alternative name is *qʰáhwalaw* 'water coming down', which can generically apply to the mouth of any stream, and is specifically another site on the Russian River.

Bokeya (ˈbōkāyä): Pdataya (pəˈdätäyä), Danokeya (däˈnōkäyä), Kanowa (käˈnōwä). There is a term *bóʔkʰeya* 'people of the west, westerners' for those who lived halfway between the coast and the Russian River, especially around the towns of Boonville and Yorkville. In some anthropological literature, and with some Indians, the term is extended to include to Boya as well. The uncertainty in use has arisen partly from the similarity in form and meaning between the two names and partly because the Bokeya no longer exist, having merged with either the Boya or the groups to the east. However, the consensus of the Yokaya and Northern Pomo is that *bóʔkʰeya* had the restricted application given above. For a tribelet between the Russian River and the coast, Gibbs (1853:112) gave a distorted Boch-hé-af (there is no f in any Western Pomo language), and Heintzelman (1855) gave Bo-kas. Other spellings have been Bokea and Bokeya.

Some of the Boya call this same group, especially those formerly at Boonville, *p̓dáˑtaya* 'downstreamers, Pdataya', and *p̓dáˑtayaʔ máˑ* 'downstreamers' land' is their word for the town of Boonville (5) and the neighboring valley. Since the place is upstream from the Boya, the name must have originated elsewhere, namely among those who in turn are called *danóˑʔkʰeya* 'upstreamers, Danokeya'. The principal village of the last named was *láˑtʰe*, on Rancheria Creek, near Yorkville (6). The name *láˑtʰe* has no readily discernible meaning; *tʰé* is 'feather', but in place-names *tʰe* is more likely to be a contraction of *batʰé* 'big (of a singular object only)' or *tʰédu* 'much, many'.

Barrett (1908:map) placed Boonville and its environs in the Northern Pomo speech area and Yorkville in the Central. What slight evidence there is—the form of local place-names and the voluntary movement of the former residents to Central Pomo rancherias—favors both being Central; the boundaries have been adjusted accordingly. A prominent village farther down the Navarro River, *tʰaˑbatʰé*, has a name more Northern Pomo in form; consequently it is maintained in that linguistic group, as Barrett had it.

A small group to the southwest of the Danokeya, and possibly to be included under the rubric Bokeya, was called *qʰnóˑwa* by the Boya. In the Boya dialect *qʰnóˑ* is 'mountain mahogany'; *qanóˑ* is the corresponding Yokaya word. The meaning of *-wa* is unknown; perhaps it is a variant of *-ya* 'people'. The name has been written Kanoa, Kan-nó-ah, and Knoya, but Kanowa is probably best. Barrett (1908:164) gives látcûpda as the most important old village site of the area. The only name for the area presently elicitable among the Boya is *lá·ča p̓da* 'ax creek' (4); since the name contains a loan from Spanish *la hacha* 'the ax', it cannot be very old. In English, the group was sometimes called the Rockpile Indians, from the name of a peak just to the south.

Yokaya (yō'käyä). The northernmost of the Central Pomo groups along the Russian River call themselves *yóqʰa·ya* 'south valley (people)'. The first known recorded version was in an 1845 Mexican land grant, in which the spelling Yokaya was used, and this is the best adaptation of the native term. Besides the primary source *yóqʰa·ya*, there are two other native terms that may have affected the great variety of recordings of the name: Northern Pomo *yo·kʰé* 'from the south' and *yo·kʰáy* 'south valley' could be the bases of the two-syllable versions Yokai, Yo-kei, Yukae, and Yukai (Gibbs 1853:112); and Central Pomo *yó·ʔkʰeya* 'southerners' may explain a variant English pronunciation of the second vowel (yō'käyō), especially common for the local alternate spelling Yokayo. Other three-syllable representations include Llokaya, Uk-a-is, Ukiah (the official name of the county seat and valley), Ukias, Ya-ki-a, Yohios, Yo-kai-a, Yokaia, Yo-kai-ah, Yokaiya, Yokia, Yo-kí-ah, Yolhios, Yukaya.

The meaning 'south valley' can be interpreted as elliptic for 'south end of the valley'; the Northern Pomo occupied the north end. A translation 'deep valley', commonly given by residents of Ukiah, seems less likely for *yóqʰa·ya* because *yó* and *yó·* mean 'south', while 'deep, below, under, lower' is *yow,* ending in a labial glide. Furthermore, *yow,* as an adjective meaning 'deep', does not precede the noun but follows it.

There is some confusion, both in English and in the Indian language, over whether the term refers basically to the people or the place. The suffix *-ya* forms names for groups of people; and in the native language, the place, Ukiah town and valley, is often referred to as *yóqʰa·yaʔ má·* 'land of the Yokaya'. However, many Indians accept *yóqʰa·ya* as the name of the place; perhaps this is due to 130 years of hearing English speakers call the place Ukiah.

The Yokaya now live principally in the town Ukiah and at the Ukiah Rancheria five miles south, although others have scattered farther. The largest aboriginal village was *šóqʰa·čal* 'east flint(?) place', on the east side of a former pond in the southeast part of Ukiah valley (7). Tatem, said to have been another important Yokaya village, is now unknown.

Lema ('lämä). To the south, at Knight's Valley, on McNab Creek, was *léma* (8). The name is probably an abbreviation of *ʔiʔléma* 'in between, middle (land)'. Lema has been applied to the small group of Indians who used to live there and has also been written La-ma, Lā'-mah, and Lima.

Shiyeko (shē'äkō). Along the Russian River, around the Largo train station, the land was called *šyé· qo* 'sugar

pine nut field' (9). This name has appeared in a variety of forms as the English designation of the small tribelet that used to live in that valley: Ciego, cīē' go, Seacos, Shiegho, Shiego, Sí-a-ko.

Shokowa ('shōkōwə), Shanel (shä'nel). There is a name Shokowa, used in some anthropological literature for the next major tribelet south. Although the native form *šóqowa* is known to the present-day Yokaya, its application is not—whether tribe, former village, or synonym for the much better known *šanél*. It is here taken to mean the people who occupied Shanel and other villages united in a rather powerful community. The name is probably formed of *šó* 'east', *qo* 'field, valley', and *-wa,* an element that appears otherwise only in the group name *qʰnó·wa*. Other representations have been Cokoa, cō'kōwa, Shokhowa, Shó-ko-ah, Socoa, and So-kó-wa.

The most important village of the Shokowa, lying on the east side of Hopland Valley, was *šanél* 'at the ceremonial house' (10) (also the name of a Northern Pomo village in Potter Valley). The name was recorded in an 1844 Mexican land grant as Sanel and that form, with the wrong sibilant, has persisted in various governmental titles. Other variants have been Canel, Sahnel, Sah-nels, Sai-nals, Sanelos, Senel, Se-nel, Sinals; but Shanel is the best anglicization. The people of Shanel in 1976 live mainly at the Hopland Rancheria and speak a dialect close to that of the Yokaya.

The area for several miles to the south is classified with this community by Stewart (1943:45ff.) and as two separate communities by Kroeber (1925:map): *qʰáhwalaw* 'water coming down' at the confluence of Pieta Creek and the Russian River (11) and *šé· p̓da* 'basket root creek' at the confluence of Cummiskey Creek and the Russian River (12).

Yobakeya (yō'bäkäyä). The name of the southernmost tribelet of the Central Pomo is recorded by Halpern (1939–1940) as *yowba·kʰeya* 'people from *yowba·*'. *yow* is 'lower' and *ba·* usually 'tail', but that meaning seems strange in a place-name; perhaps it is some metaphor relating to these people being at the lower end of the stretch of river controlled by the Central Pomo. The term appears to be the same as Ubak-héa, which Gibbs (1853:112) cites as a group between the river and the coast. Yobakeya is a good anglicization and that spelling was used by Stewart (1943:46ff.). These people were never numerous and have long been extinct.

The name of their only village (13), near the Echo station, is given by the Yokaya as *k̓alóhko,* with no meaning because it is an attempt to reproduce the sounds of the Southern Pomo name of the site *k̓ol·ok·o* 'mortar basket field'. Most evidence is that the territory was held by the Central Pomo tribelet Yobakeya at the time of White settlement, but the fact that the name is basically Southern Pomo suggests that previously it had belonged to speakers of that language.

The territory of the various Northern Pomo tribelets lay in central Mendocino County and, from a frontage of 22 miles on the coast, extended in an irregular band inland nearly 50 miles to a region on the northwestern shore of Clear Lake shared with the Eastern Pomo. To the north were the Cahto and various Yukian groups and to the south the Central Pomo. The majority of the tribelets lived in small valleys in the drainage of the upper Russian River, which flows south, and upper Outlet Creek, which flows north into the Eel River.

There was no native name for the speakers of Northern Pomo as a whole. Names of particular groups, who often spoke different dialects, were derived from the name of the valley or location where they lived. A frequent element for forming group names is *pʰóʔmaʔ*, containing the verb *pʰó-* 'live in a group'; the derivative will be anglicized here as Poma (ˈpōˌmä). Also quite freely used are *-kʰe* 'of, from' and either the independent word *čáʔ* 'person' or the element *-yaʔ* 'the one(s)', forming terminations *-kʰe čáʔ* 'person from' and *-kʰeyaʔ* 'the one(s) from'.

Coast. The Northern Pomo did not live year-round along the coast until after the encroachment of White settlers into the interior valleys, but various tribelets had their favorite coastal campsites for collecting seafood in the summer. The Mato-Poma hunted and gathered food in the drainage of Tenmile River and along the coast for nine miles north of their border. In this they shared rights with the Coast Yuki. Stewart (1943:32ff.) presents rather strong evidence that the Mato-Poma considered the land theirs. However, it is also the case that this region was the year-round, not just part-time, home territory of at least 3 of the 11 Coast Yuki groups (Gifford 1939b); consequently, the section is here maintained as Coast Yuki, as given by Barrett (1908) and Kroeber (1925). Figure 5 contains longstanding Northern Pomo names for two important sites in the region.

Farther south, the Boya considered the area around Big River as their own. When Mitom-Poma, under pressure from White settlers in the interior, took up year-round residence on the coast, about 1850, they were challenged by the Boya but defeated them in battle and thus established rights to the disputed region (Stewart 1943:37).

Important sites on the coast from north to south are

1. *kál kʰabé* 'mussel rocks'; three miles south of West-port, a series of offshore rocks, tidal channels, and pools, particularly picturesque and rich in seafood.
2. *bidá to* 'on the river'; the area at the mouth of Tenmile River.
4. *no yów* 'under the dust'; according to Barrett (1908:134), formerly applied to the north side of the mouth of Pudding Creek (3, now usually called * R̵ayán bidá* 'duck creek') and, after the coming of

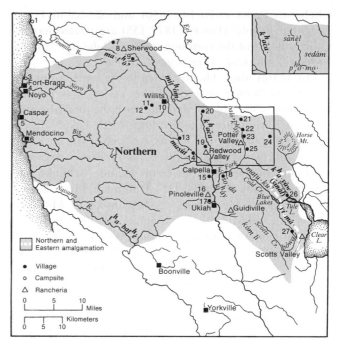

Fig. 5. Territory of the Northern Pomo. For the names corresponding to the numbers, see text.

White settlers, transferred two miles southward to the town and river Noyo (the English name being derived from the Indian).

5. *čatám* 'several jumping across'; the Caspar area.
6. *búl dám* 'trail past *búl*'; *búl* may refer to 'blowhole'. The name applies to the area at the mouth of Big River and to the town Mendocino. A trail from Mitom terminated there.

Tabate (ˌtäbäˈtā). Twelve miles inland, along the Navarro River, was the community of *tʰa· baṭʰé* 'much gravel'. No descendants of the aboriginal inhabitants are at the site and statements in earlier records are indecisive on their linguistic affiliation. Barrett's classification (1908:map) as Northern is continued here because there is no real evidence to the contrary and the name seems more Northern than Central. In Northern *baṭʰé* is 'much, many'; in Central it is 'big (of a single object)' and inapplicable to gravel; *tʰédu* is 'much'. Gibbs (1853:112) gives Tabah-téa as a tribe between the Russian River and the coast, the word apparently containing a final *-ya* or *-yaʔ*. Other renditions have been Ta-bi-tas (Heintzelman 1855), Taa-bo-tah, Tah′-bah-ta′, and Tah′-bo-ta.

Comacho or Ko-má-cho (Powers 1877:172), for Indians of this region, said to be derived from the name of a chief, is quite unknown now, although the name of a local town, Comptche, seems to be derived from it.

Mato (ˌmäˈtō). The most northerly community was at *ma· tʰóʔ* 'moldy ground', a name for Sherwood Valley and a village there; its people were called *ma· tʰóʔ pʰóʔmaʔ·*. Another name for the same region and a recent rancheria is *šibál ḍanó* 'nearby mountain' (8). Perhaps

Chebal-na-Poma (ARCIA 1856) and Shi-bál-ni Pómo 'neighbor people' (Powers 1877:155) are related names. Other villages of the community were kʰabé dile· 'among rocks' (7) and kʰalé kʰáw 'lone(?) tree' (9).

Mitom (mǐˈtōm). The next area to the south, known in English as Willits or Little Lake Valley, was miṭʰóm, containing -ṭʰóm 'splash' and mi- 'with the toes' (the area was marshy and subject to flooding). Little Lake Valley is miṭʰóm kʰáy; the town of Willits, miṭʰómaʔ (with an added verbal suffix), and the people miṭʰóm pʰóʔmaʔ. Previous renditions of these various terms include Betumke and Betumki (Gibbs 1853:634, 115), Bitóm-kai, Matomey Ki, Ma-tom-kai, Me-tum-ki, Mi-toam-kai, Mītōˈma, Mitomkai, and Mtóm-kai. Vihman (1966–1969) furnishes a second modern recording, biṭʰóm kʰáy, to compare with Halpern's (1939–1940) miṭʰóm kʰáy. The forms with initial b- instead of m- probably reflect a dialectal sound shift, or, possibly, a substitution of a verb prefix bi- for mi-.

The English name for Tomki Creek to the north and east is probably derived from this native term (Barrett 1908:128). Three villages of the Mitom-Poma were miṭʰómaʔ 'splashing with the toes' (10), na·bó, of unknown meaning (11), and čamómda 'fly's(?) trail' (12).

Masut (mäˈsōot). In the drainage of the Russian River, along Forsythe and Walker creeks and southward, was the territory of the masúʔ or masúi̯ (dialectal variants of unknown meaning). J. McKee's Maj-su-ta-ki-as (1853:144) and Gibbs's Masu-ta-kaya (1853:112) and McKee's Ma-su-ta-kéa (1851–1857, 3:634), for a tribe in this area, are probably something like masúi̯-kʰeyaʔ 'those from Masut'. Three villages of theirs were kʰo· bidá 'two creeks' (13), masúʔ (14), and čóm šadi·la 'pine ridge extending downward' (15). The last is the Choam Cha-dí-la of Powers (1877:155) and tcōˈmtcadīla of Barrett (1908:143).

Just to the north of čóm šadi·la is the modern town of Calpella, whose name is derived from that of a former chief (Barrett 1908:143). Since the chief's name is said to have meant 'mussel-bearer', it can be reconstituted as kʰál pʰi·la, consisting of kʰál 'mussels' and the verb root pʰí- 'carry', especially 'pack on the back', plus the suffix -·la 'downward'.

Komli (ˈkōmlē). In the northern half of Ukiah Valley, there lived a Northern Pomo group that, after an altercation with the Yokaya, fled eastward finally to settle among the Eastern and Northern Pomo in Scotts Valley. This event, which occurred about 1830 or 1835, is reported from several viewpoints in Barrett (1908:138ff.). Their major village, at the site of a large spring on the north side of Ukiah, is said by Barrett to have been called kōˈmlī, from kōm 'soda spring' and lī 'there'. The name is probably Řóm li 'drinking place', and it was also applied by the refugees to a temporary settlement they established by a spring in Eightmile Valley on their way eastward.

Near the site of the original Řóm li was instituted the first Pinoleville rancheria, called Řibúřibú, of unknown meaning (17). The present Pinoleville, on Ackerman Creek, is named ya· mó 'bone hole' (16) and is inhabited mainly by Indians from Potter Valley, according to Barrett. Guidiville, just southeast of Ukiah, is another Northern Pomo rancheria.

Shoda-Kay (ˈshōdä₁kī), Sacham-Kay (shäˈchäm₁kī). Just northeast of Ukiah Valley, on the lower east fork of the Russian River, lay Coyote Valley, now under the Lake Mendocino reservoir. The valley, especially the southern part, was called šo·da kʰáy 'valley in the east'. The people are listed by Powers (1877:155) as Shó-da-kai Pómo; other renditions of the place-name are cōˈdakai and Shodakhai. The northern part of Coyote Valley was known as šačám kʰáy 'live oak valley' (Vihman 1966–1969). Derived from this term, with loss of the first syllable, is the name of the principal village čámkʰaˑwi (18). Earlier versions of the names have been catcámkaū, chamkhai, Shachamkau, and tcámkawī.

Kacha (käˈchä). Farther north, in Redwood Valley, the people call themselves kʰača· 'at the flint', possibly also the name of a former village. The dominant stream of the area, the upper west fork of the Russian River, has the related name kʰačá bidá 'flint creek'. Kniffen's (1939:373) rendition as Kacha is a good anglicization; the name has also been written Katca. One of their villages was kʰabé lal 'edge of the rocks' (19). Dá-pi-shūl, given by Powers (1877:155) for a place at the north end of Redwood Valley and said to mean 'high sun', was given to Halpern (1939–1940) as dá pʰišu· 'trail's end' (20), a literal designation, for Huchnom territory lay to the north (dá means both 'sun' and 'trail, road').

Balo-Kay (bäˈlō₁kī): Shanel (shäˈnel), Sedam (sāˈdäm), Shane-Kay (shäˈnē₁kī), Pomo (ˈpō₁mō). Potter Valley, on the upper east fork of the Russian River, is called balóʔ kʰáy. Powers (1877:155) wrote it Ballo-Kai and translated it 'oat valley'; most later ethnographers have called it 'wild oats valley'. Halpern's (1939–1940) notes contain the definition of balóʔ as 'an edible shoot, like asparagus', a more probable meaning, as wild oats are an introduced species.

According to Stewart (1943:39–41), three communities inhabited the valley. The northernmost and largest was šanél 'at the ceremonial house (dance or sweathouse)'. Gibbs (1853:108) referred to them as Shanel-kaya, that is, šanél-kʰeyaʔ 'those from Shanel'. The name has also been written Canal and Canel. Ford's Salan Pomas of Potter Valley (ARCIA 1856:257), otherwise unidentifiable, could be a miswriting of the name of this group (compare the variety of representations of the Central Pomo village of the same name). Connected with Shanel were several villages, the two most important being šanél (22) and yá mo 'wind hole' (21). The people of Shanel extended their hunting range to the north side of the Eel River, beyond the territorial limit marked on figure 5, and came into frequent conflict with the Huchnom as a consequence (Stewart 1943:40).

The central part of Potter Valley was occupied by the community and village of *sedám* 'trail past the brush(?)' (23). Stewart included *šané kʰáy* 'ceremonial house valley' (24), several miles to the east, in this community, but Kroeber (1925:map) classified them separately. These are probably the people referred to as the Cha-net-kai tribe by J. McKee (1853:136). Other versions of the name have been *canē´kai* and Caneki.

Southernmost in Potter Valley was the community and village of *pʰoˑmoˑ* 'at red earth hole' (25) (Vihman 1966–1969), one source of the name of the linguistic family. The name has been rendered Paum, Poam, Pom, Pome, Pomo, Pone, and Pum, with or without a following Pomo or Poma (from *pʰóˀmaˀ*); best would be Pomo-Poma. The Po-mo´-ke-chah´ of Merriam (1955:144) is *pʰoˑmoˑ-kʰe čáˀ* 'person from Pomo'.

Gibbs's (1853:109) Bedah-marek and J. McKee's Medama-rec (1853:136) are apparently Eastern Pomo *biˑdáˑ* 'lower' (McLendon 1975:138) plus *Márakʰ* 'ceremonial house' and could refer to Shanel or some other Northern Pomo community in this area.

Three residences remain on a small rancheria in Potter Valley; most of the surviving Indians have moved to Pinoleville and elsewhere.

Matuku (mä¹toōkoō), Shinal (shĭ¹näl), Kayaw (kä¹yäw). South of Potter Valley, along Cold Creek, were the *maṭuˑkuˀ*, meaning unknown (Vihman 1966–1969). The word has been written Mah-too´-go, Matuho, Matuko, and Matuku (best). According to Stewart (1943:41), probably in the mid-nineteenth century they joined the community to their southeast in Bachelor Valley and on Tule Lake, in the drainage system of Clear Lake. This community (26) was apparently already an amalgamation of Northern and Eastern Pomo speakers. The name for their district is *šinál* in Northern Pomo, and *kʰaˑyáw* in Eastern, both meaning 'at the head'. The Northern version has been represented ceinal, cinal, and Shinal (best). The Eastern version appears more frequently in anthropological literature and has been represented Haiyau, Kaiyao, Kaiyau, Ki-ou, Ki-yow, and Xaiyáū. The Ki-yow´-bah^ch of Merriam (1955:144) is Eastern *kʰaˑyáw-bax* 'people of Kayaw'.

Survivors are at the Upper Lake rancheria and consider themselves Eastern Pomo.

Yima (yē¹mä), Bowal (¹bōwäl), Komli (¹kōmlē). To the South, in Scotts Valley, and with four miles frontage on Clear Lake, is the region *yiˑmáˑ*. In Eastern Pomo *yiˑmá* is 'gristle, sinew', and the final vowel length derives locatives (McLendon 1975:137). Stewart's (1943:41ff.) Yimaba is Eastern *yiˑmáˑ-bax* 'people of Yima'.

The Northern Pomo name, either for the same community or perhaps only for the Northern Pomo elements in an amalgamation with the Eastern Pomo, was *bówal-kʰeyaˀ* 'the ones from the west side', that is, west from the point of view of others living in the Clear Lake region, as the people were the easternmost of the Northern Pomo. The name can be anglicized without the added -*kʰeyaˀ* as Bowal, which name has appeared in some form more frequently in print than Yima. Representations of *bówal-kʰe* have been Boalke, Boilkai, and Möal-kai (Gibbs 1853:108); with the added element -*yaˀ*, it has been written Boalkea, Bo´-al-ke-ah, and Boil-ka-ya.

Joining the above toward the middle of the nineteenth century, were refugees from *Řóm li* 'drinking place', in northern Ukiah Valley. The name of these people is usually given as Komli, a good anglicization; it has also been rendered Cum-le-bah (L. Palmer 1881:35), that is, Northern Pomo *Řóm li* plus Eastern -*bax* '(people) from'. The Komli stayed temporarily in Eightmile Valley, at a spring and site that they also named *Řóm li,* before moving on eastward to join the newly formed community of Yima.

The Yima were allowed food-gathering privileges along a section of the northwest shore of Clear Lake by the *quˑłá-naˑpʰò,* but Indians from Upper Lake objected and drove them off. The Yima obtained support from the *quˑłá-naˑpʰò* and *xaˑbé-naˑpʰò* and defeated the Upper Lake Indians, thus establishing their right to use of that part of the shoreline (Loeb 1926:207–210).

Most toponyms of the Yima district are recorded only in Eastern Pomo form. An important village was *nó boˑral* (27), probably constructed of *nó* 'ashes', *bór* 'mud', and -*al* 'toward' (McLendon 1975:139, 26, 146).

The Shinal or Kayaw district and part of Yima were amalgamations of Northern and Eastern speakers (fig. 6). The previous assignment of this region exclusively to Northern Pomo seems more specific than the evidence warrants. This historical inference is that the Northern Pomo were diffusing eastward into what had been all Eastern Pomo territory. Although external conflicts were involved, the relationship between the uniting groups was peaceful. An important factor appears to have been marriage between neighboring Northern and Eastern groups to such an extent that the two peoples became closely interrelated and could easily merge (cf. Stewart 1943:41).

Northeastern Pomo

The Northeastern Pomo lived in a compact area on the eastern side of the Coast Range, primarily in the drainage system of Big Stony Creek before its confluence with Little Stony Creek (in Patwin territory), the combination flowing northward and eastward to the Sacramento Valley. They were separated from the main body of the Pomo by land that has been generally accepted as belonging to the Yuki and the Patwin. That territory was hinterland hunting ground that may not have been under the exclusive dominion of any one group. Stewart (1943:41) cites a Northern Pomo from Sedam as claiming that his people hunted in this intervening area. The

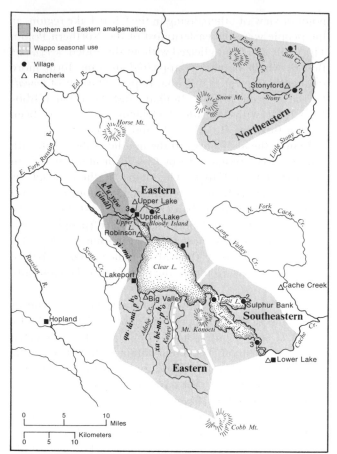

Fig. 6. Territory of the Northeastern, Eastern, and Southeastern Pomo. For the names corresponding to the numbers, see text. Upper Lake is shown in its original form (after Barrett 1908), before a 1920s reclamation project changed its shoreline by dredging and filling.

ruggedness of this zone of separation, with peaks to 7,000 feet, may have prevented permanent occupation, but it was not a complete barrier to trading parties. Pomo of the Clear Lake and upper Russian River regions, as well as Yuki from Round Valley, followed established trails across it for an important item—salt. Because of their control, or attempted control, of this economic resource, the Northeastern Pomo have also been called the Salt Pomo.

Payment was usually expected both for salt that had already been collected and for gathering privileges. However, many parties took the salt clandestinely without payment and, in the early nineteenth century, conflicts ensued known as the Salt Wars. A brief account is in Kroeber (1925:236); more details are in Barrett (1908:239–244).

The Northeastern Pomo call themselves čʰeʔeˑ fokaˑ 'salt people', and the neighboring Patwin and other Indians gave them names of similar meaning. In Northeastern Pomo, terms for groups of people customarily end in fokaˑ, constructed of fo- 'live in a group' (cognate to Northern Pomo pʰó-) plus -kaˑ, a suffix added to all words

designating animate beings. The terms Cotea and Sho-te'-ah (Merriam 1955:144) for the Northeastern Pomo are reminiscent of Central Pomo šóˑtaya 'easterners'.

The three-quarter-acre salt deposit for which the territory is best known was named čʰeʔeˑ tiʔdoˑ 'salt field' (1 on fig. 6). Their principal settlement was baʔkam taʔt̥ʰi 'chaparral village' (2).

Eastern Pomo

A reasonably accurate picture of the Eastern Pomo village-communities extant at the period of initial contact with Whites during the first half of the nineteenth century can be obtained by combining the oral historical tradition collected during the twentieth century by a number of ethnographers (Barrett, Kroeber, Loeb, Kniffen, Stewart, Merriam, Gifford), and still collectable from the oldest generation of contemporary Eastern Pomo speakers, with the two significant nineteenth-century sources of McKee (Gibbs in Schoolcraft 1851–1857, 3) and L. Palmer (1881).

Leaders of four Eastern Pomo "tribes," that is, village-communities, participated in the negotiations and signed the treaty arrived at with McKee in 1851: quˑłá-naˑpʰò, xaˑbé-naˑpʰò, daˑnó-xàˑ, and šíˑkom. A fifth Eastern Pomo village-community, the xówalekʰ, did not attend the treaty negotiations for some reason, but they are mentioned by L. Palmer (1881) and subsequent researchers. Merriam (1966–1967, 1:17) grouped the xówalekʰ with the daˑnó-xàˑ without explanation, a procedure also followed by Kunkel (1962). However, Kniffen (1939) and Stewart (1943) were told that the two groups were independent. Billy Gilbert, who was the source of Stewart's data on these groups, was a member of the xówalekʰ through his mother, but not of the daˑnó-xàˑ. Gifford (1926c) collected 23 names of individuals from daˑnó-xàˑ intermarried with, or otherwise related to, people from šíˑkom and 32 names of individuals from xówalekʰ. The father of Jim Pumpkin, Gifford's source for this genealogical information, came from daˑnó-xàˑ (but not xówalekʰ). It seems unlikely that so many individuals could consistently have been distinguished if there were not two distinct village-communities involved. The xówalekʰ seem to have fished in the spring at Bloody Island (Stewart 1943:42). It is possible that they did not attend the treaty negotiations out of fear, having been badly hurt by the cavalry attack the preceding spring.

The chief of a fifth group attended the treaty negotiations in 1851. Gibbs transcribed the name of this group as Moal-kai. This seems to have been a group that the Eastern Pomo referred to as bówalkʰeya (Northern Pomo bówal-kʰeyaʔ 'people from the west'), who are said to have lived in Scotts Valley. The western shore of Clear Lake proper and Scotts Valley, which runs parallel to this portion of shoreline but separated from it by a low range of foothills, were assigned to the Northern Pomo by Barrett (1908), but the place-names he gives for this area are mostly Eastern Pomo terms. The Eastern Pomo name for Scotts Valley is *yi·má·*, which could mean 'at the sinew'. Gifford in his genealogies of the Eastern Pomo village-community of *ší·kom* found that a number of the residents of *ší·kom* had married or were otherwise related to individuals from a Northern Pomo village in Scotts Valley that he transcribes as yima. Merriam (1966-1967, 1:17) includes in his classification of the stocks and tribes of California Ye-mah'-rah[ch] as a member of a subdivision with the Bo'-al-ke-ah (*bówal-kʰeyaʔ*), and Loeb (1926: 280) refers to the Yemabak as a Scotts Valley tribe. Merriam's and Loeb's forms seem clear attempts to represent the Eastern Pomo *yi·má·bax* 'people of Scotts Valley'. It is not clear if *yi·má·* was the Eastern Pomo name for the village-community of the Northern-Pomo-speaking *bówal-kʰeyaʔ*, or the name of an Eastern-Pomo-speaking village-community with which, perhaps, the *bówal-kʰeyaʔ* had joined. The place-names indicate that this area was used by Eastern Pomo as well as Northern Pomo. (Since the western shore was regularly flooded in winter and spring, it was not a suitable location for a permanent village, but was only used for camping.) This seems to have been an area into which the Northern Pomo were moving at about the time of contact. Barrett (1908:138-139) has collected oral historical evidence that another Northern-Pomo-speaking group associated with Scotts Valley, the *Ŕómli*, had only moved into the valley around the time of White settlement, having been forced to move from just north of Ukiah by the Central Pomo south of them. According to Loeb (1926:280) both the *bówal-kʰeyaʔ* and the *Ŕómli* intermarried with the Eastern Pomo communities of *qu·ɫá-na·pʰò* and *xa·bé-na·pʰò* to such an extent that they ceased to exist as separate groups during the third quarter of the nineteenth century. If true, this situation suggests that they were recent arrivals rather than residents for a considerable period.

The village-community of *kʰa·yáw* 'at the head', which is usually assigned to the Northern Pomo under the Northern Pomo name *šinál* 'at the head' is said by contemporary Eastern Pomo to have been a village where both Eastern Pomo and Northern Pomo were spoken and is therefore considered among the Eastern Pomo village-communities.

The various recordings of the names of these village-communities are given below; the numbers are keyed to figure 6.

1. *ší·kom* was located on the north shore of Clear Lake proper where the present town of Lucerne is located. More is known about it than any other Eastern Pomo village-community because of Gifford's (1926c) census of it. Written as cī'gōm, She-kom, Che-com, Cigom, Shigom, She'-kum, and She-gum-ba from *ší·kombax* 'people of *ší·kom*'.

2. *da·nó-xà·* was located in Clover Valley along Clover Creek to the northeast of the present town of Upper Lake. Labeled Dah-no-habe (either from *da·nó-xà·bax* 'people

of *da·nó-xà·* or a typographical error, probably introduced because this form was listed after Habe-napo, i.e., *xa·bé-na·pʰò*), Danoxa, Danoha, Dan-no'-kah, and Dinoo-ha-vah from *da·nó-xà·bax* 'people of *da·nó-xà·*'.

3. *xówalekʰ* was located just west of Middle Creek in Upper Lake Valley, about three-quarters of a mile northwest of the present town of Upper Lake. Called Xowalek, Howalek, Ho-al-lek, Quoi-lack, Hwoi-lak.

kʰa·yáw was located at the northwestern end of Tule Lake in Bachelor Valley. Both Northern Pomo and Eastern Pomo seem to have been spoken here, and there is both a Northern Pomo name *šinál* for this village-community and an Eastern Pomo one, *kʰa·yáw*. Recorded as xaiya'ū, Kayau, Kaiyao, Mayi (Eastern Pomo *ma·yíy*, a former village on the Sleeper ranch, to the northeast of Tule Lake), Haiyau, Kaiyau, Ki-yow'-bah[ch] (from Eastern Pomo *kʰa·yáwbax* 'people of *kʰa·yáw*'), ki-ou.

The exact location of the permanent village of the *qu·ɫá-na·pʰò* is difficult to determine, perhaps because Salvador Vallejo's men forced them to move from their former location when he began to run cattle in Big Valley in the 1840s. All sources seem to agree that they controlled that portion of Big Valley roughly from Lakeport to Adobe Creek, which they controlled access to. Other names are kūLa'napō, Hula-napo, KuLanapo, Bohanapwena (from *bó·xaNawi·na·*(?) 'on top of on the west water' given as name of village), Kuhlanapo, Kahibadon (from *qa·ší-ba·dòn* 'island off shore from present town of Lakeport' given as the main town), Ku'-lenap'-po, Hoo-la-nap-o.

The exact location of *xa·bé-na·pʰò* at the time of contact is unclear but seems to have probably been along Kelsey Creek, just south of the present town of Kelseyville.

The *xa·bé-na·pʰò* allowed a small Wappo group to utilize a portion of their territory seasonally (fig. 6). Variants are kabē'napō, Kabenapo, Habe-napo, Hahbenap'-po, xabenapo, Kabenapwena (from *xa·béNawi·na·* (?) 'on top of on rock'), Bidamiwina (*bi·dámiwi·na·* 'on top of the creek'), Nonapoti (*nó-na·pʰòti* 'ash-village/people'), Shabegok (*ša·bé-kókʰ* 'centerpost [of the ceremonial house] standing').

Southeastern Pomo

During the nineteenth century the Southeastern Pomo, when mentioned at all, were referred to with Eastern Pomo, Northern Pomo, or Patwin names. Barrett (1908) was the first to provide the Southeastern Pomo names for the three Southeastern Pomo village-communities of *qámdot*, *ʔlém*, and *xqóyi*.

The first published mention of a Southeastern Pomo village-community seems to have been by Gibbs (1853:109). The chief of the How-ku-ma (Eastern Pomo *xá-ku·hmà*) tribe participated in the treaty negotiations with Col. McKee in 1851. He was most likely the chief of *ʔlém* (although Barrett does give his version of *xá-ku·hmà* as one of two Eastern Pomo names for *qámdot* on Buckingham Island).

qámdot (1 on fig. 6) was located on a small island near the western shore of East Lake (an arm of Clear Lake), which was formerly called Buckingham Island and is now called Anderson Island. Gifford (1926c) and Barrett (1908) give *qámdot* as the name of the village, but it is probably the name of the whole island, since it seems clearly to contain the form *-mdot* 'island', and Merriam (1955) gives the name of this group as Hám-fo, that is, *qámfo*, from *qá + mfo* 'people'. *qa* means both a gambling game and a species of snake. Barrett gives as Eastern Pomo names for this group le'makma (lí·makʰma·, meaning unknown) and ka'ūgū'ma *xá-ku·hmà* 'swimmers, fishermen' literally 'water-people'). *xá-ku·hmà* is not now used by Eastern Pomo speakers to refer to *qámdot*. Past usages have included: ka'mdōt, Kamdot, Eastern Pomo limakmaiina (from *lí·makʰma· + wi·na·* 'on top of'?), and Le-mah-mah.

ʔlém (2), the largest of the Southeastern Pomo villages, was located on an island (now called Rattlesnake or Sulphur Bank Island) at the eastern tip of East Lake that Barrett (1908:208) describes as "a low island, covering about 35 acres, with its northern slope well wooded and its southern slope [where *ʔlém* was located] entirely open." Barrett says that the people of *ʔlém* were called ka'-mīna by the Northern Pomo and xa'-wīna by the Eastern Pomo. Actually Northern Pomo *kʰámina·* and Eastern Pomo *xáwi·na·* both mean 'water on top of' and refer to the place and not the people. Barrett gives as another Eastern Pomo term for the people of *ʔlém* ka'ūgūma (*xá-ku·hmà* 'swimmers, fishermen' literally 'water-people'). It is not now used by Eastern Pomo speakers to refer to the people of *ʔlém*. Former designations are: How-ku-ma, Elem, Eastern Pomo xaukumaiina (from *xá-ku·hmà + wi·na·* 'on top of'?), Kamina, Hawina, Kauguma, and Cow-goo-mah.

The village of *xqóyi* (3) was located on the "eastern shore of a small, low island called Lower Lake Island at the extreme southern end of Lower Lake" (Barrett 1908:207). Only slightly smaller than *ʔlém*, Barrett says *xqóyi* was called cūta'ūyōmanūk in Northern Pomo and kaūbōkōlai in Eastern Pomo. Neither term is known in these two languages in 1976 with this referent. The form credited to Eastern Pomo could be something like *xá·ba·kù·la·ya* 'those who run/fall into the water'. L. Palmer's (1881) Shoat-ow-no-ma-nook and Gibbs's (1853) Cho-tan-o-man-as (a group living at the outlet of Clear Lake but not present at the treaty negotiations) look like attempts at representing a form something like the one that Barrett attributes to Northern Pomo. This village has been termed: kō'i, xō'yī, Koi, Hoyi, and Shutauyomanok. Powers (1877) apparently discusses this group as the Makh'-el-chel, which Kroeber (1925:232) says is Patwin.

Western Pomo and Northeastern Pomo

LOWELL JOHN BEAN AND DOROTHEA THEODORATUS

Language and Territory

Culturally, socially, and linguistically the Western and Northeastern Pomo are similar peoples organized into some 25 separate, politically autonomous groups called tribelets (Stewart 1943). Five distinct language groups—Kashaya, Southern, Central, Northern, Northeastern—are described in this chapter. Oswalt (1964a) has postulated a Pomo wedge similar to the Shoshonean (i.e., Takic) wedge of southern California to explain their possible prehistoric territorial expansion. He suggests that the early Pomo lived on the shores of Clear Lake in four branches: Western, Eastern, Southeastern, and Northeastern and that "the Western Branch migrated across the range of mountains just to the west of Clear Lake over on the Russian River. There they spread north and south through the string of valleys along the course of the River so that its drainage system came almost entirely into Pomo hands" (Oswalt 1964a:419–420).

As the Western Branch spread, Yukian speakers were probably displaced. The Western Branch split into Northern and Southern groups with the latter differentiating into three languages (Kashaya, Southern, Central), while the Northern group split into several dialect units (Oswalt 1964a:420).

Environment

The area occupied by these various groups can be divided into two ecozones: coast-redwood and valley-foothill. The former is composed of a narrow land-shelf immediately adjacent to the ocean and separated from the valley-foothill zone by the heavily timbered (redwood forest) Coast Range, which closely follows the coastline. The area is cut latitudinally by the Russian River (in the extreme southern portion) and several creeks and streams.

The coast-redwood zone was the least favorable of the habitats exploited by the Pomo due to the heavily eroded nature of the coast beachline backed by an unbroken redwood forest. Further, it was restricted in the amount of edible plants and animals available. The major food and raw materials came from the ocean (fish, shellfish, snails, seaweed, sea lions, salt), the redwood forests (deer, roosevelt elk, small mammals, bark for clothing and houses), and the rivers and streams (fish, mussels). In several places along the coastal foothills stands of coastal oak were exploited in the fall while various edible bulbs, berries, roots, tubers, and seeds were available during spring and early summer. Several offshore islands were regularly visited by the coastal groups, who crossed on rafts of driftwood bound together with vegetal fiber to hunt seals and sea lions and to collect mussels (Loeb 1926:182).

Climatic factors along the coast greatly affected the human occupants. Temperatures ranged from midday summer highs of 80° F. to well below freezing during the winter. Rainfall of 40–50 inches annually was usual, and fog was common during most of the year.

Settlements in this coastal zone, determined largely by climatic factors and resource distribution, were of two basic types: permanent villages at varying distances from the ocean and seasonal campsites located along the shoreline, near river and creek mouths, and in favored areas in the redwood forest. Most permanent villages were in the inland areas (often as much as 20 miles back from the coast), and these villages appear to have had greater populations than those located near the coast. Some larger villages served as nuclei for smaller ones located nearby. These smaller villages (or subsidiary hamlets) tended to be kinship units bound closely to the larger villages through economic, social, and kinship ties.

Most of the population inhabiting this area lived near the alluvial mouth of the Russian River and along creek banks. The redwood forests were considered hinterlands, rarely occupied for periods of longer than a month. Rather, villagers made forays into them for various products, establishing seasonal campsites that were reoccupied year after year by the same kin groups. Other seasonal campsites were near salmon streams, offshore seal and sea lion rookeries, and other food-producing areas.

The valley-foothill region, bisected longitudinally by the Russian River, included the drainages of the Upper Eel River, Russian River, and Petaluma, Sonoma, and Napa creeks. The area can be characterized as primarily composed of a succession of grassy, oak-dotted valleys separated by rolling hills.

Climatic conditions were not so harsh in this region as in the coast-redwood zone. Summer temperatures occasionally ranged as high as 100° F., with winter daytime temperatures averaging 50–60° F. Rainfall was approximately 30-40 inches annually, particularly in the lower areas.

The flora and fauna were remarkably similar throughout the area. The acorn was the primary plant food available. Although the streams and rivers were fished, there was less dependence upon fish and more upon game (deer, rabbits, small mammals), which abounded in the open grassy plain of the valley.

Although settlements in this zone tended to be larger than their counterparts in the coast-redwood zone, the largest and densest populations were found in the south-central section.

Culture

Subsistence

The varied and abundant natural resources in their area the Pomo expertly used. Acorns, of which seven species were collected, were a staple. Buckeye nuts, a variety of berries, seeds from at least 15 kinds of grasses, roots and bulbs, and edible greens were gathered and eaten fresh or stored. Dried seaweed and kelp from the ocean shore were delicacies. Salt was secured from the Northeastern Pomo, who owned salt springs in their territory (Kroeber 1925:236), or was obtained from naturally evaporated seawater.

The taking of game, by individuals or in communal hunts, was one of the most important occupations of the men. It "was considered to be a matter requiring careful preparation and rigid observance of certain regulations if participants were to be successful" (Barrett 1952, 1:118–119). Group hunting took two forms: a single hunter with a deer-head mask and disguise, assisted by several drivers and packers; and the erection of a brush fence and a regular surround and drive. Hunters commonly knew every deer in the territory and maintained a balance between herds and the available vegetation to keep the animals from straying outside Pomo territory (Aginsky 1968:210).

Deer, elk, and antelope were the chief big game hunted. Rabbits and squirrels were important food resources. Many kinds of birds were taken for food or for their feathers, but a number of avian species were tabooed as food, among these the valley jay, hawks, crows, owls, meadowlark, loon, seagulls, and killdeer.

Typical weapons were bow and arrow for large land animals, the heavy spear, club for bear, and spears for seal and sea lion. Smaller animals and birds were captured by bola, low brush fences, nets, snares, and basketry traps.

Lake, stream, and ocean fish were caught in traps, with lines, or weirs. Grasshoppers, caterpillars, and larvae

NAA, Smithsonian.

Fig. 1. Northern or Central Pomo woman using a stone pestle to pound acorns in a basketry mortar. Photographed at or near Ukiah by H.W. Henshaw, 1893.

were also eaten. For details on food-securing methods, preparation, and storage, see Barrett (1952), Gifford (1967), Gifford and Kroeber (1939), Kroeber (1925), Loeb (1926), and Stewart (1943).

Technology

Implements like the mortar and pestle for grinding were usually of stone. The stone mortars were natural shapes and were used with a bottomless basketry hopper (fig. 1). Knives were made from obsidian or chert and could be attached to handles and used as axes. Bone was used more rarely for making implements, notably for awls and fishhooks.

Like their ceremonial paraphernalia, Pomo basketry techniques were characterized by great variety in type (fig. 2). Coiled ware was made in two forms (single or three-rod), twined ware in seven forms, and wickerwork was also done. The range of forms varied from very flat plate styles to almost perfect spheres. Horizontal and banded pattern arrangements predominated among decoration styles. One of the most basic characteristic features of their baskets was the use of feathers and beads for outlining or making designs (fig. 3) (Barrett 1908a).

Clothing and Adornment

Men went nude most of the time and when clothing was worn it was for some definitely utilitarian, social, or ritual purpose (Barrett 1952, 2:292). During wet or rainy

Dept. of Anthr., Smithsonian: top, 203415; bottom, 203470.
Fig. 3. Feather-decorated coiled baskets, treasured items used as gifts and offerings. top, Central Pomo (Shiyeko), surface fully covered with feathers in geometric design of yellow, green, blue, white, and red; diameter 11.8 cm; collected in 1896. bottom, Central Pomo (Danokeya), designs in red woodpecker feathers woven into natural splints, blue beads sewed over dyed splints after coiling, quail plumes around top; same scale; collected in 1890.

Dept. of Anthr., Smithsonian: a, 327998; b, 203517; c, 327996; d, 327992.
Fig. 2. Miniature coiled baskets, made for sale to basket collectors as a demonstration of high skill. a, Central Pomo (Yokaya), made by Mary Benson in 1909, diameter 4.6 cm. b, Northern Pomo (Shoda-Kay), collected in 1896. c, Northern Pomo, made by Joseppa, collected before 1925. d, unidentified Pomo, collected before 1925.

weather, men wore mantles of shredded, ripe tule (lake region), the inner bark of redwood trees (coastal region), or willow bark (interior regions). These mantles of vegetal material were worn essentially by the poorer classes, while men of wealth and importance wore ones of skins sewed together with some form of vegetal fiber (*Apocynum cannabinum, Asclepias eriocarpa, Psoralea macrostachya, Iris*).

Women always wore some kind of skirt that completely encircled the lower part of the body from the waist to the ankles. A mantle was tied about the neck and hung down to the waist to meet the skirt. Depending upon the geographical location and the wealth of the woman, the skirts were made of shredded redwood bark (coastal) or shredded willow bark (river) (fig. 4). Women also wore

291

Fig. 4. Willowbark skirt, Northern Pomo (perhaps Pomo-Poma). Length 70 cm, collected before 1900.

Fig. 5. Northern or Central Pomo man using a pump drill to perforate a shell bead. Photographed at or near Ukiah by H.W. Henshaw, about 1893.

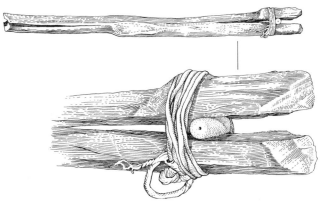

Fig. 6. Central Pomo (Yokaya) stick vise with detail showing magnesite bead in position for drilling. Length 58 cm, collected 1901.

skirts of skins, used throughout the year, and heavier bark garments as outer skirts in cold weather. On ceremonial occasions, women wore much more finely shredded skirts.

During cold weather, members of both sexes might don rabbitskin blankets, which were worn over the shoulders and fastened down the front with wooden skewers (Barrett 1952, 2:292-294). Along the coast, sea otter skins were used, while inland groups used the skins of the rabbit, puma, wildcat, gopher, and bear. Blankets and skirts were made by sewing together whole skins or woven twisted strips. Feather robes and sashes were also worn, but only on ceremonial occasions, and only by very wealthy men.

Various materials were used in making personal ornaments: discoidal beads of clamshell (fig. 5), long cylinders of clamshells, magnesite cylinders (fig. 6), brilliantly colored abalone shells, and various feathers (figs. 7-8). Belts, neck bands, and wrist bands were all woven of beads and were worn both as accessories to ceremonial costumes and as indicators of wealth and social position.

Structures

The various Pomo groups built three basic types of structures: dwelling houses, temporary shelters, and semisubterranean houses. Dwelling houses built by groups living on the coast and in the adjacent redwood belt of heavy timber (Kashaya, Central Pomo, and Northern Pomo) seem to have been primarily single-family conical dwellings of redwood bark slabs (fig. 9). These had diameters of only 8 to 15 feet and heights of 6 to 8 feet, yet among the Central Pomo they are said to have held as many as 12 people. The ground around the Central Pomo houses was surrounded by a brush fence, with the enclosed area used for drying acorns. The house

and the ground surrounding it were said to be owned by the oldest woman (perhaps the oldest in the maternal line). An obsolete form in the same area was a long, wedge-shaped slab house. Multifamily communal structures were built in the valleys inland from the redwood belt along the Russian River and around Clear Lake. These were circular, elliptical, or L-shaped and constructed of brush and grass or tule (at the lake) (Barrett 1916; Loeb 1926:158).

Temporary summer shelters built by the valley groups in the cooler foothills provided shade from the searing summer sun while permitting the easy movement of cooling breezes.

Semisubterranean structures served two main functions. In every village there was at least one small circular one, built in the spring, that was used as a sort of men's house and in which the men took daily sweat baths (Loeb 1926:159-160). A somewhat similar but much larger assembly house, averaging 70 feet in diameter, was used for dancing and ceremonials (Barrett 1916; Merriam 1955:41, 1966-1967,1:107). A special earth-covered lodge about 40 to 60 feet in diameter was used solely for housing ceremonies connected with the Ghost Dance. Occasionally, a special earth-covered lodge was built for use during the damaxii ceremony, given very rarely,

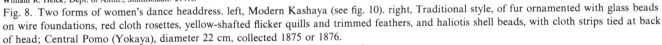

Lowie Mus., U. of Calif., Berkeley: 1-2718, 1-2719.

Fig. 7. Pair of Northern Pomo man's ear ornaments. Wood with carved and stained grooves, bead at end. Length 18.4 cm, collected by S.A. Barrett at Pinoleville rancheria *(ya· mó)* in 1902.

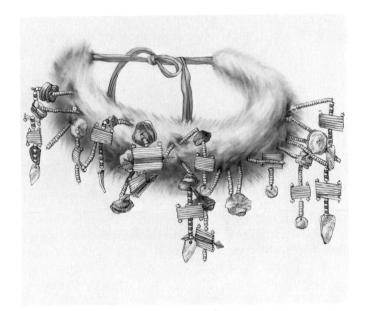

William R. Heick; Dept. of Anthr., Smithsonian: 21410.

Fig. 8. Two forms of women's dance headdress. left, Modern Kashaya (see fig. 10). right, Traditional style, of fur ornamented with glass beads on wire foundations, red cloth rosettes, yellow-shafted flicker quills and trimmed feathers, and haliotis shell beads, with cloth strips tied at back of head; Central Pomo (Yokaya), diameter 22 cm, collected 1875 or 1876.

usually at intervals of 20, 30, or even 50 years (Loeb 1926:163; Barrett 1916).

Social Organization

The Pomo generally recognized that they shared a common cultural background, the variations of which they compared and contrasted when establishing their ethnicity vis-a-vis other cultures or among themselves. Interaction among Pomo was more intense than between Pomo and others. They were, in Kroeber's (1925) terms, a nonpolitical nationality, culturally but not politically allied.

The tribelet was composed of one or more bilaterally related extended kin groups that ranged in size from 100 to 2,000 persons (Kunkel 1962). Each extended family had a headman or minor chief. The extended family chiefs together composed the principal ruling elite of the individual tribelets, functioning as a tribelet council.

The tribelets were organized into independent political units but some of these did occasionally confederate. On the Russian River a confederation of several linked tribelets combined to control some 16 miles of the river and lands adjacent to the river extending to the top of the surrounding hills. According to Kunkel (1962:287-288), seven residential kin groups of the Shokowa tribelet along the river were linked by assembly-house affiliations with one elected official, the "war chief." Kunkel (1962:285, 288) believes that the military organization of these tribelets was the primary factor binding them together and that they were the most complex of any of the Pomo groups. On another level, Pomo maintained regular military and trade alliances among themselves as well as with several non-Pomo groups (Loeb 1926).

Kin groups were the most significant social unit; the tribelet itself was a rather fragile social unit, since ambilaterality and ambilocality allowed movement of

Fig. 9. Northern Pomo (probably Mitom) houses at Big River, Mendocino Co. Photograph by Carleton E. Watkins, perhaps as early as 1860.

members from one tribelet to another. The tribelet could recombine in various ways. These kin groups were united by the ghost and secret societies and the office of chief who managed between them the political affairs of allied kin groups in a single tribelet. These groups owned assets in the tribelet territory and held some ceremonies independent of others.

The extended kin groups were composed of nuclear family hearth groups, the basic social and economic unit of the society, and averaged five to six persons. They usually lived in a multifamily dwelling for much of the year, and in separate temporary dwellings when the population of a village dispersed to seasonal fishing and collecting area.

Kinship terminology varied among the Pomo herein considered. The Kashaya, who used a Hawaiian kinship terminology, appear to be the most divergent. Omaha cousin terms are recorded for the Northern and Central Pomo, while Crow terms are suggested for the Southern Pomo (Tax 1955:5-8).

Since personal relationships among the Pomo were based primarily on kinship, relationships with nonkin were tenuous and suspect. However, a special, fictive kinlike relationship, loosely translated as 'special friend', could be established between two individuals. This was a formal relationship involving a ritual gift exchange, which contracted a reciprocal relationship, sometimes for the lifetime of the partners, and tacitly included the primary relatives of each of the partners (Aginsky and Aginsky 1967).

294 • STATUS The Pomo ranked individuals in terms of

family, background, wealth, and individual achievement. Special offices were generally inherited. Other social differences resulted from membership in the ghost society, to which most adult males could belong, and the Kuksu society, which was more select in its membership. Ritual leaders and chiefs ranked highest in prestige. Shamans, Kuksu initiates, outfit doctors (such as bear doctors), and sucking doctors ranked below them in status and wealth. Beneath these were members of the societies who regularly or occasionally served in ritual functions. Most of these men, and occasionally women, tended to be professional people.

The Pomo maintained professional positions that required apprenticeship under a sponsor, usually a kinsman, and involved formal affirmation of the secret society. The profession was practiced until passed to a successor. Professions included chieftainship, shamanic roles or doctoring including a highly developed form of psychotherapy, bead (money) making, hunting, and craft specialities such as bow and arrow making and basket making (Loeb 1926).

Among the most dramatic of these status-role positions was that of bear doctor. These individuals, male or female, possessed a special set of magical religious paraphernalia (a bear costume being the prime object) with which they were able to acquire special and extraordinary powers of movement, poisoning, and curing. The position was purchased (an unusual situation) from a previous bear doctor; it required a period of special training and considerable ritual restrictions at various times. Bear doctors acted informally as an associative group and were greatly feared and respected within their community (Barrett 1917a; Loeb 1926:335–338).

• POPULATION CONTROL   Although the Pomo exploited a rich and varied environment, they maintained a very high population density and were aware that famine could occur. Aginsky (1939:210) suggests that the anxiety of this possibility induced the Pomo to develop several techniques for population control. His cases from the Russian River are somewhat similar to Kashaya (Bean 1968). Ideally, families were kept small through sexual restrictions, coitus interruptus, infanticide, abortion, contraceptive devices, magical control, and occasionally geronticide. Some of these practices were supported by the idea that a fetus and a baby immediately after birth were not considered alive.

Aginsky (1939:214) states that the Shanel in particular practiced birth control to be able to feed the current population and that such individual action "was a traditionally accepted pattern of behavior."

Kunkel (1962) has estimated the aboriginal populations of various Pomo groups. The totals come to between 550 and 1,200 for the Kashaya, 3,950 to 6,300 for the Southern Pomo, 1,650 to 4,360 for the Central Pomo, 3,325 to 5,790 for the Northern Pomo, and about 350 for the Northeastern Pomo. His density estimates for the Western Pomo range from 1.08–1.62 to 7.94–12.71 persons a square mile (both for pairs of Southern Pomo tribelets); the Northeastern Pomo population density he estimated at 2.33.

Political Organization

The nature of Pomo chieftainship was variable with respect to the extent of the hierarchical differentiation of chiefs and the extent to which secular and sacred chiefly functions were separate and distinct roles. There are conflicting interpretations by ethnographers regarding the nature of secular chieftainship, the inheritance mode of chieftainship, the role of women as chiefs, and the importance of ceremonial chiefs.

The variations in the nature of chieftainship involved different ways of structuring authority and prestige—either secular kin-group chiefs of equal status with no other secular or ceremonial leader of greater prestige or secular kin-group chiefs of equal status who elected one of their numbers as the tribelet chief.

Barrett (1908:15–17) claimed that all blood relatives who resided in a definite village grouped themselves into a political unit under the leadership of a hereditary or "lesser captain" (hereditary kin-group chief). When a village contained several of these consanguineal units, each unit had a hereditary captain who, in conjunction with the other units' captains, functioned as a governing body. Usually one of these captains would be selected by the others to serve as the head captain (elected head of a multikin group) or head chief. He functioned primarily as an advisor, meeting and welcoming visitors, discussing in

council with the other captains matters of general public interest, making peace after conflict, and arranging and presiding over ceremonies.

Loeb (1926:236–238) defined two types of chiefs (equivalent to Barrett's two): full chiefs and "boy chiefs." Boy chiefs functioned primarily to divide and distribute foods collected by community gathering parties. A man became a boy chief by right of family and, if he proved competent, he might be elected full chief.

Kroeber (1925:250) accepted Barrett's analysis of Pomo chieftainship but expanded the scope of the head chief's authority to include satellite communities of a village. The position of "great chief" was either hereditary (Northern Pomo) or elective (Central Pomo). The kin-group chiefs formed an informal council that cooperated with the head chief.

The multiple, equal-chiefs phenomenon took two distinct forms: several chiefs heading kin-groups within one tribelet (characteristic of the Central Pomo, Valley division) with an overall chief; and loosely structured tribelets comprised of one or more single kin-group villages, with each kin-group headed by a kin-group chief (predominant pattern for the Northern Valley Pomo dialect groups and the Coast Redwood groups). Kunkel (1962) has noted a slightly different form of chieftainship among groups near the coast and along portions of the Russian River. Whereas most coastal and river groups distinguished between secular chiefs and ceremonial leaders, certain Northern Pomo tribelets fused the two roles in the single person of the kin-group chief.

Essentially, among the Pomo, there were three levels of secular chieftainship: tribelet chiefs (elected heads of multi-kin-group villages), kin-group chiefs, and assistant kin-group chiefs. The specific duties of these secular leaders varied from region to region, but generally, the tribelet chiefs arranged for and presided over ceremonies, welcomed and entertained visitors, gave advice, and held council with the kin-group chiefs regarding community welfare. The duties of the kin-group chief also varied according to area but generally included looking after the welfare of those directly related to him, and in conjunction with other kin-group chiefs, dealing with community matters. Essentially his duties and responsibilities were similar to those of the tribelet chief, except for the kin-group chief's consanguineal orientation. The assistant kin-group chiefs distributed food for feasts and substituted for the kin-group chief in his absence. By and large the various types of chiefs controlled financial aspects of trade and economics. A new chief was given money (operating capital) by his constituents, and it was his responsibility to give the largest contribution for ceremonies and to care for the aged, disabled, and unfortunate with food and clothing.

Succession to the chief's office varied among types of chieftainship, among tribelets, and possibly among kin-group chiefs within a tribelet. Kin-group chieftainships were hereditary in all tribelets. Old chiefs usually named a close relative as a successor and the kin group would ratify the choice. Assistant kin-group chiefs were usually close relatives of the kin-group chief. However, alternative succession modes were fairly normative. In most tribelets the preferred heir of the kin-group chief was the kin-group chief's sister's son, followed by the chief's sons and brothers. There were no true chiefly lineages, but rather chiefly families.

Some tribelets had women chiefs, usually the sister or daughter of male chiefs. Succession to this office was frequently hereditary and closely linked to the hereditary succession to office of the male kin-group chief. A woman chief prepared and served food at large ceremonial gatherings (Loeb 1926).

Most tribelets had a position of ceremonial chief who in actuality was master of all ceremonies (Barrett 1908). Loeb (1926) noted that many ceremonial chiefs were only in charge of certain ceremonies, such as the dances of the Ghost cult.

•PROPERTY   Like many California Indian groups, the Pomo had clearly defined concepts about land use-rights, although tribelets varied in their application of these rights. Barrett (1952,1:49), generalizing for all the Pomo, noted that certain areas and places (hunting grounds, productive fishing spots) were communally controlled and "open to all comers regardless of tribal connections." Some areas, for example, certain trees and seed-producing localities, were owned by individuals, others by nuclear families. The exact degree to which individuals owned and/or controlled basic subsistence resources is not clear and seems to have depended on the product exploited. Additionally, individuals owned all property manufactured by themselves and were free to dispose of it according to personal inclination (Loeb 1926).

In general, it would appear that there were at least three significant levels of economic ownership—nuclear families, leader-allegiance extended kin groups, and tribelets—each maintaining at least use-rights of specific resource areas.

Life Cycle

Loeb (1926:246-248) claims that the Pomo were uncertain that sexual relations alone would result in pregnancy and women employed certain magical processes to become pregnant, for example, sitting on a magical rock or drinking water from a certain spring. During pregnancy and for a prescribed time after birth, restrictions on diet, travel, food collecting and hunting, and contact with sacred items were observed by prospective parents. Birth usually took place in a special shelter where the mother and child remained for six weeks after delivery.

Children were named for deceased kinsmen after weaning or at about age one. The recipient presumably became like the person whose name was taken (Loeb 1926:259-261). Because names were considered private property, only the father and mother called the child by its real name, while relatives used relationship terms, and other people used nicknames.

Throughout childhood, boys were taught certain songs and at adolescence, about age 12, were presented with a hair net and bow and arrows. A girl's first menses was her most significant life event. It was marked by her confinement to a menstrual hut, various restrictions (on food, social isolation), and by rigorous instruction concerning her future role as a woman. Her release from confinement was celebrated, and she was given gifts by relatives and instructed in various methods of food preparation and basketmaking.

Courtship and marriage were important in the lives of Pomoans. The primary purpose of the former was sexual enjoyment and of the latter was the cementing of social and economic bonds. Marital choice offered several possibilities: polygyny, levirate, sororate, child betrothal. Marriage into other villages was common but not necessary and was restricted to nonrelatives. Perhaps the most important aspect of marriage was that pertaining to marriages between members of different Pomo dialect groups. Such intermarriages provided important economic liaisons between the various groups, and people who married into one group were often used as go-betweens or messengers to their original groups in times of peace-making settlements.

Marriages were arranged by the two families involved although the prospective marriage partners were always consulted. A girl was not usually forced into a marriage she did not want, but she could not marry against the wishes of her family. If everyone involved in the arrangements was satisfied, the boy's parents presented gifts to the girl's family and the boy moved into his prospective wife's house for a period of one month in order to become acquainted with the bride's family. After this the couple moved into the groom's house, a feast was held, and gifts exchanged. There appears to have been no invariable system of postmarital residence, but couples tended to go to one village for a while and then settle permanently in another (Loeb 1926).

Divorce was relatively easy and involved little ceremony. Any issue of the marriage remained in the home in which they were residing at the time of separation (Loeb 1926:285).

Death and mourning were handled similarly by all the Pomo. Relatives of a dying man cried and openly displayed their grief. A close watch was kept when a person appeared to be dying so that no poisoners could come near to hasten death. After death, friends and relatives brought gifts, some as donations for burning with the body, others (given later) as offerings of grievance to be returned in equivalence. The body remained in the house four days, the time required for the ghost to leave, then was taken outside and cremated. The house was then burned as were the personal possessions of the deceased, except certain sacred paraphernalia, which was either inherited or buried. Restrictions and purification were required of all relatives who handled the body. A second burning took place one year later, at which time friends and relatives brought additional gifts for offering to the deceased. The Pomo ceased to cremate as a result of White pressure sometime after 1850, although among some Pomo personal possessions continued to be buried with the deceased in the 1970s (Theodoratus 1971).

Religion

• SHAMANISM   Shamans among the Pomo were professionals who dealt in the healing arts of the society or who specialized in the ceremonial aspects of Pomo life, like the Kuksu cult. Curing specialists, called doctors, specialized as herbalists, singing doctors (or "outfit doctors"), and sucking doctors ("Cults and their Transformations," fig. 6, this vol.). Curing by the supernatural Kuksu impersonators also took place in extreme cases. Persons became shamans either through inheritance (singing doctor) or dreams (sucking doctor). Payment was made in beads and consisted of as much as one could afford. Indications are that doctors were mostly men prior to the 1870 Ghost Dance. Since the 1870s there has been an increasing number of women doctors (Theodoratus 1971:59).

Shamans warded off ills of the community in general and of individuals in particular. Illness could be caused by ghosts but was most often caused by poisoning. Leob (1926:329) doubts that much poisoning occurred among the Pomo but that the belief in it heightened their fear of it. Accounts of poisoning do exist and the Pomo seem to have been obsessed with the dangers of poisoning (Aginsky and Aginsky 1967; Colson 1974; Loeb 1926; Theodoratus 1971). All children were taught about it as a precautionary measure. Loeb (1926:334) believes that fear of poisoning had a powerful influence in shaping Pomo culture by inducing isolation, ensuring strict usage of hospitality rules, and inducing strict rules of etiquette.

After the 1870 Ghost Dance, Pomo religion curing became more closely associated with singing than before (Du Bois 1939:103). The Pomo clearly distinguish poisoning from other illnesses, and many continue to call on White doctors for illnesses in their realm of expertise and on Indian doctors for illnesses caused by poisoning (Theodoratus 1971:182–190). The fear of poisoning continues to have a strong influence over Pomo conduct. Although few in number, Pomo doctors continue to practice and curing remains an important method of treatment for some Pomo.

• KUKSU CULT   Like most north-central California Indian groups, the Pomo practiced the Kuksu, a religious complex centering around the impersonation of a god or gods, which stressed curing rituals or rites of "well-being" for the entire group. Some of the rituals stressed protection against the dangers of nature while others connoted fertility, as among the Southern Pomo, where the Kuksu

was intimately associated with first-fruit rites (Kunkel 1962).

The Kuksu ceremony, held somewhere every year but about once every seven years in a designated village, was characterized by a series of dances performed in an earth-covered dance house and involved the initiation of boys aged 10 to 12 to shamanistic, ritual, and professional roles. These initiates, along with all other previous initiates, constituted the "secret society," a ceremonial elite responsible for handling most ceremonies and public affairs. During the ceremony, members of the secret society costumed as Kuksu (or other sacred beings) instructed the initiates in religious and esoteric knowledge. Initiates assumed the name of their sponsor and often his profession or occupation as well.

In addition to god impersonation, there was a ghost-impersonating aspect of the Kuksu cult. This aspect was a religious concept older than the Kuksu and became syncretized with the Kuksu when the cult diffused into Pomo territory (Kunkel 1962; Loeb 1926, 1932). The ghost-impersonating ceremony was traditionally performed as an act of atonement for offenses against the dead (Kunkel 1962:28) but later stressed the initiation of boys into a ghost society, that is, adult status. The boys were instructed in practical customs and the proper ritual behavior required of all men.

It is important to distinguish between these two aspects of the Kuksu cult. Under the first aspect, all the tribelet's males, those who possessed "profane" knowledge, were members of the ghost society; but only certain males, those who possessed "sacred" knowledge, were members of the secret society (Kuksu).

The Pomo also had other public ceremonies concerned specifically with food and crops. These included the Lole Kilak dances, a woman's dance (the Lole) in which flowers were carried or worn by women, and first-fruits ceremonies for acorns, clover, corms, manzanita, wild strawberries, and other important foods (Gifford and Kroeber 1939:163, 212).

External Relations

The coast and valley Pomo interacted on the north with the Coast Yuki, Huchnom, and inland Yuki, who speak Yukian languages, and the Athapaskan Cahto. On the east they interacted with the Eastern and Southeastern Pomo, Patwin, Lake Miwok, and Wappo, and on the south with the Coast Miwok.

The Huchnom, Yuki, and Cahto owned the drainage of the South and Middle Eel River, the Coast Yuki that of the Tenmile River, while the Pomo controlled the Russian drainage. Mountains separated the Pomo from the Wintu. Wappo and Coast Miwok boundaries were geographically ambiguous. These boundaries seem to correlate with cultural distance; Yuki-Pomo differences are very great, while other Pomo, Lake Miwok, and

Wappo are less so. Intense conflict at the border, ritual defense as evinced in Kuksu cult differences, burial versus cremation of the dead, and drastically different basketry technology reveal the differences (Kroeber 1925).

Trade

One of the most important economic integrative mechanisms among the Pomo was the trade-feast congeries. The entire Pomo area was part of a much larger interrelated economic system that included most groups in northern California and made possible the exchange of goods, services, ceremonies, and marriage partners over a broad range of ecological and sociological zones. The nexus of this system lay in the valley zone (central to southern) and according to Aginsky (1958) formed a kind of protocapitalistic trading complex involving banking against future scarcity of items by overproduction of goods.

Various food and nonfood products of several areas thus were accessible at any one time and place to a wide range of groups through the trade-feast mechanism. For example, if the Eastern or Southeastern Pomo had an overabundance of fish they would host a feast and invite one or more groups to attend. The guests would bring magnesite and/or shell beads with them, which were presented to the host chief's spokesman. Then several days were spent feasting the guests, who enjoyed themselves by sweatbathing and gambling. Toward the end of the festivities, the host chiefs would determine how much fish they would give in return for the presented beads. The givers of fish piled the fish on the ground, and each giver took a string of beads from a pile. This piling up of fish and taking of bead strings continued until the bead supply was exhausted or the fish givers stopped. Then the guests' chief or chiefs allotted to each family an equal amount of fish.

It can be seen that this trade-feast mechanism operated to enable a community temporarily to "bank" a surplus of feed with members of other communities. By accepting an invitation to a trade-feast, the Pomo Indians who had previously "banked" food would be getting food back (Vayda 1966:498). These feasts "promoted the spreading out and equalization of consumption in space as well as time . . . and . . . served to convert inequalities in subsistence into more or less temporary inequalities in the possession of beads but equality in food" (Vayda 1966:498–499).

In addition to trade feasts, individuals and groups went on trading expeditions, not only to other Pomo groups but also to other tribes. The Central groups acted as middlemen between the Eastern and Northern, and Southern groups in the traffic of foods, manufactured goods, and raw materials. They became the market places for goods and were able to amass greater "wealth" than other groups (Aginsky 1958). By and large this wealth took the form of possession of beads, beads being a sign of position and status. One amassed beads through individual and collective efforts in the context of trading and trade-feasts.

Warfare

Warfare among the Pomo was institutionalized in varying ways. Among the Valley Pomo it was most intense, with a war chief acting as a secular leader for a number of confederated tribelets. Kunkel (1962:394) has suggested that there were several groups linked together by assembly-house affiliations in one of these confederations, with the "only official whose function seems to have pertained to all kin-groups" of the affiliated tribelets being the war leader. He was the only elected official, and it would appear that military organization was the primary factor holding these groups together. Wars often occurred in response to poaching, poisoning (witchcraft), abduction of women and children, theft of goods, or to protect or acquire prime resource areas. Some wars were precipitated by the drive to acquire high priority goods (like salt or obsidian) or territorial rights, often leading to the displacement of some groups (cf. Kunkel 1962:393–394; Loeb 1926; Barrett 1908).

Sometimes several contiguous villages, perhaps speaking different languages, united against a common enemy for the duration of hostilities. Occasionally these unions became permanent alliances, for instance, several groups of Northern Pomo with Yukis.

In preparation for battle ritual, war dances were held, prayers given, sacrifices offered, shamans consulted about the probable outcome, and omens and dreams interpreted by dreamers. The intensity of warfare varied from ritual conflict (where the battle ended with the first casualty) to annihilation of a village. Women and children on gathering expeditions were often the targets of a war party.

Cessation of hostilities and peace negotiation were complicated, involving reciprocal visits and exchange of goods between warring factions. The victors usually proposed the form and amount of settlement (Loeb 1926:203). Reparations were usually paid to the relatives of those killed. Among the Northern Pomo the peace maker was an appointee of the chief, but in most tribelets the regular chief fulfilled this function.

Prehistory

Despite the great potential for archeological investigation in the Pomo area little work has been accomplished. The contemporary Pomo connect with Phase 2 of the Late Horizon as indicated by the abundance of clamshell disk beads, which the Pomo manufactured and traded among themselves and others. They appear to have entered into the general exchange system of north-central California about A.D. 1500. Prior to that, few data are available indicating the extent or the cultural background of the occupants of the area.

History

The first contact between Pomo and non-Indians may have occurred as early as 1579 when Sir Francis Drake briefly visited the Pomos' southern neighbors, the Coast Miwok. By the late 1700s European trade goods were arriving from the San Francisco mission-presidio and the Spanish were raiding southern Pomo territory for potential converts. Simultaneously, fugitives from the missions to the south brought various aspects of Hispanic culture into the Pomo area (Forbes 1969).

By 1817 the Spanish established a mission at San Rafael (recruiting Indians from as far north as Santa Rosa in Southern Pomo territory) and in 1823 extended their influence to Sonoma in Wappo territory, establishing Mission San Francisco de Solano. Athough neophytes were badly treated and the nonsubjugated Pomo threatened reprisals, the mission succeeded in developing into a prosperous outpost of Hispanic culture. At least 600 Pomoans were baptized at Missions San Francisco de Solano and San Rafael. During this period the Spanish chroniclers characterized the Pomo as "savage," more intelligent, and more difficult to convert and control than other Indians had been.

At about the same time the Russians began exploiting Pomo territory (von Wrangell 1974; Kostromitonov 1974). In 1809 a Russian trading expedition established friendly relations with some Coast Miwok at Bodega Bay, and in 1811 the first Russian settlement in California was established at Fort Ross in Kashaya territory. In accordance with their policy of nonintervention and cooperation with natives, the Russians contracted with the Pomo for use of an area about one by two miles in extent. An agricultural colony was established at Fort Ross, and over 100 local Pomoans were employed as agricultural laborers (Essig 1933). During this period 1811–1825 many Pomos learned to speak Russian, adopted some aspects of Russian culture and religion, and occasionally intermarried with the Russians (see Oswalt 1958 for discussion of Russian loanwords).

In 1822 California became part of the newly created Mexican Republic, and drastic changes occurred throughout Pomo territory. Mexican land grants (ranches) were established deep in Pomo territory, and strict military control was exerted over the area. Colonies were established throughout Southern and Central Pomo territory, and Pomo were subject to constant raiding for capture and sale, thus bringing them into a peon working status.

Between 1834 and 1847, thousands of Pomo were captured or died as a result of increasing Mexican military campaigns. Before 1838 all Southern and Central Pomo territory was in Mexican hands, with Clear Lake, Big Valley, Sonoma and Napa valleys, and Sonora Valley (north to Ukiah and the Russian River) either settled by Mexicans or about to be settled.

By 1836 the trade in Indian slaves reached critical levels, and in 1838–1839 thousands of Pomos died during a smallpox epidemic. In 1833 a cholera (or possibly malaria) epidemic devastated many Pomo villages (Cook 1939). These diseases, plus displacement, enslavement, massacres, raids, and the beginnings of Anglo-American migration set the stage for the ever more rapid decline of the Pomo people and their cultural heritage.

During the 1850s, European economic, social, and religious institutions were active throughout Pomo territory. Settlers and fortune-seekers moved in in vast numbers. Some Pomo worked for Europeans, others were enslaved, and all were disenfranchised as a new legal system was imposed upon them. Massacres, for instance, the Bloody Island massacre of 1850 in punishment for the killing of Charles Stone and Andrew Kelsey (see Heizer 1973), not only of the Lake Pomo but also of other Pomo groups were carried out. Although the Pomo had managed to maintain, in many isolated areas, a semblance of freedom and autonomy during the Mexican period, the entrance of the Americans in greater numbers caused the entire Pomo area to be rapidly settled.

Throughout the early years of American occupation, 1850–1870, feelings against non-Europeans ran high and public efforts to eliminate local Indian populations resulted in the establishment of the Mendocino Indian Reserve near Fort Bragg and the Round Valley Reservation in 1856. Pomo were "rounded up," resettled at these reserves, and their lands immediately occupied and deeded to Whites. When the Mendocino Reserve was discontinued in 1867, Pomo interned there found themselves homeless and landless, with no legal redress.

It was during this period that the dominant economic and social format for integrating Pomos with Whites developed—a pattern of semipeonage. Most Pomos established settlements (often called rancherias) on White-owned lands, but only at the pleasure of local ranchers who used them as the principal source of cheap labor. With the agricultural industry diversifying rapidly, considerable seasonal employment was available.

Pomos worked in orchards, as fruit pickers, hop pickers, and in the grain fields as reapers. In the spring Pomos left their rancherias and went from job to job until late fall when they returned home to spend the winter living in a pseudo-aboriginal way (hunting, fishing, trapping) and practicing some attenuated forms of aboriginal ceremonies.

Several new Christian religious groups moved into Pomo territory and began missionary work. The Roman Catholic parishes expanded, Methodists held camp meetings that attracted many Indians, and various Protestant circuit riders (Baptist, Presbyterian, Episcopalian) contacted people in the more remote areas. By 1911 Colusa, Round Valley, Ukiah, Potter Valley, and Upper Lake had Christian missionaries. These missionaries were instrumental in forming Indian civil rights organizations (such as the Northern California Indian Association), purchasing homes for the needy, stopping the liquor traffic, educating children, providing medical attention and supplies, and in general promoting a pro-Indian sentiment directed toward establishing their basic rights as human beings (Taber 1911).

From the 1800s to the present, the Pomo have been the focus of various Euro-American religious interests. In the 1970s many Pomos participate in both traditional and non-Indian religions. The principal religions are Catholic (most predomonant in the Valley areas), Methodist (since 1890 in the Manchester-Point Arena area), Mormon (at the Kashia Reservation, where Mormons maintain some of the same dances and rituals as traditionalists but do them separately), Bahai (primarily Valley), and Pentecostal (throughout). In addition, there are some Russian Orthodox elements on the coast at the Kashia Reservation, but there is no longer an organized church. While most of these western religions operate in conjunction with Pomo traditional beliefs, Pentecostals and some Mormons try to exclude traditional religious practices.

Despite the attempts of these advocates of Indian rights to protect and aid the Pomo, by the last two decades of the nineteenth century the Pomo had lost 99 percent of the land they had once called home and were the recipients of an ever increasing hostility from Whites. Because of this social, economic, and political anomie, the Pomo were easy converts to the philosophies of the Ghost Dance prophets. Hundreds of Pomo flocked to this new religion and gathered in specially constructed earth lodges to await the prophesized cataclysmic destruction of the world, the demise of the "foreigners," and a return to their sacred past lifeways. Although the prophecies failed to materialize, this new religion laid the foundation for the Bole-Maru cult, an adaptive device that, during the closing years of the nineteenth century, allowed a continuance of Pomo ethnicity while simultaneously integrating Anglo-American work ethics with the older Pomo lifeways (Du Bois 1939; Meighan and Riddell 1972; Wilson 1968).

As Pomos became more familiar with the new dominant culture, and with the assistance of various White advocates, they took an active part in bettering their conditions. By the turn of the century, Pomos were actively using the courts, mass media, and White advocate groups to assist them in efforts to improve their living conditions and protect and expand their rights as human beings. For example, in 1904, the Ukiah rancheria instituted a court case to gain permanent and lasting control over 120 acres of land they originally purchased in 1881. Since 1844, the Ukiah area Pomo had been landless, forced to move from one area to another by land-hungry White immigrants (culminating in the overwhelming influx of settlers into the Russian River valley area as a result of the 1862 Homestead Act). In 1881 four Pomo "chiefs" organized a fund-raising drive among the 135 remaining Pomo (all that was left of the original 1,600 tribelet members), raised $800, and put a down payment on what eventually became the privately owned Yokayo rancheria. Within a few years the riverine-situated rancheria was a thriving agricultural commune, and its members were able to pay off the outstanding mortgage of $3,700 (Kasch 1947).

Between 1881 and 1904, the rancheria continued to prosper, so much so that it was necessary to hire a business manager (non-Indian) to handle the group's affairs. A new sense of pride and ethnic identity permeated this small community and many traditional, as well as new, fiestas were held. At one point, the rancheria was prosperous enough to distribute a $200 cash dividend among its members. But in 1904 all this was threatened. A non-Indian probate officer, acting ostensibly on behalf of the heirs of some original rancheria members, attempted to acquire ownership, for himself, of over one-half of the rancheria's acreage. The Pomo instituted a court battle culminating in a 1907 California Supreme Court decision in favor of the Indians. The Court recognized the rancheria as an unincorporated voluntary association administered as a whole as communal property and ruled that it would remain intact and protected "in perpetuity for the children of the original incorporates and their descendants" (Kasch 1947:209).

Educational activities increased rapidly. By 1910, approximately one-half of the Pomo children were in schools, albeit segregated ones; and day schools were established on the Manchester, Ukiah, and Upper Lake rancherias. Also, two government field matrons began working at Middletown Rancheria and in Lake County. Private welfare organizations (such as local auxiliaries of the Northern California Indian Association) were agitating for more public concern and action to provide better living conditions for Pomos. Still, most local White communities used Indians for cheap labor and even displaced Pomos who were residing on lands legally theirs. By this time, there were numerous nonreservation or landless Indians amounting to over 1,500 in Mendocino County alone (Taber 1911).

Such conditions continued and protests increased on many fronts. Shortly after World War I, Indian protest groups and White advocacy groups proliferated and began effectively to influence government agencies and improve general conditions for Indians. Pomos began demanding basic rights and services (such as the right to vote) and were active in the formation of various organizations (the Society of Northern California Indians, Indian Board of Cooperation) aimed at securing and advancing a peaceful and prosperous existence for all Indians, remedying unsatisfactory working and living conditions, and upgrading educational programs. Pomo leaders, such as Stephen Knight, Steve Parrish, and William Benson were among those most prominent in

Fig. 10. Essie Parrish (right) and another Bole-Maru official, Kashaya Pomos, outside the ceremonial structure at Stewarts Point rancheria. Photograph by William R. Heick, 1963.

representing Pomo to the dominant culture, while the leaders of the Bole-Maru religion (Dreamers) in each community (fig. 10) provided the Pomo continuity with their unique past. While Pomos desired some aspects of American culture, they also wanted to retain much of their own culture.

The years between the First and Second World Wars were significant for the Pomo in terms of local and federal reforms. Various studies were instituted aimed at defining problem areas and devising equitable solutions. Reforms in the areas of health, education, and welfare were instituted and new land bases were established for some landless groups. In 1924 Indians were granted full United States citizenship. With the passage of the California Jurisdictional Act of 1928 a legal entity was created allowing Indians to file suits against both the local and federal governments for past unlawful seizure of native lands.

The Pomo shared America's general economic crisis during the Depression. Social welfare and medical care programs, which had been steadily growing in the 1920s, were cut drastically, and due to the influx of White laborers from the Midwest, employment opportunities reached an all-time low. Most Pomos were struggling to survive on less than $700 average annual income for a family of five in 1936. As a result, the traditional patterns of economic reciprocity came to dominate subsistence activities. Once again, Pomos began sharing extensively with one another, and there was a marked shift away from working for Whites to working on Indian lands and hunting and collecting along traditional patterns. While California underwent a decided downward economic trend, the Pomo entered an era of relative prosperity as a result of this shift toward traditional economic patterns. Concurrent with this "revitalization" of traditional economic modes, the federal government, through programs such as the Works Progress Administration and the Civilian Conservation Corps, was able to assist the Pomos in maintaining themselves.

During this period, 1930–1940, the Pomo interactions

with non-Indian migratory workers were intense, and as noted by Aginsky and Aginsky (1947) a lateral culture-exchange occurred. During the harvest season Indians and non-Indians lived and worked side by side. Pomos became individually involved with various ethnic group members and new occupations, such as the cattle and lumber industries. Pomos learned about non-Indian food, family relations, religion, credit attitudes, habits of speech, levels of aspiration, and the idea of the strike. Concurrent with this exposure to varied economic modes, changes in marriage patterns and female-male roles occurred. Although there was internal pressure among the Pomo to limit interracial marriages, there was an increase throughout the 1930s and 1940s, with spouses drawn from Mexican-, European-, and Asian-derived Americans.

The shift in female-male roles revolved around access to and control of political and ritual offices. The first sign of this new emergence in leadership roles occurred in connection with the Ghost Dance, Earth Lodge, and Bole-Maru movements, when several women, working in concert with male political and religious leaders, became dreamers and religious leaders, roles traditionally dominated by men. The reasons for this shift were many, but all revolved around the increasingly dysfunctional nature of the more traditional male roles. As men were forced into migratory labor patterns, institutions for passing on traditional leadership roles were transferred to females.

Women gradually assumed more independence and power in religious, secular, and economic affairs.

World War II brought a new interchange of Pomo with non-Pomo. Many Pomo left the rancherias for urban employment and positions in the armed services. By the end of the war Pomo outlook had changed significantly. Young people wanted more of the material aspects of the non-Indian world and more educational opportunities, but as yet they were unable to adjust to the various changes associated with the past 15 years. The federal government began to step down from its totally paternalistic role in California Indian affairs. Several rancherias were terminated (table 1), and Bureau of Indian Affairs services were drastically reduced. The state of California was charged with health, education, and welfare responsibilities but was not prepared for, or capable of, handling the various Indian problems. As a result Pomo communities became more neglected and impoverished than ever before. The area's economy suffered a general decline while the state of California moved exceedingly slowly in responding to its new responsibilities.

Since the early 1950s Pomos have expanded their involvement in American lifeways. Various Native American organizations (Inter-Tribal Council of California, American Indian Movement, White Roots of Peace, Northern Indian California Education) have become active throughout the Pomo area and have been responsible for the increasing political, educational, and eco-

Table 1. Pomo Rancherias

County	Name	Population	Acreage	Ecozone	Language	Termination
Lake	Scotts Valley (Sugar Bowl)	25	57	Lake	Northern	Yes
Mendocino	Coyote Valley	34	100	Valley	Northern	Inundated
	Guidiville	35	243	Valley	Northern	Yes
	Hopland	109[a] 75	2,070	Valley	Central	Yes
	Manchester–Point Arena	85[a]	364	Coast-redwood	Central	No
	Pinoleville	100	96	Valley	Northern	Yes
	Potter Valley (2 parcels)	12	96	Valley	Northern	Yes
	Redwood Valley	17	80	Valley	Northern	Yes
	Sherwood Valley	9[a]	292	Valley	Northern	No
Sonoma	Cloverdale	45	27	Valley	Southern	Yes
	Dry Creek	14[a]	75	Valley	Southern	No
	Graton	3	15	Valley	Southern	Yes
	Lytton	10	50	Valley	Southern	Yes
	Mark West	4	35	Valley	Southern	Yes
	Stewarts Point (Kashia)	88[a]	40	Coast-redwood	Kashaya	No

Sources: U.S. Bureau of Indian Affairs 1969; California. Legislature. Senate Interim Committee on California Indian Affairs 1955.
[a] 1969 figures; others are 1955.

nomic sophistication evidenced by the Pomo. Simultaneously, various agencies (California Indian Legal Services, California Indian Rural Health Service) have provided funds and personnel for programs aimed at bettering conditions among the Pomo.

In the 1970s the extended family remains the principal social unit on rancherias and is integrated into the larger reservation social system through various social, economic, and religious agents or institutions. As with many non-Pomo reservations, Pomo are often split into small factionalized units, frequently based on kinship lines. In an attempt to weld together these factionalized groups, several Pomos have advanced an idea of nationalism, intending to organize an all-inclusive new Pomo nation. Unfortunately, although the Pomo social structure is as flexible in membership and allegiance as it was traditionally, it lacks the past integrative ritual mechanisms and political positions to make this pan-Pomo idea a reality.

As of 1973 there were six Western Pomo rancherias organized as independent political units, each with elected officials who conduct meetings and act as liaison personnel with the BIA and other agencies. Ten Western Pomo rancherias have been terminated (table 1) and no longer function under such an organizational structure. However, all rancherias and individuals may belong to, and participate in, various political organizations attempting to bring Pomo people together and form sociopolitical units that cooperate in a common cause. Two of these groups, the Sonoma County Coalition for Indian Opportunity and the Mendo-Lake Pomo Council, are attempting to bring the Pomo people together and to establish a formal Pomo organizational structure. If successful they will request formal recognition by the state and federal governments, thereby receiving tribal privileges for Pomo people.

Another Pomo project, the Ya-Ka-Ama (ˌyäkääˈmä, from Kashaya *yaˀkʰe ˀama·* 'our land'), located east of Windsor, Sonoma County, is an important example of Pomo self-help and self-direction. Founded by Pomo people, it is an operating farm project (funded by the U.S. Department of Labor) that trains Indians in agricultural techniques and agricultural management practices.

Traditional rituals (first-fruit ceremonies, Bole-Maru) have gradually disappeared despite a slight resurgence among the Kashaya Pomo. There, the Dreamer/culture leader has vigorously maintained some traditions and religious and philosophical principles, while ceremonial dances and songs are perpetuated through the rancheria school's educational system. Many younger children are members of the traditionalist group and perform in the ceremonial house.

The Kashia rancheria is also actively involved in ceremonial exchanges with other rancherias and hosts a variety of fiestas—acorn festival, July 4, flower ceremony, Strawberry festival (fig. 11). Whenever an event is deemed important the round house is opened and ceremonies held accompanied by ritual feasting, the wearing of ceremonial clothing, and the performing of traditional religious songs and dances. The primary function of these various ceremonies is to enhance ethnicity through emphasis on the unique and special nature of Pomo culture. Additionally, several Pomo groups perform songs and dances for non-Indian audiences, but these performances are clearly differentiated from sacred performances.

Curing rituals are also an important aspect of Pomo life in the 1970s. Several Pomo shamans are known throughout California and are sought after by both Indians and non-Indians. In 1968 several Pomo "curers" were working in concert as "doctoring teams" in the Point Arena area (Theodoratus 1971).

Curing is through sucking, dreaming, singing, and the administration of herbal medicines. Curers distinguish between two categories of disease: traditional (fright poisoning, fractures) and White (diabetes, alcoholism), but these are by no means mutually exclusive, and curers often refer a patient to non-Indian medical personnel.

Certain ritual restrictions are still observed. Among these are restrictions on the activities of menstruating women, who must isolate themselves from the community for a few days, refrain from eating certain foods, and absent themselves from any rituals.

The economic condition of Pomo is still poor in contrast to that of non-Indians in the area; however, federal funding has provided some jobs and better on-the-job training opportunities than were available in the past. Still, there is a lack of job opportunities in the more remote coastal areas and people there must often leave their homes, permanently, for employment purposes. In the early 1970s employment as farm laborers, in lumbering, in domestic services, as health and teacher aids, and in clerical and business services remained important. However, many Pomos have entered into semiskilled and skilled professions, and some are in administrative positions, particularly with Indian organizations.

Other sources of income (particularly in the more remote areas) are public assistance and social security and pensions, particularly for the elderly and indigent. These sources, although very meager, play a significant part in contemporary Pomo economy. In addition, some traditional hunting and gathering persists to supplement the economy.

Because California was to be an example for nationwide termination of federal responsibilities to Indians, many rancherias have been terminated, and during the late 1950s and the 1960s, a minimum amount of federal monies was invested in California. Most of the work done on California rancherias has occurred since 1968 under the BIA administration of R. Bennett. Since that time, money for scholarships, housing, health, and general improvement steadily increased until 1973. Simulta-

Fig. 11. Essie Parrish, Kashaya Pomo, leaching acorns on the shore of the Gualala River for food during the strawberry festival. Photograph by William R. Heick, 1961.

neously (and perhaps as a result of federal programs) there was growth of employment, education, and legal opportunities.

Most nonterminated Pomo rancherias have a Housing Improvement Program (HIP); this has included repairs and improvements on existing homes, new homes, and the introduction of trailers for living quarters. Some rancheria roads have also been improved and water improvements have been made. Several health projects are operative in the Pomo area with the California Rural Indian Health Board (CRIB) being incorporated in Lake, Sonoma, and Mendocino counties. There has been an attempt to mobilize the local health resources and bring about improvements in medical, dental, and health planning services. In addition, the state's public health service researched health conditions and acquired funds for health and training programs; both rancheria and urban Pomo have been affected.

Sources

Published ethnographic reports on the Western Pomo are abundant (Barrett 1908, 1908a, 1917, 1917a, 1933, 1952; Gifford 1923, 1926c, 1967; Gifford and Kroeber 1939; Kroeber 1925; Loeb 1926; Kniffen 1939; Oswalt 1964;

Heizer 1975b; Stewart 1943). Among several contributions by Aginsky and Aginsky is a novel (1967) containing an accurate account of the Central Pomo yearly round. Particularly important are unpublished manuscripts (Kennedy 1955; Theodoratus 1971; Kunkel 1962). Kunkel (1962) contains a great deal of information and interpretations on demography and its relations to ecology and social and political systems.

The Northeastern Pomo are very poorly known and the cultural descriptions in this chapter may not—in fact, probably do not—adequately reflect them. By the time anthropologists reached them they were much intermarried with the Patwin. That they were related linguistically to the other Pomo was discovered by anthropologists only in the early twentieth century (Barrett 1904). They were never numerous and their language became functionally extinct February 12, 1961, with the passing of Minnie Bill, the last speaker able to construct sentences. There remained in 1976 two Northeastern Pomos who knew isolated words and phrases (Robert Oswalt, personal communication 1976). The major part of what has been preserved of the language derives from three days of intensive recording in 1940 by Halpern (1939–1940). Some material was also collected by Barrett (1908), McLendon (1959), and Oswalt (1976a); Kroeber

(1932a:364-366) records a few names. Very little ethnographic research was conducted among the Northeastern Pomo. Kroeber's field notebook used during his brief visit is apparently lost (Sally McLendon, personal communication 1976); data from it is presumably incorporated in Kroeber (1925, especially pp. 224-225, 236, 1932a). Halpern's research was limited nearly entirely to the language. Barrett (1908) gathered only ethnogeographic data among this group; his other major works and those of Loeb do not reflect Northeastern Pomo data.

Modern linguistic materials, published and unpublished, on Western Pomo include Halpern (1939-1940, 1964), Oswalt (1964a, 1975, 1976), McLendon (1973), and Moshinsky (1975) on all five languages. Vihman (1966-1969) and Oswalt (1962-1965) have worked on Northern Pomo. Oswalt (1957-1975, 1958, 1960, 1961, 1964, 1964b, 1971, 1971a, 1975a, 1975b) should be consulted on Kashaya. For Southern Pomo see also Oswalt (1963-1968). For Central Pomo, include Oswalt (1958-1968, 1964b, 1971, 1971a) and Angulo (1935b).

There are several major archival resources for Pomo ethnological materials. The Anthropological Archives in the Bancroft Library, University of California, Berkeley, includes the notes of Frank Essene and Birbeck Wilson (Valory 1971). The C. Hart Merriam Collection, which includes linguistic and ethnographic data and photographs for most Pomo groups, is housed at the Archaeological Research Facility, Department of Anthropology, University of California, Berkeley (Heizer et al. 1969). The National Anthropological Archives of the Smithsonian Institution includes the ethnographic notes of J.P.

Harrington; and the American Philosophical Society Library, Philadelphia, has the notes of Paul Radin. Henry Mauldin, Lake County Historian, has a private collection of data pertaining to both present and past Pomo lifeways. B.W. and E. Aginsky have extensive archives gathered while conducting field research among the Pomo, before about 1955.

Several museums throughout the United States and abroad have collections of Pomo material culture. In the United States the larger collections are at the Milwaukee Public Museum; Museum of the American Indian, New York; Field Museum of Natural History, Chicago; Lowie Museum, Berkeley; all have photographic collections. Other collections are at the Brooklyn Museum; University Museum, University of Pennsylvania, Philadelphia; Smithsonian Institution; and the California State Indian Museum, Sacramento. The principal foreign collection is in the Muzei Etnografiyi Antropologiyi Akademiyi Nauk S.S.S.R., Leningrad. Russian sources are extensive and largely untapped (Shur and Gibson 1973). The best guide to these sources, many of which are unavailable to non-Russian scholars, is by Grimstead (1972).

In the 1960s several ethnographic films were made at the Kashia Rancheria covering basketry, games, acorn processing, ritual dances, and shamanic curing. From this footage, nine films were completed and are distributed by the University of California Media Center, Berkeley. In addition, but of restricted use, is unedited footage on these and other topics, and still photographs and artifacts manufactured and made in association with this project, all in the Lowie Museum.

Eastern Pomo and Southeastern Pomo

SALLY McLENDON AND MICHAEL J. LOWY

Language

Two of the seven Pomoan languages, Eastern Pomo and Southeastern Pomo, were spoken by a number of village-communities around Clear Lake in the Coast Range, about 100 miles north of San Francisco. These people had no names for themselves, calling themselves people, while they referred to their neighbors by directional or geographical terms such as 'the people of the north' or 'the people from *yi·má·* [Scotts Valley]'. The terms Eastern Pomo and Southeastern Pomo were assigned them by Barrett (1908).

Clear Lake is 19 miles long and nowhere wider than 7 miles (Mauldin 1945-1975). The irregular shoreline breaks it up into smaller units called Upper Lake, Clear Lake proper, East Lake, and Lower Lake ("Pomo: Introduction," fig. 6, this vol.).

The Southeastern Pomo lived around East Lake and Lower Lake, while the Eastern Pomo lived to the northwest around Clear Lake proper and Upper Lake.

The speakers of these two languages lived, then, in close geographical proximity, in what would seem to be the same general environment, and with a tradition of contact reflected by the many marriages between the two groups, which are documented in genealogies going back to at least the middle of the nineteenth century (Gifford 1926c). Yet the Southeastern Pomo and the Eastern Pomo differed in a number of ways.

Although the two languages are later stages of a single language spoken at least 2,000 years ago, they are not mutually intelligible, and the speakers of one must make a considerable investment of time and effort to acquire some sort of fluency in speaking or comprehending the other, since their vocabularies, their grammars, and their pronunciations are quite different. Second, the Southeastern Pomo were island dwellers, while the Eastern Pomo made their permanent villages back from the shoreline of the lake, along streams feeding Clear Lake that were used each spring by several varieties of fish for spawning. Third, among the Southeastern Pomo Gifford (1923:80) collected "indubitable evidence of family ownership of lands," while he was unable to find the same among the Eastern Pomo. Fourth, the Eastern Pomo and the Southeastern Pomo differed in many details of ritual and ceremonials. Finally, the Eastern Pomo and the Southeastern Pomo differed in terms of the neighboring groups with whom they were in contact—intermarrying, trading, and sharing ceremonial activities. The Southeastern Pomo were adjacent to Patwin and Lake Miwok speakers, while the Eastern Pomo were adjacent to the Northern Pomo and Central Pomo as well as the Patwin.

Settlement Pattern

There were three main Southeastern-Pomo-speaking village-communities: *qámdot* on Anderson Island (formerly called Buckingham Island) on East Lake; *ʔlém* on Rattlesnake or Sulphur Bank Island at the eastern tip of East Lake; and *xqóyi* on Lower Lake Island at the extreme southern end of Lower Lake ("Pomo: Introduction," fig. 6, this vol.).

There were five main Eastern-Pomo-speaking village-communities around the upper end of the lake: *qu·ɬá·na·pʰò* 'water-lily village/people' in Big Valley; *xa·bé·na·pʰò* 'rock village/people' in Big Valley; *da·nó-xà·* 'mountain-cut' or 'mountain-water-at' in Clover Valley; *xówalekʰ* 'city of fire' (?) in Upper Lake Valley on the western side of Middle Creek; and *ší·kom* 'blanket-standing' (?) on the north shore of Clear Lake proper where the town of Lucerne is presently located. There was one village-community that seems to have spoken both Northern Pomo and Eastern Pomo, *kʰa·yáw* 'at the head' in Bachelor Valley (Northern Pomo *šinal* 'at the head'); and possibly another, *yi·má·* 'at the sinew (?)' in Scotts Valley.

Very little is known about how the permanent villages of these village-communities were laid out. Loeb (1926:234) claims that "villages were usually scattered along a creek course with varying distances up to a hundred yards or more between houses." It is not clear which of the Pomo-speaking groups he was referring to, but it seems likely that he had the Eastern Pomo in mind, since he adds that the Eastern Pomo speaker William Benson claimed that the village-community of *xa·bé·na·pʰò* in precontact times had been located about two miles from the present town of Kelseyville on Kelsey Creek, with the houses strung out for about two miles and a ceremonial house at either end (Loeb 1926:234). The linear arrangement of houses is also confirmed for *kʰa·yáw* (McLendon 1959-1976). There is no information about the layout of Southeastern Pomo villages.

Each village-community had a semisubterranean ceremonial house, called *Márakʰ* in Eastern Pomo and *xwán* in Southeastern Pomo, and a sudatory or sweathouse, called *xó-Màrakʰ* 'fire-*Márakʰ*' in Eastern Pomo and *xócap̓a xwan* in Southeastern Pomo. These looked like gently sloping knolls, with smoke rising from the smoke hole in the center (fig. 1).

The inhabitants of the village-communities lived in dwelling houses constructed of native lake reeds locally called tules. The houses (Eastern Pomo *ká*, Southeastern Pomo *cá*) were either circular or elliptical and generally housed several related nuclear families, each with its own fire and entrance door adjacent, and all sharing storage

Fig. 1. Exterior and interior of Southeastern Pomo semisubterranean ceremonial house at Sulphur Bank *(ʔlém)*. Photograph by Pliny E. Goddard, between 1902 and 1906.

facilities, the central baking pit, and mortar stone (figs. 2-3).

There is no record of the number of dwellings at any of the Eastern Pomo or Southeastern Pomo village-communities, except for a remarkable census of the Eastern Pomo village-community of *šíˑkom,* which Gifford (1926c) was able to carry out in 1919 thanks to the extraordinary memory of Jim Pumpkin, who had been born in *šíˑkom* in 1844 or 1845 and lived there until its population was forced to move around 1871. Pumpkin was able to recall for Gifford the names and kin relations of every inhabitant of every house. As described by Pumpkin, *šíˑkom* was made up of 20 dwellings, all but two of which were occupied by two, and sometimes as many as four, families grouped around 48 fires. These 20 houses held a total population of 235 individuals.

Kunkel (1962) estimated the total aboriginal population of the Eastern Pomo at 1,260 to 2,205, and of the Southeastern Pomo at 390 to 1,070. His estimates of density range between 2.00-3.41 persons a square mile (for the *daˑnó-xà*) and 13.33-16.67 (for the *quˑɫá-na·pʰò*) for the Eastern Pomo; they are 5.27-14.46 for the Southeastern Pomo.

Environment

The Clear Lake area has a Mediterranean climate with considerable rainfall in winter and a long, hot, dry period in summer. This climate is associated with a characteristics sclerophyllous vegetation locally known as chaparral. In California, grizzly bears were particularly prevalent in this environment. Most of the region was mountainous and uninhabited.

The annual rainfall in Lake County is 21.6 inches, but from June to September rainfall amounts to only 0.53 inches (Shelford 1963:239). This variation affects the level of the lake by as much as 10-18 feet during the year, and consequently the life-style of the indigenous populations living around it, as well as the vegetation. During the winter rains, the level of the lake slowly rises, gradually flooding more and more of the lowlands adjacent to it around the main body of Clear Lake. In the surrounding mountains the rain turns to snow, which covers the mountains until the temperature begins to warm up in spring. During the spring the melting snow rushes down the creek beds in torrents to raise the level of the lake still farther. Thus the lake is at its greatest extent at the beginning of summer. During the summer, the level of the lake gradually drops, baring the shoreline flooded in winter and early spring, as water ceases to run in most of the creeks. At the beginning of the rainy winter season in November, the lake is at its lowest level.

The western shore of Clear Lake proper, from the mouth of Middle Creek to Lakeport, was a continuous stretch of tule marsh and willows alternately flooded in winter and spring and relatively dry in summer. Although

Fig. 2. The Southeastern Pomo village of ʔlém in Lake Co. with tule-covered dwelling houses in background. Photograph by R.E. Wood, probably in the early 1870s before this community moved from its precontact location on Rattlesnake or Sulphur Bank I. to the adjacent mainland.

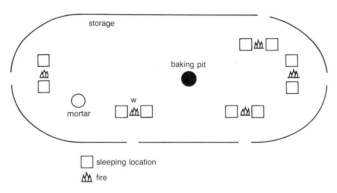

Fig. 3. Ground plan of an Eastern Pomo multifamily dwelling about 40 feet long. W, typical location for storage of a small amount of firewood. For details of occupants' kinship relations see Barrett 1916:3.

Fig. 4. John Johnson with Southeastern Pomo boat made of tules bound together with split grape vines. Length 3.96 m, the smallest of three types formerly used in this region. Photograph by S.A. Barrett, before 1915.

Barrett (1908) assigns this stretch of shore to the Northern Pomo, no permanent villages were ever located here, the area being used mainly for fish camps. The names of these camping sites are all in Eastern Pomo, and it seems likely that the Eastern Pomo shared the fishing potential with Northern Pomo speakers.

Clear Lake was apparently almost completely surrounded by a margin of tules. The extent of these tule marshes is suggested by the impressive number of uses to which the Eastern Pomo and the Southeastern Pomo put tules. They built their houses and boats of tules (figs. 2, 4); the skirts worn by women and a "mantle" worn by men were made of tules (Barrett 1952, 2:292). Men also wore

a woven-tule moccasin and legging (fig. 5). Food was invariably served on tule mats, shredded tules were used for babies' diapers and for beds, while the tender shoots and roots were eaten.

Culture

Subsistence

The Eastern Pomo and Southeastern Pomo annual cycle of subsistence was very finely adapted to the special characteristics of the environment in which they lived.

Although the lake has frequently been described as teeming with fish, the Eastern Pomo and Southeastern Pomo focused their fishing activities primarily on the spawning seasons, when the fish moved to shallow waters and large quantities could be caught in a short period of time and dried and stored for use during the rest of the year. Several varieties of fishing techniques were used, each adapted to the species of fish sought (see Barrett 1952, 1:149-156 for fishing techniques of all seven Pomo groups). At least four varieties of fish (Eastern Pomo *ša·mól* 'sucker', *ša·pʰál* 'pike', *híčʰ* 'hitch', *čʰáy* 'chay'; Southeastern Pomo *xmól, kfál, sát,* and term unknown) went up the several creeks feeding into the Eastern Pomo portion of Clear Lake to spawn in the spring when these creeks ran full of water. At least four more varieties of fish (Eastern Pomo *ša·xál* 'blackfish', *mi·qúš* 'native carp', *tóx* 'bass', *di·tʰá* 'like *tóx* but larger'; Southeastern Pomo *xqál,* term unknown, term unknown, *ʔšán*) spawned in the shallow edges of the lake.

Contemporary Eastern Pomo recall (McLendon 1959-1976) that the first fish to go up the creeks to spawn in February or early March, when the creeks were muddy and turbulent, were the suckers, which were caught with the *šá·mi·čĕ* 'conical basketry traps', which Barrett (1952, 1:152) claims were used only in the Clear Lake region.

The pikes were the next to go up, toward the middle of March, when the water was clearer, and these were speared with a fish gig. Later, when the waters became warmer, the hitch and chay went up and were caught with a long basketry trap called *ča·dár* in a brush fish dam in such large numbers that surpluses seem usually to have existed. Besides being dried, stored, and eaten throughout the rest of the year (fig. 6), they were traded to the Northern Pomo and the Central Pomo, who were invited to the lake and feted and who gave beads in return for these fish (Vayda 1966; Loeb 1926:192-194; Barrett 1952, 2:352-353).

Later still, during the last part of March and into April, when the weather got warmer, the fish went close to the edge of the lake to spawn in the flooded tule swamps there. The Eastern Pomo moved at this point to various fish camps along the lake edge, using a fish trap called *bu·xál,* and possibly nets, to catch blackfish and native carp. (After contact they began to use large seines to catch the fish spawning on the lake's edge.) The people attacked by the U.S. Cavalry, May 15, 1850, on Bloody

Sally McLendon.
Fig. 6. Eastern Pomos tenderizing dried blackfish by pounding with a stone pestle. Typical individual's meal of dried fish and acorn mush in a *tʰi·rí·bu·kù* basket on a tule mat, with Ralph Holder showing customary technique for eating mush with the fingers. Demonstration using objects in the Lake Co. Historian's collection, Big Valley. Photographs by Judy Tucker, 1973.

Brooklyn Mus.: left, 07.467.8369; right, 07.467.8342.
Fig. 5. Eastern Pomo legging and moccasin made of tule. Legging 33.7 cm long, moccasin same scale. Legging made by Nancy Graves. Collected in 1907 at *xa·bé·ma·tòlel.*

Island, were camped there fishing for these lake-spawning fish. Although the captain in charge of the cavalry troops claimed they had sought refuge on the island, Eastern Pomo accounts make it clear that they were in fact there for the important annual fishing always carried out at this time of year in this location, when they learned of the arrival of the soldiers at the southern end of the lake. It is possible that they stayed there fishing, rather than hiding in the mountains as the Eastern Pomo in Big Valley and Scotts Valley did, because the fish to be caught at this time constituted such an important source of protein that they would have been hard-pressed to do without it throughout the subsequent year.

It is unknown to what extent the Southeastern Pomo fishing practices followed this outline, although it seems possible that they utilized lake fishing more than stream fishing, living as they did on islands in the lake. Barrett (1952, 2:416) gives an account of the purchase of access to stream fishing by Lower Lake Indians who were probably from *xqóyi*.

The rest of the Eastern Pomo annual cycle was equally well adapted to their specific environment, as summarized in table 1. It is not known to what extent the table applies to Southeastern Pomo, but Kniffen (1939) felt that it was probably somewhat different.

The diet of the Eastern Pomo and Southeastern Pomo depended in part on the time of year. Fish, acorns for bread and mush, grains for pinole, and pepperwood nuts and buckeyes were stored and eaten year round. The most common daily meal throughout the year consisted of dried fish and acorn mush (fig. 6). This was supplemented with fresh meat or waterfowl when available, and fresh greens, roots, bulbs, berries, and fruits in season.

The mainland claimed by the Southeastern Pomo was divided into family-owned, named tracts on which gathering rights were the exclusive prerogative of members of the owning family, although apparently nonfamily members were permitted to hunt on these tracts. The land and its products around the main Southeastern Pomo villages on the islands were communally shared. Gifford (1923:80) was told by the Eastern Pomo that "all lands, oak trees, grass and seed places, and fishing rights were communal." He added that perhaps "their lands have been so long in American hands that memory of private ownership has been effaced." However, since Southeastern Pomo lands have been in American hands at least as long, without affecting their memory of former land ownership, it seems unlikely. Loeb (1926:197–198) claimed that some trees on Eastern Pomo village land belonged to certain families, seed- and bulb-producing fields were marked with a large pole to warn trespassers, and boat landings were private property although rights to fish in Clear Lake were universal. Since Gifford's main Eastern Pomo informant was Jim Pumpkin of *ší·kom* on the north shore of the Clear Lake, while Loeb's main Eastern Pomo informant was William Benson from Big

Table 1. Eastern Pomo Annual Cycle

Month	Activity	Residence
March	Stream fishing	Main village
April	Stream fishing by men Clover gathering by women	Main village
May	Some clover gathering Lake fishing	Scattered; a large number camped on the lakeshore
June	Root digging, tule, clams; lake fishing in early June	Scattered; camped on the lake; in hills after roots
July	Roots, tule, clams; carrying in the harvest	Main village
August	Gathering pinole seed; trips to coast and for salt	Main village
September	Pinole seed Return from trips	Main village and camp
October	Acorns	Camp
November	Continued gathering of acorns and carrying them in Waterfowl	Main village
December	Waterfowl	Main village
January	Waterfowl	Main village
February	Waterfowl until mid-month Stream fishing at end of month	Main village

Source: Kniffen 1939:366.

Valley, whose mother had been a member of the *xa·bé-na·pʰò* group, it is possible that the different claims of the two ethnographers reflect a difference in practice between the two groups.

Trade

Clamshell beads served as a medium of exchange, a standard of value, and a means of storing wealth. Gifford (1926c:378) was told that the Southeastern Pomo obtained clamshells through trade. Other authorities have described expeditions to Bodega Bay that brought these shells back in 100-pound loads. Since these authorities rarely consulted Southeastern Pomo, it is possible that Eastern Pomo and Southeastern Pomo practice differed in this respect. The shells were broken into small pieces, which were roughly shaped, drilled, and strung, then rubbed with a wet hand back and forth on a flat stone slab to grind them into smooth and even beads.

That these beads were a form of money is suggested by

Sally McLendon.
Fig. 7. Eastern Pomo men's grass game, *du·wé-qà.* left to right, Hiding the bones in handfuls of grass, revealing the bones after the opponent has guessed, and collecting the stakes (clamshell beads and magnesite cylinder) placed in front of the winner, whose bones are displayed on the ground, after all 12 counters (upper left) have been won. Demonstration using objects in the Lake Co. Historian's collection, Big Valley. Photographs by Judy Tucker, 1973.

at least three aspects of their use. First, they had standardized values. Late nineteenth and early twentieth-century accounts of the Eastern Pomo and Southeastern Pomo give the dollar equivalents of these clamshell beads, which were still recalled in 1976 by Eastern Pomo speakers, as well as the exchange value in both clamshell beads and dollars of the one- to three-inch rosy or marbled cylinders of magnesite, called Indian gold, which was mined in the Southeastern Pomo region. Second, only these two forms of wealth were gambled for in the grass game (fig. 7), which commonly brought together members of different groups as opponents. Third, these beads were used as money in the extensive trade by which the Eastern Pomo and the Southeastern Pomo linked the principal peoples of north-central California to those of the coast. Although trade was sometimes conducted by barter, buying and selling using these beads as the medium of exchange was more frequent.

The principal articles traded were foods, salt cakes, basketry materials, bows and arrows, arrowheads, obsidian blades, shells, magnesite beads, snares, belts, robes, feathers, and skins (Loeb 1926:192; Brown and Andrews 1969:41). When a village had articles to sell, the chief after consulting other family representatives invited people from another community to a trading session (Loeb 1926:193-195). The reputation of the Pomo as "great counters" (Kroeber 1925:256) is related to their trading and monetary practices. The eastern Pomo had a quinary vigesimal numeral system, while the Southeastern Pomo had a decimal system with some of the units borrowed from Wintuan languages (Dixon and Kroeber 1907). Very large numbers could be counted using a system of different-sized sticks.

Clothing and Adornment

According to contemporary Eastern Pomo (McLendon 1959-1976), men wore their hair long, with their sling wrapped around their head just above the eyebrows, so that the hands were always free but the weapon was instantly available if needed. According to Gifford and Kroeber (1939) men wore their hair tied at the nape of the

neck. Barrett (1952, 2:297), speaking of all seven language groups, describes the hair as hanging loosely or tied at the back of the neck; however, he also discusses "a specially woven hairnet made of very fine string." William Benson, the Eastern Pomo speaker consulted by Loeb (1926:270), claimed that when a boy became 8 or 10, his parents gave a feast in his natal season, and he was presented with a hairnet, elaborately made with beads if the boy was destined to become a secret society member; otherwise it was simply made of milkweed fiber and put away for ceremonial occasions.

Men wore wooden earplugs, at least on ceremonial occasions, that were "decorated either with simple pyrographic designs and beads . . . or more elaborately with feather work and beading" (Barrett 1952, 2:300, pl. 38, figs. 1-2). Women wore delicate ear ornaments of etched birdbone with feather ornamentation at one end, or feathered basketry disk and bead ornaments (Barrett 1952, 2:pl 37).

Whenever Eastern Pomo men left their village, on a trip or to hunt, for example, they carried their spear, *ba·čúy,* their bow, *šu·Múy,* and on their back, in a quiver made from a grizzly cub's hide, *qóí,* their arrows, *ba·ṭʰíy,* as well as their *čú·lú·* or hunting bag.

Although most sources claim that Eastern Pomo and Southeastern Pomo men usually went naked, Gifford and Kroeber (1939:127) record disagreement between both their Eastern Pomo informants as well as both their Southeastern Pomo informants on this point, and a few entries later the Eastern Pomo speakers claim to have used a breechclout, while both the Eastern Pomo and Southeastern Pomo speakers clamed to have used a man's apron or kilt of buckskin or rabbit or some other material. Barrett (1952, 2:414) quotes W.R. Goldsmith, an early settler at Lower Lake, to the effect that in 1858 the men (presumably Southeastern Pomo) wore breechclouts of rabbit or other skins, while the older women wore similar, slightly larger garments, and the young women had already begun to wear calico slips. Barrett (1952, 2:292) also claimed that in the lake region "the tule skirt was the regulation attire the year round and that skirts made of skins were only rarely used." As he gives only the Eastern Pomo form for skirt, it is possible that he was referring primarily to them.

According to Barrett (1952, 2:292) and Gifford and Kroeber (1939:127) Eastern Pomo wore a mantle of shredded tule tied around the neck and belted at the waist in inclement weather. All sources agree that Eastern Pomo and Southeastern Pomo men manufactured a rabbitskin blanket (Eastern *ší·č*, Southeastern *i·ʔné*), which could be worn for warmth. Although most sources agree that both groups went barefoot, Barrett describes a knee-high deerskin boot especially designed to give protection from brush, of which the fullest description was provided by Eastern Pomo speakers. He also includes an illustration of tule moccasins and leggings formerly used in the lake region (fig. 5).

Social Organization

Eastern Pomo and Southeastern Pomo societies were organized largely on the basis of kinship. Kinship determined who lived together in the communal houses and to a large extent one's adult specializations. Access to membership in the secret society was only through kinsmen, and there is considerable evidence that chiefly succession was based on kinship as well. Knowledge of the society through its folklore and oral history was transmitted through kinsmen, and kinship ties enabled the Eastern Pomo and Southeastern Pomo to move beyond the confines of their own villages into trading networks and ceremonial networks. At one point, for example, the chiefs of *ší·kom*, *kʰaˑyáw*, and *ʔlém* were all related to one another through marriage (see the genealogies in Gifford 1926c).

• KINSHIP With regard to the terms used to label cousins, the Eastern Pomo and the Southeastern Pomo had what anthropologists call Omaha-type systems. While the children of two brothers or two sisters (parallel cousins) call each other by sibling terms, children of a brother and sister (cross-cousins) call each other by terms classing the two individuals with generations above or below their own. Specifically, the son of one's mother's brother is also called mother's brother: Eastern Pomo *cʰéˑč*, Southeastern Pomo *ʔímsen*,* while the daughter of one's mother's brother is called mother's younger sister: Eastern *šéˑx*, Southeastern *ʔímxyaq*, according to Gifford (1922:105), but *ʔímxyaq q̣ta* 'mother's older sister old lady' according to Halpern (1936, 1939). However, one's father's sister's child is referred to with the same terms used to refer to a sister's child. That is, a man would call that child sister's child: Eastern *i̱áx*, also *xáˑi̱* (archaic, see McLendon 1975:119 for details), Southeastern *xáčin*,

also *wíxad* according to Halpern (1939), while a woman would call that child by terms meaning offspring, just as she would refer to her real sister's children by terms meaning offspring: Eastern *wax qaˑwí* 'my son', *wax dáhač* 'my daughter', *háriƙa* 'son!', *níƙa* 'daughter!' (in addressing them), Southeastern *wíxad* 'my son', *wímfad* 'my daughter'. There is thus no kin term in either Eastern Pomo or Southeastern Pomo meaning 'cousin' in the sense that the term has in English.

Until the 1950s the relationship of two brothers or two sisters among the Eastern Pomo continued to be a special one. Children of a brother and sister treated each other with affection, of course, but also with a certain degree of deference and respect, more like what American society considers appropriate behavior between aunts and uncles and their nieces and nephews.

In the grandparent generation, mother's mother (Eastern *qáˑč*, Southeastern *ʔímqa*) is distinguished from father's mother (Eastern *máˑč*, Southeastern *ʔímma*), and father's father (Eastern *máˑi̱le*, Southeastern *ʔímbač*) from mother's father (Eastern *káˑč*, Southeastern *ʔímcen*). As is usual in Omaha systems, mother's mother's sisters are called by the same term as mother's mother, just as father's mother's sisters are called by the same term as father's mother. Father's father's brothers are called by the same term as father's father, while mother's father's brothers are called by the same term as mother's father.

The Eastern Pomo and Southeastern Pomo kin terms deviate from what is usually described as the Omaha pattern with respect to the labeling of the siblings of parents. Father (Eastern *háriƙ*, Southeastern *wí mʔè*) is distinguished from father's older brother (Eastern *máˑi̱le*) and father's younger brother (Eastern *kéˑx*) for some Eastern Pomo speakers, while for other Eastern Pomo speakers (see McLendon 1975:117–119) and all Southeastern Pomo speakers, father is distinguished from father's brother (Eastern *kéˑx*, Southeastern *ʔímcex*). For both Eastern Pomo and Southeastern Pomo speakers, mother (*níƙ*, *wí mšè*) is distinguished from mother's older sister (*tʰúˑč*, *wí mšud*) and mother's younger sister (*šéˑx*, *ʔímxyaq*). However, according to Halpern (1939) in Southeastern Pomo any mother's sister can also be called mother, while in Eastern Pomo the terms used by mother's sisters and father's brothers in addressing the children of their siblings of the same sex follow the Omaha pattern—my mother and her sisters or my father and his brothers all refer to me and my parallel cousins in the same way, using the term for child or offspring (Eastern *wax qaˑwí* 'my boy' or *wax dáhač*, 'my girl') and when addressing us would use the address forms: *háriƙa* 'son!' (also 'father!'), *níƙa* 'daughter!' (also 'mother!').

The Eastern Pomo and Southeastern Pomo systems of kin terms differ in a number of details. The most striking point of difference, probably, is that in Eastern Pomo a

---

* All kin terms given actually translate 'my ——'. The Eastern Pomo forms are from McLendon (1975:112–121); the Southeastern forms are from Halpern (1936, 1939) and Moshinsky (1974) in the transcription of Moshinsky (1974).

basic distinction is made between a speaker's own relatives and another's relatives, by either suppletion (using two nonresemblant forms, like go:went in English), prefixation, or suffixation. Thus 'my father' is *háriǩ*, but 'his father' is *ha·me·ʔé*. 'My mother' is *ník*, but 'his mother' is *ha·mi·t̪hé*; 'my mother's brother' is *cʰé·č*, but 'his mother's brother' is *ha·mi·cʰé·*. No such distinction seems to be made in Southeastern Pomo.

Southeastern Pomo has terms for great-grandfather (*wówo*) and great-grandmother (*wóq̪ta*), but Eastern Pomo does not. Southeastern Pomo distinguishes between spouse's mother (*wí mxà*), wife's father (*wí mcàc*), and husband's father (*wí bà*), and child's spouse's parent (*t̪óʔmela*), while Eastern Pomo has only parents-in-law (*wí ma·šá·*). Both Eastern Pomo and Southeastern Pomo have terms for sister's husband (*kó·t̪, ʔímqon*) and brother's wife (*míy, wí yàqmed*). Southeastern Pomo distinguishes wife's brother (*wí mfàq*) from wife's sister (*wí mfàq bt̪ed*), and husband's sister (*wí mqàtin*) from husband's brother (*wí mxùtaq*), while Eastern Pomo only distinguishes wife's sibling (*wíma·ha·*) from husband's sibling (*wíma·qar*). Both Eastern Pomo and Southeastern Pomo distinguish older brother (*méx, ʔímmeq*) from older sister (*dé·x, ʔímdeq*), but Southeastern Pomo also distinguishes younger brother (*wí mdùtaq*) from younger sister (*wí ml̀àq*), while Eastern Pomo has a single term for younger sibling of either sex (*dú·xač*).

• DESCENT AND RESIDENCE Although Omaha systems of kin terms are overwhelmingly associated throughout the world with patrilineal descent, the Eastern Pomo, at least, seem to have had bilateral descent. That is, they reckoned descent evenly and symmetrically along both maternal and paternal lines. Residence for both the Southeastern Pomo and the Eastern Pomo was either bilocal or ambilocal. For example, the chief of *ší·kom*, *léw-t̪ʰi·rì* (his English name was Johnny Bull), seems to have practiced bilocal residence, since he is described by Gifford (1926c:335) as spending considerable time, sometimes a whole winter, at his wife's natal village, *ʔlém*, while another chief, *či·pʰá-xa·lè·*, is described as spending a year at a time at the natal village of his wife, *qámdot*. At the same time, *či·pʰá-xa·lè·*'s father, *bi·tá·*, seems to have elected to live with his wife's kinsmen permanently, chosing ambilocal residence, since he brought his second wife back to live with his first wife's family, in their house.

At *ší·kom* in 1850-1870 half the spouses were from other villages: 27 from other Eastern Pomo villages, 18 Northern Pomo, 12 Hill Patwin, 6 Southeastern Pomo, 3 Central Pomo, and 3 other Pomo or Wappo.

There seem to be no direct reports as to the principle that determined which individuals shared a communal house. However, an analysis of the kin ties binding the residents of the 20 houses in *ší·kom* in Gifford's (1926c) census reveals two striking patterns. Of the 18 houses that contained two or more fireside or hearth groups, all but one showed a consistent pattern of siblings or parallel cousins (who are terminological siblings, of course) and their immediate families sharing the communal house.

With the exception of one house inhabited solely and aberrantly by an old couple, hearth groups always included at least two generations of kinsmen, usually related as parent and offspring, or more typically, three generations, consisting of grandparents, parents, and their offspring.

The only statement as to how hearth groups were formed occurs in Loeb's description of marriage:

> The married couple kept moving from one family to the other, but when a child was expected they always went to live with the wife's family. After the child was born if either the husband's or wife's family house were sufficiently large another doorway and fireplace was installed and the married couple took up permanent residence. If neither house were sufficiently large, the married couple built one of their own (Loeb 1926:279).

There are no instances of a young couple living alone in a house in *ší·kom*, and very few examples of couples with nonmarried (and therefore presumably relatively young) children who do not also have an older parent sharing the fire with them. It would seem then that even after the birth of a child many young couples did not separate themselves from the parental fire. It is possible that only the marriage of other siblings and the arrival of their children ultimately produced such a crowd around the fire that one or more of the siblings and their spouse and children set up a separate fire and doorway.

There are several reports (McLendon 1959-1976) that boys, when old enough, consistently slept with their terminological grandfathers (either maternal or paternal, and including, of course, the male siblings of the boy's actual grandfather), when these grandfathers were without spouses. In the house illustrated in figure 3 the informant remembered that as a boy he slept with his terminological grandfather, at location A, on the opposite side of the fire from his mother and stepfather, while at location B at another fire there is another old man with a boy, who is likely to be in a grandson relation to him. This tradition seems to have resulted in a warm and affectionate bond between old man and boy and have been an extremely important source of instruction for the boy and physical assistance for the old man. The grandfathers told the boys myths, stories of their experiences as young men, and those of others they had heard during the winter months spent largely in the sweathouse while generally inculcating the ways of the Eastern Pomo world. The boy's young body kept the grandfather warmer at night, and he saw to his grandfather's comfort in a number of ways, particularly by giving him a much appreciated form of massage that involved the boy walking on his grandfather's back.

The Eastern Pomo and Southeastern Pomo practice of three or four generations of kinsmen sharing a communal house was an admirably efficient system, it seems, for simultaneously seeing sucessfully to the time-consuming and vital task of child care and education and the equally demanding task of caring for the aged, while freeing the parents, who were the most efficient food acquirers. Each communal house could be expected to have a number of older people who stayed close to the house, supervising the fire and the nonnursing children as well as various food-preparing activities and the manufacture of wealth (beads in the case of men, baskets in the case of women). This freed the younger members of the family complex with more energy and stamina for the important food-acquiring activities. They thus were able to provide the aged with the food they might have had difficulty in collecting and preparing entirely on their own. This maximization of the Eastern Pomo exploitation of the environment, in conjunction with the annual availability of croplike, storeable food sources, especially fish and acorns, made possible a remarkably high population density for hunters and gatherers. The division of labor implicit in this system also permitted the accumulation of wealth (in the form of beads of clamshell and magnesite and the beautiful, nonutilitarian feathered baskets and beaded and feathered belts) so necessary for the proper participation in births, marriages, and funerals.

Life Cycle

• BIRTH   A detailed description of the Eastern Pomo rituals and restrictions to be observed after childbirth and the subsequent caring for the child is given in Loeb (1926:251–256). There are no known sources on specifically Southeastern Pomo practices.

The child was born in its mother's family's house. Its father's mother or father's sister came morning and evening to wash the baby in a special basket called *tʰiˑríˑbuˑkù,* which was saved and given to the child when he or she grew up.

Pregnancy and the birth of a child were the occasion for an exchange of gifts between the father's family and the mother's family reminiscent of the exchange that marks marriages. The father's family gave the mother an especially valuable and beautiful necklace called *xébiˑnàr* during her pregnancy, and after the birth of the child, the mother's family presented the mother with a very valuable belt of beads, called *Múki,* and the most valuable of baskets, the *țáˑ-siˑțʰòl* (which had instead of a design the red topknots of many woodpeckers woven in), which was filled with pinole balls, all of which the mother in turn presented to the father's mother when she came to wash the baby. If the father's family was satisfied with their gift they returned the next day with two strings of approximately 800 beads each, one of which ended in a one and one-half inch long piece of magnesite, which they tied around the mother's wrists, adding a necklace too if they were very pleased. The mother wore these a day or two and then her mother removed them and gave them to one of her relatives for keeping.

For eight days after the birth of the child the father could not leave the house; then for a month he could not hunt, fish, gamble, dance, or make beads. As long as the child was nursing, both the father and the mother abstained from several varieties of fish, a number of vegetable foods, and bluejay and ground squirrel.

• PUBERTY   Loeb (1926:270–273) gives an extensive description of the special behaviors required on a girl's first menstruation. There are again no known sources on specifically Southeastern Pomo practices.

Among the Eastern Pomo, according to Loeb, the girl was isolated in a small tule structure attached to her house, where she lay on a bed of coals covered with fresh tules, purifying herself with a sort of steaming, during the whole period. She abstained from all food except acorn mush and pinole, did not scratch herself, feed herself, comb her own hair, or wash her own face. Her mother or aunt did this for her. On the fourth night or fifth morning she bathed, was given a good skirt, a string of beads, and a hairnet in which she dressed, and then was given a large, shallow basket of acorns to grind into meal, leach, and then cook. The acorn mush thus prepared was served to her family and a few friends who complimented her. The basket used for washing was saved and never used again for another purpose, unless for the first menstruation of her sisters. Such a basket seems to have been photographed by Curtis (1907–1930, 14:facing p. 68).

There was no specific puberty ceremony for boys among the Eastern Pomo, although Loeb (1926) claims boys were given a hairnet and toy bow and arrows and bathed in angelica root water at a feast given when they were 8 or 10.

• MARRIAGE   There are three sources that explicitly describe Eastern Pomo marriages (Kroeber 1925:255; Loeb 1926:277–279; McLendon 1959–1976) and one source for Southeastern Pomo marriages (Halpern 1936).

Marriage, like so much else in Eastern Pomo life and probably in Southeastern Pomo life, seemed ideally to permit individual initiative in a context of consensus. Young people seem to have made their own choices, but these choices had to be approved of, or at least agreed to, by the young couple's respective families, before a marriage could take place. There seems to be considerable agreement between the sources that, among the Eastern Pomo, two young people when attracted to each other first worked out a relationship between themselves to their satisfaction. If it seemed that their intentions were serious, the families of the two potential spouses had to determine if they were willing to support this particular alliance by taking an appropriate role in the ceremonial exchanges that celebrated a marriage.

Apparently the formal commitment to marriage began when the prospective son-in-law publicly spent the night at his bride's house, "going in as son-in-law" the Eastern

314

Pomo say. However, this was not merely a matter of individual initiative as the parents of the girl must first be willing to have him as son-in-law, to "call him son-in-law" as they say. If they refuse him the title, no marriage can take place.

All three sources agree that the exchange of presents began the next morning with the arrival of the man's relatives bringing food. The sources disagree somewhat on the relative timing of these exchanges and the items exchanged. Kroeber gives no information on the items exchanged, but Loeb (1926) and McLendon (1959-1976) agree that three types of valuables were exchanged: food, beads, rabbitskin blankets and fine baskets. The items involved had a symbolic as well as a potentially practical function. First, a valuable produced by women, food, was exchanged (Loeb says both sides gave pinole, McLendon's source says the man's side gave acorn soup, while the woman's family gave the pinole, as they do at the birth of a child). Then a valuable produced by men, beads, was exchanged, the man's family giving the woman's family the fine, small beads appropriately worn by women, the woman's family giving the man's family the large, thick beads appropriately worn by men. Last, a valuable produced by men, rabbitskin blankets, is given by the man's family, while a valuable produced by women, baskets, was given by the woman's family (see the photographs in Curtis 1907-1930, 14:facing p. 58).

Although the items exchanged all seem potentially of use in the new household, the young people do not in fact receive them. Rather it is the relatives of the husband and wife who exchange with each other and keep the items exchanged. McLendon was told that the small beads were put around the girl's neck and admired by every one for a half-hour or so and then removed by the bride's mother and put "aside or where they have hired someone to count them, so they'll know how much to pay." Benson told Loeb (1926:279) that the beads given in payment to the bride were divided up by the mother of the bride. "She kept half the beads for her side of the family and gave the other half to the father's side."

Halpern (1936) had recorded the gift by the groom's family of beads to the bride's family, among the Southeastern Pomo, which is reciprocated by a gift of baskets from the woman's family to the man's.

•DEATH   Loeb (1926:286-291) gives an extremely detailed and lengthy account of Eastern Pomo funerary practices. There is less information on specifically Southeastern Pomo practices, although it is known that both groups cremated their dead until the 1870-1880s. Death for the Eastern Pomo was the ultimate disaster, and the heartfelt grief of the surviving kinsmen was expressed in a number of institutions. Mourning began before death had actually taken place. According to Loeb, both men and women started to cry and the women scratched themselves with their fingernails from the temples down to their cheeks, often deeply enough to leave scars.

William Benson (Angulo 1935a) remembers that when he was extremely sick with whooping cough during the epidemic as a boy, his mother's mother thought at one point that he was dying and picked up a stone pestle and rammed herself in the chest with it in her grief.

According to Loeb, the body was left in the house for three or four days during which time people came in and piled gifts on the body of robes and blankets, beads and fine baskets, particularly the extravagantly beautiful feathered baskets the Pomo groups are so famous for. The relatives kept track of these gifts and gave back presents of an equal value at a later date.

The deceased was cremated in a special burning area at the edge of the permanent village on a funeral pyre, face down, with the head pointing south. During the cremation the mourners together with the chief kept the pyre encircled, crying, and throwing still more objects on the funeral pyre in their grief. The women cried and sang mourning songs, ma·xáraxè, which they continued to sing whenever they thought of the deceased during the subsequent period of mourning. Women and men cut short their normally long hair, and women rubbed little pellets of white clay into it. During this period a woman would also sprinkle pinole and acorn meal while singing the mourning songs where the deceased used to pass.

Loeb (1926) says that for important people and the young the period of mourning lasted a year and that just after the cremation, the father or a close relation came and picked up any pieces of bone not burned and reburied them. At the close of the mourning period these bones were disinterred and reburned with valuables such as beads, or the valuables were simply burned on the site of the bone interment.

Ceremonies

There are several sources of information about specifically Eastern Pomo ceremonials (Freeland 1923; Benson in Angulo 1935a; Loeb 1926:322-347, 352, 353-354; Kroeber 1925:254, 1903, 1902). Barrett's (1917) work on ceremonies includes many Eastern Pomo terms and presumably was based in part on fieldwork with the Eastern Pomo but so merges Northern Pomo, Central Pomo, and Eastern Pomo practice in its description that it is difficult to extract information as to specifically Eastern Pomo behavior. There is one source describing specifically Southeastern Pomo ceremonials (Halpern 1936).

Several lists of names of dances have been collected (Barrett 1917; Curtis 1907-1930, 14; Loeb 1926), but very little is known about the nature, timing, or reputed function of some of them. It appears that some dances could be held at any time, sometimes to mark the recovery of a seriously ill person and probably for other functions as well.

There were two major ceremonial events among the Eastern Pomo, and apparently three among the Southeastern Pomo, during the course of which a variety of dances was performed. All these were held in the spring. Benson also has described a Thunder ceremonial, *qa·líma·totow-xè*, which could be held separately in the fall, if not performed during the spring pole ceremony, which was accompanied by the appearance of Kuksu.

The most awesome was clearly the ghost ceremony, called in Eastern Pomo *qa·lúy-kà·wkʰ xé* 'ghost dance' and in Southeastern Pomo *čínamfo xé* 'ghost dance'. It seems not to have been given every year, certainly not by the same village every year. According to Freeland (1923:14) among the Eastern Pomo, the ghost ceremony was "supposed in a general way to follow not too long— several months perhaps—after the death of some important individual who might be man or woman, secret society member or not." Among the Eastern Pomo, the ghost ceremony also obligatorily involved participation by other village-communities in addition to the one at which it took place.

The *qa·lúy-kàwkʰ xé* was a ceremonial tied to the intense feelings of the Eastern Pomo around death. It involved the impersonation of the dead by specially trained and initiated men, called *ma·túči*. It took place primarily in the semisubterranean *Márakʰ*, called on this occasion *qa·lúy-kà·wkʰ Márakʰ*, but also involved the surrounding hills and village.

Loeb (1926) says Benson told him that the *ma·túči* were presided over by a man whose title was yomta. Eastern Pomo consulted since 1959 (McLendon 1959-1976) deny that this is an Eastern Pomo word, and Gifford also found in 1919 that Jim Pumpkin, himself a *ma·túči*, denied knowledge of the word. (Benson was not a *ma·túči*.) Gifford (1926c:353-354) felt that therefore among the Eastern Pomo the chiefs were probably the leaders of the *ma·túči*. yomta is in fact the Patwin word for shaman or Indian doctor, derived by the addition of a collective animate suffix *-ta* from *yom* 'power'. The spiritual leader of the New Ghost Dance (Bole-Maru) among the Kashaya and the Central Pomo is called *yómta* (although this person among the Patwin is called *bólle,* from the Patwin word for myth *bó·le,* which is also the name for the New Ghost Dance). Since Benson spoke Central Pomo as well as Eastern Pomo, having married a Central Pomo and lived in Ukiah for much of his adult life, it seems likely that he had introduced a Central Pomo form originally borrowed from Patwin with the New Ghost Dance into his description of Eastern Pomo ritual. In Eastern Pomo three categories of participants are distinguished: *qa·lúy-kà·wkʰ* 'ghosts'; *nó-qa·lúy-kà·wkʰ* 'ash ghosts' who know the secrets of handling the live coals without apparent harm; and *ma·túči* 'initiates' who know the rules for the dances and ceremonies. Benson (in Angulo 1935a) gives an account of a *qa·lúy-kà·wkʰ xé* he witnessed as a boy. This is the only known description of an actual Eastern Pomo ghost ceremony.

The first night, the ghosts made their presence known by fires in the hills surrounding the village (they are ghosts of the cremated, of course, and thus have a special, nonhuman relationship to fire) and the thunderlike sounds of dancing in the subterranean *Márakʰ*, plus occasional glimpses of flaming figures. The next morning, the captain from the knoll that is the roof of the *Márakʰ* ritually called the ghosts, who then appeared, some, at least, flaming, from the four cardinal directions, starting in the south. The chief specifically urged them to run without faltering for the health of the village and various categories of its inhabitants (Barrett 1917:408). At this point one ghost was identified by the chief as that of a recently dead man, whose relatives were instructed to line up on either side of the entrance to the *Márakʰ*. He was caught, laid down, covered with beads by his grieving female relatives, and then taken into the *Márakʰ*. All the men of the village-community entered the ghost house with the ghosts. When they were through with the ceremony inside (the timing is unclear in Benson's narrative) the women brought pinole and acorn mush, on the command of the chief, and placed it in front of the *Márakʰ* for the visiting people. The chief invited the women to eat too, and the food was divided up by the visiting chief. Everyone laughed and joked and happiness reigned, which strongly contrasted with the preceding period of seriousness and mourning. Toward evening, the rumbling thunder noise began again, and with darkness there were once again fires in the hills. Throughout the night there was the noise of thunder and dancing. Toward morning, the sounds changed, and Benson was told by his mother that the fire dance, during which the ash ghosts handle live coals and "eat" fire, was beginning. In the early morning Benson saw steaming men thrown from the *Márakʰ* where they lay until washed and revived by their female relatives. (They were apparently unconscious as a result of the sweating contest that took place at this time.) Eventually 15-20 men were thrown out, and when revived, reentered. The chief at this point announced a grass game, *du·wé-qà* (fig. 7), which was played on the west side of the *Márakʰ*. After two games had been won, the chief once again called the ghosts ritually from the roof of the *Márakʰ*. The ghosts came from all sides, the men lined up on both sides of the entrance, shouting "hu-hu-hu," while the ghosts entered (going backward) and the dancing began. After four sets of dances, the men emerged to say that the ghosts were going to do the fire dance, they were going to sweat with them, and the boys to be initiated should be brought. The following morning, after the finishing rituals, a big feast was held, after which everyone returned to their homes.

During the course of the ritual, all sources agree, the ghosts behaved in certain prescribed ways. They always talked in a special language, using Eastern Pomo lexical items and grammar, but always talking in terms of antonyms and opposites. Thus if they wanted to go on the west side, they said east side, for instance. There were in addition some ritually symbolic substitutions. The live coals that were played with and "eaten" were called *bú·* 'native potato', while the young boys to be initiated were called *mu·líy* 'young ground squirrel'. Loeb (1926:254) says that the *ma·ṭúči* were permanently forbidden to eat bluejay and ground squirrel. The young initiates were said to be "hunted" and "shot" when they were caught during the initiation. The ghosts were, on one hand, deliberately mirth-provoking in their behavior, trying to induce the participants to laugh, and, on the other hand, irascible, easily irritated into terrifying, fire-throwing anger.

The descriptions Halpern (1936) was given of the *čínamfo xé* or ghost ceremony among the Southeastern Pomo are very reminiscent of the Eastern Pomo ceremony and yet at the same time seem very different in mood and purpose. The Southeastern Pomo ritual is explicitly associated with the important sources of food in the environment—acorns, wild seeds, fish, and mammals. The movement back and forth between the wilderness area beyond the village and the ceremonial house seems concerned with the provisioning of the population more than with the supernatural forces that reside there. Although fire is used in the initiation of boys (who are called *xólnaq*), it seems to play a much smaller role than among the Eastern Pomo. It is also a ceremonial in which only men participated.

The *čínamfo xé* began with the ghosts hollering from the hills. The *x̣wán x̣ǫ́wi* 'ceremonial house-doctor' called them from the roof of the semisubterranean *x̣wán* 'ceremonial house' in a special language that was not comprehensible to the Southeastern Pomo. He told the ghosts to come putting acorns on their body. When they came, one ghost had a long pole striped with charcoal, which he threw in the air, and which was then caught by a man in the group who entered the *x̣wán* first with it. The ghosts announced which acorns they were bringing, then made motions as if shooting deer and catching fish. The second day they were called to bring the wild seeds for pinole. Again they came, announcing what they were bringing, and this time some had bull snakes. The third day they were called to bring fish of all sorts; the fourth day they were called to bring rabbits.

In addition to the ghost ceremony, the Southeastern Pomo had two other ceremonials during which the boy initiates were shot or speared in the navel as part of the initiation. Although the boys bled, they were never seriously injured. Participants claimed to have passed out when struck and come to the next day to find themselves completely well. The shooting was said to make the boys grow quickly. The two rituals were called *bqúq xé* 'spear dance' and *bṭéqal xé* 'bear dance'. In the *bqúq xé* the boys were collected on the third and last night of the ceremonial, taken outside, and then shot in the navel from within the ceremonial house. In the *bṭéqal xé*, which followed the *bqúq xé*, there were two main figures, *šállis* and his older sister *bṭéqal* (who was dressed as a bear). After a certain period of dances, *šállis* came on the north side, *bṭéqal* on the south, *šállis* speared each boy once, while two women identified as *čínamfo* stood, one on the north, one on the south, and threw beads four times. It is not clear from Halpern (1936) if this event was followed by more dancing and a second appearance of the supernaturals or whether the supernaturals appeared on the last day of the ceremony. It is also not clear precisely where the events took place, although it seems that the *bṭéqal xé* spearing took place outdoors, while the *bqúq xé* shooting seemed to involve a ceremonial structure of some sort.

The Kuksu ceremonial witnessed by Benson was held a few weeks before the ghost ceremonial he described, during the same spring, but in a different village-community. It began with an all-night dance starting at dark. The next day a bear appeared suddenly and a group of boys was made to stand in front of the dance house where the bear was running back and forth. Someone pushed a boy in front of the bear who three times knocked him over and as he got up knocked him over again. The bear then ran into the *Márakʰ* followed by the people. Inside he ran around the center pole ritually, accompanied by the sound of birds, which Benson's uncle told him came from the two little bears on either side of him. The bear climbed the center pole, turned over backward, and fell to the floor, turning over four times as he did. The bear then went to the drum at the back of the *Márakʰ* and ritually took off his bearskin and returned to sit down as a man. He was given a pipe filled with tobacco and smoked it while praying for the health of the village and its occupants. He then put on his bearskin, performed some more, and left. The children were told to go out, and while playing they saw a tall black figure approaching. This was the supernatural Kuksu, and on the occasion witnessed by Benson there seem to have been several Kuksu who herded the boys together into a *sé-Márakʰ* 'brush ceremonial house'. That night the boys (including Benson) were made to stand in a row outside, then lie down blindfolded, while their backs were ritually scratched. At dawn when they awoke, they found a group of people approaching with a long pole, which was ritually installed in a previously prepared hole in front of the entrance. Eight young men ran up the pole with stiff legs and arms (like bears) and hung there, while their female relatives pelted them with pinole balls, beads, and grain. When they came down they were washed by their female relatives and later more dancing took place, followed by a feast after the closing ceremonies.

Among the Southeastern Pomo the supernatural called *kúksu* by the Eastern Pomo is called *sqóyqyo* 'the one who cuts many'. He appeared during a spring ceremonial in which the young boys were ritually cut, but again, although sharing many details with the Eastern Pomo ceremonial, the Southeastern Pomo one had a quite different character. The *sqóyqyo* came the first day, before the *s²é ca* 'brush house' was built, was given beads, and went away. There were grown-up initiates called *q̓ówitsmfo* who entered the brush house singing and called *sqóyqyo*. He came in the morning, they shook the brush house, and he went away. On the second day the boys to be cut were brought by the *čúmfo* 'noninitiates'. From this time on the boys stayed in the brush house. The second night they sang all night, but nothing happened. If *sqóyqyo* came, he went away when they shook the brush house. On the third day, *sqóyqyo* came, and the fire tender went from house to house announcing that the boys had been cut. He cried and said "Alas, my grandsons." On the fourth day the boys played shinny, *sqóyqyo* came again and chased them into the water from where they raced to the brush house, he roughed up those he caught, but once in the brush house they were safe. They shouted, shook the house, and ultimately drove him away.

From the Eastern Pomo Barrett (1917a:444, 458, 461) collected information about men and women who could assume the powers of a bear in connection with a bearskin suit ("Cults and their Transformations," fig. 3, this vol.) and who were thought to be able to kill, for pay, a maximum of four people a year. Loeb (1926:335–337) believed that Barrett's informant was a fraud, but his own data confirm that the bear impersonators in the 'bear dance' were supposed to punish offenders in the community. The question remains unresolved (Cody 1940a); the belief may well have helped maintain social control.

Political Organization

Anthropological observers of the various Pomo groups have long struggled to understand the function of the leader the Eastern Pomo called *ká·xa·likʰ* and the Southeastern Pomo called *bálakwi*. The *ká·xa·likʰ* and *bálakwi* were by no means authoritarian and at first struck observers as having no power at all. In fact, Eastern Pomo government seems to have been achieved in large part through consensus against a shared background of expectations as to what constituted appropriate behavior in all situations. Contemporary Eastern Pomo remember being told as children by grandparents that, "in the old days there were many rules to follow," and "if you didn't follow them you'd get bad luck and get killed" (McLendon 1959–1976). There were thus sanctions, but they were not directly exercised by the *ká·xa·likʰ* or *bálakwi*, except for banishment. Rather, during the ceremonials, offending individuals could be singled out for various kinds of punishment, and it seems also to have been felt that offenses involving ritual prohibitions of various sorts would be taken care of by supernatural forces. Thus menstruating women who broke the prohibition on going for water invariably became sick and usually saw a supernatural who lived in the water, *ba·kíl*.

The function of the *ká·xa·likʰ* (and probably the *bálakwi*) seems to have been to continually remind the community of the nature of this background of shared expectations, through the example of his own behavior and through his speeches. All published sources as well as contemporary Eastern Pomo agree that the primary qualification for a *ká·xa·likʰ* was that he must be a good man. He must epitomize in his own behavior the ideal for Eastern Pomo behavior, that is, he must be good to others, observing all kinship and familial obligations willingly, graciously, but without pride or self-praise. He must be neither too poor nor avariciously rich; he must be modest but able.

The duties of the *ká·xa·likʰ* included organizing all the communal activities of the village-community, such as the spring trapping of spawning fish, the fall gathering of acorns, trading for supplemental food in the case of famine or shortage, the arranging of trade feasts with neighbors when there were surpluses of fish in the spring or of acorns in the fall, and scheduling the ceremonials, including arranging for the construction of the ceremonial house appropriate to the occasion. He apparently did these things in consultation with others, but it was his responsibility to feel out his community, arrange for a consensus to be reached, and then communicate it to the group. His seems to have been a rather difficult job, requiring great delicacy, tact, and ability, precisely because he had few direct sanctions to exercise. He seems to have carried out his functions in large part through speech making, but also by giving copious amounts of beads, sometimes from his own resources, most often collected for wealthy men in the group.

Every morning at dawn the *ká·xa·likʰ* awoke the village-community with a speech, exhorting them to be good and announcing the group activities to take place that day. At marriages, funerals, trading feasts, and all ceremonials, he opened the event with a speech appropriate to the occasion. Among the Eastern Pomo he seems always to have been a member of the secret society.

History

The Eastern Pomo and Southeastern Pomo are just to the north of the northernmost expansion of the Spanish missions in California: Dolores founded 1776, San Rafael founded 1817, and Sonoma founded 1823. That they did not escape contact is demonstrated by extensive Spanish loanwords in both languages (McLendon 1969) and by the many contemporary Eastern Pomo and Southeastern Pomo who remember having been told by grandparents of their capture by the Spanish.

There is a published account of a party of American trappers for the Hudson's Bay Company passing through the Clear Lake area in 1832 or 1833 (Work 1945). In 1841 Salvador Vallejo, who was said to own an extensive ranch in Clear Lake Valley, sent there for Indians to help in the harvesting of his grain in the Napa Valley. When they refused, he sent a small detachment of Mexican troops who ultimately massacred the men of an island village in their sweathouse. These were undoubtably Southeastern Pomo (Sherman 1945). Additional evidence that Vallejo had begun to run cattle in the lake area before 1841 comes from the Eastern Pomo chief, Augustine, who recalled that Vallejo had come some 10 years before the murder of the two abusive White settlers, Charles Stone and Andrew Kelsey in 1849 (Carpenter and Milberry 1914). Vallejo's heirs much later produced an instrument dated 1844 purporting to be signed by Manuel Micheltorena, conveying to Salvador and Juan Antonio Vallejo the land known as Laguna de Lup-Yomi (from Lake Miwok *luppu-yomi* 'rock place', the Lake Miwok name for the Eastern Pomo village-community *xaˑbéˑnaˑpʰò* 'rock-village/people') (L. Palmer 1881:4). Oral histories (McLendon 1959-1976) document that Augustine and at least three other Eastern Pomo were forced by the Spanish to become riders and herd cattle for them, for which they were recompensed with beef but no money. Stone and Kelsey were among the American settlers who took over Vallejo's cattle operations in 1847. They abused and exploited the Eastern Pomo, provoking their own deaths.

In 1850 the United States Cavalry under the command of Captain Lyons entered the lake area near Lower Lake with the specific goal of punishing the Indians for the killing of Stone and Kelsey. The Southeastern Pomo and the Eastern Pomo of Big Valley seem to have largely been able to avoid the troops, who finally massacred a group who were fishing at *baˑdónˑbaˑtʰin,* now called Bloody Island, at the northwestern end of Upper Lake. They then continued west toward Ukiah, massacring along the way other Indians who must have been Northern Pomo and Central Pomo and in no way involved in the killing.

In 1851 Col. Redick McKee was sent as Indian agent to negotiate a treaty and establish a reservation. He was accompanied by the ethnographer-journalist-linguist George Gibbs, who acted as interpreter (although he apparently knew no native languages of northern California). The treaty was never ratified by Congress and no reservation was established.

American settlement of the lake area began in earnest after 1851, with ranches being established and the Eastern Pomo and Southeastern Pomo being pressed into service on the ranches. They were gradually forced to give up the traditional sites of their village-communities, as well as much of their traditional subsistence base, since the newly arrived ranchers frequently did not welcome the Eastern Pomo and Southeastern Pomo on their homesteaded ranches, even to gather acorns, buckeyes, peppernuts, and the wild seeds used in pinole. The introduction of grazing starting with the Spanish in the 1830s or 1840s contributed to a rapid change in the plants growing, as did the American mania for chopping down trees and clearing lands. In 1870 Father Luciano Osuna purchased 160 acres in Big Valley on which he founded the Saint Turibus Mission, and to which he moved a number of the people, formerly members of the *quˑɬáˑnaˑpʰò* and *xaˑbéˑnaˑpʰò* groups, whom he had converted and baptized in large groups. The present-day Catholic church in Lakeport preserves baptismal records starting with Father Osuna's baptisms.

Although their way of life was drastically altered, the Eastern Pomo and Southeastern Pomo did not cease to maintain their identity as distinct groups, resisting total assimilation to White culture and ways, despite their adoption of much of White material culture and technology. Loeb (1926:298) claimed that among the Eastern Pomo a man who became "contaminated by alien influence" was given a position of responsibility and even made chief if of proper standing, in an attempt to "lead him back into the fold." Powers (1877:214-215) claimed the Southeastern Pomo at *xqóyi* would put to death any women committing adultery with Americans, but the accuracy of his reporting is suspect in the case of the Southeastern Pomo, since there is no evidence that he actually consulted a member of this group. The extensive settlement of the lake area by Whites was preceded apparently by their diseases. Gibbs (1853) noted in 1851 signs of smallpox on the inhabitants he encountered. Not only dread diseases like smallpox, but also diseases associated with childhood in European societies such as whooping cough, measles, and even the common cold were lethal to whole societies who had never previously been exposed to them and therefore had no immunities. Gifford (1926c) documents an infant mortality rate of 51 percent among the inhabitants of *šíˑkom* as remembered by Jim Pumpkin for the period roughly from 1850-1871. By the turn of the century tuberculosis can be documented to have killed many. The result was a drastic reduction in the size of the population in a relatively short period of time (assisted, of course, by the various massacres along the way) and the the consolidation of former principal villages and tribelets.

However, the effects of these European introduced diseases went deeper than their devastating effects on the size and distribution of the population. All the important ceremonials, most of the rituals concerning childbirth and child raising, among the Eastern Pomo at least, had as their explicit stated goal the assurance of health and well-being. Suddenly, with the arrival of the Europeans, the ceremonials must have seemed to lose their efficacy. It must have been intensely demoralizing to undergo the rigors of participation in a ceremonial and to find that the population continued to die in large numbers nevertheless.

Moreover, among the Eastern Pomo at least, virtually all illness was attributed to human causes. Either the sick person had transgressed in some way, broken some taboo and therefore become sick; or some other members of the group had reason to wish him ill and had caused the illness through a variety of techniques commonly referred to in English as "poisoning." Contemporary Eastern

Fig. 8. The Eastern Pomo dance house at *xa·bé-ma·lòlel* with *hóhoaxè* dancers. Photographed before 1902 by O.E. Meddaugh. The individuals are identified, with varying certainty, by Meddaugh's records and the Eastern Pomos William Graves (in 1949), Ralph Holder, Suzanne Moore Holder, and Sam Tooney (in 1976) as, from left to right: Tom Harness; Johnny Bull, *léw-tʰirì* (a fire eater); Dick Green, "Whiskey Head," *pʰa·šín* (the caller); Snap Bucknell, *sinápʰ* (a fire eater); and either *lí·li* or Bill Green, "Whiskey Bill," *ša·qó-ba·kàl*.

Pomo remember that at the turn of the century there was even a poison that caused tuberculosis. Thus the increased mortality was accompanied by a concomitant increase in divisive suspicions; for each death, a human agent was implied and sought.

The traditional ceremonials gradually ceased to be given. There were Eastern Pomo individuals alive in 1976 who remembered seeing Kuksu. The last Eastern Pomo ash ghost died in 1960 or 1961. But the ceremonials seem to have ceased to be given before 1900. In part the rapid depopulation must have frequently produced situations where there were not enough *ma·ṭúči* to sucessfully perform a ceremony; and the high infant mortality rate and the new range of options available to the younger generation must have left the *ma·ṭúči* frequently with the choice of transmitting the tradition to someone not perfectly appropriate in some way or not transmitting the tradition at all.

Around 1872 a new alternative presented itself. The 1870 Ghost Dance that began among the Northern

Paiute of western Nevada spread through the Patwin to the Eastern Pomo and the Southeastern Pomo. According to the Eastern Pomo of *ší·kom*, it was brought by a resident of *ší·kom* (whose father was a Patwin from Long Valley) named Poni (individual #73 in Gifford's 1926c census). According to the Southeastern Pomo it was brought to them by Lame Bill, an early Patwin prophet, together with a Southeastern Pomo named *ʔáwotu* who was also called *tó·toʔ* and was informant to Barrett (1952) and Gifford (1926c, who gives Wokox as his name).

The New Ghost Dance was called *ma·rú·* in Eastern Pomo and *ʔábk̓o* in Southeastern Pomo. Both terms mean a myth or story. In its original form it was a revivalistic movement that promised its followers that the Whites would be killed by a natural disaster and the traditional Indian ways would return again. At the center of the cult is the Dreamer, also called *ma·rú·* or *ʔábk̓o*, "who serves as the chief religious functionary and who leads the people by means of dreamed rules of ceremonial behavior" (Meighan and Riddell 1972:9). The Dreamer also doctored illnesses. Since the source of authority as to ceremonial behavior was in dreams, an alternative was provided to the breakdown in the traditional techniques of transmitting ceremonial information, and in fact many fewer personnel were required. The new religion seems to have offered a new focus of cooperation and political integration at a time of dwindling population and hostile White populations (Treganza, Taylor, and Wallace 1947: 124–125). It is usually called Maru or Bole-Maru in the ethnographic literature.

In 1872 a dance house was built in Big Valley and the *ma·rú·* was introduced. Barrett says the series of ceremonies celebrated at this time extended more or less continuously over a period of two years, Indians coming from as far away as the coast to await the end of the world. Powers (1877:210–213) has described one of these ceremonies in Big Valley during the summer of 1872.

After these ceremonies ended, the former village-communities went through a period of transition, frequently forced to move from site to site by the ever homesteading Whites. The people who had formerly inhabited Big Valley had the option of moving to Saint Turibus Mission for some security from this situation in exchange for renouncing the old ceremonials. By 1880 there were 100 former members of the *qu·łá-na-pʰò* and *xa·bé-na-pʰò* village-communities there. In 1878 and 1879 members of the former village-communities of *ší·kom, xówalekʰ, da·nó-xà·* and *kʰa·yáw/šinal* developed their own solution. They communally purchased 90 acres of land north of Upper Lake at *xa·bé-ma·îòlel* with their combined proceeds from agricultural labor for three summers. Here they built a very sucessful transitional community, organized on essentially traditional lines. By the turn of the century it consisted of 27 houses built of wood on the same model as those of the White settlers, a large wooden dance house, completely above ground (fig. 8), as well as several barns. The inhabitants had horses and buggies or wagons, practiced some agriculture in conjunction with as much hunting and gathering as was still possible, and continued to harvest crops as a group for wages. The community seems to have flourished until 1912 when several houses and the dance house were destroyed by fire. This disaster coincided with the purchase of reservation land by the government adjacent to the already held 90 acres, as well as at the Robertson Rancheria, and some of those who had lost their houses chose to move to these reservations and the free house offered by the government, rather than rebuild. This seems to have been the beginning of the decline of *xa·bé-ma·îòlel*, although a few people lingered on until after the Second World War. The year 1912 also saw the abandonment of the mission and its replacement by the Big Valley Rancheria, a tract purchased for the remaining 92 Indians in 1911. From an estimated aboriginal population of approximately 3,000 (Cook 1956:112), the Southeastern Pomo and the Eastern Pomo were reduced to approximately 431 inhabitants living in five rancherias. Table 2 summarizes the current and historical status of Eastern Pomo and Southeastern Pomo rancherias.

Since about 1910s a growing involvment in American sociopolitical processes on the part of the Clear Lake Pomo has been evident. As early as 1907 Ethan Anderson, an Eastern Pomo, won a court case giving nonreservation Indians the right to vote. Again in the 1930s concerted Indian action with the participation of Pomos from the Clear Lake region successfully eliminated segregated schools and public facilities. A general awareness of the pan-Indian movement was most dramatically reflected in Clear Lake Pomo involvement in the occupation of Alcatraz Island in 1969–1971. Various government aid programs have not appreciably changed the socieconomic position of most Eastern and Southeastern Pomo, and some bureaucratic intervention in Pomo community life has foundered on problems of religious factionalism and the Pomo view of horizontal rather than hierarchical political power and authority (Lowy 1975).

In the 1970s Eastern Pomo and Southeastern Pomo live in frame houses on the rancherias, most of which

Table 2. Eastern and Southeastern Pomo Rancherias, Lake County

Name	Population	Acreage	Ecozone	Language	Termination
Big Valley (Mission)	124	102	Lake	Eastern	Yes
Lower Lake	6	140	Lake	Southeastern	No
Robinson	45	88	Lake	Northern, Eastern	Yes
Sulphur Bank (*ʔlém*)	45[a] 13	50	Lake	Southeastern	No
Upper Lake (2 parcels)	64[a] 70	483[a] 561	Lake	Eastern	Yes

Sources: U.S. Bureau of Indian Affairs 1969; California. Legislature. Senate Interim Committee on California Indian Affairs 1955. Compiled by Lowell John Bean and Dorothea Theodoratus.

[a] 1969 figures; others are 1955.

were built by the government long ago, and many of which have since been remodeled. They own and drive cars and shop in supermarkets. Traditional foods such as acorn mush and game meat have become delicacies rather than staples. White bread and beans probably constitute the two most frequent staples of diet.

The use of Eastern Pomo and Southeastern Pomo in daily conversation is rare despite survey information that the knowledge of these languages is still held by up to one-third of the population (California State Advisory Commission on Indian Affairs 1966:67).

Many Eastern Pomos and Southeastern Pomos no longer live on the rancherias, having moved to the nearby towns, and even as far away as Chico and San Francisco. All of the Eastern Pomo rancherias were "terminated" in the 1960s. That is, the rancheria lands were divided up among the residents and others having claims to membership in each rancheria, and individual Eastern Pomos were given title to individual parcels of land. This made it possible, for the first time, for an Eastern Pomo to sell or mortgage land. It also introduced, for the first time, the necessity of paying taxes, an expense that was generally not accompanied by access to any increase in income. Many Eastern Pomos no longer live on the rancherias because they lost their parcels of land through default for back taxes, mortgage foreclosure, or payment of debts contracted through installment buying. These parcels were frequently taken over by Whites, with the result that there are a number of White families living in the Eastern Pomo rancherias of Upper Lake, Big Valley, and Robertson.

Although family income remains low for many, Eastern Pomo and Southeastern Pomo in 1975 find it somewhat easier to acquire jobs other than seasonal fruit picking and agricultural or domestic labor, which were virtually the only sources of employment until the 1960s. Some Eastern Pomo have entered college. There seems to be a revival of interest in *ma·rú·/ʔábʀo* ceremonies, particularly among the young. The setting up of an Indian Health Service Office in Lakeport seems to have provided a new focus of cooperation and communication as well as better access to health facilities.

Sources

The archeology of the Clear Lake region remains largely unknown. M.R. Harrington (1943) provides the only archeological survey (an incomplete one) of a historic village, that of *ʔlém*. Two sites, one in Southeastern Pomo territory at Borax Lake and one in Eastern Pomo territory on Kelsey Creek in Big Valley (the Mostin site), have provided samples of obsidian dated in excess of 10,000 years old. The Mostin site also included burials from which fragments of bone yielding a date (UCLA-1795A) of 10,260±340 years were taken (Eric-

son and Berger 1974; Meighan and Haynes 1968, 1970). A third stratified site of similar age is at Lower Lake, also in Southeastern Pomo territory (Fredrickson 1961, 1973, 1974). It is clear that human beings have found the Clear Lake area an attractive one for at least 10,000 years, although there is no evidence as to what, if any, relationship the contemporary Eastern Pomo and Southeastern Pomo might have to the ancient occupants of the area.

Lowy (1973) has summarized much of the published literature on Eastern and Southeastern Pomo culture. Aside from the two firsthand accounts of Gibbs (1853) and Powers (1877), the bulk of the published ethnographic information comes from the memory of four members of these groups who were consulted from the turn of the century until the end of the 1930s: for Eastern Pomo, William Benson (Loeb 1926; Angulo 1927, 1935; Freeland 1923; Kroeber 1925) and Jim Pumpkin (Loeb 1926; Gifford 1923, 1926c); for Southeastern Pomo, Wokox or *tó·toʔ* (Gifford 1923, 1926c; Barrett 1952) and Tom Johnson (Barrett 1908, 1916, 1952).

The published data are strongly biased toward material culture, food acquisition, and ceremonial activity. In addition, over 100 versions of Eastern Pomo myths have been collected (Barrett 1933; Kroeber 1911; Angulo 1927, 1935; Angulo and Freeland 1928; Halpern 1939-1940; McLendon 1959-1976). Several versions of Southeastern Pomo myths have been collected (Halpern 1939-1940; Mauldin 1945-1975; Angulo and Freeland 1928). A wide range of ethnographic topics is covered in long lists of culture traits recorded in interview sessions of a day or two (Gifford and Kroeber 1939). Gifford's (1926c) careful census reconstructing the Eastern Pomo village of *ší·kom* provides raw data for inferring much about the social and political organization of the Eastern Pomo.

Except for Gifford (1923, 1926c) and Freeland (1923), the published ethnographic sources (Kroeber 1925; Barrett 1917, 1952; Loeb 1926) merge specifically Eastern Pomo practice with that of the Central Pomo and the Northern Pomo in an attempt to describe the behavior of all seven Pomoan language groups simultaneously. The Southeastern Pomo were consulted only by Barrett (1952). One can only be sure that claims made in these sources are true for the Eastern Pomo or Southeastern Pomo if: they are specifically attributed to either of these groups, they are attributed to a named informant who can be clearly identified as belonging to one of the two groups, or the behavior described is accompanied by a native term that is, or can be, identified as an Eastern Pomo or Southeastern Pomo form.

There is very little published information on the history, acculturation, or modern conditions of the Eastern Pomo or Southeastern Pomo (on the last, Lowy 1965-1967, 1975 provide some data). Some oral historical information has been collected (McLendon 1959-1976).

322

Much more could be done. The major archival and museum collections for all seven Pomoan language groups have been discussed in "Western and Northeastern Pomo," this volume. In these collections it is usually difficult to determine which of the seven groups a given object comes from. Probably any item identified as collected at Upper Lake is Eastern Pomo. There does not seem to have been much collected from the Southeastern Pomo. Lake County Museum, Lakeport, has a quite fine collection of Pomo baskets, most of which are probably of Eastern Pomo manufacture. The Lake County historian, Henry Mauldin, has a particularily fine collection of Eastern Pomo material culture objects as well as baskets and dance regalia.

Modern studies of the Eastern Pomo language have been conducted by Halpern (1939–1940) and McLendon (1959–1976). McLendon (1975) has published a grammar of Eastern Pomo, and circulated to the Eastern Pomo a privately printed word list of 50 pages (copies of which were deposited with the Lake County Library and the Lake County Indian Health Service Office, Lakeport). Modern studies of the Southeastern Pomo language have been conducted by Halpern (1939–1940) and Moshinsky (1965–1968, 1974).

Wintu

FRANK R. LAPENA

Language and Territory

The Wintu (ˈwĭn̩ to͞o) language is quite closely related to that of the Nomlaki to the south and more remotely to Patwin, connections recognized as Powell's (1891) Copehan family. This linguistic group has also been labeled Wintun, a name sometimes restricted to the Wintu and Nomlaki alone (Kroeber 1925:354–355). The term Wintuan has been adopted here to refer to the language group of Wintu, Nomlaki, and Patwin. These languages belong to the Penutian family.

Wintu territory covered parts of what are now Trinity, Shasta, Siskiyou, and Tehama counties (fig. 1). The northern boundaries of the region are the valleys of the upper Trinity River, extending up the Sacramento River to the high divide between the Trinity and Scott rivers, to Black Butte and Mount Shasta, passing a little north of Black Fox Mountain. From the northernmost point north of La Moine the boundary runs south to about six miles south of Cottonwood Creek. On the northeast the frontier with the Achumawi comprised a strip of land several miles wide, east of Squaw Creek, which was a no-man's-land on which both peoples hunted and gathered food (Du Bois 1935:4).

Within this region the nine major groups of the Wintu are identified by names* referring to their areas: *nomti-pom* 'in-the-west-ground' (upper Sacramento valley), *wenem-em* or *wenemem* 'middle water' (McCloud), *dawpom* 'front-ground' (Stillwater), *ʔelpom* 'in-ground' (Keswick), *ƛabal-pom* 'good (peaceful) ground' (French Gulch), *nomsuˑs* 'those being west' (Upper Trinity valley people), *dawnom* 'front-west' (Bald Hills), *norelmaq* 'south-uphill people' (Hayfork), and *waymaq* 'north people' (upper McCloud River valley) (Du Bois 1935:6–9).

History

The Wintu first met White men when the expeditions of Jedediah Strong Smith and Peter Skene Ogden entered the Sacramento Valley in 1826 and 1827 (Quint 1960:15). From 1830 to 1833, a malaria epidemic, introduced from Oregon by trappers, took the lives of about 75 percent of

* Italicized Wintu words have been respelled by Alice Schlichter, in the orthography described by Broadbent and Pitkin (1964:21), substituting č for c, č̣ for č, and ł for λ.

the Indians in the upper and central Sacramento Valley (Cook 1943b:315). This demographic disaster prevented the Wintu from effectively meeting the challenge of White occupation (table 1). In 1846 Mexico granted land to Pearson B. Reading in the upper Sacramento Valley; settlers soon moved into the area, and their cattle and sheep overran the land, thus destroying vital natural foods used by the Wintu (Southern 1942:10). In 1846 Capt. J.C. Frémont slaughtered 175 Wintu and Yana (Petersen 1969:15; Southern 1942:12). After gold was discovered, American miners preempted and polluted the fishing streams and used the Wintu as laborers (Southern 1942:42–47).

In 1850 Shasta County was created. Soon thereafter, two massacres occurred. The Whites gave a "friendship feast," poisoned the food, and killed 100 Trinity Wintu. When the Trinity people tried to warn the *wenemem* Wintu, they were too late; at least 45 of the *wenemem* were killed. In 1851 the Whites tried to control the land by forcing the Wintu to the west side of Clear Creek and dynamiting a natural rock bridge crossing (Southern 1942:28). In the town of Old Shasta, miners burned down the Wintu council meeting house and massacred about

Fig. 1. Tribal territory showing extent of modern reservoirs.

300 of the people. In the same year, the Wintu consented to the "Cottonwood Treaty," which allotted them 35 square miles of land and established Reading as their agent. This "Treaty of Peace and Friendship" was formally ratified in 1852, and Reading was given $25,000 for the benefit of the Indians (Petersen 1969:15).

Fort Reading was established in 1852, but it did not prevent wrongs being inflicted upon the Wintu. In 1855 miners invaded the area around Castle Rock, polluted the streams, and assaulted the Wintu, who tried in vain to protect their land. By 1856 the east fork of Clear Creek had at least 1,000 miners (Southern 1942:36, 65). Capt. I.G. Messec and General Kibbe led regular and civilian troops against the Bald Hills and Trinity Wintu in an official "Wintoon War" lasting six months in 1858-1859. As a result, 100 Indians were killed and 300 sent to the Mendocino Reservation (Bledsoe 1885:228-280). On October 8, 1865, the Millville Resolution demanded that all Indians vacate the east side of the Sacramento River. Three days later the Churntown Declaration proclaimed all fair and honorable means be used to prevent the execution of the Millville Resolution (Petersen 1969:16; Hunt 1960:47). Nonetheless, throughout the 1860s, the Wintu were hunted down, captured, and forcibly marched to the coastal reservations.

The completion of the railroad in 1875 brought in more people and trade. Despite this increase of Whites, the Wintu underwent a period of religious revival, and many of their older practices were modified or replaced. The last two decades of the nineteenth century witnessed the last large gatherings of the Trinity Wintu at their traditional grounds (Towendolly 1966:7) and the last communal fish drive at Baird (Du Bois 1935:15). A petition by the Wintu and Yana was given to President Benjamin Harrison, who declared there was land for the Indian but did nothing to establish boundaries or offer protection of land rights (Curtin 1898:488-489). Copper-processing plants in the 1890s and early 1900s poisoned and destroyed natural vegetation and large groves of trees, and farmers of nearby regions had to file law suits against them for damages (May 1945:18).

Citizenship in 1924 did not guarantee all rights. The *wenemem* auxiliary formed during the 1920s involved themselves in land issues, tribal rolls, and local grievances

Table 1. Population Estimates

Precontact	14,250
1852	3,500
1871-1880	1,000
1910	395
1915	701
1918	500
1930	380
1971	900

Sources: Cook 1943b:97; Du Bois 1935; Toyon-Wintu Center, Inc. 1971.

of the people. It was not until 1928 that the Wintu were accepted into schools.

In 1938 work on the Shasta Dam began, and in the 1970s three dams flood Wintu territory. The dams did more to disperse the last large concentrations of Wintu than any other factor; "in the upper Sacramento and McCloud, almost the entire habitable terrain once occupied by these two subgroups of the Wintu has been inundated" (May 1945:13; Smith and Weymouth 1952:2). Termination and the allotment and parceling of land during 1952-1953 further disrupted the situation and removed the Clear Creek Reservation from trust status.

In the 1970s Wintu live widely over the United States, and they engage in vocations and activities ranging from professional sports to business and industry. Although many own their own homes and businesses, Shasta County statistics show that the largest number of unemployed, those with substandard housing, and those with the greatest health needs are Indians. Perhaps with the reacquisition of the Toyon Conservation camp (1973 Wintu tribal land) and the incorporation by the Wintu of the Toyon-Wintu Center Inc. there will be Wintu people working for the local Indian community and concerned about solving some of their problems.

In spite of much loss of their culture, traditions, and language the Wintu still maintain an appreciation of their Indian history.

The most detailed and authoritative ethnographic information available concerning the Wintu is by Du Bois (1935). The following culture sketch is based largely upon her ethnographic observations and personal accounts of Wintu informants. Where documentation is not given it will be understood to come from Du Bois (1935).

Culture

Structures

There were from four to several dozen bark houses in a village. A settlement would have from 20 to 150 people. About 50 to 70 people might have an earth lodge.

The earth lodge was circular and semisubterranean, 15 to 20 feet in diameter, with one center pole. The smoke hole was also an entrance and exit by way of a notched center post or a ladder of stick rungs lashed to the post by grapevine. The lodge was used for a men's gathering place (fig. 2), for sweating, for the shaman's initiation, and in cold weather for a sleeping place for unattached men. The dwelling was a conical bark house with poles lashed together covered with bark or evergreen boughs. The mountain Wintu dwelling was slab covered. The steam house and menstrual hut were domed brush shelters (Du Bois 1935:122-123).

Fig. 2. Men gambling in subterranean lodge at Chino village near the former town of Monroeville, at the mouth of Stony Creek. Drawing by Henry B. Brown, 1852.

Political Organization

The family was the basic unit while the village was considered the social, political, and economic unit.

Chieftainship, or more correctly, leadership among the Wintu was, in theory, hereditary from father to eldest son but only if the son's "talents and inclinations fitted him for the post" (Du Bois 1935:29). He was expected to be well informed, a good singer, and a good dancer. He had to talk to everyone, like everyone, and be liked by everyone. He had the final decision of the giving of a dance or a meeting. He sent messengers to deliver invitations and assigned rightful shares in the preparation to his people and to the guests; "he was required to know the names and relative importance of the headmen invited from other districts."

"Peace was made by an assembly of important men who met to decide upon the nature and quantity of gifts to be exchanged as compensation for the losses to both sides." "The chief did not need to hunt or fish, since a generous share of all food was his due," which he used for the different gatherings. Wealth did not guarantee leadership.

A murder demanded blood revenge. If the relatives of the murdered man did not take the murderer's life and were willing to accept blood money, "the matter was referred to the headman. If the murderer were an objectionable person or habitual troublemaker and the relatives of the deceased were vindictive, the headman might intimate that a blood revenge could be taken." Usually a purchase of the murderer's life was made. "The man, or his relatives, were expected to compensate the bereaved family. A payment for murder entailed an implicit promise of exemplary behavior in the future" and usually resulted in poverty for the murderer. A value put on the life of a young man was two to five arm-lengths of clam disk beads or dentalia.

Accidental killings never precipitated blood feuds. The murderer and his family merely joined in giving the deceased an elaborate burial. Injuries, accidental or the results of quarrels, were atoned for by gifts to the injured (Du Bois 1935:35).

In the case of theft, if the object was not recovered and the thief was known, "he was likely to be waylaid and severely mauled." If the case was referred to a headman an attempt was made for amicable settlement. If the headman knew of the thief and the object was not returned or compensation made, "the headman might arbitrarily appropriate some of his property and give it to the injured person" (Du Bois 1935:35).

Formerly, sexual immorality was severely punished. Rape of an unmarried girl was punished with death. An immoral woman might also be killed by someone hired by her parents. "If a woman refused to go to a man who had purchased her from her family, the same extreme measure might be taken, since it was felt that a woman who made no effort to be dutiful toward her parents or to love her husband would probably develop into an immoral person." A woman who left a husband who provided adequately for her and returned to her family might be killed or cast off.

Behavior of a troublemaker or fighter was often controlled by public accusations or public ridicule. A headman would sanction the waylaying and trouncing of a habitual quarreler. If these methods did not improve his behavior, he was killed.

Life Cycle

• NAMES A child received his name when he was old enough to understand what its meaning signified. "No ceremony or gifts accompanied the bestowal, nor was secrecy attached to personal names. Any relative or old person was entitled to bestow a name that was his to give through the death of a relative. This lifted the taboo on the name of the dead. If a living person gave his name to a child, he abandoned its use himself. Upon reaching adulthood, peculiar characteristics might cause the adoption of a nickname, which the individual assumed of his own accord or accepted from others." Both men and women frequently had two or three names and could have as many as seven.

It was customary after the death of parents for a woman to inherit her mother's name, and for a man to take his father's. To gain a leadership or headman position, shaman's powers, or any other social grade did not automatically involve the acquisition of a new name (Du Bois 1935:51-52).

• BIRTH A pregnant woman observed a great number of taboos. To drink from a wide-mouth jar would give the child a wide mouth. By chewing *Xerophyllum*, the grass used in basket weaving, she could produce a strong boy. She had to avoid meeting wild animals or looking too closely at fish. The most dreaded and rigorous observance was by a pregnant woman who met a bear. She had to bathe her abdomen with water, which counteracted the bad effects of the bear upon the child. To look at a rainbow would cause her child to have a flat arm or leg. She wore no clothes that had knots in them; they would

prevent or cause a difficult childbirth. To wear a necklace would cause the child to be born with its umbilical cord wrapped around its throat. A specially constructed hut or menstrual lodge at some distance away from the family dwelling was used for the actual delivery. "An older woman, usually a relative, acted as midwife." The new mother was expected to stay in the lodge for a month abstaining from flesh, salt, and cold water. The husband would observe similar food taboos. The midwife also observed these restrictions until the umbilical cord dropped off. Certain people of both sexes had the power of assisting delivery by simply laying their hands on the mother. If a woman died in childbirth, the child was frequently killed and buried with her. If a boy was born, he was immediately removed from the bad influences of the female odor or blood. The mother stood while her abdomen was kneaded to remove the remaining blood. A localized steam bath was given her as she squatted over hot rocks in a hole in the birth-lodge floor. Heated rocks were then placed on the abdomen and strips of buckskin were wound around the abdomen to restrict the size and ensure drainage of blood. The mother drank the sap of wild grape vine if her milk did not flow freely (Du Bois 1935:45-46).

The umbilical cord was tied with a human hair and severed with an obsidian knife. If the bleeding was severe, wild sunflower root, chewed wild lilac, powder scraped from the surface of fingernails, or the root of the California poppy was applied to heal the navel more rapidly. After the cord dropped off, it might be placed in a miniature basket, which was then attached to the cradle. When the child was able to crawl about, the cord could be buried. If one wished a boy to be alert and bold, the cord was tied in the split limb of a live oak tree. If one desired him to be mild and pleasant, it was tied to a skunkbush. A girl was made mild and pleasant by placing her cord in a manzanita bush or by putting it in a tiny basket that was hung from a tree facing the sun. If a child died, the cord was buried with it.

For each child, at least two baskets were made. The first was crudely woven of skunkbush. The second was carefully made of hazel and was usually initiated in ceremony. When the cradle was outgrown, it was left hanging in a tree until it disintegrated. If a small child died, its cradle or a small conical carrying basket was inverted over its body. To carry a basket of any kind upside down was considered unlucky because of this.

At the end of the mother's month of seclusion, a ceremony was observed to celebrate her return to the dwelling and the child's first entrance into it. A larger and more carefully made cradle was woven by a friend of the mother. The father gave this basket to a fast runner, who raced a short distance or circled the dwelling carrying the cradle. The child could then be brought into the house. The mother bathed before entering. The father was required to purify himself at the end of his wife's seclusion by taking a sweat bath or by washing in running water.

For one month after her return to the dwelling, the woman was supposed to refrain from intercourse. The ceremony of return was not observed by all families and was performed only in honor of the firstborn. If the first child was a girl, a woman ran with the basket (Du Bois 1935:45-47).

A boy was frequently lectured by his elders and told to "be a man" or *wi·ta*. This term of respect represented the possession of all desirable traits—skill in hunting, fishing, gambling, oratory; respect for the aged; and a democratic attitude. Adults set an example of frequent river baths usually taken before the morning meal. The steam bath was also used for cleanliness. Children frequently accompanied their elders and acquired skills by assisting them in adult occupations.

Girls were taught to sit, when in the presence of men, with their legs stretched straight out in front or else drawn up to one side. All unmarried girls wore their hair in long bangs down to their eyebrows so that men wouldn't see their foreheads. Generally they had their ears pierced and their chins tattooed in their early or middle adolescence. Ear piercing was done with a porcupine quill either by a menstruant or by a woman who for some other reason was not eating deer meat at the time (Du Bois 1935:48).

•PUBERTY   At the time of puberty, a girl notified her mother or grandmother, who then built a small brush shelter some 20 or 30 yards from the family dwelling. The girl stayed in seclusion for one to several months. The girl was not permitted to cook for herself; her diet was limited to acorn soup, prepared by the mother or grandmother. She was not supposed to leave her hut except at night. If she had to go out in the day, she covered her head with a basket or a hide. Sleep during the first five days of the first menses was forbidden, since dreams at this time were considered prejudicial to health and sanity. Above the lodge, yellow-pine bark might be burned. Its crackling was supposed to frighten away evil spirits. The girl was given a deerhoof rattle made by male relatives as a protection from evil spirits. The girl was not to touch herself and so a head scratcher was used; this could be any twig at hand. Combing her hair was forbidden. Her cheeks were streaked with vertical lines of charcoal or red and blue pigment. During the seclusion, the elderly people gave the girl advice and instruction on her future behavior. During the period of isolation young people might sing and dance outside the adolescent's lodge at night; many of the songs were obscene.

A puberty dance was generally given in the fall when food was plentiful in order to honor several girls. Neighboring villages were invited and brought food. Each arriving group danced into the village singing. All assembled in the morning and danced until about noon. The adolescents stood in the circle but did not participate. Poorer girls wore new maple-bark skirts; richer ones were

dressed in buckskin aprons and were laden with beads or seeds (fig. 3). They carried deerhoof rattles and spirally striped ceremonial staffs. If the dance was given for a single individual, it was customary for her to have as an attendant a girl who was not yet mature. The dancing and feasting continued for at least five days and longer if food was plentiful. After the first prolonged period of seclusion, the girl bathed, discarded old garments, and was at liberty to resume ordinary habits and diet. Some women abstained from meat for much longer periods (Lee 1940; Du Bois 1935:52-54).

During her subsequent menses, a woman withdrew for the period of her flow to the family menstrual lodge. Sexual intercourse was forbidden as it was considered injurious to the man. While the woman was isolated, she had her own utensils and prepared her own food. Meat, particularly deer, fish, and grease, were forbidden. Before returning to her dwelling, she bathed. A menstruant could not eat with men, especially hunters, gamblers, and shamans, because it would destroy their "power." She had to avoid sacred places for fear of being injured or carried off by the local spirit. A man could hunt and fish during his wife's illness but should not (Du Bois 1935:53-54).

When a boy shot his first deer or caught his first salmon, a feast was given by the parents. The boy was forbidden to eat any of the meat. He was required to bathe upon his return from the hunt. No other formal ceremony or observance marked a boy's maturity.

Fig. 3. Woman's front apron of buckskin and pine nuts. Length 65 cm, collected 1875.

•MARRIAGE Marriage was shown by a man and woman living together. If a young couple were known to have intercourse but were living separately, the headman of the village might publicly shame them into taking up a joint residence. A girl could go to a man's house and assist his mother in grinding acorns and gathering seeds. Her family might even urge her to undertake this course. The girl's behavior had the same implication as the man's supplying her family with game.

Monogamy was customary but men of importance were permitted two or more wives. The second wife was usually a sister or other relative of the first. The first was called 'older sister' by the subsequent spouses, and she referred to them as 'younger sister'. A man with two wives slept between them. A person of importance could acquire additional wives by purchase rather than by courtship. Residence after marriage might be either patrilocal or matrilocal, as long as an independent household was set up.

A man was not permitted to touch or get within less than three feet of his mother-in-law. A mother-in-law and a son-in-law were forbidden to joke in each other's presence. If they met on a trail they stepped out of each other's way. However, they could make ordinary requests of each other and eat together as long as they occupied opposite sides of the fire.

If a man was left widowed, his wife's family felt obligated to supply him a spouse—a sister, a cousin, or a niece. The same obligation to provide for her welfare was felt by the man's family toward a widow.

Marriage between cross-cousins and between parallel cousins was forbidden. Marriage between second cousins was not sanctioned, the belief being that offspring of related persons would be cross-eyed. The close relationships within a local group fostered marriages outside the village. Gatherings included neighboring villages and close districts. The bond of marriage gave a distinct sense of legitimacy to offspring. A child that was deserted by its father before or shortly after birth was called 'lost-flint child'. An offspring born to a woman who had been promiscuous was called 'everyone's child' or 'brush child'.

Grounds for divorce were incompatibility or adultery. As long as two people lived together they were expected to be faithful. The man or the woman might initiate a divorce. The procedure was simply to withdraw from joint residence or to establish another residence. Barrenness was not cause for separation, and in that case the wife's family was not responsible to the man for another spouse (Du Bois 1935:54–56).

•DEATH The death of an individual was mourned by the relatives as soon as they assembled. The corpse was buried the same day unless the relatives had to come from a long way. Relatives of the same sex as the deceased dressed the body in finery and placed it on a deerskin or bearskin hide in a crouching position with the elbows inside the bent knees and the hands on the cheeks. The hide was then holded and bound in a tight bundle with deer sinew or rope. The body was removed through a special opening made in the rear of the dwelling and carried to the grave.

Graveyards were about 100 yards from the dwellings. Graves, dug by the old women, were about four feet deep. Should bones from a previous burial be uncovered they were put aside, rewrapped, and reburied with the corpse.

Personal articles were placed in the grave along with the deceased's dog. There was always a basket of acorn-meal water for the soul to drink.

After the burial those who had come in contact with the corpse, mourners, relatives, and gravediggers had to purify themselves by bathing, sweat bath, or exposure to the smoke of a scrub-oak, live-oak, or fir fire.

A mourner would grieve for a year. The widow cut her hair, rubbed pitch into it, and smeared her face with a mixture of charcoal and pitch powdered over with burned and pulverized clamshells to keep it from being too sticky. The name of the deceased was not mentioned (Du Bois 1935:64–67).

War

Warfare was usually a neighborhood feud between individuals. The bonds of kinship were as a rule strong enough to prevent major bloodshed. There were three main groups hostile to the Wintu; the upper Sacramento and McCloud peoples distrusted and disliked the remote Shasta bands, the northwestern Californians on the Klamath, and the Modoc. The Shasta acted as buffers against the Modoc slave raids and considered the Wintu the bravest of their enemies because they attacked by daylight (Curtis 1907–1930, 14:76). Frequently the enemy took prisoners, which was against Wintu tradition. The Stillwater and McCloud Wintu feared and disliked the Yana to the south and east. The Stillwater Wintu were particularly unprotected because of the open plateau lands they shared with the Yana. The Bald Hills Wintus' traditional enemies were the Nomsus, who probably represented Athapaskan tribes on the western slope of the coastal range. They were on friendly terms with the Nomlaki to the south of them, although occasional quarrels did occur (Du Bois 1935:36–37).

Provocations for feuds or wars were of different degrees of seriousness. Murder and the theft of women were the most frequent causes of war. The theft of an acorn cache once caused war between the McCloud Wintu and Achumawi. Small numbers of men went to war and few individuals were killed. The weapons used were bows and arrows, clubs, thrusting spears, daggers, and slings (figs. 4–6). Elkskin armor and wooden rod armor were used (Du Bois 1935:37; Curtis 1907–1930, 14:80). Hand-to-hand fighting was avoided as much as possible. If there was hope of settlement, messengers were sent and armed parties met at a given place to arrange the terms. If a

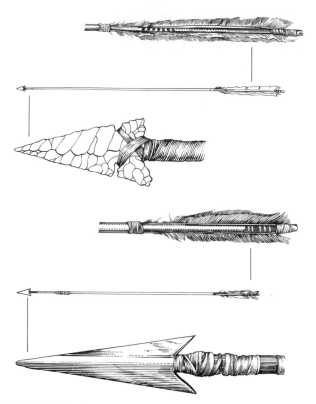

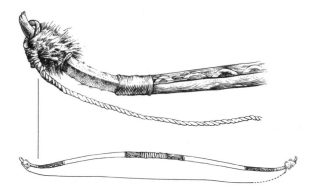

Fig. 5. Double curved sinew-backed bow with decorations in green, red, and black pigment; ends wrapped in fur; grip area wound with buckskin strips; sinew bowstring. Length 110 cm, collected in 1875.

Fig. 4. Arrows. top, Self arrow with red stone point, considered to be supernaturally poisonous, hafted with sinew; painted bands at nock end; length 85.5 cm; collected in 1885. bottom, Compound arrow with metal point hafted with sinew; painted bands at both ends; same scale; collected in 1885.

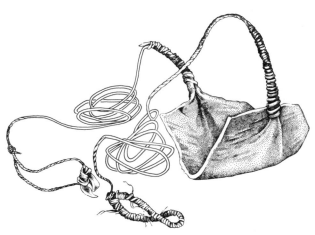

Fig. 6. Sling made of buckskin and sinew cord. Width 8 cm, collected in 1875.

combat ensued it was of a formal nature. Two lines faced each other and exchanged arrow shots. Dodging was an important technique. The victorious group took whatever valuables were available. The headman usually secured the most desirable booty. The leader of the war party did not necessarily participate in the combat but watched for those who were wounded. Scalping was practiced only occasionally. A single scalp was procured for use in a war dance. If the body of a warrior could not be brought home, it was hastily burned on the spot. If captured by slave raiders a child was told to drop a trail of leaves. The custom of shooting a prisoner to death after he had been placed on a pole seems to have been a Yana custom practiced occasionally by the Stillwater and McCloud peoples as a retaliatory measure (Du Bois 1935:39; Demetracopoulou 1940).

Trade

Generally strings of clamshell disk money, or "water-bone," and dentalia were counted. The system of measuring strings by the length of outstretched arms was used only for larger payments, such as those made to remove blood guilt.

Magnesite cylinders were also known among the Wintu and were called *mempaq xosi* 'waterbone charm'. As late as the 1930s clamshell money was so highly valued it was not offered for sale (Du Bois 1935:26).

If an object was highly admired and desired, an individual might ask outright for it. It was then presented as a gift, but with the understanding that its equivalent would be returned at once or in the near future. Barter among men was carried on occasionally in terms of clam disk money and dentalia, the only beads that men would wear. Women owned both dentalia and clam disks, but baskets were their chief medium of exchange (Du Bois 1935:24).

Another form of exchange was with craftsmen who had produced more necessities than could be utilized. A rope maker would lend a hunter a *lapči* of standard length (about 15 feet) used to make a snare. If the hunter was successful, he returned the rope with a portion of the meat or the hide. A deer hide was often the equivalent of the direct purchase of a *lapči* (Du Bois 1935:24). Very little trading was done in body paints, yew wood for bows, or obsidian. Most of these materials were acquired by the individual desiring them. If obsidian was actually traded, it was usually for objects of considerable value such as bows, arrows, and quivers. Size of the piece determined value. Intervillage and intertribelet trade was more frequent than intertribal trade.

The Shasta Indians to the north were the source of dentalia and some obsidian, in return for deer hides and woodpecker scalps. Obsidian was usually secured by the Wintu themselves from Glass Mountain, 60 miles northeast in Modoc territory. This was a semireligious and peaceful undertaking. Achumawi traded salt for McCloud Wintu salmon flour. The Stillwater Wintu and the Yana in the vicinity of Cow Creek were a source of salt for the Indians to the north and west. The clam disk money owned by the Wintu was from the south, and the farther north it was imported the more valuable it became. The Bald Hills Wintu used clam disk money as well as seeds and acorns as trade items for McCloud salmon. Dentalia traded from the north was prized throughout the tribe as an ornament. It was not so important as clamshell disks (Davis 1959; Hunt 1966).

The begging dance, *suneh*, was a means of transferring property from one person to another. In Bald Hills the *suneh* was sung and danced at a girl's puberty ceremony by a visiting group for the hosts, and the hosts then reciprocated. It could be an individual affair (Du Bois 1935:25). The Wintu considered as valuables: bows and arrows; elkskin armor; clam disk money; fisher, martin, bear, elk, buck, and otter skins; dentalia; quivers; woodcock heads; woodpecker scalps (mountain woodpecker more valuable); obsidian knives, spears with obsidian tips.

Religion

As a supreme being the Wintu spoke of ʔoleˑlbe(ˑ)s 'one who is above', nomłestuwaˑ, panti-winthuˑh 'above person', and bohem wiˑta 'the great man'.

When a man went to the river to wash in the morning, he prayed and talked to the sun. One also prayed when he smoked in the morning or evening and blew his smoke over the world. Prayer was also done before eating as one faced the sky.

The moving of the moon's reflection in the water was said to be caused by the grizzly bear that runs around in the moon. An eclipse was caused by the bear's eating the sun. Noise was made to frighten the bear away. Shooting stars or a meteorite shower was believed to be the spirits of shamans who had died and were traveling to the afterlife. Thunder was caused by a woman who violated a sacred sucker place. Thunder and lightning were twins of Grizzly Bear Woman. Northern lights were a sign of an epidemic or illness. Earthquakes were a sign of heavy snows to come in winter (Du Bois 1935:75).

A rich body of myths has been collected and published by Curtin (1898), Du Bois and Demetracopoulou (1931), Lee (1941), and Demetracopoulou and Du Bois (1932).

The first people created were part animal and part human; they lived in "old times." Several worlds came before this one; this world has been destroyed three times. An adder caused the first destruction by fire. The second destruction was by a cold north wind that blew everything away and waters flooded. The third destruction was by a flood that took the long-tail people who did nothing all day. But *haqamin iaquna* 'pounds himself with his elbow' got away. Some people were saved by going to a cave in the high mountains (Towendolly 1966:25–33). The end of the world will come when there are no more Indians, because the White people do not care for the land, or deer, or bear. They do not treat the plants right or use water or other things of nature as they should (Du Bois 1935:76).

A living person has a soul and the deceased has a spirit, which is "like a whirlwind and one can feel a chill" (Du Bois 1935:77). The soul travels northward, ascends to the Milky Way, and then journeys along this spirit trail. There is also another spirit which is one's life; it helps one think, feel, sleep, and get up; it is one's guide and dies when one dies. It is located behind the ear (Du Bois 1935:78-79). A *yaˑpaytuˑ* is a shamanistic spirit that is never seen; it lives in the hills (the word is also now the term for 'White man'). A ghost is *lolčit*.

A sacred place, *saˑwel*, could be a pot hole or a peculiarly shaped rock, often in animal form; caves, seepage holes, whirlpools in the river, and knolls were all representative of dwelling spirit sacred places. A person knew of a spirit place by the buzzing sound made there. These places were usually used by men. A sacred place used by women was the coyote *saˑwel* (Du Bois 1935:79-80).

If a person wished to gain a spirit he left his house without speaking to anyone. The spot was usually reached in the evening, and a small fire was made. If the *saˑwel* was a pool, the man bathed, lay down by the fire, and slept. After a time he awoke, prayed for whatever boon he wished, and dived into the water, attempting to reach bottom. A lucky person would find a sacred pool shallow and might find a charmstone there while an unlucky person would have difficult in reaching the bottom. After swimming and praying, he lay down again to sleep. All dreams were considered significant. At dawn the man again prayed and swam in the same spot. Prayers to the sun could not be omitted during and directly after visits to a *saˑwel*. Sometimes a man traveled from one place to another for two or three days in quest of dreams of supernatural rapport. If he dreamed of the local spirit and it seemed well disposed toward him, he might become a shaman. During the seeking of power, a strict fast was observed and the petitioner had to be naked or to wear only an apron. Upon returning to his village, he observed strict silence until he had partaken of food.

Thereafter, he was free from food taboos, although a strict person or an aspiring shaman would abstain from deer meat and salt. One could ask for shamanistic (healing, medicine, or local spirit) powers, luck in gambling or hunting, or make other requests of a sacred place.

Strangely shaped stones were kept as charms, xosi. Charms could be deer, rattlesnake, rattlesnake navel, coyote, and sucker. Flat stones two or three inches long were worn to ward off illness (Du Bois 1935:82). Charmstones could not be brought into the dwelling but had to be wrapped in grass or hide and buried or hidden at a distance from the dwellings. When the owner desired luck he went secretly to their hiding place, blew smoke on them, spat acorn meal over them, and prayed to them for success. To pat a sacred-rock place and ask for luck was called xosuna· xosi 'to make a charm for oneself'. Other charms were used but not called xosi. A shed snakeskin was treated like a charmstone. Seeds of the tamarack were strung and used for fishing luck. A root like celery, čuweči, kept sucker spirits away and was used by shamans to protect a patient from the sucker spirit (Du Bois 1935:84).

Werebeasts were animals capable of turning into humans. Werebeasts were called pʰuyqin su·s, mountain inhabitants or mountain lions, mountain boys, or bush boys. Their areas were especially avoided. There was a supernatural bird that had special powers and the feathers and quills were especially desired by shamans (Du Bois 1935:88).

• SHAMANISM The yearly initiation ceremony was abandoned in the late 1800s. This initiation took place in spring or late autumn. The ceremony began in the evening with shamans and candidates of both sexes dancing naked around a manzanita-wood fire, singing to call the spirits. A whistling sound above the smoke hole of the earth lodge announced the arrival of a spirit. This spirit entered a body usually through the ears. Then the candidate's behavior became frenzied; besides convulsions, saliva and blood might flow from the mouth and nostrils. Soon after he became unconscious, the older shaman carried him to one side of the lodge and watched over him and sang for him. After regaining consciousness, five days were spent under supervision and instruction by his seniors. During instruction, one observed a complete fast. On the last day, the new and old shamans went to the river and purified themselves. Then their bodies were painted with red, white, and black streaks to represent intrusive disease objects. All the people gathered outside the earth lodge but only the shamans participated in the dance. They danced with feather wands, skins, and other valuables for one day. Afterward, the initiates were prepared for shamanistic practices, but their success depended on their future cures and prophecies (Du Bois 1935:88-90).

Payment to the shaman was by agreement and was collected after a cure. There are three sicknesses: disease-object instrusion, soul loss, and spirit possessions. Curing was by sucking, massage, and soul capture. In the soul dance, another treatment, exorcism, is combined with extraction of disease objects (Du Bois 1935:104).

Modern shamans were called "natural doctors." Some from the early 1900s were Albert Thomas, Fanny Brown, Tilly Griffen, Charles Klutchie, Nels Charles, Jo Charles, and Kate Luckie. There were several people who rejected shamanism or had it inhibited by relatives or other shamans.

Witchcraft was treated by doctoring. Shamanistic spirits were human souls, local spirits of sacred places, animal spirits including werebeasts, and nature spirits. Lizard and sucker were the most common nature spirits (Du Bois 1935:113-114).

• GHOST DANCE The Ghost Dance movement of 1870 represents a major change in the religion and dances of the Wintu. The Ghost Dance itself was not adopted by the Wintu, but in 1871 the Earth Lodge cult, which talked of the return of the dead, the end of the world, and the protection of the faithful by use of the subterranean house, was brought by Paitla from the Nomlaki (Du Bois 1939). He gave his first dance at Baird and told the people: "The dead are returning from the east. Those not dancing will turn into rocks or animals, the world is going to change, there will be hail and then the world will catch fire; when the world ends all the living will be wiped out and the old dead will return to feast on Indian foods and talk of the world as it was before" (Du Bois 1939:54). The second dance was at puy-patk̓odi and the third at kopos-to·n.

Prior to coming Paitla stressed the need to build dance houses, and the three where the dances were given were built in response to this message. Later one was built at Old Shasta. In the spring of 1872 a group of Wintu went east to Fall River because the dead were supposed to be returning. They stayed two nights; when nothing happened, they returned home and the cult died out (Du Bois 1939:55). xonos of kopos-to·n sent the dance to the Shasta in 1872.

In 1874 Bogus Tom reached the Siletz reservation with the Earth Lodge cult from the Wintu. It was called the Warm House cult in western Oregon.

In 1872 the Bole-Maru came from the Nomlaki; it stressed an afterlife and a supreme being. Out of this developed local "dreamers" and "preachers." In 1875 the Bole-Maru was given to the Shasta. In 1874-1885, a Bole-Maru was performed at Baird and Old Shasta. In 1875-1885, Ono and Gas Point had the Bole given by Scototli, a Nomlaki who stayed in the vicinity for two or three months (Du Bois 1939:55-56).

From 1875 to 1895 a Ydalpom (waydal-pom) woman named Lus was the prime person in the development of dream dances. Dreaming of "songs" continued until 1915-1920. But the formal dream dancing probably lasted no longer than 1895 or 1900 at the latest. Dreamed songs were from deceased relatives and friends. During the dances women carried handkerchiefs and flowers in their hands. Sometimes handkerchiefs were worn around the head with a feather in it. Red stripes were put on the face. Men wore feathered skirts and painted two black stripes from shoulder to shoulder. Footdrums and skin-drums beaten with a stick provided the music. There were two chief singers; split-stick rattles and whistles constituted the rest of the musical accompaniment. Most musical instruments were traditional, including a flute of elderberry used for pleasure or serenading. The drum was new with the Wintu.

Dance innovations included: indoor dances other than the shaman's dance; square semisubterranean dance houses instead of the subterranean earth-lodge ones; footdrums; sacred striped poles and admission; dance officials, such as *čima-to·* 'fire and water keeper'; new songs and dances, such as men dancing in a circle with women in a crescent on each end.

Social Life

Dances and gatherings are both called *čonos* 'dance'. Most dances were social rather than religious. Songs were either secular or religious (Demetracopoulou 1935).

If a village found itself with a large supply of food it was customary to summon neighboring groups to gather for feasting, dancing, and games. After the pine nut and clover harvests, dances were given (Powers 1877:6). Salmon runs, rabbit and quail snaring, deer and bear hunts, and burning for grasshoppers called for large groups and were festive occasions.

The actual dances that were performed at gatherings were replaced almost entirely by the dream dances. There are three types of dances: the purely rhythmic ones like the *way-pani·ki* (round dance), *se-soyokmes,* and *sedem-čonos* 'coyote dance'; the pantomime ones, the old-time round dance *xiwi·li*, the two bear dances and to a lesser degree *hupus čonos*; and finally the unorganized horse-play performances like the *suneh,* which are the farthest removed from any ceremonial connection. These older Wintu dances are in distinct contrast to the modern cult and shaman dances (Du Bois 1935:41-42).

Gambling games were always one of the biggest events at a gathering. Competitions in prowess and skill, dancing, singing, and feasting were also part of the festivities. Men attended gatherings with all their valuables, and fortunes were won and lost in the games. Honor required an individual to continue playing as long as someone would bet against him. Three forms of hand games were played (fig. 2). *bohem ču·s* 'big wood' required about 48 hours to play. There was a single ace of bone or wood. Only a few men were on the team but those betting on them stood behind their team and assisted them in singing. Only men were allowed to play the grass game. They frequently sought supernatural power before the gathering and fasted during the game. It was played in

the winter in the earth lodges and was the most important of the gambling contests. In *xeni,* two sticks or bones were used. One had to guess which hand had the ace. Sometimes two dealers would play, each with a set of bones. Fasting was not required and only men played. Dachedope was a woman's stick game using one ace and 20 to 40 rods (Du Bois 1935:43).

Contests of physical skill and prowess included double-ball shinny, played by women, and football, which both sexes played separately. Hoop and pole was played on a hill slope. Ring and pin was played with salmon vertebrae or deerbone rings and a wooden or bone pin; one was permitted to rap the knuckles of one's opponent as many times as one had speared the vertebrae. "Throwing rocks at a goal" to see who could come the nearest was closely paralleled by a game in which saplings, about four feet long, were slid at a stake or stone. Bow shooting contests were popular. Foot races, wrestling matches, and jumping contests were common. Bets might be placed on all of these. Many string games and figures were made. Buzz was played with an oval of bark threaded with buckskin thongs. The thongs were twisted and then held in either hand and pulled back and forth to produce a humming noise.

Technology

Craft specialization among the Wintu did not run in families, as reported for the Patwin. A man became a craftsman because his inclinations and his opportunity to learn from another led him to make bows and arrows, ropes, nets, and the few other simple objects required in daily life. Out of a village of 30-50 people, approximately four specialized in fishing, which meant that they made their own spear poles, nets, and traps. Some were hunters, others were messengers; the most worthless individuals were "good only to get wood" (Du Bois 1935:21-22).

The gathering of materials and time spent to make a set of 20 arrows took approximately six months. It was believed that the bite of a small brown lizard gave great proficiency in the craft. Some craftsmen permitted themselves to be bitten repeatedly to obtain the desired skill. Lizards, salamanders, and snakes ordinarily were not touched.

It would require three or four days to gather materials necessary for a coil of rope, *lapči*. A week was required to roll the fibers. Iris was preferred as cordage material. Women could gather and shred the material, but only men did the actual manufacturing.

In tanning, a hide was soaked in water, to which deer brains might be added. The skin was then pegged down and fleshed with pumice. The thoroughness and patience expended on fleshing was thought to determine the value of the hide. The skin was next worked between the hands. Fox and other valuable pelts were not soaked but simply fleshed and worked between the hands. Occasionally gray squirrel pelts were tanned. In Bald Hills a tree moss smudge was used to color the hides; a black oak, live oak, or white oak smudge was believed to produce a brown color of successively lighter shades. Only old women might assist in tanning (Du Bois 1935:23).

Arrowhead manufacture, as practiced in the nineteenth century, was according to prescribed techniques. The craftsman split the flakes from the large pieces of obsidian by holding against an edge a piece of split deerhorn that was ground off squarely at each end. The line of the diameter of the split horn is held to cover as much of the edge of the obsidian as will make the thickness of the flake proposed to split off. Holding one end of the horn firmly against the obsidian, with the other hand holding a round, water-worn boulder, a sharp blow is given to the other end of the split horn. If successful, and the obsidian is uniform in texture, a conchoidal, leaf-shaped flake will be split off (Squier 1953:19–21). The point is finished by pressure flaking. The arrow shaft was of reed or pithy wood with a tip of hardwood inserted into the main shaft and glued with pitch of salmon-skin glue; the point was attached to this. Three bands of hawk or buzzard feathers were split and wrapped on; sometimes glue was added. Arrowpoints were chiefly obsidian. Red and white were considered supernaturally poisonous, especially red (fig. 4). Gray was good for bear; no natural poison was used. Stemmed points were used in war. Bone and blunt-tip wooden points were also used. An arrow straightener was a flat perforated rock. An arrow polisher was two flat stones with grooves, which could be held in one hand. Equisetum was used to finish it. The bow was of yew seasoned in the shade. Its back was reinforced with shredded deer sinew pasted on with salmon-skin glue (fig. 5). It was decorated with triangles in four decorative bands. The string was twisted deer backbone sinew. The bow was held horizontally or diagonally when shot. Short bows about one and one-half feet were used when entering bear dens. Other weapons were a club of heavy wood such as oak or manzanita, a dagger about 10 inches long made from the foreleg of a bear, a deer-dagger used only in fighting and worn in a man's topknot, and a quiver of whole hides used with the fur inside and hung over the shoulder that held about 40 arrows. There was no shield. A sling was used and a spear two and one-half or three and one-half feet long was used as a thrusting implement in war or in bear hunts (Du Bois 1935:124–125).

Adults used a raft to cross streams while a large basket was used to float small children or supplies across. A pole was used for guidance. A bridge, *ƙawi,* was two logs thrown across the stream. On the upper McCloud and upper Sacramento rivers there were complicated bridges lashed together by grapevine.

Fire was carried in a smoldering white oak limb or in a small bark bucket with an earth hearth. A fire drill hearth was of cedar and the drill itself was of buckeye.

The drill was turned by hand. The set was wrapped in fawnskin when not in use.

Mortars were used to grind pigments, pulverize seeds, soften meat for the elders, and grind acorns. The hopper mortar was used late in time. Some bedrock mortars were considered charmstones or sacred places. Metates were used by the Wintu. Pestles range in size from one for grinding pigment, two inches long, to one for ceremonial use, three feet long.

An awl was of bone or horn in varying sizes and used in sewing, flaking, and basketry. A wedge of horn or wood was used in splitting wood. Tree felling was done by burning with pitch and hacking away the charred area. A digging stick was of hardwood steamed straight and sharpened at both ends. It was three or four feet long. Larger sticks were used for digging graves and house pits. A hooked stick was used to pull dead branches for firewood or acorn branches within reach. A mush paddle about 30 inches long was used to take out heated cooking stones from acorn soup; it was of oak. Hairbrushes were made from the coarse fibers of the soaproot. A meal brush was made from the finer fibers; paintbrushes used for fine designs such as those on bows were feather tips. In rope making a thumb guard of mussel shell was used, while a mesh measure and a mesh shuttle were used in making nets. A carrying bag had a drawstring and was used by men only. A deep-water dip net was roughly triangular in shape, about six to seven feet in length, and held by the base of the triangle and a crosspiece between the two sides. A shallow-water dip net and a double fish net were also used. A fish trap shaped like a Wintu cradle trapped the fish in the dry end.

A harpoon was a long spear with a shaft of fir either 15–20 or 10–12 feet long with two prongs of hardwood; it was painted black with pitch darkened by bark soot. Toggles of pithy wood were about three and one-half inches long, in which a deer-bone point is thrust so as to protrude slightly. The whole is wrapped with twine and covered with pitch. The toggles cord is tied to the spear shaft.

Wooden pipes, usually of ash, were most common (fig. 7). The hole was bored by sealing a grub into the pithy

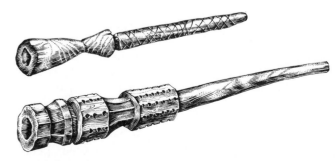

Dept. of Anthr., Smithsonian: top, 76198; bottom, 19301.
Fig. 7. Wooden pipes. top, With incised decoration, length 21 cm; bottom, with carved decoration, same scale. Both collected in 1875.

334

LAPENA

center and letting it eat its way through. The bowl and stem could be separate pieces. Stone pipes were of soft stone. The wooden stem was decorated with mink fur, strung shells, or another ornament and might be dyed with alder bark. Tobacco was collected, dried, pulverized, and stored in small baskets. As a rule, it was never chewed. A tobacco pouch (fig. 8) of deerskin was preferred when traveling (Du Bois 1935:125–130).

Wintu basketry is either openwork (fig. 9) or closework twining. Trade and gift pieces of coiling are found in the region, but the boundary for the manufacture of coiling lies between the Bald Hills Wintu and the Nomlaki. Hazel, skunkbush, and poison oak were used for warp elements. The end of the new rod is chewed and laid overlapping the old one. *Xerophyllum* grass, used as an overlay element on pine root, has a rough and a smooth side. The smooth side is used on the surface of the basket. The same is true of maidenhair. The grass or fern is inserted under the pine root, the willow warp is pulled out of the alignment, the root is laid over the warp, and the overlay element is placed over the root base. All are twisted to keep the smooth side out. When two colors like grass and maidenhair are used, the strand of the first color is not carried along under the second but is broken off after it has served to anchor the second strand. Porcupine quill work was done always in conjunction with *Xerophyllum* and maidenhair. It was rare and highly prized (Du Bois 1935:131–134).

Fig. 9. Open twined storage basket filled with grass-covered manzanita berries; detail shows construction. Height 22 cm, collected in 1873.

When a basket was finished, all the ragged weft elements were clipped. The basket was then soaked, shaped, and filled with sand until it had dried in a symmetrical form. Old baskets were occasionally re-shaped in this manner.

Grapevine or redbud splints were used to mend baskets. Willow or hazel branches were used as rims or reinforcing ribs.

Some basic basket types were: burden basket; a shallow round or shovel-shaped tray used as a sifter for manzanita or seeds, as a plate, or as a seedbeater; a shallow round plate used as a plate, dipper, or cover for containers; acorn-meal sifter; a hopper for grinding acorns that rests on a flat rock; and a cup or bowl serving basket.

Important traditional basketry designs are the quail crest, sometimes called lizard; the elbow-joint design; deer excreta; and an idealized flying geese pattern that in Wintu is variously called arrowpoint, dry leaf, or flying geese. A series of triangles set point to base is usually designated as sucker trails (Du Bois 1935:136–137).

Clothing and Adornment

Blankets were made of skins of deer, fox, or rabbit. Rabbitskin blankets were woven from one-inch strips in the Bald Hills area. Grass, boughs, or deer hides were often used as mattresses. Traditional belts worn by men were made of human hair or porcupine quill. Capes were worn by both sexes; whole deer hides were the usual material, but sewed rabbit hides were used in the Stillwater area. Men were usually naked but might wear a hide breechcloth. Women, unclothed until adolescence, wore a shredded maple-bark apron or complete skirt that hung

Fig. 8. Beaded pouch to hold tobacco or shot. Length 24 cm, collected in 1875.

just below the knees. A fringed doe or fawnskin front and back apron was used for special occasions (Du Bois 1935:120).

Other ornaments included: netted-down caps, basket hats worn by women; feather skirts and headresses (fig. 10), capes, wands, and plumes; headbands of yellowhammer feather and of strips of fox, mink, otter, or white belly fur of wolf, with perhaps a feather-wrapped quill in the band; leggings; earrings, nose pieces of shell and bone, and necklaces of olivella, abalone shell, clam disks, dentalia and pine nuts.

Piercing of the nasal septum was rare. Both sexes might undergo the operation, but it was more common for men. As in ear piercing, a twig was kept in the wound until it healed. A dentalium shell might be inserted in the septum (Du Bois 1935:48).

Men were rarely tattooed. Women applied tattooing chiefly to the chin in one to three bands running vertically from the lower lip. Although a person of any age might be tattooed, it was customary to have the operation performed at adolescence. The incision was made with a flake of obsidian, and rich pitch soot was rubbed into the

Dept. of Anthr., Smithsonian: 19272.
Fig. 10. Headress worn in dances, made of great western horned owl and white-headed woodpecker feathers and red wool-wrapped twigs with quill and bead dangles. Height 46 cm, collected in 1875.

wound. If a bluish-green color was desired, dye from a certain grass or spider web was used instead of pitch.

Knowledge

No words exist for fractions. For 20 and beyond, two different systems of counting were used, one for ordinary purposes and the other for clam disk beads and possibly also for arrowheads. In the clam disk system stones were laid to one side to keep track of the number of twenties accumulated. It was possible to count into the thousands with the Wintu method (Du Bois 1935:70).

The divisions of a day were *honhima·* 'morning', *puye·l panti nomel-łas-werum* 'middle of the afternoon', *puri·wa* 'dusk', *ke(·)nwani* 'evening', and *čipi-wenem* 'middle night'. The seasons were: *pomisim* 'winter', *ʔol-tipa* 'spring', *po·pil* 'summer', and *xaydani* 'autumn'.

Year counts were kept by a few old men, who notched sticks and planted them in a row or placed pebbles in a basket. These methods also might be used for day counts. Some old men also observed the north and south progressions of the sun between two landmarks. As the sun oscillated during the course of the year, the progression was used in association with the changes in season. Months were designated by appearances of certain animals and plants. The calendrical system was a mixture of lunar, solstitial, and seasonal observances (Du Bois 1935:68–69).

Subsistence

Hunting

Deer hunting was individual or communal. When several men hunted together the first man to graze the deer with an arrow was the owner of the carcass regardless of whether he killed it or not. Communal hunts were by invitation and lasted for about three days. Snares were set with bark tied from one tree to another. The scent of human beings on the bark drove the deer into the snare. The noose snare was suspended from a bent tree that the deer released by entering the noose. Women, children, and less-skilled people would help in communal drives by driving the game from the mouth of a canyon toward its head, beating the brush and shouting. Dogs were trained to assist in the chase. At the head of the canyon was the best marksman. One favorite spot for cliff kills was called *no·pin łalus* 'deer fall over'. Hundreds of bones accumulated at the foot of this bluff (Du Bois 1935:9–11).

The men did the butchering and passed the cuts of meat to the women to distribute to women of other households, but if the family that procured the meat wanted to give a feast, the meat was cooked and the men of the local group were invited to the feast. In a communal hunt, the leader of the hunt would carve and pass out the meat (Du Bois 1935:9–10).

Deer heads roasted separately were forbidden to young

women. Old women might eat of the head but not in conjunction with salt, water, or hot mush. The remains were covered with rocks and all who ate head meat washed their hands in a container and the water was poured over the rocks. The lower jaw of the skull was cleaned and hung in a tree to attract more deer. The fetus and uterus were forbidden to all but old women.

Various procedures for cooking deer were employed. The paunch cleaned and filled with blood and chunks of fat was roasted in hot ashes. The guts were straightened while still warm, emptied, and eaten. Sinews were cut out lengthwise. The meat was roasted in strips on hot coals. Slices from the ham were pounded with a small pestle, dampened with water, and wrapped around a clean, hot rock and laid in and covered with hot coals. A hunting party in the hills might roast a whole side or a quarter over an open fire. Meat was sometimes steamed by placing a little water and hot rocks in a cooking basket. Meat strips were laid on the rocks. A basketry tray was used to cover the cooking basket and retain steam (Du Bois 1935:10).

Brown bears were usually hunted in the fall when they were fat and sluggish. One way to get a bear was to take several friends to a den and smoke him out. If an individual was brave he could go in and slay him with bow and arrow. Communal bear hunts were done in the same fashion as deer drives. Dogs were used on the hunt. A lookout shouted information on the bear's movements. The slain bear was quartered and taken to camp where the men feasted on it. The man who initiated the hunt, not the slayer, was the host. Bear meat, because of its greasiness, was usually eaten without trying to dry it. Stillwater Wintu never ate any kind of bear.

After the feast, the hide was stretched on a square frame made by the young men. The frame was leaned against a tree in an upright position to allow the women to scrape the hide with stone flakes. By morning when the hide was fleshed, someone put the skin on and danced imitating the bear. This was the time for fun and for making requests of the bear. Both brown bear and grizzly bear hides were used as burial shrouds (Du Bois 1935:11). Black bear skins were received in trade from the mountain Yuki (Powers 1877:8).

Grizzly bears were feared and never eaten. A grizzly was allowed to rot where found. The flesh was not eaten because grizzlies ate man and one would be committing cannibalism. One should never boast of slaying a bear or a bear would kill him in the future (Du Bois 1935:12). A strong curse among the Wintu would be, "May the grizzly bear eat you!" or "May the grizzly bear bite your father's head off!" (Powers 1877:240).

In the Bald Hills area, no festivities followed the killing of a grizzly bear, but the other areas had a festival similar to that for the brown bear. If a piece of meat fell on anyone during the fleshing of the hide, he would go at once to the river and bathe. That evening the head of the animal was laid in front of a solitary singer. The people gathered in a circle while he, using his split-stick rattles, dodged back and forth, striking the head and reenacting the kill (Du Bois 1935:12).

Rabbit hunting was done communally in the Bald Hills area. There were generally three or four drives held in a season. The rabbits were divided up at camp. Snares were set and a man stationed nearby with a club. As the rabbits were caught they were killed and the snare reset. To prepare the rabbit for eating, the hair was singed off, the entrails and larger bones removed, and the carcass pounded with a flat rock and laid on coals to roast. Rabbit was also boiled and then put in a hopper and pounded into a doughy mass. This was then rolled into balls and distributed to be eaten.

Quail were caught in nets. Gophers and other small rodents were caught in snares set before their holes. Rodents such as mice were also caught in a deadfall, two flat rocks propped apart by an acorn that is parched and scraped thin. Gnawing through the acorn, the animal released the upper rock and was crushed. Ground squirrels were hunted with slings. They were also shot with bow and arrow by one man after another climbed a tree and frightened them out. Wood rats were usually hunted in winter when they were sluggish. Birds were usually hunted by the young boys using blunt arrows and hiding near springs or other places were birds were plentiful.

The usual way to cook small game was to singe it, cut off the paws and tail, and remove the entrails. The animal was then roasted in a bed of hot coals. The head was cut off and the ribs extracted along with the other large bones. The body was then pounded, bones and all. Sometimes the pounding was done before roasting (Du Bois 1935:13-14).

Grasshoppers were obtained by encircling a grassy area. The people sang and danced as they drove the grasshoppers into the center area. The grass in the center was then set afire with wormwood torches. After the blaze had subsided, the now wingless insects were gathered by both men and women. The grasshoppers were boiled in baskets, put on basket trays to dry, and then either eaten at once or mashed in a hopper and stored. Salmon flies, which swarmed on the river edge for a few days in April, were gathered early in the morning before their wings were strong enough to permit flight. They were boiled, or, if great in number, dried and saved for winter use (Du Bois 1935:14-15).

Fishing

Chinook salmon ran freely in the McCloud and Sacramento rivers. The spring run took place from middle May until October. The fall run began in the middle of October and lasted until December. The cold water, 48 to 53° F. at the hottest time of year, made for good fishing in the McCloud River all year long (Stone 1874:169). The average size of fish was approximately 20 pounds with some weighing as much as 70 pounds. Steelhead were taken in the upper reaches of the Trinity River. Suckers, which were found in all streams and creeks, were considered inferior to salmon; they weighed between one-quarter and four pounds.

Sometimes a torch was used in the communal fish drives. In a small drive no net was used, but individuals with dip nets accompanied the torchbearers and scooped out the salmon. If several villages were present as in the midsummer drives, the divisions were made among the leaders of each group, who then divided shares to each adult male. The spring catch was too rich in oil to dry, so it was usually baked in a pit lined with heated and cleaned stones on which the fish were spread in rows. They were then covered with more hot rocks and allowed to bake for a few hours. When they were removed, some of the fish were eaten. The baked fish not eaten were boned and flaked. As the fish dried out, it was pulverized into a salmon flour. The heads, entrails, tails, and bones were also dried and then pounded into a fine flour for winter use. Sun-dried fish were stored for winter use. Storage was in a wide basket with a narrow top lined with maple leaves. Dried roe and pine nuts were mixed in with the salmon flour. This food was used as a valuable trade article among the McCloud Wintu. It was exchanged principally with the peoples to the south for salt and clam disk money (Du Bois 1935:15-16). Individual fishing was usually done with a harpoon, either from the bank or from a salmon house. "The Wintūn ties together two stout poles in a cross, plants it in deep water, then lays a log out to it from the shore. At times, he constructs a booth out over the water" (Powers 1877:233-234).

Individuals had rights to certain places. This private ownership was offset by the fact that anyone might visit the owner while he was fishing and expect a present of a salmon, so that the fisherman might find himself with very little by the end of the day. This system was called mikaya from qaya 'to steal'. Salmon houses extended only as far south on the Sacramento River as Jelly, on the border between the Wintu and the Nomlaki. Women usually avoided salmon houses and could not fish or spear from them, although old women sometimes accompanied their husbands to the huts. The river-dwelling Wintu in the Bald Hills area used to invite the hill dwellers to communal fish drives. Salmon was not a staple in this area, so salmon flour was obtained by trade (Du Bois 1935:16). Steelhead were taken on the upper Trinity River in the same way as salmon.

Suckers were taken in drives during August in the creeks and shallow waters of large rivers. A weir of brush weighted down with rocks was built out from each bank. These pointed diagonally downstream and a small opening two or three feet wide was left in midstream between them. Across the opening a net was stretched. In rocky creeks, wings of stone were constructed. These drives were held in the morning. The rest of the day was spent in drying the fish, feasting, and gambling. Suckers were also caught by individuals. Children on the McCloud were given miniature harpoons and urged to spear suckers as their elders speared salmon. In Bald Hills, where fish were rarer, adults would spear small fish. Trout and whitefish were sometimes caught with a fishhook made of two thorns tied together to form an acute angle or of a nasal bone of a deer. They were also caught in traps (Du Bois 1935:17).

Fish poisoning was employed in smaller streams where isolated pools could be found or created with a rough stone dam. It was easier to do this in summer when the water was low. Some poisons used were soaproot (sakas), and ginseng (ła·rat). Men were responsible for digging the roots.

Mussels or clams were gathered by divers. Shellfish were either roasted or boiled to open the shell. The meat was eaten at once; if the supply was plentiful, it was dried in flat basketry trays for winter use (Du Bois 1935:18).

Gathering

Procuring vegetable foods was the responsibility of the women, while men were responsible for obtaining flesh foods. Women carried water. When traveling, both sexes shared in carrying paraphernalia (Du Bois 1935:23).

If a man wandering in the mountains discovered a tree heavily laden with acorns, he could claim the whole tree. If it was in an area that others might also come across, he used a stick to mark the heavily loaded branch he was claiming. If another had previously observed the tree but had failed to mark it, this new claimant could now remove one stick and place his own there, but he must pay the original claimant.

Gathering was done by the family or local group. Men climbed the trees and shook off the acorns or used hooked sticks to shake the branches. The women picked them up in burden baskets. One tree at a time was stripped. One large tree or two small ones constituted a day's work. The acorns were carried back to camp. In the evening all gathered to shell acorns. "If acorns were scarce, groups might make forays upon neighboring territories." "During gathering expeditions one woman was appointed each day to remain in camp and turn over the acorns that were being dried in the sun. In return, she received her share of the amount gathered. Acorns were stored in bark-lined pits. In Bald Hills, a chaparral bush was spread open with sticks, the whole lashed into shape with grapevines, and the interior lined with evergreen boughs" (Du Bois 1935:18).

Young women pounded the acorns while older ones sifted the acorn meal. The hopper was put on a flat rock; the calves of the legs steadied it on each side. A pestle was used to pound. Coarse meal was called si· 'teeth'. Acorn meal was leached in sand pits. Acorn soup was made by stone-boiling. As the soup boiled, it was stirred with a wooden paddle. For acorn bread, black oak and valley oak was preferred. For black oak bread, flour was leached for one day in a sand pit, removed, and dried. Flour adjacent to the sand was put in water and the sand was allowed to settle out. To bake bread a rock-lined pit was heated for nearly one day before inserting the dough. The rocks were then covered with leaves, dirt, and more rocks; finally a fire was built over the pit. The next morning the bread was done. It was of a rich consistency and would keep for months. It was distributed, like other foods, to all members of the local group. A baking was considered necessary every week or two. Valley oak acorns, to be used for bread, were put in water to mold. The moldier, the more tasty the bread was considered. Red earth was sometimes collected and soaked in water and then added to the meal. It made the batter stiffer and no leaching of the meal was necessary. The bread came out dark in color, which was a measure of its palatability. "Black bread" was a specialty of the Stillwater area where red earth was plentiful, but it was also made in other regions (Du Bois 1935:19).

Acorns were important and were used in all Wintu areas. Buckeye, found throughout Wintu country, was more plentiful in the northern section where it was the most important vegetable staple next to acorns. Manzanita berries were found throughout the region but were most plentiful in the Stillwater area. Manzanita was made into soup; the coarser part, mostly seeds, was made into cider. Indian potatoes, pussy's ears (*Calochortus* sp.), and snake's-head were gathered in May. Soaproot (toubui), was collected in June and was used for glue, pigment binder, food, and fibers for brushes. Other foods were clover, miner's lettuce, skunkbush berries, hazel nuts, pine nuts, wild grapes, and sunflower and cotton flower seeds. Some medicinals were pennyroyal, Oregon grape, soaproot, milkweed, and salt (Du Bois 1935:19-21).

Synonymy

Although the Wintu were seen and described by James Dana of the U.S. Exploring Expedition in 1841 and by John Work of the Hudson's Bay Company in 1833, the tribal name was not reported. G.W. Taggart in a newspaper article (Humboldt *Times,* Nov. 11, 1854) may have been the first to use the name Win-toon or "Mountain Diggers." The Wintu have sometimes been called Northern Wintun by anthropologists (e.g., Kroeber 1932a:256). The spelling Wintu was used at least as early as 1884 (Curtin in Hodge 1907-1910, 2:963); it derives from the Wintu word *wint^hu·h* 'person' and was proposed by Kroeber (1932a:253) as a suitable name to distinguish this group from the Patwin (Southern Wintun) and Nomlaki (Central Wintun). In English the Wintu are sometimes locally known as Shasta, and the Trinity Wintu as Trinity (Goldschmidt 1951a:316).

The Shasta referred to the Wintu as *xatukwi·wa* (Shir-

ley Silver, personal communication 1974), spelled Khatukeyu by Kroeber and Xátūkwiwa by Dixon (in Hodge 1907-1910, 2:963). The Maidu name is *winíum maydɨ* (Shipley 1963:150). Wailaki or its variants (e.g., Nomlaki *waylaka*) can mean the Wailaki proper but has also been used by Wintu or Nomlaki to refer to people of their own language living to the north (Washington 1909:93; Merriam 1966-1967,1:55). Other names applied to the Wintu in the literature usually refer to subdivisions of the Wintu and Nomlaki—tribelet names or place-names, often with the initial geographical referents *way-* 'north', *nom-* 'west', *nor-* or *no-* 'south', *puy-* 'east', or *ʔol-* 'up, above'. These names occur in a wide variety of spellings (see Powers 1877:229-242; Kroeber 1925:355-356; Merriam 1966-1967,1:52-59). Long lists of Wintu village names are given by Merriam (1966-1967, 3:266-270).

Sources

The most important, fullest, and most reliable ethnographic record of Wintu culture is by Du Bois (1935). Voegelin (1942) presents three Wintu element lists that cover in minute detail the culture of this group. This information is reliable but difficult to use on account of the method of presentation. A considerable body of Wintu mythology, collected at the same time and published by Du Bois and Demetracopoulou (1931), is important, as is a second study that not only presents 69 additional myths recorded in 1929-1930 but also explores their literary qualities and the change and stability aspects (Demetracopoulou and Du Bois 1932). Demetracopoulou (1935) published the translations of a number of Wintu songs that are of aesthetic as well as ethnographic value. D. Demetracopoulou Lee's (1943, 1944, 1944a, 1946, 1950) several analytical papers on Wintu language contribute usefully to the definition of Wintu world view. Wintu grammar (Pitkin 1963) adds further to knowledge of the Wintu language. The earliest ethnographic record of importance is a series of remarkable drawings made by the artist H.B. Brown (figs. 2, 11) in 1851-1852 of Indians and villages near Redding (in Merriam 1966-1967,1:pls. 1-5). Earlier ethnographic reporting by Stone between 1872 and 1880 when he was in charge of the federal fish hatchery on the McCloud River (Heizer 1973a:1-22) is that of an untrained but perceptive observer who was seeing the McCloud Wintu in their last days of aboriginal living. Powers's (1877) ethnographic data are more full but subject to certain errors of interpretation by a man who was a writer rather than a trained ethnographer. C. Hart Merriam compiled voluminous records, some of which are published (Merriam 1957, 1966-1967), but a great mass of second-quality linguistics and better-grade ethnogeography and ethnoscience remain unpublished in the Merriam Collection (Heizer et al. 1969). Washington's (1909) notes are brief but reliable and important.

Some Wintu word lists recorded before 1875 are printed in Powers (1877:518–534).

Archeological collections from sites in Wintu territory are in the Robert H. Lowie Museum of Anthropology, University of California, Berkeley, which also holds ethnographic collections.

There is no single account of the history of relations between Whites and Wintu.

The John Carter Brown Lib., Brown U., Providence, R.I.

Fig. 11. Chino village of subterranean dwellings and acorn caches near the former town of Monroeville, at the mouth of Stony Creek. Drawing by Henry B. Brown, 1852.

Nomlaki

WALTER GOLDSCHMIDT

Language and Territory

The Nomlaki (ˈnōm̩läkē) spoke a Wintuan language closely related to Wintu and Patwin—perhaps merely a divergent dialect of the same language the Wintu spoke—in the Penutian linguistic stock.* There were two major Nomlaki divisions, the River and Hill Nomlaki. The River Nomlaki lived in the Sacramento River valley in present Tehama County. The Hill Nomlaki occupied the foothill land to the west, extending to the summit of the Coast Range, in what is now Tehama and Glenn counties (fig.1).

Most available cultural data come from Hill Nomlaki informants. According to them, the River Nomlaki were of two groups: the *memwaylaka* 'water north language' in the north, and the *puymok* 'easterners'. The Hill Nomlaki were themselves subdivided into dialects extending along the several creek drainages: *waykeweł* (Redbank area); *waltoykeweł* (north of Elder Creek); *nomlaka* (Elder Creek to below Thomes Creek); and *noykeweł* or *kolayel* (Grindstone Creek). People from farther south were called *noymok* whether or not they spoke a related language.

At the time of first contact with Whites the Nomlaki probably numbered more than 2,000 individuals. Their numbers were heavily reduced during the first decade of contact and slowly dwindled thereafter. In the 1930s there were three rancherias of a half-dozen households each, the men serving as casual or migratory laborers. Aboriginal practices had already almost disappeared. In the 1970s only scattered descendants survive.

Prehistory

No stratigraphic archeological data in present Nomlaki territory is available to establish a succession of cultures,

but work to the south suggests a developmental sequence (Heizer and Fenenga 1939; Lillard, Heizer, and Fenenga 1939). Nomlaki culture belongs to the late phase of this sequence, as indicated by the following conforming evidence: flexed burial, burial accompanied by possessions of and gifts to the deceased, house form, clamshell disk beads, tubular magnesite beads, stone pipes with bone stems, bird-bone whistles, incised geometric designs, and acorn anvil.

Clamshell disk beads, tubular magnesite beads, and flexed burial are associated with the wealth complex of the Nomlaki. Clamshell beads were used as money; tubular magnesite beads were highly prized wealth objects; and flexed burial was associated with the practice of wrapping the corpse in a bearskin shroud, a Nomla-

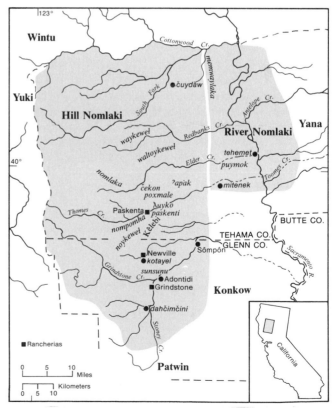

Fig. 1. Tribal territory with subdivisions, local groups, and a few important villages.

---

*Nomlaki words printed in italics have been checked by Harvey Pitkin for conformity to the orthography he developed for Wintu (Broadbent and Pitkin 1964:21), which he estimates to be an adequate representation of the Nomlaki phonological system. This orthography has been modified by substituting č for c, and by the addition of ł and X̣ (very likely the same phoneme). Vowel length was probably phonemic but cannot now be indicated since it was never recorded systematically.

ki's most valued possession. This wealth complex was in turn associated with the secret society and the pattern of occupational specialization. The evidence suggests that this wealth complex moved into the area from the south in late prehistoric times, and that it is part of that cult system of which the Kuksu of the Pomo is the best exemplar. These data support the historical reconstruction made by Kroeber (1923:306–309). The northward thrust that brought these elements did not involve conquest and population replacement but was accompanied by a gradual introduction of new population elements. It may have been associated with the spread of the bow and arrow. It introduced a fairly elaborate status differentiation in a formerly more egalitarian clan-village community system.

History

The Nomlaki were outside the orbit of the direct influence of Spanish missionary activity, though some indirect Spanish influence is indicated. In October 1808 Alférez (Ensign) Gabriel Moraga reached Glenn in Glenn County (Chapman 1921), within River Nomlaki territory. In October 1821 Luis Arguello and the diarist, Father Blas Ordáz (1958), crossed Glenn and Tehama counties. By this time the Indians told Arguello and Father Ordáz of White men who had preceded them. Arguello crossed the Coast Range, but it is doubtful that he penetrated Nomlaki territory.

In 1832–1833 the Ewing Young party crossed the area on a trapping expedition. Col. J.J. Warner described the decimated condition of the Indians of California:

The banks of the Sacramento river, in its whole course through the valley, were studded with Indian villages, the houses of which in the spring, during the day time were red with the salmon the aborigines were curing. . . . On our return, late in the summer of 1833, we found the valleys depopulated. From the head of the Sacramento to the great bend and Slough of the San Joaquin, we did not see more than six or eight live Indians, while large numbers of their skulls and dead bodies were to be seen under almost every shade tree, near the water, where the uninhabited and deserted villages had been converted into graveyards . . . (E.G. Lewis 1880:49).

This malaria epidemic of 1833 was the first serious blow Western civilization struck against the Nomlaki. Its worst toll was in the villages along the river; its effect on the Hill Nomlaki cannot be determined (Cook 1955a).

There is no evidence of direct contact between Whites and Indians until mid-century, though Dr. Charles Pickering (1848, 5:195), made contact with either River Nomlaki or Patwin in 1841 and L.T. Emmons (Pickering 1848, 8:258) was on the northern fringes of the area. Yet Goldschmidt (1951a:312) recorded informants' accounts

of raids and battles from this period.

By 1849 Tehama was a flourishing town and the impact of White civilization was felt by all the Indians of the northern Sierra Nevada and Coast Range of California. They were exploited as labor and were killed on the slightest provocation, real or imaginary. By 1851 settlers began to request that the Indians be segregated from the White population on a reservation. Others preferred to keep the Indians available for menial labor, for the principal economic asset was land and cheap labor was much in demand.

In 1851 a commission of three was appointed to make a series of treaties with the tribes of the central drainage, following a policy that was to get the Indians "down from their mountain fastnesses and place them in reservations, along in the foothills bordering on the plains." The treaties were accepted by the Indians but rejected by the United States Senate because, in the words of Congressman Joseph W. McCorkle of California, "the reservations of land, which they [the commissioners] have set apart for the different tribes of Indians, comprise, in some cases, the most valuable agricultural land in the State" (A.W. Hoopes 1932:45).

In 1852 Superintendent Edward F. Beale started the policy of establishing Indian reservations, and in September 1854 his successor, Thomas J. Henley, established the Nome Lackee Reservation on a tract of 25,000 acres in the foothills of western Tehama County between Elder and Thomes creeks.

The reservation was successful in that the Indians accepted its mode of life, learned farming and other crafts, and, according to accounts of the time, prospered. By 1856, with the threat of Indian retaliation dissipated, the settlers became covetous of the "magnificent farm of 25,000 acres" and brought pressure for its abandonment. The Nomlakis and other Sacramento valley Indians were literally herded over the mountain to Round Valley in 1863, the Nome Lackee Reservation having already been taken over by Whites. This was the Nome Cult Farm, the home of the Nomlakis' traditional enemy, the Yukis. There the sequence of conflicts was repeated and after several years a number of Nomlakis returned to settle in the foothills of their old territory, to secure a livelihood by working as farm hands.

They established a number of settlements, chiefly along the edge of the foothills in western Tehama County. In the 1870s they adopted the Ghost Dance cult, which was introduced by Homaldo, probably a Wintu, and Lame Bill, a Patwin (Du Bois 1939). A later development known as The Big Head was adopted in the early 1900s, and both rites continued to be performed as late as the 1930s. By this time there were but three rancherias left (Grindstone, Newville, and Paskenta), with probably no more than a score of households identifying themselves as Nomlaki.

Data on the history of this area are available from the

annual reports of the secretary of the interior in various dates between the years 1853 and 1864. Further materials on the area are available in Chapman (1921), A.W. Hoopes (1932), E.G. Lewis (1880), Pickering (1848), Powers (1877), Washington (1906), and Du Bois (1939).

Culture

Social Organization

Daily life centered in a village (kewel) with a population of from 25 to 200 persons under the leadership of a chieftain (čabatu). His office was hereditary in the male line, although succession was subject to review by the men of the village. The village itself was a kinship group (ʔolkapna) comprised of persons related in the male line together with their married-in wives (and a few outsiders, owing to temporary matrilocal residence). This kinship group was named and exogamous, and its members recognized kinship to any strangers who belonged to a like-named group. It was, therefore, a clan in all its major features (Goldschmidt 1948). Within the village-ʔolkapna there was a series of separate families comprised of husband, wife or wives, and minor children. These families were the food-producing and food-consuming units, but they shared food resources with their fellow village members (and ʔolkapna kin).

A diagrammatic sketch of the ʔolkapna-village (fig. 2) shows that it centers on the chief's house, which is larger than the others, toward which the individual huts of the household face. The menstrual hut is away from the water source; the dance house (figs. 3-4), where one exists, is outside the central circle.

The kinship system, recorded by Gifford (1922:97-98; see also Goldschmidt 1951a:321), equates parallel cousins with siblings; mother's brother's son with mother's brother; father's sister's daughter with granddaughter. Father's brothers, mother's sister's husband, and stepfather are equated, as are mother's sister, father's brother's wife, and stepmother.

Cutting across these spatial kinship groupings was another division, with distinguished persons according to social status. An initiatory rite (huta) introduced a limited number of adult men into a secret society. The members of this group were persons of status, having a disproportionate measure of authority in public matters and having certain sumptuary rights, especially those of engaging in trade in wealth objects that were the specific goals of this class. This group also controlled most of the skilled crafts and professions, which gave them a special source of profit and social position. Members apparently commanded the respect of their fellow initiates and obtained special privileges by their brotherhood in the organization. The wealth objects recognized by the society included furs and shell beads, and the greatest desidera-

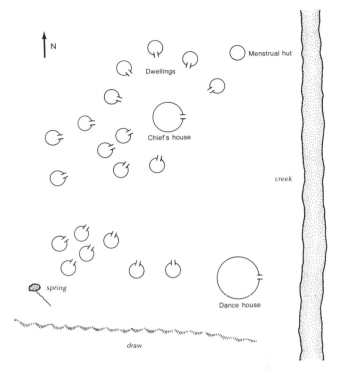

After Goldschmidt 1951a:318.

Fig. 2. Diagram of a village. The chief's house faced the stream, into which the men plunged after certain sweating ceremonials. Later houses were built near the spring, which was the source of water. The dance house was a postcontact addition, away from the remainder of the village. The menstrual hut was at the opposite end of the village from the water supply. The diagram does not represent a particular village but shows characteristic relationships.

tum was the pelt of the black bear, which served as a burial shroud. They were acquired in part by trade with neighboring tribes, the profit accruing to Nomlaki traders by virtue of enhanced value as the goods moved farther from their place of origin.

Little detail is available on either the mythic or ceremonial aspect of this group. Initiation involved an ordeal in which novices danced in a superheated semisubterranean dance house until comatose or nearly so. They also plunged into a cold stream after sweating in the ordeal. Initiates might acquire special powers (both ritualistic, such as divination, and practical, such as artisans' skills) as a result of visions obtained while comatose.

The hereditary chieftain was expected to lead the people in their daily pursuits, to harangue them with respect to moral proprieties, and to hear disputes as they arose. Disputes were also adjusted by means of warfare and feuds. In the absence of legal authority, property played an important part in arriving at settlements. Wealth property was transferred to the offended party in payment for crimes, not as a result of an established system

343

Fig. 3. A semisubterranean dance house at Paskenta. Photograph by Walter Goldschmidt, 1938.

of fines for specific criminal acts, but by negotiation between the two disputant parties. Wealth therefore played an important part, not only in the establishment of status, but also in the maintenance of law and order.

War and Trade

The cause of war was usually transgression of property rights or occasionally a murder growing out of a dispute over a woman. There was no clearly demarcated warrior class. It was not necessary to be a *huta* initiate to join the fight, but not all men engaged in warfare. Those who did fight underwent special practical and magic training, and it was said that cult members "uphold one another in a pinch" and called one another brother.

Each fighter utilized special springs in which he bathed to gain special power or protection. There were two important practitioners associated with warfare: the seer and the poisoner. It was the business of the seer to determine the proper course of action and predict the outcome. The poisoners killed people by magical means. The actual conduct of war involved surprise attacks or short pitched battles.

While warfare took place among the Nomlaki villages and especially between the Hill and river-dwelling Nom-laki, their major enemy was the Yuki of Round Valley. An analysis of nine war stories obtained from the Nomlaki and the Yuki by three ethnographers (Goldschmidt, Foster, and Essene 1939) showed certain consistent themes. The figure indicates the number of stories using that theme. A small party is attacked (8) while camping (3), gathering (2), poaching (2), or trading (2). A woman or girl returns with the news (5), a war party is formed (7), and after a period of preparation (5) either a surprise attack is made (4) or a prearranged battle fought (2). The enemy is nearly wiped out (7) with little or no loss of life (2), scalps are taken (3), and a victory dance celebrated (4). Four of these accounts purport to refer to the last Yuki-Nomlaki conflict. These accounts always claim victory for the side of the teller and always place fault with the enemy. There is no individuation of heroes, although careful reference may be made to places.

Despite the small and integrated character of the Nomlaki community, differentials in wealth and power were clearly marked. Wealth consisted in clamshell disk beads, magnesite beads, and furs and hides, particularly the pelt of the black bear. Feathers, particularly of eagle and yellowhammer, were also prized.

Trade of various kinds played an important role in the Nomlaki economy. Because of a tendency toward occupational specialization, a good deal of trade took place internally, individual families exchanging for or purchasing needed items, including food, from one another. The Hill Nomlaki acquired fish from the River Nomlaki in return for seeds and animals and also traded with the Yuki, who particularly sought salt. The Nomlaki were also a part of an exchange route extending from the Oregon border to San Francisco Bay, in which shells moved northward from the Bay region in exchange for skins, obsidian, and yew wood for bows. Some Nomlakis specialized in trading, a dangerous occupation. Clamshell beads served as medium of exchange and standard of value, though much exchange was direct barter. The beads were progressively improved to enhance their value as they moved farther from the source of supply. Trade and barter were clearly distinguished from gift exchanges, which also played an important social role, and occasionally took on a potlatchlike lavishness.

Dept. of Anthr., U. of Calif., Berkeley.
Fig. 4. Interior of semisubterranean dance house at Grindstone Rancheria. Photograph by C. Hart Merriam, May 1923.

Games

Aside from songs, dances, and storytelling, the Nomlaki had a wide variety of games. Among the sports they enjoyed were kick races, in which a buckskin ball was relayed by three players to a common goal, hockey (*weta*), in which a quoitlike loop of rope was flipped with a stick, and shinny (*kutla* or perhaps *kuχa*) in which teams of six or seven played with wooden balls struck by sticks. They had foot races, jumping, shooting, and throwing contests, and wrestling. There was also a variety of gambling games, including the hand game (*kenil*), which was a guessing game, a multiple-stick guessing game (*bohemčehu*), and dice games (*tedela* and *tela*) played by women.

Religion

To the Nomlaki, the world of reality and the world of the supernatural were inseparable, so that even the most practical undertaking was circumscribed by elaborate ritual inspired by the religious ideas with which the act was invested. Hunting, trading, warfare, and the *huta* were only a few of the Nomlaki activities that carried ritual restrictions. Every important phase of the individual life cycle required the proper ceremony to insure spiritual purity and strength of the principles involved.

The Nomlaki world was animistic. "Everything in this world talks, just as we are now—the trees, rocks, everything. But we can't understand them, just as the White people do not understand Indians." In such a world all inanimate things had to be treated with circumspection, although the inherent power of some things was far greater than that of others. People likewise had special, inherent powers; the economic and social activity of each person was believed to be determined by a talent that was supernaturally acquired. The phrase "it is given him" was used for most manifest talents, and was offered as rationale for the differences in human abilities and achievements.

It is very difficult to disentangle aboriginal religious perceptions from those with Christian influences: the single reported origin myth is clearly a syncretization. The Nomlaki apparently had a concept of Supreme Being, as did their neighbors to the north and south. There were three forms of spirits: (1) *łes,* which was variantly glossed as 'shade, shadow, ghost', which dwells within and animates the living; after death, the *łes* may be helpful or harmful; it may remain near the grave or go to the afterworld; (2) *holowit* is a ghost, an evil supernatural manifestation; (3) *yapaytu* is a supernatural manifestation whose precise nature could not be determined. There was also a variety of supernatural beasts, such as the mythical *wukwuk*. Modern informants more frequently paint these characters as devilish pranksters bent on mischief rather than as fearful beings doing harm; yet it was recognized that they occasionally killed people. The Nomlaki had a concept of heaven and expectation of an afterlife, but the characteristics are not clear.

Springs and hallowed places (*sawal*), usually inhabited by a spirit, had powers for good and evil and were of great importance to shamans, warriors, hunters, gamblers, and specific craftsmen. Some springs were said to be good; others were considered bad. They were inhabited by various spirits, who might harm a person who should not be there or benefit the visitor entitled to their powers. Each spring was visited by the person interested in its particular power, and such visits increased his luck, purified him, and strengthened him for his endeavor; a person might not visit a *sawal* to which he did not have a specific right. The afterbirth and the navel cord were buried most frequently at the hunting *sawal*. A gambler might visit a gamblers' *sawal* to insure luck and success for a son. The body of an eagle from which the feathers had been removed was buried at a special spring.

Though the world of the Nomlaki was peopled with unseen spirits having wills of their own, and nature in its many manifestations was animate, the Nomlaki were not helpless before these powers. They could influence the course of supernatural events by the use of prayer, magic, and charms. Practical acts were surrounded with special incantations and other ritual, and restrictions on behavior served to protect the Indian against these unseen forces.

• SHAMANISM   Sickness and death were caused by the intrusion of a foreign substance. This malignant object was thought to be visible and tangible, and the cure of disease lay in its proper extraction. The "pain" might be introduced into the body because of some breach of conduct (for example, "fooling with a menstruant woman") or because of the work of a magic "poisoner."

Poisons were concocted from different things. One informant claimed that dried rattlesnake fangs were the strongest poison and that lizards and bullfrogs brought about "slow consumption." Actual snake poison, which might be rolled in earwax, was said to have been used. Hummingbirds were also used for poisoning, and according to legend this bird was considered a great doctor.

Shamans acquired their powers through a rigorous initiation, the nature of which is not known. They cured by sucking out the "pain" that caused the illness; shamans could also cause illness by "throwing" pains into a person. They were thus adjuncts to warfare. Little is known of aboriginal shamans for they were replaced by the Bole doctor, who rubbed the pain from the body instead of sucking it. He did not produce a visible pain, and operated by entering a trance induced in part by smoking. This type of shaman is a historical innovation associated with the Bole-Maru cult.

The seer (ƛahit) had the power of foretelling the future. The profession was important in warfare and presumably other activities. He had no curative powers.

• CEREMONIES   The Nomlaki did not have an elaborate ritual calendar. Aside from the *huta* and the puberty dance, the only known aboriginal ritual involving the community was the spring dance (ʔoltepomčono). One Nomlaki described it as follows:

When everything is all very green, when winter is over and everything is warm and the sun is coming north, then the birds holler witwitwit, the people begin to ask, "Why can't we play a little?" Then they send word to their close neighbors that they are going to have a dance. The people ask the chief before they can give the dance, and if he agrees he will get out early in the morning and tell all the people to go hunting, fishing, and so on. He will name off the people for the various jobs early in the morning while they are outside listening.

The meat is brought to the chief, who gives each person some to be brought back prepared in the evening. Everybody gets some. At about five in the evening they start to dance . . . This is a spring dance, a play dance, a home dance. They don't gamble. It is held inside the sweat house. . . .

The dance group included two drummers, two singers, one person to call the dances, from two to six male dancers, and as many female dancers as were available. They dressed behind the drum; the singers stood in front of it, and the timekeeper in front of them with a split-stick rattle in his hands. There is a leader who "dances the girls out" of the dressing place one at a time toward the end of the dance. This is the strenuous part (Goldschmidt 1951a:364–365).

The Nomlaki had a rich store of tales. These generally were in the form of animal stories that explained the acquisition of cultural forms, such as the origin of fire or the existence of natural phenomena, such as the form of buttes. In them Coyote (*sedet*) was frequently a buffoon-hero. They are rich in imagery of death and revival and of the fabulous and not infrequently take on a ribald character.

Life Cycle

During pregnancy, both the woman and her husband were under special restrictions of a "sympathetic magic" nature. Old women served as midwives; the father was expected to cut the navel cord, which he buried at a spring to bring the child luck. Nicknames were given at birth, regular names somewhat later; but these names were not used by relatives. Children were disciplined by elders other than parents, sometimes by severe whippings.

Girls were confined at the onset of the first menses, attended by a girl who had recently undergone her puberty ceremony. They were under many restrictions, which were ended with a puberty ceremonial (*yowena*). It was a major festival, often lasting several days, involving feasting, dancing, singing (with many ribald songs), and closing with the girl and her attendant painted and resplendent in clothing and decoration, teasing the young men and enjoying being the center of attention. Although they were not confined at subsequent menstruations, women were subjected to numerous restrictions, as were their husbands.

Marriage (the ceremonial nature of which is not known) was generally arranged by the parents and involved temporary matrilocal residence and a period of bride service. Polygyny was permitted but was rare and limited to the wealthy. Marriage appears to have been easily dissolvable and could be terminated by mutual agreement. A man who left a woman without cause was expected to give presents to his wife's father, and neither was to marry for another year. The children remained with the woman.

The dead were buried in a round hole, tied in sinew rope and wrapped with a bear hide. Burial was immediately after death; mourners wailed through the night, stopping at sunrise. The possessions of the deceased were burned; a second burning of possessions took place a year later, and this released the widow from mourning and allowed her to remarry.

Subsistence

The Nomlakis lived entirely on natural products: their chief foods were acorns, grass seeds and tubers, deer, elk, rabbit and other small game, birds, and fish. The Nomlaki practiced a kind of transhumance, with each village moving to its own special area in the mountains each summer, though the base villages were not entirely abandoned.

Hunting was done either by lone individuals or in groups. All men hunted, but there were outstanding hunters and specialists. They used the bow and arrow, a knotted mahogany club, nets, snares, slings, and traps. The valley people used slings for killing birds. Deer were driven into sinew nets with 18-inch mesh, rabbits into fiber nets with 1 ¼-inch mesh, quail into or under nets stretched horizontally over poles and dropped on the feeding birds. The deer nets were about 6 feet high and made in 10-feet units; about 10 were stretched across a natural gap, the fence extended outward with a tule rope that turned the animals. Nets were privately owned. Rabbit nets were about 4 feet high and extended as much as 300 feet. Grasshoppers were also driven into a concentrated area and the grass fired. Deer and elk were also taken by running them down in relays. Bears, especially grizzly bears, were sought for their pelts. The killing required the work of specialists in the difficult art.

Boys were taught to hunt and given progressively better bows as their skill improved. A boy was prohibited from touching his first kill of any one animal; it was taken by an older person to the hunter's family for them to eat. Hunting restrictions were placed on a man whose wife was pregnant or menstruating.

Fish were taken by hand, with nets, by means of fish poisons in stagnant pools, with traps, and (on the Sacramento River where salmon were important) in weirs and with harpoons.

At least eight varieties of acorn were consumed. Some oak trees were private property. Diverse seeds and tubers were gathered by women, usually working in groups. They used a seed beater to dislodge ripe seeds into their baskets. Clover was important as a green because it provided the first fresh food in the spring. The diet was supplemented with various wild fruits and berries, pine nuts, and mushrooms. A kind of red clay was mixed with oat seeds or acorn meal and baked as bread; salt was obtained from stream banks in the spring. Tobacco was used if discovered wild; it was not cultivated.

Technology

The tools and weapons of the Nomlaki include: sinew-backed bow of imported yew or local juniper, a two-piece arrow with flint or obsidian point, flint or obsidian-bladed spear, elkhide armor, harpoon, stone and bone knives, a knobbed throwing stick of California mahogany, slings, nets of various kinds, and a wide variety of snares and deadfalls.

The Nomlaki made no pottery. In basketry, they occasionally made twined forms but more frequently three-rod coiled forms. These baskets were used for cooking, eating, storage, carrying, and diverse purposes. Rabbit-skin blankets were woven, and cradleboards that gave support to the infant's buttocks but left the legs free were also used. Clothing was chiefly of hide, men wearing a breechcloth, women skirts of decorated deerskin. Inner bark was also used for clothing. Elkhide sandals, but not moccasins, were worn.

Structures

The village headman had a house with centerpost (ʔelkel) that served not only as his residence but also as men's house and focal point of village life. Other houses (łačikel) were constructed of bent saplings tied with vine and thatched. The menstrual hut was constructed in the same manner. Woven granaries were also used. A much larger structure, the dance house (łut) is a semisubterranean, multipost structure with sod roof. In postcontact times it was associated with the introduced Ghost Dance cult, but aboriginally a smaller one had been used for the secret society initiation.

Synonymy

The linguistic family here called Wintuan was customarily called Wintun (or Wintoon) in the past, with three divisions labeled Northern Wintun, Central Wintun, and Southern Wintun. Kroeber (1932a:253) suggested that more convenient designations could be based on the word for 'person' in the three languages, yielding respectively Wintu, Wintun, and Patwin. He then sometimes referred to the Nomlaki as "proper Wintun" and pointed out that for Barrett (1908) they were the "Northerly Wintun." When the Nomlaki are called Wintun or Central Wintun, then their subdivisions may be labeled Hill and River Wintun rather than Hill and River Nomlaki (Kroeber 1932a:253, 256, 355; Goldschmidt 1951a:314). The term Nomlaki derives from the River Nomlaki name nomlaka 'west language', referring to those Hill Nomlaki on Thomes Creek whose own name for themselves was nomkewel 'west people'. These plus the neighboring waltoykewel were the main components of the "Nomlaki" of the Round Valley Reservation, who had been removed from the Nome Lackee

Dept. of Anthr., U. of Calif., Berkeley.

Fig. 5. Performer at a Big Head Dance (of Bole-Maru) representing the Big Head, a male spirit. He wears a skirt of frayed willow bark, flicker quill headbands, and a headdress of wands tipped with California poppies while carrying musical sticks made of elder. Photograph by C. Hart Merriam, Grindstone Rancheria, May 1923. Figs. 6-7 were taken at the same occasion.

Dept. of Anthr., U. of Calif., Berkeley.

Fig. 6. Performer dressed as a female spirit, wearing a headdress with a red cloth visor and flicker quill bands behind, a cloth skirt and belt, and white feather collar.

Dept. of Anthr., U. of Calif., Berkeley.

Fig. 7. Two performers near the flag pole, wearing frayed willowbark skirts and white feather headdresses and carrying music sticks.

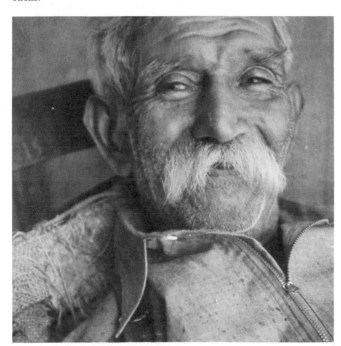

Fig. 8. Jeff Jones. Photograph by Walter Goldschmidt, 1938.

Reservation (Kroeber 1932a:265; Goldschmidt 1951a:308-311). From this usage, the term Nomlaki was extended first to refer to all those groups here called Hill Nomlaki (Hodge 1907-1910, 2:79; Goldschmidt 1951a:303, 314), and then, as here, to refer to the speakers of all dialects of Central Wintun, both Hill and River. Alternative spellings include Noamlaki, Nomee Lacks, Nome Lackees, Numleki (Hodge 1907-1910, 2:79), and Nomalackie (Round Valley Cultural Project 1974). Other names for the Nomlaki include Tehama, from the non-Indian town on the Sacramento River (Hodge 1907-1910, 2:79; Goldschmidt 1951a:243), and Titkaieno'm, the Yuki name for them (Kroeber 1925:355).

Sources

The Nomlaki have been described in detail in a single monograph (Goldschmidt 1951a:303-443), based on research in 1936. In this work, Goldschmidt sought to reconstruct aboriginal culture rather than to understand the social behavior of the surviving remnant, though for some matters, notably religious sentiment, he recorded current behavior. Archeological investigations in the area (Treganza and Heickson 1969) have confirmed those aspects of the reconstructed culture that are amenable to archeological preservation. This is somewhat remarkable in that the data were obtained from informants who had not themselves participated in aboriginal culture and Goldschmidt (1971:3) credits this to the quality of mind of his chief informant, Jeff Jones (fig. 8). Kroeber (1932a) devoted a few pages to the Central Wintun (Nomlaki) in his study of the Patwin. Data on the Nomlaki are included in general works such as Kroeber (1925), Gifford's (1922) study of kinship, Curtin (1898), Powers (1877), and Pickering (1848).

Patwin

PATTI J. JOHNSON

Language, Territory, and Environment

Patwin ('păt₁wĭn) is the native word *patwin* 'people' and was used by several tribelets in reference to themselves. It does not denote a political unity. The term was suggested initially by Powers (1877:218) as a convenient name for those contiguous groups who displayed a close linguistic and cultural resemblance but who were distinguishable from those Wintuans inhabiting the northern half of the western valley. Subsequent linguistic analyses resulted in the further division of Wintuan into Central (Nomlaki) and Northern (Wintu) Wintuan with the Patwin remaining distinct as Southern Wintuan. Wintuan speakers are classified as belonging to the Penutian language family along with the Miwok, Maidu, Costanoan, Yokuts, and presumably other groups.*

At one time Patwin occupied the southern portion of the Sacramento River Valley to the west of the river, from the town of Princeton south to San Pablo and Suisun bays (fig. 1). They were bounded on the east by Nisenan and Konkow, on the north by Nomlaki, on the south by Costanoan and Plains Miwok, and on the west by Yuki, Wappo, Lake Miwok, and Pomoans. In actuality the region so delimited was occupied by many groups usually called tribes in the earlier literature and tribelets in the later. The Patwin were also divided among speakers of many different dialects, for example, Kabalmem, Cache Creek, Cortina, Tebti (Hill Patwin); Colusa and Grimes (River Patwin); Knight's Landing and Suisun (Whistler 1976).

General territorial limits drawn by various investigators for the Patwin are essentially similar. The greatest differences lie along the eastern and southern boundaries and internally with the classification into linguistic or cultural units. Gibbs (1853b) differentiated numerous tribes from Suisun Bay to Clear Lake on the basis of language, but only the Copéh of Putah Creek from which he had collected a vocabulary (Merriam 1929) is clearly a Patwin group. Powers (1877:218) located Patwin in the lower hills of the eastern Coast Range mountain slope

* Italicized Patwin words in this article have been spelled phonemically by Kenneth Whistler. The phoneme inventory is as follows: consonants *p, t, č, k, ʔ, pʰ, tʰ, čʰ, kʰ, p̣, ṭ, c̣, Ḳ, b, d, s, h, ł, Ẋ̣, w, l, r, y, m, n;* vowels *i, e, a, o, u,* plus the corresponding long vowels, indicated by a raised dot. The tentative orthography in Broadbent and Pitkin (1964:21) lacks *čʰ* and writes the voiceless lateral *ł,* which tends to be nondistinctively affricated, as λ.

(Long, Indian, Bear, Capay, Cortina, and Napa valleys were some of the more populous), both sides of the Sacramento River several miles below Stony Creek south to just above the mouth of the Feather River, and on the west side of the Sacramento only from the Feather River south to Suisun Bay. Parts of upper Napa Valley and Coyote and Pope valleys were ascribed to other groups as were the headwaters of Cache and Putah creeks. From informants' claims of particular hills and streams, Barrett (1908) was able to more carefully delineate the western extent of the Pomoans, Yuki, Lake Miwok, and Patwin. There is general agreement that Patwin occupied a strip several miles wide along the east bank of the lower

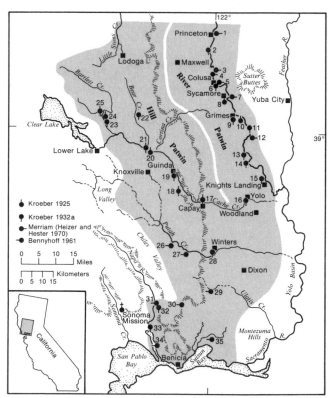

Fig. 1. Tribal territory and villages. 1, Bo'-do; 2, Katsil (*kačʰil*); 3, Si'-ko-pe; 4, Til-til; 5, Dok'-dok; 6, Koru; 7, No'pah; 8, Gapa; 9, P'ălo; 10, Nawidihu; 11, Kusêmpu; 12, Koh'pah de'-he; 13, unknown; 14, unknown; 15, Yo'doi; 16, Churup; 17, Moso; 18, Kisi; 19, Imil; 20, Lopa; 21, Tebti; 22, Sukui; 23, Ho'lokomi; 24, Tokti; 25, Tebti; 26, Chemocu; 27, Putato; 28, Liwai; 29, Ululato; 30, Soneto; 31, Napato; 32, Tulukai; 33, Suskol; 34, Aguasto; 35, Tolenas. Village names after Kroeber 1925; Kroeber 1932a; Merriam (Heizer and Hester 1970); Bennyhoff 1961.

Sacramento River. At Gray's Bend, above the juncture of the Feather River with the Sacramento, the boundary then extends to the west bank and from there proceeds in a southwesterly direction. Excluded from Patwin ownership are the Sutter Buttes on the northeast periphery and the Montezuma Hills on the southern extremity. Both are considered as unclaimed and utilized by more than one group. Sonoma Valley was once included under Patwin dominance but upon reexamination of linguistic evidence is assigned to the Coast Miwok (Beeler 1954; Kroeber 1957b). From time to time portions of the eastern and southern territorial limits have been called into question (Kroeber 1957b; Heizer 1966; Bennyhoff 1961).

From north to south Patwin territory extended 90 miles, and from east to west 40 miles. It can be divided into three physiographic regions from east to west: both banks of the Sacramento River and its attendant dense tree, vine, and brush vegetation interspersed with great tule marshes; flat open grassland plains with occasional oak groves; and the lower hills of the eastern Coast Range mountain slope rising to an elevation of 1,400 feet. Most of the population was concentrated along the river in large villages. Because much of the plains were submerged from floodwaters in winter and quite dry in summer, occupation of this region was sparse and seasonal. Tribelets in the hills lived in the numerous intermontane valleys, particularly along the drainages of Cache and Putah creeks (Powers 1874a; Koreber 1932a).

History

Some of the earliest historic records begin with the Spanish mission registers of baptisms, marriages, and deaths of Indian neophytes. At least by 1800, neophytes were taken from the Patwin settlement of Aguastos in the south-central area and probably from other villages by emissaries of Mission Dolores (San Francisco de Asís). Mission San José, established in 1797, along with Mission Dolores actively proselytized Patwin from the southern villages of Napato, Malaca, Suisun, Ululatos, Soneto, Libayto, Tolenas, Putato, Chemocu, and Topayto (Bennyhoff 1961). Mission Sonoma (San Francisco Solano), built in 1823 near the southwestern periphery of Patwin territory, also baptized neophytes until secularization of all missions in 1832–1836. Statements in early reports by explorers such as Father Abella in 1811 and Luis Arguello in 1821 (Cook 1960) suggest that mission influence was confined chiefly to the southern valleys and lowlands.

While California was still under Mexican dominance, Mariano G. Vallejo assumed military authority over Sonoma Mission and its environs, including the Indians residing there. He maintained a friendly relationship with them while they in return provided a labor force and served as a visible deterrent to others of the region who actively resented the foreign intrusions. Upon numerous occasions Vallejo sent both Indian and Mexican troops against those Indian marauders who engaged in theft of livestock or instigated trouble among the people. Chief Solano, a Patwin of considerable diplomatic skill (Lothrop 1932; Peterson 1957), became Vallejo's friend and lieutenant, often serving as his spokesman when problems arose. George C. Yount, an American who had obtained a large land grant from the Mexican government, also established himself in Napa Valley in 1832. Under Vallejo's encouragement he too formed alliances with many of the Indians about him and enlisted their aid against those who stole or promoted violence. The military atmosphere enforced by Vallejo and supported by others continued to prevail toward the termination of Mexican rule but was eroded as more and more settlers filled the region. During the 1830s and 1840s the length and breadth of Patwin territory was rapidly overtaken by both Mexicans and Americans, who under the lenient policies of the Mexican government had secured title to substantial portions of land, and by others laying claim to the region's natural resources. The Vaca and Pena families had settled on the lower part of Putah Creek in 1842, William Gordon had taken residence on Cache Creek in 1843, Gen. J. Bidwell had acquired land in the northern area in Colusa County in 1843, John and William Wolfskill had established themselves on Putah Creek in 1840–1843, Col. J.B. Chiles had settled Chiles Valley in the southern hill region in 1844, and Thomas O. Larkin held land in Colusa County by 1846 (Menefee 1873; L. Palmer 1881; J.H. Rogers 1891).

At the same time explorers such as Jedediah Smith in 1830 (Larkey 1969), John Work (1945) in 1832–1833, and Lt. George Derby in 1849 (Farquhar 1932) traversed the western Sacramento Valley and sought either to expand their knowledge of the region's potential fur resources or to determine the area's suitability for military outposts and settlement. Some approached from the north as did Work, an Englishman employed by the Hudson's Bay Company, who proceeded southward along the Sacramento River with a party of about 100 persons. Others such as the American Lieutenant Derby came from the San Francisco Bay vicinity and traveled to the east and north.

The Sacramento Valley and lower parts of the delta facing Suisun and Napa valleys received the burden of settlement while inroads into the upland reaches were less frequent and tended to occur after the late 1840s. During the 1850s and 1860s, as pressure from incoming Euro-Americans continued to increase with great rapidity, most of the Patwin who had survived the ravages of epidemics and conflict eventually either became partly assimilated into the White culture by working as laborers for the ranches or were placed upon small reservations established by the United States government.

Population

Observations of explorers and settlers (Work 1945; Bidwell in J.H. Rogers 1891; Yount in Camp 1923), mission records (Merriam 1955; Bennyhoff 1961), census reports, and ethnographic data (Kroeber 1925, 1932a) provide some clues to total population but are still quite incomplete. Nevertheless, such meager information has not obscured recording of the apparent and drastic decline experienced by the Patwin from the point of Euro-American contact onward (table 1). Missionization, casualties from military forays, and raids perpetuated by settlers in retribution for theft of livestock and for the acquisition of laborers to work the farms and ranches made significant inroads on the native population. The most dramatic reductions resulted from the malarial epidemic of 1833 and the smallpox epidemic of 1837. Cook (1955a), who has most carefully chronicled this period, estimates a decrease of up to 75 percent directly attributable to these diseases. The downward trend in population continued, and by 1923–1924 Kroeber could not find any Patwin surviving in the entire southern half of the region. Most of the few remaining were residing in or around only four communities in the Cortina and Colusa vicinities. From government rolls Kroeber and Heizer (1970) were able to trace only three to seven persons who were of one-quarter or more Patwin descent living in the Napa Valley in 1955. As of 1972 the Bureau of Indian Affairs census listed only 11 Patwins for the entire territory. All but three of the reservations (Colusa, Cortina, and Rumsey rancherias) have been terminated;

those three were described as "Wintun" and were mostly occupied by descendants of other groups.

External Relations

Historically there was a friendly exchange between the Patwin of Long Valley and the Southeastern Pomo. Long Valley Patwin could freely visit Clear Lake to fish or hunt with or without permission, depending on the particular Pomo tribelet. It was necessary to request permission when acorns or grass seeds were sought. Likewise these Pomoans would obtain permission to gather seeds in Long Valley area. Obsidian was taken from Big Borax Lake in Southeastern Pomo territory whenever the Patwin wished. Both groups in this region intermarried frequently (Gifford 1923:78–80). Northeastern Pomo on Stony Creek knew and had names for Patwin on Little Stony Creek, around the modern community of Sites. They would visit the River Patwin but only on special occasions. River Patwin did not reciprocate (Kroeber 1932a:364). Both the Lake Miwok (Kroeber 1932a) and the Wappo (Driver 1936) were closer culturally to Pomoans than to Patwin, and it may be inferred that they had less communication with Patwins. Kroeber has indicated that Valley Maidu and Patwin had considerable contact. Both Kroeber (1929) and Merriam (Heizer and Hester 1970) collected River Patwin names of villages on the west bank of the Sacramento from Nisenan informants. Kroeber's informant also knew the names of the major Patwin villages on Cache and Putah creeks and west to Napa Valley.

Many items were traded among themselves and with other tribes. Bows were a common item of exchange; Cortina people got them both from the Southeastern Pomo and from the Nomlaki to the north. At times they were traded to the Wappo. Obsidian was either brought in or gone after to the west and east. Originally, finished shell beads were traded in from the coast but later in the historic period Patwin also made them and traded in whole shells for that purpose. Flicker headbands and red woodpecker scalp belts were exchanged for beads. The River Patwin gave cordage for netting to the Hill Patwin in trade for shell beads. Magnesite beads were obtained by Hill Patwin from Pomoans. Items such as salmon, river otter pelts, and game animals were also given to the Nomlaki, who reciprocated with beads. Salt was traded to the Patwin by Pomoans (Davis 1961).

Not all relationships among Patwin tribelets and with other tribes were friendly, as Menefee (1873) noted for the Napa Valley groups. Disputes were acted upon in the manner of feuds. Provocations for battle included poaching, the most common offense, and death attributed to poisoning. Retaliation might be against the individual or group caught poaching at the time, by organized battles or by surprise attack on a village. In battles, one line of men armed with spears and bows faced an opposing line

Table 1. Population

Date	Population	Group	Source
precontact	12,500	Wintu, Nomlaki, Patwin	Kroeber 1932a
precontact	3,500	River Patwin, Valley Nisenan	Cook 1955a
1803–1827	527	Southern Patwin, 10 villages	Merriam 1955, 1970
pre-1833	15,000	River Patwin, Valley Nisenan	Cook 1955a
after 1833–1837	4,500	Wappo, Miwok, Patwin	Cook 1956:126
1843	3,000	Wappo, Miwok, Patwin	Cook 1956:126
1905–1906	185	Patwin	Kelsey 1971
1910	1,000	Wintu, Nomlaki, Patwin	Kroeber 1925:357, 883
1923–1924	200	Patwin	Kroeber 1932a
1972	11	Patwin	U.S. Bureau of Indian Affairs

from the enemy village. Each side shot arrows and hurled spears at the other. The chiefs were present but did not participate in the fighting. In an evenly matched battle the chiefs would eventually call a halt by walking between the lines and indicating the dispute was over. Peace was arranged by an exchange of material goods between the two sides. In the hill region an elk hide or armor constructed of vertical rods held together with cord was sometimes worn. Warfare seemed to be generally more organized in the hills. There are several recorded feuds for both the Hill and River people: Cortina Valley Patwin against a Pomoan group, and then again against some of the River Patwin, the Long Valley people against those of Cache Creek, Nisenan against River Patwin, and various River Patwin villages against one another (Kroeber 1932a).

Culture

Religion

• RITUAL One of the more distinctive aspects of Patwin culture was the Kuksu cult system, found elsewhere through much of north central California. Kroeber (1932a, 1939a) thought the cult may have originated with the Patwin because of its greater elaboration there; however, Bennyhoff (1961:328) reasoned that the addition of traits came from outside the area and was temporally a rather late manifestation. A main feature of the cult was the occurrence of one or more secret societies, each with its own series of dances and rituals. Membership was by initiation; among Patwin, boys from 8 to 16 years old were ritually captured, shot or speared, then isolated from the rest of the community for a short length of time during which they received instruction on the secret medicines and knowledge of the society. As noninitiates women and young children generally were not allowed to become members; an exception was women belonging to higher-status families. Among some Patwin groups women often were allowed to witness the ceremonies (Loeb 1933:208). Besides a single Pomoan group living adjacent to the Patwin and no doubt influenced by them, the Patwin were unique in possessing three secret societies. In the central California cult system, almost all groups possessed the Kuksu but only the Patwin also had both the ghost and Hesi types (Kroeber 1932a:313). The purposes of each society were slightly different although overlapping. The ghost type, called *way saltu* 'northern spirits', stressed initiating, the Kuksu emphasized curing and shamanistic functions, and the Hesi (*hesi*) elaborated on ceremonial dancing. With the River Patwin, the ceremonial cycle would begin in the fall and end in the spring with the Hesi, but among the upland Hill Patwin the Kuksu was held in the summer, as among the Pomoans, with whom they shared other ceremonial traits (Loeb 1933:214). Calling the societies to action depended upon when boys were ready to be initiated and not upon any fixed seasonal or sequential schedule.

To become a member of any of the societies a boy would be sponsored by a close relative, usually his father or maternal uncle. It was desirable though not required to belong. Membership in each society was not mutually exclusive and an adult who belonged to all three carried greater prestige. Details of each cult varied from area to area, and even from village to village, but they did have several salient features—a series of dances taking place in a special dance house, a ceremonial director, dance performers versed in the ritual who were spirit impersonators, dance regalia (headdresses of feathers and sticks, feather cloaks, bodies painted with charcoal, clay, ocher), clapper sticks or other instruments, and a log foot drum in the floor of the dance house for sound accompaniment. Onlookers would assemble for the ceremony of three days and four nights duration. There were assigned seating arrangements in the dance house for the performers and onlookers. Often the ceremony would terminate with the dancer in a state of frenzy, and with each series of dances there went a feeling of danger to the performers, in the spiritual sense. In the Hesi society there were four grades of membership based on the amount of experience and knowledge of rituals and medicines. Both the Kuksu and Hesi ceremonies were replaced or modified considerably by the adoption of a more recent variation of the Ghost Dance of 1870, the Bole (*bo·le* 'narrative; dream recited in ceremony'). Some earlier features were retained, such as the dance house, foot drum, and Moki (*mo·ki*) dancer (spirit impersonator performed by Hesi director). There were some similarities to the Ghost Dance; for example, dreams served as a vehicle for communication with spirit beings (Kroeber 1932a:308–309). In 1906 Barrett (1919a) witnessed and described a Hesi ceremony that had overtones of the Bole.

• SHAMANS Certain rituals within the cult system were of a curative benefit; however, most curing was done by shamans who acquired their power from a paternal kinsman. As with ritual knowledge, a doctor purchased his medicines and information rather than obtaining them by dreaming, although among some Hill Patwin dreaming did occur. When someone became ill a shaman was called in to diagnose and cure the disease. He would feel and press upon the patient, then obtain the appropriate medicine and administer it. At times the shaman would suck an offending object—string, for example, or often blood from cuts on the temple—but usually medicine rather than sucking was used. The shaman would stay until the patient claimed to be feeling better. A shaman was well paid for his services. If he gained a reputation for failing, he was simply no longer called but would be under suspicion as a sorcerer. A shaman was usually the only one who would handle ancient charmstones (ground stone artifacts, remnants of an earlier culture period) (Kroeber 1932a).

Political Organization

The maximum political unit was the tribelet, consisting of one primary and several satellite villages, with a definite sense of territoriality and autonomy. Each tribelet differed slightly from the next in cultural details. Dialectic boundaries were not equivalent and might encompass several tribelets. Kroeber (1932a) defined seven tribelet centers for Colusa Patwin, nine for the Grimes and two for the Knights Landing dialects. There were at least 16 Hill Patwin centers. This number represents recollections from informants' memories in 1923 and is only a partial distribution. The territory exploited by each tribelet was vaguely defined but was sometimes bounded by the limits of a small drainage (Kroeber 1932a). None of the ethnographers provides actual examples of districts, tracts, or resource ownership as Gifford (1923) has recorded for the Eastern and Southeastern Pomo, although such possession did occur.

Within the tribelet were several political and social distinctions. Each village had a chief who directed village activities. That position was the highest rank attainable and was determined by inheritance from father to son, if possible. A chief would be chosen from those eligible by the village elders on the basis of popularity and ability, but once named he enjoyed decision-making powers almost unrestricted except by concerted pressure from the villagers. His primary function was that of administrator in economic and ceremonial activities. He knew the village ownership of tree groves and fishing and hunting areas and decided when, where, and how the distribution of meat should proceed. He could require an individual family to gather or hunt a particular item such as deer. The chief presided over ceremonies, deciding when and where they should be held and which villages should be invited.

Social Organization

Gifford's (1918) analysis of Patwin kinship is the most extensive and is concerned with classification through examination of kin terms. Numerous maps are offered as graphic demonstration of the relationships with other California tribes. As Kroeber (1917) has shown, Patwin kin terms tend to merge considerably; the same term is applied to several members of the family even though they differed in age, sex, generation, and genealogical distance. This is at variance with other Wintuan, Miwok, and Pomoan groups whose kin systems reflect greater emphasis on identifying specific relationships with specific terms. There appeared to be little direct correlation of the kinship system with particular forms of marriage, descent, or personal relationships according to Kroeber (1917). It should be kept in mind that his conclusions were based on rather incomplete data. Neither Gifford

nor Kroeber could find indications of clans, moieties, or other such institutions. Marriage to the maternal cross-cousin (mother's brother's daughter) was favored but not restricted to that relationship. A taboo prohibiting speaking to one's mother-in-law was in effect for two or three years after marriage and was observed by both sexes.

As reported by McKern (1922) there were three social groupings based upon familial relationships: the paternal family, the family social group, and the household. The consanguineal paternal family was formed by a man, his children, brothers and sisters, brother's children, and so on. Residence upon marriage was matrilocal until the man acquired enough wealth to establish his own household. Until that time he was subject to the authority of the family headman. Thus the family social groups included the paternal family along with married sisters and other women whose husbands had not yet gained independent households. The family head had undisputed authority over this social group even extending to his sons once they had effected separation from their wives' people. Since unilocal residence was not a feature of either the paternal family or the family social group, the segment that did reside under one roof was the household. It included a husband and wife, unmarried sons and daughters, married daughters and their husbands and children.

Inheritance upon the death of an individual by his successors could include either personal or family properties and otherwise followed the paternal line of descent. Personal items were buried with the deceased unless they were publicly willed to a successor prior to the donor's demise. Upon the death of the headman, family possessions passed to the descendant taking his place over the family. The family as a group would retain use of these, since a family head simply functioned as an executor. Personal names were also inherited, but by the family rather than the individual. Each family also had certain medicines and rituals that were inheritable only on that level.

McKern (1922) has identified a system of "functional families" wherein certain families within a village possessed special knowledge in a ceremonial, occupational, shamanistic, or official capacity. Each such family had secret medicines, charms, and rituals that were supposed to render it more successful in its acknowledged function. Technically there was no difference in the methods employed in the actual activities from those used by nonspecialist families. Thus, for example, the salmon-fishing family used the same fishing methods as any other family; however, they were considered to have an advantage in catching salmon. They also might elect not to use their knowledge upon every occasion. Functional families were not professionals to be employed for their special skill. Every family more or less performed the necessary activities for survival and social interrelationships. Some functions were performed by the women, such as making certain types of baskets, but regardless of who did the work, the entire family was known by the name signifying their particular activity. Such specialist families carried a slightly greater prestige. Access to a family's store of secret medicines and charms was transmitted through the paternal line; however, if there was no close living relative to accept and carry on, or if the relative was unsuitable, a nonrelative could be adopted into the family to insure continuance of the specialty. Such adoptions were fully acceptable to other community members. McKern surmised that an individual could belong to more than one functional family and that probably not every village would have representatives of all families. His informants were able to provide names for 20 different functions, among them being families whose specialties were trapping ducks, making foot drums, making salt, performing certain dance ceremonies or certain shamanistic practices. There might be more than one family of the same function in a village. Shamanistic families, for example, would treat the same diseases but each had its own set of rituals and charms.

Subsistence

Hunting and fishing were done by individuals or small groups. Fish were caught by one of several types of nets, which might be attached to a single pole or to two poles that were used to guide the nets. At least two fish weirs were constructed across part of the Sacramento River, one at the village of Koru (at Colusa) and one at Saka (below Grimes). These were constructed of posts and willow sticks driven into the river bottom, which was only a few feet deep at that point. The line they formed was broken in several places by gates purposely left. Salmon or sturgeon were collected into pens behind the gates and caught with a net. A smaller salmon, perch, chub, sucker, hardhead, pike, trout, and probably steelhead were also caught by nets. Mussels were taken from the river bed. Private ownership of some fishing places required that an outsider obtain permission from the owner to fish. Many other animals were taken—tule elk, deer, antelope, bear; ducks, geese, quail, and other birds; turtles and other small animals. Either deer were shot by one man or a small group of men, one wearing a deer head decoy, or they were caught with a net. Brown bear was shot or speared. Ducks, mud hen, geese, and quail were also netted by various means. When taken, birds of prey were usually shot; their feathers were important in ceremonial regalia. Duck decoys were also used.

Turtles were roasted. Salmon and deer meat were often preserved by sun-drying, after which they were pulverized to a meal and stored for future use.

Some animals were not used as food—dogs, coyotes, some birds of prey, frogs, reptiles, caterpillars, grizzly bears, and predator animals in general. Nevertheless,

Lowie Mus., U. of Calif., Berkeley.
Fig. 2. A.C. Mitchell and wife standing next to frame structure, probably an unfinished sweathouse. Photograph by C. Hart Merriam at Katsil, Aug. 8, 1928.

many were collected, for their skins and feathers provided materials for ceremonial paraphernalia, bedding, containers, and other uses (Kroeber 1932a).

Sunflower, alfilaria, clover, bunchgrass, wild oat, and a yellow flower, all growing on the open plains, provided seeds that were parched or dried, then pounded into a meal. Seed tracts were privately owned by families.

As among many other California cultures a primary staple was the acorn. Two types of valley oak acorns, hill and mountain oak, and live oak (used rarely) were gathered. Oak groves were owned communally by the tribelet. Pulverized acorns were leached by pouring cold water over the meal spread in a sand basin. After processing it was made into soup or bread. For soup, water was added to the meal contained in a basket and heated by the stone-boiling method. The stones were stirred and removed with two oak paddles. Acorn bread was baked in a pit oven dug into the earth and lined with leaves. Buckeye, pine nuts, juniper berries, manzanita berries, blackberries, wild grapes, Brodiaea bulbs, and, in the valley, tule roots, were some of the plant foods collected at various times of the year. Bulbs were either baked or boiled; berries were eaten raw, dried and pulverized, or boiled. A complete list of plant foods was never obtained, but if other California groups can serve as an example, there were probably few edible plants that were not utilized. Each village had its own locations for these food sources, and the village chief was in charge of assigning particular families to each collecting area. Salt was scraped off rocks (in the Cortina region) or it was obtained by burning a grass found in the plains. Sometimes it was bought from the Northeastern Pomo. Tobacco leaves were dried and smoked. Tobacco was collected along the river; it was not cultivated (Powers 1874a; Kroeber 1932a).

355

Technology

Both woven rabbitskin and leather robes were constructed. Feathers were used on ceremonial headdresses (woodpecker, raven) and on highly prized belts (red woodpecker scalps) made only by certain families (McKern 1922). Netting and cordage of wild hemp (*Apocynum cannabinum*), grapevine, and milkweed (*Asclepias* sp.) fibers were important, particularly in hunting and fishing. Long burial ropes of hemp were wrapped around the body upon a person's death (fig. 3). River Patwin used temporary containers of tule. Cured animal hides served as bedding and burial robes (bear), women's skirts (deer), floor mats (deer), and tobacco sacks (fox, coyote, or wolf).

Coiled or twined basketry containers (fig. 4) were extremely important items for almost all aspects of food collection, preparation, serving, and storage; for baby carriers; and for burial accompaniment. Based on examination of 40 documented specimens from the C. Hart Merriam Collection, Dawson (1972) has identified among the coiled specimens a mush boiler, a parching or winnowing tray, a mush dipper, a container for small articles, and baskets used for burial accompaniment. All these were constructed on a foundation of three rods. Two finely worked specimens were intended as grave offerings; one is ornamented with feathers and shell beads, the other is an oval type commonly called a "canoe" basket from its shape. The twined baskets include burden baskets for carrying coarse materials, a children's basket for catching fish, a type for gathering or cleaning coarser foods like bulbs, and a mortar hopper. Seed beaters are also reported to have been made. In the construction of coiled specimens Dawson notes that the method of starting a basket was distinct from that of the nearby Pomoans, Wappo, and Yuki. Twined baskets could be worked by at least two techniques—plain twining over one or two warps, or diagonal twining. The foundation for coiled baskets consisted of peeled willow shoots with split sedge or willow roots used as the sewing strand. Designs were incorporated into the body of a basket by replacement of the primary sewing strand with ones that had been blackened by burial in mud or with split redbud shoots that provided a red color. In twined baskets the foundation or warp materials consisted of whole shoots, probably of a willow. The weft strand materials were of a split sedge root or redbud. Some of

Lowie Mus., U. of Calif., Berkeley: 1-230631B.

Fig. 3. Burial rope from Colusa area; 3-ply, made of *Apocynum*. Said to be about 100 years old in 1972. Entire length about 60 m, rope thickness about 1 cm.

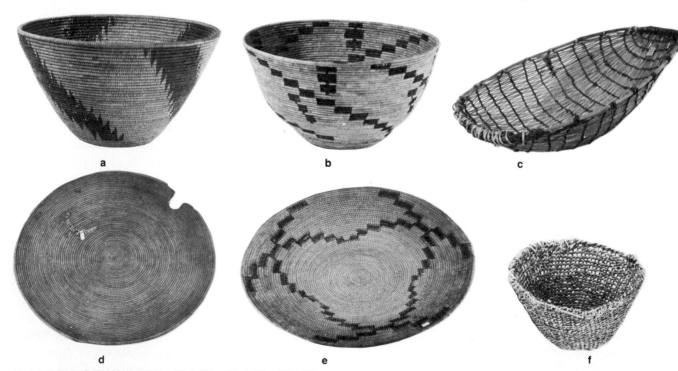

a   b   c

d   e   f

U. of Calif., Davis: C. Hart Merriam Coll.: a, 774; b, 776; c, 775; d, 765; e, 768; f, 777.

Fig. 4. Baskets. a-b, coiled cooking baskets; c, twined scoop tray; d-e, coiled winnowing trays; f, twined children's fish basket. Diameter of a, 35.0 cm, rest same scale; collected 1897–1906.

the basketmaking techniques are similar to those of the Pomoans and Wappo groups to the west of the Patwin; however, other features are more correspondent to those found among the Nomlaki, Valley Maidu, and Sierra Miwok who resided in the Sacramento Valley to the north and east and in the foothills of the Sierra Nevada Mountains.

Bone, wood, and stone were the most commonly used materials for tools. Stone flakes of various sizes served as scrapers and knives in butchering animals and dressing skins. Arrow and drill points and spearheads were shaped from obsidian and occasionally chert. Bows, besides being imported, were made locally of buckeye, juniper, or dogwood. Arrow shafts were of elderberry wood, juniper, or dogwood. Willow (River Patwin) or digger pine (Hill Patwin) provided wood for fire drills.

Tule balsa boats were constructed of large bundles of round tule bound together with grapevine to form crafts up to 20 feet long and 6 feet wide. The prow only was recurved. The craft were propelled by poling. Hill Patwin did not use boats.

To process acorns and other needs, wooden mortars of oak were used in the River area, and flat slabs of stone on which basketry hoppers fit were used in the hills. Bedrock outcroppings with mortar pits were used in the hills. The pestle was an elongated stream cobble, rarely shaped. Pooewin (southern Patwin) according to Merriam (1966–1967, 3:267) used a long pestle for pounding acorns, a short one for pulverizing meat.

Mussel shells were used as knives to cut fish and other meats into strips. Bone awls were used in the construction of basketry. Fish were speared with bone harpoons in the River area (Cook and Treganza 1947). Digging sticks of wood were utilized for recovering bulbs and tubers and for loosening earth in the construction of houses and grave pits.

Life Cycle

Information on the life cycle of the individual is fragmentary. It is reported that if twins were born both were allowed to live. At the onset of puberty a River Patwin girl would not be allowed to eat meat or fat and she would be secluded for four days. In some areas a dance was performed to acknowledge the event. For boys, sometimes there was an initiation into a secret society associated with the Kuksu cult system. For marriage, the parents served as go-betweens. A bride price of shell beads and other items was paid to the bride's parents. Patwin were usually monogamous. After a woman had given birth she underwent the same meat and fat taboo that she had observed at puberty except that it lasted for a month. Her husband also observed a meat taboo and could eat only fish. The couvade was practiced (Kroeber 1932a:271). Upon the death of her husband, a widow would blacken her face and cut her hair. She remained in this state for about one year. Infanticide was sometimes practiced when the mother died (Powers 1874a:545). The dead were buried; normally only people killed away from home were cremated. According to a Hill Patwin informant, the River people set a corpse upright, then pushed the head down, broke the back, wrapped the body in a skin, and put it in the grave. Cemeteries were usually at one end of the community. Property was buried with the dead in large quantities (probably a very recent manifestation), and in some areas it was burned near the grave. Those in contact with the Pomoans and near the San Francisco Bay did practice cremation.

Structures

Structures are the most completely described aspect of material culture. McKern (1923) recorded in detail construction methods of the four types of permanent habitation occurring in a village. The dwelling or family house could be placed anywhere, the ceremonial dance house (fig. 5) was built at a short distance to the north or south end of the village, the sudatory (fig. 6) was positioned to the east or west of the dance house, and the menstrual hut was placed on the edge of the village farthest from the dance house. All these were earth-covered, semisubterranean structures with an elliptical (River Patwin) or

C. Hart Merriam Coll., Dept. of Anthr., U. of Calif., Berkeley.
Fig. 5. Ceremonial house at Cortena Creek. Photograph by C. Hart Merriam, June 1903.

Fig. 6. Sweathouse at Katsil made and used by Joe Mitchell. Photograph by C. Hart Merriam, July 13, 1930. Dome of house retouched.

circular (Hill Patwin) form (Kroeber 1932a). All except the family dwelling were built with the assistance of everyone in the village. Family houses were built by one's paternal relatives. Materials were gathered beforehand. Digging sticks were used to loosen the earth, which was then carried away in old baskets. Earth for covering the outside was brought from outside the village while that from the pit was banked upon the outside of the rim. With everything and everyone assembled, the project might be completed in a single day. Photographs taken by Merriam and early sketches by H.B. Brown of some of these structures at Colusa have been published (Heizer 1966).

Clothing and Adornment

Men went without any covering; women wore skirts or aprons (fig. 7) of tule or shredded bark (River Patwin) or of deerskin (Hill Patwin). Rabbitskin blankets were sometimes worn but found greater favor as bedding. No hats or foot coverings were worn. Men had long hair coiled on top of the head fastened with a straight bone hairpin. They sometimes wore hair nets.

Music and Games

A clapper stick of elderberry was used in ceremonies. The flute, an elderberry tube with four holes, was played during idle times. A whistle was made but undescribed. The foot drum used in dances was usually a sycamore log, 8 to 10 feet long, split lengthwise and hollowed.

The grass game found widely over California was also known to the Patwin. Women's games included dice, shinny, and a type of ring and pin (Kroeber 1932a).

Mythology

The most complete information on mythology was collected by Kroeber (1932a:303–308), who recorded 12 tales, including eight from the River group and four from the Hill Patwin. In the origin myths both Ketit (*kati·t* 'peregrine falcon') and Sede-Tsiak (*sedew čiyak* 'Old Man Coyote') were important figures in the creation of people. The other myths are about anthropomorphized animals such as condor, grizzly bear, elk, antelope, and rattlesnake and their interactions with humans. There are three versions of the origin of the Hesi ceremonials.

Synonymy

The name Patwin (*patwin* 'people') was introduced by Powers (1874a:542) in the spelling Patweens, later written phonetically as Pat-wīn′ (Powers 1877:218). Synonymous names are Copéh (Gibbs 1853c:421), Southern Wintun (Kroeber 1932a:256), Southerly Wintun (Barrett

C. Hart Merriam Coll., Dept. of Anthr., U. of Calif., Berkeley.
Fig. 7. Women wearing skirts of skin and aprons. Drawn by H.B. Brown near Colusa on the Sacramento River, 1851-1852.

1908:81). The Nomlaki referred to them as *noymok* 'south people' (Goldschmidt 1951a:316), and the Yuki called the Little Stony Creek Patwin with whom they had contact Ku′mnom or 'salt people' (Kroeber 1932a:370).

Within the territory generally ascribed to the Patwin, numerous village names have been collected and several attempts made to identify larger politico-linguistic divisions. Powers (1877) defined 14 tribes; Merriam mapped 10 tribes, three dialect divisions, and 41 villages along the Sacramento River. Kroeber (1932a) identified 18 River and 16 Hill Patwin tribelet centers and their satellite villages, mostly in the hill region. Powers's "tribes" are linguistic units, Merriam's (1966–1967, 1) are linguistic units with territorial bounds, and Kroeber's are linguistic-political units having a definite (but unmapped) territory. Merriam's three primary dialectic divisions into Patwin, Win, and Pooewin were approximate precursors of Kroeber's cultural-environmental isolates of the southeastern, southwestern, and southern Patwin respectively. These three Kroeber (1932a:256) later reorganized into Hill (southwestern) and River (southeastern and southern) Patwin. In the linguistic classification of Whistler (1976), the dialect clusters of Hill Patwin (Merriam's Win) and River Patwin (Merriam's Patwin dialect) are grouped into a North Patwin language separate from South Patwin (Merriam's Pooewin, properly *puywin* 'east people').

There are many variations in the spelling of village and tribelet names, especially as recorded in the Spanish mission records. Those available in phonemic transcription are as follows (Kenneth Whistler, personal communication 1977): (1) from south to north on the Sacramento River were the South Patwin *yoˑdoy* or *yoˑdol* (Knight's Landing) and *hololum* and the River Patwin *paˑleli, čakidiˑhi, k̓usèmpu, nomačapin*; five tribelets near Grimes: *nowi, k̓odoydiˑhi, loklokmatʰinbe* (*loklok* 'chicken hawk'), *holwa* 'mortar', and *yali*; *kapaya* (Sycamore; on the boundary between Southern and Northern River Patwin); the Colusa complex of *kukuy, koruˑ,* and *i̇atnodiˑhi*; and *kačʰil, waytʰere* 'face the north', *ča,* and *k̓eti* ('mugwort wormwood', at Princeton); (2) in the Little Stony Creek drainage (Kabalmem dialect): *čʰuheˑlmeˑm, ʔeydiˑła* 'gnat village', and *pahka;* (3) Upper Cache Creek (*kapay*): the village of the *loˑlsel* 'tobacco people' (*alimatʰinbe* ?), two villages called *tʰebtʰi* 'confluence', with those the *loˑlsel* called *čʰenpasel* 'downstream people' at the upper of the two, and *kʰuykʰuy* 'sweet'; (4) Cortina hills: *ƛet* (or *ƛetdiˑła* 'ground-squirrel village'), *waykaw,* and *sukuy* ('bear', in Bear valley); (5) Capay valley: *koˑpe* 'root', *siča* (Rumsey), *i̇obi̇obnomeˑm* ('junco spring'; successor village to the preceding), *ʔeˑyadiˑhi* 'manzanita village', *yoˑčadiˑhi* (Tancred), *kisi,* and *moˑso* (Capay); (6) Napa valley: *napa* 'werebear; bear shaman'. Other forms are given in the lists of Powers (1877), Merriam (1955–1970), Kroeber (1932a), Barrett (1908), and Bennyhoff (1950a). Heizer and Hester (1970) have indicated the variable recordings of Merriam's village names, and Bennyhoff discusses some southern Patwin names as copied from mission records.

Sources

The Patwin have been the subject of several major cultural descriptions. Kroeber (1925, 1932a) offers the most complete overview and also includes some explicit detail. His analysis of the Kuksu ceremonial system is particularly developed. Others write more fully of architectural types (McKern 1923), geography (Merriam 1955; Heizer and Hester 1970; Heizer 1966; Bennyhoff 1961; Barrett 1908), and other aspects of the social system (McKern 1922). Merriam also describes several ceremonies as he witnessed them in the early 1900s. Powers's (1877) summary of Patwin culture is brief but one of the earliest such statements. Curtis's (1907–1930, 14:73–96) work is broader in scope; however, it is drawn principally from other published sources. A useful comparative vocabulary list is also included. Some early firsthand observations on Patwin village life were recorded by Arguello (Heizer and Hester 1970), Abella (Cook 1960), and Work (1945).

Several of the more recent studies of Patwin have been brief articles in linguistics (Bright and Bright 1959;

Bright 1960; Shafer 1961; Sawyer 1964a; Hymes 1964a; Callaghan 1964; Broadbent and Pitkin 1964). There are also 14 manuscripts by Paul Radin and one by Angulo on Patwin linguistics (see Freeman 1966). Other unpublished manuscripts include those by Halpern (in Valory 1971:23) and Gifford (in Valory 1971:28). Original Merriam field notes (1908) are housed at the Department of Anthropology, University of California, Berkeley.

Museum collections include the C.H. Merriam Collection of documented baskets at the University of California, Davis, and several other Patwin baskets at the American Museum of Natural History, New York, and Oakland Museum, Oakland, California. Taylor (1860–1863), Simmons (1905), Anonymous (1851, 1852), and articles in other northern California newspapers (see Taylor 1866; Gregory 1937) record incidents of conflict of Patwin with other Indians and Anglo-Americans and other events.

Yana

JERALD JAY JOHNSON

Language, Territory, and Environment

Yana (ˈyänə) is a Hokan language, although it is grammatically quite divergent from other members of that family (Dixon and Kroeber 1913, 1919:104; Sapir 1917:1, 17).*

The Yana inhabited the upper Sacramento River valley and foothills east of the river itself (fig. 1). The neighboring Wintun occupied all the east bank of the river, with the Wintuns' eastern boundary along the edge of the foothills (Merriam 1966-1967, 1:53-55, 76; Goldschmidt 1951a:314-315). Sapir and Spier (1943:240) and Powers (1877:275-279) suggest the Yana may have had villages or at least fishing camps on the Sacramento River. Reading's map of the distribution of the Wintun in 1852 and the observations of Henry Brown in 1851 and 1852 further indicate the boundary was along the eastern edge of the valley (Heizer 1966:52-55). Waterman's (1918:37-41) arbitrary placement of the boundary at the 1,000-feet level and Powell's (1891:135) placement of it 10 to 20 miles east of the Sacramento River undoubtedly reflect the unsettled conditions and the retreat of the Yana farther into the hills as a result of pressure from the numerically superior Wintun prior to historic conduct and from the American settlers after 1847.

Dixon (1905:124, pl. 38) included as far south as Rock Creek in Yana territory, while Waterman's (1918:map 1) southern boundary was farther north near Pine Creek. Dixon's earlier information is probably closer to the original boundary.

On the east, Yana territory encompassed the upper Deer Creek drainage through the upper Battle, Cow, and Montgomery creek drainages. Garth's (1953:map 1) inclusion of the upper reaches of the middle and north forks of Battle Creek and old and south forks of Cow Creek in Atsugewi territory does not seem reasonable; Sapir and Spier's inclusion of the headwaters of those streams in Yana territory is considered more correct.

The separation of the Yana into the Northern, Central, Southern, and Yahi divisions is based primarily on linguistic differences. The many cultural similarities between the Northern and Central divisions and their differences from the Southern and Yahi groups were clearly of secondary importance.

The southern Cascade foothills are remnants of old lava and mud flows. Lassen Peak, which is the dominant landmark on the eastern side of Yana territory, is a large volcano that was active as late as 1917. The basic rock types are primarily andesitic, basaltic, and metavolcanic in origin with some nodules of obsidian around Lassen Peak and as float in Mill Creek canyon (fig. 2).

The elevation ranged from 300 to over 10,000 feet, which provided a variety of floral and faunal resources. Much of the low-lying foothills were covered with several types of oaks and grasses, while the canyon bottoms had dense growths of vegetation. Large game—including deer, bear, antelope, and elk—as available to all the

*The best orthography for the various Yana dialects is that of Sapir and Swadesh (1960:3-5, 18-20), which differs from Handbook usage in that their p, t, k correspond to p^h, t^h, k^h and their b, d, g correspond to p, t, k.

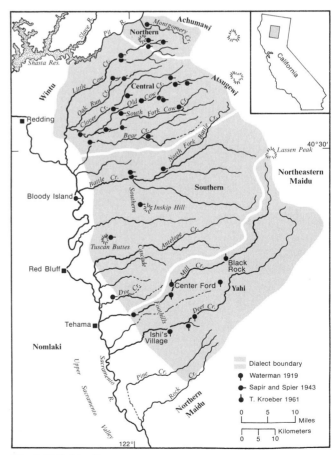

Fig. 1. Tribal territory.

361

Fig. 2. Mill Creek Canyon looking west. Home of the Yahi Yana. Photograph by Jim Johnston, July 1972.

Yana, while salmon entered most of the streams and formed an important food supplement.

The climate is relatively mild over much of the southern Cascade foothills with little snow below 4,000 feet elevation, with an average annual rainfall of approximately 54 inches at Montgomery Creek in the north to 22 inches near Rock Creek in the south. There are few days when the temperature drops below freezing, while in the summer it is often over 100°F.

History

The earliest probable contact by Whites with any of the Yana occurred in 1821. Capt. Luis Arguello, with 55 soldiers and some Indian neophytes, left San Francisco on October 18, 1821. This expedition traveled on the east side of the Sacramento River valley from Red Bluff to the vicinity of Redding and might have encountered the Yana (Bancroft 1886-1890,2:445-447). From 1828 to 1846 the Hudson's Bay Company had trapping parties in California and some of these expeditions probably had contact with the Yana along the Pit River and northeastern Sacramento valley (Leader 1928:62).

In 1837 Ewing Young and Philip Edwards led the first cattle drive from central California to Oregon. The herd followed the east side of the Sacramento valley to Red Bluff and then crossed to the west bank, and it may have been observed by the Yahi (Frank and Chappell 1881:16-17).

It was not until 1845 that the first permanent White residence was constructed in the northern Sacramento valley. This was an adobe built by R.H. Thomas at the present town of Tehama on the west side of the Sacramento River.

The Mexican government granted land to several individuals in the upper Sacramento valley in 1844. These included Bosquejo to Peter Lassen and Rio de los Ber-

rendos, or Primer Cañon, to Job F. Dye (Bancroft 1886-1890, 2:670; McCoy 1926:1). The Lassen and Dye grants were along the east side of the valley and extended into the foothills occupied by the Southern and Yahi Yana. Daniel Sill settled on part of the Lassen grant in 1846.

By 1848 the California-Oregon trail crossed Northern and Central Yana territory. Farther south the Lassen trail came into use in 1848 and traversed Yahi Yana territory on the ridge between Mill and Deer creeks (Dorin 1922:160-162). This trail was used extensively in 1849, but after the length and hardship of the route became known, it was little followed (Bruff 1949:xxxviii). Noble's Road was established in 1851; it followed the ridge between the south fork of Cow Creek and the north fork of Battle Creek and was one of the main immigrant roads into northern California (Dorin 1922:174).

The southern Cascade foothills was one of the regions in California that was least affected by early American mining and settlement. The use of the foothills as grazing lands for livestock and the establishment of hunting cabins brought the Yana into contact with the early settlers. The first major hostility took place when Capt. John Frémont attacked a peaceful gathering of Indians on Bloody Island (at the mouth of Battle Creek) in the Sacramento River in 1846. The village was supposed to belong to the Yana (Giles 1949:200-201). Occasionally the Yana retaliated by murdering a few Whites and as it became more and more difficult to obtain adequate food they began raiding cabins. There are numerous documentations of massacres in which 30 or more Yana were

Yana Population Estimates

Date	Number	Division	Source
Precontact	300-500	Northern	Kroeber 1925:339
	300-500	Central	Kroeber 1925:339
	300-500	Southern	Kroeber 1925:339
	200-300	Yahi	Kroeber 1925:341
1848	1,900	all Yana	Cook 1943b:97
1852	1,800	all Yana	Cook 1943b:97
1884	35	all Yana	Cook 1943b:97
1905-1906	121	Northern, Central	Kelsey 1971:94-95
1928	12	all Yana	Kroeber and Heizer 1970:10, 19
1935	3	Northern, Central	Gifford and Klimek 1939:78
1955	8	all Yana	Cook 1955a
1973	20	all Yana	Johnson 1973

killed (Anderson 1909:78-80; Baumhoff 1955:41-42; Apperson 1971:34, 42-43). After the 1867 massacre of 45 or more individuals on Dye Creek the bodies lay on the ground as there were not enough Yana left to bury them (Waterman 1918:51). In approximately 20 years

Lowie Mus., U. of Calif., Berkeley.
Fig. 3. Ishi, a Yahi Yana, demonstrating a rabbit call, while holding a bow and arrow ready. Photograph by Saxton Pope, 1914.

the Yana had been reduced from 1,900 individuals to probably less than 100 while the deaths of fewer than 50 settlers can be attributed to them with any degree of certainty.

Ishi (fig. 3) was an adult Yahi-Yana man who managed to live in the Southern Cascade Mountains from about 1860 until 1911 when he was discovered at Oroville, California. This remarkable person was able to leave the rocky confines of the foothills and his fear of the Euro-American settlers behind and live from 1911 to 1916 at the University of California Museum of Anthropology, which at that time was in San Francisco. He was the last known survivor of the Yahi, and in the five years he lived at the Museum he provided a wealth of information on the culture of this previously unknown group.

External Relations

The Yana were never on good terms with surrounding peoples for any length of time. The Yahi Yana were the principal enemy of the Northern Maidu, while the Yahi and Wintun were apparently on good terms; Wintun hunted and camped on lower Deer Creek in Yahi territory (Dixon 1905:206; Kroeber 1925:345). The Wintun would not have tolerated Yana settlements on the east bank of the Sacramento River (Waterman 1918:38, 40). The Stillwater and McCloud River Wintu and Achumawi feared and disliked the Northern Yana and they and the Northern Maidu considered the Yana the aggressors

(Sapir and Spier 1943:269; DuBois 1935:37; Voegelin 1942:209; Kniffen 1928:314). Sometimes the Northern Yana were on friendly terms with the Big Bend Achumawi while the Atsugewi were at one time so friendly that they could gather acorns and berries in Yana territory. This attitude changed and they became bitter enemies (Curtis 1907-1930,13:131). The Yana apparently never formed large war parties but the Northern Yana were occasionally paid to join with the Atsugewi to fight the Wintu (Voegelin 1942:210). They usually attacked another group in reprisal for poaching and to avenge the abduction of women (Gifford and Klimek 1939:85).

Obsidian was obtained from the Achumawi and Shasta and must have been already partially or completely worked as few chunks or cores are found in former Yana sites. Arrows, buckskin, wildcat quivers, and woodpecker scalps were secured from the Atsugewi; clam disk beads and magnesite cylinders, from the Maidu or Wintun; dentalium shells, from the Wintu; and barbed obsidian arrow points, from the north. In return the Yana supplied buckeye fire drills, deer hides, dentalia, salt, and buckskin to the Atsugewi; baskets to the Nomlaki; and salt to the Wintu (Sapir and Spier 1943:254-255; Gifford and Klimek 1939:82-83, 91-92, 98; Davis 1961:15-18, 33-34, 37, 44). The Wintu were occasionally allowed to gather salt from a swamp on Cow Creek but for the most part outsiders were discouraged from entering Yana territory (Du Bois 1935:25; Sapir and Spier 1943:252). Besides hostility, another primary factor for the small amount of trade was the limited range of useful minerals and other natural resources found in the southern Cascades. In addition, the Yana spent most of their time in the quest for food, thus leaving little time to devote to the preparation and gathering of materials for trade.

Culture

Ceremonial System

The mythology, symbolism, ritual, social culture and the use of wealth were little developed (Kroeber 1925:340). The practice of the seclusion of adolescent boys and certain types of feather garments could be related to the Kuksu cult; or they may be elements affiliated with the Ghost Dance, which was introduced to the Northern Yana in 1871 (Sapir and Spier 1943:285-286; Kroeber 1925:340-341). The Earth Lodge cult developed by the Wintun and Patwin as an outgrowth of the Ghost Dance was introduced to the Northern Yana in 1872-1873 and may have contained elements of the Bole-Maru (Sapir and Spier 1943:286). The chief was the master of ceremonies and gave orations from the top of the assembly house (Gifford and Klimek 1939:85). No information is available on the Southern and Yahi Yana, but the presence of the remains of what were apparently a few assembly houses indicates some organized ceremonial life probably existed among them as well (Johnson 1973:pls. 41B, 42A).

Shamans and Curing

To become a shaman an individual had to spend time isolated from the rest of the villagers. Among the Northern and Central Yana it was desirable to swim in certain pools of water in order to gain power and songs. During this time the individual had to fast, sleep little, and avoid the smell of cooking meat, fish, or other desirable foods (Sapir and Spier 1943:279-280). Novices were usually trained by older shamans (Gifford and Klimek 1939:85). The devices used by shamans included dreams, singing, pipe smoking, special net caps with feathers, special rounded luck stones, and quartz crystals, which were particularly prized (Sapir and Spier 1943:280-282; Sapir 1908). Most shamans were also doctors and diagnosed or cured by singing, dancing, and sucking out the disease object. Unsuccessful shamans were often accused of poisoning the victim or of practicing black magic and they were sometimes killed (Gifford and Klimek 1939:85). The most powerful shamans were men, while a few women were also practitioners.

Various roots were eaten or chewed and teas were drunk as medicines, and poultices were applied externally. Men used the sweathouse as a general curative or as a preventive measure. Heated rocks were used to cure many types of pains, scarification was sometimes practiced, and quartz crystals and other luck stones were also used (Sapir and Spier 1943:252-253; Gifford and Klimek 1939:85). The Yahi man Ishi said women should be in seclusion during menstruation because they could bring ill luck and sickness. He also felt the use of herbs and drugs was the province of old women and he did not hold much store in them. Most of the important Yahi cures were felt to be through magic (Pope 1920: 179-181).

Kinship and Social Status

Sometimes a young man would live with his wife's parents until after the first child was born. The Yana had a strong mother-in-law taboo for husbands and it is probable that patrilocal residence was the general rule after marriage (Gifford and Klimek 1939:83; Sapir and Spier 1943:273). Relatives were addressed in the plural as a sign of respect and friendliness while as brother and sister matured they also addressed each other in the plural. Differences of relationships were recognized via father and mother while merging of paternal and maternal lineages took place (Sapir 1918:171). The presence of a word for bastard, ostracism for illegitimacy, primogeniture inheritance of the office of chief through the male line, and secondary sex discrimination clearly indicate different status classes existed in Yana society (Kroeber

1925: 341; Gifford and Klimek 1939:84; Sapir and Spier 1943:275; Sapir 1918:171).

Political Organization

Within Yana territory numerous tribelets existed. These consisted of a major village, at which the principal chief and assembly house were located, and several smaller allied villages (Kroeber 1962:25-50). Most villages had their own chief while in Northern Yana territory at least some major villages had a chief and one or two subchiefs (Sapir and Spier 1943:274; Gifford 1928a: 681-684). Political units (probably tribelets) owned certain territories; and there was private ownership of land, seed tracts, and fishing places among the Northern Yana (Gifford and Klimek 1939:84).

The chief's status was attained through inheritance and even though he had to be from a chiefly family his wife (or wives) could be commoners. Most chiefs had at least two wives, were often rich, were the dance leaders, and were the only individuals allowed to keep vultures as pets. A chief made speeches that were suggestive but not commanding; and apparently he did not have the power to control, impose his views, or command the obedience of others. Chiefs did not have to do their own hunting as the people gave them meat and presents (Gifford 1928a:681-684; Gifford and Klimek 1939:84; Sapir and Spier 1943:274-275).

Subsistence

Deer, the most important game animals, were usually stalked by individuals who used a deer-head decoy and the bow and arrow. Native dogs were used and sometimes all the men in a village would take part in a communal hunt. Deer, rabbits, and quail were also taken with snares and among the Northern Yana game pits and deadfalls were used (Kroeber 1925:341; Sapir and Spier 1943:252; Gifford and Klimek 1939:80). The Yahi often waited in ambush at deer licks and large and small game was attracted to the hunter with a variety of calls (fig. 3) (Pope 1918:128-129). Community rabbit drives were conducted. A type of sling was used in hunting by the Northern Yana (Merriam 1907a). Various rituals were conducted to insure success in the hunt and hunters often observed taboos. Petroglyphs to influence the success of the hunt were not made (Gifford and Klimek 1939:80, 87).

Fishing was an important secondary food-procuring activity. Spears and harpoons were used to take salmon while bipointed bone gorges, seine nets, traps of willow branches, and plant poisons were used to get trout and suckers (Pope 1918:130; Gifford and Klimek 1939:80; Sapir and Spier 1943:252). Salmon were broiled on heated rocks or roasted over a fire; some were dried and stored for later use (Sapir and Spier 1943:252).

The most important food source was acorns, which were gathered in late September and October. During good years the supply would last until the next harvest but after a poor crop the Yana were often on the verge of starvation in the spring. Several varieties of oak occur in Yana territory with the black oak the preferred variety. The man climbed the trees to shake the acorns down; the women gathered the nuts and shelled them immediately. After thorough drying on tule mats, the acorns were put in storage baskets or in granaries and used as needed. They were processed into soup, mush, and bread and combined with meat, berries, and other ingredients (Sapir and Spier 1943:249-250). The bitter tannic acid was leached from the acorn meal with warm water before cooking.

Also gathered in large amounts were several kinds of roots, tubers, and bulbs. The roots and tubers were most often roasted while most bulbs were steamed. In the fall buckeye nuts were gathered, hulled, leached, and eaten soon after processing as they cannot be stored. Many stems, leaves, and bulbs were eaten raw (miner's lettuce, clover, *Brodiaea* in particular) while most of the seeds gathered were parched. Sunflower and *Clarkia* were the most important seeds while hazel, sugar-pine and digger-pine nuts, berries, and fruit were gathered in lesser quantities. Manzanita berries were eaten raw (Sapir and Spier 1943:251).

Earthworms, grasshoppers, salmon fly, and numerous small rodents were also gathered and eaten. Salt was important as a flavoring and was gathered in Central Yana territory (Sapir and Spier 1943:252). Wherever river mussels lived they were gathered; they were available in large quantities in the Pit River but were relatively scarce in the rest of Yana territory (Gifford and Klimek 1939:81). The Yana had a relative abundance of food in the fall when salmon, acorns, buckeye, deer, and other food sources were available; but during the hot summer months after the greens had shriveled and the seed plants were spent few food items were available below 2,500 feet. This search for food was probably the primary stimulus for the seasonal migration to higher elevations in search of deer, berries, and seed plants. The avoidance of the heat of the foothills in the summer may have been of secondary importance (T. Kroeber 1961: 35-37; Johnson 1973:30-31).

Technology

The Yana were located at the juncture of two major basketry traditions. To the north twining overlaid with *Xerophyllum tenax* was the primary technique used while to the south coiling and twining without overlay predominated. The Northern and Central Yana used the overlaid twining technique (fig. 4) while the Yahi had some knowledge of coiling that was similar to the Maidu. Nothing is known of Southern Yana basketry techniques (Kroeber 1925:340, 1909:236). Twined basketry with and without *Xerophyllum* overlay designs is known

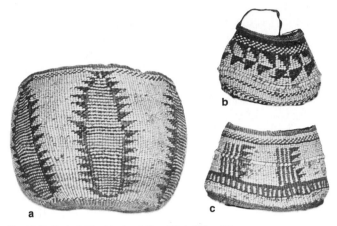

U. of Calif., Davis: C. Hart Merriam Coll., a, 815; b, 819; c, 820.
Fig. 4. Twined baskets. a, cooking; b, oval with buckskin strap on top; c, oval. Width of a, about 28 cm; b-c, same scale. Collected in 1907 from a Northern Yana woman.

from Mill Creek Canyon in Yahi territory, and twined basketry without overlay has been recovered from a shelter in Antelope Creek canyon in Southern Yana territory (Dawson 1971:1-3). It is probable that twining with *Xerophyllum* overlay was common to all Yana groups while the fewer coiled baskets noted may have been a relatively recent addition from the Maidu and Wintun. The lack of uniformity in the preparation of the materials caused the baskets to lack symmetry; the weaving was frequently not well controlled; and the edges were not carefully finished (Sapir and Spier 1943:259).

A wide variety of materials was used in basketmaking. The commonest warp materials were hazel switches and willow. Most of the weft elements were split pine roots and sedge while the overlay designs were made from white, black, and red strands against the brown pine-root background. The twined basketry was generally moderately flexible.

The designs were finished on the outside of the baskets even on trays and shallow bowls; thus the finished side was not always visible. Design elements were bold, occurring in the form of diagonals or zigzags across the whole side or sometimes in horizontal bands. Apparently the Yana seldom made isolated decorative elements, but when present the isolated designs were bold. Northern and Central Yana informants recognized 24 designs as their own after looking at Maidu and Achumawi specimens (Sapir and Spier 1943:265).

Other kinds of textiles included cords and ropes of milkweed fiber and Indian hemp. Peeled bark from trees, shrubs, and vines was pounded, shredded, and twisted into ropes and lashings. This heavier cordage was used for nets, caps, rabbit nets, skirts, and for tying objects together. Fish nets were made of milkweed string and were as long as 200 feet (Sapir and Spier

1943:257–258; Gifford and Klimek 1939:80; Merriam 1907a).

Most of the raw materials used for manufacturing tools came from within Yana territory. Digging sticks for gathering roots and bulbs were made from mahogany and oak wood. Some wedges were made of green wood while others were of antler. Fire drills were made of buckeye and were used with a cedar hearth. Tubular pipes were used and were sometimes made of ash wood. Brushes were made from soaproot fiber and scouring rush was used as arrow polishers (Sapir and Spier 1943:258–259; Gifford and Klimek 1939:81–83; Merriam 1907a).

Bows were made of mahogany, juniper, hazel, and yew with yew the preferred wood. Sinew-backed bows were preferred to unbacked specimens. Composite arrows had hardwood foreshafts of hazel, buckeye, and wild currant while solid arrows were usually of cane or serviceberry. Blunt arrows were used for birds and small game while small serrated obsidian and basalt points were used on arrows used for hunting large game (fig. 5).

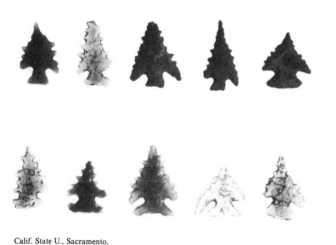

Calif. State U., Sacramento.
Fig. 5. Small serrated obsidian, basait, and glass arrow points. Length of top left specimen about 1.7 cm.

The favorite quiver was made of an otter skin with the fur side turned out (Pope 1918:111–125; Sapir and Spier 1943:268).

Principal grinding tools were the flat slab hopper mortar, shaped flat-ended pestle, unshaped unifacially used mano and slab, or boulder metates (fig. 6). Bedrock mortars were apparently not used (Gifford and Klimek 1939:97; Merriam 1907a).

Antler and bone flakers, antler wedges, bone awls, harpoon toggles, fish gorges, gambling pieces made of incised rodent teeth and gambling bones of cut deer bones were used. A few whistles of goose bone were also made. Mussel-shell spoons and scrapers were occasionally used while most of the other shell materials were obtained in trade. Most of the tool-making activities

Calif. State U., Sacramento: a, 79-1041; b, 30-914; c, 3-68; d, 9-203.
Fig. 6. Hopper mortar and pestles. a, hopper mortar base, length about 34 cm; b-d, flat-ended pestles used with hopper mortar, same scale.

took place during the winter when the Yana had a little time off from food-procuring activities (T. Kroeber 1961:38).

Life Cycle

The father and mother could not eat meat or salmon for six to eight days before the expected birth of a child or for several days afterward. They had to move to a small hut a considerable distance from the regular house and the man was not allowed to hunt or fish in the company of others. The woman's mother and one to three midwives were present. Twins and illegitimate babies were not killed at birth. After the navel cord had fallen off the parents could eat deer meat and salmon again. The husband at the birth of the first child had to perform several feats and often called on the supernatural to aid the birth. The Northern Yana apparently did not use a pitted boulder as a fertility rock even though such rocks are common in their territory. (Gifford and Klimek 1939: 83; Sapir and Spier 1943:270–271).

At puberty girls were subjected to a greater ordeal and series of tasks than boys. At her first menstruation a girl had to camp by herself, gather wood, build a fire, and sleep but little. She had to stay in a hut a considerable distance from the village. No meat or fish could be eaten, and she had to subsist on a little acorn mush and a few berries for six days. As at birth a wooden head scratcher had to be used and all utensils used by her during the confinement were thrown away (Sapir and Spier 1943:272; Gifford and Klimek 1939:83–84, 93).

Boys were sometimes sent away from the village without food. They fasted and were whipped with bow strings. At this time their ears were pierced by their fathers and sometimes the septum was also perforated (Gifford and Klimek 1939:84, 93).

Ideally marriages were to be arranged by the families of the prospective husband and wife. An exchange of gifts took place between the families. Food was exchanged and a man's suit could be rejected if the girl's family refused the gifts (Sapir and Spier 1943:273). The levirate and sororate were practiced, and though exogamy was preferred marriages could take place between villagers if suitable partners existed (Sapir 1918:173; Gifford and Klimek 1939:83). The Yana were polygynous in theory but except for chiefs they seldom practiced this form of marriage (T. Kroeber 1961:33). Various kinds of punishment were prescribed for infidelity, incest, and adultery (Gifford and Klimek 1939:87).

The three northern groups practiced inhumation while the Yahi supposedly cremated their dead. The Northern Yana would occasionally cremate when an individual died a long distance from home. The body was washed and the hair combed. It was tightly flexed and wrapped in a deerskin blanket and sewed inside; then a coarse rope was tied around the outside. After about four days the corpse was placed in a grave about five feet deep. Bows, arrows, baskets, blankets, and other objects belonging to the individual and others were placed in the grave. The house of the deceased and all the implements, food, and other materials inside were burned. Mourners cut their hair short, wore shabby garments, smeared pitch on their hair and face and put ashes on the pitch. There was a taboo on speaking the name of the dead (Pope 1918:131; Gifford and Klimak 1939:84; Sapir and Spier 1943:275; Merriam 1907a).

Structures

The Northern and Central Yana had substantial earth-covered multi-family dwellings and assembly houses. They had one center post and the entrance was through the smoke hole in the roof. The Southern Yana made little use of these earth-covered structures (Gifford and Klimek 1939:82). Conical bark houses were made of long slabs of cedar or pine bark leaned against a pole framework. Among the Northern and Central Yana these were sometimes multiple-family dwellings while among the Southern and Yahi Yana they accommodated only single families. The smaller structures had a shallow oval depression 10 to 12 feet in diameter inside and had dirt banked up three or four feet on the outside to keep the water out (T. Kroeber 1961:32–33; Sapir and Spier 1943:256). In the southern foothills the conical bark houses were apparently replaced by dome-shaped single-family structures made of poles (fig. 7) covered with branches, brush, skins, and anything else that was convenient (Powers 1877:279).

Less substantial were the menstrual lodges used in the girls' puberty rites and the thatched summer homes and temporary shelters built when on hunting and gathering trips (Kroeber 1925:340; Sapir and Spier 1943:257; Gifford and Klimek 1939:82). The Yahi often used caves for shelter (Powers 1877:279).

Lowie Mus., U. of Calif., Berkeley.

Fig. 7. Frame of Yahi house. Photograph by T.T. Waterman, about 1914.

Clothing and Adornment

Wealthy men wore buckskin leggings from the hip to the ankles in the winter while poor men wore only a simple apron. Men had elkskin hats and moccasins of deerskin. The women had a front apron or skirt of shredded bark or tules that hung down from a string of buckskin. Sometimes they also wore a back apron of buckskin. Wealthy women wore braided belts of human hair and skirts with leather tassels braided with grass that hung down in front. Sometimes the leather tassels were strung with pine-nut beads (Sapir and Spier 1943:253–254).

Juniper berries, magnesite cylinders, dentalium and olivella shells, bear claws, and clamshell disks were all used in necklaces, disks being considered the most valuable. Feather headbands, woodpecker-scalp belts, and face and body paint were also used. Deerskin robes, rabbitskin blankets, wild cat (fig. 8), coyote, and bearskin blankets were worn during cold weather and slept under. Some women tattooed their faces but this was not very common. Both sexes wore their hair long with the men usually tying it in back of the head or on top with a piece of leather while the women wore two braids or rolls in front of their shoulders that were wrapped with either mink or buckskin. The men plucked out any facial hair with a split piece of wood. Both sexes pierced their earlobes and wore in them leather thongs that were often strung with beads or other ornaments (Sapir and Spier 1943:253–258; T. Kroeber 1961: 7; Gifford and Klimek 1939:79, 88; Pope 1920:183; Merriam 1907a).

Games and Music

The Yana were apparently one of the few native California societies in which the men played double-ball shinny. Usually this was a women's game. Other games included ring and pin, cat's cradle, throwing sticks at a

Lowie Mus., U. of Calif., Berkeley: 1-19565.
Fig. 8. Cape of wildcat skins taken from the last known Yahi camp, 1908. Width about 183 cm.

stake, a child's ball game, and several forms of the grass or hand game. The last was the principal form of gambling played by men on teams (Gifford and Klimek 1939:83; Sapir and Spier 1943:277-278).

The only musical instruments described were a split-stick rattle, elderwood flute, cocoon rattle and deer-hoof rattle, while goose-bone whistles were known for the Northern Yana (Merriam 1907a; Gifford and Klimek 1939:82).

Mythology

Most of the myths appear to be elaborations of events that were believed to have happened and many carry moral messages. Most are explanatory of how the Yana came to have various customs. Thus, myths relate the origin of fire, sex, honor, death, childbirth, and marriage. The Yana did not have the water origin myths that were common to various other northern California cultures (Curtin 1898:281-484; Sapir 1910).

Synonymy

Nozi (variants: Nosi, Noze, Nozhi, Nosa) was applied to the Northern and Central Yana in early historic accounts and by Powers (1877). Anthropologists also provide Nozi as a supplementary name for the Northern Yana (Sapir and Spier 1943:242-243; Merriam 1926:16; Kroeber 1925:339; and Du Bois 1935:4). The Yahi Yana were referred to by Powers (1877) as the Kombo, which is the name given them by the Northern Maidu (Dixon 1905:124). The name Yahi did not come into use

until after the Indian Ishi was brought to the University of California in 1911. The words Yana (*yaana*) and Yahi (*yaaxi*) mean 'people' (Waterman 1918:38; Sapir and Swadesh 1960:187). The Northern Yana referred to themselves as Garii; the Central were known as Gatai. No similar terms are known for the Southern and Yahi Yana (Sapir and Spier 1943:242-243).

Each Indian group surrounding the Yana had different names for them. The Wintu living to the northwest referred to the Northern and Central Yana as Puisus 'east dwelling', Puiel Yuki 'enemy' and Noze (Du Bois 1935:4). The Nomlaki called the Yana Yuke 'strangers' while the Achumawi name for them was Tisaitei 'Salt People'. A major variant of the spelling of Yana that was used in several early publications is Yahnah (Merriam 1926:16). Many Yana names for Yana groups and their neighbors are in Sapir and Swadesh (1960:31, 215, 236, 259-260).

Sources

While Powers (1877) briefly describes the Northern Yana and Curtin (1898) includes some data on myths, it was the discovery of the camp of four surviving Yana in 1908 in Deer Creek Canyon that provoked considerable research on this tribe (T. Kroeber 1961:249). Most of the data collected pertained to the Northern, Central, and Yahi Yana with little on the Southern division (Waterman 1918:36; Gifford and Klimek 1939; Sapir and Spier 1943).

Fleeting references were made to them by some of the early trapping and exploring parties, with the greatest coverage in the Red Bluff, California, *Beacon* and other early Sacramento valley newspapers (Kemble 1962: 209-210, 226-228). Most of the articles were published between the late 1850s and early 1870s. The period between 1870 and 1900 contains an occasional story in the press in reference to the robbing of cabins and reported sighting of Indians in the vicinity of Deer and Mill creeks. Before 1911 most of the literature relates to the work of Dixon (1905), Merriam (1907a), and Sapir (1908) and to Waterman, Sapir, Pope, and Kroeber after 1911. Of principal importance are the literature and field notes that resulted from Sapir's work with Northern and Central informants in 1907 and with Ishi in 1915. Major contributions were Yana texts (1910, 1923) and linguistic work (1916, 1917, 1918, 1922, 1929a). Waterman's (1918) contribution was principally ethnohistorical; Dixon and Kroeber's, primarily linguistic (1913, 1919); and Pope's was specifically on archery (1918) and the medical history of Ishi (1920). Gifford and Klimek's (1939) culture element distributions and Sapir and Spier's (1943) work are significant.

Information on the interaction of the Yana with surrounding cultures was published by Kniffen (1928), Merriam (1926), Du Bois (1935), Voegelin (1942), Goldschmidt (1951a), and Garth (1953). Interest in the Yana appeared again with the publication of the Yana dictionary (Sapir and Swadesh 1960) and T. Kroeber's (1961) work on Ishi. McLendon's (1964) linguistic comparisons between Pomo and Yana and Apperson's (1971) personal reminiscence of Ishi and his return to Deer Creek in 1914 provide useful information.

Merriam's original field notes on the Northern Yana (Heizer 1969) are on file at the Department of Anthropology at the University of California, Berkeley. The University of California Archives of the Department of Anthropology at Berkeley house several collections of field notes by Sapir, Waterman, and Gifford (Valory 1971) and the American Philosophical Society has on file linguistic data listed by Sapir and Swadesh (Freeman 1966:385-386).

The Peabody Museum at Harvard and the Lowie Museum, Berkeley, have large collections of Yana baskets, while seven specimens are in the C. Hart Merriam collection at the University of California at Davis. The Lowie Museum also has a collection of Yahi implements collected between 1908 and 1916.

Photographs of Ishi, Yana manufactures, and a few Yana informants are at the Lowie Museum (T. Kroeber 1961; Gifford 1926: pl. 20; Waterman 1918: pls. 1-20; Pope 1918: pls. 21-37, Pope 1920: pls. 38-44).

Maidu and Konkow

FRANCIS A. RIDDELL

Language, Environment, and Territory

The term Maidu (¹mī₁dōo) as used here refers to those people also known as the Mountain Maidu or Northeastern Maidu, while the term Konkow (¹kän₁käw) refers only to the Northwestern Maidu. The third form of Maiduan speech is that of the Nisenan, also known as the Southern Maidu. The drainages of the American and Feather rivers of the northern Sierra of California approximate the extent of the area held by the Maiduan people (fig. 1).

Maidu was spoken by people living in the high mountain meadows lying between Lassen Peak and the town of Quincy some 50 miles to the south and east, probably in four dialects (American Valley, Indian Valley, Big Meadows, and Susanville). Konkow was spoken in a number of dialects along the lower reaches of the Feather River Canyon up to about Richbar, in the surrounding hills, and in the adjacent parts of the Sacramento Valley (Shipley 1963:1). Both forms are members of the Maiduan family of languages, which is classified as California Penutian. Within the Maiduan area, the dialects, in general, were quite closely related; however, the three forms of speech were mutually unintelligible at first contact.*

The Maidu inhabited a series of mountain valleys, the more important of which are Mountain Meadows, Big Meadows (now Lake Almanor), Butt, American, Indian, Genesee, and Red Clover. In each area, where winter weather would allow, permanent villages were established. In other areas, the Sierra and Mohawk valleys for

---

* The best orthography for Maidu and Konkow is that by Shipley (1963). To conform to Handbook standards, ɨ is used for Shipley's y and y for his j. The d and b are implosive. Italicized words have been respelled by William F. Shipley (Maidu) and Russell Ultan (Konkow) in this orthography. Doubtful interpretations are indicated by a question mark.

Fig. 1. Tribal territory and village locations.

Maidu: 1, *witáyim;* 2, Lone Pine; 3, name forgotten; 4, name forgotten; 5, *sumbílim;* 6, name forgotten; 7, *ràsím;* 8, *pepépem čùm;* 9, *yòlím;* 10, *wisótpinìm;* 11, *kólyèm;* 12, *čám bukùnayim;* 13, *maním báldɨ̀ɽi;* 14, *táldinom;* 15, *potádi;* 16, *kóbatásdayim;* Kotasi? (D, Ka, S); 17, *kówkòwɽi yakim;* 18, *kókitpe;* 19, *bunúk;* 20, *ʔolílimbe;* 21, *dókoꞔòk dòyím;* 22, *ʔokóno;* 23, *ʔoꞔ̀ò;* 24, *wayápom mòmí;* 25, *ʔóm koyò;* Ong-Koyo-diknom (Ka); 26, *yódawìm* (R, Ka); 27, *čakámdɨ̀ɽi;* Kushdu? (Ka); 28, *čílwam ʔínkomì;* 29, *koyóm bukúm;* 30, *čiwisi;* 31, *konók wusùpa;* 32, *kóm koyò;* 33, *yolám motò* (R, D, Ka); 34, *kòwówtàyi;* 35, *púslem koyò;* 36, *tohánom;* 37, *nòɽóm pìno;* 38, *wayápom mòmím ʔústu;* 39, *wayápom mòmím čálá hibé?;* 40, *wayápom mòmí;* 41, *píttelim* (R, Ka); 42, name forgotten; 43, *sátkini walám Ɽùmhú;* 44, name forgotten; 45, *kawa;* 46, *bábe;* Omhübe? (Ka); 47, *čàkám?* or *čákɨ̀m?;* 48, *peꞔáma;* 49, *bukúlisa ʔínkomì;* 50, *čílwam ʔínkomì;* 51, *dàsím yodá;* 52, name forgotten; 53, *boléywi;* Opüle? (Ka).

Konkow: 1, Shidawi (Kb); 2, Se-dow-we (M); 3, Sook-soo′-koo (M); 4, Muli (Kb); 5, Pah′-kem (M); 6, *čéno* (Kb); 7, Pe-dow-kah (M); 8, *čéno* (M); 9, Chan-no? (M); 10, Soo′-noos (M); 11, Sunusi (D, Kb); 12, Batsi (Kb); 13, Baht-che (M); 14, Yoot′-dok-kah (M); 15, Mo-ning-we (M); 16, Momingwi (Kb); 17, Pinuk (Kb); 18, Mau′mah (M); 19, Bo′-do (M); 20, Pake (D, Ka); 21, O′-tah′-ke (M); 22, Bay′-he-yu (M); 23; Bah-hahp′-ke (M); 24, Wah-nah′-tahm (M); 25, Tse′lim-nah (M); 26, Yow′-koo (M); 27, Yauko (D, Ka); 28, O′dawi (Kb); 29, Otaki (D, Ka); *ʔótakìmme* (P); 30, Tsulumsewi (Ka); 31, Nem′sä-wà (M); 32, *némsèwi* (Ka); 33, Ti′kus-se (M); 34, Tatampanta; 35, Tă-tan wu-ta (M); 36, *kóyo·mɽàwi;* Konkau (Ka); 37, Yu′dow (M); 38, Bahyu (D, Ka); 39, Tadoiko (D, Ka); 40, Pe-tut′-taw (M); 41, Sap′-se (M); 42, ki-dak′-te (M); 43, Utapi; Ushtupedi (P); 44, *ʔéskeni* (M); 45, Wil-lil′-lim hoo′-loo-ko (M); 46, *ʔéskeni* (R, Ka, Kb); 47, *miꞔupda·* (M); 48, *miꞔupda·* (R, D, Ka, Kb); 49, Yum-mut-to (M); 50, Olimi; 51, Taikuš (D, Ka); 52, Oltibe; 53, Koto; 54, *čéno·* 55, *sá·klemkòyo·;* 56, Wilewimkumbali; 57, Pumeku; 58, Waywushuno; 59, Bachakumlulumi; 60, Kusukuyamanimkoyo; 61, Weleudeh (P); 62, Yahankumbali; 63, Hapaiya or Hapumbasa; 64, Tatbemkoyo; 65, Tsiwopemkoyohukuma; 66, Lolingkumbali; 67, Kupno; 68, Tsamhenom; Tsambahenom (L, Ka); 69, Seleskoting; 70, Lowingkoyo; 71, *pókpoɽo;* 72, *hámsɨmkòyo·;* 73, *pókpoɽo* (M); 74, Hule; 75, Ukiali; 76, Lolosimboda; 77, Dimidoli; 78, Sukleli or Tobewimhukuma; 79, Shilteamomahukuma; 80, Bistamcha; 81, Kawitumtumi; 82, Taiwaia; 83, Tsaktomo (Ka); 84, Shushumlami; 85, *píye·to;* 86, *tá·yimɽòyo·;* 87, Hayembenke; 88, Pahumi; 89, *čá·mpɨ̀li;* 90, *tá·yimɽòyo·* (M); 91, Omolkoyo; 92, *ʔá·lemyɨ̀da;* 93, Shudokoyoloma; 94, Lasito; 95, Bipyan; 96, Tokoto; 97, Pambisku; 98, Pamtali; 99, Pulewi; 100, Palangkumbali; 101, *tó·toɽumi; tó·tommà?a* (D, Ka); 102, *tó·tomʔɨ̀sti;* 103, Tsitsimpakani; 104, Manimkaipa; 105, Yowitoma; 106, *síto;* 107, Benkumkumi (R, D, Ka); 108, *píwbe;* 109, Watchahu; 110, Munmunpani; 111, Hikinimkumbali; 112, *yínomɽùmbali* (R); *yɨno* (Ka); 113, Kotano; 114, Watama; 115, Pikimkumi or Pikingkumbali; 116, Dowoli; 117, Wonomkoyo; 118, Hokoma (Ka); 119, *pólomkòyo·;* 120, Piudusi; 121, Yakiowa; 122, Lukumbuni; 123, Titikyani; 124, Chikimaisa; 125, *kálkalyà·ni;* Kalkalya (D, Ka); 126, *séwimɽùmbali;* 127, Chichi; 128, Lumlumi; 129, Kukumbisi; 130, Kulaiapto (D, Ka); 131, Tsuka (D, Ka); 132, Witakasi; 133, Chatono; 134, *ʔá·lemɽùmbali;* 135, Yuhemui; 136, Ta′a; 137, *holholholto(m);* *holholto* (D, Ka); 138, Yumam (D, Ka); 139, Botoko (D, Ka); 140, Wabusi; 141, *ʔólolokpa·* (R, Ka); 142, Botok (Kb); 143, Taichida (Ka); 144, Hincho; 145, Bauka (D, Ka); 146, Bieyem; 147, Tomcho (Kb); 148, Bupumkumi.

The following villages in the Oroville region cannot be located: Naka; Nikdompakani; Onihiula; Pokibay; Shumemheno; Tekteka; Tsunpem.

Sources: Riddell 1960–1974 (unmarked, except with R in the case of duplication); Dixon 1905 (D); Kroeber 1925 (Ka); Kroeber 1932a (Kb); Merriam in Heizer and Hester 1970 (M); Powers 1877 (P); Swanton 1952 (S).

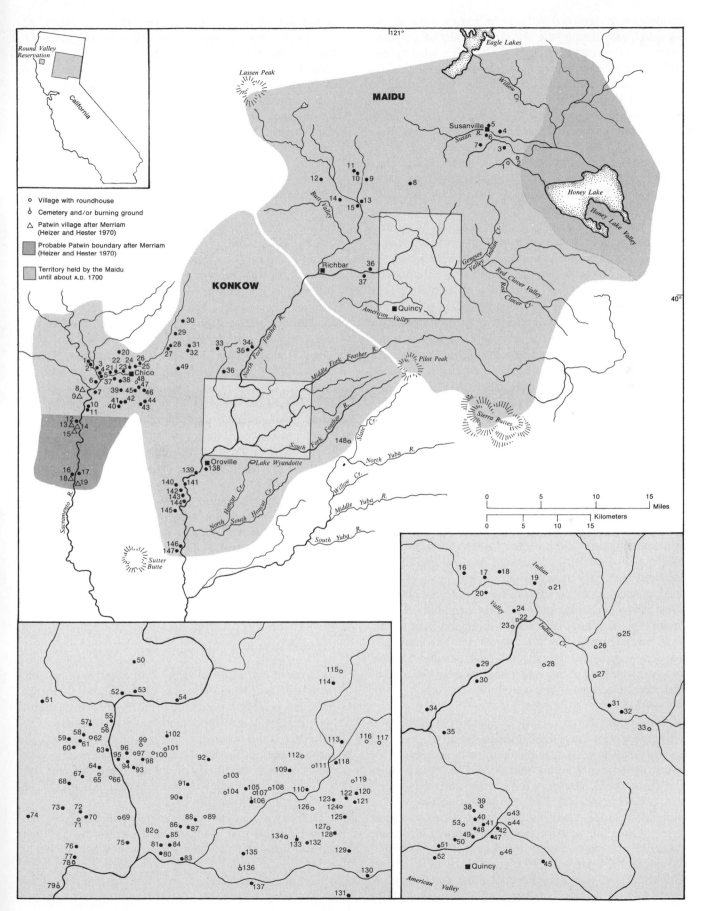

MAIDU AND KONKOW

example, only seasonal villages or camps were in use, occupied only during the warmer months of the year. Each of the other valleys had one or more villages, and the people in each were, to a degree, considered as a separate social entity. For example, those living in American Valley were known as the *silóm maʔá,* from *silóm koyó,* their name for the valley. Those living in Indian Valley were the *tasáy dɨm,* after *tasím koyó,* their name for that valley; and those living in Genesee Valley were the *yetámmetom maʔá* after *yetámmetom,* their name for Genessee Valley. It is evident that group differentiation for the Maidu was dictated by geographical considerations (Riddell 1968).

The northern portion of Maidu holdings is an area typified by a juniper-sage environment; however, demonstrating that portions of this region were economically productive is the archeological recording of an unnamed, abandoned village three miles east of Susanville with some 22 observed house pits remaining. Susan River and Willow Creek, with their sloughs, meanderings, and tributaries, support extensive meadows and marshes before flowing into Honey Lake, thus providing a superb habitat for fish and waterfowl. In addition, the ever-important acorn-bearing oak groves are within easy collecting distance.

Whereas the Maidu occupied an area generally 4,000 feet above sea level or higher, the Konkow territory included a portion of the Sacramento Valley floor and a section of the sierra foothill east of Chico and Oroville. The valley floor generally presented a vast savanna environment in which grasses and oaks formed a natural parkland.

The climate of the Konkow region was characterized by a wet winter and a dry summer season; in winter there were occasional freezing temperatures, and fog and rain occurred with varying intensity.

As to tribal territory, some difference of opinion might exist between the Maidu and their neighbors, Paiute, Achumawi, Washo, and Yana, although certain prominent physiographic features were used as boundary markers to generally delimit the Maidu territory. Border areas of value for hunting and gathering might be used by both the Maidu and their neighbors by consent or by incursion.

The Maidu penetration into the Great Basin was greater in earlier times than at the first American contact around 1850 (see fig. 1). By their own admission, the Maidu at some earlier date held all of Honey Lake Valley and its environs. At some time in the relatively recent past, possibly circa A.D. 1700, the Maidu withdrew to the west side of Honey Lake, and the vacated area was taken over by the Paiute. Although the Maidu traditionally claim the area, they cannot name any villages and few physiographic features. This is in contrast to the Paiute who are able to give explicit details of use and village and camp names, as well as being able to name all the

significant physiographic features (Riddell 1960). Although this loss was apparently relatively insignificant to the Maidu, the gain to the Paiute certainly was of considerable importance as the marshlands of the mouth of Susan River at Honey Lake, as well as two hot spring areas, provided new territory of higher economic potential than the strictly sage desert environment from which the Paiute emerged. In fact, groves of oaks on the western edge of Honey Lake in the vicinity of Milford became directly available to the Paiute for the first time.

The Konkow people derive their name from the anglicization of the native term *kóyoˑmǩàwi* 'meadowland' (see Hodge 1907-1910, 1:725). The division line between the Konkow and their Maiduan neighbors, the Nisenan, lacks clarity for a diversity of reasons, among which is the early decimation by disease, slaughter, and removal of people who would be in a position of authority on the subject. Also, it seems probable that the boundary between the two groups did not have quite the same importance as it might have between the Konkow and Nomlaki, for example. In fact, the people living along Honcut Creek, between the Yuba and Feather rivers, appear as possibly being dialectically transitional between the Konkow and the Nisenan (Kroeber 1925:393). The line may have gone from the Feather River up Honcut Creek to the North Fork of Honcut Creek and up the latter to its headwaters at Wyandotte Lake, and then sharply east to the North Yuba River and then northeasterly up Slate Creek to its headwaters at Pilot Peak.

The Konkow were divided into several village communities: Kewsayoma'a (*kíwsewimàʔa*), *yínommàʔa,* Totoma'a (*tóˑtommàʔa*). The last two, along with several others now forgotten, composed a larger unit called *táˑyi* 'west people'. (Merriam gives a number of divisions for the Konkow and Maidu that provide a somewhat different set of boundaries from that given here; cf. Heizer 1966:42-43.)

External Relations

In terms of cultural similarities and differences between the Maidu and Konkow on the one hand and their non-Maiduan neighbors on the other, there are few outstanding elements of difference and many of similarity. One difference is the occurrence of the Kuksu cult among the Konkow but not among the neighboring Yana or among their kinsmen, the Maidu. They did share this cult trait with the Nisenan and many non-Maiduan central California people (Dixon 1905:322).

Differences recognized by the people themselves stem from language and locational considerations. Although the Maidu and Konkow territories were laced together by a network of trails, it would have been unusual for a person living in a village to go more than 20 miles from home during his lifetime. This distance might have been somewhat greater among those Konkows living within the flat Sacramento Valley. Mountain people are recorded to have been driven west to a low elevation in the foothill area because of famine during a harsh winter. The lowland people were reported to have responded with compassion, possibly because their distant mountain kinsmen were, in that instance, few in number and thus posed no threat according to informant Tom Epperson (Riddell 1960-1974).

Although an individual may not have traveled far, trade items were widely distributed from village to village and from group to group. Such items changed hands at intervillage gatherings through the hand game, a form of gambling. Trade of local goods for those more common to other areas also took place.

Settlement Pattern

A settlement pattern of "village communities" (Kroeber 1925:398) served as the only political organization of the Maidu. A village community was recognized as an autonomous unit and consisted of several adjacent villages. Central to the village community was the village displaying the largest *kúm* (Konkow *kúmi*), a semisubterranean earth-covered lodge (fig. 2) provided as a ceremonial assembly chamber. The central village, although not always the most populous, was probably the residence of the most authoritative man of the village community, who used the *kúm* as a regular dwelling (Kroeber 1925:397). Among the Maidu and Konkow, this headman was primarily an advisor and spokesman (Dixon 1905:224). The separate villages were self-sufficient and not bound under any strict political control by the community headman. The central location around the largest assembly chamber of one village was primarily for ceremonial and subsistence activities.

On a basis of five persons in a house and seven houses in a village, precontact village population can be estimated at 35 persons. The number of villages in a community varied, but it is estimated that the group size did not exceed 200 (Kroeber 1925:397). Each village-community, therefore, probably consisted of from three to five villages. A village-community owned and defended a known territory, which was a common hunting and fishing ground for all members of the community. In the mountains, the Maidu villages were segregated into existing valleys, and each village-community was well defined. Because the Konkow, in the northwestern foothills, settled in a more widely dispersed pattern along river canyons, the territory of a single community was less determined (Kroeber 1925:398).

In the mountain environment of the Maidu, soft-bottomed glacial valleys were covered with snow during the winter months. Melting snow transformed the valleys into spongy meadow or marsh and sustained a heavy river flow during the summer season (Kroeber 1925:396). The Maidu "selected sites along the edges of these valleys, and rarely lived out in the middle of the level stretches" (Dixon 1905:175). Archeological evidence, too, shows that the village sites were located above the meadow or marshy valley floor (Riddell and Pritchard 1971). This placement provided excellent views of the surrounding country and enabled the dwellings to be constructed among a mixed coniferous forest. The winter months were difficult; preserved and stored food provided the main sustenance. Some families moved to lower elevations for the winter; however, most groups of Maidu remained in the permanent village sites throughout the winter months (McMillin 1963:63).

In Konkow territory, the Feather, Yuba, and American rivers wind their way through the northwestern foothills carving deep, narrow canyons. The Konkow settlements were situated by preference on the ridge, high above the rivers and generally on small flats on the crest of the ridge, or part way down the canyonside (Dixon 1905:175). Sites were further located on elevated knolls in reference to attack and defense considerations.

Subsistence

The Konkow followed a yearly gathering cycle that took them away from their winter dwellings on the river ridges. In the summer, they journeyed up into the mountains for hunting, and dried deer meat was brought back to the winter villages. Food gathering during the spring took the Indians into the valley areas to collect grass seeds, especially wild rye (Duncan 1964:15). At the summer camps the Konkow constructed a roofless, circular brush enclosure large enough to house three or four families, which could also be used for ceremonies. There was a fireplace in the center and two openings oriented toward the east and west or south (Voegelin 1942:62). Maidu knowledge of the native flora and fauna was complete. Most plants and animals had multiple uses serving subsistence, religious, and material necessities. They utilized the flora and fauna to the fullest: the root, stems, leaves, and seeds of plants and the flesh, skins,

NAA, Smithsonian.

Fig. 2. Konkow semisubterranean earth-covered dance house at Chico. Photograph by Henry W. Henshaw, 1893.

horns, bones, and hoofs of fauna were used for specific items of food, shelter, clothing, tools, and medicine.

Women and children gathered nuts by hand and collected seeds with the aid of a seed beater. The seed beater was used to strike the grass or plant head causing the seeds or grass head to fall off into a tray-basket held underneath (Dixon 1905:187). Both nuts and seeds were transferred, after gathering, to burden baskets held on the back by a shoulder or head strap.

Acorns provided by oak species were the primary source of nut meats. Three varieties were distinctly preferred: those from the black oak (*Quercus kelloggii*), the canyon or golden oak (*Quercus chrysolepis*), and the interior live oak (*Quercus wislizenii*). Two other species are particular to the northeastern mountain region: huckleberry oak (*Quercus vaccinifolia*) and bush chinqua-pin (*Castanopsis sempervirens*) (McMillin 1963:35–36).

The acorn flour was bitter because of tannin in the acorns and had to be made edible by leaching with warm water. Flour was spread over the interior of a flat, shallow excavation in sand. Cedar sprigs laid over the flour prevented it from being disturbed as warm water was poured into the basin. As the water seeped through the meal, it was absorbed by the sand. This was repeated numerous times, each time using hotter water, until the bitter tannin was leached out. The dough was then cooked with water by adding hot stones to the cooking basket to form a soup, or if thicker, mush. Bread was made from the dough by wrapping it in oak (Dixon 1905:187) or wild grape (Duncan 1964:78) leaves and baking under a pile of hot stones. "The resulting bread is very solid and heavy, resembling almost a lump of putty, and is, like the soup and mush, almost tasteless" (Dixon 1905:187).

In the foothills the Konkow gathered nuts from the digger pine (*Pinus sabiniana*). The nuts were eaten whole or ground into flour and the shells made into beads. The Maidu used the mountain species, sugar pine (*Pinus lambertiana*) and yellow pine (*Pinus ponderosa*). They ate the nuts plain or cooked into a soup or patties. Hazelnuts (*Corylus cornuta*), the nut of the buckeye (*Aesculus californica*), and wild nutmeg (*Torreya californica*) were other nut-meat sources. The buckeye nut had to be processed, as the acorn, but it took more thorough leaching to remove the poisonous, bitter-tasting prussic acid. The nutmeg required even more processing, and these nuts were first cracked and then buried in the ground for several months. They were then dug up and roasted in ashes (Dixon 1905:188).

The Maidu and Konkow drank a wild mint tea and manzanita cider. The cider was prepared in large quantities by crushing manzanita berries and mixing with water to form a stiff dough. The dough was placed on a willow sieve over a soup basket. Water poured over the dough dissolved the sweet berry flavor. The resulting liquid was a light amber color and had a strong, sweet taste not unlike that of apple cider (Dixon 1905:191).

Roots were eaten raw, roasted, boiled, dried, or pounded and mixed with berries, then baked in small, flat cakes (Dixon 1905:189). A digging stick aided in gathering roots and bulbs. This was a straight stick, a yard or more in length, with one end hardened by fire. Utilized roots included blue camas (McMillin 1963), the Indian root, cattail root, and the tule root (Duncan 1964:47, 76, 77).

Yellow jacket larvae, angleworms, locusts, grasshoppers, and crickets were caught and eaten. To gather locusts and grasshoppers, a fire was started around a large hole in a meadow and the insects were driven into the pit and collected in quantity. They were eaten dry or roasted and were stored for use during the long winter months (Dixon 1905:191).

Eels were speared and the meat was cut into small pieces and stewed. Salmon were caught with a salmon-gig, fashioned from bone or antler, and dried by hanging on a pole. The whole fish when dried was pounded into a coarse powder, stored in baskets, and eaten dry (Dixon 1905:185). The Konkow regarded the first salmon catch of the season as an occasion for ceremony. The first fish had to be speared by a shaman, and after it was cooked each man ate a piece. Only then was fishing begun in earnest (Dixon 1905:198).

Fishing was also accomplished with the use of nets or fish traps. The nets varied in size with heavy or light cord woven into a large or small mesh, depending on the use of the net. The Maidu nets were of the bag type, which were held open at the mouth by a piece of elastic willow wand. A pole tied to the opposite side of the net mouth was raised when fish entered, thus closing the mouth and trapping the fish. Seine nets of the Konkow were large and capable of stretching across the width of a stream (Dixon 1905:143, 147).

Animals, as a food source, were hunted or captured. Of the species available in the Maidu and Konkow environments, only the coyote, dog, and wolf were not eaten. The Konkow also did not eat bear and mountain lion. Buzzards were avoided, as were lizards, snakes, and frogs (Dixon 1905:185).

Hunting necessitated knives, spears, bows and arrows. Hard black basalt was used for knives and spears. The stone was fastened to a handle of wood and secured with pitch. Spearpoints were inserted in the end of a wooden spearshaft, pitched and wrapped with sinew. Arrow points were made from obsidian, which was obtained through trade. Silicate material was also used, and some came from a cave near Oroville. The Table Mountain Cave was regarded as sacred, and a person going to get flint brought with him offerings of meat and beads for the spirits. Exploitation of this resource was somewhat controlled, and "a person was allowed to take only as much flint as he could break off at a single blow" (Dixon

1905:133). Having obtained the stone, the person in respect had to crawl out backwards. Bad luck or poor quality stone would result if these customs were not followed.

The Maidu, living in the mountains, depended much more on game than did the lowland people and, thus, became more skillful hunters (Dixon 1905:192). Good hunting dogs were highly prized. Hunting could be attempted as a single or collective (deer drives and bear hunts) effort.

The grizzly bear was hunted for its hide, which was used in ritual dances. In the spring a ceremony was held in the front of the cave of a bear nearing the end of his hibernation. In the ceremony, the men addressed the bear, instructing it to stand up and let them shoot, as its life had already been paid for. The participants concealed themselves behind trees in the vicinity of the cave. The first man would approach the bear and shoot one or two arrows. He then ran, with the bear in pursuit, to the hiding place of another hunter. This continued until the bear, his body full of arrows, finally succumbed (Dixon 1905:194).

Deer could be hunted alone, but were more often caught during large deer drives. Such a hunting effort involved great numbers of men, lasted several days, and ranged over a large extent of land. Deer were either driven over a steep cliff or routed along their favorite runways and then shot by concealed hunters. Squirrel, rabbit, and elk were shot with arrows. The elk were followed for days and killed with arrows when exhausted. Rabbits were caught in nets and then clubbed to death. Quail were snared along known runways. Because it brought bad luck, the eagle was never shot. Geese and duck were either shot or caught in nooses that were hung by a cord above the water's surface (Dixon 1905:192, 195).

Meat was prepared by baking or roasting. Fire was started with a buckeye fire drill, which was twirled between the palms of the hands to ignite dry grass and tinder wood (Dixon 1905:191, 181). In baking, rocks placed in a hole were heated by a fire and then the fire was raked out. The meat, wrapped in broad, flat maple leaves, was placed in the pit and the hot stones were piled on top. The hole was filled with earth, and in one or two hours the meat was ready. For roasting, meat was placed directly on the coals (Dixon 1905:191; Duncan 1964:32).

The hides of animals were used for clothing, for adornments such as headbands and belts, and for sinew for tools. Tanning was an occupation of the women. Bone or stone scrapers were used to remove hair and the hide was then placed on a slanting post set in the ground. A cake of dried deer brain was dipped into warm water and rubbed over the skin. Following this, the hides were soaked in water, wrung out, and rubbed down before a fire until dry (Dixon 1905:142).

Salt was obtained from local salt deposits but was not used extensively (Dixon 1905:191). Among the Konkow, other condiments used included dandelion, deerbrush flour, hazelnuts, watercress, wild garlic, and onion (Duncan 1964:12).

Culture

Clothing and Adornment

Although the climate of the Maidu and Konkow environments differed considerably, the same clothing was worn by both groups and did not vary with the seasonal temperatures. All year around, the clothing was scant. In the heat of summer, men, as a rule, went naked or wore only a breechcloth of buckskin (Dixon 1905:155). Women wore an apron skirt consisting of two tassels in front and back. In the foothills, the tassels were of grass or of willow or maple bark. In the mountains, the apron was made of buckskin or bark.

Moccasins were worn only by the Maidu. In the severe cold of winter, grass was stuffed inside to give added warmth. Moccasins were of unsoled deer skin. They were sewed with a seam up the front and reached above the ankle. For protection against the snow, an additional piece of deer hide was worn from the ankle to the knee. This legging was worn with the hair side in and fastened at the knee and around the bottom of the moccasin. Snowshoes were also used in winter (fig. 3) (Dixon 1905:162–163, fig. 34; Kroeber 1925:405).

Robes of deer or mountain lion skin were worn with the fur side in, draped over the shoulders. Older men in the mountain area wore a netted cap called the ʔolé (Konkow wĭkaˑ) This was used during dances to attach ceremonial headdresses. Maidu women wore as a head covering a basket hat or cap made of tules in a manner characteristic of those worn by the Achumawi, Klamath-Modoc, and Sahaptin women. Thus, they differ from those worn by the Shasta, Yurok, and Karok (Dixon 1905:162).

The Maidu wore their hair long and left hanging loosely, while the Konkow cut their hair shorter. Soaproot was used for washing, and hair was trimmed with a hot ember. Beaten pine cones and porcupine tails were used as hairbrushes. The Konkow men plucked beard and mustache growth, while the Maidu did allow mustache growth that was slight (Dixon 1905:163).

Ornaments were of shell, bone, feathers, and wood (Dixon 1905:164). Necklaces were made from colored shell and dentalia. Women pierced their ears and wore ear ornaments (fig. 5) of bone or wood with woodpecker scalps or quail tips attached. Men pierced the septum of the nose and wore one or two woodpecker feathers. Among the Konkow, the nose was pierced as a part of the initiation into the secret society.

Paint was made of white or red clay, a red stone, fir tree fungus, or charcoal. It was applied before ceremonial

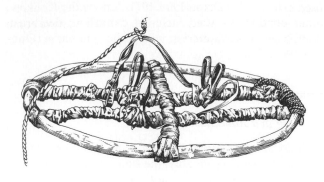

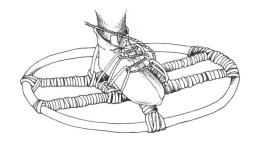

after Dixon 1905: fig. 34.
Fig. 3. Maidu snowshoes.

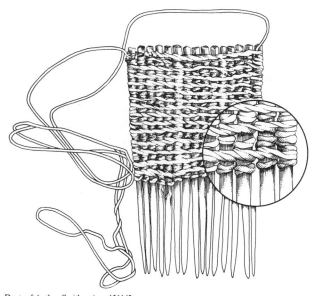

Dept. of Anthr., Smithsonian: 131142.
Fig. 4. Konkow comb. Whittled wood splints fastened together by twined cord. Length 11.5 cm; collected 1889.

dances, and the patterns were simple dots and rough streaks. The Maidu tattooed by puncturing the skin with fish bones, pine needles, or bird bones. Then a red pigment was rubbed into the skin. Men were more often tattooed with patterns of vertical lines on the chin or a single vertical line rising from the root of the nose. Tattooing was also applied to the breast, arms, and

376

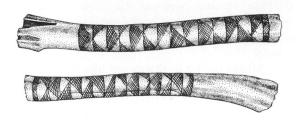

Dept. of Anthr., Smithsonian: 2638, 2640.
Fig. 5. Ornaments worn in pierced earlobes. Bird bones with design incised and filled with dark pigment. Average length 13 cm; collected 1838-1842.

abdomen. The Konkow tattoo designs were made by cutting the skin with sharp flint or obsidian, then rubbing the area with charcoal or a reddish pigment. Women were more elaborately tattooed with three, five, or seven vertical lines on the chin. Lines or dots were occasionally applied to the backs of the hands (Dixon 1905:167).

Structures

Three dwelling structures were used as the seasons varied during the year. The semisubterranean earth-covered lodge (fig. 2) and the conical bark dwelling were used only for four or five months beginning in November (Dixon 1905:175). In the summer, shade shelters were constructed close to hunting and gathering sites off and away from the main village. The summer shade was built on upright poles supporting a flat roof of oak branches and leaves. There were no walls and there was space enough for ceremonial activities.

The semisubterranean multifamily winter living and assembly house was constructed in spring when the ground was soft (Voegelin 1942:182). It was of circular ground plan, was excavated to a depth of about four feet, and had a diameter of 20 to 40 feet. The earth removed was used later as a part of the roof cover.

The dwellings which the Konkow built above the river canyons were, as among the Maidu, of three structural types. The semisubterranean lodge, excavated in the spring when the earth was soft enough for digging, was constructed in a form somewhat different from its Maidu counterpart (Dixon 1905:169).

Technology

Basketry was both an art and a necessity. Twining was used for burden baskets, milling or mortar baskets, storage or dish baskets, seed beaters, and fish traps. Material varied with the species available in the environment. The Maidu used roots of yellow pine and bear grass (*Xerophyllum tenax*), together with the roots of the common brake (*Pteridium acquilinum*) or the stems of the maidenhair fern (*Adiantum pedatum*). The Konkow used willow (*Salix* spp., including *S. hindsiana*) or the redbud (*Cercis occidentalis*) with shoots of hazelnut (*Corylus cornuta*) forming the radial elements in burden baskets.

RIDDELL

The Konkow used a simple twining while the Maidu used a twining with a double overlay. Designs were worked in with different colored sewing splints made from redbud, willow, and pine root dyed black with charcoal (Dixon 1905:145–146). Patterns were simple diagonals, either parallel or zigzag (Kroeber 1925:414).

Coiled basketry was more complicated (fig. 6). These baskets were very firm and water-tight. They were normally either a brownish red or black on a white or neutral background (Kroeber 1925:414). A bundle of three twigs was coiled tightly to another bundle with the sewing splint. The separate bundles of three were joined together by passing the sewing splint over the first three twigs and then under the upper twig of the bundle below. Baskets were made in varying sizes, with a proportionately varied stitch.

The Maidu make a twined overlay design, but only on their burden baskets. This idea was possibly taken up from their northern neighbors. The Konkow do not use overlay designs on their twined baskets, although in general the technical aspects of Konkow twining are similar to those of the Nisenan and the Maidu. The

Konkow usually employ diagonal twining for burden baskets and weave designs into them that may have come from coiled basket antecedents and from the ancient-style horizontal band patterns. The Nisenan do not use the

Dept. of Anthr., Smithsonian: top left, 328035; bottom, 313252; top right, 131104.
Fig. 6. Maidu coiled baskets. right, Basket woven with red woodpecker feathers, rim decorated with quail plumes and shell beads; diameter 22 cm, collected 1889. center and left, Same scale; collected before 1921.

Dept. of Anthr., Smithsonian: 131099.
Fig. 7. Konkow carrying sack. Knotless netting of 2-ply milkweed fiber cord with leather strap; detail shows construction of rim. Length 38 cm; collected 1889.

377

MAIDU AND KONKOW

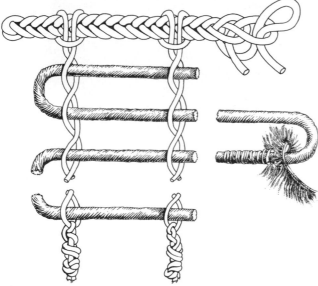

Fig. 8. Maidu feather blanket. The weft cord is closely wrapped with webs of feathers stripped from their shafts. The warp cords are attached to a braided cord on the upper edge of the blanket and are twined to hold the continuous weft cord. They are finished on the lower edge by knotting. The feathers used are wood duck, mallard, and Canada goose. Width 108 cm; collected 1841.

coiled-type patterns for their twined baskets. Konkow burden baskets are so similar in design and weaving to Pomo and Patwin that they are nearly indistinguishable. In overall appearance they are more closely related to these two groups than they are to their Nisenan kinsmen (Lawrence Dawson, personal communication 1974).

The tule mat was made from the rushes along rivers and served as seats, beds, roofing, and doors (Kroeber 1925:415). Tule leaves were used shredded for skirts, rafts, mats, beds, coverings of the summer shelter, dance headdresses, and doors (Dixon 1905:148, 198, 292, 304). In a twined form, they were used as sacks, mats, headbands, and in basketry (Voegelin 1942:62, 80, 102, 198).

Other textile art included blanket making (fig. 8). Woven rabbit skin, wildcat skin, and geese and crow skins were used as blankets and robes. Feather work was created for dancing implements, headdresses, belts (fig. 9), and ornamental ropes. Feather plumes were made by tying the feathers to small sticks that were then bound and decorated with strings of beads.

Transport

Since the rivers of the foothill region were too swift for navigation, the Konkow did not manufacture watercraft, although the Maidu used canoes in the mountain regions. There were dugout boats made by burning out the center of logs. Single paddles or poles were used for steering. In addition to the canoe, simple log rafts were constructed for crossing rivers.

Fig. 9. Konkow woman's dance belt. Buckskin covered with woodpecker scalps; abalone pendants attached along lower edge. Length 103 cm; collected 1889.

RIDDELL

Tobacco

Tobacco (*Nicotiana attenuata*) was the only cultivated plant. Pipes were one piece and tubular. An elderwood pipe was used for social gatherings or bedtime smoking. A stone pipe was smoked by shamans for ceremonies where tobacco was used as an offering (Voegelin 1942:92–93).

Political Organization

•LAW AND PROPERTY   Land for fishing and hunting was held in common. Any member of the village community could procure food from the defined tribal territory. The boundaries of the community property were guarded by different pairs of men selected each week to protect against poachers. They wore a single magpie feather upright on the top of the head. The men were selected for their steadiness of temper and good judgment. The underbrush was kept clear by burning in order to make hunting easier and to define territory in war. Within the common land, certain families could claim fishing holes as their own and if any other tribe member wished to use the private property, permission had to be secured. Among the Maidu, it was common for families to erect and own private deer fences. The fishing holes and deer fences were inherited in the direct male line (Dixon 1905:224–227).

Other property was owned by men or women according to need and service. The men owned their hunting and fishing implements such as nets, bows, arrows, spears, canoes, clothing, and knives. The *kúm* was also the property of the male. Women owned those materials necessary for housekeeping, cooking, and gathering. Baskets, utensils, acorn pestles, mats, blankets, digging sticks, seed beaters, and basketmaking supplies were among the woman's possessions. Due to the custom of burning all the personal property of a man at his death, there was little to be inherited. Those things that were not destroyed went first to the eldest son and then the rest was shared by the other children (Dixon 1905:226).

Theft of material possessions within the tribal community was punished by reprisal. If the thief was caught, he had to pay the aggrieved with something of equal value. If the thief did not pay, the aggrieved had the right to kill him. Theft or murder committed on the person of another tribal community was not regarded as wrong and involved no blame or punishment by the home people. The most important means of dealing with murder was by blood revenge. In both intertribal and intratribal murder, the victim's family had the right to kill the murderer. Effort was made to kill the offender in the same way that the original victim lost his life. The same weapons were used, the same wounds inflicted. Among the Konkow, the murder could be appeased by payment if the victim's family was willing to bargain. According to custom, if the offense was between two villages, parties from both sides, dressed in war dress, met and sat at conference until a price was agreed upon. The customs were the same for the Maidu, except that the murderer had to fast, eating no acorns or meat. Often, even after a price was paid, blood revenge was exercised. When a woman was killed, the aggressors often gave a woman of their own village or tribe to the aggrieved in order to avoid blood revenge or reprisal (Dixon 1905:227).

Oaths of any kind were not given, perhaps were not necessary, as evidenced by the Konkow belief, "the man with a crooked tongue is like the man with the crooked arrow." Lying was therefore avoided but it was not usual to curse another man. "The worst that could be said to a person was to wish that a snake might bite him" (Dixon 1905:227–228).

•LEADERSHIP   The group headman played a relatively minor role in village community organization and was not selected by inheritance. Rather, he was chosen through the aid of a shaman who conveyed the choice of the spirits to the people. The chief was chosen for his maturity, wealth, ability, and generosity. He could also be removed by the word of the shaman, again a messenger of the spirits (Dixon 1905:223–224).

The Konkow chief was primarily an advisor; he was responsible to a council composed of elder members of the Kuksu cult. His duties in war involved leading his tribe into battle. The chief could declare war and, among the Maidu, could negotiate for peace. The chief had special rights to the ceremonial earth-covered lodge as his place of residence, and it was often burned at his death. There were no redistribution advantages; the chief hunted and received food as did other members of the village community. In addition, he provided food for visitors and ceremonies; apparently he depended on support from relatives and possibly others to do this. The chief directed communal activities of deer drives, fishing, and gathering (Voegelin 1942:106).

War

Most warfare involved feuding between villages within a village-community or between village-communities. Often war was associated with blood revenge and could be avoided by meeting a demanded price as restitution. There were also traditional foreign enemies to contend with. To the north, the Maidu had conflicting interests with the Washo, Yana, and Achumawi but were on better terms with the Paiute. The Konkow fought the Yana (Dixon 1905:205–206).

Raiding and ambush were the most common tactics as there was little feeling of tribal unity. At times, several villages would band together against a common enemy but these unions were only temporary. Attack was usually at dawn, and warning of an attack was given with smoke signals and fire. On the battleground, the men stood with their side to the enemy and kept in constant motion to dodge arrows, which were often poisoned.

Spears, sticks, and slings were also employed in fighting. Elkhide armor covered the body from the knees to the shoulders. Straight round sticks of mountain mahogany were also made into armor; these were bound into the form of a waistcoat with a high collar that enabled the warrior to withdraw his head entirely from an approaching wave of arrows (Dixon 1905:205).

The Konkow were known to torture their captured male enemies. If the prisoner were an ordinary person, women were allowed to take part in the ceremony that led to the eventual death of the prisoner. If he were an important or influential person, only the men took part and the ceremony was led by the shaman. Here the victim was shot with arrows. In the warfare of the Maidu, male prisoners were usually killed. The slain were then scalped and the scalps were suspended on a pole on the return of the warriors to their village. Women were carried off by their captors but usually escaped after a short time. Slaves were not common, although often the captured women would serve in the families of the enemy until they could escape (Dixon 1905:206–207).

Trade

Trade was with immediate neighbors who could provide goods that the Maidu and Konkow could not ordinarily obtain. The Konkow secured from neighboring groups shell beads, pine nuts, and salmon. In return they gave arrows, bows, deer hides, and several sorts of food to Maidu and to the Wintuan peoples. The Maidu traded with the Achumawi despite their mutual enmity, giving bows and deerhides and receiving beads, obsidian, and a green pigment for dye. In exchanges, beads were counted individually, not by the string. Currency was a standard circular, disk-shaped shell bead. These beads, when traded, were often rough and the Maidu performed much of their own bead finishing. Strung clamshell disk beads and baked magnesite cylinder beads were also highly prized. The Konkow received abalone shell from the Wintuans, which went primarily into ear ornaments and necklace pendants rather than currency. Dentalia were valued highly and were too rare for use as standard money (Dixon 1905:201–202; Kroeber 1925:399, 421).

Life Cycle

• MARRIAGE   Marriage was simple, being established by the couple living together. The customs of initial courtship differ somewhat between the Maidu and Konkow. Common to both groups were the practices of patrilocal residency and the levirate. There was no rule of exogamy; in either group a man was free to wed within his village but usually went elsewhere to find a wife. Before residing permanently in the husband's village, the married couple lived for a time with the bride's family, and the new husband rendered service to them by providing food. After this initial service it was not uncommon for the husband to occasionally provide for his wife's family, and

it was considered an advantage to see a daughter married to a good hunter. In both groups chiefs or rich men had many wives. According to the practice of levirate, a man had first claim to his wife's sisters; if he failed to exercise his right, it passed to his brother (Kroeber 1925:403). Divorce in both groups was simply a matter of the wish of either party involved.

Among the Konkow, when a man wanted to marry he repeatedly visited the girl's home and engaged in topical conversation with her father. He then brought gifts of his own hunting and fishing efforts, and if these were accepted, he visited once more. This time, without further discussion, the couple was given a separate bed and were considered married. They continued to reside in the girl's home for a few months before taking up their patrilocal residence. The Maidu courtship was somewhat more abrupt. A man would visit a girl's family and plan to spend the night. If the girl did not want him, she would sit up all night. Her decision was greatly influenced by her parents, and an important consideration was of the man's worth as a good provider. After the initial decision, the couple resided for a time in the girl's home and the husband provided the family with fish and game (Kroeber 1925:401).

• BIRTH   A woman took considerable care during her pregnancy; she ate no meat or fish and, during the last part, did not leave her home. At this time, the husband was restricted from hunting and fishing. Among the Maidu, the parturient was assisted by a midwife and remained in her dwelling house or the summer shade shelter for the delivery. The Konkow woman left the village and went to a secluded spot outdoors to deliver her child. She was assisted by an old woman of the village and gave birth in a sitting position. To hasten delivery, hot herbal teas were administered and immediately after birth, heated stones would be placed on the mother's abdomen. The afterbirth was buried directly by the Konkow, while among the Maidu it was kept, wrapped in skin, grass, or bark, until the navel cord dropped off (Voegelin 1942:115). The child was immediately washed with warm water and the umbilical cord was cut with a sharp shell. The Maidu carefully preserved the cord and tied it to the baby's cradleboard (Dixon 1905:228–230).

Following the birth, the parents abstained from labor and the father did not hunt or fish. The period of rest and quiet for the new parents varied. The Maidu couple remained at home until the remnants of the umbilical cord fell away. The Konkow father remained at home while his wife stayed in the menstrual hut until she could again walk easily. In the case of a stillborn child, these restrictions were more severely enforced. The Konkow husband would fast for one month, and his wife remained in seclusion and fasted for three months. The Maidu husband and wife went off into the mountains for some months; the man returned alone while the woman stayed behind for additional seclusion. It was considered unlucky by the Konkow to give birth to twins. The mother often was killed with the children (Dixon 1905:230).

Until a child was about two or three years old, its designation was "boy," "girl," or "baby." The Konkow gave a name that either fit a characteristic of the child or pertained to some circumstance at the time of birth. Names were descriptive, such as 'snoring bird' or 'climbing girl'. The woman's name was changed at puberty, childbirth, and again at old age. The male received a new name on entering the Kuksu cult or secret society. These were given by older members and would be characteristic names such as 'wing-tied-up', 'pine-nut-eater', 'stick-it-in-the-ear', or 'licking-head'. In the Maidu families a child might be named after a deceased relative one year after the death, as this would remove the taboo placed on the dead person's name (Dixon 1905:230–231).

• PUBERTY At the first menses, the Konkow girl observed several restrictions while she remained quietly at home. She did not eat meat or fish and was fed only acorns, seeds, and roots by her mother. Five vertical, parallel stripes, alternating red and black, were painted on each cheek. When the last marks were removed, the girl was considered ready to marry.

At adolescence, a close friendship between two Indian girls among the Konkow is noted as being relevant to the female puberty rites. The older of the two served as the attendant for the younger who was experiencing her first menstrual period. On the first day, the girl and her friend stood with heads covered in the center of a ring of pine needles. These were set on fire and the two girls had to escape and run a short distance away. They then returned to the circle of women. There was much singing and laughter and they were given a warm bath. Afterward all retired to the girl's house, and at nightfall dancing and singing began and continued for five nights, lasting each night until dawn. The old women would sing and dance a ceremonial dance called the *wúlu* (Maidu *wulú*), which tells of their desire that the girls have eternal youth. Since, according to tradition, old people were eaten by the crow or *ʔáˑk̄a* (Maidu *ʔaʔá* or *k̄ák̄a*), one song in translation reads, 'put the two girls on the bridge so the crow cannot get them' (Densmore 1958:48; Dixon 1905:233–234).

The Maidu girl, at the first day of menstruation, journeyed with her mother into the mountains. She observed strict food restrictions and had to eat from her own dishes and drinking vessels. A scratching stick was used, and during the entire period the girl carried with her a deer-hoof rattle. At the end of the first day, the mother and child built numerous fires in the hills to signal to the village below that the ceremonies were to begin. They returned to the village where relatives had assembled and the dancing and song was begun outside around a large fire. The girl joined in the dances and at their finish the deer-hoof rattle was thrown to the girl, who ran off from the circle at top speed, signifying the end to that evening's dancing. The dances continued for four more

nights. After two nights of rest, the girl's ears were pierced at dawn of the eighth day. Dancing resumed that night and continued the following night. The morning of the tenth day, the girl painted her body in red, black, and white and joined in the *wulú* dance in which only the women took part. At noon the girl was bathed and the remainder of the day was spent in feasting. At the subsequent period, one month later, the entire ceremony was repeated and ended with a final dancing of the *wulú* (Dixon 1905:236–237).

There were no formal boys' puberty rites for the Maidu. The Konkow initiation of boys into the secret society took place at age 15 or older and could be considered a ceremony of adolescence rites. These new members were called *yéphoni*. The shaman, as head of the *yéphoni*, received from the voices of spirits the names of those to be initiated. It was to his advantage to name "bad" men so that they would not be inclined to harm the society. After a meeting or ceremony in the dance house, the shaman would attempt to capture those chosen by closing the door of the chamber. The candidates would attempt to escape while all others were made to leave. The doors were again shut and the shaman distributed to each candidate a wand that was hung up inside the dance house. The ceremony continued as a sacred acorn and birch-seed meal was sprinkled on the hair of each boy. The shaman ran around the initiates with a stick from the fire and then sprinkled water upon them. He called for food, and goods were distributed among the old and new members. One initiate was appointed to give a feast on the following day. The new members were then taught the dances of the *yéphoni* and during this time observed restrictions involving a taboo against eating any flesh and the use of a scratching stick. The ceremonies and dance lessons lasted for eight days, at the end of which new names and the wands were given to the initiates. Each was allowed to wear a netted cap as an insigne of membership. Following the eight days of initiation each new member gave a feast, and so there was a period of continued merriment (Dixon 1905:322–326).

• DEATH In the mythology, it is related that the Creator Wanome (Konkow *wóˑnommi* 'immortal [one]') brought death to the people although he originally did not want the Indians to die. Coyote, who is spoken of in many myths, wanted the people to die because he wanted burials and memorial burnings. When Coyote's own son died he tried to made Wanome bring him back to life, but Wanome made his final decision: "You wanted it this way, and this is the way it will be from now on" (D. Hill 1969:5). And so, the Maidu and Konkow observed burial customs and the latter participated in an annual mourning ceremony during which goods and materials were displayed and burned.

The Maidu and Konkow acknowledged the existence of the soul, which they referred to as "heart." At a person's death it was said that "his heart has gone away"

(Kroeber 1925:439; Dixon 1905:259). The soul left "like wind" from the mouth of the Konkow and then had to retrace every step taken in life. During this journey it haunted well-known places. The Milky Way was a path to the other world that the soul could follow after its time of haunting the past world. The good souls followed the left-hand fork of the Milky Way, which led to the "Heaven Valley." Bad people were changed into rocks and bushes. When a Maidu died, his soul stayed for a time and "blew about" crying constantly. The soul then left for the other world and was guided by deceased relatives toward the east, where the Creator lived, and passed through a gate into a paradise of food and pleasure (Dixon 1905:261–262).

Burial was the method of corpse disposal for both the Konkow and the Maidu. The Konkow dressed the body in the finest clothing and placed it in a flexed position in a bear skin. It was buried facing the west, along with some food and material possessions. The Maidu dressed their dead in beads and feathers and wrapped the body in otter skin. The body was buried in an extended position facing the east. Personal property and gifts were tied into a bundle and placed in the grave (Dixon 1905:243–244). Cremation was used by the Konkow when a person died away from home, the ashes then being carried back to the village and buried there.

Initial mourning customs were practiced by both groups. This may be accounted for by the belief that the soul stayed in among the people before journeying to the other world. The Konkow widow and widower cut their hair short and covered themselves with a mixture of pine pitch and charcoal. The widow remained in the house all day and spent her time weaving baskets that were to be burned during the annual mourning celebration. The widower refrained from gambling or dancing until after participation in the burning ceremony (Dixon 1905:243–244). Among the Maidu, only the women usually showed outward signs of mourning by covering themselves with the pitch and cutting the hair short. Men would do the same only on the occasion of the death of their father.

The mourning anniversary of the Konkow was an elaborate means of generating offerings to the dead and an economic exchange of material goods. When a person died his house and belongings were initially burned. Then, once each year for usually five consecutive years, the deceased's family participated in the anniversary burning ceremony during which they displayed, exchanged, and burned material goods that were prepared during the year for the ceremonies. Each village community had a designated burning ground ruled by a shaman of one of the villages. At the death of a family member, the mourners paid for a "string" with beads, furs, or food. The arrangement of the beads on the string indicated the family's membership to a particular burning ground where they would participate in the next burning cere-

mony. If another family member died in this time, the necklace was worn for five years following the most recent death. At the end of five years, the necklace was returned (Dixon 1905:246).

On the first evening of the mourning anniversary rites, the mourners cried at the graves of the deceased, which were then covered with "flour" and then with earth. The second evening, all proceeded to the designated burning ground, which was a circular enclosure 50–100 feet in diameter and surrounded by a brush fence. Each family brought its own poles, which were designed to display the materials made for burning (fig. 10). The poles were planted on the north and south sides of a central fire. A period of bargaining ensued during which many materials were exchanged and a family might elect to burn poorer materials in exchange for higher quality goods. The fire was lit by an old man and the shaman delivered an invocation. For the rest of the ceremony the mourners danced about the fire and cried out for their departed; there was much wailing and singing. At this time it was also believed that the ghosts or souls of the deceased could be seen to dance slowly about the fire. The ceremony climaxed when the poles were lifted down and the material goods removed. These were thrown into the fire and the mourners would enter a period of frenzy. The ceremony ended as the shaman instructed the people to go back to the dance house for the remainder of the day. There the mourners would engage in celebration; they were instructed to "eat, gamble, and make merry" (Dixon 1905:245–250; Kroeber 1925:431).

Religion

A background to the Maidu and Konkow cosmogony, numeration, superstitions, and religious life may be found in the content of the creation myth. The myth involves an initial meeting between the Creator or Earth Initiate and Turtle. Turtle was floating upon a raft over the surface of the earth, which was at that time covered only with water. From the sky, a radiant Earth Initiate descended and sat in the raft with Turtle. A conversation followed during which Turtle requested land and the Creator asked how he would be able to create dry land. To provide the land Turtle dived for mud and returned six years later. The land expanded at the word of the Earth Initiate and he then was able to instruct his sister the sun and his brother the moon to travel the skies and provide the land with light. He called forth the stars, birds from the air, trees, and animals and provided the great oak tree with its many varieties of acorns. He made man, whom he called *kúksu*, and woman, named Morning Star Woman, from dark red earth mixed with water. The Earth Initiate expressed the desire that the men and women he created live easy lives and he gave them a means of eternal life. This done, he left the earth for the world above.

Coyote, a mythological troublemaker, who involved himself in various Maidu and Konkow myths, arrived to

Amer. Mus. of Nat. Hist., New York.

Fig. 10. Poles with clothing and baskets attached to be burned by mourners to honor the dead and for their use, as part of the Konkow annual mourning ceremony. Photograph probably by S.A. Barrett, near Mooretown, 1904.

learn how easily the people were living. Coyote said, "That is no way to do. I can show you something better. We will have a mourning ceremony and burn property." It was for this objective that Coyote brought death to the people.

kúksu, on the instruction of the Earth Initiate, taught the people how to cook and hunt, gave them their laws, dances, and festivals, and then they were suddenly made to speak many different languages. *kúksu* sent them to all different parts of the world and they became the forefathers of different Indian tribes (Gifford and Block 1930:85-91).

The world created by the Earth Initiate was believed to be a flat, circular island floating on the surface of the sea. The Creator stretched ropes to anchor the land mass. The number of ropes used for this security differs according to the numeration beliefs and the geographic directions recognized among the Maidu and Konkow. The Maidu saw the earth anchored by five ropes stretching to the north, south, east, west, and northwest. Five was considered the sacred number and it was to the above five directions that the Maidu oriented himself. The Konkow practiced the ritualistic Kuksu cult and believed in the number four, which was a characteristic sacred number among the cult. The Konkow oriented themselves to the four directions from which the supportive ropes of the earth were stretched: north, south, east, and west (Dixon 1905:264-265).

Natural, climatic phenomena were explained in reference to variations of a myth concerning how fire was brought to the people. In general, fire was kept by a man and his daughters and, after Lizard discovered fire, it was stolen from the sentinel bird guarding it and brought back by a group of animals. In the race to bring the fire to man, Thunder and his two daughters, Rain and Hail (Northwind is also referred to as a daughter of Thunder), are seen as the pursuers. Stars were soft like buckskin, and the constellations were given names and purposes. Falling stars were thought to be "taking or carrying fire" and the rainbow was believed to be the urine of Coyote (Dixon 1905:265).

Mythology deals with numerous animals such as the hummingbird, lizard, dog, rattlesnake, and coyote. The coyote is noticeable in most myths, and there are Coyote stories that trace adventures of this character who is seen as opposite of the benevolent and wise Creator. Coyote is a trickster, and he causes most of the original creations to be modified to their present and less ideal states as utilized by man in daily life. There are stories concerning his roguish sexual adventures.

Charms were employed to stop storms or to bring rain or protection. Burning feathers, wild pepperwood, or oak leaves would stop a storm. Smoking or praying ceremoniously was the recourse during the periods of drought. Thunder was heard when a person was bitten by a rattlesnake or when a great man died or a woman had a miscarriage. Charms used to insure luck in hunting were in the form of stones found inside a deer and were worn about the neck. The shaman used charms to "rub out" pains of illnesses. Gambling charms were stones that were found and kept because of unusual shape or color. Roots could also serve as good-luck charms (Dixon 1905:266-267).

The Maidu and Konkow environs were occupied by mysterious powers and spirits. These lived in natural geographic sites such as rocky peaks, cliffs, rapids, waterfalls, and mountain lakes and also in the sky. Each shaman had one or many of these spirits as his guardians and sources of power (Dixon 1905:265).

The shaman was an important figure in Maidu and Konkow society. Since there was no complex political organization, the shaman, with his mysterious powers and spiritual communication, provided a sense of unity among the village community. He functioned in the festivals, Kuksu cult ceremonies and dances, and political relations with other tribes. He also served as a medical doctor, capable of healing the sick or causing sickness to fall upon an individual or entire village. The Maidu shamans inherited their office. The son, only following the death of his father, would become very ill and after a period of ceremony within the dance house he left the village and spent some months in the mountains where he met and won the favor of the spirits who were to be his guardian powers. These were thought to be the same spirits as identified with the father and were sometimes the ghosts of kinsmen. Among the Konkow there was a tendency toward hereditary shamanism, although there were defined methods for a person to become a shaman without family predecessors. The Konkow distinguished between dream shamans, who held assemblies in the dance house that were primarily clairvoyant proceedings, and the doctor shamans, who possessed the greater powers of healing or of causing sickness. The Maidu recognized only the all-powerful shaman who inherited his powers. Shamans underwent a period of instruction from older shamans and learned the art of curing "pains." This involved the sucking out of disease-causing agents that the shaman would display, like bits of wood, stone, bones, teeth, or small live animals. Shamans were not totally benevolent. They were known to possess different magical poisons that they administered by, for instance, touching or casting a shadow on the person they intended to kill. The pains a shaman sucked out of a person might be used against him later. Female shamans were known to be primarily malevolent and caused great trouble with their numerous poisonings (Dixon 1905:267–283). Among the Konkow there was also the Kuksu cult, the leader of which was also a powerful shaman. The cult functioned primarily as a ceremonial and dance organization rather than as a group involved in tribal politics or warfare. The Kuksu cult had spirit impersonations and followed a dance cycle in which dances were representative of the different spirits. The dances began with the Hesi Dance (Valley Konkow *hési*), which was celebrated in late September or early October. This feast lasted three to four days; only the men were allowed to participate. The next dance was the Waima or Duck Dance, also only celebrated by the men. This was followed by the *pá·no* 'grizzly bear' Dance, in which the women and chief participated. The Oleil (Maidu *ʔolél* 'coyote') Dance lasted 48 hours and was called the chief's dance. The Kaima was performed by old people while children 8 to 10 years old were taught by verbal explanation. The *móloko* 'vulture' Dance was performed by women. In the *sími* 'deer' Dance, the dancers dressed to impersonate deer. The Aki (Valley Konkow *ʔá·ki*) was a ceremony for the increase of the acorn crop in which the dancers wore costumes much like that worn in the Hesi, but the women were allowed to take part in this dance. The cycle concluded with the repetition of the Hesi Dance in May. These dances were known among the Maidu although there was not the connection with a Kuksu cult. Dances were held inside the dance house. The large ceremonial dances such as the Hesi were usually followed by festivities, including gambling, straw games, and races (Nelson 1909a:5).

Knowledge

The Hesi Dance cycle marked off the year's passing but was not the only means of designating annual divisions. The Maidu and Konkow recognized four seasons and a further subdivision into moons or months. The four seasons were spring, *yóm mení* (Konkow *yóhmèní*) 'flower month'; summer, *kǎwkati* 'dust, earth'; autumn, *sém mení* 'seed month'; and winter, *kóm mení* 'snow month'. The Maidu divided the year into 12 moons, beginning in the spring. Each lunation had a name and meaning such as 'big month', 'ground-burning moon', or 'bread moon'. The Konkow referred to nine moons beginning their year in autumn. Some of the meanings given to the names of the months were 'seed moon', 'big-tree freeze moon', and 'little-tree freeze moon' (Dixon 1905:217–218).

Music, Games, and Art

Music and song accompanied the ceremonial dances, social dances, and game dances. Drums were called *kílemi* (in Konkow) and were made of a huge log usually of sycamore. Its sound was said to be "like the sound made by the bear." The rattles were named *wasóso* (in Maidu) and suggested the sound of swishing pebbles. Rattles, which were used by shamans, were also important in the adolescent rites of the Maidu girls. These were often made of green elder wood with the pith removed. A musical bow was played by holding one end in the mouth and tapping a single long string with the nail of the index finger. Flutes and whistles were used for melody (Densmore 1958:12–13). Song and dance were a form of amusement. A jumping dance was performed to the words, "I jump down and dance, then I jump back up and dance" (Densmore 1958:322). A dance using a sliding step was enacted by two men carrying bow and arrow and pretending to shoot.

A hand or grass game played by the men was a popular form of gambling. Bone cylinders were hidden in the hands under a bundle of grass. These cylinders were in pairs, with one bone marked, the other unmarked. The game was played by guessing which hand held the unmarked bone. The gamblers sat opposite one another, and large quantities of goods were wagered on the results (Densmore 1958:43). A game much like football was played between the men of two villages. Players stood in parallel lines and tried to kick a buckskin ball stuffed with deer hair to the goal, which was two poles set at the ends of the lines. The winning team was the one that reached the goal first. The women played a similar game, except that ropes or sticks were tossed toward the goals by means of a long pole (Kroeber 1925:419).

Art forms were recognized in basketry, bead work, and feather work. The only object decorated with paint was the bow. A greenish-blue pigment was applied with a feather tip to make a design that "looked like a snake" (Dixon 1905:221). In addition, there is poetry, as recognized in the words of a Maidu chant:

> The world above
> in the on-top land
> mortal men wanting to talk
> on your dark trail
> by power, pour (it) over hither.
> Superb superb
> tobacco smoke drift away
> you will inhale deeply, drying
>   out your throat
> Thus is that land (Shipley 1963:81).

History

Maidu and Konkow life was little affected by White contact until after the gold discovery at Coloma in 1848. In 1808 Gabriel Moraga explored up the Sacramento River to the lower reaches of the Feather River, in close proximity to Konkow country. In an expedition up the Feather River in 1820, Capt. Luis A. Arguello gave the river its name (El Rio de Las Plumas) (McGowan 1961). In 1828 Jedediah Smith with his band of trappers spent several months in Konkow territory (Sullivan 1934:74). From 1828 to 1836, brigades of Hudson's Bay Company trappers visited Konkow territory trapping fur-bearing animals. Michel Laframboise and John Work (Leader 1928) were leaders of such groups of trappers, both of whom spent the winter of 1833 at the Sutter Buttes to avoid high water. Capt. Charles Wilkes of the United States Exploring Expedition sent boats up the Sacramento River to a Konkow village in 1841 (Wilkes 1845, 5:185).

Captain John A. Sutter established New Helvetia, now Sacramento, in 1839. Although Sutter's Fort was in Nisenan territory, it provided a focal point for ultimate penetration into the lands of the Konkow and Maidu people by settlers and then gold seekers. In 1844, Gov. Manuel Micheltorena issued to two Americans grants to land in Konkow territory, not far from the present city of Chico. A year earlier the first group of overland immigrants led by Lansford Hastings passed through Konkow country on their way to Sutter's Fort. So-called Indian haters in this party fired on the Indians as they went through the area (Bidwell 1906:75–79). In 1847 John Bidwell (D. Hill 1970:26) wrote to John Sutter that 82 White people lived in the upper Sacramento Valley. It was in this year that Bidwell moved out of Sutter's Fort and began to develop his domain in the Chico area.

Probably the first of many disasters to befall the Konkow was an epidemic of what may have been malaria, which decimated them in 1833 (Cook 1955a:322). This was a blow from which the natives never effectively rallied. What disease did not do the influx of thousands of gold seekers after 1849 did. By this time even the remote Maidu country was overrun with exploring parties and gold hunters. First into the Maidu heartland, except possibly for occasional mountain men, was Peter Lassen, who reached Honey Lake in 1850 (Bruff 1949). By this time the barriers were down and the Maidu and Konkow soon became aliens in their own land. The miners hired Indians to work for them but usually paid them poorly for their work. In ensuing years the Konkow people worked as ranch hands and farm laborers.

With the arrival of the Whites with their livestock and farms, the Konkow and Maidu ecological balance was upset. Food sources formerly available became extinct or scarce or otherwise unavailable. The Indians began killing and eating the settlers' livestock; and retaliation by the settlers, miners, and immigrants was swift and excessive. Often defenseless and innocent groups of Indians were killed by excited White men when oxen or other livestock were missed. It is true that the Indians, too, killed the newcomers with or without provocation; however, it was most often the Whites who did the killing.

In 1850, in an attempt to settle conflict between Indians and Whites, Congress authorized treaties to be made with the Indians to place them upon reservations. The Konkow signed a treaty that would have given them a limited portion of their own land (D. Hill 1970:40–46). Senators from California opposed ratification of these treaties and further demanded that the Indians be removed from the state. The issue as far as the Konkow were concerned was resolved when a reservation was established at Nome Lackee in 1854 and some Konkow were removed there in 1855 (McGowan 1961:137). Throughout the 1850s and 1860s Indian "trouble" flared up, but by 1870 resistance by the Indians was essentially at an end. In 1863 mounted soldiers marched 461 Indians to Round Valley Reservation; 32 Indians died or were killed on the way. This two-week trek is still remembered by the survivors' descendants (D. Hill 1970:74–78).

As regards Maiduan population (in this case only the Konkow and Nisenan) and its decline, the following figures (adapted from Cook 1943a) clearly show that the coming of the Whites was a great disaster:

Aboriginal	8,000
1846	8,000
1850	3,500–4,500
1852	5,000
1856	2,300
1865	1,550
1880	1,000
1910	900

To the 1910 figure can be added an estimate of 200 Maidu to make a total of 1,100 Maiduan people (Maidu, Konkow, and Nisenan).

Kroeber (1925) estimates that the Maiduan people (including the Nisenan) numbered 9,000 aborigines. Of this number probably two-thirds were Maidu and Konkow, with the Konkow total probably somewhat greater than the Maidu. The Konkow homeland nearly coincides with the present political boundary of Butte County, while that of the Maidu coincides with Plumas County. Indians in Butte County in 1940, 1950, and 1960 numbered 261, 207, and 421, respectively. Many of these are Konkow with varying degrees of Indian ancestry. For Plumas County the censuses for the same years recorded 235, 218, and 240 Indians. A large proportion of them are Maidu, both full- and mixed-blood. An undetermined number of Maidu live in adjoining Lassen County and would thus increase the Maidu total by somewhat less than 100 people more.

Possibly one of the best sources of information regarding the number of people claiming California Indian ancestry is the listing of those California residents who filed applications for enrollment to participate in the distribution of the California Judgment (Indian Claims) funds in 1973. The number who filed from Butte County was 1,435, from Plumas 422, and from Lassen County 375. Not all these claimants were necessarily Maidu or Konkow, nor necessarily full-blood Indians.

The present condition of surviving Konkow and Maidu Indians is essentially the same as for other California Indians. They have a very high unemployment rate, poor housing and sanitation, and a low level of educational achievement. Economic advancement is slow in part due to the difficulty of acquiring loans for improving housing, for establishing small businesses, and for improving livestock, water supplies, or land resources. Heartening in the case of the Maidu and Konkow is a renewed interest in their traditional values and cultural expression. The former shame felt by these people in being Indian has changed to pride. One tangible manifestation of this is the vigorous continuation of the annual Maidu Bear Dance held each spring at Janesville. The affair is attended by Indians of numerous tribes, but the two-day gathering is primarily a Maidu-sponsored ceremony. Attempts at the preservation of their language, ceremonies, and the art of basket making, for example, coupled with their pride in being Konkow and Maidu, indicate a continuing struggle for personal and tribal identity and advancement.

Synonymy

The Maidu have been referred to as: Mai'-deh and Mai'-du (Powers 1877), Meidoos (Powers 1874), Midu (Merriam 1904), and Pujunan (Powell 1891). Their name is from their self-designation *maydɨ* 'person' (Shipley 1963:149).

The Konkow have been called: Cancons (Keane 1878), Cancow (ARCIA 1874), Caw-Caw (ARCIA 1868), Con-Con's (ARCIA 1870), Con-Cous (ARCIA 1867, 1868), Con-Cow (ARCIA 1863, 1864); Concow (Round Valley Cultural Project 1974), Cou-Cows (ARCIA 1864, 1865), Cow-Cow (ARCIA 1868), and KănKau (Curtin 1885).

The Konkow term *nótoꝁòyo·* refers to the Maiduan people from Quincy in the south to Susanville in the north—the Maidu proper. As *kíwsewimmà'a* the Konkow designate the people on the Middle Fork of the Feather River and up to Belden on the North Fork.

Sources

The primary source of information on the Maidu is the excellent work done by Dixon (1905). An earlier source of merit is that of Powers (1877). Kroeber (1925) is a good and generally available source containing data gathered on the Maidu from a number of early sources to provide a synthesis of their life and culture. Details of village locations and other ethnogeographic information are provided by Riddell (1968). Sensitive works by Robert Rathbun (Coyote Man 1973, 1973a) deal with aspects of Maidu life and mythology in a less formal, academic manner than has been done by others.

Sources for the Konkow that give the best coverage include, of course, Kroeber's works (1925, 1932a). Aspects of Konkow life and culture are found in D. Hill's (1970) ethnohistoric study, an ethnogeography by Riddell (1960–1974), and Rathbun's (1973, 1973a) publication.

The language of the Maidu and Konkow has been treated in considerable detail by Shipley (1963). Possibly the best tool for those interested in the Maiduan people is the bibliography prepared by Wilson and Towne (1972), which, while not complete, is quite extensive and is annotated.

Only limited professional archeological work has been done in Maidu territory (Riddell and Pritchard 1971). Archeological work done in the Oroville area, thus referable to the Konkow (Olsen and Riddell 1963), has resulted in a tentative archeological chronological table that gives a cross-dating with areas contiguous to the Konkow.

Nisenan

NORMAN L. WILSON AND ARLEAN H. TOWNE

Language, Territory, and Environment

The Nisenan (ˈnēsə͵nän), sometimes referred to as the Southern Maidu, were the southern linguistic group of the Maidu tribe. The word Nisenan (*nisena·n* 'from among us; of our side') was used as a self-designation by the Nisenan who occupied the Yuba and American river drainages.

Nisenan together with Maidu and Konkow form a subgroup of the California Penutian linguistic family.* Kroeber (1925:393) distinguished three dialects of Nisenan—Northern Hill Nisenan, Southern Hill Nisenan, and Valley Nisenan—although it is possible to make finer dialectal distinctions (see "Native Languages of California," this vol.).

The Nisenan territory was the drainages of the Yuba, Bear, and American rivers and the lower drainages of the Feather River (fig. 1). The western boundary was the west bank of the Sacramento River, a few miles upstream from the mouth of the Feather River southward to a few miles below the confluence of the American River. The northern boundary has not been clearly established due to the similarity of language to the neighboring groups (Kroeber 1925:393). The first true Nisenan was spoken in the drainage of the Yuba. The eastern boundary was the crest of the Sierra Nevada. The southern boundary was probably a few miles south of the American River with a large area between the American and Cosumnes rivers occupied by the Miwok to the south (Bennyhoff 1961: 204-209).

The west-east orientation of Nisenan landscape varied from the plain of the Sacramento River near sea level to 10,000-foot peaks on the Sierra crest, bisected with intermittent and year-round streams. East of the river is a flat, oak-studded grassland with denser vegetation along the streams and marshes. About 15 miles from the river the land rises into foothills covered with grasses, oak, pine, and chaparral, grading into oak and conifer forest, bisected by deep canyons supporting year-round streams. Above 5,000 feet are dense stands of conifers, rocky exposures, and small, grassy meadows. This entire region supported abundant game, waterfowl, fish, and plant resources.

The Nisenan recognized several political divisions within their territory, accepting the leadership of the headman of a specific village during times of major decisionmaking, group hunts, and ceremonies. The river-plain encompassed three such tribelet areas, each densely populated with several large villages. It is not clear which villages exercised major influence.

One center was at the mouth of the American River extending east a few miles and north and south on the Sacramento River. Pusune (*pusu·ne*) was an important village. Another center was at the mouth of the Bear River including the valley drainage of the Bear and a stretch of the Feather River. One major village was Hok. A third area was at the mouth of the Yuba River and reached the northern Nisenan boundary.

Hill Nisenan, between the Cosumnes River and the south fork of the American River near Placerville, formed another tribelet with strong affiliations with groups living in the lower drainages of the American River and in ridges that lay along the south fork of the American.

People occupying the ridges between the Bear River and the middle fork of the American River, including the ridges between the middle fork of the American and the Bear, formed another tribelet area. The territory of the upper drainages of the Bear and the Yuba rivers also is identified as forming another tribelet (Littlejohn 1928:10-15).

Few Indian villages existed on the valley plain between the Sacramento River and the foothills; the area provided hunting and gathering grounds for the valley people.

External Relations

Nisenan had few contacts outside their tribelet area of influence. These contacts were limited to trade, warfare, and ceremonial gatherings (Beals 1933:365).

Native communication followed the large streams, so familiarity was to the north and northwest in the Sacramento Valley. The San Joaquin portion of the valley was unknown to the Nisenan. Groups tended to identify themselves along physiographic lines, which were defined in the valley by stream systems and in the mountains by ridges. The Valley Patwin, Northern Maidu, and Valley Nisenan seem to have shared a consciousness of cultural

* Nisenan words cited here in italics have been transcribed by Richard Smith in the phonemic system described in Uldall and Shipley (1966), with the substitution of ɨ for their y and y for their j. Words not recorded by Uldall and Smith appear here in roman, with Kroeber's [ü] being interpreted as ɨ.

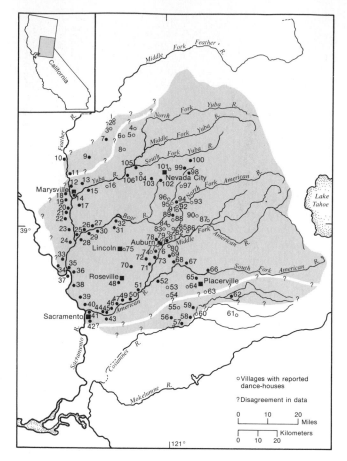

Fig. 1. Tribal territory with selected major villages. 1, Chichimbupu; 2, Manoma; 3, Onehuyan; 4, Mominku; 5, Polomyan; 6, Kaloma; 7, Helto; 8, Tuhu; 9, Toto; 10, Bayu; 11, Honkut; 12, Tomchoh; 13, Kulu; 14, Yupu; 15, Chiemwie; 16, Onopoma; 17, Taisida; 18, Molokum; 19, Mimal; 20, Sisum; 21, Hok; 22, Yukulme; 23, Popo; 24, Ollash; 25, Holloh; 26, Lelikian; 27, Intanto; 28, Homiting; 29, Talak; 30, Mulamchapa; 31, Bushamul; 32, Shutamul; 33, Yokol; 34, Olo; 35, Wollok; 36, Leuchi; 37, Nawe; 38, Wishuna; 39, Totola; 40, Pusune; 41, Momol; 42, Sama; 43, Yalisumni; 44, Sekumni; 45, Kadema; 46, Kishkish; 47, Yamankudu; 48, Pichiku; 49, Ekwo; 50, Shiba; 51, Yodok; 52, Yukulu; 53, Bamon; 54, Polunkit; 55, Chitokpakan; 56, Wapumni; 57, Kutba; 58, Komyan; 59, Opok; 60, Miminik; 61, Chletisu; 62, Chikimisi; 63, Ilemo; 64, Wuhulak; 65, Ekelepakan; 66, Tumeli; 67, Koloma; 68, Chapa; 69, Okilkil; 70, Bakacha, 71, Odayan; 72, Tete; 73, Opule; 74, Piuhu; 75, Bamuma; 76, Kotomyan; 77, Hu'ul; 78, Molma; 79, Bisian; 80, Siyakayan; 81, Chulku; 82, Didit; 83, Penui; 84, Popokemul; 85, Hakaka; 86, Watas; 87, Hempamyan; 88, Wemea; 89, Oyema; 90, Hembem; 91, Koyo; 92, Sumyan; 93, Palampenonu; 94, Soloklok; 95, Kaubusma; 96, Tuyi; 97, Siponi; 98, Ustuma; 99, Wokodot; 100, Kushna; 101, Tetema; 102, Hi'et; 103, Tsekankan; 104, Kayempaskan; 105, Yamaku; 106, Panpakan. These names have been anglicized wherever possible on the basis of the spellings in Kroeber 1925, 1929. Sources: Bancroft 1874-1876; Beals 1933; Bennyhoff 1961; Delano 1854; Gudde 1933; Hodge 1907-1910; Kroeber 1925, 1929, 1932a; Lienhard 1941; Littlejohn 1928; log of the ship *Alert*, 1841; Merriam 1966-1967; Powers 1877; Riddell 1972; Sacramento Claims 1928 (45 Stat. 602); Schoolcraft 1860; Sutter 1939; Wilkes 1849; Wilson 1957-1963.

similarity and an attitude of common cooperation and defense (Kroeber 1929:255-256).

Hill Nisenan knew the names of many of the major Valley Nisenan villages along the rivers due mainly to travel outside the local area by large groups of men for trading and fishing. Women and children rarely ventured outside their territory.

Black oak acorns, pine nuts, manzanita berries, skins, bows, and bow wood were traded to the valley people for fish, roots, certain grasses, shells, beads, salt, and feathers. Hill Nisenan traded acorns and shells for Washo seed beaters and dried fish from Pyramid Lake. Trade also brought into the area shell, magnesite, steatite, and obsidian from the west and obsidian from the east. Property was exchanged by local groups through gambling and settlement of disputes.

Settlement Pattern

The village or community group that controlled a certain territory and acted as a group in decisionmaking, ceremonies, and food gathering ranged from small extended families of 15 to 25 people to large villages of several families numbering over 500 (Kroeber 1925:831). This group occupied a village site or a cluster of small settlements around a large village. One village usually played a dominant role in this social-political organization. Its headman had the authority to call upon the surrounding villages in social and political situations. Relations were friendly but arguments occurred over trespass, hunting rights, and ceremonies. Family feuds might cause withdrawal of a family from a village; they would move to an adjoining village or establish a new settlement. Tensions occurred between tribelets over trespass, social crimes, insults to leaders, and gambling. Killing of Auburn/Nevada City men at Roseville in the 1820s caused deep-seated hatred of these people, and the epidemic of 1833 was explained as being caused by hill shamans sending bad air into the valley to avenge the killings (Payen 1961a:23; Wilson 1957-1963).

Valley Nisenan built their villages on low, natural rises along streams and rivers or on gentle slopes with a southern exposure. Villages varied in size from three to seven houses to 40 to 50 houses. Houses were dome-shaped, 10 to 15 feet across, and covered with earth, tule mats, or grasses. Brush shelters, supported by upright poles, were used in the summer and on food-gathering rounds (Kroeber 1925:407-408).

The dance house (*ƙúm*), located in major villages, was a semisubterranean structure, excavated to a depth of three to four feet, constructed with heavy beams and two or four main posts, with a covering of brush, tule, and earth. A smoke hole was at the top and the door usually faced east (Beals 1933:344). A plank drum was placed over a pit opposite the entrance. Another village structure was the acorn granary. The sweathouse, built similar to a *kúm* but to accommodate four or five men, was used for curing and purification. Caves are rare; however, a few occupied rockshelters, one ceremonial cave, and a sweating cave have been reported in Nisenan territory (Payen 1961a:22).

Hill Nisenan villages were located on ridges and large flats along major streams. They were smaller than in the valley, and it was common for family groups to live away from the main village. Houses were conical-shaped and covered with slabs of bark, skins, and brush. Brush shelters were used in the summer. Most villages had bedrock mortar sites.

Other sites included seasonal camps, quarries, ceremonial grounds, trading sites, fishing stations, cemeteries, river crossings, and battlegrounds.

Nisenan territory was crisscrossed with well-established trails, and the Nisenan gave most physical features a local place-name. They had intimate knowledge of their tribelet area and its boundaries.

Subsistence

The Nisenan area offered abundant year-round food sources. Food-gathering quests were based on seasonal ripening but hunting, gathering, and fishing went on all year with the greatest activity in late summer and early fall. They did not depend on one crop but gathered many different staples.

Seasonal harvests could be personal or communal property. Much activity and social behavior such as status, sharing, trading, ceremonies, and disagreements were important adjuncts to the gathering and distribution of food.

Extended families or whole villages of hill people would gather acorns. Men would hunt while the women and children gathered the nuts knocked from the trees. Buckeye nuts, digger and sugar pine nuts, and hazelnuts were also gathered.

Acorns were removed from the granary, cracked on an acorn anvil, and shelled. They were ground into flour using a bedrock mortar and a soaproot brush to control scattering (fig. 2). After leaching to remove the tannin (fig. 3), the flour was cooked in watertight baskets. During the cooking process fire-heated stones were lifted with two sticks, dipped in water to clean them, and then dropped into the cooking basket. Enough mush and soup was prepared for several days.

A headman could ask for acorns for a ceremony or a family in need. There were lazy people who never had enough acorns. These people would not be helped and they would often move in with relatives at another village during the winter (Wilson 1972:36).

Roots, dug with a digging stick in the spring and summer, were eaten raw, steamed, baked, or dried and pounded in mortars and pressed into cakes to be stored for winter use. Wild onion (chan), wild sweet potato

Fig. 2. Lizzie Enos using a soaproot brush to sweep back into the mortar acorn meal scattered during pounding. A Maidu winnowing tray lies nearby. Photograph by Norman Wilson, Oct. 1958.

(sɨkum), and "Indian potato" (dúbus) were most desired. Wild garlic was used to wash the head and body, and wild carrot (ba) was used as medicine (Littlejohn 1928:30).

Grasses, herbs, and rushes provided food and material for baskets and clothing. Seeds were gathered using a seed beater and tray. They were parched, steamed, dried, or made into mush.

Many varieties of native berries, wild plums, grapes, and other native fruits were eaten. Manzanita berries were traded to the valley or made into a ciderlike drink.

Game was roasted, baked, or dried.

Deer drives were common with several villages participating, the best marksmen doing the killing. A circle of fire could be used where the animals were driven to the center and killed. Deer were also hunted using deerskin and antler decoys, snares, and deadfalls. They were run down in soft ground or snow. Antelope was taken by the surround, drives, and flag decoys. Elk was usually killed along waterways in soft ground.

Much ceremony surrounded the bear hunt. Black bears were hunted in the winter. Lighted brands were used to drive them from their dens. Grizzlies on the valley floor were greatly feared and rarely hunted (Wilson 1972:34).

Wildcats and California mountain lions were hunted for food and their skins.

Rabbits and other small game were killed with sticks and blunted arrows. Traps, snares, nets, fire, and rodent hooks were also used. In the valley and foothills nets were made into a fence where driven rabbits were entangled and clubbed. Other small animals were caught and killed except the coyote. Drives usually took place in late spring. The catch was divided by the man in charge of the drive.

Weirs, nets, harpoons, traps, and gorgehooks, as well as tule balsas and log canoes were used in fishing. Fish were poisoned using soaproot and turkey mullein or driven into shallow water and caught by hand. Freshwater clams and mussels were obtained in the big rivers. On

Fig. 3. Lizzie Enos leaching acorn meal. A bedsheet is placed in a sand basin and surrounded with pine needles. The meal is put in the sheet and warm water is poured over it. Photograph by Norman Wilson, Oct. 1958.

the lower courses salmon and sturgeon were netted and speared. Suckers, whitefish, and trout were caught at higher elevations. Waterfalls were traditional eel-fishing stations; Salmon Falls, on the south fork of the American River, was one such location (Wilson 1972:35).

Birds were taken with arrows, nets, snares, traps, and nooses. Owls, vultures, and condors were not killed. Feathers and birdskins were used for regalia, clothing, and decoration.

Grasshoppers were gathered in meadows in the summer. They were chased into conical pits by drivers beating the grass. A smoking grass bundle was thrown into the pits for killing. They were soaked in water and baked in an earth oven. A light crushing with a handstone on a basketry tray broke off the wings and legs, which were winnowed away. They were eaten whole, crushed into a meal, cooked like a mush, or stored (Wilson 1972:36). A ring of fire was also built to creep through the

underbrush roasting the grasshoppers and other insects (Wilson 1957–1963).

Larvae and pupae as well as ants and other insects were eaten. Some were gathered for medicinal use and for poisons. Lizards and frogs were also eaten (Powers 1877).

Salt was taken from springs near Lincoln, Cool, and Latrobe. It was also obtained from a plant with cabbage-like leaves gathered in the summer.

Culture

Clothing and Adornment

Clothing was scant and adornment moderate. Men went naked or wore a breechclout of deerskin or pounded wire grass. The women wore short aprons made of wire grass, tule, or shredded maple or willow bark.

Fur blankets and skins were worn by Hill Nisenan while bird-feather robes were more common to the valley

Fig. 4. Captain Tom of Auburn wearing a rabbit-fur robe, flicker quill headband, a stick with woodpecker scalps and flicker feathers, and an abalone gorget. Photograph probably by A.W. Chase, before Aug. 1874.

Ears were often pierced at infancy as was the nasal septum of some women. Tattooing was accomplished with pine needles and juice of a blue flower. A three-line tattoo was most common for the women.

Bead necklaces of steatite, clamshell, and whole olivella shells, as well as abalone pendants were traded from the Patwin and Maidu. Bead value depended on kind, size, number, and quality (fig. 5) (Kroeber 1925:421, Littlejohn 1928:35). Pine nut and seed necklaces, and flowers attached to cordage were worn by the woman.

Body painting using overall dots or streaks was common. White clay, red ocher, and charcoal provided three colors.

Technology

Stone objects included knives, arrow and spear points, club heads, arrow straighteners, scrapers, pestles, mortars, pipes, and charms. Basalt, steatite, chalcedony, jasper, and obsidian were used. Pressure and percussion flaking, grinding, and pecking were methods of manufacture. Bowl mortars were valued but informants stated that neither they nor their ancestors ever made them (Wilson:1957-1963).

Wood was mainly for utilitarian objects. Simple bows were two to three feet long and sinew-baked. Grass

Fig. 5. Captain Tom's wife wearing 10-yard necklace of 1,160 "money" beads made of clam (probably *Saxidomus* sp.) and a deerskin girdle and headband decorated with abalone. Photograph probably by A.W. Chase, before Aug. 1874.

people as protection from the cold. Rabbit robes (fig. 4) required about 40 skins, cut into strips, and were woven on a framework of pegs on the ground (Wilson 1972:35). Duck feathers were wrapped into two-ply cordage and woven into blankets. "Shawls" of round-stemmed tule were also worn by the men (Kroeber 1929:260).

Snowshoes consisted of a circular hoop of willow or redbud with two crosspieces tied with sinew.

Men wore their hair long, allowing it to hang loose, tucked under a netted cap, or held back by a band of fur. Women had long hair, either loose or tied with a band. Men sometimes grew beards. A sharp stone or glowing ember was used to cut the hair. Whiskers were pulled using a shell. Soaproot was used to wash the scalp and hair.

knives, skin-dressing tools, and digging sticks were used. Wooden mortars were common in the valley.

Arrows were simple and compound. Shafts were made of willow, arrowwood, or cane and the foreshaft made of hardwood. Blunts and pointless arrows were reported. They were painted and fletched with hawk feathers.

Preparation of skins was done by women. After the hair was removed with bone or stone scrapers, the skins were soaked and rubbed with deer brains. They were not smoked. Bags for equipment, quivers, bow cases, and clothing were made. Sinew was taken from the back or leg of a deer.

Tule provided material for mats. Cordage and netting, made from the fiber of milkweed and hemp, ranged from thread size to rope one-half inch in diameter. It was used for rabbit and fish nets, seines, netted caps, snares, ropes, carrying nets, and tumplines.

Balsa canoes of round or triangular-stemmed tule and a single log or two logs tied with grapevine with a simple, flattened deck were used. These were pushed with a pole 12 to 15 feet long. Composite paddles were used with a single blade lashed to a shaft.

Baskets were coiled clockwise on a three-rod foundation of willow. Burden baskets and seed beaters were twined. All Nisenan girls learned basketmaking, but its construction fell to the older people as a winter activity.

Basketry material was gathered during the year with willow and redbud preferred. Shoots of hazel, roots of yellow pine and common brake, and stems of maidenhair ferns were used. The base color of baskets was practically white when new but changed with use to a pleasing yellowish-white or cream. Designs were imbricated generally of a reddish-brown color. A triangular decorative feature might represent an arrow point, mountain, or a tree to different basketmakers.

Women measured their basket designs for symmetry with a knotted string. Evenness of stitch, composition, and geometric accuracy were admired.

Baskets for storage, cooking and processing, "show," traps, cradles, cages, seed beaters, and winnowing were woven. Small feathered "treasure" baskets were special.

Life Cycle

Hill Nisenan women were assisted by old women, usually relatives, during childbirth. The mother remained quiet for several days being careful no cold air or cold water touched her. Taboos prevented parents from eating salt, meat, or grease, and from working, combing hair, or rubbing the eyes; all these activities were believed to cause damage to the child (Faye 1923:35; Beals 1933:368).

The baby was put into a "first" cradle made of tule, which was disposed of in a week or two, and the baby was then placed in a regular cradleboard. After 16 days a feast was prepared and the baby displayed to relatives (Beals 1933:368).

A girl was isolated in a menstrual hut for first menses. She fasted for 16 days and was not allowed outside alone. She could not touch her body but used a scratching stick. She could not step on a log or stick for fear of being bitten by a snake. On the sixteenth day she was bathed and a celebration was held. In subsequent menses the girl abstained from eating meat, salt, and fat for four days and slept in a menstrual hut. Husbands had no food restrictions. If they hunted, anything shot died in an inaccessible place. Women could talk to their husbands but could not touch their hunting equipment (Beals 1933:369).

Marriage customs varied. In the valley gifts sent to the girl's parents included beads and shells, but usually food was presented to prove the man's ability to provide. Consent of the girl was usually obtained before the man's intentions were made known to her family. If accepted, the man lived with the girl's family and hunted and fished for them. After six months they went to live with his people. In the mountains, the man made his intentions known and hunted and fished, bringing the results to the girl's home. A separate bed would be made and the couple considered married. A man might simply come to visit and stay. If the girl did not approve, she would discourage the suitor from joining her.

Child betrothal, of children the same age or a young girl promised to an older man, was practiced (Kroeber 1925:400; Beals 1933:370–371).

Residence was usually patrilocal but couples could make a residence choice.

Time before remarriage varied from six months to three years with a man permitted to marry sooner. A woman could marry her husband's brother but no other close relative. Permission and advice were obtained from the dead spouse's family (Beals 1933:372).

Divorce was by the desire of either party. Adultery was the most common cause. A man justifiably killed his wife's lover or walked out. He avoided his ex-spouse but maintained friendly relations with the family except the sister-in-law. Children belonged to the husband's family and were often adopted by the grandparents. When a widow remarried, her husband supported her children.

Mother-in-law taboos prevailed. In the valley the two would neither converse nor look at each other. If the mother-in-law met her son-in-law she would cover her head (Kroeber 1925:402).

Disposal of the dead was by cremation. Property was burned with the deceased and the house moved or destroyed. Burning usually occurred the morning following death. Friends and relatives wept and wailed. Bones and ashes were gathered and buried in the cemetery (Kroeber 1929:265; Faye 1923:37; Beals 1933:376; Wilson 1957–1963). Preinterment burning and primary burial were rarely practiced. After the burial the relatives returned to their houses and continued crying and wailing. A mixture of pitch and acorn black was used on the widow's face and hair and she often cut her hair as a sign of mourning (Kroeber 1929:265; Faye 1923:37).

When a person died away from his village, the body was cremated at the death site and the remains returned to the village. It was important to be buried at the village of birth.

Political Organization

The headman or captain served as an advisor to a village or associated villages but each extended family had its leader who assisted the village headman. The headman had little direct authority, but when supported by the villagers and the shamans his word was mandatory. If he proved unwise he could be replaced. Chieftainship was usually hereditary, but a headman could be chosen by the villagers. He often named his successor, making an assistant before his death. It was possible for a female to succeed if no competent or favored male relative were available. The headman advised his people, restrained them from trespass, called and directed special festivities, arbitrated disputes, saw to the welfare of his people, and called family leaders into council. He acted as official host at ceremonial gatherings and supervised accumulation, preparation, and distribution of food (Beals 1933:359-360).

His food was supplied by the village. He had considerable wealth and often several wives. The village attitude is summed up in the expression: "Everyone wants their chief to have a good name" (Beals 1933:360).

Each community or group of communities controlled its territory, including hunting and fishing grounds. Certain fishing sites, oak groves, and specific trees were family-controlled. Deer-drive fences and blinds were the property of the people who erected them.

• LAW AND PROPERTY   Men owned nets, hunting equipment, canoes, their clothing, and the house if occupied by one family; if inhabited by several families it was property in common to the heads of the families. Women owned their clothing, baskets and basketry material, mats, cooking and food-processing equipment (Littlejohn 1928:33-34; Wilson 1957-1963).

Men hunted, fished, trapped, built houses, and made weapons and tools. Women gathered, prepared, and cooked food; dressed skins; made clothing and baskets; and cared for the young. Children were trained in their respective roles at about eight years of age.

Gifts were common, and sharing and generosity were admired traits. Loans and debt payments were practiced, and feuds were often generated over misuse of this trust (fig. 6).

Dishonesty and cruelty were seldom forgiven and resulted in avoidance. Theft was overlooked if restitution was quickly made but killing resulted otherwise. Minor food thefts were ignored. Murder or rape was followed by retaliatory killing of the guilty or, preferably, a close relative or friend. A person often hired a shaman to do

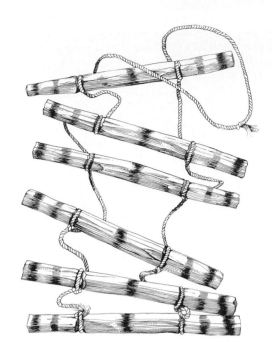

Dept. of Anthr., Smithsonian: 21474.

Fig. 6. Dunning sticks. Wood whittled and painted with red and black pigment, tied with milkweed fiber string. These were tossed into a debtor's house by the creditor, as a reminder that the debt should soon be paid. Average length of sticks 9.5 cm; collected 1876.

the killing. The shaman was not accountable if he publicized the name of the person hiring him immediately following the killing. Payment for crimes could be arranged by the headman (Beals 1933:364).

• WAR   Large-group, organized warfare was uncommon. Differences were usually caused by trespass and ranged from random feuds between families to raids and surprise attacks. Often challenges were sent and battleground and time agreed upon before the battle. A surprise attack against the enemy was made at daybreak. Reliance was placed on dodging arrows in open warfare, and constant dancing movements were made.

Men were taken prisoner only to be killed. Women prisoners became part of the captor's household (Faye 1923:43-44; Beals 1933:366-367; Wilson 1957-1963).

Religion

All natural objects were endowed with potential supernatural powers. One informant remarked "that a tree could kill you if it wanted to" (Beals 1933:379). This power might be used to bring "luck" with the possession of certain "medicines." A lucky individual differed from a shaman only in degree and in not being formally initiated. The Nisenan world contained many supernatural beings and ghosts. It was believed that people would go to the west at death (Beals 1933:379-380).

Some people believed that the world was always here but in different form; others told of everything being made by someone and that the birds and animals were

Field Mus., Chicago.

Fig. 7. Event at a Maiduan, possibly Nisenan, feast. Woman preparing acorn mush while holding a mush stirrer in her left hand. Photographed about 1900–1910. Figs. 8–10 show other events at the feast.

Field Mus., Chicago.

Fig. 8. Men carrying basket of mush using a rope tied around the outside of the basket.

Field Mus., Chicago.

Fig. 9. Shaman blessing the food.

Fig. 10. Baskets of acorn mush, loaves of bread, and sacks of flour ready for distribution.

once human. Still others spoke of a flood that killed the first people because they were not good. In creation stories there was an Earth Creator and a culture hero who actually created the earth, and Coyote, the trickster, who created death and conflict from a once-perfect existence (Kroeber 1929:275–276; Beals 1933:379–382).

The Nisenan calendar named only the six winter months. Stars were little known, but they recognized and named the Big Dipper, morning and evening stars (Beals 1933:357).

• CEREMONIES   Resistance to discuss their religion, disruption, the epidemic of 1833, and reported variations in practices make detailed descriptions difficult. However, certain central systems hold true for the Nisenan nation. Gifford (1927:220–223) divided Nisenan religious ceremonies into three strata. The earliest was indigenous dances. The second stratum came from the north; all dances were performed in the dance house, indicating they were of the generic type called Kuksu or god-impersonating. The latest stratum was introduced about 1872; it was a revival of the Kuksu religion adapted to the Ghost Dance religion.

The major religious system of Central California, the Kuksu cult, appeared in varied form. Cult membership was limited to persons initiated and instructed in its esoteric rites. The disguised dancers represented spirits of deities (Heizer 1962:11–12).

Other religious ceremonies included the mourning ceremony, known as the "cry" or "second burning," an annual ritual to the dead performed in the fall (Wilson 1957–1963). In the mountains this ceremony was conducted at a traditional location away from the village. There was a central pyre or fire surrounded by a brush wall within which the dancers and mourners performed, burned property, wailed, and cried. After the ceremony, gambling, feasting, and games occurred. Little is known about the mourning ceremony of the Valley Nisenan. Accounts by early travelers note large gatherings, wailing, and faces covered with ashes.

Important dances were the Kamin Dance (k̓ámhin) performed in late March for the first clover or beginning of spring; Weda (wéda) or Flower Dance of late April; Lole Dance (ló·le) in honor of the first fruits; Dape (dáppe) or Coyote Dance; Omwulu or Rabbit Dance; Shamans' Dance; Nemusla or Big Time (ném húsla 'big festival'), where people came from some distance; and Husla (húsla 'festival'), a local festive dance (Gifford 1927:233–238).

• SHAMANISM   The Nisenan had two types of doctors or shamans, curing and religious. Both used the dance house in their performances. Curing doctors or yomuse (yómmise· pl.), had limited contact with the spirit world and could be either sex (Loeb 1933:180). They were in possession of certain charms and medicines contained in their doctor's kit. They diagnosed by feeling, then sucked at the area of pain and removed the offending object. This could be a dead fly, a clot of blood, or a small bone or stone that was taken from the mouth, displayed, then buried immediately. A woman shaman with a good heart was often preferred to a man because she was considered less likely to use poison (Kroeber 1929:273–274). In curing, the shaman drank his "medicine" before administering it to alleviate the fear of poisoning. Shamans were paid only if they cured the patient and the amount was decided by the patient.

Doctors poisoned people by throwing pains (*sila*), by touching them with charms, or by simply letting their shadow fall on a person (Loeb 1933:181).

The Shamans' Dance was held in the spring. The sucking doctors danced around an outside fire trying to see who was the strongest or "which had the loudest voice" (Loeb 1933:180).

The religious doctor or oshpe gained control over the spirits by dreams and through esoteric experiences. He represented the supernatural and was a dominant figure in the ritual of the dance house. It was believed that a shaman could conjure up spirits and voices of the deceased.

Other specialized shamans were poison doctors, bear doctors, singing doctors, weather shamans (called ʔáyk̓aiʔ, the name of the Creator), and rattlesnake doctors (Kroeber 1929:273–274; Wilson 1957–1963).

Music, Games, and Art

The most important musical technique was the human voice, individual and group. Instruments accompanied singing and were used in dances and ceremonies. These included the flute and musical bow, clapper sticks, whistles, bull-roarers, cocoon rattles, split-stick swishers, and the foot drum.

Games were part of most social gatherings and included hand and guessing games, ball games, and games of skill such as target shooting, arrow dodging, foot races, rock throwing, wrestling, and a form of stick and ball game. Agility and trickery were heartily applauded and gambling on contestants was common.

Petroglyphs are found in the foothill areas consisting of dots, lines, geometric and curvilinear forms, pecked and grooved on natural rock faces. Paint may have been used (Payen 1959:66). Other forms of art included incising on birdbone, basket designs, feathers for decoration, and the use of paint especially on ceremonial objects.

History

Early contact with the Spanish was limited to the southern edge of Nisenan territory and most knowledge came from early penetrations of Spanish into Plains Miwok territory and minor explorations across their land.

By 1776, José Canizares had explored Miwok territory. Soon after, systematic removal to the missions and resistance by Miwok occurred on the southern border of the Nisenan. In 1808 Gabriel Moraga crossed Nisenan territory. In 1813 a major battle was fought between the Spanish under Luis A. Arguello and the Miwok, near the mouth of the Cosumnes River (Cook 1960:265).

No record exists of the Nisenan being removed to the missions. They did receive escaping missionized Indians into their area, as well as pressures of displaced Miwok villages on their southern borders.

In the late 1820s American and Hudson's Bay Company trappers began trapping beaver and establishing camps in their territory. This occupation was peaceful.

In 1833, a great epidemic, believed to be malaria, swept through the Sacramento Valley (Cook 1955a:308). This sickness was disastrous to the Valley Nisenan, wiping out entire villages. Survivors retreated into the hills. It is estimated that 75 percent of the native population died in this epidemic, and only a shadow of the Valley Nisenan was left to face the settlers and gold miners who soon followed (Cook 1955a:322).

Capt. John Sutter first settled in Nisenan territory in 1839. He had few problems with the remaining Nisenan. After making alliances with the Miwok villages on the Cosumnes River, he moved them close to the fort. Through persuasion and force he soon had most of the remaining Valley Nisenan on peaceful terms.

The mountain people were little affected by the epidemic or early settlers although their lands were crossed by Whites. But with the discovery of gold, the lands of the Hill Nisenan were overrun in a period of two or three years. James Marshall discovered gold near the Nisenan village of Culloma in 1848, and soon thousands of miners were living in the area. Widespread killing, destruction of villages, and the persecution of Nisenan, called Diggers by Whites, quickly destroyed them as a viable culture.

The few surviving Nisenan lived at margins of foothill towns and found work in agriculture, logging, ranching, and domestic pursuits.

In the 1870s there was a resurgence of native culture and modified ceremonalism under the influence of the Ghost Dance revival. This movement ended in dissolution in the 1890s. By the 1930s no living Nisenan could recall the times before White contact.

In the 1960s the condition of these Indians is described by low educational attainment, high unemployment, poor housing and sanitation, a high incidence of alcoholism, violent crimes, and suicide. Many have disappeared into the mainstream of White culture through marriage and movement to new areas.

The 1960 United States census (see California State Advisory Commission on Indian Affairs 1966:54) reported 1,321 Indians from the counties that the Nisenan originally held as their territory but with no tribal identification. Sacramento County listed 802 Indians, of which only three or four were known descendants of the Valley Nisenan. El Dorado, Nevada, Placer, and Yuba counties in the 1970s have several Hill Nisenan families who are descendants of the mountain people, can speak their language, and retain some knowledge of the earlier lifeways. A few people still make baskets and practice other Nisenan customs; but for all intents, the old ways are lost. Some of these people participate in pan-Indian activities and enjoy private celebrations and gambling games, and many are active in social movements and organizations to better the Indian situation in the White culture.

Synonymy

The English term Nisenan derives from their self-designation *nisena·n* 'from among us, of our side' (Uldall and Shipley 1966:86, 222). The spelling Nishinam (or Ní-shi-nam) was used by Powers (1874b:21-31, 1877:313-330), Dixon (1910b:75), Merriam (1904:914), and Kroeber (1925:391-442). Merriam (1904) also cited Nis-se-non, and Kroeber (1925) Nisinan. Merriam (1966-1967, 1:19) adds Nis'-sim Pa'-we-nan and Nis-se Pa-we-nan. Only the form Nisenan is used by Littlejohn (1928:1), Kroeber (1932a:266, 376), Wilson (1957-1963, 1970:124), and Riddell (1972:1). Faye (1923:35-57) and Gifford (1927: 214-257) called the group Southern Maidu, while Loeb (1933:140-206) called them Valley Nisenan or Southern Maidu and Beals (1933:335-413) referred to the Nisenan and Southern Maidu.

Maidu names for the Nisenan are reported as Tainkoyo, Tanko (both presumably for *tá·nkɨ* 'Hill Nisenan'), Tankum, Tan'köma (both these probably for *tɨkɨ·mmà?a* 'Valley Nisenan') (Dixon 1905:128, 1910b; the phonemic spellings for Konkow from Russell Ultan, personal communication 1974). A Nisenan village named Tanku is located by Kroeber (1932a:268) at the mouth of the Feather River; others call this village Wo'lok.

Writers of the mid-nineteenth century often referred to the Nisenan according to the names of their villages, which was the traditional manner of self-identification by Central California Indians. Hoc (Hock, Hok), Culloma (Coloma, Culooma, Koloma), Kiske, Yuba (Uba, Yupu) are among the major villages that appear in the literature in a variety of spellings. The village most often referred to was Pusune, which according to Dixon (1910b) was a Nisenan settlement near Barnard Slough between the American and Sacramento rivers. Among the spelling variants of this name are: Pu-su'-ne, Pu-su'-na, Poosoonas, Pushune, Puzhune, Puzlumne, Pūjuni (all these in Dixon 1910b, citing original sources), and Pujune (Kroeber 1929:256). Powell's (1891:99) label Pujunan for the Maiduan linguistic family was based on Pūjuni from Hale (1846:630-632).

The derogatory term Digger is still in the 1970s sometimes used in reference to the Nisenan as well as other Central California Indians (Heizer 1974:xiv-xv).

Sources

Kroeber's (1925) general work on California is the base point for reading about the Nisenan, but other ethnographic descriptions are important (Kroeber 1929, 1932a; Faye 1923; Beals 1933). Studies of special topics include Nisenan geography (Littlejohn 1928), religious ceremonies (Gifford 1927), the Kuksu cult (Loeb 1933), and Nisenan environment and subsistence (Ritter and Schulz 1972:1-58).

Descriptions of Nisenan life after contact are provided by Bryant (1849:265-272), Buffum (1850:40-51), Delano (1854:248-320), and Cook (1943b:16). Cook (1955a:316) gives some population estimates for the contact period. Little has been written on the twentieth-century Nisenan.

Nisenan linguistics are best represented in a grammar (Uldall 1930), and in a text and dictionary (Uldall and Shipley 1966). Culture element distribution lists are most complete in Voegelin (1942:49-162).

Representative museum collections in California are found at the State Indian Museum, Sacramento; Lowie Museum of Anthropology, Berkeley; The Oakland Museum, Oakland; and the University of California, Davis. Collections are also housed at the National Museum of Natural History, Smithsonian Institution, Washington.

An extensive annotated bibliography of the Maidu containing most published and unpublished sources on all Maidu groups, including the Nisenan, with historic and ethnographic references has been compiled by Wilson and Towne (1972). Kenton's (1972) bibliography surveys Maidu archeology. These are the most complete lists of sources for the in-depth researcher on Nisenan.

Eastern Miwok

RICHARD LEVY

Language, Territory, and Environment

The Eastern Miwok (¹mē₁wuk or ¹mē₁wäk) comprise one of the two major divisions of the Miwokan subgroup of the Utian language family. The Eastern Miwok peoples belonged to five separate linguistic and cultural groups, each having a distinct language and culture. The Bay Miwok or Saclan occupied the eastern portions of Contra Costa County extending from Walnut Creek eastward to the Sacramento-San Joaquin delta. The Plains Miwok inhabited the lower reaches of the Mokelumne and Cosumnes rivers and both banks of the Sacramento River from Rio Vista to Freeport. The Northern Sierra Miwok occupied foothills and mountains of the Mokelumne and Calaveras river drainages. The Central Sierra Miwok occupied the foothill and mountain portions of the Stanislaus and Tuolumne drainages. The territory of the Southern Sierra Miwok embraced the upper drainages of the Merced and Chowchilla rivers.

The five Eastern Miwok languages have been assigned to three distinct groups on the basis of their phonological history and structural and lexical similarity. Plains Miwok and Bay Miwok are each the sole member of a distinct group while the remaining three languages (Northern, Central, and Southern Sierra) make up a Sierra Miwok language group (Callaghan 1971).*

There appears to have been internal dialect differentiation within at least three of the five Eastern Miwok languages. Central Sierra Miwok was spoken in two dialects, West Central Miwok and East Central Miwok (Freeland 1951:9). A line of cleavage seems to separate Southern Sierra Miwok into two dialect areas, one centered upon the Merced River drainage and the other on Mariposa Creek and the Chowchilla and Fresno rivers. Speakers of the Merced River dialect used a retroflex s as the reflex of Proto-Sierra Miwok *ṣ while speakers of the Mariposa-Chowchilla dialect used h (Broadbent 1964:13-14; Merriam 1966-1967, 3:326; Callaghan 1972). There also appears to have been inter-

nal dialect differentiation within Plains Miwok (Callaghan 1972).

Lexicostatistic data suggest that the Western Miwok languages and the Eastern Miwok languages have been separated for approximately 2,500 years. Plains Miwok separated from the Sierra Miwok languages about 2,000 years ago. The internal time depth of Sierra Miwok is approximately 800 years (Levy 1970b).

The classification of the Miwok languages and the lexicostatistic chronology suggest that the ancestors of the Miwok have been resident in the central California delta region for a long period of time. The occupation of the Sierra Nevada and its foothills is probably a much more recent event.

In discussing the geography of Eastern Miwok territory from a political point of view a number of different and hierarchically arranged units must be recognized. At the grossest level of analysis the five languages and their constituent dialects embrace a certain prescribed physical territory. Such language areas (Bay Miwok, Plains Miwok, Northern Sierra Miwok, Central Sierra Miwok, Southern Sierra Miwok), while of very great importance to anthropologists and other students of Miwok culture, were of little interest to the Miwok themselves. The Plains Miwok, for example, though they spoke a common language, were not in any sense a single people, but rather a number of separate and politically independent nations that happened to share a common language and a common cultural background.

The foremost political unit of the Miwok was the tribelet. Each tribelet was an independent and sovereign nation that embraced a defined and bounded territory exercising control over the natural resources contained therein. The nationality of a Miwok, then, was a statement of his tribelet membership. Within each tribelet were several more or less permanently inhabited settlements and a larger number of seasonally occupied campsites used at various times during the seasonal round of hunting, fishing, and gathering activities.

The only other unit of political significance to the Miwok was the lineage. Lineages were localized and named for a specific geographical locality. In most cases these lineage localities were the permanently inhabited settlements of the tribelet. Each tribelet, then, included a number of lineage settlements. Among the Sierra Miwok the population of these settlements was probably about

* Phonemic orthographies have been worked out for Central Sierra Miwok (Freeland 1951:1-9; Freeland and Broadbent 1960:v) and Southern Sierra Miwok (Broadbent 1964:11-32). The inventories for these two languages are essentially the same. Forms taken from these sources are here italicized and a few standard Handbook symbols have been substituted: *i* for the high central vowel, *y* for the alveolar semivowel, and *č* for c.

25 persons on the average. Plains and Bay Miwok lineage settlements were probably larger.

Knowledge of the number and names of Eastern Miwok tribelets and lineage settlements is fragmentary. For the Bay and Plains Miwok there are mainly the names of tribelets with little or no information on lineage settlements within most tribelets. The locations of Bay and Plains Miwok tribelets given in figure 1 are based on studies of ethnohistoric documents from the Spanish colonial period (Schenck 1926; Cook 1955, 1960, 1962) and on a map of the area drawn by a Spanish missionary in 1824. Attempts by twentieth-century ethnographers to obtain information on tribelet locations in the delta area produced only incomplete and conflicting testimony since there was tremendous depopulation and relocation of people and consequent loss of geographical knowledge

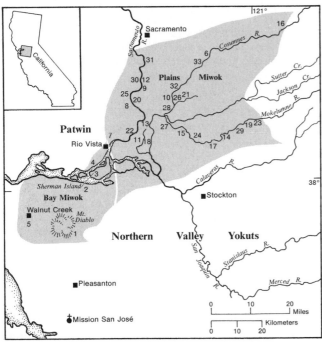

Fig. 1. Bay and Plains Miwok tribelets. Years during which baptisms took place and total number recorded are given.
Bay Miwok. 1, Bolbon, 1803-1813, 67; 2, Chupcan, 1804-1812, 103; 3, Julpun, 1806-1827, 149; 4, Ompin, 1811-1812, 108; 5, Saclan, 1794-1798, 20.
Plains Miwok. 6, Amuchamne, 1834-1835, 13; 7, Anizumne, 1812-1825, 244; 8, Chucumne, 1816-1825, 369; 9, Chupumne, 1828-1836, 8; 10, Cosomne, 1826-1836, 84; 11, Guaypemne, 1821-1834, 41; 12, Gualacomne, 1825-1836, 57; 13, Junizumne, 1813-1836, 119; 14, Lelamne, 1821-1836, 22; 15, Locolomne, 1826-1834, 52; 16, Lopotsimne, 1824, 1; 17, Muquelemne, 1817-1835, 143; 18, Musupumne, 1818-1828, 46; 19, Noypumne, 1827-1834, 6; 20, Ochehamne, 1829-1836, 428; 21, Olonapatme, 1834-1835, 14; 22, Quenemsia, 1811-1828, 185; 23, Sakayakumne, 1839, 1; 24, Seguamne, 1821-1835, 47; 25, Siusumne, 1827-1836, 14; 26, Sotolomne, 1828-1834, 12; 27, Tauquimne, 1815-1828, 73; 28, Tihuechemne, 1820-1836, 35; 29, Tusealemne, 1825-1835, 10; 30, Ylamne, 1818-1836, 74; 31, Hulpumne, no baptisms; 32, Newachumne, no baptisms; 33, Shalachmushumne, no baptisms. All data from Merriam (1968).

during the nineteenth centry (Merriam 1907; Kroeber 1908c).

Knowledge of Sierra Miwok ethnogeography, on the other hand, is largely confined to simple lists of lineage settlements or hamlets with very little information on tribelets and the tribelet memberships of the various lineage settlements. Locations of lineage settlements for the Sierra Miwok peoples have been determined by ethnographers (Merriam 1907, 1966-1967, 3; Kroeber 1925; Gifford 1917a) during the early twentieth century. Some reconstruction of tribelet membership of these settlements is attempted in figure 2. The reconstructions are based on a number of considerations. All Miwok tribelets had the same name as their principal or capital lineage settlement. Capital lineage settlements have been identified by references in ethnographic literature to the presence of a chief in the community or the presence of an assembly house in the community. Settlements within a tribelet are usually located in close physical proximity to one another.

The Eastern Miwok inhabited four rather distinct biotic areas: the valleys of the inner Coast Range, the delta-plains region of the central valley, the Sierra foothills, and the Sierra Nevadas. The Bay Miwok were located in the inner Coast Ranges in the vicinity of Mount Diablo and extended northeasterly from there into the delta of the Sacramento-San Joaquin river system. Most of the delta and the plains along the Cosumnes and Mokelumne rivers were the territory of the Plains Miwok. The foothills and higher mountains of the Sierra were the home of the Sierra Miwok.

A number of differences between Plains Miwok culture on the one hand and Sierra Miwok culture on the other seem to be correlated with their differing ecological contexts. While the most notable examples of cultural difference are exhibited by material culture and subsistence practices, there were probably also significant differences in sociopolitical organization. The Bay Miwok probably were culturally more like the Plains Miwok than the Sierra Miwok.

Prehistory

Knowledge of prehistory varies from one group of Eastern Miwok to the next. A fairly good picture of the prehistory of the Plains Miwok area is available, but knowledge of the Sierra Miwok peoples is fragmentary. Linguistic evidence indicates a considerable time depth for Eastern Miwok, arguing that the ancestors of the Eastern Miwok occupied the delta region during the Middle Horizon of California prehistory. The Miwok occupation of the Sierra Nevadas, on the other hand, appears to be considerably more recent and probably occurred after the beginning of the Late Horizon. The Mariposa archeological complex is probably identifiable with the Sierra Miwok (Bennyhoff 1956) and appears to

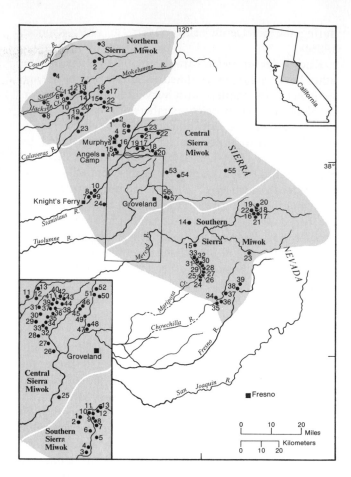

Fig. 2. Sierra Miwok lineage settlements.
Northern Sierra Miwok. Settlement clusters may correspond to tribelets. Omo Ranch Area: 1, Omo; 2, Noma; 3, Chik-ke′-mĕ-ze (M). Plymouth Area: 4, Yule. Sutter Creek Area: 5, Chakanesü; 6, Yuloni; 7, Seweusu. Buena Vista Area: *8, Upüsüni. Jackson Area: 9, Tukupesü; 10, Polasü; 11, Tă-woo-muz′-ze (M); 12, Yu′-yut-to (M). Westpoint Area: 13, Tumuti; 14, Sopochi; 15, Heina; *16, Künüsü; 17, Penkensü. Rail Road Flat Area: 18, Ketina; 19, Monasü; *20, Apautawilü; 21, Kaitimü; *22, Hechenü. San Andreas Area: 23, Hutasü.
Central Sierra Miwok. 1, Sasamu; 2, Shulaputi; 3, Katuka; 4, Humata; 5, Yungakatok; 6, Alakani; 7, Tuyiwünu; 8, Keweno; 9, Tulanachi; 10, Oloikoto; 11, Wüyü; 12, Tipotoya; 13, Loyowisa; 14, Akutanuka; 15, Kosoimunonu; 16, Newichu; 17, Hangwite; 18, Wokachet; 19, Tulsuna; 20, Sutamasina; 21, Takema; 22, Hang-e′-we-ĕ (M); 23, Kawinucha; 24, Singawunu; 25, Hochhochmeti; 26, Siksikeno; 27, Sopkasu; 28, Akankaunchi; 29, Suchumunu; 30, Kotoplana; 31, Poktono; 32, Akawila; 33, Kahp′-pah-nin′-nah (M); 34, Ko-tup′-plan-hah (M); 35, Chakachino; 36, Wakache; 37, Akankaunchi; 38, Kuluti; 39, Pota; 40, Pā′-pah-lā′-no (M); 41, Wolangasu; 42, Tel′ula; 43, Tunukchi; 44, Kesa; 45, Hung′-ah (M); 46, Tā′-les-sā′-nah (M); 47, Pasinu; 48, Pangasemanu; 49, Sukanola; 50, Sukwela; 51, Teleseno; 52, Hunga; 53, Olawiye; 54, Kulamu; 55, Hechhechi; 56, Pigliku; 57, Sala.
Southern Sierra Miwok. Settlement clusters may correspond to tribelets. Merced River Miwok: 1, Sayangasi; 2, Ko′-yo-che (M); 3, Alaulachi; 4, Kuyukachi; 5, Angisawepa; 6, Hikena; 7, Owelinhatihü; 8, Wilito; 9, Kakahulachi; 10, Awal; 11, Yawokachi; 12, Kitiwina; 13, Sisochi. Bull Creek Miwok: *14, Sopenchi. Bear Creek Miwok: 15, Sotpok. Yosemite Miwok: 16, Hokokwito; 17, Kumaini; 18, Macheto; 19, Notomidula; 20, Lesamaiti; 21, Sakaya; *22, Awani. South Fork Miwok: 23, Palachan. Mariposa Miwok: 24, Chahm-hahn′-che (M); 25, Lĕ′-ham-mit-te (M); 26, He-hut-to-che (M); 27, Tin-pă′-nah-che (M); 28, Nok′-too-tah-che (M); 29, Nochuchi; 30, Wahk-kal′-loo-tah-che (M); 31, Kasumati; 32, Pe-loo′-ne-che (M); 33, *palpalya? (B). Chowchilla Miwok: 34, Nowach (=now·oč, B); 35, Olwia; 36, čihči? (B); 37, Wehilto; *38, Wasema (=wasa·ma?, B); 39, Hitch-ă-wet-tah (M) (=hičwe·ta?, B).

Sources: Kroeber 1925 where unmarked, Merriam 1907 (M), and Broadbent 1964 (B). Lineage settlements known to have had either a chief or an assembly house in the late nineteenth or early twentieth century are preceded by an asterisk.

be chronologically contemporaneous with the Late Horizon sites elsewhere in central California.

History

The Eastern Miwok were first contacted by Spanish exploring expeditions to the Sacramento-San Joaquin Valley in the second part of the eighteenth century. With the depletion of the population in coastal areas, where Spanish missions were established, the attention of the missionaries shifted to the conversion of interior peoples—the Bay Miwok, the Plains Miwok, and the Valley Yokuts. The Bay Miwok were the first of the Eastern Miwok to undergo missionization, with the first recorded Bay Miwok converts coming from the Saclan tribelet to Mission San Francisco in 1794. Plains Miwok converts from the westernmost delta begin appearing in the Book of Baptisms of Mission San José in 1811. It appears that many Bay Miwok and Plains Miwok tribelets disappeared through the combined effects of removal of the population to the missions and epidemics, which killed many thousands of persons in the central valley in the first half of the nineteenth century.

Most of the Bay and Plains Miwok converts were taken to Mission San José. The Plains Miwok were by no means willing converts; there are several accounts of Christian Indians fleeing the missions and returning to their villages in the delta. Military expeditions were sent to bring the

fugitives back to the mission establishments. At first the Indian response was to hide from the soldiers in the tule swamps of the delta; but as hostilities increased and the Miwok learned techniques of warfare from the Spanish, several tribelets participated in a series of Indian wars that involved systematic raids upon missions and ranchos to obtain horses. Considerable amounts of culture change must have been involved in the development of these raiding practices (Heizer 1941b). Previously independent tribelets seem to have acted in concert to resist incursions of the punitive military expeditions and raids, changing their subsistence economy to one based on extensive consumption of horse meat. Plains Miwok militarism grew during the 1820s and 1830s until they and their Yokuts neighbors to the south posed a substantial threat to the Mexican settlements in the coastal areas (Cook 1960, 1962).

The arrival of substantial numbers of Europeans and Americans in California during the 1840s opens a third period of Eastern Miwok history. New diseases reached California with the advent of fur trappers, gold miners, and settlers; and relations between the Sierra Miwok and the miners soon became hostile. Plains Miwok people in the valley became involved in agricultural work on the big land-grant ranchos that were established in this period. The Ochehamne tribelet of the Plains Miwok, for example, were employed by John Sutter at Sutter's Fort (Forbes 1969). For a brief period during the first year or two of the gold rush the Miwok were heavily involved in gold mining. A number of Southern Sierra Miwok and Yokuts tribelets supplied labor for J.D. Savage's gold-mining operations in the Big Oak Flat district, but as the number of miners increased large mining operations were shut down and Indian participation lessened (Mitchell 1949). Cook (1943b:106) has found records to indicate killings of at least 200 Miwok by the miners during the period 1847-1860.

With the annexation of California by the United States there began a policy of confiscation of Indian lands. Although treaties were signed by members of a few of the Eastern Miwok tribelets (Heizer 1972), the treaties were never ratified by the U.S. Senate. A few groups of Sierra Miwok were removed to the Fresno area but most of the Miwok population remained in rancherias scattered throughout the Sierra Nevada foothills. During the latter part of the nineteenth century and the early part of the twentieth, Miwoks living on the rancherias in the foothills subsisted partly by hunting and gathering and partly through seasonal wage labor on farms and ranches in the foothill area. Reliance on cash income increased throughout this period and dependence on hunting and gathering diminished. The last survivor of the Guaypemne (also rendered Wipa or Guaypen), whose home lay on Sherman Island in the delta area, was located and interviewed by C. Hart Merriam in 1905 (Merriam 1966-1967, 3:367-369). A description of the miserable life of the surviving Miwoks at Murphys in the 1930s has been written by Burrows (1971), an account that could apply to each of the little remnants who eked out their lives on the edges of the Sierran towns.

In the early part of the twentieth century the federal government acquired by purchase and through executive order a number of small parcels of land (ranging from 2 acres to over 300 acres) as reservations for some rancherias of Plains Miwok, Northern Sierra Miwok, and Central Sierra Miwok. No reservations were established in Southern Sierra Miwok territory, and rancherias there as well as in other parts of Eastern Miwok territory received no official recognition by the federal government. Many persons of Miwok descent still lived in Sierra Nevada foothills in the 1970s.

Population

It is difficult to assess the population of the Eastern Miwok in both aboriginal and postcontact times since no

adequate census of the Miwok has ever been made (table 1). The bulk of information regarding the population of the Bay and Plains Miwok derives from historical documents, particularly mission baptismal records (Merriam 1955, 1968) and accounts of military and religious expeditions into the central valley (Cook 1955, 1960, 1962). The main techniques of estimating the aboriginal population of the Sierra Miwok, on the other hand, rely on population densities and square mileage figures or on the number of lineage settlements present in a given area. Another complicating factor in the assessment of aboriginal population is that it is impossible to estimate populations of all Eastern Miwok groups at the same point in time.

The Bay Miwok were the first of the Eastern Miwok peoples to be missionized. The first baptisms of Bay Miwok occurred in 1794 and the last in 1827; the vast majority occurred between 1805 and 1812. Transcripts of baptismal records (Merriam 1955, 1968) indicate a total of 447 baptisms from the five Bay Miwok tribelets; however, numbers of baptisms are not a very good indicator of the total population since many persons died of introduced diseases before being baptized. There is only one direct estimate for the population of a Bay Miwok settlement. On April 3, 1776, members of an exploring expedition visited a village near Antioch. Anza (1930:144) estimated the population of the settlement at 400 persons. The settlement visited probably belonged to the tribelet referred to in the mission books as Chupcan. The mission records indicate a total of 103 baptisms, implying that only 25 percent of the population was baptized. If the same proportion holds for other Bay Miwok settlements then the total aboriginal population of the Bay Miwok was about 1,700 persons.

The Plains Miwok, too, were subject to missionization in the early part of the nineteenth century. The first Plains Miwok baptisms are recorded in 1811 from the Quenemsia tribelet on Sherman Island. Missionization proceeded among the Plains Miwok until the end of the mission period in 1834. During the period from 1811 to 1834 over 2,100 Plains Miwok baptisms are recorded in the baptismal records. Almost all the Plains Miwok were taken to Mission San José, where they constituted the largest single ethnic group. As noted previously, the

Table 1. Population

Date	Population	Source
1805	19,500	estimate
1852	4,500	Cook 1943b
1856	3,000	Cook 1943b
1910	670	Cook 1943b
1930	763	Cook 1943b
1951	109 (on reservations)	California. Legislature. Senate Interim Committee on California Indian Affairs 1955

number of baptisms for any given group falls far short of the actual population. Cook's (1955) studies of aboriginal population in the delta, which rely on accounts of military and religious expeditions, suggest an aboriginal population of approximately 11,000 persons for the Plains Miwok. On the average, then, only about 20 percent of the inhabitants of Plains Miwok settlements were baptized. Plains Miwok tribelets were rather populous for central California, averaging about 400 persons each. The population density of the Plains Miwok was probably the highest of any group in aboriginal California, averaging over 10 persons a square mile (Baumhoff 1963).

Assessments of the aboriginal populations of the three Sierra Miwok groups is even more difficult than the calculation of Bay and Plains Miwok populations. Cook (1955) estimates populations of various geographical areas within the Sierra Nevada, basing his estimates on village lists compiled by Kroeber (1925), Gifford (1917a), and Merriam (1902-1930). Baumhoff (1963) has reanalyzed Cook's data to arrive at populations of 2,100 and 2,700 respectively for the Central Sierra Miwok and the Southern Sierra Miwok. Lack of adequate data on Northern Sierra Miwok settlements makes population estimates risky, but the population was probably about 2,000 persons.

The total aboriginal population of the five Eastern Miwok peoples thus amounts to 19,500. Severe population decline characterized all of the nineteenth century. Kroeber (1925) estimated the population of the Eastern Miwok in 1910 at about 700 persons. The number of persons of Miwok descent living in 1970 is difficult to assess. There has probably been a substantial increase during the twentieth century, but without an adequate census there is no way of determining the Miwok population.

Subsistence

The Eastern Miwok lacked both cultivated plants (except tobacco) and domesticated animals (other than the dog). The main focuses of subsistence were the gathering of wild plant foods and the hunting of mammals. Abundance of seed-bearing annuals and ample forage for deer, antelope, and tule elk were insured by annual burning (in August) of the Miwok lands.

The Sierra Miwok traveled to higher or lower elevations during various seasons of the year to obtain foods not found in the vicinity of their permanent settlements. The inhabitants of the Transition Zone forest moved to higher elevations in the Sierra during the summer months, following the deer. People in the foothill country would occasionally visit the plains of the central valley to hunt antelope and tule elk, species that are absent from the mountains.

Gathering of wild plant foods varied with seasons and locality. Greens were usually gathered in the spring and were used as a supplement to the diet of acorns stored since the previous fall. Seeds were gathered from May through August and were the major staple during this part of the year. After the August burning of the land the attention of the people turned to collection of digger pine nuts and finally in late fall and early winter to the all-important acorn crop. Quantities and types of animal foods also varied seasonally. Meat consumption was greatest in the winter months when consumption of plant foods (with the possible exception of mushrooms) was limited to stored foods.

• PLANT FOODS   The most highly prized and most important plant foods were the several varieties of acorns gathered by the Miwok. Seven different varieties of acorns were used by the various Eastern Miwok peoples. The acorns of the valley oak (*Quercus lobata*) were most important to the Plains Miwok while interior live oak (*Q. wislizenii*) and blue oak (*Q. douglasii*) in the foothills and black oak (*Q. kelloggii*) in the higher mountains were most important to the Sierra Miwok. Acorns were usually allowed to ripen and fall off the tree of their own accord, but sticks were occasionally used to knock them from the branches. The acorns were then gathered in burden baskets.

Nuts used included buckeye (*Aesculus californica*) laurel (*Umbellularia californica*), hazelnut (*Corylus cornuta* var. *californica*), digger pine (*Pinus sabiniana*), and sugar pine (*Pinus lambertiana*), the most important of which were pine nuts and buckeyes. Digger pine nuts were gathered both in the spring when green and in September when ripe. Buckeye nuts were not a prepared food, being used primarily in years when the acorn crop failed.

Seeds also formed an important part of the Eastern Miwok diet. The following species were used by the Central Sierra Miwok: wild oats (*Avena barbata*, a European weed), balsam root (*Balsamorhiza sagittata*), dense-flowered evening primrose (*Boisduvalia stricta*), ripgut grass (*Bromus diandrus*), redmaids (*Calandrinia ciliata*), painted cup (*Castilleja* sp.), Fitch's spikeweed (*Hemizonia fitchii*), clarkia (*Clarkia unguiculata*), summer's darling (*Clarkia amoena*), farewell-to-spring (*Clarkia biloba, C. purpurea*), gumweed (*Madia gracilis*), tarweed (*Madia elegans, M. sativa*), buena mujer (*Mentzelia* sp.), skunkweed (*Navarretia* sp.), valley tassels (*Orthocarpus attenuatus*), California buttercup (*Ranunculus californicus*), and a number of unidentified species.

Roots of various kinds were also important in the Eastern Miwok diet. The Central Sierra Miwok used the following species: ookow (*Brodiaea pulchella*), harvest Brodiaea (*B. coronaria*), white Brodiaea (*B. hyacinthina*), golden Brodiaea (*B. lugens*), white mariposa lily (*Calochortus venustus*), squawroot (*Perideridia gairdneri*), anise (*Perideridia kelloggii*), eulophus (*Perideridia bolanderi*)

Saint-John's-wort (*Hypericum formosum*), corn lily (*Veratrum californicum*), and a number of unidentified species.

Many species of plants were used as greens. The Central Sierra Miwok ate: columbine (*Aquilegia formosa* var. *truncata*), milkweed (*Asclepias fascicularis*), white goosefoot (*Chenopodium album*), western larkspur (*Delphinium hesperium*), larkspur (*Delphinium* sp.), horseweed (*Conyza canadensis*), tibinagua (*Eriogonum nudum*), alum root (*Heuchera micrantha*), wild pea (*Lathyrus vestitus*), rose lupine (*Lupinus densiflorus*), broad-leaved lupine (*L. latifolius*), common monkey flower (*Mimulus guttatus*), musk flower (*Mimulus moschatus*), miner's lettuce (*Montia perfoliata*), twiggy water dropwort (*Oenanthe sarmentosa*), sweet cicely (*Osmorhiza chilensis*), sheep sorrel (*Rumex acetosella*), green dock (*Rumex conglomeratus*), clovers (*Trifolium ciliolatum, T. wormskioldii, T. tridentatum*), mule ears (*Wyethia helenioides*), and many other species.

Berries did not constitute a major portion of the diet. Madrone (*Arbutus menziesii*) and manzanita (*Arctostaphylos viscida, A. tomentosa, A. manzanita*) berries were used in the production of an unfermented cider by the Central Sierra Miwok. The Central Sierra Miwok ate nine-bark berries (*Physocarpus capitatus*), chokecherries (*Prunus virginiana* var. *demissa*), wild plums (*Prunus subcordata*), wild Sierra currants (*Ribes nevadense*), gooseberries (*Ribes roezlii*), blackberries (*Rubus vitifolius*), nightshade berries (*Solanum xantii*), and wild grapes (*Vitis californica*) raw; but blue elderberries (*Sambucus cerulea*) and toyon berries (*Photinia arbutifolia*) were always cooked before eating.

A number of different varieties of mushrooms were consumed but none has been specifically identified.

•ANIMAL FOODS   Mule deer (*Odocoileus hemionus*) was the most important mammal in the foothills and mountains. Tule elk (*Cervus nannodes*) and pronghorn antelope (*Antilocapra americana*) were most important to the Plains Miwok but were occasionally hunted by the people of the foothills who journeyed to Plains Miwok or Northern Valley Yokuts territory for this purpose. Black bear (*Ursus americanus*) and grizzly bear (*Ursus horribilis*) were hunted by the Sierra Miwok. Blacktailed jackrabbits (*Lepus californicus*) and cottontails (*Sylvilagus audubonii, S. nuttallii, S. bachmani*) were hunted with nets in the summer. Beaver (*Castor canadensis*), gray squirrels (*Sciurus griseus*), ground squirrels (*Spermophilus beecheyi*), and woodrats (*Neotoma* sp.) were also eaten.

The most important game birds for the Sierra Miwok were the valley quail (*Lophortyx californicus*) and the mountain quail (*Oreortyx pictus*). Waterfowl were of considerable importance to the Plains Miwok. Bandtailed pigeons (*Columbia fasciata*), red-shafted flickers (*Colaptes cafer*), jays, and woodpeckers also served as food.

Fishing was very important in the Plains Miwok economy and locally of significance in the Sierra Nevada.

Salmon were the dominant food fish for the Plains Miwok, and trout held a similar position in the mountains. The Plains Miwok also fished for sturgeon. Lampreys were caught by all of the Eastern Miwok.

A number of insects, most prominent among which were grasshoppers and yellow jacket larvae, served as food. River mussels, freshwater clams, and species of land snail were also used as food.

A number of animal species were avoided as food. The Plains Miwok never ate grizzly bear, black bear, fox, or wildcat, although all of these species were seen as fit food by the Sierra Miwok. Some species were avoided by both the Plains and Sierra Miwok: dog, coyote, skunk, eagle, great-horned owl, road runner, and all types of snakes and frogs (Aginsky 1943:397–398).

•SALT   The Eastern Miwok obtained salt from a number of different sources. A number of saline springs were exploited. Salt was also obtained in trade from the Mono Lake country east of the Sierra Nevada. A third source was salt obtained from a plant belonging to the Umbelliferae. The plant was gathered along the lower course of the San Joaquin River and was burned to release salt. Linguistic evidence suggests that the Plains Miwok obtained salt in trade from the Costanoan peoples to the west.

•TOBACCO   Two species of tobacco (*Nicotiana bigelovii, N. attenuata*) were used by the Eastern Miwok. Most tobacco was obtained from plants that grew wild, but seeds were sometimes planted. The cultivated plants produced bigger leaves and had better flavor.

Tobacco was smoked in tubular pipes made of oak, ash, maple root, manzanita, or elder. Smoking was usually reserved to males; women smoked only to cure bad colds.

•GATHERING TECHNIQUES   Different techniques were used in the gathering of plant foods. Acorns and pine cones were dislodged from the branches of trees with poles of various sorts. They were then gathered into burden baskets for transportation. Roots were dug from the ground with a digging stick made of mountain mahogany or buckbrush wood. The point of the digging stick was hardened by fire.

There were two general methods used in gathering seeds. Most kinds of seeds were collected with a seed beater and burden basket. The seed-bearing head of the plant was bent over the mouth of the basket and the plant was beaten with the seed beater, dislodging the seeds. A second method was used in obtaining seeds from red maids, summer's darling, and farewell-to-spring. The entire plant was collected and spread on a granite outcrop or similar flat hard surface. After the plants had dried for a sufficient length of time they were beaten to dislodge the seeds onto the surface of the rock. The plants were then removed and the seeds swept together with a soaproot brush (fig. 3).

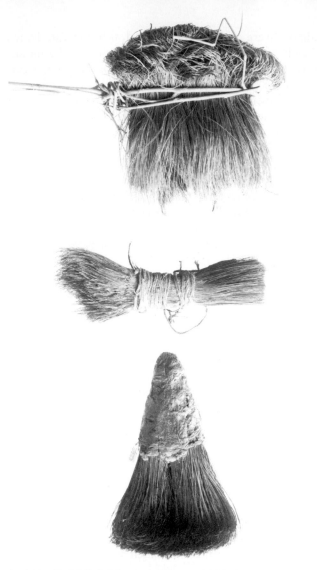

Fig. 3. Soaproot brushes for meal or hair. Top, coarse fibers from soaproot bulb bound with a twig, in order to have soaproot juice or pitch applied for a handle; center, brush bound with twine; bottom, brush bound with string covered with an adhesive. Length of top 14.5 cm, rest same scale; collected 1906.

• HUNTING Deer was by far the most important animal hunted. Deer were hunted both communally and individually. Communal methods included surrounding an area, driving deer over a cliff or into a net, and surrounding an area with a series of small fires. Individual methods included stalking while wearing a deer's head disguise, shooting from blinds alongside a deer trail, and running a deer down. The last method involved the hunter chasing a deer for a day or more until the animal tired sufficiently for the hunter to approach at close range.

When deer were killed communally the meat was divided among all the males participating in the hunt. Meat from an individually killed deer was distributed to the hunter's consanguineal and affinal kin. Consanguines were given the legs, and affines the remainder of the animal.

Elk and antelope were hunted in the lower foothills and plains. Both of these were stalked by hunters wearing a deer's head disguise. Antelope were also hunted communally by being approached by groups of hunters from two directions.

Grizzly bear and black bear were hunted by the Sierra Miwok. They were usually hunted communally by a party of a dozen or more.

Rabbits were second only to deer in terms of the quantity of meat they supplied. The main method of taking rabbits was a communal rabbit drive in which the entire population of the village participated. People chased rabbits into a net where they were clubbed by waiting hunters. The net was three or four feet high and 300–400 yards long.

• TRAPPING Traps and snares were the dominant means of taking small game. Snares were also used for deer but never for elk or antelope. A deadfall trap was used for woodrats. Both valley quail and mountain quail were taken by means of a brush fence with snares set in the openings. A snare trap baited with an acorn was used to catch band-tailed pigeons, jays, and flickers. Woodpeckers were taken by plugging most of the holes in a grove of trees and capturing the birds that entered the remaining holes. Ducks and other waterfowl were captured with nets used in two distinct ways. One method was to pull the net over the ducks while they were feeding and the second was to quickly raise a net in the path of a group of flying ducks.

• FISHING Fishing was most important to the Plains Miwok and the people who lived along the main courses of the larger rivers in the foothills. The main method of capturing fish was with nets, of which four different types were used. Dip nets were used in deep holes in rivers. Seines were used in large rivers and sloughs where the movement of water was relatively slow. Seines were usually used in conjunction with the tule balsa. In the nonnavigable waters farther upstream the set net replaced the seine. A casting net was also used.

There were several additional methods used in taking fish. The Plains Miwok caught sturgeon with hook and line. Two-pronged harpoons were used for salmon. Whitefish were taken with an obsidian-tipped fish spear. Basketry fish traps were used, sometimes in conjunction with a stone weir (Aginsky 1943:453). Fish were stupefied with crushed buckeye nuts and soaproot.

• STORAGE A number of factors allowed the Eastern Miwok to store large quantities of food. Acorns were stored in acorn granaries (fig. 4). Most other foods (seeds, greens, grasshoppers, quail, dried meat and fish) were stored in large flat-bottomed storage baskets of twined weave.

Acorns and seeds required no advance preparation for storage. Greens and grasshoppers were steamed and then dried for storage. Quail, deer meat, and fish were dried either by exposure to the sun or to the heat of a fire.

Fig. 4. Yosemite Miwok acorn granaries. Photograph by Adam Clark Vroman, about 1900.

• COOKING   Meat of large mammals was usually cut in strips and broiled directly on the coals of the fire. Birds, fish, and small mammals were roasted whole in the ashes of the fire. The earth oven was used for both baking and steaming. Bulbs, greens, and grasshoppers were cooked in the earth oven.

Seeds were generally eaten as pinole. Pinole was prepared by first winnowing the seeds with a winnowing basket. The seeds were cooked by tossing them with live coals in a basketry tray. The cooked seeds were then ground into flour with the mortar and pestle. This flour or pinole was eaten dry or made into mush depending on the kind of seeds involved.

The most complex process involved the preparation of acorns. The acorns were first shelled. They were placed on an acorn anvil and struck with a hammerstone. The meats were then ground in the bedrock mortar with a cobblestone pestle. A soaproot brush (fig. 3) was used to sweep the meal into a pile. The next step involved the sifting of the meal in a closely coiled discoidal basket. The sifted meal was placed in a shallow basin of sand, and water was poured on it to leach the tannin from the meal. The first application of water was cold and the temperature was gradually increased until about 10 applications of water had been made (at which point the water used would be quite hot). The leached meal was used to prepare four kinds of dishes: soup, mush, biscuits, and bread.

Acorn mush and acorn soup were prepared by boiling the leached meal in baskets. Hot rocks, lifted from the fire and placed in a cooking basket containing water and meal, were stirred with a looped mush stirrer or paddle to prevent scorching of the basket. As the rocks cooled they were removed from the basket and placed in a basket of water to be rinsed. The quantity of water used determined whether acorn mush or acorn soup was made. The soup was like a thin gruel in consistency while mush was much thicker.

Acorn biscuits were prepared by extended cooking of acorn mush. As it cooked a dipper was used to remove a portion of the mush and pour it slowly back into the cooking basket from about two feet above the basket. When the desired consistency was achieved the basket was placed in a running stream to cool the ingredients, which solidified to form biscuits with approximately the consistency of a gelatin dessert.

The acorn bread (either leavened or unleavened) of the Plains and Northern Sierra Miwok was baked in the earth oven. The Central Sierra Miwok prepared acorn bread by placing freshly leached acorn meal on a hot stone, turning it as it cooked.

Buckeye nuts, too, were inedible in their natural state. They were ground into meal and leached with repeated applications of cold water. The leaching process lasted 18 hours of more.

Culture

The aboriginal culture of the Eastern Miwok as portrayed here is based upon information given to ethnographers by Miwok people living in the early twentieth century, 100 years or more after the first contact with European cultures. The data on material culture is based upon Barrett and Gifford (1933) except where otherwise noted.

Technology

• HUNTING IMPLEMENTS AND WEAPONS   The principal tools of hunting and the primary weapons of war were the bow and arrow. No protective armament (neither shields nor armor) was used in warfare. Bows were usually made of the wood of the incense cedar in the territory of the Sierra Miwok. In some areas the wood of the ash (*Fraxinus latifolia*), oak, willow, pepperwood, maple, or hazel was used (Aginsky 1943:408–409, 456). Most bows were of the sinew-backed variety. Several layers of sinew were glued to the back of the bow with an adhesive made from the root of a species of soaproot.

Arrows were made in a number of different types. The arrows used in war and in hunting large game had a foreshaft designed to remain implanted in the victim even when the main shaft was removed or broken off. Ordinary hunting arrows had no foreshaft, the arrowhead being attached directly to the main shaft. Headless arrows were used in hunting small game, birds, and fish. Arrows usually had three-feather radial fletching. In most cases the feathers of the redtailed hawk were used. Throughout the territory of the Plains and Sierra Miwok arrowheads were made with a concave base, at times with side notches. Laurel leaf points were used only by the Plains and Northern Sierra Miwok (Aginsky 1943:409).

Several tools were employed in the manufacture of bows and arrows. Shaping of the bow was done with an obsidian flake and a scraper made from the leg bone of a deer. Fine finishing of both bow and arrow was done with abrasive stone and with pieces of scouring rush (*Equisetum arvense*). Arrow straighteners were of two types, a perforated type made of manzanita, maple, or stone and another type consisting of a single piece of steatite with a transverse groove. Two kinds of antler chipping implements were used in the manufacture of arrowheads. Once the flake had been removed from a core with the hammerstone, the larger of the two antler implements was used to perform the rough chipping. A smaller antler tool was used for finer finish work and for side-notching. The arrowhead was held on a buckskin pad while the flaking was being done.

Arrows were kept in two sorts of quivers. A storage quiver consisting of a buckskin bag was used for storage of arrows in the owner's home. On hunting trips a quiver of fox or otter skin, open at both ends, was carried.

An obsidian-tipped spear with a mountain mahogany shaft about seven feet long was used in warfare.

• BASKETRY The Eastern Miwok manufactured both twined and coiled basketry. The foundation of coiled baskets and the warp and weft of twined baskets were usually made from willow. Redbud served as the wrapping element in coiled basketry. Basketry of the Plains

Dept. of Anthr., Smithsonian: 313077.
Fig. 5. Sierra Miwok coiled granary basket. Diameter 53.4 cm; collected before 1920.

and Northern Sierra Miwok resembled that made by the peoples of north-central California, while the basketry of the Central and Southern Sierra Miwok was stylistically akin to that of the Yokuts and Numic peoples.

Twined basketry included the seed beaters and burden baskets employed in gathering seeds, triangular winnowing baskets, openwork sifters of several different shapes, globose storage baskets, basketry cradles, and rackets used in a ball game.

Coiled basketry included plate-form winnowing trays, parching baskets, and truncated conical baskets of several varieties (fig. 5), which were used to cook and serve acorn mush.

• OTHER TEXTILES Mats were made and used extensively only by the Plains Miwok. Two kinds of tules were used in their manufacture. Matting served primarily as a floor covering.

Cordage was made from several plants: milkweed (*Asclepias* spp.), *Fremontodendron californica,* and Indian hemp (*Apocynum cannabinum*). String was made by placing bundles of fibers on the thigh and rolling them downward with the right hand. Fish nets and net bags were made from milkweed string. Milkweed and hemp string were also used in the manufacture of braided and twined tumplines used for carrying baskets.

Woven blankets were made of rabbitskin strips or, more rarely, duck or goose feathers. The strips of skin or feathers were attached to cordage warp strands while the weft consisted of cordage alone.

• SKIN DRESSING Dressing of skins was the work of men. Deer hides were staked out on the ground, scraped when necessary, and allowed to dry for a few days. The hide was then soaked in water for a couple of days. After the soaking the hide was treated with pulverized deer brains, soaking in a solution overnight. The hide was then pulled and rubbed to make it pliable. A deer tibia scraper was used to remove hair from the hide.

In preparing bear skins rotten wood was applied to the skin to absorb the fat. A wooden defleshing tool was used to lossen adhering flesh from the hide. Bear skins were not softened but were allowed to dry stiff and hard.

• NAVIGATION At lower elevations on navigable rivers the tule balsa was the principal water craft. About 20 bundles of tules were normally used. Rigidity was obtained through the use of two willow poles for gunwales and about eight external ribs, also made of willow. The tule balsa was propelled with one or more wooden paddles.

In the Sierras the only form of water craft was a pair of logs lashed together to form a raft. The raft was used primarily for crossing streams, while the tule balsa received much more general use.

Clothing and Adornment

Young children wore no clothing. Women wore a one-piece wraparound dress of deerskin in Northern Sierra

Dept. of Anthr., U. of Calif., Berkeley.

Fig. 6. Family of Bill Howard, Chowchilla Miwok. Short hair of older woman is probably an indication of mourning. Photograph by C. Hart Merriam, Mariposa, Sept. 1902.

NAA, Smithsonian.

Fig. 7. Saclan Miwok women with tattooing on chin and neck. Lithograph (Choris 1822) based on lost watercolor by Louis Choris, 1816.

Miwok territory. In Central Miwok territory women wore two-piece skirts of deerskin or grass skirts consisting of front and rear aprons. In Plains Miwok territory women wore skirts of shredded tules. Men wore buckskin loin cloths. In cold weather both men and women wore robes of dressed skin (deer, bear, mountain lion, coyote, and sometimes buffalo) or blankets of rabbitskin or feathers.

The hair was worn long, being cut only upon the death of a close relative as a sign of mourning (fig. 6). The hair was brushed with a soaproot fiber brush and washed every few days with the lather of the soaproot plant. The hair was sometimes allowed to flow loosely but a headband of beaver skin, a piece of string, or a feather rope was sometimes used to tie the hair back. Hair nets were worn only on special occasion by most people; only chiefs wore them every day.

Tattooing was practiced by both sexes and usually consisted of straight lines extending from the chin (fig. 7) to the navel. Tattooing was done when a person was about 12 to 15 years old. A sharp piece of obsidian or flint was used as a scarifier and ashes were rubbed into the cut areas for pigmentation.

Fig. 8. Northern Sierra Miwok house, aboriginal in form but built of sawed lumber with shingle roof. Photograph by C. Hart Merriam at Hachanah Rancheria near Rail Road Flat, Oct. 1905.

Body painting was done primarily on ceremonial occasions. Red, white, and black paints were used. Red paint came from a mineral source in the territory of the Eastern Mono (Owens Valley Paiute), white from locally obtained chalk, and black from charcoal.

Both the earlobes and nasal septum were pierced in childhood. Young children of both sexes wore flowers in their pierced ears. Adult women wore earrings of beads and shells. Adult men wore earplugs made of bird bone with white feather protruding from the ends. Nose sticks were made of either polished bone or shell.

The Eastern Miwok practiced head deformation. The head was flattened in the back by the hard cradle. The forehead was pressed and rubbed from the center to the sides to produce a short flat head. Flattened noses were also desirable, and mothers would press an infant's nose to insure flatness.

Structures

The Eastern Miwok made four distinct kinds of dwellings. The dominant form of house in the mountains was a conical structure of bark slabs. Three or four thicknesses of bark slabs were arranged to form a cone that had no internal supporting posts or framework. At lower elevations the principal house type was a thatched structure. Poles were arranged in a conical framework, and a thatch of brush, grass, or tules was applied externally. These simple thatch structures were also used on hunting and gathering expeditions in the mountains during the summer. A conical house of tule matting was used at lower elevations in Central Sierra Miwok territory. Tule mats were tied to a framework of poles. A semisubterranean earth-covered dwelling was also used at times as a winter house. Only richer men built such houses among the Plains Miwok.

Houses had a centrally located hearth where some of the cooking was done. An earth oven was usually located

Fig. 9. Casus Oliver, Muquelemne Miwok, at entrance to roundhouse at Buena Vista, near Ione. Photograph by C. Hart Merriam, Oct. 1905.

LEVY

Dept. of Anthr., U. of Calif., Berkeley.
Fig. 10. Interior of roundhouse at Buena Vista. Taken same occasion as fig. 9.

next to the hearth. The floor of the house was covered with digger or western yellow pine needles; mats and deerskins used as bedding were placed directly on top of this. Chiefs and important men sometimes had beds made of poles and bearskins for bedding.

The Miwok built two sorts of assembly houses, a large semisubterranean type (fig. 9) that was the focal point for most ritual and social gatherings of the community, and a circular brush structure that was used for mourning ceremonies held during the summer months. The semisubterranean earth lodge was built over a pit 40–50 feet in diameter and three to four feet deep (fig.10). Four center posts supported a conical roof, the bottom edge of which rested upon the edges of the pit. Over a lath of closely placed cross sticks a layer of brush was placed. The brush layer was covered with a layer of digger or western yellow pine needles. The final roofing material was a layer of earth, which covered the structure. A centrally located opening at the top of the earth lodge served as a smoke hole. The earth lodge was entered by a door on one of the sides rather than through the roof.

The circular brush assembly house was a much simpler structure. It was roofed with brush or pine needles and was considerably smaller than the earth lodge. The covering material was applied in a thin layer, which allowed summer breezes to cool the occupants.

The sweathouse was from 6 to 15 feet in diameter and was built over a pit that was two to three feet deep. The structure was conical in shape and was covered with layers of brush, pine needles, bark, and earth. The sweathouse was used for the curing of disease and for purification before going deer hunting.

Other structures built by the Miwok included a small conical hut used by newly menstruating girls and aged people and a conical grinding house built over a bedrock mortar to permit grinding in bad weather. Special acorn granaries were built for the winter storage of the acorn crop. Granaries were cylindrical and up to 12 feet high and 5 feet in diameter (fig. 4). The walls of the granary were composed of upright poles to which were laced hoops of grapevine and small vertical poles. The interior lining was made of grass with a layer of twigs and brush placed in the bottom of the structure.

The unit of ultimate political sovereignty among the Eastern Miwok was the tribelet. These tribelets were also units of ethnic and linguistic differentiation. The population of a tribelet ranged from about 300 to 500 persons among the Plains Miwok. Sierra Miwok tribelets seem to have been somewhat smaller in population size, probably ranging between 100 and 300 persons. Each tribelet owned a definite and bounded territory and the resources of that territory.

With the coming of Whites and the subsequent decline in population there ensued a period of political realignment and, probably, consolidation of what had been previously independent tribelets. The precise number of tribelets and the exact extent of their territories is, therefore, difficult to determine.

Each tribelet contained several physically distinct settlements or hamlets. Each of these settlements was named. The tribelet as a whole went by the name of the principal settlement, the capital of the tribelet, where the chief resided. The tribelet capital contained the assembly house, which was regarded as the personal property of the chief. The assembly house was the site of all important religious ceremonies and other major social events. The authority of the chief extended over all the settlements within the tribelet.

Each of the tribelet's settlements appears to have been the headquarters of a localized patrilineage. These patrilineages bore the name of the settlement at which they originated and usually occupied that locality. Gifford's data suggest an average population of about 21 persons for each of these settlements (Cook 1955:35). Speakers acted as representatives of the tribelet chief to the various settlements. The authority of the speaker was limited to the settlement.

• OFFICES   The focus of legal and political authority in the tribelet was the tribelet chief. The office of chief was a hereditary one, passing in the male line from father to son. In the absence of a male heir the chieftainship would pass to the chief's daughter. When the heir to the chieftainship was a minor the deceased chief's wife (the child's mother) acted as regent. The chieftainship was the property of a single patrilineage within the tribelet and all members of that patrilineage or "royal family" were called by the same term as the chief (Gifford 1955:262; Aginsky 1943:431).

The chief acted as an advisor to the people and manager of natural resources. It was his responsibility to prevent trespass upon the hunting and gathering territory of the tribelet and to determine the best time at which to begin the acorn harvest. The chief acted as arbitrator in disputes and had final say in settling arguments. Chiefs were also responsible for sanctioning the killing of criminal offenders such as poisoners or witches (Aginsky 1943).

The chief was a wealthy man and acted as the official host for the tribelet. Chiefs acted as sponsors for religious and social gatherings by providing food for the guests and underwriting a large proportion of the costs of producing the ceremonies. The approval of the chief was necessary before any public ceremony could be held. Chiefs delivered speeches at all public ceremonies (Aginsky 1943).

Chiefs had considerable control over the external relationships of the tribelet. The chief issued invitations to attend ceremonies to the chiefs of surrounding tribelets. Chiefs also acted as war leaders, though they did not participate in actual combat (Aginsky 1943).

Chiefs had a number of special rights associated with their office. The chief did not do his own hunting but was supplied with meat by his son and other members of the patrilineage. These hunters were usually young unmarried men who resided with the chief during their service as hunters. Chiefs also seem to have been differentiated from commoners by virtue of their possessions. Chiefs and their wives and daughters wore buckskin belts decorated with woodpecker scalps and olivella disk beads. Chiefs had bearhides for seats and bedding and might also have elevated sleeping benches (Gifford 1955; Barrett and Gifford 1933).

There were two other major political offices in Miwok society—speakers and messengers. Speakers made proclamations from the roof of the assembly house announcing to the people of the village edicts of the chief

Lowie Mus., U. of Calif., Berkeley: top, 1-10360; bottom, 1-24328.

Fig. 11. Top, invitation string, with knots showing the number of days before the ceremony begins, collected 1906; bottom, model of necklace of wormwood leaves tied around the neck of a mourner at the funeral of a close relative, worn until the next annual mourning ceremony or until it wears in two, collected 1923. Length of top, 57.5 cm, other same scale.

pertaining to the gathering and preparation of food. Speakers were also responsible for soliciting contributions of food and obtaining ritual paraphernalia in preparation for a ceremony as well as the actual distribution of food during the festivities (Gifford 1955:264, 268–269). According to Merriam's informants the office of speaker was an elective one and there were speakers for each of the settlements in the territory of the tribelet. The speakers functioned as subchiefs having authority only in the settlement where they resided, serving as representatives of the chief (Merriam 1966–1967, 3:348, 355).

The primary duties of the messenger were to deliver invitations (fig. 11) to attend ceremonies to the chiefs of surrounding tribelets and to act as official announcer on ritual occasions by addressing guests from the top of the ceremonial house. The office was hereditary, passing in the male line.

A number of minor officials aided the chief. These included the hunters who provided him with meat for his own personal use and for ceremonial occasions, fishermen who provided salmon in the same way, four ceremonial cooks who prepared meat for religious and social events, servers who distributed food to guests at ceremonies, and a fire-tender for the assembly house (Gifford 1955:264).

Other offices seem to have existed in some areas of Miwok territory. There were apparently moiety chiefs in at least some sections of Northern Sierra Miwok and Southern Sierra Miwok territory (Aginsky 1943:430, 461). War chiefs, distinct from the tribelet chief, are known from some areas in Central and Northern Sierra Miwok territory (Aginsky 1943:433; Gifford 1955:264).

Social Organization

• MOIETIES   The Eastern Miwok believed that all living things belonged to one or another of two distinct categories. These two categories of things or moieties are an important part of Miwok social organization since people by virtue of their lineage membership fall into one of these two halves of the world. The two "sides" were called land and water or were referred to by the names of important and representative animal members. The Southern Sierra Miwok used bluejay and grizzly bear as representatives of the land side and coyote as representative of the water side. The Central Sierra Miwok used bluejay as representative of the land side and frog as representative of the water side (Merriam 1966–1967, 3).

The personal names of the Central Sierra Miwok contained an implied reference to an object or animal species that belonged to the same moiety as the person named. Personal names of people in the water moiety frequently referred to deer, salmon, water, and valley quail. Personal names of people belonging to land-moiety lineages frequently referred to bear, farewell-to-spring, and chicken hawk (Gifford 1916b).

The moieties were intended as exogamous units. About 75 percent of Central Miwok marriages followed this rule (Gifford 1916b).

The moieties also played a part in a few Central Miwok ceremonies. In funeral ceremonies (fig. 11) it was the duty of members of the opposite moiety to prepare the corpse. During the ritual washing that concluded the mourning ceremony people of each moiety were washed by members of the opposite moiety. Girls of opposite moiety exchanged dresses at the time of the girls' puberty ceremony. During the ahana ceremony of the Central Miwok, dancers were given presents by members of the same sex and opposite moiety (Gifford 1916b).

• LINEAGES   Lineages were of primary importance from a political and economic point of view. Miwok lineages were local groups, lineage settlements, where a number of agnatically related men and their wives and children resided for the better part of the year. Lineage members cooperated in the exploitation of economic resources. One important ceremony of the Central Sierra Miwok, the pota, was closely connected with lineages. The lineage holding a pota erected three poles with effigies of lineage members attached. People from the opposite moiety attacked the effigies, which were defended by other lineages of the same moiety as the host lineage (Gifford 1926d).

• KINSHIP   The kinship terminological systems of the Eastern Miwok peoples are all closely similar; they are all of the Omaha type and are in many respects similar to the terminological systems of the Wintuan, Yokuts, western Miwok, and Pomoans. There are small differences, however, between the Plains Miwok and the Sierra Miwok. The Sierra Miwok systems fall into two groups; the Northern and Southern Sierra systems form one group, while the Central Sierra Miwok stand apart (Gifford 1922).

Trade

The Eastern Miwok participated in a trade network that involved the flow of goods across ecological boundaries. There were four major physiographic and ecological areas in south-central California: the Coast Range mountains and adjacent littoral, the central valley, the Sierra Nevada, and the western edge of the Great Basin. The trade network in which the Eastern Miwok participated is characterized by movement of goods from east to west and west to east running at right angles to the generally north and south orientation of the physiographic areas. The Costanoan peoples occupied the Coast Ranges, the Plains Miwok and Northern Valley Yokuts occupied the central valley, the Sierra Miwok occupied the Sierra Nevada, and the Washo and Eastern Mono held the adjacent portion of the Great Basin.

Salt and obsidian originating in the Great Basin were traded westward to the Sierra Miwok and from them to the Plains Miwok in the central valley. Olivella and haliotis shells originating in Costanoan territory moved eastward. Valley-dwelling peoples imported bows from both the people to the west in the Coast Ranges and the people to the east in the Sierras. Basketry was also an important item of exchange, usually moving in both directions between contiguous groups of people.

For a full listing of items exchanged by the Eastern Miwok see Davis (1961).

Religion

• SHAMANISM   A number of different types of shamans were recognized by the Miwok. Shamanism, like many other offices in Miwok life, was inherited patrilineally. The shaman's skill emanated from a combination of instruction by an older shaman and the acquisition of supernatural power. The spirit doctor or sucking shaman held an important place in Miwok religion. Spirit doctors obtained their power through dreaming during normal sleep, through vision quests and the use of datura, and through trances. Spirit doctors cured their patients by locating disease objects (with the aid of guardian spirits obtained in the vision quest) and removing them by sucking. Spirit doctors engaged in contests at mourning ceremonies to see whose power was greatest. The victors were successful in poisoning their opponents and subsequently cured them.

Herb doctors were concerned primarily with the administration of medicinal plants as cures for less serious diseases. Deer doctors had the power to foretell the success of the hunt, to attract fawns, and to locate deer. Rattlesnake shamans performed at rattlesnake ceremonies by handling snakes. Weather shamans had control over the weather and could cause rain and wind to start or stop. Bear shamans performed at public ceremonies and had bears for their guardian spirits.

• CEREMONIES   Quite a few distinct ceremonies have been described by Gifford (1955) for the Central Sierra Miwok. Though possessing many elaborate ceremonies, the Eastern Miwok lacked completely the secret-society type of cult system that was present in many areas of north-central California. The number and kind of ceremonies held in any given Miwok village was determined by the position of the village within the tribelet (the most important ceremonies were held only in the capital lineage settlement) and by the geographical location of the tribelet (a wider variety of ceremonies was held in the tribelets closest to the central valley).

The Central Sierra Miwok recognized two categories of ceremonies. What may be termed "sacred ceremonies" involved the use of elaborate and highly potent ceremonial costumes usually consisting of robes and headdresses of feathers. Mishandling of this ritual paraphernalia could cause sickness in either the performers in the dance or the audience. "Profane dances," on the other hand, were seen primarily as entertainment and posed no threat to the participants, since little or no ritual paraphernalia is associated with these ceremonies.

Sacred ceremonies of the Central Sierra Miwok people living in the hills at places such as Murphys, Angels Camp, Bald Rock, and Groveland during the later nineteenth century were largely indigenous and were relatively few in number. Central Miwok people at Knight's Ferry during the same time period produced a large number of sacred ceremonies, both of indigenous origin and introduced. The introduced ceremonies were brought to Knight's Ferry by a "dance teacher" from Pleasanton named Chiplichu, as part of a major religious revival known as the Ghost Dance. The date of introduction was probably about 1872. A second dance teacher introduced similar dances to the Northern Miwok community at Ione at approximately the same time.

There was a much smaller number of profane ceremonies in both Central Sierra Miwok areas. These seem to have been largely indigenous (Gifford 1926a, 1955).

Mythology

Eastern Miwok mythology resembles closely that of other peoples of south-central California, especially that of the Yokuts and Costanoan peoples. The major characters of Eastern Miwok mythology are Coyote, Prairie Falcon, and Condor. Condor is the father of Prairie Falcon, and Coyote is Condor's father and Prairie Falcon's grandfather. Many Eastern Miwok myths relate the victories of Coyote and Prairie Falcon over monsters that formerly inhabited Miwok territory.

Synonymy

Gatschet (1877:159) and Powell (1877:535) classified the Miwok and Costanoan peoples together under the rubric Mūt′sūn, the name of a Costanoan tribelet. Powell (1891) later recognized the distinctness of the Miwok and used the word Moquelumnan (adapted from Latham 1856; cf. the place-name *muké·lumne·ʔ* in Northern Sierra Miwok, Freeland 1951:183) as a designation for the Miwokan language family, for which Merriam (1907:341) used the term Me′wan. The name Miwok has been fairly consistently employed in the literature either to apply to the Miwokan family or to refer specifically to the Eastern Miwok alone. It is from Central Sierra Miwok *míw·ɨ·k* 'people, Indians' (Freeland 1951; Freeland and Broadbent 1960), evidently introduced by Powers (1873:322, 1877:346) at first as Meewoc.

The language here called Bay Miwok (a term taken from Bennyhoff 1961) has also been called Saclan. Plains Miwok is referred to as Mew′ko by Merriam (1907:338). Northern Sierra Miwok is termed Northern Me′wuk by Merriam (1907:338) and Amador by Barrett (1908b). Southern Sierra Miwok is called Central Me′wuk by Merriam (1907:341) and Mariposa by Barrett (1908b).

Sources

The only general account of Miwok culture is given by Kroeber (1925). Also useful in general terms are Merriam's (1955, 1966-1967) ethnographic notes and Aginsky's (1943) culture element distribution lists. Material culture is covered by Barrett and Gifford (1933). Social organization of the Central Sierra Miwok is described in a number of articles by Gifford (1916b, 1926d, 1944). Central Sierra Miwok ceremonies have been described by Gifford (1926a, 1955). Eastern Miwok mythology is reported by Merriam (1910), Gifford (1917), and Barrett (1919).

Major descriptive accounts of the Central Sierra Miwok language (Freeland 1951; Freeland and Broadbent 1960) and the Southern Sierra Miwok language (Broadbent 1964) include grammars, texts, and dictionaries. Historical materials relating to the early part of the nineteenth century have been assembled by Cook (1955, 1960, 1962). More recent periods in Miwok history have remained unstudied. The prehistory of the Sierra Miwok area has been reported by Bennyhoff (1956), Elsasser (1960), and Fitzwater (1961-1962, 1968a). Plains Miwok prehistory is detailed in Lillard, Heizer, and Fenenga (1939).

Coast Miwok

ISABEL KELLY

Language and Territory

Miwok (^{1}mē$_1$wôk), one of the California Penutian languages, consisted of several contiguous and two discrete groups (Merriam 1907:pl. XX; Kroeber 1925:pl. 1; Callaghan 1970:map facing title page). The discrete groups were Lake Miwok, which lay to the northwest of the main body, and Coast Miwok, which lay to the west. Coast and Lake entities were comparatively close linguistically (Callaghan 1970:1).

The Coast Miwok territory centered in Marin and adjacent Sonoma counties (fig. 1). For them, Barrett (1908:303–314) recognizes two dialectic groups: Western, or Bodega, and Southern, or Marin, with the Southern further divided into valley and coast.* There was no overall tribal organization. A large village had a headman, but if settlements were grouped into meaningful, named clusters, these have not been recorded. Published terms, which might refer to such groups, seem to be chiefly expanded village designations.

Several well-known place-names in the area today derive from Coast Miwok (Merriam 1916:118): Cotati (kót·aṭi 'to punch') (TS)†; Olema, dubiously translated as 'lake' (TS); Olompali (ʔólom 'south') (TS); Tamalpais (támal páyiṣ 'west hill' or 'coast hill') (TS); Tomales (támal 'west, coast, west coast') (TS). Marin, Novato, and Nicasio are said to have been names of local chiefs (Merriam 1916:118); all sound Spanish.

History

From two famous sixteenth-century voyages, Drake in 1579 (fig. 2) and Sebastian Rodriquez Cermeño in 1595, come tantalizing accounts of what presumably was contemporary Coast Miwok culture (Kroeber 1925: 275–278; Heizer 1947; Heizer and Elmendorf 1942). Not until the latter part of the eighteenth century are there

again records of visits of Europeans to the area. Beardsley (1954,1:15–18) has summarized these and earlier visits and has culled from the accounts the ethnographic information.

In 1811 and 1812, the well-known Russian colony was set up at nearby Fort Ross, to exploit sea-otter resources, and Bodega served as its port (Bancroft 1886–1890, 2:630). Several decades before the Russian penetration, the mission onslaught was launched with the founding, in 1776, of the mission at San Francisco. From this base and successively from missions at San Rafael (1817) and Solano-Sonoma (1823), forced evangelization took place, with attendant dislocation of population and disintegration of the culture. The final blow was the Anglo appropriation of 1846. The early years of American exploitation focused on lumbering, dairying, and agriculture, and at least some of the few surviving Coast Miwoks found work in the sawmills and in the fields.

Local archeology is of interest principally because it seems to have produced concrete evidence of the Cermeño visits, and the resulting reports (Heizer 1941; Meighan 1950; Meighan and Heizer 1953) concern chiefly iron spikes and sherds of Ming porcelain and an undated coarse stoneware. Beardsley (1954) provides information relative to the less glamorous artifacts attributable to native Coast Miwok culture in late precontact and early historic times.

• POPULATION   Even in aboriginal times, the Coast Miwok population was small. Kroeber (1925:275) guessed a total of 1,500 persons. Figures published subsequently by Cook (1943:181–183, 1943b:99, 105) doubtless are as well documented as is possible today:

Aboriginal times	2,000
1851 (1852?)	250
1880	60
1888	6
1908	11
1920	5

The shocking decimation of the California Indian population has been a recurrent theme in a number of studies by Cook (1940, 1941, 1943, 1943a, 1943b, 1943c). By the early 1930s, there were perhaps three individuals predominantly Coast Miwok in blood, two being informants Tom Smith and María Capa Frías. A number of

*The orthography developed for Bodega Miwok by Callaghan (1970) can be brought into line with Handbook standards by substituting y for j and č for c and by using the raised dot to mark long vowels and long consonants. Italicized Coast Miwok words have been respelled in this orthography by Callaghan; question marks indicate her surmises for forms that do not occur in her dictionary. Words left unchanged in the author's spelling have tc for Callaghan's č, ts for c, ' for ʔ, and sometimes i for y and u for w. Kelley's ü represents one of the five vowels of Callaghan's system, her t represents either t or ṭ, and she normally does not note length.

† Information from Tom Smith, a speaker of the Bodega dialect, is marked thus. See Sources.

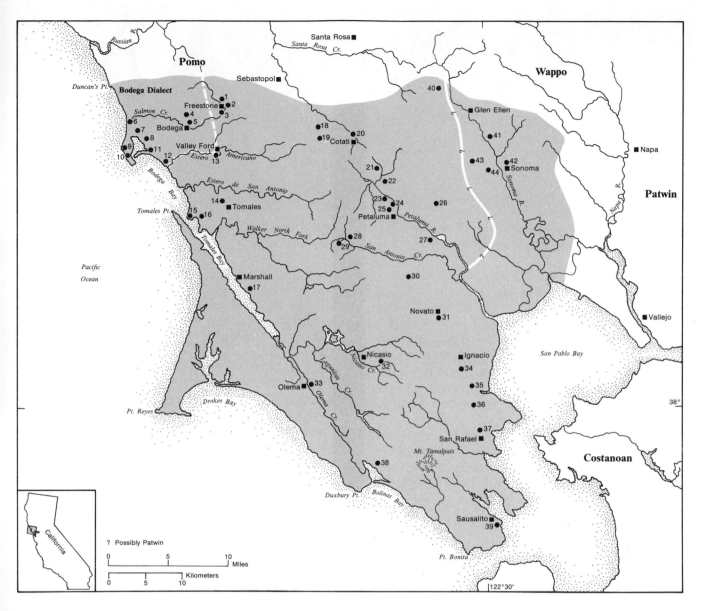

Fig. 1. Tribal territory and villages. 1, pakahuwe; 2, patawa yómi; 3, ʔóye yómi; 4, suwutene; 5, kén·e kó·no; 6, pulya-lakum; 7, ho-takala; 8, helapattai; 9, tiwut-huya; 10, tokau; 11, hime-takala; 12, awachi; 13, ewapait; 14, utumia; 15, sakloki; 16, shotomko-wi; 17, ʔéč·a kúlum; 18, uli-yómi; 19, páyin ʔéč·a; 20, kót·aṭi; 21, susuli; 22, tulme; 23, tuchayelin; 24, likatiut; 25, etem; 26, péta lú·ma; 27, wotoki; 28, melé·ya; 29, amayelle; 30, olompolli; 31, čóik ʔéiče(?); 32, ʔéč·a támal; 33, olema-loke; 34, puyuku; 35, shotomoko-cha; 36, ewu; 37, awani-wi; 38, bauli-n; 39, liwanelowa; 40, lúmen laká·lu(?); 41, wúki líwa; 42, huchi; 43, tuli; 44, temblek. All names from Kroeber (1925); those italicized have been respelled by Catherine Callaghan.

persons today have some Coast Miwok blood but apparently no knowledge of native culture and no interest in it. Effectively people and culture have disappeared.

Culture

Subsistence

Terrain was in part coast—low-lying, or with cliffs, and with extensive bays, lagoons, sloughs, and marshes—and in part, open valleys alternating with low hills. Mount Tamalpais was the point of highest elevation. Vegetation ranged from salt-marsh plants to grasses, oaks, red-

woods, and pines; animals, from sea foods to deer and bear. In short, resources were diversified and well suited to an economy based on fishing, hunting, and gathering.

The annual cycle is clear. Some animal foods, such as deer and crab, were available all year. Winter and early spring were times of shortage, when stored dried acorns and seeds, plus kelp (čól·a) (TS) were the mainstay. Nevertheless, there were salmon runs; mudhens were available, and in late winter, geese. In spring, small fish stranded at low water in pools on the rocks were collected, and another kelp (háṣkula) (TS) was eaten. Villages were adjacent to shore, lagoon, or slough; but

415

Fig. 2. Imaginary depiction of Coast Miwok Indians welcoming Francis Drake to California, June 1579. This is the earliest known illustration intended to show California Indians. Engraving published by Theodor de Bry (1599:pl. 5).

come summer, attention shifted to the hills for hunting and for gathering of vegetable products.

Marine foods were important. Sea mammals were not eaten, but there was heavy reliance on fish. Surf fish were caught in a circular dip net; bay fish, in a seine strung between two tule balsas. Only for bullhead was a line with gorge used. Steelhead and salmon were taken during the winter runs. Then small weirs, with elongated, socklike traps, were built in shallow water for use during the return downstream of the fish. Otherwise, a dip net or a stabbing spear was employed for salmon. Eels were netted or were poisoned by introducing a root (*Marah fabaceus*) into pools on the rocks. Of shellfish, only mussels and several kinds of clams were important as food. The relative abundance of shellfish and game were indicated clearly by TS, who said bear was scarce; deer not plentiful, but more common than bear; rabbit more prevalent than either; but that they "ate more clams than rabbits." Bear, elk, and deer were the large

game animals; rabbit, cottontail, wood rats, gophers, and squirrels, the small ones. Land birds were trapped or netted, some for food, some for the feathers. Aquatic birds were varied and plentiful.

Sexual abstinence was required several days prior to fishing or hunting, and these activities were suspended during the wife's menstrual period and following birth of a child. A deer hunter lived on acorn mush and pinole for two days prior to the hunt and ate no saltwater food except kelp. There were diverse ways of obtaining hunting luck, ranging from song and food offerings to amulets.

Acorns were basic; for mush (*húlki*) (TS), those of the tanbark oak were preferred; for bread, those of the valley oak. The leached meal was boiled with hot stones to make mush; or it was mixed with water and red earth, made into a cake, and baked as bread (*číp·a*) (MC)‡ in

‡Information from María Copa Frías, a speaker of the Marin dialect, is marked thus. See Sources.

416

KELLY

the earth oven. Buckeye fruits (ʔúunu[?]) (TS, MC) also were leached and prepared as mush, eaten with salt. Cakes were made from the fruits of the pepperwood, or they were prepared as a beverage "like chocolate." A large variety of seeds was harvested and eaten as pinole, not as mush. Greens were eaten fresh or cooked; edible roots were rather limited, as were fruits. Two kinds of edible kelp were noted.

Tobacco (káyaw) (TS, MC) was "strong, heavy," and was gathered along Healdsburg and Santa Rosa creeks, in South Pomo country. All adult males smoked; a few women, mostly elderly, indulged sparingly. The tubular pipe was of elderberry, held at an angle in the mouth. Two kinds of datura were known. One (monoi) (TS, MC) may have been *Datura stramonium*. For the other, túlwač(?) (TS, MC) (evidently from Spanish toloache, derived from Nahuatl), there is no herbarium specimen, and apparently the plant was not local.

Structures, Clothing, and Manufactures

The dwelling was conical and grass-covered, built on a frame of two forked, interlocking poles of willow or driftwood, against which additional poles were leaned, and with light, flexible poles lashed horizontally to the skeleton. To the horizontal wands bunches of grass, rush, or tule were tied, shinglelike, with lupine-root cordage. TS denied that the house was semisubterranean, but a central hearth was excavated slightly and surrounded with stones; it was immediately beneath the smokehole, which was covered with a sealskin during the rains. A grass or tule mat hung at the doorway, and mats spread on the floor were the only furnishings except a grass "pillow" (háwi) (TS). A dwelling accommodated 6 to 10 persons, who slept with feet to the fire.

Large villages had a sizable sweathouse, circular, dug four or five feet into the ground. Forked posts were set around the perimeter, their tops flush with the surface and connected by poles to a large forked post in the center of the pit. Transverse sticks were placed on the poles, then brush, grass, and earth. The entrance was gallerylike, with a drop. Although not really a male dormitory, the sweathouse was a social and work center for men.

In populous settlements, the so-called secret societies had a ceremonial chamber, or dance house, of essentially the same construction as the sweathouse. That of the society including both sexes was perhaps 15 feet in diameter and excavated two feet deep. The chamber of the female society was smaller and was roofed with grass or tule, without earth covering.

Body clothing was scant. Men sometimes wore a deerskin loin cloth (hú(·)li or húl(·)i) (TS), which may have been a double apron tied at the waist; sometimes it was an unhandy ankle length. A tule or deerskin "shirt" was simply a sleeveless shoulder throw. Women used a double apron of fringed deerskin or of small tules split with

the hand. MC had heard that the skirt (láw·a, now 'dress') (TS, MC) was of deerskin, hair side out, not fringed, and open on one side; in short, not a double apron. Skins of jackrabbits or other small animals were cut in strips and held together with loose twining of lupine cordage to make blankets, apparently used also as capes. Neither sex wore footgear, and the use of the woman's basket cap is doubtful.

TS thought women wore the hair long, with a part in the center and three braids, one in the rear and one over each shoulder. MC had heard that both sexes bundled the hair up in the rear, wrapped it around the head, tied it in place, and secured it with a hairnet. Men let the beard grow (fig. 3). Clamshell disk beads were used as

Fig. 3. Man of the Guimen tribelet according to the artist Louis Choris. Watercolor, 1816.

adornment but were more important as currency. To indicate civil status, widows and widowers wore a necklace of any kind of lightweight shells. Some thought ear perforation contributed to longevity. "A few old men and some old women had tattooing on the chest," done with a sharp bone and poison-oak charcoal (fig. 4). Feathered wristlets and belts were popular for dress occasions, and the dance costume must have been positively elegant.

Manufactures in wood were limited to the hollowed-log foot drum, shaped by burning, to the double-bladed balsa paddle, and perhaps to the mush stirrer. Stone work must have been well developed. Boulders found on the beach were adapted as mortars. Charms (tcila) (TS) for luck in hunting or fishing were of polished stone (fig.

417

NAA, Smithsonian.

Fig. 4. Woman of the Numpali tribelet according to the artist Louis Choris. Lithograph based on lost original watercolor, 1816.

5), sometimes perforated; and a long, retouched obsidian blade (tcita) (TS) was a hunting amulet, indispensable if bear were the quarry. A general utility knife was of green chalcedony; the butchering knife and arrow points were of black obsidian, which was purchased with clam beads from the Wappo. The stone was broken in Wappo country and usable pieces brought back, to be worked locally.

Disk beads of clamshell were used as money. The shells were broken, shaped roughly, perforated (with the pump drill in use as far back as TS could remember), strung, then rubbed on a stone to refine shape and give polish.

Most cordage was two-ply, of lupine (tsópogo) (TS) (*Lupinus chamissonis*) root; sometimes such twine was combined to make heavy, three-ply rope. Nets were manufactured by the men, who measured the mesh on the hand or with an oak gauge (témen) (TS).

Basketry was well developed. Primarily a woman's work, a man might make burden baskets and mortar hoppers, and normally he made the special willow container for his hunting equipment. Techniques were both coiled and twined, the former, to some extent, "for show." Varicolored motifs were mentioned, and Pomo-like, boat-shaped specimens were remembered—with ornament of red (woodpecker) and white (duck) feathers, and quail tips, plus haliotis and clamshell pendants. Other coiled baskets included the mush bowl, cooking basket, hopper, and parching tray. The last three seem also to have been made in twined stitch. Other twined bas-

kets were: the conical burden container, in open or closed stitch; storage baskets; presumably the sifter for meal; and doubtless the body of the cradle. The technique used for the seed beater remains undetermined.

The bow was the chief weapon; it was backed with sinew, usually from the wing of the brown pelican, and it may have been recurved. The string was of sinew or of lupine cordage; one end was fixed, the other, noosed. Release was primary. All arrows had three feathers; a long arrow was for game and a short one, about 18 inches in length, "for fight." Those for small game were merely sharpened shafts; others had an obsidian point. Weapons also included a sling (láwik) (TS) with a pocket of deerskin and a bola (hitcila) (MC) for ducks, made by tying a heavy bone to each end of a cord.

Property and Intertribal Relations

There was a strong feeling for property. TS remarked casually that some villages staked their territory and shot trespassers and that one who crossed the Pomo boundary near Freestone was asked for clamshell money and "he has to pay, too." Land, as such, was not private property, but certain food-producing trees (oak, pepperwood, buckeye) were, as were hunting, fishing, and clam-digging rights to some tracts.

The chief claimed several kinds of feathers (cf. Gifford 1926a:397) used for dancing gear; pelican skins with feathers were largely his, but not exclusively so. Captured "eaglets" belonged to the man who removed them from the nest. Individuals' possessions, such as arrows and split-stick clappers, bore ownership marks. Every transaction involved payment: transport of the head of a slain bear and its subsequent disposition; permission to hunt or fish on private preserves; acquisition of a song or amulet for luck; initiation into both secret societies; use of the dance house for a girl's puberty rite; admission to dances, with a refund to disgruntled members of the audience; instruction, even by a relative, in any skill, such as dancing, singing, curing, crafts; and doctoring attention of all kinds, including that of poisoning an enemy.

Such emphasis on property conceivably relates to the highly developed monetary system based on disk clamshell beads (píspi) (TS); archeologically, the prevalence of such beads seems to be "late" (Beardsley 1954, 1:44). There were thin, thick, and extrathick beads, all of uncooked shell. The Coast Miwoks owned the clam beds that provided all neighboring peoples with shell, yet seem not to have derived any particular advantage from such potential monopoly. For strung clam beads, there were formal measures, which TS could not recall. Magnesite cylinders *(čupú·ṭa[?])* (TS) purchased in Lake County, presumably from the Pomos, were "our gold." One an inch long was worth two yards of clam money. Haliotis shell was prized for ornaments but seems not to have formed part of the monetary system. Individual attachment to property is revealed by the simple state-

418

ment that the victim of a "poisoner" could be cured, "but it took too much money. [Most] would rather die than spend the money" (TS).

Despite an ample supply of clamshell currency, there is no indication of vigorous trade. Such money bought venison, obsidian, and magnesite cylinders from the Pomos and yellow paint and obsidian from the Wappos. Sometimes the Coast Miwoks went to Wappo country to collect medicinal plants. They went also to South Pomo territory: to Sebastopol for turtles and willow for basketry; there and to Santa Rosa for angelica; to Healdsburg for one kind of datura (monoi); to Healdsburg and Santa Rosa creeks for tobacco. There was no mention of payment in connection with such forays and, in reciprocity, South Pomos visited the coast to fish and to dig clams.

Relations with (presumably Missions) San Jose and San Leandro were amicable and apparently related to the Pleasanton ferment of the 1870s (Gifford 1927:220–221, 229–230; Du Bois 1939:114–115). The language there was called kekos or tüstüko and was unintelligible to MC, although her maternal grandmother could communicate in it. Such linguistic divergence does not agree with Kroeber's comment (1908a:26) that, in later times, Mission San Jose was primarily Miwok in speech, dialect not specified.

Although these facts of intertribal relations seem amiable, MC summarized relations with neighbors in terms that suggest hostility: "The Tomales people didn't like the Nicasio people; the Nicasio people didn't like the Healdsburg [South Pomo] or Petaluma people; the Marshall people didn't like the Bodega people; and nobody liked anybody else." Except for Healdsburg, she was speaking of fellow Coast Miwoks.

On journeys, people traveled single file; "the woman always walked ahead . . . packing a basket of household stuff. The man walked behind, packing nothing—only his bow" (MC). Both sexes used the conical, twined burden basket and the carrying net, but the first was utilized chiefly by women; the second, by men, primarily for fish. Heavy loads, including a child in a cradle, were borne by chest tumpline, with a protective pad of vegetable material.

Bays and lagoons were crossed on a raft of three or four logs tied together or on a tule balsa (lógo-sáka 'tule boat') (TS) of several bundles of rushes. The balsa was either punted or paddled. MC mentioned the double-bladed paddle, which is confirmed by two old reports (Beardsley 1954, 1:17).

Sociopolitical Organization

Strong suggestions of moiety organization, presumably vestigial, link Coast and Lake Miwok with the main body of Miwok (Gifford 1916b; cf. Loeb 1932:119). Such dichotomy is reflected primarily in the real, or yali,

personal names, classed either as Land (yówa yómi 'land home') or Water (líwa yómi 'water home') (TS).

In practice, inconsistencies were enormous. One man is said to have changed his name, putting himself in the opposing "home"; another had two names, one Land, one Water. Often, full siblings did not bear names of the same persuasion. Moreover, there is no indication that "moiety" affiliation was exogamic or that it operated in kinship terminology, funeral observances, inheritance, games or the selection of an "old relative" to teach skills. Upon occasion, seating in the dance house was by "moiety." In the Bear Dance and its aftermath, the man selected to handle the head and cook and distribute the meat was of the same "home" as the hunter; "they leave other people alone" (TS). Furthermore, tule effigies, representing the dead in certain Bird Cult performances, were made by people of one "home" and shot at by those of the other (cf. Gifford 1926a:397).

There was no overall tribal organization. A large village had a chief (hóypuh), and the post was not hereditary. He "took care" of the people, offered advice, and harangued them daily, addressing them personally, not through a crier or orator (cf. Heizer 1947:270). The old chief and four elderly women tutored an incipient headman; and when the successor was ready to take over, the incumbent withdrew or a poisoner was hired to liquidate him.

There were two important female leaders. One (hóypuh kulé(·)yih or hóypuh kul(·)éy·ih 'woman chief') (TS) probably was more significant than data indicate. She handled the Acorn Dance, dominated the sünwele Dance, and was deeply involved in the Bird Cult. The second female leader (máien) was a genuinely key person: "máien bosses everyone, even hóypuh" (TS). Theoretically, she was head of the women's ceremonial house and hóypuh was head of the mixed dance house, "but máien did all the work." She bossed construction of a new dance house; had wood hauled for festivals; superintended preparation of fiesta food; sent out invitation sticks for dances, and, in some cases, selected the performers.

If the memory of TS is to be trusted, the selection of a new máien took place following the dance for the investiture of a new wál·ipoh 'doctor'. He chose "the best-looking girl . . . the best dancer." She accompanied him to the hills for two days and two nights, during which time she was thought to die and return to life, as the wál·ipoh himself already had done.

Illness and curing

Illness was common, but the real scourge was poisoning or fear of it. "Do-it-yourself" efforts were popular, and four kinds of professional poisoners were for hire, the price ranging from 15 to 100 shell beads. Poison was not exclusively magical; iris root was known to be toxic, as was the dried, pulverized flesh of an unidentified animal called "mountain fish."

There were several doctoring specialists; one treated a girl at first menses, another was a snakebite practitioner. Otherwise, TS recognized five kinds of doctors: *wénen ʔápi* ('medicine-expert'); *temnép·a*; *wákel ʔápi*; wilaksi (roughly the equivalent of the Pomo "outfit doctor"); and *wál·ipoh* (poisoner as well as curer and thought, moreover, to be a dead man returned to life). Certain kinds of equipment (fig. 5) and curing techniques were identified with each practitioner, but the material is too detailed to be described here. Some doctors sucked; most sang, and certain songs were accompanied with the cocoon rattle, split-stick clapper, or bone whistle. A doctor's buckeye "stick" (yawi) (TS), with charmstone attached, was useful in diagnosis.

The "old dancers"—men or women—were considered more effective than doctors in treating illness. One of the chief functions of the dance was therapeutic, yet it seems unwarranted to speak of a "secret society of medicine

men" or "a shamanistic society" (Loeb 1933:229). Many members of the so-called secret societies did not attempt to cure.

Life Cycle

Restrictions during pregnancy were few, but eating clams was discouraged, lest closure result (TS). After a woman bore three children, subsequent offspring might be killed, by stepping on a stick placed across the throat of the newborn infant (MC). This procedure seems to have held more in theory than practice.

Birth apparently took place in the menstrual hut. The parturient lay on her back, and the infant was received in a cavity dug in the ground and lined with dry grass. A fire burned nearby, or the woman lay on a "hotbed" (húp(·)a) (MC), with grass placed over hot stones. The husband apparently remained secluded in the sweathouse.

The new mother used a scratching stick and ate no meat until the umbilical cord fell (MC). She avoided dry fish, but fresh fish and kelp were acceptable (TS), although pinole and acorn mush were the preferred foods. Salt was eaten sparingly. The infant's father also observed food taboos. He bathed and did not smoke, hunt, or fish.

If, at first menses, a girl already belonged to the dance house (secret society), she informed the máien of her condition and remained with her four days. A nonmember stayed home, usually in a small, conical hut. She did not wash hands or face, and she used the hairbrush and scratching stick. She ate acorn mush and avoided fresh meat but could eat dry meat, fish, and salt. She drank water directly from a basket cup. Occasionally she was led outside, her face covered. A special practitioner sang

Lowie Mus., U. of Calif., Berkeley: a, 1-157492; b, 1-157491; c, 1-157472; d, 1-157493; e, 1-157486; f, 1-157485; g, 1-157487, h–j, 1-157497 a–1-574499; k, 1-157490b; l, 1-157715; m, 1-157716; n, 1-157495; o, 1-157481; p, 1-157500; q, 1-157713; r, 1-157482; s, 1-157483; t, 1-157478; u, 1-157473; v, 1-157496; w, 1-157494; x, 1-157488, 1-157490, 1-157497b, 1-157714.
Fig. 5. Tom Smith's singing doctor outfit used for curing and poisoning. Collected and described by David W. Peri about 1950. a, split-stick wand; b, clapper-stick rattle; a–b alternating black and red painted bands with quartz crystal inserted; c, red-shafted flicker wing with haliotis and clamshell disk, used to brush away illness at the joints; d, cocoon rattle with bird-quill handle, never used to poison; e–g, a bundle consisting of three items of four each used to indicate cardinal direction; e, golden eagle tail feathers, f, ocherstained wooden pegs from underground ghost house; g, flicker tail feathers; h–j, quartz crystals, h used for curing severe illnesses; k, buckskin pouch containing ocher and charmstone; l, mortar and pestle used to grind pigments; m, mortar and pestle used to grind herbs and crystal dust; n–o, charmstones used to cure "water sickness"; p–q, obsidian hide scraper and skinning knife received from a rival doctor (a bear doctor) after T.S. cured her victim; r–s, obsidian blades used to cut patient for sucking blood to determine if patient is ill; t–u, cloth pouch with pockets appliquéd with maru dream designs; o, r, s, partial contents of pouch t; v, bird wing-bone whistle used to awaken spirits; w, bamboo double whistle with burned-in design; x, buckskin wrappers for some of above paraphernalia. Length of a, 56.5 cm; b–x, same scale.

over the girl, remaining outside but adjacent to the hut. At the conclusion, the girl jumped in cold water, and a (circle?) dance was held for her.

MC claimed that mature men always wanted to marry young girls and often had the youths poisoned, to eliminate competition; because of the chronic threat of poison, a girl's parents dared not reject a suitor. There was no local exogamy, and the matter of "moieties" and cousin marriage is unclear; however, siblings and first cousins were not distinguished in kinship terminology, so the possibility of cousin marriage is slight. There was a special form of address between individuals and their parents-in-law (MC), and the "joking relationship" prevailed between a man and his brother's wife and his wife's sisters.

At death, the body was lashed to three long poles and carried to the nearby cremation grounds, where corpse and litter were burned (TS). Property, including most shamanistic equipment and shell money, ordinarily was burned, but it might be spared if the deceased left numerous children. Except for wailing (Merriam 1907:355), no extravagant demonstration of grief was mentioned (cf. Heizer 1947:265). A mourner cut his hair and threw it into the water, and the name of the dead was taboo indefinitely. There was no outright mourning ceremony, unless the poló·lo(?) Dance (Loeb 1932:117) and the manufacture of clay and tule figures representing the dead be so considered.

Death, resurrection, ghosts, and poison form an interrelated cluster of recurrent themes touching many basic aspects of Coast Miwok culture: male tribal initiation, selection of the female leader (máien), "moiety" alignment, doctoring, various dances, and the Bird Cult.

The boys' initiation was essentially a male tribal rite. When he was six or seven years old, every lad had to submit to a stint of training in song and dance lasting perhaps several days. At the end, the neophytes performed to demonstrate their new skills.

Prior to this dance, four human effigies—three male, one female—were made of clay. They were about a foot tall and were dried and clothed. Said to represent "dead relations," all the figures belonged to the Land "home" and from them the boys' rite took its name of ʔú·ti kanká(·)wul 'they dance the child (doll)' (TS); TS thought wali' (Loeb 1933:table 1) synonymous. Before the boys danced, four women, each clasping a clay figure, entered the ceremonial house through the smoke hole and danced with the "dolls." They danced again the fourth night, after which the effigies were left outside to disintegrate.

On the first and fourth nights, several wál·ipoh doctors appeared. They treated the ailing who presented themselves and jocosely offered poison to the neophytes. Each wál·ipoh held a boy rigid, over the fire, which he circled four times; and, on the fourth night, he tossed the lads out the smoke hole.

This is what Loeb (1932:115-116) calls the "Ghost ceremony." For him, the "ghost" aspect referred to impersonation by the wál·ipoh, but Kelly (1931-1932) indicates the wál·ipoh were not regarded as ghost impersonators but were believed actually to have died and returned to life. Moreover, association with the dead was stronger than Loeb realized, because of the clay figures representing the demised.

Membership in the secret societies involved another kind of initiation. There were two societies: one, mixed; the other, with women only. Adolescents or adults were eligible for membership and the entrance fee was modest. Novices were trained inside the dance chamber or in the hills and learned the use of costumes and regalia, dance steps and songs, and the society "talk," ʔís·ak máč(·)aw 'true or honest speech' (TS). The hóypuh and máien directed activities, and there were special officers, such as drummer, fire tender, cleaning woman, and so on. Many, but not all, dances were sponsored by the secret societies, and at most of them the ailing were treated.

Dances

They danced because "they wanted to have a good time. If someone was sick, they danced to cure them. If nobody was sick, they danced anyway . . . " (TS). There seems to have been a regular dance calendar that TS could not recall; it could not have been rigid, for sometimes dances were held at the request of a sick person who hoped to be cured.

Dancing took place on the slightest provocation. Informal, individual "dancing" and singing were obligatory when even a small game animal was killed. There were dances or ceremonies related to the capture and release of "eaglets," to the Bird Cult, to the bear, deer, and salmon, to hunting luck, and to harvest. At one special performance, a doctor demonstrated his control of snakes. Still other dances were held: to install a new chief; jointly, to recognize a new wál·ipoh doctor and select a new máien; and to mark the end of the boys' initiation. Of the remaining dances, some were sponsored by the secret societies, some not; some involved impersonation, some not.

In kúksuy (?), wilani, and tsúkin Dances, only men danced; in others, both sexes, and occasionally a woman was the head dancer. On special occasions, there were feats of ventriloquism and magic and of fire eating. Clowns attended some performances, talking "backwards" and otherwise entertaining the audience with their antics. Clapping might be the only accompaniment, but usually the foot drum was used, and singers and dancers carried one or more musical instruments. Sometimes the chorus was all male.

With certain exceptions, the dance costume for both sexes was a pelican coat made from the skin of a brown or white bird. A slit along the inside of each wing inter-

sected with a full ventral cut; presumably additional slits freed the head and legs, so that the skin was peeled off in one piece. The wing slits were sewed to form sleeves and the jacket, tailored to measure, was closed with three haliotis "buttons" (cf. Gifford 1926a:396). Other feathered garments were made on a net foundation of puluti (*Heracleum lanatum*) (TS) and included a rear apron (siliwa) (MC) for men, a cape, and a sort of bertha. The kilak and kúksuy(?) impersonators were naked except for paint and headgear. Feathered headdress was chiefly of three kinds: flicker strip, headband with upstanding black feathers, and "hornlike" tremblers. Staves or canes of various kinds, pelican wings, deer cannon bones, bundles of feathers, and tufts of grass constituted dance paraphernalia.

It is difficult to distinguish "sacred" from profane and secret-society dances from others. Unfortunately, TS was unable to provide a classification. Some dances he declared "no good": pololo, hiwe, and ṣúy·a. We know little of the pololo except what Loeb (1932:117-118) has published. Women wailed, both sexes impersonated the dead, and Loeb considers it a "memorial dance." The hiwe Dance was marked by weeping followed by malaise, and the ṣúy·a seems to have been akin to mass hysteria. Women returning from gathering seeds and roots in the hills started the dance, becoming "kind of crazy, with the hair hanging down in the face and blood coming out of the mouth" (MC). Participants had visions and lost consciousness, and MC described the dance as "a kind of fit." It, or something similar, might account for the extraordinary performance witnessed by Francis Drake's party in 1579 (Heizer 1947:285-286). Of the song texts Kelly recorded, Heizer (1947:275) reproduces a line of the ṣúy·a as suggestive of that given in the Richard Madox account of Drake's visit. Furthermore, this visit took place in June and might have coincided with the women's summer ṣúy·a, which MC thought took place in May. It is possible, however, that ṣúy·a and hiwe, as well as ṣóli 'dream' Dances are late and belong to the 1870 Ghost Dance cluster, as do the le-huye and polo-hote (ball throw), to judge from their names (Du Bois 1939:73-75, 88, 95-96, 99, 110-112, 115, 133).

There was no impersonation in the following: Acorn Dance, pákah ká·wul 'flower dance', wí·law wál·i ká·wul 'hot season (summer) dance'; táyih ká·wul 'man dance'; koyane (song, or singing); Salmon Dance, and one of the two Bear Dances. Most of these were associated with game, hunting luck, or first fruits. Animal impersonation characterized a second Bear Dance, the Deer, and possibly the Coyote Dances. Fox and Skunk Dances are known by name alone.

The remaining dances for which there is information seemingly centered on spirit impersonation, a term more accurate than "god impersonation." Included are: kilak, kuksui, so'oto, soto (apparently two dances with almost the same name), sünwele, tiwila, tsúkin, way·iko(?), and wilani, as well as ṣóli and ṣúy·a. Of these, ṣóli, sünwele, way·iko(?), and wilani referred to air or wind spirits. Doubtless all these spirit-impersonation dances were associated with secret societies.

Religion and ritual

Over the primeval water, "Coyote shook his walik—something like a blanket, of tule—to the south, east, north, and to the west. The water dried and the land appeared" (MC). Coyote (wüyóki) (TS) (ʔóye ʔóy·is [?] 'old man coyote') (MC) came from the west alone, followed by his grandson, Chicken hawk wál·in ʔápi (TS, MC). Coyote turned "his first people" into animals and made others, some of mud, who "might be the Sebastopol people" (South Pomos), some of sticks, who became the Coast Miwoks. He was responsible for menstruation and for death.

The dead leapt into the ocean at Point Reyes and followed a "kind of string leading west through the surf," to a road behind the breakers. This took them farther west, to the setting sun, and there they remained with Coyote in the afterworld (úte-yomigo, or úte-yomi 'dead home') (MC).

TS felt Coyote intervened little in current affairs, but MC was sure her elder relatives had prayed to him. Occasionally, TS spoke of lí·le 'up, top', the "man who watches the hole in the sky." Otherwise, there was no reference to celestial perforation, and Loeb (1932:120) probably is correct in considering lí·le a "modern concept." In addition, there were large numbers of supernatural beings—some ghosts, some nature spirits; of the spirits, some were underground and some above ground, and many were associated with the air or wind.

Song, ritual fasting, continence, and prayer were involved in many enterprises. There were constant petitions for luck or power, terms which TS used synonymously, although the solicited agency was vague. A small food offering marked the beginning of every meal, and at one of the chief's speeches, bread, mush, and pinole were cast into the water, into the fire, and into the bush (MC); acorn-meal offerings were associated with the Bird Cult.

The Bird Cult was one aspect of the special attitudes toward certain animals, especially the bear and various birds. A hunter sang all night and prayed to the bear. Or he dressed as a bear and conversed with his ʔá·mo 'younger sibling' (TS), the bear, requesting luck in hunting and fishing. Ritual requirements surrounded butchering, packing the carcass, cooking and distributing the meat, and disposing of the head of a slain bear. Of the four men hired to attend to these matters, the leader was of the same "moiety" as the hunter. Presumably there were bear shamans in former times, but bear impersonators, as my informants knew them, were simply bandits, male or female, disguised in order to rob and kill.

The local Bird Cult ties nicely with ones that Gifford (1926a) describes for other Miwok. TS reported special observances associated with the condor, móluk(?); duck hawk (o'olela); pelican, both the brown (tsépula) and white (tsoló·l[?]); chicken hawk (wál·in ʔápi); American goldfinch (tsupitc); flicker (hótca); and robin(?) (tsaptsáp). These were "outside" performances, quite different from the usual dance-house, spirit-impersonation functions. Poles were set up, the number depending on which bird was involved, and on them were hung tule figures (tú·ne) (TS), male and female, about 2.5 feet tall. These were associated with the dead and with "moiety" division; for example, in the Condor ceremony, the effigies belong to the Land "home" and were shot at by people of the Water "home."

Quite different was the capture of young birds that TS called eagles (hopa) although they may actually have been a kind of hawk (Merriam 1905-1929:6). The "eaglets" were brought to camp and reared; when they grew the feathers were pulled; and the birds were released ceremoniously, with dance and song.

Music and Games

Most songs were personal property that was bought and sold. There were songs for curing, and for luck in hunting, fishing, and gambling. Love songs were sung by men and women.

Excepting the elderberry flute, musical instruments were considered effective in curing: the hollow-log foot drum; cocoon rattle, split-stick clapper, and bone whistle. The bull-roarer also was therapeutic, but was primarily for luck; it was used mostly by men but not exclusively so.

Both sexes played hockey with a wooden ball. The women's dice game was based on six sticks a foot long; the up-turned "white" faces were counted. Far more important was the grass game (hani) (TS, MC), played by men and women, in which two players hid, each with a pair of duck bones about three inches long. One bone, tied with a string, was called táyih 'man'; the other, plain, kuyéy·ih 'old woman' (TS). A bunch of grass in the hands concealed the bones, which the hiders shuffled in front or behind the back. Opponents tried to guess the relative position of the marked bones. The usual game was for 12 counters; a "big game" was for 16. Gambling was associated with hockey and the grass game. Luck was sought chiefly through amulets; some thought consumption of datura useful; in the grass game, the hiders sang to kawátak ("the grass-game man") (TS), asking for success.

Children played with dolls of mud or sticks, with acorn buzzers, and with pebbles used as jacks. MC remembered string figures.

Knowledge

Numeration was decimal; four, rarely three, were ritual numbers.

A month was called *pul(·)ú·luk* 'moon' (TS, MC), and the "old headman counted the days of the month; he had about 20 sticks . . . maybe 25," each representing a day. Similar sticks, called tcúki (TS), were sent to neighboring villages as invitations to dances. Knotted cords were not used in time reckoning.

The seasons were: spring, *wéyan túp·e* 'ground come out' (TS, MC); summer, *wí·law wál·i* 'hot season' (TS, MC); winter, *ʔómcu wál·i* 'winter (short day?) season' (TS). No name could be recalled for fall. Time of day was expressed by the position of the sun (*hí·*) (TS), thus: *hí·n ków·a* 'sun or day middle, noon' (TS). The sun and moon were not anthropomorphized, and "the old people paid no attention" to solstices. A lunar eclipse was called pulúluk-yo (MC); a solar eclipse was *hí·n múke* 'sun gone' (MC), and it was said a bear was eating the sun (cf. Loeb 1926:228). A red dawn presaged rain, but a red sky at sundown meant the dead in the west were burning seeds and that it would not rain.

MC gave the cardinal directions thus: *ʔólom* 'south', *ʔá·la* 'east', *kánwin* (?) 'north', *hélwa*(?) 'west'. Little was remembered concerning constellations, but the Big Dipper was tceno (MC), the same as the hooked staff used for gathering fruits (cf. Loeb 1926:228). The morning and evening stars were male (TS). An earthquake (yówa-ünówits 'ground-shake') (TS) was caused by a "man," underground, lying face down, arms stretched before him. When he moved his fingers the earth trembled.

Many beliefs related to animals, especially birds. Nocturnal birds were associated with bear impersonators; they and blackbirds had close rapport with a *wál·ipoh* doctor. The meadow lark was "dangerous," could speak "any" language, and sometimes insulted people. Something called a "mountain crab" (pái'is-mulus) (MC) could be dried to make a hunting amulet, but it lived with the rattlesnake, hence acquisition was difficult. "Mountain fish" lived underground but sometimes were found in trees; dried and pulverized, they were added to food as poison.

Synonymy

Nomenclature is confusing. The summary below is based on Powell (1891:93), Hodge and Kroeber (1907:941-942), and Barrett (1908:301-303, 307-314), plus Merriam (1907:353-356) and Kroeber (1925:274).

In the first place, Miwok (also Meewoc), Moquelumnan, and Mewan refer to the entire language "family" and include not only Coast Miwok, but Lake, Valley, and Sierra congeners. Merriam lumps Lake and Coast Miwok in a unit that he calls Inneko.

In the second place, more specifically, Powell recognizes two "divisions" of Moquelumnan: Miwok and Olamentke, the latter what is now called Coast Miwok. Merriam gives Hookooeko the same meaning but divides it into three "tribes": Olamentko (about Bodega Bay), Lekahtewutko (between Freestone and Petaluma), and Hookooeko (the area adjoining Lekahtewutko on the south). The repetition of Hookooeko, with distinct meanings, is unfortunate, as is the close resemblance of Olamentko to Powell's Olamentke, each of different application.

In addition, a great many terms—most, it would seem, derived from village or place names (Kroeber 1925:274)—sometimes are used as if they had tribal significance: Baulines (Bolinas), Bollanos, Chokuyem (Chocuyen, Tchokoyem, Tshokoyem), Guiloco (Guilos), Guimen (Guymen), Jukiusme, Likatuit (Lecatuit, Licatius, Lecatiut, and other variants of Merriam's Lekahtewutko), Nicassias, Numpali, Olamentke, Oleomi, Olumpali (Olompalies), Petalumas (or Yolhias), Sonomi, Tamal (Tamallos, Tamalanos, Tumalehnias), Timbalakees, Tulare(s), and Utchium.

Sources

This chapter is based principally on Kelly's field notes (1931-1932), for which the informants were Tomás Comtechal, called Tom Smith (TS) (fig. 6), of Bay (Bodega dialect) and María Copa Frías (MC) (fig. 7), originally of Nicasio (Marin dialect).§ Most data come from the first named, who was the elder and better informed.

§Attention should be called to two recent "compilations" that appear as Chapters I and II of Number 6 of Treganza Museum Papers, of the San Francisco State University. Although the volume bears an imprint date of 1970, it did not appear until early in 1973, some months after the Department of Anthropology of that university had been informed that I was preparing this article.

Several comments are in order. Data used in these two chapters are taken directly from my field notes, which had been deposited for safekeeping with the Department of Anthropology, University of California, Berkeley. Eventually, custodianship passed to the Lowie Museum, the staff of which imprudently released three photocopies of the notes (each of approximately 500 pages, single-spaced typed) to representatives of the Treganza Museum, who signed an agreement specifying that the material would not be published without written consent. Needless to say, the compilations just mentioned were not authorized by the Lowie Museum and certainly not by me.

Chapter I, signed by Saichi Kawahara, consists of 65 pages, of which 35 are "ethnographic extracts"; these list, without reference to dialectic group, all mention in my notes to plants and animals and their uses. Chapter II, attributed to Linda and M. Curtis Mannion, is even more exasperating. In its "preface," the Mannions show themselves to be unacquainted with even the brief article on the Coast Miwok in Kroeber (1925). Unaware of dialectic groups and even of major boundaries, they suggest that "not all the informants were of the Coast Miwok group." Since my informants were two only, each of a different dialectic group, this explains why field notes were carried on paper of different colors, as two separate, complementary ethnographies. It also explains why to the Mannions the notes seemed "not originally organized to be easily used" and why there were "many contradictions." The solution was to lump all data concerning material culture, plus some aspects of language and society, and to "order" them according to the Murdock scheme, thus losing all attribution to individual informants and to dialectic groups. Apart from the preface, the Mannion "contribution" consists of about 30 pages, exclusively of verbatim excerpts, out of context, from my field notes.

The Treganza Museum and San Francisco State University are not to be felicitated for a botched, subprofessional job and particularly not for a conspicuous breach of personal and professional ethics.

Fig. 6. Tom Smith (Tomás Comtechal). Photograph by C. Hart Merriam, 1927.

Fig. 7. María Copa Frías. Photograph by C. Hart Merriam, 1927.

Both, more fluent in Spanish than in English, spoke largely in the present tense, and direct quotations have been left thus. Published material on the Coast Miwoks is limited in scope and volume (Merriam 1907, 1916; Barrett 1908; Kroeber 1925; Loeb 1932). Loeb's data come in part from informant TS. Du Bois (1939) has published Kelly's field material relative to the 1870 Ghost Dance, and Heizer (1947) has cited scattered in-

formation from it in connection with the Drake landing. A dictionary from the Bodega dialect of Coast Miwok has appeared (Callaghan 1970).

Lowie Museum of Anthropology, University of California, Berkeley, has a few Coast Miwok ethnographic specimens. Archeological artifacts from the zone are in the Lowie Museum and at California State University, San Francisco, in the Treganza Anthropology Museum.

Monache

ROBERT F. G. SPIER

Language, Territory, and Environment

The Monache (mō'nä₁chē) were not a single people but comprehended at least six tribal groups: the Northfork Mono ('mō₁nō), the Wobonuch ('wōpô₁nôch), the Entimbich ('entĭmbĭch), the Michahay (mĭchä'hĭ), the Waksachi (wäk'sä₁chē), and the Patwisha (pät'wĭshə). No federation or nation linked these independent tribes, which were distinguished from their Penutian-affiliated Foothill Yokuts neighbors primarily in language, although some units among them were bilingual. The Monache, often called the Western Mono, shared a distinct language in the Western branch of the Numic family with their neighbors to the east, the Eastern Mono and the Owens Valley Paiute (Lamb 1958; see "The Numic Languages," vol. 11).* The Monache refer to themselves in their own language as *nɨ·mmɨ* 'person, people' and in English as Mono (Lamb 1958:96–97, personal communication 1975; Gifford 1932:16; Kroeber 1925:584).

The social and cultural identity of these tribes was primarily linguistic and locational. They differed from the Foothill Yokuts and the Southern Sierra Miwok (sometimes called Pohonichi) in language, with the possible exception of the "transitional" Michahay and Waksachi (Gayton 1948, 2:213, 254). The Monache differed from the Eastern Mono in being located west of the Sierra Nevada crest and in acculturation to the California scene (fig. 1).

The Northfork Mono were readily distinguished from other Monache by isolation, being separated from the Wobonuch by the essentially unattributable terrain between the headwaters of the San Joaquin and Kings rivers. Gayton (1948, 2:254) discusses a group of unorganized kin groups, evidently without tribal identity, that may have been in this region.

The Wobonuch are recognized as a unit even though their constituent tribelets were more or less independent. The organizing force may have been the example of

* The sound system of the Northfork dialect of Monache has been analyzed by Lamb (1958a). The orthography he describes (substituting a few symbols to accord with Handbook practice) includes the stops *p*, *t*, *k*, *q*, *kʷ*, *qʷ*, *ʔ*; the affricate *c*; the spirants *s*, *x*, *h*; nasals *m*, *n*; semivowels *y*, *w*; front vowels *i*, *e*; back unrounded vowels *ɨ*, *a*; back rounded vowels *u*, *o*. Vowel length can be written with a raised dot; long fortis consonants can be written double.

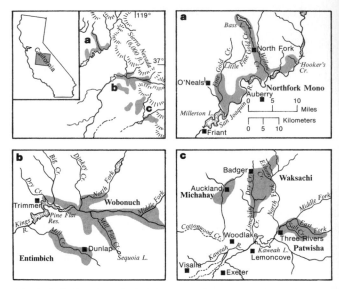

Fig. 1. Tribal territory including: a, Northfork Mono; b, Wobonuch and Entimbich; c, Michahay, Waksachi, and Patwisha.

Foothill Yokuts, such as the Choynimni, to the southwest.

The major affiliation of the Entimbich is still open to question, whether Monache or Yokuts. Gayton (1948, 2:254–255), who probably had the best basis for judgment, inclines to the view that the tribe had lineages derived from both peoples but may have originally been Yokuts. The Wobonuch had been infiltrating Entimbich territory since 1875 (Merriam 1930).

The Michahay, Waksachi, and Patwisha (whom Kroeber 1925:586 calls Balwisha) are deemed basically Monache (Numic-speaking) peoples who have partially absorbed Yokuts culture. As with the Entimbich, the classification chosen verges on being arbitrary until better information emerges. All of these peoples, like their neighbors along the western Sierra slope, were markedly bi- or multilingual.

The Monache were a second tier of aboriginal groups occupying the western slope of the Sierra Nevada. At lower levels along most of the same territory were Foothill Yokuts tribes, from the Chukchansi of the north to the Wikchamni at the southern end of the Monache range. The Foothill Yokuts occupied lands from the valley edge up to about 3,000 feet elevation (essentially the Upper Sonoran life-zone). The Monache lived principally between 3,000 and 7,000 feet elevation (corresponding mostly to the Transition life-zone) but were able to move unhindered to higher elevations. They crossed the Sierra crest on trading expeditions at elevations between 11,000 and 12,000 feet.

The Northfork Mono moved about—seasonally, by reason of a death, or simply for variety—within a home territory centered on the North Fork of the San Joaquin River. Some hamlets were on the adjacent Fine Gold Creek and others were at Hooker's Cove on the San Joaquin. A detailed list of their settlements is furnished by Gifford (1932:18, 57-61).

The Wobonuch lived along various forks of the Kings River from its confluence with its own North Fork upstream. On the North Fork there were habitation sites up to the present Black Rock Reservoir. North of the river they evidently shared the stretch between Trimmer Springs and the confluence of the North Fork with the Tuhukwaj, one of the untribalized Monache groups. Mill Flat Creek, which drained Sequoia Lake into Kings River, was the location of at least two villages; from this area the Wobonuch were forced southward to the vicinity of Dunlap by sawmill operations in the twentieth century.

The Entimbich lived to the south and west of the Wobonuch and at a lower elevation, one comparable to that of Foothill Yokuts. Their principal village was at the present town of Dunlap and was shared beginning with the twentieth century with some displaced Wobonuch. Other sites lay down Mill Creek to its junction with White Deer and Rancheria creeks. Below that point was Foothill Yokuts (Choynimni) territory (Gayton 1948, 2:254-258).

The Michahay lived on the headwaters of Cottonwood Creek north of the present town of Auckland. The Patwishas' westernmost village lay on the left bank of the Kaweah River just below the confluence of its North and Middle Forks, close to the present town of Three Rivers. Eastward Patwisha territory probably extended up the Middle Fork of the Kaweah to Salt Creek or the East Fork (Gayton 1948, 1:58, map B).

The Waksachi territory was higher than that of Michahay and Patwisha, centering on Eshom Creek, a minor tributary of the Kaweah River's North Fork. Other Waksachi sites were along Dry Creek and Limekiln Creek from the present town of Badger downstream for 15 miles (Gayton 1948, 2:212-214, map E).

External Relations

All the Monache maintained close relationships with their neighbors, whether Monache or not. These external contacts included trading, traveling, intertribal assemblies for ceremonies, visiting, incursions into others' territories or common territory for resource exploitation, and marriage.

Intertribal coresidence should be considered a form of external relations, for it must have accelerated linguistic and cultural diffusion. For example, at the village of Tušao, about four miles northeast of Auckland, the Michahay, Waksachi, and Chukaymina lived together. The first two tribes are considered transitional Yokuts-Monache, but the last is unequivocally central Foothill Yokuts (Gayton 1948, 2:213).

Captive eagles (less commonly vultures or other birds) were displayed and danced over. The captors of these moiety-affiliated birds were given money and gifts, ostensibly the property of the captive. Groups went from village to village and from tribe to tribe to participate and to secure birds (Gifford 1932:39-41).

The joint use, by Waksachi, Patwisha, and Wikchamni (a Foothill Yokuts tribe), of uninhabited lands north of present Three Rivers for hunting and foraging illustrates another type of contact (Gayton 1948, 2:213).

The Monache generally traded with their Numic relatives on the east side of the Sierra Nevada, with trading expeditions moving in both directions. The exchange was principally in natural products with acorns being moved eastward while pine nuts, obsidian, and rabbitskins went in the other direction. In addition to securing items for their own use, the Monache were also middlemen in trades between the Yokuts proper and the Eastern Mono.

Hostilities involving the Monache and other tribes usually stemmed from injuries, often attributed to malevolent shamans, occurring to individuals. These people or their survivors sought revenge, usually by killing the person held responsible and sometimes his family as well. Occasionally a third party might become involved through harboring a fugitive or aiding one bent on revenge. Rarely did such incidents lead to wholesale hostilities.

The cultural summary that follows is based on data for the Wobonuch insofar as it is tribally specific, with notice taken of variations among other Monache.

Subsistence

Hunting, fishing, and the gathering of wild-plant foods were the basis of Monache subsistence. Their pursuit called for seasonal movements to various elevations on the Sierra slopes. The Northfork Mono also visited the eastern slope of the Sierra to gather pine nuts, while other Monache traded with Eastern Mono to secure the nuts.

Deer, which were a prime staple, were taken by stalking in a disguise, by driving into an ambush, by tracking a deer until it became exhausted, and by trapping with a spring-pole device that caught the deer by the leg. Deer were customarily shot with bow and arrow to kill them. Sharing of meat and other products was mainly voluntary and done more commonly by the better hunters.

Bears were hunted by rousting them from caves in the spring of the year. The bear's exit was retarded by poles held by members of the hunting party while a bowman shot at the animal. A solo hunter might track and shoot a bear, but this was a very dangerous method. To kill a bear at a regular feeding place, a temporary platform was built in an oak tree where the hunter concealed himself all night. At dawn the bear came to feed beneath and was shot. He might climb the tree in his rage or simply stagger away. The hunter shared the meat with his family and those who helped him with the platform and retrieval of the carcass.

No special ritual precautions accompanied the hunting of deer or bear. Animals were not addressed before, during, or after the kill. Some skilled hunters were thought to have special (supernatural) powers derived from Cougar.

Ground squirrels and rabbits were smoked from their holes or pulled out by twisting into their fur a long flexible stick. They and other small game were trapped between two flat stone slabs propped apart by a stick resting on an acorn.

Pigeons were snared, by the Michahay and Waksachi, from booths on the ground near a feeding place or in a roosting tree. Decoy pigeons, which were tame and kept in basketry cages, were used to lure wild pigeons within reach of a noose on a pole. Each bird, as caught, was quickly drawn into the booth to have its neck wrung so as not to disturb other feeding birds. Booths were privately owned and the decoys were bought and sold.

The Wobonuch built weirs on Mill Flat Creek to catch fish during seasonal runs. A fish harpoon was also used in fishing. The Waksachi used neither weir nor spear but did poison small streams with the mashed remains of an unidentified plant. Freshwater mussels were known as food, although they are found only in the San Joaquin valley, outside the usual range of the Monache.

Acorns and pine nuts were basic to the diet. Acorns were generally obtainable in the lower parts of the Monache range. They were stored in elevated granaries

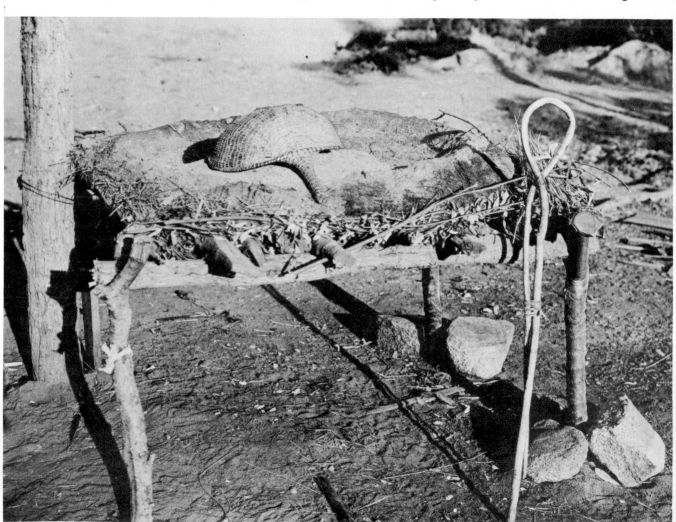

Fig. 2. Waksachi platform for leaching acorn meal, in Eshom Valley. Seed beater is on top of platform; wood mush stirrer used to lift cooking stones from boiled food leans against front. Photograph by C. Hart Merriam, Oct. 1903.

near the house and shelled as required. The Michahay additionally stored acorns in a circular bin built of poles and mats directly on the ground. After being shelled, ground in bedrock mortars, and leached (fig. 2), acorns were cooked in baskets to a mush that was eaten when cold and congealed.

Manzanita berries yielded a beverage when water was poured through a mashed mass held on a sieve. Insects, grubs, and seeds were parched with hot coals in a winnowing basket before being eaten. Yucca and other roots were collected and roasted. Honey was relished when found.

Culture

Technology

Obsidian (volcanic glass) was the principal material for knives, scrapers, and arrow points. It was imported, sometimes as tool blanks, from the Eastern Mono and sometimes resold, rough or finished, to Yokuts tribesmen. Evidently one source for obsidian used by northern Monache was in the vicinity of the present Devil's Postpile National Monument.

Plain self-bows of California laurel wood and sinew-backed recurved bows of juniper were made, the former being in common use. Both were three to four feet long by two inches wide and used two-ply sinew strings. Four kinds of arrows were known: for birds, for small game, for big game, and for war. Bird arrows were alderwood, self-pointed or with cross-points, and often unfletched. Small game arrows had cane shafts with a wooden foreshaft and were self-pointed and fletched. Big game arrows had cane shafts and stone points and were fletched; the point was insecurely fastened so that it remained in the wound. War arrows were similar to big game arrows, though shorter, and had their obsidian points securely lashed and glued (Gayton 1948, 2:218-219). Arrow poisons of deer liver, either rotted or envenomed by rattlesnakes, were reported for the Wobonuch (Gayton 1948, 2:261).

Small goods included a carrying net with a tumpline, commonly a man's item. Men made a feather fire fan of vulture or hawk tail feathers used at the hearth or when smoking animals from their holes. A soaproot brush was important to all grinding of foods on bedrock mortars (fig. 3) to sweep the scattered bits together. A looped stick mush stirrer, similar to that of the Yokuts, lifted spent stones from cooking foods. Pine tongs or a pair of pine sticks put the heated stones into the cooking baskets. Steatite vessels (fig. 4) are reported for both the North-fork Mono and the Wobonuch (Gifford 1932:25; Gayton 1948, 2:266).

In general, Monache basketry is quite like that of the Foothill Yokuts, with the resemblances stemming from an exchange of types. Gifford (1932:26) observes that

Fig. 3. Jane Whaley, Wobonuch, using a boulder pestle in a bedrock mortar. Winnowers and soaproot brush are at her feet. Photograph by C. Hart Merriam, at Kings River, Sept. 1930.

twined cooking baskets occurred commonly among the Northfork Mono, though rare among Miwok and Yokuts. His view is possibly supported by Gayton's (1948,1:18-19, figs. 2-3) summary of Yokuts and Monache types, but unfortunately her sample is drawn heavily from the groups that should be compared to Yokuts generally and so is not definitive. The Chukchansi Yokuts are known to have used twined mush baskets (Gayton shows coiled mush baskets) and possibly coiled ones as well; but they were, after all, next neighbors to the Northfork Mono (R.F.G. Spier 1954:figs. 14-15, 24, 38). Baby cradles (fig. 5) among the Monache were of the so-called Mono type, a flat trapezoidal base of crossing small sticks held by twining and a hooplike hood with attached sunshade (Gifford 1932:pl. 8; Gayton 1948, 2:273). This

Fig. 4. Northfork Mono steatite cooking vessel. Height about 10.2 cm, collected 1918.

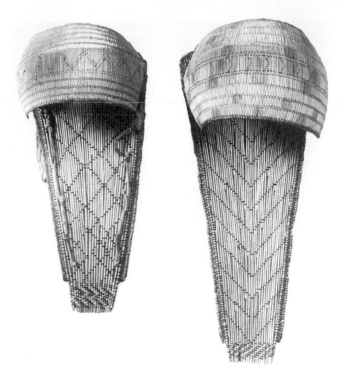

Lowie Mus., U. of Calif., Berkeley: left, 1-21716; right, 1-21717.
Fig. 5. Twined cradles. left, For female, length about 63 cm; right, for male, same scale. Collected 1918.

style made inroads among the Foothill Yokuts (in the nineteenth century?) to the extinction of the classic cradle on a forked-stick base (Kroeber 1925:534–537, fig. 48d). A Michahay-Waksachi informant described to Gayton (1948, 2:234) a hybrid style that had the Mono back and sunshade superimposed on the Y-shaped forked Yokuts base, a usage that further stresses the transitional nature of these tribes. Designs on cradles reflected the sex of occupants, among the Northfork a chevron for boys and a zigzag for girls (Gifford 1932:pl. 8).

Other basketry products included: twined burden baskets (fig. 6), seed beaters, sieves, and fan-shaped winnowers; and coiled mush, storage, or washing baskets, winnowing trays, gambling trays, and treasure baskets—a

Lowie Mus., U. of Calif., Berkeley: left, 1-19720; right, 1-10493.
Fig. 6. Burden baskets. left, Close twined seed carrier, diameter 56 cm, collected 1915. right, Diagonal twined openwork basket, primarily used for carrying acorns, same scale; collected 1906.

430

Yokuts specialty, the so-called Tulare bottlenecks (Kroeber 1925:531, pl. 50a; Gayton 1948, 1:18–19).

Pottery was made by the Monache, except those at Northfork, by a coiling technique. The resulting vessels were fired in a pit, with a period of preheating on its edge. Larger pots were used for boiling meat (Gayton 1948, 2:226, 265). The making of pottery was shared with central Foothill Yokuts, to whom it evidently diffused, but was not a generalized Yokuts trait (Gayton 1929).

The Monache made cordage of sinew, milkweed fiber, and various barks such as willow bark. All were rolled on the thigh in the absence of a spindle. The vegetable twines were worked into nets and tumplines in addition to common fastenings (Gifford 1932:28; Gayton 1948, 2:226). No woven textiles were natively made.

Structures

The dwelling houses of the Monache ran to three types: a conical house with an excavated floor, an oval house with a ridgepole, and a conical bark-covered house with a center post (fig. 7). The first two types were shared with Foothill Yokuts, while the last was primarily Monache as the bark was only available at higher elevations (Gifford 1932:20; Gayton 1948, 2:215–216, 260).

The conical house was 6 to 12 feet in diameter and its floor was excavated to a depth of a foot or more. The basic frame poles were set inside the depression and brought together at a ring at the top (forming a smoke hole). Lighter poles were set between and the whole held by encircling willow withes. The exterior was thatched with grass and fine willow twigs. The doorway, about five feet high, was covered with a mat tied to a side pole. Inside a fire burned in a central depression in the floor. The house had no interior divisions or furnishings.

The oval house had diameters of 10 to 15 feet by 17 to 20 feet and its floor at ground level. A ridgepole was supported by forked posts set at two-thirds of the long diameter. Poles leaned against the ridge and the forked post tops. Grass was thatched over the withes that held the poles, with an unthatched slot at the ridge to serve as a smoke exit. The doorway, with a mat door leaned in place, was on a long side.

The conical bark house, with unexcavated floor, had a few large poles placed against a forked center post and roped in place. (Occasionally two posts and a short ridge beam were used.) Slabs of cedar bark were laid against the poles and tied as necessary. Earth was often banked around the lower wall. Smoke evidently found its way out through the cracks. Size was similar to the other conical house.

The sweathouse, usually one to a village but not present in every hamlet, was the other major structure. The Wobonuch-Entimbich and the Michahay-Waksachi both used a two-post foundation. The general construction was similar to that of the oval house. A lintel resting on short posts held the shortened roof poles above the

Fig. 7. Conical bark-covered house, Northfork Mono. Photograph by C. Hart Merriam, Oct. 1902.

open doorway, which was about three feet high. There was no closure. Earth was taken from within the sweathouse to put over the outside. The fire, using no heated stones or steam, was either just inside the doorway or just outside. The single-post sweathouse, reported for the Michahay and Waksachi, had an excavated floor, poles laid up to a central forked post, fine sticks over the base, and an earth cover (Gayton 1948, 2:217, 259–260). The Northfork Mono had a sweathouse described as "like the dwelling, but covered completely with earth" (Gifford 1932:20). Their house was a conical type with an apex ring and an excavated floor. The sweathouse was a gathering place for men who sweated usually in the late afternoon and took a quick dip in the stream that it faced. Women stayed away from the sweathouse, but boys sometimes played there and might stay around to listen to old men's stories. Single men might sleep in the sweathouse.

Other structures included an acorn granary built of sticks and matting on a raised platform about six feet off the ground. The Michahay additionally had a tall cylindrical bin made of poles set directly in the ground.

Around the poles was a willow mat, added turn-by-turn as the bin was filled. The whole was three feet in diameter and eight feet high. A shade, formed by brush piled on a horizontal frame between four corner posts, was a common adjunct to every house. Rows of shades were built around the dance ground when major ceremonies were planned.

Settlement

Settlements were generally small and loosely organized. The Northfork Mono had no principal village; instead there were a number of hamlets ranging from one to eight huts with an average of three huts and 13 people per place (Gifford 1932:17–19). The Michahay-Waksachi had no village plan; an individual built wherever he pleased. By contrast, a Wobonuch informant claimed that their villages had houses, facing south, southeast, or southwest, set in a semicircle with the local chief and messenger living in the center houses (Gayton 1948, 2:216, 260).

Transport

When moving camp temporarily the women carried household goods in burden baskets supported by a   *431* tumpline over the head. A coiled basketry cap, for this purpose only, was worn under the tumpline. Men used a carrying net with a tumpline that they placed across the upper chest and the deltoid muscles at the shoulder. Infants in cradles were carried atop the loads of elders or by older sisters.

The Wobonuch used a raft of two or three logs with a brush or mat decking to carry household goods, game, or a nonswimmer across a stream. If the stream was fordable one man pushed the raft, otherwise two swimmers propelled it. A basketry boat, four feet in diameter, coiled, flat-bottomed with flaring sides, was a common family possession. It could carry infants or light valuables. No canoes, paddles, or poles for rafts were known (Gayton 1948, 2:266).

Training in swimming was part of the education, and toughening, of children. They learned a breastroke with a scissors kick.

Clothing and Adornment

There is no clear account of everyday dress of the Monache. By implication both men and women may have worn breechclouts and/or aprons front and rear for the women. Gifford (1932:29) reports two-piece dresses of buckskin worn by the women. Perhaps this was a double apron.

While people normally went barefooted, the Michahay and Waksachi bought moccasins from the Eastern Mono. The Wikchamni (Foothill Yokuts) and Patwisha had a moccasin (which they made?) (Gayton 1948, 2:217, 1:65–66).

People ornamented themselves with plugs in pierced earlobes. Formerly they also pierced the nasal septum for a shell bead. Tattooing on the face was appropriate for both sexes, while some women carried facial tattoos down the throat and onto the chest. Tattooing had no special significance or ritual aspect, but patterns were standardized (Gayton 1948, 2:218).

Painting was reserved for ceremonial and comparable occasions. Colors were red, black, white, and dark blue, with some pigments obtained from Eastern Mono. Each major lineage among the Wobonuch and Entimbich had its characteristic paint pattern, mostly on the face, for both sexes (Gayton 1948, 2:264–265).

Life Cycle

Pregnancy was marked by no special behavior for either prospective parent. Birth took place in the house with the parturient's mother or any other competent woman relative in attendance. A shaman might be called in the event of a difficult delivery, but he aided mostly by his presence. The umbilical cord was cut with a cane knife, and the baby was washed in warm water and placed on a forked-stick (Michahay only?) cradle. The mother remained quiet and on a restricted diet for several months. A taboo on meat remained in effect for three months until the mother was ritually cleansed by her mother-in-law and other female relatives of the child's father (Gayton 1948, 2:233–234, 272–273).

In theory a child was named by and for his or her paternal grandparent of the same sex, but in genealogies this alternate generation naming is not borne out. Personal names had no meaning of which people were conscious; nicknames were common and often referred to some trait of the individual (Gifford 1932:46–49; Gayton 1948, 2:234, 273).

A girl's puberty was marked by use of a scratching stick during the first period or two. Her parents might put on a little cleansing ritual at which she was ceremonially washed and garbed in such new clothes and ornaments as the family could afford. Menstruating women were not segregated, but they could not cook or have intercourse.

Marriages were prevailingly monogamous, but polygyny was permitted and occasionally practiced by the wealthy. The levirate and sororate were found, but not compulsory; too hasty a remarriage was thought to risk death.

Unions between cototemites were permissible if no other relationship was known. Cousin marriages were definitely prohibited. Negotiations toward a marriage were initiated by the groom's parents who exchanged gifts with those of the potential bride. Both principals would be pubertal age or older. If the proposal were satisfactory the principals would be informed or consulted; they usually agreed with parental judgment. Temporary matrilocal residence was followed by patrilocal or neolocal residence with frequent short visits home by the bride. No bride price is reported for the more southerly Monache, but among the Northfork Mono it was paid to a girl's father or some other paternal relative in his absence (Gifford 1932:31).

A divorce was possible when irreconcilable differences arose or when a husband simply deserted his wife for another woman. No return of prenuptial gifts was made.

Behavior between parent-in-law and child-in-law was circumspect, with some avoidance and the use of formal address in speech. The taboo was somewhat relaxed through the years but never vanished.

The Monache contracted intertribal marriages with their kind and with the Yokuts. A Waksachi informant stated that they never married Eastern Mono on the grounds that the latter were not welcome as permanent residents (Gayton 1948, 2:235). Such marriages do seem to have been infrequent. Gifford's (1932:35) survey of marital habits showed a very low percentage of intertribal marriages by the Northfork. Of 199 marriages recorded, 9 were to foreigners: 2 to Eastern Mono, 4 to Monache other than Northfork, and 3 to Chukchansi.

Death, of all life crises, evoked the most substantial social response. When a person was seen to be dying women gathered around and began weeping while the tribal messenger went to inform relatives. Disposal of the body came 24 to 48 hours after death. Before contact with Whites cremation was common; it continued to be used for those who died away from home so that the ashes might be transported for burial. The fire was built and tended by friends or a corpse-carrier, a public functionary who was paid. Personal possessions were sometimes burned and the house of death was customarily abandoned. The ashes and unburned bones were gathered and placed in water, according to a Michahay-Waksachi informant, or else buried in a basket in the local cemetery (Gayton 1948, 2:236, 274).

Digging of a grave was commenced immediately on a death. Testimony differs on who dug the grave, with the corpse-handler, professional mourning singers, and relatives of the deceased being named. The first two would have been paid for their services. Personal effects were often buried with the flexed, wrapped body. The corpse lay on its back, head to the west.

The extent and length of mourning were not prescribed but varied with closeness of kinship and other bonds to the deceased. Widows were expected to mourn about a year or more, others a shorter term. Hair was often singed short and the person allowed to become disheveled and dirty. Mourners were subject to food taboos and were socially withdrawn. A "little" mourning ceremony was held, at the individual's discretion, to mark termination of that status. The mourner's chief, with the assistance of his messenger, made arrangements for the visit of members of a reciprocating family from another tribe who came along with their chief and his messenger. After some preliminaries, the mourners were washed and reclothed by the reciprocants. The affair lasted only a day or two and was evidently more developed among the transitional Yokuts-Monache than among the unequivocal Monache (Gayton 1948, 2:238, 275). The annual mourning ceremony, which pertained to all mourners of a tribe, is described below.

Social Organization

Of the Monache under consideration only the Northfork are reported as having possessed moieties (Gifford 1932:34-37). In this social feature they resembled the neighboring Foothill Yokuts and Southern Sierra Miwok (Gayton 1945:410). Each Northfork moiety, in which membership was derived patrilineally, was in two divisions, perhaps reflecting the coalescence of the Northfork from several smaller units. The moieties each had chiefs who occupied a hereditary office and might be members of any of three divisions; the fourth division was not eligible to furnish a chief. Only one division of the four was able to furnish an assistant chief so that members of one moiety were forced to hire their assistant chief from the other moiety. The totemic affiliations of these officials contrast with those among the Yokuts and more southerly Monache in that the chief is nominally associated with the eagle but might have another creature as his

personal totem. The assistant chief, on the other hand, must be drawn from the moietal division having the eagle as its principal totem. The contrasting practice has chiefs uniformly associated with the eagle while the assistant chief (usually a messenger) commonly has the dove as his totem.

In general, and notably in recent times, the moieties had rivalrous and reciprocal relations in games, feasts, and ceremonies. It was noted that at some distant date the four divisions were cross-paired in funerary and mourning observances thus creating, for this purpose at least, two intersecting pairs of moieties. In the twentieth century the social fabric has "shrunk" so that any person not of one's group, even from another tribe, may be placed in the role of a reciprocant in some of these same circumstances.

Lineages were the major kinship units reported for the Monache, except the Northfork among whom some of their functions fell to the divisions of the moieties. Lineages were exclusively patrilineal. Each lineage was recognized as having a totemic creature—prevailingly birds rather than animals—that was referred to as a member's "pet" (literally 'dog') (Gayton 1948, 2:231, 272). The Eagle lineage provided the tribe with chiefs while the Roadrunner or the Dove lineage furnished the chief's messengers. The lineage totems were distinct from whatever supernatural aids the individual managed to acquire for himself; the former came through the accident of birth while the latter were gotten by active effort.

The principal officials of the Monache were the chief and the messenger, but their functions were not everywhere the same. Among the Northfork the chief headed a moiety, not a settlement, so there were two chiefs simultaneously in office (Gifford 1932:41). The more southerly Monache tribes, the Michahay-Waksachi and the Wobonuch-Entimbich, had chiefs who led the people of a village. Again, more than one chief might have been in office at a time, but they were necessarily in different communities. However, not every settlement was large enough to rate a chief. Both north and south the chieftainship was patrilineally inherited, passing to a younger brother or an eldest son, but transmission was tempered by considerations of individual ability and personality. Other members of the chief's immediate family, presumably those who might conceivably have been inheritors, also bore the title of chief although they did not so act. (This circumstance may have led to confusion about leadership on first contact with Whites in that persons were deemed to have the authority implied by their titles.) Secondary chiefs were reported among the Michahay-Waksachi who were appointed by the chief and assisted him financially with major ceremonies (Gayton 1948, 2:230-231).

Gayton (1948, 2:270) has summarized the duties of a Monache chief: "He decided upon the time for ceremonies, as none could be held without his consent, suggested the time to move, saw that the needy were fed and sheltered, and sanctioned the killing of malicious shamans or, presumably, other evil-doers. His power was by no means absolute but was that of a benevolent or paternal governor who advised rather than ordered."

The messenger was drawn from the lineage that held the Roadrunner as its totem, with secondary recognition of the Dove as a totem. Among the neighboring Yokuts, from whom Gayton (1948, 2:271) considers the office to have been derived, the Dove is the messenger's totem. Unlike the Monache chiefs, the messengers possessed a mark of office—an eight-foot-long cane with red-painted bands and a string tied to the top—by which they were immediately recognized. Although the record is unclear the string apparently kept track of time, as the days before a ceremony. The duties of the office were "to take messages to and from his chief, or between other people who cared to hire him; to supply his chief with wood and water; to give orders around the village; and particularly at ceremonies direct proceedings, supply wood and water, prevent quarrels, and direct the dancing or entertainment routine" (Gayton 1948, 2:271). In addition to the chief's messenger there were others, generally his subordinates, some of whom aided shamans. Messengers were regularly paid for their services.

Religion

The Monache generally believed in the supernatural powers possessed by totemic and tutelary spirits, powers that might be employed by persons who had the proper experiences and skills. The powers of the totemic spirits were of value and concern to all, with particular spirits being those associated with lineage or moiety. Tutelary spirits were often sought on an individual basis. Success in this quest could lead to recognition as a shaman. Even those persons who did not seek such distinction were inclined to possess, if possible, some lesser powers for themselves as leading to success in life.

The Monache shamans counted fewer specialists in their ranks than did those among the neighboring Yokuts (Gayton 1948, 2:275), but Gifford (1932:50) reports bear and deer shamans among the Northfork. A major function of shamans was curing illness, often by removal of supposed intrusive objects. The ability to cure carried with it the ability to make ill or to kill and there were frequent suspicions and accusations of malevolent shamans. Shamans usually operated independently when curing but were believed to consort in groups at times when engaged in malicious behavior. Cannibalism, exhumation of the dead, poisoning, and acts of magic were attributed to shamans. Anecdotes of shamanistic malevolence suggest vicious individuals operating on their own account rather than as hirelings of others (Gayton 1948, 2:279-280).

The power of flying was believed possessed by ordinary persons who had the proper talismans. Flight was not sustained, but the person progressed in great leaps being invisible as he passed through the air. Each leap cost the power in one talisman; however, it could be shared with someone in the same adventure. Flight was allegedly employed when one was in great danger from an enemy (Gayton 1948, 2:276).

Datura was taken in an annual spring ceremony among the Michahay-Waksachi and Entimbich, but at personal convenience among the Wobonuch. The narcotic was known and used among the Northfork as well. In the ceremonial circumstance the date was set several months ahead so that the participants could observe a meat taboo. Adolescent boys and girls drank the infusion, perhaps only once in their lives, to assure a good life and knowledge of the supernatural world. Adults occasionally, and some powerful shamans annually for a decade, might join them. The six days of the ceremony, under the leadership of a knowledgeable man, saw segregation of the participants, their observance of a restricted diet, prayerful consideration of the datura spirits, and the climax of drinking the infusion. The drinkers danced before spectators until they fell unconscious. Until he had fully recovered each participant was attended by two aides to keep him from injuring himself (Gayton 1948, 2:245-247, 281-283).

The Bear Dance and related ideas of bear supernaturalism were stronger among the Wobonuch and Entimbich than among the Michahay-Waksachi. Men of the Bear lineage who, through dreaming, had Bear as a personal helper gave dance performances imitating movements of the bear. Additionally, it was believed that such men might transform themselves into bears in order to harm those whom they disliked or to travel quickly without being molested. The Northfork also had bear shamans and a lively interest in bears (Gayton 1948, 2:248, 283-284; Gifford 1932:50-51).

The annual mourning ceremony was held more or less regularly though the frequency was linked to deaths and the affluence of the mourning families, who paid most of the costs (Gayton 1948, 2:249-252, 286-289; Gifford 1932:43-45). The early fall is reported for the Wobonuch-Entimbich and was a likely time for other tribes as well. After consultations the chief sent his messenger to other tribes with announcement of the occasion and its date. The visitors brought little beyond their blankets and were furnished food, firewood, and shelter by the hosts.

During the ceremonial week little happened on the first four days other than morning and evening weeping by old women. Paid singers accompanied the weeping. The evening sing might also be the occasion for the mourners to parade with the baskets, money, and other gifts that they would distribute after the ritual washing. The fifth evening sometimes saw a contest of powers between shamans, a feature imported from neighboring Yokuts who might also furnish the performing shamans. On the sixth night a fire was built in the dance plaza (the first unless there had been a shamans' contest) and the hosts and reciprocant tribesmen lined up facing across the area; nonreciprocant visitors watched from the ends. Several periods of intense crying, singing, and parading occurred. Ultimately some of the goods that the mourners provided and had been carrying came into the possession of the reciprocants. Other items, especially effigies of the deceased, were burned. With them was supposed to vanish the mourners' grief. Baskets of money and other gifts were given to the chief of the reciprocants for distribution to his people; it was at this time that the mourners' chief and his henchmen might have to make up deficits in the payments. This payment might follow the ritual washing on the final day of the ceremony instead of following destruction of the effigies.

The last (often seventh) day brought ritual washing of the mourners by the reciprocants. Although special attention was paid to those actually bereaved the entire tribal group was included. The washers supplied fresh clothes to those whom they cleansed and received in return the handsome washing baskets. Finally, a feast was spread that broke the fast of the mourners. As a postlude there was sometimes a performance by Yokuts *huhuna* dancers who customarily sought hidden money and were laid low by "shots" from powerful shamans (Gayton 1948, 2:289).

Those who reciprocated as washers and mourners in this ceremony stood in a regular relationship. Tribes were traditionally so ranged, with the Wobonuch and Entimbich reciprocating, for example. However, there are some indications that families, even of the same tribe, may have been so allied. Confusion has been added to the scene in the twentieth century by the contraction of this aspect of social organization so that people are uncertain of lineages, their relations to totems, and the link of both to moieties where present.

The Monache were central to the introduction of the Ghost Dance of 1870 west of the Sierra Nevada. A Northern Paiute missionary brought the cult to an enthusiastic audience among the Northfork. The resulting dance, evidently in the spring of 1871, drew participants from among both Monache and Foothill Yokuts from as far south as the Entimbich. Singers, who learned the songs on this occasion, toured to the south, spreading the gospel. The Entimbich were moved to sponsor another large dance in Eshom Valley, a convenient place though actually Waksachi territory. Some converts put on a dance at Tule, which was attended by Southern Valley Yokuts; and dances, large and small, followed in that area. The large dances ceased in 1873 and private observances were abandoned by 1875 (Gayton 1930a).

The Ghost Dance performance involved a round dance by both sexes, circling clockwise, to their own clapping and a repetitive song from male singers. The dancers danced primarily in the evening, with resting, swimming, games, and general socializing through the days of an assembly lasting as long as a week. The dance itself was continued to exhaustion; while resting the dancers might hear an exhortation from a leader. As the efforts of the 1870s had failed to bring back the dead, the 1890 revival of the Ghost Dance had no impact among the Monache (Gayton 1948, 2:252-253, 289-290).

History

Kroeber (1939a:154, map 19) indicates the foothills of the Sierra Nevada—Foothill Yokuts and Monache territory—as among the most densely inhabited in California. The aboriginal population exceeded 70 persons a square kilometer (about 180 a square mile). By 1910 an estimated 6 to 9 percent survived (Kroeber 1925:887, fig. 72).

The population estimate for 1770—4,000 persons—included both the Monache and the Paiute (Western and Eastern Mono), with 1,500 believed surviving in 1910. Another estimate for 1770 places 1,000 Monache in the Kern River area. If approximately 10 percent survived into the twentieth century, then this would accord with the 1950 population of the consolidated tribes at the Tule River Reservation. The Monache of the Northfork area were thought to total 154 (in three communities) in 1950 (Tax and Stanley 1960).

Most accounts of the Monache have sought to reconstruct the native life of precontact or early contact times; consequently, their modern situation is not well studied. Survivors are evidently living on the Tule River Reservation, east of Porterville, California, where they are in close contact with some remaining Yokuts. Merriam (1966-1967, 3:412-416) visited the reservation in 1903 and recorded the condition of its inhabitants. The modern reservation is organized with a tribal council, headquarters, store, and camping lands for rental to nonmembers. Both Protestant and Catholic churches are found in the area.

Synonymy

The Monache have been known as Monachi (Kroeber 1925:584), Monos (Powers 1877:396), and Western Mono (Gifford 1932:15). Various Penutian-speaking Californians named their Numic eastern neighbors with words similar to Mono; Monache may perhaps have been derived from a version with a Yokuts suffix used in that language to refer to the Western Mono and Owens Valley Paiute (Lamb 1958:97). Another possible source may be Southern Sierra Miwok, where *mo·na-* refers to 'Mono person or language'; however, a form *mo·naʔčiʔ* with the suffix meaning 'people of (a place)' is not attested (Broadbent 1964:257, 288).

Monache were called *nutʰaʔa* (plural *nutʰšawayi*) by their Yawdanchi Yokuts neighbors (Kroeber 1963:225, phonemicized). This term, spelled Nūtʰha by Powers (1877:396), and the form nuta'wi (plural nutsa'wi) from

435

another Yokuts dialect (Gayton 1948, 2:145) is basically directional, rather than tribal, as it means 'uplanders, easterners' and was also applied, by some Yokuts, to their more eastern Yokuts neighbors (Kroeber 1925:584). Entimbich have been called Em'-tim'-bitch (Merriam 1930) and Intimpeach (Royce 1899:955) as well as other variant but easily recognizable spellings. Michahay occurs in the plural as Michahaisha or Michahayisa (Kroeber 1925:480). Northfork Mono have been identified as Nim or Neum (Merriam 1955) from the Monache self-designation ni·mmi. Patwisha has been variously spelled Padoosha, Pot'-wish-ah (Merriam 1955:168, 1930:497), Pal-wis-ha (Royce 1899:782), and Balwisha (Kroeber 1925:586). Variations of Waksachi include Wuksache (Merriam 1955:168), Wack-sa-che (Royce 1899:782), and their Wobonuch name, Pa'ohabi (Gayton 1948, 2:254). The Wobonuch have been known as Woponutch, Wä-pon-nutch, and Wo-pung'-witch (Merriam 1955:168, 174, 1930:497).

Sources

Two prime anthropological sources for the Monache are sections of Gayton (1948) and Gifford (1932). Additional notes are found in Merriam (1966–1967, 3). Kroeber (1925) offers very little on the Monache.

Topical studies in the conventional literature include Gayton on pottery making (1929), chiefs and shamans (1930), the Ghost Dance of 1870 (1930a), and social organization (1945). Gayton and Newman (1940) discuss myths. Gifford's broader studies in social organization (1916a, 1918) and Driver's culture element survey (1937) contain pertinent information.

There is virtually no writing about the Monache apart from that primarily devoted to the Yokuts. This circumstance reflects the close association of these two groups of tribes and the consequent difficulty of dealing independently with the Monache.

Tubatulabal

CHARLES R. SMITH

Language, Territory, and Environment

Tubatulabal (təˌbătləˈbäl) is both the name of a group that aboriginally inhabited a portion of California's southern Sierra Nevada foothill region (fig. 1) and the name of the language that they spoke. Three discrete bands (Pahkanapïl, Palagewan, and Bankalachi) originally composed the Tubatulabal group, with only the Pahkanapïl surviving the intensive White settlement of their territory that began in 1850. The bands' similar and mutually intelligible dialects collectively formed the Tubatulabal language, formerly classified as the Kern River branch of the Shoshonean stock but now considered to be a separate subgroup of the Uto-Aztecan family.* The name Tubatulabal 'pine-nut eaters' was applied to the Pahkanapïl and Palagewan by their western (Yokuts) and southern (Kawaiisu) neighbors and by themselves; the Bankalachi (a Yokuts term) were called Toloim by the other Tubatulabal bands.

The Tubatulabal habitat was the drainage area of the Kern and South Fork Kern rivers from their sources near Mount Whitney to approximately 41 miles below the junction of the two rivers. The area, roughly 1,300 square miles, is mainly mountainous; elevations range from 2,500 to 14,500 feet. Terrain of the northern two-thirds, lying in the Sierra Nevada, is mountainous, with peaks rising over 8,000 feet. Interspersed among them are numerous meadows and small lakes. The southern one-third of the area is broken by three connected valleys, each drained by a river: the Kern valley, the South Fork Kern valley, and the Hot Springs valley. The valleys lie at 2,500 to 3,000 feet elevation, and summers are hot and dry, with temperatures of 100°–115°F. not uncommon (Voegelin 1938:10). Winters are cold and rainy with temperatures a consistently cool 32°–70° F. Snow falls occasionally in the upper reaches of the Kern and South Fork Kern valleys, and the mountains are blanketed under heavy snow from November until March.

The valleys are characterized by a Transition Desert grassland and Interior chaparral-Upper Sonoran vegetation pattern (Munz and Keck 1959:11–18), that is, primarily various grasses, cactus, scrub oak, willows, cottonwood, and toward the valley edges, juniper and

*The spellings of all italicized Tubatulabal words are by the author, in the more recent form of C.F. Voegelin's orthography (1935, 1958).

piñon in the South Fork Kern valley and oak and pine-sugar pine in the Kern valley. In the northern mountainous portions are subalpine and alpine communities of hardwood trees (Klyver 1931:8).

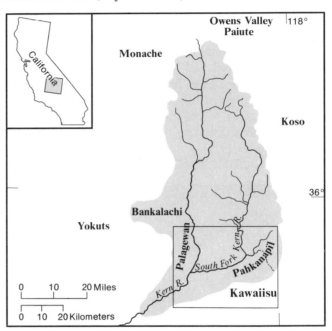

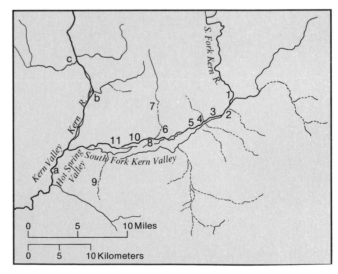

Fig. 1. Tribal territory with hamlet locations. Palagewan hamlets: a, pašgeštap; b, cuhka·yl; c, ho·lit. Pahkanapïl hamlets: 1, ʔu·u·pu·lap; 2, čebu·nun; 3, ʔomomïp; 4, ʔomomïp; 5, yowolup; 6, yïtiyamup; 7, kolokum; 8, tušpan; 9, pa·da·ẓap; 10, ha·halam; 11, ʔumu·bi·lap. (Hamlets after Voegelin 1938:42).

Varied fauna includes rabbits, squirrels, deer, mountain lion, mountain sheep, coyote, skunk, California brown bear, white-faced geese, mallard and canvasback ducks, teals, coots, quail, pigeons, a variety of smaller birds, trout, whitefish, suckers, catfish, minnows, and freshwater mussels.

History

Little is known concerning the Tubatulabal prior to 1850. They say they have always inhabited the Kern valley region and their mythology contains no migration tales (Voegelin 1938:9). Archeological investigations have shown that the majority of historic and prehistoric hamlet sites were located near the confluence of the Kern and South Fork Kern rivers (Wallace 1970). The cultural pattern revealed is one of small bands that periodically entered an area, used locally available materials for tools, gathered and hunted, and then returned to larger dwellings along the rivers. The earliest cultural horizon definitely attributable to the Tubatulabal is about A.D. 1450, but several cultural horizons underlie the Tubatulabal materials and may date as early as A.D. 1 (Anonymous 1971).

The Tubatulabal were first visited by Europeans in 1776 when Francisco Garcés explored the lower reaches of the Kern valley (Coues 1900:280). In this same year guides for Father Pedro Font encountered a group of Indians (possibly Palagewans) a few miles south of the Kern–South Fork Kern River junction (Font 1930, 4:390). During the next 50 years, the Tubatulabal, on trading trips to the California coast, came into contact with the Spanish at San Buenaventura mission. By 1850 White settlers had established ranches in all three valleys, and in 1857 the Kern River gold rush began, displacing many Indians. In 1858 some Pahkanapïl moved from the Hot Springs valley to the eastern end of the South Fork Kern valley to escape White domination (C.R. Smith 1968–1972).

In 1862 a few Tubatulabals joined an Owens valley Paiute band in anti-White hostilities in the Owens valley. The following year, American soliders responded to pleas from White ranchers who complained that their milkcows were being stolen by the Tubatulabal: 35-40 Tubatulabal men were massacred in the Kern valley. By 1875 most Tubatulabal men were employed by White ranchers, and in 1893 the surviving Pahkanapïl and Palagewan were allotted land in the Kern and South Fork Kern valleys.

From 1900 to 1972 many Tubatulabals moved to the Tule River Indian Reservation (fig. 2), north of the Kern

Fig. 2. Dan Williams of Tule River Indian Reservation. Photograph by C. Hart Merriam, Sept. 1935.

Fig. 3. Steve Miranda and family at Weldon Rancheria, Kern Valley. Photograph by C. Hart Merriam, May 1932.

valley region, and to towns and cities throughout California. The majority of men remaining in the Kern valley area (fig. 3) in 1972 were employed as cowhands, while some women worked as secretaries or bookkeepers.

Population estimates for the Tubatulabal prior to 1930 are tenuous. Kroeber (1925:608) estimates a precontact population between 500 and 1,000, and at contact in 1850 Voegelin (1938:39) estimates a population of 200 to 300. The 1972 field census (C.R. Smith 1968–1972) showed 29 full-blood Tubatulabals (15 females and 14 males, ages ranging from infant to over 75) and 14 half-blood Tubatulabals (9 females and 5 males, all under 35 years old) still living in the Kern valley area. Seven Tubatulabals, all three-quarter blood, live in other areas of California. The population decline between 1850 and 1972 is related to: the 1863 massacre, the 1902 measles epidemic, the 1918 influenza epidemic, and loss of cultural identity through intermarriage with non-Indians and subsequent migration from the area.

In 1972 little remained of aboriginal Tubatulabal culture. Only six people still spoke the language, all of whom were over 50 years old. The Tubatulabal lived and worked much as their non-Indian neighbors did. Aboriginal cultural practices were almost nonexistent: several people still traveled into the foothills to gather piñons, but only for use as a delicacy; salt grass was gathered by some, but mixed with water and sugar, cooked into a stiff dough, sun-dried, and used by children as all-day suckers; the burning of the dead's clothes was still done; the one surviving shaman was still sought out to cure all but the most serious illnesses; and a witch still lived and practiced witchcraft.

Culture

Sociopolitical Organization

The Tubatulabal were loosely organized into three politically discrete bands each with its own "chief": the Pahkanapïl (living along the South Fork Kern riverbanks), the Palagewan (residing in the Kern River valley), and the Bankalachi (situated a few miles west of the Palagewan in Yokuts territory—see fig. 1). Although each band lived apart from the others during the winter, strong feelings of relationship obtained among them, and visits and intermarriages were frequent. Each band had a high degree of internal unity, but interband political solidarity was lacking. Only in times of warfare might the bands join together and then only for the duration of hostilities.

Each band was composed of a number of mobile family groups who roamed widely during the greater part of the year and settled down during the winter in semipermanent hamlets near the rivers. These hamlets, often inhabited for several years by the same families, consisted of two to six households; each household comprised a single, biological, bilateral family, neither markedly paternal nor maternal (Voegelin 1938:43). The family also included any widowed parents, and depending upon the marriage form, sons-in-law or, less frequently, daughters-in-law. A more precise definition of family structure cannot be made because of the lack of evidence.

Marriages, essentially economic transactions between the two families, were of two types: gift exchange and groom service. In the former, a man and woman agreed to marry. The groom's parents paid the bride's parents $30 to $40 (on the basis of the 1850 value of gold at $12 an ounce) in clamshell money. They then presented his parents with baskets, acorns, and various gifts. Marriage ritual and postmarital residence rules were absent, but the newlyweds usually established residence near the groom's father's house.

In a groom-service marriage a man obtained permission to marry from the woman's parents and lived with them and assisted in all activities until the birth of the first child. Then the couple was free to live anywhere they chose. Occasionally child betrothal occurred, including gift exchange at the time of betrothal or when the intended couple reached marriageable age (20 for males, 18 for females).

Marriages between lineal and/or collateral kin within two ascending or descending generations were considered grave moral offenses. Since the households comprising a single hamlet were usually interrelated by blood, either matrilineally or patrilineally, this rule made the hamlets exogamous units. There were no formal rules of exogamy or exogamous units above the hamlet level.

• OWNERSHIP OF GOODS   Like most societies, the Tubatulabal were territorially based, claimed property rights in land as communities, and recognized certain natural geographical boundaries as marking off local group territories (Hoebel 1966:415). However, unlike many California Indian groups, the bands did not claim exclusive possessory communal rights over the land they identified as their home range. Although each band identified with a geographical area, the members freely searched other bands' domains for food. Permission from the appropriate band chief was usually sought although it was not required.

Weapons and implements for individual use were owned by their creator and permission was required for their use by others. Houses were owned by the household head, usually a man, and upon his death the house was either burned or vacated. When both a man and his wife died the house might continue to shelter the oldest son and his family. If left vacant, anyone could occupy it; the original owners surrendered all rights to the house when they vacated.

Since most personal possessions were destroyed after death, there was little inheritance: occasionally some of a man's property (bows, arrows) would not be destroyed

439

but pass to his brothers or sons; a woman's awls, knives, and some baskets went to her sisters or daughters. However, a husband never inherited his dead wife's belongings nor she his.

• CHIEFTAINSHIP Each band's chief (*timiwal*) possessed limited authority. His main duties were as counselor, arbitrator, and band representative. He received messengers from other groups, arranged for wartime allies, assembled war parties and their leaders, negotiated peace settlements, arbitrated intraband disputes, admonished or ordered the death of shamans suspected or proved to be witches, and acted as the model Tubatulabal for the others.

A *timiwal* was usually appointed. Upon his death the eldest males from the different hamlets assembled to select a new one. An attempt was made to name a man who was honest, of sound judgment, even tempered, over 40 years old, wealthy, and skilled in arbitration. Although any man with these attributes was eligible, a dying chief usually named a son or brother as successor, subject to the old men's approval.

If the people felt the incumbent *timiwal* was unsatisfactory the individual most instrumental in mobilizing replacement was the *hiliʔidac* 'clown; dance manager'. During ceremonies or at other times the *hiliʔidac* passed among the people, criticized the *timiwal*, and called for action to replace him. Inherited from father to son, the position of *hiliʔidac* involved serving as a clown at ceremonies where he danced backward and spoke unintelligibly to alleviate the solemnity of the ceremonials.

Life Cycle

• BIRTH During pregnancy a woman was expected to work hard to ensure her, and her baby's, health and well-being and to ensure a swift and easy delivery. During the last month of pregnancy she refrained from eating meat or salt; otherwise her husband would be unable to find game while out hunting.

An older female relative and the expectant father attended the birth. A shallow trench was dug (either inside or outside the house, depending upon weather conditions), a fire built in it, stone slabs laid over the fire, followed by a layer of earth and a final covering of tule mats. At delivery the pregnant woman knelt on the mats and the attendant pressed on the woman's stomach, pushing the baby out and onto the mats. If a breech presentation was suspected, the pregnant woman was suspended upside down, the fetus righted itself, and the woman reassumed the kneeling position for a normal delivery.

Following birth mother and child remained in the trench six days. For one month following delivery the mother ate no meat, salt, or grease: otherwise her blood would thicken and she would die. Her husband observed this same taboo until the child's navel healed, and he refrained from sleeping with his wife for two to four months following the birth.

A barren woman who desired children could take various herbal medicines to correct the problem. A pregnant woman who did not desire a child could either abort by drinking an infusion of mistletoe or commit infanticide. Occasionally practiced, infanticide was considered a grave moral offense, but the transgressor was not punished.

• PUBERTY Both boys' and girls' adolescence rites were lacking. At a girl's first menses she refrained from eating meat, salt, and grease for one month; thereafter she observed this taboo only for the length of her menstrual period. Shortly after attaining puberty both sexes were encouraged to drink a decoction of datura to obtain a long and healthy life.

• DEATH When a person died the body was kept in the house overnight. The next day two old women corpse-handlers (*ʔuhuyahm*) wrapped the body in tule mats, removed it from the house, and buried it in a shallow grave away from the hamlet. Certain of the deceased's survivors were under a meat taboo (the ingestion of which was considered equivalent to eating the corpse) until the *huyudil* 'face-washing' ceremony. At the *huyudil* the closest surviving relative's face was washed in plain cold water by a nonrelative from another hamlet to remove the taboo.

At the *huyudil*, which took place within one year following the death, the mourner announced when the mourning ceremony (*muyil*) would be held. At the *muyil*, held within two years following the burial, a tule image of the deceased plus most of the deceased's possessions were destroyed. Attending relatives and friends were provided with food and entertainment during the six-day ceremony performed by male dancers (*mulwin*) and singers (*ayanalipil*).

War

Although not a markedly aggressive people, the Tubatulabal bands engaged in hostilities against neighboring groups (Kawaiisu to the south, Koso to the east, and Yokuts to the west). The motive was always revenge for their neighbors' previous attacks. Wars lasted one to two days, and casualties were light. Attacks came at dawn and attempts were made to kill men, women, and children as they slept. When all arrows were spent or night fell the battle ended and the attackers returned home. Prisoners and scalps were taken and torture was not practiced. When possible a dead enemy's weapons were taken home for display and use.

The settling of hostilities was a chief's duty. He met with the enemy leader, discussed the incidents that precipitated the war, and then promised, and expected a reciprocal promise not to fight again.

Trade

Trade was both short- and long-range. Men and women

440

traveled in couples or in small groups as far west as the California coast or as close as the next hamlet. Such journeys are known to have been made in the 1850s, but whether they were made in pre-White times is not known. On long trips, through a system of silent trade, "they exchanged the piñons, balls of prepared tobacco, and other commodities they had brought with them, for lengths of white clamshell disks" (Voegelin 1938:3), which served as money among many southern California Indian groups. Tubatulabals strung the clamshells on native twine and stored them in basket money-jars. During the winter, when certain commodities (dried meat and fish) were low, people borrowed strings of clamshell money to purchase needed supplies. No interest was charged, the borrower returning the amount borrowed as soon as possible.

Music, Games, Dances

Tubatulabals made a few simple musical instruments: three varieties of rattles; a quill whistle; a flute made from an elderberry stalk, used by men for personal amusement; a musical bow; and bull-roarers, used by boys as toys.

Several games were played and most involved betting on the outcome: the women's dice game (wi·ša·išt), played with pine pitch–filled half-walnut shells set with white shell fragments; the men's shinny game (pa·wa·šil) where opposing teams attempted to drive a wooden ball, by means of sticks, through each other's goalposts; and the men's hoop-and-pole game (howi·l), in which opposing sides attempted to shoot arrows through a hoop sent rolling by the opponents. A nonbetting game was the making of string figures during winter evenings. The figures were representations of objects or animals and short stories were told while making the figures.

Professional male dancers and singers performed at mourning and face-washing ceremonies and the singers also performed at dances. At other times, both men and women danced, usually a round dance. They moved in concentric circles around a fire with the women on the inside; or a line of women moved sideways right to left while the men danced around the fire.

Religion

The Tubatulabal lacked any concept of a supreme deity. However, the concept of a dying benefactor was part of their belief system and related to the use of jimsonweed. According to Tubatulabal legend, jimsonweed was once a man who turned himself into the plant, instructing the people to dig and use his roots, to cure sickness or poverty or to aid in obtaining supernatural help. No form of worship was attached to the plant or its use. Rather, the plant's medicinal properties and its use in obtaining supernatural power and longevity were emphasized.

The Tubatulabal world was inhabited by various supernatural spirits, in both human and animal form. These spirits, together with certain animals (coyote, bear, deer, rattlesnake, owl, hawk) and shamans' helpers (usually dead relatives' ghosts) were referred to as yu·mu·gi·wal. Though not necessarily malevolent, all were treated with respect, tinged with fear.

Among the Tubatulabal, Coyote was both a culture hero and a trickster. As culture hero he remade the earth after the flood, obtained water and fire for the people, regulated the division of labor, and caused death to enter the world. As trickster, he played the role of liar, cheat, and dupe (C.F. Voegelin 1935a:199, 207, 209, 211).

Dreams were interpreted as actions performed by the soul (šu·nun), which resided in the head. During dreams the soul left the body and as such was vulnerable to attacks by malevolent shamans. Precautions were taken to ensure dreamless slumber by the ingestion of tobacco. Upon death, the soul left the body and assumed human form. In this state it was called ?a·bawinal 'ghost', 'devil' and traveled during the day in dust spouts. Although usually harmless, ?a·bawinal were occasionally evil shamans' helpers sent to cause harm or death.

• MYTHOLOGY Tubatulabal myths are predominantly Great Basin in character (Gayton 1935:588, 595), animal motifs being all-important. Many relate to the first peoples' adventures and their subsequent transformation into animals at the end of the mythological age (C.F. Voegelin 1935a). Myths were recounted at ceremonies or at a skilled narrator's home, but only in winter, as rattlesnakes would bite both hearers and tellers if told at other times.

• SHAMANISM Among the Tubatulabal both men and women could be shamans (?a?a·ʐowa·l, plural; ?a·ʐowa·l, singular) but only if born with shamanic abilities. No amount of practice made one a shaman, and not all those born with the ability desired the responsibility. Male shamans had curative and witching power, women only witching power. A shaman was assisted by supernatural guardian-helpers (large birds and deer for curing shamans; coyotes, a dead relative's ghost, rattlesnakes for witches) who either helped curing shamans in the diagnosis and treatment of illness or aided witches in carrying out their evil machinations. All misfortune and all deaths except those resulting from wars were attributed to witchcraft, and witches were the most feared members of the community.

Curing shamans began their careers by acquiring a supernatural helper through fasting and the ingestion of jimsonweed. This helper taught the shaman curing songs and rituals. As the shaman gained wisdom he began to cure illnesses as well as diagnose them. Cures were effected through dancing, singing, blowing tobacco smoke over the patient, sucking at the affected area to extract the cause of the illness, and administering herbal remedies. Cures, performed publicly inside the patient's home, lasted all night. The shaman privately conferred with his supernatural helper regarding diagnosis and treatment. Curing shamans held high status and their prestige grew with the number of cures performed. However, if a shaman failed continuously he might be exposed to accusations of witchcraft and to possible execution. The ʔaʔaˑ˳zowaˑl frequently engaged in contests of power against one another either at ceremonies or at special shamanic gatherings held for the purpose of displaying their power. At these gatherings the contestants would "shoot" invisible objects at one another.

Structures

Aboriginal Tubatulabal material culture was simple but efficient. Shelter types varied according to season and activity. During the winter, circular, domed, brush- and mud-covered, one-family houses (*mohošt*) were used. Furnishings were few: tule mats as ground cover, piles of tule mats for beds, bearskins and deerskins for blankets.

During warmer months shade shelters (*komaˑl*) under which the family worked, ate, and slept were built. These unwalled structures had a brush roof supported by four vertical poles and two horizontal beams. A larger *komaˑl*, with the addition of two brush walls, was built for several families' use during ceremonies.

At the piñon grounds a large, circular, corrallike brush enclosure (*hoˑyat*), 30 to 50 feet in diameter, with three- to four-feet-high brush walls, was built. Here several families slept, ate, and stored supplies. A *hoˑyat* was also built at hamlets for dances to provide a camping area for guests and performers.

Associated with most hamlets was a large, ovoid sweathouse (*muˑšaht*). The framework was of oak branches; the sides and roof were built up with logs, poles, and brush, then covered with dirt. Located near a natural pool or dammed stream, the *muˑšaht* served as a sudatory for men, women, and children. Sweatbathing was done in the evening, men and women bathing separately. After bathing, the bathers plunged into the nearby pool.

Clothing and Adornment

During hot weather men went naked and women wore aprons, front and back, of tanned deerskin. During colder periods tanned buckskin vests, aprons, and sleeveless coats were worn by all. While hunting and gathering during the dry season, men and women wore buckskin moccasins with pitch-smeared soles. Buckskin sandals with double-layer soles were worn while roasting piñons to protect the feet from the fire.

Only women, clowns, and shamans wore ornaments or decorated their bodies. Women attending dances painted their faces red or white and wore shell-cylinder noseplugs, white clamshell or olivella-shell necklaces and earrings. Women also tattooed themselves, using a cactus spine to prick the design and charcoal for the dye. Shamans and clowns painted their faces in red and white

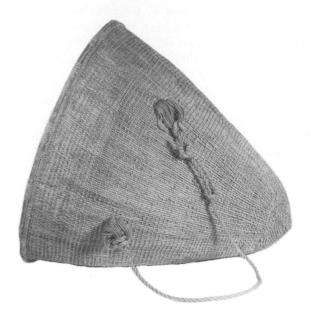

Lowie Mus., U. of Calif., Berkeley: 1-19815.
Fig. 4. Twined pack basket. Collected 1916; length, about 60 cm.

Lowie Mus., U. of Calif., Berkeley: 1-19823.
Fig. 5. Coiled flat sifting basket. Collected 1916, diameter 39.5 cm.

stripes, shamans when engaged in power contests, clowns when performing during cermonies.

Technology

Women made baskets (fig. 4) and pottery. In fashioning coiled and twined baskets they used split willow or tree yucca roots for the starter and deer grass (*Muhlenbergia*

442

SMITH

Lowie Mus., U. of Calif., Berkeley: 1-20944.

Fig. 6. Coiled basketry bowl with smoother, more finished work face on the interior. The four colors—black, red, buff, and white—are characteristic of the tribe's finer coiled work. Collected before 1900. Height 26 cm.

rigens) as foundation material. Only coiled ware (figs. 5, 6) carried designs—usually snakes, or human or geometric figures. Tree yucca roots were used for red designs, pods of devil's claw (*Proboscidea*) for black ones. Basket traps and, after the introduction of the horse, saddles and saddle blankets, were woven with tules. At the piñon grounds women wove basket jars using piñon nuts strung on native twine.

Pots were made from a red clay available in the South Fork Kern valley. No temper was added to the clay and all work was done by hand. Pots were built up by stacking clay rolls on top of one another and pinching them together; they were then sun-dried and fired in an open fire until they turned a gray-black.

Bows were of two types: a sinew-backed bow (strung with sinew) and a self-backed bow (strung with native twine). Arrows (fig. 7) were compound and of two types: the war arrow, about 34 to 36 inches long, with a wooden foreshaft tipped with shouldered stone points, set into a cane mainshaft with feather fletching; and

Lowie Mus., U. of Calif., Berkeley: 1-19803.

Fig. 7. Arrow straightener with two grooves, collected in 1916. Length 11.3 cm.

hunting arrows, similar to war arrows, but longer (48 inches) and either untipped or tipped with loosely fitting obsidian points. Arrows were carried in a sacklike quiver of untanned antelope, coyote, or wildcat skin.

A variety of nets, traps, snares, and throwing sticks was made for taking small game. For fishing a variety of tools included basket traps, nets, bone and wood pronged harpoons, fishhooks, and stone-and-wood corrals.

For dismembering and skinning game a large, unhafted stone knife was used. A smaller, hafted knife was used for all other cutting jobs while a scraper made from a deer's entire lower leg bone was used to dehair skins prior to tanning. Large splinters from a deer's leg bone butted with asphalt lumps were made into awls for flaking stone implements. For sewing and basketmaking a smaller awl, made from a barrel cactus spine, was used.

In gathering and preparing plant foods prior to cooking, women used digging sticks, wooden and stone mortars and pestles for pounding, and slabs and rub stones for grinding. The pounding was done at both the piñon and acorn-gathering areas, while the grinding was restricted to hamlet sites.

Subsistence

The Tubatulabal subsistence economy was based entirely on hunting, fishing, and gathering. Due to geographical placement, Tubatulabal plant food resources were more abundant and varied than in many other areas of California; within their territorial limits Tubatulabals exploited two staple crops, acorns in the Greenhorn Mountains and piñon nuts on the Sierra Nevada's eastern slopes. Since piñons normally mature biennially, the presence of acorns (six varieties) greatly supplemented the Tubatulabals' food resources. The successive maturation cycles of the two nuts (piñons in the early fall and acorns in the late fall) enabled the Tubatulabal to utilize both crops.

Acorns were gathered from the ground, sun-dried, and stored in elevated granaries near hamlets. Piñon cones were knocked from the trees, gathered, and piled on a brush fire to force them open. The nuts were pried out, sun-dried, and cached in circular stone-lined pits about five feet in diameter and two and one-half feet deep, located near the piñon-gathering areas.

In addition to acorns and piñons a variety of small seeds, shoots, leaves, bulbs, tubers, and berries was collected. Small seeds (chia, wild oats, *Mentzelia*) and berries (juniper, manzanita, gooseberries, boxthorn berries) were gathered by women using seed beaters and catch baskets. Roots of tule and cattail and bulbs (*Calochortus* sp.) available for March through May were collected by women using digging sticks.

Plant food was cooked by boiling, parching, roasting, or baking in pit ovens. Parched seeds and roasted piñons, after being ground into meal, were mixed with water to form a thick gruel, which was eaten warm or cold. Shelled acorns were pounded into flour (fig. 8), leached in warm water, mixed with water, boiled into mush, and eaten with meat. Berries were eaten fresh, boiled, or pounded into a thick mass, mixed with water, shaped into cakes, sun-dried, and stored. After reconstitution in water they became a beverage.

Roots, tubers, and bulbs were peeled and then either eaten raw or else sun-dried, pounded, mixed with water, and boiled into mush. During the summer honey dew sugar was collected from the stalks of cane (*Phragmites communis* var. *berlandieri*) where aphids deposited it. The stalks were cut and flayed, the crystals collected, winnowed, cooked into a stiff dough, sun-dried, and eaten with acorn and piñon gruel. Saline crystals, found on *Distichlis spicata*, were obtained in a similar manner, mixed with water, and drunk as a refreshment or laxative, but never used as a seasoning. Rock salt, obtained by the men from dry salt lakes on the northern edge of the Mojave Desert, was used for seasoning and for preserving meat.

Large game (deer, bear, mountain lion, mountain sheep, antelope) was hunted with the sinew-backed bow. Hunting techniques included stalking, use of blinds, and chasing game toward concealed hunters. Annually, the Tubatulabal joined with neighboring tribes (Yokuts, Kawaiisu) in communal antelope drives in the San Joaquin valley. Smaller game, with the exception of rabbits, was not actively hunted. Rather, traps, snares, or spring-loaded nets were set out for squirrels and mice and checked daily. Rabbit hunting, a communal affair, was carried out by two techniques: firing the brush cover in various sections of the valley floor and shooting the animals as they attempted to escape, or stringing nets across canyon mouths and driving the rabbits into nets and shooting them. Birds (quail, pigeon, teal, coot) were taken with the bow, hunters concealing themselves in blinds built near nesting areas or water holes.

Fish were second only to acorns and piñons in economic importance. Most fishing was done by individual men except in July when several hamlets engaged in communal fishing. Stones were placed in the rivers arranged in a keyhole shape with the narrow end left open. The sides were built up with willow branches and stones to a level above the water's surface. Men were stationed along the outside of this "corral" while men downstream waded toward the open end driving the fish into the "corral." Inside, two men caught the fish and tossed them onto the banks, where women clubbed them to death.

Large game was skinned while still warm, and the meat was brought back to camp to be broiled, roasted, or stewed for immediate consumption or salted and sun-dried for storage. Small game was either skinned or de-

Lowie Mus., U. of Calif., Berkeley: 1-19800.

Fig. 8. Brush of soaproot fiber used either for flour or hair, collected in 1916. Length 15 cm.

haired by singeing and then cooked in the same manner as large game. Birds were plucked and gutted, then cooked by broiling or roasting. Fish were cleaned and roasted whole to be eaten or salted and sun-dried to be stored. Freshwater mussels were roasted in their shells.

• DIVISION OF LABOR   The more strenuous but intermittent tasks, the hunting and most fishing, were men's jobs. Women attended to less strenuous but more time-consuming tasks. This labor division was established during the mythological age when the women lost an arrow-shooting contest to the men through Coyote's trickery. However, not all tasks were sex specific. Men and women worked together during piñon collecting and corral fishing and an older man and his wife might prune tobacco plants together.

• TOBACCO   Two species of tobacco (*šoʔogont*) grow wild in Tubatulabal territory: *Nicotiana bigelovii* and *N. attenuata*. In early summer women stripped off the side shoots to encourage larger leaf growth. The plants were pruned twice more, then the leaves were stripped from the plants, sun-dried, sprinkled with a water–pine nut mixture, wrapped in willow shoots, and sun-dried. After 10 days the leaves were pounded into a fine powder, mixed with water, and formed into balls. Tobacco was mixed with lime and chewed, smoked, snuffed, eaten, or diluted with water and drunk as an emetic before retiring to ensure a dreamless slumber (Voegelin 1938:36–38). Both men and women used tobacco, but only very old women smoked it.

Synonymy

The earliest generic appellation for the Tubatulabal was Kern River Indians (Henly 1857). The Palagewan (C.F. Voegelin 1935, 1935a, 1958) band was called Polokawynahs (Bancroft 1874–1876), Pal-li-ga-wo-nap' (Powers

1877), and Pallegawonap (Gatschet 1879:411).

The Pahkanapïls were variously termed Ku-chi-bich-i-wa nap' (Powers 1877), Ti-pa-to-la-pa (Powers 1877), Pa-kań-e-pul (Merriam 1904), and Bahkanapul (Kroeber 1907b).

As a unit, Palagewan and Pahkanapïl were recorded as Te-bot-e-loƀ-e-lay by Merriam (1904) before being called Tubatulabal by Kroeber (1907b, 1925).

The Bankalachi (C.F. Voegelin 1935, 1935a, 1958) had been referred to as Toloim by the other Tubatulabal bands and were so called by Kroeber (1925).

Sources

The primary anthropological sources for the Tubatulabal are Voegelin's ethnography (1938), C.F. Voegelin's grammar (1935) and texts (1935a), Kroeber (1925: 605-610), and C.R. Smith's (1968-1972) field notes. The first four works are available in most university libraries and Voegelin's volume gives a detailed and explicit description of all known facets of Tubatulabal culture prior to 1850.

Between 1938 and 1968 no ethnographic fieldwork was carried out among the Tubatulabal. Only a limited amount of archeological research has been conducted in the Kern River area. The most extensive was done in 1947 by a field crew from the West Coast Projects, River Basin Surveys, Smithsonian Institution (Fenenga 1947), who made a surface survey of 17 square miles east and north of the Kern and South Fork rivers' confluence. Since 1947 only sporadic archeological activity has occurred: several surface collects (Griffin 1963); an excavation of a rockshelter by a field party from the University of California at Los Angeles; a salvage project by Fresno State College; and a surface survey by UCLA (Wallace 1970).

Yokuts: Introduction

MICHAEL SILVERSTEIN

The named groups discussed in the next three chapters, numbering approximately 40, were classified together under the term Yokuts (ˈyōˌkuts) by Powers (1877:369) and others. However, Hodge (1907–1910, 1:807–808) used Powell's (1891:90–91) term Mariposan Family for the linguistic grouping of these dialects and, by the then current fashion, of these people. This usage, based on the incorrect precedent (Latham 1856:84) of locating Yokuts in the region of Mariposa County, has since been abandoned (see Kroeber 1925:488). The Yokuts language is demonstrably a member of the California Penutian family of languages (Dixon and Kroeber 1919; Pitkin and Shipley 1958; Silverstein 1972), which includes four other diverse families of central and coastal California: Miwok, Costanoan, Maiduan, and Wintuan. Of these, Miwok and Costanoan are sometimes grouped together into a Miwok-Costanoan or Utian family ("Native Languages of California," this vol.).

Yokuts dialects, of which only a handful were spoken in 1974, were remarkably homogeneous, given the great geographical spread of their extension. Following Kroeber (1907:309–315, 1963:236–238), who based his classification on a 22-dialect lexical survey, the main division is into a Valley division of dialects, and a Foothills division, based on the geographical location of most of the speakers. This linguistic cleavage is distinct from, and should not be confused with, the cultural-geographical divisions Northern, Southern Valley, and Foothills, represented in the following chapters. Certain northern Valley-type dialects (Chukchansi, Kechayi, Dumna) were spoken by people who were culturally Foothills tribes, and certain southern Foothills-type dialects (Tulamni, Hometwoli, Chuxoxi) by people in the valley south of Tulare Lake. In general, within smaller linguistic groupings, the geographically closest tribes spoke linguistically closest dialects. For example, judging from manuscripts of Father Arroyo de la Cuesta (Beeler 1971:74–75) and the evidence of Kroeber (1959a), Northern Yokuts groups, as represented by Nopchinchi, are linguistically closest to the Chawchila, substantially documented by Newman (1944). With the exception of Yawelmani, spoken by latecomers into the southern Yokuts area, and the isolated Palewyami, all the better-known dialects at the southern and southeastern edge of the family have acquired central slightly rounded vowels *i̵, ë, ë·;* and these with Palewyami have acquired the velar nasal ŋ, all of

these sounds being clearly Uto-Aztecan (or Great Basin) in origin (Dixon and Kroeber 1919:82–83; Kroeber 1963:229; Silverstein 1970). Yawdanchi and Wikchamni have usually shifted inherited Yokuts *l to t, but they keep distinct the two affricate series c, cʰ, c̓ and č, čʰ, č̓. Yawelmani shifts the č-series to ç, çʰ, ç̓, and all other major dialects merged both series to č, čʰ, č̓, Chukchansi having further merged these partially with s. Such correspondences make dialect and tribal names vary from dialect to dialect; for example, yaẃlančʰiʔ in Yawelmani is equivalent to yaẃtančʰiʔ in Yawdanchi and Wikchamni.

The general Yokuts sound system, with these qualifications, includes the consonants p, pʰ, p̓, t, tʰ, t̓, t̪, t̪ʰ, t̪̓, k, kʰ, k̓, one or two sets of affricates as above, s or š, ṣ, x, m, m̓, n, n̓, w, w̓, y, y̓, l, l̓, h, ʔ, and the vowels i, i·, e, e·, a, a·, o, o·, u, u·. Newman (1944:13–20) describes this system in more detail, and all further research and reinterpretation of older sources is based on his analysis. Newman uses b, d, ḍ, ȝ, ʒ, ǯ, g for the Handbook p, t, ṭ, c, ç, č, k, and these latter symbols for the aspirates here written pʰ, tʰ, t̪ʰ, cʰ, çʰ, čʰ, kʰ. The transliteration is easily accomplished.*

The word Yokuts is an English rendering of the general term for '(Indian) person' or 'people' in the westerly, or Valley dialects. The stem appears in Yawelmani, the best recorded dialect, as yokʰoč̓, and in other Valley dialects (like Tachi), with regular sound correspondences, as yokʰoč̓. The plural form yo·kʰič̓a or yo·kʰič̓a means 'relatives' (Newman 1944:84, 148, 213; Kroeber 1963: 187). In many Foothills dialects, such as Wikchamni, yokʰoč̓ means 'thigh' and person is may. Many other Foothills dialects use the word tʰaʔatʰ(i) for 'person'. However, all three of these designations contrast with native terms for non-Indians, variously borrowed from the words Mexican(o) and American(o) (Kroeber 1963:187, 212). They contrast also with the term for smaller-sized units '(people of a) village', tʰipʰis or tʰipʰiš (Newman 1944:216; Kroeber 1907:244). The earlier Spanish sources, cited in the chapters that follow, refer to the Yokuts in general as Noche or some variant of this and, especially in the later period of Franciscan missionary activity, as Tulareños. Noche, again probably from

---

* Italicized Yokuts words have been respelled in this orthography by Silverstein and (for the Foothill and Northern Yokuts chapters) by Geoffrey Gamble.

the Valley dialects, is a native term for 'friends', a distinctively plural form attested as *noč^he·-*, from the singular *no·č^ho·-*. Tulareños, used for San Joaquin Valley Indians especially, comes into regional Spanish from Aztec and means 'people of the cane brakes' (Beeler 1971:19).

The names of individual Yokuts groups, tribes, or tribelets that appear in the following chapters come from the early Spanish sources as well as from various impressionistic recordings of English speakers. In most cases, the sounds of Yokuts have been approximated by the orthography. In the Spanish sources, the alveolar series of sounds, *t, t^h, ṭ*, is only sometimes distinguished either from the affricates, *ç, ç^h, ç̣* or *č, č^h, č̣*, or from the dental stops, *t, t^h, ṭ*. When they are, they appear spelled as "thr" or "ths" (for example, by Garcés, Muñoz, Arroyo de la Cuesta; cf. Beeler 1971:51–61). Thus the *nop^ht^hinṭ^hi* appear as Nupchenche, Noptinte, and, most accurately, as Nopthrinthres. Similarly, the common Yokuts sounds *x* and *h* have various confusing hispanicized spellings such as j, g, h, according to the sounds that precede and follow. Hence the Northern Yokuts village sites spelled Jusmite(s) and Tugite(s) in the sources can be identified with the known stems *xosim-* 'north' and *t^hoxil-* 'plains, south', which are common stems in place or tribe names. The Spanish sources virtually never indicate vowel length or glottalization. With the exception of Newman and his successors, all tribal and place-name transcriptions are deficient in one or more of these respects and must be subjected to interpretation in light of knowledge of the sound system and structure of words.

The majority of place-names that can be interpreted in this manner have reference to a geographical formation, such as Wowol (*wit^hi-)čoló·win* 'island, open plain' (Kroeber 1963:197), or represent the locative case form, ending in -(*i*)*w*, -(*u*)*w* or -(*a*)*w*, -(*o*)*w* of some formation, plant, or name of an activity, such as Yawelmani *t^hinl-iw* 'where the animal hole is, at the animal hole' or *čiṅ ewh-iw* 'at the place of many shades' (*čiṅiw-* 'to be in the shade'). A few names seem to be derived from tribal names, like Chunut *č^huṅt^h-aw* 'where the Chunut are, among the Chunut' and a few from the general words for structures, like Tachi *č^hi?* 'house'. Probably few of these latter types are genuine native place-names.

Tribal names, which all must have had both singular and plural forms, are cited in these chapters in the form given by tradition, sometimes singular and sometimes plural. The plural formations expressed by vowel changes are highly complex, but rather regular (Newman 1944:204–214; Kroeber 1963:221, 224–228). The name Yawelmani is a plural, *yaẁelmani*, the singular of which is *yaẁlamni?*, while Wikchamni represents a singular, *wik^ht^hamni*, the plural of which is *wik^hat^hmina*. It is very difficult to give convincing etymologies to the roots of these names, though a few obvious ones, like Hometwoli—*xomet^h-wol-i* (pl.), *xoṁ t^h-iṅ in* (sg.) 'people (person) from the south' from *xomo·t^he·-* 'south' (Newman 1944:220)—encourage the search through meager vocabularies. Several suffixes are recognizable in these names, for instance, -(*?a*)*m*, -*me·n*/-*min* 'one who has something' and -*iṅin* 'person of a place', in their various forms with change of vowels. It is clear linguistically that many names are very ancient and were used in several dialects; whether they always were proper names referring to exactly the same people, or were geographically relative, is unknown.

447

Southern Valley Yokuts

WILLIAM J. WALLACE

Territory and Environment

Yokuts tribes inhabiting the southern or upper end of the San Joaquin valley, from the lower Kings River to the Tehachapi Mountains, formed the nucleus of a culture that differed in significant respects from that of the northern and foothill tribes. Many of the peculiarities can be attributed to ecological factors, for the Indians had worked out a mode of life that was closely integrated around the natural circumstances of their unique lake-slough-marsh environment (Gayton 1946; Beals and Hester 1958). External stimuli, particularly from the south, and local innovations account for other localized typical traits.

The Southern Yokuts homeland comprised Tulare, Buena Vista, and Kern lakes, their connecting sloughs, and the lower portions of the Kings, Kaweah, Tule, and Kern rivers (fig. 1). Adjacent to all these waters lay an extensive swamp or tulare, which shrank and expanded seasonally. Besides providing an inexhaustible supply of animal and plant foods, the contiguous rivers, sloughs, and lakes served as a waterway for travel.

Were it not for the rivers that entered the southern San Joaquin valley from the Sierras to the east, this land would be little more than a desert, or at best semidesert, for it receives only 5 to 10 inches of rain annually.

On passing over the valley floor, the rivers fan out into a labyrinth of channels that feed into three shallow lake basins, located on the lowest part of the broad flatland. Twice each year they discharge their waters into the

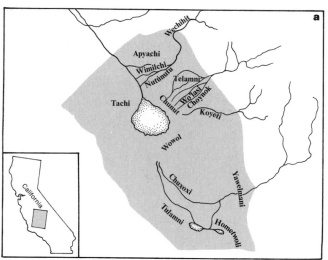

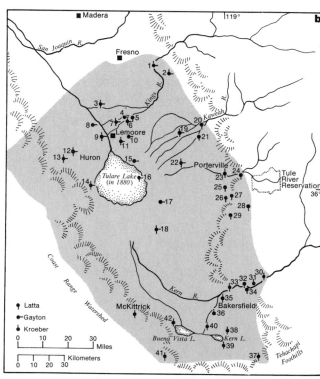

Fig. 1. Tribes (a) and villages with tribal affiliation (b). Wechihit: 1, Musahau; 2, Wewayo. Apyachi: 3, Wohui. Nutúnutu: 4, Honotan, *xo·nowtʰan* 'always going'; 5, Kadistin; 6, Chiau, *ċiy(a)w* 'where the bones are' (K); Chiyi, *ċiy* 'bones' (G); Chiou (L). Wimilchi: 7, Ugona, *ʔuko·na(ʔ)* 'drinking place'. Tachi: 8, Telweyit, *tʰelwe·yitʰ* 'summit lake'; 9, Chi, *cʰiʔ* 'house' (K, G); Heinlen Chi (L); 10, Gaiwashiu; 11, Waiu, *wayiw* 'at the (Tulare) lake'; 12, Golon; 13, Udjiu (also Poso Chana, L); 14, Walna; 15, Yimel, *yimel* 'catch fish by hand'. Wowol: 16, Wititsolowin (G); Chawlowin (L); 17, Yiwomni; 18, Sukwutnu (also Dulau, K). Telamni: 19, Waitatshulul (K); Waitachuiyui (G). Wo'lasi: 20, Dawaw Nawshid; 21, Chuntow. Choynok: 22, Chiuta (K, G); Cheuta (L). Koyeti: 23, Chokowisho (K), Chokowesho (L); 24, Tenalu; 25, Chetetik Nowsuh; 26, Pahpahwits; 27, Ahsaw; 28, Kiahlu; 29, Hawscheu. Yawelmani: 30, Shoko, *ṣokʰɔw* 'windy'; 31, Konoilkin, *ʔonow ʔilk̃in* 'at the falls of the water'; 32, Hawsu; 33, Tsineuhiu (K); Tsinehiu (L); 34, Wawcoye; 35, Woilo (K); Woilu (L); 36, Kuyo; 37, Tinliu, *tʰinl(iw)* 'where the animal burrow is'. Hometwoli: 38, Loasau; 39, Pohalin Tinliu, *pʰo·halin tʰinl(i)w* 'at the ground squirrel hole' (also Sihetal Daal, K); 40, Halau. Tulamni: 41, Hoschiu; 42, Tulamniu, *tʰulamniw* 'where the Tulamni are'; 43, Wogitiu (K); Wogatiu (L). The following villages cannot be located. Chunut: Miketsiu; Chuntau, *cʰuṅtʰau* 'where the Chunut are'. Nutúnutu: Hibekia. Chuxoxi: Tahayu. Sources: Kroeber 1925 (K); Gayton 1948 (G); Latta 1949 (L).

lakes. First comes the rain-flood, in January to March, followed in early summer by runoff from melting Sierran snows. Besides scanty rainfall the southern valley suffers from extremely long and hot summers, with temperatures often rising above 100°F. Winters are fairly mild.

A marsh and aquatic flora of extraordinary exuberance once covered the entire wetlands. Typical were the luxuriant growths of tules, as much as 10 or 12 feet high, which dominated vast tracts of damp and waterlogged ground to the complete exclusion of other species. On drier stretches tules gave way to scattered sage, greasewood, and bunchgrass. Except for a fringe of cottonwoods, sycamores, and willows lining the river channels and sloughs, the region was treeless. Oaks did not extend far into the valley floor.

The lake and marshland sheltered an enormous variety and abundance of wildlife. Here thousands of aquatic birds resided the year around, to be joined in the winter by migratory ducks and geese in untold numbers. The waters teemed with fish and turtles and beds of freshwater mussels. Great herds of pronghorn antelope and tule elk browsed on the surrounding dry plains, and mule deer came down from the mountains in winter. The region harbored many smaller mammals and birds too, notably jackrabbits, ground squirrels, and quail. Insects, particularly mosquitoes, swarmed about the lakes and marshes.

Prehistory

Signs of human presence in the lake country go back in time at least 8,000 years. A deeply buried stratum on the western shore of Buena Vista Lake, radiocarbon-dated at 6000 B.C., contained a meager range of stone artifacts best suited for killing and butchering big game (Fredrickson and Grossman 1966; Grossman 1968). The southern shore of Tulare Lake has yielded a number of early-type projectile points, some of the fluted variety (Riddell and Olsen 1969). Evidently bands of hunters frequented the area at an early date, preying on the herds of large game animals. To a subsequent period belong remains uncovered at some depth in sites on Buena Vista Lake. Typical artifacts comprise seed-grinding implements, suggesting a shift from a hunting to a food-collecting economy. (Fredrickson 1965:1-2). The third archeological period includes the cultures of the Yokuts Indians and their immediate antecedents (Gifford and Schenck 1926: 113-118; Wedel 1941:153-154). By this time the native inhabitants had worked out a diversified subsistence pattern through wider exploitation of the natural foods, plant and animal, of their lakes and marshes. They also had developed a culture of greater material wealth and lived in bigger settlements. The duration of this period, originally estimated at only three centuries, A.D. 1400-1700 (Wedel 1941:143), may have been nearly 2,000 years (Fredrickson 1965:3; Fredrickson and Grossman 1966:2).

At the beginning of the historic period at least 15 Yokuts groups inhabited this watery area, each speaking a separate dialect of the Yokuts language (Kroeber 1925:478-483; Latta 1949:21-33; Swanton 1952: 523-526). Tulare Lake and its shores were divided among three tribes. In order from north to south, these were the Tachi, Chunut, and Wowol. North of Tulare Lake, on the south side of the lower Kings River, in a country formerly a mass of sloughs and swamps, lived the Nutúnutu. Separated from them by the river channel were the Wimilchi, who occupied the northern bank. Farther upstream, also on the north side, came the Wechihit. The Apyachi, a little-known group somehow associated with the Tachi, lived north of the Kings River at its outlet slough. The Choynok represented the southernmost of three tribes on the flaring delta of the Kaweah; north of them were the Wo'lasi and the Telamni. The Koyeti inhabited a land of swampy sloughs on the lower Tule River. The Tulamni held possession of Buena Vista Lake with the Chuxoxi north of them occupying the channels and tule-lined sloughs of the Kern River delta. On smaller Kern Lake were the Hometwoli. To the west, the Yawelmani held an extensive strip of territory.

It has been estimated that Yokuts political units averaged 350 persons each (Kroeber 1962:38), giving a total aboriginal population of 5,250 for the 15 southern San Joaquin Valley tribes. A much higher figure, 15,700 (table 1), has been calculated, based on estimates or head counts for various villages made by Spanish exploring expeditions in the early nineteenth century (Cook 1955). These are not necessarily accurate because there is no way of knowing how many persons had flocked to see the strangers or, in some instances, fled because they feared the soldiers.

Subsistence

The Southern Valley Yokuts followed a mixed economy that emphasized fishing, hunting waterfowl, and collect-

Table 1. Population Estimates

Area	Aboriginal	1850
Tulare Lake	6,500	1,100
Tachi, Chunut, Wowol		
Lower Kings River	2,000	900
Apyachi, Wimilchi, Nutúnutu, Wechihit		
Lower Kaweah River	3,800	800
Telamni, Wo'lasi, Choynok		
Lower Tule River	800	320
Koyeti		
Lower Kern River	1,300	280
Yawelmani		
Buena Vista Lake	1,300	280
Tulamni, Chuxoxi, Hometwoli		
Total	15,700	3,680

SOURCE: after Cook 1955.

ing shellfish, roots, and seeds. Fishing remained productive through most of the year. Of the varieties of fish regularly available, lake trout, which attained a good size, were most prized as food; chubs, perch, and suckers, taken in large numbers, were considered less palatable. Steelhead and salmon entered the rivers, sloughs, and at times, Tulare Lake, as did a great fish, evidently the sturgeon.

Fish were caught in many different ways. Nets, often of considerable length, with one end attached to a pole on land, were dragged by a tule raft that moved in an arc toward the shore. Diving for fish with hand nets was a common practice, and collective drives forced them into stick pens erected in the shallows. A wide and flat tule raft designed to pass over very shallow water and with a spearing hole at the center was employed on Tulare Lake by Tachi fishers. Fish were also speared through holes cut in the great natural mats of tules that accumulated along the lakeshores. Scaffolds for spearing, often covered with a booth, were built out from the banks of rivers and sloughs. Other methods of capture included the use of conical basketry traps, catching with the bare hands, and shooting with bow and arrow (a very casual activity). Fires kindled at night helped to attract fish. Angling, reported only for the Nutúnutu (Driver 1937:63), may have been unknown in aboriginal times. A crushed plant, turkey mullein (*Eremocarpus setigerus*), dropped into quiet water caused stupefied fish to rise to the surface where they were easily picked up. Freshly caught fish were usually broiled on hot coals. When a considerable catch had been made a portion of it was sun-dried.

Geese, ducks, mud hens, and other waterfowl were taken in snares set up among the tules and captured with long-handled nets as they flew overhead. Frequently they were hunted from fishing rafts by men who threw loose tules over themselves so they could approach within easy bowshot of their unsuspecting prey. Special devices and techniques—spring poles with triggers set underwater, arrows provided with tule rings for skipping over the surface, and stuffed decoys—had been developed for capturing aquatic birds. When flocks of geese were heard approaching on dark nights, piles of brush were fired. Upon seeing the flames, the geese swooped down and in their bewilderment were easily killed. Eggs were taken from the nests of ducks and geese.

Large quantities of mussels were gathered and steamed on beds of tules. Turtles also furnished much food. They were stabbed under the throat with a sharp stick, put on coals and roasted. Curiously, the Southern Yokuts showed a repugnance to the idea of eating frogs, a potentially rich source of nutriment. They did, however, enjoy dog flesh and may have reared these domestic animals for eating (Powers 1877:379). Relatively few insect foods were consumed.

Wild seeds and roots provided a large portion of the sustenance. A starchy flour for mush was prepared from dried and pounded tule roots. Tule seeds, knocked off into a basket with an open-twined seed beater, were also ground into meal. Seeds of grasses and flowering herbs were harvested and treated in much the same fashion. The small nutty roots of grassnuts were roasted whole or mashed into meal. Tender leaves and stems of certain plants were relished. In the spring, clover ranked high as a subsidiary food. Fiddle-neck and alfilaria in the young and tender stage were eaten with salt. Acorns, the standby of most California Indians, were not easily available. Each year the Tachi journeyed to the neighborhood of Kingston to obtain their supply or traded fish for acorns with tribes to the east.

Only a minor share of the native diet came from land mammals and birds. Lesser game was mostly taken in snares or traps, though both birds and smaller mammals were shot with simple, unbacked bows and wooden-tipped arrows. Wild pigeons, lured by live decoys to booths concealing hunters, were taken by means of a noose on a stick. During mass hunts held in the barren lands hundreds of jackrabbits were driven into long nets. As they herded the rabbits before them, the hunters hurled short sticks at the running animals to kill or cripple them. Ground squirrels and other burrowing rodents were smoked or drowned out of their holes or prodded out with pointed sticks. The Southern Valley Yokuts rarely ventured out into the open country to prey on the herds of antelope and elk. They did shoot them from blinds when the animals came to the lakes and sloughs to drink (Mayfield 1929:34–35) as well as setting nooses attached to spring poles along the runways in the tules where elk habitually sought water. When an elk's horns became entangled in one of the loops, the animal was stabbed to death with a spear or shot with arrows. Sinew-backed bows and stone-headed arrows, the same as those used in warfare, were employed in big game hunting.

The various foodstuffs were cooked in different ways. Ground tule root and other meals mixed with water were stone-boiled in baskets. The hot stones were placed in the basket with two green twigs and removed from it with a looped stick that also served for stirring. Meat and fish were broiled on coals or roasted in ashes. Both vegetable and animal foods were baked in small earth ovens. Since firewood for cooking was scarce it had to be eked out with dried tules. Salt derived from salt grass seasoned many dishes.

Culture

Structures

The rich food resources of their land permitted the southern tribes to occupy permanent residences for most of the year. These were of two types. Smallest and least elaborate were the single-family dwellings with oval floor

450

Fig. 2. Tachi single-family summer house southeast of Lemoore. Two-post frame construction covered with tule mats. Photograph by C. Hart Merriam, June 1903.

plan (fig. 2); large tule mats covered their wooden frameworks. The floors were not excavated in the lake area since moisture or flood water would seep or flow in. Within the community the houses stood in a single row. More distinctive were the long, steep-roofed communal residences of the Tulamni, Hometwoli, Wowol, and probably Tachi, which sheltered 10 families or more. Sections of the big mat-covered structures were apportioned to individual families, each with its own fireplace and door. Cooking and other domestic activities commonly took place beneath a shade porch roofed with tule mats, which extended entirely across the front. Little in the way of furnishings existed inside the houses—beds raised on wood frames and padded with tule matting, mats covering the floor, and family belongings hanging from the rafters or leaning against the walls.

Other structures included mat-covered granaries, their bottoms raised off the ground to prevent moisture from settling in them. When a tree was available one or more storage bins was set up in its branches. Supplies of dried fish, roots, seeds, and other foods were kept in the granaries. In every settlement stood at least one communally owned sweathouse in which the men did their daily sweating, and, on occasion slept. This was a sudatory of the usual dirt-covered variety, not over 15 feet in length. There was no structure for dances or rituals.

Clothing and Adornment

Clothing was minimal. Males wore a breechclout, generally cut from deerskin, or went about naked. Women had the standard California female costume, a narrow fringed apron in front and a larger back piece, fashioned from various materials—tules, marsh grass, mud hen skins, or rabbitskins. Conditions of extreme cold led both sexes to wrap themselves in skin cloaks of mud hen or rabbit. As blankets these provided warmth on cool nights. Mostly the people went barefoot; simple moccasins of deer and elk skin were put on only when traveling in rocky, brushy

country. Men wore no head covering but women donned basketry caps when they had burdens to carry. Males and females allowed their hair to grow full length and, normally, to hang loosely. To keep it out of the way while at work, both sexes gathered it together under a string. Tattooing was rather sparingly done. Women had lines, zigzags, and rows of dots, chiefly down the chin and across from the corners of the mouth. Only a few males possessed tattooings. Early in life the earlobes and nasal septa of boys and girls were pierced for the insertion of wood, bone, or shell ornaments.

Technology

Considerable dependency upon tule as a source of raw material characterized Southern Valley Yokuts handicrafts. Stems of this plant served for the manufacture of baskets, cradles, and many other items. Supplies of several essential substances such as wood and stone were either absent or in short supply in the lake country and had to be acquired through trade.

As elsewhere in California basket weaving dominated the industrial arts. The baskets varied in form and use, the chief ones being bowl-shaped cooking containers, conical burden baskets, flat winnowing trays, seed beaters, and necked water bottles (fig. 3). Mostly they were twined. An unusual ware, peculiar to the Tachi and possibly their neighbors, had a spiral foundation of tules

Fig. 3. Tachi twined tule water bottle. Diameter 25 cm.

Fig. 4. Meal sifting tray with foundation of tule and weft of fiber. Diameter 55.5 cm; collected 1907.

bound with string (fig. 4). The Tulare Lake peoples and others dwelling in the tulare may not have fabricated coiled baskets, obtaining them instead by an exchange of goods with Plains Yokuts (Gayton 1948, 1:16).

The remainder of the lake peoples' equipment showed no special technical merit. Evidently none of the tribes manufactured clay vessels, though some uncertainty surrounds the Telamni, Wo'lasi, and Choynok because of their proximity to pottery-making groups (Gayton 1929:249). Many basic articles such as digging sticks, fire drills, mush stirrers, and bows were fashioned from wood; but this craft remained poorly developed. Work in stone was likewise quite undistinguished. Knives, arrow-points (fig. 5), and scraping tools were chipped from various imported lithic materials, including obsidian.

Stone mortars and pestles were secured in trade. Wooden mortars, many if not all brought in from the outside, frequently took the place of the more typical stone vessels. A few useful items, notably sharp-pointed awls, were made of bone. Tanning animal skins represented a minor activity. Cordage, rolled by hand on the thigh, usually was made of milkweed fibers.

Marine shells, used in the manufacture of money and articles of personal adornment, were secured in their natural state from coastal peoples, collectively known as t^hok^hya. Perforated clamshell disks passed as currency and long cylinders of the same material had high value. Beads of olivella and other shells and abalone pendants were made into necklaces (fig. 6).

Transport

Having no beasts of burden, the Yokuts traveled on foot or, preferably, by water. Canoe-shaped rafts or balsas of dried tules lashed together constituted the only watercraft (fig. 7). An average-sized balsa comfortably held six persons and their possessions (Gayton 1948, 1:21). The tule rafts were propelled by means of long poles. When not in use the craft were drawn out of the water and allowed to dry (Merriam 1966-1967, 3:428-429). Back-packing was the method for transporting loads on land. Women consistently bore the heaviest burdens, filling large conical baskets supported by a strap across the forehead with family belongings and food. A brimless basketry cap protected the forehead from the tumpline band. Men carried loads in nets held upon the back by a chest strap (fig. 8). Light things such as containers of water, resting upon a ring of tule, grass, or bark, were borne upon the head by females.

Social Organization

The biological family composed of a husband, wife, and their offspring formed the basic domestic and economic unit in Southern Valley Yokuts society. Another key grouping comprised the patrilineal totemic lineage. A

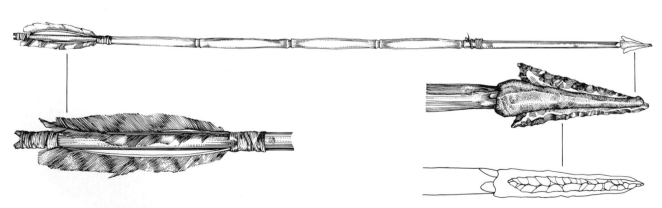

Fig. 5. Compound hunting arrow. Glass point hafted with sinew to hardwood foreshaft and covered with asphaltum; feathers attached to reed main shaft with sinew. Length 83.7 cm; collected in 1875.

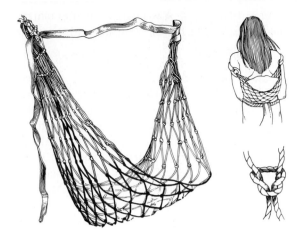

Fig. 8. Carrying net. Milkweed two-ply cordage with hide carrying strap inserted through a ring covered with cotton cloth. Used for carrying wood or large bundles. Extended length 125 cm; collected in 1875.

Fig. 6. Necklace of golden eagle beaks with abalone and glass beads, and a bear claw hanging from fiber twisted with eagle down. Total length 45.5 cm; collected in 1875.

totem symbol peculiar to his paternal line was transmitted by a father to all his children; it was an animal or bird that no member would kill or eat and that was dreamed of and prayed to. The mother's totem, while never passed on to her offspring, received respectful

Fig. 7. Tule balsa made by Bob Bautista, a Tachi Yokuts. Photograph taken at the mouth of the Ventura River about 1920, possibly by John P. Harrington.

treatment from them and her husband. Families sharing the same totem formed an exogamous lineage. The lineage had no formal leader nor did it own land. It was a mechanism for transmitting offices and performing certain ceremonial functions. Members had mutual loyalties and gave aid when called upon.

The lineage totems of the Nutúnutu, Tachi, Wowol, and Chunut were traditionally connected to one of two patrilineal moieties. For example, the Tachi assigned Eagle, Crow, Killdeer, Raven, Antelope, and Beaver to the *tʰokʰelyuwič* or West moiety and Coyote, Prairie Falcon, Ground Owl, Great Horned Owl, Skunk, Seal, and several other species of hawks and owls to the *nutʰoˑwič* or East moiety (Gifford 1916a:294). Hence a man who had Crow as his lineage symbol belonged to the *tʰokʰelyuwič* division. Eagle represented the *tʰokʰelyuwič* moiety (though more often Crow was the eponym) and Coyote the *nutʰoˑwič* side (Gayton 1948, 1:28).

The halving of society made no real difference in the daily life of the Yokuts villagers, for it was only on certain occasions that the duality came into operation. Moiety members formed opposing teams for games and in mourning rites the two social units acted reciprocally, as they did in first-fruits ceremonies. When one of the primary totem animals, Eagle or Coyote, was killed, it became the duty of the moiety to which it belonged to redeem the body by making a payment of shell money and to bury it properly.

Moiety exogamy was customary but not obligatory. Despite the fact that they called all fellow members "relative," the Tachi and Chunut permitted marriages within the divisions if no blood tie was known (Gayton 1945:419). Ordinarily a child followed the paternal moiety, but the rule was not rigid. In a large family a husband occasionally "gave" his wife one or two of their children, who then assumed the duties and taboos of their mother's

453

unit (Gayton 1948, 1:28). A woman, even after marriage, continued to associate herself with her father's moiety.

Political Organization

No overall political unity existed within the several Southern Valley Yokuts tribes. Rather they were split into self-governing local groups or miniature tribes, averaging 350 members (Kroeber 1962:38). Each had a special name for itself and spoke a different dialect. To the tribe belonged a strip of territory, about 250 square miles (Kroeber 1925:474). The land was owned collectively and every tribal member enjoyed the right to utilize its resources. However, in some localities, tracts that yielded plentiful supplies of seeds were claimed by individual women.

Some of the political units constituted a single village; more often there were several settlements, of which one was the largest and recognized as dominant. The names and approximate locations of almost 50 Southern Yokuts settlements are known (fig. 1) (Kroeber 1925:478-484; Gayton 1948, 1:8-9; Latta 1949:8-28, 45-47; Swanton 1952:523-525). The communities tended to be stable, and the people lived for most of the year in their villages. Disruption of community life began in the late spring or early summer when families left for several months to gather seeds and other wild plant foods, shifting camp locations with the change of crops.

Certain official positions within the villages were associated with the totemic animals and hence available only through patrilineal inheritance. Most important was that of chief in the Eagle lineage. His duties were many: he set the time for and directed the great mourning ceremony and other celebrations, mediated disputes, sanctioned the killing of evil sorcerers and other antisocial persons, authorized families to go on seed-gathering and trading expeditions, played host to visitors, and assisted the helpless and indigent. Considerable wealth accrued to the headman for he profited from trading transactions, shared payments received by shamans and entertainers, and loaned money at high interest; however, his patriarchal obligations drained off part of his wealth and he was not necessarily the richest man. An able chief was known and respected among neighboring groups, but his actual power was limited to his own tribe. Normally a son followed his father in this office but a younger brother or brother's son might succeed to it. A chief's daughter or sister occasionally took over.

Dual chieftainship prevailed in the Tachi tribe. Each settlement had two chiefs, one for each moiety. The authority of the pair was reckoned substantially equal; at least they were expected to exercise it in cooperation. But the tʰokʰelyuwič headman of the Eagle lineage was accorded a certain precedence (Kroeber 1925:496).

A herald or messenger of the Dove lineage acted as the chief's assistant. At large gatherings he supervised food distribution and gave commands during ceremonies. While on official visits the messenger carried a long cane with a string of beads attached to the top. Another position, hereditary in the Magpie line, constituted that of spokesman or crier. The chief paid this official to make his announcements.

Friendly and even intimate relations generally prevailed between the local groups. They exchanged hospitality in connection with religious ceremonials and the Tulare Lake peoples freely shared their plentiful resources with outsiders (Mayfield 1929:29). Certain enmities did exist, however, and armed conflicts occasionally broke out. Some small wars and feuds went on, for example, among the tribes dwelling around Tulare Lake and their valley neighbors to the north on the lower San Joaquin River (Gayton 1930a:59). The tribes seem to have acted as units in warfare and sometimes allied with one another against a common foe. There was no regular war chief. Any brave man, particularly one with Raven as a supernatural helper, led the party. Often battles were prearranged by messengers (Gayton 1948, 1:10-11), but surprise attacks took place too. Signal fires were lighted during military campaigns. Fighting occurred on a small scale and rarely more than two or three persons were killed. Doctors were particularly sought out as victims, and their corpses were flayed and impaled. Heads of slain warriors were taken. Little ritual activity accompanied warfare. No dance of incitement preceded a battle and no victory dance followed.

Life Cycle

The Southern Valley Yokuts, like all peoples, believed that certain crucial periods in the life of the individual required special care and attention. The occasions regarded as significant were: birth, a girl's puberty, and, particularly, death.

• BIRTH   A prospective mother, although she continued her normal household duties, took precautions to ensure a safe and easy delivery. The Tachi mother, for example, avoided eating meat products, limiting her diet pretty much to roasted tule roots (Gayton 1948, 1:30). During childbirth, which took place in the family dwelling, a woman squatted on tule matting, grasping a stake. The husband was not present during his wife's travail; she was attended by a midwife. If labor became difficult or prolonged, a shaman was called in. To hasten delivery he placed a bear's paw or its claws on the woman's abdomen. The fetus, frightened by parts of such a ferocious animal, hurried to leave the womb (Driver 1937:135). Immediately after parturition the female attendant cut the umbilical cord and bathed the newborn. When the navel stump dropped off it was put in a little skin bag, suspended around the infant's neck. To rid her of the effects of childbirth, the mother lay on a bed of hot stones and ashes for about two weeks. A purification observance and bath followed.

After an infant's birth the parents took extreme care lest their actions be detrimental to its well-being. The mother ate no meat or salt for 30 days, drank no cold water for 10, left her hair uncombed, and avoided scratching herself with her fingernails, employing instead a piece of bone or stick. Cooking for the family, basket weaving, and traveling were forbidden for a couple of weeks, or, in some tribes, for as long as two months. For his part, the father observed a mild form of the couvade. He remained quietly indoors and refrained from hunting, sweating, smoking, and gambling. Meat products, salt, and cold water were tabooed to him until the remnant of the cord dropped from the child's navel.

A baby's first cradle was made of soft tule (see "Basketry," fig. 6b, this vol.). Later the child was bound to a forked-stick frame, upon which it remained day and night with only brief periods of freedom until the age of walking. Naming took place three of four weeks after birth, at which time the parents served food to guests who came bearing gifts. Lineage names were bestowed by maternal as well as paternal relatives. As in most primitive societies the nursing period lasted more than a year. Other foods were gradually introduced along with the mother's milk until complete weaning occurred. Adultery by either parent was thought to sicken a nursing child.

•PUBERTY At the time a girl experienced her first menses, she remained indoors until the discharge of bloody fluid ceased. The menstruant abstained from eating meat and salt and drinking cold water. She scratched herself with a stick rather than her fingernails. Neighbors were invited to a feast at the termination of the girl's period, but no public ceremony was held. Confinement inside the house and the same restrictions on eating and behavior prevailed during subsequent menstrual periods. Girls may have been tattooed shortly before or at about puberty.

The coming of age of a boy received no attention. The Yokuts have been credited with an initiation into manhood and tribal status that centered around the drinking of a preparation of crushed datura roots (Kroeber 1925:502; Latta 1949:197); however, for the southern valley tribes at least the taking of the decoction was not connected with a puberty rite comparable to that of other southern California tribes.

•MARRIAGE When a youth reached marriageable age, his kin took the initiative by offering presents to the family of a suitable girl. The gifts included clothing, shell money, and other valuables. If the potential bride and her family proved in accord with the plan, they in turn gave baskets, food, and additional products of female labor. The marriage pact concluded with a feast. Sometimes such arrangements were made before the two individuals involved had reached puberty. All the Southern Valley Yokuts had strict rules barring unions between blood kin, and a couple known to be even remotely related could not wed without incurring unfavorable comment. Members of the same lineage, all actual or assumed kinsfolk, were not supposed to marry. It was customary but not compulsory for a man to seek a wife outside his own moiety. Polygyny, though allowed, occurred infrequently, the chief more often than others having two wives.

For about a year a newly wed couple lived with the wife's parents. Then they moved permanently to the husband's father's home or set up their own dwelling nearby. Restrictions on social intercourse with parents-in-law were in force. A definite taboo precluded any conversation between a man and his wife's mother; restraint also marked the relationship between a woman and her father-in-law. Marriages were easily dissolved. Infidelity, laziness, quarreling, and a woman's barrenness led to their breakup.

The division of labor between a married couple followed the usual California pattern insofar as the husband hunted and fished while the wife supplied the vegetal fare. The man also wove nets and manufactured implements of wood, bone, and stone. To the wife's lot fell the duties of cooking, housekeeping, and child care. She also wove the baskets and mats. In housebuilding, males erected the framework and gathered the tule stalks that women made into mats for covering.

•DEATH Upon death, the body was almost immediately readied for burial by paid undertakers, generally male transvestites. The corpse, tightly bound, was placed with the head to the west or northwest in a grave dug in a cemetery outside the village. Various personal effects of the deceased were interred with the body and a dog was sometimes sacrificed. Though burial represented the primary means of disposal, cremation was practiced in special cases, such as individuals who died away from home or shamans. Among the Tachi, everyone of any social consequence was burned (Kroeber 1925:499). The charred bones were gathered together and buried in the regular graveyard.

Mourning affected only the dead person's immediate kin. The widow cut her hair, stopped washing her face, and remained in seclusion until a private mourning ceremony was held. The favorite Yokuts ritual impositions, abstention from meat and salt, applied to her. Female blood relatives likewise cut their hair. Meat and salt remained taboo to all bereaved, and male relatives did no hunting until the family mourning rite took place. The name of the deceased was never again mentioned in the presence of his kinsfolk. The levirate and sororate were sometimes followed.

To ward off the danger of the dead person's return, a short prayer was addressed to him (Kroeber 1925:509):

> You are going to another land
> You will like that land
> You shall not stay here.

It was believed that the soul left the grave two days after death and traveled westward (or northwestward) to the afterworld. A narrow bridge that moved up and down and spanned a broad river had to be crossed before entering (Gayton and Newman 1940:14). Conditions in the land of the dead were reversed. Its inhabitants slept by day, danced and enjoyed life at night; food was abundant and in inexhaustible supply; the living smelled foul to them (Gayton 1948, 1:31). Relatives lived in the same domestic groups as in life.

The private or family ceremony that marked the end of the mourning period took place in the third month following a death. The deceased's kinsmen sent shell bead money to the chief of the opposite moiety, along with a request for him to make the necessary arrangements. By the end of six days the chief had assembled much food and had appointed a person to wash the faces of the male mourners. Following the ritual washing, a sumptuous feast was eaten.

Games

When not occupied with more serious concerns adults often played games, most frequently competing against members of the opposite moiety. Both males and females were addicted to gambling. The hand game, accompanied by singing, was enjoyed by either sex. Women threw dice consisting of half-shells of walnuts (fig. 9, see also "Foothill Yokuts," fig. 9, this vol.) or split sticks. Matching lines drawn on the ground underneath a basketry tray represented a men's game of chance. Teams of males contended in shinny, ball or stick races, and hoop and pole contests. Women competed in the first two of these. The object of a favorite Chunut pastime, engaged in only by men, was to toss a ball or shoot an arrow through a ring fastened to the top of a long pole. Other pleasures included dancing joined in by the two sexes and attendance at major festivals. Storytelling afforded a favorite form of evening entertainment for adults and children alike.

Smoking tobacco in a short length of cane, usually at bedtime, provided a diversion for males. The tobacco consisted of a wild variety gathered locally. Moistened tobacco mixed with lime from burned shells was eaten, often just to "feel good" but also by persons seeking supernatural power.

Fig. 9. Women's dice. Walnut shells filled with asphaltum inset with abalone shell. Average diameter 2.5 cm; collected in 1875.

456

Curing

Minor ailments were treated with home remedies. To prevent a cold in the chest, red clay was smeared liberally over that part of the body. For a bad cough, horehound was boiled in water and the liquid drunk. Apparently the fall became a season of widespread and debilitating sickness for the lake and marsh dwellers (Derby 1933:42; Gayton 1946:257). Whether this resulted from contaminated or alkaline water, heat stroke, tularemia due to increased handling of rabbits and ground squirrels, or to another cause remains unknown. In serious cases of illness the people had recourse to a medicine man.

Religion

Southern Valley Yokuts religion was not rich in group ceremonials. The rital honoring the tribal dead ranked as the most conspicuous religious festival. Usually this took place annually, but sometimes a year was skipped depending on the number of deaths, the financial condition of the bereaved families, and other circumstances (Driver 1937:139). The six-day affair, participated in by outside local groups, was held in the summer or fall. Such a major ceremony involved the entire tribe; guests came by the hundreds. A symbolic "killing" and reviving of a costumed dancer, an intertribal shamans' contest, the use of effigies of the dead, the burning of property, and ritual washing of mourners by visiting chiefs of the opposite moiety all formed part of the observance. It concluded with feasting, merriment, and gambling.

Much less spectacular were the first-fruit rites. These observances, which pertained to seeds and berries, seem to have been scrupulously celebrated but remained unelaborated. All seeds were classified as belonging to the $t^hok^helyuwič$ moiety, whereas berries were $nut^ho\cdot wič$. When berries ripened, the $nut^ho\cdot wič$ people gathered some and presented them to $t^hok^helyuwič$ members who thereupon ate them. The $nut^ho\cdot wič$ were then free to eat berries, hitherto taboo. The $t^hok^helyuwič$ performed a similar act as each seed crop became ready for harvesting.

Another group ritual centered around drinking a preparation of crushed datura roots. The drinking occurred in the spring, never later because of the belief that the plant became too strong as the year progressed. Young adults, 18 years of age or thereabouts, of both sexes took the mixture under the direction of an elderly man to gain long life, health, prosperity, rapport with a spiritual helper, and other benefits (Gayton 1948, 1:38; Driver 1937:136). While recovering from the stupor induced by the datura, they experienced visions and foresaw events. No one was compelled to take the concoction and a few individuals never did; others, in contrast, drank it more than once. As with all Yokuts festivals, the datura rite ended with a feast.

Other public ceremonials remained in the hands of the medicine men and were in essence demonstrations of

Fig. 10. Bob Bautista, Tachi medicine man, performing a "spring dance." Photograph by John P. Harrington, about 1920s.

their magical skill. A seed-growing dance was performed each spring by one or two shamans who sang and made plants magically appear. During this display the villagers queried them about wild seed crops for the coming year.

Group ceremonials took place in the open, never in a dance house or enclosure. The characteristic costume (fig. 10, see also "Eastern Coastal Chumash," fig. 3, this vol.) comprised a short skirt of eagle down twisted into strings of milkweed fiber tied to hawk feathers and a tall headdress of magpie tail plumes encircled at the base by crow feathers (fig. 11). The headdress was placed on top of a headnet covered with down. Celebrants' faces were often painted with patterns symbolizing their totems (Gifford 1916a:294; Gayton 1948, 1:20-21). Religious paraphernalia included the cleft-stick rattle, also used to beat time for pleasure dances, and the medicine man's cocoon rattle. Many ritual acts were habitually performed as part of the public observances. They included reciting short prayers, making offerings of seed meal, tobacco, or eagle down, and singing sacred songs. All of them could be done separately and not as part of a larger whole. The ritual number was six. Mourning and datura

observances lasted six days; other ritual and mythological references to the number also occurred.

Various beliefs and practices centered around the weather. Plummet-shaped charmstones, thought to be natural objects, which abounded in the lake region, were manipulated to bring rain. To stop thunder, a dog was whipped until it yelped and then turned loose. Most Yokuts feared wearing shell ornaments during a thunderstorm. If caught out in bad weather a man ripped off his adornments and threw them away. An eclipse was interpreted as the devouring of the moon (or sun) by some creature, probably Coyote. On this occasion, old Tachi women sang, danced, and begged that a little of the orb be left to them.

The Southern Valley Yokuts had no organized priesthood. The only real religious specialists were the shamans, almost always males. Power came to them unsought in a dream or vision, or through deliberate quest, most commonly from animals or monsters inhabiting the water. To obtain a revelation, a prospective Tachi medicine man bathed nightly for a whole winter in a pool,

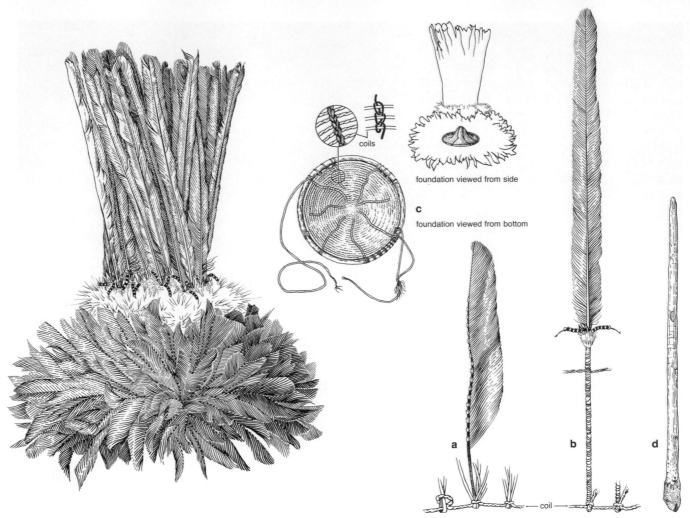

coils

foundation viewed from side

c

foundation viewed from bottom

a

b

coil

d

Dept. of Anthr., Smithsonian: 200090.

Fig. 11. Medicine man's headdress. Detail a, of split crow feather with notched shaft; b, magpie tail feather wrapped with red wool, base of feather ornamented with mink fur, red wool, and black and white beads; c, construction of foundation, wood outer rim with continuous coil of cord to which feathers are attached; d, wood skewer to secure headdress on head. Height of headdress 38 cm; collected at Tule River Reservation in 1898.

spring, or waterhole until the creature dwelling in it met him face-to-face and gave specific instructions. The man who accepted supernatural help prayed and fasted for a long time. He secured certain talismans, perhaps parts of the creature that aided him or objects that it directed him to collect.

Most important from the ordinary person's point of view was the shaman's ability to heal the sick. Doctoring regularly lasted two days. On the first visit the practitioner made a diagnosis. After consulting with his supernatural helper, he returned the next day to affect a cure by feigning to suck a disease object out of the patient's body. Bloodletting was often joined with sucking. Shamans received large fees and not a few displayed a mercenary attitude by demanding more money while the healing was still underway. Supposedly they had caches, each guarded by a beast of some sort, where their accumulated wealth lay hidden. Often medicine men

drank a datura preparation to determine who would fall ill or die. They then doctored the unfortunates in advance.

But shamans did more than practice curative and preventative medicine. They dominated the religious life by taking a leading role in many public rituals. Through frequent public display of their miraculous powers they inspired awe in the minds of the villagers and thus maintained their standing. A system of reciprocal relations frequently existed between chief and medicine man (Gayton 1930). The chief received part of the doctoring fee. In turn he protected the shaman from violence at the hands of avenging relatives of patients he failed to cure. But even strong support from the chief might fail to save the life of a chronically unsuccessful practicioner or one suspected of sorcery. A deeply rooted belief held that a medicine man could turn his power at will to evil purposes and kill victims by shooting magical missiles into their bodies. If suspected of repeatedly doing harm to

458

his fellows, a shaman was executed, quite likely with the sanction of the chief, who hired the killers.

The lake peoples do not seem to have had shamans who concentrated their efforts upon controlling the weather or rattlesnakes, as did the southern foothill tribes. They did posses one class of specialists, the bear doctors. These individuals had the ability to transform themselves into bears, the species from which their supernatural aid came, and to survive successive killings while in this form. The function of the bear shamans remains unclear. Only the Tachi attributed special curative benefits to their singing and dancing (Kroeber 1925:516).

A doctor's power differed only in degree from that acquired from a spiritual helper by many men and older women. Ordinarily the tutelary, an animal or bird, appeared unsought to a person in a dream. For others it came while under the influence of datura or as a result of having eaten tobacco in a deliberate quest. If a visitant appeared during a dream, a man walked some distance from his house, smoked a little tobacco, and cast crane feathers on the ground (Gayton 1948, 1:31). Even if he did not wish to have private power a man performed these acts, for to ignore the being who offered it caused illness. If the dream helper was accepted, a fast was maintained through the following day. Once a compact had been formed, the sense of intimacy between a person and his particular species became deep (Gayton 1946:267). Such a relationship conferred general good fortune or certain specific abilities or successes on the recipient. Cooper's hawk was regarded as the bestower of particularly strong power (Gayton 1948, 1:31).

The Yokuts relied primarily on their individual patrons, and other spiritual beings seldom entered into their religious consciousness. Local spirits, some potentially malevolent, inhabited various spots. Water babies, characterized by long black hair, lived in local ponds and people did not like to encounter them. A big snake equipped with a human head dwelt underground. If he liked an individual he appeared before him. And there were other strange creatures (Gayton 1948, 1:37).

Literature, Music, and Art

The Southern Valley Yokuts had not developed a complex mythology nor arranged their sacred stories in any sort of orderly system. Most tales dealt with a prehuman people who bore animal and bird names and who later transformed themselves into the actual species. The origin myth began with the world covered with water (Kroeber 1907a:195; Latta 1936:19-26; Gayton and Newman 1940:11). Eagle summoned various aquatic birds to dive for mud. Teal, the smallest duck, or Mud Hen succeeded in fetching a little but perished in the effort. Eagle molded the mud with seeds that swelled when wet to form the earth. The creation of mankind was practically disregarded, the mythical account centering upon the reaction of the first people to the event. Likewise, the beginnings of cultural institutions received little attention. Stories were told of the theft of fire and sun, mainly through the instrumentality of Coyote, and of the origin of death. Other tales comprised recitations of the adventures of the prehistoric race. An idea that had taken special hold concerned a man's visit to the land of the dead in pursuit of his wife.

Music found primary expression in the songs that accompanied rituals. Characteristically the lyrics were sparse and highly allusive (Hatch 1958:49). The cleft-stick rattle accompanied most singing. Other musical instruments included the cocoon rattle, bone and wood whistle, flute, and musical bow. Nothing corresponding to a true drum existed.

The graphic and plastic arts were not developed. Decorative patterns woven into baskets constituted the chief artistic achievement. Painting found representation in the lines and other motifs employed in facial and body adornment and applied to articles of daily use. Designs found on the walls of rockshelters in the western foothills and Coast Range may have been painted by Southern Valley Yokuts. The lake peoples made no sculpture in wood or stone.

History

The Southern Valley Yokuts were encountered by the Spaniards soon after they settled in California. In the fall of 1772, Pedro Fages led a little band of soldiers through Tejon Pass and down into the southernmost part of the San Joaquin valley. He visited a native village on the shores of Buena Vista Lake before making his exit westward to San Luis Obispo (Fages 1937:72-76). The next visitor was the intrepid friar-explorer, Francisco Garcés in 1776, who kept a detailed diary of his journey (Coues 1900). The Spaniards appear to have seldom set foot in the lake country during the next three decades. Reports of expeditions in search of deserting soldiers and runaway mission neophytes exist, but these are vague.

Active exploration begain in the second administration (1802-1814) of Gov. José de Arrillaga, who was eager to extend the Spanish sphere of influence and gain a foothold in the hinterland (Cutter 1950:57). The Church joined forces with the governor, for the Franciscans looked upon the tulare with its substantial Indian population as a fruitful place for future missions. Beginning in 1806 several expeditions were sent into the interior (Gayton 1936; Cook 1960); however, the Spaniards never succeeded in conquest, probably because the impotency of their crumbling New World empire prevented them from taking advantage of the knowledge gained by the various exploring parties. The course of native life appears scarcely to have been altered by these casual contacts.

No very considerable portion of the lake tribes ever seems to have come under control of the Franciscan missionaries. Some Tachi, Telamni, and members of other tribes were settled at Soledad, San Luis Obispo, San Antonio, San Juan Bautista, and at other missions. It remains uncertain how exhaustively the Franciscans drew on the various local groups or how long certain of them were under mission influence.

More significant was the infiltration of runaway mission neophytes. During the early decades of the nineteenth century the southern valley became a rendezvous for Indian converts fleeing from the discipline of steady and directed work at the coastal mission establishments. Their presence had far-reaching consequences, for the fugitives introduced alien practices from their half-forgotten cultures and others they had learned from the padres. From them the local peoples acquired a taste for horseflesh; later they wanted horses to ride. Aided by apostate neophytes, the Yokuts began making forays against the mission and rancho herds. They raided so successfully that they became known as the "Horsethief Indians."

In the turbulent period (1822-1846) when California formed part of Mexico, expeditions into the valley continued, but they were very largely punitive. Rancheros organized campaigns for the purpose of recovering stolen livestock, punishing the thieves, and capturing slaves. No ranchos were established in the lake country and the Mexican influence on the tribes appears to have been slight, except for an 1833 epidemic, which may have been malaria of unusual severity (Cook 1955a:303). The outbreak devastated the native population, with an estimated mortality rate of 75 percent.

Cultural breakdown and the near-total disappearance of Indians from the upper San Joaquin valley came with the annexation of California by the United States. The lake country, lacking gold, did not experience an invasion by the first wave of immigrants, the gold seekers. But settlers soon overran the country and Indian lands passed into private hands. The process of dispossession proved relatively easy, since the native people, unwarlike, discouraged, and apathetic, failed to offer any effective resistence. Their open valley habitat made them extremely vulnerable and there was no way for them to escape the full brunt of civilization. Minor Indian raids on outlying ranches occurred occasionally, and serious consideration was given to setting up a military post near Tulare Lake to protect the settlers east of San Luis Obispo from these incursions and to control the tribes inhabiting the borders of the lakes and the slopes of the Sierra Nevada (Derby 1933:29). The post was not established. In 1851 the tribes agreed to relinquish their lands for reservations and payments in goods, but the treaty was never ratified by the United States Senate (Heizer 1972:26-37).

A pitiful remnant of the southern valley peoples went to the Tejon reservation established at the base of the Tehachapi range and a few to the Fresno reservation located on leased land near Madera. Despite the comparatively large sums appropriated to equip and maintain them, the reservations never proved a success. Tejon was abandoned in 1859 and the Indians were taken to Tule River, where after another removal the Tule River Reservation was set apart for them in 1873. By 1905 the reservation population numbered only 154, mostly members of the Southern Valley Yokuts tribes (principally Yawelmani and Tachi) with a few foothill natives (Curtis 1907-1930, 14:153). A settlement for Tachi was established near Lemoore, north of Tulare Lake, and scattered families continued to live in their original localities.

More and more the tribes became dependent upon Whites for their livelihood. These years of hand-to-mouth existence proved difficult and demoralizing and they reacted to their unhappy state by turning enthusiastically to a revivalistic movement, the 1870 Ghost Dance. The cult's doctrine, which promised the return of dead relatives, absolution from sickness and death, and a life of peace and prosperity, had great appeal. Local Ghost cult dances were held every month or so for almost two years before disillusionment brought the movement to a rapid decline. Probably it was this disenchantment that stopped the 1890 Ghost Dance from penetrating the region.

In 1970 approximately 325 Yokuts lived on the 54,110 acres of the Tule River Reservation (California State Advisory Commission 1966:81-82). Their economy was fairly good and relatively stable due to employment of most of the men in the lumber industry and to income from payment for timber owned by the Indians and from leasing grazing lands. Because logging employment is seasonal, during the off season loggers drew unemployment compensation. Other men picked fruit, as did some women, and did ranch work in the valley. Although the reservation's soil was said to be fertile and the water supply adequate, no one gardened and only a few families kept domestic animals. Great variation in housing existed, but most dwellings were quite modest. The educational level remained low with a small minority of the young graduating from high school. Recurrent social problems included excessive drinking of alcoholic beverages and intragroup jealousies and friction, primarily of an economic nature. Yawelmani became the reservation's lingua franca (Newman 1946:222).

The hundred or so Tachi at Santa Rosa Reservation, a 170-acre tract near Lemoore, were much more impoverished, their land consisting of an alkali flat unsuited to agriculture or animal husbandry. Tachis worked at a variety of jobs, mostly as farm laborers. Frequent trips in search of jobs took families away from Santa Rosa for days or weeks, and working as farm laborers provided contact with other Indians, who frequently visited the reservation, as well as with Mexicans and other peoples.

By 1972 no one from the reservation had graduated from high school, nor had any of the Indians become tradesmen or artisans (Hatch 1958:47). Housing consisted of about three dozen shacks in poor repair.

Only bits of the old Yokuts life persist and each year, as the elderly die, even these vestiges disappear.

Synonymy

A diversity of names exists for the various Southern Valley Yokuts political divisions. Often a group designation given by one writer was never mentioned by any other; nevertheless, there is agreement on certain names, and although the spelling differs, the pronunciation in these instances is about the same. The following listing is arranged under the anglicized spellings used by Kroeber (1963:237), except that ch replaces his ṭ. The next items in each entry are the pronunciations in Yokuts, as provided by Michael Silverstein (personal communication 1973) in an attempt at transcriptions appropriate for the dialect spoken by each group whose name is given. Here the singular form is given first, followed by the plural. After these pronunciations appear major spelling variants from Kroeber (1925), Powers (1877), Hodge (1907-1910), Merriam (1902-1932 and in Heizer 1966), and Latta (1949).

Tachi, *i̯ačʰčʰiẏ, i̯ačʰeˑčʰaẏi*, Ta'-chi, Tah'-che, Atach, Atache, Dachi, Laches, Tadji, Talches, Ton-Taches.

Chunut, *čʰuṅutʰ, čʰuṅoˑtʰatʰi*, Chu'-nut, Choo'-nut, Chohonuts, Chonot, Chusute.

Wowol, *woˑwal, wuwoˑwali* (or *wowoˑwali?*), Wah-wol, Woo-wells, Wowal, Wowod, in Spanish Bubol or Hubol.

Nutúnutu, *nutʰuˑnutʰu?, nutʰantʰisa*, No-toan'-ai-ti, No-to'-no-to, Mon-to-tos, Na-too'-na-ta, Notonatos, Noton-toos, Notoowthas, No-tow-too, Nutonetoos.

Wimilchi, *wimilčʰi?, wimeˑlačʰi*, Ho-mel-ches, Mowelches, Ne-mil-ches, Was-mil-ches, We-mal-che, We-melches, We-mol-ches.

Wechihit, *weˑčʰixitʰ, wičʰeˑxatʰi*, Wi'-chi-kik, Wechikhit, Wa'-cha-kut, Wa-cha-et, Wa-cha-hets, Wa-che-ha-ti, Wa-che-nets, Wa-che-ries, Waches, Wechahet.

Apyachi, unknown, probably begins *?a-*, Apiachi, Apaichi.

Choynok, *čʰoẏṅokʰ* (or *čʰoẏṅukʰ*), *čʰoẏeˑṅakʰi*, Choinok, Choi'-nook, Chenooks, Cho-e-nees, Cho-e-nook, Cho-e-nuco, Choi-nuck, Choinux, Cho'-nook, Choo'-enu, Chóinoc.

Wo'lasi, *wo?lasi(?), wo?wulasi* (or *wo?wolasi*), Wo'-wul, Wo'ladji, Wo-la-si, Wowulasi.

Telamni, *tʰeˑlamni(?), tʰeẏeˑlamni*, Te'-lum-ni, Tadum'-ne, Talame, Tal-lum-nes, Tedamni, Telam, Telame, Telamoteris, Telomni, To-lum-ne, Torim.

Koyeti, *kʰoẏeˑtʰi(?), kʰoẏeˑtʰatʰi*, Ko-yet'-te, Co-ye-te, Ko-ya-ta, Ko-ya-te, Ko-ye-to, Kuyeti.

Tulamni, *tʰulamni(?), tʰulalmina*, Too-lol'-min, Tulamne, Too-lol-min, Tu-lum'-ne.

Chuxoxi, *tʰuxoxiy, ṭuxoˑxayi*, Ṭuxoxi, Tuhohi, Tohohai, Tohohayi, Truhohayi, Truhohi.

Hometwoli, *xoṁtʰiṅin, xoṁetʰwali*, Po-hal'-lin-Tin'leh (not a tribal name, but the village *pʰoˑhalintʰinl(i)w*), Ham-met-wel'-le, Humetwadi.

Yawelmani, *yaẁlamni?, yaẁelmani*, Yauelmani, Tin'-lin-nen (village designation, not the tribal name), Ya'welmani, Yow'-el-man'-ne, Tejoneños, Tinlinin, Yowedmani, Yowenmani, Yowlumne.

Sources

The published literature on the Southern Valley Yokuts is not very voluminous due to the early decimation of the Indians and the rapid disruption of their native culture. The best-known and most accessible historical records are those of Pedro Fages (1937), Father Francisco Garcés (Coues 1900), and Lt. José Maria Estudillo (Gayton 1936). Additional accounts have been assembled by Cook (1960). Interesting insights into the life of the Tulare Lake people have been provided by Thomas Jefferson Mayfield (1929), who lived for nearly 10 years among the Yokuts.

Ethnographic descriptions, based on questioning aged informants about customs, most of which had been long discarded and had to be reconstructed from memory, are by no means complete. The Yokuts as a whole are treated by Powers (1877), Curtis (1907-1930, 14), Kroeber (1925), and Latta (1949). Gayton (1948, 1) deals specifically with the Southern Valley tribes. The culture element distribution study for the Southern Sierra Nevada (Driver 1937) contains trait lists for the Nutúnutu, Tachi, Chunut, and Yawelmani.

A few publications describing some particular aspect of Southern Valley Yokuts life have also appeared (Hatch 1958; Merriam 1966-1967, 3). Additional details can be found in monographs devoted to regional or tribal studies of certain topics (Kroeber 1907a, 1962; Gifford 1916a; Latta 1936; Gayton and Newman 1940).

Northern Valley Yokuts

WILLIAM J. WALLACE

No large section of California is so little known ethnographically as the lower or northern San Joaquin valley. The lack of information concerning the aboriginal inhabitants of this region is due to their rapid disappearance as a result of disease, missionization, and the sudden overrunning of their country by American miners and settlers during the gold rush years. Most of the native groups are now completely gone; the others are represented either by small remnants living among other tribes or by a few isolated survivors. It was too late to gather much useful information from the people themselves when the period of intensive study of California Indian populations began, so that most of what can be learned about them must be extracted piecemeal from the writings of explorers, military men, missionaries, and other early travelers. Unfortunately these accounts contain distressingly few details of aboriginal life. The scraps of information recorded in historical documents can in some instances be augmented by the slim and deficient archeological record.

Territory and Environment

Before the coming of the Whites, the lower valley was inhabited by the northernmost tribes of Yokuts Indians. Generally speaking, Northern Yokuts territory extended from near where the San Joaquin makes a big bend northward to a line midway between the Calaveras and Mokelumne rivers (fig. 1). The northern limit of their land, the dividing line between them and the Plains Miwok, has been a subject of controversy, with the dispute centering upon the classification of several of the northernmost groups (Chulamni, Yatchicumne, Tawalimni), variously identified as Yokuts or as Miwok (Merriam 1907:350–351). The best evidence at hand seems to leave little doubt that the Chulamni tribe, including its village called Yatchicumne (Yachik), was Yokuts while the Tawalimni were Miwok (Barrett 1908b:345; Kroeber 1908c, 1959a:3, 1963:237; Bennyhoff 1961:214). The crest of the barren and desolate Diablo Range probably marked the Yokuts's western boundary; to the east their country extended to the juncture of the broad plain of the San Joaquin with the foothills of the Sierra Nevada.

The sluggish San Joaquin River, with its maze of channels, often abandoned to become sloughs, formed

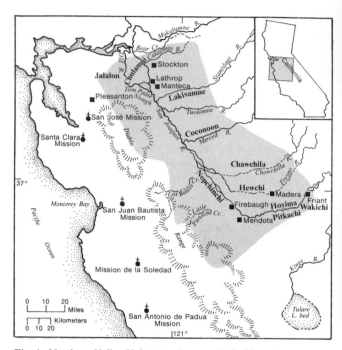

Fig. 1. Northern Valley Yokuts territory and tribal locations.

the core of the Northern Yokuts homeland. As the river, lined with natural levees, meanders northward, it collects a vast amount of water from its primary tributaries, the Fresno, Chowchilla, Merced, Tuolumne, Stanislaus, and Calaveras, which originate in the Sierra Nevada and feed one by one, at right angles, into the main stream. Extending back from the riverbanks, often for as far as the eye could see, were expanses of tule-choked marshes. Beyond the marshes lay level or undulating, virtually featureless plains, much broader on the eastern than on the western side. The west plain, situated in the lee of the coastal mountains, is more arid and furnishes not a single permanent stream. East and west, low hills, in irregularly disposed lines, border the plain.

Apart from the wetlands, which were heavily overgrown with tules and marsh grass, the natural vegetation of the valley floor tended to be sparse. In its original condition the plain formed a grassland, enlivened in the spring with many flowering herbs. Stands of trees remained restricted to narrow ribbons of sycamores, cottonwoods, and willows along stream courses and to groves of valley oaks in well-watered localities with rich soil.

In contrast to the rather limited plant growth, animal life was present in unusual variety and abundance, both in the water and on the land. The river and sloughs were well stocked with fish, mussels, and pond turtles; migratory waterfowl nested by the thousands amongst the tules. Immense herds of two large browsing animals—tule elk and pronghorn antelope—found ample forage on the plains and at the fringes of the marshes. The elk and antelope shared the plains with many smaller mammals and birds, including jackrabbits, ground squirrels, and quail. There was also an exuberance of insect life, particularly of mosquitoes, which bred in the standing water.

Though the climate as a whole can be characterized as mild and equable, summer days can become excessively hot, with temperatures rising to 100°F. and beyond. And the winter, the rainy season, can have cool or even bitterly cold days. The valley is semiarid, averaging 10-15 inches of rainfall annually.

Despite certain disadvantages, such as periodic flooding of the bottomlands, intense summer heat, and the ever-present annoyance of mosquitoes, the lower San Joaquin provided a favorable environment for aboriginal habitation. It is not surprising therefore that the ancestors of the historic Northern Yokuts (and populations before them) chose to settle there. The archeology of the northern valley is too imperfectly known to provide details regarding the time of entry and length of tenancy of the region by Yokuts, but what little information does exist indicates that they were relative latecomers.

Four archeological sites in the delta, a vast complex of islands and tule marshes where the San Joaquin and the Sacramento rivers meet, have produced materials that can almost certainly be attributed to Yokuts groups (Bennyhoff 1961:83). Articles of White as well as native manufacture occurred at three of the localities, proving their occupancy continued into historic times; no Caucasian-made objects turned up during the limited excavations made at the fourth. The native artifacts, though corresponding in a general way to those characteristic of the closing aboriginal period (Late Horizon, Phase 2) of the delta, form a cultural unit quite distinct from that found farther north on the Mokelumne and Cosumnes rivers in territory held by Plains Miwok Indians. Apparently the local differentiation of cultures had its beginnings in a previous prehistoric phase (Late Horizon, Phase 1) dating back beyond A.D. 1500.

Archeological findings from the west side tell nearly the same story. Excavations at habitation sites in western Merced and Fresno counties have revealed an artifact assemblage belonging to the Yokuts groups who inhabited this part of the valley into historic times (Olsen and Payen 1968:65-66, 1969:39-40; Pritchard 1970:45). These materials have been assigned to the interval between A.D. 1500 or 1600 and Spanish contact, 1800-1815. An earlier assemblage that shows close links to the Late Horizon, Phase 1 complexes of the delta probably represents an antecedent stage of Northern Yokuts culture. So far, too little archeological work has been done on the eastern side of the San Joaquin, south of the delta, to tell much about Yokuts occupancy of this section.

One interpretation of the linguistic data supports the view that the Yokuts were comparatively recent arrivals in the northern valley, suggesting that they originally did not range beyond the main bend of the San Joaquin (Kroeber 1959:269-277). Then, starting about 500 years ago, pressure from Numic-speaking Monache from across the Sierra Nevada, who began to enter the San Joaquin drainage, caused tribes on the upper river, and perhaps on the Kings as well, to spread over the valley floor, mainly toward the north. Movement northward, a gradual process taking a couple of centuries, considerably extended the limits of Yokuts territory at the expense of Costanoans, Miwok, or both, who had hitherto occupied the country.

By the time Spanish expeditions began penetrating the interior of California in the early nineteenth century, the Yokuts had firmly established themselves in the northern valley, for the exploring parties reported encountering their settlements in the delta, along the San Joaquin, and on the main tributary rivers. Obviously they had prospered and multiplied because their villages are described as being well stocked with food and populous. No precise idea of the size of the aboriginal population of the region can be arrived at from the early Spanish accounts, but two estimates allow for an approximation. The first, based partly on figures culled from documentary sources and partly on analogy with stream-mile densities for known populations on the Merced and Kings rivers, placed the total at 25,100 (Cook 1955:49-68). Not counted were Indians living in the arid district west of the San Joaquin. The second calculation, established from an evaluation of available major food resources, resulted in a higher figure of 31,404 (Baumhoff 1963:221). Both estimates far exceed the 11,000 inhabitants enumerated previously for the entire valley (Kroeber 1939a:137) and the 18,000 for the Yokuts as a whole (Kroeber 1925:883).

The native population was not evenly distributed. Rather, it was clustered in a narrow strip of land bordering the San Joaquin and its main tributaries. A density of 10+ persons a square mile, equal to that anywhere in aboriginal California, has been computed for the waterways (Baumhoff 1963:map 7). By contrast, a density of only two or three inhabitants for each square mile is allowed for the plains. The overwhelming bulk of the plains people lived on the more hospitable eastern side of the river. To the west, the population, concentrated on semipermanent watercourses well within the foothills (Hewes 1941:125), was much sparser.

Subsistence

In their general mode of life, the northern valley tribes closely resembled the Yokuts groups occupying the southern half of the San Joaquin. Yet there were cultural differences. Part of these stemmed from the nature of their food supply. The northerners had greater access to two important dietary resources—salmon and acorns—than did their southern neighbors and, as a consequence, placed considerably more dependence upon these products. Other dissimilarities, as in religious practices, had their origin in influences emanating from the north.

Given their close identification with the river, it is not surprising to learn that the Northern Yokuts gained much of their livelihood through fishing. Salmon, mentioned in several historical accounts (Cook 1960:242, 260), must have been the most sought-after fish. Fall spawning brought great numbers of king salmon into the San Joaquin and its primary feeder streams; the same species frequented the San Joaquin and Merced again in the spring (Baumhoff 1963:174). There were other fish too. Huge white sturgeon ascended the main river (Rostlund 1952:map 3); and river perch, western suckers, and Sacramento pike, none with flesh of high quality, were to be found at all times of the year. Knowledge of the native techniques employed in capturing the various kinds of fish is very fragmentary. Reference is made to the use of small dragnets equipped with stone sinkers (Cook 1960:242). Another device that seems to have been utilized consisted of the bone- or antler-tipped harpoon (Bennyhoff 1950:312–316). This instrument could not have been wholly effective in the San Joaquin's frequently muddied waters. Fishing from tule rafts was probably practiced. Part of the catch was preserved by drying (Cook 1960:270).

Next to fishing, fowling must have been the most important source of flesh food. Geese, ducks, and other aquatic birds, present in almost profligate abundance, offered easy prey to the hunter, and their taking must have played a key role here as around Tulare and Buena Vista lakes in the southern valley. But, strangely enough, the written records contain no mention of their capture by the Indians. Spanish chroniclers took notice of the immense herds of antelope and elk, although they again made no reference to their killing and eating by the northern valley peoples. Big-game hunting probably constituted a marginal rather than an important subsistence activity.

The harvesting of wild plant foods was of prime significance. Acorns were gathered in quantity from the groves of valley oaks, ground into meal, and cooked in the usual form of a thick soup or gruel (Cook 1960:242, 264). Valley oaks do not grow in dense stands, but, because of their huge size and abundant crops, the yield of individual trees is prodigious, amounting to 300–500 pounds or more in a good year (Baumhoff 1963:165).

Tule roots, in unlimited supply, were also gathered and ground into meal. In addition, the Indians foraged for seeds. One variety, described as resembling rice, was cooked in the form of white loaves. Evidently the Northern Yokuts followed the widespread native custom of setting fire to the vegetation in an effort to improve the following year's seed crop (Cook 1960:242, 248).

Dogs were the only domesticated animals kept in aboriginal times. They may have been reared, as in other Yokuts tribes, primarily for eating. Captured wild animals, such as young deer, were occasionally raised as prized pets (Cook 1960:260).

Culture

Clothing and Adornment

What sort of clothing the natives wore can only be guessed, for early travelers failed to describe native costume. In keeping with the generally amiable climate and with California Indian custom, it must not have been very elaborate. Necklaces of marine shells were favored for personal adornment, with olivellas most preferred (Olsen and Payen 1968:10–11, 1969:5–7; Pritchard 1970:28). The shells were secured in trade from coastal tribes or picked up during excursions to the seashore.

Structures

The usual dwellings consisted of small, lightly built structures, covered with tule stalks, apparently woven into mats. An 1819 chronicler described the habitations he observed in a recently deserted village on the San Joaquin as "composed solely of the same tules, with their ends bent [? *dobladas sus puntas*] like those I had seen on

NAA, Smithsonian.

Fig. 2. Chulamni man with three lines tattooed on his chin. Lithograph (Choris 1822) based on lost watercolor by Louis Choris, 1816.

the shores of the river and sloughs" (Gayton 1936:83). Archeological work has brought to light a few additional facts. Round to oval, hard-packed dirt floors, 25–40 feet across and sunk two feet below ground level, have been exposed at settlements once tenanted by Yokuts in both Merced and Fresno counties (Olsen and Payen 1968:38, 1969:36; Pritchard 1970:31–40). From the combined information it seems sufficiently clear that the shelters corresponded in construction and design to the single-family dwellings of the upper San Joaquin valley, the type being an oval framework of light poles pulled together at the top, to which was attached large tule mats. The elongated multifamily houses erected by some Southern Yokuts groups seem not to have been built. Within the community, the individual residences were scattered about, without any perceptible order (Gayton 1936:83). The arrangement differed in the southern valley, where houses stood in a single regular row.

Besides dwellings, there appear to have been two other kinds of structures—the sweathouse and the ceremonial assembly chamber. Comparable characteristics suggest that remains unearthed at an archeological site on Little Panoche Creek in Fresno County are those of an earth-covered sweathouse (Olsen and Payen 1968:36). Very likely each community possessed one or more of these typical buildings. Seen at the above-mentioned deserted San Joaquin river village was "a sweathouse of considerable capacity" (Gayton 1936:83). This may well have been an earth-covered ceremonial lodge of the Central California variety, for Spanish visitors to the native settlements habitually called such edifices "sweathouses." Actually the ritual chamber was built like the sudatory, but on a much more ample scale. Surviving portions of what must have been a large (84 by 93 feet) communal structure were found in a former Indian village on Los Banos Creek in Merced County (Pritchard 1970:32–35). The possible presence of the ceremonial earth lodge among the Northern Yokuts is of more than passing interest because of its close connection elsewhere in aboriginal California with a specialized cult system. No buildings for dances or rituals were constructed by the southern San Joaquin tribes.

Technology

Little concerning arts and crafts can be gleaned from the written records, and as far as is known, no ethnographic examples have survived in museums or in private collections to illustrate the kinds of articles manufactured and the technical processes employed. Basket weaving, native California's foremost handicraft, undoubtedly supplied a wide assortment of containers as well as other items. Carbonized fragments, preserved archeologically at the Los Banos Creek site, demonstrate knowledge of the coiling technique and of a peculiar sort of work in which a spiral foundation of tules was bound with string (Pritchard 1970:41–42). The latter has been reported only

for the Tachi of the Tulare Lake region, who used it in fabricating mealing trays. Various twining techniques must also have been utilized. Mats, too, were woven (Cook 1960:248, 250). The common material used for matting in the San Joaquin valley consisted of tule stalks.

Specimens dug from the ground show that local craftsmen fashioned a wide range of essential tools and implements from stone. For pulverizing acorns, roots, and seeds they made stone mortars and pestles. Wooden mortars may also have been used. Hand- and milling stones were manufactured, but with less frequency. Arrowpoints, knives, and scraping tools were chipped mostly from pieces of chert, jasper, and chalcedony, obtainable locally. Obsidian, an imported substance, saw only sparing use. Still other stone tools included simple hand-held hammers and choppers. Mammal bones supplied artisans with a second important raw material. Of the bone tools, the awl, used primarily in the manufacture of coiled baskets, occupied the most prominent place in the domestic kit. Earthenware vessels, prepared by Yokuts living in the foothills and possibly by a few valley tribes (Gayton 1929:249, fig. 3), do not seem to have been made; however, trade pieces occasionally reached the Northern Yokuts, for potsherds occur sporadically in their homeland (Olsen and Payen 1968:55–56; Pritchard 1970:17).

Travel and Trade

Rafts fashioned by lashing together bundles of tules provided the means of water transport (Gayton 1936:83). The light and buoyant watercraft probably served fishermen as well. Even though the nature of the country strongly favored movement from place to place by water, travel by foot was by no means neglected. Straight, beaten paths running through meadows and along riverbanks were observed by a Spanish exploring party on the lower Merced and Tuolumne rivers (Cook 1960:240).

The Northern Yokuts also journeyed into the territory of adjoining peoples. Well-traveled trails struck west into the land of the Salinan in the Coast Range (Gayton 1945:409). In historic times mounted Yokuts bands made regular visits to Monterey Bay in Costanoan country (Pilling 1950). Whether these excursions occurred in pre-Spanish times is uncertain.

Trade relations were maintained with other peoples. From the Miwok, the Northern Yokuts obtained baskets and bows and arrows; in return they gave dog pups (Barrett and Gifford 1933:270). Mussels and abalone shells were received in exchanges of goods with Costanoans. It is not known what the Yokuts bartered for these products.

Social Organization

No fragment of evidence bearing on Northern Yokuts social units has been preserved in the original chronicles; however, chances are strong that society, as elsewhere in

465

California, was built on the family. Too, there is reason to believe that the lower San Joaquin Indians divided the population into two interacting halves. Their association with fellow Yokuts to the south as well as with upland Miwok, both of whom possessed a totemic moiety system based upon patrilineal descent, render it likely that this form of organization prevailed among most if not all of them (Kroeber 1925:493).

A few random references to social usages are contained in the documentary sources. One custom—extending lavish hospitality to visitors—stands out. Guests were entertained generously and kindly, being warmly welcomed, provided with mats to sit on, invited to partake of food, and given presents (Palóu 1926:130; Cook 1960:248-250). The display of friendliness included the sprinkling of seeds over the arrivals by an old woman. Also alluded to is the familiar institution of the berdache or transvestite (Gayton 1936:81).

Political Organization

There were miniature tribes of 300 or so people. Any attempt at this late date to determine the correct number and designations of these local groups and to accurately fix their territories is beset with great difficulties. Even so, many of the tribes mentioned in the written records of the Spanish-Mexican period can be named and approximately placed (fig. 1). In the delta region, probably extending from the lower Calaveras River through the tule swamps west of the main river channel to Tom Paine slough, lived the Chulamni (including the Cholbones, the Nototemne, and the Coybos, mentioned in the early records). Farther south, a long stretch of territory, from about opposite the mouth of the Merced down to the big bend of the San Joaquin at Mendota, was held by the Nopchinchi. An area on the Stanislaus below the foothills and east of the main river was inhabited by the Lakisamni, including the Leuchas, a tribe thought to have lived around Manteca. Of uncertain situation is the lower valley of the Merced. A Spanish exploring expedition noted villages along the river, but the chronicler failed to list a tribal name (Cook 1960:248). The "Coconoon" reported in this general region in later times may have been a composite group, made up of fragments of several tribes. Below the Merced came the Chawchila, on the plains along the several channels of the Chowchilla, and the Hewchi, who held the north side, or perhaps both banks, of the lower Fresno. On the north side of the San Joaquin where it flows across the lowlands before turning north lived the Hoyima; on the opposite bank were the Pitkachi, and farther upstream, the Wakichi. Additional tribal designations are given in the documentary sources. Quite possibly some of these represent different names for the tribes mentioned above; others apparently refer to village sites or to the inhabitants of a particular place. Open to doubt is Kah-watch-wah, meaning 'grass nut people,' an appellation for a local group said to have occupied the San Joaquin below the Pitkachi and around the towns of Firebaugh and Mendota (Latta 1949:14). This may well be a descriptive rather than a tribal name.

A headman guided each tribe; references to such leaders occur with some frequency in the early records. In some instances the Spaniards referred to a particular tribe or its main village by the name of its chief. A second office appears to have been that of messenger or herald (Cook 1960:249-250).

It is plain that most of the members of a tribe congregated in one principal settlement, and here the headman dwelt. Often this community bore the same name as the tribe. Thus, the village of Nupchenche constituted the main settlement of the Nopchinchi tribe and Pitkachi (Pizcache) that of the Pitkachi. Quick head counts and estimates, both subject to high potential error, place the populations of the cardinal settlements at 200-250 or more (Cook 1955:51, 1960:253-254). Smaller communities, some mere hamlets containing two or three houses, also existed.

Settlement

Most settlements, at least the principal ones, sat perched on top of low mounds, on or near the banks of large watercourses (Schenck 1926:132; Schenck and Dawson 1929:308; Cook 1960:242, 259, 285). The elevated positions helped to keep the inhabitants, their houses, and their possessions above the waters of the spring floods. A strong tendency toward sedentary life, fostered no doubt by the abundant riverine resources, was evident, with the same sites occupied for generations. Flooding posed the chief threat to a fully stationary existence. Rampaging rivers, swollen by melting Sierran snows and heavy rains, periodically overflowed their banks and drove the villagers to even higher ground. Disruption of community life also occurred seasonally when the local group broke up into smaller units for the harvesting of wild plant products. Generally, a handful of aged persons remained behind when the more active members went off to gather acorns and seeds (Cook 1960:251, 264).

War

Originally the Northern Valley Yokuts were not prone to warfare and the various tribes lived in peace with one another; however, petty hostilities did arise, as illustrated by the conflicts between peoples living on the San Joaquin and those occupying the shores of Tulare Lake (Gayton 1930a:59). Warriors painted their faces and bedecked themselves with feathers before entering an affray (Chapman 1911:19; Cook 1960:259). Their primary war weapon consisted of the bow and stone-tipped arrow, probably carried in a skin case (fig. 3) (Mahr 1932:365). Before commencing the battle, combatants hurled insults back and forth (Cook 1960:259). In Hispanic times, as missionaries and soldiers drew near a

Fig. 3. Chulamni men with bow, arrows, and animal skin quiver. Lithograph (Choris 1822) based on lost watercolor by Louis Choris, 1816.

village, its inhabitants often fled into the tule swamps and woods or took refuge in an inaccessible spot (Gayton 1936:83; Cook 1960:249, 250, 260, 263, 270), sometimes dismantling their houses and removing their possessions before abandoning the settlement. The general impression gained is that they were following a long-established native custom of retreating rather than fighting. Lighting fires to signal the approach of a potential enemy may also have been an aboriginal habit (Gayton 1936:83).

Religion

Not much is known, or perhaps can be known, about the lower San Joaquin Indians' religious beliefs and practices. Statements by members of bordering tribes suggest that they participated in two widespread Californian ritual systems—the datura and the Kuksu. Sierra Miwok informants declared that their Yokuts neighbors on the Stanislaus had a ceremony centering around the drinking of a decoction prepared from the roots of the datura plant (Kroeber 1925:502); and a sketchy account of such a ritual, as followed by Valley Yokuts living between Madera and Friant, was obtained from a Monache Indian (Merriam 1966–1967, 1:68–69). The plant roots contain an alkaloid that produces stupor and visions. In the southern valley, young adults drank the mixture in order to gain various supernatural benefits (Gayton 1948, 1:38).

Evidence for participation in the north-central California god-impersonating cult, known as Kuksu, is not altogether satisfactory. Though the Miwok attributed many of their observances of the Kuksu type to their Yokuts neighbors of the adjacent valley (Kroeber

1925:371), at least some of these came from a postcontact community near Pleasanton in Alameda county, which was made up of former San José Mission neophytes who included Coast Miwok converts (Gifford 1926a: 399–400). The Pleasanton settlement included Costanoans and Plains Miwoks as well as Yokuts. Their geographical position, between and in contact with tribes who followed the Kuksu (Kroeber 1925:371), and their building of large earth-covered structures of the kind in which the god-impersonating ceremonies were regularly held increase the likelihood that the Northern Yokuts had assimilated at least the essentials of the colorful and exciting cult. The Kuksu, probably the most vivid expression of California Indian religious life, did not extend into the upper San Joaquin.

Solemnities connected with the crises of life—birth, puberty, and death—almost surely figured prominently in the religion. But apart from the manner of disposing of the deceased, no information on these observances has been found. When a Northern Yokuts expired, his body was cremated or buried in a flexed position (Olsen and Payen 1969:39; Pritchard 1970:30–31). This difference in custom cannot be readily accounted for, though mixed cremation and burial was not exceptional in aboriginal California (Gould 1963:155–158, map 2). Inhumation was the usual practice in the southern valley, with cremation reserved for tribesmen who died away from home, shamans, and, among the Tachi, persons of any consequence (Kroeber 1925:499). Whether the lower San Joaquin peoples shared their southern kinsmen's obsession with death and mourning has not been determined.

Since shamanism was strongly developed in native California, it can be taken for granted that the various river tribes had their full quotas of practitioners who treated disease by supernatural means.

History

Contacts with Whites proved disastrous for the Northern Valley Yokuts. The sequence of events leading to their decline closely parallels that in several other parts of the state. First, in the Spanish-Mexican period, 1769–1846, there was a gradual erosion of the aboriginal culture, coupled with a progressive decline in population. Then came rapid and nearly total destruction in the years immediately following the American conquest of California and the gold rush.

For most of the tribes, their initial encounter with outsiders came in the first decade of the nineteenth century when Spanish expeditions began to actively explore the delta and lower San Joaquin valley. The explorations, by land and water, were accomplished by small, often poorly equipped parties (Cutter 1950:ii), composed of a few soldiers, an officer, and a priest. Indian auxiliaries, who acted as guides and interpreters, sometimes accompanied them. Usually, the Yokuts greeted the soldiers and padres warmly, though now and then, warily, or even with hostility (Cook 1960:259). A few persons—old women mainly, an aged man or two, an adult in dying condition, or a sick child—were baptized in their native villages. These sporadic contacts affected the Indian manner of living only in a minor way, if at all.

The process of extinction and cultural breakdown commenced when the valley peoples were drawn into the mission system. As native populations in the vicinity of their coastal establishments became exhausted, the Franciscans gathered converts from farther and farther inland. Intensive proselytizing among the lower San Joaquin tribes began around 1805 and continued into the early 1820s. Sizable numbers of them were taken to the San José, Santa Clara, Soledad, San Juan Bautista, and San Antonio missions (Merriam 1955:188–225, 1968: 48–77). Whether the neophytes came willingly or by force is not always clear.

Compelled to work at strange tasks and subjected to the restrictive routine and severe discipline of mission life, many of the newly baptized Indians deserted and returned to their interior homes. Soldiers were regularly sent to bring them back. The pursuit of the runaways seems to have been motivated not so much by a desire to punish the fugitives and to keep them in subjection as it was to ward off their allying themselves with wild tribesmen in forays against the mission herds. For the fugitives had imparted to their unconverted brethren, along with other mission ideas and Spanish colonial ways, a taste for meat. Raiding parties—many organized and led by exneophytes—began to prey on the herds. Because of the ease with which horses could be driven off, their flesh became preferred (Heizer 1941b).

To offset the growing threat of the unchristianized natives as well as to convert them, proposals were put forth to extend the mission system inland (Beattie 1929, 1930). Several exploring expeditions were sent out to choose likely spots for the establishments. Yet, despite continued efforts by the Franciscan padres, supported at times by the civil authorities, the interior chain of institutions never materialized.

Disruption of aboriginal life did not end with the change of flag in 1822 from Spanish to Mexican, though the new government made no serious effort to penetrate the San Joaquin. Ranching was instituted at several points on the west side and at the delta fringes, but the rest of the valley remained in its pristine state. The hostility of the interior tribes and the increasing boldness and effectiveness of their horse stealing discouraged settlement beyond. As the Indians became hungrier for horse meat, they began to range farther and farther west and outlying ranches in Coast Range valleys became constant targets for their depredations. Dozens of retaliatory expeditions were sent out by local officials. These met with very little success: some natives were killed, a few villages were burned, but the thefts of livestock continued unabated. Posses were organized by individual ranchers who had lost animals. Often these turned into slave-raiding parties, which brought back women and children to serve as laborers and domestics.

The Mexican period witnessed two events of importance for the northern valley tribes—a sudden and sharp drop in their numbers and the secularization of the mission establishments. Already the native population had suffered a progressive decline, due to the drawing off of converts to the missions and to European diseases against which they had little resistance. Decimation occurred in the summer of 1833 when a terrible pestilence swept the valley and claimed thousands of lives. So great was the catastrophe that entire communities disappeared and certain tribes were virtually wiped out. The disease, evidently transmitted by beaver trappers from the Columbia River, has been identified as malaria (Cook 1955a:303–308).

Under pressure from the outset of Mexican rule, the Franciscan missions, in 1834, became converted into ordinary parish churches, their neophytes freed from the complete supervision of the padres, and much of their lands released for other utilization. Many of the missionized Indians returned to their former homeland, though not necessarily to the precise villages or localities from which they had come. Some organized themselves into polyglot communities, made up of members of different tribes. Like the runaways before them, the exneophytes aided and abetted horse stealing.

Considerable tribal and territorial readjustment was set in motion. Surviving fragments of tribes amalgamated and boundaries shifted. By 1830, for example, the Miwok had acquired control of former Chulamni territory on the Calaveras (Bennyhoff 1961:319). Tribal movements had occurred earlier. In response to attacks on their villages by Spanish soldiery, the Leuchas who had formerly lived west of the San Joaquin crossed to a less vulnerable position on the east bank (Cook 1955:59).

Annihilation of the Indians came a few short years after the American conquest of California in 1846, largely as a result of the 1849 gold rush and its aftermath. While the northern San Joaquin was not gold country, thousands of prospectors bound for the southern mines passed through it, relentlessly pushing aside any natives in their path. After the initial upheaval, the rich soils of the delta and valley attracted many exminers to farming. As they filled up the district, the remaining Yokuts were driven off their hunting and food-gathering lands.

The process of dispossession proved relatively easy. The settlers forcibly ousted or murdered families or communities. Sometimes the tribesmen were roused to acts of resistance or retaliation, but they showed little tendency toward concerted opposition. Atrocities were committed by both Whites and Indians. The military failed to deal effectively with the problem.

With this situation at hand, plans for a reservation system were drawn up in 1850 (C.B. Leonard 1928). Bowing to the inevitable, the headmen of surviving groups signed treaties by terms of which they ceded all the land they owned or claimed (Heizer 1972). Only three Northern Yokuts tribes—Hewchi, Chawchila, and Pitkachi—were among the signers; a possible fourth, the Coconoon, seem to have been a composite political unit. For the land cessions, the government set aside fairly adequate reservations.

Pressure from the new state of California prevented the treaties from being ratified by the United States Senate. The rejection of the treaties left nothing for the unfortunate little tribes to do except drift about, scrabbling for a living as best they could, since they had already been moved off the surrendered land and White settlers had encroached upon the promised reservations. Some found refuge on ranches where they worked as laborers. Usually held in low esteem by their employers, who complained that they were shiftless and dirty, addicted to drink, and undependable, the Indians were poorly paid and housed and practically held in bondage. Finally, conditions became so bad that federal authorities took cognizance of the situation and set aside tracts of land for them, including leased acreage on the Fresno and the Tule River Reserve.

The subsequent vicissitudes of the northern San Joaquin tribes duplicate those of the majority of native Californians. In the 1970s their representatives live scattered among Whites or other Indians. Most have lost their identity, and it is only by hard search that a few can be found. The survivors live generally in obscurity and poverty on the fringes of the White society.

Synonymy

Only a relatively small number of village names have been recorded. In the following list (based on Kroeber 1925:484–486; Schenck 1926:137–141; Cook 1955:51, 67, 1960:283, 289) the villages are arranged by tribe. Tribal names are given first in the anglicized spellings used by Kroeber (1963:237), but with ch for his ṭ. Next, and in italics, are the Yokuts pronunciations of the tribal names, where known, as provided by Geoffrey Gamble (personal communication 1974). After these are some major variant names from older sources.

Chulamni, *čʰulamni*, Chulamne, Cholbon, Cholovomnes, Nochochomne, Nototemne.
Yachik (near Stockton)
Wane (near Stockton, just below landing)
Pescadero (on southwest side of Union Island, a mile or two northeast of Bethany)
Jusmites
Tugites
Tomchom (name of chief)

Nopchinchi, *nopʰṭʰinṭʰi*, Nopṭinchi, Noptinte, Nupchenche.

    Cheneches (probably opposite mouth of Mariposa Creek, north of Los Banos)

    Malim (upstream from Cheneches)

    Nupchenche

    Catucho

    Copicha (opposite mouth of Chowchilla)

    Tape (near or just south of great bend of San Joaquin)

Lakisamni, *lakʰisamni,* Leuchas.

    Lakisamne

    Leuchas

    Pitemis (Aupimis)

East side of San Joaquin, from vicinity of Manteca to just below mouth of Merced, tribal name unknown or uncertain.

    Cuyens

    Mayem

    Bozenats (probably name of chief)

    Taitones (may be larger unit, including more than one village)

    Aplagamne (may be larger unit, including more than one village)

Lower Merced, tribal name uncertain.

    Chineguis

    Yunate

    Chamuasi

    Latelate (on south bank)

    Lachuo (on south bank, west of Latelate)

Chawchila, *čʰawčʰila*, plural *čʰaweˑčʰali* (also recorded as *čʰawšila, čʰaweˑšali* and as *čawsila, čaweˑsali*).

    Shehamniu (on Chowchilla, apparently at edge of plain, some miles below Buchanan)

    Halau (at Berenda)

Hewchi, *hewčʰi*, plural *hewačʰinawi*, Heuchi.

    Ch'ekayu (on Fresno, four miles below Madera)

Hoyima, *hoyima*, plural *hoyeˑyami*, Hoyma.

    K'eliutanau (on creek entering San Joaquin from north)

    Moyoliu (above mouth of Little Dry Creek)

Pitkachi, *pʰitʰkʰaṭʰi*, plural *pʰitʰeˑkʰaṭʰi* or *pʰitʰaˑkʰaṭʰi*.

    Pitkachi (Pizcache)

    Kohuou (near Herndon)

    Weshiu (on slough)

    Gewachiu (downstream from Kohuou)

Wakichi, *wakʰiyčʰi*, plural *wakʰeˑyačʰi*.

    Holowichniu (near Millerton)

Sources

The very meager body of knowledge about the Northern Valley Yokuts is furnished primarily by Spanish military men and missionaries who preserved glimpses of the life and customs of the groups with whom they came into contact. In the early nineteenth century small parties of soldiers made frequent forays into the San Joaquin valley to seek converts and mission runaways, to find favorable sites for an inland chain of missions, and to pursue and punish horse thieves. The commandants of these little expeditions and/or the priests who accompanied them kept diaries or made reports. None of the accounts is very illuminating ethnographically, but taken together, they provide a fund of useful information on tribal and village names, locations, and numbers. The majority of the documentary sources have been made easily available in translation (Chapman 1911; Palóu 1926; Gayton 1936; Cook 1960). Data on the placement of tribes and villages and the aboriginal population have been assembled from the written records (Schenck 1926; Cook 1955; Bennyhoff 1961).

Further facts may be contained in the replies made by padres at 19 of the Franciscan missions to a questionnaire on native customs distributed by the Spanish government in 1812; however, because the neophytes at any one establishment were drawn from different tribes, speaking diverse languages, none of the material can be with confidence attributed to the Northern Valley Yokuts. Copies of 18 of the padres' answers, known as *Preguntas y Repuestas,* are contained in the Santa Barbara Mission Archives (Geiger 1949, 1953). Transcripts of the documents made in 1877 are available in the Bancroft Library, University of California, Berkeley. Most of the replies have been translated and published singly; they have been treated as a whole only by Kroeber (1908a).

Due to the early decimation of the native dwellers of the lower San Joaquin, it was not possible for later ethnographers to fill out the deficiencies of the contact-period documentary sources. A few vocabularies exist, from which the linguistic affiliation of the various northern tribes can be established (Kroeber 1907, 1908c, 1959a, 1963). The Chulamni vocabulary recorded by A. Pinart in 1880 at Pleasanton is reprinted in Merriam (1955:133–138) accompanied by a discussion of its identification, with references to the literature. For prehistory, there is a general summary pertaining to the northern valley (Schenck and Dawson 1929), a few detailed reports for the west side (Olsen and Payen 1968, 1969; Pritchard 1970), and little else.

Foothill Yokuts

ROBERT F. G. SPIER

The Foothill Yokuts are a group of about 15 named Yokuts tribes who occupied the western slopes of the Sierra Nevada from the Fresno River southward to the Kern River (fig. 1). A further division into Northern Foothill (including the Chukchansi, Dumna, Kechayi, and Gashowu of the Fresno and San Joaquin river drainages), Central Foothill (including the Choynimni, Chukaymina, Gawia, Yokod, Wikchamni, and Yawdanchi of the Kings, Kaweah, and Tule river drainages), and Southern Foothill (primarily the Palewyami of the Poso Creek drainage) has been customary (Kroeber 1925; Gayton 1948). Problems of tribal synonymy do not loom large, but the enumeration of tribes is complicated by extinctions, the substantial independence of small groups of people, and confusion from the marked differences between singular and plural forms of tribal names. Kroeber (1925:478–482) has named at some length the

tribes of the foothills, and later authors have substantially agreed with him in their names and locations (Swanton 1952:523–525).

The several Yokuts tribes have sometimes been called "subtribes" or "tribelets" in order to reserve the tribal label for all the Yokuts. However, there was no Yokuts nation or any overarching political unity of these tribes within recorded times. The number of the Yokuts tribes, perhaps as many as 50, and the marked differences between peoples only a few miles apart make it unlikely that close alliances existed. This unusual situation, in the California context, is discussed briefly by Kroeber (1925:474–475). The distinctions between groups were most obviously linguistic and territorial; the people of one group spoke a distinct dialect of the Yokuts language and were the denizens of a particular place. Cultural differences were on a grosser scale, as between northern

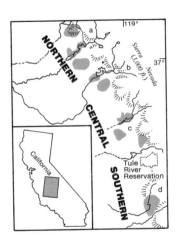

Fig. 1. Tribal territory including: a, Chukchansi, Dumna, Kechayi, and Gashowu tribes; b, Choynimni and Chukaymina tribes; c, Gawia, Wikchamni, Yokod, and Yawdanchi tribes; d, Palewyami tribe.

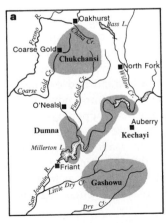
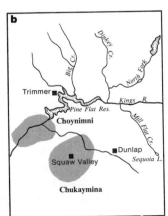
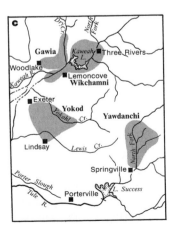
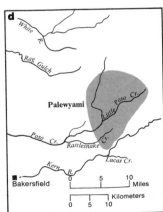

471

and southern foothill peoples or between the foothill and valley Yokuts. It is possible to offer a generic cultural description that applies, with only minor exceptions, to all the Foothill Yokuts.

The individual identity of each Foothill Yokuts tribe is based primarily on residence in a recognized territory, use of a dialect of the Yokuts language, and practice of a way of life slightly different from that of its neighbors. Of these differences, the territorial one is most obvious and the others less clear. Each tribe inhabited one or several villages that were collectively central to the tribal lands. That is, the areas around these villages were considered to be home and to be exploited more or less exclusively by their residents. It appears that generally the territory of a tribe lay within one or two drainage systems, with creeks or valleys forming the stems along which villages were located. It must also be recognized that major rivers, such as the Fresno or the San Joaquin, were often nominal boundaries between tribes. However, the division of Foothill Yokuts tribes into Northern, Central, and Southern groups (a classification of questionable native origin) clusters tribes that fall within a major river drainage, so the boundary effect of rivers was probably more potential than real.

Most of the Yokuts identify more strongly with their individual tribal name or with that of the home village than with the generic Yokuts entity. The tribal names are not necessarily translatable, but the village names often refer to a plant or other physical feature of the location.

Even though intertribal marriages were frequent, at least in the nineteenth and twentieth centuries, and some involved alliances with non-Yokuts peoples, there still existed a strong tribal identification with the father's group. It is difficult to say whether the tribe or the village was the paramount unit of affiliation, but it was probably the tribe. People did move from village to village during a lifetime but remained within the tribe except for outmarriages by the women.

The unity among Yokuts tribes was not so strong as to preclude extra-Yokuts relations locally. The Chukchansi, northernmost of the Foothill Yokuts, had close alliances with the Southern Sierra Miwok, so much so that there is confusion about the tribal affiliation of some border villages. The Central Foothill Yokuts came into increasingly close contact with the Monache in the latter half of the nineteenth century.

Environment and Territory

The Sierra Nevada foothills rise, in 15 to 25 miles, from the San Joaquin valley floor (300–400 feet above sea level at its eastern edge) to elevations over 6,000 feet. Although the major streams generally flow westward or southwestward, their tributaries are irregular in direction and reflect a disorderly arrangement of ridges and valleys.

The rivers have cut few deep gorges so that it is feasible to follow the streams, too swift for navigation, on foot. This habitat includes two major life-zones: the Upper Sonoran, from 600 to 3,300 feet; and the Transition, from 3,300 feet to 6,200 feet. Above the Transition zone lay the more difficult environment of the High Sierra, which had few resources and did not encourage settlement. Most settlements for the Foothill people were between 2,000 and 4,000 feet. Thus a short journey afoot took an individual down to the San Joaquin valley floor or up through the coniferous forests. This close spacing of markedly differing zones broadened the scope of readily available resources.

Tribal boundaries among the Foothill Yokuts were somewhat vague. Streams formed the axis of tribal settlement as often as the boundary. In the Northern Foothill area tribal locations were disrupted by the activities of the Mariposa Battalion in 1851 (Eccleston 1957). Finally, the Yokuts tribes often gathered together or shared ranges during certain seasons of the year (Gayton 1948, 2:159).

Subsistence

The subsistence of the Foothill Yokuts was based on hunting and gathering with fishing as a supplement. Deer, quail, and acorns were prominently mentioned by informants. Beyond these mainstays there were many sources of food: pine nuts, ground squirrels, rabbits, wild oats, manzanita berries, ducks, trout, mussels, and wasp grubs among others. Importantly, the distinctive feature of subsistence was not a dependence upon one abundant resource, but the omnivorous character of the diet. As Kroeber (1925:523–526) has pointed out this diversity gave protection against famine as all these sources were unlikely to fail simultaneously.

Deer were killed with the bow and arrow following still-stalking, driving (sometimes with fire), or an ambush from a booth at a permanent waterhole. Deer disguises, using head, antlers, and skin, are reported as having been used by all Foothill Yokuts except the Chukchansi. There is no evidence for the trapping of deer.

Quail were taken by extensive trapping and by shooting them as they roosted in trees. The quail traps called for substantial community effort, as reported among the Chukchansi. A fence, like a miniature stockade, was made of sticks closely set in the ground and extending upward to a height of a few feet. Noose traps, powered by a bent stick under tension, were set in openings in the fence at intervals of 20 to 50 or more feet. The ground-feeding quail would attempt to walk through these openings rather than fly over the obstacle across their path. These fences, reported as having been as long as a mile, yielded a good supply of birds when regularly patrolled.

472

Acorns were gathered from the ground and shaken from trees, some of which were claimed as private property. Green acorns were peeled with the teeth and sun-dried; they kept longer in storage than acorns gathered dry, up to five years. Dried acorns had their shells cracked by being placed on a pitted anvil stone and struck with a hammerstone (fig. 2). The dried acorns were pounded into a meal in a bedrock mortar located near the village or habitation. (These granite outcrops with deeply worn holes serve today to identify the locations of aboriginal residence sites.) The acorns to yield a day's supply of meal were usually pounded at one time. The resultant meal was then leached to remove the bitter tannic acid, using either a sandy basin on the ground or one elevated on a platform of small sticks (R.F.G. Spier 1956). Acorn meal was baked into cakes but more commonly was cooked into a mush using a basket and heated stones.

Salmon were taken by spearing along the major rivers in the fall. They were eaten fresh and strips of flesh were sun-dried for storage. Other fish were caught using weirs of stones or willows across a stream with a basket trap or sack in the small opening. Fish were driven into the weir by wading about or the use of a brush drag (Powers 1877:376). As intermittent streams dried up during the summer, fish were stupefied in the resulting pools by poisoning them with pounded buckeye fruits. In the same context fish might also be caught by hand or scooped ashore with baskets. Salmon fishing was primarily a man's task, while fishing for smaller fish and for shellfish involved women as well. There is little evidence to indicate marked ownership of fishing places; the major streams on which they were located were often tribal boundaries so probably some sharing took place.

NAA, Smithsonian.
Fig. 2. Eda Ichow cracking acorns on soapstone anvil. Photograph by Click Relander, 1938–1939.

Culture

Technology

Before the coming of Europeans the Yokuts had no use of metals. Their stone working, both chipped and ground, was primarily in obsidian (partly from the east slopes of the Sierra Nevada), granite and quartz (available locally), and soapstone (from sources in the foothills). Ethnographic studies came too long after contact to record much of stone working in the making of cutting tools; metals had taken over the scene. However, the making of mortars and pestles of granite and of acorn anvils and stone-boiling stones from soapstone continued into the twentieth century.

The Foothill Yokuts bows were both plain (self) and sinew-backed, often from mountain cedar (juniper) and strung with sinew. Length was from three and one-half feet to about five feet with the shorter bows being backed and broader. Evidently neither bow had any substantial reflex curve. Though a Chukchansi informant supplied a description of the making of a sinew-backed bow, the bulk of these bows were obtained from the Monache (Gayton 1948, 1:73). Powers also reported a trade in bows (quoted in Gayton 1948:73).

Arrows were composed of a stone point, a wooden foreshaft, and a wooden or cane shaft in varying combinations. In some wooden-shafted arrows the shaft itself was pointed and heat-hardened. Cane arrows regularly had wooden foreshafts or points. Stone points were attached to a foreshaft. All arrows were regularly feathered. Evidence conflicts on the nature of war arrows, which may have been more or less lethal than hunting arrows. Kroeber (1925:530) suggests that war arrows lacked stone points, but Gayton (1948, 2:219), writing of Central Foothill Yokuts, clearly states the opposite.

Stone arrow points are regularly described by Kroeber and Powers as of "flint." There is no reason to find this literally true as the Foothill Yokuts seem to have made wide use of obsidian and quartz for this purpose. Obsidian is said to have been obtained by trade from the Valley Yokuts of Tulare Lake who, in turn, must have obtained it from elsewhere; Gayton (1948, 1:73) suggests the Coast Range. Other obsidian came semifinished from the Eastern Monos (Owens Valley Paiute) (Gayton 1948, 2:219).

Crafts among the Foothill Yokuts were completely simple except for basketry. In this circumstance they did not differ greatly from many California tribes.

Tanning of hides was rudimentary. Beyond simple scraping and working of the skin there was use of deer brains, cooked or moistened, to produce an oil tan. Ashes assisted in the dehairing of skins. Long strips of scraped rabbit skins were twisted or allowed to twist as they dried, resulting in a furry rope that was woven into a blanket. Tanning was commonly done by men.

The looped-stick mush stirrer was a characteristic domestic implement that continued to be made and used, 473 at least to 1950, by those Indians who still stone-boiled acorns. The implement was formed from a single stick bent back on itself to form a small loop (about five inches in diameter); its overall length was about 30 inches. The artifact seems to be shared by the Yokuts more with peoples of Nevada than with other Californians.

Both wooden bowls and wooden mortars (fig. 3) are attributed to the tribes of the northern foothills (Aginsky 1943:407; Kroeber 1925:528), but they evidently did not loom large as household goods since baskets and bedrock mortars were abundant.

Pottery of a utilitarian nature was made by the Central Foothill Yokuts tribes. There is a questionable report of pottery among the Chukchansi of the Northern foothills (Aginsky 1943:458), but elsewhere it was evidently absent. The distribution of the craft suggests that it reached the Yokuts by way of the Monache (Western Mono) from the Eastern Mono of Owens Valley (Gayton 1929:250). The ware was sand-tempered (often naturally), substantially undecorated, and usually formed of concentric coils smoothed upon their neighbors. The products were mostly bowls with flat bottoms, flaring straight sides, and slightly incurved rims. Small bowls and tubular pipes, for tobacco smoking, were hand modeled. The craft was entirely in the hands of women, but not all women knew it.

Basketry of good quality was made by all the Foothill Yokuts although Kroeber (1925:532) considers that of the northerners to be inferior. Both twined and coiled baskets were made with the former technique employed

NAA, Smithsonian.
Fig. 3. Woman pounding acorns in an oak mortar and open-end basket hopper. Photograph by Click Relander, about 1938-1939.

for openwork products, such as sieves, winnowers, and cages. However, a generic cooking basket was produced by close twining. The coiled baskets placed slightly more stress on appearance than did the generally utilitarian twined products. Finish was better, decoration somewhat more elaborate, and the types included those made as gifts or for display. Gayton (1948, 1:18-19) illustrates seven types of twined baskets and nine types of coiled baskets; in her tabulation, those of the Wikchamni and Michahay pertain to tribes of the central foothills. Basketry patterns tend to be horizontal on baskets, or circular in the instance of trays, and prevailingly of simple geometric forms (steps, zigzags, triangles) in bands or zones, although anthropomorphic designs were also used (fig. 4). Kroeber (1925:533) offers a series of Yawdanchi designs and related comments. Coiled baskets, most notably the "Tulare bottleneck," also called a "treasure basket" (fig. 5), and gambling trays are characteristic of Foothill Yokuts. Only in the late nineteenth century was the technique of coiling employed to a significant degree by the Valley Yokuts.

Cradles for infants were a special and changing category of basketry. Evidently the common form of the past (in the early nineteenth century?) was built on a Y-shaped foundation formed by a forked stick. The frame had several crosspieces or a cross-lashing and was often padded with a tule mattress (Kroeber 1925:fig. 48d; Gayton 1948, 1:86). This style gave way before one after a Monache model, which was a flat trapezoid of vertical parallel sticks twined laterally. The cradle had a hoop or band of similar twined work that extended forward over the infant's head. On top of the hoop might be added a twined sunshade. The sex of the cradle's occupant was indicated by the decorative pattern on the hoop and the back of the cradle. There is some confusion about the correlation of markings with the sexes: Kroeber (1925:536) found parallel diagonal lines on a boy's cradle and zigzags on a girl's, as did R.F.G. Spier (1954:117, 121); Gayton (1948, 2:188) reports that zigzags marked a boy's cradle and diamonds a girl's. One is led to conclude that the idea of marking was widespread but that the marks themselves were locally variable.

Cordage was made from milkweed (*Asclepias*) fiber rolled into a two-ply string by action of the palm on the bare thigh. Hemp or dogbane was used to make another fine string. Rough cord or rope was twisted from the inner bark of willow.

From cords were made carrying nets and the tumpline with which these nets, carrying baskets, and some cradles were carried on the back. The carrying nets were produced by a knotting technique. The tumplines and similar belts that supported breechclouts and aprons were made by sewing back and forth through a series of parallel, twisted cords. Gayton (1948, 1:83-85, fig.13) has illustrated some of these techniques in detail.

Fig. 4. Woman coiling a basket with multiple foundation of grass. The basket with anthropomorphic designs contains a bone awl. Photographed on Tule River Reservation about 1900.

FOOTHILL YOKUTS

Fig. 5. Coiled "treasure basket" with rattlesnake design. Decorated with quail topknot feathers and red wool yarn around the shoulder. Height, 17 cm; collected about 1900.

Rabbitskin blankets, prized as warm bedding, were made locally and derived from trade with the Monache. Skins of other small animals and some birds (ground squirrels, ducks, quail) were similarly treated, but each blanket was made solely of one kind of skin. When intended for blanket use, and this was the prime use of rabbitskins, the animal was skinned by removing the skin as a tube. From the scraped and dried tubular skin was cut a long strip, around and around the tube. These strips were twisted and allowed to double back on themselves, producing a four-stranded furry rope. The ropes, laid out parallel, were sewed across through the twists. There is some question about the use of a frame to suspend the twisted ropes while being sewed, but in any case the frame was not a true loom and the technique was not true weaving (Gayton 1948, 1:81–82).

Structures

The structures of the Foothill Yokuts included: a conical dwelling (fig. 6) in at least two forms, a flat shade or

Fig. 6. Chukchansi brush house on China Creek near Fresno Flat. Photograph by C. Hart Merriam, Sept. 1902.

Fig. 7. Wikchamni ramada, or sun shade, on the Kaweah River near Lemon Cove. Photograph by C. Hart Merriam, Aug. 1902.

ramada (fig. 7), a sweathouse, and a hemispherical shade (grinding booth) (fig. 8).

The conical houses were 12 to 15 feet in diameter with a height slightly less than that. The floor might be excavated to the depth of a foot but was otherwise unmodified. The framing, of two-inch poles set into the ground and brought together at the top of the house, was strengthened by three circumferential hoops tied on the inside. In the central foothills the top of the frame had an interior ring that defined the smoke hole. The Chukchansi technique was unusual; they tied their framing pieces together at the apex, without a ring, and left a hole over the door as a smoke exit. The exterior of the house was covered with a thatch of local materials (such as tarweed or pine needles) and/or with slabs of pine or cedar bark held in place with encircling lashings (according to the Chukchansi). The Yawdanchi are reported as having used tule mats as the house covering, a Valley Yokuts trait (Kroeber 1925:522).

The doorway was sometimes equipped with a small overhanging rainshed (as among the Chukchansi) and closed with a hanging mat. Inside the door by a distance of several feet, which placed it substantially under the overdoor vent or the apex smoke hole, was a small fire. It was mainly fed by a long log, gradually pushed in through the doorway. Back from the fire were beds of pine needles on which people sat and slept with their feet toward the fire.

The flat shade had five posts, one at each corner and one in the center, set into the ground with their tops connected by smaller poles and sticks to form a base for piled brush. The structure was about 10 by 15 feet and 7 feet high. The ground beneath was not specially treated but became hardened with use. The shade was built in the vicinity of dwellings as a shaded outdoor living and work place and occasionally a hot-weather sleeping place. Such shades were often used as the sole dwelling when away temporarily from the home village during the summer. (Summer rains in the foothills are exceedingly

476

rare; rains from thunderstorms fall sporadically in the higher Sierra.) Powers (1877:513) observed a Chukchansi mourning ceremony held on a ground bounded on three sides by a row of these shades that served as camps for the celebrants.

The sweathouse came in two forms according to its size and the locality. The northern Foothills Yokuts, as reported for the Chukchansi, built a circular structure (18 feet in diameter, up to 8 feet high) with a low conical roof. The floor was excavated to several feet below grade and a frame of heavy oak timbers erected. Roof beams of saplings held a layer of brush, which was then covered with earth. The doorway was in the lower portion of the roof wall with the fire close inside. A smoke hole was left at the top of the roof. There is some question about the presence of a central post to hold up the structure. Logically there must have been one, but it is not mentioned in Gayton's account, which instead notes the possibility of use of the Miwok four-post design (Gayton 1948, 2:186). However, the four-post design was for the Miwok earth lodge, not their sweat lodge (Barrett and Gifford 1933:200-206).

The Central Foothills Yokuts had two forms of sweathouse. The smaller (about 15 feet diameter) was circular and had a center post. In many respects it seems like that of the Chukchansi, lending support to the supposition of a center post in the northern structure. The larger sweathouse (about 20 feet in major diameter) was more elliptical and had two main posts supporting a short center beam. Against the beam and the forks atop the main posts were radial poles reaching beyond the edge of the excavation to form rafters. On these a haphazard layer of sticks was laid to support brush and earth. The doorway was not closed but its location, side or end, is uncertain. There was no smoke hole but the fire was just inside the doorway, which doubled as a smoke vent (Gayton 1948, 1:60-61).

Foothill Yokuts sweathouses used only the heat of the fire; no heated stones or steam was employed. The men, with women and children excluded, sat close along the walls and talked or sang while they sweated. Each sweat was followed by a plunge into a nearby pool or stream. Late afternoon was the time for a favored predinner sweat, but a morning session was added if time permitted.

The sweathouses, between sessions, were warm places to relax in cold winter weather. Women evidently went into the houses for this purpose when no men were around; there was no absolute taboo on their presence in the structures. These were merely men's places. Men and boys might sleep in the sweathouse when quarters were crowded at home. Young, single men regularly stayed at the sweathouses. Any village would have one or two sweathouses that were quasi-public structures. They were built, usually at the instigation of the chief and always with his permission, by a group of interested men. One

established no special right by building a sweathouse but had made a civic gesture.

The hemispherical shade was a light, temporary structure built by women for shelter from the sun. A half-dozen flexible poles were set in the ground along a semicircular arc and their tips drawn together and tied. Loose brush or mats were placed on these poles to shade the work place. A shade of this type, sometimes called a grinding booth, was set up over the granite outcrops where bedrock mortars were located (fig. 8).

Lowie Mus., U. of Calif., Berkeley.
Fig. 8. Mary Pohot working at a shaded bedrock mortar. Photograph by Anna H. Gayton, April 1925.

Settlement

There was little organization to Foothill Yokuts settlements. Although Kroeber (1925:522) reports that the Yawdanchi of the central foothills built their houses in rows, there is no evidence of such regularity elsewhere. People built their houses according to individual choice without even consistency as regards door facing. If two houses belonged to one larger family then the doors would face each other. The location of modern houses on the sites of traditional villages, such as the Chukchansi village at Picayune, suggests that formerly houses were built 100 or more feet apart but within view. Sharing of springs, bedrock mortars, sweathouses, and swimming places would tend to hold people within a small area. However, the modern population of a place like Picayune is perhaps one-fifth of that in the early nineteenth century. If the area of the community even approaches that of the past, the density will be much lower and give a spurious air of spaciousness about the settlement.

Transport

Travel among the Foothill Yokuts was on foot and loads were carried on the back. Women often made use of a twined conical burden basket that was stiffened with soaproot juice and equipped with loops for the attachment of a tumpline. A carrying net was also used with the tumpline. Men did not seem to have employed these carrying aids.

Rivers were crossed by swimming by those who were able. A breaststroke was widely employed by the Yokuts and evidently learned during the instruction and toughening of young boys and girls at adolescence (Gayton 1948, 1:104, 2:266). Those unable to swim and household goods were taken across on rafts made of two logs lashed together. The raft was pushed by a wading man if the water was shallow, otherwise by two swimming men. At least the Northern Foothill Yokuts also made use of a basket boat that was coiled, flat-bottomed, and as much as four feet in diameter. This basket, pushed by a swimming man, ferried babies and small goods.

Clothing and Adornment

The general pattern of dress among the Foothill Yokuts included a garment worn at the waist from puberty on. Older men might go naked as suited their convenience. Both men and women made some use of a deerskin breechclout that was long enough to have the end, front and rear, hang over the supporting belt as a short apron. Chukchansi women are reported to have worn a two-piece skirt (instead of the breechclout?) with a grass front and a buckskin back (Kroeber 1925:519). The shoulders of both sexes, in inclement weather, might be covered with an animal skin that had been tanned complete with fur. The cape's overlapping front sometimes was held in place with a skewer. Also the rabbitskin blanket, primarily used for bedding, gave protection in cold weather.

Footgear was not habitually worn by either sex in any season. Rude moccasins were made at one time, but informants' accounts of their construction are vague. They seem to have been little more than a hide wrapped around the foot and secured at the ankle by thongs. Moccasins of better quality were imported from the Eastern Mono on the other side of the Sierra Nevada. Sandals, consisting of several layers of sole-shaped pieces of hide, were fastened on with thongs. Of whatever kind, foot coverings were for hunting and travel purposes and women may not have worn them at all.

Men's hair was worn long with a part in the middle. At work or when hunting the hair might be held with a string at the nape of the neck. The hair was also confined by a turbanlike net in order that it might be dressed for ceremonial occasions. Women's hair was likewise worn long. The hair of both sexes was singed short during periods of mourning.

Tattooing, by charcoal rubbed into cuts, was common among Foothills Yokuts women, rarer among men. Most frequently tattooed was the chin, from the corners of the mouth toward the rear and downward. Additionally women might have designs continued down the throat onto the chest and abdomen. Both men and women in the central region sometimes had a mark on the inside of the lower right forearm that was related to the situs of the wearer's supernatural power (Kroeber 1925:520-521, figs. 45, 46; Gayton 1948, 1:69-70).

Piercing of the earlobe by men was reported as having been done in the distant past. The nasal septum was pierced, but there is some conflict between authorities as to who did it. Probably both men and women had the option.

Gayton gives the essentials of ceremonial garb as a feather headdress and feather skirt. Additional ornaments of feathers, beads, skins, and rattles are shown in sketches of shamans and dancers (Gayton 1948, 1:68, fig. 8).

Life Cycle

The life cycle was essentially simple in that it recognized only common and major steps in life.

•BIRTH From the definite onset of pregnancy the expectant mother observed several food taboos: on meat, salt, hard or dried foods. (The meat and salt taboos were common in all circumstances of ritual hazard or abnormal status, such as in mourning, shamanistic performance, and ritual preparation for a hunt). Her activities were not substantially restricted until an easing of work in the final days before delivery. The prospective father observed the meat taboo and refrained from deer hunting, gambling, and tree felling.

The birth itself occurred in a dwelling, although reports of an earlier use of another, special structure are to be found. The parturient was assisted by her mother, her sister, an aunt, or her mother-in-law. No man or childless woman was allowed to be present except that a male shaman might be called in instances of difficult delivery. There were some older women who possessed supernatural powers enabling them to ease a birth. Occasionally a child was born away from the house, at trailside, without assistance. This circumstance was not considered extraordinary although remembered.

On birth the baby was taken by an assisting woman, the cord cut about two inches from the abdomen and tied with sinew. The baby was washed in a basket of warm water, then wrapped in old deerskins. The cradle for the first child was made by the paternal grandmother after its birth. With the advent of the Monache-style cradle, which took longer to make than the older Y-framed type, the cradle came to be made in advance of the birth. Presumably its decoration had to wait until the birth had taken place in order to be sex-appropriate.

Disposal of the umbilical cord and afterbirth was variable locally and among regions. The Chukchansi of the northern foothills buried the cord, put it in an anthill, or hung it in a tree. In the central foothills one found that the cord was thrown in the river or buried in an anthill. In general there was thought to be a connection between the mode of disposal and the continuing welfare or disposition of the child. The anthill location assured industry. The river protected against stomach illnesses. The tree, a young and vigorous one being chosen, assured the growth of the child.

The child was named within a few days or weeks of birth. The name was conferred by the paternal grandmother or another senior paternal female and was customarily that of an older relative in the male line. While some names lack meaning, others denote objects, animals, or acts. The name was used in direct address and reference from early childhood on through life. An exception to continued use of the name was imposed by the taboo on the name of the dead. When a person's namesake died another name was taken or one already recognized came into exclusive use.

• PUBERTY Puberty was recognized in girls by the onset of the menses at which time the girl was made to observe a bland meatless diet. No segregation occurred, and the girl was required to use a scratching stick instead of her hand. The girl might be betrothed, though not irreversibly, at puberty; marriage would take place some years later. The future husband and his mother came as guests of the girl's mother bringing gifts to the girl. In exchange the visitors received gifts of food. The youngsters were urged to accept the arranged marriage, but no return of gifts was made if it did not take place eventually.

Adolescents of both sexes were toughened by nightly swims during the winter. The youth was roused from sleep three times during the night and sent forth to get wet. Persons of strong character continued to take at least one nightly swim after reaching adulthood. A daily swim, at daybreak, was a part of everyone's normal personal hygiene.

From early adolescence onward children were instructed in the useful, sex-appropriate arts by their parents. Older people, or those without children, often taught stories, songs, moral behavior, and etiquette.

• MARRIAGE Marriage among the Foothill Yokuts properly took place only between those who were not demonstrably related in any degree. Even unions between distant cousins were objects of scorn. In the northern foothills, as among the Chukchansi, marriage was additionally regulated by the custom of moiety exogamy.

Preliminaries to marriage often went back to the betrothals resulting from interfamily visits at the girl's puberty. If the girl accepted the gifts brought by a young man and his mother, she made a substantial commitment to marry him at some later time. The intended groom and his family usually took the initiative, but a girl might indicate to her parents some young man in whom she took an interest. The gifts constituted, effectively, a bride price, and there was some grumbling if the gifts were not returned should the girl refuse to marry. On his part, the young man incurred a serious obligation to marry if he

should sleep with his intended. He also was obliged to hunt for his prospective parents-in-law's table when affairs had reached this stage. A temporary or trial marriage had been established, but it was terminated at a rather indefinite time among the Central Foothill peoples. The northern tribes seem to have celebrated the marriage with a little feast for which food was furnished by both families, the only persons present.

Patterns for postmarital residence seem uncertain and variable. The visits of the betrothed husband, the frequent lack of a definite celebration of the marriage, and the probable residence of the pregnant young wife at her mother's house all contribute to this picture. Eventually the new family lived with the husband's parents or in their community.

Plural marriages occurred in which a man had two wives at a time. While both wives might be in the same village, they usually lived separately or in different settlements. No formal ranking of wives occurred, but favoritism was manifest in the division of time and support between them. Only exceptionally was a marriage of one woman to two men reported, in this instance in the central foothills.

Divorce was discouraged by the pressure of relatives but could occur on the volition of either party. Grounds for divorce included infidelity (especially of the wife), barrenness combined with refusal to countenance a second wife, improvidence, sloth, garrulousness, slovenliness, and general incompatibility. The wife with several children was left in possession of the house and its furnishings. The wife might return to her parental home with very young children. Older children sometimes went to either grandparental home. The stepchildren were thought to belong to the second marriage of the parent who retained them. There were few fixed rules governing property and children involved in a divorce, but the details were settled, case by case, by the affected families.

Remarriage of divorced and widowed individuals was permitted. The custom of the levirate was reported as common among Central Foothill Yokuts but denied as occurring among the Northern tribes. The sororate was found rarely, only among the Central groups. In each instance the bereaved person did not remarry until some time after the spouse's death.

• DEATH When a death was impending the relatives in other villages were summoned by the moiety chief's messenger. The funeral was delayed, but not more than a few days, until the relatives assembled. The corpse was washed and dressed, usually by a female relative, and the bereaved wept over it. Professional corpse-handlers (whose character and occurrence remain obscure) joined in the lamentation and prepared the funeral pyre or dug the grave. Cremation was supplanted by inhumation, evidently in response to Whites' urging, during the mid- or late nineteenth century. There were indications that both practices were known aboriginally in Foothill territory. Following cremation the bones and ashes were gathered in a basket for secondary burial. In both disposal practices valuable goods, primarily baskets and beads, were placed with the dead to be destroyed or buried.

Mourning was conducted both privately and publicly. The private ceremony might follow immediately on a death, as among the Chukchansi, or several months later, according to Wikchamni sources. In the north private mourning accompanied the disposal of the dead, while the southern ceremony marked the end of deep mourning. Women singed short their hair in mourning, its shortness being in direct proportion to closeness of relationship to the deceased, and often pitched the face and chest on which dirt accumulated. Men did comparatively little to make obvious their grief. Meat was taboo to mourners, as was participation in public ceremonies.

A mourning ceremony, held at various intervals despite its label as "annual," was the occasion of public mourning for the dead and of the release of mourners from their restricted status. Testimony about the frequency of this ceremony is vague and often contradictory. It may have been annual when tribal life flourished several centuries ago and become intermittent in recent times. Some Northern Foothills informants suggested that it was held for each death at the request of the bereaved family. The extensive preparation and great expense of the ceremony make this individualization seem improbable. Yet Powers (1877:383–391) attended part of a major ceremony held for the deceased sister of a chief. The generality seemed to call for a ceremony every year or two, held for several families.

Organization of the ceremony was by the bereaved families in conjunction with the chief and his messenger. The families collected food, goods for gifts and trade, and money. Word was sent through the chief's messenger, a fortnight to three months in advance, to intended participants. A temporary camp, consisting of shelters around a dance plaza, was constructed. Preparations were substantial as this was a major occasion, bringing together hundreds or even thousands of individuals from several Yokuts tribelets and possibly even non-Yokuts tribes.

The duration of the ceremony was approximately six days and nights, with emphasis on events of the evenings. The first days saw the arrival of guests; and activities included games, footraces, and dancing. Gambling also took place but was conducted away from the ceremonial site. The mourners might not participate in any of these activities until ritual washing ended their mourning status.

The middle of the ceremonial period saw the performance of the *huhuna* Dance, in which specially endowed costumed male dancers found money that had been hidden in the dance area. When all the money had been found the dancer was struck down supernaturally by a shaman of the host group. The dancers were carried

Dept. of Anthr., U. of Calif., Berkeley.
Fig. 9. Women playing a gambling game with walnut dice (see also "Southern Valley Yokuts," fig. 9, this vol.). Photograph by C. Hart Merriam, near Fresno Flat, 1902.

senseless to one side where host spectators laid strings of money over them and wept. Soon a shaman of the dancers' tribes revived them and "shot" down the attacking shaman who was, in turn, revived by one of his fellows. The dancers kept the money except that paid to the accompanying singers. The shamans were paid by their respective chiefs. The entire performance lasted a day (Gayton 1948, 1:68, 127–128). The *huhuna* Dance seems to have been most characteristic of the Central Foothill Yokuts. It is reported for the Kechayi of the Northern Foothills but not among the Chukchansi. However, the Chukchansi accounts were disorganized and fragmentary and the dance may have been present prior to recent cultural disintegration.

A shamans' contest was a common part of the mourning ceremony, more frequently than the *huhuna* Dance; such contests also occurred on other occasions. Shamans of one tribe were paired, as opponents, with shamans of another tribe. The contestants paraded onto the dance plaza from opposite ends and ranged themselves in two facing rows. Each shaman had a fire in which he smoked the basketry tray that he used to catch magical "shot" from the sun. At a signal each shaman caught his shot from the sun and then directed it against his opponent. He did this repeatedly until his rival fell or he himself was brought down. Fallen men were carried to a shade where each was revived, whether by his direct opponent or by another shaman is not clear. As the contest between the last pair ended, the host chief caused money and gifts to be collected from his people and given to the chiefs of the performing shamans. This donation was accompanied by tears from all present. Evidently some strings of bead money were given directly to shamans as they lay unconscious.

There was some belief in trickery accompanying the revival of fallen shamans. If not properly treated the shaman might die in a few days or a month and improper treatment might be deliberate. Also a shaman might be left unconscious on the grounds that he could not be cured. Rivalries and enmities between chiefs and associated shamans were deep and bitter (Gayton 1930).

The mourners had been crying at intervals during these days, as befitted their status. On the last day or next to last day, the mourners were ceremonially stripped and washed. Their hair was cut and they were clothed in new garments provided by the washers. The host chief declared, in one of his many speeches throughout the ceremony, that their mourning was ended and called for rejoicing. A feast, social dancing, and games followed to terminate the ceremony.

Throughout the mourning ceremony two principles were operant: reciprocity of relationships and payment for services. The Northern Foothill Yokuts world was divided into two parts that interacted. Each tribe had two major social divisions—moieties—in which membership was hereditary (Gayton 1945). Among other reciprocal duties that the moieties bore toward each other were those connected with the mourning ceremony; each moiety washed the mourners of the other. In practice the moiety divisions had intertribal equivalence and the host and guest tribes were also considered to stand in a similar reciprocal relationship; such intertribal relations were found in the absence of moieties, as among the Central and Southern Foothills people. The tribes with which such interactions existed were traditionally linked, as were certain lineages (within each moiety) paired intertribally with other lineages.

In the mourning ceremony singers, dancers, shamans, messengers, managers, money lenders, and washers were all compensated for their services. Most of the money and goods came primarily from the mourning families and secondarily from their tribesmen. Payment did not in all instances mean a profit: for example, the washers furnished the washing baskets and the new clothing for those washed. This reciprocation was considered an even exchange. The lending of money and exchange of goods was a pronounced feature of the ceremony among the Central Foothill Yokuts.

Social Organization

Lineages, with membership inherited in the paternal line, were found among the Foothill Yokuts. Each lineage had a totem (common totems: Eagle, Falcon, Dove, Crow, Magpie, Bear, Cougar, Bluejay, and Rattlesnake) that gave potential strength and wisdom to members of the group (Gayton 1945:415). The totem was treated respectfully by its followers and should be redeemed (ransomed) by them if brought in dead or alive by a hunter of another lineage. Respect was also shown the totems of other lineages within the moiety (if this social unit were recognized) or to the totems collectively of the moiety when constituent lineages were lacking.

Tribal offices, primarily of the chief and the messenger, passed within the lineages from father to son. Noninheriting children often used the title although daughters could not transmit it to their children. (In the disturbed social situation of cultural collapse it was found among the Chukchansi that the title of messenger was assumed by a woman, but she was deemed unable to transmit the title, hence to be the last of a line.) Specific lineages were also the source of quasi-official functionaries who performed ceremonies for general tribal benefit. These specialists attended to the increase of the acorn crop and to the prevention of rattlesnake bite, among other activities.

Gayton offers a map and a list of occurrence of patrilineal lineages among Yokuts and neighboring tribes. All the Foothill Yokuts tribes under discussion, except possibly the Gashowu, for whom adequate data were lacking, are shown to have had these lineages (Gayton 1945:419).

Moieties occurred less frequently than lineages among the Foothill Yokuts. Only the tribes of the Fresno, San Joaquin, and Kings river drainages are believed to have possessed this dual organization. The Central Foothill Yokuts of the Kaweah and Tule River areas and the Southern Foothill Yokuts of the Kern River drainage had only lineages.

The animal world, in totemic reference, was divided between the moieties: the *tʰoxelyuwič* or *tʰokʰelyuwič* (western, downhill, downstream) and the *nutʰoˑwič* (eastern, uphill, upstream). Through assignment of his lineage totem, inherited patrilineally, to a moiety, the individual's membership was determined. The collective lineage totems, numbering 6 to 16 in the various tribes, were those of the moiety and were treated with some respect by all members of that group. Each moiety had its own chiefly lineage, Eagle for the *tʰoxelyuwič* and Coyote for the *nutʰoˑwič*, which became by extension the general totem of the moiety. The Eagle lineage also provided the tribal or community chief (presumably the same individual as the moiety chief). The chief's assistant, called a messenger, came from the Dove lineage of the *nutʰoˑwič* moiety, thus preserving the principles of reciprocity and balance.

The moieties were nominally exogamous, but genealogies show less than total observance of this mandate. Perhaps 70 percent of marriages were exogamous.

Moieties played their most important role in the reciprocation of the annual mourning ceremony. As this ceremony involved a host tribe and a guest tribe, with customary pairings observed, the moiety service was rendered across tribal lines as well as moietal lines. When no moieties were present, each tribe as a whole was a reciprocant, either mourner or guest.

Political Organization

Chiefs were preeminent among tribal officials. Each tribe had several chiefs, usually at least one in each of its villages. No individual chief was paramount and in matters affecting the whole group called upon his fellow chiefs for concurrence in his judgment. A chief's status derived from his lineage totem (Eagle), his office, and his wealth. Although chiefs were called upon to contribute heavily to communal undertakings such as the seasonal round of ceremonies, were obliged to feed the poor, and were expected to offer hospitality to visitors, they also had special sources of income. When a chief was invited to bring a shaman or a special dancer (such as a *huhuna* dancer) to a ceremony he was paid as an inducement. (He might have to pay the dancer, but usually the dancer received the bulk of his compensation from audience contributions.) People who had received alms often gave the chief small gifts when their lot improved, even if only temporarily.

Eagle down was an important ingredient in religious activities and much sought after. Only a chief could approve the killing of an eagle. The carcass was bought by the chief from the hunter and then the down, leg bones, and tallow were sold to those persons wanting them.

Because he entertained visitors the chief was a focal point for trading. All persons entering the tribal area went first to the chief's house to state their business. The chief's wealth made it possible for him to buy and then retail a trader's wares.

The chief's executive powers were limited. He set the dates for events on the ceremonial calendar. He gave permission for revenge killings, but only after consultation with other chiefs and senior men. He was not a war leader although he did engage in intertribal negotiations.

The messenger was the right-hand man of the chief, without whom the chief could not function. This office, tenanted by someone from the appropriate lineage (Dove), saw to the execution of the chief's errands and orders. The messenger brought news of a coming event and told the people to make appropriate preparations. The messenger was involved when a family decided to end their formal mourning period with a ceremony, which must be sanctioned by the chief. The messenger was a source of intelligence for the chief and commonly his confidant. It was generally believed that a messenger was also a shaman and therefore capable of going everywhere unmolested. In fact, it seems that messengers did pass quite freely without molestation. This office had its perquisites, mostly the fees paid by the recipients when carrying news or information. Gayton (1930) suggests that at times the chief and messenger could form a predatory pair and enrich themselves at public expense.

Religion

The uniting of all Foothill Yokuts, or even the people of one tribe, in the worship of a commonly recognized deity was not found. Yet religious feeling—a sense of awe and a recognition of the supernatural world—was common. All adults had some experiences (primarily hallucinatory) that paralleled, in a minor way, those leading to shamanism. Many people felt that they had, usually as a result, some minor grant of "power," that is, supernatural assistance, that would aid them personally or could be turned to social benefit (such as locating game animals or alleviating minor ailments.) There were daily acts of both commission and omission that would avert harm and bring good fortune.

The shamans and those whose experiences approached the shamanistic derived their powers from spirit animals comparable to those recognized as lineage or moiety totems. These creatures were the supernatural counterparts of living animals and shared many attributes. A person who had had repeated and vivid dreams about these conventional sources of supernatural assistance would turn to established shamans for information, interpretation, and possibly instruction. There was no formal organization of shamans.

In the northern foothills the drinking of a datura infusion was part of an annual spring cleansing and curing ritual. Participants fasted for six or more days before the event and for a similar time afterward. They paid an old man to prepare the weed for them to drink. The hallucinations induced made it possible for the drinkers to see the sicknesses from which they or others suffered and to brush the illness off for removal and burial. Datura was recognized as a potent substance and a possible source of death by the Choynimni. They were especially reluctant to drink it other than in the spring (Gayton 1948, 2:150-151). The Wikchamni of the central foothills had a more elaborate observance. The dietary restrictions preceding drinking were longer, as long as two months, and the postevent restrictions likewise longer. The principal drinkers were adolescents who engaged in this once-in-a-lifetime event in quest of good health, long life, and possible supernatural information, but adult men might repeat participation annually to acquire additional supernatural power. Although they drank as a group, each participant had his own blanket, drinking basket, and two senior women as sponsors. The women took care of their ward as the infusion rendered him unconscious; after an initial coma of 12 to 18 hours, the participants could become active and run away or injure themselves. Drinkers had revelations of causes of illness, sources of individual power, and the evil doings of malevolent shamans. They could share this information only with those family members, often most of the kindred, who had likewise fasted. Recovery from the occasion was signaled, after 12 days, by a small feast held by families of participants (Gayton 1948, 1:120).

Datura was also used as a poultice on serious wounds and as an anesthetic, internally, after a short fast, in cases of fractures.

The Ghost Dance of 1870 made a considerable impression among the Northern Foothill Yokuts and, slightly later, among the Central Foothill Yokuts, from whom it diffused to Valley Yokuts and in the direction of the Chumash, via Fort Tejon. The introduction from the Paiute came to the Monache of the North Fork of the San Joaquin River in 1871. Missionaries from here conducted a series of small dances along the foothills to the south. These activities resulted in two major dances, one at Saganiu, a site on the North Fork of the San Joaquin River in Monache territory, and the other in Eshom Valley, on the headwaters of the North Fork of the Kaweah River. At the former were gathered people from the Northern Foothill Yokuts and the Monache of local and central foothill origin. The Eshom Valley dance about 18 months later, in the fall of 1872, attracted tribesmen from the Monache of this area, the Central Foothill Yokuts groups, and some from the Southern Foothill Yokuts and Valley Yokuts.

Local dances were held throughout the region with diminishing frequency for the next several years. By 1875 the Ghost Dance had been abandoned and the revival of 1890 failed to penetrate the region even though news of it must have reached the Yokuts through their Monache neighbors. Gayton (1930a) has written a special study of the Ghost Dance in this area in addition to its mention in her ethnography of the Yokuts and Monache (1948, 1:131, 2:152, 174, 203).

Twentieth Century

In the mid-twentieth century the aboriginal culture of the Foothill Yokuts has been greatly changed by more than 100 years of contact with Europeans. Isolated individuals still use parts of the native diet, such as acorns; some still make baskets (fig. 10). However, native housing has been replaced by European-style structures, native foods generally by store-bought foods, native clothing by manufactured clothing, and so forth. The social structure has crumbled so that the offices of chief and messenger mean virtually nothing, if recognized at all. People are vague and unsure about moiety and lineage affiliations, even when phrased in totemic terms.

Although some Foothill Yokuts may be residents of the Tule River Indian Reservation, east of Porterville, most live in hamlets or isolated dwellings scattered through their traditional territories. In a few instances, exemplified by the Chukchansi community of Picayune, near Coarse Gold, there remains a recognized Indian

NAA, Smithsonian.

Fig. 10. Cecile Silva *(yame·sut)* coiling a basket. Photograph by Geoffrey Gamble, June 1974.

community on the site of a precontact settlement. The Picayune community together with that near Oakhurst had an estimated population of 112 persons in 1950 (Tax and Stanley 1960). However, modern reservoirs, such as Bass Lake and Millerton Lake on the San Joaquin River, Pine Flat Reservoir on the Kings River, and Lake Kaweah on the Kaweah River, have inundated important areas of native inhabitation. The points at which rivers reach the plains are attractive both as dam and dwelling sites, with the modern use obliterating the old.

The number of people has dwindled to half or less that of the pre-White period, and scattering has made these survivors even less apparent. Precise figures are impossible to secure, but the Chukchansi in 1950 were close to 150 individuals based on genealogical data. However, Chukchansi informants gave counts as low as seven, considering as true Indians only full-blood Chukchansis in their own generation. The Wikchamni of the Kaweah River claimed a precontact population of 5,000 but had been reduced to 40 when Merriam (1966–1967, 3:409) visited them in 1902. Parallel circumstances probably occur in other Foothill tribes.

Modern Foothill Yokuts live in the style of poor Whites in the same region. They are irregularly employed, often as agricultural labor, and welfare payments loom large in their economy. The older people, usually women, receiving public assistance are often the focal point of an extended family.

Synonymy

The general name Yokuts derives from the Valley word for 'person' or 'people', but most of the Foothill tribes said *may*(*i*) or *tʰaʔatʰ*(*i*) instead.

The following list of Foothill tribes is arranged according to the anglicized spellings used by Kroeber (1963:237), except that his Gawya and Wükchamni are here Gawia and Wikchamni. The second items in each entry are the pronunciations in Yokuts, first in the singular form and then in the plural, as provided by Geoffrey Gamble (personal communication 1974). After these appear some of the major spelling variants from earlier sources.

Ayticha, *ʔaytičʰa, ʔayetačʰi,* aiʔkitca, Kocheyali.

Bokninwad, *pokʰninuwat, pokʰenwati,* Bokninuwad.

Choynimni, *čʰoŷnimni?, čʰoyeṅmaṅi,* Choinimni, Cho-e-nim-na, Chainimaini.

Chukaymina, *čʰokʰoyemni?, čʰukʰaymina,* Chukaimina, Cho-ke-min-nah, Chokimauves.

Chukchansi, *čʰukʰčʰansi?, čʰukʰatniša,* Shukshansi, Chookchances, Chukchancy.

Dalinchi, *taʔlinčʰi, taʔelnaši.*

Dumna, *tumna, tumaˑniša.*

Gashowu, *kašowu?, kašwuša,* Kosh-sho-o.

Gawia, *kaˑwiya(?), kaweˑyaŷi,* Gawya, Kawia (not to be confused with the Takic-speaking Cahuilla).

Kechayi, *kʰečʰayi?, kʰečʰeˑwali,* Ka-chi-e.

Kumachisi, *kʰumačʰisi, kʰumečʰwati.*

Palewyami, *pʰaleẃyami, pʰaleẃyami,* Paleuyami, Padeuyami, Peleuyi, Paluyam, Pal-la-a-me, Paloyama, Pal-lah-wech-e-am.

Toltichi, *tʰoltʰičʰi, tʰoleˑtʰačʰi.*

Toyhicha, *tʰoyxičʰa, tʰoyeˑxačʰi.*

Wikchamni, *wikʰtʰamni, wikʰatʰmina,* Wükchamni, Wukchumni.

Yawdanchi, *yawtančʰi, yawetčʰani,* Yaudanchi, Yaulanchi, Yawedentshi.

Yokod, *yowkʰot, yuweˑkʰati,* in other dialects Yokol, i.e. *yowkʰol, yuweˑkʰaĺi.*

Sources

Based on field research begun during the middle 1920s, Gayton (1948) is the most recent full-scale study of these people, with at least half devoted to Foothill peoples. Kroeber (1925) devotes four chapters to data gathered two decades earlier. Latta (1949), the result of 25 years' work by a skilled amateur ethnographer, emphasizes Valley rather than Foothill Yokuts.

Specialized studies with substantial bearing on the Foothill Yokuts include Newman (1944) on languages and Gayton and Newman (1940) and Rogers and Gayton (1944) on myths. Gayton also published papers on pottery making (1929), chiefs and shamans (1930), the Ghost Dance of 1870 (1930a), social organization (1945), and culture-environment integration (1946).

Two historical accounts of early Indian-White contacts are available for the Northern Foothills. Bunnell (1911) has passed through several editions. The diaries of Eccleston (1957) concern the Mariposa Indian War of 1850-1851. The foothill territories of most Yokuts received little attention, from a historical view, because they lay beyond the southern limit of the gold rush country, which was roughly the line of the San Joaquin River.

Costanoan

RICHARD LEVY

Language and Territory

The term Costanoan is a linguistic one; it designates a language family consisting of eight languages. In 1770 the Costanoan-speaking people lived in approximately 50 separate and politically autonomous nations or tribelets (fig. 1). Each tribelet had one or more permanent village sites. During various seasons of the year parties went out from the villages to temporary camps at scattered locations in the tribelet territory to engage in fishing, hunting, and collection of plant foods. The average number of persons in a tribelet was approximately 200. Tribelet population seems to have ranged from about 50 to about 500 persons. The larger tribelets usually had several permanent villages; frequently these were located in close proximity to one another.

The ethnic groups recognized by the Costanoan themselves were sets of tribelets who spoke a common language and lived in a contiguous area. Many of the tribelets within an ethnic area were distinguished from one another by slight differences of dialect. This is particularly true in the Rumsen and Awaswas ethnic areas.

The languages comprising the family and their locations in 1770 were approximately as follows. Karkin was spoken in a single tribelet on the southern edge of Carquinez Strait and appears to have had approximately 200 speakers. Chochenyo or East Bay Costanoan was spoken among the tribelets occupying the east shore of San Francisco Bay between Richmond and Mission San José, and probably also in the Livermore Valley, by about 2,000 people. Tamyen or Santa Clara Costanoan was spoken around the south end of San Francisco Bay and in the lower Santa Clara Valley and seems to have had about 1,200 speakers. Ramaytush or San Francisco Costanoan was spoken by about 1,400 people in San Mateo and San Francisco counties. Awaswas or Santa Cruz Costanoan was spoken among the people living along the ocean shore between Davenport and Aptos in Santa Cruz County; its speakers numbered about 600. Mutsun was spoken among the tribelets of the Pajaro River drainage and seems to have had about 2,700 speakers. Speakers of Rumsen numbering about 800 occupied the lower Carmel, Sur, and lower Salinas rivers. Chalon or Soledad was spoken by about 900 people on the Salinas River (Levy 1970).

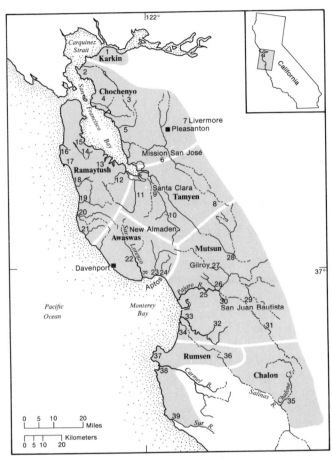

Fig. 1. Ethnic groups and tribelets (late 18th century). Tribelets: 1, *karkin* (Los Carquines); 2, *xučyun;* 3, (Palos Colorados); 4, (San Antonio); 5, *lisyan;* 6, *ʔoroyšom* (San Francisco Solano); 7, *šewnen* (El Valle); 8, (Santa Ysabel); 9, (Santa Clara); 10, (San Juan Bautista); 11, (San José Cupertino); 12, *puyšon* (Arroyo de San Francisco); 13, *lamšin* (Las Pulgas); 14, *salson* (San Matheo); 15, *šipliškin* (San Bruno); 16, *ramay* (Cañada de las Almejas); 17, *satunumno* (San Egidio); 18, *kotxen* (La Purísima); 19, *ʔolxon;* 20, *kaxasta* (San Antonio); 21, *čitaktak* (San Juan); 22, *sayant* (San Juan Capistrano); 23, *ʔuypi* (San Daniel); 24, *ʔaptos* (San Lucas); 25, *ʔawsayma;* 26, *xuristak;* 27, *kulu·listak* (San Bernardino); 28, *ʔorestak;* 29, *kotetak;* 30, *xumontwaš;* 31, *paxšin;* 32, *mutsun* (La Natividad); 33, *wačron;* 34, *kalenta ruk;* 35, *čalon;* 36, *ʔensen* (Los Sanjones); 37, *ʔačista* (San Carlos); 38, *ʔičxenta* (San José); 39, *sarxenta ruk* (R. del Sur). Names in parentheses are Spanish designations.

The eight branches of the Costanoan family were separate languages (not dialects) as different from one another as Spanish is from French. They form a language   *485* continuum. Except for the close relationship between Awaswas and Chalon, each language was most closely related to its geographically contiguous neighbors. The ordering of languages in the continuum was approximately the following: Karkin-Ramaytush-Chochenyo-Tamyen-Awaswas-Chalon-Mutsun-Rumsen. The eight Costanoan languages form a language family since they are more similar to one another than to any outside language (Levy 1970).*

The closest linguistic relatives of the Costanoan were the Miwok languages; together they form a Miwok-Costanoan or Utian family within the Penutian stock (Callaghan 1967; Pitkin and Shipley 1958).

History

Linguistic evidence suggests that the ancestors of the Costanoan moved into the San Francisco and Monterey Bay areas about A.D. 500. They probably moved south and west from the delta of the San Joaquin-Sacramento River system. Linguistic evidence indicates that they were then in contact with speakers of a Hokan language that shared some vocabulary with ancestral Pomoan and Esselen. This long-extinct Hokan language probably occupied at least a portion of the territory into which the Costanoan expanded (Levy 1972a).

The above postulated movement of Costanoan languages into the San Francisco area seems to coincide with the appearance of the Late Horizon artifact assemblages in archeological sites in the San Francisco bay region. The ancestors of the Costanoan were probably the producers of the artifacts contained in the Late Horizon components of the archeological sites of the San Francisco bay area (Levy 1972a).

The Rumsen were the first of the Costanoan peoples to be encountered by Spanish exploring expeditions. The Sebastián Vizcaíno expedition arrived at Monterey in 1602 and recorded some description of the Rumsen. Manila galleons may have stopped occasionally at Monterey between 1602 and the founding of Monterey by the expedition of Gaspar de Portolá in 1769, but little is known of this period in Costanoan history (Broadbent 1972:46–48). Accounts of expeditions that explored Costanoan territory between 1769 and 1776 provide important information on settlement pattern, population, subsistence, and material culture.

Seven missions were established within Costanoan territory between 1770 and 1797. Analyses of mission

Expeditions in Costanoan Territory 1769–1776

Expedition	Dates	Sources
Portolá	Sept. 26–Dec. 13, 1769	Crespí 1927; Portolá 1909; Costansó 1911
Fages	Nov. 21–Dec. 4, 1770	Fages 1911
Fages-Crespí	Mar. 20–Apr. 5, 1772	Crespí 1927:275–303
Anza I	Apr. 17–22, 1774	Anza in Bolton 1930, 2:1–130, 213–243
Rivera	Nov. 23–Dec. 13, 1774	Palóu 1930
Anza II	Mar. 9–Apr. 14, 1776	Font 1930; Anza in Bolton 1930, 3:1–200
Moraga	June 17–24, 1776	Moraga 1930; Palóu 1930a

baptismal records demonstrate that the last Costanoan tribelets living an aboriginal existence had disappeared by 1810 (Cook 1943, 1957; Levy 1969, 1972). During the mission period, 1770–1835, the Costanoan people experienced cataclysmic changes in almost all areas of their life. As a result of introduced diseases and a declining birth rate the Costanoan population fell from 10,000 or more in 1770 to less than 2,000 in 1832 (Cook 1943, 1943a). The aboriginal subsistence economy was largely replaced by the agricultural economy of the missions. Many ritual and social activities were discouraged or prohibited by the missionaries at some missions.

Another profound change involved the comingling of the Costanoan with peoples of differing linguistic and cultural background during the mission period. The following peoples were brought to the seven missions in Costanoan territory: Esselen (San Carlos, Soledad), Foothill Yokuts (Soledad), Southern Valley Yokuts (Soledad, San Juan Bautista, Santa Cruz), Northern Valley Yokuts (Soledad, San Juan Bautista, Santa Cruz, Santa Clara, San José), Plains Miwok (Santa Clara, San Jose), Saclan Miwok (San Francisco), Lake Miwok (San José), Coast Miwok (San José, San Francisco), and Patwin (San Jose, San Francisco) (Levy 1969, 1972).

The mission period is documented in the books of baptisms, deaths, and marriages of the various missions; annual reports of crop production and censuses; diaries of exploratory and punitive expeditions; the replies to an *interrogatório* or questionnaire of 1812 by the missionaries at various missions; and the accounts of the various European seafarers that called at San Francisco and Monterey during this period.

The Costanoan experienced a second cataclysmic change with the secularization of the missions by the Mexican government. Most natives gradually left the missions to work as manual laborers on the ranchos that were established in the surrounding areas. During the next few decades there was a partial return to aboriginal religious practices, particularly shamanism, and some

---

* Italicized Costanoan words are written in a phonemic orthography worked out by the author. All the languages have the stops p, t, ṭ (with allophones [ṭ] and [č]), č, k, and ʔ; the continuants s, š, x (with allophones [h] and [x]), m, n, l, and r; the semivowels w and y; and the vowels i, e, a, o, and u. Vowel length (shown with raised dot) is phonemic. In addition, ṣ occurred in Mutsun, Rumsen, Awaswas, Chalon, Ramaytush, and possibly Karkin.

return to food collection as a means of subsistence (Harrington 1921). Several multiethnic Indian communities grew up in and around Costanoan territory composed of the people who had been living at the missions when these were secularized. Such a community at Pleasanton, for example, was composed of Chochenyo, Plains Miwok, Northern Valley Yokuts, Patwin, and Coast Miwok. There were similar communities at Monterey and San Juan Bautista and probably at other locations as well.

These communities gradually shrank in size as the young people moved away and the old people died. The only extant statements made by the Costanoans themselves about their culture were made to ethnologists in the period from 1878 to 1933. These form the basis for the culture sketch that follows.

It is difficult to estimate the exact number of persons of Costanoan descent who were living in 1973. Galvan (1968:12) estimates approximately 130 Ohlone descendants in the San Francisco bay area. Thompson (1957) located over 100 persons of probable Costanoan descent in a linguistic survey of the areas formerly inhabited by the Awaswas, Mutsun, Rumsen, and Chalon. Judging from these two partial figures, the total number of persons of Costanoan descent in 1973 was probably considerably more than 200.

The Costanoan languages were probably all extinct by 1935.

In 1971 descendants of the Costanoan united in a corporate entity, the Ohlone Indian Tribe, and received title to the Ohlone Indian Cemetery where their ancestors who died at Mission San José are buried. "No official governmental recognition has ever been given to the Costanoans: No reservation has ever been set aside for them. No special emoluments, federal funds, or aid of any kind whatsoever has been given them at any time. They have still not been paid by the federal government for lands taken from them during the Gold Rush. They are still waiting for the justice due them as the native people of this land, who owned the land and loved it and cared for it" (Galvan 1968:12).

Culture

It is extremely difficult to fix an exact point in time to which all the statements made about Costanoan culture presented below apply. Information from expeditions between 1769 and 1776 must be combined with statements of Costanoan people recorded by ethnographers in the 1920s and 1930s to produce a rounded picture of Costanoan life. Another limiting factor is that the ethnographers who recorded the statements of Costanoan people about their own culture were primarily interested in the precontact culture and not the modified version that existed during the mission period and afterward.

Some of the material in this sketch is derived from the field notes of Harrington (1921, 1929-1930). The only major publications that have been derived from Harrington's work are his culture element distribution lists (Harrington 1942), used as the principal source for the following ethnography, and his letters to C. Hart Merriam concerning his work of 1929 to 1930 (Merriam 1966-1967, 3).

Harrington's principal Chochenyo informant was Maria de los Angeles Colós, who learned what she knew of Chochenyo culture from her maternal grandmother and grandfather. Harrington's principal Mutsun informant was Ascensión Solarsano de Cervantes. Bedridden and dying of cancer, this woman spent the last months of her life telling Harrington of the social institutions, beliefs, medicinal practices, and language of her people.

Political Organization

The basic unit of Costanoan political organization was the tribelet. Each tribelet consisted of one or more villages and a number of camps within a tribelet territory. This type of organization was practically universal in aboriginal California (Kroeber 1962). Evidence for this organization is present in the Books of Baptisms of the missions which received Costanoan converts (Merriam 1955:217-225, 1968:11-62). The Book of Baptisms of Mission San Francisco, for example, refers to a "Lamchin" nation (that is, tribelet) and three rancherias (that is, villages)—Lamchin, Cachanigtac, and Ssupichum—in or of the Lamchin nation. Lamchin, thus, was the name of both the tribelet and the principal village of the tribelet.

Territorial boundaries of tribelets were defined by physiographic features. Anza (in Bolton 1930, 3:129) found that the Costanoans who accompanied his expedition were unwilling to step beyond the limits of their territory because of the hostility of neighboring groups.

Tribelet chiefs might be either men or women. The office was inherited patrilineally, usually passing from father to son. When there were no male heirs the office went to a man's sister or daughter. Accession to the office of chief required the approval of the community. The chief was responsible for feeding visitors; providing for the impoverished; directing ceremonial activities; caring for captive grizzly bears and coyotes; and directing hunting, fishing, gathering, and warfare expeditions. In all these matters the chief acted as the leader of a council of elders (Harrington 1933:3).

The chief and council served mainly as advisors to the community. Costanoan ideas of personal freedom precluded the existence of any type of institutionalized coercive power. Obedience to a higher authority was rendered only in time of war. Duran and Fortuny (1958:274) described the attitudes of the Costanoan: "Outside of these [war leaders and shamans] they do not recognize any subordination, either civil or political, or

COSTANOAN

487

even domestic, but each one lives and does whatever his inclination may be, without anyone interfering with another."

A chief's envoy, mentioned in Pinart's vocabulary of Rumsen (Heizer 1952:8) argues for the presence of the office of speaker. The bearded man who delivered a speech to the members of the expedition led by Capt. Fernando Rivera y Moncada, inviting them to come to a village (Palóu 1930:439), was probably such a speaker. Speakers probably assisted the chief in collecting property to be used in ceremonies and in extending invitations to neighboring tribelets.

Kinship and Social Organization

In general the kinship and social organization of the Costanoan was very much like that of the Salinan, Chumash, Takic, and Numic groups to the south and differed markedly from that of other Penutian groups. Households were large for California, averaging 15 persons at Mission San Carlos (Broadbent 1972:62) and about 10 at a village in Gilroy Valley (Palóu 1930:404–405). Palóu (1924:64) notes that sororal polygynous marriages occurred and that the cowives and their children resided together in a polygynous household. Households consisting of patrilineally extended families were also a Costanoan practice (Harrington 1933:3).

The Costanoan were grouped in clans (Harrington 1933:3) and divided into deer and bear moieties (Harrington 1942:12).

In several matters of kinship terminology some of the Costanoan groups resemble the Salinan and Yuman peoples to the south more than they do the other Penutian peoples of central California. Children are classified in three different ways by the various Costanoan groups. The Mutsun and Rumsen, like the Yumans, possess a three-term system: man's son, man's daughter, woman's child. The Chalon, on the other hand, and their Antoniaño Salinan neighbors have a two-term system: son, daughter. The Chochenyo and Awaswas have four-term systems: man's son, woman's son, man's daughter, woman's daughter.

The Chochenyo and Rumsen have two terms for grandparents—grandmother, grandfather—like the Wintuan, some of the Yokuts, and some of the Miwok. Mutsun and Awaswas may have had the type of grandparent terminology employed by the Yumans, Numic groups, and Pomoans. Chalon possessed two terms for grandchildren—son's child, daughter's child—aligning the Chalon with the Salinan and Yumans. Both Mutsun and Awaswas have two terms for grandchild and may well have possessed the same grandchild terminology as the Chalon. The Rumsen and Chochenyo each have a single term meaning grandchild.

In both Chochenyo and Rumsen father's brother and mother's brother are terminologically equated in a single uncle term. Likewise, mother's sister and father's sister are terminologically equated. This lineal terminology has no equivalent in central or southern California. The nearest ethnic group with a lineal system is the Yurok of northwest California. Unfortunately, Costanoan cousin terms are virtually unknown.

The terminological equation of nephew-niece with various consanguineal and affinal kin throws some light on possible marriage forms among the Costanoan. The Chochenyo equate children-in-law with nephews and nieces, suggesting cross-cousin marriage. The Awaswas, Chalon, Mutsun, and Rumsen equate nephews and nieces with grandchildren, suggesting the practice of wife's brother's daughter marriage.

The Mutsun, Awaswas, and Chalon kinship terminologies appear to be the most divergent of the Costanoan groups. Rumsen and Chochenyo, on the other hand, have probably been more conservative in maintaining the original Costanoan system. The three divergent terminologies appear to have been heavily influenced by the Salinan.

Warfare and Trade

Warfare is commonly mentioned in the historical materials relating to the Costanoan. Wars were waged both among the various Costanoan tribelets and with Esselen (Broadbent 1972:73), Salinan (J.A. Mason 1912:181), and Northern Valley Yokuts (Langsdorff 1968:195) tribelets. Infringement of territorial rights seems to have been the most frequent cause of war. Warfare was conducted either by surprise attack or by prearranged meeting (Broadbent 1972:73).

Captives were usually killed; only young women were spared (Duran and Fortuny 1958:274). The heads of enemies killed in battle were placed on a pike and displayed by the victors in their villages (Kroeber 1908a:25). Raiding parties burned the villages of their enemies (Palóu 1930a:402). The bow and arrow were the chief weapons of war (Font 1930:328); no shields or armor were used (fig. 2).

The Plains Miwok, Sierra Miwok, and Yokuts were probably the main trading partners of the Costanoan. The Costanoan supplied mussels, abalone shells, salt, and dried abalone to the Yokuts and olivella shells to the Sierra Miwok (Davis 1961:23). Some linguistic evidence for trade also exists. The Plains Miwok, who probably obtained all their bows in trade (Powers 1877:352), have borrowed the word for bow from either the Chochenyo or the Tamyen. The Plains Miwok word for salt is also a loanword from Costanoan. One of the Esselen words for salmon may be a borrowing from the Chalon Costanoan. The Rumsen and Chalon languages share the word for rabbitskin blankets with Salinan.

The only definitely known import of the Costanoans was piñon nuts, which were obtained from the Yokuts (Davis 1961:23). Linguistic evidence suggests that the

Fig. 2. Costanoans fighting a mounted Spanish soldier. A thatched house is to the right. The women are wearing tule front aprons, buckskin rear aprons, and otter skin robes. Pencil drawing probably by Tomás de Suria, 1791.

Chochenyo obtained clamshell disk beads from the east. The Chochenyo word for clam disk beads is similar to the Plains Miwok, Sierra Miwok, Nisenan, and Konkow terms and may be a loanword from a Miwok language.

Religion

Prayers and offerings played an important part in the religious life of the Costanoan. Prayers offered to the sun were accompanied by the blowing of smoke toward the sky (Palóu 1930:425). Offerings consisted of seeds, tobacco, or shell beads. The Chochenyo made offerings of shell beads to appease a spirit who inhabited a whirlpool in San Francisco Bay (Harrington 1921). Small feathered sticks were used as charms to promote good luck in hunting or fishing ventures. Offerings were frequently attached to the tops of poles. Among the items mentioned as being offered in this fashion are tobacco leaves (Kroeber 1908a:25), feathers (Abella and Lucio 1924:148, 151–152), strips of rabbitskin (Font 1930:368), feather headdresses (Harrington 1921), and capes made of grass (Palóu 1930:440). The capes seem to constitute a mortuary offering but "pole offerings" were probably not limited to this context.

Dreams played an important role in Costanoan religion (Duran and Fortuny 1958). A person's dreams probably served as an important guide in directing his or her future actions. The known omens included twitching of leg muscles, which meant that one would go somewhere. A bird entering a house, a bird hovering in one's path, or a dog howling near a house were bad omens. The call of the great horned owl (*Bubo virginianus*) foreboded death (Harrington 1921).

• SHAMANISM Shamans controlled the weather and could cause the rain to start or stop. They cured disease by cutting the skin of the patient, sucking out disease objects, and exhibiting the disease objects to the onlookers. Herbs were also used by the shamans in curing of disease and shamans were hired whenever people were seriously ill (Duran and Fortuny 1958). Diagnosis of disease was accomplished by the singing and dancing of the shaman. Shamans also conducted performances to insure good crops of acorns, an abundance of fish, or the stranding of whales (Palóu 1924:62). Much of the shaman's power depended upon performance of dances and ceremonies.

Witchcraft was largely the province of grizzly bear doctors. Rumsen grizzly bear doctors wore bear skins and had bear teeth and claws filled with poison with which they killed their victims (Merriam 1966–1967, 3:373). The Chochenyo believed that bear doctors killed their own mothers, fathers, and siblings. They were rarely pardoned when discovered and were killed by shooting with arrows (Harrington 1921).

• CEREMONIES Several dances are mentioned in Merriam's Rumsen vocabulary: medicine man's dance, devil's dance, bear dance, coyote dance, dove dance, and puberty dance (Broadbent 1972:79). Among the Chochenyo dances were the Hiwey, Loole, Kuksu, and Coyote Dances (Harrington 1921). The repertoire of dances tallies closely with those described for the Salinan (J.A. Mason 1912:177–179).

The Hiwey and Loole dances form a pair. The Hiwey was an all-male dance; the Loole was danced by women. The Chochenyo Hiwey doctor wore a flicker feather headdress and a skirt of crow or raven feathers. His face and arms were painted and he had a live snake wound on his forearm and down feathers sprinkled on his face. He sang, yelled, and danced leaping through the fire. Embracing the trunk of a tree he talked to the "devil" causing the earth to tremble. The Hiwey doctor cured all kinds of disease. Little is known of the Loole except that the dancers wore a headdress of flicker feathers (Harrington 1921).

Dances were held in brush dance enclosures (Font 1930:326; Merriam 1966–1967, 3:373) or large assembly houses (Crespí 1927:219).

Music

Stylistically Costanoan music falls into the California-Yuman musical area. The music of this area is characterized by the use of a relaxed, nonpulsating vocal technique and the presence of the "rise," a type of form and melodic movement (Nettl 1954:2, 18–19).

Music was usually, if not always, connected with ritual and myth. Songs were employed as hunting or love charms, in dances and ceremonies, and in the telling of myths (Broadbent 1972:79).

The wind instruments of the Costanoan were whistles and flutes. Whistles were made of single bird-bone tubes. A wooden whistle is mentioned in Henshaw's (Heizer 1955:171) vocabulary of Rumsen. Flutes were made of alder (*Alnus* sp.) and were blown from the end (Broadbent 1972:78).

The percussion instruments of the Costanoan were rattles. The split-stick rattle was a piece of laurel (*Umbellularia californica*) wood (Broadbent 1972:78) with a single longitudinal cut; it was played by striking against the palm of the hand (Font 1930:366). Cocoon rattles were made by attaching cocoons to a wooden handle. The Costanoan did not use the log foot drum of north-central California (Broadbent 1972:79).

The only stringed instrument was a musical bow, which was played by plucking the string with the fingers.

Mythology

The culture hero of Chochenyo mythology was Duck Hawk, the grandson of Coyote. He traveled the country killing monsters and made the earth a safe place for humans to live. Coyote advised Duck Hawk in all that he did; Coyote was the chief of the animals (Harrington 1921).

Coyote figures prominently in the mythology of the Rumsen. He taught the arts of subsistence to the people. Coyote is also a trickster who is constantly trying to deceive the other characters in the myths (Kroeber 1907a:199–202).

Costanoan mythology is closely related to that of the Yokuts and Salinan. The Chochenyo Duck Hawk is clearly the equivalent of the Prairie Falcon of the Yokuts (Kroeber 1907a) and Salinan (J.A. Mason 1918). The Rumsen story of the flood and the creation of men and women (Kroeber 1907a:199–200) is closely paralleled in the mythologies of the Yawelmani Yokuts and the Salinan (J.A. Mason 1912:187).

Life Cycle

As soon as a child was born the midwife tied the umbilical cord with string and bathed the baby in cold water to remove the vernix caseosa. The mother bathed in the ocean or in a stream (Rollin 1959:114). For several days following birth the mother and child lay together on a mattress of leaves in a pit lined with rocks that had been heated in the fire (Amorós 1950:472, 482).

During the next few weeks the mother followed a special diet. Drinking of cold water; eating of meat, fish, and salt; and lifting of heavy objects were all taboo for her. During this period the ears of the baby were pierced. Babies were normally nursed for 18 to 20 months (Rollin 1959:115), during which time the parents abstained from sexual relations.

Upon reaching puberty girls began to observe the customary menstrual practices. During menstruation meat, fish, salt, and cold water were all taboo. The woman was confined in a corner of the dwelling.

Upon reaching puberty boys were initiated into a datura society. Datura was administered to the boys in order to produce visions.

Costanoan marriage was relatively informal. The only economic exchange taking place at the time of marriage was a gift (usually of minor value) to the bride's kin from the groom and his kin (Broadbent 1972:66; Duran and Fortuny 1958:271). After marriage the couple went to live in the groom's father's house (Harrington 1933:3). In the event of divorce the children remained with their mother (Palóu 1924:64).

A corpse was buried or cremated on the day of death. Inhumation was the practice of the Chalon and probably also of the Rumsen (Jayme 1929:26; Broadbent 1972:72). The Chochenyo and Ramaytush usually cremated the dead, but inhumation occurred when there were no kinsmen to gather wood for the pyre (Harrington 1921; Kroeber 1925:469; Duran and Fortuny 1958:273). Widows and perhaps other female kin cut their hair with

490

knives or burned it off with live coals, smeared their faces and heads with ashes or asphalt, and beat themselves on the head and breast with pestles (Broadbent 1972:72). In some instances the beating resulted in death (Harrington 1921). Most or all of a person's belongings were buried with him or destroyed. A widow remained in confinement for a year after the husband's death.

The dead were believed to go to a land across the sea. The names of dead persons were not spoken until formally bestowed anew upon another individual. Kinship terms were modified with a special suffix when reference was made to deceased individuals. Mourning ceremonies were probably held annually for all the people who had died during the year.

Subsistence

The Costanoan insured a sustained yield of plant and animal foods by careful management of the land. Controlled burning of extensive areas of land was carried out each fall to promote the growth of seed-bearing annuals (Crespí 1927:57–273; Galvan 1968). This annual burning retarded the growth of chaparral species and prevented the accumulation of large quantities of dead plant material, which would have posed a serious fire hazard. The judicious use of burning also increased the available grazing areas for deer, elk, and antelope and facilitated the gathering of acorns that ripened after the burning took place.

Acorns were probably the most important of the plant foods used by the Costanoan. Four species of oak stand out as relatively important. Coast live oak (*Quercus agrifolia*) and valley oak (*Quercus lobata*) were probably most important in terms of the quantities of acorns produced. Tanbark oak (*Lithocarpus densiflora*) was considered superior to the other species because of the whiter meal that it produced. California black oak (*Quercus kelloggii*) was also used.

Straight poles were used to knock acorns loose from the limbs of live oaks. The acorns were ground to produce meal that was leached to remove the bitter tannin. Acorns were consumed either as mush or in the form of acorn bread. The Chochenyo made acorn bread by wrapping balls of thickened mush in alder leaves and baking them.

The nuts of buckeye (*Aesculus californica*) were also leached to remove bitterness and made into mush, but they were considered an inferior food. The nuts of the California laurel (*Umbellularia californica*) were eaten either raw or cooked. Hazelnuts (*Corylus cornuta* var. *californica*) were also eaten (Palóu 1924:63).

The seeds of a number of plants were roasted by tossing them with live coals in basketry trays. Among the species used were dock (*Rumex* sp.), tarweed (*Madia* sp.), chia (*Salvia columbariae*), and digger pine (*Pinus sabiniana*). The seeds of the holly-leaf cherry (*Prunus ilicifolia*) were ground to produce a meal that was eaten.

Berries eaten included blackberries (*Rubus ursinus*), elderberries (*Sambucus* sp.), strawberries (*Fragaria* sp.), manzanita berries (*Arctostaphylos* sp.) gooseberries (*Ribes* sp., subgenus *Grossularia*), madrone berries (*Arbutus menziesii*), and wild grapes (*Vitis californica*). Toyon berries (*Heteromeles arbutifolia*) were always cooked by the Chochenyo.

Roots eaten included two species of wild onion (*Allium* sp.), cattail roots (*Typha latifolia*), an herb called chuchupate (*Lomatium californicum*), amole (*Chlorogalum pomeridianum*), wild carrots (*Daucus pusillus*), and a number of unidentified species.

Young shoots of three varieties of clover (*Trifolium* sp.), chuchupate, and thistle were eaten. The pollen of common tule (*Scirpus acutus*) was made into balls and baked. Cider was made from the berries of manzanita (Harrington 1921; Merriam 1966–1967, 3).

Large animals eaten by the Costanoan included black-tailed deer, Roosevelt elk, antelope, grizzly bear, mountain lion, sea lion, and whale. The most important method of hunting deer was stalking by individual hunters. The hunter wore a deer's head as a disguise and imitated a feeding deer in order to approach his prey. The flesh of stranded whales and sea lions was roasted in earth ovens and was highly prized for its fat content (Palóu 1924:62–63).

Other mammals eaten included dog, wildcat, skunk, raccoon, brush rabbit, cottontail, jackrabbit, tree squirrel, ground squirrel, woodrat, mouse, and mole. Rabbits were hunted communally with nets and straight rabbit clubs. Mice were captured by deadfall traps. Woodrats were secured by burning their nests and ground squirrels were driven from their burrows by blowing smoke into the burrows with a feather fan.

Waterfowl were the most important birds in the Costanoan diet. The species eaten by the Chochenyo were the Canada goose (*Branta canadensis*), snow goose (*Chen caerulescens*), white-fronted goose (*Anser albifrons*), American widgeon (*Anas americana*), pintail (*Anas acuta*), mallard (*Anas platyrhynchos*), green-winged teal (*Anas crecca carolinensis*), shoveler (*Anas clypeata*), and American coot (*Fulica americana*). Ducks and geese were captured in nets with decoys of tules or stuffed bird skins used to lure them into position (Harrington 1921).

Other birds eaten included mourning dove (*Zenaida macroura*), robin (*Turdus migratorius*), California quail (*Lophortyx californicus*), and hawks. Eagles, owls, ravens, and buzzards were not eaten. Cagelike traps of twigs were used to capture quail; bolas consisting of two pieces of bone tied to a string were used in hunting birds.

The most important fish were steelhead (*Salmo gairdnerii*), salmon (*Oncorhynchus* sp.), sturgeon (*Acipenser* sp.), and lampreys (*Entosphenus tridentatus* and possibly *Lampetra ayresi*). Many other species are mentioned in the vocabularies but are not specified as eaten; among the identifiable varieties are sardine, shark, swordfish, and trout. Salmon, steelhead, and lampreys seem to have been very important to the Costanoans living on the San Lorenzo and Carmel rivers. Sturgeon and salmon were caught in the Carquinez Strait area in seine nets (Font 1930:370–372). Dip nets were used by the Chochenyo to catch an unidentified species of fish (Harrington 1921). One very efficient method of catching fish was attracting them to bonfires at night and spearing them. Basketry fish traps were also employed (Crespí 1927:280). Fish poisoning with amole and *yerba del pescado* (probably turkey mullein, *Eremocarpus setigerus*) (Harrington 1921) and hook and line fishing were also practiced.

All varieties of reptiles appear to have been eaten but frogs and toads were not.

Insects eaten included yellow jacket larvae, grasshoppers, and caterpillars. Honey and wasp larvae were obtained by killing the bees and wasps with smoke blown into the nest with a fan of hawk feathers (Harrington 1921). Mollusks were of considerable importance in the coastal areas of Costanoan territory. Mussels, abalone, octopus, and a number of unidentified aquatic species were used for food.

Structures

The most common type of dwelling was apparently a domed structure thatched with tule, grass, wild alfalfa, ferns, or carrizo (fig. 2). The thatch was held on a framework of poles with pole binders tied with willow withes. The doorway was rectangular, and the fireplace was located in the middle of the house. The Ramaytush and the Rumsen also made conical houses of split redwood or redwood bark (Kroeber 1925:468; Crespí 1927:219). When dwellings became flea-infested they were burned (Broadbent 1972:62).

A small sweathouse was constructed by excavating a pit in the bank of a stream and building the remainder of the structure against the bank. Rumsen sweathouses accommodated six to eight persons (Broadbent 1972:62). Both men and women sweated in the sweathouse but the children were excluded (Harrington 1921).

Dance enclosures were circular or oval in shape and consisted of a woven fence of brush or laurel branches about four and one-half feet high. There was a single doorway and a small opening opposite it (Font 1930:326; Merriam 1966–1967, 3:373).

An assembly house on Gazos Creek impressed the members of the Portolá expedition. It was a domed structure (probably thatched) and was large enough to accommodate all 200 inhabitants of the village (Crespí 1927:219).

The Rumsen and the Awaswas located their permanent settlements away from the ocean shore and situated them on high ground (Broadbent 1972:63; Williams 1890:47).

Assembly houses or dance plazas were located in the center of the village with dwellings around the periphery (Crespí 1927:219; Font 1930:368). Sweathouses were located along a stream bank near the villages.

Technology

Tule balsas were the watercraft of the Costanoan; they were propelled with a double-bladed paddle (fig. 3) (Heizer and Massey 1953). Stone anchors are mentioned by Font (1930:370). Balsas were used for transportation and for fishing and duck hunting.

Both sinew-backed and self-bows were made by the Costanoan. Bowstrings were made of either sinew or vegetable fiber. Arrows had three-feather radial fletching attached with asphalt, a cane shaft, and a hardwood foreshaft. Arrowheads were made of stone or bone; for some types of arrows the foreshaft served as the only head. Nets were used in hunting quail, ducks, and

Coll. Sir John Galvin, Dublin.

Fig. 3. Tule balsa with men using double-bladed paddles. Figure in middle wears blanket of woolen cloth woven at the mission. Watercolor by Louis Choris, 1816.

rabbits. Quivers of fox skin were used by the Chochenyo (Harrington 1921).

Rocks and minerals provided the raw material for many stone tools. A wide variety of sedimentary and metamorphic rocks were used in implements such as manos, metates, mortars, net sinkers, anchors, and pipes. Minerals used in the manufacture of chipped-stone tools included chert and obsidian. Chert was quarried at a number of localities in Costanoan territory and obsidian was obtained in trade.

Minerals were also used as coloring agents in body paints. White pigment was obtained from a type of clay. Hematite and cinnabar provided red pigment. Hematite was quarried in the Oakland hills and cinnabar was mined at New Almaden. The Costanoan had excavated a tunnel between 50 and 100 feet long by the middle of the nineteenth century. Wars were fought between Awaswas and Tamyen groups over the right to use the deposits. The cinnabar of New Almaden was known over much of northern California, and parties from as far away as the Columbia River journeyed to Costanoan territory to obtain it (Heizer and Treganza 1972; Harrington 1921).

Cordage was made from the fibers of milkweed (*Asclepias fascicularis*), Indian hemp (*Apocynum cannabinum*), or nettle (*Urtica* sp.). It was made by both men and women by rolling the fibers on the thigh.

Blankets were woven of strips of sea otter (fig. 2), rabbit, or duck skin. Tule mats and animal skins served as bedding (Harrington 1921; Broadbent 1972:62).

Acorns, buckeye nuts, and seeds were ground in several different types of mortars. Stone mortars included bedrock mortars, portable stone mortars, metates, and hopper mortars. Wooden mortars were hollowed in the side of logs. Small mortars were used for paint and medicine. Pestles were made of stone or wood.

Most Costanoan basketry was twined rather than coiled. The materials employed in making baskets were willow (*Salix* sp.), rush (*Juncus* sp.), tule (*Scirpus* sp.), and the roots of "cut-grass." Baskets were ornamented with abalone pendants, quail plumes, and woodpecker scalps (fig. 4) (Broadbent 1972:63; Harrington 1921; Merriam 1966–1967, 3:374, 381).

Many types of baskets were used in the collection, preparation, and storage of food. Seed beaters were used to remove seeds from plants. Basketry traps were employed in the catching of fish. Collected food was carried on the back in conical burden baskets; a small basketry bottle was used for carrying water. The hopper portion of the hopper mortar was basketry. Seeds and acorns were winnowed, parched, and sifted with baskets. Baskets were sometimes used in the leaching of acorn and buckeye meal. All boiling was done in basketry utensils. Dippers and mush bowls were also baskets. Water jugs, cradles, and food storage containers were all made of

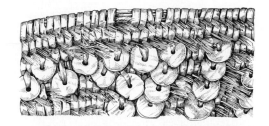

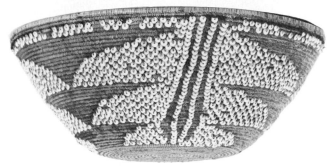

Dept. of Anthr., Smithsonian: 313234.

Fig. 4. Coiled basket covered on outer surface with olivella shell beads, black quail feathers, and red acorn woodpecker feathers, probably 18th century. Diameter 30 cm.

basketry (Broadbent 1972:63; Merriam 1966–1967, 3:393–394).

Baskets were also used as trinket containers, in which items such as sewing materials were stored (Broadbent 1972:63). Awls were made of bone or wood (J.A. Mason 1916:434).

Other household utensils included soaproot brushes used in preparing meal from acorns, a paddle for stirring food, and shell spoons. Rib bones and split cobbles were used in fleshing skins; skins were dressed with brains and wood ashes on an inclined post.

Clothing and Adornment

Costanoan men and boys usually went naked. Women wore aprons. The small front apron was made of netting or braided tule or grass. The larger rear apron was made of buckskin (fig. 2) or sea-otter skins. In cold weather both men and women wore robes that were fastened under the chin with a piece of cord. Robes were made of rabbit skin, sea-otter skin, duck feathers, or buckskin. Men sometimes covered their bodies with mud to keep warm in cold weather. The Costanoan went barefoot and wore no hats (Harrington 1921; Broadbent 1972:57).

The hair was worn either long or cropped to four or five inches. Women wore their hair with bangs cut in front and the remainder of the hair hanging freely. Men with long hair either braided it or tied it on top the head with a buckskin thong (fig. 5). While some men wore long, flowing beards, most removed facial hair with wooden tweezers or a pair of mussel shells. Chochenyo men sometimes removed facial hair with a hot coal (Broadbent 1972:57; Harrington 1921).

Fig. 5. San Francisco mission Indians at a gambling game. Men wear hair tied with thongs. Note the strings of shell beads being wagered and the wooden gaming sticks. Watercolor by Louis Choris, 1816.

Tattoos were registered on the face, forehead, and arms (fig. 6). Paints worn in nonritual contexts were applied to the face and body. Grass, flowers, feather ornaments, and earrings were worn in the pierced ears. A bone ornament was worn in the pierced nasal septum by some men. Necklaces of olivella shells and abalone pendants were also worn. Other ornaments were made of feathers and beads (Harrington 1921; J.A. Mason 1916:433-435; Heizer 1955:162).

Games

Games and gambling were favorite amusements of the Costanoan. A ball race was played in which a wooden ball was kicked along a course. Shinny was another favorite game, in which a wooden puck was struck with curved sticks. Other games included the hoop-and-pole game, a dice game with half-round wooden sticks, and the hand game (fig. 5).

Synonymy

Costanoan is derived from the Spanish word *Costaños* meaning 'coast people'. Two other terms were used earlier to designate the Costanoan languages, Olhonean

and Mutsun. Olhonean is ultimately derived from the name of a tribelet, ʔolxon, located on or near San Gregorio Creek in San Mateo County. The name Olhone first appeared in print in Beechey's account of his 1826 visit to San Francisco; he spells it Alchone and Olchone and makes the statement that the Olchone inhabited the seacoast between San Francisco and Monterey (Beechey 1968:76, 78). The Oljon tribelet contributed converts to San Francisco Mission between 1786 and 1790 (Merriam 1968:19). The San Francisco Mission records locate Oljon on the coast south of the Cotegen tribelet, which held Purísima Creek. Mutsun was the name of a village at a place called Natividad (probably La Natividad land grant) in the hills between the Salinas and Pajaro rivers (Merriam 1968:15, 19, 33).

No native name for the Costanoan people as a whole existed in aboriginal times, since the Costanoan were neither a single ethnic group nor a political entity.

The only previous set of names used to designate the Costanoan languages was devised by Kroeber and based upon identification of linguistic groups with particular missions in the historic period. Kroeber (1925) used the names Monterey, Soledad, San Juan Bautista, Santa Cruz, and San Francisco to refer to the groups here

Coll. Sir John Galvin, Dublin.

Fig. 6. Neophytes at San Francisco Mission. Woman is tattooed on chin and upper body. Detail from watercolor by Louis Choris, 1816.

designated respectively as Rumsen, Chalon, Mutsun, Awaswas, and Ramaytush. Under the rubric of Santa Clara Costanoan Kroeber included the speech of the Costanoans at Missions San José and Santa Clara (peoples here designated as Chochenyo and Tamyen). Kroeber assigned the northern portion of Chochenyo territory and the adjacent Karkin and Saclan lands to a group called Saclan. Beeler's (1955, 1961) linguistic studies of

vocabularies collected by Arroyo de la Cuesta have demonstrated that Saclan is a Miwok language and that Karkin must be recognized as a separate and distinct language within the Costanoan family.

Etymologically the names Karkin, Tamyen, Mutsun, Chalon, and Rumsen are simply names of tribelets and villages whose usage has been extended to embrace larger linguistic and cultural entities that were aboriginally unnamed. Chochenyo is the Mutsun name for the people living north of Santa Cruz (Merriam 1966–1967). Ramaytush is the name used for the inhabitants of San Francisco peninsula by the Chochenyo of the east bay. Ramay was the tribelet that held the northern end of the peninsula. Awaswas is the Mutsun name for the Santa Cruz people (Merriam 1966–1967).

Sources

Primary sources of ethnographic information on the Costanoan fall into five major categories: accounts of the exploring expeditions that traversed Costanoan territory from 1769 to 1776, replies of missionaries to the *interrogatório* of 1812, accounts of seafarers who visited the seven missions in Costanoan territory, ethnographic data collected by anthropologists between 1900 and 1935, and statements of the Costanoan themselves. The explorers' accounts contain a good deal of ethnographic information that can be located in time and space with a relatively high degree of certainty. The replies of missionaries to the *interrogatório* (Abella and Lucio 1924; Amorós 1950; Duran and Fortuny 1958; Jayme 1929) and the accounts of seafarers (Langsdorff 1968; Lapérouse 1959; Beechey 1968), on the other hand, fail to ascribe the ethnographic practices observed to specific ethnic groups (Costanoan, Esselen, Miwok, Yokuts, or Patwin). Small amounts of ethnographic material were collected by Kroeber (1907a) and Merriam (1968). The most extensive single body of Costanoan ethnographic and linguistic material is the field notes of Harrington (1921, 1929–1930). The only publication that has presented this material is Harrington's (1942) Central California Coast culture element distributions. Two brief accounts of Costanoan history (Galvan 1968; Williams 1890) contain the point of view of the Costanoan themselves.

Esselen

THOMAS ROY HESTER

Language and Territory

On the basis of very fragmentary data, the Esselen ('esələn) language has been placed in the Hokan stock (Dixon and Kroeber 1913; Sapir 1917). Linguistic summaries have been published by Henshaw (1890) and Kroeber (1904a). The Esselen linguistic data consist primarily of several short vocabularies, including those published by La Pérouse and Galiano, Duflot de Morras (both summarized in Kroeber 1904a), Arroyo de la Cuesta (1821) and Pinart (in Heizer 1952). Taylor's (1860–1863, 13) word list is a Rumsen Costanoan vocabulary and not, as thought by him, of the neighboring Esselen. Kroeber (1904a) states that then-extant material was unsatisfactory for grammatical studies. In 1902 he had made an attempt to obtain additional Esselen word lists, but the only informant he could locate was an aged Costanoan woman living at Monterey who could recall only six Esselen words. In 1908 Kroeber was able to add to the Esselen data a single sentence that he found in a Spanish document. The only substantial contribution to Esselen linguistic research since then has been the publication of Alphonse Pinart's 1878 manuscript, containing a list of 134 Esselen words (Heizer 1952). Two sources on Esselen not yet studied in 1975 are an extensive manuscript discovered in the Naval Archives, Madrid, in 1973 and some notes recorded by J.P. Harrington in 1936–1937 and now in the Department of Linguistics, University of California, Berkeley.*

Clearly, the Esselen are among the least-known groups in California. They inhabited a thickly wooded, mountainous environment on the south-central California coast, south of the present city of Monterey (fig. 1). Although the extent of their territory is not well defined, it definitely included the upper drainage of the Carmel River and extended south to the vicinity of Junipero Serra Peak (elevation 5,844 feet) and west to the Sierra de Salinas. A 25-mile stretch of this territory bordered on the rocky Pacific coast, from Point Sur to Point Lopez. Total area claimed by the Esselen is estimated to have been 580 square miles (Cook 1943:186). This would include the drainage of the Big Sur River, which Levy (1973) believes was occupied solely by Costanoan speakers. The Salinan

* Until all these materials have been studied no systematic orthography can be suggested for Esselen words, which are here cited in the spellings of the original sources.

peoples bordered Esselen territory on the south, and there were Costanoan groups on the northern and eastern boundaries. Cook (1974) made a careful survey of the baptismal registers for San Carlos (Carmel) and San Antonio missions and from the recorded natal villages of neophytes has reconstructed the territory of the Esselen. Cook's map is substantially the same as figure 1 except that Cook places the northern limit of the tribe on the coast along Little Sur River.

Knowledge of Esselen villages and settlement pattern within the defined territory is quite limited. Sebastián Vizcaíno, who in 1602 was the first European to visit Indians in the Monterey area, noted that there were both coastal and inland villages. Hodge (1907–1910,1:438) notes that some Esselen groups lived in the coastal ranges

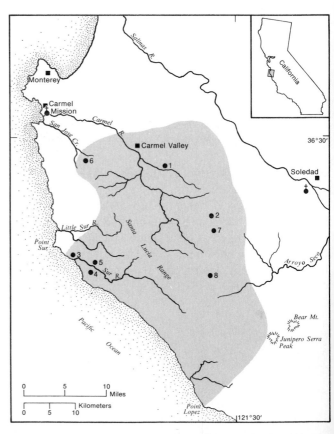

Fig. 1. Tribal territory and villages or possible villages. 1, Capanay; 2, Ippimeguan; 3, Jojopan; 4, Ecgeagan; 5, Eslanagan; 6, Echilat; 7, Hash-show'-wen; 8, Agua Caliente. Village names after Merriam 1902/1933–1934; Levy 1973; Pilling 1948.

paralleling the littoral. Costansó (1910) records that in the year 1769–1770 the natives of the Monterey area (probably Rumsen) were observed living in the hills about one and one-half leagues from the beach. There is some evidence (Pilling 1948:96) that the Esselen moved their villages every few years and usually reoccupied former village sites.

Known Esselen villages are few, and there is considerable confusion as to their identity and locations. Recorded villages, some of which are plotted in figure 1, include Agua Caliente (Tassajara Hot Springs), Exse'ein 'the rock', Capanay, Ippimeguan, Ekheya (in the mountains), Echilat, Xaseum and Pachhepes (both in the coastal ranges), and Hash-show'-wen (near the present town of Jamesburg). A list of 20 additional Esselen villages has been published (Hodge 1907–1910,1:438), but it is far from certain that these can actually be linked to the tribe. Levy (1973) states that the village of Jojopan, sometimes considered to be Esselen, must be attributed to the Costanoan. Similarly, there is confusion about the possible Esselen villages of Eslanagan and Ecgeagan, purportedly located on opposite sides of the Carmel River (Kroeber 1925:545); Levy (1973) believes that Eslanagan (or Eslenajan), a "tribelet," was actually situated on the Salinas River at Soledad and that Ecgeagan was somewhere in the Santa Lucia Range. Kroeber (1925:545) lists the village of Ensen as belonging to the Esselen, but Levy's more recent work affiliates it with the Rumsen Costanoan.

Levy (1973) has recognized six Esselen "tribelets": Excelen (near the town of Carmel Valley; eight subsidiary settlements), Echilat (Santa Lucia Mountains), El Pino (on the lower Arroyo Seco; three subsidiary settlements); Cuchunu (also on the Arroyo Seco; one subsidiary settlement); Eslenajan (near Soledad Mission), and Tucutnut (on the Carmel River; one subsidiary settlement).

Culture

Sometime in the early decades of the nineteenth century, the Esselen became culturally extinct, the first of the California Indians to so vanish. Thus it is almost impossible, given the paucity of reliable data, to define the nature of this small tribe. Early accounts make it evident that the Esselen were different from both their Salinan and Costanoan neighbors (Balbi 1826; Kroeber 1904a), although it is difficult to determine whether or not this distinction was made on other than linguistic grounds. There is some slight evidence that the Esselen were culturally more similar to the Rumsen Costanoan, but there are no specific details. Kroeber (1925:545) characterized the Esselen as "distinct mountaineers." Unfortunately, the bulk of information on Esselen culture was obtained from informants (primarily Costanoan) who had only vague recollections of Esselen lifeways.

When Vizcaíno visited Monterey Bay in 1602, he observed "numberless Indians" (Bolton 1925:92), but these probably included members of both Esselen and Costanoan groups. Kroeber (1925:545) estimated Esselen population at between 500 and 1,000, while later calculations by Cook (1943:186) and Levy (1973) place the figure at 750. As of 1928, it was believed that a possible Esselen descendent (of one-quarter Indian blood) was living in the Carmel area (Kroeber and Heizer 1970:12). Cook (1974:11) estimates the aboriginal population at 1,300 and the population density at 2.1 persons a square mile.

Data on Esselen subsistence often come from sources that may have confused the activities of this tribe with those of the adjacent Rumsen. However, it is probably accurate to say that both groups exploited similar resources, including those found in both inland and maritime environments. Vizcaíno (in Bolton 1925:92) notes that the Indians at Monterey "most commonly eat, besides fish and crustaceans . . . acorns and another nut larger than a chestnut [buckeye?]." During the visit of the ships *Sutil* and *Mexicana* in 1792 (see Navarrete 1802), it was observed that the "Eslen and Runsien" gathered seeds that were stored for winter use and also engaged in hunting and fishing. During the year 1769–1770, fishing was not a major subsistence endeavor, as wild game was plentiful; Costansó (1910) indicates that fishing was done only when hunting prospects were poor. A poison made from "man root" (a wild turnip, *Marah* sp.) was used to stupefy fish (Pilling 1948). Disguises and imitations of animal behavior were used as hunting techniques. According to Kroeber (1904a:54–55) and Pilling (1948:96), other items in the Esselen diet were various seeds and plants, including roots, dandelions, "cherry stones," and buckeyes. Skunks and dogs were eaten, and rabbits were roasted on sticks. Lizards were caught with grass snares.

The informant Isabella Meadows (Pilling 1948) has reported that the Esselen of Agua Caliente made abalone-collecting trips to Aulon Point near Pacific Grove. After the abalone had been obtained, the meat was removed from the shell and strung on bulrushes to be dried.

Information on Esselen material culture is a patchwork of scattered references, amplified somewhat by inferences based on the extant word lists. A general ethnographic description of the Indians of the Monterey Bay area appears in papers by Kroeber (1908a) and Broadbent (1972), and while most of the data in these two ethnographic sketches are specifically referable to the Rumsen Costanoan, much is no doubt also applicable to Esselen culture.

Subsistence-related artifacts included winnowing baskets, small basketry jugs or bottles, roasting pans for roots, arrows, knives, pestles, and mortars. Clothing consisted of rabbitskin robes or coats (rabbitskin blankets were also made) and tule aprons; at times, the Esselen were said to go naked. They made baskets (shape and size

497

unknown), using tule and "grass" roots as foundation materials. The women also wove mats. Tule reed rafts were possibly the only watercraft used by the Esselen until dugout canoes were introduced in the historic era.

Nothing of substance is known of Esselen social life customs. There are brief mentions of dances and of mythical "night spirits" (Kroeber 1925:545), but no details are available. An adulterous wife was either repudiated or was handed over to her lover for an indemnity, which usually equaled the cost of the acquisition of a new wife for the wronged husband. According to Navarrete (1802), the Esselen believed that they were transformed into owls at death. With the passing of a chief, there was a four-day mourning ceremony involving the entire tribe. Participants cut off their hair and covered their faces with ashes. The corpse was shrouded with cloth and beads. Other information on disposal of the dead has been provided by Isabella Meadows (in Pilling 1948:96). She states that the body of a person with no friends was unceremoniously placed in the woods and forgotten. When the deceased had a few friends, the body was interred. Very popular persons were cremated at death. In all instances, the hut of the dead person was destroyed.

The aboriginal existence of the Esselen ended with the construction of Mission San Carlos Borromeo de Monterey in June 1770. The mission was later moved (December 1770) to a new site called Eslenes in the Carmel Valley and became known as San Carlos Borromeo del Carmelo (Lewis 1910:427). The bulk of the Esselen population was gathered into this mission (some may have been taken to the Soledad mission). Esselens were described by the Spanish as friendly and generous people; they supplied the mission with wild game and helped the garrison make adobes for use in mission construction (Vallejo 1875,1:55). After 20 years of mission life, the Esselen apparently existed in a degraded state, for in 1792 the Indians of the San Carlos mission were characterized as "the most stupid as well as the ugliest and filthiest of the natives of America" (Navarrete 1802:164). If this is an accurate description of their condition at that time, it is no surprise that Esselen culture completely disappeared within the course of a few decades.

Prehistory

Given the paucity of written data on the Esselen, archeology is the only avenue of research that may eventually provide more information on this extinct cultural group, since the archeological potential of the Esselen area has not been fully exploited. The files of the Archaeological Research Facility, University of California, Berkeley, contain records on a number of archeological sites in what is considered to be Esselen territory. There are many sites on the coast, especially in the Point Sur area. These include a number of small sites that are primarily eroded sand dunes with exposed hearths, chipped-stone artifacts, and shell debris. Bedrock mortars are sometimes located near these sites. Some of the coastal sites are more extensive and can perhaps be termed village sites; occasionally, cemetery areas are associated. Site Mnt-64 is located on the Molera Ranch near Point Sur in the general vicinity of the possible Esselen village of Jojopan (fig. 1). This site is an occupation refuse mound 40 yards in diameter and three to four feet in height. The direct historical approach might be quite effectively applied at such a site.

In the mountainous interior, bedrock mortar sites are particularly common; one such site attributed to the Esselen is illustrated in Breschini (1972). The frequency of bedrock mortars reflects a heavy dependence on vegetal foods by the aboriginal population (probably Esselen). There are also occupation sites in the narrow stream valleys, which have yielded chipped-stone artifacts, mortars, pestles, and food remains (particularly the shells of mussel and abalone). Burials are sometimes found in these sites, and cremated bone is recorded at several sites. Rockshelters in the interior often contain rock art—both petroglyphs and pictographs—and occasionally, occupational deposits are found. One rockshelter, the Isabella Meadows site, was excavated by Meighan (1955a). It remains as the only fully reported archeological site in the Esselen area. The occupation at the site extended well into the historic era, and many of the objects found there can undoubtedly be linked to the Esselen. One very interesting discovery was that of a burial of a small Indian child, perhaps dating from about 1825. Glass trade beads were found with the burial. The child (believed to be a girl) was wearing an olivella shell bead pubic apron, a leather headband, a possible cordage hair net, a string of beads made from the chitinous leg segments of beetles, and various shell ornaments.

Also recovered from the site, and possibly of Esselen manufacture, were fragments of a large, closely twined burden basket; cordage made of apocynum fiber, animal skin, and twisted bark; arrow shafts and hardwood foreshafts; fire drills; a wooden awl; fire pokers; abalone shell containers (used for holding asphaltum); shell ornaments; worked antler tines; and a few stone artifacts. Meighan (1955a:25-26) has used the data from Isabella Meadows rockshelter to develop a general model of Esselen culture, much of which closely fits information derived from written sources. Meighan believes that the Esselen lived in small family groups, migrated regularly (occupying favored camp sites), and exploited both littoral and interior resources. He suggests that many of the Esselen spent the fall season in the interior.

Synonymy

If the Esselen had a single term that they used as a designation for the entire tribe, it has not been discovered. The rubric Esselen is probably derived from the name of a major village, perhaps Exse'ein or the place called Eslenes, which was the site of the San Carlos mission. In any event, the early Spanish extended the term to include the entire linguistic group (Kroeber 1908a:20). A variety of names has been used to refer to this group, including Eslen or Eslenes (Navarrete 1802), Ecclemach, Excellemaks, Aschatliens (Balbi 1826; Taylor 1862), Excelen, Ecselen, Escelen, and Ensen (Kroeber 1908a:20).

Salinan

THOMAS ROY HESTER

Language

The Salinan (sə'lēnən) language is tentatively included in the Hokan stock (Powell 1891; Sapir 1921a). The definitive study of the language is by J.A. Mason (1918) although considerable substantive research had been done by Sitjar (1861), Arroyo de la Cuesta (1821), and Kroeber (1904a). Jacobsen (1954-1958) studied it prior to its extinction.*

Mason's research demonstrated the existence of two mutually intelligible Salinan dialects, one associated with the northern division of the tribe (Antoniaño), and the other with the southern division (Migueleño).

The Salinan peoples occupied a rugged, mountainous area on the south-central California coast. The interior is dominated by heavily wooded hills and mountains of the South Coast Ranges, and there are sheer cliffs and rocky beaches along the Pacific littoral. Additional environmental data can be found in J.A. Mason (1912:104).

The actual extent of the territory inhabited by the Salinan is not at all certain. Henshaw and Kroeber (1910:415) attribute to them a very large area, stretching "from the sea to the main ridge of the Coast Range, and from the head of the Salinas drainage to a short distance above Soledad." However, J.A. Mason (1918:102) believes that the Salinan boundaries were somewhat more restricted, with the most definite northern boundary marked by Junipero Serra (Santa Lucia) Peak, and from that mountain "generally northeast to the Yokuts boundary and southwest to the sea in the vicinity of Lucia." Levy (1973) sets the northern boundary of the Salinan in the Salinas River valley, 10 to 12 miles from Mission San Antonio de Padua. There were Costanoan and Esselen groups on the northern boundary, Yokuts to the east, and Chumashan peoples on the southern border.

On the basis of linguistic data and the accounts of the Spanish missionaries, it seems fairly certain that there were two major divisions of the Salinan. The northernmost were gathered into the Mission of San Antonio de Padua, and thus became known as Antoniaños. According to Merriam (1902/1933-1934) their territory extended from Junipero Serra Peak to the divide between the San Antonio and Nacimiento rivers. The southern division became associated with the San Miguel mission and were called Migueleños. Unfortunately, there are no data on the extent of their territory.

Records at both missions refer to "Playanos" or 'beach people'. This group, apparently few in number, possibly constituted a third division of the Salinan, but nothing of substance is known of them.

External Relations

Trade was a major factor in relationships between the Salinan and surrounding peoples. Various sources make it clear that the Salinan were on friendly terms with the Yokuts (especially those groups around the Tulare lakes). The Yokuts permitted the Salinan to visit and fish in the lakes, while the Salinan allowed them access to the littoral (J.A. Mason 1912:108). There was much trade, with the Yokuts receiving shell beads and unworked shells from the Salinan, for which they exchanged saltgrass salt (cf. Heizer and Rapoport 1962), obsidian, seeds, lake fish, and possibly tanned antelope and deer skins (Baldwin 1971).

With their Chumash neighbors to the south, the Salinans carried on at least some trade, obtaining univalve columella ornaments, wooden dishes, and steatite vessels. However, there seems to have always been much hostility between the two groups.

There was an even greater degree of hostility between the Salinan and the Costanoan groups on their northern border, and it is probable that this enmity stemmed from trade competition. Pohorecky (1964:15) postulates that the boundary between the Salinan and the Costanoan marked a sort of trade barrier and that these two peoples were "competitors for that rich inland trade-market where marine shells were a premium commodity" (ibid.:25). The southernmost of the Costanoan groups

---

* A rather detailed and reasonably accurate, although old-fashioned, description of the Salinan sound system is presented by J.A. Mason (1918:7-13). Much of this can be equated with the modern phonemic orthography—tentative in some aspects—worked out by William H. Jacobsen, Jr., which can be summarized as follows. There are just five vowels, *i, e, a, o, u,* which occur short and long(·). The stops occur in a voiceless series (in which following aspiration is not significant): *p, t, ṭ, k, ʔ;* a glottalized series, *p̓, t̓, ṭ̓, k̓;* and a voiced series (with fricative allophones) *b, d, g.* Voiceless fricatives are *s, š, x, h.* The nasals *m, n,* liquids *l, r,* and semivowels *w, y* have voiceless allophones; and [ŋ] is an allophone of *n.* Stress, ´, is phonemic. Italicized Salinan words in this chapter are Mason's forms mechanically converted (with some doubts about vowel length) by Jacobsen into his own orthography.

were reputed to be the greatest extratribal foes of the Salinan (J.A. Mason 1912:108).

Settlement Pattern

J.A. Mason (1912:106–108) lists and discusses a number of Salinan villages, most of which cannot now be accurately located. Another list of villages, extending to 44 manuscript pages, was prepared by C.H. Merriam (on file, Archaeological Research Facility, Berkeley). From these two compilations it is possible to locate 21 villages (fig. 1).

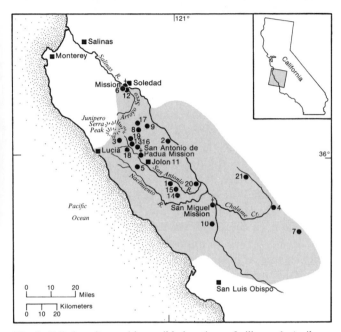

Fig. 1. Tribal territory with possible locations of villages. 1, Assil (*násil*); 2, Atnel (*ʔatnél*) or Chuclac; 3, Chacomex (*ǐša·xoméš*); 4, Cholami (*ǐšolám*); 5, Chuguilim or Chuquilin; 6, Chuttusgelis (Levy 1973 suggests this village is Esselen); 7, Cuia; 8, Ejcita; 9, Ginau or Genau; 10, Him'-se-en'; 11, Jolom (*holón*); 12, Palo Caido (may be identical with Ginau); 13, Papuco; 14, Patzác; 15, Sapaywis (*sapé·wis*); 16, Skătĭtâ'gi; 17, Squem; 18, Tĕssospĕ'k; 19, Tilacusam; 20, Tsho-hwal (*ǐšóxwal*); 21, Tĕcau'mistram. Village names after J.A. Mason 1912; Merriam 1902/1933–1934. According to Merriam's list, the villages of Lajolle, Lachayuam, Lit, Lizul, and Ssamacen are on the east side of the Salinas River, across from Atnel; more specific locations are not known.

Nothing substantial can be offered regarding Salinan settlement pattern. Fages (in J.A. Mason 1912:106) notes that there were 20 villages within a 20-mile radius of the San Antonio mission. There were also occupation sites along the coast (sometimes said to be on the shore or beach), and others were located inland along creek and river banks or on the floodplains. No permanent sites were situated in the coastal ranges, but there were probably hunting and foraging camps in these locales.

The major village of the Migueleños was said to be *ǐšolám* (or Cholami) at the site of present-day Cholam. There were several important Antoniaño villages, includ-

ing Skătĭtâ'gi, Tĕssospĕ'k, Ko'ic. One informant, a Rumsen Costanoan woman living at Sur, told Merriam that the Salinan "headquarters" was a big rancheria at or near the present city of Salinas.

Culture

This discussion of Salinan culture is general; consult J.A. Mason (1912) and Harrington (1942) for details.

In subsistence, emphasis was placed on the collecting of vegetal foods, particularly acorns. Acorns were stored in willow-twig granaries before being processed (in a stone mortar) and leached. Other plant foods included wild oats, sage seeds, berries, mescal, and wild fruits. Salinan informants could not recall the use of digging sticks. Mammals hunted and eaten by the Salinan include deer, bear, and rabbits. The rabbits were hunted with nets by the Migueleños. Meat was roasted, baked, or dried. Cooking baskets and earth ovens were used in food preparation. Fishing was done by both coastal and interior groups.

Little survives of Salinan material culture. There are a few baskets (fig. 2), including a collection in the Robert H. Lowie Museum of Anthropology, Berkeley. There is a variety of sizes and shapes, and coiling and twining appear to be the major techniques of manufacture (J.A. Mason 1912:146–152). Pinart (in Heizer 1952) has provided sketch profiles of basket types recorded in 1878.

Stone work by the Salinan can only be inferred from the limited archeological research in the area. Flaked stone artifacts include projectile points, scrapers, and choppers. Pecked and ground stone objects include bowl mortars, pestles, metates, basket mortars, stone bowls, notched pebble net sinkers, and arrowshaft straighteners. Ornaments are of steatite and serpentine. Bone and shell tools were also manufactured, especially bone awls and wedges and, on the coast, C-shaped shell fishhooks.

Other equipment of the Salinan were wooden-hafted stone knives, wooden mortars, wooden combs and food stirrers, and dippers made from gourds. Weapons consisted of self- and sinew-backed bows up to four feet long. Arrows were of cane and had hardwood foreshafts; specialized bird-hunting arrows were used.

Houses were domed and up to 10 feet square, constructed with a pole framework covered with tule or rye grass. Communal structures and dance houses are reported but not described. Semisubterranean sweathouses were built. There are conflicting data as to the use of menstrual huts.

Clothing included tule aprons, rabbitskin or otterskin cloaks, and basket hats. Hair was shoulder length and tied at the neck. Personal adornment consisted primarily of body painting and possibly tattooing. The Migueleño perforated the nasal septum. Ear ornaments were fashioned of abalone shell.

501

Fig. 2. Twined baskets with crossed warp pattern. Collected by J. Alden Mason at the Salinan settlement near Jolon, about 1910.

Shell beads of mussel and abalone formed the basis of Salinan currency, and value depended on the color of the individual shell. Long beads from a distant, unknown source were most valuable. Generosity with property was considered a virtue. However, both Salinan divisions were noted for high interest rates charged on loans of currency: "In their wild state, usury consisted of the daily augmentation of the value of the amount lent" (Kroeber 1908a:18).

Women retired to a specially built hut to give birth. At birth, the umbilical cord was severed and the baby was washed in a spring; the afterbirth was buried. Women returned to normal activities in two days. Young Salinan boys were instructed by their fathers, while the teaching of girls was left to their mothers, at times aided by berdaches. With the exception of local village endogamy, marriage was exogamous. There was a marriage feast for the girl; however, there was no formal marriage ceremony. Divorce was common; one cause was infertility, usually ascribed to the female. Several forms of prostitution were permitted.

At death, the most distinguished dead were cremated among the Antoniaños and the house of the deceased was burned, followed by brief abandonment of the village. There does not seem to have been an annual mourning ceremony. Among the Migueleños, the corpse was wrapped in skins and the possessions were ceremonially burned. Additional data are given in J.A. Mason (1912:167) and Baldwin (1971:134).

The data on kinship are very poor. See summaries by J.A. Mason (1912:169-172), Gifford (1922), and Harrington (1942).

The bone game, found in many aboriginal groups in the western United States, was popular among the Salinan. Other games were ball races, shinny, games of strength, and possibly hoop-and-pole games.

Dances were usually performed by individuals, although group dances were often part of festivities following construction of a communal dwelling. J.A. Mason (1912:158) has described the character of Salinan singing.

Musical instruments were cocoon rattles, wooden rasps, rattles and flutes of elderwood, musical bows, and bone whistles. Merriam (1902/1933-1934) notes the use of a drum, made by stretching a hide over a frame.

The golden eagle appears to have been the chief deity (possibly related to the Chingichngish cult of the Chumash). Prayers were offered to the sun and moon. The Migueleños believed that the soul left the grave after three days and traveled over the ocean. There was a puberty ritual for boys that involved the use of datura (toloache); no ceremony was held for girls.

Shamans played an important role in bloodletting and black magic and were specialists in poison. However, their chief function was in curing disease. There were also weather and grizzly bear shamans.

Chief medical treatments were bleeding, scarification, and the use of herbs and sweatbaths. White willow was used as a cure for fever, and toloache was used as a drug in tending broken bones. Merriam (1902/1933-1934) records the use of datura for relief of pain, especially burns and broken limbs.

A substantial collection of Salinan myths has been published by J.A. Mason (1912,1918). Cosmogonical myths show heavy Christian influence. There is a series of adventure myths, with Prairie Falcon and Raven as the culture heroes. One tale relates a rainmaking contest between a mission priest and a shaman; this was won by the shaman when he caused a great downpour. There are explanatory myths, accounting for the origin of mescal, of different languages, and of the "theft of fire." Stories of actual events included an eclipse of the sun, an earthquake at Cholam and a three-year famine.

Calendrical and numerical systems were present among the Salinan, as was a system of linear measures. A knowledge of astronomy is indicated by native names for stars and constellations.

Villages or village groups were the major sociopolitical units and were autonomous; they often feuded with one another. There is evidence for the existence of clans, with a patrilineal chief and family descent, and there is a suggestion of Bear-Deer moieties. According to Harrington (1942), chiefs ruled solely over their village or village group and were accorded status through primogeniture. A new chief, however, required community approval. Among the Migueleños, the chief was always a wealthy man. J.A. Mason (1912:173) states that the chief was selected for his courage and was approved by the older men of the village. This implies that he was both the ordinary and war chief. In most of California these two offices were separate.

Prehistory

As in the case of their Esselen neighbors, Salinan prehistory remains virtually unknown. Four major archeological investigations have been carried out, but none of the excavated sites shows any clear cultural stratigraphy, and there is as yet no chronological control over cultural development in this region. The best available studies of the archeology in the Salinan territory are by Pohorecky (1964), Howard (1972), and Baldwin (1971). There are both inland and coastal sites, including small temporary camp sites and villages with deep midden deposits. Bedrock mortar sites are common, as are groups of petroglyphs and pictographs (usually in rockshelters).

History

In July 1771 San Antonio de Padua became the first mission to be established in the Salinan area. Salinan population at the time of European contact is estimated at close to 3,000 (Cook 1943). The Salinan were found to be a friendly and charitable people and the mission grew rapidly, becoming the largest of the California missions in 1790. Neophytes were primarily of the northern division of Salinans (Antoniaños), and there were a few "Playanos."

Mission San Miguel was founded in July 1797 and also expanded rapidly, having a population of 1,076 neophytes in 1814 (Lewis 1910a:449). Most of the neophytes were of the southern Salinan division (Migueleños), but 'beach people', Yokuts, and northwest Chumash were also recruited.

Once the Salinan were brought under the aegis of the missions, they were not permitted to resume their aboriginal life-style. Instead, they were taught agriculture and stock raising and were employed at weaving tasks. They apparently adapted easily to mission life and were said to be well dressed and orderly. The Indian quarters at San Antonio de Padua were excavated by Howard (1972); the recovered artifacts indicate rapid acculturation of the Salinan neophytes.

The mission existence caused a tremendous decline in Salinan population, which fell to fewer than 700 by 1831. There was a strong datura cult in the mission, and "orgies" were reported (Cook 1943:152). Indian healers

still operated. Vices of the Salinan at this time were described by Fathers Martin and Cabot (in Engelhardt 1929) as "sensuality, idleness and telling lies."

In the nineteenth and early twentieth centuries, Salinan survivors continued to live in the vicinity of the two missions. Population decrease accelerated greatly after secularization of the missions, with 350 Salinans at San Miguel in 1840 and only 30 in 1842; at San Antonio in 1842, there were 150 Antoniaños. By the 1880s Henshaw (in Powell 1891:101) estimated Salinan population at about 12. When Kroeber, Mason, and Merriam worked among the Salinan in the early twentieth century, there were only three Salinan families, all living northwest of Jolon. The most data exist on the Encinales family (Olive Wollesen, personal communication 1973), descendants of Eusebio Encinales, an Antoniaño born in the Santa Lucia Mountains. Another family is represented by Flujencio Santana (fig. 3), an informant consulted by J.A. Mason in 1910.

The California Roll of 1928 showed 36 Salinans, including 21 claiming to be of the Antoniaño division and 14 Migueleños (Kroeber and Heizer 1970:13). Among these were Pedro Encinales, son of Eusebio; his wife, Francesa Gambuscera Encinales; and their seven children including daughter, Josepha. In 1933, research by Merriam indicated that the sole surviving members of the Antoniaño division were three sons and a daughter of Eusebio Encinales: Felipe (born 1856), Eusebio (known as Tito, born 1858), Josedo Dolores (born 1874), and Maria. The wife of Tito Encinales was a remarkable Migueleño woman, Maria de los Angeles Ocarfu Encinales, who died in 1936 at the age of 127. Also located at this

Lowie Mus., U. of Calif., Berkeley.
Fig. 3. Flujencio Santana. Photograph by J. Alden Mason near San Antonio Mission, Sept. 1910.

Fig. 4. Dave Mora (Antoniaño Salinan) and his wife Maria Mora (Migueleño Salinan). Photograph by C. Hart Merriam near Jolon settlement, about 1933.

time by Merriam was David Mora, the husband of Maria Encinales (fig. 4), and Maria Bylon, a Migueleño living in Toro Creek Canyon. Although genetic descendants of the

Salinan are still living, Salinan culture can be described as ethnologically extinct.

Synonymy

The Salinan linguistic stock was named by Latham (1856) and Powell (1891), both of whom derived the name from the Salinas River. Kroeber (1925) states that no designation for the tribe was remembered or recorded. In his unpublished manuscripts, C.H. Merriam uses the term En'-ne-sen exclusively; according to one of his informants, this was the name of the Salinan headquarters at or near present-day Salinas.

Sources

The best sources on the Salinan are the studies of J.A. Mason (1912, 1918) and Harrington (1942), both of which are available in major public and college libraries. There are brief summaries by Henshaw and Kroeber (1910), Kroeber (1925), and Wollesen (1972). A sizable corpus of unpublished data on the Salinan was compiled by Merriam (1902/1933–1934) including over 100 pages of vocabulary.

Chumash: Introduction

CAMPBELL GRANT

Language and Territory

The Chumash ('choo͞,măsh) were known to Henshaw and other early investigators as the Santa Barbara Indians. The first reference to their language (Latham 1856) noted that the dialects of Santa Barbara, Santa Ynez, and San Luis Obispo were related. Powell (1891) later referred to the dialects of the region as Chumashan.

Beginning in 1878 with the Chumash vocabularies collected by Alphonse Pinart (Heizer 1952), considerable information on their languages was recorded from surviving Chumash. There were at least six Chumash languages (fig. 1): Ventureño (probably including Castac), Barbareño (probably including Emigdiano), Ynezeño, Purisimeño (these four forming a Central group of more closely related languages), Obispeño, and the Island language. Whether the interior Cuyama spoke a different Chumash language is uncertain (Beeler 1970:14, Beeler and Klar 1974).*

Geographically, the Chumash occupied the region from San Luis Obispo to Malibu Canyon on the coast and inland as far as the western edge of the San Joaquin valley. In addition, they occupied the Santa Barbara Channel Islands—San Miguel, Santa Rosa, Santa Cruz, and Anacapa.

History

For such a large and important tribe, there is remarkably little documented history. The Chumash were docile and friendly to the Spanish and readily went into the

---

* All the Chumash languages have been extinct since the death of Mary Yee, the last native speaker of Barbareño, in 1965. Materials on most or all the languages were provided by late 19th- and early 20th-century investigators, especially John P. Harrington, and by the work of Madison S. Beeler with Yee during her last year. According to Beeler (personal communication 1974), "the differences among the various Chumash languages, at least those that constitute the Central group, were lexical and inflectional rather than phonological." Thus a single orthography should suffice for all of them—that of Beeler (1970:15–16), which conforms to Handbook standards if *h* is substituted for the raised comma, and *i* replaces ï. The italicized Chumash words in the following chapters have been rewritten by Beeler in this orthography; the spellings of those with a question mark following are less certain. The principal difficulties are that early recorders rarely recognized glottalization and did not hear the difference between *k* and *q,* so that words from sources other than Harrington and Beeler cannot be accurately transliterated in these regards. Most of the Chumash words that Beeler was unable to identify are written in a Spanish-based orthography.

mission system that ended their native culture. Before anthropologists became interested in them, there were few Chumash left with any knowledge of the ancient life patterns; therefore, the ethnological record is slim.

The diaries and journals of the Spanish explorers who passed through the Chumash territory do remain, and in their writings can be glimpsed these interesting Indians before their destruction. The Chumash were the first major group of California Indians to be discovered by Europeans. On October 10, 1542, Juan Rodríguez Cabrillo, on an exploring trip up the coast, landed near the present site of Ventura. Cabrillo visited many points on the mainland and on the Channel Islands and noted the names of many of the settlements. The next brief contact was 60 years later when Sebastián Vizcaíno entered and named the Santa Barbara Channel.

In 1769 an expedition under the command of Capt. Gaspar de Portolá passed through the Chumash coastal region heading north to find Monterey Bay, reported by Vizcaíno in 1602. With him were Lt. Pedro Fages, the engineer Miguel Constansó, and the Friar Juan Crespí. All four wrote valuable accounts of the appearance and activities of the Indians. There are several more contemporary accounts before the turn of the nineteenth century: the 1775 diary of Father Pedro Font, diarist of the Juan Bautista de Anza expedition; Father Francisco Palou's account of 1778; the 1791–1792 journal of the naturalist José Longinos Martínez; and in 1793 the first account of the Chumash in English by Archibald Menzies, the naturalist of the George Vancouver expedition.

Those early historical accounts describe only the heavily populated Santa Barbara Channel coast. For all other areas in the Chumash territory, the scanty references to Chumash people and places in the mission records must be used in combination with the archeological evidence for a picture of Chumash life.

In 1772, San Luis Obispo, the first of the Franciscan missions in Chumash territory, was founded. Four others soon followed: San Buenaventura (1782), Santa Barbara (1786), La Purísima Concepción (1787), and Santa Ynez (1804). By the early 1800s, the entire Chumash population, with the exception of those who had fled into the mountains and the inland valleys, had come into the mission system. The Spanish missionaries were determined to make industrious farmers and artisans of the Chumash and taught them the trades that made the

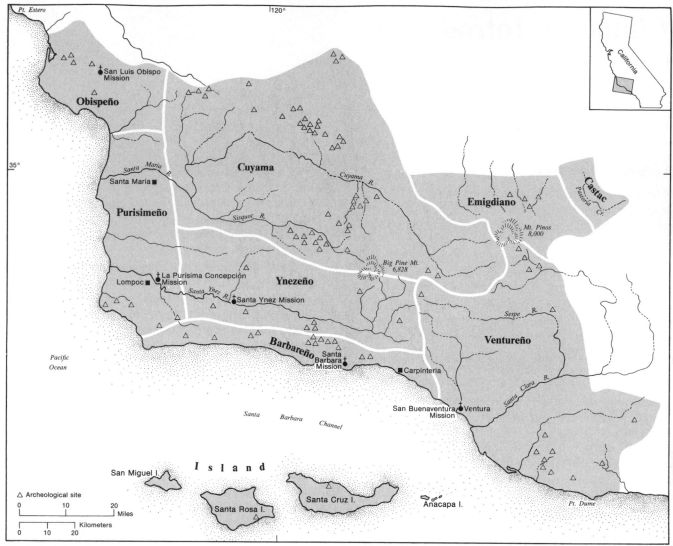

Fig. 1. Tribal territory with dialect areas and rock-art sites indicated. After Kroeber 1925; Grant 1965.

building and maintenance of the great mission establishments possible.

One-fourth of the 21 missions in California were devoted to the spiritual welfare of the large Chumash population, yet further historical reference to them is mainly confined to vital statistics in the mission registers. Some information on the Chumash during the mission period is found in the *interrogatorios*, or questionnaires, that the mission padres were required to send to the civil authorities in Mexico.

The mission period in the Chumash region lasted from 1772 until 1834, when the missions were secularized. In 1831 the Chumash registered at the five missions numbered 2,788, with 726 at the Santa Barbara mission (A. Forbes 1839). This was a great decline from the large population described by the explorers. Many of the original Chumash, of course, had simply migrated into the interior to escape the tedious mission life; but the basic cause for the population decline was the mission system itself, which crowded the neophytes into com-

pounds near the presidios and mission buildings, where they were daily exposed to the European diseases for which they had no immunity. Smallpox and syphilis were the major killers but even the common cold would rapidly develop into some deadly form of pulmonary disease.

Kroeber (1925:551) thought that the original population might have been between 8,000 and 10,000 for the entire Chumash area, including the interior and the islands. Cook and Heizer (1965:21) considered Kroeber's figures far too low and estimated (on the basis of 15 people in a house and 46 villages) that the 1770 population of the mainland channel area was between 18,000 and 22,000. In their village count, Cook and Heizer included 22 archeological Chumash sites (Rogers 1929) not mentioned by the explorers. Brown (1967:79) places the figure at 7,000 for the coastal region with 15,000 for the entire Chumash area. According to King (1969:map 1) the 1770 Barbareño population in 26 rancherias was between 4,300 and 6,700. The same map gives a total

Chumash population for all areas at between 10,700 and 17,250.

The Chumash made one attempt to escape the deadly benevolence of their Spanish masters. In 1824, driven to desperation by mistreatment by the mission soldiers and the endless toil, the neophytes revolted at Santa Barbara, Santa Ynez, and La Purísima. After brief hostilities in which several Indians and Spanish were killed, many natives fled to the Tulares (the lower San Joaquin valley) to take refuge with the Yokuts (Cooper 1969). Numbers were subsequently persuaded to return to the missions, but in 1833 a party of American fur trappers found a village of the renegade Spanish-speaking Chumash living near Walker Pass in Kern County raising corn and riding horses (Leonard 1839).

The intention of the secularization of the California missions in 1834 was to transform the mission centers into Pueblos; the Indians, with their knowledge of trade and agriculture, would become Mexican citizens in these Pueblos. Civil administrators would oversee the orderly changeover and allot land to all the former neophytes. What actually happened was far different. With the removal of authority, many Chumash fled to the interior and others refused to labor for the Mexican rancheros. Those who attempted to farm for themselves were harassed by the Whites and driven off the land. Those that remained at the missions were enslaved by the administrators (P. Wallace 1971:3).

In effect, the missionary system, having destroyed the native culture, now turned the survivors loose to fend for themselves. There is no record that the promised land or property was given to the Indians at the time of secularization, although in the 1840s some small parcels were given to individual Chumash. This land was soon lost through gambling or traded to Whites for whiskey and blankets. By 1838 drunkenness among the Chumash was widespread and continued to be a problem for many years (P. Wallace 1971:5). Many finally found work on the large ranches acquired by Mexican citizens through grant or by purchase from the mission administrators.

Disease continued to decimate the remaining Chumash and in 1844 a serious epidemic caused the death of most of the Purísima Indians. From the earliest Spanish contact the Chumash blood had been mixed with that of the Spanish and particularly the mestizos, so that by 1900 very few full-blooded Chumash were alive.

With the coming of the Anglo-Americans in 1847, the lot of the Chumash continued to deteriorate. They were exploited as cheap labor or ignored except when drunk and disorderly or when caught stealing horses. The Chumash that remained near the settlements worked as vaqueros, house servants, or farm laborers.

In 1855 a small piece of land (120 acres) was set aside on a creek near Santa Ynez Mission and 109 Chumash were settled there. This reserve, known as the Zanja de Cota (now reduced to 75 acres), eventually became the

Mission Chumash Population Following Secularization

	San Buenaventura	Santa Barbara	La Purísima	San Luis Obispo
1834	636	556	900	264
1835			400	
1839	300			
1840	180	250	170	170
1842				100
1844		300	200	
1845	200		50	60
1854		117		
1856		55		

SOURCE: P. Wallace (1971:48–50).

Mission Records

Mission	Years	Baptisms	Deaths	Difference
Santa Barbara	1834–1842	109	360	−251
Santa Ynez	1834–1850	265	401	−136
La Purísima	1835–1845	56	284	−228

SOURCE: Engelhardt (in P. Wallace 1971:48–50).

Chumash Population Since Contact

Date	Population
1770	8,000
1832	2,471
1842	1,656
1852	1,107
1865	659
1880	336
1920	74

SOURCE: Cook (1943a:40). Estimates based on 1832 mission records with the assumption that birth rate was 4% a year and death rate was 8%.

smallest official Indian reservation in the state. In 1972 about 40 mixed-blood Chumash occupied the land, with doubtless many more scattered about in southern California who have no knowledge of their ancestors or traditional culture (Lloyd 1955; Gardner 1965; Heizer 1970).

Synonymy

The name Chumash was arbitrarily chosen by Powell (1891) from the word used by the Coastal Chumash for Santa Cruz Island and its inhabitants, Mi-tcú-mac, or the Coastal Chumash word for the Santa Rosa Indians, Tcú-mac. Each regional group had its own name for itself. The Santa Rosa Islanders called themselves Hĕl-a-wac-skú-yu; the Barbareño, Wal-wa-ren-na; the Ynezeño, A-la-hu-la-po; and the Ventureño, Mitc-ka-na-kan (Heizer 1955:115).

Sources

Source materials covering the first contacts between the Spanish explorers and the Chumash are abundant. These original accounts are available: Cabrillo (Wagner 1929), Vizcaíno (Wagner 1929), Fages (1937), Constansó (1911), Crespí (1927), Font (1930), Palóu (1926), Longinos Martíncz (1961), Vancouver (Menzies 1924).

The Pinart and Henshaw Chumash vocabularies are published in the University of California Anthropological Records (Heizer 1952, 1955). Linguistic research on Chumash is surveyed in Beeler (1970) and Harrington (1974). There is a chapter on the Chumash in Kroeber (1925). Landberg (1965) contains a valuable study of the Chumash subsistence patterns. There is much ethnological information in the culture element distribution lists of Harrington (1942). Rogers (1929) describes many archeological sites along the channel. Drawings and photographs of paintings from all Chumash areas are available in Grant (1965). Father Engelhardt of Santa Barbara Mission wrote the histories of the five Chumash missions (1923, 1930, 1932, 1932a, 1933). They contain scveral of thc carly cightccnth-century Spanish *interrogatorios* with ethnographic information.

Extensive Chumash bibliographies are found in Landberg (1965), Grant (1965), E.N. Anderson (1964), and Heizer, Elsasser, and Clewlow (1970).

Eastern Coastal Chumash

CAMPBELL GRANT

The Coastal Chumash are divided into three linguistic-geographic entities: Barbareño, Ynezeño, and Ventureño.

The Barbareño occupied the narrow coastal plain from Point Conception to Punta Gorda in Ventura County (fig. 1). Directly behind the coastal shelf, the chaparral-covered Santa Ynez Mountains rise sharply to over 4,000 feet. The region enjoys a year-round mild climate and here the major concentrations of Chumash were found.

Chumash speaking the Ynezeño dialect occupied the middle and upper drainages of the Santa Ynez River between the Santa Ynez and San Rafael mountains. To the west, their territory was bounded by a north-south line roughly five miles east of La Purísima Mission. The climate is typical of the inland valleys, with hot summers and cold winters.

The Ventureño Chumash country was mainly mountainous with the exception of the Oxnard plain between Ventura and Point Mugu. The rancheria of Maliwu on the east side of Malibu Creek was the easternmost of the coastal Chumash villages (Kroeber 1925:pl. 48). The northern region includes the headwaters of the Ventura and Santa Clara rivers and is extremely rugged with several peaks rising to over 8,000 feet.

These three groups shared a common culture and the descriptions of the Barbareño can be applied to the other linguistic divisions except where differences are noted.

Barbareño

The first description of the Chumash was recorded by Juan Rodríguez Cabrillo in 1542: "They were dressed in skins and wore their hair very long and tied up with long strings interwoven with the hair, there being attached to the strings many gewgaws of flint, bone, and wood" (Bolton 1925:27). Font in 1775 noted other details:

The dress of the men is total nakedness. For adornment only they are in the habit of wearing around the waist a string or other gewgaw which covers nothing. . . . Some of them have the cartilage of the nose pierced, and all have the ears perforated with two large holes in which they wear little canes like two horns as thick as the little finger . . . in which they are accustomed to carry powder made of their wild tobacco . . . (1930:250–251).

Fages in 1775 described cold weather clothing: "The men go clothed with a large cloak made of the skins of cony, hare, fox, or sea otter; the garment reaches the waist, the captain only being allowed to wear it reaching to the ankle . . ." (1937:32). For additional warmth, the Chumash made blankets by twisting strips of bird and rabbit skin and weaving these strips together. The men often carried netting around their waists that served to carry small objects.

The women wore two knee-length skirts made of pieces of buckskin, one in front and one behind, the

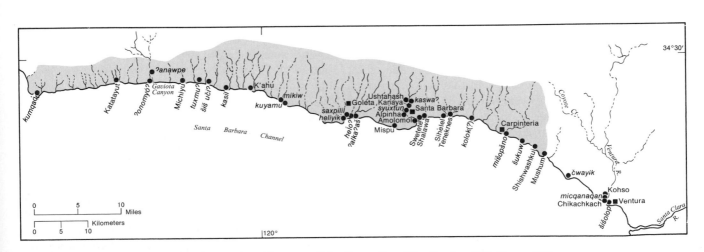

Fig. 1. Historic (after 1770) coastal settlements from Ventura to Point Conception. After Kroeber 1925; Brown 1967.

edges of which were fringed and ornamented with snail shells and cut pieces of abalone shell. The women wore their hair in bangs combed forward over the forehead, the rest worn loose down the back. Both sexes wore necklaces of shell, bone, and steatite and the women wore earrings of shell and stone. Body painting was done extensively by the Chumash, each rancheria having a distinctive pattern so that each group could be distinguished when they gathered for a dance or ceremonial function. Explorers noted that some of the men kept their beards plucked with clamshell tweezers but this was by no means universal.

All the early writers were impressed by the Chumash. Fages in 1775 noted that they were "of good disposition, affable, liberal, and friendly toward the Spaniard" (1937:47). Palou in 1778 found them "extremely intelligent and skillful" (1926, 3:232).

Structures and Settlement

The Chumash houses were much admired by the Spanish, and Longinos Martínez (1961:52) described their appearance in 1792:

These Indians live in communities and have a fixed domicile. They arrange their houses in groups. The houses are well constructed, round like an oven, spacious and fairly comfortable; light enters from a hole in the roof. Their beds are made on frames and they cover themselves with skins and shawls. The beds have divisions between them like the cabins of a ship, so that if many people sleep in one house, they do not see one another. In the middle of the floor they make a fire for cooking seeds, fish, and other foods, for they eat everything boiled or roasted.

The hemispherical houses were made by driving strong pliable poles into the ground and then arching them into the center where they were tied. Then a very thick covering was applied of interwoven grass. Much use was made of reed matting for mattresses, flooring, and for creating room divisions and doors.

Crespí (1927) wrote that some of the houses he entered would hold 70 persons. Another account speaks of houses 50 feet in diameter.

There is ethnographic evidence that stools made of whale vertebrae were often used and that tule, carrizo grass, wild alfalfa, and fern were also used for thatching.

In every village there were one or more sweathouses. These were semisubterranean and made of poles and earth. Entrance was through an opening in the roof by way of a ladder (Menzies 1924:325).

The Chumash villages along the channel were usually built on high ground where a stream ran into the ocean or on the borders of a slough area. A typical village consisted of several houses, a sweathouse, store houses, a ceremonial enclosure, a gaming area, and a cemetery usually placed well away from the living area.

When Cabrillo was visiting the Chumash in 1542, he recorded many of the coastal village names from the Ventura River to Point Conception. The explorers of the late eighteenth century describe 21 of these, of which only 17 were inhabited (Brown 1967:74).

Heizer (1955:194–195) lists 36 villages (from Chumash sources collected by H.W. Henshaw in 1884) between Malibu Canyon and Point Conception. Some of the most important with their present locations are: *kasil* (Refugio Beach), *mikiw* and *kuyamu* (Dos Pueblos), *heloʔ* (Mescaltitlán Island) (Goleta Slough), *syuxtun* (Burton Mound, Santa Barbara), *mišopšno* (Carpinteria Creek), *šukuw* (Rincon Point). Crespí and the other journalists of the Gaspar de Portolá expedition gave descriptions and population estimates of the villages between Assumpta (Ventura) and Point Conception (Brown 1967:16–48):

Village	Population	Houses	Canoes
ʔonomyōʔ (Gaviota) (Heizer 1955)	300	52	7
tahiwaš	400	80	15
mikiw and *kuyamu* (Dos Pueblos) (Heizer 1955)	1,100	120	10+
Goleta Slough Towns: *saxpilil̀*, *heloʔ*, Geliec, Alcas	2,000	100+	16+
syuxtun (Santa Barbara) (Heizer 1955)	600	40+	10
mišopšno (Carpinteria)	300	38	7
šukuw (Rincón Pt.)	300+	60	7

Social and Political Organization

The Chumash villages, known to the Spanish as rancherias, were composed of patrilineal descent groups. Harrington (1942:32) maintains that the Chumash had totemic clans but Henshaw (in Heizer 1955:149), who took ethnological notes in 1884, found no evidence of the clan idea.

Crespí in 1769 observed that "all the towns have three or four captains, one of whom is head chief" (1927:38). Font in 1775 noted the status conferred by canoe ownership (similar to northwestern California wealth emphasis): "Among the men I saw a few with a little cape like a doublet reaching to the waist and made of bear skin, and by this mark of distinction I learned that these were the owners and masters of the launches [see fig. 2]. . . . When it [the canoe] arrived at the shore ten or twelve men approached the launch, took it on their shoulders still loaded with the fish and carried it to the house of the master or captain of the launch . . ." (1930:252–259).

According to Harrington (1942:33), each village had at least one chief and the position was hereditary patrilineally but subject to village approval. Sometimes

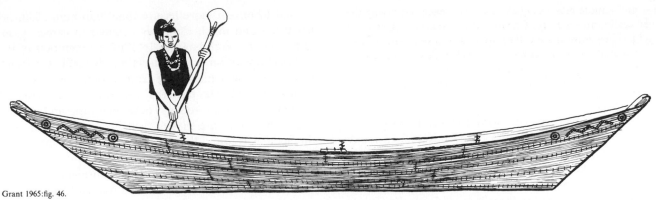

Grant 1965:fig. 46.

Fig. 2. Planked canoe. Length 6.9 m. Based on eyewitness accounts by Pedro Font in 1775 and Archibald Menzies in 1793. Drawing by Campbell Grant.

daughters or sisters of deceased chiefs inherited the position. The account of the Cabrillo expedition recorded one example of this (Bolton 1925:29). Harrington (1942:33) wrote that a chief could rule over a village or group of villages. The power of such chiefs or captains was strictly limited. Besides their function as war leaders, they would preside at ceremonies and would receive gifts for their services. Each village had prescribed hunting and seed-gathering areas and only the chief could grant permission for other villages to gather or hunt on his village territory.

Life Cycle

Lieutenant Fages in 1775 noted the method of childbirth practiced by the women near the mission of San Luis Obispo. The woman would make a small hole in the ground wherever she happened to be when the labor pains began. The hole would then be warmed by fire and lined with straw. Here the woman would await the birth. After the birth, the nose of the child was flattened, and then the mother bathed herself in cold water (1937:49).

Longinos Martínez in 1792 recorded a birth practice that shocked the early Spanish: "In this region they have the notion that unless they have an abortion at their first pregnancy, or if the child does not die immediately, they will never conceive again. Hence they murder many babies with the efforts they make, the blows they give themselves, and the barbarous medicine they take in order to induce an abortion, so that some of the women die and others are badly injured" (1961:56).

There is little information in regard to the Chumash puberty rites but Harrington (1942:36–37) has some details. During the puberty period, girls were forbidden to eat meat or grease and they could not look into a burning fire. Boys were taken out at night and given a strong liquor made of pounded toloache (*Datura*) root mixed with water, to induce visions. An identical ceremony was practiced by the southern Yokuts.

With the exception of the chiefs and captains, the Chumash men had only one wife. A new bride was purchased from her parents with gifts such as some beads, an otter skin, or a blanket (Engelhardt 1930:35). Henshaw (in Heizer 1955:148) noted that a girl could marry in her own village or in another. Adultery was punished by whipping. Polygamy was only for the favored few (Fages 1937:33).

Longinos Martínez in 1792 described a typical cemetery: "Above each grave they erect a board, some three varas long and half a vara wide, painted in black and white squares, and a pole three or four times as tall as the board, painted in the same colors, on top of which they usually place trophies; if the dead man was a fisherman, hooks and lines; if a hunter, bows and arrows, etc. They also lay lengthwise over the grave the rib of a whale, bent like a bow. The cemetery is enclosed by a high stockade" (1961:62). In his excavation of Burton Mound at Santa Barbara, Harrington (1928:134) noted that slabs of whalebone made of crosscut rib sections and whale scapulae had been used to line some graves. The whalebone markers mentioned by Longinos Martínez were still evident in the second half of the nineteenth century and were an aid to the curio looters who stripped so many of the Chumash cemeteries.

Lieutenant Fages in 1775 gave a detailed account of the mourning ceremony:

When any Indian dies, they carry the body to the adoratory, or place near the village dedicated to their idols. There they celebrate the mortuary ceremony, and watch all the following night, some of them gathered about a huge fire until daybreak; then come all the rest (men and women) and four of them begin the ceremony in this wise. One Indian smoking tobacco in a large stone pipe, goes first; he is followed by the other three, all passing thrice around the body; but each time he passes the head, his companions lift the skin with which it is covered, that the priest may blow upon it three mouthfuls of smoke. On arriving at the feet, they all four together stop to sing I know not what manner of laudation. Then come the near and remote relatives of the deceased, each one giving the chief celebrant a string of beads, something over a span in length. Then immediately there is raised a sorrowful outcry and lamentation by all the mourners. When this sort of solemn response is ended, the four ministers take up the body, and all the Indians follow them singing to the cemetery . . . (1937:33–34).

The bodies were placed with the head toward the west, face down, and tied in a flexed position. In many cemeteries, reburial was practiced, with bodies being moved to make room for new ones. Offerings such as bowls, pestles, beads, weapons, and charmstones were included. In many graves there was evidence that bowls and mortars had been deliberately broken at the time of burial.

Small canoes of stone, bone, or wood have been found with infant burials. A Chumash informant said that they were to help conduct the small soul into the other world.

Social Culture

The large number of smoking pipes found in burials suggests a general addiction to the strong native tobacco (*Nicotiana attenuata* and *N. bigelovii*). The typical Chumash pipe is a tapering tube of steatite, usually fitted with a bird-bone mouthpiece. The Chumash used tobacco in another way, as "a confection of wild tobacco and lime, which when chewed, strengthens them as they say; but if they go to excess, it intoxicates them . . ." (Engelhardt 1932:18).

The early Spanish noted that the Chumash were not inclined to anger and cruelty and that any form of punishment was rare. For theft, the culprit was brought before the chief and made to return the goods or something of equal value. Disputes between village men were sometimes settled by the disputants facing one another and exchanging blows with their sweat scrapers until someone drew blood.

Only a few instances of taboos have been recorded (Engelhardt 1930:34):

The pagans, especially the old men cling to many of their superstitions. For instance, a fisherman will not eat of the fish or of the venison, rabbits, hares, etc. which he caught, believing he will in that case catch no more. In order to win at a play of chance, he must fast for some days; and if he loses, he imagines that the winner fasted more. The husband may not touch his wife until the child can stand alone on its feet, otherwise he shall have no more children. When the wife is delivered of a child, the husband must abstain from meat for some time, lest the child die.

Nearly all the early writers commented on the presence of transvestites among the Chumash, remarking that there were two or three such men in each village, who "are called *joyas*, and are held in great esteem" (Fages 1937:33).

The ease of life along the channel, afforded by the abundant food supply and the benign climate, gave the coastal Chumash more leisure time than many California tribes and much time was devoted to games, gambling, singing, and dancing. In 1769 the members of the Portolá expedition were entertained by their Chumash hosts. Prominent men came from various villages, each painted in different patterns and carrying bunches of feathers and hollow reeds. These men sang and danced to the rhythm of the shaken reeds for several hours and the Spaniards found the effect pleasing but interminable (Crespí 1927:168).

The Chumash had no drums. The musical instruments were flutes of elder wood or bone (blown from the end over the edge), the musical bow, whistles of cane and bone, the bull-roarer, and rattles of split sticks, sea shells, turtle shells, and bunches of deer hoofs.

A flat area for dancing and ceremonials was an important part of each village and Fages in 1775 described a dance at such a spot: "The women go to them well painted, and dressed as has been described [with antelope hide skirts], carrying in both hands bundles of feathers of various colors. The men go entirely naked, but very much painted. Only two pairs from each sex are chosen to perform the dance, and two musicians, who play their flutes. Nearly all the others who are present increase the noise with their rattles . . . at the same time singing, very displeasing to us" (1937:36).

The Chumash played all the games familiar to the southern California Indians, including shinny, with a small ball of hard wood. After the shinny game, the entire team retired to the sweat lodge (Robinson 1846:94).

They also played a variation of the hoop and pole game. A small hoop made of tied rushes or bark was rolled along the ground, and the contestants tried to throw a long pole through the rolling hoop.

The Chumash were great gamblers and the men were constantly wagering shell money, which they kept strung around their topknots. A favorite was the ancient game of hiding a stick behind the back and having the opponent guess which hand held the stick. A gambling game played by women was the dice game. The dice were snail or walnut shells filled with asphaltum. There is no Chumash account of the playing of this game, but the dice are identical with those used by the Yokuts (Latta 1949:130–131) and the Chemehuevi (Kroeber 1925:598). The Chumash also had gaming sticks made of split wood seven inches long and pointed on one end, which were probably cast like the walnut dice to see whether the flat side fell down or up.

Warfare

The early Spanish invariably found the Chumash gentle and friendly, a quality that led to their undoing as they entered the fatal mission system without a struggle. Only once, in the abortive revolt of 1824, did they take up arms against their Mexican masters.

There is evidence that Indians from the mountains and the interior valleys made forays against the coastal Chumash. On August 18, 1769, the Portolá expedition traveling between present-day Carpinteria and Santa Barbara saw two burned villages, Paredon (*kolok* [?]) and Montecito (Saluhaj). The Indians told the Spaniards that the mountain Indians had attacked these villages three months earlier and had killed all the people. Another burned settlement was seen later farther to the west (Crespí 1927:164).

At the Santa Barbara Museum of Natural History, there are a number of skulls and other bones with flint arrowheads imbedded in them that have been excavated from channel cemeteries. It is impossible to say who the raiding Indians were, though the inference is that they were non-Chumash and might have been Takic speakers or Yuman Mohaves from the Colorado River. It is known that the latter made periodic visits to the coast (Señán 1962:126).

Among the Chumash, the cause for war could be the infringement of a village hunting and gathering preserve, the refusal of a chief to accept an invitation to a feast or dance, or the avenging of witchcraft.

Warfare was arranged formally as opposed to the surprise raid. The aggrieved group would send a messenger to arrange a meeting at a certain place. Here both parties met, throwing feathers in the air and shouting their battle cries. An Indian from one side would then step forward and fire a series of arrows at the other side. Then one from the other side shot off an equal number.

Religion and Shamanism

Almost nothing is known of the religion of the Chumash. The diaries of the explorers and the *interrogatorios* of the missionaries afford a few glimpses. In 1542 Cabrillo (in Bolton 1925:30) wrote: "They have in their pueblos large plazas and have an enclosure like a fence; and around the enclosure they have many blocks of stone set in the ground, and projecting three palms above it. Within the enclosures they have many timbers set up like thick masts. On these poles they have many paintings, and we thought that they worshipped them, because when they dance, they go dancing around in the enclosure." Longinos Martínez in 1792 noted that at all the rancherias, the Chumash would plant a stake about three feet high on the highest and most open area and fasten a bunch of feathers to the top of the stake. Longinos Martínez thought that this primitive shrine was worshiped by the people as a symbol of the unseen power that provided them with seeds, fish, and all needed things. No amount of ridicule by the Spanish would sway them from this belief (1961:53).

Father Olbés of the Santa Barbara mission, in his report of 1813, recorded the name of the Chumash deity as Sup (i.e., *šup*). They had no figure or idol to represent this deity but would honor him and show their gratitude for his favor by strewing seeds and feathers in various areas. These offerings were a token of acknowledgment to *šup* for his bounty (Engelhardt 1923:96).

The deity *šup* is certainly identical with Achup or Chupu worshiped by the Purísima Chumash. In 1801 a messianic movement occurred at the Santa Barbara mission following a severe epidemic of pneumonia and pleurisy that killed many Indians. An Indian woman neophyte had a vision in which Chupu appeared to warn her that the pagan Indians would all die if they allowed themselves to be baptized and that the Christian Indians would also die if they did not pay tribute to Chupu. The movement was endorsed by all the Channel Chumash settlements and the Mission Indians. A neophyte revealed the plans of the movement to the Spanish and as the epidemic lessened, the movement died (Heizer 1941a; Stickel and Cooper 1969:13).

The worship of Chupu persisted for some time; in the 1820s the neophytes often built little shrines of sticks and brush on which they hung bits of cloth and various objects. On the inside of the shrine, they would place tobacco and other offerings as gifts for the unseen spirits. The missionaries severely punished any Chumash caught practicing such a reversion to their pre-Christian beliefs (Woodward 1934:120-121).

Kroeber (1925:567-568) places the origin of the Chingichngich religion with the Gabrielino, possibly on Santa Catalina Island and spreading east, south, and possibly north into Chumash territory. This native cult based on the use of toloache has been described in detail among the Juaneño Indians by Father Boscana (Harrington 1934). One of the Chingichngich ceremonies centered about the panes, a giant bird described as resembling the vulture only larger (the California condor). Today the Chumash territory is the last haunt of the condor (Barbareño *wit*, Ynezeño *ʔalmiyiʔ*) and Ventureño rock paintings often show men in bird costumes that might represent the condor. In the coastal Chumash area, ritualistic figurines of steatite have been found, often representing killer whales. According to Kroeber (1925:938), these and also rock paintings may have been used in connection with the toloache cult.

As in other parts of California, the chief function of the shaman was the curing of disease. In the Chumash area, according to Harrington (1942:39-42), the shaman (fig. 3) was invariably a man, who employed singing, herbs, and a medicine tube for sucking out the foreign object presumed to be causing the sickness. His power was derived from a guardian spirit that appeared to him during a trance or vision. There were rattlesnake shamans, who had the ability of handling rattlesnakes; weather shamans, who could control the weather; and grizzly bear shamans, who had the power to turn themselves into bears and kill enemies. The contents of an archeological example of a shaman's fetish bundle are listed by Olson (1930:19): "painted fabric or basketry containing two perforated stones, five awl or spatula-like batons with quartz crystals set into the open ends, three loose quartz crystals, two steatite pipes, a small incised steatite dish, and a number of beads, pendants, curious shells, etc."

The most interesting objects employed by the Chumash shamans were the charmstones. Though widely known among the other California tribes, the Chumash type was distinctly cigar-shaped and averaged about six inches in length. The material was a hard, close-grained rock and the pieces were carefully worked and polished. In the Santa Barbara area, they were considered very powerful sorcery stones and the shamans would arrange them in a circle of 20, then shove them violently together and sprinkle water over them (Yates 1889).

Rogers (1929:410) occasionally found the beaks of swordfish near the heads of male skeletons. At a late historic site, he found such a beak undisturbed and protruding above and forward from the face of the skeleton. Above and below the skull lay a thick sheet of overlapping triangular abalone shell ornaments pierced as though for attachment to some material. Rogers postulated that the man had been dressed to represent the swordfish. There were traditions that the Chumash revered this great fish because it drove ashore the whales so important for food and cultural material (Mohr and Sample 1955). Such an occurrence has not been recorded in historic times and it would appear that the stranding of whales had no connection with swordfish.

Technology

The early Spanish explorers were impressed by the Chumash craftsmanship. When the Juan Bautista de Anza expedition passed through the channel villages in 1775, Font noted the fine basketry, many articles such as trays and boxes skillfully made of wood, and the finely finished objects in stone. Above all he was astonished by the planked canoes, so skillfully made with the most primitive of tools (Font 1930:261).

• STONE   The finest objects made by the Chumash were of steatite. Its resistance to heat made it ideal for cooking receptacles. The pre-Spanish Chumash made no pottery and all cooking was done in heavy steatite ollas and on comals (flat cooking stones, like skillets) (fig. 4). Small, highly finished bowls to hold beads and prized possessions were made of the dark-colored steatite and often decorated on the rim with tiny flat shell beads inlaid on asphaltum. Other objects made of polished steatite are carved beads, medicine tubes, smoking pipes, effigies of whales, and a very curious artifact shaped like a small hay-baling hook and sometimes called a "pelican stone." Charmstones are sometimes made of steatite, though more often they are of stone not found in the coastal area, such as alabaster, schist, granite, and other rocks capable of taking a fine finish.

514

Fig. 3. A man wearing the ceremonial costume of a shaman. The dance skirt has strings of milkweed (*Asclepias*) fiber with eagle down twisted in and feathers attached to the lower ends. The entire costume is identical to that of a Yokuts shaman (in Latta 1949:202). Photograph by Léon de Cessac, 1878.

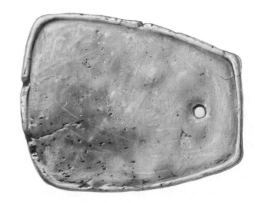

Fig. 4. Steatite slab for baking. A hooked stick inserted in the hole served as a handle to remove the hot stone from the fire. Length 32.0 cm, collected 1883.

The major steatite quarries were on Santa Catalina Island, territory of the Gabrielino (Schumacher 1878). The Chumash traveled to the island by canoe to obtain the steatite but whether they made the ollas at the quarries or traded for the roughed-out olla blanks from the Gabrielino is not known. There are some deposits of the fine-grained steatite in inland Santa Barbara County, and nodular pieces of unworked steatite have been found at a Chumash village site in the San Rafael Range.

Sandstone was much used by the Chumash artisans in the manufacture of large flaring storage bowls with up to eight quarts capacity. Mortars and pestles are abundant in burials but the most interesting type of mortar is the basket mortar where a bottomless funnel-shaped basket is attached to the upper surface of a flat boulder with asphaltum.

Asphaltum was an indispensable material to the Chumash. It occurs in natural seeps all along the channel. With it, they attached shell inlays to stone, caulked their canoes, sealed their water baskets, and fastened arrow and spear points to the shafts (Heizer 1940:74).

The Chumash made very fine projectile points of chert and occasionally of obsidian, obtained by trade with tribes to the east. The points are typically triangular with a notched base or leaf-shaped with a rounded base. The Chumash did not have the pump drill but used a slender sharp flint set in the end of a wooden shaft that was rotated between the palms.

A characteristic Chumash artifact, often made of sandstone, is the perforated or "doughnut" stone. These stones average about four inches in diameter with the drilled hole about an inch in diameter. Its principal use was as a weight for digging sticks (Heizer 1955:152). The perforated stones vary greatly in size (from one ounce to seven pounds) and undoubtedly served a variety of purposes (Heizer 1971:64–67).

• WOOD The outstanding technological achievement of the Chumash woodworkers was the *tomol*, or planked canoe (fig. 2). The Spanish were unanimous in praising these craft:

They are very carefully made of several planks which they work with no other tools than their shells and flints. They join them at the seams by sewing with very strong thread which they have, and fit the joints with pitch. . . . Some of the launches are decorated with little shells and all are painted red with hematite. In shape they are like a little boat, but without ribs, ending in two points . . . In the middle there is a somewhat elevated plank laid across from side to side to serve as a seat and to preserve the convexity of the frame. Each launch is composed of some twenty long and narrow pieces. I measured one and found it to be thirty six palms long and somewhat more than three palms high. In each launch . . . ordinarily not more than two Indians ride one in each end. They carry some poles about two varas long which end in blades, these being the oars . . . (Font 1930:252–253).

The canoes varied from about 12 feet to over 30 feet in length and were remarkably light (two men could easily carry an average-sized one). In these craft, the Chumash could quickly reach their fishing grounds and make long voyages, not only to the Santa Barbara Channel Islands but to Santa Catalina Island and even as far as remote San Nicolás, 65 miles from the mainland. For splitting the wood into planks, wedges of whalebone were employed (Heizer 1938; E. Robinson 1942).

The explorers noted wooden plates and bowls (fig. 5) made from the roots of oak and alder and boxes made of small planks sewed together. Costansó in 1769 described some fine bowls: "wooden plantes and bowls of different forms and sizes made from one piece, so [skillfully] that not even those turned out on a lathe could be more successful" (Costansó 1911:193). Seeds were generally ground in wooden mortars by the Coastal Chumash but only the stone mortars have survived (Menzies 1924:325).

The Chumash men carried in their hair small flint knives (fig. 6) fastened to a handle of straight polished wood inlaid with shell. Two types of arrows have been

Musée de l'Homme, Paris: top, MH 82-30-84; bottom, MH 82-30-85.
Fig. 5. Carved oak bowls. Top specimen has shell inlay along rim, maximum diameter 15 cm; bottom has 22 cm rim diameter. Collected in the Santa Ynez Valley in 1878 by Léon de Cessac.

Dept. of Anthr., Smithsonian: 20502.

Fig. 6. Flint knife set in wooden handle. The handle was at one time probably decorated with shell inlaid in asphaltum. Length 15.7 cm, collected 1876.

recovered from dry caves in the Chumash territory. One was the type made of a single piece of wood sharpened at one end. The other is the typical southern California two-piece arrow with the mainshaft of carrizo grass (*Phragmites communis*) and the foreshaft of hard wood, to which is attached the chert point with asphaltum and sinew.

• BASKETRY   Chumash basketry was outstanding in decoration and workmanship and examples were avidly collected by the early Spanish explorers and settlers (Dawson and Deetz 1965; Kroeber 1905c). The Chumash utilized many types of basketry in their everyday life. Water was stored and carried in basketry bottles (see "Interior Chumash," fig. 1, this vol.) ingeniously waterproofed on the inside. According to a Ventura Chumash (Craig 1966:210), some pulverized asphaltum was placed in the finished container and a number of round stones about two inches in diameter were heated and dropped into the neck of the bottle. These were then rolled about, melting the tar and forcing it into the weave of the basketry.

The Chumash weavers used both the coiling and twining techniques. In the coiled ware, there were basin-shaped baskets for food preparation, large burden baskets, olla-shaped baskets for storing seeds, and nearly flat circular trays for winnowing and parching (fig. 7). The finest work and decoration were reserved for trinket baskets for small possessions (Dawson and Deetz 1965).

The twining method was employed for water bottles, seed beaters, and coarsely woven basin-shaped baskets, probably strainers. In addition there were basketry cradles, hoppers for grinding mortars, bait baskets for fishing, and large twined tule mats for floor covering and wrapping.

• SHELL AND BONE   The Chumash made much use of shells, particularly the abalone (*Haliotis*) abundant along the channel. The inner mother-of-pearl surface of the abalone was cut into spangles of various sizes and shapes and attached to garments. It was used lavishly as inlay material on stone, bone, and wood. The circular fishhooks were often fashioned from abalone shell. The entire shell was commonly used as an eating dish after the row of siphon holes was plugged with asphaltum.

The keyhole limpet (*Megathura*) was a favorite material for hair ornaments and the univalve (*Olivella*) was universally used for bead material. The giant Pismo clam (*Tivela stultorum*) was ground into beads and disks for money. The money disks were strung and traded by length, standard length being the circumference of palm and outstretched fingers. Slender drilled tubes of clamshell up to three and one-half inches long were highly prized as money and were sometimes worn by both sexes in the pierced nasal septum.

Whalebone was utilized for wedges, abalone pries, burial markers, and grave liners (Harrington 1928:134). Sweat scrapers were made of deer and bear bones as well as swordfish bills. Long bone beads were used as spacers in many necklaces. Flutes and whistles were made of bone, the whistles usually of deer tibia (Elsasser and Heizer 1963:59). Needles, awls, fishing hook barbs, and harpoon heads were fashioned from bone.

• CORDAGE   The Chumash made excellent rope and twine. The bulk of their cordage was made from yucca. For a more pliable string, Indian hemp (*Apocynum*), nettle (*Urtica*), or milkweed (*Asclepias*) was employed. The heavier cordage was used for things such as canoe anchor ropes or harpoon lines. The lighter twine served for fish nets, carrying nets, bowstrings, and all manner of tying and securing.

Subsistence

The most important single food source was the acorn, mainly from the California live oak (*Quercus agrifolia*). It was gathered in the fall and stored for year-round use. The shelled nuts were ground into meal and cooked as mush or in some form of cake.

Pine nuts, especially of the piñon pine (*Pinus monophylla*), were a favorite food. Islay, the wild cherry (*Prunus ilicifolia*), was bruised in a mortar and boiled. The cattail *Typha* gave seeds and flour from the roots for making pinole, a gruel or paste. Berries, mushrooms, and cress were gathered in season to vary the diet.

The Chumash prized the amole, or soap plant (*Chlorogalum* sp.). The bulb was roasted and eaten, the green bulb furnished lather for washing, the dry husks could be frayed and bound into brushes, and the crushed plant was used as a fish poison. Berries of the California laurel

left, Southwest Mus., Los Angeles: 811-G-1709; right, Field Mus., Chicago: 103131.

Fig. 7. Coiled baskets. left, Necked "treasure basket" collected before 1937; right, parching tray, collected before 1920, diameter 34.9 cm.

(*Umbellularia californica*) were roasted. The chia sage (*Salvia columbariae*) produced a tiny oily seed that was made into flour or a very nutritious form of pinole.

The Chumash gathered many types of seeds with a basketry seed beater, a fan-shaped implement with which grass and weed seeds were knocked off into a wide-mouthed basket.

For hunting, the basic weapon was the bow and arrow (the self-bow or sinew-backed bow), and with it the Chumash killed animals such as the California mule deer, coyote, and fox. Smaller animals were usually taken with snares and deadfalls. Flat, curved throwing sticks were used to kill rabbits during communal rabbit drives. All the game birds were regularly harvested, particularly migratory ducks and geese on the lagoons. From canoes, the hunters pursued large marine mammals—seals, sea otters, and porpoises—and killed them with harpoons. Bowers (1878:319) quotes a Santa Rosa Indian informant who stated that the islanders killed whales and ate the blubber raw. He was probably referring to porpoises or pilot whales, as the California gray whale (*Eschrichtius gibbosus*), which was abundant in the channel during the winter migration, grew to 45 feet in length and was too dangerous an animal to be captured by the Chumash in their light canoes. It would appear likely that the Indians utilized the dead and ailing whales that were occasionally stranded along the channel. Though Chumash tradition credits the swordfish with the ability to drive the whale ashore (Rogers 1929:410), there are numerous reports of packs of killer whales (*Orcinus orca*) attacking baleen whales, tearing at their lips and tongues, and often killing them (Scammon 1874:90; R.C. Andrews 1916:198–200). The benefactor of the Chumash in this instance was probably the killer. Steatite effigies of these voracious toothed whales (see "Island Chumash," fig. 2, this vol.) have been recovered from channel and island burials.

Mollusks were an important food source and, except for the seasonally toxic mussel, were eaten the year round. The enormous shell middens along the channel are made up of shells such as the California mussel (*Mytilus*), the horse clam (*Tresus*), the gooseneck barnacle (*Mitella*), and the jacknife clam (*Tagelus californianus*). The very important mollusks, the Pismo clam (*Tivela stultorum*) and the various abalones (*Haliotis* spp.), though a major food source, seldom appear in middens as their shells were utilized as material for beads and ornaments.

The Santa Barbara Channel provided an inexhaustible supply of fish such as the shark, bonito, yellowtail, black sea bass, rockfish, halibut, anchovy, and barracuda. Larger fish were harpooned; the smaller ones were caught in seines and dip nets of twisted vegetable fiber or with hook and line. Trout were taken by poisoning still water with the soap plant (*Chloragalum*) or the turkey mullein (*Eremocarpus setigerus*).

Intertribal Relations

The Chumash shared many cultural traits with the people in adjoining territories. To the north were the Hokan-speaking Salinans. To the northeast were the Yokuts of the Penutian linguistic group. To the southeast were the Takic-speaking Gabrielino and Fernandeño. Of their neighbors, the Gabrielino were culturally the most similar, sharing a maritime environment and economy.

Trade was active between the Chumash and nearby tribes. The mainland Chumash supplied the Salinans with steatite, wooden vessels, and beads (Davis 1961:29). They traded white pigment, shell beads, Pismo clam, abalone, olivella, limpet and cowrie shells, and dried sea urchin and starfish to the Yokuts for black pigment, antelope and elk skins, obsidian, salt, steatite, beads, seeds, and herbs. They supplied the Tubatulabal with asphaltum, shell ornaments, steatite, and fish in exchange for piñon nuts. They traded seeds, acorns, and bows and arrows with the Island Chumash for chipped implements, fish-bone beads, baskets, and basaltic rock for digging-stick weights. The Kitanemuk obtained wooden and shell inlaid vessels from the Chumash. From the quarries of the Gabrielino on Santa Catalina Island the Chumash obtained the all-important steatite vessels, but there is no record of what they gave in return.

Rock Art

The rock paintings (see "Interior Chumash," figs. 3, 4, 5, this vol.) of the Chumash Indians are the most interesting and spectacular in the United States. The paintings almost invariably are abstract, but when life forms are represented they are highly stylized and imaginative. A feature of the more elaborate paintings is the multiple outlining of figures, especially the concentric circle and "cogged wheel" motif. A well-preserved example of this style was illustrated by Mallery (1886:pls. 1, 2). This site is the well-known Painted Cave of San Marcos Pass, a few miles from Santa Barbara. Most of the 12 known Barbareño painted sites are within a few miles of the Painted Cave along the summit of the Santa Ynez Range. Without exception they are near water, and bedrock mortars are often found in the immediate vicinity. As to their meaning, Kroeber (1925:938) suggests that the coincidence of southern California rock art with the area of the toloache religion points to a possible association.

In the Luiseño area, abstract paintings were made by girls during puberty rites (J.H. Steward 1929:227), and it can be presumed that a similar motivation was connected with some of the Chumash paintings. It can be theorized, based on known shamanistic practices in other parts of the world, that most of the Chumash pictures were ceremonial and made by or under the direction of shamans.

The idea that the painted sites represented shrines or sacred spots is suggested by their location, which almost invariably is a remote area in the coastal range high above the population centers. The extraordinarily fanciful character of many of the paintings suggests that they were painted by persons under the influence of the powerful hallucinogen, toloache (Grant 1965:63–64).

Ynezeño

The Chumash under the jurisdiction of Mission Santa Ynez (Ynezeño) and Mission San Buenaventura (Ventureño), especially those living in the inland mountains, are far less well documented than the Barbareño. Their material culture was quite similar to that of the Channel Chumash, but the people in the interior river valleys lacked an ocean-oriented economy and placed more emphasis on hunting and gathering.

In 1798 Father Esteván Tapís and Capt. Felipe de Goyocoechea crossed the Sierra Mescaltitlán (Santa Ynez Mountains) from Santa Barbara to locate a new mission site roughly halfway between La Purísima and Santa Barbara. Striking the river, they passed through two rancherias, Tegueps (*teweps*) and Calabuasa, before arriving at the village of Alajuapa, where the mission was eventually built. During a survey to check on the number of Indians in the area, Tapís recorded 14 rancherias, all within 7 to 36 miles of the proposed mission site. The largest settlement had 50 houses and the smallest eight. Tapís estimated that the average number of Indians in a house was four and arrived at a figure of 1,008 for the Santa Ynez settlements (Engelhardt 1932:3–4).

No descriptions are available on the size of the houses that Tapís saw but they must have been much smaller than those on the channel, where Cook and Heizer (1965:21) estimated the average number of people in each house at 15. In 1769 the Portolá expedition diarists estimated the populations and counted the houses in the villages between Rincón Point and Point Conception. The average number of people in a house was eight (Brown 1967).

Before the establishment of Mission Santa Ynez in 1804, Tapís requested troops to safeguard the mission as there was trouble with some of the interior Indians. He noted that the Chumash rancherias nearest the Tulares (Yokuts territory), in the southern San Joaquin valley, were of a bad disposition; and Indians from them would often murder people from other villages suspected of witchcraft. In 1801 a group of these Indians set fire to a small rancheria near Tegueps on the Santa Ynez River and killed five persons. The victims were related to the chief of *kuyamu* on the coast, who was attributed responsibility for a severe epidemic that had taken many lives (Engelhardt 1932:7).

By the end of 1804 only 112 Indians had been baptized and it had become apparent that there were not enough local gentiles, or unconverted Indians, to support a large mission establishment. As a result, converts were sent to the new mission from the two nearby missions. In 1806 there were 570 Chumash at Santa Ynez Mission, 132 from Santa Barbara and 145 from La Purísima. The baptismal registers show that eventually the mission had converts from many coastal and mainland rancherias and settlements on *limuw* (Santa Cruz Island). In 1831 the Chumash population at Mission Santa Ynez was 436 (A. Forbes 1839).

There are eight known rock art sites in the Santa Ynez River drainage. Several are along the crest of the Santa Ynez Range near San Marcos Pass and near permanent springs. The others are on small streams flowing into the river. The recency of some Chumash paintings is demonstrated by several examples from this region. A site in the Nojoqui Valley was illustrated by Mallery (1893:63–67) with a number of the design motifs. Eighty years later, in 1973, the panel is barely recognizable due to the natural erosion of the soft sandstone.

Another example of late prehistoric or historic rock art was recovered at the site of the Chumash rancheria Saca on Alamo Pintada Creek. A rock slab with crosses and centipede motifs was found in a layer of mission-period material (Deetz 1964). Also at this site was a large serpentine boulder with pit-and-groove markings, a type of petroglyph rare in Chumash country.

Ventureño

On October 12, 1542, Cabrillo landed near the Indian rancheria of *sisolop* (present site of the city of Ventura) and the Spaniards saw their first Chumash. He took formal possession of the country, noting that "there came to the ships many very good canoes, each of which held twelve or thirteen Indians . . . the interior of the country is a very fine valley and they made signs that there was . . . abundant food" (Bolton 1925:25). Cabrillo named the settlement Pueblo de las Canoas. The Spanish were entertained with a feast of bonito by the hospitable Chumash, who traded many objects for the glass beads of the explorers.

The 1769 Portolá expedition traveling north to Monterey from San Diego first encountered the Ventureño Chumash at the rancheria of Santa Clara (near present Fillmore). Their houses resembled the rectangular, mat-covered houses of the adjacent Takic speakers but they had many artifacts of types the Spanish later described from the coast. Portolá, following the Santa Clara River to the coast, arrived at *sisolop* and recognized it as Cabrillo's Pueblo de las Canoas, described two centuries earlier. He named it Assumpta. The explorers all commented favorably on the appearance of *sisolop* as the largest and best-laid-out rancheria they had seen since leaving San Diego, with 30 large houses and 15 canoes. In 1782 Father Junipero Serra established the second Chumash mission, San Buenaventura, at *šišolop*.

Away from the ocean, most of the settlements in the Ventura region were not large. On their return trip south in 1770, the Portolá expedition passed through the Conéjo Valley east of *šišolop* and Costansó noted four small villages in the area. At one of these the Spanish were entertained and were given roasted mescal (yucca) to eat. The villagers appeared "very poor and thin" (Costansó 1911:314–317). The Ventureño region was well populated, especially along the Santa Clara and Ventura rivers and Calleguas Creek. Kroeber (1925:pl. 48) shows 28 villages; and King (1969:map 1) locates 41 settlements and estimates the total Ventureño population in 1770 at between 2,500 and 4,200. Many of the Chumash rancheria names persist in the Ventura area as names of modern towns or localities: *šatiƙuy*(?) (Saticoy), Matilja (Matilija), *ʔawḣay* (?) (Ojai), *seƙspe* (?) (Sespe), *šohmus*(?) (Somis), *šimiyi*(?) (Simi), *muwu*(?) (Mugu), and *kayewaš*(?) (Calleguas).

Archeological investigations in the Ventura area have demonstrated that the high material culture of the coastal Chumash diminished in direct ratio to its distance from the seashore. The inland excavations have mainly yielded generalized Chumash artifacts technically inferior to those produced on the coast.

In the mountainous inland regions, the most interesting Chumash remains are the rock paintings that generally occur in wide-eroded sandstone shelters away from permanent settlements. A few such sites in the Santa Monica Mountains have paintings on rough conglomerate surfaces but the finest work is on sandstone. The rock art of the area is confined to the Santa Monica Mountains, the Simi Hills, and the mountainous headwaters of the Sespe and Piru creeks. The subject matter is quite unlike the elaborate polychrome abstract patterns and geometric motifs in other Chumash areas and is mainly concerned with fantastic anthropomorphic and zoomorphic creatures. A characteristic of this region is the small scale of most of the figures. Many of the Mutau Flat site motifs are only a few inches high; and at sites in the Sespe drainage (Grant 1965:pls. 18, 24) and near Boney Mountain in the Santa Monica Range, there are similar tiny figures painted with great care (Gibson and Singer 1970). A curious motif at all three sites is a bird that looks very much like a man in bird costume— possibly the California condor, mentioned by Boscana (Harrington 1934) as revered by the Juaneño. The paintings and associated artifacts suggest ceremonial activities possibly connected with deer hunting. There is only one example of a deer being pictured in the Chumash region. That painting is high in the Santa Monica Range at a site that also has the only known example of European horsemen painted by a Chumash. Excavations near several of these painted sites (Eberhart and Babcock 1963; Gibson and Singer 1970) indicate they were seasonal seed-gathering and hunting camps.

Prehistory

During the 1870s and 1880s, there was extensive looting of the Chumash cemeteries along the Santa Barbara Channel and very rich finds of artifacts were made, for sale mainly to private collectors. It was not until the 1920s that anything approaching systematic excavation was undertaken (Harrington 1928).

Rogers, who had been Harrington's assistant in his work at Burton Mound, made extensive excavations between Carpinteria and Gaviota, recognizing two earlier cultures, which he called the Oak Grove People and the Hunting People. The former were characterized by settlements on high ground away from the sea, prone burial, semisubterranean huts, large elliptical metates and oval manos, rectangular cooking stones, crude points, and fist axes. The Oak Grove culture in the channel area has been radiocarbon dated at over 5000 B.C. (Owen 1964).

Rogers's Hunting People were quite different. There was no trace of houses but they made many well-shaped projectile points, sandstone bowls, mortars, pestles, and baskets. The Hunting People buried their dead in a flexed position, head down. By A.D. 1000 the whole area was in the possession of the Chumash, who had supplanted, amalgamated with, or developed from the Hunting People. The complex culture of the Chumash, Rogers called Canalino (People of the Channel), a term that has proved confusing and is no longer used (Rogers 1929).

Olson (1930), Orr (1943), and others have done stratigraphic work in the Chumash cemeteries near Santa Barbara and many artifacts, including fragments of the planked canoes described by the explorers, have been recovered in such excavations. There is almost no archeological knowledge of the Yneceño sites in the Santa Ynez Valley beyond that provided by casual pot hunting. Excavations at the coastal Ventureño sites have demonstrated that the climax area of the Chumash culture was centered near Santa Barbara with grave offerings less elaborate in ratio to distance from this center. Inland sites were small with artifacts reflecting a simple hunting-gathering economy.

Obispeño and Purisimeño Chumash

ROBERTA S. GREENWOOD

Language, Territory, and Environment

Obispeño and Purisimeño are geographic and linguistic subdivisions within the larger Chumash cultural family. These names were assigned to the two groups reflecting their attachment to the missions founded among the Indians, San Luis Obispo de Tolosa in 1772 and La Purísima Concepción in 1787. The native identities do not survive, except that Purisimeño were called ʔaxmú (?) by their eastern neighbors at Santa Ynez (Merriam 1966–1967, 2:252). The language spoken by the Obispeño, the most northern of all the Chumash, was quite divergent from the Central Chumash languages (including Purisimeño).

Both groups were coastal people dwelling along an exposed outer shore, although the boundaries are far from precise (fig. 1). The eastern borders of most intense occupation followed the coastal mountains along lines such as the Santa Lucia and San Rafael ranges. Inland, the border between the Chumash and the Salinans is uncertain on the Carrizo Plains—a pattern suggesting intermittent, seasonal, or special-purpose occupation. On the north, the Obispeño periphery has traditionally been drawn at Point Estero, although material remains such as quartz crystals, line sinkers, painted rocks, burial of the dead, and petroglyph sites attributed to the Chumash are archeologically demonstrable as far north as San Carpojo Creek near the Monterey County line within Salinan linguistic territory. To the south, the Purisimeño lands probably extended at least to Point Conception; certain named villages easterly along the Santa Barbara Channel sent neophytes to both La Purísima and Santa Barbara Missions.

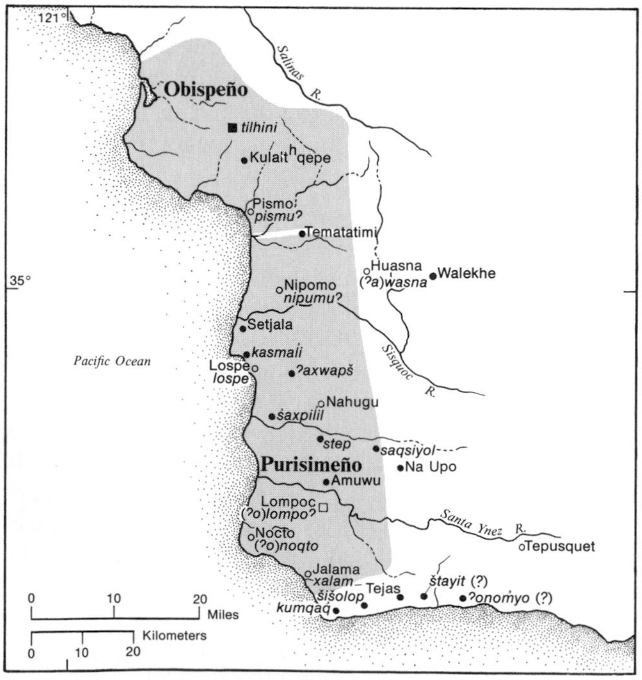

The Obispeño and Purisimeño shared a common environment characterized by narrow coastal terraces with occasional sand dunes, small valleys, and a rocky outer shore swept by winds and fog. It is a habitat of great variety at an interface of northern and southern plant associations and warm-water and cold-water marine life, yielding an abundance of wild plant foods, land and sea mammals, fish, birds, and molluscan resources, all of which were utilized from the earliest periods.

History

Both historical accounts and ethnographic studies present less evidence for this area than for the Santa Barbara Channel. There is no indication that Juan Rodríguez Cabrillo's ships made a landing in San Luis Obispo County. Pedro de Unamuno entered Morro Bay in 1587, and Sebastian Cermeño visited San Luis Obispo Bay in 1595. The procession of Gaspar de Portolá traversed the area in 1769, leaving the coast north of Pismo and traveling overland to Morro Bay. Father Juan Crespí reported seeing no houses whatever, although 60 Indians greeted them with a gruel made of roasted seeds (Engelhardt 1933:7). Lt. Pedro Fages came to the Los Osos Valley in 1772 to hunt bear. None of the diarists describes any large or populous villages such as those seen along the channel. Instead, they mention "very small towns," or small groups of Indians whom they assumed to be nomads because they did not see houses.

Since structures have been revealed by excavation, for example, a house floor 30 feet in diameter at Morro Bay within putative sight of the Portolá camp (Clemmer

Fig. 1. Tribal territory and prominent villages. Place names indicated by open circles are still in use. Some place-names after Whitehead and Hoover 1974.

1962) and "roasting pits" in the Cuyama Valley (Martin and Satow 1971), it is possible that certain villages had flourished and declined before the years of exploration. Certain named archeological sites, such as Schumacher's "Wa-le-khe" on the Santa Maria River (1875:345), do not appear among the rancherias in the records of either San Luis Obispo (Merriam 1955:201-210) or La Purísima Missions (Merriam 1968:90-92, 1970:31-39). The Chumash component of a large permanent village on the coast at Diablo Canyon has a radiocarbon date of A.D. 930 ± 50, lacks historic materials altogether, and cannot be identified by any Indian name (Greenwood 1972). Comparison of the explorers' population estimates with analysis of the mission records suggests that the effects of the first European contacts on a population already falling or dispersing were detrimental even before the missions were founded.

Purisimeño Population

Rancheria	Location	Houses	1769 Canoes	Population	1796 Population
(ʔo)noqto	Pedernales	10	0	60	50
Silimastus	Jalama	20-30	0	150	81
šišolop	Cojo	24-50	5-6	150	150
Texa	Santa Anita	20	3	115	55
štayit (?)	Bulito	25-50	3-5	200	86
ʔonomyóʔ	Gaviota	50	7	300	164

SOURCE: Brown (1967:16-22, table 2).

By 1803 conversions in the coastal villages had already penetrated so deeply into social structures that the decaying settlements, already stricken with high mortality, were barely inhabited. The final wave of baptisms resulted in the ultimate abandonment of many villages (Brown 1967:50-51). At San Luis Obispo, none of the 23 larger rancherias (those with 15 or more baptisms) produced any new neophytes after 1804 (Merriam 1955:201-210). By 1838 the Indian population at Mission San Luis Obispo had declined from its 1803 peak of 919 to 170; at La Purísima, the 1804 peak of 1,520 had fallen to 120. In 1845 La Purísima was abandoned by all converts (Engelhardt 1908-1915, 4:151, 529, 570).

According to the Roll of 1928 compiled by the Bureau of Indian Affairs, there were no Indians living at that time who traced their descent to La Purísima Mission converts, and only four—all of mixed ancestry—who claimed to be survivors of San Luis Obispo neophytes (Kroeber and Heizer 1970:13-14). The Rolls of 1950 and 1970 do not specify tribal origin. While not all Indians did register financial claims, it is likely that those few lineal descendants who may survive demonstrate an admixture of blood and loss of their native culture and languages.

The explorers' accounts support mission statistics that suggest a difference in settlement pattern north of Point Conception. In contrast to the populous and structurally ordered villages along the channel, population density in historic times decreased toward the north. While Santa Barbara Mission listed six rancherias with more than 100 converts (two of these over 300), La Purísima had only three with more than 100 baptisms (Brown 1967:95); and the largest rancheria at San Luis Obispo (Te-ma-ta-ti-mi) contributed only 59 neophytes (Merriam 1955:208). Estimates of regional density in 1770 support the same conclusion: for the Purisimeño, 45 to 70 persons in 100 square kilometers (38.25 square miles), and for the Obispeño to the north, 25 to 45 individuals (Heizer 1960:fig. 4). Although each settlement was smaller, there probably were more of them in the north. Santa Barbara received neophytes from 93 named rancherias, whereas San Luis Obispo, with many fewer baptisms, lists 142 place names (Merriam 1955:191-210).

While most of them are unexcavated, it is significant that very incomplete surface surveys had already located 140 archeological sites by 1972 in the area between San Luis Obispo and Morro Bay bounded by the Chorro Valley and See Canyon, an average of at least one site in a square mile. Thus, the land was not always sparsely occupied and the northern Chumash may be regarded, not simply as an impoverished group on the margin of the channel climax, but as descendants of an ancient areal tradition that already embodied the multiresources adaptation of the linguistically defined family.

Culture

By the time of historical contact, witnesses agree that most of the houses were small, round, and domed, with some people apparently living in the open. There is no mention of the houses arranged in rows such as seen along the channel (Brown 1967:5). Underground dwellings were reported near Morro Bay, each a round hole roofed over with branches and large enough to hold 12 people (Wagner 1929:146-147). Archeological evidence supports observations that twin or split villages frequently existed on opposite sides of streams or other features, possibly reflecting the moiety system of native California.

Coinciding approximately with Point Conception and the southern boundary of the Purisimeño are certain shifts in material culture items. Not only was this the limit of large towns in 1770, but it also marked the northern extent of the wooden planked canoe. Cermeño had noted the tule balsa at San Luis Obispo Bay in 1595, but there is no evidence for the fragile plank vessel on the outer coast in early historic times. Font recorded that six Obispeños were escorted to Santa Barbara in 1776 to purchase two canoes with glass trade beads. These may not have been the first, since Fages men-

521

tioned plank canoes in the bay in 1775, but the replacement of the balsa by the wooden boat was probably not much earlier (Heizer and Massey 1953:301). Use of the canoe flourished only where shore and water conditions permitted, and its presence or absence is not regarded as a criterion for the Chumash definition.

Archeological evidence demonstrates that the Indians did exploit the marine food resources of the area back to the earliest occupation of the coast at least 9,000 years ago (Greenwood 1972). But since local conditions never favored the canoe, the people always depended more upon harvesting tidal pools and shallow waters by hand, traps, poles, nets, and ultimately the hook and line, rather than developing a deepwater finfishery. The shell fishhooks (fig. 2) of the northern coast are distinctive: a small J-shaped form typically made of mussel shell without groove, shank, barb, or knob but sometimes notched for line attachment and a larger type that is circular and commonly made from abalone, but also lacking groove, shank, or knob. The Purisimeño are credited with using salted sardines for bait and catching larger fish with hooks made from cactus spines (Wagner 1929:242).

The diagnostic Chumash projectile points of the Santa Barbara Channel came late to these provinces. The small triangular form with concave base and the small leaf shape do occur, but there was a longer survival in the north of such early forms as large stemmed and side-notched points, and possibly the atlatl. As late as 1587 Unamuno described elder-wood "javelins" with oak

points hardened by fire (Wagner 1929:147). Within the food preparation inventory, the milling stones used in the earlier years tended to be either flat or shallow, rather than deeply basined as in the south. In later years, the globular stone bowl gave way to a straight-walled vessel with flaring sides and flat base and rim. Rims were occasionally grooved, scalloped, or inlaid with shell ornaments. Cordage bags, flat basketry trays, and wooden grinding troughs were also described (Wagner 1929:147, 161). A very abundant artifact is a cobble or broken rock of hand size with one or more small pits. These articles may have aided in cracking either mollusks or acorns (Harrington 1914–1915).

Steatite objects were less common than along the channel. Beads and ornaments paralleled southern forms, with somewhat less variety of shapes in the abalone items. Beads appear as inlays on stone vessels, bone whistles (fig. 3), and baskets. Incising occurs on bone beads, shaft straighteners, and stone tablets; and punctate designs are seen on bone beads and whistles. Clam and mussel disk beads appear later than those made from the purple olive.

Mortuary customs include cemeteries within the villages with interments positioned in seated posture, flexed on the back, or flexed on the side. Painted stone grave markers (Pilling 1951:197–198) and tablets (Engelhardt 1933:51) have been described. One individual was delegated to carry the corpse to the cemetery and open the grave; the ritual included songs, ceremonies, and a distribution of beads to all who assisted (Kroeber 1908a:17). Grave goods frequently included quantities of shell beads and ornaments, whistles, bone tubes, unmodified whole shells, slabs of stone or whale bone, lumps of pigment, as well as utilitarian items. The occurrence of these goods in differential quantities nonspecific by age or sex implies a ranked social system. When Schumacher (1875a:219) excavated 300 to 400 burials in 1874 at Kesmali (*kasmali̯*) (Purisimeño), Nipomo (*nipumuʔ*) and Tematatimi (Obispeño), and Walekhe

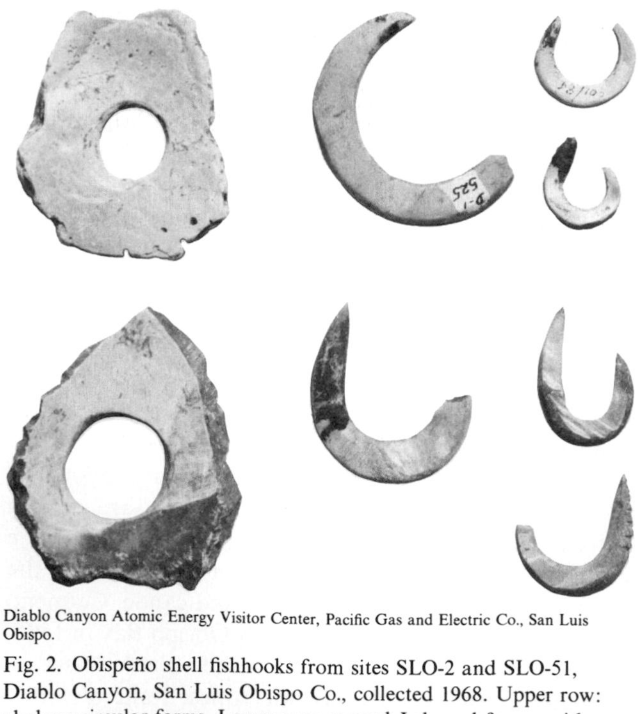

Diablo Canyon Atomic Energy Visitor Center, Pacific Gas and Electric Co., San Luis Obispo.

Fig. 2. Obispeño shell fishhooks from sites SLO-2 and SLO-51, Diablo Canyon, San Luis Obispo Co., collected 1968. Upper row: abalone circular forms. Lower row: mussel J-shaped forms, with lower right showing notched shank for line attachment. Specimens on left in each row are unfinished. Top left specimen is 3.2 cm, remainder same scale.

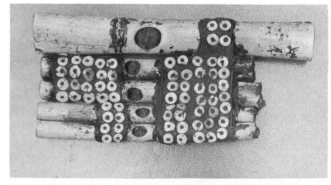

Diablo Canyon Atomic Energy Visitor Center, Pacific Gas and Electric Co., San Luis Obispo.

Fig. 3. Obispeño five-tube bone whistle with shell beads inlaid in asphaltum. Collected at site SLO-2, Diablo Canyon, San Luis Obispo Co., 1968. Longest tube 11.2 cm.

(Interior), he considered the contents so similar that it was not necessary to attribute the items to the specific villages. He found the skeletons flexed on the back and frequently disturbed by later interments. Among the offerings were painted stone slabs, globular stone bowls with small mouths, conical pipes, a variety of small stone dishes showing traces of color, glass beads, and imported pottery.

Obispeño chiefs were said to have many wives and also the right to divorce them (Heizer 1955:149). Social rank was derived from wealth, and all made offerings of food, goods, and beads to the chief (Kroeber 1908a:17).

Items without obvious subsistence function include imperforate charmstones or plummets; quartz crystals; incised stone tablets; and single (fig. 4), paired, or multiple whistles (fig. 3) variously made of bird, coyote, or mountain lion bone. Wooden flutes are ascribed to the Obispeño (Kroeber 1908a:16). Rock-art sites occur in Purisimeño and Obispeño territory as far north as San Simeon, although less frequently than in the southern provinces. As elsewhere, they occur away from the immediate coast, apart from large or permanent villages, and suggest ritual or special purpose activities.

Although material culture items generally reflect those known on the Santa Barbara Channel, the most obvious trade relations aside from the Catalina Island steatite are with the Interior. The Obispeños supplied the Yokuts with asphaltum and the shells of abalone, clam, limpets, and periwinkle, receiving in exchange pottery and possibly obsidian (Sample 1950:4, 20). One known route passed from the coast up the Santa Maria-Cuyama river drainage to the southern San Joaquin valley (Davis 1961:map 1). The northern Chumash could also have been direct or intermediary suppliers of univalve columella ornaments, wooden dishes, and steatite vessels to the Salinans, and of shell beads, dried fish, and sea otter furs to the interior, receiving in return deerskins, acorns, and grasshoppers.

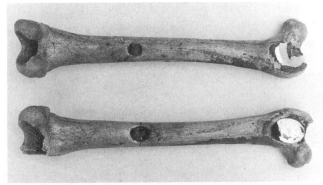

Diablo Canyon Atomic Energy Visitor Center, Pacific Gas and Electric Co., San Luis Obispo.

Fig. 4. Obispeño whistles of mountain lion bone with abalone inlays. Collected at site SLO-2, Diablo Canyon, San Luis Obispo Co., 1968. Length shown 26.3 cm.

Archeological evidence verifies not only that the number of Indians was rapidly decimated by missionization, but also that the culture itself disintegrated rapidly. The decline was not a uniform process; at La Purísima, chipped-stone artifacts related to male activities such as hunting, skin dressing, and weapon manufacture disappeared rapidly from the barracks assemblage, while continued persistence of basketry tools and food preparation equipment suggests that the female role suffered less disruption (Deetz 1962-1963:186).

Ethnographic accounts of the Obispeño and Purisimeño lack the wealth of detailed observation recorded for the channel coast. The women wore their hair with bangs over the forehead, and either loose or tied up behind; the men had perforated earlobes (Engelhardt 1933:30). There is agreement on skin robes and basketry caps. Cermeño described the Indians at San Luis Obispo as naked, bearded, and painted with stripes on their faces and arms (Wagner 1929:161). The padres confirmed the efficacy of the Obispeño plant remedies and their use of purgatives, emetics, and hot baths (Engelhardt 1933a:49).

In 1914-1915, Rosario Cooper, the last Obispeño speaker, described witchcraft cured by fasting, singing, scarifying, and bloodletting; beliefs in the sun, moon, stars, bear, and coyote; and dances associated with the swordfish and coyote, the former with a feather costume. An offering of feathers, beads, and tobacco was thrown to the swordfish at Avila. She knew a game played with wild walnuts filled with brea, and material culture items such as a broom made from split juncus stalks, sleeping mats, a foxskin quiver, and use of white clay as a shampoo (Harrington 1914-1915). Harrington's (1916) work in the Purisimeño area was devoted primarily to recording place names and linguistic data. The replies from this mission to the *interrogatorios* of 1811 have been lost (Engelhardt 1932a:39).

These two groups occupied lands among the least well known in aboriginal California. Since it is now too late for ethnography, most of the information will ultimately be revealed by archeology. It has long been assumed that this area was a late and attenuated reflection of the Santa Barbara Channel climax. A newer hypothesis is that the explorers did not traverse an empty or impoverished territory but an area once populous, which had already begun to decline. The Obispeño and Purisimeño shared with the broader Chumash culture those traits relevant to their own environment, adapting and enlarging upon an ancient base already long reliant on the littoral resources. The cultural lines were drawn more sharply by the ecological boundaries separating the southern Purisimeño area from the channel or the outer coast from the interior than by the linguistic subdivisions defining the Purisimeño from the Obispeño or the Obispeño from the Salinans.

523

Island Chumash

CAMPBELL GRANT

There are four islands forming the southern flank of the Santa Barbara Channel (fig. 1). From east to west they are Anacapa, Santa Cruz, Santa Rosa, and San Miguel. Their distance from the mainland varies between 12 and 30 miles. During the continental glaciations, the seas were lowered and the Santa Barbara Channel Islands were connected as a peninsula to the mainland and formed an extension of the Santa Monica Mountains. Mammoths and other life forms migrated westward onto the peninsula, and when rising sea levels isolated them, many terrestrial organisms underwent endemic evolution (Valentine and Lipps 1967:32). Examples of this are the dwarf mammoth of Santa Rosa Island and the fox, skunk, and mice that have deviated from the mainland varieties through long isolation. In addition, plants such as *Lyonothamnus*, known from Miocene and Pliocene fossils on the mainland, still grow on Santa Rosa and Santa Cruz island as island ironwood (*Lyonothamnus floribundus*). By the end of the Pleistocene epoch approximately 10,000 years ago, the sea level was stabilized at present levels.

The climate for most of the year is mild but the islands are subject to very strong winds, especially in the winter. Rainfall is somewhat less than on the mainland and averages about 12 inches near sea level and 20 inches a year on Santa Cruz (central valley at 200 feet elevation).

Juan Rodríguez Cabrillo visited the islands in 1542 and his account states (Bolton 1925:34): "The Indians of these islands are very poor. They are fishermen; they eat nothing but fish; they sleep on the ground; their sole business and employment is to fish. They say that in each house there are fifty souls. They live very swinishly and go about naked."

San Miguel

San Miguel is the most westerly of the islands and is separated from Santa Rosa Island by a strait three and one-half miles wide. It is roughly eight miles long, averages about two miles wide, and covers 14 square miles. The formation is mainly marine sandstone with some hard ridges of volcanic rock. Most of the island averages about 200 feet in elevation with two central hills of 850 feet. There are no running streams and only one fairly good spring (at Cuyler Harbor) and a few seeps of fresh water. Originally the island was covered with a dense growth of brush such as sumac and manzanita, but much of the vegetation has been destroyed by overgrazing of sheep and cattle, and erosion is severe (Bremner 1933:9). Much of the island is covered by immense sand dunes, constantly shifting through wind action. The landing area is Cuyler Harbor on the northeast coast, the safest haven on any of the islands in a severe windstorm. The island periodically supports large herds of sea lions, elephant seals, and in former times, sea otters.

On October 18, 1542, Cabrillo's little fleet of two ships anchored in Cuyler Harbor and severe storms kept them there for a week. Cabrillo recorded the Chumash name for the islands as Ciquimuyu. The Spaniards named it La Posesion, and after Cabrillo's death there it was named Isla de Juan Rodríguez (Bolton 1925). The name

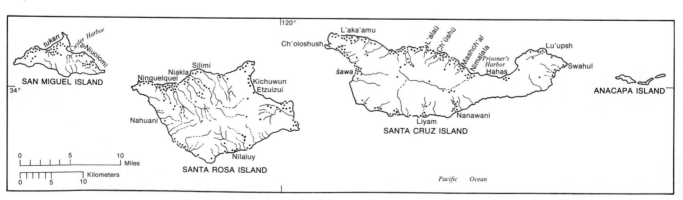

Fig. 1. Historic settlements and archeological sites. After Kroeber 1925; Rogers 1929; Brown 1967.

for San Miguel Island according to Pinart's Santa Cruz Island vocabulary is Tukkan (Heizer 1952:51), *tukan*. Sebastián Vizcaíno was in the channel in 1602 and renamed Cabrillo's La Posesion, Isla de San Bernardo. The final naming was by Capt. George Vancouver who was at Santa Barbara in 1792 and referred to the most westerly island as San Miguel (from a Spanish chart) (Vancouver 1798).

Brown (1967:map 1) shows two rancherias on San Miguel—Toan (*tukan*) and Niuoiomi. The Santa Barbara Mission records for 1786-1825 note 43 baptisms from Tucan (San Miguel) in 1788 and two in 1803 (Merriam 1962). King (1969:map 1) estimates the population of these two settlements at from 75 to 140.

In the 1870s there was a great interest in Indian curios and San Miguel Island became a favorite collecting area as the strong prevailing winds were constantly shifting the sand dunes to expose burials. The actual burials were in the shell middens, some of which were of great size. The first known collector on San Miguel was W.G.W. Harford of the U.S. Coast Survey (now the National Ocean Survey), who was on the island in 1872 and 1873. William H. Dall, also of the Coast Survey, and Paul Schumacher collecting for the Smithsonian Institution and the Peabody Museum were there in 1875. In 1877 Léon de Cessac was on San Miguel and the following year, Stephen Bowers, a well-known pot hunter.

Schumacher (1877), who excavated just west of Cuyler Harbor, observed that the burials were similar to those on the mainland and that whalebone slabs (made of rib sections) lined certain important burials and that whale vertebrae marked the location of some graves.

No further excavations were undertaken on San Miguel for many years, perhaps because the indiscriminate digging on the island had ruined the sites for serious archeological study; however, in 1919, the Museum of the American Indian, Heye Foundation, collected on the island for six months (Heye 1921). Twenty-three sites, mainly near the north shore, were excavated, and 343 individual burials were found. In spite of the heavy digging in previous years, the Heye expedition found a wealth of artifacts and many undisturbed burials. The dead were buried in flexed position, face up, while the usual mainland position was face down.

The artifacts testified to the islanders' dependence on fishing and the hunting of marine mammals. There were great numbers of the circular abalone fishhooks as well as parts of composite bone fishhooks. Many fine projectile points were recovered, including a chipped harpoon point. Since there is no steatite on the islands, the great number of steatite artifacts found by the Heye expedition demonstrates an active trade with the mainland Chumash across the channel or direct contact with the steatite sources on Santa Catalina Island. Of the typical mainland steatite objects (fig. 2), only the hooked "pelican stones," cooking ollas, comals, and arrow straighteners are missing. The relative scarcity of sandstone cooking vessels and complete lack of steatite vessels indicates that the cooking of fish, shellfish, and marine-mammal meat was done over open fires. The perforated stones (fig. 3) were abundant and most were made of steatite where the mainland types are predominantly sandstone.

Fig. 3. Perforated steatite stone. The use of such objects is unknown; they may have been digging-stick weights, club heads, fish-net sinkers, shaman's paraphernalia, or game stones. Diameter 11.0 cm; collected 1875.

Mortars and pestles of standstone were excavated and were probably traded, as the sandstone on San Miguel is not suitable for the purpose. One mortar was made from the hollowed vertebra of a whale.

Charmstone-shaped artifacts were grooved on one end and showed asphaltum marks where they had been attached to fishing lines or nets. Whalebone (fig. 4) wedges, abalone pry bars, and clubs (possibly for use in killing seals) were found in the middens.

Beads (fig. 5) of many types and materials were recovered; most were found in infant burials. Many clamshell pendants had punched-hole designs. Fragments of bas-

Fig. 2. Steatite whale effigy. Length, about 17.2 cm.

Santa Barbara Mus. of Nat. Hist., Calif.: NA-CA-SBA-27-3c-1.

Fig. 4. Whale-bone spear straightener. Length, about 39.6 cm; possibly Coastal Chumash.

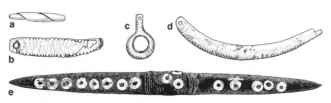

Dept. of Anthr., Smithsonian: a, 18187; b, 26249; c, 18185; d, 18320; Santa Barbara Mus. of Nat. Hist., Calif.: e, NA-CA-SBA-131.60-6a-1.

Fig. 5. Shell ornaments and charmstone. a, univalve shell columella; b-d, haliotis; e, steatite charmstone decorated with shell and asphaltum, length 15.2 cm; a-d, same scale.

ketry hats and sea-grass aprons were recovered from female burials.

Rogers (1929:262-268) did a surface survey of San Miguel and found site concentrations all along the north shore and inland south of Cuyler Harbor. With only a few short breaks, the sites along the north shore were continuous. The immense numbers of abalone shells in the middens led Rogers to conclude that abalone were the San Miguel Islanders' chief diet, whereas on the mainland, this mollusk was much scarcer and seldom seen except as a finished ornament.

San Miguel Island is now the property of the U.S. government and currently is used by the navy as a missile target area.

Santa Rosa

Santa Rosa is the most westerly of the two big channel islands and lies midway between San Miguel and Santa Cruz. It is 18 miles long and 11 miles wide, with an area of 84 square miles. The land is basically a series of rounded hills rising in some instances to 1,500 feet and covered with grass, brush, or cactus. The shoreline cliffs are low, and along the eastern coast there are long stretches of beach. There are a number of well-watered canyons and some wooded areas of oak and pine. There are small intrusions of igneous rocks but the island is composed mainly of sedimentary rock.

Cabrillo, on October 18, 1542, tried to double Cabo de Galera (Point Conception) and failing, sailed south to discover Santa Rosa and San Miguel Islands. He named them both Islas de San Lucas and counted six villages.

The Santa Cruz Chumash name of the island is Huimal or Guima (Heizer 1955:115; Merriam 1970:45)—i.e. *wima?*.

The mission baptismal registers of Santa Barbara, San Buenaventura, La Purísima, and Santa Ynez all list Indians from the islands among the converts, and from these lists it is possible to identify six and possibly seven rancherias of 1770. The largest of these settlements were Etzuizui, Silimi, and Nilajuy (Merriam 1962, 1970). The majority of the Santa Rosa Islanders were sent to La Purísima Mission. According to King (1969:map 1), the Santa Rosa population in 1770 was between 490 and 790.

There is little ethnographic information on the Santa Rosa Chumash, but according to Henshaw (Heizer 1955:151-158), a man marrying out of his village was never allowed to return. The villages were generally friendly. Bows and arrows were obtained from the mainland. The islanders were most skillful in chipping stone implements and this formed their stock in trade. (There was abundant igneous rock on the islands, for fine flaking.)

Bristles of the sea lion were used as needles and as perforators (for the tubular clamshell money). The Santa Rosa Islanders sharpened the edge of the abalone and wore it around the neck as a scraper (sweat scraper?). Abalone shell was polished by rubbing on a piece of stretched skin. Long curved pendants were made of the edge of the abalone shell and used by the young girls as head scratchers. The children were taught to swim when small and could stay in the water all day.

After the burial of a Santa Rosa man, the hair of the widow was cut off and she was compelled to visit the grave at stated intervals. The widow also observed a prescribed diet. The period of widowhood lasted one year after which the woman was at liberty to marry any man from her village. The marriage ceremony consisted of the couple's eating mush together out of the same dish, after which they were husband and wife.

According to a Santa Rosa Island Chumash, these islanders hunted whales with spears and ate the blubber raw. This report of Chumash as whale hunters is not supported by any other ethnographic or archeologic data. Most food was eaten without cooking. They worshiped the sun, the crow, and the swordfish. They believed that the swordfish as well as the killer whale drove the whales ashore (Bowers 1878).

Possibly the planked canoes of the Chumash developed out of a dugout-type canoe. There is some evidence that such boats were still being made occasionally into historic times by the Chumash. Harrington (1942:11) lists both dugouts and ocean balsas from Barbareño informants, and Daniel Hill, who went to Santa Barbara in 1822, described dugouts made from tree trunks with stone axes. They were about 30 feet long and four feet wide (Woodward 1934:119).

Informants told Henshaw that at the time of the great earthquake of 1812, which seriously damaged the missions, the Indians were terrified and were easily persuaded by the padres to leave Santa Rosa and come to the missions. The mission baptismal registers (Merriam 1962, 1970) list 102 Santa Rosa converts for the period 1786–1825.

Most of the archeological stone, bone, and shell artifact types known from the mainland were present on Santa Rosa, but as on San Miguel Island, there were no fine sandstone bowls, steatite ollas, arrow straighteners, hooked stones, or medicine tubes. There was much reburial but in the undisturbed burials most of the bodies were placed on the left side with the left hand under the head. Often great masses of olivella shells were placed with the body, and in reburials many skulls were filled with the shells. The middens contain chiefly mussel shell with some abalone, and seal bones were abundant. There were many milling stones and mullers apparently mixed with late Chumash material but as Jones (1956) did no stratigraphic work, no conclusion on cultural change can be drawn from his data. In the midden burials clean sand was placed in the prepared grave pits. There were great numbers of flint microlith bladelets, often found in sizable groups, with a burial. These small tools average only two centimeters in length and were used as drills set in the end of wooden spindles to drill holes such as those in the tiny olivella beads so often found imbedded in asphaltum on decorated objects (fig. 5). Basket mortars were present as well as fragments of asphalted water bottles. One curious burial area was in a cave where 55 graves were excavated. All open burial areas were marked by large stones and whale bones. At the site of the historic rancheria of Silimi Jones counted 20 house rings.

Rogers (1929) noted that the larger settlements on Santa Rosa were along the north shore where locations are ideal with abundant nearby water. The inland settlements appeared to be seasonal camps. On the north shore there were frequent house rings plainly defined by circular ridges of midden. Rogers counted 18 villages concentrated into five major settlements on the north coast. Of these, three are identifiable on Kroeber's map (1925:48), Siliwihi (Silimi) at Green Canyon, Niakla at Soledad Canyon, and Numkulkul (Ninquelquel) at Corral Canyon.

At Kichuwun on the north side of Ranch House Creek, Rogers found camp debris 12 feet deep above a two-feet section of mixed burials. Canoe wood was found on the asphaltum plugs from the drilled holes. He also dug the site of Nilaluy at Johnson's Lee on the south coast. It had been badly looted but there was one house ruin in fair repair, made of four arched whale ribs and seven posts of split ironwood. Smaller horizontal poles encircled the uprights, forming a domelike shape. The whole had been thatched with sea grass.

Orr (1960) named two early cultures as Dune Dweller and Highland. These both occurred on the northwest coast. The former lies in the sand-dune area, and the Highland occurs farther back from the sea. Early Dune Dweller is characterized by sitting-up burials, red-painted skulls, perforated stones, and absence of grinding implements. This period had radiocarbon dates secured from abalone shell of 4870 B.C. to 5450 B.C. The Late Dune Dweller culture is dated at 2150 B.C. to 1050 B.C. and features flexed burials in clean sand and abundant grave goods, including Gypsum Cave-type points.

The Highland culture suggests seasonal camps of the Dune Dwellers as mortars were present but few other artifacts. There are few burials and scanty middens though over 100 sites were recorded.

Orr's earliest Chumash date of 640 B.C. comes from charcoal from a sweathouse. He excavated a number of Chumash sites on the northwest coast, possibly part of the big settlement of Niakla (Kroeber 1925:48). Orr (1968) noted the tremendous amount of olivella beads in the burials (also reported earlier by Jones 1956). There were great numbers of microblades.

The only rock painting on Santa Rosa Island is in a cave on the north side of the island—faint unrecognizable patterns in red and black. One petroglyph of the pit-and-groove type was found in Jones's Cave on the south coast. The elaborate Chumash art of the mainland may be late in time and therefore did not affect the islanders before their culture was destroyed by the missionaries.

In private hands since the end of the mission period, Santa Rosa Island was in 1972 a cattle ranch owned by Vail-Vickers Corporation.

Santa Cruz

Santa Cruz Island is the largest and in many ways the most interesting of the Santa Barbara Channel Islands. It is about 25 miles long and the greatest width is about seven miles. The total area is 96 square miles. The island is very rugged and appears like a mountain range rising from the sea from a distance. The wide western half of the island is divided into two mountain ranges; the highest peak has an altitude of 2,400 feet. Between the ridges is a long well-watered central valley created by a fault, with side canyons wooded with oak, pine, and island ironwood. The north shore is cut by many deep, narrow, wooded ravines, some with small permanent streams, which make east-west travel extremely difficult. This shore has a number of small cobble beaches between high sheer cliffs; and the sea is quite calm in the summer months, making ideal landing conditions for the Chumash canoes. In the winter, severe southeast and northwest winds make even the two best anchorages, Pelican Bay and Prisoner's Harbor, hazardous. On the exposed south coast the cliffs are not so high and there are a

527

number of sandy beaches but the surf is often heavy. About 55 percent of the island is composed of Tertiary volcanic rocks, andesite, basalt, and rhyolite. The balance is evenly divided between metamorphic and sedimentary rocks (Bremner 1932:14–26). Seasonally, certain beaches are occupied by large herds of seals and sea lions. Like Santa Rosa, this island has been privately owned since the end of the mission era, first as a sheep ranch and later as a cattle ranch.

Cabrillo in 1542 noted 10 rancherias on Santa Cruz (Limun, i.e. *limuw*[?]), but none resembles known settlements of the mission period and the names do not even sound like Chumash words. On the other hand, Cabrillo listed six villages on Santa Rosa (for which he gives the native word Nicalque), three of which are identifiable with known villages on Santa Cruz: Maxul (Maschal), Xugua (*šawa*), and Nimitopal (Nimalala) (Kroeber 1925:554).

In 1769, Juan Perez, commanding the *San Antonio*, one of Father Junipero Serra's supply ships, headed for San Diego, became hopelessly lost, and found himself among the Santa Barbara Channel Islands. They put into the present Prisoner's Harbor on Santa Cruz to get a supply of water. While there, Father Juan Vizcaíno left a walking staff mounted with a metal cross at the village. It was returned by the Indians and the island was named Santa Cruz to commemorate the event (Vizcaíno 1959:iv).

Although ethnological information on Santa Cruz is slight, the Chumash names for the island (*mičʰumaš* or Limun i.e. *limuw*[?]) and for its 12 villages are recorded in the mission baptismal books. In 1884 Juan Pico, a Chumash informant, gave Henshaw the locations for these settlements (Heizer 1955:197). The mission records (Merriam 1962, 1970) list 511 Santa Cruz natives that were dispersed among the various missions, chiefly Santa Barbara and San Buenaventura. The largest number (161) came from the rancheria of Ishguagel (Swahul) at the extreme eastern tip of the island. The last Chumash were removed to the missions in the 1830s from the Prisoner's Harbor rancheria, Nimalala (Schumacher 1877:42). According to King (1969:map 1), the Santa Cruz Island population in 1770 was between 925 and 1,450.

Santa Cruz Island has a very large number of archeological sites, only a few of which have been systematically excavated. Along the north shore, every point and headland is white with midden shell and there has been much pot hunting since the 1850s.

In one month in 1875 Schumacher (1877) excavated over 700 burials at seven sites. He noted that the middens on the headlands, so conspicuous from the sea, were invariably shallow and represented camp areas and that the burial middens were at the village sites near permanent water.

Both Bowers and de Cessac collected on Santa Cruz in the 1870s. De Cessac made a large collection of microliths (bladelets and burins of brown chert, the latter previously unknown in California) (Heizer and Kelley 1962). De Cessac also found flint quarries in the interior of the island and caves that had served for shelter and burial (Hamy 1951:8). Outhwaite (1913) mapped 86 sites.

The first systematic survey of Santa Cruz (Rogers 1929) recorded more than 100 sites with major concentration of villages around the 12 known historic rancherias. The Chumash settlements can be located on Rogers's survey map.

Henshaw (in Heizer 1955:197)	Kroeber (1925:pl. 48)	Approximate location
L,acoyamu	La'ka'amu	West Point
L,alale	L'alalü	Diablo Point
Ch,heshe	Ch'üshü	Platt's Harbor
Mashchhal	Mashch'al	Pelican Bay
Nimatlala	Nimalala	Prisoner's Harbor
Jajas	Hahas	Chinese Harbor
Lu upsh	Lu'upsh	Scorpion Cove
Suajel	Swahül	Smuggler's Cove
Nanawany	Nanawani	Coches Prietos
Liyam	Liyam	Willows
Shawa	Shawa	Christy's Harbor
Ch,oloshush	Ch'oloshush	Forney's Cove

In one site at Valdez Cove two steatite ollas were found containing baby burials. At a number of points along the cliffs, there was evidence that large fires had been burned over a long period, possibly signal fires to guide the canoes in to the villages after dark. Rogers also excavated Coches Prietos, where he found steatite ollas, rare on the islands, an immense number of whale bones, and the ruins of a house partly built of whale ribs. At Christy's Harbor, there were many villages and Rogers found quantities of shallow mortars, several dog burials, and one burial with a spear point imbedded in the skull.

Olson (1930) excavated on Santa Cruz in 1927 and 1928. His work contained the first stratigraphic information on the Island Chumash, as well as tables on the frequency of artifact occurrence. He divided the Santa Cruz archeology into Early Island and Late Island periods. The Early was basically characterized by the presence of bone pendants and charmstones and the absence of circular fishhooks, steatite ollas, and comals. In the Late period, there was an increased use of steatite and ollas and comals came into use. Olson recorded 120 sites in addition to the 86 mapped by Outhwaite in 1913. Olson's material was studied by Hoover (1971), who recognized three main phases dating roughly from 4000 B.C. to the first Spanish contact in 1542.

On the islands woven sea-grass matting has been recovered from graves. It was used for the same purposes as tule matting on the mainland.

There are only two known examples on Santa Cruz of rudimentary rock art. At Dick's Cove on the north shore, there is a rock inscribed with parallel scorings and in Olson's Cave near Orizaba Cove there is a painting mainly of red parallel lines.

Basically the Island culture is the same as that of the mainland but differs in showing a much greater dependence on fishing and the gathering of shellfish. There is less use of steatite and the large sandstone bowls of the mainland are almost unknown.

Anacapa

Anacapa, the smallest of the Santa Barbara Channel Islands (1.1 square miles), lies 12 miles off the coast and six miles east of Santa Cruz Island. It is actually three small islands, six miles long in all, and is composed of volcanic rocks overlaid with sedimentary deposits. Essentially the island segments are flat-topped plateaus 90 to 300 feet high bounded by high vertical cliffs in most areas. Seals and sea lions occur on East Anacapa and on the north shore of the island are shallow rock formations excellent for abalone gathering.

The island was uninhabited at the time of Cabrillo's visit, and in 1769 Gaspar de Portolá named it Las Mesitas. The Ventureño Chumash name for the island is Aniapa (ʔanyapax[?]) and Anacapa is a corruption of this word (Heizer 1955:115). The occupation of Anacapa was seasonal due to the scarcity of permanent water on the island. The three segments of the island have been surveyed by a number of investigators beginning with de Cessac in 1878. All sites appear to be temporary fishing camps with a few scattered burials and artifacts.

529

Interior Chumash

CAMPBELL GRANT

The Interior Chumash occupying the northern territory are virtually unknown. Few systematic excavations have been carried out in the region, ethnographic information is almost nonexistent, and there were no established missions to record vital statistics. Yet this is the area that has provided the finest of the Chumash rock paintings.

The Cuyama region is bounded on the north by the mountains separating the drainages of the Salinas and Cuyama rivers, on the south by the crest of the San Rafael Mountains, on the west by the Coast Ranges (roughly 12 miles from the ocean), and on the east by the Temblor Range and the mountains dividing the watersheds of the Cuyama and the Santa Clara rivers. The region is drained by the Cuyama and Sisquoc rivers and the Sisquoc tributary, Manzana Creek.

The Carrizo Plains are barren and waterless except for an occasional spring. The Cuyama River, rising in the forested mountains of northeastern Santa Barbara County and northwestern Ventura County, is intermittently dry except during the rainy season. In its upper two-thirds, the river is a broad sandy wash lying between the desolate Caliente Range and the Sierra Madre. Below that, the river passes through a mountainous area before entering the rolling oak and grassland country near Santa Maria. The Sisquoc River has its headwaters in high rugged forest land and carries water through the year as far as the junction with Manzana Creek.

Cuyama

The first record of the Indians in the Cuyama region is in the report of a reconnaissance from Mission Santa Ynez to the San Joaquin valley undertaken by Father José de Zalvidéa in 1806 (Cook 1960:245-247). The expedition, traveling north from the mission, passed several abandoned villages on Alamo Pintado Creek before entering the Cuyama region where the party camped at a small native settlement of three houses on the Sisquoc. This was called Olomosong and held only seven people. Zalvidéa then began the steep ascent of the Sierra Madre and enroute passed by the village of Gecp, with five houses and 11 people. The small number of people at the mountain villages may indicate that many had already gone to the missions. They then came to extensive plains (Cuyama Valley) where they found a ranche-ria called Talihuilimit of 25 Indians. One woman said she had a son at La Purísima Mission. The expedition then moved along the foothills up the Cuyama Valley and came to the rancheria of Lisahua, which had a population of 28. Cook (1960) places this settlement near the mouth of Salisbury Canyon. From this point, it is difficult to follow the route though it seems to continue along the Cuyama River with the settlements located in the south canyons. After Lisahua, Zalvidéa visited Cuia, with nine houses and 41 people; Siguecin, with over 30 inhabitants; and Sgene, with 26 people. Here the expedition left the Cuyama drainage and Chumash country as the next village, Malapoa, with 59 Indians, was in Yokuts territory on Bitterwater Creek.

In 1824 another Spanish expedition crossed the Cuyama area (Cook 1962:154-157). Capt. Pablo de la Portilla had been sent in pursuit of the runaway neophytes from the coastal missions after the revolt of 1824. His route to Lake Buenavista in the San Joaquin valley had been via the Santa Clara River and Piru Creek. Portilla's return, accompanied by many of the Chumash who had surrendered, was directly back to Santa Barbara through the mountains. He found Malapoa, the last Yokuts village, deserted. Crossing the Cuyama, they moved up a dry wash (probably Santa Barbara Canyon), past the village of Camup and crossed the crest of the mountains (near Malduce Peak). The country is very rough and Portilla wrote that "many people tired out, particularly old persons and women with children" (Cook 1962:156). Descending the south slope, they camped at a village called Casitec. The expedition followed a stream called Segua-ya (Nono Creek?) past a village of the same name to the junction of the creek and the Santa Ynez River. From there, they descended the river to the vicinity of San Marcos Pass and crossed the mountains to Santa Barbara. This information is all that is known on the settlements of the mountainous Cuyama region. The two expeditions mention 10 villages and the ones described are all small.

The first excavations in the Cuyama region were at the site of Wa-le-khe several miles up the Cuyama River from Alamo Creek (Schumacher 1875a). In 1904 the University of California acquired a collection of nine baskets that J.E. Heath had found in dry caves in the Cuyama Valley on the north slope of the Sierra Madre (Kroeber 1925:12, 53, 54). During the 1920s J.G. James,

Fig. 1. Twined water container lined with asphaltum. Height, 45 cm.

a rancher in Salisbury Canyon, recovered many perishable artifacts in the caves on and near his ranch (Grant 1964). These included tule matting, water bottles, a sieve, olla-shaped baskets, gaming trays and sticks, a seed beater, yucca netting, a yucca tumpline, a deerskin storage bag, and leather sandal soles. In one cave, buried under sand and wrapped in tule matting, James found a perfectly preserved feathered dance skirt. It had been used into historic times as there were blue glass beads attached to it.

Later, with Henry Abels, James excavated a small cemetery on Salisbury Potrero, containing about 20 burials. The offerings included most of the typical Chumash artifacts found on the coast, including steatite pipes, bowls (fig. 2), ollas, and beads; conical sandstone bowls and pestles; sweat scrapers, flutes, molded red ocher cakes; and Spanish contact material such as scissors, a

Fig. 2. Steatite bowls. Specimen at right 14 cm width.

key, and a Mexican polychrome pot. The grave goods were so abundant and varied that it seems impossible that this was a typical mountain village cemetery. Possibly these people were fugitives from the coast who had fled to this area during the mission period or retreated here after mission secularization.

In 1934 W.D. Strong of the Smithsonian Institution conducted a brief investigation of the Cuyama Valley and later of the upper Sisquoc under the guidance of J.G. James. At one canyon site he found the remains of ovoid semisubterranean lodges of juniper poles. At another site near the present town of Cuyama, a circular house was excavated that was 19 feet in diameter with four central posts. At another village site (possibly Sgene), an ovoid lodge was excavated that was 24 feet long. The ovoid houses resemble southern Yokuts-type dwellings. Nearby was a small burial area. Artifacts were rare but included basket mortars, a thin oak bowl, sandstone mortars and pestles, small notched arrow points, and beads (mainly olivella). The Sisquoc reconnaissance of 1934 located a number of rock paintings and some artifacts in dry caves such as digging sticks, fire hearths, fragments of baskets, and matting. Two villages were investigated on the upper Sisquoc but the house pits yielded little (Strong 1935).

In 1935 the Santa Barbara Museum of Natural History conducted a preliminary survey of the same upper Sisquoc-Manzana area. They found that the great number of wind-eroded caves in the Manzana drainage had been utilized as shelters or cache spots for baskets, and that where water was found adjacent to the caves, there were bedrock mortars. Rock paintings were found in many caves. A small cemetery was trenched and conical sandstone bowls and a steatite olla were found (Rogers 1937).

In 1959 the University of California at Los Angeles made a four-day preliminary survey of archeological sites in the extreme western part of the Cuyama region at the Vaquero Reservoir, which impounds the Cuyama River (McKusick and Watson 1958-1959). Twelve sites were located and local collections of grinding implements were examined. Metates and manos were rare and mortars and pestles, including basket mortars, fairly abundant. Later that year two sites on Alamo Creek were excavated (Wire 1960-1961; Smith and LaFave 1960-1961). The sites were both middens and most of the objects were broken, but the recovered material indicated that this was a peripheral Chumash culture area lacking the more specialized coastal artifacts. The middens contained many species of shells, demonstrating a constant contact with the ocean over 20 miles away.

In 1963 Finnerty and Pearson excavated a small burial area in the Carrizo Plains (Finnerty 1963). The four burials excavated were all flexed and lying face up. One had a large quantity of shell beads and ornaments over the face. These were all common types found on the coast—haliotis spangles, *Tivela* tubes and beads, and the like. The two projectile points were leaf-shaped and side-notched. Nearby a number of large conical sandstone bowls were excavated, and there was a surface find of asphalt-covered basket-coating pebbles. The importance of this small site is that it is immediately adjacent to a major complex of elaborate rock paintings (fig. 3). There has always been some doubt as to who occupied the Carrizo Plains and were the authors of the rock art. The artifacts from the rock painting area strongly indicate a Chumash settlement, and descendants of Tejón Chumash have said the Carrizo was Chumash territory as far west as Soda Lake (Latta 1949:30).

The Chumash rock paintings certainly reach their highest development in the barren Carrizo Plains region. It appears probable that this highly developed art form of polychrome abstract designs had its beginning in the petroglyph art of the desert Numic speakers to the east, particularly in the Coso Range area of Inyo County. In the mountains between the Coso region and the Kern River to the west, there are paintings that resemble the desert abstract pecked style. Farther west in the Yokuts territory, the basic style remains abstract but the paintings are much more elaborate and many are polychrome. The closest Chumash to the southern San Joaquin Yokuts were those living in the Carrizo Plains and the Cuyama Valley, both berry areas that lay on trade routes to the coastal region. Latta (1949) gives an account by a Yokuts woman of a Yokuts trading expedition that met a group of Coastal Chumash somewhere in the Cuyama Valley or the Carrizo Plains. It is possible that the Interior Chumash in whose territory the trading took place sometimes acted as middlemen in such traffic. Certainly they traded directly at times with their channel kinsmen.

The Chumash apparently acquired the rock-painting tradition from the Yokuts and developed it to its highest point (fig. 4). Toward the Santa Barbara Channel the paintings decrease in complexity and numbers, and it is very likely that rock painting along the channel had scarcely begun before missionization destroyed the native culture.

Kern Co. Land Company.
Fig. 3. Polychrome pictograph on a large isolated sandstone outcrop in the Carrizo Plains, San Luis Obispo Co., site SLO-79. Colors are red, black, white, yellow. Photograph by von Petersdorff, 1894. This panel and adjoining sections, over 100 feet long, have since been destroyed by vandals.

532

Fig. 4. Painted Cave near Santa Barbara, site SBa-506. Brownish red, black, and white pictographs on grey sandstone. Photographed about 1930.

Emigdiano

Territory of the Emigdiano is a peripheral Chumash area that is difficult to define; the boundaries given can be only approximate. Roughly, it lies in the extreme southwest corner of Kern County. On the north it is defined by a line drawn roughly from Grapevine to the Mount Abel road and including all the north-flowing streams from the Mount Abel-Tecuya Mountain region. On the east it is marked by Castac Lake and on the south by a line somewhat south of the Cuddy Valley Road.

For the location of some of the Emigdiano rancherias, there is the 1806 journal of Father Zalvidéa (Cook 1960:245-247), who visited Tacui (Tecuya), a village of 23 inhabitants on Tecuya Creek. Later his party passed by the rancheria of Casteque (Castac, *kastɨq*) on the north shore of Castac Lake, at the head of Grapevine

Canyon. Zalvidéa noted that his party "found no Indians for they were all away at their fields of Guata" (ibid.: 247).

Some additional information on the Emigdiano settlements was obtained in 1905 by C. Hart Merriam. Sasau was a rancheria on the north shore of Castac Lake. Lapau was a large settlement at the mouth of the Cañada de las Uvas (Fort Tejon Canyon), and Takuyo was in Tecuya Canyon. All three were villages of the Castac tribe which Zalvidéa misunderstood as a village name. At the Santa Barbara mission ranch, San Emígdio, on San Emígdio Creek, there was a Chumash rancheria named Tashlipunau and the Indians bore the same name (Merriam 1966-1967, 3:429-436). According to Merriam's informants, the Tashlipunau at San Emígdio spoke a dialect similar to the Santa Barbara area while the dialect of the Castac people from the Tejón area was more similar to Ventureño. Kroeber lists another settle-

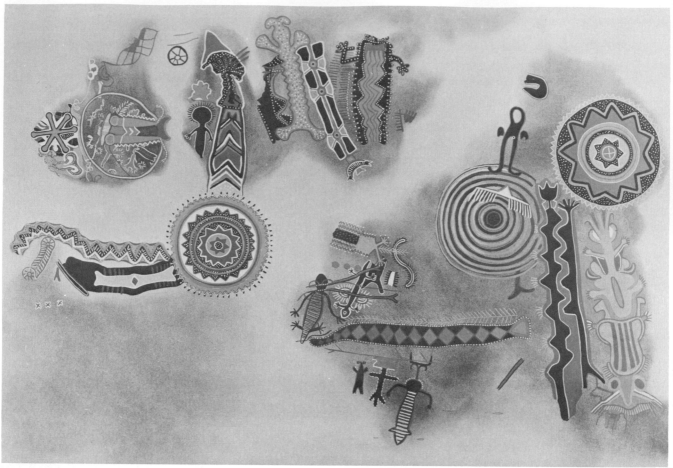

Grant 1965: pl 27.

Fig. 5. Polychrome pictograph, Pleito Cr., Kern Co., site CG-K2. It shows considerable overpainting to the right where cruder work is overlaid with elaborate designs. The painting originally covered most of the cave walls, but wind has eroded all but these paintings on the ceiling. Facsimile by Campbell Grant.

ment on upper San Emígdio Creek—Kamupau (1925: map 1). The Yokuts knew the Chumash on their southwestern border as Tokya.

There is literally no ethnological or archeological information on the Emigdiano, though a story is recorded about them from a *muwu* Chumash. A Tejón (Emigdiano) woman had married a *muwu* man and came to live on the coast. She was unfaithful to him and was killed by being shot to death with arrows; her body was burned according to the *muwu* custom. About 400 Tejón Indians came to the coast to avenge the death of the woman and in the battle over 70 killed. The *muwu* Chumash did not take scalps but cut off the right hand of slain enemies (Bowers 1897).

The population of the interior Chumash area is difficult to estimate but the meager ethnological and archeological records would indicate a population of over 1,000 in the Cuyama region and several hundred in the Emigdiano region.

There are few rock paintings in the Emigdiano region,

though one cave near the rancheria of Tashlipunau contains the most elaborate Chumash painting (fig. 5) known and ranks as the finest example of prehistoric rock art in the United States.

Most of the Chumash rock paintings are located in the Cuyama region and in the mountainous part of the Emigdiano region. The flowering of a complex ceremonial art tradition in this remote area of peripheral hunters and gatherers sharply contrasts with the coastal Chumash, where technical excellence in the working of stone, wood, and bone was apparently accompanied by the most meager religious ceremonialism. As Kroeber (1925:568) puts it: "It is possible that the [coastal] Chumash were really inferior to the speculating Shoshoneans in power of abstract formulation. Such differences in national spirit exist in California, as witness the Shoshonean [i.e., Takic] Luiseño and Yuman Diegueño [Ipai-Tipai]. The technological abilities of the Chumash do not by any means prove an equal superiority in other directions."

Tataviam

CHESTER KING AND THOMAS C. BLACKBURN

Language

On the basis of a short word list collected in 1917 by John P. Harrington of the Smithsonian Institution, Bright (1975a) has concluded that the Tataviam (tə'tävēyəm) language may be "the remnant, influenced by Takic, of a language family otherwise unknown in Southern California," or, more likely, that it is Takic (but not, apparently, Serran or Cupan). The second hypothesis receives support from ancillary comments made by some of Harrington's Kitanemuk informants as well as from ethnohistoric and archeological data. In 1776 Francisco Garcés followed the usage of his Mohave guides and referred to all the people living along the Mohave River, in the San Gabriel and San Fernando valleys, along the upper reaches of the Santa Clara River, and in the Elizabeth Lake region—thus the Tataviam and their Takic neighbors—as the Beñeme. The Kawaiisu called the Kitanemuk, the Vanyume, the Tataviam, and presumably the Serrano and Gabrielino pitadɨ 'southerners' (Zigmond 1938); the Chemehuevi name Pitanteme(we) 'Vanyume' (Carobeth Laird, personal communication 1975) may have had a similar range of application. Garcés (1965) and Fages (1937) both considered the Tataviam similar to their southern Takic neighbors in dress, political organization, and language. Archeological evidence, such as the types of artifacts used in social interaction and the internal organization of cemeteries and villages, also indicates that the Tataviam resembled neighboring Takic groups. Archeological data suggest that the Tataviam began to differentiate from other southern California Takic speakers around 1000 B.C. It is at this time that cremation as a mortuary practice begins to predominate in those areas occupied ethnographically by Takic-speaking peoples. By historic times the Tataviam language was so distinct that one of Harrington's Kitanemuk informants expressed the opinion that it was as foreign to him as English and certainly less easily understood than the San Fernando Valley dialect of Gabrielino.

Territory and Environment

The Tataviam lived primarily on the upper reaches of the Santa Clara River drainage east of Piru Creek, although their territory extended over the Sawmill Mountains to the north to include at least the southwestern fringes of the Antelope Valley (fig. 1). The major portion of the Antelope Valley itself was probably held by Kitanemuk and Vanyume speakers. The Tataviam were bounded on the west by various Chumashan groups: to the northwest, at Castac Lake, lived the Castac Chumash; to the west, on Sespe Creek, were the seŕspe Chumash; and to the southwest, at kamulus (a village recorded at San Fernando Mission under its Chumash name), lived a mixed Chumash-Tataviam population. The Tataviam were bounded on the south by various Gabrielino-speaking groups.

Most of the Tataviam region lies between 1,500 and 3,000 feet above sea level, with a minimum elevation of about 600 feet on the Santa Clara River near Piru and a maximum elevation of 6,503 feet at Gleason Mountain. The core of this area, and indeed of the Tataviam territory itself, is comprised of the south-facing slopes of the Liebre and Sawmill mountains. In southern California generally, the degree of exposure to sunlight present on a slope and the corresponding rate of evapotranspiration are important determinants of various types of vegetation. The nature of the slope-exposure in the Tataviam region is such that the Tataviam themselves probably relied more heavily on yucca as a major staple than did neighboring groups. However, the plant and

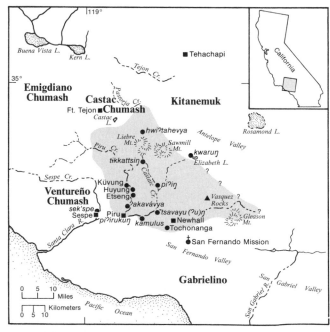

Fig. 1. Tribal territory and villages.

535

animal associations in the territory of the Tataviam were otherwise generally similar to those exploited by neighboring Takic speakers.

External Relations

Little is known about the social and political interaction that occurred between the Tataviam and other groups, although the presence of north-south enmity and east-west amity relationships similar to those found throughout southern California in protohistoric times seems likely. In 1776, for example, Garcés asked the chief of the Cuabajay (apparently the Castac Chumash) with whom he was staying to cease waging war against the people living on the upper Santa Clara River. Archeological data indicate that the Tataviam participated in economic transactions similar to those engaged in by both adjacent Takic groups and Yokuts groups farther north. During the postmission period, the few surviving Tataviam often intermarried with the Kitanemuk, with whom they seem to have interacted most intensively at that time. They also participated in and attended Chumash fiestas and ceremonies on occasion. Future analyses of mission record data will undoubtedly clarify and perhaps modify what little information is available on Tataviam external relations and internal organization.

Settlement Pattern

Until the mission registers are thoroughly analyzed, it will not be possible to make a definitive list of all Tataviam villages inhabited in early historic times nor to estimate population size with any degree of accuracy. Known Tataviam village names (given in their Kitanemuk forms) and their locations are as follows:

tsavayu(ʔu)ŋ, San Francisquito (probably equivalent to Chumash takuyamaʔm).

piʔirukuŋ, Piru (called pi·δúkʰùŋ in Tataviam).

piʔiŋ, near Castaic reservoir.

ʔakavávya, probably the site of the main village in the area prior to founding of historic Piru (called kaštu in Ventureño Chumash and El Temescal in Spanish).

Etseng, on Piru Creek, above ʔakavávya (Kroeber 1915a:774); probably the same as the Zegueyne of the mission records.

Huyung, on Piru Creek, above Etseng (Kroeber 1915a:774); probably the same as the Juyubit of the mission records (for which other spellings are in Merriam 1968:97).

Tochonanga, near Newhall, mentioned in mission records (e.g., in Merriam 1968:101).

kwaruŋ, perhaps the Tataviam name for Elizabeth Lake, whose occupants apparently were called mɨmɨyam by the Kitanemuk. The village of Quariniga mentioned in a Spanish diary of about 1808 (Cook 1960:256) may be the same place.

During the Mexican period, the Tataviam also lived at Küvung above Huyung (Kroeber 1915a:774), at La Liebre ranch or hwiʔtahevya, and at tɨkkattsiŋ (which may be a Tataviam name) on upper Castaic Creek. They also evidently lived with Chumash at Pastoria Creek during the American period.

On the basis of archeological and ethnohistoric information, Tataviam villages appear to have varied in size from large centers with perhaps 200 people to small settlements containing 10-15 people. The two or three large villages were maximally dispersed in relationship to one another; very small villages were adjacent to these larger villages, while intermediate-size villages of 20 to 60 people were dispersed in between the major centers. At the time of historic contact the total Tataviam population was probably less than 1,000, even if the Elizabeth Lake area is included in the estimates.

Culture

Archeological data indicate that foodstuffs were obtained and prepared in much the same way as neighboring groups. The primary vegetable foods in order of importance were the buds of Yucca whipplei (which were baked in earth ovens), acorns, sage seeds, juniper berries, and berries of islay (Prunus ilicifolia). Small mammals, deer, and perhaps antelope comprised the major animal foods.

There are no data on Tataviam social organization that might serve to differentiate them from Kitanemuk or Gabrielino. However, some interesting information that tends to suggest major similarities among Tataviam, Chumash, and Gabrielino ritual organization was recovered from Bowers's Cave between Newhall and Piru (Elsasser and Heizer 1963). This site contained ritual paraphernalia identical to that described ethnographically by Ventureño Chumash as being used by secret-society members (ʔantap) in the performance of ceremonies. Like their southern neighbors, the Tataviam also apparently held their annual mourning ceremony in the late summer or early fall and used open circular structures at the site. The Gaspar de Portolá expedition of 1769 recorded the presence of a number of people associated with a brush enclosure when they passed through the area in August (Palóu 1926). Pictographs in Tataviam territory also have strong similarities to those found in adjacent areas.

History

By 1810, virtually all the Tataviam had been baptized at San Fernando Mission. By the time secularization occurred in 1834, the descendants of most of the missionized Tataviam had married members of other groups, either at the mission or in the Tejon region. By 1916 the last speaker of the Tataviam language was dead, and any real opportunity for collecting firsthand information on this obscure group had vanished forever.

Synonymy

While the term the Tataviam applied to themselves is unknown, their Kitanemuk neighbors called them *táta·viam,* related to their words *ta·viyɨk* 'sunny hillside' and *ata·vihukwaʔ* 'he is sunning himself'. The upper Santa Clara River drains an area in which south-facing slopes are a dominant characteristic of the terrain. Thus *táta·viam* might be roughly translated as 'people facing the sun' or 'people of the south-facing slope'. The Vanyume name for them may have been the same, for Kroeber (1907b:140) recorded the term Tatavi-yam from a Vanyume woman long resident among the Mohaves as the equivalent for the Mohave name Gwalinyuokosmachi 'tule sleepers' who lived in tule houses on a large lake. These people Kroeber (1907b:136) suggested were "no doubt the Yokuts on Kern, Buena Vista, and possibly Tulare lakes." The Mohave word was recorded by Pamela Munro (personal communication 1975) as *kʷalʸəʔinʸolʸkʷəsmač* 'they sleep in the high tules', applied to the "Tehachapi Indians." Tehachapi is just north of the Kitanemuk area. However, given the near-identity of the Vanyume equivalent to the Kitanemuk term for the Tataviam, this may in fact have been the Mohave name for the same group. The San Fernando Valley Gabrielino called the Tataviam *turumkavet.*

When Kroeber (1915a) first recognized this group as a distinct entity, he applied what he said was their name in the neighboring (Ventureño) Chumash: Ataplili'ish. This term was recorded by Harrington as *ʔaɫapliliʔiš,* a name for the Gabrielino (Bright 1975a). Kroeber (1925:556, 621) later reported that Ataplili'ish was the Ventureño Chumash name for the Gabrielino and perhaps other Takic groups. Probably because he now believed his earlier name to have too broad an application, Kroeber (1925:577, 614) then called the Tataviam by what he reported to be the specific Ventureño Chumash name for them, Alliklik. Harrington (1915, 1917, 1935:84) recorded *ʔaɫlik̃lik̃ini* in Ynezeño Chumash as equivalent to Yawelmani Yokuts *ʔeʔewiɣič* and Spanish *Pujadores,* all three meaning 'grunters, stammerers' and being synonyms for Tataviam.

A vocabulary of "Alliklik Chumash" was recorded by Merriam without a date or location; Beeler and Klar (1974) have identified this as Ventureño Chumash with borrowings from Kitanemuk and suggested that it represents the speech of at least the northernmost extension of the region Kroeber (1925:pls. 1, 48) labeled Alliklik. To avoid further confusion it seems preferable to apply the name Castac Chumash to this region, about which almost nothing else is known. Merriam (Beeler and Klar 1974) used the name "Kas-tak (Chumash)," Harrington recorded *kaštɨk* as a village name in Ventureño Chumash (Bright 1975a), and Spanish sources referred to the group as Cuabajai (Beeler and Klar 1974) and Castequeños. The coastal Ventureño Chumash name for the dialect of the Castac region was *ʔaɫkuʔli,* and for the inhabitants, *ʔiʔaɫkuʔli* (Harrington 1915).

Sources

Ethnographic notes collected by Harrington (1913, 1916a, 1917) from his Kitanemuk, Chumash, Gabrielino, and San Bernardino Mountains Serrano informants regarding the Tataviam are the basic source for this chapter.

The San Fernando Mission registers remain one of the most important sources of data yet to be investigated in regard to village size, distribution, and intermarriage patterns. The early observations of Garcés and the members of the Portolá expedition provide further important information on the Tataviam. Other data are probably present in archival materials.

Archeological data for much of the area were systematically gathered by Richard Van Valkenberg in the early 1930s; his notes are on file at the Los Angeles County Museum of Natural History. Important data were also obtained during salvage excavations at Castaic reservoir from January 1970 to June 1971. Under the auspices of the Los Angeles County Department of Parks and Recreation, data from archeological research carried out in the Vasquez Rocks area have been synthesized with the results of previous work done on the upper Santa Clara River (King, Smith, and King 1974).

Gabrielino

LOWELL JOHN BEAN AND CHARLES R. SMITH

The Gabrielino (gäbrēəl'ēnō) are, in many ways, one of the most interesting—yet least known—of native California peoples. At the time of Spanish contact in 1769 they occupied the "most richly endowed coastal section in southern California" (Blackburn 1962–1963:6), which is most of present-day Los Angeles and Orange counties, plus several offshore islands (San Clemente, Santa Catalina, San Nicolas). With the possible exception of the Chumash, the Gabrielino were the wealthiest, most populous, and most powerful ethnic nationality in aboriginal southern California, their influence spreading as far north as the San Joaquin valley Yokuts, as far east as the Colorado River, and south into Baja California. Unfortunately, most if not all Gabrielinos were dead long before systematic ethnographic studies were instituted; and, as a result, knowledge of them and their lifeways is meager.

Language, Territory, and Environment

Gabrielino was one of the Cupan languages in the Takic family, which is part of the Uto-Aztecan linguistic stock (Bright 1975).* Internal linguistic differences existed, Harrington (1962:viii) suggesting four dialects and Kroeber (1925), six. Harrington's four-part division includes: Gabrielino proper, spoken mainly in the Los Angeles basin area; Fernandeño, spoken by people north of the Los Angeles basin, mainly in the San Fernando valley region; Santa Catalina Island dialect; and San Nicolas Island dialect—although according to Bright (1975) insufficient data exist to be sure of the Cupan affiliation of the San Nicolas speech. There were probably dialectical differences also between many mainland villages, a result not only of geographical separation but also of social, cultural, and linguistic mixing with neighboring non-Gabrielino speakers.

The names Gabrielino and Fernandeño (fernän'dā-ₗnyō) refer to the two major Spanish missions established in Gabrielino territory—San Gabriel and San Fernando.

* Italicized Gabrielino words have been written in a phonemic alphabet by Kenneth C. Hill, on the basis of John Peabody Harrington's unpublished field notes. The consonants are: (stops and affricate) *p, t, ç, k, kʷ, ʔ;* (fricatives) *s, ṣ, x, h;* (nasals) *m, n, ŋ;* (approximants) *v, ð, r, y, w.* Stressed vowels are *i, e* [ɛ]*, a, o* [ɔ]*, u,* which may occur long or short; in unstressed syllables the vowels are only *i* [e]*, a,* and *u* [o].

It was to these two missions that the majority of the Indians living on the coastal plains and valleys of southern California were removed.

Although the major outlines of Gabrielino territorial occupation are known, the fixing of definitive boundaries is difficult. Generally, Gabrielino territory included the watersheds of the Los Angeles, San Gabriel, and Santa Ana rivers, several smaller intermittent streams in the Santa Monica and Santa Ana mountains, all of the Los Angeles basin, the coast from Aliso Creek in the south to Topanga Creek in the north, and the islands of San Clemente, San Nicolas, and Santa Catalina (fig. 1). The area thus bounded encompassed several biotic zones (such as Coast-Marsh, Coastal Strand, Prairie, Chaparral, Oak Woodland, Pine) and, following Hudson's (1971) studies, can be divided into four macro-environmental zones (excluding the islands): Interior Mountains/Adjacent Foothills, Prairie, Exposed Coast, and Sheltered Coast. Each area is characterized by a particular floral-faunal-geographical relationship that allows delineation of subsistence-settlement patterns "according to the macro-environmental setting." The interior mountains and foothills, according to Hudson, comprise an area of numerous resources including "many small animals, deer, acorns, sage, piñon nuts, and a variety of other plants and animal foods." Settlement-pattern studies

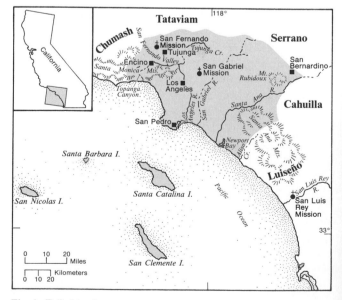

Fig. 1. Tribal territory.

(Hudson 1969) indicate the existence of both primary subsistence villages occupied continuously (perhaps by multiple clan groupings) and smaller secondary gathering camps (small family unit occupation) occupied at various times during the year, depending upon season and resource. All settlements in this zone, as well as in the other zones, were situated near water courses.

The Prairie, the area flanking the interior mountains on the north, east, and south, had as its predominant food resources acorns, sage, yucca, deer, numerous small rodents, cacti, plus a wide variety of plants, animals, and birds associated with marshes (Hudson 1971). Sites (both primary and secondary) were distributed throughout, but always near water courses or springs. The exposed coast from San Pedro south to Newport Bay was an area of concentrated secondary subsistence gathering camps with no primary subsistence villages immediately adjacent to the coast, but rather located inland. Various shellfish, some rays, sharks, and fish were the important food resources, while the offshore kelp beds (prime fishing areas for tuna and swordfish) were used year-round, especially in late summer and early fall. The sheltered coastal area stretching from San Pedro north to Topanga Canyon was characterized by primary subsistence villages located on the coast and secondary subsistence sites concentrated inland near areas of plant-food abundance (like sage stands and acorn or pine nut groves). The resources of this area were primarily marine (fish, shellfish, rays, sharks, sea mammals, and waterfowl), and "it is likely that some ecological elements of this region were also present in Area III (Exposed Coast), depending upon geographical features and weather" (Hudson 1971:56).

Climate varied according to locality, but average July temperatures along the coast ranged from approximately 68° F. to 76° F., with average January temperatures for the Gabrielino area as a whole ranging between 40° F. and 52° F. In the mountains, especially above 7,000 feet, temperatures often dipped as low as 30° F. in the winter (accompanied by snow), while summer temperatures on the prairies occasionally rose as high as 100° F.

While average annual precipitation in the twentieth century is generally less than 15 inches, as much as 40 inches is known in the higher mountains; and it is assumed that a similar pattern existed in precontact periods. The predominant climatic type is Hot Steppe, but near the coast and inland in the foothills and mountains the climatic type is warm Mediterranean. The predominant vegetation associations throughout most of the mainland area are grass and coastal sagebrush, especially in valley bottoms, and chaparral at higher elevations. Over 89 percent of Gabrielino territory was within the Sonoran life-zone, an extremely rich zone, while the balance was Forest Transition along the higher slopes and peaks of the San Gabriel and Santa Ana mountains.

The islands presented a different environmental picture. On San Nicolas Island, called ṣo·yŋa in Gabrielino, 75 miles southwest of Los Angeles, there were virtually no land mammals and a scarcity of exploitable floral resources. However, the little (32.2 sq. mi.), semidesert, windswept island was "particularly favored by the occurrence of abundant sea mammals" in the surrounding sea (Meighan and Eberhart 1953:113), including California and Steller sea lions, harbor seals, sea otters, and northern elephant seals. Additionally, the island was rich in sea fowl, while several different species of fish abounded in the surrounding sea. But the most important meat source was shellfish (rock scallops, mussels, several kinds of limpets, sea urchins), obtainable in large amounts along the island's rocky shoreline. From the hundreds of mortars and pestles (fig. 2) found on the island it is assumed that some plant material was prepared (some parts of the island supported trees, brush, mosses, grasses), but early Spanish references indicate mortars were also used in processing dried abalone meat.

The settlement pattern on San Nicolas is remarkably consistent through time. Villages were located either on sand dunes within 200 yards of shoreline or at considerable elevation above sea level inland on the island's central plateau. The determining factors in settlement pattern were access to the beaches or sea, fresh water (limited to a few springs in the inland's northwestern corner), and elevation affording an unobstructed view. From archeological research it appears that the densest

Dept. of Anthr., Smithsonian: top, 18670, 18698; bottom, 21887.
Fig. 2. Utensils for food preparation. top, Sandstone mortar and pestle collected at San Nicolas Island, diameter of mortar 23.5 cm; bottom, soapstone pot collected at Santa Barbara Island, same scale.

occupation of the island occurred in the few centuries preceding Spanish conquest, with a population of 600–1,200 at any one time (Meighan and Eberhart 1953).

Santa Catalina Island, called *pimu·ʔa* by the Gabrielino, is predominantly mountainous, with very limited plant resources (sparse, thin grasses, small shrubs, a few species of cacti) and few land animals (mainly deer, ground squirrels, foxes). There appears to have been limited use of migratory waterfowl, and quail, abundant today, may have also been used. However, as with San Nicolas Island, the major food resources were marine animals: fish, shellfish, and sea mammals. According to Meighan (1959:401) there was not just a "heavy dependency on sea mammals, but a specialized maritime economy which exploited dolphins and porpoises to a great extent." Permanent habitation sites were located mainly along the coast with interior sites not much more than trail-side camps occupied for very short periods. Although very little is known about the aboriginal inhabitants of the island, on the basis of archeological research at one of the coastal headland sites, Little Harbor, it has been established that the island was occupied as early as 2000 B.C. by a sizable number of people, because the Little Harbor site is areally large and the layers of cultural material are deep.

Very little information is available concerning habitation patterns on San Clemente Island, but the environmental situation is essentially identical with that of San Nicolas and Santa Catalina. As Kroeber (1925:620) noted, "the local culture on San Clemente . . . was clearly connected with that of Santa Catalina, perhaps dependent upon it; and Catalina was pure Gabrielino in speech." Therefore, cultural patterns were probably fairly similar to the mainland, or at least to those of Santa Catalina.

History

Population estimates for the Gabrielino are next to impossible to make. Possibly more than 50 or 100 mainland villages were inhabited simultaneously with an average population in each village of 50–100 at the time of contact with Europeans. Early Spanish reports indicate a range of village population between 50 and 200 people. At Tujunga in 1797 there were 90 full-time residents, Crespí (1927) counted over 200 at Yangna (*ya·ŋa*), and Forbes (1966:139) states that the village at Encino had a population of at least 60 permanent residents but over 200 people were present to greet the Spanish explorers. Later reports that give very low population figures, such as those of Hugo Reid and those from the Spanish mission baptismal records, probably reflect the results of inroads made by introduced disease prior to the actual arrival of Spaniards. Pablo Tac, a neophyte from San Luis Rey Mission, reported that the Indians in that area had suffered severe population loss

from disease several years prior to Spanish entry into the area (Tac 1930).

According to the archeological record, the Gabrielino were not the first inhabitants of the Los Angeles basin but arrived around 500 B.C. (as part of what Kroeber has called the Shoshonean [Takic-speaking] wedge), slowly displacing the indigenous Hokan speakers. By A.D. 500 dialectical diversification had begun among the Gabrielino. Permanent villages were established in the fertile lowlands along rivers and streams and in sheltered areas along the coast; and population expanded with many of the larger, permanent villages having satellite communities lying at varying distances from them and connected through economic, religious, and social ties. Kroeber (1925) believed that the Gabrielino cultural pattern encountered by the Spanish in the eighteenth century had crystallized as early as A.D. 1200 and shortly before the Spanish arrived in force about 1770 the population had grown in excess of 5,000.

As early as 1542 the Gabrielino were in contact with the Spanish, for in that year Juan Rodríguez Cabrillo became the first Spaniard to set foot on Gabrielino soil. This first contact, at which the Indian women and children fled and men armed themselves with bows, was peaceful; and when the Spaniards returned in 1602, under Sebastián Vizcaíno, the Gabrielino received them with hospitality. However, it was not until 1769 that the Spaniards took steps to colonize within Gabrielino territory. Several land expeditions were dispatched to locate suitable mission sites, and by 1771 four had been built. But relations with the Indians disintegrated; their population dwindled (due to introduced diseases, dietary deficiencies, forceful reduction); and by 1900 they had ceased to exist as a culturally identifiable group (see table 1).

Culture

Clothing and Adornment

The Gabrielino, described as being "a race which . . . was genetically stable, physically hardy, and attuned to the conditions of its environments" (B.E. Johnston 1962:28), were for a short period considered by the Spanish as a special race of "White Indians" because of their light skin color. Older women used liberal amounts of red ocher paint on their faces to retard the browning and wrinkling process caused by sun and wind. Younger women also used the red paint as a rouge to make themselves more attractive. Tattooing, using thorns of flint slivers as the agent and vegetable charcoal as the dye, was common practice. Before puberty, girls were tattooed on their foreheads and chins, while adult women had tattoos covering an area from their eyes down to their breasts. Men tattooed their foreheads with vertical and/or horizontal lines.

Table 1. History

1973	Some residents of San Gabriel claim Gabrielino heritage.	1800	Most Gabrielinos missionized, dead, or fled to other areas with scattered numbers in area. More non-Gabrielinos brought into Gabrielino missions (e.g., Serrano, Luiseño, Cahuilla, Ipai-Tipai).
1925	Some remnants of Gabrielino songs and culture recorded by J.P. Harrington at Pala Indian Reservation.	1797	San Luis Rey active, growing, expanding.
1903	C. Hart Merriam, A.L. Kroeber, and others work with the few remaining Gabrielinos. A few years later J.P. Harrington begins Gabrielino research as does Constance Goddard DuBois.	1796	Because of poor economic conditions in missions and Spanish communities, neophytes arranged to use traditional Gabrielino subsistence methods to help feed the general populace. Gabrielinos also are major labor force in Pueblo of Los Angeles and outlying ranches and farms.
1860–1900	Smallpox epidemic further reduces Gabrielino population except for isolated families and Gabrielinos living in remote areas. Gabrielino culture is now only in the minds of a few people.	1786	Revolts in areas outside Gabrielino area. Spanish control firm only within a 20-mile radius of Los Angeles.
1852	Hugo Reid publishes *Indians of Los Angeles County*. His wife, Victoria (d. 1868), is a Gabrielino and a prominent person in the Los Angeles area. B.D. Wilson publishes report on Indians of southern California and recommends better treatment for Indians. This report is ignored.	1785	Indian protests, revolts are frequent, culminating in a major revolt led by Toypurina, a chief's daughter. Increased segregation of Indians from *gente de razón* attempted by government. Most Gabrielinos become a peasant class working for missions or a landed gentry. Apartheidlike policy dominates Spanish-Indian relationships.
1840–1850	Most Indians in Los Angeles area are other Mission groups, but a few Gabrielino still in the area. Some Gabrielino language, some rituals and games, traditional crafts and economic modes still maintained, but in very attenuated forms. Gabrielino is until this period the lingua franca for Whites and Indians. Clamshell beads still used as money; baskets and steatite artifacts still being used by Europeans and Indians. Smallpox epidemics decimate all tribes in the area.	1779	Social organizations of missions crystallized as the positions of councilmen and alcaldes are established—elected by neophytes. Conflicts between military and church become acute as each vies for authority over Indian labor.
		1778	Mass conversions of villages begins, as certain chiefs become converted, drawing many of their followers with them.
1833	Missions secularized, become refuges for aged, infirm. Most Gabrielinos are laborers for gentry class or landowners themselves (very rarely). Gabrielinos are scattered as far north as Monterey and south to below San Diego, while many are living with groups in the remote interior.	1771	Mission San Gabriel established, slowly integrates a few Gabrielinos into the mission. Many nonconverted Gabrielinos integrate into economic and social life of Spanish, but not religious life.
1800–1833	Missions grow, ranches expand, most Indians firmly in peasant class or fugitives. Diseases (among Indians) still killing many; armed raids conducted by Spanish against escaped neophytes and those Indians still not converted.	1769	Gaspar de Portolá expedition crosses Gabrielino territory and interacts with Gabrielinos. European disease probably decimating populations already. Conflicts among Gabrielino begin almost immediately. Conversions slow.
		1602	Spanish explorers visit Santa Catalina.
		1520	Spanish explorers visit Santa Catalina.

Men wore their hair long, parted in the middle, and either falling straight or braided in the back and doubled upward, fastening onto the head with a cane or bone pin. The women's hair was also long and free, with bangs, and frequently adorned with flower garlands. When in mourning women either singed or cut their hair as a sacrifice and as a demonstration of their feeling of loss. To keep their hair glossy and free of parasites, clay was applied to the head, left to dry, and then broken off. In those instances where baldness was a problem, various plants were reduced to charcoal, ground into paste, and rubbed into the scalp once in the morning and again in the evening for as long as necessary to restore the lost hair. Daily bathing for everyone was rigorously adhered to, and usually done before sunrise, with everyone drying out by the fire as breakfast was prepared (B.E. Johnston 1962).

Men and children usually went naked, while women wore aprons of either deerskin or the inner bark of willow or cottonwood trees. Occasionally capes of deerskin, rabbit fur, or bird skins (with feathers intact) were worn, especially in cold or wet weather. Except in areas of rough terrain when yucca fiber sandals were donned, everyone went barefooted. At night robes of deerskins or twisted strips of rabbit fur woven together with milkweed or yucca fiber were used as blankets. On the islands and along the coast, otter skins were used for the same purposes. Ritual costumes (worn during dances by warriors, chiefs, shamans) were colorful (with plummage from different birds, fur, shells, and beads used as decoration) and elaborate and included feather headdresses, feathered capes and skirts. Uncovered skin was brightly decorated with paint.

Technology

The majority of Gabrielino material culture, although perishable and rarely lasting more than a few years, reflected an elaborately developed artisanship, with many everyday use items decorated with shell inlaid in asphaltum, rare minerals, carvings, and painting, and comparable in quality and excellence to that of their northwestern neighbors, the Chumash. Perhaps the best-known items of Gabrielino material culture are the objects made of steatite, obtained in finished or raw form by most mainland groups from the Indians of Santa Catalina Islands, where a veritable steatite industry flourished. The steatite was used in making animal carvings, pipes, "ritual" objects, ornaments, and cooking utensils (figs. 2–3). The last were considered of such value (because of their being made of steatite) that when a cooking pot broke, it was either mended with asphalt or a handle was attached to the largest piece, which was then used as a frying pan. Other food preparation items included bedrock and portable mortars, metates, mullers, mealing brushes, wooden stirrers, paddles, shell spoons, bark platters, wooden bowls (often inlaid with haliotis shell), and pottery vessels, made by coiling technique and paddle and anvil (Blackburn 1962–1963).

A variety of tools was made, including saws made from deer scapulae, bone or shell needles, fishhooks and awls, scrapers, flakers (of bone or shell), wedges, hafted or unhafted flint or cane knives, and flint drills.

Baskets were made by the women from the stems of rushes (*Juncus* sp.), grass (*Muhlenbergia rigens*), and squawbush (*Rhus trilobata*) with a three-color patterned decoration (Harrington 1942:20–23). Coiled wares included mortar hoppers; flat baskets used as plates, trays, winnowers, shallow carrying or serving baskets; storage baskets; and small globular baskets used to keep trinkets in. Closework and openwork twining was used to make deep or globular-shaped baskets, or for baskets used in leaching, straining, or gathering. Ceremonial baskets, urn-shaped and choke-mouthed, were used for grave offerings (Merriam 1955:84; Blackburn 1962–1963).

Weapons included three forms of wooden war clubs, self- and sinew-backed bows, tipped (stone or bone) and untipped cane arrows (simple or compound), wooden sabers, throwing clubs, and slings used for hunting birds and small game (Blackburn 1962–1963).

Structures

Houses were domed, circular structures thatched with tule, fern, or carrizo (fig. 4). For groups located near the sea, the doorways opened seaward, to avoid the north wind (Harrington 1942:10). B.E. Johnston (1962) noted that the Indians' houses were, in some cases, "so spacious that each will hold fifty people." On Santa Catalina, Costansó (1911) described houses of more than 60 feet in diameter, with three or four families living in each one. Other structures commonly found in villages included sweathouses (small, semicircular, earth-covered buildings used for pleasure and as a clubhouse or meeting place for adult males), menstrual huts, and a ceremonial enclosure, the *yuva·r*. A *yuva·r* was built near the chief's house and was essentially an open-air enclosure, oval in plan, made with willows inserted wicker fashion among willow stakes, decorated with eagle and raven feathers, skins, and flowers, and containing inside the enclosure painted and decorated poles. Consecrated anew before every ceremony, these ceremonial enclosures were the centers for activities relating to the Chingichngish cult. An image representing the god Chingichngish occupied a special "sacred" area within the *yuva·r*, and on the ground near the image was a sand painting representing the cosmos, with figures of the Sun and Moon predominating. Only very old men or very powerful ones (chiefs, priest-shamans) were allowed in this inner sanctuary. Another building, similar in structure and design to the *yuva·r* but never consecrated, was sometimes built and used for instruction and practice for upcoming ceremonies (Blackburn 1962–1963; Heizer 1968).

Dept. of Anthr., Smithsonian: top, 382666; bottom, 18349.

Fig. 3. Soapstone artifacts with carved grooves, possibly comals. Used to heat water in baskets, the hot stone was manipulated by a stick through the hole. top, Length 15 cm, collected at San Clemente Island; bottom, same scale, collected at Santa Barbara Island.

542

Santa Barbara Mission, Calif.

Fig. 4. Mission San Gabriel Arcangel with thatched Indian house in foreground. Painted by Ferdinand Deppe, 1832, after his sketch made June 1828 during a Corpus Christi procession.

Social and Political Organization

The intricacies of Gabrielino social organization are unknown, and only a rudimentary outline of basic organizational features can be presented. It appears that a moiety system similar to that of other southern California Takic speakers existed, but it seems not to have functioned viably in controlling socioeconomic interrelationships.

Almost nothing is known of the nature and texture of adult life among the Gabrielino. There seem to have existed at least three hierarchically ordered social classes: an elite (having a specialized language) including chiefs and their immediate family and the very rich; a middle class, or those from fairly well-to-do and long-established lineages; and a third class comprising everyone else, with those individuals engaged in ordinary socioeconomic pursuits. Some individuals owned real estate, and property boundaries were marked by painting a copy of the owner's personalized tattoo on trees, posts, and rocks. These marks were almost equivalent to the owner's name and known not only to other Gabrielino but also in many cases to members of non-Gabrielino groups. Engelhardt's (1927a:100) comment that pictures of animals were drawn on tree trunks may refer to this boundary-marking process.

Villages (that is, tribelets) were politically autonomous, composed of nonlocalized lineages, often segmentary in

Title Insurance and Trust Company, Los Angeles.

Fig. 5. Village at Jurupa Rancho, base of Mt. Rubidoux, near San Bernardino inhabited by Cahuilla, Serrano, and probably some Gabrielino refugees. Photograph by C.C. Pierce, 1890.

nature. Each lineage had its own leader and at various times during the year fragmented into smaller subsistence-exploitation units that went out seasonally to collect resource items and then return to the villages.

The dominant lineage's leader was usually the village "chief" (*tumia·r*) whose authority was legitimatized by the possession of the sacred bundle, the link between the sacred past and the present and the material, temporal representation of the Gabrielinos' raison d'être and the primary embodiment and focus of "power." Often several villages were allied under the leadership of a single chief. For example, at San Pedro the largest village, *ṣua·ŋa* 'place of the skies', was the political center for a cluster of other villages located nearby and its chief was the political leader for these associated villages. Succession to chiefly office was usually through the male line, a chief's eldest son assuming the office subject to community approval. If a direct line-of-descent male replacement was unavailable or unacceptable, a new chief was selected by the community elders from the same kin group as the previous chief. If there were no satisfactory male candidates, a woman, usually a sister or daughter of the previous chief, was appointed. According to Hugo Reid, regardless of who became the new chief, his or her name was changed to correspond to that of his or her village, with the addition of a special suffix (Heizer 1968).

New chiefs occasionally had more than one wife, were about 30–35 when they became chief, and often were the political heads of multiple village confederations. A chief's most important duties were to administer community solidarity and welfare and to act as the guardian of the sacred bundle. In the former sphere of action the chief arbitrated disputes, supervised tax collections ("gifts" from the people used principally for consumption by guests at ceremonies), led war parties, concluded peace treaties, and acted as the "model" Gabrielino. To help in these activities, the chief had several assistants: an announcer, treasurer, general assistant (who often delivered moral lectures to the people), and messengers (usually two, with excellent memories, especially trained and kept until they "wore out").

In addition to the chief, others who held authority positions within the community were shamans and the *ta·xkʷaʔ*. The latter was responsible for the management of the elaborate mourning ceremonies among other things and oversaw the distribution of food following communal hunts. But it was with the shamans that perhaps the greatest power existed, sometimes even greater than the chief's. For, as Reid pointed out, even chiefs had no jurisdiction over shamans because they "conversed with the Great Spirit" and could be punished only by other shamans.

Shamanism

A shaman obtained his power directly from the supernatural through dreams or visions, often caused by the ingestion of datura. During these trancelike states an animal or object with energizing power would appear to the person and henceforth be his power aid. Following this stage, the prospective shaman entered a period of apprenticeship under proved shamans and was taught various aspects of the profession.

A shaman served mainly his own village and possessed the ability to cause as well as cure illness. Curing was accomplished by various techniques (herbal therapeutics, body manipulation, bloodletting, sucking, blowing smoke, hypnosis) and a wide variety of magical, power-invested paraphernalia. The basic instrument was a board with rattlesnake rattles attached to it (Blackburn 1962–1963) worn by the shaman, plus dried animal skins, curiously shaped rocks, plant roots, sparkling stones, rare minerals, as well as surgical implements such as obsidian blades. These objects not only were considered as having power in and of themselves but also were felt to be particularly efficacious in concentrating power in a particular area.

In addition to their function as curers, shamans also served as diviners, guardians (supernatural) of the sacred bundle, locators of lost items, collectors of poisons used on hunting and war arrows, and rain makers. Most possessed second sight, several had the ability to transform themselves into bears (in order to travel rapidly) and to handle fire with impunity, and some were able to witch people living at great distances. For example, among the Fernandeño, a shaman wishing to witch or kill a person prepared a four-sided ground painting, roped it off, and then stood in the center holding 12 radiating strings, the ends of which were held by 12 assistants. When the shaman shook the strings, the ground quaked and the person he had in mind fell ill and could eventually die (Kroeber 1925:626).

However, if a shaman became too malevolent and practiced evil against his own people, other shamans convened and stripped him of his power. Women could also acquire considerable power and at least in one instance exert this power politically as in the case of Toypurina, who led a significant revolt during the eighteenth century against the Spanish at Mission San Gabriel (Temple 1958).

Life Cycle

• MARRIAGE Information about aboriginal Gabrielino marriage and residence patterns is practically nonexistent, and what data are available are sketchy and confusing. It appears that marriages were usually between individuals of nearly equal social rank, especially in the case of leading families, with the marriage partners coming from different lineages (lineage exogamy). Occasionally parents, while their children were quite young, would promise them in marriage (child betrothal), but usually "when a person wished to marry, and had selected a suitable partner, he advertised the same to all his relations, even to the *nineteenth cousin*. On a day appointed . . . they [the males] proceeded in a body to the residence of the bride," where she and all her female relations were assembled, and presented shell beads to the bride's relatives (Heizer 1968:25). A few days later the bride's female relatives visited the groom-to-be's home, presented his male relatives with food stuffs, and set the date for the wedding ceremony. On the appointed day the bride, adorned with beads, paints, feathers, and skins, was carried by her relatives to her future husband's home. Friends and neighbors accompanied the bridal party singing, dancing, and strewing the ground with gifts. Halfway to the groom's house the procession was met by his relatives who took on the role of carrying the bride the rest of the way. Upon arrival, the bride was placed beside her new husband, and baskets of seeds were liberally poured over both bride and groom to signify a rich and bountiful future life. A festive dance was held at which warriors and hunters performed in full costume; then everyone departed leaving the couple "to enjoy their 'Honey Moon' according to usage." From this date forward the wife was forbidden to visit her relatives, but they could call on her at any time (Heizer 1968:26).

Except in the case of chiefs who practiced polygyny, a man usually took only one wife at a time. If, during the course of married life, a husband ill used his wife, she could complain to her family, who would return to the husband his family's "bridal gifts," and the woman was then free to return to her own home. If a wife was barren or unruly, her husband could send her home and his family's "gifts" would be returned. In the case of a wife's infidelity the husband could beat or kill his wife or, if possible, claim the wife of his wife's lover.

The Gabrielino traced their most important kinship ties through males (patrilineal descent) with an individual's social rank, value, and status in part dependent upon wealth possession (family and self) and heredity. Sharp distinctions were made between families in different classes both within and beyond the lineage. In the kinship terminology, what little data are available suggest a Dakota system with Iroquois cousin terminology.

• BIRTH   Every time a woman gave birth both she and the child were ritually purified by sweatbathing for three consecutive days. During this period certain dietary restrictions were observed by the mother, and not until her child could run was she free to share her husband's bed (Heizer 1968).

The birth of a child to a chief was an occasion of special ritual and included dancing by old women who lauded the newborn's future renown and a ceremonial washing of the baby. Children were treated with such

love, devotion, and fondness by their parents that the Spanish missionaries were astounded and commented that the children were treated like "little idols" (B.E. Johnston 1962).

• PUBERTY   As a child grew she or he was expected to show deference to those older—never to pass between adults or to interrupt their conversation. When a girl reached puberty—an occasion for joy and happiness—she underwent a purification ceremony similar to that of women at childbirth. During the ceremony she was the center of dancing and singing in her honor and was formally presented to society as an eligible, marriageable woman. She was not allowed to eat meat during the ceremony; was lectured on proper female conduct (in order to insure her popularity); and was instructed to be industrious, bathe daily, be hospitable, and be without deceit at all times. During the ceremony a sand painting was made depicting certain cosmological-supernatural beings, the significance of whom was explained to the young woman so she could better understand her place, role, and function (as well as that of her society in general) in the overall scheme of creation.

It is not known with certainty if all young males underwent a puberty ceremony. Blackburn (1962-1963:34) notes that some adolescent boys were involved in a complex ceremony, one resembling the toloache cult of their neighbors. While there is little specific documentation concerning the Gabrielino cult, all indications point to Santa Catalina Island as the traditional home of the Luiseño, Cahuilla, and Cupeño toloache ceremonies (Kroeber 1925:620); and it is assumed that their toloache rituals are survivals of a much more elaborate Gabrielino ceremony.

• DEATH   When an important person died a piece of flesh from his or her shoulder was eaten, the person so doing gaining some of the deceased's power while the deceased was assured of a quick passage to the heavens to become a star (B.E. Johnston 1962; Harrington 1920-1930). This was in contrast to ordinary people who, when they died, went underground and danced and feasted forever. On the mainland the corpse was wrapped in a blanket (one used by the deceased during life); relatives assembled for ritual wailing and dancing; and after three days the corpse, along with most of the deceased's personal possessions, was burned. This disposal practice was in contrast to that practiced by at least one of the island groups, those of Santa Catalina. Here the dead were buried with artifacts used during life; the recurrence of certain tools in certain assemblages may indicate that there were vocational guilds on the island. Often dogs would be buried over the body.

Those possessions of the deceased not destroyed or buried were kept for use in the annual mourning ceremony, the biggest event celebrated in the year. Held in the fall following the acorn harvest, eight days were spent instructing the inexperienced in correct ceremonial procedure, songs, and dances (Harrington 1920–1930). The beginning of the ceremony was signaled by the construction or consecration of the *yuva·r,* the special ceremonial enclosure, followed by ceremonial feasting. Over the next seven days there was a great deal of visiting, dancing, singing, and feasting. Dancers, adorned with hawk and eagle feathers and with their faces, necks, and thorax painted, reenacted various sacred time events, their movements governed by shaman-priests, who watched from the sidelines. On the fourth day a ritualist brought forth all the children born during the year and the chief gave them names selected from their fathers' lineages. On the fifth day life-size images of the deceased were made, the men's images usually decorated with bows and arrows, the women's with baskets. Either on the evening of the fifth day or during the sixth day, an eagle-killing ceremony was held accompanied by special dances and songs.

In the predawn light of the eighth day the images were brought into the *yuva·r*, carried by the dancers while they performed, then thrown onto a fire along with personal items saved at the time of death. The annual mourning ceremony is one of the typical elements of California culture and possibly developed from the Gabrielino and spread to most, if not all, other southern California groups.

Subsistence

Men carried out most of the heavy but short-term labor; they hunted, fished, assisted in some gathering activities (fig. 6), conducted most trading ventures, and had as their central concerns the ceremonial and political well-being of their families and homes. Large land mammals were hunted with bow and arrow, while smaller game were taken with deadfalls, snares, and traps. Burrowing animals were smoked from their holes and clubbed to death, while rabbits were taken in communal hunts with nets, bow and arrows, and throwing clubs (Blackburn 1962–1963:24). For hunting sea mammals harpoons, spearthrowers, and clubs were used. Deep-sea fishing or trading expeditions between island and mainland were undertaken from boats made of wooden planks lashed and asphalted together. However, most fishing was carried out from shore or along rivers, streams, and creeks and involved the use of line and hook, nets, basketry traps, spears, bow and arrow, and vegetal poisons.

Women were involved mainly in collecting and preparing most floral and some animal food resources and production of baskets, pots, and clothing. When old, they shared with old men the task of teaching, supervising, and caring for the young (Blackburn 1962–1963; B.E. Johnston 1962).

Fig. 6. Rojerio, chorister at Mission San Fernando, gathering cactus fruit. Photograph by C.C. Pierce, July 1898.

External Relations

War

Although nineteenth-century writers often characterized the Gabrielino as timid and peaceful, the earlier chroniclers paint a different picture. A state of constant enmity existed between some coastal and prairie-mountain groups. Engelhardt (1927a:20) noted that intervillage conflicts among the Gabrielino were so frequent and of such intensity that inland Gabrielino were effectively prevented by coastal Gabrielino from reaching the sea for fishing and trading purposes. This concern with war as more than a defensive or rare occurrence is further supported by the occurrence of reed armor, war clubs, swords, and large and heavy bows used for warfare, as well as the hunting of big game. While these "wars" were not lengthy, they were deadly and often involved several villages. Those villages allied through marriage ties (and hence economic and religious bonds) usually actively supported one another in armed conflicts. Furthermore, it was not uncommon for a village planning a "war" to send ceremonial gifts to villages with whom it did not have close ties in hopes either of entering into an alliance of mutual help or at least of ensuring the villages' neutrality.

Armed conflict could arise for a number of reasons: failure of a chief to return a gift during a ceremony (that is, breaking the economic reciprocity system), abduction of women, trespassing, or sorcery (it was generally assumed that neighboring groups were using supernatural powers for harm). In the event of potential conflict, a war council was called by an official crier (smoke signals were also used to call people from distant villages) with all potentially involved villages attending, and the pros and cons of going to war discussed. A decision to go to war was not lightly made, since warfare involved not only the warriors, but also old men, women, and even children. The chief led the war party and, while on maneuvers, was followed in order by able-bodied warriors, old men, women, and then the children, the last two groups carrying the food and supplies (Heizer 1968).

Every attempt was made to surprise the enemy, descending upon his villages and killing, or occasionally capturing, as many people as possible. Bows and arrows and war clubs were the primary instruments of warfare. The clubs were of hard, heavy wood, often with bulbous heads and sharp conical projections, with a length up to three feet. During battle the women gathered up arrows shot in their direction and gave them to the men to shoot back. Wounded, if left on the battlefield, were killed by the opposition. If prisoners were taken, their fate varied: males were tortured in front of the entire village population, beheaded, and scalped, the scalps later dried, cured, and placed on display in the yuva·r. Women and children, if not also killed, were enslaved, their only chance of freedom being escape or recapture by their own people. Occasionally it was possible to buy back captives, but this seems to have been rare (Heizer 1968).

Feuds

More common than warfare, and involving considerably less people, were the feuds that passed from father to son, often for many generations. Hostilities were vented through ritualized "song fights," some lasting as long as eight days. Songs, obscene and insulting in nature and sung in the vilest language possible, were accompanied by stomping and trampling the ground, symbolizing the subjugation of the opponent (Heizer 1968).

Interpersonal disputes were adjudicated by the village chief. If the dispute involved members of the same village, the chief heard testimony, examined evidence, then passed a binding judgment. If the quarrel involved parties from two different villages, each party's chief conducted a separate hearing among his own people, then met with each other to pass sentence. If they were unable to issue an acceptable joint statement, a third chief was summoned to hear the two chiefs' arguments, then make a final, unappealable judgment—unappealable, that is, short of open armed conflict or sorcery (Heizer 1968).

Intermarriage

Yet by and large, interpersonal, intra- and intervillage relationships were amicable. Gabrielino villages were often located immediately adjacent to non-Gabrielino ones, and intermarriage was common. For example, at Corona, the Gabrielino village of Paxauxa lay directly across Temescal Creek from a large Luiseño village, and intermarriage between the two was common. Forbes (1966) reports that the people of the Gabrielino village of Tongva intermarried with the people of at least 13 other villages, including Yokuts, Chumash, and Serrano. This arrangement is not unusual, since the Gabrielinos were part of a widespread ritual congregation union "which existed between all Cahuilla, Serrano, Luiseño, and Gabrielino clans" (Bean 1972; Strong 1929). Since this was the case, relationships were usually friendly among members of these different groups.

Trade

Intra- and intergroup exchange was brisk and common, with people, goods, and ideas flowing in many directions and in some cases, for long distances. From the inland Serranos the coastal Gabrielinos obtained acorns, seeds, obsidian, and deerskins in exchange for shell beads, dried fish, sea otter pelts, shells, possibly salt, and steatite (obtained by coastal Gabrielinos from those living on the islands). Through middlemen located in interior southern California—such as Cahuilla, Chemehuevi, Mohave— shells from coastal sections controlled by Gabrielinos were traded as far east as central Arizona. Ruby has noted that Cibola White ware (A.D. 1000) from the Southwest has been found in Gabrielino territory, while shells and steatite have been found in Pueblo sites. It is likely that southern California and the Southwest "were engaged in a series of reciprocal exchanges, regularized by the establishment of trading partnerships . . ." (Ruby 1970:96, 266–267), perhaps as early as A.D. 600–800. Most trading was usually of the barter type, but when this was not feasible or desirable, strung olivella beads, considered legal tender throughout most of southern California, were used to transact business (Ruby 1970).

The principal trade item, both among the Gabrielino and for export to other groups, was steatite. Available in great quantities on Santa Catalina Island, steatite was traded, in rough or finished form, to many groups (Chumash, Yokuts, Ipai-Tipai, Luiseño, Serrano, and via the Chumash to the distant Tubatulabal). Most of the steatite was used to make palettes, arrow straighteners, ornaments, and carvings of animal or animallike beings. From archeological and ethnographic accounts it would appear that the Gabrielino received traders, possibly at trading centers, from other groups rather than journeying out to distant peoples (Harrington 1920–1930). In some business transactions knotted cords were used as mnemonic devices for recalling figures and quantities and intricacies of past or pending transactions.

Perhaps the most important "item" originating in the Gabrielino territory that found its way to non-Gabrielino groups and significantly influenced them was the set of associated religious beliefs and rituals called the Chingichngish cult (see "Cults and their Transformations," this vol.).

Religion

Less is known concerning the Gabrielino religious system and beliefs than those of their neighbors. Several different creation stories exist. One relates to the god Qua-o-ar—compare the Luiseño-Juaneño *kʷáʔuwar,* one of their names for Chingichngish (Harrington 1933b:139, phonemicized). He created the world out of chaos, fixing it upon the shoulders of seven giants created for this purpose (Heizer 1968:19). Following this, Qua-o-ar created animals and then humans from earth, and then ascended to the afterworld. B.E. Johnston (1962:41) recorded a different creation story whose prime characters were Heaven and Earth. The two were respectively brother and sister who, through six different creations, made all of the world; then Earth gave birth to Wiyot (*wuyoˑt*), "an animate being, but different from the rational kind, and irrational" (B.E. Johnston 1962:41). Wiyot ruled the people for a long time but eventually was killed by his sons because of his cruelty. Following his death, the people met to discuss what things in the world could be used as food. As they enumerated the wild food "a new leader appeared to them, at first seeming like a phantom or an evanescent vision . . . announced himself as a greater chief [than Wiyot]. . . . He called himself Chungichnish [Chingichngish†] and gave a great speech in which he set the future course of tribal law and religion. [He] delegated powers and responsibilities to certain persons [shaman-priests]. . . . The god also created out of mud . . . a new race" of people and instructed them in new life-ways. Following this, Chingichngish began to dance and slowly ascended into heaven (B.E. Johnston 1962:42-44).

By the time the Spanish arrived in Gabrielino territory the belief in Chingichngish had apparently spread to neighboring non-Gabrielino groups (Luiseño, Ipai-Tipai, Cupeño, Juaneño), becoming intimately involved with the toloache cult. The belief in Chingichngish had become highly formalized and ritualized involving the erection of "temples" (sacred enclosures where elaborately decorated poles and banners were erected and an image of Chingichngish was placed) into which only old men possessing great "power" could enter, lengthy and elaborate ceremonies, and offerings of food and goods not only to Chingichngish but also to Sun and Moon (B.E. Johnston 1962).

The exact nature of Sun and Moon are not known, but they have enjoyed almost as much attention and devotion

as Chingichngish. Whenever sand paintings ("maps" of the Gabrielino cosmology) were made, representations of Sun and Moon figured predominantly in them (Harrington 1920-1930). In addition to these cosmological beings, the Gabrielino also recognized the sacred beings characterized as Crow, Raven, Owl, and Eagle. The Eagle emerges as a central figure in the remote past, a great and wise chief who, when dying, told the people he would become an eagle whose feathers were to be used in all rituals (Harrington 1920-1930; Kroeber 1925).

Little else is known about Gabrielino mythology. In the few stories, often of fragmentary nature or imbued with non-Gabrielino (European) elements that survive, predominant themes include revenge, transformations to escape bad events, severe punishments for selfishness or disrespect, and "deliberate or artistic incoherence, both as regards personages and plot" (Kroeber 1925:625).

Prime life values included respect for age, maleness, and above all, secrecy: "Whenever they tell the truth they think some slight damage may result to them or they might loose something good. They conceal it [truth] every way. In this matter, they have no other motive than their own convenience" (Engelhardt 1927a:104).

The four cardinal directions (North, East, South, West) were named, while the year was divided into two parts (according to the solstices) with 10 moons. Several stars were named (usually animal names), the Pleiades were considered to be sacred time maidens, rainbows conferred good luck while ball lightning conferred bad luck, whirlwinds were evil spirits, and springs and lakes the dwelling places of potentially malevolent spirits (B.E. Johnston 1962; Heizer 1968).

Synonymy

The Gabrielino of the Los Angeles area called themselves *kumiˑvit* (cf. *kumiˑ* 'east') and were so referred to by the Fernandeños, who were known to the Gabrielino as *paṣeˑkʷarum* (cf. *paṣeˑkŋa* 'San Fernando').

The Spanish group name Gabrielino first appears, spelled Gabrileños, in a report by Loew (1876) and has been intermittently applied to the aboriginal inhabitants of the Los Angeles area since that time. Another spelling is Gabrieleño (Hodge 1907-1910, 1:480). Other names, for which Hodge gives some early attestations, are Kij (B.E. Johnston 1962); Kizh (Heizer 1968); Tobikhars (B.E. Johnston 1962); and *tumámqamalum,* a Luiseño word related to *tumáˑmik* 'north' (though 'northerners' in general is *tumámkawčum*) (William Bright, personal communication 1974; Kroeber in Hodge).

Sources

The major published sources on Gabrielino are B.E. Johnston (1962), the published forms of the Hugo Reid letters that contain valuable footnotes (Heizer 1968; W.J.

---

† Chingichngish and Chungichnish are spellings of the Luiseño name *čiŋíčŋiš* (dialect variant *čaŋíčŋiš*); no corresponding Gabrielino name has been recorded.

Hoffman 1885), Engelhardt (1908-1915, 1927, 1927a), Harrington's culture element distribution list (1942) and work on Chingichngish (1933b), Kroeber (1925), and Blackburn (1962-1963). Various articles in *Masterkey* and the UCLA Archaeological Survey Reports should be consulted.

The principal archival collections containing ethnographic, linguistic, and historical data are at the University of California, Berkeley (A.L. Kroeber Papers, C.H. Merriam Collection); Huntington Library, San Marino, California (H.N. Rust Collection); Los Angeles County Museum of Natural History (especially the Thomas W. Temple Collection); the National Anthropological Archives, Smithsonian Institution, Washington, D.C. (J.P. Harrington Collection contains the largest amount of ethnographic and linguistic data on the Gabrielino); and the Southwest Museum, Los Angeles (especially Bernice E. Johnston Collection). Artifacts are described in detail by Blackburn (1962-1963) and are housed at various institutions throughout the United States—Los Angeles County Museum of Natural History; Santa Barbara Museum of Natural History, California; Lowie Museum of Anthropology, University of California, Berkeley; San Diego Museum of Man, California; Peabody Museum of Archaeology and Ethnology, Cambridge, Massachusetts; Field Museum of Natural History, Chicago; Museum of the American Indian, Heye Foundation, New York; and Smithsonian Institution. In Europe there are artifacts in the Musée de l'Homme, Paris. Photographs of Gabrielino peoples are rare and most are in local or private collections. The Southwest Museum and the C. Hart Merriam Collection have a few photographs of Gabrielinos taken around 1900 plus a few sketches from the late Mexican period.

Luiseño

LOWELL JOHN BEAN AND FLORENCE C. SHIPEK

Language

The term Luiseño (lōowĭ'sā̗nyō) derives from the mission named San Luis Rey and has been used in southern California to refer to those Takic-speaking people associated with Mission San Luis Rey. The term Juaneño (hwä'nā̗nyō) derives from Mission San Juan Capistrano and has been used to refer to the Takic speakers associated with that mission. These designations have been used since the Spanish occupation of California. Although Kroeber and Harrington separated Juaneño and Luiseño on the basis of linguistic differences, later studies (R.C. White 1963:91) indicate that they are ethnologically and linguistically one ethnic nationality, which here will be termed Luiseño.

The Luiseño language (along with Cupeño, Cahuilla and Gabrielino) belongs to the Cupan group of the Takic subfamily (Bright and Hill 1967; W.R. Miller 1961; Bright 1975). This subfamily, which also includes Serrano and Kitanemuk, all of southern California, was earlier called Southern California Shoshonean; it is part of the widespread Uto-Aztecan family.

Like most California groups, the Luiseño probably had no name for their own nationality, although they may sometimes coin names to satisfy outside investigators. Quechnajuichom and Puyumkowitchum, suggested as possible names for themselves (True 1966:43), seem not to be. The former is a Spanish spelling of *qéčŋaxwičum* 'people of San Luis Rey Village', and the latter is presumably *payó·mkawčum* 'westerners' (probably as used by inland Luiseños to refer to coastal dwellers).*

External Relations

The development of a separate Luiseño culture is clearly evident in archeological patternings that are locally distinct. This complex, which has been divided into San Luis Rey I (A.D. 1400–1750) and II (A.D. 1750–1850), shows the long-term development of a society that in the second era added components (for example, pottery and cremation urns) from neighboring groups (Meighan 1954).

External relations with neighboring ethnic nationalities were conservative. The Luiseño tended toward an isolationist policy except when expanding, which they did through warfare and marriage. They were considered by their neighbors to be dangerous and warlike expansionists, an opinion supported by their more highly developed warfare structure incorporating war leadership duties in the hands of the *nó·t,* or chief, and an initiated warrior class.

The Luiseño shared boundaries with the Cahuilla, Cupeño, Gabrielino, and Ipai peoples on the east, north, and south respectively. The Cahuilla, Gabrielino, and Cupeño share cultural and language traditions with the Luiseño. The Yuman Ipai have a different linguistic and cultural background but shared certain similarities in social structure (patrilineality as a basic form of social organization) and exchanged some religious practices with the Luiseño.

Luiseño social structure and philosophy were similar to the other Takic-speaking tribes, but they diverged in having a more rigid social structure and greater population density. The differences are clearly seen in: (1) extensive proliferation of social statuses, (2) clearly defined ruling families that interlocked various rancherias within the ethnic nationality, (3) a sophisticated philosophical structure associated with the taking of hallucinogenics (datura), and (4) elaborate ritual paraphernalia including sand paintings symbolic of an avenging sacred being named Chingichngish (*čiŋíčŋiš* or *čaŋíčŋiš*). The common spelling Chinigchinich for this name copies an eighteenth-century attempt to write the Juaneño form *čiŋíčŋič* (Boscana 1933).

Territory and Environment

The territory of the Luiseño comprised 1,500 square miles of coastal southern California (R.C. White 1963:117). Along the coast it extended from about Agua Hedionda Creek on the south to near Aliso Creek on the northwest. The boundary extended inland to Santiago Peak, then across to the eastern side of the Elsinore Fault Valley, then southward to the east of Palomar Mountain, then around the southern slope above the valley of San Jose.

---

* The orthography used for Luiseño words here is that of William Bright (1968). The preceding two paragraphs are based on data provided by him. The spellings of Luiseño words in the text have been corrected by Bright, Sandra L. Chung, or Pamela Munro, with the assistance of Villiana Hyde. None of them was able to identify the ritual here called aputs.

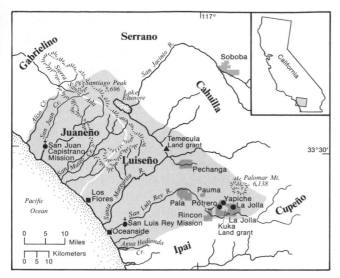

Fig. 1. Tribal territories with reservations and land grants.

From there the boundary turned west and returned to the sea along the Agua Hedionda Creek (fig. 1).

The territory of the Luiseño (excluding the Juaneño) included most of the drainage of the San Luis Rey River and that of the Santa Margarita River immediately to the north. Their habitat thus covered every ecological zone from the ocean, sandy beaches, shallow inlets, marshes, coastal chaparral, lush interior grassy valleys, extensive oak groves, up to the pines and cedars on the top of Mount Palomar. The Juaneño portion extended from the sea to the crest of the southern continuation of the Sierra Santa Ana. For the Luiseño as a whole, territorial elevations ranged from sea level to 6,000 feet on top of Mount Palomar.

Summer temperatures averaged from below 68° F. at the coast to above 85° inland, while winter temperatures averaged about 52° along the coast to 40° in the mountains. The average annual precipitation varied significantly, ranging from below 15 inches at the coast to 40 inches at Palomar Mountain. The Hot Steppe is the prevailing climate type found along the coast and extends inland along the river valleys into Riverside Basin. The uplands of the Santa Ana Mountains and Palomar Mountain had a warm Mediterranean-type climate with summer thunderstorms and winter snowfalls over Palomar Mountain. This diverse environment provided a more abundant and variable subsistence than most areas in southern California.

Settlement Pattern

Sedentary and autonomous village groups, each with specific hunting, collecting, and fishing areas, were located in diverse ecological zones. Typically these were in valley bottoms, along streams, or along coastal strands near mountain ranges. Villages were usually in sheltered coves or canyons, on the side of slopes in a warm thermal zone, near good water supplies, and in defensive locations.

Each village area contained many named places associated with food products, raw materials, or sacred beings. Each place was owned by an individual, a family, the chief, or by the group collectively. Trails, temporary campsites, hunting sites, areas for rabbit or deer drives, quarry sites, and areas for ceremonial use and gaming are examples of places owned by the community as a whole.

Group economic activities were restricted to the particular areas owned by the village, and family gatherings were confined to family-owned areas. Only with the express permission of the other group or family could gathering be done on territory other than one's own. Most inland groups also had fishing and gathering sites on the coast that they visited annually when tides were low or when inland foods were scarce from January to March. Each year for the acorn harvest (October–November) most of the village population would settle for several weeks in the mountain groves to collect acorns, hunt game animals, and collect whatever else was locally available. However, most of the Luiseño foods were available in locations within a day's travel of the village.

Culture

Ownership and Property

Ownership and property, both tangible and intangible, ranged from communal, that is, village, to personal property. At the most general level all members of the village collectively owned the whole area and all its contents. Trespass against this property was explicitly forbidden, boundaries were marked, and the area was protected by physical combat as well as supernatural means. Trespass was a major cause for war.

Within these collectively owned areas, the village chief supervised specific areas for group hunting and gathering. The produce from these areas was under the chief's control and was used for public occasions. R.C. White (1963:124) also describes "gardens" that were owned by individual household groups for subsistence, for example, clusters of cactus, oak trees, other food plants, medicines, or tobacco. These privately owned areas, also with marked boundaries, were inherited patrilineally or could be given to another by the owner. The concept of private property was important and violation of trespass on these areas was seriously punished.

Other private property included the house (owned by a family head), capital equipment, treasure goods (ritual equipment, ceremonial and trade beads, other ceremonial paraphernalia), eagle nests, songs, and other nonmaterial possessions. Individual material possessions were usually destroyed upon the death of an individual, so that his spirit could take all to the spirit world. Songs and knowledge had generally been taught to a successor—a son, son-in-law, or nephew—who had shown the prerequisite innate abilities to handle that form of knowledge.

Subsistence

The principal game animals were deer, rabbit, jackrabbit, woodrat, mice and ground squirrels, antelope, valley and mountain quail, doves, ducks, and other birds, including some songbirds. Most predators were avoided as food as were tree squirrels and most reptiles. Coastal marine foods included sea mammals, fish, crustaceans, and mollusks (especially abalone). Trout and other fish were caught in mountain streams (Sparkman 1908:200).

Acorns were the most important single food source; six species were used. Villages seem to have been located near water resources necessary for the leaching of acorns. Grass seeds were the next most abundant plant food used. Other important seeds were manzanita, sunflower, sage, chia, lemonade berry, wild rose, holly-leaf cherry, prickly pear, lamb's-quarters and pine nuts. Seeds were parched, ground, and cooked as a mush in various combinations according to taste and availability. Greens such as thistle, lamb's-quarters, miner's lettuce, white sage, and tree clover were eaten raw or cooked or sometimes dried for storage. Cactus pods and fruits were used. Thimbleberries, elderberries, wild grapes, and wild strawberries were eaten raw or dried for later cooking. Cooked yucca buds, blossoms, and pods provided a sizable increment to the food resources. Bulbs, roots, and tubers were dug in the spring and summer and usually eaten fresh. Mushrooms and tree fungi provided a significant food supplement. Various teas were made from flowers, fruits, stems, and roots for medicinal cures as well as beverages. Tobacco and datura (or toloache; Luiseño náqtumuš) were collected for sacred rituals because of their hallucinogenic qualities and were also used as medicines.

Fire was used as a crop-management technique as well as for community rabbit drives. The annual return from certain wild foods and useful plants—grass seed, some greens, yucca, and basket grasses—was maintained by burning at least every third year.

Food Sources

	Inland Bands		Coastal Bands	
	R.C. White 1963	Revised	R.C. White 1963	Revised
Acorns	25-50%	25-45%	10-25%	15-25%
Seeds	15-25	20-40	5-10	20-40
Greens	10-15	10-12	5-10	5-10
Bulbs, roots, fruits	10-15	10-13	10-15	10-15
Game	15-25	15-20	5-10	5-10
Fish and marine animals	0-5	0-5	50-60	20-35

Technology

Tools for food acquisition, storage, and preparation included an extensive inventory made from widely available materials. A few items were traded from specific localities, such as steatite bowls from Santa Catalina Island and obsidian blanks or points from either northern or eastern neighbors.

Hunting was done both individually and by groups. A shoulder-height bow was used with fire-hardened wood or stone-tipped arrows, which were carried in a skin quiver. Felsite and quartz points were made using deer-antler flakers. Deer were stalked with deer-head decoys or were tracked and run down. Community deer drives were held when quantities of meat were wanted. Small game was caught with the curved throwing stick (fig. 2), rabbit nets, slings, traps, or the spring-pole or pit type of deadfall.

Mus. of the Amer. Ind., Heye Foundation, New York: 5/468.
Fig. 2. Luiseño wooden throwing stick for hunting rabbits. Length about 65 cm, collected before 1916.

The bows for war were similar to those for hunting. In addition to the bow and arrow, weapons included a small hand-thrusting war club, large war clubs, broad-bladed thrusting sticks, lances, and slings.

Near shore ocean fishing was done from light balsa or dugout canoes. Seines, basketry fish traps, dip nets, hooks of bone or haliotis shell, and possibly harpoons were used. Mountain-stream fish were caught with traps, nets, or poisons.

Coiled and twined baskets were used in food gathering, preparation, storage, and serving (fig. 3). The basket type, shape, and size varied according to the purpose for which it would be used: small hand-held berry and bird-egg-gathering baskets, water-carrying bowls, storage baskets, and large round-bottomed carrying baskets. Coiled baskets were usually decorated with a darker tan, red, or black geometric design. These were very finely and artistically made and are to be found in many collections under the general area term "Mission Indian baskets" (Kroeber 1924).

A large shallow tray was used for winnowing chaff from grain or for sorting coarse from finely ground meal. Openwork twined baskets were used for leaching tannic acid from acorn meal. Basins formed in fine sand could also be used for leaching acorn meal.

Depending upon the size and quantity of the items to be stored, clay and basketry storage containers varied in

Dept. of Anthr., Smithsonian: top, 313023; bottom, 313172.

Fig. 3. Coiled baskets. top, Juaneño meal tray; bottom, Luiseño feast basket with black elder dyed design. Diameter of top 38 cm, collected in 1900.

size from small bowls to baskets or jars large enough to hold several bushels. Acorn granaries were made of intertwined willow boughs set on a flat rock base.

Net pouches of two-ply cordage were made for handling the fruit and young pads of cactus. Net or skin pouches and bags were also used to carry small game and other foods. Large back-carrying nets were used with a tumpline around the forehead bearing on a coiled basket cap. Infants were carried on a cradleboard frame made of willow boughs.

Seeds were ground with handstones on shallow unshaped basin metates of fine-grained granite (fig. 4). The same granites were made into shaped or unshaped mortars and pestles for pounding acorns or small whole game. Bedrock mortars and metates were generally located near village sites, especially inland. A basket hopper was attached to new or shallow mortars. Medicines, tobacco, and datura roots were ground in stone bowls usually painted red and white for ritual purposes.

Food was cooked in wide-mouthed clay jars over fireplaces or in earth ovens wrapped with clay or leaves. Game was roasted in coals. Seeds were parched by shaking with coals in shallow pottery or basket trays; heated stones were dropped into food held in baskets, pottery jars, or soapstone bowls for boiling.

The pottery was made by paddle-and-anvil technique and fired in shallow open pits. Simple line decoration was either painted or incised with a fingernail or stick.

Decoration was rare. Relatively few shapes were made: shallow dishes, bowls, hemispherical bowls, wide- and narrow-mouthed jars, ladles and dippers, and miniatures. A double-mouthed pot was used as a water jar.

Other utensils for food preparation included wooden food paddles, brushes, tongs, tweezers, steatite bowls and cups, and wooden digging sticks. Also a variety of ground-stone, pressure-flaked, or percussion chipped-stone tools were made for cutting, prying, scraping, drilling, and pounding (True 1966).

Ritual equipment included small spherical sacred stone bowls for grinding and drinking datura or tobacco; ceremonial blades of obsidian, clay figurines with "coffee bean" eyes; sacred wands with abalone or crystal insets (fig. 5); ritual head scratchers for puberty ceremonies; eagle-feather headdress, dance skirts, and shoulder bands; head and hand plumes of owl or raven feathers, and ceremonial blades.

Shamans' equipment included tubular soapstone or clay pipes for smoking, purification, and sucking disease rituals. Some had enlarged bowls and cane stems. Shamans also had magical power stones of quartz, tourmaline, and other crystals; magical swallowing sticks; a syringe of deer bladder with a cane nozzle; and special shamans' bundles.

Other ritual equipment included the ground paintings representing the cosmology, image of sacred beings, and of deceased persons; funeral pyre and cremation pits; funeral poles; and offering baskets.

Structures

Houses were primarily conical, partially subterranean thatched structures of reeds, brush, or bark, whichever was available locally. Domestic chores were done in the shade of nearby brush-covered rectangular structures known by the Spanish term *ramadas*. Round, semisubterranean, earth-covered sweathouses (fig. 6) were important for purification and curing rituals. A ceremonial structure, the *wámkiš*, was a centrally located area within the village that was enclosed by circular fencing. Sometimes within this area there was a raised altar upon which was a skin-and-feather image. Ceremonies were held inside the *wámkiš* and ritual and paintings were made in front of it.

Adornment

Personal ornaments were made of bone, clay, stone, shell, bear claws and, later, glass. Beads or pendants were made of these as well as of mica sheets, bear claws, deer hooves, and abalone shell. Bracelets and anklets were made of human hair. Men wore ear and nose ornaments made of cane or bone, sometimes with beads attached. Cloaks and robes were made of deerskin, otterskin, or rabbitskin strips, wound on lengths of fiber, and put together by a twined weft. Yucca-fiber sandals and deerskin moccasins were worn. Body painting and tattooing for men and

Fig. 4. Juaneño woman in front of adobe house grinding with mano and metate. An earth oven is behind her under the sunshade. Copyright and possibly photographed by Herve Friend, 1892.

women were ritually significant. Semiprecious stones were commonly used, such as quartz, topaz, garnet, opal, opalite, agate, and jasper. Women wore twined cedar-bark double aprons.

Music and Games

Musical instruments included bird-bone and cane whistles; cane flutes; split-stick clappers; rattles of turtle shell, gourd, or deer hooves; and bull-roarers. Gaming equipment included bone and wood cylinders with stretched rawhide loop and counters used in the peon game, dice, painted or incised split sticks for women's gambling games, wooden ball and sticks for the ball-and-stick game, ring and pin, acorn tops, cat's cradle strings, hoops and pole, and wooden balls.

554   Fig. 5. Luiseño ceremonial wand, wood handle with remnants of abalone inlay, obsidian point. Length 61.8 cm, collected before 1923.

Title Insurance and Trust Company, Los Angeles.
Fig. 6. Luiseño sweathouse on Soboba Reservation. Photograph possibly by C.C. Pierce, about 1885.

Social and Political Organization

Women collected most of the plant resources, and men hunted the large game and most of the small game and fished; but there was no rigid sexual division of labor. Work activities often overlapped. Men aided in acquiring acorns and other plant foods by helping with heavy work associated with them, such as knocking acorns from the trees. They sometimes collected plant foods on hunting expeditions. Women, in turn, sometimes hunted and trapped small game and collected shellfish.

Aged women stayed at home to care for children, teaching them arts, crafts, and knowledge necessary for adulthood while active women were busy collecting and processing foods. Older men were most active in ritual, ceremonial affairs, making political decisions, and teaching selected young men. They were skilled net makers and arrow makers; they manufactured much of the capital equipment used in hunting as well as creating much ceremonial paraphernalia.

Children were involved in productive activities at the earliest possible age, boys and girls working with adults as they learned. Older, unmarried girls assumed some care for younger siblings. Men tended to have exclusive responsibility for ritual and sacred affairs, while women made food preparations for ritual affairs and performed supplemental dancing and singing.

Each Luiseño village was a clan tribelet—a group of people patrilineally related who owned an area in common and who were politically and economically autonomous from neighboring groups. The entire social structure is obscure. It does not appear that they were organized into exogamous moieties such as were the Cahuilla, Cupeño, and Serrano (Strong 1929:291). They may have been loosely divided into easterners (mountain-oriented peoples) and westerners (ocean-oriented peoples) (Strong 1929:288-289). R.C. White (1963:163-174) sees a possible moiety structure but the evidence is highly inferential. R.C. White (1963:173-178) and Strong (1929:287) agree that the "party organization" or grouping of lineages for reciprocal performance of ritual is a result of the recent drastic decline of population and the loss of ceremonial leaders without trained replacements.

The hereditary village chief (*nó·t*) held an administrative position that combined and controlled religious, economic, and warfare powers (Boscana 1933:43). He had an assistant (*paxá?*) who acted to relay orders and information and who had important religious ceremonial duties also. There was an advisory council of ritual specialists and shamans, each with his own special area of knowledge about the environment or ritual magic. These positions were hereditary with each man training a successor from his own lineage who showed the proper innate abilities (R.C. White 1957:5-6). These specialists were also members of the cultic organization of Chingichngish and shared special access to ritual and supernatural power forms. There was a multiplicity of specialist roles under the *nó·t* and *paxá?* such as the leaders of the rabbit hunt, deer and antelope drives, expeditions to the sea, as well as a specialist in each major food crop.

The more populous villages along the coast and in the larger valleys undoubtedly had a more complex structure than did the smaller settlements in the little valleys, which seem to have contained fewer lineages (Strong 1929).

Kinship terminology and marriage rules, in addition to the social structure, have been changed so extensively by the overlay of the Roman Catholic incest rules and external linguistic, political, and economic factors that the aboriginal or contact-period usage, rules, and structure are extremely obscure.

Luiseño kinship terminology had a Dakota structure (R.C. White 1963:168) and kin terms occurred only with possessive prefixes (Kroeber 1917:348). There was a tendency toward paired reciprocal terms that indicated equal relationship distance, with the diminutive ending on the younger of the pair (Kroeber 1917:351). For example, *-ka?* 'grandfather' and *-ka?may* 'grandson' (*-may* being the diminutive). This tendency affected all terms of grandparents, great-grandparents, father-in-law, brother-in-law, and cousin classes. The Luiseño had bifurcated merging for aunts and siblings with distinctions being made according to relative age of the parent's siblings (R.C. White 1963:168). Other features included merged terminologies for grandparent's siblings of the same sex; siblings were differentiated by age and sex, as were parallel aunts and uncles; nephews and nieces were recognized by age of connecting relative and sex of speaker; cross-nephews and -nieces were merged as well as parallel nephews and nieces.

At a child's birth the *nó·t* of the mother's lineage performed the *ṣúlaxiš* ceremony, which confirmed the child to the householding group and the patrilineage (R.C. White 1963:165). Extensive dietary and activity restrictions were imposed upon both father and mother for about a month.

At puberty boys and girls underwent initiation rituals during which they were taught about the supernatural beings governing them and punishing any infractions of the rules of behavior and ritual (Sparkman 1908:221, 225). They were taught to respect elders, to listen to them, to give them food, not to eat secretly, to refrain from anger, to be cordial and polite to in-laws, to follow rituals exactly and respectfully or be subject to punishment and death by the messengers of Chingichngish (rattlesnake, spider, bear, and sickness). The boys' ceremony included the drinking of toloache (datura), visions, dancing, ordeals, and the teaching of songs and rituals. The girls' ceremony included advice and instruction in the necessary knowledge for married life, "roasting" in warm sands, and rock painting.

Marriage was arranged by the parents of children, sometimes at infancy. Girls were married shortly after their puberty ceremonies took place. Luiseños suggest an important concern was that spouses not be closely related, although R.C. White (1963:169-170) suggests that cross-cousin marriages may have been the norm prior to Spanish Catholic influences. Important lineages were allied through marriage. Elaborate marriage ceremonies and a bride price accompanied marriage. Residence was generally patrilocal. Polygyny, often sororal, was practiced, especially by chiefs and shamans. Divorce was not easy, but possible; widows could remarry, preferably a classificatory "brother" of her deceased husband, as a husband might marry a classificatory "sister" of his deceased wife.

Marriage was utilized as an instrument of ecology and economics. Reciprocally useful alliances were arranged between groups in differing ecological niches, and became springboards of territorial expansion, especially following warfare and truces (R.C. White 1963:130). In the twentieth century, marriages of Luiseño women into neighboring reservations have extended Luiseño influence among their neighbors, for instance, among the Cupeño and Ipai and Tipai, and on Soboba reservation.

Death was a major concern to the Luiseño. They observed at least a dozen successive mourning ceremonies. After a *tuví·š* or ritual washing of clothes, a smoking purification of relatives was held and various related clans were invited to an image-burning ceremony, which ended formal mourning. Feasting took place, and food and gifts were distributed to guests. A special ceremony, the eagle killing, was held to commemorate the death of a chief.

Ritual provided dramatic enactments and reciting of sacred oral literature in which ritual was initially ordained. The rituals functioned to control environment, emulate the experience of sacred persons, and guarantee their positive responses. Ritual also aided in the control of knowledge-power, which resided in varying degrees in the Luiseño world. Rituals were strictly governed by rules and procedures administered by religious chiefs and shamans, who comprised a hierarchical power pyramid dominated by the village chief, an assistant, a council, and a secret society, which included most adult males in the village. They articulated ritual and controlled hunting, harvest, warfare, in fact, all major activities of village life. The rituals are connected with the Chingichngish cult.

Most participants in rituals were paid. A guest ritual leader and his assistants—from another village or moiety—officiated. Great quantities of food and treasure goods were distributed at these affairs. R.C. White (1963) has recorded over 16 kinds of ceremonies. In addition to rites for the dead there were rites of passage—naming, birth, puberty, death, installation of new office holder. Other rituals controlled the environment, for instance rainmaking or increase of food crops or animals. Still others involved social and political controls both within and between villages, like peace making between individuals or groups.

Principal rituals conducted by the *nó·t* and his organization were: (1) *má·ni pá·ʔiš*—datura drinking, (2) *ʔántuš*—ant ordeal of puberty, (3) *nó·tuš*—pole climbing, (4) *méyiš*—hunting purification by smoke, (5) *mó·raxiš*—eagle-feather dance, (6) *pé·niš*—eagle killing, (7) aputs (Boscana in Harrington 1934:41)—fertility dance, (8) *háyiš*—moon racing (fertility?), (9) *čúyiš*—mortuary, clothes burning, (10) *tó·činiš*—mortuary, image burning, (11) *tuví·š*—clothes-washing at birth and death, (12) *wiqéniš*—female puberty, (13) *péwluš*—marriage, (14) *né·tuš*—conception, (15) *čélaxiš*—peace among individuals (*čéla-* 'observe ritual silence'), (16) *náwtiš*—peace between parties (lineage groups) or tribes.

Sand painting was a significant ritual-cosmological component associated with most rituals; although utilized by several southern California groups, the paintings are best documented for the Luiseño. The paintings (*turó·hayiš*) were made at boys' initiation rites, girls' initiation rites, and death rites for initiates of the datura cult. Each painting represented various aspects of the universe, for example, the Milky Way, all-encompassing night and sky, sacred beings, and spiritual phases of the human personality, especially the punisher-beings representing Chingichngish (fig. 7). These art forms were destroyed when the ritual was finished. They were only occasionally made in the 1970s.

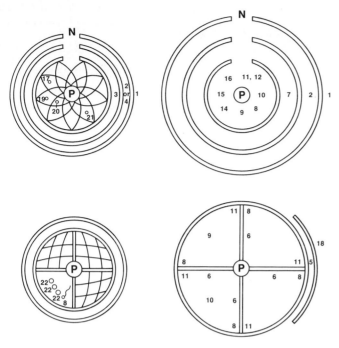

after Kroeber 1925:662.

Fig. 7. Sand paintings. Elements include: 1, Milky Way; 2, night or sky; 3, root (of existence); 4, our spirit or soul; 5, world; 6, hands (arms) of the world; 7, blood; 8–16, avengers and punishers sent by Chingichngish; 17, sea; 18, mountains; 19, plant hill; 20, boil or abscess; 21, four avenging animals; 22, ceremonial baskets (may be actual objects); N, north; P, pit symbolical of death and burial of ashes, the abode of the dead, or navel of the universe.

After contact, Luiseño ceremonial leaders began to die out. Lineages that no longer had ceremonial leaders and *paxá?* or requisite ritual paraphernalia associated, for ritual purposes, with lineages that did. The groups resulting from this process are now called "parties" to distinguish them from traditional ritual units (Gifford 1918).

Cosmology

Luiseño cosmology centered about a dying-god motif and around *wiyó·t,* a creator-culture hero and teacher who was the son of earth-mother (*tamá·yawut*). It was he who established the order of the world and was one of the first "people" or creations. The death of *wiyó·t* was brought about by another of the first "people." This death changed the nature of the universe and led to the creation of the existing world of plants, animals, and men. The original creations took on the various life forms now existing. Some remained in contact with their descendants, while others went to different levels of the universe. After the death of *wiyó·t* the "people" gathered and worked out solutions for living, including the adoption of the present spatial organization of "species" for living space, and a chain-of-being concept that placed each species into a productive, hierarchically arranged and mutually supportive relationship with all others. Thus the problems of food and space were solved by the accept-

ance of predatorship and death for all beings and things: rocks and trees lived on top of the ground, gophers lived under, men ate deer, and deer ate grasses (R.C. White 1957:9).

The disposal of the body of *wiyó·t* affirmed the concept of death and established funeral ritualism. It also ended the formation of prescribed knowledge that was given to each species. The remaining knowledge that *wiyó·t* threw away upon his death was known as residual knowledge. Formulated knowledge, the prescribed knowledge given before his death, became the exclusive possession of the ritual officials. Residual knowledge could be sought and acquired by anyone who had the innate ability consistent with that form of knowledge-power (R.C. White 1957:6, 8).

The acquisition and use of knowledge-power was required to be kept secret and there were constant admonitions not to divulge knowledge-power because misfortune and death would follow. The negative consequences of the misuse of knowledge-power or its potential use by an enemy made any careless sharing of knowledge unthinkable. People with knowledge-power had the right to receive more in the distribution of goods (thus ensuring a higher degree of survival in cases of shortages). Knowledge, because of its dangerous nature, was transmitted only reluctantly after the recipient had demonstrated his ability to handle that form. It had to be used specifically and unvaryingly according to set procedures and on the appropriate occasions. Failure to follow set rules at appropriate times resulted in loss of control over the particular kind of power being used and brought grave consequences to the entire community (R.C. White 1957:4).

The rank-order system in society and nature depended upon the natural innate knowledge-power adhering to a species or individual. For people, the innate ability varied with individuals, accruing most often to the families of powerful individuals. An attitude of complete fearlessness was seen to be the satisfactory state of mind for acquiring knowledge-power.

History

Although several earlier European explorers observed the Luiseño, first contact with Europeans was in 1796 when the Gaspar de Portolá expedition arrived and San Diego Mission was founded to the south. In 1776 a mission was established at San Juan Capistrano, and 22 years later San Luis Rey Mission was founded.

R.C. White (1963:104) estimates that there were 50 Luiseño villages, with a mean population of about 200 each, thus suggesting a population of 10,000 people in contrast to Kroeber's (1925:646, 649) estimate of 4,000–5,000 people. At no time have published population figures been reliable, since many individuals and some villages were never part of the mission or reserva-

Table 1. Population

Date	Total	Men	Women and Children	Reservation Residents	Source
Precontact	10,000				R.C. White 1963
1828	3,683	1,598	2,085		Mission Records
1856	2,500–2,800 (19 villages)				ARCIA
1860	1,011				U.S. Census Office 1880
1865	1,047	536	511		ARCIA
1873	975 (10 villages)				ARCIA
1881	1,120				ARCIA
1885	1,142				ARCIA
1889	901				ARCIA
1894	784			417	ARCIA
1895	948			272	ARCIA
1914	983			983	ARCIA
1925	841			841	ARCIA
1940	721			402	ARCIA
1960	1,757			564	BIA, Sacramento

tion system; therefore, the figures in table 1 may consistently be considered as minimums. Recent counts are further skewed by the mixture of tribal groups on some reservations, for example, Pala.

Upon contact, European ideas and diseases immediately began to spread throughout the Luiseño population. Living conditions at missions and on the ranchos accelerated the population decline.

Some coastal village people were moved into mission environs. Over a period of years, Indians were brought from progressively more distant villages into San Juan Capistrano Mission where they were taught the Roman Catholic faith, Spanish language, farming skills, animal husbandry, adobe brickmaking, carpentry, and other European crafts.

The policy at San Luis Rey Mission was to maintain Luiseño settlement patterns. The priest, Father Peyri, visited villages to hold masses, perform marriages, and supervise agricultural activities; but traditional economic methods remained as the basic subsistence mode, and leadership continued for the most part as it always had.

In 1834 missions were secularized and the attendant political imbalance resulted in Indian revolts and uprisings against the Mexican rancheros, who were using many of the Indians as serfs. Many left the missions and ranchos and sought refuge among inland groups, while a few individuals acquired land grants—Kuka, Temecula (fig. 8), La Jolla—and entered into the mainstream of Mexican culture. Several Indian pueblos were established for some of the San Luis Rey Indian rancherias, among them Santa Margarita and Los Flores, by the Mexican government. These pueblos were intended to be governmental units within the Mexican political system. Most of them disappeared under Mexican rancho pressures; Los Flores, for example, was sold to Mexicans.

Most Luiseño villages, however, continued to maintain their traditional orientation with the addition of wheat and corn agriculture, irrigation, orchards, and animal husbandry.

For the purposes of political and economic controls, the leadership roles that had been established in the mission period, such as *generales, capitanes,* and *alcaldes,* continued to exist and operate with political and economic, rather than religious, mechanisms. These new leaders operated in addition to religious leaders and acted as liaisons between the people and Europeans (fig. 9).

With the entrance of Anglo-Americans into California, Luiseños were displaced from more of their lands (for instance, Temecula, 1859–1877). Conflicts between Indians and encroaching Whites finally led to the investigation and establishment of executive-order reservations for some villages (for example, Pala, Potrero, La Jolla, Yapiche) in 1875. Other Luiseños were evicted from their homes and dispersed at random, some going to reservations, others to nearby towns or ranches.

Civil rights and federal protection were minimal until 1891 when the Act for the Relief of the Mission Indians established trust-patent reservations and initiated a bureaucratic management of them. Agents, teachers, medical personnel, Bureau of Indian Affairs day schools, and Indian captains, judges, policemen, and Indian courts were established. The stated function of this system was

Fig. 8. View of Pechanga showing houses of the Temecula. Palomar Mountain is in the background. Photograph by C.C. Pierce, about 1895.

to develop a self-supporting population, which would eventually be assimilated into the mainstream of American life. Special educational institutions, day schools, and boarding schools such as Perris School, Sherman Institute, and the Carlisle School, and private boarding schools such as the Roman Catholic Saint Boniface were established to adapt Indian children to the American culture. Under the provisions of the Dawes Act a land-allotment program was established to provide land for individuals. During this time there was a concerted program against traditional authority by the federal government, which insisted that all tribally elected persons (captains, judges) must be approved by the local Indian agent. Furthermore, Indian policemen and other Indians were often employed in positions of power without regard to local feelings.

Indians continued to support themselves by farming, ranching, and various forms of wage labor, supplemented by hunting and gathering wherever still available.

Some Luiseños vigorously protested the Bureau of Indian Affairs management of the reservation, and by 1919 the Mission Indian Federation and other instrumen-

tal voluntary associations were formed to solve new problems. In 1934 the Indian Reorganization Act was rejected by Luiseños because it did not allow sufficient home rule. Nevertheless, bureaucratic control increased as federal activities on Indian reservations were expanded. The complication of the Depression affected economic life and increased bureaucracy, but considerable support to Indians came from federal agencies such as the Civilian Conservation Corps Indian Service and from economic-aid programs such as the reimbursable cattle program.

Commencing with World War I, many Indians entered the service or migrated to urban areas for defense industry jobs. Reservation activities diminished, but personal incomes increased as new jobs were available and markets improved for agricultural products. At the end of the war a resurgence of farming and cattle raising by the returning servicemen, along with increased job skills and opportunities, led to higher levels of income for most Luiseños.

Pressures for termination of federal involvement in Mission Indian affairs, which had been building since the

Fig. 9. Capt. Pedro Pablo and his headmen from Pauma at Pala for a tribal meeting. Photograph possibly by C.C. Pierce, about 1885.

1930s, reached a peak in the 1950s. Luiseños assumed active leadership, both for and against this program. It was vigorously discussed and partially averted. In 1953, with the passage of Public Law 280 (67 Stat. 588-590) federal services were reduced to the maintenance of the trust status of the land. A period of chaotic legal problems developed because Public Law 280 did not spell out the exact areas of responsibility of states and counties in regard to law enforcement and use of Indian trust lands. Neither the public agencies nor the Indians were adequately apprised of the new relationships of Indians to local, state, and other federal agencies and the consequent changes in responsibilities.

In spite of the confusion engendered by Public Law 280, or because of it, a resurgence of local self-government and self-determination occurred. Reservation groups began to write articles of association and establish formal membership requirements in terms of degree of relationship to original members. With the beginning of the federally funded programs in the late 1960s, such as low-cost housing, manpower training, and Office of Economic Opportunity grants, the Luiseño began establishing new forms of local organizations in order to participate and take advantage of programs. Since pro-

gram funding required large populations, new organizations were developed to include several reservations, Luiseños as well as others. Luiseño participation and leadership again became prominent in state organizations such as the Intertribal Council of California, county organizations such as the Tribal Chairmen's Association of San Diego County, and regional groups such as the All-Mission Indian Housing Authority. The Luiseño appear to be more generally involved with these types of organizations than most other Indian groups in southern California. Consequently an exceedingly complex proliferation of organizations, committees, and boards working with new governmental and private agencies has developed. Some reservations belong to none, some to one or several reservation-based groups, and some to all. Final authority on any reservation is the entire adult membership. These other groups have no authority inherent in themselves in regard to the reservations. Many of the same individuals sit on several boards, but this does not indicate coordination or closeness between organizations.

Some county or state organizations have had "an Indian" appointed in order to have some Indian input into the policy level: San Diego County Welfare Council,

County Human Relations Committee, County Office of Economic Opportunity, Public Employment Program, and some local school boards.

Then there are federally funded programs that have a board of directors elected from or appointed by various member reservations on the local level or from sections of the state on the state level. The Intertribal Council of California is an example of such an Indian organization. California Indians Legal Services is another organization funded by the Office of Economic Opportunity. It is given loose policy direction by a board composed of Indians appointed from various sections of the state and several lawyers appointed by the bar association. It hires lawyers and their staffs and consultants to provide legal assistance to Indians in California. The All-Mission Indian Housing Authority has all the powers of any "housing authority." It requires a legally certified resolution to join passed by the majority of members of a reservation. To have housing on tribal land under the All-Mission Indian Housing Authority, the tribe must develop a housing area plan and lease that portion of the reservation to the Housing Authority for 50 years.

United States Public Health Service, Indian Division, is responsible for safe domestic water supplies and sanitary disposal of sewage. Individual health is the individual's responsibility. California Rural Indian Health serves only the five reservations in the northern part of the county and receives federal funds through the State Public Health for transporting people to doctors and some health education classes. The South County Business Managers supervise an unfunded outpatient clinic for which they have obtained volunteer services. Mission Indian Development Corporation was set up by the Bureau of Indian Affairs to serve all southern California reservations but in fact serves only the Luiseño.

Cultural Persistence

Most Luiseño bands were in the 1970s enrolled on the reservations at La Jolla, Rincon, Pauma, Pechanga, Pala, and Soboba. In 1970 approximately one-third of the enrolled Luiseño resided on the reservations. Most others lived within a 20-mile radius in towns or on other reservations. A few lived in Los Angeles and other parts of California. Less than 1 percent lived in more distant areas. Some nonreservation Luiseño live in San Juan Capistrano and Oceanside. They are only vaguely organized as groups. The reservation groups are structured with elected councils, formal membership rolls, and articles of association.

Occupations are primarily in semiskilled or skilled categories, such as electricians, carpenters, cattle raisers, farmers, firemen, defense workers, domestics. Some are in professional positions such as teachers, professors, engineers, certified public accountants. Programs for the aged

and indigent, Medicare services, social security, and unemployment compensation are available on the same basis as for any other California citizen. Planning for improved housing and economic development of resources is actively taking place on all Luiseño reservations.

During the 1930s the Bureau of Indian Affairs day schools for southern California were gradually closed and before 1950 both grade-school and high-school students were in public schools. Educational achievement is highly valued and sought out. In the 1960s, numerous young people entered colleges throughout the state, and many adults were returning to college.

Most Luiseño in the 1970s were practicing Roman Catholics but retained an attenuated form of their precontact religion (fig. 10). Approximately 10 percent belong to Evangelical, Church of Christ, or other Protestant denominations. Pala Mission is active with the Verona Fathers servicing a Catholic chapel on each Luiseño reservation. A Roman Catholic elementary school has many of the Luiseño children enrolled at Pala. Major Catholic festivals are celebrated; and baptism, confirmation, marriages, funerals, and memorial services are important to most Luiseños. Protestant churches are active on La Jolla and Rincon reservations.

The original Luiseño culture persists in many forms, although it is sometimes not readily apparent to the outside observer. Philosophical assumptions (R.C. White 1957) are maintained as are certain rituals and shamanic practices. Surviving ceremonies include initiation for cult candidates, installation of religious chiefs, funerals, and clothes burning (R.C. White 1953).

While the Luiseño language is spoken by only a few elderly people, there is a revival of interest among the young and language classes have been organized. A language text has been written by a Luiseño, Villiana

Fig. 10. Indian graveyard at Pala with personal possessions or gifts on top of the graves. Photograph probably by C.C. Pierce, about 1900.

Hyde (1971). Traditional amusements such as peon games and secularized songs and dances are continuing; Luiseño foods such as acorns, yucca, and wild game are still eagerly sought. Some traditional medicines and curing procedures are practiced, and traditional political concepts still function, although in new forms. Attitudes toward property, sexual roles, knowledge, power, isolationism, and leadership continue.

In the late 1800s fiestas celebrating saints' days for each reservation became a major activity for each Luiseño reservation, involving interreservation visitors for one, two, or three weekends of each year. These fiestas were active until about the 1920s when they were discouraged, sometimes forbidden, by the BIA. They had become a major mechanism for interreservation economic exchange as well as ceremonial, social, and political activities. They were revived after World War II on some reservations for social and fund-raising purposes.

A traditional feature indicating vigorous persistence is the peon game, a complex guessing game involving two competing groups of four players each and a referee supported by singers and magical formulas to acquire luck. To win the game, 16 counters must be acquired by guessing the ways in which black and white peons are held hidden in the hands by the opposing team. Large amounts of treasure goods and food stores were formerly wagered. Now large amounts of money are wagered on these games, which are played during fiestas. Teams represent families, and sometimes language groups or reservations. Both men and women play. The winning team and their backers are rewarded by large wagers. Individual players are renowned in the local Indian community if they possess peon skills.

Synonymy

The Luiseños (both Juaneño and Luiseño proper) have been known by a variety of terms. The earliest use of the term Luiseño appears in Arroyo de la Cuesta (1821) and was used as the name for the language spoken by a group of Chumash living at San Luis Obispo Mission about 1821-1837. This term was later applied to the Indians living at San Luis Rey Mission (Coulter 1835:67). Pablo Tac, a young Luiseño man, gave several names for the inhabitants of Luiseño territory: Quechnajuichom (translated as 'the inhabitants of Quechla', that is, San Luis Rey), Sanjuaneños, and San Luiseños (Tac 1952:87). Couts (ARCIA 1857:240) termed them San Luisenians, and variations of this term continue: San Luis Indians (Winder 1857:124), San Luis Rey (ARCIA 1872:682), San Luiseños (Bancroft 1874-1876, 1:460; Tac 1952:87; B.D. Wilson 1952), San Luisieños (Bancroft 1874-1876, 1:460). Kroeber (1907b:145) gives the terms Ghecham and Khecham (alternative spelling) for the Luiseños, the term being derived from *qéč* 'Mission San Luis Rey'; for

this Harrington (1933b:97) gives Juaneño *qé·ʔeč*, Luiseño *qé·ʔeš*. These terms appear to be the same as those given by Gatschet (1879:413) and Shea (1855:108): kechi and kechis respectively. In 1907 Kroeber termed the Indians living near Mission San Juan Capistrano Juaneño. Boscana's name for them, Acagchemem, appears to be a spelling of Juaneño *ʔaxáčmeyam* or Luiseño *ʔaxášmayam* 'San Juan Capistrano people', derived from the name for the mission town, *ʔaxáčme*, Luiseño *ʔaxášmay* (Harrington 1933b:102). In the 1970s Luiseños tend to use the term San Luiseño when referring to themselves or to identify and call themselves by reservation or clan names.

Sources

Historical sources on Luiseno begin with observations by Cabrillo in 1542 and Vizcaíno in 1602. Later overland Spanish explorers (Portolá, Fages, and Mariner) described villages and activities. Mission records from San Luis Rey and San Juan Capistrano contain accounts of baptism, birth, marriage, and death. Ethnographic descriptions exist in the answers to *interrogatorios* as well as in various writings, of which Boscana's accounts (1933; see also Harrington 1934) are the most valuable. A neophyte's description (Tac 1952) adds further valuable ethnographic and historic data. Various archival resources were drawn upon by Engelhardt in his histories of various missions (1908-1915, 2, 1921, 1922, 1923, 1927). B.D. Wilson (1952) and the National Archives Luiseño files provide data about these people after the American conquest of California. In later years various federal commissions reported on the conditions of Luiseño peoples (Jackson and Kinney 1884; Smiley Commission 1891).

The earliest ethnographic account is that of Henshaw in 1884 (Henshaw 1972); the major ethnographic works begin with Sparkman (1905, 1908, 1908a), Du Bois (1904a, 1908a), and Kroeber (1906, 1908d, 1909b, 1917, 1925). They set the basic ethonographic frame to which other scholars have contributed. Gifford (1918, 1922) and Strong (1929) analyzed kinship, social organization, and ritual. Harrington, who collected extensively in the 1930s and 1940s, published (1933a, 1933b, 1934a) important new ethnographical and linguistic data. R.C. White (1963) established a new interpretation of Luiseño settlement pattern, social organization, and philosophy.

Major archival resources are: United States National Archives (War Records, Department of Pacific; Bureau of Indian Affairs files); John P. Harrington Collection, National Anthropological Archives, Smithsonian Institution; Sparkman papers, Anthropological Archives, Bancroft Library, University of California at Berkeley; and the C.H. Merriam Collection, Archaeological Research Facility, University of California at Berkeley. Major collections of Luiseño artifacts are held at the Museum of the American Indian, Heye Foundation, New York; American Museum of Natural History, New York; the Smithsonian Institution; San Diego Museum of Man; Lowie Museum of Anthropology, Berkeley; and the Southwest Museum, Los Angeles. Other archival and considerable photographic materials are available at the Huntington Library, San Marino, California; additional material can be found at the San Diego Historical Society Junipero Serra Museum, the San Diego Public Library, and in San Diego County records.

563

Kitanemuk

THOMAS C. BLACKBURN AND LOWELL JOHN BEAN

Language, Territory, and Environment

The Kitanemuk (kĭ'tänə,mŏok) were a small group located principally in the Tehachapi Mountains at the southern end of the San Joaquin valley. They spoke a Serran language of the Takic family (Bright 1975).* Their neighbors to the north were the Yokuts (essentially a valley people); in the hills to the west were the Chumash; to the south were the Tataviam, with whom the Kitanemuk shared the western end of the Antelope Valley; and to the east in the higher Sierra Nevada were the Kawaiisu. The Kitanemuk were thus primarily mountain dwellers, although during cooler seasons of the year they did range into the arid lowlands to the south (fig. 1).

Precise data on village locations, demographic characteristics, and political organization can no longer be obtained.

External Relations

Harrington (1917) suggests that considerable interaction took place among Kitanemuk villages, as well as between the Kitanemuk and groups such as the Chumash, Tubatulabal, and possibly the Kawaiisu. Their relationship with the Yokuts and Tataviam was one of enmity, while an amity relationship seems to have linked the Kitanemuk with the Chumash and Tubatulabal in a complex trading and ritual alliance. In addition, the Mohave and Quechan visited frequently for trading purposes. Intermarriage seems to have occurred with all groups. The Kitanemuk were significantly influenced by their northern and western neighbors, particularly in the realm of ritual, mythology, and shamanism; in fact, they appear to have culturally resembled these groups more than their linguistic kin—the Serrano, Cahuilla, and Chemehuevi.

History

No significant archeological work has been done in the Kitanemuk area. Francisco Garcés may have visited a

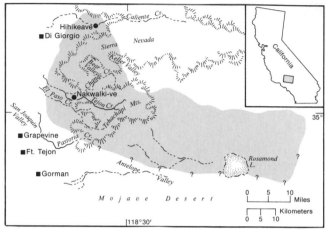

Fig. 1. Tribal territory and known villages.

Kitanemuk village in 1776, but little other historical information on these people is extant (Coues 1900). They were apparently assimilated into Missions San Fernando, San Gabriel, and possibly Ventura (San Buenaventura). Some Kitanemuks were certainly present at Fort Tejon during the 1850s and were later probably resident on the Tule River Reservation. Some were attending ceremonies as late as 1869 at San Fernando, Piru, and Saticoy (Blackburn 1974). When Harrington interviewed the few surviving Kitanemuks in 1917, they were living at Tejon Ranch; others may have formed part of the Indian population on the Tule River Reservation, where apparently some of their descendants reside still. Many Kitanemuks worked as laborers on local ranches after Fort Tejon ceased to be an active post.

No population figures are available on the Kitanemuk during any part of the historic period; however, comparisons with similar groups suggest that 500–1,000 people would be a reasonable estimate in view of the size of the territory that they occupied.

Culture

Subsistence

The general ecological adaptation and subsistence technology of the Kitanemuk differed little from that of their neighbors to the north or west; some data are available in Kroeber (1925:611–619) and Harrington (1942).

---

* The Kitanemuk language is extinct; it is known chiefly from Harrington's (1917) field notes. Italicized Kitanemuk words are in Harrington's (nonphonemic) orthography, except that q, č, and y (in their usual Handbook values) are substituted for his special symbols, i represents his ə, ç replaces his tr and tšr, ṣ replaces šr, and doubled consonants or a raised dot replace his macron to mark length.

Fig. 2. A wattle and daub house with wood shingles, probably Kitanemuk, at Tejon. Photograph by Edward S. Curtis in 1924 or before.

Structures

It seems probable that the communal dwelling described by Garcés (Coues 1900) was actually a special ceremonial structure of the kind used for the mourning anniversary.

Life Cycle

• BIRTH   Women gave birth at home, sitting upright, attended by a midwife. The navel cord was cut with a cane knife and the baby washed. A hole was dug, filled with hot coals, and covered with dirt and a mat on which mother and child lay. The mother drank only warm water and for three months avoided eating meat, fat, and salt. The afterbirth was buried where no one would step on it, often in a corner of the house. If the mother wished another child but of opposite sex, the afterbirth was turned inside out. Newborn babies were placed in an elliptical, troughlike cradle until they were a month old, then in a regular cradle. Shortly after birth a name of someone long dead was given. Sometimes a name was given by both parents, so that the infant had two names.

• PUBERTY   At her first menses a girl was often lashed with nettles by her mother, then washed with hot water containing pounded estafiata (a plant species); she was also given some to drink. A woman paid by the mother painted the girl's face and upper torso red with white spots and painted black stripes on her cheeks. Then the girl ran back and forth between two rocks about 150 feet apart, chased by a woman chosen for her industriousness.

Next the girl was taken to a small isolated hut constructed by her father. Here she remained for four months with an elderly kinswoman. The structure had a fireplace; wood was supplied by male kin, and the women slept on one side of the door. The girl left the hut only to urinate, with her head covered, looking at no one. Food was brought to her; she could not eat chia, salt, meat, or fat; all food and water was warm. She was forbidden to bathe. Her life would be seriously shortened if she did not observe these restrictions. After the period of confinement the girl was bathed by her mother, and the restrictions were ended.

When her first regular menstruation occurred the girl abstained from meat and fat for a month and used a specially constructed scratching stick of wood or abalone shell; she also lay face down on a bed of nettles for three days. At each subsequent menses the girl dieted and used the scratching stick for a week. After marriage she used the stick only prior to childbirth.

Girls were never given datura. In the winter months one or more boys would be given an infusion of *ma·niç* (datura) so that they might acquire supernatural power, usually in the form of an *aˀatsiδunast* or dream-helper. A man referred to as *pinɨhpa* 'their captain' was in charge. The drug, taken one evening after fasting, induced a coma for a day or two. Upon awakening the boy was given a lump of tobacco to hold in his mouth; this rendered him briefly unconscious. When he awakened the *pinɨhpa* asked him what he had seen, for example,

565

whether he had seen or spoken to some animal or bird, or had seen nothing (in which case the process was still regarded as beneficial). Before dawn on the following day the *pinihpa* took the boy to an isolated place in the hills or to a shrine to pray, taking seeds, tobacco, feather down, and beads as offerings. These were placed in five piles on the ground in the form of a cross. The *pinihpa* prayed to the boy's animal helper, saying: "These things are for you, for you gave your power to this man—now he is your friend." After this the boy abstained from meat, avoided people, did not bathe, and lived in a specially constructed house for a month; he also prayed frequently in the hills. He was then considered a man, and his dream-helper was henceforth his friend and protector.

When a man killed his first deer, it was brought home and laid on a mat in his parents' house. Guests were invited who placed gifts, like beads, beside the deer. The mother prepared food and it and the deer meat were divided among the guests. The heart of a deer was reserved for old men.

• MARRIAGE   Some marriages were arranged by a couple's parents, but most by the couple themselves. The boy's parents called on the girl's parents with gifts; if accepted, the two were "engaged." During the engagement the boy took presents (food or other gifts) to the girl and her parents. Finally the girl's mother prepared a feast and invited guests, who brought gifts such as baskets and other household goods. The couple lived with the boy's parents until the wife became pregnant, at which time they moved into their own house. Girls married about the age of 20 and boys somewhat later. Divorce was uncommon, and polygyny has not been reported.

• DEATH   At death the body was taken to the chief's house. The chief paid for the wake, which lasted for several days. Only old people were allowed to attend the wake or the funeral. Songs were sung (accompanied by deerhoof rattles) during the night, and people wept after each song. The body, doubled up and tied, was wrapped in a mat by hereditary morticians (old women called *titiyim*, from *tiyt* 'spirit' or 'devil'). In the morning, the *titiyim* carried the body to the cemetery; as they neared it, one of them cried out to warn the dead of their arrival. They circled the cemetery three times counterclockwise before approaching a grave previously excavated by some men with digging sticks. At the grave the skull of the corpse was broken open with a stone and one of the *titiyim* gave each mourner a tiny portion of the brain to eat.

The body was then placed in the grave with valuables, and the dirt pushed in with baskets, which the *titiyim* kept. When the mourners returned home the *titiyim* and singers were given food and money to divide.

For a month the mourners ate no meat or fat. At another wake, clothes and other personal possessions of the deceased were burned in a hole outside the house, and presents of food and money were exchanged. Widows put soot on their faces, which was not washed off until the next mourning anniversary. If a man's wife died, a second wake (called *nihnic*) was held at the end of a year. The man presented a sum of perhaps $40 (contributed in part by his relatives who attended the wake) to his deceased wife's parents. The *paka*ʔ made a speech during the wake, and then the man was free to marry again. During the wake the chief announced the time of the next mourning anniversary (called *wáqac*); these were usually held at four- or five-year intervals because of the expenses involved. They lasted a week and were held in a special horseshoe-shaped ramada called a *hororkinat* constructed near the village. The chief sent invitations to others by messenger; only invited people came. As guests approached the village they were met by messengers of the host chief, given food, and escorted to the ramada. They entered the ramada dancing and were then shown to a place within, where they were to live. Guests brought no food with them, but each chief gave money to his messengers to deposit on a mat along with the money supplied earlier for the fiesta by the host chief. Thus the guests contributed to the hosts for expenses. When all had arrived, the host *paka*ʔ spoke and stated the purpose of the fiesta, after which everyone wept. Each day dances were held in the patio until nine or ten o'clock at night. Most people then retired, although some played peon, a hand game. An effigy (called *tsahira*) was constructed by followers of one of the guest chiefs, upon orders of the host chief, on the morning of the final day of the fiesta. It contained personal belongings of all who had died recently. These were brought by relatives and held by the host chief for use in the effigy, which had a human form. The arms held two of the ceremonial *kakait* and *mahivat* wands. The body, made of cloth, was covered by strings of beads. It was carried by four men from guest villages followed by men carrying baskets on sticks to be burned. Women of the host village came behind throwing nuts, seeds, baskets, and beads to the spectators. Three times they went around a fire that had been built in a nearby pit. Then the effigy was placed on the fire, and the mourners began throwing the baskets, beads, and other property on as well. A guest catching something could keep it. After the burning, the pit was filled and a special dancer was ordered to dance over it to erase all trace of it. Simultaneously, the *niciminits* ceremony was held, in which the *paka*ʔ of the host village distributed money and a pair of *kakait* and *mahavit* wands as pay for washing those in mourning. Each invited chief directed certain of his people to wash mourners. The mourners stood in a group, and the washers took them money (less in amount than that just paid by the host chief) and new clothing. The mourners' faces were washed and they were dressed. Many guests then left, though some stayed and danced that evening, leaving the following morning. The dancers, the *paka⁷*, the messengers, and the men who made the effigy were all paid by the host chief.

When a chief died a special gravepole called a *kutumɨts* was prepared prior to the *wáqaç*. Men went to the mountains to cut and trim a pole about 20 feet long and 6 inches in diameter. This was painted with horizontal stripes of red, white, and black, carried to the patio of the ramada, and laid on the ground on mats. People threw beads or seeds on it, from which the workmen took their pay. The pole was erected in the center of the patio with strips of cloth and feather banners (which the workmen later claimed) hanging from it. After the fiesta, the pole was taken to the cemetery, where baskets with holes in their bottoms were inverted and slipped over the pole. Two ceremonial wands were fastened to the top so that they projected upward forming a V; the pole was then erected at the head of the chief's grave.

A very similar ceremony was observed and described among Gabrielinos and Serranos by C.H. Merriam about 1906 (Merriam 1955:77-86).

Wands presented to visiting chiefs at the *wáqaç* and placed on the *kutumɨts* poles were obtained by trade. The *kakaɨt*, obtained from the Tubatulabal, were made from peeled yucca stalks about two feet long. Quail topknots were attached to them at one-inch intervals, and bunches of white eagle down were fastened to one end. The *mahivat*, obtained from the coast, were about two feet long and a quarter of an inch thick, painted red. The wide ends were indented and had shell inlaid in the wood, while the opposite ends were pointed. These wands were kept carefully stored away with other ritual gear in a huge basket; some chiefs might have to borrow some from others.

Social Organization

Although few data are available on the nature of Kitanemuk kin and local groups, the close similarities between Kitanemuk and Cahuilla kinship terminologies suggest the presence of some form of the patrilineage system found elsewhere in southern California (Strong 1929:5-35). However, lineage affiliations do not appear to have been of concern to Harrington's (1917) Kitanemuk informants, and they definitely insisted on the absence of moieties.

Like other Takic-speaking groups, the Kitanemuk were patrilineally organized; however, they did not have the typical totemic moiety structure, nor were lineages totemic. Social ranking and prestige systems were certainly well developed. Each village had an administrative elite involving a chief (*kíka⁷y*), a ceremonial manager (*paka⁷*), two messengers (*wana⁷ypats*), as well as shamans, diviners, and other ritualists.

Shamanism

Shamanistic abilities derived from a relationship with one or more *a⁷atsitam* or dream-helpers, which was acquired after ingesting a hallucinogenic (either datura or a species of ant), and symbolized by an *aqʷaçɨmuk* (talisman) worn around the neck. Only certain individuals had the personality or interest to develop the several relationships necessary for exceptional power. A shaman (*tsaç*) was paid for curing, which he did during an all-night ceremony, dancing and calling on his dream-helpers for aid. Powerful shamans were able to bring rain, make an animal skin come alive, and cause miniature animals to appear on their arms while dancing. They also performed at major ceremonies like the mourning anniversary. There were also diviners called *⁷ɨnnannat* or *maçike⁷*.

Most men acquired a dream-helper at the adolescence ritual; those who wished additional power could acquire it by taking ants. After a three-day fast, a boy consulted an older man, who took him to a secluded spot in the hills. The boy would lie down and the other man would drop ants into his mouth for him to ingest. The boy went into a coma for several hours. After he awoke, the old man prayed, describing what the boy had seen and referring to mythological figures such as *çannɨqpa* and *tsúqqit*. The boy then wore a talisman symbolic of his dream-helper, such as a falcon's head or a quartz crystal. Hummingbird was a good dream-helper for a warrior, since the bird flew too fast to be hit by an arrow. A man with three or four helpers, such as Bear, Thunder, or Hummingbird, had exceptional powers and could cure the seriously ill.

Major illnesses were treated by professional shamans, but most people knew a variety of medicinal substances that could be used for curing. Datura and tobacco or *tsivu⁷* were perhaps the most important plants used in this way. Tobacco was pounded into a fine powder with lime, inducing a temporary intoxication (and possibly hallucination) before vomiting occurred. Red ants were used for women having complications during menstruation or after childbirth; they were allowed to bite the body or were swallowed. It was believed that anyone who failed to take ants after stating his intention to do so would die. Other plants used for medicine included the herbs chuchupate, romerillo, and saltpeter. Certain mineral pigments were also considered to have medicinal properties.

Most people had sacred sentient stones (*tɨsaɨt*) in their houses to protect them from storms, or to place in water to be drunk as a medicine. These stones, variously shaped, were obtained from the coast. They were kept wrapped with offerings of eagle down, seeds, beads, and tobacco; the offerings were changed yearly at the winter solstice.

There were shrines (*nahwinits*) on hills, near trails, or in other isolated places that consisted of a cleared space with five small piles of earth in the center in the form of a cross about six feet across, representing the earth. Offerings of seeds, down, tobacco, or beads were deposited by anyone passing by, coming to pray, or at the time

567

KITANEMUK

of the summer and winter solstices. It was believed that theft from a shrine would cause death.

The Kitanemuk believed in the existence of malevolent bear shamans, men whose identities were unknown. They had special costumes endowed with supernatural powers in which they dressed for the purpose of killing people secretly and for pay. In these costumes they resembled living bears. They sat inside and guided the costume with reins made from the hair of dead people. With this device a bear shaman was believed able to travel great distances in a short time.

Beliefs

The Kitanemuk probably had names for the lunar months; they definitely observed both summer and winter solstices. A new year began after the winter solstice; the word *tɨvaç*, like the Central Chumash word *šup*, meant both 'year' and 'world'. During solstices, adults collected feather down and beads to give to the *paka?*, who deposited them at a shrine and prayed. The sun was felt to be wild and angry on the morning of the winter solstice, so people stayed indoors to avoid being killed. Solar and lunar eclipses were not particularly feared, except by pregnant women who hid indoors.

A soul or spirit (*tɨyt*) could appear in various guises: as a human, a whirlwind, or as moving lights at night. If one rubbed dog's tears in his own eyes one could see *tɨyt* all around. A falling star was a sign that a chief was dying somewhere. Owls were considered birds of ill omen.

Mythology

Kitanemuk mythology was a mixture of elements, many of which had their origin among the Chumash, Yokuts, or Gabrielino. The universe was originally created by *çannɨqpa*, a being who formed earth and sky and made the *urehatam táqqátam* 'first people' by breathing on clay images of them. These people included the ancestors of the present birds and animals, the most important of which were five brothers and a sister. The brothers were named *yuqaqat* (the eldest), *pitsurayt, hukaht, papamaṣ,* and *pamasyɨt,* and the sister *tsúqqit.* The siblings created five superimposed worlds, the smallest on top and the largest (that in which people now live) on the bottom. This world was circular and floated on a surrounding ocean supported by two gigantic serpents whose movements caused earthquakes. Later there was a great deluge that covered all but the tops of the highest mountains. All First People were drowned or turned to animals with the exception of the six siblings, who were safe in their home at *a?iykitsa tɨvat,* a beautiful place in the south where flowers bloomed continually and it was never hot. Although the brothers lived apart from their sister, *hukaht* began to visit her secretly and *tsúqqit* became pregnant. She gave birth to Hummingbird, and *hukaht* was punished for his incest by having his arm and leg bones removed so that he could no longer move. After that

tsúqqit had many children, the ancestors of people living now. She was the wisest of the siblings and taught her children everything they needed to know in order to survive, such as making tools and baskets, hunting, preparing tobacco, and making the *yɨvar* or sacred enclosure. *yuqaqat* sent them off in different directions, telling each man to marry a certain woman, and where to live and what language to speak. Thus different tribes of people were created. *tsúqqit* and her five brothers still lived at *a?iykitsa tɨvat,* and prayers were frequently addressed to her while facing south.

The land of the dead, *tɨypea,* was located in the east. A few people had gone there and returned to tell their friends. The normal round of activities was reversed there, for the spirits slept during the day and played, danced, and sang all night. *tɨypea* was a very beautiful place; there was always plenty to eat, and spirits never aged. The chief of *tɨypea* was *tameat* or Sun, who lived in a shining house with two daughters. They appeared old, but never aged. Sun played peon every night with *tsúqqit,* with Moon as referee; if *tsúqqit* won it was a bountiful year, but if Sun won many people died and there were wars.

The rainbow, the colors of which were those of various seeds and flowers, was held up at both ends by *pahikyɨt* or Morning Star, a woman with hair so long it reached her heels. She was the grandmother of the three Thunders. Evening Star was a man. The Kitanemuk universe was quite anthropomorphic.

There was a race of dwarfs (with adults the size of a small boy) called *?anuhnusi táqqátam* who lived somewhere to the north. The Kitanemuk also knew of the Central Chumash *?elyeẁun* or Swordfish, whom they called *papamašryam.* These were eight brothers who lived in a house under the sea near Mugu, sleeping all day and dancing all night. Light was supplied by a creature called *kočeanat,* with an upper torso like that of a man, and a lower body consisting of a burning brand. He sang while the brothers danced. During each song the brothers took turns racing three times counterclockwise around the world. They also hunted whales, tossing them back and forth like balls until they died, then throwing them up on shore. There were also *páppahavim,* dangerous beings that roamed around after dark (equivalent to the Central Chumash *nunašɨš*).

Chumash influences can be seen in a number of other Kitanemuk stories. In one myth, Falcon and Raven met an ogre with a basket of hot tar on her back. When she tried to throw them into it, they sat on a bow stretched across its mouth and then set the tar on fire, killing the ogre. Another myth concerned a boy whose parents were killed by a cannibal bird and a bear, and who was then raised by his grandmother. He finally killed both bird and bear, and then frightened his grandmother with the bear's skin.

568

Fig. 3. Marcelino Rivera and his sister, with children in front of sun shade at Tejon Ranch. Photograph by Maurice Zigmond, 1937.

Synonymy

According to Kroeber (1925), "a synonym of Kitanemuk is kikitanum or kikitamakar," words that may stem from ki- 'house'. Garcés refers to a group called the Cuabajai, who may be the Kitanemuk or, more probably, the Tataviam. In Yokuts (perhaps Choynok or Chunut) they were called Mayaintalap 'large bows', which would be *maỷʔin ịalap* in Yawelmani Yokuts (Geoffrey Gamble, personal communication 1975); the Tubatulabal called them Witanghatal; the Chemehuevi, Nawiyat; and the Mohave, Kuvahaivima. In more recent times Whites have called them Tejon Indians, a term that was applied to a number of groups located in the Tejon Ranch area.

Other Indians have referred to them as the Haminot, from a characteristic Kitanemuk expression meaning 'what is it' (Kroeber 1925).

Sources

The only historical mention of the Kitanemuk is contained in Garcés's 1776 account (Coues 1900); however, the tribal attribution may be incorrect, since there seem to be certain discrepancies between it and the ethnographic data collected by J.P. Harrington. Harrington's (1917) notes contain the only extensive body of information on the Kitanemuk (fig. 4). These field notes provide the material for this chapter except where otherwise noted. Merriam (1955:77–86) collected scattered linguistic data. There are brief ethnographic notes by Kroeber (1925) and the culture element distribution list by Harrington (1942). No artifact collections containing Kitanemuk materials are known; an extensive ethnobotanical collection assembled by Harrington is available for study.

NAA, Smithsonian.
Fig. 4. Magdalena Olivas wearing basketry cap and beads. Photograph by John P. Harrington, about 1917.

Serrano

LOWELL JOHN BEAN AND CHARLES R. SMITH

Language, Territory, and Environment

The small ethnic nationality called Serrano (sə'rä₁nō), from a Spanish term meaning 'mountaineer, highlander', aboriginally occupied an area east of present-day Los Angeles. The name Serrano has also been used, in a broader sense, for a group of languages in the Takic family: Serrano, Kitanemuk, probably Vanyume, and just possibly Tataviam. The term Serran has been introduced (Bright 1975) for the linguistic group consisting of Serrano and Kitanemuk, as contrasted to the other, more distantly related Takic languages Gabrielino, Luiseño, Cahuilla, and Cupeño (a group Bright calls Cupan).*

It is nearly impossible to assign definitive boundaries for Serrano territory due both to Serrano sociopolitical organizational features and to a lack of reliable data. As Strong (1929) noted, the Serrano were organized into autonomous localized lineages occupying definite, favored territories, but rarely claiming any territory far removed from the lineage's home base. Since the entire dialectical group was neither politically united nor amalgamated into supralineage groups, as many of their neighbors were, one must speak in terms of generalized areas of usage rather than pan-tribal holdings (Strong 1929).

Very little is known of the Vanyume, a sparse and poor population living along the Mojave River. Whether they spoke a dialect of Serrano or a separate Takic language cannot be determined from the brief word list available (Bright 1975; Kroeber 1907b:139-140). Politically they seem to have differed from the Serrano proper, for example, in enjoying friendly relations with the Mohave and Chemehuevi, who were enemies of the Serrano (Kroeber 1925:614-615). The number of Vanyume, never large, dwindled rapidly between 1820 and 1834 as the Spanish collected southern California Indians in various *asistencias* and missions (Beattie and Beattie 1939); well before 1900 the group was extinct.

Most researchers place Serrano groups in the San Bernardino Mountains east of Cajon Pass, at the base and north of these mountains in the desert near Victor-

ville, eastward as far as Twentynine Palms, and south to and in the Yucaipa Valley (fig. 1). The area thus described varies considerably topographically (elevations ranging from about 1,500 feet in the desert to over 11,000 feet in the mountains) and in plant-animal community associations. The desert floor and valley region passes from Lower Sonoran through Upper Sonoran, the latter region being confined to a narrow strip on the mountains' eastern slopes, and above 5,000-6,000 feet the forest Transition life-zone predominates. Rainfall varies as does topography with water almost nonexistent in the desert areas while in the lower foothills are found perennial seeps, streams, and occasionally small lakes. Available foods include, but are not restricted to, mountain sheep, deer, rabbits, acorns, seeds of various grasses, piñon nuts, bulbs and tubers, shoots and roots, berries, mesquite. The principal vegetation at lower elevations on the mountains' southern sides is coastal sagebrush and chaparral while to the east and north in the desert there is a sparse covering of edible plants, the most important being barrel cacti and Joshua trees. The mountains' inland slopes support, at successively higher elevations, Great Basin sagebrush, juniper, piñon pine (whose nuts provided a valuable food resource), and minor conifers, types of relatively little value in the dietary plans of the Serrano (Kroeber 1925; Strong 1929).

Most village-hamlets were in the foothill Upper Sonoran life-zone while a few were out on the desert floor (near permanent water sources) or in the forest Transition zone. As Benedict (1924:368) points out the availability of water on a year-round basis was, to a large

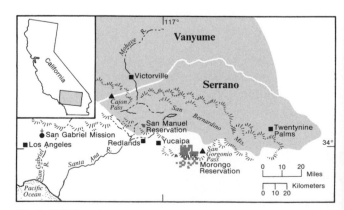

Fig. 1. Tribal territory.

---

* Italicized Serrano words have been rewritten by Kenneth C. Hill in the phonemic orthography he developed (K.C. Hill 1969), with a few symbol substitutions in accord with Handbook standards: χ is here written x̣, χʷ is xʷ, ñ is nʸ, ł is lʸ and v is β. Vowels with a dot beneath are retroflex.

extent, the determining factor in the nature, duration, and distribution of Serrano settlements.

Subsistence

The Serrano, like their neighbors, were primarily gatherers and hunters and occasionally fishers. The women were responsible for most of the gathering, while hunting and fishing were the province of males. The primary vegetable staples varied with hamlet locality: acorns and piñon nuts for groups living in the foothills; honey mesquite and piñon nuts plus yucca roots, mesquite, cacti fruits, for those living in or near the desert. These principal foods were supplemented by various other roots, bulbs, shoots, and seeds, particularly chia (*Salvia columbariae*), which was periodically burned over to increase its yield. Desert groups annually traveled into the foothills to collect nuts of various kinds and to trade with their kindred desert fruits and seeds for products not available in the desert (Kroeber 1925; Strong 1929; Drucker 1937; Benedict 1924).

Principal game animals taken were deer, mountain sheep, antelope, rabbits and other small rodents, and various birds, quail being the most important and desirable game bird. The most commonly used hunting implements were bows and arrows for large game and curved throwing sticks, traps, snares, and deadfalls for smaller game and birds. Occasionally, communal deer and rabbit hunts would be held, especially during the annual mourning ceremony; and communal acorn, nut, and mesquite gathering expeditions involving several lineages amalgamated under one lineage leader's authority were not uncommon (Benedict 1924:391-392; Drucker 1937; Bean 1962-1972).

Meat was prepared by baking in earth ovens; by boiling in watertight baskets containing water, meat pieces, and heated stones; or by parching from tossing it with hot coals in shallow trays. Bones were boiled and the marrow extracted and eaten. Blood was drunk either cold or cooked into a thick consistency and then swallowed (Bean 1962-1972). Surplus meats, as well as some vegetable foods, were sun-dried and stored for later use. Plant foods were eaten raw or cooked, depending upon type. Precooking processing included grinding (with metates) or pounding (with mortars of stone or wood), or parching (principally seeds). Primary food processing utensils included flint knives, stone or bone scrapers, pottery trays and bowls, baskets, horn and bone spoons and stirrers, as well as mortars and metates (Strong 1929; Bean 1962-1972; Drucker 1937; Benedict 1924).

Culture

Structures

Because settlement location was determined by availability and accessibility of water, most Serranos lived in small villages situated near water sources. Individual family dwellings were usually circular, domed structures built of willow frames covered with tule thatching. These homes were occupied by a husband and wife (or wives), their unmarried children (if female), usually married children (if male), sometimes the man's parents, and occasionally a widowed aunt or uncle. Although not common, sometimes a single individual would erect a house for his own personal use, usually in the mountains, the use of which depended upon the individual. Although the family house had a central fire pit, the house served primarily as a sleeping and storage area with most daily, routine household activities taking place either out in the open or under the shade of a ramada. The ramada is a wall-less structure with a roof of thatched willow poles supported by four or more posts placed vertically in the ground (Drucker 1937; Benedict 1924; Kroeber 1925).

In addition to family residences and ramadas, most Serrano villages had a large ceremonial house where the *ki·ka?*, or lineage leader, lived. The ceremonial house was the religious center for each lineage or lineage-set. Lineage-sets consisted of two (or possibly more) lineages joined to one another through ties of marriage, economic reciprocity, and, most important, through joint participation in ritual. Lineages in a lineage-set shared the ceremonial house and the sacred bundle (the raison d'être for the Serrano). Further, they were obliged to have their ceremonies codirected by the *ki·ka?* from one lineage and locality and his assistant the *paxa·?* from another (Strong 1929).

Other village structures included granaries and sweathouses, the latter being located immediately adjacent to pools or streams, if possible. Sweathouses were large, circular, semisubterranean, earth-covered structures supported by willow-pole frames and thatching and having only one opening, the door. A fire was built in the center of the sweathouse and men, women, and children would gather inside to cleanse their bodies by sweating. Following the sweat everyone would take a dip in the nearby water (Strong 1929; Bean 1962-1972).

Technology

Technologically, the Serrano were very similar to their neighbors, particularly the Cahuilla. Shells, wood, bone, stone, and plant fibers were used in making a variety of implements including lavishly decorated baskets (Smith and Simpson 1964), pottery, rabbitskin blankets, awls, arrow straighteners, sinew-backed bows, arrows, fire drills, stone pipes, musical instruments (rattles of turtle or tortoise shell, deer-hoof rattles, wood rasps, bone whistles, bull-roarers, flutes), feathered costumes, mats (for floor and wall coverings), bags and storage pouches, and cordage (usually of yucca fiber), and nets (Drucker 1937; Bean 1962-1972).

The Serrano were loosely organized into exogamous clans, which in turn were affiliated with one of two exogamous moieties, *tukʷutam* (Wildcat) and *wahiʔiam* (Coyote) (Strong 1929). The exact nature of the clans, their structure, function, and number are not known, but Strong (1929) was able to determine that each clan was the largest autonomous political and landholding unit with the core being the patrilineage and that included were all males recognizing descent from a common male ancestor plus descendants and wives of these males. However, in marrying women retained their own lineage names and at times participated in ceremonies of their natal groups (Strong 1929:17). According to Strong (1929:14) there was no form of pan-tribal political union among the clans, all bonds being strictly ceremonial in nature with clans aligning themselves with one another along lines of economic, marital, or ceremonial reciprocity, a pattern common throughout southern California. In addition to forming bonds with other Serrano bands (that is, clans) they also formed alliances with Cahuilla, Chemehuevi, Gabrielino, and Cupeño clans (Strong 1929; Bean 1962–1972).

A clan's titular head was the *kiʼkaʔ*, a hereditary position to which great psychic importance was attached, since the *kiʼkaʔ* was, in addition to his other duties, the one ceremonial and religious leader of the clan. The office passed preferably from father to ablest son but under unusual circumstances could pass to the wife of the previous *kiʼkaʔ* (Strong 1929; Gifford 1918). The duties of the *kiʼkaʔ* included determining when and where to collect or hunt and ascertaining and naming the times for, and presiding at the various ceremonies. He lived in the clan's *kiʼč ʔatiɬʔaç* 'big house', where all ceremonies took place, the sick were brought for healing, and novice shamans performed prior to their acceptance as full-fledged curers (Strong 1929).

The *kiʼkaʔ* was assisted in his ceremonial affairs by the *paxaʼʔ*, also a hereditary office passing from father to son. The *paxaʼʔ* took charge of the sacred bundle (*möʼʔč*) containing all ceremonial paraphernalia, notified the people when ceremonies were to take place, carried shell money between groups for ceremonial purposes, and attended the division of shell money and food at all ceremonies. This *kiʼkaʔ-kiʼč ʔatiɬʔaç-paxaʼʔ-möʼʔč* complex was standard among most southern California Takic speakers, but the Serrano clans were unique in that the clan or clans of one moiety had the *kiʼkaʔ* and house while those of the opposite moiety possessed the bundle and the *paxaʼʔ*. For example, the *maʼriŋaʔ* clan of the Coyote moiety retained the ceremonial house and *kiʼkaʔ* and called the ceremonies, while the *paxaʼʔ* of the *mihenʔniam* clan of the Wildcat moiety presided at the ceremonies and kept charge of the sacred bundle, its display and use during the ceremonies. This may be a reflection of the lateness of investigation by non-Indians and represent cultural disintegration and hence amalgamation of formerly separate groups. Alternatively, Strong (1929:19) suggested "a further extension of the moiety idea wherein the partial moiety reciprocity of the more southerly groups is further accentuated by an actual division of the all-important priest, house, and fetish concept. Thus the clan of the opposite moiety with whom intermarriage is most common becomes an integral part of the ceremonial unit, and the cooperation of both groups becomes necessary for any ritualistic activity." Which theory is closer to the truth is at present unknown; however, the economic implications are significant and are comparable to those for the Cahuilla.

Life Cycle

Immediately following birth both mother and child were placed in a heated pit where they remained for several days, observing food taboos and leaving only long enough for the pit to be reheated and for the mother to take care of personal body functions. On the second day following birth the child's grandparents held a feast for clan members and distributed presents (Strong 1929).

When boys and girls of prominent families reached adolescence special ceremonies were held for each. The girls' ceremony, waxan, included "pit roasting," ingestion of bitter herbs prepared by the *paxaʼʔ*, observation of certain dietary restrictions, and instructions on how to be good "wives." The ceremony was, for the most part, public and held at the same time as the boys' ceremony. Girls from less prominent families were initiated at private ceremonies attended by the immediate family only (Strong 1929).

The boys' ceremony, tamonin, in addition to boys from prominent families, included those boys who had outstanding personalities. The *paxaʼʔ* presided and was assisted by the clans' shamans. Datura was prepared in secret in a special mortar, made into a decoction, and ingested by the initiates at a secret place away from the village. The boys were brought into the ceremonial house where they danced around a fire until falling into a trance state. They were then laid out near the fire and allowed to sleep off the effects of the drug. While sleeping the boys would have visions that were later interpreted by the shamans and used as sign posts for the boys' future lives. Afterward special songs were learned by the boys and feasting and gifting took place (Strong 1929).

Prior to Spanish domination, the Serrano practiced cremation almost immediately following death with most of the deceased's possessions destroyed at the same time. Within one month the deceased's family held the mamakwot, a night of singing and dancing at which certain possessions of the deceased were burned (Strong 1929).

Annually, a seven-day mourning ceremony was held at which time several other ceremonies took place. The first two days of the ceremony were spent preparing the foods and gifts that would be consumed or given away during the next five days. On the third night the sacred bundle was brought forth and shown to the assembled clans gathered in the *ki·č ʔatiɬ ʔac̣*. On the fourth night a naming ceremony was held for all children born in the preceding year (or since the last mourning ceremony was held, whichever was longer) and gifts were distributed to the assembled clans' members by the children's families. On the fifth night a special eagle-killing ceremony took place. Raised in the *ki·č ʔatiɬ ʔac̣* for this purpose, the eagle had its feathers removed and saved to be used later in decorating the images of the dead. The following day the mourning families constructed the images, which were life size, made of tule, and dressed in clothes of the deceased. On the evening of the sixth day an eagle dance was held, much like that of the Cahuilla, Luiseño, and Gabrielino, in which a dancer dressed in eagle feathers whirled around the ceremonial house simulating the movements of the eagle. All through the night singing and dancing continued, and gifts and shell money were distributed. In the morning the images were burned (Strong 1929).

Religion and Shamanism

The Serrano shaman *hʷọ·mč*, like most southern California shamans, was "psychically" predisposed for his possessions and acquired his various powers through dreaming, assisted in this process by the ingestion of datura (Strong 1929; Bean 1962–1972). Shamans were mainly curers, healing their patients through a combination of sucking out the disease-causing agents and administering herbal remedies (Benedict 1924).

Serrano cosmogony and cosmography closely parallel that of the Cahuilla. There are twin creator gods, a creation myth told in "epic poem" style, each local group having its own origin story, water babies whose crying foretells death, supernatural beings of various kinds and on various hierarchically arranged power-access levels, an Orpheus-like myth, mythical deer that no one can kill, and tales relating the adventures (and misadventures) of Coyote, a tragicomic trickster-transformer culture hero (Bean 1962–1972; Benedict 1924).

History

Except for a few field surveys (primarily by the San Bernardino Museum staff) there have been no significant archeological research projects to determine the relationship between the Serrano historic and prehistoric periods. However, statements by Hicks (1959), Campbell (1931:39), and Haenszel (1957) provide a useful introduction to possible Serrano archeological assemblages.

Although contact with Europeans may have occurred as early as 1771 (when Mission San Gabriel was established) or 1772 (the date of Pedro Fages's trip into

Serrano territory), Spanish influence on Serrano lifeways was negligible until about 1819 when an *asistencia* was built near Redlands. Between then and secularization in 1834 most of the western Serrano were removed bodily to the missions (Beattie and Beattie 1939:366), after which too few remained to reestablish their native lifeways. In the region northeast of San Gorgonio Pass, Serrano culture survived more fully, and it is these groups who preserve what little remains of Serrano native cultural patterns (fig. 2).

top, San Bernardino Co. Mus., Redlands, Calif.: Smith Coll.; bottom: Dept. of Anthr., Smithsonian: 313225.
Fig. 2. Coiled storage baskets. top, Made by Jesusa Manuel and her daughters, San Manuel Reservation, about 1927, with design said to represent natural formation on mountain above Arrowhead Hot Springs, Santa Barbara Mountains; diameter 40.7 cm. bottom, Made by Marie Martina, Morongo Reservation, 1906; same scale.

In 1975 most Serrano lived on two southern California reservations (Morongo, San Manuel), participating in ceremonial and political affairs with other native Californians (mainly Cahuilla, Cupeño, some Luiseño) on a pan-reservation rather than strictly Serrano basis. Only slightly over 100 people claim Serrano descent, reduced from a precontact figure between 1,500 (Kroeber 1925:617) and 2,500 (Bean 1962–1972), and even fewer speak their native language; however, all recall with pride their history. Ethnic identity is strong and they remain a readily identifiable cultural entity.

Synonymy

The Serrano have been referred to by a multiplicity of terms. Hodge (1907–1910, 2:512–513) cites 46, mainly appellations given to the Serrano by their neighbors. Examples are Maringints and Pitanta, Chemehuevi terms for different divisions, and Marayam, a Luiseño word. The Gabrielino called the Serrano *kuko·mkar* or *qaqa·yvit*(?), while the Cupeño name for them is *təmámkawičəm* 'people to the north'. Gatschet (1879) notes that the Serrano call themselves Takhtam (*ta·qtam*) 'men', while Kroeber (1925) gives Kaiviatam (*qai·βiatam*), a derivative of the word for 'mountain', as the Serrano translation of the Spanish *serrano* 'mountain dweller' (from *sierra* 'mountain range'). Barrows (1900) recorded the termCów-ang-a-chem as a native Serrano word for the Serrano people as a group, but it may in fact be Cahuilla, based on their word *qáwiš* 'rock, mountain' (Kenneth C. Hill, personal communication 1975).

The name Vanyume is Mohave and the source of the term Beñeme, which Francisco Garcés in 1776 applied to all the Serran peoples. The last known speaker of the language gave Möhineyam or Möhinyam as their name for themselves, but Kroeber later dropped the term because of its resemblance to Mohiyanim, a local group of the Serrano proper (Kroeber 1907b:135, 140, 1925:614).

Sources

The most extensive and reliable written sources on the Serrano are Strong's (1929) monograph, Kroeber's (1925) handbook, Benedict's (1924, 1926) articles, and Drucker's (1937) culture element distribution list. Archival resources range from a rather extensive set of field notes collected by J.P. Harrington (at the National Anthropological Archives, Smithsonian Institution) through the more recent work of Paul Chase and Lowell Bean. The San Bernardino County Museum, Bloomington; Bancroft Library, University of California, Berkeley; the Huntington Library (especially the Wieland collection), San Marino; and the Malki Museum, Morongo Indian Reservation, all have some artifact or photographic collections. They also house field notes collected by various researchers.

Cahuilla

LOWELL JOHN BEAN

Language and Environment

Cahuilla (kə'wēyu) is the name given to a group of south-central California Indians. The term is of uncertain origin but may be from their own word *káwiya* 'master, boss' (Kroeber 1925:693; Hansjakob Seiler, personal communication 1974). Their language belongs to the Cupan subgroup of the Takic family of the Uto-Aztecan stock; among the four Cupan languages, Cahuilla is more similar to Cupeño than it is to Luiseño (Bright and Hill 1967; Bright 1975).*

The Cahuilla area was topographically complex: mountain ranges interspersed by passes, canyons, valleys, and desert, with elevations from 11,000 feet in the San Bernardino Mountains to 273 feet below sea level at the Salton Sink. The Cahuilla occupied most of the area, from the summit of the San Bernardino Mountains in the north to Borrego Springs and the Chocolate Mountains in the south, a portion of the Colorado Desert west of Orocopia Mountain to the east, and the San Jacinto Plain near Riverside and the eastern slopes of Palomar Mountain to the west (fig. 1).

Valleys, passes, and foothills blended into the mountain ranges with the lower desert areas. Alluvial fans led into canyons averaging 4 to 16 miles in length and several miles in width; these in turn led into mountain valleys flanked by high scarps. Consequently, separate and distinct environmental zones were formed, each with its characteristic life-zones (table 1): Lower Sonoran, Upper Sonoran, Transition, and Canadian-Hudsonian (Hall and Grinnell 1919; Grinnell and Swarth 1913).

Seasonal extremes of temperature, precipitation, and wind patterns caused dramatic differences in the relative abundance of flora and fauna from place to place and time to time. Dry winds affected food potential and increased the incendiary potential of the plant cover, while high velocity winds accompanied by sandstorms were common (Ryan 1968).

* Modern linguists have used several equivalent phonemic orthographies for Cahuilla. Those described by Bright (1965a) and in more detail by Seiler (1957) are readily converted to Handbook standards by the following substitutions (Bright's symbol is given first, then Seiler's, and finally the Handbook equivalent): qw, kʷ, *kʷ;* xw, xʷ, *xʷ;* ly, ĺ, *lʸ;* ñ, ñ, *nʸ*. Bright and Seiler show vowel length with a double letter, while a raised dot is used here. Italicized Cahuilla words in the Handbook are written in this orthography, after respellings provided by Hansjakob Seiler.

During some years abundant water was available, while in other years serious drought conditions prevailed, inhibiting plant growth and causing decreases in the faunal population. Permanent springs and tinajas were common; lakes appeared occasionally; and rivers, streams, springs, sloughs, and marshy areas were subject to considerable variation in water potential throughout the year. Periodic desert lakes extended to 60 miles in length and were formed by melting snows, torrential rains, and overflows from the Colorado River. When the water table was low deep, walk-in wells were dug in the sand (A.S. Evans 1889; Ryan 1968; Shepard 1965; Lawton and Bean 1968; Nordland 1968; Bean 1972).

Territory

The Cahuilla area, located near the geographic center of southern California, was bisected by a major trade route, the Cocopa-Maricopa Trail, and was at the periphery of two others, the ones labeled Santa Fe and Yuman. Natural boundaries such as the Colorado Desert separated the Cahuilla from the Mohave, Halchidoma, Ipai and Tipai; the mountains, hills, and plains separated them from the Luiseño, Serrano, and Gabrielino.

These peoples interacted regularly by intermarriage, trade, ritual, and war. The Cahuilla shared a common tradition with the Gabrielino and other nearby Takic speakers, such as the Serrano and Luiseño. Of these, the Gabrielino and Serrano were most intensively involved with the Cahuilla (Bean 1972:69; Kroeber 1925: 578-580).

Villages

Villages were usually situated in canyons or on alluvial fans near adequate sources of water and food materials, where a degree of natural defense was afforded from strong prevailing winds.

The area immediately surrounding the village was owned in common by the lineage, while other lands were divided into tracts owned by clans, families, and individuals. Networks of trails used for hunting, trading, and social visiting interconnected villages. Numerous sacred sites marked off by petroglyphs and pictographs were associated with each lineage village.

Movement out of permanent villages was for specific purposes such as hunting, gathering, trade, ritual, or

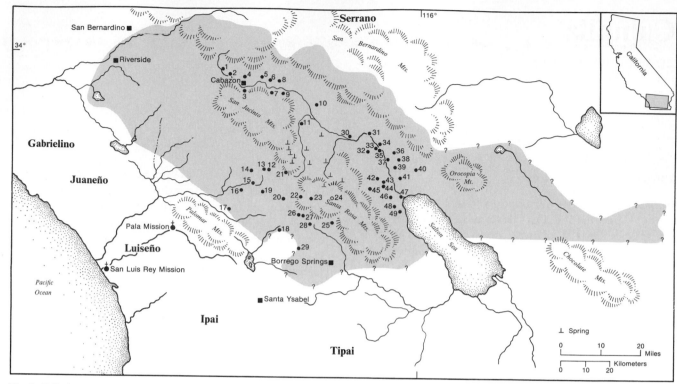

Fig. 1. Tribal territory and villages. 1, *aýkat;* 2, *písataŋa;* 3, *húvana;* 4, *wáqsiš;* 5, *pálakna;* 6, *hévina;* 7, *téčaŋa;* 8, *wánikik;* 9, *wáqina;* 10, Palm Springs; 11, *pánik;* 12, *páwata;* 13, Pastawha; 14, *sáwvelpa;* 15, *páwi;* 16, *wíyasmal;* 17, *áwaŋa;* 18, *číya;* 19, *máwet síwpa;* 20, *páwki;* 21, *pál písa;* 22, Natcúta; 23, *síwiw;* 24, Old Santa Rosa Indian Ruins; 25, Ataki, 26, *tépaŋha;* 27, Wilīya, *sáwivel* (or *sáwʔvel*); 28, *sáwiš;* 29, *páčawal;* 30, *káviniš;* 31, *pál téwat;* 32, *iłʼ čúŋhaluŋi;* 33, *pál sétaxat;* 34, *pál sétamal;* 35, Coachella; 36, *pál áyil;* 37, Thermal; 38, *áwal páčava;* 39, *túvakiktem hémkiʔ;* 40, *máyswat héla·nat;* 41, *pál múluqalet;* 42, *máwl míʔi;* 43, *témal síkalet;* 44, *pál híłʼiwet;* 45, *púičekiva;* 46, Alamo; *pál púni;* 48, Agua Dulce; 49, *túva, ú·lišpači.*

Table 1. Environment

Zone	Altitude	Significant Habitats	Plant Foods	Animal Foods	Percent of Tribal Area	Percent of Diet Acquired in Zone
Lower Sonoran	−200 to 3,500 feet	Sand dune–creosote, creosote–palo verde, cholla–palo verde, rocky slopes, agave–ocotillo	Cacti, palm, mesquite, agave, Mohave yucca, screwbean, catsclaw, Mariposa lily, desert lily, ephedra, corn, beans, squash, melons	Deer, rabbit, antelope, mice, rats, mountain sheep, reptiles, insects, larvae, fish, quail, doves, ducks, roadrunners	60	25
Upper Sonoran	3,500 to 6,300 feet	Piñon-juniper, chaparral	Cacti, agave, mushroom nolina, yucca, piñon, oak, juniper, manzanita, sugar bush, tule, various grass seeds, chia, cattails, wild onion, wild rose	Deer, mountain sheep, rabbits, rats, mice, reptiles, insects and larvae, fish, quail, dove, roadrunners	28	60
Transition	6,300 to 9,000 feet	Coniferous forests, meadows	Oak, elderberry, service berry, manzanita, wild cherry, yucca, tule, various grass seeds, chia, cattail	Mountain sheep, deer, pack rats, squirrels, mice, chipmunks, fish	7	15
Canadian-Hudsonian	9,000 to 10,000 + feet	Alpine	Few	Deer, mountain sheep, rabbits, squirrels, mice, some reptiles	5	less than 1

Source: Bean 1977

Fig. 2. Dome-shaped brush house in the desert. Photograph by Edward S. Curtis in 1924 or before.

social visiting. Houses and other structures in a village were situated to take advantage of water sources and ensure privacy. The largest number of people left for the greatest amount of time during the acorn-collecting season, when most village members moved for several weeks to acorn groves.

Buildings varied in size from brush shelters to dome-shaped or rectangular houses (fig. 2), 15–20 feet long depending on the individual family's needs, and ceremonial houses (fig. 3). The home of the *nét* 'chief', usually the largest, served many purposes. It was located near a good water source and usually built alongside the ceremonial

Fig. 3. Rectangular ceremonial house on Soboba Reservation. Photograph by C. Hart Merriam, Oct. 1901.

CAHUILLA

house (used for rituals, curing, and recreational activities). A communal men's sweathouse and several granaries were also located within the village, clustered around the ceremonial house or homes (Bean 1972:70-75; Strong 1929; H.C. James 1960; Barrows 1900; Kroeber 1925).

Culture

Subsistence

Hunting was the occupation of adult able-bodied men who stalked their prey, chased it, hid in blinds, maneuvered the animals into striking range of their arrows, chased them down trails into pits, or exhausted them so they could be clubbed to death. Rabbits and other small game were shot with bow and arrow; stunned or killed with throwing sticks; captured in nets, snares, and traps; or acquired by firing bush clumps (Bean 1972:64).

Butchering and skinning was done by men, cooking by women. Meat was roasted, boiled, or cut into strips and sun-dried. Bones were cracked to extract marrow or crushed and ground into a powder and mixed with other foods. Blood was either drunk fresh or cooked and stored in a leather pouch or sections of gut (Bean 1972).

Diversity of habitat produced a floral domain of immense variety consisting of several thousand species of which the Cahuilla remember using several hundred for food, manufacture, or medicine (Bean and Saubel 1972). The most important were: acorns (six varieties of oak), mesquite and screw beans, piñon nuts, and the fleshy bulbs of various types of cacti. These were supplemented with a variety of seeds, wild fruits and berries, tubers, roots, and succulent greens (Bean 1972).

Proto-agricultural techniques and a marginal agriculture existed among the Cahuilla. Corn, beans, squashes, and melons of the types used by the neighboring Colorado River tribes were the most commonly raised (Lawton and Bean 1968).

Other plants provided construction materials for houses, while over 200 plants were used to cure diseases, decrease infections, and stimulate physical activities (e.g., tobacco and datura) (Bean and Saubel 1972).

Grinding acorns and dried berries was done in stone mortars with stone pestles; stone manos were rolled on stone metates to grind hard seeds as well as soft foods like piñon nuts; and wooden mortars were used to pulverize soft, fibrous foods like honey mesquite. Flourlike materials were then sifted in baskets to segregate the larger particles from the flour, and the larger particles were reground. This was usually the duty of women. Parching, performed in a basket or pottery tray, preceded grinding. Leaching acorn meal, which was essential, was done in baskets or sand basins. Yucca, agave, and tule-potatoes were baked in stoned-lined ovens or pits. Sun-drying allowed for preservation of fruits, blossoms, and buds.

Various foods were cooked in baskets, or sometimes in pottery, with liquid.

Preservation was facilitated by hermetic sealing of perishable foods with pine pitch. Large granaries were used for storing enormous quantities of food, such as acorns (figs. 4-5); and ollas were used to store seeds. In times of famine natural caches, the food stores of rodents and birds, were raided for food (Bean 1972).

Title Insurance and Trust Company, Los Angeles.
Fig. 4. Woman filling a granary with acorns. Photograph possibly by C.C. Pierce, about 1900.

Title Insurance and Trust Company, Los Angeles.
Fig. 5. Large granary for storing mesquite beans at Torres-Martinez Reservation. Photograph by C.C. Pierce, 1903.

Technology

Baskets were made of a grass (*Epicampes rigens*) for the warp, a reed grass (*Juncus robustus* or *Rhus trilobata*) for the weft, and either elder or suede species for black dye. Yellow, red, brown, and greenish colors were obtained from different portions of juncus.

Coiled wares were of four types: flat baskets for plates or trays for winnowing; shallow baskets—receptacles for food or for parching corn or seeds; deep baskets, large and shaped like inverted cones used for carrying along with a net; and globular, flat-bottomed baskets used to keep small utensils and trinkets. Cosmologically significant beings (*núkatem*) such as eagle, lightning, and stars were the most commonly used motifs in basket design (Bean 1972; Kroeber 1925).

Cahuilla pottery was often painted and incised. It was a light, thin, brittle red ware made by coiling narrow cylinders of ropes of clay. This was then patted between a smooth, rounded stone and a wooden paddle. Five principal forms of pottery existed: small-mouthed jars (fig. 6), cooking pots, open bowls, dishes, and pipes (Kroeber 1908b).

Stone implements (besides the mortars, pestles, and metates) included the arrow straightener, fashioned from soapstone and incised with linear designs having magical connotations and indicating ownership (Kroeber 1908b).

Bows of willow or mesquite were narrow, thick, and strung with a mescal fiber or sinew. Arrows varied in shape, size, and design, depending upon the use to which they were put (Kroeber 1908b).

Ceremonial implements included charmstones, bull-roarers, clappers, rattles, feathered headdresses and wands, and eagle-feathered skirts worn by ritualists (fig. 7). The principal ceremonial object was the *máyswut* (or

Fig. 7. Sylvestro Saubel dressed as an Eagle Dancer. He is wearing a skirt and cape of eagle feathers and is holding what appear to be ceremonial wands. Photographed before 1905.

máyswat), which was brought out of the ocean by Coyote. Known as "heart of the house," the *máyswut* was passed from clan leader to his successor in the paternal line (Bean 1972; Bean and Saubel 1972).

Clothing included sandals, made of mescal fibers soaked in mud to whiten them and held to the foot with strips of the same fibers or buckskin (fig. 8). Mescal and yucca fibers were used to make rope and cordage. Women wore skirts made from mesquite bark, skins, and tules. Mesquite bark was also used as diapers for babies. Men usually wore a loincloth and hide shoes or sandals (fig. 9). Warmth was provided by blankets or rabbitskin strips woven together (Kroeber 1908b).

Games and Music

Games had an important place in Cahuilla society, men's involving very strenuous physical activity where endurance and ability to withstand physical punishment were

Fig. 6. Earthenware jar with painted design in yellow ocher. Diameter 32.0 cm, collected in 1876.

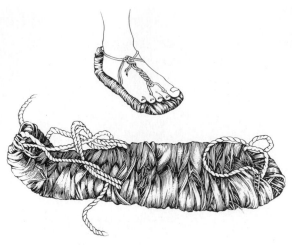

Dept. of Anthr., Smithsonian: 219341.

Fig. 8. Sandal made of a fiber cord foundation, toe and heel loop, and woven bunches of yucca fibers. Worn only on rough or thorny ground. Extended length 33.0 cm, collected in 1875.

basic to the winning of the game. Moiety played against moiety, lineage against lineage, and individual against individual, with wagers placed on the outcome of many games. Men engaged in foot races, demonstrated their skill with the bow and arrow, and played the guessing game *taxnénŋiľ* 'hiding each other' (called *peón* by the Spanish). Women favored foot races, juggling, guessing games, cat's cradle, top spinning, jackstones, and balancing objects.

Music pervaded all activities. Tribal cosmology and history were recorded in songs, and songs accompanied games, secular dances, shamanic activities, and hunting and food-gathering activities. Musical instruments included the flute (made of elder); whistles; pan-pipes; flageolets (made of bone); and rattles of turtle shells, deer hoofs, split sticks, seashells, gourds, and dried cocoons. Most musical expression was vocal (Bean 1972).

Hygiene and Diseases

Bodily cleanliness was emphasized; regular bathing and sweating were routinized (Strong 1929:138). There was

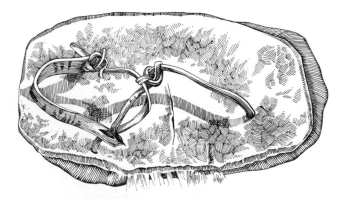

Dept. of Anthr., Smithsonian: 207604.

Fig. 9. Rawhide sandal with a double sole. Length 26.5 cm, collected in 1900.

concern for the proper cleaning of cooking utensils, mortars, manos, baskets, and ollas, because the presence of foreign particles on any of this equipment was considered a great disgrace.

Diseases frequently mentioned are bronchial infections, gastrointestinal disorders, tuberculosis, hepatitis, infections in wounds and sores, blood poisoning, rheumatism, and arthritis. Trichinae and tularemia may also have caused health problems because of ingestion of poorly cooked meats or by handling game that had been infected. Infanticide was condemned among the Cahuilla, but private and individually determined cases of infanticide by suffocation are recalled (Bean 1972:81).

Social and Political Organization

The Cahuilla, a nonpolitical, cultural nationality speaking a common language, recognized two nonterritorial, nonpolitical patrimoieties, *túktem* (Wildcats) and *ʔístam* (Coyotes) (adapted from Kroeber 1962). The Cahuilla were organized into political-ritual-corporate units (clans) composed of 3–10 lineages, dialectically different, named, claiming a common genitor, with one lineage recognized as the founding one. Each lineage within the clan cooperated in defense, in large communal subsistence activities, and in performing rituals. Founding lineages often owned the office of ceremonial leader, the ceremonial house, and a ceremonial bundle (*máyswut*), while other ceremonial offices were distributed throughout the lineages. Although each lineage owned a village site and specific resource areas, most of the clan territory was open to all Cahuillas (Bean 1972:85–86).

The office of lineage leader (*nét*) was usually inherited from father to eldest son and wherever possible kept within a direct line of descent. The *nét* was responsible for the correct maintenance of rituals, care of the ceremonial bundle, and upkeep of the ceremonial house (*kíš ʔámnawet* 'big house'). He was an economic executive, determining where and when people gathered foods or hunted game, administering first-fruit rites, and storing collecting goods for community use (ceremonial, subsistence, or exchange to other groups). He knew boundaries and ownership rights and adjudicated conflict with binding decisions. His sanctioning authority was the *máyswut*, the symbolic representation of the lineage and the link between the sacred past and the present. He met with the *nét*s from other lineages concerning land use, boundary disputes, marriage arrangements, trade, warfare, and ceremonial decisions.

The *nét* was assisted in his ceremonial, administrative, and adjudicative functions by the *páxaʔ*. This office tended to be hereditary, the *páxaʔ* arranging the details for proper order and performance of many rituals and seeking out and punishing anyone who transgressed ritual rules. He told ceremonialists when to perform, contacted the people who were to contribute food, instructed them in what to bring, and saw to it that protocol was maintained in the proper distribution of food and gifts during ceremonies.

A *háwaynik* or *háwawaynik* 'ceremonial talker, singer' was a songleader and ceremonialist who possessed and sang ceremonial songs used at rites of passage and intensification. Song cycles were long and complex, some requiring several days to perform. The *háwaynik* trained assistant singers and dancers so mythical events could be enacted.

Among the most revered and simultaneously feared members of the community were the *púvulam* 'shamans' (singular *pú·l*). These individuals, always male, through the manipulation of supernaturally acquired power cured illness (naturally or supernaturally caused), divined, controlled natural phenomena such as rain, created food, witched, acted as guardians during ceremonies (keeping away ghosts, malevolent spirits, evil beings or evil power), and in conjunction with the *nét* and *páxaʔ* exercised political authority over the community at large. Especially powerful shamans, called *páʔvuʔul*, were able to transform themselves into animals, and unlike the *púvulam*, could kill a person instantly through supernatural means. However, a shaman's status was secure only through reaffirmation of his power through public and private demonstrations of abilities (fig. 10).

Shamans formed an elite group in society, acting together along with the *nét* and *páxaʔ* as leaders who expressed opinions and made decisions, especially in times of disasters and epidemics. The *nét* and *púvulam*, controlling the political structure by weaving it into a tightly interacting group, thereby increased their power over the community. Thus, an association of *púvulam* cut across clan and lineage boundaries to form an interclan, intertribal association of power-oriented persons.

A diviner (*tétʔayawiš* or *tétʔayawniš* 'dreamer') foretold future events, found lost objects, located trespassers on clan or lineage property, and located game animals and new food sources.

Persons who secretly possessed supernatural power were called nenananiš. They had no formal position in the social hierarchy. Many women are said to have possessed supernatural powers and to have used them to effect magical control over others or predict future events.

The *tíŋʔayvaš* or *tíŋʔaywet* 'doctor', in sharp contrast to the other statuses in Cahuilla society, was not necessarily connected with supernatural power. Most were women who learned their medical lore from some other *tíŋʔayvaš* or shaman. As they learned through experience and became known and trusted in the community, they were employed in their profession. A *tíŋʔayvaš* was middle-aged or older and possessed great knowledge concerning medicinal herbs and the specifics for various conditions or ailments, such as childbirth, wounds, broken bones, or intestinal discomfort.

Malki Mus., Banning, Calif.

Fig. 10. Salvador Lopez, a shaman, at the dedication ceremony of the Malki Museum. He was the last of the fire eaters and is shown here with hot coals of mesquite in his mouth. Photograph by Bill Jennings, Feb. 1965.

• MARRIAGE AND KINSHIP Spouses, selected by parents from members of the opposite moiety, were from families unrelated within five generations. An ideal husband was responsible to his kin obligations, skilled, and diligent in economic pursuit or religious acumen. Young girls were expected to be hard working, get along well with their in-laws, produce food efficiently, and bear male children. Upon marriages the husband's family presented gifts of food and goods to the wife's kin group, and she was brought to the house of the boy's parents and taught wifely duties by her mother-in-law. When a child was born, a long-range economic and social alliance between two families was established, characterized by frequent reciprocal exchange of gifts of food and treasure goods. Most marriages occurred between Cahuillas but some crossed cultural boundaries, for example, Luiseño, Chemehuevi, and Gabrielino.

Divorces were difficult unless a wife was sterile, incorrigibly nonproductive, or lazy. A spouse's death did not destroy the partnership between families, since sororate and levirate rules were often activated.

Kin relationships, memorized by everyone while young, were based on criteria of age, sex, lineality, affinity, sex of speaker, sex of connecting relative, and perhaps locality. The system, Dakota with Iroquois terminology and bifurcate merging of parents and their siblings, was particularistic with a minimum amount of merging (Bean 1972:93; Kroeber 1908b; Tax 1955).

Formal joking relationships existed between kin in the form of verbal jokes, horseplay, and ribald references. These correlated closely with the principles of kin determination and basic Cahuilla values, as age, generation, and lineality determined the nature of the relationships.

Familiar kin terms (equivalent to daddy and mom) were also used. These were limited to collateral, affinal, or female lineal relatives, thus often people who lived outside ego's village.

Proper social and economic role distinctions were clearly reflected in the Cahuilla kinship system, which extended beyond the nuclear family to embrace relatives five generations removed from ego. Further extensions were accomplished affinally. Corporate assets, rights, and responsibilities within the lineage were determined by the rules of kinship (Gifford 1918).

Emergency conditions such as widowhood and orphanhood with their economic consequences were taken into account within the system. Older brother's social role was that of surrogate father to his younger brothers. Differentiation of age and directness operated to insure the equitable and clearly defined distribution of corporate goods and regulated decision-making powers within the lineage (Bean 1972).

• LAW AND PROPERTY Cahuilla law, embodied in oral literature, provided Cahuilla administrators with precedent and authority for proper behavior and punishment. Laws were reinforced through ritual, story, anecdote, and action. Supernaturally imposed automatic retribution was expected when actions went against tradition, but more direct sanctions ranged from individual ridicule to public execution.

Ownership of the territorial units was established by boundaries marked by petroglyphs, stones, or geographic features and by oral traditions, which set the precise boundaries. Clan territory was jointly owned by all members. Each lineage owned particular sections of land (village sites, food-gathering and hunting areas, areas of raw materials), traditional stories, songs, and anecdotes. Subsistence and ritual equipment were also owned by individuals and could be sold or loaned (Strong 1929).

War and Trade

Disputes were usually over economic resources because of poaching or trespassing or because a lineage failed to fulfill its responsibilities in the reciprocal ritual system. Sorcery against another lineage, personal insults, kidnapping of women, nonpayment of bride price, and theft were other reasons for going to war, but armed conflict was attempted only when all other efforts failed. The *nét* or a skillful warrior served as a temporary war party, and a community ritual was performed before and after conflict. Combat usually involved ambush, and weapons used were war clubs and bows and arrows with poisoned arrowheads (Bean 1972).

Trade, between individuals and groups, occurred frequently with some Cahuillas specializing as traders, visiting as far west as Santa Catalina and east to the Gila River to get goods. Gabrielino traded steatite, asphaltum, and shell beads for food products, furs, hides, obsidian, and salt. Rituals and songs were also exchanged. Tourmaline was acquired from the Luiseño and Joshua tree blossoms from the Serrano of the Mojave Desert. Colorado River people exchanged agricultural products (corn, melons, squash, gourds), turquoise, and grooved axes. Craftsmen exchanged their wares—such as baskets, pottery, bows and arrows, and eagle-feathered skirts—for service and goods. Shell beads provided a general medium of exchange (Service 1966).

Cosmology

Cahuilla cosmology recognized ʔívaʔal, a power or energy source, as the creative force of a systematic but potentially unstable and unpredictable universe. Although ʔívaʔal was neither good nor bad, it was quixotic and therefore made all things subject to unpredictable change. Because of the unpredictable nature of ʔívaʔal, the all-pervasive and intense feeling of apprehension of the Cahuilla toward the present and future was a realistic orientation to an environment full of real and continual changes.

The presence of power explained all unusual talents or unusual events and differences in cultural attainment, and all phenomena that contained ʔívaʔal were capable of negative and positive actions. Individuals were prepared to deal with contrasting qualities in all phenomena, and since man was an intregal part of nature and the universe was an interacting system, an ecological ethic existed that assumed any action affected all other parts of the system (Bean 1972).

A number of beings inhabited the universe and some were active in Cahuilla affairs as symbols reminding the people of the "early times," while others were associated with the control of ʔívaʔal (e.g., tákuš, kutyáyʔal). The téwlavelem, or soul spirits, existed in the body of the living and had a separate existence after an individual's death. Then they went to the land of the dead (télmekiš), east of Cahuilla territory, where all téwlavelem and those núkatem lived (first people created) who no longer dwelt on earth. Most téwlavelem reached télmekiš after arduous ritual on both the part of the living and themselves. Messages were passed from télmekiš to the living, so the téwlavelem were directly involved in Cahuilla social life—advising, sanctioning, and aiding those still on earth (Bean 1972).

Cahuilla values were clearly related to basic environmental and economic circumstances. Tradition was authority, and the past was the referent for the present and future. Correct behavior and access to power were correlates of one another, and innovative actions were seen as potentially dangerous. Oral literature was quoted to assess the value or appropriateness of taking action in crisis situations.

Old age was a criterion for privilege, power, and honor. The Creator Gods struggled to establish who was the older. *múkat,* the successful one, demonstrated that older people were more cautious, precise, and orderly and had more creative power than did the younger people. Elders functioned as repositories of knowledge and lore that fostered adaptation to a diverse and sometimes harsh environment. The aged taught the values and skills necessary for successful adult life and for survival of the young. Older women made baskets and rabbitskin blankets and nets, ground seeds, and performed other time-consuming tasks. They taught young girls the techniques and values of womanhood. The older men manufactured arrowheads, bows, rabbit sticks, and hunting nets. They taught boys the traditional values of the society as well as the intricacies of hunting techniques, which fostered the maximum learning for successful adulthood.

Reciprocity was a pervasive value. A well-balanced and rigidly enforced system of reciprocal relations operated at every level of society as well as throughout the universe. Each Cahuilla was taught and encouraged to share possessions, food, and capital equipment. It was proper to give and receive, neither action requiring much formal recognition. Failure to reciprocate was a serious breach of behavioral norms, one punished by public sanctions and ridicule. Accompanying reciprocity were fairness and equality. Lineages and clans reciprocated in collecting privileges by invitations to collect and hunt in one another's areas when surpluses were apparent.

Doing things slowly, in an orderly procedure, deliberately, and thinking about all the ramifications of one's actions were stressed to every Cahuilla. Haste and misplaced sympathy resulted in inappropriate actions in the realities of the world. Rituals were required in the attempt to control and eliminate error anticipated in an unpredictable world.

Integrity and dependability in personal relations were sought constantly and were evident in the manner in which Cahuillas presented information to one another. Actions were expected to be as explicit and direct as possible in order to reduce misunderstandings while simultaneously being correct.

That secrecy and caution in dealing with knowledge was always necessary is repeatedly reflected in Cahuilla oral literature and everyday life. The judicious use of knowledge brought praises and reward; failure generated severe punishment.

Ritual

Ritual was a constant factor in the life of every Cahuilla—always directly ahead or immediately finished. Some rituals were scheduled and routine, while others were of a sporadic and situational nature. Strong (1929) and Bean (1972) have described most Cahuilla rituals in detail. Of the 10 or more types of ritual, the most significant were the *núkil* (annual mourning ceremony), eagle ceremony, certain rites of passage (the most important being birth, naming, adolescent initiation, marriage), public performances announcing status changes of adults (e.g., when a new *nét* assumed office), and rituals aimed at improving subsistence resources. The central focus of most of these rituals was the performance of cosmologically oriented song cycles that placed the universe in perspective and reaffirmed the relationship of the Cahuilla (both the individual and the collective) to the sacred past, to the present, to one another, and to all things.

History

It is likely that the Cahuilla were both aware of and affected by European institutions well before the Spanish first passed through their area in 1774, the Juan Bautista de Anza expedition. That first contact found them hostile to Europeans. Subsequently, Europeans used sea routes to populate California, because the Quechan Indians closed the land route in 1781. The Cahuilla consequently had little direct contact with Europeans except for those baptized at missions in San Gabriel, San Luis Rey, and San Diego and thus integrated into the mission system. In 1819 several *asistencias* were established near the Cahuilla area (San Bernadino, Santa Ysabel, Pala); and Cahuillas became partially involved with the Spanish and adopted some Spanish cultural forms—cattle, agriculture, operations, trade, wage labor, clothing, language, and religion (Beattie and Beattie 1939).

A conservative estimate of the aboriginal Cahuilla population is 3,600 (Hicks 1931). Bean (1972) has suggested that the population may have been as high as 6,000 to 10,000 (table 2) based on an estimate of 80 lineages. Government census figures of Indian villages in the 1850s in which several villages were said to have numbered from 150 to 300 persons (Harvey 1968:190) support this estimate. The larger number seems possible when more lacustrine conditions prevailed.

European diseases probably affected Cahuillas even before contact. Settlement patterns were only slightly changed as Cahuilla lands were used for cattle grazing. Some Cahuillas worked seasonally for the Spaniards and would return to their villages. By the time of the American invasion of California, the Cahuilla still maintained their political and economic autonomy. A principal function of leaders at the time was to articulate the Cahuilla peoples to Europeans, as it had been in the past

Table 2. Population Estimates 1770–1970

Year	Population	Source
1770	6,000	Bean 1972
	2,500	Kroeber 1925
1860	3,238	County of Los Angeles Census 1860
1863	(Smallpox epidemic)	
1865	1,181	Harvey 1968:193
1883	1,036	Harvey 1968:193
1888	463 (Cahuilla, Los Coyotes, Morongo, and Agua Caliente only)	Harvey 1968:193
1891	1,156	Harvey 1968:193
1892	1,262	Shipek 1971
1955	535	H.C. James 1960
1970	1,629	U.S. Bureau of the Census 1971

with other Indians. When the Americans came to California they were involved with conflicting strategies but maintained their political and economic autonomy. Leaders like Juan Antonio and Cabeson represented them in treaty negotiations in 1851 and acted as liaison between their culture and Americans in legal, economic, and political affairs. The grestest blow to Cahuilla culture and society came in 1863 when a smallpox epidemic killed a large number. From that time on the Cahuillas were in a more dependent and defenseless condition vis-a-vis Americans, who were coming in increasing numbers to their area (Beattie and Beattie 1939; Phillips 1971).

From that time until reservations were established in 1877 and until federal supervision became close and intensive in 1891, the Cahuillas remained for the most part on their own lands, making a living in combination with aboriginal techniques, wage labor, and the like. After 1891 their economic, political, and social life was closely supervised by the federal government. Government schools were opened in which young Cahuillas were trained in rather menial roles, Protestant missionaries became influential, and much traditional Cahuilla life was altered. Cahuilla cultural institutions were generally suppressed, particularly religious and political ones. Despite this, Cahuillas were successful in maintaining a diversified economic strategy until the allotment programs divided lands into such small parcels that agricultural development was difficult (Bean 1972).

From this time until the 1930s, the Cahuilla were variously supported from their reservation land bases—subsistence farming, cattle, leasing lands—and wage labor, Indian Service employment, and the like. The

reservation political organization was closely controlled by Indian Service personnel residing on the reservation. This supervision was constantly protested by reservation peoples as well as formal protest organizations that cross-cut reservations, like the Mission Indian Federation. The Indian Reorganization Act resulted in increased political autonomy. The Second World War affected labor patterns; and immediately following, partial termination of federal supervision for California Indians forced Cahuillas to become more involved in health, education, welfare, and economic development from local to federal levels. Reservation governments (elected councils) had to rely less upon Bureau of Indian Affairs gratuities and services (Bean 1972).

In the 1960s new opportunities from federal resources became available. Various programs financed by the Office of Economic Opportunity and other agencies significantly changed conditions of health, education, and welfare for Cahuillas.

There were approximately 900 people claiming Cahuilla descent in 1974; most of these were enrolled on one of several reservations (table 3; "History of Southern California Mission Indians," fig. 1) organized as political and corporate units administered by elected business committees in conjunction with the Bureau of Indian Affairs. They also have committees that aid in the day-to-day administration and provide advice and consent capacities to the group (Bean 1972).

Each reservation interlocks with a network of other reservations in temporary and permanent associates. Consequently, some belong to county-wide, state-wide, and national Indian organizations like those for Mission Indians (see "Luiseño", this vol.).

Occupational specialization among the Cahuilla includes independent businesses, such as cattle raising and farming, as well as secretarial, civil-service, construction, teaching, public-health, blue-collar, and social-work positions. Generally, Cahuillas in the 1970s acquired income from a variety of sources, private lands, and businesses, as well as tribal enterprises when it is feasible. The economic situation appears to be rather poor, but the diversified way in which Cahuillas acquire income may obscure the actual nature of economic income.

The economic situation of the Cahuilla is complicated by the nature of land ownership and location in areas far from markets, water, service roads, and job opportunity. However, economic development plans have been instituted on most reservations. For example, Los Coyotes Reservation has opened a campground facility, and others have written economic development programs (Bean 1977).

Religious affiliations are mixed; most Cahuillas are practicing Catholics, but some are Protestants. Some reservations are still served by the Verona Fathers from Santa Ysabel Mission; others, by priests in local commu-

Table 3. Population and Land Status

Reservation	Tribal composition	1970 population[b] total/reservation	1975 Land area (acres)[c] total	allotted	Economic resources
Agua Caliente, 1891[a]	Cahuilla	164/164	25,899		real estate
Augustine, 1891	Cahuilla-Chemehuevi	2/0	(616) [d] 342	150	agriculture
Cabazon, 1876	Cahuilla	22/6	(2,160) [d] 1,153	548	agriculture
Cahuilla, 1875	Cahuilla	89/23	18,272		agriculture, recreation, real estate
Los Coyotes, 1889	Cupeño-Cahuilla	106/42	25,050		timber, recreation, real estate
Morongo, 1876	Serrano-Cahuilla-Cupeño	652/242	(32,254) [d] 30,957	1,286	agriculture, cattle, recreation
Ramona, 1891	Cahuilla	2/0	560		cattle grazing
Santa Rosa, 1891	Cahuilla	61/7	11,093		recreation, cattle grazing
Soboba, 1883	Cahuilla	314/178	5,036		recreation
Torres-Martinez, 1876	Cahuilla-Chemehuevi	217/42	(31,696) [d] 18,223	6,881	recreation

[a] Date of executive order establishing reservation.

[b] U.S. Bureau of the Census 1971.

[c] U.S. Bureau of Indian Affairs, Southern California Agency 1975. Figures rounded to nearest acre.

[d] Amount of land originally set aside. Theoretically, nonallotted reservations have not lost any land. To determine approximate amount of land alienated from allotted reservations, subtract 1975 total from figure in parentheses.

nities. Cahuilla traditional religions are dominant in funeral ceremonies.

Educational opportunities have increased in recent years, and the level of achievement has advanced rapidly. More Cahuillas are graduating from high school, and many are in college programs, both academic and trade oriented. Adult education programs enjoy vigorous participation.

Residence varies from reservation to reservation. Most Cahuillas live off the reservation, because of water conditions, job opportunities, and the like; but most express a desire to live and occupy the reservations, which are the principal land and identity base for all generations. Settlement patterns on reservations are dispersed. Cahuilla society is extending its identity to a general pan-Indian order while maintaining a sense of ethnic identity that is still Cahuilla (fig. 11). Cahuillas are becoming more organizationally adept in Indian and non-Indian political and economic strategies, transferring traditional organizational principles very frequently to new conditions (Bean 1977). This is especially so in the relationship with state and federal bureaus that are

involved with the Cahuillas in addition to the Bureau of Indian Affairs (Bean 1972).

Important institutions have been developed to supplant and serve needs that others have not served adequately. The Malki Museum, Morongo Indian Health Clinic, and Torres-Martinez Historical Society are examples.

Although somewhat modified, many traditional values continue in the 1970s to operate in economic, political, and social affairs, though institutions for enforcing them are not conspicuous. Traditional foods are sometimes used, especially at ritual or social events, like fiestas. Kin relationships, especially in the extended family, remain important, and among a few families kin terminology and attendant role behavior is still used. Traditional concern for individualistic ownership of productive goods remains an important value, as does reciprocity.

In religious affairs funeral ceremonies and memorial services for the dead, directly related to the *núkil* ceremonies (Bean 1972), are practiced. Only two reservations still maintain ceremonial structures, while at other reservations any available structure is used. The ceremonies

585

Malki Mus., Banning, Calif.

Fig. 11. Gene Pablo chipping an arrowpoint. Photograph by Bill Jennings, at Morongo Reservation, Aug. 1965.

are reduced in content, but the basic patterns—singing the creation epic and feting guests— are maintained.

Some personal rituals (e.g., menstrual) are still observed. Traditional supernatural power techniques for acquiring "luck" and influencing the use of power malevolently continues in some interfamily and interpersonal relations. One traditional game *(taxnénɲilʸ)* is still frequently practiced, using traditional equipment and songs. Wagering remains an important feature of this game, and players receive considerable prestige by demonstrating their skill at it. Various nonreligious songs and dances are remembered. Bird songs are sung on some holidays and at fiestas. A few other song types are remembered but rarely performed.

Until recently, Cahuilla was a dying language with only older people speaking it with fluency. However, language classes have started in some communities and a few families are teaching the language to their children.

On the Morongo Reservation the Cahuilla have established the Malki Museum, a repository for artifacts and ethnographic knowledge ("History of Southern California Mission Indians," fig. 3, this vol.; Bean 1977).

Synonymy

The Cahuilla refer to themselves as *ʔívitem* or *ʔívilʸuwenetem* meaning the people who speak *ʔíviʔat* or *ʔívilʸuʔat*, which is what they call their language. Their closest neighbors, the Cupeño, call the Cahuilla *íswətim* 'wolves' (which is one of the Cahuilla clans) or *támikawičəm* 'people from the east'. They are also called 'easterners' by the Luiseño (*kʷímkačum*) and the Gabrielino (*kumiˑtaraxam*).

They have also been known by the following names: Cowela, Cowillas, Dancers, Danzarines, Gecuiches, Hakwiche, Jecuches, Jecuéche, Jecuiches, Kahuilla, Kahweaks, Kah-we-as, Kahweyahs, Kauvuyas, kau-yaíchits, Kavayos, Kavwaru-Maup, Koahualla, and Tecuiche (Hodge 1907–1910, 1:669); Cahahaguillas (Bean and Mason 1962); and Coahuillas (Barrows 1900).

Sources

A wealth of archival resources is available on all periods of Cahuilla history. The J.P. Harrington ethnographic notes in the National Anthropological Archives in the Smithsonian and letters and correspondence of agents, missionaries, and historians at the Huntington Library, San Marino (H.N. Rust, William Weinland, Cave Couts, Grace Nicholson, George and Helen Beattie Collections) are valuable. The Bancroft Library, University of California, Berkeley, has numerous resources covering all periods, the most significant of which are the D.P. Barrows Collection, the Anza Expedition Reports, numerous state and federal documents, Estudillo Papers, provincial state papers, and papers from various missions in California. Other institutions holding materials are the Southwest Museum, Los Angeles; Museum of Man, San Diego; Malki Museum, Morongo Indian Reservation; National Archives, Washington, D.C.; and the Library of the Museum of the American Indian, New York.

An extensive bibliography of Cahuilla materials is listed in Bean and Lawton (1967), while descriptive accounts of material culture, social organization, ritual, and myth are available in Barrows (1900), Strong (1929), Kroeber (1908b, 1925), Hooper (1920), H.C. James (1960), Curtis (1907–1930, 15), Bean (1964, 1972), Bean and Lawton (1965), and Bean and Saubel (1972). The works of Bean, Curtis, and James provided new interpretations and data on both aboriginal and historical matters. Several intensive linguistic studies have been done, the most comprehensive being Seiler (1957, 1958, 1965, 1967, 1970) and Bright (1965a).

Several books on the Cahuilla of the 1800s are available, in particular Bean and Mason (1962) and Phillips (1971).

There are five main museum collections of Cahuilla material items: Malki Museum; Lowie Museum of Anthropology, University of California, Berkeley; Southwest Museum; Museum of the American Indian; and the

National Museum of Natural History, Smithsonian Institution, Washington,

There is little archeological material on the Cahuilla. Only tentative surveys have been accomplished revealing settlement patterns, trail complexes (Meighan 1958-1959; F. Johnston 1967; Ruby 1961-1962), and petroglyphs.

Much of this chapter was drawn from Bean (1972), particularly the sections on social and political organization and cosmology.

Cupeño

LOWELL JOHN BEAN AND CHARLES R. SMITH

Language and Territory

The Cupeño (kōō'pā͵nyō), one of the smallest linguistic groups in sourthern California (less than 750 people), occupied an area more or less circular in shape about 10 miles in diameter in a mountainous area at the headwaters of the San Luis Rey River and encompassing the broad open valley of San Jose de Valle. The Cupeño language belongs to the Cupan subgroup of the Takic family of Uto-Aztecan (Bright and Hill 1967; Lamb 1964). Within Cupan, Cupeño is closer to Cahuilla than to Luiseño. As the Cupeño were bordered on the south by the Yuman-speaking Ipai, a few Yuman linguistic elements appear in their language.*

Ecologically, Cupeño territory was quite similar to that of the Luiseño, but unlike them, the Cupeño had no direct access to the sea coast. Their principal foods were acorns, small seeds, berries, cactus fruit, deer, quail, rabbits, and other small mammals.

Prior to 1902 the Cupeño occupied two permanent villages: *kúpa* (at the base of Hot Springs mountain) and the smaller and more linguistically mixed village of *wilákalpa* (fig. 1). Although united by marriage and social intercourse, the two villages were politically independent. Table 1 describes the relationships of moiety and clan within the villages. The clans were bound by social, religious, and territorial ties; but each maintained its distinctness, had its own gathering areas, and usually had its own clan leader.

Culture

Cupeño social organization was complex and represented the amalgamation of several historically different

* Several orthographies have been used for Cupeño. Perhaps the most representative is the "morphophonemic" level orthography in Jacobs (1974). An orthography modified for use by nonlinguists, emphasizing maximum pronouncibility with mimimum need for rule application, is in Hill and Nolasquez (1973). Italicized Cupeño words in this Handbook have been respelled by Jane H. Hill (with doubtful spellings indicated by parenthetical question marks) using the Hill-Nolasquez orthography with the following substitutions of symbols to agree with Handbook standards: *e* for Hill-Nolasquez ɛ, ə for their e, raised dot for vowel length where Hill-Nolasquez write a double vowel, č for ch, š for sh, ṣ for sh, *k*ʷ for kw, *x*ʷ for xw, *q*ʷ for qw, ʔ for ', δ for d, γ for g, *n*ʸ for ny, ŋ for ng, *l*ʸ for ly. *R* is a continuant while *r* is a flap; these and *f*, δ, γ are relatively rare sounds that appear in words borrowed from Spanish and English. Stress is marked ', where Hill-Nolasquez underline the vowel.

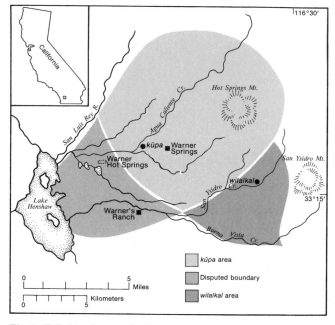

Fig. 1. Tribal territory and villages.

groups—an amalgamation that began as early as A.D. 1000–1200 and resulted in a new tradition, rooted in Cahuilla customs but "changed by an intricate interaction with the peoples around them" (Hill and Nolasquez 1973:i). While maintaining the complex Cahuilla social organization of exogamous moieties, patrilineal clans, and ceremonial exchange parties, they acquired some of the Chingichngish religious rituals from the Luiseño, to which they added an "older complex of funerary rituals" while exchanging and adopting ceremonies with the Ipai (Hill and Nolasquez 1973:i).

The most productive food-gathering spots were owned by clans, with the intervening areas free to all for both hunting and gathering. Each clan was headed by a *nə́t*, an office that usually passed from father to eldest son. If that son was thought unfit, a younger son or an uncle in a collateral line might serve as *nə́t*. The *nə́t* kept the clan bundle and lived in the clan's ceremonial dance house. His duties included controlling trade with non-Cupeño groups, regulating production and distribution of goods, articulating intra- and interclan relationships, deciding when ceremonies would be held and who would be invited, and collecting and distributing goods and gifts to

Table 1. Moieties and Clans

Village	Moieties	Clans	Supposed Origin
kúpa	Coyote (íslʸam)	kávalim[a]	Cupeño
		pəmtəmʔa	Cupeño
		túlnikčam	
		təmáxawəčim	Cupeño
	Wildcat (túktam)	sivimúʔatim	Ipai-Tipai
		áwlinvaʔačim	Ipai-Tipai
		takáʔatim	Luiseño
wilákalpa	Wildcat (túktam)	čútnikat	Ipai-Tipai
		tə́švikiya	Cahuilla

[a] The sáwvəlim clan is a group of Cahuilla who moved from Los Coyotes canyon about 1840. Since that time they have lived with the kávalim clan on their lands and subject to the kávalim clan leader's authority.

guests at ceremonies. Everyday affairs concerning an entire village were discussed by all the nə́t until a mutually satisfactory decision was reached.

The clan leader's assistant was the kutvə́ʔvaʔaš, a hereditary office, passing in a lineage as did clan leadership. In addition to being an administrative assistant the kutvə́ʔvaʔaš performed certain organizational functions at ceremonies, saying prayers and distributing goods.

Sometimes a nə́t would also be a shaman, although this did not have to be the case. Shamans were powerful, respected, and often feared members of their community. Their supernatural power, acquired individually through trances and dreams, enabled them to hear and understand natural and supernatural phenomena, divine, cure, and witch. Certain powerful shamans could influence crop growth, while especially powerful ones could transform themselves into deer or bears (Hill and Nolasquez 1973: 91; Gifford 1918:209).

Most marriages were parentally arranged, a boy's parents selecting the prospective wife, exchanging gifts with the girl's parents, and taking the couple to the nə́t of the boy's clan, and in his presence holding a feast and distributing gifts. Postmarital residence was usually patrilocal.

Children were born away from the villages and brought back when they were about two to three weeks old. At a later date they were given names at special naming ceremonies given by any clan having several children to name (Strong 1929:254). When girls were between 9 and 10 years old they underwent a puberty ceremony, each clan hosting its own, while boys between 10 and 18 went through an initiation ceremony. Both rituals signified the transition from child status to adult status.

Perhaps the most significant ceremonies for all involved were those held in connection with deaths in the clan. The first was actually a series of three ceremonies: the burning of the deceased body almost immediately after death; the burning of all the deceased's possessions a few weeks to several months later; and the annual or biannual image-burning ceremony, which devoted as many as eight days and nights to feasting, dancing, and singing and which culminated with a burning of images of all those who had died since the last ceremony.

Another ceremony held in memory of the dead was the eagle-killing ritual, held once a year, usually by the kávalim clan since they owned the only eagle nest, and hence the rights to the eagle, in Cupeño territory. If no kávalim clan member had died the eagle was given to the opposite-moiety clan in which deaths had occurred. This ritual gift was only a small manifestation of a much larger economic-ritual reciprocity organization operating throughout southern California and the functional equivalent of the "elaborate shell money exchange" found in northern California (Strong 1929:263).

Cupeño cosmology and values were essentially like those of the Cahuilla. The world was divided into three parts—below, on, and above the earth; and everything was created by təmáyawət and múkat, the twin creator gods. Most tales and myths involve the activities of the "old ones," those who lived before the Indians. Animals figured predominantly in Cupeño tales with Coyote assuming the traditional trickster-transformer role he occupied in most forms of Takic mythology. One unique Cupeño cosmological figure was a giant rabbit, a key figure in the origin tale of the kúpa clans.

History

When the Cupeño were first encountered by Europeans in 1795 they probably numbered between 500 (Kroeber 1925:689) and 750 persons (Bean 1973). From 1795 until 1810, the Cupeño had little direct contact with the Spanish; but in the next 10 years asistencias were built, cattle grazed on their lands, Europeans used the hot springs as a health spa and meeting place, and a chapel was erected at kúpa. During this period and continuing throughout the Mexican and American periods, Cupeños worked in serflike relationships to their "over lords." Shortly after United States takeover of California, a kávalim nə́t, Juan Antonio Garra, attempted to organize a revolt among all southern California Indians to either kill or drive out all foreigners. The attempt failed, Garra was executed, and kúpa was burned (Evans 1966). In the late 1890s, with their population less than 225, the Cupeño were faced with a new threat: the "owners" of Cupeño territory wanted them (Cupeños) removed. After several years of litigation, public protest (reaching national concern), and studies, the California Supreme Court ordered the Cupeños removed to Pala Reservation in Luiseño territory (see "Impact of Euro-American Exploration and Settlement," fig. 5, this vol.; fig. 2).

By 1973 less than 150 people claimed Cupeño ethnicity. Few spoke their native language, and little or nothing

Fig. 2. One of the houses that the Cupeño were moved into at Pala Reservation after their eviction from Warner's Ranch. Photograph possibly by J.O. Means, June 1928.

Fig. 3. Man with a woven yucca-fiber pack blanket. Photograph by Charles F. Lummis, about 1890s.

remained of precontact lifeways, although there was some ritual involvement in funeral ceremonies, both intra- and interreservation.

Synonymy

The word Cupeño is of Spanish derivation, adopting the native place-name *kúpa* and appending Spanish *-eño* to mean a person who lives in or comes from *kúpa*. It does not appear in the literature until 1906 (Morrison 1962:28) when Hudson called the Indians living at *kúpa* (then called Warner's Ranch) "Cupeños or Warner's Ranch Indians." Other terms applied to the Cupeño are: Jajopín, a 1795 Spanish spelling of Ipai-Tipai *xaˑkupin* 'Warner's Hot Springs' (J.J. Hill 1927:1; Couro and Hutcheson 1973:19); *xəkʷač*, the Ipai-Tipai name for the tribe (Boas 1896:261; Couro and Hutcheson 1973:20); Agua Caliente; Warner's Ranch Indians (Hodge 1907–1910, 1:27); Kupaŋakiktum, kupa-ngakitom, and cupanga-kitoms (renderings of the Cahuilla name for those living at *kúpa*) and tochil (the *wilákalpa* group) (Gifford 1918:192, normalized; Kroeber 1925:689; Forbes 1965:327); Jecuiche (Forbes 1965:327), a name also applied to the Cahuilla; chay mukatem (Harrington 1925–1928, normalized); and Qakwat (Bean 1973).

Sources

Written observations describing the Cupeño begin as early as 1795 with the writings of the Spanish explorer Juan de Grijalva (Wagner 1942). B.D. Wilson (1952) described briefly general living conditions among the

Cupeño, and Jackson and Kinney (1884) focused national attention on the deplorable living conditions forced upon the Indians of soutlᵊrn California (including the Cupeño) by the Americans. Between 1890 and 1902, Charles Lummis (1902) and the Sequoya League worked with the Cupeño in preparing a legal brief for a government report on the question of Cupeño removal.

Fig. 4. Juan Chutnikat demonstrating method of carrying a wooden mortar in a net. Photograph by John P. Harrington in 1925 or before.

BEAN AND SMITH

Anthropologists who have visited the Cupeño since 1909 have written on the following topics: Kroeber (1925), a general ethnography; Gifford (1918), the basic social definition of the amalgamated Cupeño community; Faye (1928), linguistic and ethnographic studies; Strong (1929), a study more in-depth than previously; Harrington (1925-1928), linguistic and ethnographic fieldwork; Hill (1969, 1970, 1972) and Bright (1965a), linguistics; Hill and Nolasquez (1973), oral tradition and oral literature; and Bean (1973), ethnographic and ethnobotanical studies. Unfortunately, no archeological research has been conducted in Cupeño territory.

Institutions that have collections of Cupeño material culture and/or photographs of Cupeño peoples include the Smithsonian Institution, Washington (baskets, yucca fiber blankets [fig. 3], photos) and the Cupa Cultural Center, Pala Reservation (a representative collection of material culture augmented by photos). The most outstanding photographic collection is in the San Diego Museum of Man, San Diego, California, while both the Lowie Museum of Anthropology, Berkeley, and the Museum of the American Indian, Heye Foundation, New York, have smaller photographic collections.

Archival documents are concentrated at the Bancroft Library, University of California, Berkeley (Juan José Warner Reminiscence, Paul L. Faye Papers); the Kupa Cultural Center, Pala Indian Reservation; the Malki Museum, Morongo Indian Reservation; the Junipero Serra Museum, San Diego; and the National Anthropological Archives, Smithsonian Institution, Washington (John P. Harrington field notes).

Tipai-Ipai

KATHARINE LUOMALA

Tipai ('tē₁pī) and its cognate Ipai ('ē₁pī) are names meaning 'people' that since the 1950s anthropologists have begun to use instead of Diegueño (de¹gā₁nyō) and Kamia to designate closely related, Yuman-speaking bands that, in the sixteenth century, when contact with Europeans began, occupied nearly the entire southern extreme of the present state of California and adjoining portions of northern Baja California. Except among casually horticultural Kamias, they lived on wild plants, supplemented with more small than large game, and, in places, fish.

As used here, Ipai, the northern dialectical form, covers Diegueño divisions formerly called Northern (or Northwestern) and Coastal and the northern parts of Western and Mountain Diegueño. Tipai, the southern form, covers Southern (or Eastern or Southeastern) Diegueño, Kamia, Bajeño (or Mexican) Diegueño, and the southern parts of Western and Mountain Diegueño. These divisions, hazily defined by anthropologists, have cultural and environmental differences shading into one another.

The Mission Indians of southern California include Diegueños. San Diegueño is an eighteenth-century Spanish collective name for bands living near the presidio and mission of San Diego de Alcalá, established 1769, first of a coastal chain of Franciscan missions. The name became extended to culturally and linguistically related bands south and east of the mission, including unchristianized, isolated, American bands and Mexican bands converted by Dominicans. Calling Imperial County bands Kamia unnecessarily questioned their relationship to other Diegueños, particularly Tipais.

The name Diegueño signifies whatever homogeneity distinguishes these Indians collectively from others. The names Tipai and Ipai, concise and native in origin and usage, reflect the presence of at least two principal, but overlapping, cultural and linguistic divisions.

Aboriginally lacking organized social and political unity, the autonomous, seminomadic bands of over 30 patrilineal, named clans, some hostile to one another, had no native tribal name (Luomala 1963). Nor did an individual band have a name. A person identified himself by his clan and by the settlements that the clan, led by male heads of families, fairly regularly, if intermittently, occupied during a year. Because clans were localized, except in Imperial Valley, clan name implied, albeit imprecisely, band and territory. Localization continued perhaps longer after missionization among more Tipais than Ipais.

A band or tribe not his own, a person also described by clan or by stereotype, habitat, or direction in relation to himself. Thus, reference to kʷətxal connoted mountain-dwelling runaways from clan discipline. Residents east of the speaker's terrain were ʔənʸkipa· 'eastern people'; there were also ʔəwik 'western', and kəwa·k 'south', or if south of the Mexican border, ʔəxa·kəwa·k 'southern water'. (The expression "he belongs to a different water" and numerous place-names mentioning water highlight its importance for campsites.) More broadly, residents in the northwestern sector of Ipai range were ʔəlʸkipa· connoting 'people over there'; southerners were kuməya·y. From this word, which is also applicable to certain northern clans for reasons now unclear, originated the term Kamia.

Needed is information on the tribal name people themselves prefer. Although nonpejorative, the native meaning of ti·pay and ʔi·pay encompasses both human beings and certain flora and fauna, for instance, white sage and eagles. That, since the 1940s, occasional Tipais and Ipais have employed Kameyaay as their tribal name shows the absence of a standard term to express twentieth-century tribalism.

Language

Their language, still designated Diegueño and classified in the Yuman language family, Hokan stock, has especially distinguished these bands from speakers of different Yuman languages flanking them west of the Colorado River and those of the Takic language family bordering them in northern San Diego County.* Since the 1940s linguists have confirmed the long-recognized presence of two principal dialects with many subdialects and have discovered that speakers at territorial extremes have great

* Italicized Diegueño words are in the phonemic orthography described in detail by Langdon (1970:25–49), except that č has been substituted for her c. Otherwise her symbols correspond to Handbook standards (consonants with subscript dot are alveolar, contrasting with dental equivalents). Italicized Diegueño words have been rewritten by Langdon in this orthography. However, for most uses, she prefers the practical orthography described and used by Couro and Hutcheson (1973).

difficulty communicating with each other. Although specialists differ on the names and exact geographical boundaries of these dialects, their descriptions are basically similar (Langdon 1970:1–9).

Ipai is spoken from the Pacific through northern and central San Diego County south of Takic speakers. Mesa Grande and Santa Ysabel exemplify Ipai-speaking villages. Southward it shades into Tipai at communities like Jamul, Campo, Manzanita, and Cuyapaipe, and also in Imperial Valley. In the peninsula, variation, slight at San Jose and Neji, increases southward. A third dialect has been hypothesized, therefore, to include Ha'a, San Jose de la Zorra, La Huerta de los Indios, and Ensenada. At Santa Catarina is an enclave of three Tipai-speaking families.

Children in western Baja California in the 1960s still learned Tipai first; adults acquired Spanish as a second language. In American California, the number of native speakers continually declines. Mesa Grande in the 1960s had a dozen, yet an Ipai recalled that in 1891 when he was 14 he spoke only Diegueño. Older people, knowing Spanish and English from mission or reservation schools, speak Diegueño and a smattering of another Yuman or Takic tongue, perhaps a rote-learned, borrowed chant in a myth-song cycle.

Territory and Environment

Ipai-Tipai territory extended protohistorically from approximately 33° 15' latitude in the north, with the San Luis Rey River mouth a landmark, to about 31° 30' latitude in the south, with Todos Santos Bay a likely marker. Fluidity of boundaries is indicated by Spanish missionaries finding, in the north, that Luiseños encroached south of the river mouth, displacing Ipais toward Agua Hedionda in the south; Tipais ranged into the valley between Sierras de Juárez and San Pedro de Mártir, where Dominicans established Santa Catalina Mission. From the Pacific, people ranged inland across San Diego and Imperial counties to about 115° west longitude, with Sand Hills a landmark (see fig. 1). Except immediately south of the border, Mexican Tipais were split by other Yuman-speakers into a western contingent between the Pacific and lower slopes of Sierra de Juárez, and an eastern, along sloughs between Cocopa Mountains and the Colorado delta.

The eastern boundary, from the southern end of Salton Sea, irregularly fronted other Yuman speakers, who often migrated because of feuds or changes in the Colorado floodplains, where most planted gardens. The easternmost Tipais lived along sloughs like New River and in the adjoining desert, not along the Colorado except protohistorically when a few resided among Quechans. The eastern Baja contingent, consisting of northern slough Tipais supplemented historically with refugees from western Dominican missions, roved south down sloughs and intermingled with delta Yuman speakers.

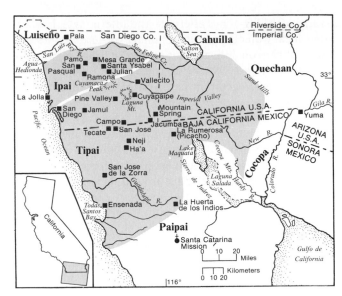

Fig. 1. Ipai and Tipai tribal territories.

On their north, Ipais encountered, from west to east, Takic-speaking Luiseños, Cupeños, and Cahuillas. As with eastern Tipais, cultural and physical intermingling that often obscured ethnic identity was accelerated during the European period.

Topographically, this territory transverses from west to east: coast, mountain, and desert. From flat or sloping coastal belt, a granitic uplifted fault block rises through a transition zone of plateaus, each higher than the preceding. Elevation climaxes in the central mountain belt, the Peninsular Range, which relates, separates, and modifies each adjacent belt. The highest peak in the Cuyamaca and Laguna mountains, American California, is over 6,500 feet. Like the foothills, the mountain belt is cut by narrow canyons, rocky hills, and flats. Its steep eastern scarp, with either rocky cliffs or, at Jacumba pass, only slightly less abrupt boulder-strewn slopes, ends in Colorado Desert, below sea level. Here is Salton Sink that modern irrigation, absent from eastern Tipai horticulture, transformed into fertile Imperial Valley. Indian bands, perhaps including Tipais, found it hospitable for about 400 years because of its 300-mile-round, freshwater Lake Cahuilla. It evaporated or became saline by approximately A.D. 1450.

In comparable peninsular topography, the peaks are in the Sierra de Juárez, of the same chain as Laguna Mountains. Its eastern scarp; the desert, Laguna Salada, below; and eastward, the Cocopa Mountains, were ordinarily not Tipai lands but Paipai or other Yuman.

Landscape shaped the travel of each seminomadic Tipai and Ipai band toward seasonal changes in altitude from valley bottom to mountain slope.

This region, although arid or subarid with Mediterranean climate of winter rains (mountain snow) and summer drought, provided varied wild plants for food and raw materials. Upper Sonoran, Lower Sonoran, and

593

Transitional life-zones alternate and intermingle. In each zone, local water supply, directional exposure, and topography of canyon, hill, and flat created stairlike microhabitats with characteristic flora and fauna.

The largest vegetation belt west of the desert was the Upper Sonoran chaparral with the predominant chamiso (*Adenostoma*) associated with oaks *(Quercus)*, wild lilac (*Ceanothus*), elderberry (*Sambucus*), and the like. Tipais in southern San Diego County and Mexico had more opuntias, yuccas, agave, and other xerophytic plants than Ipais northward. For Tipais around Jacumba and descending to Imperial Valley, southern chaparral gradually gave way to bush desert and true desert of the Lower Sonoran. East of the chaparral on dry mountain slopes were spottily distributed junipers and piñons. At higher altitudes grew Transitional flora such as yellow pine in open forests. Along the Pacific were beach and marsh plants, and, inland, grasslands and salvias. Historically, chaparral and introduced wild oats replaced unidentified native bunch grasses, which became extinct.

Prehistory

Tipai-Ipai ancestors were not the first Indians attracted to this land. Others had come even before it had acquired natural characteristics familiar to later residents (Willey 1966). About 20,000 years ago, people lived along the coast and left flint scrapers and choppers made of pebbles. About 10,000 years later, in the cool, pluvial, terminal Pleistocene and early Recent geological ages, other bands, also relatively unspecialized, exploited particular niches for food. Coastal shell middens attest to intensive fishing and fossicking. Inland campsites provide evidence for hunting big game, which was dismembered with heavy stone choppers; hides were processed with flint scrapers. Their improved tools appear in campsites between the coast and former lakes and marshes in the present Mojave and Colorado deserts.

Around 7000 B.C., perhaps from this foundation, slowly emerged two western cultural traditions, the Desert and the California Coast and Valley. Both, with many local types of plant collecting, hunting, and fishing, eventually became represented among later residents in a way to question (Kroeber 1939a:43-44, 193) whether to classify the historic Tipai-Ipai culture in the Southern California culture area (predominantly a California Coast and Valley base with specializations from the Southwestern area) or in the Peninsular culture area (predominantly a Desert base). According to the geographical sector or set of customs emphasized—that of Tipais for the Peninsular area or of Ipais for Southern California—either tradition may be stressed.

These two traditions arose as glaciers retreated and people adapted to ever drier, hotter weather. After many fluctuations, modern flora, fauna, temperatures, and topography gradually developed. Southeastern and Baja California localities, once traversed by numerous bands seeking plants and game abundant around marshes and streams, became deserts. Early sites of the Desert tradition, subsequently typical of Great Basin and eastern California tribes, including the Tipai, show by baskets and by numerous metates and mullers (formerly rare or absent) people's increasing dependence on wild plant foods, especially seeds to be parched or nuts and even bones to be ground into flour. Small, chipped-stone projectile points for darts are clues, like later arrow points, to meat mostly from small game—anything alive and not taboo—and uncommonly a large animal like a deer. Caves and probably pole-and-brush huts provided shelter. In this culture Tipais and Ipais would probably have felt at home.

After 1000 B.C. in the Arizona region local adaptations to severe desert conditions spread into adjacent parts of the Californias. Later to be incorporated into historically known Tipai-Ipai culture were new types of mortars and metates, deeper floors for huts, and cremation. Around A.D. 600, two great changes modified the collecting-hunting traditions. Lower Colorado River people, inspired probably by indirect contact with Middle American horticulture, began to plant maize, beans, and gourds in floodplains, and, later, to make pottery. Attenuated, these two practices reached southeastern California, although trade had perhaps brought pottery earlier.

By A.D. 1000, these lower Colorado River tribes were, possibly, Yuman speakers, who, wandering east from the southern Californian coast into the Mojave region, had spread south along the river. A few, dislocated perhaps by Lake Cahuilla's evaporating, turned west over the mountains either to rejoin remaining bands or to form the nucleus of later Tipai-Ipai groups. Evidence depends on scanty archeological data and comparison of languages, mythology, and legends recorded only after 1540 when Spaniards arrived at the river and its historic period began; nonetheless, basic cultural patterns of historic Tipais and Ipais were deeply rooted in those of their predecessors in this area, whoever they were.

History

Through historical circumstances, Tipais and Ipais have remained within protohistoric boundaries during successive Spanish, Mexican, and Anglo-American control, partly through the absence of foreign effort before 1769 to alter their life and before 1821 to colonize extensively. More important, to Christianize them and teach them agriculture and crafts, San Diego Mission, initially unable to irrigate the large fields required to feed numerous resident neophytes, seized instead a few Ipais to convert while they lived and worked at the mission, released them, and captured others. Moreover, conversion was slow in the first decade. Of all mission tribes in the Californias, Tipais and Ipais most stubbornly and vio-

594

lently resisted Franciscan or Dominican control. Severe, sedentary, mission regimen with disruption of seminomadic routine adjusted for survival in familiar microhabitats triggered uprisings. Twice within the first six years attacks on San Diego Mission ended with fatalities. In 1775, a year after its relocation away from the presidio, about 800 people from some 70 villages united to burn the mission; among the dead was a priest, the only martyr in the California missions.

Nonetheless, in 1779, the mission had 1,405 neophytes (1,559 in 1811) living nearby. After 1818 establishment of the Santa Ysabel branch mission permitted interior Indians to become neophytes without moving far from their native homes. In 1821 a community of 450 lived near Santa Ysabel.

In 1834, 13 years after its independence from Spain, Mexico secularized the missions. To make them Mexican farmers and colonists, Indians were to get half the mission lands, but only to use, and were to work on community projects. Those who received lots soon lost them. Secular administrators, ignoring their responsibility to the Indians, functioned like feudal lords. Ipais and Tipais became serfs, trespassers on ancestral lands, rebels, or mountain fugitives. Their fate was similar if their hunting-gathering tracts or new gardens planted with mission seed fell within any large land grant Mexico made to attract settlers. A few Mission Indians secured such grants.

United States control was heralded for Ipais in 1846 when Gen. S.W. Kearny fought the California Rangers at San Pasqual. At first, Indians received little federal government attention. A treaty at Santa Ysabel in 1852 with 22 headmen of "the nation of Dieguino Indians" was rejected by the United States Senate. White settlers seized Ipai-Tipai lands as California boomed after the Civil War and gold was found at Julian in 1870. Indian efforts to secure legal titles or have Mexican titles acknowledged failed. Non-Indian efforts to have land set aside for them, as at fertile San Pasqual, merely hastened White squatting. After Ipais had already been forced off the best lands where the more acculturated were successful ranchers, an executive order in 1875 established the first Tipai-Ipai reservations, mainly where native villages still existed. Reservations were inadequate for the aboriginal economy or the more common mixture of old and new. Overgrazing and diversion of water, including underground resources, had destroyed grassland and woodland. Grazing on coastal grasslands, source of food seeds, had been a factor in Indian attacks on the old mission.

Helen Hunt Jackson, who investigated the situation in 1883 as a special federal agent, recommended removal of all White settlers from reservations and patenting of lands to Indian residents. No action resulted except to authorize the Indian Bureau to remove squatters with

military aid. Jackson wrote the novel *Ramona* (1884) to arouse public opinion and help Mission Indians.

Having no reservation, coastal Ipais, first and hardest hit by civilization, lived in San Diego slums, camped in nearby hills, or drifted to the less populated peninsula, where Tipai history resembles that of the north (Cuero 1968). In San Diego County the isolated mountain bands that were always outside mission and reservation systems continued like others to live within protohistoric boundaries, but less traumatically, and preserved more of the old culture longer. By the 1890s many men and women, industrious but poorly paid, labored on ranches, in mines, and in towns, but returned as in the 1970s to reservations for fiestas. In 1968 the Tipai-Ipai had 12 reservations and shared Pala Reservation with Takic speakers. Imperial County Tipais shared reservations with other tribes.

Native, aggressive perseverance and independence were again demonstrated in the 1930s when the Mission Indian Federation, formed for self-government with captains, judges, and armed policemen, challenged federal authority. The Federation and a counter organization called Southern Mission Indians have divided people as bitterly as probably the Franciscan missions originally did. As then, factionalism has contrarily fostered tribalism, aboriginally absent or nascent. Equally spirited has been reaction to mid-twentieth-century changes in federal and state Indian policy. The social structure in 1972 with respect to federal, state, county, and local agencies is essentially similar to that of the Luiseño.

Roman Catholicism has remained the dominant Christian faith. Since 1948, one or two priests, Sons of the Sacred Heart order, have ministered on the reservations. After secularization in the 1830s, the Santa Ysabel *asistencia,* like the San Diego mission, fell into ruins. For some 60 years converts led only by one of their members and an occasional visiting priest conducted services in makeshift shelters. The bitter narratives, still passed on orally, that keep alive memories of Franciscan harsh treatment are balanced by affectionate recollection of priests like Father Edmund La Pointe, who from 1903 until his death in 1932 devoted himself to the people and rebuilt Santa Ysabel Mission. The active role of Indian lay leaders, which has continued into the 1970s, has been, with their congregations' critical reactions, significant in fitting together meaningfully the Christian and native rituals.

At various reservations including those of neighboring tribes where friends and relatives live, a major recreation has long been the religious and secular fiestas that uniquely syncretize Indian, Spanish, Mexican, California frontier, and contemporary American customs and beliefs. Tipai-Ipai talent for synthesis was already evident when Davis in 1903 described their Fiesta de las Cruces, at Santa Ysabel Mission (Quinn 1964:24–25). Annually on November 14, hosted by Santa Ysabel Indians for hundreds of people, this harvest festival reunited scat-

Table 1. Population

Year	Total	Male	Female	Remarks	Source
1828	1,711	931	449	At mission stations only	San Diego Mission Record
1856	ca. 2,500				Annual Report, Commissioner of Indian Affairs (ARCIA)
1860	1,571	891	680	24 villages counted; 24 known but uncounted	Federal census
1873	886+			9 villages, mission area only; no Southern Diegueno	Archives, Catholic Indian Missions
1883	731			Many nonreservation uncounted hereafter	ARCIA (reservations)
1885	745				ARCIA (reservations)
1894	591	310	269		ARCIA (reservations)
1895	640				ARCIA (reservations)
1913	910				ARCIA (reservations)
1914	785				ARCIA (reservations)
1925	817	446	371		ARCIA (reservations)
1932	871	460	411		ARCIA (reservations)
1940	957	492	465	Last regular annual BIA census; only 782 were reservation residents	ARCIA (reservations)
1968	1,322			Only 435 were reservation residents	Sacramento Area Office Directory, Bureau of Indian Affairs

Compiled by Florence Shipek, 1972.

tered kinsmen and friends for barbecued meals, old and new games and sports, thanksgiving processions, and prayers for rain.

Warfare

Although agressive, Tipais and Ipais initially were less warlike than the Colorado River tribes. Traditionally, clans feuded over women, trespass, murder, and sorcery. Ambushing a lone trespasser or chasing the enemy away was satisfaction enough for most people. Before obtaining Spanish guns and horses, men went on foot with bows, poniards, and clubs—heavy and curved for slashing, forked for thrusting. Legends, based probably on exceptional historical cases, dramatize scalping, victory dances, and warrior purification. Warlikeness intensified in the Mexican period. The territory, dangerous until mid-nineteenth century, had raids on mission and presidio herds, and battles either against neighboring tribes with native or Mexican leaders or against Mexicans with neighbors as allies. Slough-dwelling Tipais, who early joined alliances of warlike River Yuman tribes (most often with Quechans), fanned war fever with western congeners as foreign pressure mounted (Woodward 1934a; Forbes 1965).

Population

Estimates of Tipai-Ipai population in either California, or both, between 1770 and 1970 undergo revision through data previously unknown or disregarded as irrelevant. Kroeber's (1925:712) estimate for 1770 of a standing population of 3,000 was based on San Diego Mission having in 65 years baptized approximately 6,000 persons and on three generations to a century. His Bajeño estimate was 710. While he recognized Diegueño dogged physical survival and resistance to missionization, his estimate ignores the unbaptized. Also, continuing research indicates that the efficient seasonal exploitation of varied ecological niches could prehistorically have supported double or triple the estimated 3,000. Imperial Valley Tipais totaled perhaps a few hundred aboriginally; in 1849 a New River chief had 254 Tipais under him (Gifford 1931:16). In 1957 Tipais of western Baja California totaled around 250 (Hinton and Owen 1957:88).

Table 1 shows population trends within the range of San Diego Mission influence, which reached perhaps only one-third of all Tipai-Ipai territory. Many inhabitants were never counted either by missions, Franciscan or Dominican, or by governmental censuses. Some villages never moved to reservations, or went to mixed reservations such as Pala, or joined relatives in Baja California or among Quechans, Cocopas, and Paipais. Incorrect tribal designations for certain reservations render particularly unreliable the 1890–1910 figures in the annual reports of the commissioner of Indian affairs; however, these figures in table 1 are tribally identifiable because individual village totals were reported. Even so, between 1873 and 1968, approximately 200 could be added to each total because San Pasqual residents, who did not occupy the reservation designated for them, were incorrectly reported. For 1968, estimates account for about half the reservation totals recorded in the Sacramento Area Office Directory, Bureau of Indian Affairs. Actual membership figures when given reflect specific reservation enrollment, mainly before 1960, the official date of enrollment, and thus exclude children born later.

Culture

Settlements

No list exists of all settlements, names, locations, dates of existence, estimated population, and composition. Clearly incomplete are lists of less than 60 for American California (Henshaw 1907). By 1795 San Diego Mission, with neophytes from 33, had explored at least 25 more villages, mostly north of Pamo.

Many villages were only campsites that a band occupied in its territory during a year. A Tipai of the Jacumba-Campo region who estimated that his clan, one of the largest, numbered 750 to 1,000, recalled over 19 settlements occupied during the 1850s; earlier the clan had begun to permit two friendly clans to occupy sites in its territory (Spier 1923:301–302). By a "permanent rancheria" nineteenth-century observers apparently meant that more band members gathered there for more months than at their other campsites. At Pamo at least three Ipai clans wintered together but dispersed in the spring into the Mesa Grande region (Gifford 1918:172). Any campsite might have residents "off season" (Woodward 1934a:145).

A campsite was selected for access to water, drainage, boulder outcrops or other natural protection from weather and ambush, and abundant flora and fauna of that ecological niche. Former house sites where avoided through fear of ghost-caused illness; houses were burned following a death.

Structures

Structures varied according to locality, need, choice, and raw materials. A summer village needed only a windbreak, trees, or a cave fronted with rocks. Mountain oak groves often had substantial shelters and platform-supported, covered granaries such as the conical, coiled "bird's nest" basket and the pole-and-brush box. In winter villages (fig. 2), well sheltered at low elevation, each cluster of dwellings, scattered for privacy and advantageous use of landscape, belonged to a man and his married sons.

A dwelling, with its floor slightly sunken, was a dome or gable set on the ground (fig. 3). A withe-tied pole framework (fig. 4) had brush thatch covered with grass and earth. A dome's two small, arched, opposite entries were directioned to avoid wind. Fire was made on the floor. A gable's mat-covered rectangular opening faced east, the ritual direction. Attached was an unroofed windbreak for outdoor work and summer cooking, and nearby a granary. Slough dwellers built Quechan-type rectangular, sand-covered houses, a large one for the chief, and in the desert put palm-leaf thatch on four poles. Some mountain Tipais wintered in large caves or bark-roofed, pine slab huts.

Village-owned structures were ceremonial. Clans jointly harvesting agave or piñon had a rock-supported, brush fence circling a leveled dance ground. Persisting, for fiestas, into the 1970s were the brush dance circle and the rectangular, flat-roofed, brush shelter, sometimes walled. For karuk ceremonies when images of the dead were burned, a semicircular shelter with an open eastern front and two flag poles faced a brush dance circle with a pit at the far end. Sweathouses were of minor importance.

Political Organization

Each band, an autonomous tribelet, had a clan chief and at least one assistant chief. Positions, where inherited, went to eldest sons, or if none, to brothers or, rarely, to widows. Additionally, Pamo had a village chief selected by consensus (Gifford 1918:168). Imperial Valley Tipais, having no clan chiefs, had a tribal chief like Quechans, among whom have been chiefs of Tipai descent (Gifford 1931:50–51; Forbes 1965:343).

A chief, because of knowledge of custom and people, directed clan and interclan ceremonies, lectured on their significance, admonished people on behavior, advised about marriages and their dissolution, resolved family differences, and appointed a leader for an agave expedition or a fight. His assistant delivered his messages and implemented his orders. A chief's mainly noncoercive approach was perhaps altered historically when capitanes ordered assistants to flog nonconformists.

The position of hunt master generally passed to the holder's eldest, or most capable, son. Consensus among participants determined the leader of a communal rabbit hunt, of shamans' dances (when not led by the clan chief), of specific dances in a series. Male and female dance leaders took turns to present their specialty. No sodalities existed.

Although property concepts recognized a band's communal claim to land and springs within boundaries identified by natural landmarks and its right to kill thieves and trespassers, they required that water be available to all and cached foods consumable by those in need who intended to reciprocate. Also a large clan might claim a weaker's property, such as an eagle nest. The nest, theoretically clan property, might practically be one family's, often the chief's, which had inherited the nest and rearing of its captured eaglets for ceremonial pur-

597

Fig. 2. Ipai thatched brush house on stone foundation. Photograph by Edward S. Curtis at Santa Ysabel, 1924 or before.

Fig. 3. Tipai camp at Vallecito. Pencil sketch by John W. Audubon, Oct. 23, 1849.

NAA, Smithsonian.

Fig. 4. Angel Quilpe, Tipai, standing in front of the framework of a house he made for John P. Harrington. Photograph by Harrington at San Diego, 1925.

NAA, Smithsonian.

Fig. 5. Four Tipai men with feather headdresses and body paint, and 2 Tipai women in calico skirts and plaid shawls. Photograph by Francis Parker at Tecate, 1880s.

poses. Clans gathered unevenly distributed food and materials, like agave, regardless of which owned the land. A clan, or sometimes an individual, might claim a specific song cycle or chant.

Families, like individuals, owned and disposed of what they had made and obtained, but custom might impose limitations as on a hunter. No tangible goods were inherited; everything had to be burned with its dead owner or later. Giving away rather than burning certain possessions developed when horses and other European things became common.

Clothing and Adornment

Clothing, like other tangible possessions, was minimal. Children and men went naked. To hold objects a man wore a waist cord, sometimes with pendant twigs. Women wore a two-piece or a single apron. To protect her head from her packstrap from which her carrying net hung, a woman wore a round twined cap; a man had a coiled cap. For travel, people wore padded-sole sandals of agave leaves. Cold-weather robes, doubling as bedding, were of rabbitskin, willow bark, or buckskin.

Hair hung long with bangs at the forehead except for boys and mourners. Imperial Valley Tipais, like Quechans and some Campo or Jacumba imitators, wore long pencillike rolls. A man plucked whiskers with his fingers. A woman, chin tattooed, daily decorated her face with red, black, and white designs. Male facial painting and tattooing were probably nineteenth-century innovations (fig. 5). A child's pierced ears carried round, deer-shank bones. An adult Valley or upland man hung from his nasal septum, pierced when a boy, a pendant or inserted a stick. Special, but still simple, costumes and adornment appeared at ceremonies.

Subsistence

• ANNUAL CYCLE   A band's seasonal travel was vertical, following the ripening of major plants from canyon floor to higher mountain slopes. Two or three families would arrive at a campsite, joined later by others, to gather, process, and cache seasonal vegetal food. Simultaneously they obtained their secondary source of sustenance, meat, from fauna either permanent residents at the place or migrants like themselves for the harvest. When winter began, people returned to a sheltered foothill or valley. Slough dwellers, apparently lacking campsites as stable as other Tipais, moved according to variable conditions of sloughs and ripening wild plants.

After months of preserved vegetal food and limited game, March through May provided welcome buds, blossoms, and potherbs from canyons and lower foothills. Some people left in May for agave ("mescal"). In early June they dried ripening cactus fruits to store in foothill caves. From June through August wild seeds ripened, and at higher altitudes wild plums and other fruits. Imperial Valley Tipais gathered mesquite pods in July. Elsewhere men, women, and children worked far into the night from September through November in higher altitudes to gather and preserve acorns and sometimes piñon nuts. Men also hunted deer, rodents, and birds feeding on nuts. When snow fell they returned to the winter village.

• GATHERING At least six species of oaks provided acorns, the staple for all except Valley Tipais who dried mesquite pods or pounded the beans into flour. Second in quantity was flour ground from seeds of species of sages (especially *Salvia columbariae,* chia), of grasses (including pigweed, peppergrass, flax, and buckwheat), of cacti, and of fruits. Valley Tipais made flour from seeds of *Cyperus erythrorhizos, Atriplex torreyi,* and other plants.

Fresh foods included watercress, miner's lettuce, two kinds of clover, young stalks and roots of yucca, many grasses, and shrubs. Fresh or dried blossoms and buds of clover, rose, cacti, and agave flavored food and water. Berries, common west of the desert, were from manzanita and elderberry, with juniper limited. Two species of plum and three of cherry were gathered. Relishes included wild onion. Agave, yucca, and cacti like chollas, barrel (bisnaga), and prickly pears grew near the border. From infrequent marshes came foods like tule roots and pollen.

Women and girls, major collectors and processors, used simple but effective means and equipment. Because they did not climb they picked from the ground or knocked down acorns, piñon cones, and mesquite pods for collection into baskets or net bags, struck off seeds with sticks or seed beaters, and with stick tongs picked cacti into mesh bags to roll spines off on the ground. The meat from cracked and hulled acorns was stored in granaries, with some immediately pounded and ground into flour with a stone pestle in bedrock or portable stone mortars shielded with basketry hoppers. Only a really good wife, one man said, could pound into flour large hard acorns from burr oaks. Only a really nice grandmother, his wife added, would graciously eat her granddaughter's lumpy mush. After winnowing the flour, women leached out the tannin. They did the same for bitter seeds like those of plums.

In parching her threshed and winnowed seeds a woman tumbled them with hot coals in a broken pot, or with a mush paddle she stirred the seeds mixed with heated granite fragments in an olla set on three stones over a fire. After further winnowing she stored the seeds in a covered pottery jar.

From preserves or freshly ground flour she cooked mush, cakes, and stews with meat and vegetables in pots set on the fire. Game she roasted on coals or in ashes and ground some bones into meal for gruel. Requiring many, varied, and specialized containers (fig. 6), she also obtained materials for baskets (more often coiled than twined) and plainware or decorated reddish-brown pottery (fig. 7) (made by the paddle-and-anvil method) while gathering plant foods.

• HORTICULTURE Desultory imitators of River Yuman farmers, Imperial Valley Tipais planted maize, beans, teparies, and melons in newly flooded land. When upland kinsmen visited them, they gave them seed to plant (Drucker 1937:5). However, hosts and guests readily

Dept. of Anthr., Smithsonian: 19478.
Fig. 6. Gourd water vessel with leather casing. Height 18 cm; collected 1875.

abandoned the chance to harvest if news came of plentiful wild plants and game.

Women transplanted wild onions and tobacco to more convenient locations and planted wild tobacco seeds for a better product. (Only men smoked, using a clay pipe distinctively angled with a flange under the bowl for ease in holding.) Grasslands were deliberately fired to improve the seed yield. Despite this marginal interest, horticulture was not seriously undertaken until Europeans disrupted the traditional economy. By the 1850s some remote, nonmissionized bands had peach trees and patches of maize, melons, and pumpkins; but they left gardens

Dept. of Anthr., Smithsonian: 19728.
Fig. 7. Clay pot, painted and wrapped with strips of bark. Diameter 22.5 cm; collected 1875.

600

unattended to continue their seasonal round. Missionized Ipais developed good ranches with gardens, orchards, and livestock.

• HUNTING Most meat came from rodents. Lizards, some snakes, insects, and larvae were also eaten. During winter, and in families without a deer hunter, rodents and birds were the only game. Old people and boys obtained them alone or in informal parties. Woodrats, driven from nests with poles, were shot with bow and arrow, or caught in fall traps set with acorn bait. Rabbits, their burrows fire-circled, were killed with bow or curved throwing stick. Or a pocket net was set on each side of a run. The aboriginal (now extinct) small dog, the only domesticated animal, rounded up game or flushed it from holes.

Lured with a bunch of weeds, doves, geese, quail, some hawks, or other birds unconnected with restrictive beliefs were caught with slip loops or shot with arrows fitted with crosspieces. Quail were hand-caught when cold and wet, or smoke-blinded. Mockingbirds and roadrunners were caged for pets.

Coastal and slough bands ate much fish, taken with bows, nets, hooks, and other devices. They had tule balsas. Foothill people sometimes joined them to fish, but mountain dwellers were indifferent.

Not many men were hunters of large game. Highly respected, they knew practical techniques, animal habits, hunters' signal codes, star lore, rituals, six-month calendars, mythology, songs, and an ideal hunter's behavior toward people and animals. Men made their own weapons and equipment or got them from experts knowledgeable about rites to insure success. A good hunter tested grandsons on rats before he taught them about rabbits. He taught only the most promising boy about large game.

Important milestones for such a boy were his first deer and his first trip with a party under a hunt master. A party, preferably of consanguineal kin, represented two generations, the older to carry equipment and pack meat home, the younger to hunt. One hunter was always a tracker, one a trail-sitter, or there might be two of each. Ground paintings depict the Mountain Sheep, three stars of Orion, being trailed by a hunter, a large star in the east, with trail-sitters represented by two other stars (Luomala and Toffelmier 1934; Waterman 1910:350, pl. 24; Spier 1923:319–320, 358).

Before a trip a hunter studied his dreams, fasted, drank only warm thin gruel, and avoided women. He always avoided corpses. His first deer he gave away outside the family. He sent a paunchful of meat home to old people and shared as directed by the hunt master with his companions, the clan chief, the shaman, and anyone to whom obligation existed. The ideal hunter watched proudly while others ate his game.

If a desired commodity was uncommon or absent in a clan's range, supplements came by expeditions to localities where it was plentiful, visits to friendly clans, and

trade. Travel was connected with social and religious dances and games. In May, expeditions converged at large agave patches near Vallecito or Mountain Spring. Although Mexican Tipais had more agave than the American, their customs were similar. In the work, more often by men than women, the agave was baked in a communal, covered pit, each group with its supply separate. By-products included sap, stored in small ollas, to later blacken faces of images and mourners. Baked agave was sun-dried, pounded, and flattened to be taken home. A fermented agave drink, a late introduction, might be prepared. At Mountain Spring, where people stayed until June, social dances included a song series called Tipai. When clans harvested piñon nuts at Picacho, Mexico, they performed the Piñon Bird Dance, named for jays that also noisily congregated in late autumn. Lead singers, a man and a woman, had a gourd-rattle accompaniment. These apparently social dances may have had first-fruits ritual significance.

Trade

Tipais and Ipais traded more frequently with each other than with unrelated tribes; however, major intertribal trails, such as the Yuma, crossed their territory between the lower Colorado and the Pacific. Spaniards, who like later newcomers used Indian trails, marveled how rapidly news, goods, and people circulated between river and coast. In 1540 Juan Rodríguez Cabrillo at San Diego Bay and Hernando de Alarcón on the Colorado River encountered Indians who had already heard, from inland tribes, accounts about Spaniards in the Southwest (Bolton 1925:23; Hammond and Rey 1940:147). In 1604 Juan de Oñate found Yuman speakers in the lower river area with "good and sweet oak acorns" traded from tribes to their west as part of a network of intertribal trade between the seacoast and as far east as the Zuni (Bolton 1925:270–280). In the 1770s Spaniards, either tracking Indians escaped to the east from coastal missions or seeking land routes from Sonora west to the Pacific, learned details of trails and trade in Ipai-Tipai territory in both Baja and Alta California (Bolton 1930, 2; Forbes 1965). American use of Indian trails was highlighted in 1849 by gold rush miners streaming west past the Amiel Whipple party journeying east from San Diego to determine the international boundary at the Gila-Colorado juncture; soon this and other Indian trails were surveyed for stage and railway routes (Whipple 1941, 1961; Hayes 1929; Davis 1961).

Coastal Tipais and Ipais traded salt, dried seafood, dried greens, and, for eyes of images, abalone shells, for inland acorns, agave, mesquite beans, and gourds (Cuero 1968:33).

In their exchanges, Tipais around Jacumba and Campo provided greater variety but perhaps Imperial Valley Tipais gave more quantitatively, for upland kin enjoyed wintering with them to eat their garden produce and fresh fish. Valley Tipais, in turn, helped themselves to granite for pestles, steatite for arrow straighteners, and red and black minerals for paint. They traded to get yucca fiber for sandals, agave fiber and juncus rushes for image frameworks, and eaglets or feathers. Those permitted to catch an eaglet themselves must surely have been of the same clan as that owning the eyrie. Cocopas, also wanting eagle feathers, brought salt and, for image teeth, clamshells. Historically, an eagle or its feathers traded for a horse (Gifford 1931:29 ff.; Spier 1923:349).

Manufactured items that Valley Tipais got upland included carrying nets, basketry caps, and winnowing trays. They also craved seed flour or acorn flour and processed agave. So did Quechans who exchanged them for wild black grapes and dried fish. Like Tipais they preferred upland, seed-grown, wild tobacco to their own (Gifford 1931:34 ff.; Luomala and Toffelmier 1934, 1962).

The frequent, long visits between Imperial Valley Tipais and upland, particularly Jacumba-Campo, Tipais developed a distinctive Diegueño subculture, the Tipai. The totaling of similar and dissimilar traits (Gifford 1931:83–85) among Kamias, Diegueños, and Quechans, which shows Kamia culture as more Quechan than it is Eastern and Western Diegueño, tends to obscure effects of continuing interaction, which introduced desert products and Quechan-learned customs to upland Tipais, and through them a little to Ipais. Ipais disseminated their adaptations of Takic innovations among Tipai neighbors from whom diluted variations sometimes reached the desert.

Life Cycle

• BIRTH Pregnancy and childbirth required a couple, especially the wife, to scratch themselves only with a stick and avoid salt, fat, meat, and cold water. The husband, sometimes before but generally during and after the birth, refrained from work, including hunting and, among eastern Tipais, gardening. The couple had followed similar customs during the wife's menses and before marriage during puberty ceremonies. The mother, lying in an outdoor, heated, and sage-lined pit with kinswomen nearby, was repeating, with fulfillment, her puberty rite; now instead of lying with girl friends she had her infant. Taboos ended with ritual purification by warm-water bathing, fumigation in fragrant smoke, and sometimes, emetics.

Twins, a blessing, were believed supernaturally gifted; the creators, *tu·čaypa·* and Yokomatis, were twins, as were the culture heroes, the *ča·wp·*. Relatives celebrated any birth with gifts of bedding, food, baskets, and pots. A child, playing with clay dolls (fig. 8) and miniature objects, imitated adults under grandparental direction. The two generations, while teasing and playing with each other, also contributed substantially within their ability to household needs.

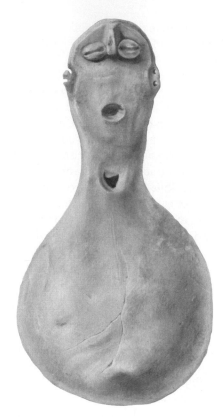

Dept. of Anthr., Smithsonian: 19739.
Fig. 8. Pottery doll, hollow and containing two pebbles. Loops of strung glass beads are missing from pierced ears. Height 17.3 cm; collected 1875.

• MARRIAGE Young people married outside their father's clan. Extension of exogamy to include the mother's clan may reflect missionary influence. Families preferred mates from clans they knew, even though feuding. Monogamy was more common than polygamy; but occasionally two brothers shared a wife or exchanged wives, and sisters shared a husband. Brothers-in-law and sisters-in-law joked together, and a widower preferred to marry his wife's sister or kinswoman, a widow her husband's blood or clan brother. A bride's parents entered into a special relationship with the groom's parents that ideally involved the older couples' lifelong deference to each other with frequent exchange of gifts and favors and concern for the success of the younger couple's marriage.

Marriage at puberty was arranged by parents. A Tipai boy brought game to the girl to demonstrate his ability. After marriage their parents informally exchanged presents. Ipais, having a progeny price, envied a family with daughters, its bridewealth of food, rabbitskin blankets, and later, horses, and many sons-in-law to visit. Approved residence was with the groom's clan in a separate shelter near his parents. If parents waived the price and got a son-in-law to live near them the bride's brothers mercilessly teased him. Either spouse readily divorced for incompatibility, laziness, or sterility.

• PUBERTY Unlike marriage and childbirth, puberty and death received public attention. Guests came from other clans to honor a group of individuals of similar status—adolescent girls (less often boys) and persons dying since the last image ceremony. Less public were the cremation and mourning anniversary of an individual.

The girls' "roasting" rite, absent among Imperial Valley and some western Mexican Tipais, was to promote a girl's future welfare and her self-confidence as a woman. Two or more girls, at or near puberty, remained a week, except for chaperoned trips to relieve themselves, in a pit with fragrant branches carpeting heated rocks. After a purifying tobacco drink, a girl lay face down, with face painted black, basketry cap and garland on her head, human-hair bracelet, and scratching stick. A warmed, crescentic stone between her legs supposedly insured easier future motherhood. Elderly women, who also gave practical instruction, danced, without instrumental accompaniment, around the pit as they sang song cycles or new songs. They tattooed each girl's chin; in old age when she dribbled food she would still look nice and her spirit would fly straight to the afterworld. On abandoning the pit, girls watched as guests feasted and rejoiced (Rust 1906; Waterman 1910:285–290; Luomala and Toffelmier 1934, 1962).

Mexican Tipai girls, after private observances, met at public rites to be tattooed while boys had their nasal septums pierced. Only boys in Imperial Valley had a public ceremony; mountain Tipai boys, indifferent imitators, had their septums pierced during a mourning ceremony or girls' rite. Valley girls had private observances at which their tattooing was done (Gifford 1931; Drucker 1941).

Perhaps just before Franciscans arrived, Ipais learned from Takic groups to give adolescent boys and adult men who wished it a vision-producing drink of toloache root (*Datura meteloides*). Each one who drank it was attended by an older initiate who, while people sang under the chief's direction, guided him through dances. Nearing collapse, the boy was allowed to sleep in order to dream of his future animal guardian. Gradually recovering, he was painted, learned more ritual from local and visiting experts, began a partial fast supported by a hunger belt, raced, underwent ordeals, received a feather head plume and dance stick, and studied a colored ground painting. He insured longevity, it was thought, if he spat into a hole in the painting and jumped from stone to stone on a netted anthropomorphic figure in a pit. This, when filled carefully to avoid dust, became the site of what foreigners miscalled the War Dance because dancers stamped and grunted vigorously. More likely, it concerns *čaˑwp*, Ball Lightning, younger of similarly named twins. After exhuming his father who told him to rebury him, death being eternal, he accidentally let grave dust rise between his toes; thereby sickness came to mankind (Waterman 1910:293–305).

• DEATH A corpse, extended with head to the south (the afterworld) or the east, was cremated in a pyre over a pit watched by a kinsman or paid fire tender. Imperial Valley Tipais, like Quechans, later filled in the pit. Others gathered ashes, bones, and unburned fragments of property into a pottery water or seed jar, capped it, and hid it in the mountains, with a metate, broken to release its spirit to serve the dead (C.G. Du Bois 1907b; E.H. Davis 1921; Heye 1919; Myrkrantz 1927).

For cremation there might be wailing, speech making, all-night singing of song cycles, and gift exchange with nonrelatives from friendly clans. Corpse-handlers and relatives observed customary taboos with subsequent purification. Mourners cut their hair, blackened their faces, and never mentioned the person's name again. Women saved their hair for an image.

Customs of mourning ceremonies sometimes merged. A family or lineage, if means permitted, held a mourning anniversary, or clothes-burning, for an individual a year after death to assuage grief and insure the spirit's nonreturn for possessions. Things not burned earlier, or new such as used in life, were burned after guests, holding clothes symbolizing the deceased, had given the spirit one last dance accompanied by wailing and song cycles. In return, grateful relatives gave guests presents. Historically, the ceremony has combined old elements with Catholicism (Kessler 1908; J.A. Woodward 1968).

To commemorate clan members—male, female, old, young—dead since its last observance, the *kǝṛuk* or image ceremony was a clan's major public event. Preferably in late summer or fall, after years of accumulating food, goods, and regalia, the *kǝṛuk* was held, directed by the clan chief and lasting four to eight days. Every night around a fire before the ceremonial shelter, painted and ornamented male and female guests danced with images of the dead as hosts scattered gifts, historically of currency, cloth, and baskets, to nonrelatives. Each image (fig. 9), as lifelike as possible, had a matting framework, plumped with grass, and was painted and finely dressed with traditional decorations and, historically, new European garments and currency ornaments. Imperial Valley Tipais used an image in the anniversary rite. Finally, at dawn, images, regalia, and new goods were piled in a pit or in the shelter and burned (E.H. Davis 1919).

Religion

• SHAMANISM Tipais first learned toloache customs around the 1850s from Ipais. They and Ipais might regard an initiate, eligible to participate in shamans' dances and possessor of ritual knowledge, as a shaman. Recognizing individual differences, people judged each pragmatically. Toloache was believed to stabilize an inherent talent and insure its lifelong enhancement. A man, and a rare woman, might take it only to learn a specific song series or to get luck, usually in gambling. This was particularly the case among Valley Tipais who

603

Fig. 9. Jim Qualsch, Tipai medicine man with funeral images. Photograph by Edward H. Davis at Campo, 1918.

took a leaf concoction without ritual, sometimes in a group under a shaman who had taken it for visions and curing skill (Gifford 1931:73). Infrequent "born" shamans were believed able to transform themselves into their guardian animal, with rattlesnake and bear feared. Some shamans specialized in weather control (Spier 1923:311–325).

A more broadly trained shaman might concentrate, for example, on herbalism, dream interpretation, and hunting large game while acquiring a general background in other subjects. One such man, after a year's instruction when he was 10, took toloache and had five stereotyped dreams—about his new sexual name; arm-encirclement symbolizing all knowledge and the world, perhaps like Ocean Monster; guardian animal (mountain lion); five magic crystals for communing; and First Woman, grandmother of *ča·wp*, primal hunter who named and marked all animals whereby they lost their *ti·pay* ('human') nature. A feast introduced the young shaman to the public (Toffelmier and Luomala 1936).

Among supernatural causes of disease and death were sorcery by evil shamans, who might be killed to protect a community, and psychological disorders, often with erratic sexual behavior, resulting from possession by Bullet Hawk spirit. A curer reversed an evil shaman's actions. For nervous disorders he used confession, dream interpretation, a form of hypnotism, herbs, and practical advice on diet and behavior. Curing by blowing on a patient and sucking also were common.

• MYTHOLOGY   Like the named song cycles with their dances, ground paintings were based on mythology shared with neighboring Yumans and Takic speakers, who, however, lacked Tipai-Ipai symbolism of colors and directions, in which east-white paired with west-black and north-red with south-blue (or green). Paintings, symbolism, clan organization, and pottery making linked these southern California and neighboring bands with the Southwestern culture area.

Locally and idiosyncratically variable like much Tipai-Ipai culture, mythology tells of *tu·čaypa·* and Yokomatis, sons of Earth Mother (First Woman) and Primal Water (later Sky when lifted by his sons). They created man, other life, heavenly bodies, and culture. Their pets were foxes. The noble elder twin, who sickened from water poisoned by Frog, died despite Eagle's and Mountain Lion's care. At his cremation Coyote stole and ate his heart. Frog is now abhorred, Eagle and Mountain Lion revered, and Coyote distrusted. Wishing to mourn the dead properly, the animal people sent for Ocean Monster, a snake, who hoarded knowledge and encircled the world. When he filled up the ceremonial shelter, they burned it. From his heart, blood containing song series and other learning spattered on clans now claiming them. This was at Wikami, identified with a local mountain or with Avikwame in Mohave territory. Some of these mythological details or those about *ča·wp* and others are depicted in ground paintings made by Ipais for girls and boys and by Tipais for male toloache initiates (see "Mythology," fig. 2, this vol.). They are cryptically mentioned in song cycles, important for recreation and religion (Waterman 1908, 1909, 1910; C.G. Du Bois 1901, 1904, 1905, 1907, 2:129–133).

• CEREMONIES   Incorporated usually in *kəɾuk* but not limited to it were special performances, more often among Takic-influenced Ipais than Tipais, with only rare details in the valley. Stereotyped songs ridiculing the dead of other clans were sung, usually by old women. At any assembly, shamans exhibited singly or in contests magical tricks but they collaborated in religious dances. In the Fire ceremony (fig. 10) they ritually extinguished a fire with hands and feet. In the Eagle Dance, honoring a dead chief or shaman, they sorrowfully killed a tamed eagle (later its feathers were removed, its body cremated like that of a person, and its death mourned). To honor

604

Fig. 10. Rafael Charley, Ipai medicine man, with ceremonial swallowing-stick and wand in his hat. The swallowing-stick was used at the conclusion of the Fire ceremony, which always followed another ceremony such as the toloache (Waterman 1910:325-338). Photograph by Edward H. Davis at Mesa Grande, 1903-1904.

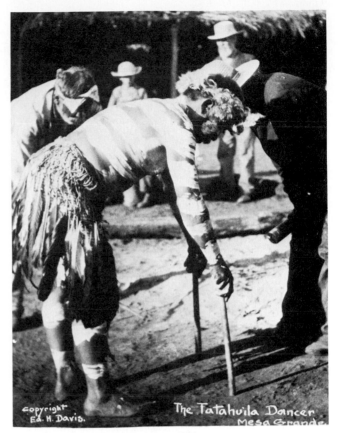

Fig. 11. Ipai Tatahuila Dancer or Whirling Dancer wearing eagle feather kilt strung on a cord. Photograph by Edward H. Davis at Mesa Grande, 1908 or before.

a dead colleague, each shaman, painted with a design relating to his vaguely totemic guardian animal, crawled and imitated it. In the War Dance, Ipai shamans at every rise in pitch (characteristic of Yuman music) raised each closed fist in turn. The Whirling Dance had a star performer, painted in white stripes and decked in eagle-feather kilt and owl-feather headband, who paused occasionally to whirl in place (fig. 11). Except for infrequent basket scraping, pottery, tortoise-shell, or gourd rattles provided accompaniment, with the deerhoof rattle (fig. 12) essential for *kəɾuk* (C.G. Du Bois 1905a, 1907a, 2:135-138, 1908; Waterman 1910; Spier 1923:326-327).

Betting, instituted by primal twins, characterized recreation at ceremonies, as in the men's guessing game of peon, the women's stick-dice game, and the hoop and pole, shinny, and other ball games.

Synonymy

Ipai and Tipai

Ipai: from *ʔiˑpay* 'person, Indian' in the dialects of the northernmost groups (Mesa Grande, Santa Ysabel, Inaja, San Felipe, San Pasqual, Campo) (Langdon 1970, personal communication 1973). Recorded as Ipai (Kroeber 1925:710; Joel 1964:99; Langdon 1971:150), Ipaye on the 1851 expedition (Bartlett in Gatschet 1877a:392).

Tipai: from *tiˑpay* 'person, Indian' in the Baja California dialects and some of the southern United States dialects (Margaret Langdon, personal communication 1973). Recorded as Tipai' (Spier 1923:298), Tipai (Gifford 1931:17, for Kamia or Imperial Valley bands; Joel 1964:99; Langdon 1971:150).

Directional, descriptive, place-name, and clan-name prefixes, and occasionally suffixes, combined with Tipai or Ipai present problems of identification (Kroeber 1925:710; Spier 1923:298). However, directional prefixes usually refer to neighboring related bands, not to neighboring tribes. The following may include recorders' misunderstandings. Diegueño *ʔəwik ʔiˑpay* 'west people' or *ʔəwik kupaˑy* 'person from the west' (Margaret Langdon, personal communication 1973) seems to be reflected

605

San Diego Mus. of Man, Calif.: Jessop 4704.

Fig. 12. Deer-hoof rattle with fiber handle. Length 18 cm; collected before 1932.

by Awik-upai (Kroeber 1925:710). Diegueño ʔənʸaˑk 'east' (Margaret Langdon, personal communication 1973) appears in Inyak-upai, the name for neighboring "Yuma (or Yum)," probably Imperial Valley Tipais (Kroeber 1925:710). Diegueño kəwaˑk 'south' (Margaret Langdon, personal communication 1973) is reflected in Kawakipai (Waterman 1910:272), Kawak-upai "sometimes" with reference to neighbors; for example, Mesa Grande Diegueño are Kawak-upai with reference to Luiseño, as are San Felipe Diegueño with reference to Cupeño, whereas the Campo Diegueño are Kawak-upai with reference to San Felipe (Kroeber 1925:710). Ikwai-niL tipai' 'blackwood people', Cuyamaca Mountains local group (Spier 1923:298; cf. nʸilʸ 'black', tiˑpay 'people', Margaret Langdon, personal communication 1973). Mél è-páie (1849 expedition in Whipple 1851, 1961:82). M'te pai ya oowai, Tipai self-name at La Huerta de los Indios (Hinton and Owen 1957:99; cf. Yahano below). Tis-se'-pah is an unidentified Yuman tribal group in north-central San Diego County, different from Kam'-me-i, Yu'man, Diegueño, and Es-kah'-ti within the Ipai-Tipai range, and from Mohave (Merriam in Heizer 1966:41, maps 5, 14c; note that 14c here overlaps Kroeber's 21r, Cupeño, in Heizer 1966:map 4).

Diegueño

Of the three major spellings—Dieguiño, Diegueño, and Yahano—the first two occur written with or without the tilde. Variant spellings represent either misprints or writers' idiosyncratic hearing or recollection of written forms.

Dieguiño: in 1769 Junipero Serra, having established Mission San Diego de Alcalá, wrote "Dieguino" in a letter (Coues 1900, 1:207) to refer to Indians in or immediately around the mission and thus established a spelling that dominated in Spanish, Mexican, and Anglo-American official records, memoirs, and newspapers for some 125 years continuing as an alternative form to the end of the nineteenth century. The most frequent variation in spelling was to eliminate u and either retain the i following it or substitute e or ee or, less commonly, a. An uncommon alteration was to replace the final o with either a or e. The same writer frequently used more than one spelling. Earliest known published examples of major, recurrent, variant spellings of Dieguino are: Dieguina in the *San Francisco Herald,* June 1853 (Bancroft 1874-1876, 1:457); Diegeeno from an 1849 expedition (Whipple 1851, 1961:23 ff.); Diegeno (Bartlett 1854, 2:7); Diegino from an 1854 expedition (Whipple et al. 1856; Whipple 1941:206); Diegene (Greene 1870:93). Apparently not misprints but variations usually of one writer only include Diagano, Diegano, Diegena, Diegmons, Digenes, and Diogenes.

Diegueño: Americans first used Diegueño alternatively to Dieguino and its variant spellings. The earliest published or manuscript use of this spelling occurred during the early 1870s and by the early 1900s, it was well established as the standard form. Hayes (1929:299), who died in 1878, used it at least once in an undated essay. Gatschet (1877a:384) perhaps gave authority to the spelling by applying it to the name of the dialect spoken by "Comoyei" settled near San Diego and by criticizing American customary incorrect spelling as Diegeño whereas to him San Dieguno and Diegueño were the only correct forms. "Dieguno" may be a misprint as was Schoolcraft's similar spelling (1851-1857, 2:100). Bancroft (1874-1876, 1:402) writes Diegueño.

Ya-ha-nos: in 1870 Romero gave the name to Hayes (Woodward 1934a:140) as the "true name of this nation." It represents Indian pronunciation, still heard into the 1960s, of "Diegueño."

Ya-ha-moes: apparently a variant pronunciation from "an old Indian" to Hayes (Woodward 1934a:148). M'te pai ya oowai: Tipai ("Southern Diegueño") self-name at La Huerta de los Indios, Baja California (again probably Indian pronunciation of Tipai-Diegueño, meaning Diegueño people) according to Hinton and Owen (1957:99). Llégeeno: 1849 expedition, Whipple (1851, 1961: 23, 31) alternated this spelling with Diegeeno, perhaps as a composite spelling of his pronunciation of

LUOMALA

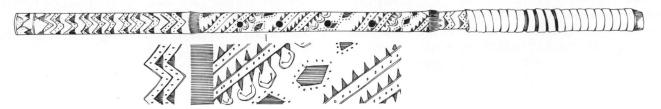

Dept. of Anthr., Smithsonian: 19756.

Fig. 13. Cane end-blown flute, incised and rubbed with brown pigment. The upper end is wrapped with red fabric tape. Length 66.5 cm; collected 1875.

eighteenth-century written Spanish "Dieguino" and his Diegueño, mission-trained guide's pronunciation of the d as ya, which Whipple quixotically spelled with the Spanish ll. Margaret Langdon (personal communication 1973) recorded *yegé·n*, another variant of the Spanish word incompletely assimilated into the Diegueño sound system.

Kamia

The Diegueño word *kaməya·y* or *kuməya·y*, perhaps once meaning 'the steep ones, those from the cliffs' (Langdon 1975a:68), lies behind many orthographic variants recorded from 1775 to the present as the name for themselves used by Diegueño groups from the Pacific coast to the Colorado River—but not including the Ipai or Northern Diegueño, and perhaps not including most of those Tipai now in Mexico (Hedges 1975; Cuero 1968:7; Langdon 1970:1, 1975a). In 1973 some of the Diegueño of southern San Diego County stated a preference for Kumeyaay as their own name, establishing the Kumeyaay Tribal Affairs Office in El Cajon and the Kumeyaay Corporation (Hedges 1975:77; Langdon 1975a:69).

Quèmeya, Quemayá, Quemeyá: 1775, Garcés (Coues 1900, 1:165 ff.) and Font (1933:131) report this as the name "Yumas" gave to a western Colorado River floodplain and sierra people who "extend to . . . San Diego"; Gifford (1931:2) identified them as "Eastern Diegueño"; occasionally, in 1775, Garcés (and Font follows) continues as in his earlier expeditions, through his confusion and actual Indian mixture and resemblances, to call this same people Mountain Cajuenches (Kohuana), Jecuiche (Hakwichya, Cahuilla), "Indios Serranos," and other names. Quemayab, Quemeyab, Quemexa: 1770 and after, Font's map and copies use these variant spellings of Quemeyá (Bancroft 1886-1890, 1:263, 274; Coues 1900).

Camillar, Camillares (pl.): in 1781 (Fages 1913:175 ff.), Velásquez (in Bancroft 1886-1890, 1:454). During the early 1780s Spaniards apparently preferred this spelling to that of the earlier Quemayá for the same people. Camilya: this spelling (Bourke 1889:176) perhaps reflects one pronunciation of the written Spanish ll; Bourke (1889) seemingly mingles his Mohave informant's data with material from unidentified Spanish records.

Como-yéi: on an 1849 expedition, Whipple (1851, 1961:31) alternates Quemeya with Como-yei for a predominantly Colorado Desert-New River people mixed with Cuchan and "Diegeeno." Whipple's other 1849 spellings are Comoyah, Comoya, Comoyeé. Co-mái-yàh and Comoyátz are variant spellings of Comoyei from an 1854 expedition (Whipple et al. 1856:16). Gifford (1931:3) identified Comoyatz as "(Kamia?)." Comeya: a form from Bartlett (1854, 2:7, 179) used by Henshaw and Hodge (1907) in discussing the synonymy. Gifford (1931:3) identified Bartlett's Comeya people as Diegueño and not Kamia. Comedás: from Fröbel (1859:511), equated by Gifford (1931:3) with Kamia people. Ko-mo-yah: "group of Kam'-me-i" (Merriam in Heizer et al. 1969:23).

Kamiai: Southern Diegueño self-name "sometimes" (at Campo, Manzanita, Jacumba) or northern Diegueño name for San Pasqual group. Kamiyahi: alternate Southern Diegueño self-name "sometimes" with Kamiai (Kroeber 1925:710, 725). Kamiyai: refers to "a Kamiyai at Campo" (Waterman 1909:43).

Kam'me-i, Kam'me-i': in "(Diegueno)" vocabularies Kam'me-i informants are from near Yuma, Colorado Desert, and southern San Diego County; with Ă-whah'kō-wahk (unidentified) from Manzanita, Campo, Mesa Grande, and El Cajon; with A-whah'-kah-wahk, from San Diego and Campo. A-wah'-kah-wahk and Ă-whah'-kō-wahk are unidentified terms that seemingly mean 'foreign southerners' with reference to Tipais south of the Tipai informants (according to Merriam in 1903 in Heizer et al. 1969:23, 31, 45; Heizer 1966:41, map 5).

Kamia: this spelling evidently reflects *kamyá*, the Mohave and Quechan name for their western neighbors, which they probably borrowed through Cocopa from the Diegueño form *kaməya·y* (Langdon 1975a:69). Thus Kamia is the "Mohave name" according to Kroeber (Henshaw 1907); "easternmost Diegueño," along "back channels of the Colorado in Imperial Valley, and sometimes . . . on the main river. The Diegueño consider the Kamia Diegueño, and the other Yuman tribes call the Diegueño Kamia, sometimes with the addition of a suffix such as ahwe, foreign, remote" (Kroeber 1943:24); "so-called Yuman Diegueño" (Gifford 1918:156). "Both [Eastern Diegueño and Imperial Valley Kamia] call the

607

Eastern and Western Diegueño Kamia also, distinguishing them merely as western Kamia" (Gifford 1931:2, 11). Kamya is the Quechan name for Eastern (southern) Diegueño; the Quechan included the western (northern) Diegueño with the Takic Cahuilla under the name Hakwichya, "to whom alone it properly refers" (Kroeber 1925:724–725). Gifford (1918:156, 1931:1 ff.) tentatively separated Kamia and Diegueño as did Spier (1923:328) and Kroeber (1925:710, 723 ff.). Forbes (1965) applied the name Kamia to all Tipais and Ipais.

kumáθa: "the people of the mountains west of the Imperial Valley" according to the Maricopa, that is, Kamia or southern (eastern) Diegueño or both (Spier 1933:11). Kŭmiai: northern Diegueño name for southern Diegueño (Spier 1923:298).

Kamia'-ahwe, Kamia ahwe: Mohave name to distinguish western Diegueño from Kamia (Kroeber 1925:710, 724). Kamia-akhwe: Mohave name for 'foreign Kamia' (Henshaw and Hodge 1907:330). Axua, Axüa: (Hardy 1829:368; Henshaw and Hodge 1907); Hardy's Axua are "Comeya"; according to Gifford (1931:3), Axua are "probably Akwa'ala" and according to Forbes (1965:250–251), "probably Cocopas, with some Paipais."

Others

Cumana: a lower Colorado River people, Alarcón, 1540 (Hammond and Rey 1940:140ff.). Although Gifford (1931:86) thinks it "unlikely" that the Cumana were Kamia, Forbes (1965:96) believes that "the stem *Cuma* would seem to be related to certain of the names given the Kamias, such as *Kuma'ca.*"

I'-um O'otam: in 1883, a Pima applied the term to "a Yuma- and a Comoyei-Indian" Gatschet (1886, 3:98). Yum: "New River Indians" (Heinzelman 1857:42). Yuma Diegueño: Kamia (Gifford 1918:156). The tendency existed to lump lower Colorado River and New River Indians as Yum or Yuma or to distinguish some as Yuma Diegueño.

kičámkawičəm, Kichamkuchum, Kichamkochem: Luiseño and Cupeño name meaning 'southerners', for Diegueño (Jane H. Hill, personal communication 1974; Kroeber 1925:710).

Clan or rancheria names are occasionally misinterpreted as applicable generally for Ipai or Tipai especially if a given rancheria was on a major trail or if a given clan was well represented on one or more rancherias visited by Europeans. The following examples may not be readily identifiable by reference to lists of known rancherias or clans in Kroeber (1925:710, 719) and Gifford (1931) or are otherwise confusing.

Cuñeil, Cuñeiles (pl.): people "bounded by San Diego and by the disembouement" of the Colorado River, 1775–1776, Garcés (Coues 1900, 1:444, 450); "evidently Yuman," and seemingly "identical with the Comeya, but Garcés mentions the latter, under the name Quemayá, as

if distinct" (Hodge 1907–1910, 1:372), "probably Paipai" (Joel 1964:101). Cunyeel: Font's map, 1777 copy (Coues 1900) shows Cunyeel in north-central Baja California between 31° and 32° north latitude and 115–117° west longitude; with Quemeya between 32° and 33° north latitude and 115°–117° west longitude; 1777 map (Bancroft 1886–1890,1:263) writes Cunyeil and Quemexa. Cuñai: (Orozco y Berra 1864:353). Kuneyil, Kunyil: name in "Comeya" dialect means 'all men', 'people', Gatschet (in Hodge 1907–1910, 1:372). Kwainyi'L, KwinyiL: (Spier 1923:300, 304, fig. A); Tipai-Ipai clan name meaning 'black' (Gifford 1931:11, 13). Cuñeil is probably the clan name KwinyiL. Gimiel may be variant spelling.

Gimiel: "all the Indians of the missions above Santa Gertrudis are undoubtedly Yuma in their family relations. . . . Those of Santa Catalina, San Pedro Martyr, and San Miguel, and Santo Tomas, such as the Guyemuras, and Gimiels, were nearly pure Yumas, as were those of San Diego" (Taylor 1869:53–54); "about Santo Tomás and San Miguel, near the modern pueblo of Ensenada, dwelt the Gimiels, doubtless a subtribe of the Yumas" (North 1908:239).

Gueymura: a Diegueño rancheria (Henshaw 1907:390).

Junir, Jurin: Velásquez, 1785, with Fages met these Indians at La Palma, between San Sebastian and San Felipe rancherias. Forbes (1965:224) calls them Kamias. The name is unidentified.

KwatL, E'kwaL: Baja California group "allied to State of California group . . . possibly the Akwa'ala or Ekwa'ahle known to the Mohave" (Spier 1923:302–305). KwatL/koʔaL/, meaning 'hide', 'skin', is the name of a Tipai clan of Imperial Valley, southern San Diego County, and Baja California. Kwatl Kumiyai: Kwatl subdivision of Kumiyai at Santa Catalina (Meigs 1939:85). Quathl-met-ha: 1868, Thomas (Gatschet 1877a:370), Quechan word for New River people, written as Kuathlmet'-ha by Gatschet. Yaka-kwal: "extinct group which resided around Santo Domingo Mission" (Hinton and Owen 1957:93).

Sources

Major ethnographic syntheses based on both older research and new fieldwork are Kroeber (1925) and Curtis (1907–1930, 15), the latter with excellent photographs. General field surveys are Spier (1923) on Southern Diegueño and Gifford (1931) on Kamia culture; Drucker's (1937, 1941) element lists on Tipai and Ipai regions are highly informative. Numerous reports on religion and mythology by Davis, DuBois, and Waterman have been cited. Luomala and Toffelmier (1934, 1962) secured shamanistic and other data. Among several archives with documents are San Diego Museum of Man Scientific Library; San Diego Historical Society Junipero Serra Museum; and University of California at Berkeley. The San Diego Museum of Man has the Constance G. DuBois collection of photographs. Museums with extensive collections of artifacts include the Museum of the American Indian, Heye Foundation, New York; Lowie Museum of Anthropology, University of California, Berkeley; Los Angeles County Museum of History and Science; and San Diego Museum of Man.

History of Southern California Mission Indians

FLORENCE C. SHIPEK

Sociopolitical developments in the twentieth century among the Mission Indians of southern California reflect the continuation of the ability of the various ethnic nationalities to make a variety of successful and repeated adjustments and adaptations to what has been characterized as a "most unstable, erratic and unpredictable" environment (Bean 1972:35). Starting with the entrance of the Spanish into California in the late eighteenth century, other human elements entered the environment bringing new political and religious organizations and new technology, plants, and animals. These new elements instituted a drastic new period of instability and change that has not abated.

The Spanish crops, weeds, domestic animals, and elements of technology were rapidly integrated into the subsistence pattern and spread beyond the perimeters of Spanish control. Domestic animals changed the plant ecology as the original seed-food grass disappeared and was replaced by European grasses and weeds (E. Anderson 1956:763). Overgrazing brought a period of accelerated erosion and lessened surface water availibility. Antelope and bear disappeared; mountain sheep and mountain lion have become almost extinct; deer were reduced in range and numbers. Access to coastal food was reduced.

Internal sociopolitical mechanisms adjusted to population reduction, mission interference, and regulation in the lives of coastal bands. New officials, appointed by the Spanish, became the intermediaries for Spanish orders (Tac 1958:19). These officials continued to function as intermediaries under Mexican political rule and also became economic entrepreneurs controlling the Indian labor force for the Mexican ranchos. They continued in these functions even after the American entry into California in 1846. Slowly, the functions of the religiously sanctioned native individuals who administered social, political, economic, and ritual matters (Bean 1972:105) were reduced to control of only ritual activities; the political-economic activities of the past disappeared and the Indians entered the newly available economic niches in the changed human environment (Shipek 1971a:26).

The rate and amount of change varied with ease of access from White settlements. The more rugged mountain and desert reaches of Cahuilla (Bean 1972:17-18) and Ipai (Shipek 1954-1973) territory remained relatively undisturbed until 1870, some until 1910. Between 1870 and 1910, encroachment by American settlers brought loss of the best farm and grazing lands and finally encapsulation of some bands upon reservations under bureaucratic controls.

By this time, the term Mission Indian had come to include all those Indians whose ancestors were in the Spanish missions from San Francisco south to San Diego at the Mexican border and also those portions of these groups whose ancestors had remained free of the missions in the mountains and deserts to the east of the coastal strip, except for those Indians along the Colorado River. Many of the mountain and desert Indians hate the term and insist upon the use of their band names or the tribal designation of Cahuilla or Kumeyaay.

The reservation of land for Indian occupants began in 1875 with an executive order by President Ulysses Grant. These and additional lands were finally given legal trust patent status between 1891 and 1913, under the "Act for the Relief of Mission Indians" passed by Congress in 1891. A list of the reservations with date of establishment and other basic data is given in table 1 and figure 1.

These reservations are relatively small, scattered over southern California, variably located with reference to water supply, rainfall, quantity and quality of land, and differential access to non-Indian population concentrations. Indian populations varied in size, in amount of contact and displacement that had preceded encapsulation, population reduction and recovery rates, amount of land available per person or per family, as well as in family skills and specialist status from the past. Each reservation became an individual unit that has had its unique conditions and particular history, which tend to make generalizations difficult and to produce exceptions and variances at specific levels. However, in response to generally similar external pressures and bureaucratization, the various groups have tended to modify their sociopolitical and economic structures in convergent ways (Sutton 1967, 1975).

Economic Change

While the economic status of the Mission Indians has not determined the social and political changes, these changes can only be understood in conjunction with the economic conditions.

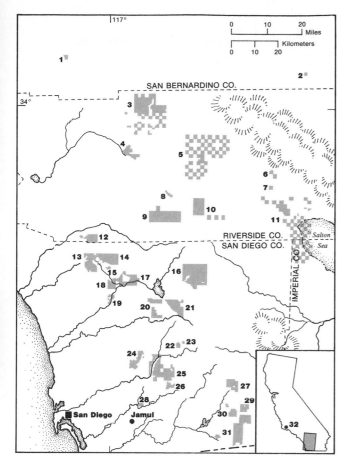

Fig. 1. Southern California Reservations: 1, San Manuel; 2, Twenty-nine Palms; 3, Morongo; 4, Soboba; 5, Agua Caliente; 6, Cabazon; 7, Augustine; 8, Ramona; 9, Cahuilla; 10, Santa Rosa; 11, Torres-Martinez; 12, Pechanga; 13, Pala; 14, Mission Reserve; 15, Pauma-Yuima; 16, Los Coyotes; 17, La Jolla, 18, Rincon; 19, San Pasqual; 20, Mesa Grande; 21, Santa Ysabel; 22, Inaja; 23, Cosmit; 24, Barona; 25, Capitan Grande, 26, Viejas; 27, Cuyapaipe; 28, Sycuan; 29, Manzanita; 30, La Posta; 31, Campo; 32, Santa Ynez.

Throughout the entire period of American encroachment, 1846 to 1911, the Mission Indians continued to support themselves. Rations from the Indian agency were negligible. As farming and livestock subsistence decreased due to loss of land, people turned to wage and subsistence labor on ranches and in towns. When title to their lands was secured by the creation of trust patent reservations under the 1891 Act for the Relief of Mission Indians, a resurgence of farm activity began. Indians planted crops and orchards and raised livestock and poultry, not only for subsistence but also for cash sale. They continued to form a major portion of the labor pool for local agriculture; cattle ranching; fruit ranching; road building; stevedoring; and unskilled, semiskilled, and some skilled labor activities. Negligible quantities of agency rations were distributed only on a temporary emergency basis or to disabled and aged from 1891 until 1932 and the Depression period. Even then, the proportion of rations and aid was low compared to self-produced income through the Depression and to the close of the bureaucratic period in 1954.

From 1900 to 1949, Bureau of Indian Affairs agricultural statistics for Mission reservations are comparable to agricultural statistics for small ranches and farms in southern California (Shipek 1954–1973). For example, similiar crop yields per acre and income per farm family are found. This comparability was maintained in spite of the diminution of water supplies as rivers, streams, and springs were progressively impounded and diverted above reservations. The Indians were making continual adjustments to economic conditions and water loss, changing crops, labor methods, and marketing facilities to gain the maximum return for the labor expended.

World War II extended travel and helped in the development of new skills through Indian participation in war production and the armed forces. With the close of the war and return to the reservations, farm activity expanded. However, a prolonged drought through the next 20 years made dry farming impossible. Meanwhile riparian waters had been diverted into other river basins and onto farms around the reservations. Reservations had already been pumping ground water, but as water tables were lowered through use, the adjoining ranches with more easily obtained capitalization were sinking deeper wells and drawing water off more rapidly. As irrigation water from any source became scarce, farming was reduced and abandoned. Some reservations even lost domestic water supplies.

Increased off-reservation work was sought, but the drought combined with increasing mechanization had reduced the number of local farm-labor jobs available. Mechanization in local business, construction, and industry had also reduced the overall demand for unskilled and semiskilled labor. This portion of the Indian labor force was unemployed and without adequate job opportunities. Those Indians in the more skilled trades and professions and those who had been willing to work in the cities or at indoor jobs continued as before. The reservations became the refuge for the unemployed and the retired. A search for retraining opportunities for adults and new types of training for youths began. However, this 1950–1965 period of changing job-skill requirements coincided with the withdrawal of Bureau of Indian Affairs school and training services to California Indians. The states and counties were neither prepared to handle nor aware of the specific problems that faced Indian people.

Indians came to be stereotyped as lazy by the public due to what was easily visible on the scattered reservations—unused (that is, unusable) farm lands and the unemployed (that is, unemployable) fraction of the Indian population.

Table 1. Indian Trust Land, 1973

Reservation	Tribe	Acreage Tribal	Allotted	Estimated Residents	Estimated Membership[b]
Augustine, 1893	Cahuilla	341.80	160.49	0	2
Cabazon, 1876	Cahuilla	1,153.21	548.32	4	22
Cahuilla, 1875	Cahuilla	18,272.38		23	89
Morongo, 1877	Cahuilla, Serrano	30,956.69	1,300.81	260	578
Pechanga, 1882	Luiseño	2,860.78	1,228.02	33	220
Ramona, 1893	Cahuilla	560.00		0	1+
Santa Rosa, 1907	Cahuilla	11,092.60		14	61
Soboba, 1883	Cahuilla	5,035.68		185	314
Torres-Martinez, 1876	Cahuilla	18,223.16	7,026.13	43	217
San Manuel, 1893	Serrano	653.15		19	50
Twentynine Palms, 1895	Chemehuevi	162.13		0	12
Santa Ynez, 1901	Chumash	99.28		41	169
Public domain, Santa Barbara Co.			160.00		
Barona, 1932	Ipai (Diegueño)	5,180.66		125	156
Campo, 1893	Kumeyaay	15,010.00		40	103
Capitan Grande, 1875	Ipai (Diegueño)	15,753.40		7	309
Cuyapaipe, 1893	Kumeyaay	4,100.13		2	5
Inaja-Cosmit, 1875	Ipai (Diegueño)	851.81		0	21
La Jolla, 1875	Luiseño	7,588.16	639.90	41	280
La Posta, 1893	Kumeyaay	3,672.29		0	4
Los Coyotes, 1889	Cahuilla	25,049.63		51	106
Manzanita, 1893	Kumeyaay	3,579.38		6	69
Mesa Grande, 1875	Ipai (Diegueño)	120.00		24	261
Mission Reserve,[a] 1903		9,470.82		0	
Pala, 1875	Luiseño, Cupeño, Ipai (Diegueño)	6,547.48	1,185.58	273	447
Pauma-Yuima, 1892	Luiseño	253.76		100	
Rincon, 1875	Luiseño	3,612.04	353.75	115	345
San Pasqual, 1910	Ipai (Diegueño)	1,379.58 ♪		21	214
Santa Ysabel, 1875	Ipai (Diegueño)	15,526.78		110	300
Sycuan, 1875	Kumeyaay	370.55	269.45	31	37

Source: Riverside Area Field Office records, Bureau of Indian Affairs.

[a] Intended for Pala and Pauma peoples; not trust-patented to them as of 1973.

[b] 1969 data.

Table 1. Indian Trust Land, 1973 *(Continued)*

Reservation	Tribe	Acreage Tribal	Acreage Allotted	Estimated Residents	Estimated Membership[b]
Viejas (Baron Long), 1939	Ipai (Diegueño)	1,609.00		121	127
Public domain and purchased property, San Diego Co.			1,461.82		
Agua Caliente, 1896	Cahuilla	26,523.37[b]	equalized value allotments	74	117
Jamul, 1912	Kumeyaay			20	50

[b] 1969 data.

Land Tenure

Understanding political and social activities also requires understanding the continuity of land ownership concepts among the various Mission Indian nationalities. All had concepts that included individual and family ownership and inheritance of specific resources as well as the undivided ownership of others and interband use of still other resources. The allotment program, or the division of reservation land by the Bureau of Indian Affairs into tracts to be owned by individual Indians, was opposed only after it became apparent that traditional ownership patterns and existing improvements were not primary considerations in this division. Some Indians lost portions of their already developed land held under the traditional private ownership concepts (C.G. Du Bois 1908a:159; Bean 1960-1971; Shipek 1954-1973). Thus, the cause of this opposition was the arbitrary taking of land from one individual Indian owner and giving it to another Indian. This was not opposition to or lack of understanding of the concept of private individual land ownership.

Elsewhere in the United States, the allotment program resulted in the loss of two-thirds of Indian lands from Indian ownership and the destruction of tribal governments (T.H. Haas 1957:15). In southern California, this loss of Indian trust land and the destruction of tribal government has not occurred. In southern California, less than 25 percent of the allotted acreage had been taken out of trust by 1973, and some of this out-of-trust, or fee-patent, land is still in the hands of Indian owners (Shipek 1976). Thus, less than one-fourth of the trust land has been lost by Indians as compared to two-thirds lost elsewhere in the United States. Tribal governments have not been damaged by this loss nor by the allotment programs other than as a temporary source of factionalism.

From the inception of the reservations, use of the land for income purposes has been related to the overall water supplies. Residence or lack of residence upon a reservation was related not only to the amount of water available for farming but also to accessibility to jobs governed by distance of good roads, and more recently by the presence or absence of domestic water supplies. A family does not have to reside on or use either allotted or unallotted land in order to maintain ownership, inheritance rights, or band membership. Social, religious, and political activities, as well as tribal governments, continue regardless of the location of the residence of members. Over 90 percent of the members live within about a 500-mile radius and maintain personal contacts and tribal activities.

Political Activity

During the period preceding the formation of trust-patent reservations, that is, 1860 to 1891, the Indians had discovered the advantages of using "advocates" (Bean 1977) to plead their causes. They had learned that their own "elected" official intermediaries must meet the approval of the exterior powers and that they could not faithfully and satisfactorily represent the interests of the band. Under bureaucratic regulations, in order to lead their own lives, they found it necessary to continue to pit advocates against bureaucratic controls and advocates against each other in such a way that gradually there came to be a negation of government. The term advocates is used to mean those well-meaning individuals or organizations who will "take up the battle" for an Indian band or Indian individual's rights. While they have been of some service, they frequently do not understand the full problem, tend to increase factionalism, see only their own idealized conception of "Indians" or "Indian beliefs," and even sometimes have their own hidden advantage to be gained by advocating some course of action to the Indians or to the government.

Power groups formed that sometimes used equally oppressive methods to combat unsympathetic officials and restrictive regulations. People were divided between those who felt advantage could be gained by cooperating with Bureau of Indian Affairs policies and those who demanded immediate elimination of the Bureau. Most of the Mission Indians were satisfactorily managing their own economic affairs in spite of bureaucratic red tape and interference. Some homes and land had been bought outside of the reservations by Indians. Many resented wardship status and felt that federal control was degrading. Termination of federal trust status and controls became the battleground.

When a termination bill was finally proposed in 1954–1955, the provisions were such that a majority of people realized that passage of the bill would be a disaster to all and could result in the probable loss of lands. The Indians united in opposition, again invoked advocates, and managed to kill the termination bill.

In the meantime, however, Public Law 280 had been passed in answer to the demands for an end to bureaucratic controls. Public Law 280 removed all Bureau of Indian Affairs services from the Indians as a people. They became eligible for all the state and county services and subject to all the laws on the same basis as any other citizen of California except for the Bureau of Indian Affairs maintenance of the trust status of existing trust lands and minor aspects of "traditional" use and tenure rights. They already paid all the same taxes as any other citizen except for the property-tax-free status of these trust lands.

It was common in the mid-1950s to hear supposedly informed people state that "identifiable Mission Indians" and Indian reservations would disappear within 20 years. Actually the passage of Public Law 280 was a turning point in the development of effective reservation self-government and organized Indian political action as opposed to the effective use of advocates. While factionalism and the use of advocates continued, the Indians were also searching for new sources of information and new advocates to deal with the totally different external political powers and governmental apparatus. The Indians were no longer dealing with one centralized agency but with multiple agencies, located in several counties, operating under different county laws and regulations. The old power factions used so effectively to negate Bureau of Indians Affairs controls were inadequate to deal with this diffuse situation.

The services to be obtained from the counties were primarily personal services, such as general law enforcement, county agricultural extension service, state employment service, new construction safety inspection, as well as Department of Public Health and Welfare Services. That is, the services shifted from the Bureau of Indian Affairs to county responsibility were the normal public services available to any citizen and were to be received upon the same basis of eligibility as any other citizen. These also included the right to receive general welfare, old-age pension, blind aid, disability pension, aid to needy children, unemployment relief, county hospitalization, and testing of well water for safe drinking, for example. Many individual difficulties, injustices, and inequities occurred due more to misunderstandings on both sides than to any other cause. Many county depart-

ments, officials, and personnel did not know that the Indians were now under their jurisdiction and the Indians were not all aware of their rights and the procedures necessary for obtaining services.

The Indians also began to realize that some valuable privileges had been lost. They began to request specific laws to recover these privileges, such as year-round hunting and fishing rights upon their reservations. Other laws needed modification, such as placing a clause in the state civil code that would legalize existing custom marriages as they had previously been recognized by the Bureau of Indian Affairs (Shipek 1968).

Other than the personal welfare services or law enforcement for major crimes, the reservations were left in a vacuum of government. While advocates were still around telling reservation members what "they ought to do" or "what would be best for them," no county, state, or federal government was doing anything to or for the reservations. Social disorganization was acute. The previous goal of a major faction, the elimination of total personal and reservation control by the Bureau of Indian Affairs, had been achieved, but no new goals were in sight.

New nationwide federal programs came into existence during the 1960s. The Economic Development Administration, the Office of Economic Opportunity, and various housing and educational programs were among these. All the programs were based upon criteria of need and required large numbers of people and also legal formal organizations of people for participation. While Indian reservations were included in the categories of groups to be served, the programs were not written specifically for reservations or for the specific conditions that existed for southern California reservations. Some 32 relatively small Indian communities are scattered over 5 counties and several hundred miles. Each always had its own membership and government or lack of government. Each has always guarded jealously its independence, self-determination, and right to self-government. There were no interreservation organizations through which action or even communication could be channeled and through which these new programs could be activated for southern California reservations.

As local reservation leaders began examining these programs, they became aware that no single reservation was large enough to qualify for the programs. They also became aware that they did not have the proper legal organization on most reservations to qualify. The majority of reservations had consistently refused to participate in the Indian Reorganization Act, recognizing that government control was simply being masked under the form of an elected tribal council and constitution. Most refused to write constitutions that would turn authority over to a "representative" elected government. Instead they had developed an unwritten form in which the elected council and spokesman were simply administrators who could only carry out specific actions or make statements specifically authorized by the membership.

Since 1968, the reservations have sought to develop new organizations that would be capable of meeting new situations; many ways have been tried. Some reservations adopted constitutions of the representative-government type, following the model offered by the Bureau of Indian Affairs (Fay 1970, 1970a). Others sought different models. There was a search for information about methods and procedures for legal written forms of government, such as different types of constitutions, articles of association, and ordinances.

Some interreservation organizations—for example, Mission Indian Development Corporation, Inter-tribal Council of California, and California Rural Indian Health Program—had been sponsored by outside agencies with the participation of a few leaders from some reservations. Originally these organizations and their programs were viewed as new sources of income, power, and position outside the reservation community for the individual participants. They were classed as agencies to be fended off and negated in their interference in Indian lives. Each program was offering some type of panacea for their problems. The people, in general, exercised their usual cautious approach and looked for the hidden "catch." They were demanding facts but were deluged with glowing accounts and propaganda. They were looking for the social costs to themselves in terms of time, effort, land use, cash outlay, impingement upon their independence of action and their lives and values in addition to the promised benefits. They wanted unbiased sources of information.

A few leaders approached the University of San Diego just as the university was seeking ways to provide useful services to the local area. With funding cooperation from the California State Coordinating Council for Higher Education, a program of community development education was made available to the San Diego County reservations. It was directed to the land-based groups, worked through reservation councils, supplied requested information and documents, and instituted classes in governmental forms and methods, bookkeeping, accounting, community planning, housing programs, and economic development. As classes, seminars, and workshops were held for organizations and reservation members, participation in some interreservation organizations increased. These, then, became more effective in bringing services to reservations that desired them. Active participation in reservation government increased. Constitutions were written to formalize the existing administrative-executive model that retained decision-making powers in the hands of members. This is a practical model for reservations with small total memberships varying from 4 to 150 members.

One small band, Jamul, had never been recognized as Indians by the Bureau of Indian Affairs and had never had its lands reserved. They had lived as a village, or band, by "squatting" on their small cemetery and partially on an adjoining ranch. The band organized formally, wrote a constitution, and obtained recognition and membership in the Inter-tribal Council of California. Following this, they were recognized in November 1975 by the Bureau of Indian Affairs, which then offered its services to the band.

Another band, Mesa Grande, has had an unusual and complicated land-title problem, which has prevented any form of development. The band elected a committee with instructions to solve the problem. This committee acquired copies of historical documents, developed a statement of the problem, and obtained the cooperation of the Department of Interior in conducting an impartial investigation leading to a title solution.

Interreservation organizations began to be formed by Indians themselves to obtain and manage new programs. For example, the South San Diego County Health Clinic Board was formed by the southernmost reservations when the local U.S. Army Reserve Hospital unit offered outpatient clinic services of medical and dental personnel. The Board members found a building on a centrally located reservation, then leased, renovated, furnished, equipped, and operated it. They arranged for the Bureau of Indian Affairs to fund a community college class on the reservation to train clerical and medical aid person-

Fig. 2. Kumeyaay Tribal Affairs Office with part of the staff and part of the Board of Directors. An outgrowth of the Southern San Diego County Reservations organization, this office acts as an agency to provide the many small reservations with community action programs. left to right: Joseph J. Benintende, Administrator of the Community Action Program; Louis Gunn; Andy McReynolds; Peggy McReynolds; Tony J. Pinto of Cuyapaipe; Rosalie P. Robertson of Campo Reservation. Photograph by Florence Shipek, Dec. 1975.

615

nel. Following this, they organized a blood bank committee and developed a blood bank account. This is a system of credit accounting for covering cost of blood needed by any member of the group establishing the account.

From these experiences, the southern reservations have formed Kumeyaay, Inc., a formal, nonprofit organization incorporated under the state laws of California (fig. 2). Utilizing this organization, the member reservations are developing their own plans and programs, then joining in seeking funds, technical aid, and program management.

These political developments among the Kumeyaay have been paralleled by similiar developments among the other reservations, both along ethnic nationality lines and crossing them for specific purposes. Interreservation organizations and boards have become complex as they have proliferated. Some of the more widespread organizations are the All-Mission Indian Housing Authority, Inter-tribal Council of California, and California Rural Indian Health Program (funded by the U.S. Department of Health, Education, and Welfare). The California

Indian Education Association, Native American Students, and the American Indian Historical Society (founded by a Cahuilla), which are more pan-Indian in character and purpose, include many Mission Indians as members.

Economic developments on the reservations have been paralleling the political. La Jolla (Luiseño), beginning in 1969, and Los Coyotes, in 1972, developed excellent recreational facilities that are sources of tribal income as well as of individual employment. Pala Reservation has its own tribal housing program and has also developed an industrial park facility. Some reservations have begun range-improvement programs or specialty orchard-development plans. Others are exploring for economic development solutions that will be compatible with their location, home-use patterns, and access roads.

Along with these political and economic changes, there has been a resurgence of interest in their own languages, history, and past culture. Museums have been founded: Malki Museum on Morongo Reservation (fig. 3) and the

Malki Mus., Banning, Calif.

616   Fig. 3. Entrance to the Malki Museum, with a southern California brush house in the foreground. Photograph by Don Morehouse, Dec. 1975.

Fig. 4. The dedication ceremony of the Cupa Cultural Center, Pala Reservation. The dancers were Pala children who attended classes in language, culture, and history of the Cupeño at the Center. Cultural material from the original home of the Cupeño (Warner's Ranch) is on display. Photograph by Nancy Bercovitz, May 1974.

Cupa Cultural Center on Pala Reservation (fig. 4). Cultural history classes have been held for a number of groups. Language classes have been held on many reservations and in nearby towns for several years. Margaret Langdon and Roderick A. Jacobs of the Department of Linguistics of the University of California at San Diego developed the formal linguistics framework for the class materials in response to the desires of the communities and with their full support. Malki Museum began an extensive program of publication in California anthropology and texts for the language classes.

As a part of this resurgence, Indians demanded that the public stereotyped image of their existence at "the lowest level of human culture," which has existed in school books, be replaced by a recognition of the competences of their culture and their own adaptability. While this demand resulted from and used the recent writings, papers, and lectures of anthropologists involved in detailed studies of their cultural adaptive mechanisms and culture history, the interest, decisions, and actions have been entirely the Indians' own.

Conclusion

Problems will continue to exist concerning the development of reservation lands, Indian-federal government relationships, and Indian-local government relationships. The difference will be that the Indians have been developing effective organizations to handle their problems and no longer need to pit advocates against the government and against other advocates in order to manage their affairs. They have been learning to be effective politically as well as economically within the framework of twentieth-century institutions, modern contractual forms of government, business relationships, and voluntary organizations. Instead of fighting "the system" and fending it off, they are learning to make "the system" produce the desired results: better housing, roads, sanitation, water supplies, health, education, and income. They have been developing better representation and communication to all levels of government.

In sum, it might be said that the central core of values and the organizational concepts that underlay their original successful adaptation to the unstable physical environment of southern California has enabled the

617

Indians to continue to maintain their identity and to adjust not only to a drastic change in their human environment but also to entirely different forms of technology, economic, political, and religious life. These central conceptual aspects of their various adaptations include independence and individuality (Fages in Engelhardt 1920:122), flexibility (Luomala 1963), secrecy and categorization of knowledge (R.C. White 1963:144, 149), industriousness, order, precision, moderation, and caution (Bean 1972:73-79).

Prehistoric Rock Art

C. WILLIAM CLEWLOW, JR.

The first record of prehistoric rock art in California was made in 1850 by Bruff (1949:423-424), who sketched part of an extensive panel of petroglyphs in Snowstorm Canyon, Lassen County, while being menaced by local Indians. Bruff, like many early writers on the subject, mistakenly referred to the petroglyphs as "hieroglyphic symbols, perhaps of Egyptian origin." This was once a common error in the study of New World rock art; however, subsequent research has clearly demonstrated that this art is in no way related to writing of any sort and that it has no connection with any Old World glyphic systems.

Anthropological attention was first called to California rock art by Mallery (1893), whose interests ranged over rock art of the entire nation. His work was followed by Kroeber (1925:936-939), who noted that some areas of the state, particularly those occupied by tribes with "Shoshonean" (i.e., Uto-Aztecan) linguistic affiliations, were unusually rich in rock-art sites. J.H. Steward (1929), who conducted the first comprehensive study of rock art in the state, was the first scholar to delineate the basic style areas. Most students of rock art have followed Steward's insight to focus upon single style areas or regions for intensive analysis. Excellent interpretive reports have been produced on the art of specific regions such as the Great Basin style area of eastern California (Heizer and Baumhoff 1962), the Coso Range of Inyo County (Grant, Baird, and Pringle 1968), the Chumash area near Santa Barbara (Grant 1964a, 1965), and the Central Sierra region (Payen 1966).

In 1948 Heizer began a comprehensive study of California rock art that aimed at amassing as much data as possible about the sites and their associations. In the many years of the project's duration a great deal of information was collected and is on file at the Archaeological Research Facility, Berkeley. Completed in 1971, this analysis resulted in a quantification and refinement of Steward's work, and a redefinition of California rock-art style areas (Heizer and Clewlow 1973).

Two basic types of rock art occur in California. The first is painted art, found at sites where the rock surface has been applied with pigment or paint of one or more colors. Painted sites are referred to as pictograph sites, and each individual element is referred to as a pictograph. The second type is rock art that has been pecked or abraded, or, less commonly, ground into the surface where it is presently visible. Sites with this type of art are called petroglyph sites, and the individual designs or elements are referred to as petroglyphs. Petroglyphs have a wider distribution and occur with more frequency than do pictographs in California. The two types of art usually occur separately, but there are cases where they occur at the same site or in the same element of a site. This usually takes the form of a pecked or abraded element being painted over with pigment.

Any given petroglyph or pictograph site is made up of one or more elements or design units such as circles, rakes, or human figures. Style areas in California are based on the description of each rock-art site in terms of its component elements. While it is possible to segregate California rock art into categories utilizing large numbers of specific elements, the most productive analytical

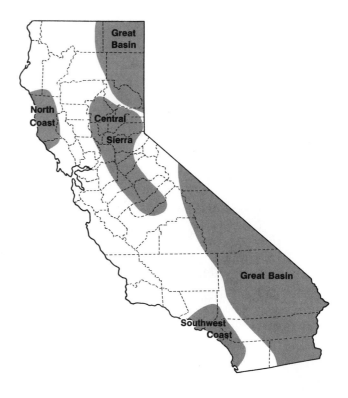

Fig. 1. Petroglyph style areas.

619

results have been derived when a relatively small number of general elements were employed in the sorting process. In the following discussion, style areas are based on segregation of the art into five major element categories. These are Human, Animal, Circle and Dot, Angular, and Curvilinear. Although many of the figures are highly stylized or abstract, if they are at all recognizable as animal or human, they are classed as such. The Circle and Dot category refers to individual elements comprised of one or more concentric circles with a dot or sphere inside, not unlike traditional "bull's eye" targets. Angular elements are geometric or subgeometric designs that consist of roughly linear segments joined at angles. Curvilinear elements are geometric or freeform designs comprised mainly of nonlinear or wavy elements joined by curving lines.

Style Areas

Rock art is known to occur in at least 1,000 sites in 39 of the 58 counties of California. Counties for which no rock art data are on record are Alameda, Alpine, Colusa, Del Norte, Glenn, Kings, Marin, Napa, San Benito, Santa Cruz, San Joaquin, San Mateo, Solano, Sonoma, Sutter, Tehama, Ventura, Yolo, and Yuba. Four counties (Contra Costa, Santa Clara, Shasta, and Tuolumne) have so few sites that they are not amenable to stylistic discussion. Most of the counties for which no rock art has been

recorded are situated in the alluvial Sacramento and San Joaquin valleys, where suitable rock outcrops do not exist. Some areas of the state where appropriate rock outcrops occur are, nonetheless, practically devoid of recorded rock-art sites. In some cases this is merely a reflection of inadequate search. In other regions, like Los Angeles and Orange counties, a great many rock-art sites have fallen victim to urban expansion and were engulfed by the megalopolis before they could be recorded. In still other areas, prehistoric man, for whatever cultural or ecological reasons, did not leave behind his artistic efforts in the form of rock art. In fact, one of the most fascinating aspects of prehistoric rock art in California is its tendency to appear in a highly developed form in one area and to be completely absent from the cultural inventory of a neighboring geographical province or temporal unit.

In spite of its lack or scarcity in some areas, extensive portions of California are abundantly endowed with rock-art sites. It is these regions that form the nine main stylistic areas. There are four petroglyph style areas: Great Basin, Central Sierra, Southwest Coast, and North Coast. The five painted style areas are: South Coast Range Painted, Santa Barbara Painted, Southwest Coast Painted, Southern Sierra Painted, and Northeast Painted. The style areas of California rock art are shown in figures 1 and 2.

Great Basin Petroglyph Style

The Great Basin petroglyph style* is the most widely distributed of the California rock-art styles, being reported in Lassen, Mono, Inyo, San Bernardino, Riverside, Imperial, and Modoc counties. The style was named in 1958 and subdivided into two substyles: Great Basin Curvilinear, and Great Basin Rectilinear (Baumhoff, Heizer, and Elsasser 1958). These were slightly refined in a later work into Great Basin Representational, and Great Basin Abstract, which included Curvilinear and Rectilinear subcategories (Heizer and Baumhoff 1962).

Two qualities characterize the style in California. The first is the fact that all five element categories occur consistently in each county where the style is present. Second, Angular and Curvilinear elements predominate, with Curvilinear being always the more common, recalling J.H. Steward's (1929:228) remark that this style "has most in common with petroglyphs in other parts of the western hemisphere, especially in its abundance of curvilinear designs."

Heizer and Baumhoff demonstrated for the first time that Great Basin petroglyphs are functionally related to

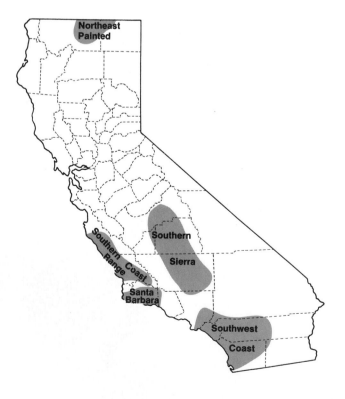

Fig. 2. Pictograph style areas.

---

*Although this style is outside the culture area delimited for tribal California, it is included here for comparison.

stood as part of the economic pursuit of hunting large game (deer, antelope, and mountain sheep)" (Heizer and Baumhoff 1962:239). This hypothesis was subsequently confirmed in studies of rock art in the Owens valley area (Werlhof 1965) and the Coso Range, where the petroglyphs present evidence of a sheep-hunting cult that became so successful that it ultimately was instrumental in eradicating its primary prey, the bighorn sheep (Grant, Baird, and Pringle 1968). Great Basin-style petroglyphs in California are almost always associated with migratory game trails, winter grazing areas, or favored hunting or ambush areas; and they are clearly linked with hunting and hunting magic (figs. 3, 4).

On the basis of archeological associations and stylistic evolution, the Great Basin petroglyph style in California dates from about 1000 B.C. to A.D. 1500. Only the Central Sierra style has an equivalent antiquity and duration.

after Heizer and Clewlow 1972:fig. 24a.

Fig. 4. Example of Great Basin petroglyph style from site Iny-205, showing bow and arrow, atlatl, and big horn sheep.

Fig. 3. Petroglyph from site Iny-279, Great Basin style, depicting big horn sheep and a "medicine bag" in the lower left corner. Photograph by Campbell Grant, before 1962.

Central Sierra Petroglyph Style

The Central Sierra petroglyph style is found in a large area of the central Sierra Nevada and adjacent foothills in all or part of the counties of Amador, Butte, Calaveras, El Dorado, Madera, Mariposa, Merced, Nevada, Placer, Plumas, Sacramento, Sierra, and Stanislaus. The region has generally been considered of minor importance, with a few rock-art sites that were stylistically related to other areas (cf. Kroeber 1925:937; J.H. Steward 1929:219). While it is true that there is some stylistic influence from the Great Basin pecked and the Southern Sierra painted styles, there is nevertheless sufficient cohesion within the Central Sierra petroglyph corpus for it to be granted a stylistic unit. The style is characterized by a near absence of Human and Animal representations and a higher incidence of Circle and Dot than is found in the Great Basin style area. Moreover, Central Sierra-style sites tend to have either a preponderance of Angular or Curvilinear elements, with one being represented and the other excluded, or vice versa, at any given site. This contrasts with Great Basin-style sites where both Angular and Curvilinear elements usually occur in abundance.

The most comprehensive study of Central Sierra style petroglyphs was done by Payen (1966), who identifies at least seven substyles in the area, which are dated at between 1000 B.C. and A.D. 1500 (ibid.:72–73). This estimate is quite reasonable, accounting for archeological factors as well as stylistic affiliations. Many of the Central Sierra sites are associated with game trails and seem to be part of the magico-religious aspect of big-game hunting. Some sites may have been tribal boundary markers, and others were fertility-oriented representations of female genitalia, possibly connected with increase magic (Payen 1966, 1968; Payen and Boloyan 1963; E. L. Davis 1961).

North Coast Petroglyph Style

The North Coast petroglyph-style area is limited to Humboldt, Trinity, Lake, and Mendocino counties, which encompasses a small region centered on the North Coast Range. Stylistically, the petroglyphs may be described as completely lacking any Human or Animal elements; they take the form of angular incisions or random scratches on soft boulders. These incisions seem to have been placed upon the stones in a haphazard manner (fig. 5). The North Coast style area was occupied by ethnographic groups who conducted at least two different ceremonies involving the scratching or incising of rocks and boulders. One of these practices, found among the Tolowa, Karok, and Hupa, was concerned with rain control (Driver 1939:364; Goddard 1903–1904, 1904). The other was found among the Pomo, where women wishing to conceive would incise boulders in a fertility-enhancing ceremony (Barrett 1952; Loeb 1926; Aginsky 1939). Heizer (1953a) has summarized data on both the "rain rocks" and the "baby rocks" of the North Coast style area. In all probability the North Coast style appeared late, around A.D. 1600, and lasted into the historic period.

Dept. of Anthr., Archaeo. Research Facility, U. of Calif., Berkeley.
Fig. 5. Petroglyph from site Men-437, North Coast style. Photograph by Martin Heicksen, July 1963.

Southwest Coast Petroglyph Style

The Southwest Coast petroglyph style applies to the pecked rock art of the extreme southwest corner of California in San Diego, Orange, and Los Angeles counties. This region is best known for its elaborate pictograph style, but the petroglyphs, although clearly related to the painted art, form a separate stylistic entity. The style is characterized by the consistent presence of Angular, Curvilinear, and Human elements and the near absence of Animal and Circle and Dot elements (fig. 6). It thus has clear connections with the Southwest Coast painted

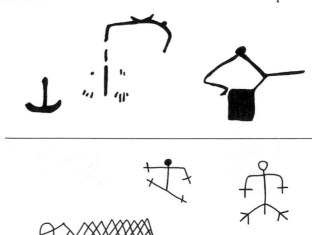

after Heizer and Clewlow 1973:fig. 104e, j.
Fig. 6. Example of Southwest Coast petroglyph style from site Lan-164.

style and is also stylistically related to the Great Basin and Central Sierran petroglyph styles. These stylistic connections suggest that at one time the Southwest Coast petroglyphs were associated with game-hunting magic.

This style probably dates from about 500 B.C. to A.D. 900 or 1000, terminating at about the same time that the Southwest Coast Painted style begins (Heizer and Clewlow 1973).

Northeast Painted Style

In extreme northeast California, in Modoc and Siskiyou counties, is an area with a heavy concentration of pictographs known as the Northeast Painted style[†] area. Both J.H. Steward (1929:221) and Grant (1964a:34) have pointed out the resemblance between the style of pictographs in this area and those around Santa Barbara and in Tulare county. A number of the renderings are polychrome, featuring one color to outline figures of another hue, remarkable insects, triangles, zigzags, and sun disks. Stylistically, it might be noted that Human and Animal figures, while not abundant, are consistently present. The same is true of Circle and Dot elements (fig. 7). Angular elements are very common, with Curvilinear ones predominant, linking the area stylistically to the Great Basin petroglyph style as well as to the Santa Barbara and Southern Sierra Painted style areas (Heizer and Clewlow 1973). No direct ethnographic evidence exists to aid in interpretation, but it may be assumed by analogy that some of the sites were painted in connection with ceremonies, possibly of a fertility nature. The style probably dates to the period A.D. 500–1600.

The area has received very little attention by students of rock art (cf. Lathrap 1950; Hoover 1968; Pilling 1948) and was considered by J.H. Steward (1929:234) to be "marginal." No Circle and Dot elements appear in this style area, a fact that separates it from the Santa Barbara pictographs farther south. The style consists almost entirely of Angular designs, with some Human and Animal figures. Grant (1964a:34) notes that the "designs are chiefly linear, with some polychrome in red, black, and white."

According to Grant, there is strong circumstantial evidence that most California pictographs were painted as part of a ceremony, either by shamans or under their guidance. "They are often hidden in the most remote and inaccessible places, and were certainly not for display as art for art's sake" (Grant 1964:40). This assessment applies almost certainly to the South Coast Painted style pictographs, which date A.D. 1000–1600.

Southwest Coast Painted Style

In the extreme southwestern corner of California, in Orange, San Diego, Riverside, and Los Angeles counties, another concentration of prehistoric rock paintings occurs referred to as the Southwest Coast Painted style area. Almost all the elements are Angular, consisting of diamonds, chevrons, zigzags, and other geometric motifs (figs. 8 and 9). Curvilinear elements, such as wavy lines, are common, and Human figures occur consistently. Almost no Animal or Circle and Dot elements appear. Most of the designs appear on the vertical surface of isolated boulders (Grant 1965:113) and seem to be asso-

after Heizer and Clewlow 1973:fig. 166d.

Fig. 7. Example of Northeast Painted style from site Mod-23. Solid areas are red, heavy stippled areas black, light stippled areas yellow, other area blue where indicated.

South Coast Range Painted Style

In an isolated section of Monterey and San Luis Obispo counties a concentration of rock-art sites occurs that has been named the South Coast Range Painted style area.

†Although this style is outside the culture area delimited for tribal California, it is included here for comparison.

after Heizer and Clewlow 1973:fig. 246a.

Fig. 8. Example of Southwest Coast Painted style from site SDi-33.

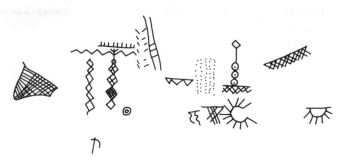

after Heizer and Clewlow 1973:fig. 246b.

Fig. 9. Example of Southwest Coast Painted style from site SDi-31, color red.

ciated with ethnographic village sites (True 1954:69). Occupied ethnographically by the Cahuilla, Cupeño, Ipai-Tipai, Luiseño, and Serrano tribes, this territory is of particular interest because of ethnographic accounts that report the use of rock painting in girls' puberty ceremonies (cf. C.G. Du Bois 1908a; Sparkman 1908; Strong 1929; Kroeber 1925:674–675; J.H. Steward 1929:227). This area presents a rare instance where ethnographic accounts of rock-art use are available. The style may be assigned dates from about A.D. 1300 or 1500, to the ethnographic period.

Santa Barbara Painted Style

The most spectacular and best-known pictographs in California are those of the Chumash region of Santa Barbara and Ventura counties. They have been desig-

nated the Santa Barbara Painted style. Many of the pictographs are polychrome, and, stylistically, the group may be characterized as emphasizing Angular and Curvilinear elements in roughly equal proportions. Circle and Dot elements, in the form of large "suns" and "targets," are common as are Human figures, often clearly shamanistic, and Animals, especially centipedes and marine motifs, the latter presumably reflecting the maritime orientation of coastal Chumash culture. Figure 10 is an example of this pictograph style (see also "Interior Chumash," figs. 3–5, this vol.). The Santa Barbara Painted style has been the subject of considerable scholarly attention (Frederick 1901; Strong 1935; Eberhart and Babcock 1963; Rozaire 1959a). The most intense study has been from Grant (1960, 1964a, 1965), who has analyzed the style in terms of its seven ecological subareas, discerning five substyles of painting within the region. The coastal sites exhibit very simple paintings, while inland, in higher, less accessible country, the designs are increasingly sophisticated and complex, an observation that led Grant (1965:76–79) to conclude that some sort of magico-religious or shamanistic motivation accounts for the manufacture of most of the sites within the style area. Using evidence from subject matter (the appearance of horsemen in one pictograph), radiocarbon dating, erosion rate, and artifact association, Grant (1965:96) has concluded that the style began no earlier than A.D. 1000. Deetz (1964) recovered a portable pictograph in a Chumash village with an associated date of around A.D. 1800, a date that was probably terminal for the style.

after Heizer and Clewlow 1973:fig. 269.

Fig. 10. Example of Santa Barbara Painted style from site SBa-526. Solid areas are red, stippled areas black.

Southern Sierra Painted Style

The Southern Sierra Painted style area lies in the dry foothill country of Kern, Fresno, and Tulare counties. It is often referred to in the literature as the Kern-Tulare or Tulare style. Most of the elements are Curvilinear, with Angular motifs also heavily represented. Many of these are not simple but are combined into series of "complex patterns" (Grant 1964a:34). Human and Animal figures are notably present, and Circle and Dot designs appear consistently. Stylistically, the Southern Sierra Painted area is quite closely related to the Santa Barbara style, the main difference being the preponderance of Angular designs in the Santa Barbara region. It also bears some similarities with the Northeast Painted and Great Basin pecked style areas. Figure 11 is an example of Southern Sierra Painted style pictographs.

The function of the Southern Sierra pictographs is difficult to ascertain. Voegelin (1938:58–61) noted a number of sites that he was told were made by "brownies," while Gatschet (1883:73) and Merriam (1966–1967, 3:412) were informed that local Indians did not paint rocks. From stylistic analogy it seems probable that the pictographs were made in connection with shamanistic practices, as well as magico-religious accompaniments of hunting big game. Grant (1964–1965:87) concurs in this view, which is supported by Gayton's (1948:113) observation that painted rocks often marked shamans' caches. The Southern Sierra may be the oldest of the California painted styles, possibly dating from A.D. 1 to 1600, with most sites probably painted between A.D. 500 and 1200.

after Heizer and Clewlow 1973:fig. 356d, g.

Fig. 11. Example of Southern Sierra Painted style from site Tul-89. Solid areas are red, stippled areas black.

Basketry

ALBERT B. ELSASSER

Among the textiles arts of native California, basketry is beyond any question the most highly developed, and compared with that of other regions of North America, the basketry of California Indians must be judged to be of the highest quality. Many tribal groups did not utilize pottery at all before White contact, but even those who had pottery, such as the Cahuilla and Luiseño in southern California, also produced a range of basketry forms similar to that of the peoples living farther north. It is thus possible to describe California basketry as a single unit, even though there were great numbers of detailed differences apparent from group to group.

If there is any one factor underlying the suggested unity of California basketry, it almost certainly must be found in the acorn-processing complex that obtained with little variation throughout the region. Gathering, carrying, storing, milling, and cooking of acorns, from north to south, were all performed in approximately the same way; and the similarity of procedures reflected in the forms of the baskets that otherwise remotely related groups employed.

Another characteristic feature of California basketry taken as a whole is that in any tribe only a small portion of available material for warps and wefts was utilized (Kroeber 1909:249), and the choice seems to have only a partial relationship to the botanical differences in the several physiographic provinces occupied. Beyond this, however, numbers of remarkable variances in details of form, manufacturing techniques, or in decoration have been noted, sometimes among closely neighboring groups. While there is no ready explanation for these discrepancies, they may profitably be looked upon as forming a simple corollary to the well-known cultural and linguistic separatism of California Indian groups, even those occupying the same environmental subareas.

Despite the minute differences in basketry observable from group to group (table 1), there are several features with a comprehensive regional distribution rather than sporadic individual tribal occurrence or random spread. Thus, while all groups surveyed here made twined baskets (fig. 1), the people in northwestern California employ this technique exclusively: they have no coiled basketry. Groups to the south can be said to have a preference for coiled baskets (fig. 2), although the Pomo,

the best known of the California basket makers, employ twining and coiling in about equal measure. Only among the Pomo and their neighbors did men weave baskets, and they occupied themselves only with certain kinds of openwork twining (Kroeber 1909:243).

Other examples of regional differences may be cited where simple choices are involved, as in direction of weft

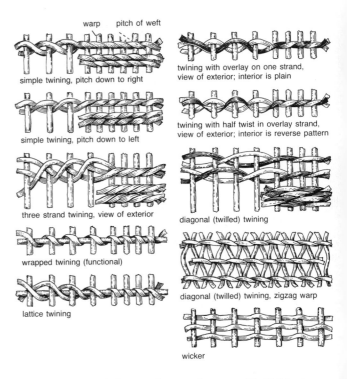

Fig. 1. Twining techniques and nomenclature used in California baskets.

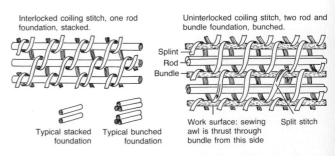

Fig. 2. Coiling techniques and nomenclature used in California baskets.

Table 1. Variety and Distribution

Ethnographic group (north to south)	Basic Techniques	Types and usages	Materials	Ornamentation	Dyes	Remarks
Tolowa (Driver 1939)	Twining: plain, 2-strand, lattice twining (reinforcing band); openwork, closework; starts: T1; selvages: T5, T9	B-T, Csg-T, Cft-T, Cs-T, F, H-T, Hm-T, Sg-T, Sw-T, Crs-a	WpT-Cory,[1] Sal; Wft-Cory, con	Ba; Ov-Xer, Adi, Woo, por	Aln, Eve	[1] stained on some openwork
Karok (Driver 1939; O'Neale 1932)	Same as Tolowa	B-T, Csg-T, Cft-T, Cs-T, F, H-T, Hm-T, J, Sb-T, Sg-T, Crs-a	WpT-Sal; WfT-con, Vit, Cory	Same as Tolowa	Same as Tolowa	
Yurok (Driver 1939; O'Neale 1932)	Same as Tolowa	Same as Karok	WpT-Cory,[2] Sal; WfT-con, Sal	Same as Tolowa	Same as Tolowa	[2] stained on some openwork
Wiyot (Driver 1939)	Same as Tolowa	B-T, Csg-T, Cft-T, Cs-T, F, H-T, Hm-T, Sb-T, Sg-T, Crs-a	WpT-Cory,[3] Sal; WfT-con, Cory	Ba; fea; Ov-Xer, Adi, Woo	Aln, soil	[3] stained on some openwork
Hupa, Chilula,[4] Whilkut[4] (Driver 1939)	Same as Tolowa	Same as Karok	WpT-Cory, Sal; WfT-con, Vit, Cory, Sal	Same as Tolowa	Same as Tolowa; Hupa-Ber	[4] not enough data
Mattole (Bear River) (Driver 1939)	Twining: plain, 2-strand, lattice (reinforcing band); openwork, closework; starts: T1; selvages: T5, T9	B-T, Csg-T, Cft-T, F, H-T, Hm-T, Sb-T, Sg-T, Crs-a	WpT-Sal; WfT-con	Ba; Ov-Xer, Adi, Woo	Aln	
Sinkyone (Driver 1939; Nomland 1935)	Twining: same as Mattole Coiling: 1-rod foundation (rare)	B-T, Csg-T, Cft-T, Cs-T, F, H-T, Hm-T, Sb-T, Sg-T, Sw-T, Crs-a	WpT-Cory, Sal; Wft-con, Cory	Ba(zigzag); fea; Ov-Xer Adi, Woo	Same as Mattole	
Nongatl (Driver 1939)	Twining: same as Mattole	Same as Sinkyone	Same as Sinkyone	Ba; Ov-Xer, Adi, Woo	Same as Mattole	
Lassik (Essene 1942; Kroeber 1925:pl. 24)	Twining: plain, 2-strand, openwork, closework; starts: T1; selvages: T5, T9	B-T, Csg-T, Cft-T, Cs-T, F, Hm-T, Sb-T, Sg-T, Crs-c	Same as Sinkyone	Same as Nongatl	Same as Mattole	
Wailaki (Essene 1942)	Twining: Same as Lassik. Coiling: 3-rod foundation, split-rod foundation (probably from Yuki)	B-T, Bt, Csg-T, Cft-T, Cs-T, F, Hm-T, Sb-T, Sg-T, Crs-c	Same as Sinkyone	Same as Nongatl	Same as Mattole	
Chimariko (Driver 1939)	Twining: plain and 2-strand only types known	B-T, Cft-T, Cs-T, F, H-T, Hm-T, Sb-T, Sg-T, Crs-a	Same as Sinkyone	Same as Nongatl	Same as Mattole	
Shasta[5] (Dixon 1907; Voegelin 1942)	Twining: plain, diagonal, 2-strand, 3-strand; openwork, closework; starts: T1; selvages: T5, T6, T7	B-T; Csg-T, Cft-T, Cs-T, F, H-T, Hm-T, Sb-T, Sg-T, Sw-T, Crs-a,c	WpT-Cory, Sal; WfT-con, Vit, Cory, Cer	Be; Ba; Ov-Cer, Xer Adi, Woo, por	Aln, Eve	[5] basketry similar to Klamath River groups
Atsugewi (Voegelin 1942)	Twining: plain, diagonal, 2-strand, 3-strand; openwork, closework; starts: T1, T3; selvages: T5, T7	B-T, Csg-T, Cft-T, Cs-T, F, H-T, Hm-T, Sb-T, Sg-T, Crs-c	Same as Shasta	Be; Ba; fea[6]; Ov-Cer, Xer, Adi, Woo, por	Same as Shasta	[6] used sparingly

Table 1. Variety and Distribution *(continued)*

Ethnographic group (north to south)	Basic Techniques	Types and usages	Materials	Ornamentation	Dyes	Remarks
Achumawi (Voegelin 1942)	Twining: plain, diagonal, 2-strand, 3-strand; wrapped twining; openwork, closework; starts: T1, T3, "hourglass shape" from Modoc; selvages: T5, T7, T10	B-T, Csg-T, Cft-T, Cs-T, F, H-T, Hm-T, Sb-T, Sg-T, Wb-p,[7] Crs-c, Crl-d, e	WpT-Cory, Sci,[8] Sal; WfT-Phr,[8] con, Vit, Cory, Sci,[8] Sal	Be; Ba-Pte, Sci[8]; Ov-Xer, Adi, Woo, por	Same as Shasta	[7] E. Achumawi, probably from Paiute [8] N. Achumawi, probably from Modoc
Cahto (Driver 1939; Essene 1942)	Coiling: 1-rod, 2-rod and splint, and 3-rod foundations; starts: C1, C3; selvages: C7, C9. Twining: plain 2-strand, 3-strand; openwork, closework; starts: T1; selvages: T5, T7	B-T, B-C, Csg-T, Cft-T, Cs-T, Cs-C, F, H-T, Hm-T, Sb-T, Sg-C, Crs-c	FoC-Corn, Cory, Cer, Sal; SeC-Corn, Cer, Car; WpT-Cory, Sal, WfT-con, Sal	Ba-Cer; fea; Ov-Cer, Xer; gap	Same as Shasta	
Yuki Huchnom Coast Yuki (Driver 1939; Essene 1942; Kelly 1930a)	Coiling: 1-rod, 2-rod and splint, and 3-rod foundations[9]; starts: C1, C3 selvages: C7, C9 Twining: plain, 2-strand, 3-strand; openwork, closework[10]; starts: T1; selvages: T5, T7, T11	B-T, B-C, Csg-T, Cft-T, Cs-T, Cs-C, F, H-T, Hm-T, Sb-T, Sg-C, Sw-T, Crs-a, c	FoC-Corn, Cory, Lon, Cer, Sal; SeC-con, Corn, Cer, Car; WpT-Cory, Sal; WfT-con, Corn, Vit, Cory, Sal	Be; Ba-Cer, Car; fea (on coiling only)	Aln	[9] double-coil foundation also known (J.A. Mason 1912:147) [10] lattice twining attributed to Huchnom—reinforcing rods
Pomo (Barrett 1908a; Gifford and Kroeber 1939; Essene 1942)	Twining: plain, diagonal, 2-strand, 3-strand, lattice twining, wrapped twining; openwork, closework; starts: T1, T2; selvages: T5, T6, T7, T11. Coiling: 1-rod and 3-rod foundations; starts: C3, C4, C5, C6; selvages: C7. Wicker seed beaters	B-T, Bt, Csg-T, Cft-T, Cs-T, Cs-C, F, Hm-T, Sb-T, Sg-T, Sg-C,[11] Sw-T, Sw-C, Crs-b	WpT-con, Cory, Sci, Sal; WfT-con, Vit, Cory, Cer, Car, Sci, Sal; FoC-Cer, Sal; SeC-Pte, con, Cer, Sci, Car	Be; Ba-Cer, Pte, Car, Sci; fea (mainly on coiling); smal; gap	Aln, Rhd	[11] boat-shaped baskets of varying sizes, rare elsewhere
Wappo (Driver 1936)	Twining: plain, diagonal, lattice; openwork, closework; starts: T1; selvages: T5, T7. Coiling: 1-rod and 3-rod foundations; starts: C1, C3, selvages: C7, C8.	B-T, Csg-T, Cft-T, Cs-T, F, Hm-T, Sb-T, Crs-b	WpT-Sal; Wft-con, Cer, Sal; FoC-Sal; SeC-Cer, Car	Be; Ba-Cer, Car; fea	Aln	
Lake Miwok Coast Miwok (Gifford and Kroeber 1939)	Twining: diagonal, lattice; openwork, closework. Coiling: 1-rod and 3-rod foundation	Similar to Pomo and possibly to Patwin	Similar to Pomo and possibly to Patwin	Similar to Pomo and possibly to Patwin	Similar to Pomo and possibly to Patwin	

Ethnographic group (north to south)	Basic Techniques	Types and usages	Materials	Ornamentation	Dyes	Remarks
Wintu (N. Wintun) Nomlaki[12] (C. Wintun) (Du Bois 1935; Gifford and Kroeber 1939; Goldschmidt 1951a; Voegelin 1942)	Twining: plain, diagonal, 2-strand, 3-strand, lattice twining on reinrods; openwork, closework; starts: T1, T3; selvages: T5, T9, T11. Coiling: 3-rod foundation.[13]	B-T, Csg-T, Cft-T, Cs-T, H,[14] Hm-T, Sb-T, Sg-T, Sw-T, Crs-c	WpT-Cory, Sal; WfT-con, Vit, Cory, Rhd, Cer, Sal; FoC-Cer, Sal; SeC-Cer	Be; Ba-Cer; Ov-Xer, Adi, por; Smal	Aln, Eve	[12] not enough data; resembles Pomo or Patwin [13] not developed among Wintu; traded from Nomlaki [14] not developed; modeled after Shasta
Patwin (S. Wintun) (Gifford and Kroeber 1939; Kroeber 1932a)	Coiling: 1-rod and 3-rod foundations; starts: C1, C4; selvages: C7, C8. Twining: plain, diagonal, 2-strand, lattice, wrapped twining; openwork, closework; starts: T1; selvages: T5, T11.	B-C,[15] Csg-T, Cft-C, Hm-T, Sb-T, Sb-wicker, Sg-C,[16] Sw-T, Sw-C, Crs-b	FoC-Car, Sal; SeC-Cer, Sci; WpT-Sal; WfT-con, Vit, Car	Be; Ba-Cer; fea	Same as Pomo?	[15] coiling in culinary baskets distinguishes Patwin from Pomo, who used more twined ware [16] some boat-shaped vessels
Yana: Northern,[17] Central,[17] Southern[18] (Gifford and Klimek 1939; Sapir and Spier 1943)	Coiling: 3-rod foundation. Twining: plain, diagonal, 2-strand, 3-strand, lattice-twined reinforcing rods; openwork, closework; starts: T1, T3; selvages: T5, T7, T10, T11	B-T, B-C, Csg-T, Cft-T, Cft-C, Cs-T, Cs-C, F, H-T (N. Yana only), Hm-T, Sb-T, Sw-T, Crs-c, Crl-f	FoC-Cory; SeC-Cer; WpT-con, Cory, Sci, Sal; WfT-con, Cory, Cer, Sal	Ba-Cer; fea; Ov-Cer, Xer, Adi; Smal	Eve, red earth	[17] basketry most resembles Wintu or Nomlaki [18] not enough data; resembles Maidu
Maidu Konkow Nisenan (Dixon 1902a, 1905; Voegelin 1942)	Coiling: 3-rod foundation; starts: C1, C4; selvages: C7, C10. Twining: plain, diagonal, 2-strand, wrapped; openwork, closework; starts: T1, T3; selvages: T7, T8, T10, T11. Wicker.	B-C, Csg-T, Cft-T, Cft-C, Cs-C, F, H-T,[19] Sb-T, Sb-wicker,[20] Sg-C, Sw-T, Crl-d, h	FoC-Cer, Sal; SeC-Cer, Sal; WpT-Ace, Sal; WfT-con, Vit, Cer, Sal, Xer (used as double-weft)[19]	Ba-Cer, Pte; fea (from Pomo?); Ov-Xer, Adi,[19] Smal		[19] N. Maidu only [20] Nisenan only
Costanoan[21] (Harrington 1942; J.A. Mason 1912)	Coiling: 3-rod foundation; starts: C1, selvages: C7. Twining: plain, diagonal, 2-strand; openwork, closework; starts: T1; selvages: T11	B-T, Csg-T, Cft-C, Hm-T, L, Sb-T, Sg-T, Sw-T,[22] Wb-P, Crl(?)	FoC-Sal; SeC-Pte, Car; WpT-Sal; WfT-Car, Sal	Be; Ba; fea		[21] not enough data [22] unique scoop-shaped tray
Esselen (Meighan 1955a)	Coiling. Twining: WpT-Sal; WfT-Car, Sal	Few data; probably like Costanoan	Few data; probably like Costanoan	Few data; probably like Costanoan	Few data; probably like Costanoan	

Table 1. Variety and Distribution (continued)

Ethnographic group (north to south)	Basic Techniques	Types and usages	Materials	Ornamentation	Dyes	Remarks
Salinan[23] (Harrington 1942; J.A. Mason 1912)	Coiling: 1-rod, bundle foundation, also double-coil foundation; starts: C1; selvages: C7, C8 (2-strand diagonal overstitch). Twining: plain, 2-strand; openwork, close-work; starts: T1; selvages: T5, T6, T11	B-C, Csg-T, Cft-C, H-C, Hm-C, Sg-T, Sw-T, Sw-C, Wb-a, Crl-f, h	FoC-Muh; SeC-Cla, Pte, WpT-Sal; WfT-Sci	Be; Ba-Pte; fea; Smal	Sam	[23] resembles Yokuts basketry
Yokuts (Aginsky 1943; Driver 1937; Gayton 1948; Latta 1949)	Coiling: bundle foundation; starts: C2; selvages: C8. Twining: plain, diagonal, 2-strand, 3-strand; openwork, closework; starts: T1,[24] T3, T4; selvages: T5, T10, T11	B-T, B-C, Csg-T, Ca, Cft-T, Cft-C, Cs-C, F, H-C, Hm-C, Sb-T, Sg-T, Sg-C, Sw-T, Sw-C, Tul, Wb-p, n, Crl-d, e, f, g, h, some with hoods	FoC-Muh, Cer, Sci, Sal; SeC-Pte, Cla, Cer, Car; WpT-Cory, Sci, Sal; WfT-con, Vit, Car, Cer, Sal	Ba-Cer, Yuc; fea; Smal	Same as Salinan	[24] some with wrapped cordage partial warp in one direction
Sierra Miwok Plains Miwok[25] (Aginsky 1943; Barrett and Gifford 1933)	Coiling: bundle, 1-rod, 2-rod, 3-rod foundations; starts: C2; selvages: C7, C8. Twining: plain, diagonal, 2-strand; openwork, closework; starts: T1, T3; selvages T5, T10, T11	B-T, B-C, Csg-T, (soaproot sealing), Cft-T, Cft-C, Cs-T, F, H-C (rare, probably borrowed), R, Sb-T, Sg-C, Sw-T, Tul, Wb-P, Crl-e, f (hooks at end, unique to Miwok)	FoC-con, Muh, Cory, Iri, Rht, Sal; SeC-con, Ace, Cer, Car, Rht, Sal; WpT-Cory, Sal; WfT-con, Vit, Cory, Ace, Cer, Sal	Ba-Cer, Yuc; fea; Smal		[25] not enough data [26] bundle is Yokuts influence from south; 3-rod foundation is Maidu or Washo influence from north
Monache[27] (Aginsky 1943; Driver 1937; Gayton 1948; Gifford 1932)	Coiling: bundle, 3-rod foundation; starts: C2; selvages: C8. Twining: plain, diagonal, 2-strand; openwork, closework; starts: T1; selvages: T10, T11	B-T, B-C, Csg-T (soaproot sealing), Ca, Cft-T, Cft-C (from Yokuts), Cs-T, Cs-C, F, H-T and H-C (rarely used), Sb-T, Sg-C, Sw-T, Sw-C, Tul, Wb-P, Crl-d,e	FoC-Muh, Cer, Sal; SeC-Cer, Car, WpT-Cer, Sal; WfT-Cer, Car, Sal	Ba-Cer, Pte, Yuc, Car, Pro; fea; Smal		[27] resembles Yokuts basketry
Tubatulabal[28] (Driver 1937; Voegelin 1938)	Coiling: bundle foundation; starts: C2; selvages: C7. Twining: plain, diagonal, 2-strand; openwork, close-work; starts: T2, T3; selvages: T10, T11	B-T, B-C, Csg-T, (soaproot sealing), Cft-C, F, H-C, Hm-C, Sb-T, Sg-C, Sw-T, Sw-C, Tul, Wb-P, n, Crl-f, g, h	FoC-Muh, Cer, Sal; SeC-Cer, Car, Sal, Yuc; WpT-Sci, Sal; WfT-Cer, Car, Sci, Sal	Ba-Pte, Yuc, Pro; fea		[28] basketry resembles S. Yokuts
Chumash[29] (Dawson and Deetz 1965; Harrington 1942; Kroeber 1924)	Coiling: 3-rod, bundle foundation; starts: C1; selvages: C7. Twining: plain, diagonal, 2-strand, 3-strand; closework; starts: T2, T4; selvages: T5[30]	B-C, Csg-C, Cft-C, Cs-C, H-C, Hm-C, Sb-T, Sb-C, Sb-twilled wicker, Sg-C, Sw-C, Tul, Wb-a, Crl-f, h	FoC-Muh, Rht, Jun; SeC-Rht, Jun, Car, Sci, WpT-Jun, Sci, Sal; WfT-Rht, Jun, Sci	Be (doubtful); Ba-Jun, Rht; fea (doubtful), Smal	Dal, Sua	[29] influenced by Yokuts and Takic, Numic, and Tubatulabalic tribes [30] not enough data

Ethnographic group (north to south)	Basic Techniques	Types and usages	Materials	Ornamentation	Dyes	Remarks
Gabrielino[31] (Harrington 1942; Kroeber 1924)	Coiling: 3-rod, bundle foundations; starts: C1; selvages: C7. Twining: plain, diagonal; closework.	B-C, Csg-C, Cft-C, H-C, Hm-C, Sb-T, Sg-C, Sw-C, Wb-a, Crl-f, i	FoC-Muh, Jun; SeC-Rht, Jun; WpT-Jun; Wft-Jun	Ba-Jun, Rht; Smal		[31] not enough data
Luiseño[32] (Drucker 1937; Kroeber 1924)	Coiling: 2-rod, bundle foundations; starts: C1; selvages: C7, C9. Twining: plain, 2-strand; openwork; starts: T1; selvages: T7	B-T, Csg-C, Cs-T, Cft-C, F, H-C, Hm-C, L, Sb-T, Sg-C, Sw-C, Crl-f, i	FoC-Muh, Jun; SeC-Was, Jun, Rht; WpT-Jun, Rht; WfT-Jun, Rht	Ba-Jun; Smal	Sam, Dal, Rub, Sua	[32] basketry resembles Cahuilla
Serrano Kitanemuk[33] (Benedict 1924; Drucker 1937; Harrington 1942)	Coiling: bundle foundation; starts: C1; selvages: C7, C9. Twining: plain, diagonal, 2-strand; openwork, closework	Csg-C, Cft-C, Cs-C, H-C, Hm-Ch, Sb-T, Sg-C, Sw-C, Tul (Kitanemuk only), Wb-p (Kitanemuk only), Crl-f, i	Same as Luiseño	Ba-Jun, Rht; Smal	Sam	[33] related in some respects to San Joaquin Valley basketry rather than to that of S. Calif.
Cahuilla Cupeño (Barrows 1900; Drucker 1937; Kroeber 1908b, 1924; Schumacher 1879)	Coiling: bundle foundation; starts: C1; selvages: C7, C9. Twining: plain; openwork	Csg-C, Cft-C, H-C, H (Great Basin twined among Cahuilla), Hm-Ch, L, Sb-T, Sg-C, Sw-C, Crl-f, i	FoC-Aga, Muh, Jun; SeC-Was, Rht, Jun, Sci; WpT-Art, Jun, Rht, Sal; WfT-Art, Jun, Rht	Ba-Jun; Smal	Sam, Dal, Sua	
Ipai -Tipai (Drucker 1937; Spier 1923)	Coiling: bundle foundation; starts: C1; selvages: C7, C9. Twining: plain; openwork, closework (including soft textiles in basketry shape). Wicker (cradle hoods)	Csg-C, Cs-C, H-C, H (Great Basin twined), Hm-Ch, Hm (old basket with bottom cut out), L, Sb-T, Sg-C, Sw-C, Crl-f, i	FoC-Aga, Muh; SeC-Rht, Jun; WpT-Rht, Jun; WfT-Rht, Jun	Ba-Jun		Same as Cahuilla, Cupeño

ADDITIONAL SOURCES: Kroeber 1925, Merrill 1923

C - *coiled work*; T - *twined work*

C1 wrapped segment of basic foundation material, often shredded, with wrapping continued in use as basic sewing element
C2 wrapping material length (sometimes folded upon itself) formed into spiral, with open end incorporated into (bundle) foundation
C3 twined, for example, modified crosswarp start
C4 overhand knot of shredded foundation material; less flexible material (such as willow) may then be incorporated as foundation
C5 perforated shell disk bead serving as base for starting spiral and beginning of wrapping
C6 use of basic foundation material as keel for first coil, as in boat-shaped baskets
T1 crosswarp; ordinary 2-strand weft baskets may have 3-strand wefts at beginning
T2 crosswarp; with sets of warps twined or wrapped together, then crossed as sets
T3 fan-shaped tray start: warps bent over into single warp section near center of fan (outer edge of tray)
T4 hank of start material splayed out radially, acting as form of crosswarp start; common on water bottles
C7 "self-coiled" rim with tapered end foundation
C8 same as (7) but with "overstitching"—additional sewing course (1 or 2 strands) around rim
C9 "self-coiled" with blunt-end foundation, often with 3 or 4 backstitches
C10 selvage incorporating thickened wrapped or sewed rim
T5 simple trimming off of warp ends; last (border) weft courses on 2-strand weft baskets may be 3 strand, for strengthening
T6 warps bent to one side, usually in pairs, becoming weft strands for simple twining or braiding over succeeding sets of warps
T7 warp ends turned down and taken up in basic weft courses, inside or outside of basket
T8 warps turned back inside, leaving loop for elements used in lashing on rim hoop
T9 warps' ends turned to one side and plaited over one another (usually on hopper mortars and seed-gathering or carrying baskets)
T10 coiled or lashed selvage; warp ends turned to one side, becoming like foundation bundle, usually with rim hoop associated
T11 rim hoops sewed or wrapped with ordinary weft materials or tied on with string or hide thongs (usually with hopper or seed-gathering baskets)

Types and Usages

B - boiling vessels, including small-sized serving baskets and scoops or dippers
Bt - bird traps, twined
Csg - carrying or seed-gathering baskets
Ca - cage, with or without lid, twined
Cft - circular, fan- or ovoid-shaped, flat or shallow trays for various purposes
Crs - sitting cradle - a, northwestern California "toe" type; b, Pomo "deep" type; c, northern California variant of Pomo type; d, sex of child designated
Crl - lying type cradle - e, basketry; f, with wooden frame and slats or cross-rods; g, with woven tule mat provided; h, Y-frame; i, U-ladder
Cs - circular (subconical or spheroid) storage baskets
F - fish traps, twined
H - hat or cap
Hm - hopper for stone mortar; h, started on a hoop
J - Jumping Dance basket, twined
L - leaching vessel, twined
R - racket (for ball game), twined
Sb - seed beater
Sg - small round or globular vessel used as tobacco or work basket and sometimes called "treasure" or "fancy" basket
Sw - winnower or sieve
Tul - "Tulare bottle necked" or treasure basket, coiled
Wb - water bottle, twined - p, pitch seal; a, asphalt seal; n, no sealing material (some specimens)

Materials, Ornamentation, Dyes

Ace - bigleaf maple (*Acer*)
Adi - maidenhair fern (*Adiantum*)
Aga - agave (*Agave*)
Aln - alder (*Alnus*)
Art - wormwood (*Artemisia*)
Ba - banded designs (wrapping or weft elements)
Be - shell beads or ornaments attached
Ber- barberry, Oregon grape (*Berberis*)
Car - sedge, slough grass (*Carex*)
Cea - deer brush (*Ceanothus*)
Cer - redbud (*Cercis*)
Cla - bunch grass (*Cladium*)
con - conifer roots, usually split (*Picea, Pinus, Pseudotsuga, Sequoia*)
Corn - dogwood (*Cornus*)
Cory - hazel (*Corylus*)
Dal - parosela (*Dalea*)
Eve - wolf moss, lichen (*Evernia*)
fea - feathers
FoC- coiled foundations
gap - banded decoration with deliberate break or gap
Iri - iris (*Iris*)
Jun - rush (*Juncus*)
Lon - honeysuckle (*Lonicera*)
Muh - deer grass (*Muhlenbergia*)
Ov - overlay twining (background or banded designs)
Phr - reed (*Phragmites*)
por - porcupine quills, split
Pro - devil's horn (*Proboscidea*)
Pte - brake fern (*Pteridium*)
Que - white oak (*Quercus*)
Rhd - poison oak (*Rhus diversiloba*)
Rht - squaw bush, sumac (*Rhus trilobata*)
Rub - blackberry (*Rubus*)
Sal - willow (*Salix*)
Sam - elderberry (*Sambucus*)
Sci - tule, bulrush (*Scirpus*)
SeC - coiled sewing elements
Smal - "small element" decoration
Sua - sea blight (*Suaeda*)
Vit - grape vine (*Vitis*)
Was - desert palm (*Washingtonia*)
WfT - twined wefts or rimming materials
WpT - twined warps
Woo - giant fern (*Woodwardia*)
Xer - squaw grass (*Xerophyllum*)
Yuc - yucca (*Yucca*)

pitch in twining or in direction of work, use of interlocking or noninterlocking stitches, or use of split or nonsplit stitches in coiled basketry. Table 2 shows graphically that northern or central California groups show divergences from northwestern and from southern California, both in twining (pitch of weft in both directions, for example, for Pomo, Wappo, and Maidu) and in coiling (work direction, interlocking stitch and split-stitch use). There is no clear rationale for these peculiar distributions in either environmental or historical terms, al-

Table 2. Techniques

Ethnographic group	Pitch of weft (Twining)	Work direction† (Coiling) to left	to right	Interlocking stitch (Coiling)	Noninterlocking stitch (Coiling)	Split stitch‡ (Coiling)
Tolowa	/					
Karok	/					
Yurok	/					
Wiyot	/					
Hupa	/					
Mattole*	/					
Sinkyone	/					
Nongatl	/					
Lassik	/					
Wailaki	/		A		A	C
Chimariko*	/					
Shasta	/					
Achumawi	∧					
Atsugewi	∧					
Cahto	/		A		A	C
Yuki	/		A		A	C
Pomo	∧	A		B,A(x)	C	B
Wappo	∧	A		B,A(x)	C	B
Lake Miwok*		A		B,A(x)	C	C
Coast Miwok*		A		C		B
Wintu	/					
Nomlaki*		A		B		C
Patwin	\	A		B,A(x)	C	B
Yana	∧	B	C		A	C
Maidu	∧	A				A
Costanoan*	∧	A				A
Esselen*	∧					
Salinan	/		A		A	
Yokuts	/		A		A	
Sierra Miwok	/	A		A		
Plains Miwok*	∧ arch.	A				A
Monache	/	B	C		A	
Tubatulabal	/		A		A	
Chumash	∧		A		A	C
Gabrielino			A		A	
Serrano and Kitanemuk*			A		A	
Luiseño	/		A		A	
Cahuilla	/		A		A	
Ipai-Tipai	∧		A		A	

SOURCE: Lawrence E. Dawson, personal communication 1974.

* Baskets known in small or poorly documented samples.

† As viewed by the weaver. Direction of work in twined basketry, as the weaver views it, is almost always to right, in all tribes. Probably left-handed persons in any group would account for the rare exceptions.

‡ Stitches split by awl on back face of basket (opposite "work surface").

(A) predominant usage, (B) used in large part, (C) minor usage.

x single-rod foundation.

∧ Both directions, but with qualifications, such as different directions on different types of baskets.

/ Down to left.

\ Down to right.

arch. Known from archeological remains only.

though it has been suggested that the direction of work in coiled basketry is conditioned by whether the awl is inserted from the outside or the inside (top, as looked upon from above) of the basket (Kroeber 1925:415). In twined basketry, the direction of work is determined by the consistent, region-wide practice of holding the bottom of the basket toward the (usually right-handed) weaver (Kroeber 1909:239).

History

Seed-grinding implements of stone in dated archeological sites that do not contain perishable materials show definite analogies with those found among ethnographic groups who utilized such implements together with basketry in food preparation. This, plus evidence from dry archeological deposits, mostly in the Great Basin, indicates that basketry was employed in California at least 5,000 years ago. It is not known, and perhaps can never be determined, which particular technique—twining or coiling—was first known in a given area. Maps of North America showing the various regions in which one or the other of these basic techniques was practiced (cf. Weltfish 1930:456) offer little in way of resolving the question. To the north and east, at least, basketry of the subregions of California (for example, the region for exclusive twining in northern California) tends to resemble that of the non-California neighbors.

Archeological evidence based upon textile impressions on baked clay balls probably used in the stone-boiling of acorns in baskets and the near absence in deposits of bone awls suitable for manufacturing coiled baskets both suggest that in ancient central California only twined basketry was known or it was at least predominant. At a date estimated around 1000 B.C. coiled basketry was introduced, possibly in connection with a major population displacement originating ultimately in the Great Basin to the east (Heizer 1949:28). Baumhoff and Heizer (1958) later suggested, however, that certain fine coiled basketry found in dry caves in the Great Basin was derived from "outlands," perhaps even central California, at about the same time level (about 1000 B.C.).

In southern California, bone awls offer the main approach to the question of precedence of twining over coiling in prehistoric times. Unfortunately the evidence here is by no means clear, since it must necessarily rest upon the positive identification of "awls" as true basketry awls rather than as remnants, for example, of fish gorges or other implements (cf. Harrison and Harrison 1966:79). Wallace (1955:220) indicates the paucity of any bone implements in early archeological deposits in southern California, although they occur frequently in later ones. It seems likely that coiling occurred at a later time at least in coastal southern California than in central California. Numerous dry cave finds in the Santa Barbara region, all seemingly late (estimated A.D.

1500–1800) are of twined basketry, although coiling was not lacking concurrently (see Mason 1904; Elsasser and Heizer 1963). Rozaire and Craig (1968:131) have described coiled basketry impressions on asphalt from a southern California open site dated by carbon 14 at about A.D. 1530 (King, Blackburn, and Chandonet 1968:94).

Techniques and Materials

In addition to technical traits, other elements having specific areal distributions in either the north or the south are outlined in table 1. For example, overlay twining and lattice twining are both confined to northern California, while wicker work is apparently randomly distributed (for instance, among the Pomo and the Ipai-Tipai). Information in table 1 pertaining to other techniques, forms, or usages of widespread or common occurrence, and to materials, including dyes, has been obtained largely from analysis of baskets in the collections of the Lowie Museum of Anthropology, University of California, Berkeley. These baskets were mostly acquired beginning about 1900 by ethnographers such as Kroeber (1909, 1924) and many of his students. Barrett (1908a) is especially noted for his work on Pomo basketry. O'Neale (1932) and Merrill (1923) were other specialists who made outstanding contributions to knowledge about the collections in the realm of technique, decoration, or material analysis.

Types and Usages

•CARRYING OR SEED-GATHERING BASKETS Usually wide-mouthed, conical or "rounded-conical" vessels with stout rim hoops, integral or added, were used in collecting seeds. Fitted with some kind of carrying strap (heavy cordage, or more recently, leather or cloth), approximately the same kinds of vessels were used as carrying baskets (fig. 3a; see also "Monache," fig. 6, this vol.). Depending upon the burden, whether of small or large seed such as acorns, or any other type of goods, twined carrying baskets were in open or close work; if closework, a soaproot sealing agent was sometimes used, as among the Miwok and Mono. In southern California, carrying and gathering baskets were predominantly made with the coiling technique.

•HOPPERS FOR STONE MORTARS Almost all the California groups discussed here used stone slabs with shallow central depressions (fig. 3b-c) for grinding seeds or other plant materials like manzanita berries. Exceptions were the Sierra Miwok and Monache, who regularly used bedrock mortars not requiring hoppers around the holes to contain the ground meal. The Luiseño in southern California employed hopper baskets on slabs but discarded the hopper when the hole in the stone was ground to a certain desired depth.

A regional difference between twining (north) and coiling (south) has been noted for basketry hoppers. Reinforcing upper rim hoops were common, and several southern California groups, such as the Cahuilla and Ipai-Tipai, started the manufacture of a hopper with a (basal) hoop. Asphaltum or pine pitch was often used for more secure attachment of the basket to the stone slab than could be obtained by mere pressure of the arms or legs while the basket was in use.

• TRAYS, SEED BEATERS Plaque forms served a variety of purposes, for example, as shakers or sifters in northwestern California, where small flat or shallow round trays with ground acorn meal placed upon them were shaken or tapped, perhaps with a deer leg bone, to separate fine from coarse meal. A larger flat basket was used in the same region to catch or receive the sifted acorn meal (fig. 3e). Among the Yokuts an almost flat coiled basket (fig. 3f) was employed as a winnowing implement in preparing acorns. A basket of this kind also could

serve as a parching tray for other small seeds, and some gambling trays as well followed approximately the same design.

Openwork twined, circular, flattish trays were used by Klamath River peoples in northern California for serving salmon (cf. Goddard 1903-1904: pl. 21). Circular flat trays also were employed as serving baskets among south-central California groups.

For beating seeds from dried inflorescences into gathering baskets, the Ipai and Tipai frequently used wooden sticks, and the Cahuilla had a sort of frame, not really a basket, for the purpose. More common, to the north at least, were well-made flat or shallow baskets (fig. 3d), sometimes resembling open-ended winnowing trays with handles provided, and with few exceptions woven in the twined technique (see Kroeber 1925:701, pl. 29). It is clear from this sequence that the southern California groups were not much interested in elaborating seed beaters. On the other hand, one example (see

Mus. für Völkerkunde, Berlin: a, IV B 7271; Lowie Mus., U. of Calif., Berkeley: b, 1-3033; c, 1-1200; e, 1-2485; f, 1-211533; Dept. of Anthr., Smithsonian: d, 203268.
Fig. 3. a, diagonal twined seed-gathering basket with close-coiled hoop selvage, Pomo; b, twined basketry hopper in place on mortar stone, selvage type T5 (see table 1), Pomo; c, twined basket hopper with reinforcing rods applied to lattice-twining technique, upper selvage type C7, Yurok; d, seed beater, wickerwork, Pomo; e, twined tray used to receive acorn meal as it is sifted, Hupa; f, wide-spaced coiling winnowing tray, Yokuts type. Diameter of f, 46.3 cm; a-e, same scale.

"Cahto," fig. 3, this vol.), from the Cahto in northern California, shows a glaring exception to the usual northern Californian weaving art: it is a carelessly made but functional implement that would hardly allow even an attempt at decoration.

• STORAGE BASKETS Large subglobose or subconical vessels with tapering walls (large flat bottoms and relatively narrow mouths) were most commonly used for storage of food such as acorns. Obviously other household articles or delicate ceremonial equipment often needed to be stored temporarily or for prolonged periods, and baskets of suitable sizes could be adapted for these purposes (fig. 4a).

Among the Miwok and other foothill Sierra groups there were thatched outdoor acorn granaries. These, and the southern California outdoor granaries made without textile process (Kroeber 1925:700), as well as pottery vessels in the south, made large storage vessels of basketry almost unnecessary. This happened to be true especially in regions where twining was infrequent (cf. Kroeber 1925:448).

At the lower end of the size scale were found in most households small vessels, serving, for example, as to-bacco containers or as "work baskets" (fig. 4c), that is, as reticules for basket makers and trinket or "treasure" baskets (fig. 4b, d). These are usually called small globular baskets in the ethnographic literature.

The coiled, bottle-necked, relatively small shouldered vessel (fig. 4e) almost certainly belongs in the category of treasure baskets since it is not characteristically a container for liquids. Nevertheless it has been nicknamed "Tulare bottle" in many descriptive works. Its center of distribution is roughly the south-central region—among the Yokuts, Monache, Tubatulabal, and Chumash. The inland groups usually decorated the shoulder with feathers or colored yarn, while the Chumash did not. Among all four groups baskets of this sort were often referred to as "money baskets," as they were repositories of shell-bead money.

• WINNOWING AND LEACHING The usual process of sifting acorn meal throughout California was by shaking on a close-woven basket rather than passing it through a fine-mesh screen. Sieve baskets proper were utilized for some purposes, such as separating husks from mealy parts of manzanita berries, which could be used as an

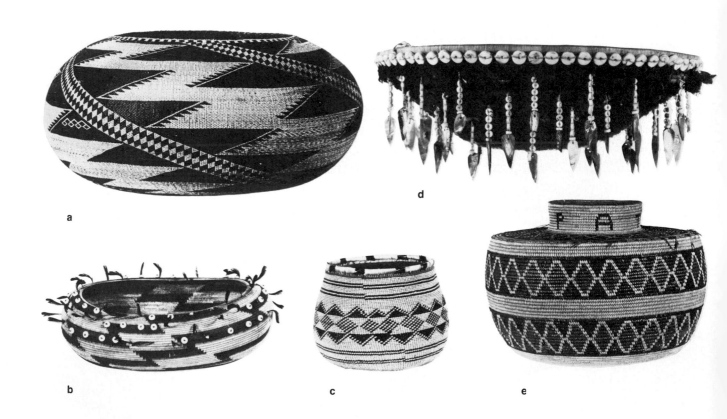

a

d

b

c

e

Mus. für Völkerkunde, Berlin: a, IV B 7269; Lowie Mus., U. of Calif., Berkeley: b, 1-70767; c, 1-26815; d, 1-20867; e, 1-70523.
Fig. 4. a, diagonal twined storage basket, Pomo; b, coiled "boat-shaped" basket, probably for trinkets, shape unusual in Calif. except among the Pomo; c, modern "fancy" basket, twined, with wrapped rim, not done in traditional fashion, and criticized by Karoks for inexcusably poor "stepping of rows," Karok; d, fancy coiled basket, almost completely covered with feathers, clamshell beads, and abalone pendants, Pomo; e, coiled narrow-necked basket "Tulare bottle," with addition of colored yarn on shoulder and Latin letters woven into neck, Yokuts type. a, diameter about 87 cm; b, diameter 25.5 cm; c, e same scale as b; d, diameter about 15.6 cm.

ELSASSER

addition for acorn soup. Gayton (1948:18) illustrates an openwork sieve of the type that was probably so used.

Circular flat trays intended to be used as winnowers for acorns were not so common in the entire region as the ovoid-shaped, usually twined trays such as those shown in figure 5a. Of these the more openwork trays were used as winnowers while the closework ones could serve either as winnowers or as acorn meal sifters (fig. 5b).

Leaching baskets are, in a sense, sieves. In some regions, especially in southern California, twined, circular, shallow vessels had acorn meal placed in them and water poured over them so that unpleasant elements in the acorns could be leached away. Obviously these baskets had to be of a certain sized openwork, or some other means such as a lining of leaves had to be employed to control the flow of leaching water through the vessel.

• BOILING AND SERVING UTENSILS Cooking of acorn gruel in a basketry vessel by placing heated stones in it and agitating them so that the vessel itself would not be burned was the most common method practiced in California. This technique obviously required sturdy watertight baskets, which were made in a range of sizes and shapes (fig. 5c; see also "Wiyot," fig. 3, this vol.) Small vessels of this type were sometimes used not for cooking but for serving food (fig. 5d), and among the Yuki and some of their neighbors flat-bottomed vessels resembling small boiling baskets were also used in seed parching with hot coals (see "Cahto," fig. 2, this vol.). Baskets used in this fashion can be distinguished by the frequent appearance of burn marks from hot coals, just as well-used boiling vessels can be recognized by acorn meal imbedded in their walls. Among Klamath River groups such as the Yurok, where overlay twining was used heavily, boiling baskets represented an exception, since on such vessels the double wefts were used only sparingly (Kroeber 1925:310).

Scoops or dippers resembling small serving baskets were used for pouring water over acorn meal to be leached and also for scooping acorn mush out of the cooking vessel. In northern California such baskets were twined and usually undecorated while in central and southern California they were coiled and decorated.

• FISH AND BIRD TRAPS Twined basketry fish traps are recorded from most regions of California, though they are probably more heavily emphasized in the north. Shapes and sizes vary, although elongate, openwork specimens used by the Pomo are the most remarkable (cf. Kroeber 1925:pl. 33).

Only from the Pomo are reported twined bird traps that are similar in construction to the elongate type of fish trap. A tubular openwork twined basket with closed

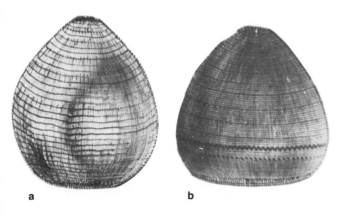

Lowie Mus., U. of Calif., Berkeley: a, 1-21699; b, 1-21698; c, 1-1761; d, 1-1772; e, 1-198299; f, 1-19436.

Fig. 5. a, open twined winnowing basket, Monache; b, close twined meal sifter or shaker, also used as winnower, Monache; c, twined boiling basket, Karok; d, twined food-serving vessel, Karok; e, openwork twined basket used as a woodpecker trap, Pomo; f, twined bottle, asphaltum applied to neck and shoulder, chumash. a, height about 59 cm; b, same scale; c, diameter 32 cm; d-f, same scale as c.

end was used to take woodpeckers, for example, which were unable to turn around or back up once they entered the tube (fig. 5e). The same principle applied to fish traps, which were placed in small stream currents.

• WATER BOTTLES   True water bottles (not "Tulare bottles") had a fairly wide distribution in south-central California (the San Joaquin River drainage) and in southern California, although pottery users like the Cahuilla and Ipai-Tipai probably rarely or never made this kind of basketry vessel. Water bottles sealed with asphaltum or pitch otherwise seem to be one of the few kinds of twined vessels used by people like the Chumash. They and their south coastal neighbors may have needed water containers in extensive maritime activities connecting them with the Channel Islands, which are not noted for plentiful supplies of spring or stream water for drinking. Many twined water bottles sealed with asphaltum (fig. 5f) have been recovered from late prehistoric dry caves in Chumash territory (cf. Mohr and Sample 1955a).

• CRADLES   Not all California cradles may properly be called "baby baskets." Some cradles have wooden frames and usually do not incorporate any basic basketry techniques in their manufacture. These are the "U-ladder" type (see Kroeber 1925: pl. 39b) of the Tipai-Ipai; the cradle with two long supporting rods bent forward at the top, adaptable either as hooks for hanging or as hood supports (Kroeber 1925: pl. 39f) of the Miwok; and the "Y-frame" of the Yokuts and Tubatulabal (fig. 6a) and its variants, for instance, among the Maidu (Kroeber 1925: pl. 40o, n). The Y-frame types sometimes include a twined tule mat or a soft-tule mat cradle such as that used by the Tachi Yokuts (fig. 6b). Kroeber (1925: 536) suggested that the wooden cradle with cross rods is originally trans-Sierran, including southern California.

All wood-framed varieties are so-called lying cradles; the Y-frame examples were almost always hoodless, and the U-ladder hoods (of wicker work, as among the Ipai and Tipai) are structurally separate from the frame. Lying cradles are characteristic of southern and central California. Besides the nonbasketry types already discussed, the Yokuts, Monache, and Miwok had a number of twined basketry lying cradle forms, with hoods (see "Monache," fig. 5, this vol.) and without hoods (fig. 6b-e).

In northern and northwestern California the sitting cradle of twined basketry prevailed. The principal forms among these were "boat-shaped," with rounded bottom or "toe" and carrying loop at the heel or top, as used primarily in northwestern California (fig. 6f); the "Pomo type" with horizontal loop used by the Pomo and their neighbors (fig. 6g); and the variant of the Pomo type, a flaring bowl with a loop handle at one end (fig. 6h) found among the Shasta and Wintu (Kroeber 1925: 248;

Cody 1940:91). Hoods were occasionally used with sitting cradles, but were not ordinarily an integral part of the body of the cradle. A little cone of separate openwork basketry could be hung or tied so as to allow a skin or mat to be laid in front of the child's face.

• HEADGEAR   Fine-overlay twined hats with a low, almost convex profile (fig. 7a-b) were worn habitually in northern California and may represent the culmination of the weaver's art among the Klamath River peoples (see also "Wiyot," fig. 2, this vol.). Oddly, their neighbors to the south, for example the Pomo and most of the Maidu groups, did not wear hats.

The southern California coiled hat is higher than the northern form, shaped like a fairly tall frustum (fig. 7c). Generally southern women wore hats only when they were carrying a load with a carrying strap or tumpline (Kroeber 1925:700).

• SPECIAL-PURPOSE BASKETS   Probably the most elegant coiled baskets in California were those adorned with colorful feathers and often shell beads or ornaments, made chiefly by the Pomo Indians (fig. 4d). These were frequently given as gifts and, besides serving as treasure baskets, were also destroyed in fires in honor of the dead.

The baskets usually designated "presentation" or "dedicatory" were made in fine coiling by "Mission Indians" such as the Chumash. These often were made with inscriptions, for example, the Spanish royal coat of arms (fig. 7d), woven into them (Nuttall 1924). They indicate that the Indians 50 years or so after the first Franciscan mission influence began to be felt were still carrying on a revered tradition with grace and enthusiasm, not to mention consummate skill.

Jumping Dance baskets were used in the dance by that name among the Klamath River tribes. They are cylinder-shaped, with longitudinal openings in the top and are sometimes called "purse baskets," probably because they resemble in general shape the hollowed elk-antler money purses of the same tribal groups (fig. 7e). However, Kroeber (1925:56) stated that these vessels contain only grass stuffing and are for display only during the dance. The Yurok, for example, attach no symbolic significance to them.

Some Yokuts and Monache groups had rattlesnake shamans who kept the snakes in bottleneck baskets

Lowie Mus., U. of Calif., Berkeley: a, 1-10363; b, 1-10731; c, 1-10944; d, 1-10235; e, 1-10216; g, 1-2362; h, 1-2307; f, Goddard 1903-1904: pl. 21.

Fig. 6. Cradles. a, Y-frame cradle for girls, with tule mat, Tubatulabal; b, twined soft tule mat lying cradle, Yokuts; c, twined lying cradle, Monache; d, twined lying cradle with two transverse strengthening rods, Miwok; e, twined lying cradle, with strengthening hoop, which may be vestige of former wooden formation, Miwok; f, sitting cradle with toe and loop at heel, Hupa; g, "deep" type sitting cradle with horizontal circular head loop, Pomo; h, sitting cradle with hoop rim at top serving as carrying loop, Wintu. Length of a, 109 cm; b-h, same scale.

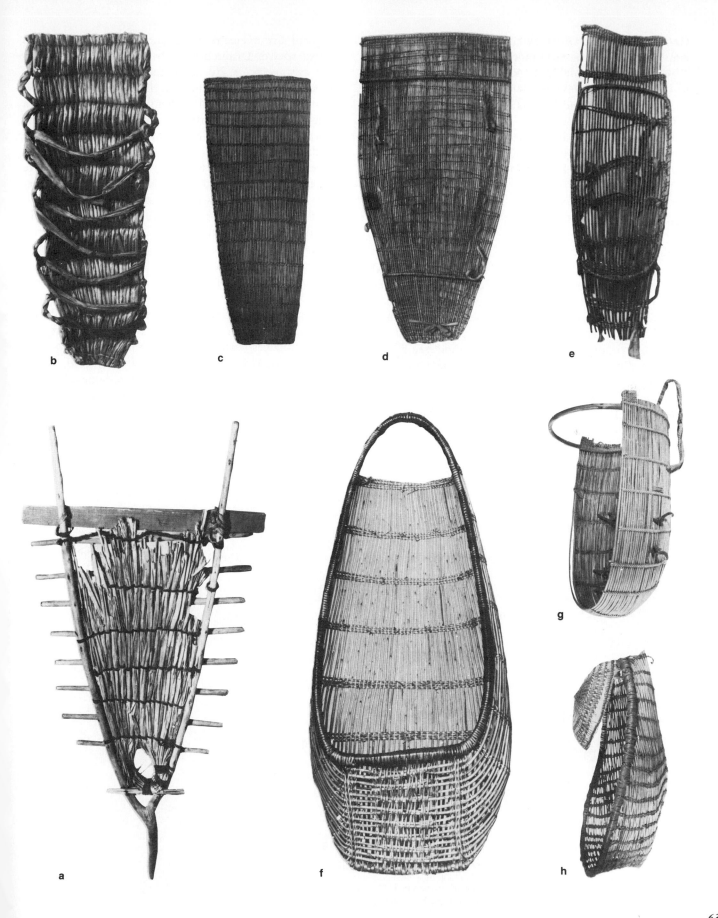

b   c   d   e

a   f   g

h

639

(Driver 1937:104). Other twined baskets, such as those employed in hunting wild pigeons, are reported for the Yokuts (Gayton 1948:221). Another "hanging basket" or cage, with lid (Gayton 1948: 18) was probably used by both Monache and Yokuts for keeping birds such as eaglets.

For a women's ball game, roughly resembling lacrosse, Barrett and Gifford (1933:254) describe basketry bats resembling seed beaters (fig. 7f) used by the Sierra Miwok.

Ornamentation

Beyond insertion of feathers (see fig. 4b) or, occasionally, colored yarn or porcupine quills, and superficial addition of shell beads and ornaments, most basketry decoration is produced by use of contrasting colored weft materials, dyed or of natural hue. In northwestern California, the region of predominant twining, patterns are always produced by the overlay method (see fig. 1). Probably redbud (*Cercis* sp.) is the most common of the naturally colored wefts, but of course choice of weft material varies from region to region.

Kroeber (1909:241) states that horizontal banded arrangement of designs is common for plain twining while diagonal arrangement is characteristic of the twilled twined weave. Distinctions between banded and diagonal arrangements are not noted in table 2; both arrangements are simply labeled "banded." Another layout, referred to as "small element" is sometimes used in design description, referring to isolated "patch" decoration, which may occur in regular though discontinuous bands (cf. fig. 3b).

Design elements (see fig. 8) throughout the region are named, but Barrett (1908a) makes the point clear, especially with the Pomo, who are excellent exemplars, that design elements came first and the naming afterwards. The designs therefore have little or no symbolic significance. In most groups, names frequently denote animals or parts of the body, although in the north zigzag, stripe, and spotted (speckled) designs are also well known (Kroeber 1909:245). Some exceptions to the symbolic conceptions of designs are seen in the use of sex-distinguishing marks on Monache cradles and in certain Pomo practices, such as in the break (dau, i.e. *dám* in Central Pomo) of a pattern in an encircling band, so that "the maker will not be afflicted with blindness"; in the insertion of yellowhammer quills in coiled bands as a preventive charm in cases where a woman works on a basket during her menstrual period; and in the introduc-

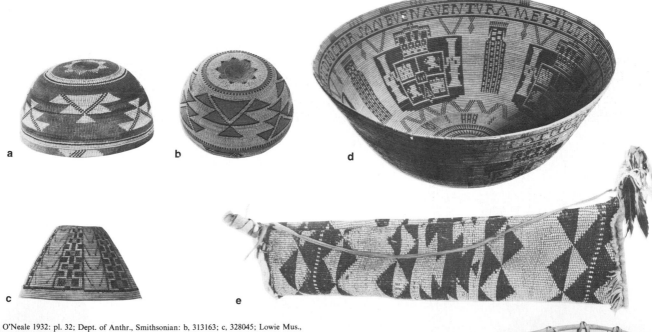

a, O'Neale 1932: pl. 32; Dept. of Anthr., Smithsonian: b, 313163; c, 328045; Lowie Mus., U. of Calif., Berkeley: d, 1-22478; e, 1-20825; f, 1-10363.

Fig. 7. a, women's twined cap with overlaid pattern, Hupa; b, widow's twined cap with overlaid pattern, Tolowa; c, women's coiled cap, showing the more conical appearance of the southern Calif. style in contrast to the more rounded northern Calif. cap, Yokuts; d, coiled "presentation basket," including woven-in Spanish royal coat of arms and inscription in Spanish, Chumash; e, Jumping Dance basket, for display during dance, Hupa; f, openwork twined racket for women's ball game, Miwok. Diameter of a, 19.0 cm; b-f, same scale.

After Barrett 1908a.

Fig. 8. A portion of the designs used in Pomo Indian basketry representing elements with arbitrary, nonsymbolic names probably typical of most Calif. groups. Examples of names of elements are: a, arrowhead, butterfly, large spots, turtleneck; b, quail plume band, butterfly and/with quail plumes; c, ant-design crossing, deer-back crossing, potato-forehead crossing; d, deer-back, potato forehead.

tion of an initial design (shaiyoi, perhaps *šayó·y* of Northern and Central Pomo), which is also connected with religious beliefs (see Kroeber 1909:242).

Dyes were used mainly for wefts, especially on overlay materials, in twined basketry or on sewing elements of coiled basketry. These elements are sometimes dyed (black) by burial in soil.

Conclusion

Data on California basketry assembled here are derived almost entirely from one nearly comprehensive collection at the University of California, supplemented by reports in publications relating directly or indirectly to it. A.L. Kroeber was principally responsible for forming this collection and devoted a great deal of time to analysis and description of many of its components. For that part of California considered here, he made numerous references to four principal areas of basketry manufacture: (1) Northwestern—Klamath River region, (2) Northern—including Pomo and Patwin, (3) South Central—generally San Joaquin River drainage, (4) Southern—including Tubatulabal, Cahuilla, Chumash, and Ipai-Tipai. Lines of demarcation for these areas are fuzzy, since there has demonstrably been interchange of various customs associated with basketry across these and other lines; for example, Tubatulabal basketry shows parallels to that of the Great Basin on the one hand and to Yokuts Indians of the San Joaquin River drainage on the other.

Kroeber's ideas about California Indian basketry first took formal shape in the early twentieth century, but the thrust of his observations then, despite further research by himself and others, has not been significantly altered. The mass of summary detail presented here tends to bear out his most pointed impression, that the basketry exemplifies "the tremendous predominance of unmotivated custom and habit over conscious utilitarian, artistic, or religious purpose" (Kroeber 1909:249). This statement ostensibly does not suggest an unawareness by the Indians of artistic talent or utilitarian drive but indicates a high level of residual aesthetic sensibilities in an essentially functional medium.

Basketry reached one of its high points of artistic achievement, worldwide, in native California, and the traditions of the weaving craft have by no means disappeared. High-quality basketry is still being produced in the 1970s by several Indian groups throughout the region, although in total volume or variety, production has been drastically reduced from former times.

Sources

Probably the most nearly complete collections of documented California Indian basketry are on two campuses of the University of California, at Berkeley and at Davis. Collections at Berkeley, referred to most frequently in this chapter, were assembled principally by A.L. Kroeber and S.A. Barrett, while the Davis collection was made almost entirely by C. Hart Merriam. The catalogue of the Merriam collection is especially valuable, with nearly every specimen accompanied by provenience data, photographs, and supplementary descriptive material, such as name of weaver and explanation of design.

Other considerable assemblages of California baskets are at the Southwest Museum, Los Angeles; the Museum of Man, San Diego; the National Museum of Natural History, Washington, D.C.; Milwaukee Public Museum; the American Museum of Natural History, New York; Field Museum of Natural History, Chicago; and the Peabody Museum of Archaeology and Ethnology, Harvard University.

In Europe, the Museum für Völkerkunde, Berlin; the British Museum; and the Musée de l'Homme, Paris, are known to have some excellent California baskets in their collections. The Musée de l'Homme holds what is probably the oldest known California basket, a coiled and bead-decorated specimen collected about 1780, which was made by a central California tribe (Heizer 1968a).

Music and Musical Instruments

WILLIAM J. WALLACE

More often than not California Indian music formed part of another function and was indulged in only seldom for sheer pleasure or spontaneous self-expression. Above all it served as an indispensable adjunct to religion; hardly a ceremony or ritual act was performed without its appropriate songs and instrumental accompaniment. Music also had a place in nearly every other aspect of tribal culture, including social life, subsistence, recreation, and warfare.

Vocal Music

As with other North American tribes, music was vocal rather than instrumental. The occasions for singing were many and varied and the native peoples employed distinctive songs for every one of them. Each tribal ceremony had its own songs, interspersed with dancing, prayers, and other ritual performances. Another large body of tunes aided in healing the sick. Besides these, there were songs to ensure success in hunting, gambling, warfare, and other pursuits, to accompany social dancing and courtship, as well as lullabies, laments for the dead, and many others. A curious class of derisive songs as used by southern California tribes to heap ridicule on members of rival clans (Strong 1929:80-81). Oftentimes singing was interwoven with story telling, the narrator inserting short ditties here and there in myths or tales to characterize one of the figures or to express some emotion or striking thought of a character.

Group singing, often with one person leading, predominated. Choruses were made up of male voices, female voices, or a combination of the two. Rarely, as in the Wikchamni Yokuts hand game, a group of women "answered" a group of men (Gayton 1948,1:91-92). Solos were sung by both males and females and not infrequently the melody was divided between a solo and a chorus. Although both sexes vocalized, male singers were greatly in the majority and performed more often in public. Only a few classes of songs, such as lullabies, acorn-grinding tunes, and the Yuki girls' puberty songs, were rendered exclusively by women. All adults knew how to sing but a few naturally showed more aptitude and took the lead in introducing tunes or carried on as soloists. Accomplished performers received high praise and esteem. In the Hupa Brush Dance those with exceptionally good voices were often encored.

A large share of the songs represented common property, known and sung by any member of the tribe. Others, owned by individuals or social groups, had more limited circulation. Luiseño cosmological songs, as an example, represented treasured possessions and could be sung only by those persons who had inherited them. Songs supposedly received in dreams were individually owned. Among the more important dream-inspired songs were those used in treating the sick. Typically a medicine man received his curing songs directly from a spirit during a dream experience along with instructions for their employment.

Compositions did not pass from singer to singer or from generation to generation in an exact and unchanging form even though an effort was generally made to keep sacred songs close to their original form. Little latitude was tolerated in the presentation of serious tunes and performers took unusual care to be error-free. The Luiseño believed that misusing or misperforming a sacred chant could bring supernatural punishment. To insure close adherence to tradition, Pass Cahuilla boys aged 6 to 12 were subjected to five or six days of intensive drilling in their clan songs. No such strictness attached to ordinary tunes and each singer, consciously or unconsciously, could give a song a novel twist by omitting, adding, embellishing, or even improvising. Even so, it seems that innovations occurred within the framework of the local style and were rather minor in nature.

Usually the native songs were quite brief, some of only 20 to 30 seconds duration. If they were longer, it was from repetitions or stringing together a series of short melodies. To illustrate, a set of Hupa White Deerskin Dance songs, each lasting 50 to 60 seconds, took 15 minutes to present (Goldschmidt and Driver 1940:110). Exceptions to the customary brevity include Cahuilla commemorative songs for the dead, every one of which took many minutes to present. The Cahuilla and neighboring tribes also favored long song cycles founded on elaborate creation myths.

Few songs were designed to tell a well-rounded story or for that matter to be very informative. Rather, the accompanying word materials tended to be minimal, obscure, and repetitive. The cryptic character of aboriginal lyrics can be demonstrated by Tachi Yokuts songs that averaged no more than two or three phrases, totaling 10 to 12 syllables. Allusions and symbolic phrases abounded in the song texts with the listeners left to identify the veiled references. A good sample is the one-line Luiseño song (Strong 1929:293):

> North, east, south, west, the hair lives.

This is comprehensible only if it is understood that hair is symbolic for spirit and the directions refer to the hair ropes at the four corners of the sand painting representing the world, which was prepared for the boys' initiation rite. Another example of the highly figurative style is the Tachi Yokuts shaman's song (Hatch 1958:51):

> Where will I go
> I will go in [at the place]
> Where green scum is on the pool.

To be able to supply what was missing, the auditor had to know the story of a famed shaman's experience. Supposedly, as a young man, he went to the edge of Woodlake (where the green scum is on the pool), dived in, and visited the underwater camp of a great medicine man.

Repetition was a prevailing characteristic of native lyrics. Syllables, words, phrases, or entire songs were reiterated either exactly or in slightly modified form. A Wintu dream song will serve as an illustration. First came two alternating verses in a low tone (Demetracopoulou 1935:484):

> It is above that you and I shall go;
> Along the Milky Way you and I shall go;
> It is above that you and I shall go;
> Along the Milky Way you and I shall go.

Next came a variation of the theme in a higher key:

> It is above you and I shall go;
> Along the flower trail you and I shall go.

Then back to the tune of the first verse:

> Picking flowers on our way you and I shall go.

A good deal of symbolism is also evident in this song. "Above" refers to the land of the dead and the Milky Way is the route over which spirits of the dead passed in arriving at their last resting place.

Not infrequently the diction of the songs differed markedly from normal speech. Certain words, modified to conform to the rhythm or melody, assumed an unusual form, thus making it hard to grasp their significance. Other expressions were so obsolete or archaic as to have no remembered meaning. Words or lyrics borrowed from an alien language were often used. Several Cahuilla songs, for example, were in the Serrano language and Luiseño songs contained foreign words, presumably Gabrielino. Names and words of Atsugewi shamanistic songs were understood only by the guardian spirits to which they were addressed.

Many songs contained meaningless syllables. These comprised chains of easily vocalized syllables such as the he yo, he yo, he yo of a Pomo Kuksu tune. The vocables were not spontaneous but were fixed for a particular tune and varied considerably from tribe to tribe. Often song texts consisted entirely of utterances such as in the girls' puberty song presented by Yuki women (Foster 1944:182–183):

> e, o, e, o, e, o, e, o, è, ó.

Another slightly altered:

> e he o, e he o, e he o
> e he o, e he o, è ó.

Like the first it ends with a startling exhalation. Another sample piece is the Achumawi song of Cloud Maiden in the myth of the Silver Fox Man and Cloud Maiden (Merriam 1928:20):

> he hi na   we na   we na
> he hi na   we na   we na
> he hi na   we na   we na

Vocables formed only part of other songs, frequently introductory and final elements like the hinini of a Wintu love song, which was repeated an indefinite number of times. Or a line of meaningful words alternated with one made up of meaningless syllables as in the Wikchamni Yokuts composition, sung by a medicine man for the entertainment of onlookers and to make money for himself (Gayton 1948,1:117):

> Kingfisher, Kingfisher, cover me with your power
> Sho ho sho ho na na het na na het
> I am circling about [as a kingfisher while hunting].

Songs were presented in a simple straightforward manner. Rhythm was well marked and usually a composition consisted of a single melody. The singing of one or more independent melodic lines was practically absent except for some occurrences of the "drone" type, in which a melody was accompanied by a sustained note on a single pitch. No real attempt was made at part singing or harmonization.

Vocal techniques varied somewhat in different parts of native California. Throughout the central section the singer's voice moved uniformly in a smooth, relaxed manner without much tension or pulsation. Somewhere, in the majority of tunes, came an interruption of the general melodic trend by material with a higher pitch (the "rise"), followed by the original to close the song. The range of melody was small, moving not far above or below the principal tone. The closely similar singing style of the southern tribes exhibited a simpler rhythmic pattern and even less vocal tension but was formally more complex. The rise portion of a song tended to be progressive whereas in central California it consisted of the same material transposed up an octave.

Clearly affected by influences from the North Pacific Coast, the vocal style of the northwestern Californians showed a more elaborate rhythmical pattern and a wider range of intonation and richness. Songs were delivered from a moderately tense and pulsating throat. In the great ceremonies, a soloist's voice often leaped an octave or more to a powerful note and then tumbled downward in a series of slides. The accompanying chorus maintained a simple drone with a long note that bore no melodic relation to the strain. The mode of singing of tribes living in the north-central part of the state such as the Yana, Yahi, Achumawi, and Atsugewi afforded considerable contrast by its extreme simplicity.

Instrumental Music

Aside from tunes like lullabies and work songs, singing without instrumental accompaniment was quite rare. The instruments provided a short introduction and closing and marked the rhythm; they were not intended for producing melody. Mixed combinations of instruments were unusual but not unknown. Men made and played the various musical devices.

The typical aboriginal instrument was the rattle, which occurred in one form or another over the entire state (table 1). The most widely used type comprised the clapper made from a short length of soft wood (fig. 1 c-g). One end of the stick was split and the pith removed; the unsplit end served as a handle. When shaken the free ends clashed together, giving forth a clacking noise. Constructed on the same principle but with the top pared down into a number of slender rods were the clappers of the Hupa and some of their neighbors (fig. 1a-b). The cleft stick functioned in a variety of ways. Hupa men kept time with it while singing at the girls' adolescence ceremony, while in central California it accompanied almost any dancing or singing, both pleasure and ceremonial. Pomo shamans manipulated a special variety in their curing rites.

Another common form of rattle consisted of a bunch of hoofs or dewclaws of deer loosely fastened to a wooden or bone handle and arranged so as to strike together and create a sharp clicking sound (fig. 2). Over much of California the deerhoof rattle figured in rites held when girls attained the status of women. But in southern California it functioned in two quite different ways. Luiseño hunters shook the rattle to assure success before setting out in pursuit of deer; the Chumash, Kitanemuks, Fernandeños, and Gabrielinos employed it in mourning ceremonies. For two northwestern groups, the Tolowa and Sinkyone, it had a more frivolous purpose—the accompaniment of gambling songs.

Container rattles with small objects placed inside were also popular. Moth cocoons furnished the material for the greatest number of these (fig. 3). Tiny pebbles, seeds,

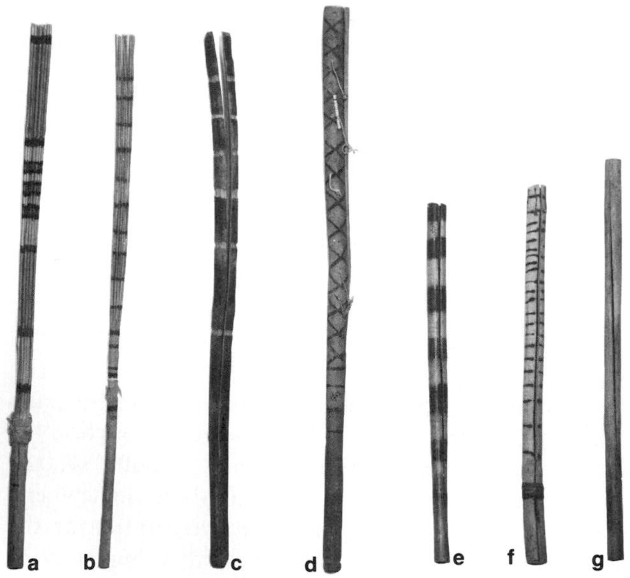

Lowie Mus., U. of Calif., Berkeley: a, 1-14603; b, 1-1511; c, 1-692; d, 1-2682; e, 1-13987b; f, 1-12192; g, 1-10050.

Fig. 1. Clappers, single and multiple. a-b, Hupa; c-e, Pomo; f, Wailaki; g, Miwok. Length of a, 61.0 cm; b-g, same scale.

Lowie Mus., U. of Calif., Berkeley: 1-2453.
Fig. 2. Deer-hoof rattle. Tolowa. Length 35.5 cm.

644

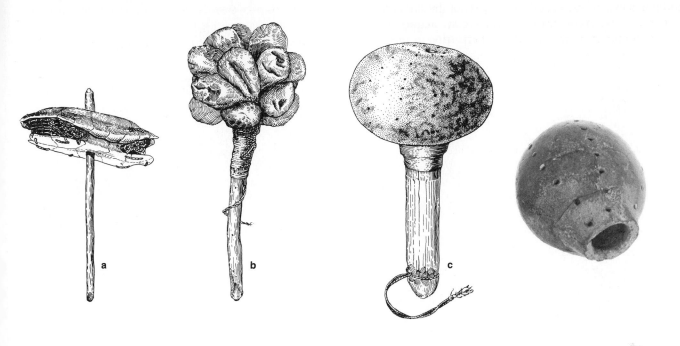

Fig. 3. Rattles. a, Tipai-Ipai, turtle shell with cordage mesh, length 19.9 cm, collected 1902; b, Pomo, moth cocoons; c, Cahuilla, gourd; all same scale.
Fig. 4. Pottery rattle. Tipai. Diameter 6.7 cm.

or even shell beads were inserted into the dried envelopes after the pupae had been removed. The cocoons were then mounted singly or in clusters upon handles of wood, bone, or quills. Most often the cocoon rattle functioned as a shaman's accessory, but it also saw service in group ceremonials. This form of rattle had a wide distribution in the central section but was absent in parts of northern and southern California. At the southern end of the state rattles made of dried gourds, turtle shells (fig. 3), or, rarely, pottery (fig. 4) replaced the cocoons as religious paraphernalia.

Whistles were employed by practically all tribes. The most familiar form comprised a straight bone tube with the lower end plugged by pitch or asphalt (fig. 5). Leg or wing bones of large birds supplied the preferred material with rodent, deer, elk, or even human bones less frequently utilized. Whistles were also manufactured from hollowed sections of soft-grained wood and cane. Each

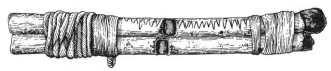

Fig. 5. Double whistle of bone with incised design, bound with cord. Yuki. Length 13.1 cm.

instrument had a single hole, generally at or near its center, which was partially stopped with a plug. Central Californians sometimes bound together two whistles, each with a contrasting pitch, to form a two-toned instrument; and there were exceptional examples of a succession of graduated tubes. Whistles were blown during ritual dances and by shamans while treating patients.

Drums were strikingly absent over much of California though various substitutes were used to mark rhythm. These percussion devices included a convenient plank that was stamped, kicked, or beaten with a canoe paddle, an inverted basket that was rubbed or thumped, and two sticks tapped together. In aboriginal times the Indians knew only the big foot drum and its use remained restricted to a group of central tribes who shared a god-impersonating cult. Made with considerable care, the foot drum consisted of a hollowed half-section of log, placed convex side up over a trench dug at the rear of the great semisubterranean assembly house. The pit served as a resonance chamber. When stamped on by the drummer's bare feet in cadence with the singers or thumped with a heavy club, the log reverberated with a deep compelling boom. The foot drum was treated with extreme reverence and replaced only when it became rotten. Skin-headed drums did not penetrate into California until the historic period. A rectangular wooden box covered with hide served as an accompaniment to gambling songs in the northwestern part of the state (fig. 6). The Shasta, Achumawi, and Atsugewi acquired a shallow tambourine from some northern tribe in recent but possibly pre-White times.

Fig. 7. Wood flute with incised design. Pomo. Length 37.5 cm.

Fig. 6. Captain Jack, a Yurok of Requa, using a contemporary gambling drum. Photograph by Ruth or Harry Roberts, about 1925.

Fig. 8. Pomo man playing a flute. Possibly photographed by S.A. Barrett, about 1915.

Only two instruments—the flute and the musical bow—were divorced from singing, and these represented the only ones capable of producing melodies. The native flute was a wooden or cane tube, pierced by a horizontal row of holes on its upper surface and with the mouth end trimmed down to a fairly sharp edge (fig. 7). Holding the instrument at a 45-degree angle or nearly vertical, and to one side of his mouth, the player blew across the thin end, opening and closing the finger holes to form the various notes of the sweet and plaintive melodies (fig. 8). Flute playing, universal or nearly so in California, constituted a favorite leisure pastime of young men and served as an aid to courtship.

The musical bow, the native people's sole stringed instrument, was a simple contrivance, consisting of a thin strip of wood with a string stretched between the two ends to give it a shape like an ordinary shooting bow. Not often, the instrument was fitted with two strings. A modern form has a tuning peg for adjusting the string's tension. One end of the wood, and sometimes the string, was grasped firmly by the teeth or the bow was held before the open mouth, which acted to amplify the sound. When set in vibration by plucking or tapping with the fingers or a stick or piece of bone, the taut string emitted a feeble noise. A skilled musician could create a combination of notes by different shapings of the mouth. Barely audible, the instrument was twanged

by a man absorbed in meditation or as a restful form of self-entertainment. A Chukchansi Yokuts played it to express a quiet sadness while grieving for a dead relative or friend. The Northwestern Maidu considered the bow's faint sound suitable for conversing with spirits and restricted its use to medical practitioners. Of wide but scattered distribution, the custom of playing the musical bow extended from northern to southern California. Now and then an ordinary bow was temporarily converted into a music-maker.

To many California Indians, the bull-roarer served as an important sound-producer, though hardly as a musical instrument. This device, in its usual form, consisted of a flat slab of wood, tapered to one end, with a stout cord passed through a hole at the opposite (fig. 9). When swung rapidly at arm's length, its blade rotated and gave forth a humming or roaring noise that carried a good distance. Except for a block of northwestern tribes, the use of the bull-roarer was quite general. It is a curious fact, however, that while the instrument possessed a sacred or magical character in some groups, others looked

Fig. 9. Wooden bull-roarer with rawhide thong. Tipai. Length 68.7 cm, collected in early 1920s.

646

WALLACE

upon it merely as a child's toy. The bull-roarer's weird sound, heard during solemn rites, symbolized thunder to the Pomo and Yuki; the Sinkyone and Cahto twirled it to invoke rain; and the Cahto, to bring fair weather, too. The majority of central Californians, on the other hand, regarded the bull-roarer as a plaything. Throughout southern California its roar summoned people to religious events and provided a starting or stopping signal during them. An Ipai-Tipai headman occasionally swung the contrivance to warn his people of an impending danger.

The 1970s

The native songs and musical instruments are no longer heard in much of California. As Indian customs gave way to new ones adopted from Western civilization, the tribal music fell into disuse, altered, or was replaced. Indians in the coastal strip from San Diego northward to beyond San Francisco Bay who fell under the influence of Franciscan missionaries quickly learned to sing hymns and to play Spanish instruments, and most of them abandoned their own songs and musical devices.

Table 1. Distribution of Musical Instruments

	Split-stick Rattle	Deer-hoof Rattle	Cocoon Rattle	Turtle-shell Rattle	Gourd Rattle	Bone Whistle	Wood or Cane Whistle	Foot Drum	Flute	Musical Bow	Bull-roarer
Tolowa		X				X	X		X		X
Yurok		X				X	X		X	X¹	
Wiyot		X				X			X	X¹	
Hupa	X	X	X			X	X		X		
Chilula	X	X				X	X		X		
Karok	X	X	X			X	X		X	X¹	
Mattole	X		X			X			X	X¹	
Nongatl	X					X			X		
Lassik	X	X	X			X			X		
Sinkyone	X	X	X			X	X		X		X
Chimariko	X								X		
Shasta		X				X			X		
Achumawi		X	X			X			X	X¹	
Atsugewi	X	X	X			X			X	X¹	X
Cahto		X				X	X	X	X		X
Wailaki	X	X					X	X	X		
Yuki	X	X	X			X	X	X	X		X
Wappo	X		X			X	X	X	X		
Pomo	X		X			X	X	X	X	X	X
Wintu	X	X	X			X	X	X²	X		X
Nomlaki	X		X			X	X	X	X		X
Patwin	X		X			X	X	X	X	X	
Yana	X	X	X			X	X		X		
Maidu	X	X	X			X		X	X	X	X
Nisenan	X	X	X			X		X	X	X	
Miwok	X	X	X			X	X	X	X	X	X
Monache	X	X	X			X	X		X	X	X
Tubatulabal	X	X	X			X			X	X	X
Yokuts	X		X			X	X		X	X	X
Costanoan	X					X			X	X	X
Salinan	X		X			X	X		X	X	X
Chumash	X	X	X	X		X	X		X	X	X
Gabrielino	X	X	X	X		X	X		X	X	X
Luiseño	X	X	X	X	X	X	X		X		X
Kitanemuk	X	X	X	X		X	X		X	X	X
Serrano		X		X		X	X		X		X
Cahuilla	X	X		X	X	X	X		X		X
Cupeño	X	X		X	X		X³		X		X
Ipai-Tipai	X	X		X	X		X		X	X	X

¹ Ordinary hunting bow.
² Introduced with modern religious cult.
³ Recent.

Along the northern coast and in the great interior of the state, the decline proceeded at a slower speed. In a few isolated areas a fair amount of aboriginal music has survived. But it is less frequently performed and changes are discernible. Though a minimum of hybridization seems to have taken place between Indian and Euro-American music, alien rhythms, melodies, and forms can be detected in some native songs and new instruments have been adopted or the old ones modified. White influence has probably been greater in an indirect rather than in a direct fashion. The throwing together of different groups on reservations and the mobile life as farm laborers followed by many California Indians has led to mutual borrowings of songs and blendings of styles. Intertribal exchange was not, of course, a new thing, though its tempo certainly increased. Not only the music itself but also the purpose and customs pertaining to it altered. With the Tachi Yokuts, for instance, music-making has become dissociated from religious solemnities that are no longer observed.

The decay of native music continues apace. Few younger Indians give attention to their ancestral songs, accepting in their place folk, country, or modern tunes. Pan-Indianism, in which increasing numbers of California Indians are participating, has led to a revival of interest in Indian customs and institutions, but the music associated with this movement is synthesized from elements derived from diverse cultural sources and bears little relationship to the aboriginal. Today, knowledge of the old music exists largely in the minds of a few aged persons and with their passing will be irrevocably lost.

Sources

California Indian music represents a neglected field of research and there is no comprehensive survey of the whole field. Too few ethnologists have given consideration to music as a significant component of culture, generally treating it incidentally as a by-product of other work. A large body of material collected with the phonograph and more modern recording equipment is available in the Lowie Museum of Anthropology, University of California, Berkeley; Southwest Museum, Los Angeles; Library of Congress; American Museum of Natural History, New York City; and the Archives of Traditional Music, Indiana University, Bloomington. Much of it has not been analyzed or even searched through. Ethnological publications contain scattered notations of melo-

dies, occasional song texts, and descriptions of musical instruments. Information on the cultural background of music is often scanty. Song texts have been gathered also as expressions of literary art, partly for their ethnographic value, partly for linguistic purposes.

Technical studies of aboriginal vocal music and musical styles have been handicapped by the relative lack of trained ethnomusicologists. The first serious investigations were undertaken by Herzog (1928) for Yuman, including Ipai-Tipai, and by Roberts (1933) for Luiseño and Gabrielino. Further studies have been published by Densmore (1939, 1958) for Valley Maidu; Hatch (1958) for Tachi Yokuts; Heidsick (1966) for Luiseño; Angulo and Béclard d'Harcourt (1931) for Karok, Shasta, Achumawi, Pomo, and others; and Pietroforte (1965) for Yokuts and Western Mono. The most ambitious project was undertaken by Peter Abraham who analyzed the musical styles of several central (Pomo, Miwok, Patwin, Maidu) and northwestern (Hupa, Karok) groups. Unfortunately the results of his work were never published. Statements on California styles are included in two general treatises on native North American music (Roberts 1936; Nettl 1954) and in a discussion of California culture areas and intensifications (Kroeber 1936:113–114). The melodic structure of the songs of the major northwestern California ceremonials has been analyzed (Kroeber and Gifford 1949:135–136). Much more data will be required to define tribal and regional styles, which at present are only suggested in the literature.

Knowledge of musical instruments, though not totally satisfactory, is more complete. Descriptions of aboriginal music-making devices, often quite detailed, are contained in nearly all tribal monographs and their tribe-by-tribe occurrence is recorded in the Culture Element Distributions lists. A brief article on native instruments (Waterman 1908a) and a statement on the regional occurrence of various types (Kroeber 1922:277–278) are available. Many specimens are preserved in anthropological museums but they have been little studied and data are often lacking to tell about methods of construction, tuning, if any, and the exact method of playing. Further, there remains a need for exact tonometric analyses of the various kinds of instruments.

Acculturation of the Indian music has not been studied systematically. The musical conquest of the mission tribes by Franciscan friars has been described (Silva 1941), and changes in Tachi Yokuts songs noted (Hatch 1958).

Natural Forces and Native World View

ROBERT F. HEIZER

The Pit River Council proclamation to the president and people of the United States in June 1970 declared: "No amount of money can buy Mother Earth; therefore, the California Land Claims Case has no meaning. The Earth is our Mother, and we cannot sell her." What did the Pit River Indians mean by this?

The perception that individuals have of who they are in a world of other men and nature, what their existential and normative values comprise, and the reasons why these values are important as a basis for behavior are all aspects of what is called "world view."

Ethnographers in California from the time of Powers's (1877) pioneering work compiled a tremendous body of culture facts. But ethnography was generalizing and aimed at objectivity so that only rarely does one encounter in the literature reports that discuss the matter of personality, of how individual humans saw themselves in a world of everyday activities that operated in parallel with the world of spirits of nature. In short, the published ethnography is deficient in the kinds of explicit information needed to define these Native Californians' world views, for there must have been many of these among the 500 or so tribelet societies.

California, despite the proposals of some theoreticians who talk about aboriginal confederations, international alliances, and far-flung trade networks, was a region holding a large number of societies that had limited knowledge, understanding, experience, and tolerance of neighboring peoples. California Indians, while perhaps knowing individuals in neighboring tribelets, for the most part lived out their lives mainly within their own limited and familiar territory. Nothing illustrates more the deep-seated provincialism and attachment to the place of their birth of California Indians than the abundantly documented wish for persons who died away from home to have their bodies (or their ashes if the distance was too great) returned for burial at their natal village. Living out the span of existence from birth to death within an area bounded by a horizon lying not more than 10 or 15 miles from one's village and not having talked to more than 100 different persons in a whole life must have made one's world small, familiar, safe, and secure (Kroeber 1925:145, 213, 395; Gifford 1932). As if to emphasize or reinforce this sense of localization, many (perhaps all) tribes put their children through a drill of learning the group boundaries. Powers (1877:109–110) explains:

The boundaries of all tribes . . . are marked with the greatest precision, being defined by certain creeks, cañons, bowlders, conspicuous trees, springs, etc., each of which objects has its own individual name. It is perilous for an Indian to be found outside of his tribal boundaries, wherefore it stands him well in hand to make himself acquainted with the same early in life. Accordingly, the squaws teach these things to their children in a kind of sing-song. . . . Over and over, time and again, they rehearse all these bowlders, etc., describing each minutely and by name, with its surroundings. Then when the children are old enough, they take them around . . . and so faithful has been their instruction, that [they] generally recognize the objects from the descriptions of them previously given by their mothers. If an Indian knows but little of this great world more than pertains to boundary bush and bowlder, he knows his own small fighting-ground intimately better than any topographical engineer can learn it.

Indians not only lived close to nature but also felt intimately an integral part of it. The attribution to animals of higher intelligence and human qualities and emotions was common. In most mythologies it was animals who occupied the earth before man, and these myth-time beings lived, felt, and talked like men, created the earth for man, and provided man with many of the necessities of life (fire, food) as well as some of the undesirable features (death). In northwestern California it was believed that everything humans did was derived from the way it was done in myth times. Originally the world was populated by a prehuman race of people who worked out how everything should be done. They waited until the present people appeared, taught them everything they knew, and then turned into animals, plants, rocks, and mountains (Harrington 1932:8).

The Yurok, like all other California tribes, had a rich mythology. Some of this was just removed from historical anecdote and may have derived from actual persons and events of the fairly recent past, perhaps one to two centuries ago (Spott and Kroeber 1942). Most of it was pure myth, which often concerned a prehuman race called the wo·gey, in which all sorts of remarkable things occurred. All Yurok knew these myths and professed to believe that the incidents related did actually happen in this mythical past. One myth incident concerned a dog who spoke to a human, and this was a portent of the person's death. The living Yurok never spoke to dogs, and when asked why they said, "The dog might answer."

It is doubtful that any Yurok actually believed that his dog would answer with human speech if talked to; nevertheless, the Yurok acted upon this half-belief in myth as the rationalization for certain human actions in real life.

Other actions by living people have a basis in belief referring to ritual contamination. For example, the Yurok never drank the water of the Klamath River. They gave as their reason the fear that the river water might be poison and cause illness and even death. When asked what kind of poison, the Indians answered, "Someone upriver may have thrown into the stream a dead dog or a human fetus." Such objects are impure and contaminated; even in a stream the size of the Klamath River they were thought to be powerful enough to contaminate it ritually and adversely affect a person who drank the water.

One other example to show how human actions were dictated by belief comes from the Yurok. They smoked a tobacco that was native to the area, but they never smoked tobacco that they picked from plants growing wild; only tobacco that they had planted and tended themselves was safe to smoke. The reason was the possibility that the wild tobacco might have grown in the disturbed earth of a grave, and since corpses were highly contaminated, impure, and dangerous, it would have been dangerous to smoke tobacco that came from a plant growing on a grave. In fact, tobacco is a ruderal, that is, a plant that readily volunteers in disturbed earth; and it is quite probable that in the past the Yurok observed that tobacco plants tended to appear in graveyard areas and in time the two became associated. Thus, some objective botanical observation is combined with native magical belief and customary practice (Kroeber 1925:88; Harrington 1932:78-79).

Natural phenomena require some explanation, and in native California these usually were provided in the form of myths. Thus, the phases of the moon, eclipses, earthquakes, shooting stars, thunder, and the like are all accounted for. If these explanations do not agree with ones advanced by astronomers, meteorologists, and geologists that does not matter; as explanations they accounted satisfactorily for what would otherwise have been unknown and dangerous.

The Indians' relationship to the environment was guided by certain basic beliefs. Man shared his existence with plants and animals and felt responsible for them (cf. Goldschmidt and Driver 1940:112; Goddard 1903-1904:87). In each of the numerous forms of plants and animals there existed a soul or spirit, much like that of man's, so that all three were thought of as part of the whole of nature. Many tribes believed that men after death became transformed into animals (Powers 1877:59; Merriam 1909a). This idea may be linked with that of the immortality of game animals (Kroeber 1925:68). When man hunted, he thanked the spirit of the deer for its assistance. By respecting other forms of life man did not abuse his relationship to them. Conservation of resources helped insure the continued supply of all the things man needed, so that wasteful killing was rarely, if ever, practiced. One took what he needed and expressed appreciation, rather than acting as though what was available in the way of food and materials was simply there for the taking. Without these attitudes the California Indians could have laid waste to California long before the Europeans appeared.

Distinctive habitats (oceanshore, foothill, valley, lakeshore) yielded different foodstuffs, and as a result the cultural practices and appliances for food taking varied. Some of these responses have been studied. Beals and Hester (1960) have provided a useful ecological typology of California Indians; Gould (1975) has described in detail the Tolowa territory microhabitats and techniques for exploiting these. Underlying these there seem to have been various highly organized rituals and practices that controlled or regulated the human exploitation of resources. In effect these were resource management systems. For two analyses of such systems see Swezey (1975) and Swezey and Heizer (1976). Some concepts of the relationships between man and plants, and how plants enter into belief and ritual, are attested in the ethnobotanies from different tribes, for example, Karok (Schenck and Gifford 1952), Yuki and Pomo (Chesnut 1902), and Cahuilla (Barrows 1900; Bean and Saubel 1972).

A good illustration of the Indian concept of man's relationship to natural things is a statement by Kate Luckie, a Wintu, recorded in 1925:

People talk a lot about the world ending. Maybe this child [pointing to her eldest child] will see something, but this world will stay as long as Indians live. When the Indians all die, then God will let the water come down from the north. Everyone will drown. That is because the white people never cared for land or deer or bear. When we Indians kill meat, we eat it all up. When we dig roots, we make little holes. When we build houses, we make little holes. When we burn grass for grasshoppers, we don't ruin things. We shake down acorns and pine nuts. We don't chop down the trees. We only use dead wood. But the white people plow up the ground, pull up the trees, kill everything. The tree says, "Don't. I am sore. Don't hurt me." But they chop it down and cut it up. The spirit of the land hates them. . . . The Indians never hurt anything, but the white people destroy all. They blast rocks and scatter them on the earth. The rocks says, "Don't! You are hurting me." But the white people pay no attention. When the Indians use rocks, they take little round ones for their cooking. The white people dig deep long tunnels. They make roads. They dig as much as they wish. They don't care how much the ground cries out. How can the spirit of the earth like the white man? That is why God will upset the world—because it is sore all over. Everywhere the white man has touched it, it is sore. It looks sick. So it gets even by killing him when he blasts. But eventually the water will come (Du Bois 1935:75).

Goldschmidt (1951a:430) writes that the Nomlaki recognized the forces of nature and believed that all nature was capable of willful acts, usually potentially evil ones. The world of mountains, lakes, springs, caves, and forests was viewed as animate and therefore ever ready to intercede in human affairs. There was also a supernatural world of unseen beings who might affect the course of the life of men. To mitigate the potential of interference with human plans, ritual was practiced, even for the most practical and mundane human activities. The Nomlaki said, "Everything in this world talks, just as we are [talking] now—the trees, rocks, everything. But we cannot understand them, just as the White people do not understand Indians."

The Wintu hunter must possess both skill and luck to kill deer. A man who had lost his hunting luck did not say "I cannot kill deer any more," but rather "Deer don't want to die for me." The Yurok believed that "a hunter's success is brought not by his own cunning, but by the favor he can win from his game by respectful treatment" (Kroeber 1925:68). A Pomo hunter before going out rubbed his body with aromatic angelica and pepper tree leaves, believing that by so doing he would not be molested by the spirit of the hills (Loeb 1926:171).

Maintaining a stable world in which man could continue to live was managed by the Maidu through the male secret society. A myth explains how and why the secret society was established by *wó·nommi* the Creator:

> Until now you have let all your boys grow up like a wild tree in the mountains; you have taught them nothing; they have gone their own way. Henceforth you must bring every youth, at a proper age, into your assembly house, and cause him to be initiated into the ways and knowledge and ways of manhood. You shall teach him to worship me, and to observe the sacred dances which I shall ordain in my honor. Keep the sacred dance house, as I have told you, while the world endures. Never neglect my rites and my honors. Keep the sacred rattle and the dances. Worship me in the night and not in the daylight. Then shall your hills be full of acorns and nuts; your valleys shall yield plenty of grass seed and herbs; your rivers shall be full of salmon, and your hearts shall be rejoiced (Loeb 1933:165).

One can scarcely find a better illustration of the Indian concept of the mythical world that is blended with the actual, physical earth than in the world map of the Yurok (see "Mythology," fig. 1, this vol.). The small bounded earth known to the Yurok is there—the land with the Klamath River flowing across it, and the edge of the great saltwater ocean. For the rest it is all mythical, but in the Indian mind as real as the palpable earth. The Pomo (Loeb 1926:300) hold the same idea of the earth as floating in an ocean with the sky dome arching over it all like a gigantic bowl, and something very similar is reported for the Sierra Miwok (Merriam 1910:19). And far to the south among the Luiseño and Ipai-Tipai there are actual cosmological maps drawn with the colored earths that portray visible physical features of mountains, the sea, islands, the moon, sun and stars with supernatural and ordinarily invisible spirits (see "Luiseño," fig. 7, this vol.).

Cosmological instability seems always to have been a threat hanging over the heads of men. Eclipses of the sun or moon were generally thought to be due to a monster (often a frog or bear) devouring the luminary. In order to frighten away the monster people beat sticks on the houses, hit dogs to make them howl, and shouted their loudest. And, of course, the noise-making activity was always successful. The Wintu gathered up all the food and water in the village and threw it out after an eclipse, giving as the reason that some of the blood from the chewed sun or moon might have spattered on it and thus contaminated it. While nobody could see the blood, it might nevertheless be there, and the food-water disposal ritual was merely to play it safe. Throughout native California taboo and ritual served the purpose of controlling or stabilizing an unstable earth, which was populated both by men and animals as well as supernatural spirits. The earth-firming or world-renewal ritual was practiced as a formal cult in northwestern California (Kroeber and Gifford 1949) basic to the Kuksu cult of north-central California (Kroeber 1925:383-384). Native ritual in pre-White California was a continual check on and affirmation of the mechanism of natural forces.

Earthquakes were usually thought to be caused by a giant, at times the Creator who, while sleeping underground, rolled over (Spier 1923:329).

Shooting stars were thought by the Wintu to be the spirits of dead shamans who were doing a little traveling in the afterlife. The Northern Lights were thought to be a portent of epidemic illness that would later visit the village. A dust spiral near the house was interpreted as the presence of the spirit of a dead relative; to pacify this ghost, whose presence was unwelcome, some acorn meal was sprinkled near the spot where the dust spiral appeared (Du Bois 1935:75 ff.). Such omens were part of the beliefs of all California tribes.

Pomo world view seems to inhibit goal-oriented behavior through having strong anxieties deriving from living in a world full of potential dangers coming either from other individuals or supernatural powers (Loeb 1926:302-304). Taboos were common and were strictly observed as a means of protecting persons from interference from supernatural powers. Observing taboos could prevent illness or death, but they did not improve one's lot; this neutralized the threat of supernatural action and was therefore an anxiety-reducing device. There was always the possibility of unwittingly breaking a taboo, and if so punishment was automatic but not necessarily immediate. Therefore, bad luck, illness, or death of a child, for example, was taken as a sign that a taboo was broken. Such beliefs presumably would amplify anxiety feelings (Colson 1974).

Loeb's (1926:246) Northern Pomo informant believed that "a woman can't get children simply by having sexual intercourse. She must do something else besides. She has to make use of a certain tree or rock, or the sacred dolls or bull snake. She must also pray." It is likely that the Pomo did recognize that sexual intercourse was required to have children but that in addition they believed that other activities were necessary to complete the process. Small clay dolls were put in miniature cradles and treated like actual babies. Certain sacred rocks were scratched and the dust was rubbed on the body accompanied by prayers and ritual motions. The Eastern and Northern Pomo had a baby-getting ritual involving a bull snake brought from the hills by a performer of the ghost ceremony. The snake was thrown into the crowd. A woman desiring to have a child raised her dress and wrapped the snake around her thighs. A certain Northern Pomo spring was called *kawí kʰá* 'child water'. A married woman wanting a child drank this water. A Central Pomo spring named *ǩúˑqá* 'child water' contained mud that was taken and rubbed on the body of a woman wanting to become pregnant. The Pomo had many kinds of pregnancy taboos; for instance if the woman looked at the sun or moon, she would delay the birth of the child. Neither the husband nor wife could kill rattlesnakes; if they did so the child would have a harelip. A pregnant woman did not lay her hand on her stomach; if she did so she could not give up the navel cord. All kinds of special food taboos were observed. Fish were tabooed since the fish would take up all the water in her and cause her death. Many of these taboos are supposed to determine the character of the unborn child. Twins among California tribes were variously considered as abnormal in one way or another. Among the Maidu they were ill-omened, and both were killed as well as the mother. Among some tribes no particular note is made of them; in others one would be killed in the belief that they would fight when they grew up.

Morality can be construed as an element of world view. This aspect of behavior rises to the fully conscious level in some groups where moralistic precepts were openly spoken of and formed the basis for interpersonal behavior. For the Luiseño, ethical principles were formulated in a ritualistic context in the form of addresses given to boys and girls who were being initiated into adulthood. The ethical or moral principles must be observed lest, as the people were warned, supernatural avengers would punish them with sickness or death. The impending punishment was, in short, concretely physical rather than merely one of incurring the displeasure of the supernatural spirit overseers of men. The "sermon" addressed to boys at their ritual induction into manhood when they are gathered around the sacred sandpainting went:

See these, these are alive, this is bear-mountain lion; these are going to catch you if you are not good and do not respect your elder relatives and grown-up people. And if you do not

believe, these are going to kill you; but if you do believe, everybody is going to see your goodness and you then will kill bear-mountain lion. And you will gain fame and be praised, and your name will be heard everywhere.

See this, this is the raven, who will shoot you with his bow and arrow if you do not put out your winnowing basket. Harken, do not be a dissembler, do not be heedless, do not eat food of overnight (i.e. do not secretly eat food left after the last meal of the day). Also you will not get angry when you eat, nor must you be angry with your elder relatives.

The earth hears you, the sky and wood mountain see you. If you will believe this you will grow old. And you will see your sons and daughters, and you will counsel them in this manner, when you reach your old age. And if when hunting you should kill a hare or rabbit or deer, and an old man should ask you for it, you will hand it to him at once. Do not be angry when you give it, and do not throw it to him. And when he goes home he will praise you, and you will kill many, and you will be able to shoot straight with the bow. . . .

When you die your spirit will rise to the sky and people will blow (three times) and will make rise your spirit. And everywhere it will be heard that you have died. And you will drink bitter medicine, and will vomit, and your inside will be clean, and illness will pass you by, and you will grow old, if you heed this speech. This is what the people of long ago used to talk, that they used to counsel their sons and daughters. In this manner you will counsel your sons and daughters. . . .

This is the breaker; this will kill you. Heed this speech and you will grow old. And they will say of you: He grew old because he heeded what he was told. And when you die you will be spoken of as those of the sky, like the stars. Those it is said were people, who went to the sky and escaped death. And like those will rise your soul . . . (Kroeber 1925:684).

The sermon addressed to the girls ran along similar lines, but it emphasized female pursuits:

See, these are alive; these will think well of you if you believe; and if you do not believe, they are going to kill you; if you are heedless, a dissembler, or stingy [they will kill you]. You must not look sideways, must not receive a person in your house with anger; it is not proper. You will drink hot water when you menstruate, and when you are pregnant you will drink bitter medicine.

This will cause you to have your child quickly, as your inside will be clean. And you will roast yourself at the fire (after childbirth) and then your son or daughter will grow up quickly, and sickness will not approach you. But if you are heedless you will not bear your child quickly, and people will speak of your heedlessness.

Your elder relatives you must think well of; you will also welcome your daughters-in-law and your brothers-in-law when they arrive at your house. Pay heed to this speech, and at some future time you will go to their house, and they are going to welcome you politely at their house . . . (Kroeber 1925:685).

In these sermons or counseling sessions, in which young people participated at the great event in their lives when they were fully prepared to be impressed, was taught consideration for elders (giving food and respect to them freely), refraining from anger, being cordial and polite to one's relatives-in-law. Observing these was a guarantee that you would grow old in good health and have children who honored you, and when you died to have your spirit go to live in the sky. Persons who were heedless of these principles would be bitten by the rattlesnake or spider or be killed by the "breaker," or might vomit blood, become lame, acquire a wasting cough, have their eyes become granulated, and bear children who were sickly. The avengers were the messengers of the all-powerful, all-seeing Chingichngish—an impersonal, unseen power who knew all and would arrange for revenge through an inexorable causality. Note also that there was no mention of certain antisocial acts such as theft, assault, rape, witchcraft, or murder. These are apparently behavioral extremes that were too obvious to be cited on the list of tabooed acts. Probably they were rare, even absent for the most part; or if they occurred and the perpetrator was known, it was up to living people, rather than a remote deity, to settle with the person who committed the act by arranging for his death. According to Kroeber, it is only written codes that mention the worst crimes. "The Indian, beyond taboos and cult observances, centers his attention on the trivial but unremitting factors of personal intercourse; affability, liberality, restraint of anger and jealousy, politeness.

He . . . sets up an open, even, unruffled, slow, and pleasant existence as his ideal. He preaches a code of manners rather than morals. He thinks of character, of its expression in the innumerable but little relations of daily life, not of right or wrong in our sense. It is significant that these words [right and wrong] do not exist in his language. In California, at least, the Indian speaks only of 'good' or 'bad' . . ." (Kroeber 1925:684).

A deeper analysis of the Luiseño theory of knowledge (*ʔayálkawi-š*) has been presented by R.C. White (1957). This knowledge has, by itself, supernatural qualities, and the possessors desire from it supernatural powers. It was through *ʔayálkawi-š* that the grand system or order of the universe—of people and nature—was seen in cosmogonic terms (cf. Bean 1972).

These are the kinds of concepts Native Californians developed to understand their worlds and to serve as guides for their behavior in them. Europeans destroyed or radically altered much of the environment and introduced by force or precept very different ways of conceiving the relations of man and nature. Ancient and efficient ecologies were disrupted before adequate and sympathetic records could be made that would promote understanding of what must have been a whole series of different integrated native philosophical systems.

653

Mythology: Regional Patterns and History of Research

ROBERT F. HEIZER

Although there are a few briefly recounted native myths recorded from the mission period (Boscana 1846) and from gold rush times (H. B. D. 1859) the first substantial collection of complete myths was that by Powers (1877). Bancroft (1874-1876, 3) had also collected a number of myths. Powers gives one or two full-length myths from the following California tribes: Karok (1877:35-43), Yurok (59-64), Tolowa (70-71), Hupa (80-85), Mattole (110-112), Yuki (144-145), Pomo (162, 182-183), Wappo (200-203), Patwin (226-227), Achumawi (272-273), Maidu (288-305), Nisenan (341-345), Sierra Miwok (358-360, 366-368), Yokuts (383-384), and Tubatulabal (395-396). About 1900 there begins to appear in print a comprehensive body of myth. Formation of the American Folklore Society encouraged more recording, as did the systematic ethnographic survey of California Indian cultures by the Department of Anthropology of the University of California at Berkeley, the findings being in large part reported in the American Archaeology and Ethnology series. Ethnologists outside the university also made important contributions; among these were John P. Harrington, R.B. Dixon, Constance G. Du Bois, Jeremiah Curtin, C. Hart Merriam, and E.S. Curtis.

Kroeber (1904b) early attempted to characterize regional styles of mythology and repeatedly referred to tribal myths (1925). Gifford and Block (1930:15-75) in a collection of myths preface their retold tales with a general introduction that still stands, nearly a half-century later, as the best survey of themes and styles. Gayton's (1935) useful summary of myth plots and their extra-California occurrences provides, though incidentally, a broad synthesis of myth types. Demetracopoulou (1933) discussed the Loon Woman myth among the tribes of northern California, and Loeb (1933) summarized the creator concept of the same tribes. These surveys are most useful but they are rare.

There are regional patterns of myths in California native culture—Northwestern, Central, and Southwestern. Sharings of myths and myth elements among California tribes and those of the Great Basin, Southern Plateau, Northwest Coast, and Colorado River have been shown by Gayton (1935).

Northwestern California

The mythology of Northwestern California stands apart from the rest of California. It is intimately connected with the central motives of the living people through the device of detailing the experiences of a prehuman race of immortals that occupied the earth, made it ready for man, and established in the mythic past the order of all things to be followed in the human present. Thus, dentalium shell money, which looms very large in the thoughts of men anxious to become rich (Kroeber 1925:20-52; Gould 1966), is elevated to the rank of a deity or "almost a creator." But there are no creation myths in Northwestern California; the prehuman race of spirits did not create humans but merely organized life and its specific routine for them when humans appeared as the proprietors of the land (Gayton 1935:584). The existence of earth and what it holds, including humanity, is simply taken for granted. While one might argue that this is a kind of philosophical short-circuiting, at the same time there is implicit in such belief some sort of automatic and ordained world pattern in which humanity is only one of the many elements, and not even the most important of these. Such beliefs come close to the revealed testimony of the Old Testament, and the parallel here is even more striking when one considers Goldschmidt's (1951) persuasive argument on the similarity of the European Protestant ethic and capitalism to the Yurok view of life and money. Kroeber (1925:5, 73-74) characterizes Yurok myths as slight in stirring plot and suspenseful narrative; strong in elegaic emotion; full of examples of affection, homesickness, pity, and attraction to the place of one's birth; and with an overriding concern about the acquisition of wealth goods that would give a man status and influence in his society. Myth here, in short, is a direct reflection of the actual way of life and outlook and values of a people. Erikson's (1943) psychoanalytic interpretation of Yurok culture is interesting but scarcely credible if taken literally. Waterman (1920) shows how intimately Yurok toponymy is connected with myth characters' actions and events (fig. 1). Since no other study of native geography is so detailed, it is impossible to know whether myth and topography were as closely interwoven among any other tribes. However, it can be said that the mythology of all tribes refers frequently to local natural features (mountain peaks, rivers, unusual geological formations) within the tribal territory (see "Achumawi," fig. 8, this vol.), and it is the "internalization" that gives the impression that the my-

654

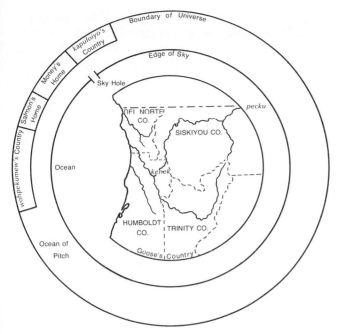

after Waterman 1920: fig. 1.

Fig. 1. Diagram showing the Yurok conception of the world. A composite made by Waterman derived from testimony provided by native informants.

thology has been regionally present for a considerable length of time.

Yurok myths (Spott and Kroeber 1942; Kroeber 1975; Cody 1941; J. Sapir 1928) often detail the exploits of important characters such as *wohpekumew* 'widower across the ocean', who made many things in the world the way they are now; *pulekuk*ᵂ*erek* 'down-stream sharp', who destroyed dangerous monsters and instituted the taboo on women entering the sweathouse; *mewomec*, a bearded dwarf who carries acorns on his back and is the master of vegetal abundance; and *seɣep* 'coyote', whose actions as spoilsport are of lesser consequence to humans than elsewhere in California.

The Northwestern California tribes have developed a major cult system called World Renewal, whose manifestation is in a series of dances, some larger and more important than others. The main ones are the Deerskin Dance and Jumping Dance (see "Hupa, Chilula, and Whilkut," figs. 11–12, this vol.) (Kroeber 1925:53–75; Kroeber and Gifford 1949; Goldschmidt and Driver 1940; Goddard 1901a, 1904). Myths explain the origin of these dances and account for their localization by reference to specific named spots. Although the dances are public affairs, each must be preceded by the recitation of a formula by a person who knows and owns the correct one for the special occasion. These formulas are nothing more or less than myths (Kroeber 1925:69–73; Kroeber and Gifford 1949:3, 76–77; Goddard 1904). For myths of the Wiyot see Kroeber (1905a, 1908) and Reichard (1925); for the Karok, Harrington (1931, 1932), Angulo and Freeland (1931b), and Olden (1923); for the Hupa,

Wallace (1948); for the Yurok, Thompson (1916), Spott and Kroeber (1942), and Graves (1929); for the Chilula, Goddard (1914a); for the Cahto, Goddard (1909); for the Lassik, Goddard (1906); for the Wailaki, Goddard (1921–1923); for the Bear River, Nomland (1938: 118–123); for the Sinkyone, Nomland (1935:170–174) and Kroeber (1919); and for the Shasta, Dixon (1905a, 1910), Burns (1901), and Farrand (1915).

Central California

The mythology of Central California, as might be expected in view of the size of the area and diversity of tribes, is variable. Gayton (1935:595), who concluded that Central California mythology shared few tales with bordering culture areas, refers to "a comparatively discrete nucleus in central California composed of the Miwok, all the Yokuts tribes, the Salinan, and probably Costanoan, Lake Miwok, and Patwin, which appears to be rather aloof from the surrounding regions." A true creator of the world exists in Wiyot myth in the person of *ku ratəri kakwìt* 'that old man above', and the same supreme god is found among the Cahto as the Thunder god, among the Sinkyone as *nagayčo* 'great traveler', the Yuki as Taikomal, the Eastern Pomo as *maˑrúmʔda*, the Wintu as *ʔolelbes*, and the Maidu as *Kódoyapè* 'Earth Maker' (Kroeber 1925:119, 155, 182–183; Loeb 1933). Animal characters are especially common in the myths of Central California tribes, and they are referred to as the "first people" (Gifford and Block 1930:47; Merriam 1910:17). In the Central area there are stories of a primeval flood when everything was water and the solid earth and man were formed from a bit of mud that the Earth Diver (usually a turtle) brought up from the bottom. The manner of creation of humans is varied but in one form or another it is almost universal in this area (Gifford and Block 1930:79–120; Gayton 1935:588). Also present, but sporadically, is the idea of a succession of world destructions by flood or fire (Kroeber 1925:206), a myth theme that was particularly important among the faraway Aztecs of Central Mexico. Coyote as a myth character at times engages in acts that turn out to be to man's advantage, but more often he is the trickster or marplot who causes death and imposes unfortunate hardships for man in what would otherwise have been a perfect world. In importance as a myth person, as well as in the effect of his actions on man's fate and possessions, Coyote is often equal to the more lofty and distant creator.

The concept of a high god or supreme being among American Indians was once a subject of considerable anthropological interest (Schmidt 1926–1949, 2:57–72, 5:37–68, 1936; Dangel 1927, 1928, 1934; Satolli and Tentori 1941; Loeb 1933) and the Pomo and Yuki creators have been particularly cited in this connection.

In north-central California among the tribes that practiced the Kuksu cult (Kroeber 1932a:312–419; Loeb

1932, 1933) the mythology is quite definitely linked through spirits named in myth, who are present, in impersonated form, as dancers in the ceremonies. Some ritual dances are probably myth reenactments (Kroeber 1925:385). In its most fundamental aspect the Kuksu resembles that of the World Renewal cult in that its purpose was "to bring rains, nourish the earth, and produce a bountiful harvest; perhaps also to ward off epidemics, floods, earthquakes, and other disasters" (Kroeber 1925:383).

South of the god-impersonating Kuksu tribes, among the Costanoans, Esselen, Miwok, and Yokuts, the anthropomorphic creator is lacking. His place is taken by a pantheon of animals—Eagle at the top, Coyote his chief assistant, and then Falcon, Hawk, Condor, Owl, Fox, Roadrunner, Antelope, Deer, Hummingbird, and Raven (Gayton 1935; Loeb 1926). This distinction allows a division into a northern (Kuksu-related) and southern subtype of Central California mythology. The Yokuts and Miwok totemic moiety system (Kroeber 1925: 453–457, 493–496; Gifford 1916a) naturally lent itself to a connection with myth since the animals in both spheres are the same. Yokuts myths are replete with tales of contests between animals who are also totems, and once again there is the intimate association between myth as invented history and human events.

Central California mythology is abundantly reported: interior Miwok (Barrett 1919; Gifford 1917; Freeland and Broadbent 1960; Lehmer 1929; Merriam 1910), Lake Miwok (Freeland 1947), Yokuts and Monache (Hudson 1902; Gayton and Newman 1940; Gifford 1923a; Kroeber 1907a; Rogers and Gayton 1944; G.W. Stewart 1906, 1908), Maidu (Dixon 1900, 1902, 1903, 1912), Pomo (Angulo 1927, 1935; Angulo and Freeland 1928; Barrett 1906, 1933), Tubatulabal (C.F. Voegelin 1935a; Voegelin 1938:53–55), Achumawi and Atsugewi (Angulo and Freeland 1939a; Curtin 1909; Dixon 1908; Merriam 1928), Wappo (H.R. Kroeber 1908; Radin 1924), Yana (Curtin 1898; Sapir 1910, 1923), Wintu (Curtin 1898), Yuki (Gifford 1937; Kroeber 1925:182–183, 206–207, 1932a; Schmidt 1926–1949, 2:57–72, 5:37–68, 1936), and Salinan (J.A. Mason 1912:186–196, 1918:59–120).

Southwestern California

Native myths south of the Yokuts in the region from the Chumash through the Gabrielino, Cahuilla, Luiseño, Juaneño, and Serrano to the Ipai and Tipai are different from those to the north in Central California. Southwestern California mythology is phrased in more abstruse language and concepts, which often border on the philosophical. Frequent reference is made to the human spirit, to the relation of life and death, to the soul, and to the earth-female and sky-male duality, which are concepts that do not occur in the tribal mythologies of Central and Northwestern California. The Luiseño origin myth has been compared to the Polynesian form. It speaks of an

original void—no sky, no earth, no water, but just empty space. In this space there became two clouds. One was called Vacant and the other was called Empty. They were brother and sister. This brother and sister kept changing into different forms, until finally the brother became Sky and the sister became Earth. The union of Earth and Sky produced objects and animals who were people, and who later transformed into the actual objects (red paint, baskets, flat throwing sticks for killing rabbits, water, mud). After the early acts of creation the first people migrated from one place to the next, finally arriving in their homeland areas. An all-powerful god, *wiyó·t*, rules the people, but he dies through magic and is cremated. His body departs to live in the form of the moon, and he ordains by his death the nature of the mourning ceremony. The demise of *wiyó·t* institutes death in the world. There is later born a person, conceived of as a god, named Chingichngish, who instructs the people in ceremonial rites and the preparation and taking of the narcotic datura plant, which is administered to boys at their puberty initiation (fig. 2) during which they are addressed with a long moralizing sermon (Kroeber 1925:648–688). This myth, with different names for the characters involved according to the tribe, is referred to as the "dying god" theme; it extends across Southern California to the tribes on the Colorado River (Kroeber 1925: 788–792).

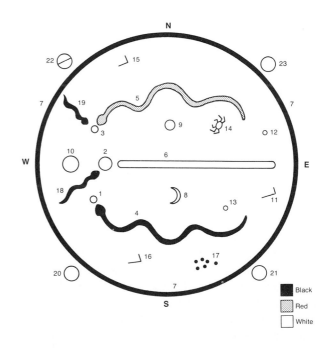

after Waterman 1910: pl. 25.

Fig. 2. Map or diagram of the world as conceived by the Ipai; formed with colored earths and used during the boys' initiation ceremony. 1–3, datura mortar and pestle; 4–5, rattlesnake; 6, Milky Way; 7, world's edge (perhaps black); 8, new moon; 9, full moon; 10, sun; 11, coyote; 12, buzzard star; 13, crow; 14, black spider; 15, wolf; 16, mountain sheep or Orion; 17, Pleiades; 18, black snake; 19, gopher snake; 20–23, mountains.

The Chingichngish god is the center of a cult, and it has been suggested (Kroeber 1925:656, 1959:291; R.C. White 1963:136) that the idea of this lofty deity with his moral teachings may derive from Christianity through some missionized Indian. The origin of the Chingichngish cult is traceable to the Gabrielino, and it may have spread secretly, without the Franciscan padres being aware of it, from one mission to the next as far south as San Diego, and northward through the Chumash and Yokuts to the southern Sierra Miwok.

In Southwestern California, as a parallel accompaniment to the major rituals (annual mourning ceremony and Chingichngish cult) are song cycles (Kroeber 1925:657-660), the words of which are full of mythological allusions. Here again there is undoubtedly a historical connection with the song cycles of the Colorado River tribes (Kroeber 1925:784-787).

Myths of the Mission Indians (Gabrielino, Juaneño, Luiseño, Cahuilla, and Ipai-Tipai) have been published (C.G. Du Bois 1901, 1904, 1904a, 1905, 1905a, 1907, 1908a; James 1902, 1903; Henshaw 1972; Kroeber 1906, 1925:622-626, 637-639, 677-680; Heizer 1968:49-68; Hooper 1920:364-378; Sparkman 1908a; Waterman 1909, 1910:336-342; Woolsey 1908). The Chumash are still poorly represented (Heizer 1955b); the Serrano are treated by Kroeber (1925:619) and Benedict (1926).

Comparative Literature

WILLIAM J. WALLACE

Because the California Indians lacked any form of writing, their literature was oral, that is, it passed by word of mouth from one person to another and from one generation to the next. Certain old people, usually men, their memories well stocked with tribal lore, were the recognized storytellers. They held forth at night by the fitful light of a fire in an assembly house, chief's dwelling, or other large structure with their audience stretched out around them. Often a narrator prolonged his tale telling for a good part of the night.

It was the practice to tell stories, at least the more serious ones, only at night because of the belief that harm would befall the narrator if he related them at any other time. According to the Yuki and Pomo the one who recounted a serious tale in the daytime would become hunchbacked. Winter was regarded as the only proper season for storytelling by many tribes. North-central California Indians as well as the Yokuts and Tubatulabal feared to relate tales in the summer for to do so would attract rattlesnakes. Simple tales could be told to children by a parent or grandparent at almost any time, however.

Storytelling represented a dramatic and musical performance as well as an oral one. Narrators identified themselves with the characters in their tales, imitating their actions with appropriate movements and gestures, mimicking their voices, and singing the verses they were supposed to have sung. Though he told the same stories many times over, the skilled raconteur received utmost attention. Everyone listened eagerly and enjoyed the narratives as much as before. The auditors expressed surprise and amazement at miraculous happenings and responded with roars of laughter to amusing incidents.

The stories were recounted in a traditional form. Often there were set openings and closings. *ʔuknî·*'once upon a time' or 'they were living (there)' formed the initial element in many Karok stories that tailed off into short prayers for food (Harrington 1932; Bright 1957:167). The Tubatulabal drew upon a small stock of units for the beginnings and endings of their tales (Voegelin 1948). Pomo myths demanded the ritualistic closing, "from the east and the west may the Mallard girls hurry and bring the morning," which was supposed to make daylight come quickly (Barrett 1933:43). Stereotyped or set phrases, such as the often-repeated Tubatulabal "it is said," were frequently employed. A favorite literary device was repetition, applied to persons, beings, or events. Characteristically the frequency of reiterations depended upon the number held sacred by the tribe.

Listening to stories provided one of the most popular and satisfying pastimes for both adults and children. But this activity had serious purposes too. It imparted lessons to the young at the same time it amused them, for accepted standards of behavior were illustrated and made known by the stories. And the sacred narratives justified the existing social system or accounted for the traditional rites and customs of the various tribes.

Origin Myths

Stories dealing with the world before it attained its present state had a prominent place in the oral literature of most California tribes. Such narratives furnished explanations for the origin of the earth, of mankind, and of culture.

Ideas varied in different regions; for instance, the concept of any kind of creation was wholly lacking among the northwesterners. Their myths began with the assumption that the earth was already in existence and looked much as it did in aboriginal times. On it lived a former race, conceived of as very human in nature and habits, but endowed with supernatural powers. These beings were held responsible for nearly everything existing in the Indians' world, or origins were explained simply by growth or appearance during this earlier prehuman epoch. They went away across the ocean when humans appeared.

Myths of central California reflected a greater interest in the genesis of the world and attributed its making to the will of a creator. Very usual were the ideas of a primeval ocean and an already existing divine being sending an animal or bird to dive for a few grains of sand or a little mud, from which he created the earth. In the north-central part of the state a high god or "One-who-is-above" made the world, whereas Eagle, assisted by other animals, accomplished this task in the south-central region.

The origin story of the southern extremity of the region told of two quarreling brothers born at the bottom of a great sea. They emerged from the waters to make land, people, the sun, and moon and to institute customs. Of different order was the Luiseño cosmogony, which led back to a time of shapeless nothingness. Sky, a male, and Earth, a female, brother and sister, developed in this void. They became the first parents, for from their incestuous union were born all things—the spirit of man, animals, sun, trees, rocks, and so on. In the beginning these things were really people and later were changed into the various phenomena.

The coming of humans seemed to have held lesser concern than the establishment of the world. To the northwest tribes, man merely sprang into existence, the signal for his arrival being smoke on the mountainsides. A specific creation from sticks, feathers, or, in a few cases, clay, accounted for man's appearance in much of California. His maker was sometimes conceived of as human in form, at other times as an animal or bird, most frequently Coyote. Farther south, the Ipai-Tipai described the first human as being fashioned of clay by the elder of two creator brothers. The Luiseño regarded people as the offspring of Earth Mother and Sky Father. More correctly it was the human soul or spirit that was brought forth by Earth Mother, not the actual physical body.

Some native stories served to account for the way of life the Indians knew. Such narratives were especially important in the northwest where they clustered around the deeds of a great culture hero, of whom the Hupas' Lost-across-the-ocean was a typical example (Goddard 1904:123-134). Manlike in form, he belonged to the prehuman race. Stories told of Lost-across-the-ocean included one about how he liberated salmon from a woman who kept them locked up and another of how he initiated the modern method of childbirth, women previously having been cut open at the time of delivery. He also ridded the earth of several cannibals. A peculiarity of this character was that he often displayed disagreeable traits and stooped to the most vile actions to gratify his own personal whims.

The establishment of culture held narrative interest for relatively few central California tribes. Coyote was frequently portrayed as the inaugurator of customs. The Pomo Coyote, for example, performed many good deeds such as giving people food and implements and destroying monsters. But he committed evil acts too, introducing illness so he could doctor patients and thus gain riches, and bringing on a deluge when angered. The southern Californians likewise devoted slight attention to the beginnings of tribal life. Luiseño stories, as far as they dealt with cultural origins at all, pictured the arts, crafts, and customs as having been taught by Wiyot, a semidivine hero, or as springing into people's minds at the time of his death and funeral. Most Ipai-Tipai culture, according to myth, emanated from a gigantic, ocean-dwelling snake who had swallowed all learning. When the serpent came ashore, the tribesmen, terrified by his bulk, set him afire and as he burst everything flew out.

Origins of celestial bodies received slight notice. Practically all Indians who discussed the inception of the sun and moon regarded them as objects obtained and placed in the sky after man himself came into being. The central tribes usually accounted for the sun's presence by theft from a far-off people. Southern California myths described the manufacture of the orbit out of clay or spittle. The story of greatest interest about the moon was told by the Luiseño. They declared it the reincarnation of the culture hero, Wiyot, the first individual to die and to be resurrected, hence setting the example for mankind. Explanations for the existence of stars, seldom met with in northwestern and central California, were common enough in the south where the constellations were considered to have once been people.

The origin of numerous other things was accounted for. Nearly all, if not all, the tribes explained the coming of death. Generally these explanations took the form of a controversy as to whether people should live forever or die. Especially prominent in central and northern California, though lacking in the south, were stories of the acquisition of fire.

Miscellaneous Myths

Many other kinds of myths were related in one part of California or another. Narratives describing the covering of the earth by a sudden flood occupied a prominent place in the literature of the central tribes. Stories of the earth's destruction by fire occurred sporadically. No very consistent ideas concerning the revival of the world after these catastrophes were found in the myths.

Migration stories, set in the mythical age, were related by the southern Indians. Beginning with the coming into being of the world and mankind, they recounted tribal wanderings from the far north, or in the Ipai-Tipai myth, from a mountain on which human creation took place. No migration narratives of any sort occurred in central or northwestern California, where the various tribes assumed that they had sprung into existence or were created in the very localities in which they lived.

Trickster and Animal Tales

A series of stories revolving around Coyote, though set in prehuman times, had none of the high seriousness of the origin myths. In these Coyote was portrayed not as a creator or culture hero, but as a wily and rascally trickster, greedy, erotic, and boastful, one moment a cunning schemer, the next a gullible dupe. His attempts at deceit to gain his ends turned out badly more often than they succeeded. Coyote's foolish escapades, which caught the imagination of young and old alike, were recounted to entertain. Often they did point a moral, yet this was taken rather lightly. Trickster tales enjoyed their greatest popularity among the central tribes. They were less frequently related in northwestern California and, with the exception of the Tubatulabal and Serrano, not at all in the southern half of the state.

Meant also for amusement were animal tales. As in the myths, the animal characters spoke, thought, and behaved like humans while retaining their own creature faculties. The stories were short and simple, involving a single incident. Occasionally an explanation of a species' peculiarities (for example, why the wood rat has small eyes and white feet) formed part of a tale. Animal stories also moralized mildly. They were widely told only in central California.

Stories of Humans

A good number of native stories had their setting in the more recent human period. The figures in them were distinctly men and women rather than supernatural beings or animals and the background was that of tribal life. To be sure, the purely fanciful occupied a large place and little distinction was made between the real and unreal. The Avenger of the Cupeño tale, for instance, recounted the adventures of an extraordinary yet earthly hero who defeated his enemies by slinging a magical bearskin that became a real bear at them (Strong 1929:270–273; Gifford and Block 1930:251–253). Events that fell even farther beyond the range of things experienced by the Indians included journeys to worlds outside the one they lived in. A Cahuilla tale described how two brothers ascended to the skyland in search of wives, and a Hupa narrative related the experiences of a young husband who went to the underworld and brought back his dead wife. Popular throughout California were tales of the theft of a wife or other relative by some evil monster.

Of a different order were narratives derived from actual events. These, as a rule, contained little or nothing that was marvelous or grotesque, although they were not always free of exaggeration. Some were historical or pseudohistorical and told of recent happenings (Goldschmidt, Foster, and Essene 1939); others had a legendary character and described peoples and events of the more distant past (Spott and Kroeber 1942:210–219). Actually no dividing line could be drawn between the two classes for to the Indians one imperceptibly shaded into the next. War stories from two opposing tribes (Nomlaki and Yuki) demonstrate how current events became legends within a few decades (Goldschmidt, Foster, and Essene 1939). Though they undoubtedly had their origin in actual conflicts and were related as truthful chronicles, the details had become blurred and distorted and each tribe had set its stamp on the accounts so that they no longer represented real battle records. The subject matter of the historical and legendary narratives strongly reflected tribal interests.

Stories Borrowed from Europeans

A few stories of obviously foreign origin had crept into the repertories of California Indian narrators. Fruito the Gambler, related by the Costanoans, came from a Spanish folk tale (Gifford and Block 1930:302–303). An acculturated version of the well-known Tar Baby story (of African provenience) told by the Shasta had Coyote as its focal character. The making of woman from man's rib in versions of the Ipai-Tipai and Shasta creation showed that biblical episodes had infiltrated the native mythology. Introduced material—personages, objects, ideas, and phraseology—from Western civilization turned up in a number of tales.

Poetry and Formulas

A discussion of the oral literature of native Californians would not be complete without mention of poetry. On the whole, verse was not highly developed. It was always sung and most songs were extremely brief and frequently contained meaningless syllables or obscure words. Rhyme was never found but other repetitive forms took its place.

Song texts, on occasion, did possess a good poetical quality. A Wintu love song embodied in appropriate language both imagination and sentiment (Demetracopoulou 1935:492):

> Before you go over the snow-mountain to the north,
> Downhill toward the north,
> O me, do look at me,
>
> You who dwell below the snow-mountain,
> Do look at me.

Some of the finest verse, rich in figurative language of a metaphorical or allusive sort, was found in ceremonial songs of the southern tribes. The following excerpt from the Cupeño creation song, which divided into verses naturally by a slight rhythm or tune change at each division, is a good example (Joughlin and Valenzuela 1953:17–18):

> *Creation Song*
>
> Desolate it was
> Desolate it was
> Desolate the Earth.
> First they appeared,
> First they came out,
> First Mokat,
> First Tamayowit,
> These the chiefs,
> These the ancients.
>
> His heart roared.
> His heart thundered.
> Water, mud roared.
> Then outside toward the door
> They themselves lay;
> Mokat outside
> And Tamayowit.

Where it was bare
Where it was lonely
Themselves they laid
Where dust was
Where mist was.

First they appeared.
First they lay there;
First Mokat,
First Tamayowit.
Then they put down
The things they brought:
This tobacco,
This Toloache.

Far away, Far away
They died,
Mokat and Tamayowit.
Then the people
They cut their hair
They cut their hair.
And he, too, cut his hair in mourning
Weeping Roadrunner.

My heart gives out, gives out.
My heart turns over, turns over.
My heart goes down to the underworld.
My heart goes down to the underworld.
My heart goes to the ocean.
My heart dics in the ocean.
He is buried.

Magical formulas, from a few to many lines long, were an important form of verbal composition in northwestern California. They consisted of stereotyped sets of words either in the form of a myth or a dramatic dialogue. They seem not to have been memorized absolutely for their effect derived from the sense of the words rather than letter-perfect recitation. Formulas served many specific purposes—curing the sick; gaining success in hunting, love, or war; and acquiring wealth, to mention a few. The central feature of each important public ceremony was a recitation of how the ritual had been established by the ancient race of supernatural beings. Formulas were considered personal property and were inherited in families. A stiff charge was made for their rendition.

Other forms of oral expression attained no significant development in native California. Short fixed prayers were sometimes resorted to, but no great emphasis was placed upon them. Popular sayings, such as riddles, and proverbs were unknown.

Sources

A considerable body of myths and tales of the California Indians has been assembled. Basic contributions were made by Kroeber (1905a, 1907a, 1908), Dixon (1902, 1910), Goddard (1904), C. G. Du Bois (1901, 1906), and Curtin (1909). These consisted of collections of tales and discussions of relationships between various tribal mythologies. The record of native Californian literature became greatly enlarged through the labors of faculty members and students of the University of California Department of Anthropology, among them Gifford (1917), Barrett (1919, 1933), Gayton (Gayton and Newman 1940), Du Bois and Demetracopoulou (1931), and Voegelin (1948). Aside from this organized effort, independent collectors such as Merriam (1910, 1928), Harrington (1931, 1932), Benedict (1926), Angulo (1935), and Angulo and Freeland (1928) added to the store of available material.

Several summaries have appeared, such as Kroeber (1907a) and Alexander (1916). Gifford and Block (1930) compiled an excellent anthology, which included comparative statements on the various categories of stories. Nine stories are retold by T. Kroeber (1959). The areal affiliations of California folktales were discussed by Gayton (1935).

No systematic account of aboriginal poetry has been compiled but details are found scattered through the numerous ethnological publications devoted to California Indians. Good samples of magical formulas were collected by Goddard (1904) and Sapir (1927).

Cults and Their Transformations

LOWELL JOHN BEAN AND SYLVIA BRAKKE VANE

The major religious systems of native California are commonly known as the World Renewal, Kuksu, and toloache (ʔantap and Chingichngish) cults. The Ghost Dance, the derivative Bole-Maru and Dream cults, and the Shaker Church are developments after European contact (fig. 1). The philosophical concepts underlying these traditions are not dealt with directly in this chapter since they have been described elsewhere (Bean 1975; Bean 1976; Blackburn 1975; Kroeber 1925; Loeb 1932). Many local smaller traditions of tribes not included in these prominent traditions, such as bird cults (Gifford 1926a), Peyote religions, ancient prehistoric religious systems, girls' adolescent rites, war dances, funeral rites, or the basic shamanic tradition that underlies all the native religious systems are not discussed in detail, nor are the effects and adaptations of Christian denominations, such as Roman Catholicism, Methodism, Mormonism, and Pentecostalism considered except briefly. All these continue to bridge the old and the new among many native California Indians in the late twentieth century.

The major religions mentioned above established common philosophical assumptions that served to integrate large numbers of people into social, economic, political, and ritual networks of considerable dimensions, including many thousands of people and sometimes hundreds of communities. In most of the groups that participated in these networks, initiation into religious secret societies was a sine qua non for elite or leadership status. Initiatory rites, accordingly, served as formal educational institutions in which the existential and normative postulates of these societies were imparted to each generation of elites. These religious-political leaders served as administrators and statesmen of early California—boundary players in the broad-ranged network of social systems encompassing many political and several language groups.

Entry into and status within these religious societies usually correlated with the wealth and the social background of an individual as well as his or her social, intellectual, and technological skills. In fact, some religious societies (e.g., ʔantap among the Chumash) controlled professions and displayed some of the characteristics of craft or guild associations determining who could enter certain trades or have usufruct and possessory rights to certain property (Blackburn 1974; Goldschmidt 1951).

These religious systems were intimately involved in the economic aspects of California societies in that ritual events were usually associated with the production and distribution needs of each group and its neighbors. Rituals prescribed by the rules of each system served also as interchange events where goods were transferred or exchanged and rights and privileges to economic goods and services affirmed (Bean 1972; R.C. White 1963; Bean and King 1974; Kroeber 1925). These same ritual events, of course, demonstrated to all in splendid dramatic fashion the religious and philosophical assumptions of each individual society, thereby serving as ethnicity maintenance devices that separated each group from its neighbors while binding many groups together as ritual congregations.

As these religious systems developed through time the institutions associated with them became increasingly complex and formalized, more efficiently integrated both within individual political groups and among neighboring groups, and more institutionalized (Kroeber 1971a; Bean and King 1974; Heizer 1964). They may have been in full development as much as a millennium or more before White contact. Intergroup integration was facilitated by ritual rules requiring religious leaders of groups other than the local group to participate in its rituals. Such rules brought about the development of many major religious centers, which were also centers of economic, social, and political interaction. These were found throughout California; for example, in northwestern California World Renewal rites were celebrated at 13 ritual centers (Kroeber and Gifford 1949), while in southern California the Chumash (King 1971:35-36) and the Gabrielino (B.E. Johnston 1962) also had such ritual centers. In other areas apparently the centers were not usually permanent ones; rather, each community became a ritual center for the time it hosted its reciprocating comembers of a ritual congregation (Bean 1972).

All these religious systems had strong roots in a shamanic tradition. Shamans, having control of "altered states of consciousness," were religious specialists in charge of the relationships between man and the supernatural in all California societies, in effect philosophers. In some societies, especially those where religion was less formally organized, their vocation was theoretically thrust upon them, and their knowledge was acquired by direct communication with the supernatural. In effect, of

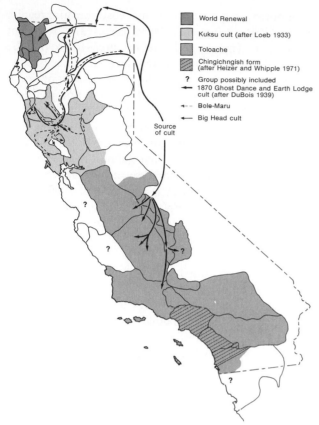

World Renewal
Kuksu cult (after Loeb 1933)
Toloache
Chingichngish form
(after Heizer and Whipple 1971)
? Group possibly included
←— 1870 Ghost Dance and Earth Lodge
cult (after DuBois 1939)
←-- Bole-Maru
←— Big Head cult
Source
of cult

Fig. 1. Major religious systems of Native California.

course, traditional knowledge provided basic formats upon which individual, creative shamans worked. A priestlike role for religious specialists, in which knowledge was acquired by formal education, was more common in the great religious systems described here (Kuksu, ʔantap, World Renewal, Chingichngish). Where these religious systems were not operative, one finds networks or informal associations of religio-political specialists cross-cutting cultural and political boundaries and involving social, economic, and political behavior similar to that of the major religious systems. Among some groups (Atsugewi, Achumawi, Tubatulabal), these networks were informal with little visible structure while in areas of clan and lineage structure (Miwok, Yokuts, Cahuilla, Serrano, Tipai, Maidu) they were more institutionalized, serving to create socioeconomic ties in less favorable ecological settings, the degree to which these systems were institutionalized correlating markedly with economic and ecological potentials. In the most favored environments the formation of the great religious systems was possibly one of the ways in which economic and political interchange between more populous groups competing within the most favorable eco-niches was established and thus was a factor in the establishment of social systems that could maintain dynamic equilibrium over long periods of time.

To some degree these major religious systems may also have been devices for political expansion, the fear of competing neighbors bringing about the formation of ritual, political, and economic alliances (ritual congregations) in order to reduce potential conflict situations over scarce resources, particularly after population density reached optimal levels. By providing for routinized peaceful interactions between groups of differing and disparate ecological potentials, trade agreements, marriage alliances, and other intergroup institutions were maintained, renewed, made, and reaffirmed so that goods, services, and wealth were more equitably or at least more predictably spread among neighboring groups (Bean and King 1974).

World Renewal

The World Renewal religion and its rituals were the most striking aspect of the religious practices of the Karok, Yurok, Hupa, Tolowa, and perhaps of the Wiyot, whose culture had largely disappeared by the time ethnographers appeared on the scene. These rites were imbedded in a religious system that extended to the north among the peoples of northwestern America as far as Alaska. It was characteristic of this larger group to have status explicitly based on the possession of wealth and its reciprocal exchange in a complex of ritual feasts and to maintain a rigid philosophical system comparable to the Protestant ethic (Goldschmidt 1951). The World Renewal system was an aspect of this larger system that was in its details unique to California even though the basic ideas upon which it was based were more widely distributed (Kroeber and Gifford 1949).

The Tolowa, Karok, Yurok, Hupa, and Wiyot lived along the northwestern California coast from the mouth of the Mad River to that of the Trinity River and along the rivers and streams as far inland as Inam on the Klamath River. They resided in small villages, hemmed in by forested mountains, an environment with a wealth of plant and animal resources, but one in which unpredictable floods, earthquakes, and forest fires were as threatening to humans as a whole as disease and accident were to individual humans. In these nations, a network of male priests officiated at annual cycles of rites that were considered essential to the maintenance of world order, the health of individuals, productivity and availability of plants, animals, and fish, assistance from spiritual beings, prevention of natural disasters, and the like. Women shamans acted in curing capacities, especially for psychosomatic phenonema (Kroeber 1925; Kroeber and Gifford 1949).

Floods, earthquakes, fires, disease, and accidents were alike in being manifestations of power wielded by extrahuman forces, often as a result of improper actions on the part of humans. Tradition decreed that only the performance of appropriate rites could restore the world to an orderly and predictable state, with man in some degree of control. These rites had been established or demonstrated by the Immortals at the time of creation. Their teachings were incorporated not only in the language, customs, and ritual lore of the people, but also in the esoteric narratives and dialogues that prescribed for the sacred ceremonies and had the power to recreate what the Immortals had originally done. These formulaic narratives and dialogues were repeated by a priest in each ritual center, acting out a story of what the Immortals had done in early times of creation in several precise locations, sometimes separated over some distances, where the original events had occurred, and in the exact fashion prescribed by tradition. The death and rebirth of the world were in part reenacted in the rebuilding of sacred structures (sweathouses, ceremonial houses, dance arenas), the creation of the sacred fires, the erection of stone walls related to shamanic power acquisition rites, or the sacred pile of sand in which priests might stand for part of the rite. Kroeber and Gifford (1949:128) reveal the traditional "rites of passage" structure of the ritual when they note that "at Rekwoi and presumably at the three other Lower Yurok Jumping dances which rebuild an 'ancient' sweathouse, the new timbers are buried and otherwise treated like a corpse." That is, separation and liminality are indicated. After the ritual, both the priest and the dancers who helped him, in part by stomping the "newly created" earth to firm it, went through rites of purification, retiring from public view and dancing before reappearing as their profane selves (Kroeber and Gifford 1949).

The rites conducted by priests and their assistants were esoteric, sacred, and secret, parts of the World Renewal cycles. They were accompanied by one or both of two major dance cycles: the White Deerskin Dance and the Jumping Dance. The former involved the ceremonial use of an elaborately decorated hide of the rare albino deer (see "Hupa, Chilula, and Whilkut," fig. 11, this vol.), apparently a condensed symbol of birth (whiteness), the male principle, and the beneficient spirit of the deer. The dance lasted as long as 16 days and worked up to a stirring climax of dancing and an elaborate display of wealth, where potential power became active, kinetic (Kroeber and Gifford 1949).

The Jumping Dance participants wore woodpecker-scalp headbands and carried sacred dance baskets (see "Hupa, Chilula, and Whilkut," fig. 12, this vol.). As in the White Deerskin Dance, the performers were men, usually young, and they danced in place standing side by side, with two or three of them who sang well doing the singing from their places in the center of the line (Kroeber and Gifford 1949).

The dance host invited neighboring peoples to the ritual center, thus integrating thousands of people from several language groups into large ritual congregations. The host needed wealth, power, and networks of wealthy friends and followers to organize the event. He needed to own or borrow requisite ceremonial costumes and regalia used by dancers (who displayed them) and sufficient dentalium bead money and other resources to provide the food for the feasts that accompanied the dances. The wealthy came into their estates by inheritance or personal acquisition, often by legal suits. The dance houses themselves were inherited (Kroeber and Gifford 1949).

These rituals had first-fruits rites implications as well as served as a time when the recently deceased were remembered and mourned. First Salmon rites were part of the World Renewal system at several ritual centers, as was the Acorn Feast, with a woman priest officiating among the Hupa. The *keᵽel* dam-building ceremony, at the peak rather than the beginning of the salmon season, was also a World Renewal rite of the Yurok (Kroeber and Gifford 1949).

In the dances, it was customary for the downstream village peoples in the vicinity of a ritual center to alternate with and compete with upstream people, the upstream and downstream directions being the predominant ones in northwestern California, as they were in the San Joaquin Valley, where these directions were involved in moiety characteristics (Kunkel 1962). The northwestern peoples may have had an incipient moiety system reflected in this competition during dances. The dances were timed so that the dark of the moon coincided with either the end or the climax of the dances (Kroeber and Gifford 1949). It should be noted that this orientation was also a characteristic of bead-money exchange and exchanges of women in the area (Gould 1966; Chagnon 1970).

Priests represented Immortals in some of the ceremonies but did not impersonate them; that is, there was no thought that they were transformed into deities. However, during the rite the priest, who went through extensive purification before and after performing the ritual, was secularized. He purified himself by separation and fasting. During the rite he abstained from water, since drinking interfered with his esoteric function of world renewal, and avoided sexual encounters, as sexual behavior was antithetical to wealth acquisition (Erikson 1943). Social distance was maintained between the priest and the people; it was also taboo to look at him or make loud noises near him.

Karok and Yurok priests had male assistant priests, and the downriver Yurok had both male and female attendants as well, perhaps a measure of the various groups' relative stratification. The assistants, attendants, and the Karok sweathouse singers seem to have been incipient secret-society members. Priests, and possibly their aides, had to come from families who "owned" secret formulas. It was a remunerative position since the individual who put on the dance was paid. Tobacco, "incense," and the powerful angelica root were used during the rites. Apparently, tobacco smoke and dancing were equivalent to "cooking," symbolizing transformations to new forms (Kroeber and Gifford 1949).

Curing shamans were usually females who sought power by fasting, abstaining from water, and prolonged dancing to attain a trance or dreaming state and a spiritual guardian who provided the power to diagnose and cure. They were assisted by experienced shamans, or "doctors," often their mothers or grandmothers; this form of shamanism also ran in families. Part of the ritual included procedures requiring heat, just as the girls' puberty rite did. Spott and Kroeber (1942:155) suggest that the pain had to be "cooked." It is possible that the "cooking" was also directed at the shaman, who was being made into a higher-status being (Lévi-Strauss 1964:334–338). In northern California the sign that a shaman had attained power was bleeding from the mouth or nose, orifices in opposition to the vagina from which came the blood that signified the woman's elevation to adult status. It is significant that the shaman, dance leaders, and others of high status were assumed to go after death to join the Immortals in a pleasantly ordered "heaven" whereas the ordinary person after death went to an underworld or to the west where they ate rotten salmon and other unfit food and engaged in brawls or fights, that is, their afterlife was disordered, having the same high entropy as menstrual blood (Kroeber and Gifford 1949).

Kuksu

The religious system that anthropologists have generally referred to as the Kuksu cult was an interwoven cluster of subsystems common to the peoples in the San Francisco Bay area and the Sacramento and northern San Joaquin valleys and adjacent hill area. It included the Pomoans; Coast, Lake, and Plains Miwok; Patwin; Valley Nisenan; Hill and Valley Maidu; Cahto; Yuki and Huchnom. These peoples developed secret societies of learned men (and occasionally women) who underwent complex rites of passage and formal instruction to signify their elevation to and warrant their holding of leadership positions. They administered and led cycles of rites and ceremonies, usually including curing, singing, and dancing, in which elaborately costumed members of the society or societies represented transformed divinities, ghosts, or spirits. They thus recreated sacred time and in one way or another restored their people to the unsullied state that had prevailed at the time of creation (Loeb 1932, 1933; Kroeber 1932a).

There were few activities common to all peoples in this area since a variety of religious customs and beliefs, many of them prevalent in adjacent areas, were interwoven to create a complex recognized by all its constituent members. Available data suggest that the religious customs and beliefs of any given people within the Kuksu area varied considerably over time, although the Kuksu reli-

gion generally may have been several thousand years old. What distinguished the religion was its complexity and formalized organization rather than any given ritual feature of it. Most of the peoples who practiced it had one or more secret societies (ghost, Kuksu, Hesi, Aki) whose members were socially, politically, and economically superior to nonmembers (women, children, and many male commoners were excluded from membership). Most of them had ceremonies in which gods, spirits, or ghosts were impersonated (returned to earth) and some of them, notably the Cahto, Yuki, Huchnom, Eastern Pomo, Valley Maidu, Hill Maidu, and Mountain Maidu, maintained a concept of an anthropomorphic creator that was otherwise found only among the Wintu and Nomlaki directly north of the Kuksu area. The religion as a whole had no native designation and is called Kuksu because the god most widely impersonated is called *kúksu* in Eastern Pomo and similar terms in other languages—an indication of the fundamental identity of the various forms of the religion (Loeb 1932, 1933; Kroeber 1932a).

The individualistic character of the religion as practiced in any local group meant that the religious system provided boundaries that bolstered individual group identity. At the same time it was an open system in which traits were exchanged with some neighboring peoples. It was mandatory to invite neighboring groups to ceremonies, a custom whereby ritual reciprocity requirements alleviated the stress of competition for resources and helped reduce conflict. In addition to the reciprocity, which took the form of gifts both received from and given to the guests at ceremonies, it was customary to engage in gambling, trade, and other social activities during the course of ceremonial events (Loeb 1932, 1933; Kroeber 1932a).

The secret societies that were so prominent in Kuksu religions were a mechanism identifying persons and the privileges they enjoyed. In some areas a man could not function fully as a member of society without belonging to at least one secret society. In groups where every man was not a member, those who were had access to more power, information, wealth. The same applies to women where they were secret-society members. Membership in the societies was conferred upon chosen young people on the basis of both birth and achievement, but there was a tendency for membership to run in families, often passed ambilineally, a possible indication that the secret societies were used to strengthen affinal relationships and thus constitute intervillage alliances.

The explicit purposes of the secret societies varied. In some areas the initiation of young people and their training seems to have been a major stated goal; in others the goal was "world renewal," first-fruits recognition, curing, or initiation of economic activities appropriate to the time of the year (Loeb 1932, 1933; Kroeber 1907d, 1971a; Swezey 1975). Whatever these ritual goals the primary function was administrative.

The most elaborate versions of the Kuksu religion were to be found among the most heavily populated river valleys where there were the most abundant supplies of material resources and the greatest access to information brought by traders and other travelers (Loeb 1932, 1933; Kroeber 1932a).

Kuksu was impersonated by a secret-society member strikingly costumed, including a special headdress that varied from group to group, sometimes being a crown or top-knot of eagle or buzzard feathers and sometimes, apparently, a basket headdress with projecting feather-tipped wands that was the precursor of the so-called Big Head of the later Bole-Maru cult. These were frequently symbols of valuable food products, such as acorn or manzanita, which were bestowed as gifts each year to the leader of the group giving the rite. Kuksu's body was painted black among the Pomoans and other western peoples and covered with black feather capes among the central valley peoples. He was more anthropomorphic among the western peoples, where he was associated more often with a divinity than in the east, where he was to a degree associated with the moon (Loeb 1932, 1933). In the east he also had more birdlike attributes. In peripheral groups, where he was known by other names, he took only minor roles in rituals. In the Sacramento River valley and in the Sierra foothills, Hesi and Aki (more complex forms of ritual societies) societies replaced or existed alongside Kuksu societies. These had incorporated Kuksu traits, and almost always had vestiges of Kuksu impersonation (Kroeber 1932a; Loeb 1932).

Over most of the area where the Kuksu system prevailed, there also existed a lower ranking society, perhaps on older tradition, whose members impersonated the spirits of the dead. These spirits were considered to live in the area where they had lived as human beings, but in the forests and with the order of things reversed; they slept in the daytime and worked at night, for example. To see a ghost was dangerous and a cause of illness, especially for uninitiated young persons, so that one role of the ghost impersonators was to cure illness so caused. Ghost impersonators wore feather decorations (sometimes representative of disease-causing beings) and carried long black poles; their bodies were painted in red, black, and white stripes (Loeb 1932). They were thus condensed symbols of life and death and mediators between the dead and the living as indicated by the color symbolism and the allusions to heaven and earth. The dances, in another sense, were a way of opposing the relatively uncontrolled power of the spirits of the dead with the relatively uncontrolled power of adolescent boys under orderly, rhythmic conditions that brought both under greater social control. Thus, both boys and ghosts became "civilized."

Ghost societies seem to have served some of the same functions as annual mourning ceremonies in other parts of California and did not occur where annual mourning ceremonies for the dead were held. In the Sacramento River valley the River Patwin had "running spirits" who went into ecstatic trances and behaved in extraordinary and erratic fashion, perhaps being possessed by the ghosts they represented (Kroeber 1932a).

The major public role of ghost societies was usually the initiation of young people, that is, the conduct of the rite of passage to transform adolescents into fully participant members of the tribe. This was true of the Yukian peoples, most of the Pomoans, the Maidu, and the Coast Miwok. The ghost societies of the Northern and Northeastern Pomo and the Wappo did not initiate all boys and thus were more clearly involved in the formation of an elite class (Loeb 1932; Kroeber 1932a).

Initiation into the Kuksu was more dramatic and often included dangerous experiences or the acquisition of dangerous knowledge. In groups to the northwest and southeast boys were initiated, and where the Hesi society was the strongest, girls underwent Kuksu initiations. Within the society there were ranks and many positions associated with ceremonial roles to be achieved, there being at least three ranks of Kuksu membership: novice, initiate, and director. The last was apt to have a high rank in secular as well as sacred society (Kroeber 1932a).

In some groups the ghost and Kuksu societies were merged; among other groups traits common in adjacent areas were merged with the Kuksu system. For example, the bear "impersonation" that occurred in the Northwest was represented among some of the Pomoans (figs. 2–3), the Coast Miwok, and the Patwin where Bear society initiations were held annually. In Patwin groups Bear or an analogous "north spirit" society was sometimes a third level of elite secret society (Loeb 1932; Kroeber 1932a).

Sally McLendon, from L.S. Freeland.

Fig. 2. William Benson, Eastern Pomo, in bear doctor's costume. Photograph by Roger Sturtevant, 1931.

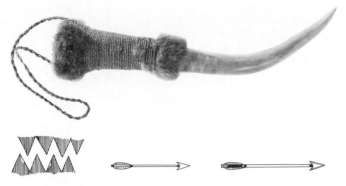

Dept. of Anthr., Smithsonian: 252887.
Fig. 3. Ceremonial dagger of polished and incised elk antler with the hilt wrapped with fiber cord and otter fur. Worn by an Eastern Pomo bear doctor around the neck or suspended from the belt. Detail shows incised decoration. Length 18 cm. Made by William Benson in 1908.

In the Sacramento Valley there were Hesi societies into which all or most boys were initiated. The name may be from Nomlaki, for the Valley Konkow word *hési* was borrowed, with the ceremony, from the Nomlaki (William F. Shipley, personal communication 1976). Within the Hesi society there were as many as 10 or 12 ranks to be achieved by payment and performance. Members were paid for enacting ceremonial roles, the acting not requiring the acquisition of esoteric knowledge; they paid to learn the esoteric knowledge that permitted them to direct performances and for the right to sit in a hierarchy of seating sections within the dance house. Where the Hesi religion was practiced, the dance costumes were extremely elaborate and a bewildering variety of dances was performed in a series of ceremonial events. The dance leader in a Hesi ceremony impersonated a bird divinity; he was termed *mo·ki* in Patwin and, from that, *mó·ki* in Konkow. Kuksu was often only one of many other animal-spirit impersonator performers (Kroeber 1932a).

The Hesi society not only celebrated the usual seasonal events, such as first-fruit rites, but also conducted a cycle of dances to animal spirits. The esoteric information that might have clarified the meaning of these song and dance cycles has for the most part not appeared in the anthropological literature. The last members of the secret societies who knew it may have taken it to the grave with them (Loeb 1932, 1933).

The Hill Maidu, instead of the Hesi society, had the Aki society (Loeb 1933); the Valley Konkow word was *ʔá·ki* (William F. Shipley, personal comunication 1976). The northwest Maidu at Chico had both Hesi and Aki cycles. The foothill and valley Nisenan and Maidu had annual mourning ceremonies and no secret ghost societies.

The most sacred Kuksu society dances were Coyote, Condor, and Hawk Dances. Coyote figured in the myths of many peoples as creator, usually one of twin creators,

the younger brother of a more remote creator firgure. He possessed attributes of intelligence, cleverness, and positive creativity, as well as negative attributes. The Condor and Hawk, as well as other predatory birds, were power symbols and in the south central valley and in southern California they often were considered as powerful deities. Bean (1975) has pointed out that such members of the animal kingdom are often at the high points in the cosmological order of native Californians.

The Kuksu also served as a recruitment process for medicalists, but not uniformly or universally. There was generally more than one kind of medical specialist, at least one of whom was a sucking doctor. The training of doctors was often a function of the secret-society initiation rite; in other instances, sucking or other kinds of doctors received their training solely through individual spiritual experience (Loeb 1932, 1933; Kroeber 1932a).

Toloache

The use of narcotic plant materials to facilitate the acquisition of power from sources accessible only in altered states of consciousness is widespread in the Americas. In California, the ritual and ecstatic use of tobacco was almost universal, and even among people who practiced no other agriculture, tobacco was diligently planted and cared for (Kroeber 1925).

Another plant with more dramatic narcotic properties, datura, commonly known as jimsonweed or toloache (from the Nahuatl *toloatzin,* through Spanish), is native to large parts of the Americas. In California, as in parts of Mexico and Central and South America, toloache was used in ritual hallucinogenic and medicinal contexts. Physiologically, any part of the datura plant is toxic as well as vision-producing. It was used with due safeguards since its use can result in coma or death. Even when taken in safe dosages, the psychedelic state that results can be frightening, and those who took it needed to be watched and guided carefully through the experience. The development of the uses of this plant for medicinal and psychedelic purposes was a significant technological achievement (Gayton 1930a; Bean 1972; Kroeber 1925).

A precise delineation of its use in California is difficult since societies that use it were no longer fully functioning by the time ethnographers investigated them. The fullest description of the datura-based religion designated the toloache cult in the anthropological literature are for the Yokuts (Gayton 1930a), Luiseño, and Cahuilla (Strong 1929; C.G. Du Bois 1908a). This cult is apparently a very old religion common to the peoples of south-central and southern California, while the datura plant itself was known and used (but apparently not in a toloache cult complex) by peoples as far north as the San Francisco Bay region and thence eastward into the Sierra Nevada. Among those ethnic nationalities known to have used datura in religious or medical contexts are the southern

Californians Ipai, Tipai, Luiseño, Juaneño, Serrano, Gabrielino, Cupeño, Tubatulabal, and Kitanemuk plus various other groups (Miwok, Costanoans, Salinan) (Gayton 1930a), and, outside California, the Chemehuevi, Kawaiisu, Quechan, Mohave, and Cocopa.

Two major religious subsystems developed out of the toloache cult in coastal California: the Chingichngish religion among the Luiseño-Juaneño, Gabrielino, and Ipai-Tipai peoples and the ?antap religion among the Chumash (Kroeber 1925; Blackburn 1974).

The use of datura was frequently correlated with leadership positions and almost always with professional orientation or social rank. For example, the Cahuilla *páxa?*, Serrano *paxa·?*, and Luiseño *paxá?* was an official whose major role was the administration of the boys' initiation ceremony. He and the shamans (whose assumption of shamanic powers was accomplished through the mediation of datura) were important members of the men's council that controlled the affairs of the tribe. A young man's initiation ceremony was held when a number of uninitiated young men, the accumulated food resources, or the development of internal social stresses stimulated this ruling group to undertake the necessary preparations (Strong 1929; Gayton 1930a; Kroeber 1925).

Prior to initiation the young men were separated from their families and taken to a secluded place. After appropriate purification rites, they were given an infusion of datura root (fig. 4), then encouraged to dance until falling into an unconscious state. When they awoke, they were in a trance state in which they saw colorful, symbolic, and emotionally meaningful visions under conditions controlled by the *páxa?* and his assistants. During the ensuing weeks the boys were taught clan songs and dances, and at the end of the week a ground painting depicting cosmological concepts was made and explained. The datura drinking was the esoteric part of longer rites, which varied in detail from group to group. However, such ceremonies were the core traits of the toloache religion of the Luiseño-Juaneño, Cahuilla, Ipai, Tipai, Cupeño, and Gabrielino. Among these groups the ceremonies were performed for all boys while among their northeastern neighbors, the Serrano, only boys of "elite" families were so initiated (Strong 1929).

Toloache was drunk by shamans as part of most of the religious ceremonies in the southern California tribes; it gave access to sources of power needed for healing, divining, diagnosing, dancing, and singing for long periods; for long hunts; for sharper vision; and for sorcery. Shamans in several groups tested their powers during the Eagle Dance by engaging in a contest to see who could kill the sacred eagle by "shooting" it with toloache. In these particular instances the toloache appears to have been personified power (Strong 1929; Harrington 1942).

The Monache and Yokuts who lived in the San Joaquin basin and the southern Sierra foothills took

Southwest Mus., Los Angeles.
Fig. 4. Fred Magee, Luiseño, with basketry sieve used in making toloache infusion. He wears an eagle-feather skirt. Photograph by Josephine P. Cook, before 1942.

toloache in group rites held in the spring. To take it was an individual decision and its use was not confined to boys and men; women also took it. Before the ritual the participants fasted for 40 days. A professional "pharmacist" prepared the toloache drink and administered it. Those who took it in this rite were also kept dancing until they were unconscious. The visions experienced upon "awakening" gave information about what was causing illnesses or trouble as well as about the location of lost objects and a guide to them (Gayton 1930a; Kroeber 1925:504).

These same groups occasionally used datura on an individual basis to assure luck in gambling, to cure certain illnesses, and to attain personal visions (Gayton 1930a). In the south the use was more a "part of a ritual which initiated the participants into a ceremonially and politically self-conscious unit" (Gayton 1930a:57). The farther away from the southern California center of the toloache religion one went, the less distinct and important the use of datura became. Among the Central Miwok, Gayton (1930a) reports that sungazers, a species of ritual participants, engaged in "contests" in which they "shot" each other with toloache, each side seemingly "dying" in turn.

ʔantap

Among the Chumash, toloache use in the protohistorical period centered in the secret society, ʔantap, which takes its name from that of its members. All tribal leaders were ʔantap. This society presided at ceremonies in which the sun, as a male and threatening deity, and the earth and her three aspects (wind, rain, fire) were worshipped (Blackburn 1974:104). A symbolic association between such powerful deities in whom power was concentrated and the ʔantap who had a monopoly on the sources of power and wealth among the Chumash can be discerned. In fact, a major Chumash deity, a female one, bore the same name as the Chumash word for toloache (Blackburn 1974), *momoy* in Ventureño and Ynezeño.

The Chumash had important ceremonials of the world renewal type at harvest time and at the winter solstice, timing them by means of a lunar calendar reset twice a year at the time of the solstices. An astrologerlike official named newborn children, reported problems to the chief, and administered toloache (Blackburn 1974:104).

Shamans used toloache for mediating with supernatural sources of power in various contests. For example, they were thought to have used charmstones in connection with toloache rites having to do with curing, bringing rain, or assuring success in war or fishing (Grant 1965:66–68). Such rites apparently were also common as far north as the Santa Clara valley and inland among the Yokuts (Blackburn 1974:100).

The visions of the participants of toloache rites may have been the basis of numerous cave paintings found in the mountains in the Chumash area and in other parts of southern California, but this is not certain. These are abstract works of art probably representing symbolically various supernatural beings in Chumash cosmology as well as the individual dream helpers employed by shamans. They may also have represented the good and evil aspects of power in forms that were in the visual idiom of the people for whom they where painted. The very presence of paintings in sacred sites increased the power inherent in the place (Grant 1965:91–92).

Chingichngish

A second variation on the toloache religious system was the Chingichngish religion, which may have developed from conditions arising from European contact, perhaps a "crisis cult" developed in reaction to European diseases that were decimating Gabrielino and Luiseño groups prior to 1776. Others have theorized that this branch of the toloache religion developed as a result of contact with Christian deserters or castaways, since many of its central features are reminiscent of Christian themes (R.C. White 1963). C.G. Du Bois (1908a:76) suggests that Chingichngish "had every requisite of a conquering faith. It had a distinct and difficult rule of life requiring obedience, fasting, and self-sacrifice. It had the sanction of fear. . . . It had an imposing and picturesque ritual. And above all it had the seal of inviolable secrecy. . . ."

The religion is traditionally supposed to have diffused from Pubunga (near Long Beach) in Gabrielino territory where a shamanlike hero named Chingichngish taught a new body of beliefs that became syncretized with preexisting beliefs and practices. He was assimilated into Luiseño religious literature as creator of the Luiseño and their laws and ceremonials, after he had transformed the people created by *wiyó·t*, the earlier creator, into spirits. He provided a more explicitly moral normative order than had hitherto prevailed and enforced this order by creating a new class of spirits, the "avengers" (rattlesnake, spider, tarantula, bear, sting ray, raven), who were assigned to watch that people obeyed his laws and to punish wrongdoers. Raven had the special assignment of reporting ceremonial mistakes, disobedience of the rules of life, and incorrect revelation of secrets to the god Chingichngish (C.G. Du Bois 1908a).

So well were the secrets of the religion kept that the esoteric knowledge of its dogma and ritual have only come to light after acculturation processes have left so few who practice it that these elderly people prefer to leave some record of it rather than letting it be completely lost. That it has lasted as long as it has in the face of great odds means that it provides some bulwark against the encroachment of the invading culture complex, thus helping a people to survive. In the 1970s the cult is active at Rincon and Pauma reservations in southern California.

The Chingichngish doctrine is to be found in the songs of the Luiseño sung during their great initiation and annual mourning ceremonies. It has been blended in with rites common to the toloache religion and the traditional Luiseño religion. Its primary center was among the Luiseño-Juaneño, Gabrielino, and Ipai-Tipai peoples. These peoples have the most extensive recorded repertoire of sacred music and dances among California peoples, although their not having developed a comparable complexity in ceremonial regalia deluded early anthropologists into an assumption that they had a simpler religious system than existed elsewhere.

Postcontact Religions

In the south coastal region of California, Roman Catholicism was introduced beginning in 1769. Although some native Californians were Christianized only by force, others accepted the new religion apparently because the Spanish demonstrated possession of kinds of power that appeared desirable. The acceptance of Christianity did not mean that native religious systems disappeared.

Native religious ceremonies persisted alongside Catholicism, often tolerated by the priests under the guise of "secular" events, but sometimes carried out secretly. The extreme decrease in native population in the last part of the nineteenth century and the concomitant "melting pot" philosophy on the part of the Anglo-Americans were more destructive to native religious systems than Catholicism. Protestant missions that were permitted to proselytize within Mission as well as non-Mission groups often were the agents of the prevailing pressures toward acculturation, because Protestant missionaries, like the Catholic priests, tended to equate native gods and culture heroes with the devil. However, unlike many of the priests, Protestants were intolerant of syncretism. Many aspects of native religions died out because there were no longer ritualists to organize, lead, and participate in them. Their disappearance was often due to death, especially of the elites, loss of native value systems that defined the ceremonial roles as worthwhile, and pressure from Whites who denied worth to native beliefs and ceremonies.

To a greater degree than is generally realized, native religious systems persisted, some of them to the present, having been transformed by various degrees to fit a changing socioeconomic system, largely under the direction of native shamans. The first major event signaling a reorientation of native religious systems came to public attention as the Ghost Dance of 1870, a messianic movement originating among the Nevada Paiute, where a prophet announced the end of the world and/or the return of the dead, along with the destruction of all White people and the return of the world to the Indians. The religion spread rapidly in northern California and Oregon, attracting large numbers of native peoples to dances held at ritual centers, often in the semisubterranean earth-covered dance houses where Kuksu rites had been held. These structures figured for some groups as the means by which natives would be saved during the predicted world holocaust. When the predicted disaster failed to occur, the Ghost Dance died out except in the area where the Kuksu religion had been practiced and among certain adjacent peoples, especially the Miwok and the Nomlaki. Here it survived in the form of a reanimated Kuksu religion in forms compatible with the new social and economic realities. The Ghost Dance demonstrated that by traveling longer distances, a feat made practical by the adoption of the horse as a mode of transportation, native peoples could reestablish some of the underlying structure of their social system through the ritual, which provided spiritual reassurance, contact with the mythic as well as the sacred past, and contacts with one another across the now-weakened intertribelet ethnic boundaries, so that they could make common cause in a troubled time. The Ghost Dance also legitimized the authority of the individual Dreamer, as opposed to the cult or hereditary leader, and it was this feature that was directly responsible for the innovative offshoots of the Ghost Dance. Group participation was emphasized by incorporating all members of the community more directly into the sacred order—men, women, and children (Du Bois 1939; Gayton 1930a).

Shortly after 1870, a variation of the Ghost Dance known as the Earth Lodge religion spread from the northern Yana, where it originated, to the Nomlaki, Hill Patwin, Northeastern Pomo, other Pomoans, Wappo, Coast Yuki, Sinkyone, Lake Miwok, Coast Miwok, Cahto, Wintu, Achumawi, Shasta, and various Oregon tribes. As the new ideology traveled, new Dreamers arose who added some embellishments and deleted others. The original doctrine stressed the importance of earth lodges as an escape from world destruction. At least nine large new earth lodges were built at religious centers in the Pomoan area. The "return of the dead" concept was minimized here, whereas in the northernmost parts of the state, the return of the dead was considered a more important purpose of the rituals (Du Bois 1939).

With the aggregation of peoples from various groups assembled in the Pomoan area in expectation of a crisis, and the people adjusted to the idea that any individual might have a dream that would bring information from the creator, the stage was set for further innovations. The most lasting innovation was the Dreamer or Bole-Maru religion (fig. 5). The name Bole-Maru was coined by

Lowie Mus., U. of Calif., Berkeley.
Fig. 5. Dancers (Big Head in center) of the Bole-Maru religion. Northeastern Pomo at Stony Creek, Colusa County. Photograph by C. Hart Merriam, July 1907.

670

BEAN AND VANE

combining two names for the cult, Hill Patwin *bo·le* and Eastern Pomo *ma·rú·* (Du Bois 1939:1), both of which are used to designate the Dreamers, who conducted the ceremonies, and apparently originally also the myth or dream that was recited. Two Hill Patwin Dreamers originated this form of the religion, which spread to the Pomoans, southern Hill Patwin, and the Maidu at Chico. It was most elaborate in north-central California where it emphasized traditional dualistic concepts, which were sometimes integrated or compared with the Christian concepts of heaven and hell, God and the devil. Its doctrine forbade drinking, quarreling, stealing, and disbelief. The dance house pole, important as a symbol of the world's center, a path that connected humans with this ultimate source of power, became more important than in the Kuksu religions; its meaning intensified rather than changed. Its decorations changed; cloth in addition to feather pennants was used. Cloth in addition to feathered costumes was also worn, and clamshell jewelry continued to be important (see "Western Pomo and Northeastern Pomo," fig. 8, this vol.). In ritual costume designs new postcontact elements appeared, such as crosses and hearts (Meighan and Riddell 1972), but they are rigorously defended as truly Indian-inspired by today's dreamers. Bole-Maru Dreamers also assumed some of the healing and diagnostic functions of the older religions (fig. 6), but more significantly they became the practical philosophers adapting a new cosmological scheme for the people of this area.

Another innovation was the ball dance, in which participants threw a multicolored cloth ball back and forth, the ball apparently representing among some groups the sacred colors of the universe. Otherwise, most of the Bole-Maru dances were modifications of Kuksu and Hesi ritual dances. A major change from the past was the diminishing importance of secret societies with a concomitant increase in total community (men, women, and children) involvement. As time passed, the end-of-the-world concept faded, and it became customary for the dream function to be concentrated in the hands of dreamer specialists, who took on many of the shamanic roles of traditional times. In the twentieth century, the Bole-Maru is a striking example of a religion that persists in a form adapted to present conditions.

The Ghost Dance of 1890, which originated among the same group as that of 1870, had relatively little effect in California. A number of people vigorously proselytized for it, but most native groups were apparently "immune" to it, some because of the earlier disillusionment, some because the derivative versions (Bole-Maru) of the earlier dance vigorously persisted, some because traditional religions were still relatively intact. It may have been significant that native Californians in 1890 were in comparatively fortunate economic situations and were well articulated with the dominant society while still

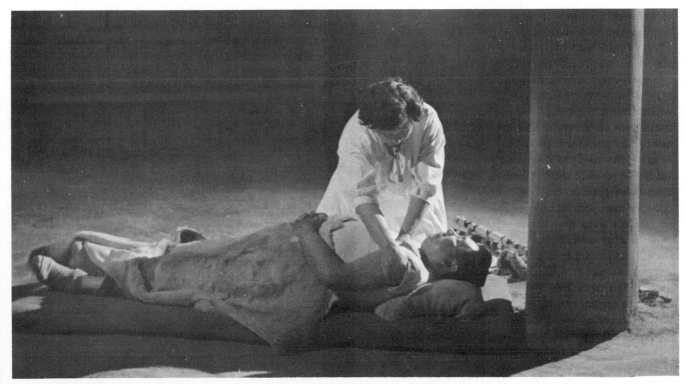

Fig. 6. Essie Parrish, Kashaya Pomo shaman and Bole-Maru Dreamer, performing as a sucking doctor in the dance house. Photograph by William R. Heick, June 1963.

CULTS AND THEIR TRANSFORMATIONS

maintaining their own ethnicity to a considerable degree. Thus there was little need for any form of nativistic movement (Mooney 1896).

In the 1920s, the Shaker Church, a nativistic movement that originated in Washington in the 1870s, spread to northwestern California (Barnett 1957:75-78), particularly among the Hupa, Yurok, Tolowa, and Wiyot. Its doctrine and practices have changed over the years, being derived from varying accommodations reached between Shakers who have individually received power and messages from God, usually during a trance state characterized by body and hand trembling or shaking. The doctrine has features similar to those in Catholic and Protestant Christianity. These are found in its ritual, regalia, music, and architecture (Barnett 1957).

The major emphasis of the Shaker Church is on faith healing, carried out in homes or in the church. The broad outlines of healing ritual are somewhat institutionalized, being similar to those used by the traditional shamans of the Yurok, Hupa, and Karok. Participants sing and dance to the sound of bells ringing, the bells being "played" as if they were native instruments such as rattles or clapping sticks. Melodic lines are primarily Indian, and the lyrics are a mixture of Christian and native components (Barnett 1957).

Church services are conducted by a minister or by any Shaker, and usually include an exhortation, confessions, and healing. In all church activities the individual has a great deal of individual freedom to innovate within a structured context. These particular characteristics are much like the traditional northwestern California curing techniques and religious practices (Barnett 1957).

Shaker healers also conceive of illness as a "pain," as did the traditional shamans of this area, and they use techniques for curing similar to precontact practices. As in the Bole-Maru religion, healing power is used only for the good of others; the negative aspect of power is played down (Barnett 1957). Significantly, these healers function in a context where traditional types of witchcraft still exist, a phenomenon probably still present in all California groups in the 1970s.

Shaker "big doings" at Easter and in August suggest some of the functions of World Renewal ceremonies in that they are thought to involve the restoration of the world to well-being as well as of the individual to health. The Bole-Maru ceremonies are also variations of world renewal and first-fruit rituals, and Bole-Maru believers hold a Strawberry festival (see "Western Pomo and Northeastern Pomo," fig. 11, this vol.) in the spring and an Acorn Festival in the fall. Other groups still maintain a variety of traditional dances and fiestas; in southern California funeral and special rites commemorating the dead are performed among most groups. The Inter-tribal Council of California has begun to put on state-wide dance events. In all of these there are echoes of the precontact religious events, including the World Renewal ceremonies of the northwest, the annual mourning services of the southern California peoples, the First Salmon or First Acorn festivals or rites of many smaller "little" traditions, and the great dance cycles of the Kuksu religion. The world is still being renewed for native Californians, and their identities as native peoples are resurgent.

Social Organization

LOWELL JOHN BEAN

The nature of social organization in native California has been the subject of research by anthropologists since the beginning of the twentieth century, and a picture of increasing complexity has emerged as one scholar after another has added seminal concepts. The earlier view that California Indians were rather simple folk has been replaced by a realization that they were hunters and gatherers whose peculiarly complex social systems were similar to those of horticulturalists and some agriculturalists with presumably greater technological advantages. This development of social mechanisms apparently allowed for a maximal use of resources across ecological and political boundaries.

Basic Social Units

Perhaps the most important contribution to understanding political California was the discovery by Gifford (1926d) that the lineage was the principal political and corporate unit in much of California; however, Californianists no longer subscribe to his suggestion that lineages were the universal political unit and where they were lacking they had once been present (Kunkel 1974). Kroeber (1925) approached the problem of social organization differently, noting in his earliest writings that the nature of political life in California was sufficiently different from other areas of North America that a special explanatory model was necessary. He saw the "tribelet" as the basic landowning group, pointing out that the "so-called tribes" in California were usually nonpolitical ethnic nationalities, defined as a cultural unit—a group of people sharing a language, culture, and history, and, to some degree, philosophical concepts. Variations from this common pattern occurred on the Colorado River and in the northwestern part of the state. He suggested that the tribelet (or village community) was the equivalent of the tribe among some other American Indians, since it was usually the largest group over which any one person, leader, or chief had recognized authority and was the largest autonomous group. An able chief might be known and respected and listened to among neighboring tribelets, but his actual following was generally limited to his own tribe.

In any strict usage, the word "tribe" denotes a group of people that act together, feel themselves to be a unit, and are sovereign in a defined territory. Now, in California, these traits attached to the Masut Pomo, again to the Elem Pomo, to the Yokaia Pomo, and to the 30 other Pomo tribelets. They did not attach to the Pomo as a whole, because the Pomo as a whole did not act or govern themselves, or hold land as a unit. In other words, there was strictly no such tribal entity as "the Pomo"; there were 34 Pomo miniature tribes (Kroeber 1962:38).

Kroeber suggested there were probably over 500 tribelets, estimated conservatively at between 100 and 500 persons in each group. A higher maximum of 1,000 persons seems now more reasonable (see table 1), and the estimated number of tribelets may be reduced as more encompassing social structures are recognized. Among the Cahuilla, for example, 50 or more lineages were organized in approximately 12 sibs or tribelets. The recognition of political confederations further alters the total number of these autonomous groups.

Tribelets were composed of varying types of family and household groups comprising parents, children, collateral, lineal, or affinal relatives, and sometimes nonrelatives. Kroeber (1962) suggested that the average family size was 7 or 8, with a range of 5 to 10. Tribelets varied in structural form. In south-central and central California, patrilineages were usually the basic corporate groups within a tribelet and occasionally one formed the tribelet itself. Often several lineages were linked into clans, or, as among the Tipai-Ipai, a tribelet was composed of persons from several unrelated lineages, one of which was dominant. Descent in these groups was traced three to five generations.

The population density of precontact California groups varied in different ecologic conditions, the least advantageous environments supporting smaller numbers of people (fig. 1). Population density of tribelets probably ranged from 0.5 each square mile up to the Yokuts and Chumash maximum of 10 or more persons a square mile. Tribelet territories ranged from the Miwok low of 50 square miles to as much as 6,000 square miles. The traditional ethnographic model postulates that each group expanded to the greatest extent that the requirement for cohesiveness permitted, thus lowering subsistence competition and conflict. A more modern model attributes the equilibrium between resources and population to a complex system of socioeconomic checks and balances involving, for example, ritual reciprocity, exogamy, and trade feasts.

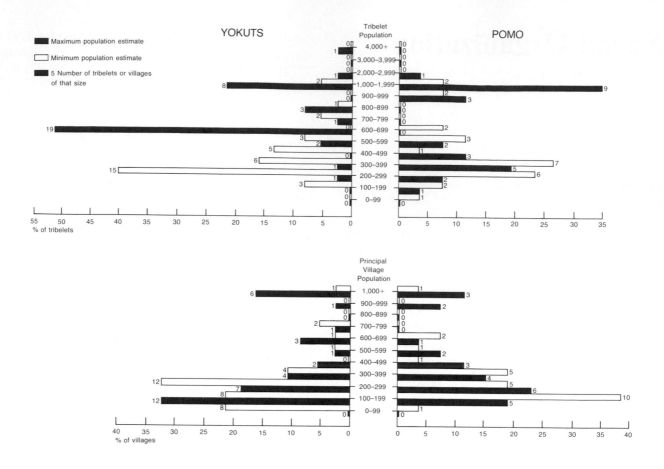

Fig. 1. Proportional distribution of populations. Based on maximum and minimum estimates of population in a fixed number of tribelets and principal villages. Source: Kunkel 1962, 1974.

There was usually a central town that served as a political, ritual, and economic center, and several subordinate smaller settlements. Council meetings and legal or legislative debates were held at the principal village, where large caches of food, goods, and treasure were also maintained. The settlements were variously occupied permanently or seasonally. Often each had a chief, usually the head of a lineage or extended family or, where kinship was less important as in northwest California, a wealthy man. The basis of political authority varied from ranked inherited chieftainships within a tribelet to situations where one or more wealthy and powerful men were titular cochiefs (Kroeber 1962).

The two major variations to the California pattern noted by Kroeber were the Colorado River and northwest California areas. The Tolowa, Hupa, Chilula, Wiyot, Karok, and Yurok on the lower Klamath River shared a cultural tradition resembling the Northwest Coast and had forms of social organization that had not developed the sociopolitical rigidity and complexity of central and southern California. In northwestern California political organization was characterized by extreme fractionalism (Kroeber 1962:43), the tribelet was a loosely connected set of separate settlements, and the people clustered in a town or village that did not have

the sense of cohesiveness and continuity found in other areas. Individualism or atomism was the rule, and their style drew status, prestige, honor, or renown from the possession (usually inherited) of property. Each man strove for himself and his family (within certain class boundaries), not for the community as a whole. Competition rather than cooperation was emphasized as an ideal, although certain ritual safeguards against flagrant individualism were imposed by the religious and legal system. These characteristics are not in themselves unique to northwestern California, but they stand out because of the relative lack of sociological and ritual modifiers that other groups used to avoid the harshest effects of competition, individual achievement, and capitalistic effort.

Two forms of organizational style were used in California tribelets. The lineage principle was the primary device in the area south of San Francisco and perhaps in the Sacramento River delta, with some exceptions (Tubatulabal and perhaps the Chumash). Kunkel (1974) has argued that northern California tribelets generally were composed of ambilocal residential corporate kin groups and that villages were composed of multikin groups, not modified lineages that have been disturbed by historical process, as Gifford (1926d) supposed, or imminent clans as argued by Goldschmidt (1948). In central California each village had one or more chiefs, each the head of a kin group composed generally of ambilaterally related people, sometimes, as with the Pomo, with a matrilineal and matrilocal bias.

Another pattern existed in the Sacramento valley where villages consisted of one or more extended residence groups with patrilocal tendencies. People were linked patrilaterally in the chiefly succession and in the inheritance of property, and descent tended to be patrilineal (in contrast with the Pomo) and associated with Omaha kinship terminology. However, there were no corporate unilineal groups such as those common in southern California (Kunkel 1974).

In the northwestern part of the state the Hupa, Yurok, Karok, Tolowa, and Wiyot also favored patrilocal residence. Their settlements consisted of one or a cluster of residential kin groups led by a wealthy man and including his extended family and various collateral kin and hangers-on (Kunkel 1974). The exact patterns of social organization in north-coastal and northeastern California are unclear; the general northern California pattern appears to differ significantly from that of southern and south-central California, where the unilineal principle provides the focus for clearly defined and rigid corporate groups, rather than loosely organized tribelets based upon ambilateral extended family forms that result in highly flexible, fluid corporate groups based upon residence rather than on kinship itself (Kunkel 1974).

Political confederations have been suggested for the Chumash (for whom L. B. King 1969 has even suggested "nation-states"), Pomo, Miwok, Patwin, Shasta, Gabrielino, Tipai-Ipai, and Salinan. Thus, the thrusting upward in sociopolitical integration in historic times is probably not, as Gifford (1926d) argues, a product of European influences. Other levels of organizational structure connected these confederations. Trade, ritual, and military alliances or associations correlated rather neatly with ecological parameters over all of California. In northern and central California stable trade and military alliances seem to have involved at least three tribelets, often members of different ethnic nationalities, whose ecological potential was mutually useful—for example, as ocean, river, foothill, and mountain peoples allied for mutual exchange and protection. These alliance structures appear to have taken advantage of and been limited by ecological factors as they extended to the naturally imposed limits within an area. Thus, in northern and north-central California the distance from the coast inland to the mountain ranges is short. There another interlocking alliance picks up and extends eastwards, while in southern California alliances extended across deserts and mountains through passes from the Pacific Coast into Arizona and New Mexico. At least three chains crossed this broad area together, linking the Tipai-Ipai with the Quechan; the Gabrielino with the

Cahuilla, Halchidoma, and Cocopa-Maricopa groups; and the Chumash with the Yokuts and Mohave (Forbes 1965:80). There are indications also of north-south alliances on the coast, from the Gabrielino to the Chumash and the Salinan, and from the Miwok to the Southwestern Pomo (Heizer 1968; Landberg 1965; Loeb 1926).

Intermediate in level between the political confederations and the alliance systems (which sometimes were coterminous) there were ritual congregations associated with the jimsonweed cult, which linked each southern California tribelet with other tribelets and ethnic nationalities (Bean 1972). The Kuksu and World Renewal rituals may have done likewise for central and northern California groups (Kroeber and Gifford 1949).

Interface Centers

Cross-tribelet interfacing appears to have commonly involved peoples within a radius of 50 to 75 miles in rituals or trade feasts, which sometimes brought several hundred to several thousand people together. Cultic centers for the World Renewal system where a few centers or towns held the rituals for a large area are a case in point (Kroeber 1925). Another is recorded among the Yokuts where Lt. José Maria Estudillo (Gayton 1936:75-76) reported about 3,000 people at a single ritual mourning ceremony. Similar centers are described for the Chumash (Point Mugu), Gabrielino (Povongna), and Tipai-Ipai (Pamo) (Heizer 1968; L. B. King 1969; Shipek 1954-1971). While communities of this sort hosted trade fairs or mourning ceremonies, for example, they simultaneously served as nodes or centers for intense sociopolitical and economic interaction. The economic equilibrium maintained over this network included as many as a dozen or more villages or tribelets, in two or more nationalities and across several ecological zones such as coast, foothills, and riverine-mountain. These partners in social interaction (along with the well-developed money systems in native California) are the most important social devices for exploiting economic resources in the area, since they expanded the amount and diversity of energy potential of every tribelet to include part of the resources of most of their neighbors (Bean and King 1974).

Levels of Organization

Thus native California can be understood as having a series of organizational systems of increasing generality. At the local level were tribelets—corporate groups based on residence and/or kinship and composed of one or more villages or settlements under the authority of one or more chiefs. Two or more tribelets were sometimes federated under a single political authority, as among the Shasta (Holt 1946), Miwok, Chumash, Gabrielino (Heizer 1968), Tipai-Ipai (Shipek 1954-1971), and Salinan (J. A. Mason 1912). More generally, local groups were interconnected by temporary, nonformalized eco-

Table 1. Demography by Habitation Zone

Yokuts	Tule Swamp	Oak Forest	Foothill	Total
		Zone		
Tribelets	9	7	21	37
Totem groups	92	92	134	318
Totem groups per tribelet	10	13	6	7
Area (sq. mi.)	3,900	630	2,440	6,970
Population total	4,570–10,600	2,200–6,900	6,810–15,000	13,580–32,500
Population density	1.2–2.7	3.5–11.0	2.8–6.2	2.0–4.7
Tribelet population	508–1,178	315–986	324–714	367–878
Totem group population	50–115	24–75	51–112	43–102

Pomo	Lake	Valley	Coast-Redwood	Total
		Zone		
Tribelets	7	12	7	26
Kin groups	23	50–55	24–29	97–107
Kin groups per tribelet	3	4–5	3–4	4
Area (sq. mi.)	429	1,480	1,440	3,349
Population total	2,010–3,755	6,500–11,440	2,930–6,360	11,440–21,555
Population density	4.7–8.8	4.4–7.7	2.0–4.1	3.4–6.4
Tribelet population	287–536	542–953	419–909	440–829
Kin group population	87–163	130–208	122–219	118–201

SOURCE: Kunkel 1962.

nomic exchanges and by formal secular associations such as the trade feast partners that related the Sherwood Pomo and the Coast Yuki. Ritual associations also linked tribelets, through shared use of permanent ritual centers and in congregations of various tribelets for periodic ritual and economic exchange. At a still broader level, several groups might share common belief systems in the jimsonweed, Kuksu, and World Renewal sacred societies and cultic organizations. Also, tribelets in different environments might be linked in amity-enmity alliances, often across ethnic boundaries (such as the links between the Gabrielino, Cahuilla, and, outside California, the Halchidoma Maricopa).

Moiety organization

Gifford (1926d) was one of the first scholars to appreciate the presence and sociological significance of the moiety concepts in native California. In 1918 he noted the presence of totemic moieties in south-central and southern California and in Arizona from north to south. They are found among the Miwok, Monache, Central Yokuts, Salinan, Kitanemuk (?), Serrano, Cahuilla, Cupeño, and Luiseño. It is possible that the Gabrielino are the point of origin for the concept, according to Strong (1929). Among these groups moiety exogamy was associated with moiety ritual reciprocity and consequently served to define potential marriage alliances as well as religious, economic, and sometimes military associations. These, accompanied by rules forbidding marriage within five generations, created very extensive social networks among neighboring groups, since marital partners were necessarily sought from a wide sociological and ecological base.

Totemic associations are often connected with taboo or privileged relationships to animals or birds that signal social relationships—ritual and economic privileges or responsibilities. Yokuts cases are rather clearly documented by Gayton (1930), where totems could not be exploited by those they symbolized. So, a person holding these totemic statuses was responsible for the proper care and keeping of the totem animals on earth. Among the Yokuts they were obliged to redeem the totem animal from any person killing or capturing one, by paying a price and subsequently providing the proper burial or disposition of the body. This system maintained the man-land-animal balance in nature so that totemic guardians would continue to cooperate with man on earth. It further acted as a means of economic redistribution, since an individual controlled valuable totems (for example, the economically valuable eagle feathers) and since an ambitious or lucky hunter could thus gain an extra economic advantage.

There are indications that among some Yokuts, Gabrielino, Kitanemuk, Chumash, and Juaneño there was a pseudomoiety structure like that found among central California groups (Strong 1929).

In central California and some southern California groups pseudomoieties functioned in social and ritual activities, but they did not control economic exchange as they did in south-central and southern California. The Pomos and their neighbors possessed these pseudomoieties—so called because they are not based on descent per se, although they do sometimes determine what part of a village a person lives in and his position in the ceremonial round house. The populations of these villages were usually divided into two, such as east-west, north-south, or upriver-downriver. Apparently an individual could choose the side he wanted to join, which was often the side of his mother's brother. This arrangement was consistent with the kind of flexibility found in marriage residence, kinships, and inheritance of any important position (Loeb 1926).

Marriage

Marriage was a closely regulated institution. Girls were usually married shortly after puberty to boys not much older than themselves. Great difference in age between spouses was rare, but it could happen, especially if the husband was a wealthy or powerful man.

As with most institutions in California, wealth and kinship were fused. The wealthy of high rank usually married their children into comparable families. The extreme example of this situation occurred in northwest California where the "personal worth" of an individual was measured in terms of "bride price." Thus among the Yurok, although status could be achieved, still a child's position depended on that of his parents and on the nature of their marriage, and especially on the size of bride price involved (Kroeber 1925). A 'bastard', abused and ostracized throughout life, was someone whose parents' union had not been legitimized by a bride price (Valory 1970). The northwest examples should not be seen as exceptions so much as extreme examples of patterns found throughout the state. Among most peoples birth determined social rank and women were used in a complex system of economic and political strategies for the long-range benefit of their own families or lineages. Lineage rank or other factors as well as wealth influenced an individual's personal worth rather than bride price per se (Bean and King 1974).

Throughout the state generation rules determined the boundaries of spouse selection. Close relatives were not suitable for marriage, except possibly the mother's brother's daughter among the Miwok. Marriage to any relative within three to five generations was discouraged, the specific number of generations depending upon the particular group. In the southern half of the state, where lineage system and moiety were the principal articulators of social relationships, individuals could not marry within their lineages, clans, or moieties, nor within the given number of generations prescribed by a generation rule. Consequently, the average tribelet was virtually without potential spouses for its own members, who thus necessarily married into neighboring tribelets, establishing affinal relationships across group boundaries. Exchanges of economic goods and the ritual participation that articulated economic and political life were usually ordered by kinship obligations. In war and peace marriages influenced who would be attacked, the relative intensity of combat, and the like.

Most men had only one wife but might divorce and remarry several times during their lifetimes. However, polygyny was generally accepted throughout California and there are rare scattered references to polyandry (Gifford 1923). Generally it was considered proper for a chief to have more than one wife simultaneously, a reflection of the economic and political needs of his office. Shamans also commonly had more than one wife, because they possessed sufficient wealth to support more

than one, and families were willing to ally with them. As with chiefs, polygyny marked their greater social prestige as men of power.

Where multiple wives were permitted, a man often married two sisters, an arrangement the wives preferred to the alternative of sharing household responsibilities with someone not related to them. This sororal polygyny is frequently reflected in kinship terminology where the mother's sister is thought of as a surrogate mother and sometimes called by the same term. A similar reflection often occurs in the term used by a husband for his wife's sister.

Alliances and proper child care were also encouraged through the practice of the sororate and the levirate. The custom of marrying the sister of a deceased wife protected the interfamily relationship and presumably promoted a positive continuity in child rearing, which would not be expected without it. However, the sororate was rarely an absolute rule, the woman in this case having more of a voice in the matter than with an initial marriage. The success of a previous marriage alliance was no doubt a determining factor.

The levirate was probably the more common and comfortable form; since it did not require the socialization of new personnel, it more easily protected the interfamily alliance structure and the child-rearing aspects of the marriage. Marriage was not only an economic mechanism; it had political and class-maintaining functions as well. In all tribes there were frequent instances of marriage with other ethnic units, for example, Shasta with Modoc (Holt 1946), Luiseño with Tipai-Ipai (Shipek 1954-1971). In a Gabrielino case, one village (Tungva) had intermarriages with 13 other villages, three of which belonged to foreign language groups—Chumash, Yokuts, and Kitanemuk (Forbes 1965).

Since marriage was a matter of concern to families, individual desires were often subordinated to group needs, and divorce, which would disturb the economic and political alliances set up by marriages, was discouraged. There are frequent examples of the difficulties of personal adjustment, especially of the bride, frequent runaways and subsequent forced returns until absolute incompatibility was established. A man divorced a woman with greater ease than vice versa. Usual reasons were sterility, laziness, or sexual infidelity. Cruelty on the part of the husband or his family was the principal reason for a woman leaving her husband. An expectation that a wife would eventually be protected from an unfavorable marriage by her own kin served as a safety mechanism for the wife, since a woman usually retained some basic rights within her own kin group.

Classes

The ethnographic literature of California documents the frequent incidence of class distinctions expressed in behavior and in native terms for statuses such as wealthy

677

person, commoner, poor person, drifter, or the like. It appears that a tripartite system existed in most groups, characterized by elites or nobility, commoners, poor, and sometimes with a fourth class of slaves or vagabonds (Bean and King 1974; Foster 1944; Gayton 1945; Gifford 1939b; Goldschmidt 1951a; Kroeber 1925; Loeb 1926; Ray 1963; Garth 1953).

These classes or ranked positions were stabilized by the fact that upper-class people in the chiefly families tended to inherit rank and capital resources. They controlled the distribution of political and ritual privileges and the economic surplus that was often associated with these privileges. They maintained special knowledge and their speech often involved special refined usages that set them apart from others. They tended to marry among themselves, and their rank was also justified in cosmological and normative postulates.

These were not completely closed class systems, for there were mechanisms for some social mobility. Individuals could increase their social rank by manipulating economic affairs, the classic but not unique example being in the northern part of the state among the Yurok and Tolowa. Shamanic roles, although they tended to be controlled through inheritance or secret societies, were theoretically open to any person with special talent and the ambition and the willingness to assume the arduous responsibilities. If they were individuals approved by the elites, they could become shamans, becoming wealthy and entering actively into ritual and political institutions that controlled society.

The class distinctions were tied to family traditions as a rule. McKern's (1922) description of the functional families among the Patwin was an early recognition of what now appears to have been generally true: craft and political and religious specializations were often family or lineage linked and ranked. Subordinate classes were also firmly linked to lineages or families as among the Yurok, Cahuilla (Bean 1972), Atsugewi (Garth 1953), Tipai-Ipai (Luomala 1963), Chumash (L.B. King 1969), and Yokuts (Gayton 1945). It is clear that members of different kinship groups had differential access to status positions and nonegalitarian behavior was more often the case than not. It is now evident that in most tribes a rigid and authoritarian social structure prevailed and that differences in rank were usually inherited.

• CHIEFS Chiefs were economic administrators, managing the production, distribution, and exchange of goods. They were usually subordinate to no other authority, although they were variously influenced by councils, secret-society officials, shamans, and other officials and wealthy men. Since his primary function was to control the collection, distribution, and exchange of food stores, money, and valuables for the benefit of the group, the chief needed ties with other corporate groups. Every group was in danger of occasional food stress unless there were economic exchange arrangements with other corporate groups. Intermarriage, ritual alliances, gift giving between chiefs, and other reciprocal acts symbolized the sealed agreements that corporate administrators maintained with one another.

Chieftainship or headmanship was generally hereditary and it consistently correlated with wealth. If a man were not conspicuously wealthy before he assumed office, he soon gained wealth as the economic administrator of the tribelet. A candidate for the chieftainship, however legitimate by hereditary standards, was replaced by a more suitable person (usually by a brother or another son of the previous chief) if he was clearly unsuitable in temperament and talent, or unwilling to serve.

The chief lived in relative luxury compared to other men; his house and household were conspicuously large, his clothing was extravagant, and his possession of regalia or signs of office, shell-bead money, food stores, and treasure goods was greater than others'. He was usually released from ordinary labor—although not among the Atsugewi—and was supported by the community, inasmuch as his many functions required a freedom from ordinary routines (Garth 1953). He was a man of prestige, feared and respected. He usually married several women, often from different tribelets, who were daughters of other chiefly or wealthy families, thus providing himself and his children with kin among the elite of other communities. Occasionally the role of the chief extended to a confederation of tribelets. The groups in this confederation might constitute the entire membership of an ethnic nationality, as among the Shasta (Holt 1946), or they might not.

In postcontact times many chiefs used their traditional role to bring together large numbers of people. They were recognized by European authorities, and were able to carry on negotiations with Europeans so that a more successful accommodation was accomplished, since they could negotiate from a greater power base.

• SHAMANS The religious function of the shaman is discussed at greater length in the chapter on world view and cults. Shamans were the principal religious functionaries throughout the state; they frequently assumed priestly status and the role was often carried simultaneously with others. Shamans specialized in various activities, and a man might be a chief and shaman, engaging in various types of medical and psychiatric services, divination, and the control of natural phenomena. Shamans were integral to the political, economic, and legal institutions. Gayton's (1930) classic description of the close integration of chiefs and shamans in political and economic institutions applies generally to the entire state.

Shamans usually ranked second only to chiefs in authority and prestige, but they were more often criticized than political leaders. It was generally assumed that they were both malevolent and benevolent, although some argue that this is a matter of differing philosophies or conceptions of the role between professionals and laymen (Handelman 1972). Shamans were paid for their services. Their roles tended to be inherited and maintained in family lines, although inheritance was not so rigidly determined as that of chiefs.

• COUNCIL AND MANAGERS   The chief was assisted by managers or administrators who were usually associated with the ritual or cult systems, since it is through ritual that many economic and political affairs were articulated in native California. Thus in addition to the obvious administrators such as assistant chief and messenger, there were honorific positions such as dancer or singer.

These bureaucrats usually composed the council of "elders" who provided advice and consent to chiefs. These councils existed at each level of sociopolitical organization. Above the tribelet level, tribelet chiefs formed councils. At the tribelet levels councils were composed of subchiefs within the group—lineage leaders, extended family chiefs, and other officials depending on the individual social structure of each group. At the lineage level the chief, his assistant, and officials comprised the council. Since age as well as succession rules usually were basic criteria for bureaucratic roles, councils tended to be composed of elders (men over 40 seems to have been normal) who were frequently close relatives of the chief, since, while bureaucratic positions were not necessarily inherited, they did tend to be passed along in family lines, especially in the chiefly family. Thus, a chief often had considerable administrative experience before he assumed his position (Bean and King 1974).

In council, consensus was considered an ideal. It appears that decision making was accomplished for the most part in an informal manner so that consensus could be overtly realized without public conflict. The shaman was often used to "bless" the meeting, to divine a propitious occasion for a meeting, and perhaps to bring supernatural knowledge and opinion into the process. On occasion, when conflict was still unresolved, expert opinion or higher opinion was brought to bear on the group by calling in higher-level chiefs—a village council, the tribelet chief, or a chief of another tribelet.

Chiefs' assistants (subchiefs, boy chiefs) were found in most groups. Their principal duties were to communicate between the people and the chief. They sat in council meetings in a judicial capacity, acted as chiefs in the absence of a chief, and often succeeded him in office. They often acted as masters of ceremonies at ritual events and took care of protocol when visitors came to the village.

Since chiefs required information from the community and the outside, the assistant chief or subchief often acted as a messenger or reported to the chief. In more complex societies this was a separate role, so a chief's messenger was appointed by the chief because of his

ability to talk and his "powers of observation." Beals (1933) describes Nisenan "native gossip columnists" who traveled to other villages at night and reported their activities to the chief the next day. Traveling singers and traders also acquired sociopolitical data, which they reported to their chiefs. These various officials were found either permanently or occasionally in all California societies. Among the Yokuts the office was restricted to a particular lineage and had a totemic symbol. For the Patwin, several chiefs' assistants are listed (Gayton 1945; Kroeber 1932a; T. King 1972).

Several bureaucratic or managerial roles were commonly found either separately or in combination among other groups such as clowns, dance managers and other ritualists, peacemakers, and war chiefs. The clownlike jester made fun of the chief, acted disrespectfully, and sometimes pointed out the chief's foibles to the public. His burlesque role served to emphasize the usual respect that was due the chief. This position was often incorporated in another such as the chief's assistant, and it was frequently inherited (Kroeber 1932a).

Since ritual was so pervasive in California, the role of ritual manager was indeed important. In some groups it was clearly separated from that of chief, in others the chief or his immediate assistant was the principal ritual manager. Where secret societies and sacred roles were less clearly integrated, as among some Pomo groups, or where secular powers were present, it was a role separated from political office.

War chiefs and peacemakers or negotiators were usually temporary offices. A skilled warrior was often selected as war chief by the council or by the chief. Chiefs rarely assumed this role, nor did they usually engage in combat; they were expected to seek peace, but a peacemaking role was sometimes formalized into a ranked position (Kroeber 1925; Loeb 1926).

• SPECIALISTS   Professionalism or occupational specialization outside of the activities described above created status differentiation and provided economic advantages for many. Although most people could discharge most mundane tasks, there were those who specialized because of ability or training or birth, sometimes monopolizing the activity or craft that brought them prestige and wealth. The degree of specialization varied from one tribe to another in direct proportion to ecological advantages and population density. Specialists occurred in all groups in occupations such as trading, basketmaking, and clamshell-disk manufacture; but in some societies specialization was more casually developed or more dependent on ability or personal choice than on training or inheritance (Bean and King 1974; Goldschmidt 1951a). In the more complex societies "craft guilds" were established, which controlled an industry. In central and southern California as well as the south coastal area, entrance into a guild was by purchase. In the Chumash case, one author infers that upon the death of a guild member, the right to produce the craft reverted to one guild and was resold to a new member (L.B. King 1969).

More moderate controls have been described for the Patwin, Nomlaki, and Pomo (McKern 1922; Goldschmidt 1951a; Loeb 1926) in which "functional families" controlled an activity and shared a spiritual guardian. One or at best a few members practiced the specialization. In other groups the craft tended to be inherited from parent to child, but it could be sold to another person.

Craft techniques were often kept secret; Beals (1933) suggests that Nisenan craftsmen practiced in the privacy of their homes late at night so they would not be observed. Some craftsmen exchanged their products for other goods and were often completely relieved from other subsistence activities: the Clear Lake Pomo money maker is an example (Gifford 1926c:386). In other societies they simply acquired a more prestigeful and economically advantageous position by expanding their income base. In the northwest area rich men had slaves to do their manual labor for them so they could spend their energy making luxury items to reinforce their wealth (Willoughby 1963).

Women were less involved in specialized activities than men—except for basketmaking, midwifery, and herbalism. Women were sometimes shamans, especially in the northwestern groups such as the Yurok, Hupa, Tolowa, and Karok (Driver 1939).

In central and apparently in coastal southern California, specialists stood as a class between the nobles (the chiefly families) and the commoners, protected by religious institutions or proscriptions attached to their crafts in the form of guardian spirits or membership in a secret society. They are somewhat analogous to medieval burghers, the first townsmen, since it appears that they clustered somewhat in larger towns, which tended to be trade centers where their crafts would have more ready markets. In central California where community residence was more flexible than in other areas such as southern California where there were lineage-based corporate residence groups, it is likely that urban clustering was more possible. The ability to select residence may have been important for the development of urban tendencies (Kunkel 1974).

• COMMONERS The category of commoner or ordinary person refers to those without rank, who are not conspicuously important either in terms of wealth, talent, or other position. They are visible primarily in contrast to others who are described so frequently, and to their inferiors, who are described infrequently but in negative terms. The impression of this majority of the population is that they were a ruled class, highly intimidated by their social superiors who controlled spiritual, economic, and religious institutions that the ordinary people were expected to support by donation (taxes), gifts, and various fees imposed by specialists and managers. It is more

than simply supporting a few administrators; it appears that with a few exceptions, they supported an elite class (Bean and King 1974; Garth 1953; Kunkel 1962; Loeb 1926; McKern 1922; Ray 1963).

Especially in lineage-based societies, the ordinary person was frozen by an almost feudal situation to his land of birth, since there was little opportunity for geographic mobility and little escape from the restrictions and controls of his own local group. At best he could migrate through a kinship tie to another village where relatives would support his social placement, or he could become a vagabond or wanderer who might be allowed to reincorporate in a new fixed group.

Commoners were generally reluctant to travel (Kroeber 1925). They were provincial in thought and tied mainly into local social networks. There were some itinerant commoner entertainer-traders and the like who were exceptional, since commoners usually did not have the protection of high status or numerous kinfolk of rank in other communities. Travelers were as welcome and safe as the prestige of their village and its chiefs and the status of their own kin or formal trading partners, who resided in foreign areas and who protected them. Thus people of high rank were the specialists in cross-cultural interaction (culture brokers or boundary players).

Commoners had a set of traditions and values somewhat different from their "betters." Their knowledge was of the ordinary rituals, of the "folkloric" little traditions rather than the esoteric aspects or great traditions of their culture. They shared a dependence on the people of power, provided them with deference, and recognized their right to rule by tradition and divine right, supernatural power implied by rank and shared philosophies that pictured them as sometimes beneficial and fair and occasionally malevolent and exploitive.

• LOWER CLASSES The presence of lower classes has been generally unrecognized except in the literature on northwest California, where Kroeber (1925) and others detailed very precisely the dynamics of social mobility. Luomala (1963) has described a social status among the Ipai that may very well have been typical in much of the state: the kʷətxal or vagabonds, "an aggregate of nonconforming individuals who congregated seasonally without organization identification." They were people who sometimes infiltrated stable lineages as social poseurs, allowed fictive membership if they were useful to the group. Luomala found that there was a generational continuity of these "morally loose" people who behaviorally were also associated with irresponsibility, theft, and the like. One irregularity in descent affected subsequent generations so that a chain of disregard by legitimate sib members developed and a classlike situation prevailed (Luomala 1963:296-298).

The presence of this sort of social situation in much of the state (there are Atsugewi, Tolowa, and Nomlaki examples) suggests that this "class" accounts for many peculiarities and conflicts in the literature about social organization. It explains what happens to deviant individuals—surely they were not all socialized into the system as "proper" people or accepted despite their deviancy through institutions such as institutionalized transvestism, slavery, or severe legal sanctions (Drucker 1937a; Garth 1953; Goldschmidt 1951a).

• SLAVERY In northern and southern California certain tribes institutionalized slavery in a manner reminiscent of the Northwest Coast culture area. The Karok, Hupa, and perhaps the Wappo kept slaves, who were usually taken from other ethnic groups in raids. The Shasta acquired Atsugewi slaves through the Modoc. While slavery was generally not a hereditary status, sons of slaves tended to have lower status than children of ordinary or wealthy people. Oftentimes slaves were eventually returned as part of a negotiation between groups in conflict, and escape was apparently common (Driver 1939; Garth 1953; Holt 1946; Kroeber 1925).

• SPECIAL ROLES In those societies where the family, extended family, or lineage was the primary means of articulating social relationships, and where trust was rarely extended beyond these units, the role of trading partner, special friend, or fictive kin was a very important device to extend their social, psychological, economic, and political networks to larger areas.

These roles are most clearly described for the Pomo and other central California groups, but they were also important elsewhere (Loeb 1926). Among the Cahuilla a special friend was called by the same term used for a fellow moiety member (Bean 1972). Among the Pomo the special friend is a ritually established relationship cemented by the exchange of a valuable gift, usually a feather basket, and the relationship is considered to be quite a special one involving a sociologically primary relationship (Loeb 1926).

Trading partners were found throughout the state, and the relationship was sometimes reinforced by intermarriage. A high level of trust and reciprocity was assumed, and often the service of liaison to one another at least formally superseded a profit motivation. Thus, the advantages of the nonprofit, reciprocal economic relationships generally found within the extended family or lineage in native California are extended to a foreign group.

Summary

Population density, extensive social scale, and societal complexity were not developed just from efficient technology (such as the protoagricultural techniques of burning, irrigation, pruning) and a fortunate environment, which provided an extraordinary amount of energy potential (Bean and Lawton 1973). Rather, specific social institutions served to increase productive resources and redistribute energy in such a way that sociocultural complexity in California is truly analogous to that customarily found in horticultural and agricultural societies. The mechanisms were:

(1) Economic and political alliances, which were extended by marriage rules (three to five generations) and/or moiety exogamy so that each corporate group (tribelet) had affinal relationships in several other groups with differing economic potentials;

(2) Ritual and kinship obligations, which required that at any ceremony ritualists and relatives from other corporate groups would be invited. Obligatory giving and receiving, fee payments, and opportunities for formal trading occurred in these contexts;

(3) Administrative rights to the production and distribution of goods, which were publicly acknowledged for certain persons and sanctioned through membership in secret societies or in the roles of chief, shaman, craft specialist, and the like;

(4) Exchange of goods to mutual advantage during formal or informal trade feasts between politically separate groups living in different ecologic areas;

(5) A banking procedure that was implicit in all these situations where subsistence goods could be transformed into treasure goods, money, or craft goods.

Some features of social organization may be summarized as follows, under Murdock's (1949:224–259) labels for types of social organization.

Eskimo social organization. Wiyot, Chimariko, Atsugewi, Yana. Nuclear family the functionally dominant social group; bilateral descent, bilateral extension of incest taboos; monogamy predominant; kindreds and demes frequent; low population density with associational flexibility.

Hawaiian social organization. Yurok, Hupa, Karok, Sinkyone, Coast Yuki, Southwest Pomo, Nisenan, Monache, Tubatulabal, Foothill Yokuts. Bilocal extended families; bilateral kinship reckoning, with bilateral extension of incest taboos; limited polygyny; bilateral demes frequent; generation terms for nephews and nieces. Murdock (1949) suggests that most California kinship systems were originally of the Hawaiian type.

Yuman social organization. Wintu. Unilocal residence; tendency toward bifurcate merging kinship terminology. Murdock (1949) suggests that weakly developed lineages among some Wintu represent a transitional state between Hawaiian and Dakota or Omaha systems.

Dakota social organization. Luiseño, Serrano, Cahuilla, Cupeño, Tipai-Ipai. Patrilocal families; Iroquois cousin terminology, bifurcate collateral merging terms for aunts and nieces; lineage, clan, or moiety exogamy; sororal polygyny common; levirate and sororate; patrilineal descent; lineages usually the basic corporate groups; sometimes clans (Cahuilla, Cupeño, Tipai-Ipai); moieties among Serrano, Cahuilla, Cupeño.

Omaha social organization. Northern Pomo, Eastern Pomo, Nomlaki, Patwin, Wintu, Miwok, Lake Yokuts,

Valley Yokuts. Kinship terminology overrides generation differences; perhaps matrilateral cross-cousin marriage among Miwok and others; kinship group as the production and distribution unit; patrilineal descent; Baumhoff ("Environmental Background," this vol.) suggests that this type is associated with high population density, as in the Sacramento River area, and its occurrence among the Lake and Valley Yokuts supports this hypothesis.

Crow social organization. Wappo, Southern Pomo. Lineality takes precedence over generation in kinship terminology.

Sexual Status and Role Differences

EDITH WALLACE

All California Indian tribes distinguished between the statuses and roles of men and women, assigning to each sex special tasks, duties, and prerogatives. The pattern of sex dichotomy reveals a remarkable similarity from one end of the state to the other though some interesting deviations occurred and a certain amount of flexibility was allowed. Social differentiations between males and females were not restricted to status and role but extended to dress and decorations, names, seating postures, manner of carrying burdens, etiquette, recreation, and in the Yana tribe, speech. Yana men spoke fully and deliberately to fellow males; where women were concerned, they preferred a reduced or clipped style of utterance (Sapir 1929a). Women used only the latter, whether addressing males or females.

Economic and Domestic Life

Food-getting tasks were variably allotted with each sex contributing substantially to the support of the family. Everywhere in California wild plant foods formed the mainstay of the native diet and women obtained the bulk of these. They collected acorns—the primary staple—pine nuts, seeds, berries, roots, and greens. In the fall when the year's supply of acorns and pine nuts had to be harvested within a short period, they got considerable help from men and boys who climbed the trees to shake down the acorns and pine cones or knocked them down with poles. In some groups the males assisted in picking up and carrying home the products. Occasionally men aided in gathering other vegetable foods.

Fishing, the importance of which varied locally, was predominantly a male pursuit. Women sometimes caught fish, but as a rule by distinctive techniques, as with baskets (Monache, Foothill Yokuts) or only in shallow water. Both sexes shared the work of stream or lake fishing. As an example, Achumawi women and children drove the fish into nets held by men (Curtis 1907–1930, 13:136). Shellfish and crustaceans were regularly procured by women and girls as were insects, larvae, and grubs, supplementary foods for many Californians. Communal insect hunts, in which everyone participated, were undertaken too; and now and then men went out to search for a particular species.

Hunting, which nowhere furnished the major portion of the food supply, was exclusively a male activity. Incidents of women engaging in the catching of large mammals have been noted but these were exceptions. Women did help in a minor way during rabbit drives, which were essentially masculine enterprises.

Rules governing the division of labor in food getting proved more stringent for women than for men. Males were freer to take part in ordinarily feminine activities such as harvesting edible plants, and reports of husbands helping their wives are surprisingly numerous. Women were barred from hunting, and to a lesser extent, from fishing. Their exclusion from these pursuits was frequently bolstered by supernatural beliefs.

Most household duties fell to the women (fig. 1). Customarily they fetched wood (fig. 2) and water, although men were drawn into service as water carriers, particularly if the source lay far away, or as fuel gatherers, dragging in the heavier logs. The preparation of foodstuffs—grinding seeds (fig. 3), pounding (fig. 4) and leaching acorns, and the like—as well as their preservation were definitely feminine tasks. Normally women did the cooking, but Yana husbands made the roasting pits, collected the fuel, and cooked the fritillary and other roots and tubers that their wives had gathered (Sapir and Spier 1943:250–251). Atsugewi and Wikchamni Yokuts men regularly broiled meat (Garth 1953:141; Gayton 1948:76).

The mother played the principal part in the upbringing of children; however, other members of the household, including the father, were expected to take a turn in looking after them. A man performed all these domestic tasks if his wife fell ill or under other special circumstances. Frequently, menstruating women were prohibited from cooking for others, so a man was obliged to take over.

Craftsmanship was separated strictly along sex lines. Women wove the indispensable baskets (O'Neale 1932). It is noteworthy that the California Indians left this, the most advanced of their handicrafts, to females (fig. 5). Men had no hand in basket weaving other than fashioning coarsely twined fish traps and other forms used exclusively by them and, in some tribes, baby cradles. Usually the making of clothing was deemed women's work, though among the Cahto and Wailaki men fashioned the garments (Loeb 1932:48, 89). Males did all manner of woodworking and tended to make most, if not all, articles of bone, stone, horn, and shell. In addition they wove nets, prepared much of the cordage, and manufac-

Fig. 1. Cupeño woman of Warner's Ranch washing clothes under a sunshade. Photograph by G.P. Thresher, 1898.

tured luxury items. Generally there was little individual craft specialization. Each person made his or her own objects, though an unusually skilled worker found some demand for his wares, such as the Pomo chippers of obsidian arrowpoints (Loeb 1926:179).

Collaboration of the sexes did occur. The building of family dwellings, for instance, regularly involved joint effort. But even here a division of labor ensued, for men did the heavier jobs—digging the house pits and post holes, cutting and preparing the timbers—while women gathered the covering materials and did the thatching.

Social Life

The position of women in California Indian society, though favorable, hardly equaled that of men. The system of marriage, the prevailing pattern of residence with the husband's people, the custom of tracing descent through the male line, and male control of important property—all gave men a strategic advantage.

Parents regularly contracted marriages for their chil-

dren. Even so the wishes of the young people were not ignored and no effort was made to force a boy or girl into a distasteful match. Furthermore, owing to the homogeneity of cultural standards, the advantages of a particular choice made by relatives were likely to be the same as those valued by the potential spouses. Industriousness and proficiency in day-to-day work appropriate to the sex concerned were stressed as desirable qualities. When a Tolowa man thought of taking a wife he looked to see if her hands were rough and scratched. If they were, he was convinced of her capacity for work and the match arranged (Du Bois 1932:253).

Some financial consideration normally accompanied marriage. The practice of paying bride price, the transfer of wealth items from the bridegroom's kinsfolk to those of the bride, occurred everywhere in California, but its import differed according to locality. The northwestern tribes made of it a definite commercial and negotiated transaction, the absence of which constituted a serious injury to the girl's family and reflected on the children

WALLACE

Fig. 2. Mary Major, Hupa, hauling firewood in a pack basket. The basket cap protects her head from the heavy load held by the tumpline. Photograph by A.W. Ericson, before 1903.

Fig. 3. Tipai-Ipai woman from near Cuyamaca grinding with mano on metate. A basket tray catches any fallen food. Photographed about 1905.

resulting from the marriage. In the central part of the state, the bride price coexisted with obligations on the part of the bride's relatives to make complementary gifts, usually of lesser value, though often nearly equal exchanges took place. To the south, the transaction again became more one-sided with the groom's kin being obliged to turn over a handsome amount to the girl's parents. The California Indians emphatically did not regard the bride price as derogatory to the wife's status. To the contrary, it served as a recognition of her economic and social worth. Nor was there any question of outright purchase, for the "bought" woman was never regarded as a chattel and a husband never could sell his wife.

The taking of plural wives was the prerogative of any man. Actually only a small minority—chiefs, wealthy men, great hunters—had more than one spouse. Contrarily, no tribe in native California granted freedom to the woman to acquire two or more husbands simultaneously.

Permanent residence after marriage was regularly patrilocal. In most parts of the state a newly married couple lived for a time with the wife's family but sooner or later took their place with the husband's people. Only among a few Pomo groups and the neighboring Huchnom did the pair settle permanently with the bride's kin. Naturally the spouse who did not have to shift residence enjoyed the advantage of remaining in familar physical and social surroundings.

Headship in the family rested with the man and the wife was expected to show deference to him. She never ate before her husband had eaten, and frequently the sexes dined apart. On the trail the man walked ahead and his wife followed. If something was to be trans-

Fig. 4. Nomlaki woman pounding acorns in basket mortar. Drawn by H.B. Brown at Tehama on the Sacramento River, 1852.

Fig. 5. Tipai-Ipai woman making a basket. The fibers used for stitching are soaking in the pail to make them more pliable. Photographed about 1904.

ported (food, clothing, or an infant), the woman carried it. Actually, a husband's authority was far from absolute and a woman was her own mistress in provinces such as food gathering, house managing, and child rearing. A capable and determined wife often exerted considerable influence in the family or even dominated.

Either partner could abandon the other for cause, but divorce, never resorted to lightly, was probably more easily achieved by the husband than the wife. The requirement, as among the Yurok, Tubatulabal, and other tribes, of a refunding of the bride price made separation more difficult for a woman. Sometimes her kin were unable or unwilling to return it.

Almost everywhere in the state descent was counted through the male line. Certain Pomo groups were exceptional in giving priority to the female in kinship. For an unknown reason, Pomo women appear to have enjoyed an unusually high status. Besides the disposition to ma-

trilineal descent, there were titular female chiefs, admission of a few women to the sacred male secret society, and ownership of a house occupied by several families by the oldest wife.

Although the husband's kin was ordinarily stressed in native California, the wife's family was by no means ignored. Recognition of her relatives could be seen in a number of customs, such as the manner of bestowing children's names. Each Pomo youngster, for example, received two names, one conferred by the mother's brother and the other by a paternal uncle. In special circumstances acknowledgement of the female line took a peculiar form among the Southern Yokuts. Customarily a boy or girl assumed membership in the paternal moiety, but in a large family a man sometimes "gave" his wife one or two of their offspring who eventually joined the wife's moiety (Gayton 1948:28).

As for ownership of property, that of land rested with

686

WALLACE

the lineage (male kinsmen who formed an autonomous political unit) or the larger tribelet, both male oriented (Kroeber 1962). Most land was held communally and used jointly by all members of the group. Separate proprietorship to given tracts did obtain, however. Perhaps the extreme in private ownership prevailed in northwestern California where individuals or families held title to choice fishing spots, hunting areas, and oak groves.

Movable property was generally individually owned on the principle that a person had a right to whatever he or she had produced, and only here did women enjoy equal property rights with men. A woman's ownership of her clothing, ornaments, household utensils, and other belongings was clearly recognized, as was her exclusive right to dispose of them at will. Both males and females controlled incorporeal property such as sacred spells, songs, and other possessions of a magico-religious nature. Commonly, special tracts passed to males whereas personal possessions went to individuals who could use them. A man's tools, weapons, and valuables were inherited by his sons or other male relatives; things made and used by a woman went to her daughter. Rules of inheritance were simplified in many tribes by the custom of destroying or burying most of the decedent's effects.

Mention should be made of an exclusively male social institution, the sweathouse, found everywhere in the California cultural province. This structure served as a clubhouse to which men retired almost daily to cleanse themselves, to refresh aching or fatigued bodies, to engage in idle conversation, and to discuss serious matters. As an exclusive preserve of men, the sweathouse seemed to represent among other things a place of sanctuary from females.

Political Life

Normally, women played little part in political affairs. The office of chief or headman, which except for the northwest, was universal, tended to be hereditary in the male line, passing from father to son. If the deceased chief's son proved not fitted for the office, it went to the chief's brother or other male kin. Quite exceptional was the Pomo succession in the mother's line. Usually the headman's eldest sister's son was chosen if he possessed the necessary leadership qualities (Loeb 1926:238).

Women occasionally assumed leadership. An instance of female chieftainship in Chumash territory is reported in an account of Juan Rodríguez Cabrillo's 1542 voyage along the west coast of North America (Henshaw 1879:309). Among the Central Miwok, when a male heir was lacking, a woman succeeded to the office through paternal descent (Gifford 1955:262). Or, if a headman died when his son was only a child, the boy's mother acted as regent until he reached maturity. If a Yuki chief left no son, his sister served until a male successor could be appointed (Foster 1944:177). Female chiefs were obeyed exactly as were men.

A specific female relative of the chief—wife, mother, or sister—often occupied a privileged social position and performed special duties. A Yuki headman's wife aided him by supervising female tasks connected with preparation for "big times" (Foster 1944:177). In certain Takic-speaking groups the wives of chiefs, along with their children, were known by titles; this fact argues that they received considerable deference (Kroeber 1925:833).

Under native law, an equality of treatment was handed out to both sexes, and the claim of a woman was no less than that of a man. However, the balance of legal prerogatives probably weighed in favor of males, since responsibility for action against legal offenses rested with the person harmed or his immediate family, and it was the man's duty to seek redress. Even though the rights of a Yurok woman were by no means curtailed by her sex, it was her husband or her kin who pressed the claim and received damages for her, although only as her natural guardian (Kroeber 1925:22).

The waging of war fell to men with women playing little part in the conflicts. In the northern part of the state, they carried on ceremonies at home during the campaign or joined in a victory dance when the men returned. Yuki women and older men, unable to fight, went with the war party to shout encouragement and to aid the wounded (Foster 1944:189). Women and children, though not active participants, often became the victims as captives or casualties during attacks upon their villages. Even though warfare seldom rose to any considerable consequence, the fact that the men were the warriors and wielders of weapons stood for a certain preeminence.

Religious Life

Women did not share as freely or as fully in the religious life as did men. This debarment was clearly evident in the great public rituals of the northwestern and central Californians. The performers in the World Renewal ceremonials of the northwest were males. Corresponding conditions have been described for the elaborate god-impersonating rites held in central California. The masquerading and dancing of the two Pomo spirit-impersonating cults—the Ghost and Kuksu—took place in an earth-covered dance house from which females and uninitiated boys were excluded. The "devil-raising" performances held in connection with this structure were antifeminist, carried on for the purpose of terrifying women (Loeb 1926:162). Females may have suffered fewer disabilities in southern California, for there they took an active part in the memorial for the dead, the most important tribal ceremonial.

Although women were not admitted to participation in the major sacred rituals to the same degree as men were, they often had important functions in lesser solemnities. Four to six selected females pounded acorns for the Acorn Ceremony held each fall by the Hupa (Goddard 1903-1904:80), although the priest in charge was a man. Rituals performed exclusively by women were rare in California.

Strict and demanding sanctions were directed against women because of the religious uncleanness that the Indians associated with menstruation and childbirth. Taken very seriously, these rules compelled abstinence from customary activities and certain foods and, often, isolation. At first sight some of these restraints appear to connote a measure of female inferiority; however, it is doubtful whether such a feeling had anything to do with the taboos, which were based upon magico-religious considerations. Men too came under negative rules, though less stringent and binding, during their wives' menstrual period and when a child was born.

In the field of shamanism, females suffered fewer handicaps. They dominated the profession in northwestern California; men could enter it but rarely did. Elsewhere the ratio of females to males varied with the tribe, though overall there tended to be more men doctors, especially in the southern half of the state. Attitudes toward female shamans varied. The Tubatulabal always regarded them as malevolent (Voegelin 1938:62); an ill Nisenan preferred a woman doctor with a "good heart" because she was considered less likely to invoke witchcraft (Kroeber 1929:274). A Chukchansi Yokuts female shaman, suspected of evildoing, suffered the same fate as a male (Gayton 1948:210).

Very frequently women took a hand in treating lesser illnesses. They administered herbal medicines or other home remedies, often accompanied by the recital of a magical formula. Midwives were always women but male shamans were summoned to handle difficult births.

Aesthetic Life

The artistic achievements of the California Indians were modest. Intricate basketry designs, woven by women, represented the highest form of expression (fig. 5). Particularly noteworthy were the Pomo baskets covered with feather mosaic (Barrett 1908a:141-145). Men contributed relatively little in the way of art objects. Northwesterners carved in wood and horn (Kelly 1930). Carving was absent in the remainder of the state except for a section of the southern coast where simplified sea mammal representations were cut from soft stone. Males probably painted and pecked the vast majority of designs seen on rock surfaces over nearly all of California, though some in the southernmost part of the state were painted by girls at the close of puberty ceremonies (Strong 1929:257, 299).

Men took the leading role in music. While both sexes vocalized, male singers were greatly in the majority and performed more often on public occasions. Men made and played the various instruments (fig. 6).

Males also dominated the field of oral literature. The

NAA, Smithsonian.
Fig. 6. Hackett, a Karok, playing a bow. Photographed by John P. Harrington at Catimin, 1927-1928.

narrators, particularly of myths, were men, although an occasional woman raconteur held forth.

Conclusion

The California Indians, like nearly all peoples, had a traditional system of allotting different tasks to males and females. On the whole the work seems to have been fairly equally distributed between the sexes. Yet both Wintu males and females felt that women did more work than men (Du Bois 1935:24). It was true that they were more constantly employed, for the men sometimes spent hours or even whole days in leisure. Mostly women performed their duties cheerfully and faithfully, rarely complaining. But a Tolowa matron with an air of grievance stated that men lay in the sweathouse all day while their wives worked very hard (Du Bois 1932:254).

The two biological groups had different roles in social life, politics, and religion as well. Even though a male bent existed in all of these, the position of the California Indian woman in the family and community was a respected one and she enjoyed a large measure of freedom and independence. Surely one of the basic reasons for her high status lay in the essential and many-faceted part she played in the domestic economy.

Boys and girls learned from family, friends, and others the duties and norms appropriate to their sex. Almost from the first days of life, different forms of behavior were expected of them and many child-training practices were geared toward teaching the young their proper sexual roles. Yet not all individuals were successfully steered toward their culturally defined places in society; in nearly every tribe a few males gave up the struggle to conform to the masculine role, wore female clothes, and followed the occupations of women (Willoughby 1963:table 6). Apparently there were women who reversed the sex roles too (Gifford 1931:56; Voegelin 1942:134–135), but information on them is scanty.

Sources

The data concerning the statuses and roles of the sexes, particularly those of women, are meager and indefinite, making it difficult to define accurately the place of male and female in the native cultures. Monographs and articles dealing with the various tribes contain bits of information as do Kroeber (1925) and Curtis (1907–1930, 13, 14, 15). The division of labor is the only topic that has been adequately treated (Willoughby 1963). The facts that aboriginal conditions were rapidly obscured by European influences and that some of the earliest observers were liable to the suspicion of having misinterpreted what they saw (Harrington 1934:29–30) add to the difficulty of forming a clear picture.

Trade and Trails

ROBERT F. HEIZER

Aboriginal trade is defined here as the purchase or exchange of objects between individuals of one tribal group and individuals of a different tribal group, that is, trade on an intertribal basis. Intratribal trade between villages or between tribelets within a tribal group was common but is not treated here. Nearly all ethnographic treatments of California tribes contain details of this kind of internal exchange.

There is no good evidence for specialists in trade—that is, professional traders—and there is no information on the existence of regular markets. At times certain individuals or groups may have engaged more frequently in trade than others by reason of having control over a desirable and scarce resource such as a salt spring, flint exposure, or obsidian deposit, but the occupants of such villages in no recorded instance made procurement and marketing of a resource their primary activity. Further, certain large villages situated at some strategic spot near a tribal boundary may have developed into "import-export centers" where certain desirable goods were handled, but markets in the sense of places where traders regularly came with exchange goods are not known.

Trading between tribes occurred either on the occasion of friendly visits as guests or participants in a ceremonial performance to which outsiders were invited or between villages of different tribes situated near the common border. The so-called Pomo trade feasts (Vayda 1966) were a means of goods exchange (food, sumptuary objects, utensils) that allowed surpluses of one group to be bartered for the surpluses of another—a redistributive mechanism among neighboring tribes who had more goods (usually food) than they needed (Loeb 1926:192 ff.; Chagnon 1970:10–13). Social status and prestige were also involved in the trading that took place when different tribal elements got together for a ceremonial performance. One inhibition to such trade was the unfriendly relations that often obtained between near-border villages of different tribal groups (Loeb 1926:194).

Friendly relations between such groups were an encouragement to intertribal trade, especially when the main territories held by each tribe lay in ecologically distinctive zones that produced items desirable to a neighboring group that lacked them. Kroeber (1925:236) gives an account of a party of Clear Lake (Eastern or Southeastern) Pomo who journeyed about 1830 to the salt-spring area held by the Northeastern Pomo where they intended to combine trading for salt with a dance. The Clear Lake party was attacked in the sweathouse and all but two men killed. After 10 years the Clear Lake people took revenge by ambushing a party of Northeastern Pomo fishermen. This incident, unimportant by itself, can be taken as indicating that normal trade relations between the two groups were interrupted for at least a decade and probably more, in view of the known tendency for such feuds to smolder for very long times, breaking open into hostility on occasion until the cause no longer seemed so important as it was to resolve the altercation and normalize relations.

The most common form of trade was a one-for-one exchange of items; next most common was the purchase of items for currency in the form of shell beads.

The ethnographic record contains much information on intertribal trade, which has been collected and summarized by Davis (1961). The following list of items traded between tribes in California is summarized from an extensive accumulation of documented statements by native informants. Full documentation can be found in Sample (1950) and Davis (1961).

Number of recorded ethnographic instances
of items traded to another tribe.

Foods

Salt	37
Acorns	22
Fish	20
Miscellaneous vegetables	14
Pine nuts	12
Mollusk meats	9
Seaweed and kelp	7
Miscellaneous seeds, nuts	6
Animal meat	5
Miscellaneous fruits, berries	4
Insects	3

Beads and ornaments

Marine shell beads	28
Dentalium shells	23
Clamshell disk beads	22
Whole or broken marine shells	20
Magnesite beads	6
Shell ornaments	3
Miscellaneous beads (nut, berry, mollusk, stone)	16

Household items

Baskets	38
Pottery	2
Tule or fiber mats	2
Hot rock tongs	2
Steatite vessels	2
Stone mortars, pestles	1
Digging sticks	1
Wooden bowls	1

Clothing and regalia

Hides and pelts	34
Pigments and paints	12
Rabbitskin blankets	6
Tailored skin clothing	6
Woodpecker scalps	5
Moccasins, sandals	6
Skin or fur robes	5
Yellowhammer feathers	3

Industrial materials

Obsidian	19
Basketry materials	5
Steatite	5
Horn (for spoons)	3
Asphaltum	3
Sinew	1
Pottery clay	1
Bow wood	1
Pumice stone	1

Finished artifacts (except baskets, clothing)

Bows	26
Arrows	9
Stone arrowheads, knives	6
Dugout canoes	5
Wooden fire drills	4
Cordage, nets, packstraps	3
Sea lion harpoon heads	1
Gourd rattles	2

Miscellaneous

Tobacco	6
Tobacco seeds	4
Dogs	3
Smoking pipes	1
Seeds for planting	2
Slaves	1

The most frequently attested trade items were marine-shell beads including dentalium and whole or fragmentary marine shells (91 instances), then baskets (38), and salt (37), and in decreasing order, hides and pelts (34), bows (26), acorns (22), fish (20), and obsidian (19). Swanton (1907:446) says that shell beads and animal skins were the most common trade items among North American Indians considered as a whole.

The list of exported trade items may be divided into two classes: luxuries and necessities. All foods listed are classed as necessities, as are, arbitrarily, half the household items, clothing, regalia, industrial materials, finished

artifacts, and miscellaneous items—a total of 30. The balance (beads and ornaments and the remaining half of the groups of items cited above) gives a total of 27 luxury forms. A division such as this is arbitrary, but granted its logic, one could argue that about half the intertribal trade was involved with securing things or materials for which some local substitute could have been found. Trade in luxury items would seem to provide a good argument for the exchange to be long practiced.

Shell beads are the most anciently documented trade item, the evidence being the occurrence at Leonard Rockshelter, Pershing County, Nevada, of a string of about 50 large spire-ground *Olivella biplicata* beads dating from about 6600 B.C. whose source was the Central California coast. Implied by the presence of a complete string of olivella beads some 250 miles from their source are intervening peoples who passed these items on by intertribal trade. Obsidian implements recovered from graves of the Windmiller culture in sites on the lower Mokelumne River dating from 2000 B.C. prove to be made of obsidian from deposits at Mount Hicks, Bodie Hills, and Casa Diablo in Mono County about 150 miles to the east and from Napa County deposits about 60 miles to the west. Assuming that obsidian and shell beads moved through intertribal trade these two examples indicate that this was going on for a very long time.

Other archeological examples of long-distance exchange are known. Grooved stone axes of Puebloan origin are found widely throughout California (Heizer 1946). Cotton blankets (Kroeber 1910a, 1925:934; Gifford and Schenck 1926:104–112; Heizer 1941c:187) and decorated pottery of several types also of Southwestern manufacture have been found in southern California sites (Ruby and Blackburn 1964; Forbes 1961; Gladwin and Gladwin 1935:204; Walker 1945:193; Davis 1961:13). Such exotic items can only have traveled so far north and west of their homeland by intertribal trade. The Mohave figured importantly as middlemen in this east-west trade (Farmer 1935; Heizer 1941c), which is a well-documented one (M.J. Rogers 1941; Brand 1935; Colton 1941; Tower 1945). Numerous species of marine shells (haliotis, olivellas, and pecten were favorites) traveled from the Pacific shore across the Colorado Desert and River into the Southwest in prehistoric times (Brand 1938; Gifford 1949; R. Ives 1961; Fewkes 1896; Henderson 1930). Shells (olivella, haliotis) and finished beads and ornaments from the coast of Central California were traded during the last 4,000 years across the Sierras into western Nevada (Bennyhoff and Heizer 1958; Grosscup 1960:37–40; Tuohy 1970). Not to be confused with prehistoric trade is the importation of abalone (haliotis) shells from Monterey to the Northwest Coast by European sea otter fur traders in the late eighteenth century (Heizer 1940a; Taylor 1862b). A long-distance resource procurement instance is that of the Walla Walla who, at least as early as 1800, came south through Oregon to the

Sacramento Valley to secure vermilion (that is, cinnabar) from the spot that was later known as New Almaden in Santa Clara County (Heizer 1942). Since the Walla Walla expeditions, which were being carried out up to 1848, involved horses and the distance between the Columbia River and New Almaden is great, these may not go back into the prehistoric period.

The tribes of northwestern California secured dentalium shells in some quantity from Oregon tribes to the north, the original source lying at Quatsino Sound on Vancouver Island. Details of this long-distance trade are lacking.

Trade routes were along trails that ran from one village to another; or if their course was continuous (that is, cross-country), as through the southern California desert, the line of march lay from one tank or spring to another. There are examples of intervillage trail "systems" within delimited tribal areas for Yurok (Waterman 1920), Wiyot (Loud 1918:pl. 1), Pomo (Kroeber 1925:pl. 36), and Monache and Southern Valley Yokuts (von Werlhof 1961). The trails from one village to another may extend into the territory of neighboring tribes and from there to adjoining tribes. These intertribal articulations in their totality produced what in effect were long-range trade routes along which traders usually traveled only short distances but the goods they carried would be passed on, at times for hundreds of miles from their original source. Trails going over the Sierra Nevadas into the Great Basin followed open areas and avoided as much as possible difficult terrain. It is alleged that many of the trans-Sierran trails follow game migration routes, and this seems probable but has not been proved. All the main Sierran passes were used as crossing points in this east-west communication (Hindes 1959). Many Indian trails later became wagon roads and ultimately modern highways or railroad routes (Davis 1961:4-5; Anonymous 1959). Some prehistoric trails across the dry desert areas of southern California were still visible in the mid-twentieth century (Weaver 1967:pl. 1; Johnston and Johnston 1957:pl. 1). Trails are often marked by votive stone piles or cairns on which each passerby threw a stone or a few shell beads for luck (Goddard 1913; Davis 1961:7) and in the southern California desert by scatters of potsherds left by ancient litterers (Taylor 1862a; Harner 1957; Weaver 1967). That California Indians at times had quite precise knowledge of the geography of lands that lay beyond their own tribal borders—a fact that implies firsthand acquaintance with "foreign territories"—is shown by their ability to make "sand maps" that were crude topographic renderings (Heizer 1958a).

Davis (1961) has written a thorough study of trade among California Indians and has plotted the known or inferred trail routes (fig. 1). North-south trails combine to form a continuous line of communication from the Mexican border to the Oregon line. In part these run along the coast, but the main routes lie in the valleys of

Fig. 1. Aboriginal trade routes (after Davis 1961). The base map of tribal areas is somewhat diagrammatic, so the relations between trails and tribal boundaries may not be precisely accurate.

the Coast Ranges and the great interior valley. East-west trails run from the Pacific shore across the Coast Ranges into the interior valley and across the Sierra Nevadas through the main passes into the Great Basin. The scarcity of trails in parts of the mountainous Sierra Nevadas and Klamath Mountains and in desert Southern California may reflect the low density of population as much as the terrain that was difficult to move in or across freely. It has been too little emphasized that much, possibly all, of the long-distance visits of interior peoples to the coast for securing desirable items (salt, kelp, fish, mollusk shells) such as is reported for Valley Yokuts treks to the Santa Barbara and Monterey coast (Pilling 1950; Gayton 1948,1:7-9; Grant 1965:73; R.G. McClellan 1872:205; Powers 1877:382; Shuck 1869:299) or visits of interior Pomo to the coastal margin (Loeb 1926:176-177) may have been instituted in the historic period only after White domination had disrupted the aboriginal system of territoriality. Note that the Yokuts coastal visits were made by mounted Indians (Pilling 1950) and that Kniffen (1939:387) says that the Southwestern (Kashaya) Pomo visits to Bodega Bay to secure clamshells for making bead money did not happen until "modern times." Much about prehistoric trade will be discovered by archeologists who recover, identify the place of origin of raw

692

materials such as obsidian and flint or finished items such as shell beads and ornaments, and determine their age. Some of this information will be new in the sense that ethnographic records do not report trade in these items in prehistoric times. For this reason, depending too heavily on ethnographic analogy as a guide to studying prehistoric trade items and routes reflects the situation at or soon after the beginning of the historic period. The tribal distribution map of California shows a multiplicity of tribal entities and discontinuous distributions of speakers of various language families. These tribal-linguistic placements must have been effected by migration, at times compounded by the factors of warfare, disease, and the like, all of which might upset relations between neighboring tribes to the extent that trade would no longer be practiced. Thus, an almost infinite number of precise intertribal relationships may have obtained during the thousands of years of native history of California, and any new information on the details will come from the work of archeologists. The most complicating feature of reconstructing prehistoric trade relations, of course, is the fact that most of the items traded were perishable and would leave no palpable evidence for the archeologist to find.

Intergroup Conflict

THOMAS McCORKLE

The kind of organized, armed conflict among members of relatively small, stateless societies such as California Indian groups has been termed "primitive" war. Some 117 separate cases of armed conflict between California groups were analyzed, and it was found possible to develop generalizations as to levels of group responsibility for aggressive acts, causes of conflicts, types of engagements, numbers of casualties, roles of captives and booty, settlement procedures, and apparent function of armed conflict for four fairly distinct and contrasting regions within the state. Most cases cannot be dated securely, but it seems likely that all conflicts here used as case material occurred during the nineteenth century, when all groups were in contact with Europeans. A half-dozen cases reveal direct influence of Whites, and some others involve the use of firearms obtained from Whites. Nonetheless, the material presented bears the mark of native societies relatively uncontaminated by European influence.

Coverage is limited to four areas: the northwestern coastal Yurok and their neighbors (13 conflicts); the Pomo-Wappo region just north of San Francisco Bay (23 conflicts); the San Joaquin Valley Yokuts, Western Mono, and Tubatulabal (7 conflicts); and the Quechan and Mohave of the lower Colorado River (33 conflicts). Northeastern peoples such as the Klamath and Modoc are excluded as belonging to an area whose center lies outside California, as are the Paiute, Washo, Koso, and Eastern Mono. Peoples of the central coast (Costanoan, Esselen, Salinan), the Chumash, and the Takic-speaking groups all lost their independence very early and provide few reliable-looking accounts of actual conflicts. There are numerous accounts (some 23) for the Yuki- and Wailaki-speaking peoples who lived south of the Yurok and north of the Pomo. This region was one of only two in California where people took pleasure in rough sports and intergroup conflict; however, most of the practices of these peoples fall somewhere between those of the Yurok and the Pomo and add little to knowledge of the several sets of principles that can be derived from the data. Two Sacramento Valley tribes (Wintu, Maidu) yield data on at least another 18 accounts of actual conflict, but attitudes and customs of the area are less clear-cut manifestations of those of the Pomo. Thus, there is a total of 76 separate conflicts plus very abundant ethnographic material on the four areas chosen for major em-

phasis. Presented here is a summary of native conflict in these four areas and an assessment of "primitive" war in California contexts.

The Yurok and their Neighbors

Yurok (fig. 1), Tolowa, Hupa (fig. 2), Chilula, Whilkut, Chimariko, Karok, Wiyot, Shasta, and Bear River

NAA, Smithsonian.

Fig. 1. Yurok man from the village of Weitchpec. An animal-skin quiver on his right side hangs from a strap around his neck. One arrow is engaged in the bow while the next is held between his teeth. His right hand holds an iron sword apparently modeled after a cutlass of the 18th century. Drawn by Seth Eastman after lost original sketch by George Gibbs, October 1851.

Calif. State U., Humboldt.

Fig. 2. Captain John, Hupa, dressed for battle. His left hand holds a typical close-combat California weapon, the short thrusting spear with an obsidian point. Under his right arm he carries a quiver made of a whole animal skin. The deerskin wrap, the grass-filled deerskin-covered headband, and the dentalium necklaces are typical of northwestern California. Behind him is a sweathouse. Photograph by A.W. Ericson, about 1890s.

INTERGROUP CONFLICT

groups all have been reported as contestants in armed conflict. A few cases involve clashes between opposing Yurok groups; otherwise adversaries are reported as members of single tribes or coalitions of tribes against other single tribes or coalitions. It is important to note that none of these peoples operated as organized tribes under full-time chiefs. Instead individual aggressors plus their nearest kin made up the contending groups, and it was kin groups that were held responsible in cases of damage, whether or not as a result of armed conflict (Kroeber 1925:22ff.).

Motives for armed conflict are given as "poisoning" (or sorcery), homicide, and "personal enmities." But in view of the fact that law of the type best known for the Yurok prevailed in the whole region prescribed that every injury or offense must be compensated for exactly (Kroeber 1925:22ff.), it seems likely that actual or alleged failure to pay legitimate damages underlay most calls to arms.

There were no battle lines or pitched battles. Usual engagements were attacks on individuals, loosely organized fights between kin groups, or surprise raids on villages. In the last case, houses belonging to kinsmen of the raiders might be spared. Reported casualties in numbers of slain were light, ranging from "some" (two) to "many" (up to 13). Enemy property was not appropriated (Spott and Kroeber 1942:204). Young women sometimes were carried off as captives but were likely to be returned to their kin at time of settlement (Wallace 1949:9).

Settlement procedures were strictly according to Yurok law, and seem to have been adhered to in all reported cases save one, where the Yurok refused to pay for the death of a Shasta (Spott and Kroeber 1942:200). Settlement was arranged through go-betweens who arranged the amount of payment in property or shell money for each individual injury. Damages were not canceled out; instead every aggrieved party received his full settlement (Kroeber 1925:49). Under this system the "victorious" kin group was required to make the greater payments (Wallace 1949:11), and this burden probably fell most heavily on the wealthy men who were respected and influential in these wealth-oriented societies.

It seems that war in this region served, as Wallace (1949:12) says, a double purpose, enabling people to express anger over some offense that could not be satisfied by the usual legalistic means and also having the effect of strengthening and reaffirming the ties that bound kin groups together. It also appears that regional, intertribal adherence to the unwritten law that each injury must be exactly recompensed limited armed aggression, since restraint served to save wealth goods that would have to be expended at the settlement marking the end of hostilities.

Sources for 13 conflicts of the Yurok and their neighbors are available (Curtis 1907–1930, 13:40–41; Goddard 1914:269, 1914a:351–352; Kroeber 1925:51, 126, 140; Nomland 1938:105; Spott and Kroeber 1942:200, 203–205; Wallace 1949:10).

Pomo and Wappo

Most reported conflicts for the Pomo-Wappo region involved some Pomo village or local group fighting against another Pomo group. The Pomo (fig. 3) also fought against local groups of neighboring Wappo, Patwin, Wintu, and Yuki. Traditional enmity is reported as existing between the Pomo of Canel and the Huchnom (Loeb 1926:210).

In this region to the north of San Francisco Bay political organization was developed to a point where there were chiefs over two or three villages, and villages were capable of acting as units, though according to Kroeber (1925:228, 250) dialect groups were not. Some chiefs acquired title through election, others by descent. They were influential, but unanimity was sought in making important decisions.

NAA, Smithsonian.

Fig. 3. Pomo man holding bow in shooting position. Two arrows for his next shots are between his teeth, and the remainder are in the animal-skin quiver under his arm. His armor consists of rods of willow or hazel shoots closely twined with cordage, in two layers—an outer, vertical one and an inner, horizontal one. Photographed about 1900.

McCORKLE

Sense of territory was strongly developed in Pomo culture, a feeling that was shared to some degree by their neighbors. Each political unit laid definite claim to certain hunting grounds, boundaries of which were well known and well marked. Individual families laid claim to certain oak or manzanita trees, which were blazed with family markings; and a woman who found a new place to gather vegetable food might also lay claim to that place as her individual or family property (Loeb 1926:97).

Two-thirds to three-quarters of recorded conflicts seem to have begun with economically motivated disputes over hunting or fishing rights; acorns; salt; or theft of personal property such as finery, deer snares, or accumulated acorns. Other conflicts arose over slaughter of women who crossed boundary lines to gather produce, over homicide, or over alleged "poisoning" (or sorcery).

Types of engagements included surprise attacks on villages and, in cases where chiefs were unable to negotiate a settlement, formal battles, whose time and place were agreed upon by both groups in advance. In battle members of the two parties formed opposing lines with emphasis on hurling insults and dodging missiles. There were no hand-to-hand engagements. When one member of one party was wounded, this "losing" party often fled.

Casualties in surprise attacks might have numbered as high as 25 or even 50 deaths (Loeb 1926:205, 211). Ten is the largest number reported killed in a battle (Driver 1936:215), and battles sometimes ended with no one having been killed at all. According to Loeb (1926:203), women and children were sometimes captured and later, when they had learned the language, adopted into the local tribe.

Settlement was through negotiations, with chiefs of the rival groups sometimes aided by other chiefs acting as peacemakers. Gifts were exchanged regularly, but it does not appear that these were meant as payment for damages, as did occur among the Yurok. In several cases rights to hunt, fish, or collect salt were gained or lost (Driver 1936:215; Kroeber 1925:236) and in at least two cases local groups made territorial gains at the expense of adversaries (Kroeber 1925:220, 225).

Sense of property was strong among the Pomo and their neighbors; it seems clear that a principal function of armed conflict in their region was to improve or to consolidate the economic position of the small, local political group.

Sources for 23 conflicts among the Pomo, Wappo, and their neighbors are available (Barrett 1908:265-266; Driver 1936:214-215; Gifford 1923:80, 1926c:342; Gifford and Kroeber 1939:198; Kroeber 1925:220, 235, 236; Loeb 1926:205-297; Revere 1849:109; Stewart 1943:33, 52).

Yokuts, Monache, and Tubatulabal

The peoples of the San Joaquin Valley and adjacent Sierra Nevada foothills were organized into a large number of tribelets consisting of several villages, each tribelet having a distinctive tribal name and speaking a distinctive dialect (Gayton 1930:365). Chiefs, usually of the eagle moiety, were hereditary leaders who were served by messengers and by shamans whose sorcery was an instrument of the chief's authority (Gayton 1948:390, 408-409). The position of chief as a dignified and judicial manager of affairs was one validated by legendary history (Gayton 1930:369). The idea of sorcery was a commonplace, like bacteria in Western society (Gayton 1948:409). Not all shamans were harmful, but a chief would give permission for a malevolent shaman to be killed if it became apparent that he was maliciously destroying people (Gayton 1930:381, 1948:112). The chiefs themselves did not take part in armed conflict.

The Monache, who may have been late intruders from the eastern side of the Sierra Nevada, have the reputation of being somewhat more aggressive than the Yokuts, but in recent times the two peoples have been similar enough to be described together, as for example in Gayton (1930, 1948).

The Tubatulabal, linguistic relatives of the Mono, seem also to belong with this group, and together, these three peoples must have constituted something like one-sixth of the total native population of California, yet the records include very few circumstantial accounts of armed conflict. It appears that these peoples were rather generously supported by their environment, and property sense in the ownership of land was little developed. Hunting or gathering was limited to the general tribal area, but neighbors who had friendly relationships with the owners simply asked permission to seek food there. Hostilities over resources of the land were rare (Gayton 1948:365); usually these broke out only when the intruders were strangers, and especially if the interlopers undertook to mark off territory for themselves (Gayton 1948:159-160). Latta (1949:3) describes one of the northern groups, the Chawchila, as the only warlike Yokuts tribe. Described conflicts occurred between Yokuts groups, between Yokuts and Tubatulabal, between Yokuts and Eastern Mono (Paiute), and between intertribal coalitions of Yokuts and Monache versus other Yokuts and Monache.

Motives in five actual conflicts included three based on invasions of food-gathering territory or theft of seeds, an adventurous raid by young men on a neighboring people, and an alleged death by sorcery where the shaman's relatives took up arms after he had been killed by indignant relatives of the dead person. A sixth case yields no clear cause for conflict. The seventh incident involved killing of several Tubatulabal men by Yokuts when they broke formation during a joint antelope hunt.

These last killings were unavenged and thus may have been perceived as deserved punishment rather than a contest at arms.

Types of engagements in the San Joaquin Valley included homicides, raids, and occasional battles that may have been fought from behind rocks and trees (Gayton 1930:383).

Specified numbers of killed range from three to seven; however, it was said that the Yokuts, in an attack on sleeping Eastern Mono intruders, killed all but one of the party, and another account reports that "half" of the fighters from three Yokuts tribelets were killed in one pitched battle. The Yokuts and Mono sometimes took scalps. It does not appear that captives were taken.

Peacemaking and peacekeeping techniques were well developed. Sometimes a chief was able to restrain angry people from becoming violent (Gayton 1930:382). The usual method of settling a difference was through a conference of chiefs of the involved groups who were likely to distribute presents (which do not seem to have represented reparations) and to decide that there should be reconciliation symbolized by joint feasting and dancing (Gayton 1930:383, 1948:10–11).

Yokuts and Monache societies apparently were generally peaceable ones with their peoples showing little enthusiasm for armed conflict. If examination of processes of enculturation were possible it might turn out that the ideal was peaceful, dignified conduct, and that there was a consistent bias against violence of any sort. Such hostilities as did accumulate seemingly were focused on shamans whom chiefs permitted to be killed, thus providing some outlet for hostile feelings. About the only kind of disruption that remained partly out of control was adventurous raiding by young men. Such raids and other conflict-generating situations could be smoothed over by respected chiefs.

Sources for seven conflicts in the Yokuts and Mono are Gayton (1930:383, 1948:10–11, 159–160) and Voegelin (1938:49–50).

Yuman Tribes of the Lower Colorado River

Although the Mohave and Quechan fall outside the California culture area covered in this volume, they have usually been treated as California Indians because they occupied territory in the modern political state. Yuman warfare is quite different from that of the tribes previously discussed as judged from 33 conflicts recorded as occurring between 1835 and 1886.

Warfare as practiced by the Quechan and Mohave, who rarely fought each other but mainly engaged in conflicts with the Maricopa and Cocopa, was a national affair. Weapons included a special "potato masher" club of mesquite wood, wooden club, wooden spear with fire-hardened tip, and bow and arrow.

Conflicts traditionally began after an auspicious dream reported by some respected warrior. Engage-ments took the form of raiding an enemy village, often followed by an arranged battle in which the adversaries faced each other in two lines. Taunts and duels between champions were followed by hand-to-hand engagement.

Casualties must have been heavy in terms of total populations. In 14 cases where death tolls are specified the greatest figure is 149 and the average 44.

Female captives sometimes were taken, but it was considered dangerous to have intercourse with them. Even after they had been purified, the river Yumans seem to have married captives only rarely. They kept them as curiosities who were given garden plots for themselves and not abused unless suspected of trying to escape (Kroeber 1925:752).

There were specialists who took and handled scalps (Forde 1931; Densmore 1932:10–13). Plunder does not seem to have been an important consideration (Kroeber 1925:272), but arable land did change hands on several occasions (Kroeber 1925:799), and the Halchidhoma and Kohuana both were harassed to a point where they left the river to live with the Maricopa.

The river Yumans may have felt anger and frustrations that were acted out in the killing of sorcerors (Kroeber 1922a:198–199; Russell 1908:44). And some such killings precipitated group conflict. But a smouldering sense of wrong does not seem a good explanation for armed aggression in this area.

Forde (1931:174) summarized the position and function of warfare for the lower Colorado area: "the explanation [for Yuman militarism] is to be sought in the deeply rooted tradition of warfare as a means for obtaining and demonstrating tribal strength. This tradition is associated with a definite technique of fighting, with particular criteria of bravery, and the use of feathered standards [as] symbols of bravery and invincibility . . . . Warfare enters intimately into the creation myth and its reenactment in ritual."

There is good evidence to support Forde's position. Future parents of boys dreamed of war bonnets and of the eagle feathers used for arrows (Devereux 1948:103). Boys were trained in arrow dodging and target shooting. They had mudball battles and were directed in attacking hornets' nests in formation. There also were sham battles in which boys, young men, and sometimes young women took part (Forde 1931:173). There were hereditary chiefs, but the war leader, the ceremonial manager, and the shaman-healer occupied the most prominent positions, and these got their power through dreams (Kroeber 1925:745). Dreams boding success in battle were among the most valued and were sung in the popular song cycles. Yuman myth and ceremonial was intimately associated with warfare (Kroeber 1925:774–776), and the creation myth includes an account of the first war party.

Sources for 33 conflicts involving tribes of the lower Colorado are available (Devereux 1951:36; Dobyns et al. 1957:53, 60; Forde 1931:162, 163; Gifford 1926b:64–66, 1931:31, 1932a:185, 1933:299, 301, 302, 1936:304–305; Ives 1861:71; Kroeber 1925:478, 746, 753, 799, 1922a:198–199, 201–202; Russell 1908:38, 42, 44; Spier 1923:299, 1933:169, 173; K. Stewart 1947:258; Trippel 1889:567; Woodward 1953).

Conclusions

When examined in terms of levels of group responsibility, causes of conflicts, types of engagements, casualties, captives and booty, settlement procedures, and apparent function, intergroup armed conflict among the simple societies of native California displays more variety than unity. The number held responsible for damage done ranges from a single individual or kin group, as in the Yurok, all the way to the entire tribe among the Colorado River tribes. Immediate cause of conflict also is quite variable, including homicide and alleged injury through sorcery, poaching, trespass, and quarrels over access to economic resources. The Yuman tribes apparently needed no immediate provocation because they fought for the pleasure and excitement fighting produced.

If killing a single individual is not counted as an armed conflict there are only two basic types of engagements—the raid on a village or group of travelers and the battle. The battle is quite variable in spirit and execution. Pomo battles were formal affairs, Yokuts battles were fought without enthusiasm from behind trees and rocks, and those of the Colorado River peoples seem to have been combinations of sport and the most serious of business.

Casualties apparently were quite low except on the lower Colorado where the ideal was for opposing groups of warriors to fight to the last man.

Neither captives nor booty was of value to the Yurok and their neighbors since they would have to be returned or, if kept or damaged, would have to be paid for up to their full value. It appears that neither captives nor booty was taken by the Yokuts or other San Joaquin Valley peoples. The Yuman tribes did carry off young women, but only for prestige and perhaps also curiosity value. The Yuki and Wailaki of the north took both captives and booty. Described by Kroeber (1925:169) as "rude and hardy mountaineers," the Yuki are reported to have killed, sold, or given away captured women. And only the Pomo (Loeb 1926:203) and the Nisenan (Beals 1933:367) are reported regularly to incorporate captive women into their own tribe through marriage.

Three of the four areas had well-developed, successful procedures for settling intergroup conflicts. The Yurok method appears most promising as a model, on paper at least, consisting of intertribal adherence to laws that required exact compensation for every injury done. However, the Yokuts method appears to have been the most successful, with nonviolent chiefs who were treated like judges and sometimes were able to halt contestants already engaged in hostile action. The Pomo also respected decisions made by their leaders.

The functions of intergroup armed conflict among native California peoples should be approached with caution, remembering that most of the material available was dredged from the memories of aged respondents long after the engagements occurred. No ethnographies were written during or soon after engagements occurred; still less was there psychological testing of nineteenth-century Indian peoples before, during, or immediately after termination of recorded conflicts.

Much of what anthropologists have thought and written about what here is called "primitive" war has been summarized by Vayda, Lesser, and Aberle (in Fried, Harris, and Murphy 1968).

Vayda (in Fried, Harris, and Murphy 1968:86–88) sought to generalize the functions of "primitive" war into six propositions. Four of these may be described as socioeconomic functions: (1) regulation of economic variables—war breaks out when inequalities between neighboring peoples reach unacceptable levels; (2) regulation of demographic levels, such as by taking captive women and children to fill out imbalances; (3) redistribution of land and of people; and (4) preventive war, to hold down the rate of offensive actions. The others are psychological: keeping anxiety and hostility from exceeding tolerable limits and diverting intrasocietal hostilities onto a suitable object like some foreign group.

Examination of the California data suggests that Vayda's first three propositions are not universally valid. In some areas, such as those of the Yuki and Wailaki, the Pomo, and the natives of the Sacramento Valley, intergroup armed conflict may well have had a function such as regulation of economic and demographic variables through redistribution of people and of economic resources. The Yurok and their neighbors did redistribute property, but this appears to have been more a function of their legal system than of warfare. And while warfare among the Colorado River tribes certainly did redistribute land and people, it seems a mistake to generalize about this in any way that suggests "primitive" war always rests on economic motivation.

Vayda's fourth proposition, the concept of preventive war, does appear to be a useful one in understanding the behavior of most native California peoples. From this generalization the Yuman tribes must be excluded. They apparently viewed war as an end in itself: sport, plus an important kind of self-realization as Quechan and as Mohave.

The psychological functions—keeping anxieties down and diverting hostilities onto suitable objects—appear more plausible than useful in the California context. No doubt all California peoples felt anxious and hostile at times, but the most frequent way of working these feelings out would appear to have been by killing some "doctor" felt to be a harmful sorceror rather than by intergroup armed conflict.

Lesser (in Fried, Harris, and Murphy 1968:92–96) takes Vayda to task for offering only equilibrium models. His most concrete suggestions consist of drawing attention to drives toward prestige and economic gain and to a proposition earlier developed by Beals and Hoijer (1965:542ff.) to the effect that what distinguishes stateless societies is absence of organized warfare aimed toward gaining control over new people and territory. Lesser adds that such societies can be characterized as ones in which intergroup conflict is waged for motives that are deeply personal. The idea of drives for prestige fits the Yuki and the Colorado River tribes but does not wear well elsewhere, especially among the Yurok and their neighbors, whose system disallows gain and discourages boasting of war exploits (Wallace 1949:2).

Lesser's suggestion that intergroup conflict in simple societies is for deeply personal motives seems plausible; however, many of the cases from Pomo, Yuki, and the Sacramento Valley involved trespassing on group territory or contests over group rights to food and other economic resources, and surely these ought to be classified not as personal but societal concerns.

Aberle (in Fried, Harris, and Murphy 1968:99–100) has contended that the aim of much warfare is to *increase* inequities, not to level them as Vayda wrote. This contention may well be true in many cases but it finds little support in the California data. Aberle's suggestion that concepts like competition, expansion, and domination should be examined fares a little better. The most warlike Californians, the Yuki and the Colorado River peoples, did like competition. Both enjoyed recounting past exploits, and the Quechan and Mohave at least apparently took pleasure in harassing (if not in dominating) the hapless Halchidhoma. Still it does not seem likely that the Yurok or the Yokuts had appreciable drives toward what is usually meant by competition, expansion, and domination.

What is it that appears most instructive in the recorded accounts of California Indian conflict in its various cultural contexts? First, Beals and Hoijer (1965: 539–565) are correct to the extent that warfare obviously motivated by desire to seize territory and to exploit subjects was not native to the several kinds of simple societies that lived in California. This is not to say that economic resources and some people and plunder did not change hands, sometimes on a "permanent" basis. It does indicate that there were no native California conquest states.

Second, what anthropologists have been saying and writing at least since 1917 (Perry 1917:2) should be emphasized—that human warfare is cultural behavior and not the uniform expression of some panhuman biological trait or psychological set. If such panhuman traits and sets exist (which is doubtful), the California data demonstrate that these are very distinctly modified by culture. Note that the very least politically organized of California peoples, the Yurok and their neighbors, have at least as strong a bias against armed conflict as do the moderately organized Yokuts. And it is the most organized peoples, the tribal Yuman groups of the lower Colorado, who take the most interest in armed conflict. There is a wide variety of attitudes toward armed conflict in native Californians—from groups who are distinctly antiwar to those that are very belligerent. Beyond doubt, war is cultural, not biological, behavior.

Finally, perhaps most striking of all is the finding that the simple societies of two regions in native California appear to have developed effective methods for limiting armed intersocietal conflicts: the Yokuts and their neighbors respected their judge-chiefs and may have enculturated their children to dislike and distrust violence, and the Yurok and their neighbors developed an intertribal legal system that prevented economic gain through violence and laid the greatest burden of reparation on those who were wealthiest and most influential.

Treaties

ROBERT F. HEIZER

The Indians of California, after their discovery by Juan Rodríguez Cabrillo in 1542, came into direct contact with a wide variety of national groups or their agents who imposed their authority: Spaniards, Mexicans, Russians, and Americans. During the period when California was a frontier outpost under Spanish control (1769–1821) no treaties as such were made with the Indians. Through practice the government of Spain assumed ownership of lands claimed by it through the right of discovery and performance of the formal Act of Possession. Resident natives were considered not as human beings in possession of land by virtue of occupation, but rather as a special appurtenance of the territory much in the same way that timber, minerals, and the climate were judged to be useful resources. For this reason the Spanish Crown did not enter into treaty relations with native peoples. It might, as in the case of Captain Palma, the leader of the large and warlike Quechan tribe, which occupied the important crossing spot of the Colorado River at Yuma on the land route from Mexico to California, make special concessions to him, distribute gifts to his tribesmen, and ask for a promise of loyalty; but such acts were not treaties. The Mexicans who secured independence from Spain in 1821 continued, as might be expected, to view Indians in frontier outposts such as California as a natural resource to be used in any manner desired. The Russians who had established a fort on the Sonoma County coast in 1812 did not enter into formal treaty arrangements with the local Pomo, but held native hostages as a guarantee of good behavior of the nearby tribes. In some areas, particularly on the northern and eastern border of Mexican settlement where contact was close with large native populations that had not been missionized, as for example in the Sonoma region, treaties were occasionally made for the sake of reducing conflict between Indians and Mexicans. Mariano Vallejo in 1836 entered into such a treaty with the Wappo and in 1837 a similar treaty was made with the Satiyomi (Wappo), whose chief was Succara (Lothrop 1932:185, 189–190).

It is with the military seizure by United States forces of California in 1846 that the California Indians, now reduced to about 100,000 from their estimated number of 350,000 in 1769 (when the first Spanish settlement was established at San Diego) encountered the particular American system of entering into treaty arrangements to secure legal title to occupied lands. Regardless of how considerate of Indian life and property the treaty-making theory of the United States government was, it can also be argued that it was a method to rationalize and abet the principle of Manifest Destiny.

"General" Vallejo, an Indian slaveholder in Sonoma County, signed, by the authority of his appointment as United States Indian subagent, a treaty with 11 groups of the southern Pomo and Lake Miwok Indians on June 1, 1848. This was not a binding act since the treaty was neither ratified nor observed, and it is merely of historical interest in being the first one of the American period (Heizer and Hester 1970:108–109). At about the same time the Swiss settler, "Captain" J.A. Sutter, who held the lands of "New Helvetia" through a Mexican land grant, had quite by accident through his associate, James Marshall, discovered gold during the building of a sawmill at Coloma on January 24, 1848. This important event occurred during the interim period of U.S. military rule between the seizure of California from Mexico in 1846 and admission of the state to the Union in September 1850. Sutter, also holding an official appointment as United States Indian subagent, realized the desirability of securing exclusive exploitative interests in what he knew must be immensely valuable auriferous placers in the Coloma-Placerville region; and with his partner, James Marshall, he entered into an "Agreement" with the Yalesumne (Nisenan) Indian occupants of the area for exclusive land rights in exchange for certain payment of food and equipment. This agreement, despite the title given it by Sutter, was in fact an Indian treaty. To legitimize it Sutter dispatched it to Col. R.B. Mason, military governor of California, stationed at Monterey, for approval. Mason refused to approve it, noting in his answer to Sutter that the United States government did not recognize the right of Indians to lease, sell, or rent their lands (Heizer and Almquist 1971:67; Heizer and Hester 1970:107–110; C. Olson 1948). It is obvious that both Vallejo and Sutter were attempting to secure exclusive title to protect the lands they were occupying at the time of American annexation (1846), through their official appointments as Indian subagents. The Sutter-Marshall "lease" is dated January 1, 1848, which would predate the discovery of gold at Coloma by 24 days. But Marshall himself in a letter written in 1856 said: "In February the Captain [Sutter] came to the mountains for the first time. Then we consummated a treaty with the Indians, which had been previously negotiated" (Hittell 1861:12).

Within the four-year span of military government (1846-1850) the discovery of gold at Coloma in January 1848 led to a massive entry of gold seekers. It is estimated that 100,000 miners were in California by the end of 1849. Military forces were too small to keep order among the newly arrived mob and between them and the resident Indians and Mexicans. Frequent conflicts with Indians in the gold-producing area indicated the desirability of protecting the Indians and removing them from the areas in which mining and farming were being carried on. The appointment of a number of Indian agents was considered by the U.S. Senate but decided against as an effective means of handling the problem. Adam Johnston was appointed Indian agent for California on April 14, 1849, and the letter of his appointment reads in part: "So little is known here of the condition and situation of the Indians in that region that no specific instructions can be given at present" (U.S. Congress. Senate Journal 1853:2). In May 1850 Johnston learned of difficulties between Whites and Indians on Bear River, north of Sacramento, and journeyed there where he encountered T.J. Green of the California militia and P.H. Burnett, elected as governor when the California voters approved the state constitution in November 1849. Johnston was informed by them that an "armistice or treaty" had been entered into with the Indians on Bear River. Johnston recommended against its approval by the federal government and his advice was followed.

Immediately upon Senate approval of admission of California on September 9, 1850, long debate occurred about what steps the federal government could and should take to remove the California Indians from contact with the gold miners since numbers on both sides were being killed. Newly seated California Sens. John C. Frémont and William M. Gwin participated. In the end the Senate approved the appointment of three Indian agents for California and passed special legislation authorizing President Fillmore to make treaties with the California tribes. All this occurred just before Congress adjourned in 1852, and it was learned only after adjournment that no appropriation had been made for the salary of the Indian agents while no persons had been specified as treaty commissioners although an appropriation of $25,000 was made to support treaty making. Accordingly, the three Indian agents whose appointment had been confirmed by the Senate (Redick McKee of Virginia, George W. Barbour of Kentucky, and O.M. Wozencraft of Louisiana) were named as treaty commissioners by President Fillmore to serve as such until they had negotiated the necessary treaties, and after which they would assume the title and duties of Indian agents.

Instructed to enter into such treaties "as seemed just and proper," their pay was to be eight dollars a day; after arriving in California they might appoint a secretary whose pay was not to exceed five dollars a day. All costs of treaty making were to be borne with the appropriation of $25,000. Meeting in San Francisco in January 1851, the three commissioners decided to travel together and meet with Indians, but after a trip together to the Sierra region it became obvious that they could never hope to meet with enough tribes if they remained together. Hostilities between Indians and Whites were raging all over the state and the need for action was obvious. It was decided, by drawing lots, that Barbour would make treaties in the district south of the San Joaquin River; Wozencraft would be responsible for the area north to the headwaters of the Sacramento River and from the Coast Ranges to the south of San Francisco Bay to the Sierra Nevada crest; and McKee would handle the Coast Range area north of San Francisco and the balance of the northern part of the state not being visited by Wozencraft. The first two treaties entered into while the three were acting as a board were adopted as the pattern. The details of the experiences of the three treaty commissioner agents are described in Senate documents (U.S. Congress. Senate Journal 1853). McKee's travels were recorded in a journal by George Gibbs and published by Schoolcraft (Gibbs 1853) and by his son, John McKee, who served as his secretary. His official diary appeared in Senate documents (U.S. Congress. Senate Journal 1853:134-195).

Each of the 18 treaties stipulated that a certain tract of land would be set aside for sole occupancy of signatory tribes and various measures to aid and improve conditions were promised—a school teacher, farmer, blacksmith, farm animals, agricultural instruments, seed, cloth, and much else. In return the Indians "forever quit claim to the government of the United States to any and all lands to which they . . . now have, or may ever have had any claim or title whatsoever." Ellison (1922) states that the proposed reserved areas totaled 11,700 square miles or 7,488,000 acres of land. The areas supposedly ceded and the intended reserved areas are shown in figure 1.

The three commissioners who arranged the 18 treaties in 1851-1852 knew nothing at all about California Indians. Their procedure was to travel about until they could collect enough natives, meet with them, and effect the treaty explanation and signing. One wonders how clearly many Indians understood what the whole matter was about. Not a single Indian signature was ever recorded; only an X mark occurs. Some treaties were agreed to by a number of Indians each of whom had a Spanish given name (Antonio, Joaquin, José, Pablo); others were signed by persons with either Spanish or native names; and a number were signed by persons who, without exception, bore native names. In the last

After Royce 1899:pl. CXIV.
Fig. 1. Areas supposedly ceded by Indians in the 1851-1852 treaties and areas intended to be reserved. Treaty designations are those used by President Fillmore in 1852.

instances it is to be doubted that an interpreter was always present who knew all the native dialects of the Indians assembled for the treaty making.

The Senate in executive session refused, on July 8, 1852, to ratify the 18 treaties, largely because of the objections of the California legislature and the California senators (Warner 1852; Coats et al. 1852; Ellison 1922, 1925; U.S. Congress. House. Committee on Indian Affairs 1922:265–272) and the dead treaties were filed. Since the injunction of secrecy was removed on January 18, 1905, the treaties have been published a number of times (for example, U.S. Congress. House. Committee on Indian Affairs 1921–1922, 1:12–15, 1928:38–85; Heizer 1972).

Two attempts have been made to identify the "tribes" recorded in the California treaties. One, by C. Hart Merriam, was made at the request of the Subcommittee of the Committee on Indian Affairs, House of Representatives, before which Merriam testified in 1926. Merriam (1926a:62) stated that of the 126 "alleged tribes" listed in the treaties half a dozen were unidentifiable, some were duplications, and that "the great majority of so-called tribes enumerated in the 18 treaties are nothing more than local bands or villages—not more than 56 of the 126 being tribes. On the other hand, in checking the treaty names against the names of the known California tribes it appears that more than 175 tribes are not included in the 18 treaties." Merriam's (1926b) worksheets have been preserved.

In 1955 R.F. Heizer and A.L. Kroeber made an independent analysis of the names of the "tribes" signatory to the 1851–1852 treaties. This was submitted as Exhibit ALK-8 in hearings before the Indian Claims Commission (allowed in 1946 under H.R. 4497), Dockets 31 and 37, in 1955. Of 139 signatory groups, 67 are identifiable as tribelets, 45 are merely village names, 14 are duplicates of names heard and spelled somewhat differently without the commissioners' being aware of the fact, and 13 are either unidentifiable or personal names (Heizer 1955a).

The Indians of California in 1928 were permitted, under H.R. 491, Seventieth Congress, to sue the federal government for compensation promised but not provided by the 18 unratified treaties that they had entered into in good faith. The attorney general of California was authorized to prosecute the suit. The suit was settled in 1944 in favor of the California Indians and a judgment of $5,025,000 was awarded. Royce (1899) lists, in the order of their dates, all land cessions and treaties between the United States government and Indians of California. The earliest of these is dated March 19, 1851 (Treaty A of the 1851–1852 unratified treaties) and was with six Southern Sierra Miwok and Foothill Yokuts tribelet groups or villages (Royce 1899:780, Nos. 273, 274 on map shown as pl. CXIV). The latest is dated October 16, 1891 and was with the Hupa and Yurok (Royce 1899:942, Nos. 400, 461 on map shown as pl. CXV).

The lands supposedly ceded to the United States by the various "tribes" with whom treaties were entered into in 1851–1852 are not specified in any of the treaty documents. The chief reason for not specifying ceded areas was obviously that the commissioners did not know, or even attempt to learn from the individual Indians with whom they were meeting, which lands their tribe or tribes owned. The Senate in 1852 might have inquired of the president whether representatives of each and every California Indian tribe had been treated with, but it apparently did not do so, presumably for the reason that the successful lobbying of the California senators had already made it obvious that the treaties would not be approved. Royce (1899:pl. CXIV) shows very large sections of the state as areas supposedly ceded by native Californians through each of the 18 treaties. There seems to be no basis whatsoever for this map beyond the vague impression of the U.S. Senate in 1852 that the California Indian tribes were agreeable to ceding to the United States the lands of California. Royce's map is, therefore, his own artifact deriving from the same assumption that the Senate made in 1852. But since it was already known in 1852 that many groups had not been treated with (cf. Gibbs 1853: 116, 119, 130), either because they had not been encountered in the course of the wanderings of the three commissioners or because through lack of interpreters no communication was possible between the Americans and numbers of groups of native Californians, it must have been obvious that the 1851–1852 treaties did not, as was implied, cover the quieting of territorial claims ("title") of the Indians then living in the state.

The treaty-making venture of 1851–1852 carried out by McKee, Wozencraft, and Barbour was intended to reduce the Indian-White confrontation on the California frontier, a point made clear from the location of the places where the treaties were made, which was either in the gold-mining regions of the Sierra Nevadas, the Klamath-Trinity-Scott River gold area, or along the main lines of communication. The treaty commissioners were unable to do more than promise the Indians they made treaties with that the government would soon establish a reservation where they would be fed, protected, and instructed in letters and useful pursuits—promises that were never honored. Even if the treaties had been ratified by the Senate, one wonders whether the many hundreds of groups who had been missed in 1851–1852 during the treaty making would have been taken care of on the 19 reserved areas that were to be set aside for the exclusive use and occupancy of those "tribes" named in specific treaties. Those groups who had been omitted from consideration would have had to be taken care of in some way.

The spate of treaty making in 1851–1852 led to nothing because of the refusal of the Senate to ratify the treaties. There were other so-called treaties, for example what Coy (1929:192–193) describes as one made between A. Wiley, superintendent of Indian affairs for California and the Hupa Indians. Commissioner of Indian Affairs W.P. Dole, in commenting on the document entitled "Treaty of peace and friendship between the United States government and the Hoopa, South Fork, Redwood, and Grouse Creek Indians," wrote to Wiley: "The relations of the government of the United States to the Indians of California do not contemplate treaties with those Indians, to be submitted by the President to the Senate for confirmation; but as it is deemed advisable to have the chiefs and leading men of the tribes in question subscribe their hands to a document which shall fully commit them hereafter, you will, after ex-plaining to them the nature of the additions or alterations now suggested, as being intended solely for their benefit, cause a copy to be signed by them, and forward it to this office" (Dole 1865:138). Apparently the distinction between what the Indians *thought* was a treaty and what the commissioner and Senate *knew* was a treaty was not explained to the Indians. The reality of the whole affair was that the Hoopa Reservation was established not through treaty but by authority of an act of Congress of April 8, 1864 (Royce 1899:832–833). Legally speaking, no California Indian tribe (among those considered in this volume) ever entered into relations based on treaty with the U.S. government. The alternative means of providing for federal protection and welfare of California Indians was that Congress authorized, in 1853 and 1855, the setting aside of seven "military reservations" on which Indians were gathered with the intention of providing them houses and a means of livelihood through farming and stock raising. These reserves were not to exceed 25,000 acres each. Their names and approximate dates of establishment are: Tejon Pass, 1853; Nome Lackee, 1857; Klamath, 1857; Tule River, 1856; Round Valley (Nome Cult), 1856; Fresno River, 1857; Hoopa, 1864; Smith River, 1862; Mendocino, 1856; Mission Indian, 1887 (Royce 1899).

The meeting of those California Indians who had survived the Spanish and Mexican occupations with the American gold miners in 1848 marked the beginning of what was to be a disastrous encounter. The Indian population was reduced in two decades (1850–1870) from about 100,000 to about 50,000, and some estimates are as low as 30,000. Much of this wantonly destroyed humanity and a great deal more of native culture would have survived if the California Indians had been protected on the reserves stipulated in the 18 treaties. But with the failure of the U.S. Senate to ratify the very treaties that they had authorized, the California Indians, who were also denied by the California legislature the privilege of citizenship, were helpless (Heizer and Almquist 1971:23–64, 120–137). In the history of California Indians no other single event (that is "nonevent") had a more rapid destructive effect on their population and culture than the about-face that the Senate made between authorizing President Fillmore on September 30, 1850, to make treaties and its failure on July 8, 1852, to ratify those treaties.

Litigation and its Effects

OMER C. STEWART

The legal status of the Indians of California and the litigation affecting them is based upon all the governmental laws concerned with California Indians from the time the Spanish explorers and missionaries arrived in the area of California. Spanish and Mexican law governing citizenship and property was accepted by the United States. In the Treaty of Guadalupe Hidalgo, July 4, 1848, the United States government pledged itself to protect rights to property and to religious and civil freedoms of Mexican citizens who elected to remain in the United States. Those citizens included the Indians of California.

Under the federal system of the United States, the state of California retained certain powers, and the majority of the California constitutional convention in 1849 voted to deprive California Indians of some of the civil rights promised in the Treaty of Guadalupe Hidalgo. Although Indians had been invited to participate, the constitutional convention voted to restrict future voting to White persons and requested that the Indians be removed from the state. In 1850 the California legislature enacted laws that prevented Indians from giving evidence in any case in which a White person was a party and authorized the indenture of Indians as uncompensated laborers to White persons. Indians were denied firearms.

At about the time that the U.S. Congress admitted California into the Union, another act of Congress (September 30, 1850) authorized the president to negotiate treaties with the Indians of California to cede and relinquish to the United States their title and interest to all lands in California. Commissioners were appointed to negotiate the treaties and 18 treaties were signed by representatives of 139 different Indian groups or tribelets between March 19, 1851, and January 7, 1852. Under the treaties 18 reservations were to be established for the Indians on which they would receive some clothing and food as well as education in the "art of civilization." The area to be reserved for Indians amounted to 8,619,000 acres (fig. 1).

As soon as the provisions of the treaties became known the legislature of California adopted resolutions opposing the ratification of the treaties; consequently, when the treaties were submitted by President Millard Fillmore to the Senate for ratification on June 1, 1852, the Senate rejected the treaties and took the unusual step of placing them in secret files of the Senate. There they remained until January 18, 1905, when the Senate voted to remove the injunction of secrecy. The failure to ratify the treaties left the federal government without explicit legal obligation toward the Indians of California.

Even without the treaties, the U.S. government recognized that it was morally and legally bound to protect the Indians of California and to compensate them for their land in which they had original Indian titles as a result of use and occupancy from time immemorial. The Supreme Court of the United States had ruled as early as 1823 (*Johnson* v. *M'Intosh*, 8 Wheat 543) that American Indians had rights of occupancy and ownership equal to the fee simple absolute title of the Whites; however, California White citizens of the nineteenth century almost completely frustrated the feeble attempts of the federal government to treat the Indians of California fairly.

Federal efforts to protect California Indians took the form of establishing executive order reservations. The first was Hoopa Valley, in Humboldt County, consisting of 116,572 acres set apart in 1864 (see table 1). Three other reservations were authorized but local opposition either delayed or blocked them. In 1873 Tule River Reservation in Tulare County (49,074 acres, later enlarged) and Round Valley Reservation in Mendocino County were established with the hope that individuals of many tribelets would move to these reservations, yet many stayed away. Some other reservations established early were Cahuilla in 1875 in the desert and Palm Springs (Agua Caliente) in 1896, both in Riverside County. In 1891 an extension to the Hoopa Reservation, designated as the Klamath Strip, was added on both sides of Klamath River from the original reservation toward the ocean.

The publication of *Century of Dishonor* (1881) and the novel *Ramona* (1884) by Helen Hunt Jackson, dealing with the plight of California Indians, pricked the conscience of America and stimulated more federal help for California Indians. Small reservations, often called rancherias, were purchased in southern California beginning with Rincon and La Jolla in 1892, Ramona and 10 others in 1893. The procedure continued and was extended throughout California until 1940 when XL Ranch was purchased for the Achumawi in Modoc County, and in 1942 Chico Colony of 25 acres for any Indians who wished to settle there. In all, 117 California Indian communities were established by the federal government

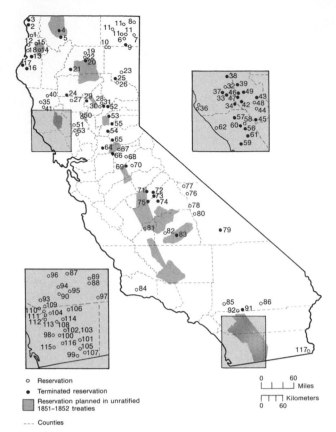

○ Reservation
● Terminated reservation
▨ Reservation planned in unratified 1851–1852 treaties
--- Counties

0   60
| | | | Miles
|⊓⊓⊓| Kilometers
0   60

Fig. 1. Reservations and rancherias. Numbers identify the reservations in table 1.

on land set aside from the public domain or purchased with federal funds. Sizes varied from the 116,572 Hoopa Reservation to a one-acre plot in Strawberry Valley, Yuba County, made available in 1914. The area of land under some federal restriction as of 1950 was 632,599.58 acres. That year a toal of 10,000 Indians listed the federal reservations and rancherias as their homes. There were 14,100 California Indians not attached to reservations (U.S. Congress. House. Committee on Interior and Insular Affairs 1953).

The Indians who signed the 18 treaties in 1851 and 1852 remembered the treaty councils. Friends of the Indians did their best to obtain compensation for the Indians as soon as federal failure was known. The reservations and rancherias were not considered as an adequate substitution.

In 1905–1906, Kelsey (1906) labored as a Bureau of Indian Affairs special agent for California Indians. Kroeber (1957a:218) wrote that "Kelsey was an attorney in San Jose who . . . had been appointed to survey the landless non-reservation Indians of California, their needs, and what might be done for them, and on whose recommendations various small tracts . . . were purchased . . . ." Eight were purchased in 1907, seven in 1908, 10 in 1909. Kelsey's lecture in San Francisco to the Commonwealth Club of California in 1909 may have been the beginning of the support of that service club for legisla-

tion to redress, in part, the wrongs done to California Indians.

Shortly after Kelsey aroused the Commonwealth Club, Frederick G. Collett started his work as a beneficent missionary among California Indians. From them he learned of their unratified treaties. Collett shifted his labors from converting Indians to the Christian faith to convincing state and federal legislators to enact laws that would allow the Indians to sue the federal government. From 1914 until his death in 1955 Collett was an active lobbyist for California Indians. Much of his support was provided by annual "dues" collected from Indians. A number of organizations joined the struggle and spent considerable effort competing with one another. In the 1920s the following groups were active in behalf of the Indians: Native Sons of the Golden West, Federated Women's Clubs, California Indian Rights Association, Inc., Northern California Indian Association, Mission Indian Federation, and Women's Christian Temperance Union (K.M. Johnson 1966:62). In 1927 the California legislature passed a bill authorizing the attorney general of California to bring suit against the United States, in the event Congress authorized such a suit. The California Indians' Jurisdictional Act became law on May 18, 1928. In the Court of Claims the number K–344 was assigned the case and the number alone often has been used to identify it.

As with all federal dealing with California Indians, K–344 was very complex and controversial. Many Indians and their attorneys opposed having the case handled by the attorney general of the state of California. On the other hand, the Jurisdictional Act of 1928 (45 Stat. 602) defined a group as the Indians of California. After unusual delays and several unsuccessful attempts to get better jurisdictional acts, on December 4, 1944, the U.S. Court of Claims awarded the Indians of California $17,053,941.98 for the 18 reservations the Indians were promised in 1851–1852 but did not receive. But from that amount the federal government deducted as an offset $12,029,099.64, the amount spent by the government for the benefit of the Indians of California over the years, including reservations. There remained $5,024,842.34. In 1950 Congress authorized the payment of $150.00 to each Indian on the corrected and updated roster of California Indians prepared under the original provisions of the act. Finally, in 1954, Congress once more amended the 1928 act to allow appeals until June 30, 1955 (68 Stat. 240). On that date, the secretary of interior approved a roll bearing 36,095 names. As of June 30, 1971, $6,408,630 judgment fund plus interest had been distributed to Indians of California in per capita payments from the case authorized in 1928. Remaining in the fund to be distributed was $1,496,246.08 as of that date.

The 1928 Jurisdictional Act, even though it brought small cash payments to all the identifiable Indians of California, did not compensate the Indians for all the lands they lost to the United States. The payment was a minimum compensation of $1.25 per acre for 8,619,000 acres promised in the 1851–1852 treaties, less the value of the 611,226 acres actually made available to California Indians in reservations and rancherias as well as any other benefit. Could the Indians be paid for the remaining 91,764,600 acres of the state of California? Indians, their attorneys, and their friends were not at all satisfied with provisions of the Jurisdictional Act of 1928, so that efforts for a more satisfactory hearing were continued.

Attorneys for California Indians, lobbyists like Frederick G. Collett, and organizations like the Indian Rights Association and the Commonwealth Club maintained pressure on the U.S. Congress for another day in court that would consider payment for the 91 million acres of California not covered by the 1928 case. California Indians were not the only ones demanding a hearing on their tribal claims. Almost all tribes had claims and dozens had retained law firms in Washington, D.C., to work for them to have their claims adjudicated.

On August 11, 1946, the Indian Claims Commission Act (60 Stat. 1049) became law and identifiable groups of Indians of the United States were allowed to present any claims against the U.S. government the Indians and their attorneys might discover and for which petitions could be filed within five years. By August 13, 1951, 23 separate petitions had been filed for some Indians of California. In 1958 Indians along the northern and eastern border of California whose lands extended into adjacent states were removed from claims of the Indians of California because they could share in recovery by their own tribal cases. These groups were the Modoc, Northern Paiute, Shoshoni, Southern Paiute, Chemehuevi, Mohave, and Quechan. For Indians wholly within the state of California there were two groups claiming to represent all the Indians of California (Dockets 31 and 37) as well as separate petitions from 46 bands of Mission Indians, Yokiah (Central Pomo), Shasta, Yana, and Achumawi. By an order of the Indian Claims Commission of July 20, 1964 (13 Ind. Cl. Comm. 369) these were all combined into Dockets 31, 37 after 20 years of legal maneuvering.

Some of the major difficulties in the litigation of the Indians of California were set forth by the Indian Claims Commission July 20, 1964 (13 Ind. Cl. Comm. 369): "This case has a long history of litigation in this Commission and in the Court of Claims. The claims of Dockets 31 and 37 were initially dismissed because petitioners were held not to be an identifiable group with capacity to sue (1 Ind. Cl. Comm. 383). The Court of Claims reversed (122 Ct. Clms. 419) and the Supreme Court denied *certiorari* (344 U.S. 856). A motion to amend the petition was granted over objection (4 Ind. Cl. Comm. 147); the claimed exclusive right to assert claims to lands in California was denied and the capacity of the Mission Indians and the Pit River Indians was upheld (6 Ind. Cl. Comm. 86); the lands claimed in other tribal claims were

separated from the lands the Commission permitted to be claimed by petitioners in Dockets 31 and 37 (6 Ind. Cl. Comm. 666); the Yokiah [Pomo], Yana, and Shasta claims were consolidated with Docket 31 and 37 for all purposes, including judgment (6 Ind. Cl. Comm. 674); after trial an interlocutory judgment of Indian title and date of taking was entered in favor of petitioners in Docket 31 and 37 (8 Ind. Cl. Comm. 1), on July 31, 1959. In Docket 347, an interlocutory judgment on the title phase (including the taking and valuation date of March 3, 1853) was entered in favor of the Pit River Indians (7 Ind. Cl. Comm. 815) on July 29, 1959."

The hearings for Dockets 31 and 37, in Berkeley in June 1954 and in San Francisco in September 1955, warrant mention. Alfred L. Kroeber, Samuel A. Barrett, Robert F. Heizer, and Edward W. Gifford were the anthropologists who testified for the petitioners. Julian H. Steward, Ralph L. Beals, W. Duncan Strong, Harold E. Driver, Erminie Wheeler-Voegelin, Walter R. Goldschmidt, and Abraham M. Halpern were expert anthropological witnesses for the Department of Justice. In the opinion of the Commission decided July 31, 1959 (8 Ind. Cl. Comm. 1) the entity "Indians of California" was recognized as an "identifiable group" and could present a case before the Indian Claims Commission, in accordance with the opinion of the Court of Claims (122 Ct. Clms. 349). The Commission ruled that 8,811,070 acres were removed from consideration because that amount of land had been granted by the governments of Spain and Mexico and ownership had been confirmed by the United States in 1851.

The Commission wrote further: "One of the most difficult, if not the most difficult, question we have to decide is what California lands the petitioners actually occupied and used for their subsistence, that is, the lands they exploited for their day to day lives." The Commission found that "the Indian groups ranged throughout their respective territories in their gathering, hunting, and fishing exertions . . . their exploitation of the available resources in a given territory required frequent and extended travel within the territories claimed . . . during a normal season [they] would visit and use the whole territory to which they asserted ownership as their exclusive places of abode" (13 Ind. Cl. Comm. 369).

In the hearing for Docket 347, Pit River Indians, evidence was presented that 60 animals were used—birds, reptiles, fish, mammals, insects (antelope to yellow jacket larvae)—which were found scattered throughout the length and breadth of the area. Waterfowl, fish, and aquatic mammals were taken from streams, marshes, and lakes. Fifty-five plants were used for food, clothing, weapons, medicines, and houses. Eagles and mountain sheep were found on mountain tops; and jackrabbits, antelope, sage hens, and sage hen eggs were obtained from the extensive sage brush plains. This evidence confirmed the opinion expressed by the Commission in Dockets 31, 37.

The July 31, 1959 (8 Ind. Cl. Comm. 1) ruling by the Indian Claims Commission that the Indians of California had "Indian title to these lands by virtue of the act of March 3, 1851" and that "the case will now proceed to a determination of the acreage . . ., less the Spanish and Mexican land grants and the reservations . . ., the value thereof as of the date of acquisition by the United States, and the question of what offsets, if any, the United States may be entitled . . ." set in motion another complex series of legal struggles.

Evaluation law suits are both very expensive and time consuming. The law firm of Wilkinson, Cragun, and Barker, attorneys for Docket 31, and the attorneys most experienced in Indian claims litigation, having gained an award of 32 million dollars for the Ute Indians, favored a negotiated settlement rather than a long, costly, and potentially dangerous legal battle. Under the leadership of Robert W. Barker, the more than a dozen other attorneys, mostly in California, representing various segments of Indians, agreed to accept a compromise negotiated settlement. Such a compromise was agreed to both by attorneys for the Department of Justice and by Barker for combined dockets of Indians of California in July 1963. The amount agreed to was 29,100,000 dollars to pay for 64,425,000 acres, the area remaining after deducting reservation lands previously paid for, land grants of Spain and Mexico, and land of border Indians having independent cases (13 Ind. Cl. Comm. 369). The compromise settlement was contingent upon being accepted by both the Pit River Indians, who had won their independent suit determining liability, and the Mission Indians with independent cases pending, as well as being approved by all the other Indians of California. The Stipulation for Compromise and Settlement and Entry of Final Judgment for payment of 29,100,000 dollars provided 26 lines for signatures of attorneys representing various groups or organizations of California Indians. All signed in 1963, except Louis L. Phelps, Attorney of Record, Docket 347, Pit River Indians.

In August 1963 conferences among the representatives of the Bureau of Indian Affairs, the Department of Justice, the Indian Claims Commission, the attorneys for the Indians, and the Indians themselves were announced. September 1963 meetings were held with Mission Indians at Riverside, Escondido, San Diego, and Los Angeles. The Mission Indians voted 1,559 "for" and 354 "against" accepting the compromise.

On September 28, 1963, a meeting for Pit River Indians was held at Alturas. Of the 760 eligible Pit River Indians to whom notices had been sent, only 187, or 24.5%, voted at the meeting. Seventy-five voted for the settlement, 105 against it, and 7 ballots were spoiled. On November 8, 1963, a mail ballot sent to the eligible Pit River Indians who had not voted on September 28, 1963, elicited an additional 221 votes: 137 "for," 83 "against," 1 "spoiled." The total vote was thus: 212 "for," 188 "against," with 8 spoiled ballots. The vote of 408 represented 53.7% of the 760 eligible Pit River Indians as of December 10, 1963.

The Pit River Indians' strong, vociferous, and persistent opposition to the settlement of the claim of the Indians of California stimulated the Indian Claims Commission to hold 15 other meetings in various parts of the state in January and February 1964, with a return engagement for the Pit River Indians, March 7, 1964, at Alturas, at which 22 voted "for" and 19 voted "against" the compromise. At Yuma, Arizona, where a few Quechan Indians enrolled as Indians of California met on March 14, 1964, the vote was 7 "for" and 9 "against," but their vote was submerged in the general group. For the 15 meetings held January to March 1964, the final totals were: 4,276 (67%) for acceptance; 2,118 (33%) for rejection; total 6,394. On March 18, 1964, ballots were mailed to the 13,369 enrolled adult California Indians who had not previously voted: 5,380 "yes" and 650 "no" for 6,030 valid ballots were returned. The final tabulation was: 11,427 (77.54%) affirmative and 3,310 (22.46%) negative, for a total 14,737 (58.8%) of 20,041 California Indians eligible to vote (13 Ind. Cl. Comm. 369). On the basis of this tally the Commission on July 20, 1964, issued its Final Determination or Judgment to pay 29,100,000 dollars to the Indians of California. Congress appropriated the amount authorized by the Act of October 7, 1964 (78 Stat. 1033).

It required over four years, until September 21, 1968, for Congress to enact the legislation, Public Law 90–507 (82 Stat. 860) to authorize the secretary of the interior to spend up to 325,000 dollars to prepare a list of Indians of California eligible to share in the award. The above law authorized the distribution of remaining funds available under the Act of 1928, plus interest, as well as the judgment and interest from the 1964 claim less costs. By November 1971, 75,000 persons had applied for enrollment in order to share in the distribution of the claims money, and the secretary of the interior had expended the $325,000 authorized in 1968 for the preparation of the roll.

As of May 24, 1972, 92,218 applications had been sent out of which 75,433 had been returned. Of these, 61,143 had been declared eligible, 4,462 had been declared not eligible. Appeals were filed by 1,709 applicants. Notices of eligibility had been mailed to 55,899 California Indians.

As of June 30, 1971, the 1964 award of $29,100,000 had been reduced by payment of attorneys' fees to $26,491,-000 but had been increased by interest less costs by $9,643,543.66 to a total of $36,134,534.66 to be added to the $1,496,246.08 remaining from the Act of 1928. Thus, as of June 30, 1971, $37,630,781.74 was available for per capita distribution to nearly 65,000 Indians of California.

STEWART

There remains to be considered the future legal status of Indian lands in California. In the 1920s, largely through the efforts of Charles De Young Elkus, the Commonwealth Club of San Francisco directed its efforts to the transfer of responsibility for Indians of California from the federal government to the California State government. Pressure to accomplish this transfer was increased following the passage of the California Indian Jurisdictional Act of 1928 (45 Stat. 602). In later years such a transfer was designated "termination" and many Indian leaders opposed the termination of federal jurisdiction. In 1936 and 1938 the superintendent of the Sacramento Agency of the Bureau of Indian Affairs submitted reports to the commissioner of Indian affairs outlining a program to definitely liquidate the U.S. Indian service in California in 10 years. BIA officials in California made similar recommendations in 1944, 1949, and 1950.

In 1947 William Zimmerman, then acting commissioner of Indian affairs, stated his approval for the immediate removal of U.S. Indian Bureau supervision of California Indians. In 1951 special agents of the BIA were dispatched to California by Commissioner of Indian Affairs Dillon S. Myers to make a local study in preparation to terminating federal responsibility. Population and acreage data in table 1 came from that study.

In 1951 the California legislature passed a resolution: "That the Legislature of the State of California respectfully memorializes the President and the Congress of the United States to dispense with any and all restrictions, whatever their nature, whereby the freedom of the American Indian is curtailed in any respect, whether as to governmental benefits, civil rights or personal conduct." Commissioner Myers prepared bills to facilitate the termination of federal supervision over Indian affairs in California on April 10, 1952 (H.R. 7490, H.R. 7491, and S. 3005), which were not enacted. In 1957 H.R. 9512 was introduced into Congress. This bill proposed a joint state and federal Indian appeals board and otherwise recommended all federal trust property in California be given to the Indians as fee patent land and then the Indians would be the responsibility of the state of California. One difficulty revolved around Indian water rights. Finally the U.S. Congress agreed to terminate the trust status of California Indian lands as requested by members of the different rancherias. On August 18, 1958, the first California Indian "rancheria bill" was enacted by the 85th Congress, H.R. 2824, which became Public Law 85-671. Forty-one rancherias containing 7,601 acres became the property in fee of 1,330 Indians (see fig. 1 and table 1). Additional rancherias and reservations may be removed from federal supervision upon request of occupants of the area and upon congressional amendment to Public Law 85-671 passed in 1958.

The enrollment to receive shares from the claims cases under the laws of 1928 and the Claims Commission Act of 1946 was completed in December 1972. Almost 70,000 Indians received $668.51 each, making the final payment near 46 million dollars (Janet L. Parks, personal communication 1975).

Table 1. Indian Reservations in California

Map No.	Reservations and Rancherias	Population 1951	Area in Acres	Tribe	Date Terminated
	Del Norte County				
1	Coast Indian Community (Resighini)	40	228	Yurok	
2	Crescent City (Elk Valley)	22	100	Tolowa	1958
3	Smith River	110	164	Tolowa	1958
	Siskiyou County				
4	Quartz Valley	40	604	Shasta	1958
5	Ruffeys	2	441	Shasta	1958
	Modoc County				
6	Alturas	12	20	Achumawi	
7	Cedarville	13	17	N. Paiute	
8	Fort Bidwell	112	3,340	N. Paiute	
9	Likely	0	40		1964
10	Lookout (2 parcels)	16	50	Achumawi	
11	XL Ranch (4 parcels)	39	8,760	Achumawi	
	Humboldt County				
12	Big Lagoon	0	9		
13	Blue Lake	22	26	Wiyot	1958
14	Hoopa Valley	600	87,496	Hupa	

Table 1. Indian Reservations in California *(Continued)*

Map No.	Reservations and Rancherias	Population 1951	Area in Acres	Tribe	Date Terminated
	Humboldt County *(Continued)*				
15	Hoopa Extension (Klamath Strip)	375	17,299	Yurok	
16	Rohnerville	30	15	Wiyot	1958
17	Table Bluff	40	20	Mixed	1958
18	Trinidad	9	60	Yurok	
	Shasta County				
19	Big Bend (Henderson)	11	40	Achumawi	
20	Montgomery Creek	1	72	Achumawi	1958
21	Redding (Clear Creek)	36	31	Undesignated	1958
22	Roaring Creek	0	80		
	Lassen County				
23	Susanville	45	30	Undesignated	
	Tehama County				
24	Paskenta	4	260	Nomlaki	1958
	Plumas County				
25	Greenville (2 parcels)	40	275	Maidu	1958
26	Taylorsville	0	160		
	Glenn County				
27	Grindstone Creek	30	80	Nomlaki	
	Butte County				
28	Berry Creek	0	33		
29	Chico (Meechupta)	40	25	Undesignated	1958
30	Enterprise (2 parcels)	14	81	Maidu	
31	Mooretown	14	160	Undesignated	1958
	Mendocino County				
32	Coyote Valley	34	100	Pomo	
33	Guidiville	35	243	Pomo	1958
34	Hopland	75	2,070	Pomo	1958
35	Laytonville	90	200	Cahto	
36	Manchester—Point Arena	85	369	Pomo	
37	Pinoleville	100	97	Pomo	1958
38	Potter Valley (2 parcels)	12	96	Pomo	1958
39	Redwood Valley	17	80	Pomo	1958
40	Round Valley	500	25,654	Mixed	
41	Sherwood Valley	0	291		
	Lake County				
42	Big Valley (Mission)	124	102	Pomo	1958
43	Cache Creek	2	160	Pomo	1958
44	Lower Lake	6	140	Pomo	
45	Middletown	21	109	Pomo	1958
46	Robinson	45	88	Pomo	1958
47	Scotts Valley (Sugar Bowl)	25	57	Pomo	1958
48	Sulphur Bank	13	50	Pomo	
49	Upper Lake (2 parcels)	70	561	Pomo	1958

Map No.	Reservations and Rancherias	Population 1951	Area in Acres	Tribe	Date Terminated
	Colusa County				
50	Colusa (Cachil Dehe)	50	254	Nomlaki	
51	Cortina	4	640	Miwok	
	Yuba County				
52	Strawberry Valley	2	1	Undesignated	1958
	Nevada County				
53	Nevada City	4	75	Maidu	1958
	Placer County				
54	Auburn	80	20	Maidu	1958
55	Colfax	0	40		1964
	Sonoma County				
56	Alexander Valley	12	54	Wappo	1958
57	Cloverdale	45	27	Pomo	1958
58	Dry Creek	14	75	Pomo	
59	Gratton	3	15	Pomo	1958
60	Lytton	10	50	Pomo	1958
61	Mark West	4	35	Pomo	1958
62	Stewarts Point	88	40	Pomo	
	Yolo County				
63	Rumsey (2 parcels)	18	141	Nomlaki	
	Sacramento County				
64	Wilton	30	39	Miwok	1958
	El Dorado County				
65	Shingle Springs	1	240	Miwok	1966
	Amador County				
66	Buena Vista	5	70	Miwok	1958
67	Jackson	5	330	Miwok	
	Calaveras County				
68	Sheep Ranch	9	2	Undesignated	
	Tuolumne County				
69	Chicken Ranch	9	40	Miwok	1958
70	Tuolumne	50	312	Miwok	
	Madera County				
71	North Fork	6	80	Monache	1958
72	Picayune	21	80	Chukchansi Yokuts	1958
	Fresno County				
73	Big Sandy (Auberry)	101	280	Monache	1958
74	Cold Springs (Sycamore)	25	160	Monache	1958
75	Table Mountain	50	160	Chukchansi Yokuts	1958
	Inyo County				
76	Big Pine	50	279	N. Paiute	
77	Bishop	500	875	N. Paiute	
78	Fort Independence	42	320	N. Paiute	
79	Indian Ranch	0	560		1958
80	Lone Pine	115	237	N. Paiute-Shoshoni	

Table 1. Indian Reservations in California (Continued)

Map No.	Reservations and Rancherias	Population 1951	Area in Acres	Tribe	Date Terminated
	Kings County				
81	Santa Rosa	82	170	Tachi Yokuts	
	Tulare County				
82	Strathmore	0	40		1964
83	Tule River	200	54,116	Yokuts	
	Santa Barbara County				
84	Santa Ynez	28	99	Mission	
	San Bernardino County				
85	San Manuel	18	653	Mission	
86	Twentynine Palms	0	161		
	Riverside County				
87	Agua Caliente (Palm Springs)	78	31,128	Cahuilla	
88	Augustine	8	616	Cahuilla	
89	Cabazon	15	1,480	Cahuilla	
90	Cahuilla	32	18,252	Cahuilla	
91	Mission Creek	1	2,560	Serrano	1970
92	Morongo	125	31,723	Serrano	
93	Pechanga	20	4,125	Luiseño	
94	Ramona	0	520		
95	Santa Rosa	10	11,093	Cahuilla	
96	Soboba	150	5,116	Cahuilla	
97	Torres-Martinez	250	30,132	Cahuilla	
	San Diego County				
98	Barona Ranch	22	5,005	Ipai-Tipai	
99	Campo (2 parcels)	63	15,010	Ipai-Tipai	
100	Capitan Grande	0	15,234		
101	Cuyapaipe	3	5,320	Ipai-Tipai	
102	Inaja and Cosmit	20	880	Ipai-Tipai	
103	La Jolla	112	8,329	Luiseño	
104	La Posta	0	3,879		
105	Los Coyotes	25	25,050	Ipai-Tipai	
106	Manzanita	27	3,520	Ipai-Tipai	
107	Mesa Grande	100	5,963	Ipai-Tipai	
108	Mission Reserve	0	9,480		
109	Pala	100	11,016	Luiseño	
110	Pauma and Yuima	70	250	Luiseño	
111	Rincon	85	3,486	Luiseño	
112	San Pasqual	8	1,343	Luiseño	
113	Santa Ysabel	40	9,679	Ipai-Tipai	
114	Sycuan	15	604	Ipai-Tipai	
115	Viejas (Baron Long)	37	1,609	Ipai-Tipai	
	Imperial County				
116	Fort Yuma	1,100	7,853	Quechan	
	Public domain allotments		130,922		
	Total	7,168	612,530		

Source: U.S. Congress. House. Committee on Interior and Insular Affairs 1953.

Twentieth-Century Secular Movements

EDWARD D. CASTILLO

While many scholars have concentrated on studies of native Californians in the nineteenth century and earlier, few have tried to deal with attempts by Indians and their White allies to make adjustments for the individual and his tribe to the rapidly changing world of the twentieth century. Nonreligious organizations of and for Indians blossomed before the turn of the twentieth century and have been active periodically since then. These organizations varied from those with exclusively White membership, to mixed Indian and non-Indian groups, and finally to all-Indian associations. The history of these groups is, in many ways, the history of the emergence of an expanding consciousness among native Californians that ultimately led to what has been termed Indian nationalism or pan-Indianism.

It is ironic and tragic that the Dawes Allotment Act of 1887 was the outcome of intense lobbying on the part of philanthropists, missionaries, and other "do-gooders" who wanted only to help the Indians. The result of this act was the forced division of the Indian communal land base, causing intense intratribal disruption resulting in lawsuits and finally in the loss of millions of acres of trust property nationally. Unfortunately, few recognized the lesson of this disastrous procedure of making policy for Indians without consulting the people who are supposed to benefit by it (Prucha 1973).

In California the earliest example of an Indian interest organization for native peoples was the legal aid provided Indians threatened by expulsion from villages situated on Mexican land grants by the Indian Rights Association of Philadelphia. This group paid all legal expenses and received a favorable judgment in this important case in 1888 (*Byrne* v. *Alas et al.* 74 Cal., 628). It was this issue, which soon reached the United States Supreme Court (*Barker* v. *Harvey*), that prompted the organization of the first Indian welfare group in California.

In 1901 the U.S. Supreme Court decided to award possession of the Cupeño village at Warner's Hot Springs to ex-governor John Downey and expel the Indians from their ancestral home. This event stirred the militant sympathies of the influential Los Angeles businessman Charles F. Lummis, who soon organized a group calling itself the Sequoya League. Among the many influential members of this organization were David Starr Jordan, C. Hart Merriam, Phoebe A. Hearst, and Frederick W. Hodge. Lummis's major concern was to persuade the government to provide a new home for the dispossessed Cupeño. Through its many powerful contacts the League pressured Congress and President Theodore Roosevelt to act. A special commission was appointed (fig. 1), including Lummis, to survey and select a new homesite for the Cupeño Indians. After a careful investigation of possible sites, including consultation with Cupeño leaders Salvador Nolasquez and Ambrosio Ortega (fig. 2), the commission selected and purchased a 3,438-acre ranch in the Pala Valley February 20, 1902. Although the Cupeño Indians attempted a last-minute appeal to the president to avoid removal they were evicted on February 20, 1903, and moved to Pala (see "Impact of Euro-American Exploration and Settlement," fig. 5, this vol.). While removal was indeed tragic the Cupeño were more fortunate than many other Indian groups who were similarly removed but cast adrift to shift for themselves. After the Cupeño removal the League became active with other tribes outside California.

The League again aided southern California Indians in 1905. The winter of that year had indeed been harsh. Facing starvation and desperate health conditions, San Diego and Riverside county Indians were supplied by the Sequoya League with emergency food and medicine. Pressure again successfully stirred public sentiment and embarrassed the Bureau of Indian Affairs into aiding these desperate peoples. The League then attempted to stimulate income for these people by acting as middlemen (without commission) in selling native baskets and crafts. The Sequoya League eventually lost its momentum; it was last active in 1911 (Watkins 1944).

Events unfolded differently in northern California. At this time thousands of Indians in the north had not yet received reservations and rancheria lands but were constantly being evicted from their villages. In response a Methodist welfare group in concert with an all-White philanthropic organization called the Northern California Indian Association purchased a farm for the Manchester band of Pomoan Indians in 1902 (Edwards and Kelsey 1904). A similar corporate-communal farm was given for the Chico Indian colony by the estate of Gen. John Bidwell to the Presbyterian Board of Home Missions. Unfortunately, this unique idea was eventually abandoned and both settlements turned over to the Bureau of Indian Affairs. Nevertheless, the idea did provide some relief for these harrassed natives and again

Fig. 1. Council of Cupeño Indians with the Warner's Ranch Commission. Photograph by Charles F. Lummis, March 17, 1902.

drew attention to the criminal neglect of numerous bands of homeless California Indians by the Indian Service.

In 1905 C.E. Kelsey, secretary of the Northern California Indian Association, was appointed as special agent of the Bureau of Indian Affairs to survey and make recom-

Fig. 2. Ambrosio Ortega, a Cupeño leader at Warner's Ranch. Photograph by Charles F. Lummis, March 17, 1902.

mendations for government support of homeless Indians in California. His report (Kelsey 1906) resulted in a congressional appropriation of $100,000 for the purchase of land and for the development of domestic and irrigation water.

In addition to land acquisition, civil rights movements began to gain momentum a few years later. A Methodist preacher named Frederick G. Collett, who was to be a controversial figure in Indian affairs throughout the next 40 years, first began his career at Round Valley in 1913. Collett organized a group called the Indian Board of Cooperation that year to aid northern California Indians in their struggles against the incompetent management and cruelties to native children by the Bureau of Indian Affairs at Round Valley. Over the next few years Collett's organization aided in Indian attempts to integrate public schools in Lake and Mendocino counties (Forbes 1969:92). Objecting to the inferior education provided by the Indian Service, native parents faced bitter opposition from local Whites. One Indian recalled: "I can remember those people on the school board yet. One woman just screamed, 'I don't want my children sitting next to any dirty Indians!' And a man yelled, 'we'll close the school.' Oh, my I'm telling you it hurt" (American Friends Service Committee 1957:14). In the early 1920s public education was "integrated" by partitioning off the classrooms and hiring a teacher for the Indians. Eventually several individual Pomoans sued the school district on their own and finally achieved their goal.

The issue of citizenship was also challenged in the courts when the Indian Board of Cooperation raised funds among Indians to support the attempt of Ethan Anderson, a Pomoan, to register to vote in Mendocino County. The case eventually reached the State Supreme Court and finally received a favorable decision, which established citizenship rights for nonreservation Indians (*Anderson* v. *Mathews*, 174. Cal., 537; 163 Pac., 902). Yet many traditionalists did not feel citizenship was a critical issue for native peoples. For instance, in 1919 the Society of American Indians, a national pan-Indian organization, held a conference in Minneapolis with the theme of citizenship (Hertzberg 1971:184). Cahuilla spiritual leader Francisco Patencio expressed these sentiments: "I hear that you want citizenship. I and my people we do not want citizenship. . . . What my people in California want is to know their reservation boundary lines. . . . My friends . . . you are different from my people. . . . for I know the thoughts and feelings of my old people" (Patencio 1943:64-65). Perhaps Patencio was more perceptive than many, realizing that voting rights and American court and justice systems would not greatly improve the lot of California Indians.

Attempts to improve living conditions were organized by the Society of Northern California Indians among nonreservation Pomoans, Konkow, Yuki, and Wailaki peoples. Under the direction of Rev. Father Raymond O.M. Cap of Saint Mary's Church in Ukiah, this group like many others combined welfare relief along with attempts to christianize (U.S. Board of Indian Commissioners 1920:69).

The early 1920s witnessed the evolution of the powerful Mission Indian Federation in southern California. The Federation was headed by a White man, Jonathan Tibbits of Riverside, but like the Indian Board of Cooperation, the Mission Indian Federation had a large body of Indian members. Non-Indians dominated many meetings and urged the membership to follow their advice. However, the Bureau of Indian Affairs soon grew intolerant of all these Indian concern groups and provoked an incident that served only to convince public opinion that indeed Indian grievances were legitimate. "At the Federation meetings expressions of ill will or hostility to the government were occasionally heard. Grievances were aired and complaints, both legitimate and trivial, were uttered. As a result and under orders of the Department of Justice, some 57 Indians were placed under arrest on the charge of conspiracy against the government. Upon arraignment they were dismissed without bail" (U.S. Board of Indian Commissioners 1922:22). These native people prepared to fight a long court case; however, with the granting of citizenship to American Indians in 1924, the government dropped all charges.

Throughout the next decade the Mission Indian Federation organized considerable opposition to allotment of reservation lands and promoted participation of women in tribal councils (fig. 3). The Federation went so far as to appoint reservation captains, judges, and police to challenge the BIA's authority. It eventually became embroiled in the land claims issues and ultimately in its bitterness called for the dismantling of the Bureau of Indian Affairs, calling all its enemies "communists" (Mission Indian Federation 1967).

Beginning in 1922 many Indian welfare organizations began separate efforts to sue the federal government over the illegal seizure of Indian lands in the nineteenth century and the failure of Congress to ratify the 18 treaties of 1851-1852. That year Collett's Indian Board of Cooperation organized "Indian auxiliaries" and began a campaign to collect $36 dues from every Indian man, woman, and child in northern California. Collett then went to Washington, D.C., and lobbied a bill that would use the Indian Board of Cooperation as a distributing agent for a per capita cash settlement of Indian claims. In November 1922, at a statewide meeting of auxiliary delegates in San Francisco, a major scandal was uncovered. Delegates were astonished to discover that a major part of the over $30,000 raised among the desperately poor Indians had been used to pay Collett's salary, travel, and personal expenses. This scandal caused many responsible leaders to break away from Collett and organize the California Indian Brotherhood. Nevertheless, Collett continued to work on "behalf of California Indians." In 1928 Collett was indicted for mail fraud as a result of his campaigns to solicit funds for his organiza-

Fig. 3. Adam Castillo, President of the Mission Indian Federation. Photographed about 1931.

tion. After two inconclusive trails Collett reportedly still attempted to collect funds for the land claims case in 1931, even though the state attorney general prosecuted the case for the Indians at no cost. In 1955 Collett was killed in an automobile accident (Heizer et al. 1969:61).

Perhaps the earliest all-Indian welfare and intertribal organization was the California Indian Brotherhood, led by the Pomoan Stephen Knight and by Albert James. Originally a group of disillusioned followers of Collett, they had acquired a membership of 3,000 native peoples from many northern California bands and tribes. Among the goals of this group organized in 1926 were: securing of small farms for all California tribes, public schooling with free lunch and clothing, and opportunities for college education for native youth (Heizer et al. 1969:61).

From 1925 until the Depression a landslide of welfare and civic groups commenced a concerted attack on the policies of the BIA, nationally and statewide. Joining Indian groups like the Brotherhood and the Mission Indian Federation, the Commonwealth Club of San Francisco, Native Sons of the Golden West, The Federated Women's Clubs, The California Indian Rights Association, The Women's Christian Temperance Union and John Collier's Indian Defense Association all pressed for reform of Indian policy and a bill that would allow native Californians to sue the government over the 18 unratified treaties. As a result of this considerable support, native peoples won the right to sue the government when Congress passed the Jurisdictional Act of 1928 (K.M. Johnson 1966).

Unfortunately the momentum of reform gained during the decade of the 1920s came to a rather abrupt end as the Depression deepened and widened throughout the American economic system. Although the New Deal's Indian reform managed to bring some relief, native California peoples grew dissatisfied over both the paternalistic Indian Reorganization Act of 1934 (almost every decision had to be approved by the secretary of the interior) and the unsatisfactory provisions of the Jurisdictional Act of 1928, which did not allow for per capita payments. Naturally, Indians, who were among the poorest people in the 1920s did not prosper in the 1930s. Much of the support of sympathetic Whites disappeared as they too became primarily concerned with survival. And finally the Second World War diverted both public and government attention from Indian affairs.

After the war, native groups in California were greatly disappointed with the outcome of their suit against the government, which granted the plaintiffs $5,024,842 after all offsets (K.M. Johnson 1966:80) in 1944. They began to organize both to amend the Jurisdictional Act of 1928 to make per capita payments and to draw up another claim against the government under provisions of the Indian Claims Act of 1946.

Native peoples discovered that little if any White support could be garnered for these issues. Instead nearly all non-Indians agreed that the federal trust and services to Indians should be ended as soon as possible. This so-called new policy was named termination. Three groups of Indians finally began separate suits against the federal government for further land claims from 1951 through 1959. In retrospect it seems unfortunate that so much Indian leadership, group capacity, and attention was focused on these claim issues in light of the unsatisfactory compromise settlement agreed to in 1964. These two issues, in which the BIA consistently and vehemently fought Indian interest, seriously crippled pan-tribal unity and left much bitterness with virtually everyone involved. While the battle against termination was important, it unfortunately diverted attention from other critical issues facing Indian peoples in California.

About 1964, as the second claims case (for lands not included earlier) came to another controversial conclusion with a compromise settlement of 29.1 million dollars, the BIA began to relent on its termination policy, and a new era in pan-tribal history began. Nationally the civil rights movement ushered in an era of social consciousness among White Americans. In conjunction with the end of the claims and termination issues among native leadership the climate was again ripe for reform in Indian affairs. In consequence a great many new pan-tribal groups organized at this time. One of the earliest of these groups was the American Indian Historical Society organized by Cahuilla tribal chairman Rupert Costo in 1964. The Historical Society early concentrated its efforts at protecting Indian burial sites as well as demanding reform in textbooks dealing with Indians. The California Indian Education Association founded in 1967 reflected pan-tribal concerns over the failure of primary and secondary education for Indian youth. Pan-tribal efforts to support college education for native youth resulted in the formation of Native American Studies departments on several major university and college campuses in California. Various Office of Economic Opportunity programs became available to reservation Indians through the creation of the Inter-tribal Council of California in 1968. Health services so long denied California Indians were restored under a pan-tribal health group called California Rural Indian Health Board organized in 1969 by Joe Carrillo, a Yokuts. Indian land issues became international news in November 1969 when a group called Indians of All Tribes occupied Alcatraz Island in the San Francisco Bay and held the site for nearly two years. Finally in a last minute effort to prevent payment for the 1964 claims settlement a group of California Indians with the support of the Achumawi tribe formed a group called California Indians For a Fair Settlement. Citing the fraudulent BIA vote among the Achumawi to accept the settlement this group representing Indians all over the state tried desperately to stop the payment and demanded instead a proposal to return surplus federal lands to the thousands of still landless California Indians. While this group failed to stop the payment, many members refused to cash the $633 payment checks and continued to demand land reform as an alternative to cash payments.

There can be no doubt that White welfare organizations have been and continue to be a factor in the history of pan-tribal associations. These groups appear to express concern and support periodically in the plight of native peoples, especially during prosperous economic times when Indian poverty and destitution stand in such shocking relief. Of course Indian concern in these matters has been constant. It is also interesting to note that in the past Whites have had considerable influence in policy making for pan-Indian groups while more modern groups have rejected this position, instead insisting on self-determination.

The issues concerning these groups have remained very much the same—land reform, cultural revitalization, water rights, quality health care, relevant education programs, and environmental concerns. While a considerable number of out-of-state Indians have chosen to live in California and have participated in many of these new organizations in the recent past, one fact must be kept in mind. All of these pan-tribal concerns among native California peoples have a single important purpose. That is to improve the quality of life for native people, as Indians themselves define a better life. That better life is not only for the individual but depends on the cultural survival of the band and tribe as well.

717

Contributors

This list gives the academic affiliations of authors at the time this volume went to press. Parenthetical tribal names identify Indian authors. The dates following the entries indicate when each manuscript was (1) first received; (2) accepted after all revisions had been made; and (3) sent to the author for final approval of editorial work.

BAUMHOFF, MARTIN A., Department of Anthropology, University of California, Davis. Environmental Background: 3/13/73; 4/22/75; 11/5/75.

BEAN, LOWELL JOHN, Department of Anthropology, California State University, Hayward. Western Pomo and Northeastern Pomo: 12/73; 3/28/76; 6/18/76. Gabrielino: 4/11/74; 10/9/74; 4/20/76. Luiseño: 9/11/72; 11/12/73; 4/21/76. Kitanemuk: 1/24/75; 6/30/75; 4/15/76. Serrano: 7/3/75; 10/15/75; 4/20/76. Cahuilla: 11/9/73; 10/9/74; 4/19/76. Cupeño: 11/19/73; 9/27/74; 4/15/76. Cults and Their Transformations: 12/16/75; 2/26/76; 4/23/76. Social Organization: 8/6/73; —; 10/11/74.

BLACKBURN, THOMAS C., Social Sciences Department, California State Polytechnic University, Pomona. Tataviam: 11/10/75; 1/22/76; 4/22/76. Kitanemuk: 1/24/75; 6/30/75; 4/15/76.

BRIGHT, WILLIAM, Department of Linguistics, University of California, Los Angeles. Karok: 5/3/72; 5/8/74; 8/27/74

CALLAGHAN, CATHERINE A., Department of Linguistics, Ohio State University, Columbus. Lake Miwok: 11/8/73; 4/11/75; 10/30/75.

CASTILLO, EDWARD D. (Cahuilla), Native American Studies Program, University of California, Berkeley. The Impact of Euro-American Exploration and Settlement: 9/24/73; 3/13/74; 10/11/74. Twentieth-Century Secular Movements: 8/27/74; 4/10/75; 4/15/76.

CLEWLOW, C. WILLIAM, JR., Institute of Archaeology, University of California, Los Angeles. Prehistoric Rock Art: 6/22/73; 9/12/73; 9/23/74.

COOK, SHERBURNE F. (deceased), Department of Physiology, University of California, Berkeley. Historical Demography: 5/12/72; 9/21/74; 9/23/74.

ELSASSER, ALBERT B., R.H. Lowie Museum of Anthropology, University of California, Berkeley. Development of Regional Prehistoric Cultures: 6/7/72; 8/24/74; 8/27/74. Wiyot: 10/19/72; 5/8/74; 8/27/74. Mattole, Nongatl, Sinkyone, Lassik, and Wailaki: 8/13/74; 10/31/74; 10/3/75. Basketry: 2/14/74; 3/14/74; 9/23/74.

GARTH, T. R., Los Gatos, California. Atsugewi: 6/23/72; 1/23/74; 8/27/74.

GOLDSCHMIDT, WALTER, Department of Anthropology, University of California, Los Angeles. Nomlaki: 7/17/72; 9/20/74; 11/3/75.

GOULD, RICHARD A., Department of Anthropology, University of Hawaii, Honolulu. Tolowa: 2/14/72; 3/14/74; 8/27/74.

GRANT, CAMPBELL, Santa Barbara Museum of Natural History, Santa Barbara. Chumash: Introduction: 6/13/72; 9/18/74; 9/23/74. Eastern Coastal Chumash: 6/9/72; 9/18/74; 9/23/74. Island Chumash: 6/9/72; 9/18/74; 9/23/74. Interior Chumash: 6/9/72; 9/18/74; 9/23/74.

GREENWOOD, ROBERTA S., Natural History Museum of Los Angeles County, Los Angeles. Obispeño and Purisimeño Chumash: 5/3/72; 9/18/74; 9/23/74.

HEIZER, ROBERT F., Department of Anthropology, University of California, Berkeley. Introduction: 11/22/74; 2/11/75; 4/19/76. History of Research: 9/17/75; 9/23/75; 4/16/76. Natural Forces and Native World View: 4/2/76; 4/4/76; 4/13/76. Mythology: Regional Patterns and History: 2/21/75; 3/12/75; 10/10/75. Trade and Trails: 1/2/74; 1/7/74; 8/15/75. Treaties: 10/24/72; 9/18/74; 9/23/74.

HESTER, THOMAS ROY, Division of Social Sciences, University of Texas, San Antonio. Esselen: 6/22/72; 1/24/75; 8/15/75. Salinan: 6/22/72; 1/24/75; 8/15/75.

JOHNSON, JERALD JAY, Department of Anthropology, California State University, Sacramento. Yana: 5/14/73; 9/13/73; 9/23/74.

JOHNSON, PATTI J., Department of Anthropology, University of California, Davis. Patwin: 11/6/72; 7/8/74; 9/17/75.

KELLY, ISABEL, Arizona State Museum, Tucson, and Tepepan, D.F., Mexico. Coast Miwok: 4/20/73; 9/25/74; 10/11/74.

KING, CHESTER, San Jose, California. Protohistoric and Historic Archeology: 6/23/72; 11/12/73; 9/17/75. Tataviam: 11/10/75; 1/22/76; 4/22/76.

LaPENA, FRANK R. (Wintu), Native American Studies/Art, Sacramento State University, Sacramento. Wintu: 9/1/72; 3/1/76; 4/20/76.

LEVY, RICHARD, Department of Anthropology, University of Kentucky, Lexington. Eastern Miwok: 5/12/75; 8/28/75; 12/30/75. Costanoan: 6/2/72; 1/3/73; 9/30/75.

LOWY, MICHAEL J., Stanford, California. Eastern Pomo and Southeastern Pomo: 3/22/76; 3/28/76; 6/21/76.

LUOMALA, KATHARINE, Department of Anthropology, University of Hawaii, Honolulu. Tipai and Ipai: 8/5/72; 5/5/75; 12/19/75.

MCCORKLE, THOMAS, Department of Anthropology, California State University, Long Beach. Intergroup Conflict: 6/26/72; 9/20/74; 9/23/74.

MCLENDON, SALLY, Department of Anthropology, Hunter College and the Graduate Center, City University of New York, New York. Pomo: Introduction: 3/22/76; 3/28/76; 4/28/76. Eastern Pomo and Southeastern Pomo: 3/22/76; 3/28/76; 6/21/76.

MILLER, VIRGINIA P., Department of Sociology and Anthropology, Dalhousie University, Halifax. Yuki, Huchnom, and Coast Yuki: 5/4/72; 9/19/75; 10/7/75.

MYERS, JAMES E., Department of Anthropology, California State University, Chico. Cahto: 6/20/72; 8/23/74; 8/27/74.

OLMSTED, D. L., Department of Anthropology, University of California, Davis. Achumawi: 8/28/72; 5/15/74; 8/27/74.

OSWALT, ROBERT L., California Indian Language Center, Kensington. Pomo: Introduction: 3/22/76; 3/28/76; 4/28/76.

PILLING, ARNOLD R., Department of Anthropology, Wayne State University, Detroit. Yurok: 8/2/72; 5/10/74; 8/27/74.

RIDDELL, FRANCIS A., Department of Parks and Recreation, State of California, Sacramento. Maidu and Konkow: 3/12/73; 8/31/74; 11/3/75.

SAWYER, JESSE O., Language Laboratory, University of California, Berkeley. Wappo: 5/5/73; 9/13/73; 8/27/74.

SCHUYLER, ROBERT L., Department of Anthropology, City College and the Graduate Center of the City University of New York, New York. Indian-Euro-American Interaction: Archeological Evidence from Non-Indian Sites: 7/10/72; 9/27/74; 10/11/74.

SHIPEK, FLORENCE C., San Diego, California. Luiseño: 9/11/72; 11/12/73; 4/21/76. History of Southern California Mission Indians: 11/9/73; 4/12/74; 4/21/76.

SHIPLEY, WILLIAM F., Board of Studies in Linguistics, Stevenson College, University of California, Santa Cruz. Native Languages of California: 9/26/72; 4/25/75; 9/19/75.

SILVER, SHIRLEY K., Department of Anthropology, Sonoma State College, Rohnert Park. Chimariko: 1/29/73; 7/9/74; 10/3/75. Shastan Peoples: 8/24/73; 8/28/74; 11/3/75.

SILVERSTEIN, MICHAEL, Department of Anthropology, University of Chicago, Chicago. Yokuts: Introduction: 8/23/74; 10/18/74; 9/24/75.

SMITH, CHARLES R., Berkeley, California. Tubatulabal: 11/28/72; 9/20/74; 9/23/74. Gabrielino: 4/11/74; 10/9/74; 4/20/76. Serrano: 7/3/75; 10/15/75; 4/20/76. Cupeño: 11/19/73; 9/27/74; 4/15/76.

SPIER, ROBERT F.G., Department of Anthropology, University of Missouri, Columbia. Monache: 6/4/73; 1/7/74; 9/24/75. Foothill Yokuts: 6/4/73; 1/7/74; 9/24/75.

STEWART, OMER C., Department of Anthropology, University of Colorado, Boulder. Achumawi: 8/28/72; 5/15/74; 8/27/74. Litigation and its Effects: 11/16/72; 2/5/75; 8/15/75.

THEODORATUS, DOROTHEA, Department of Anthropology, California State University, Sacramento. Western Pomo and Northeastern Pomo: 12/73; 3/28/76; 6/18/76.

TOWNE, ARLEAN H., Department of Parks and Recreation, State of California, Sacramento. Nisenan: 10/2/73; 8/27/74; 10/24/75.

VANE, SYLVIA BRAKKE, Department of Anthropology, California State University, Hayward. Cults and Their Transformations: 12/16/75; 2/26/76; 4/23/76.

WALLACE, EDITH, Redondo Beach, California. Sexual Status and Role Differences: 7/27/72; 9/27/74; 10/11/74.

WALLACE, WILLIAM J., Department of Anthropology (emeritus), California State University, Long Beach. Post-Pleistocene Archeology, 9000 to 2000 B.C.: 11/13/72; 9/20/74; 9/23/74. Hupa, Chilula, and Whilkut: 11/17/72; 5/8/74; 8/27/74. Southern Valley Yokuts: 4/29/74; 10/21/74; 9/24/75. Northern Valley Yokuts: 4/29/74; 10/21/74; 9/24/75. Music and Musical Instruments: 2/27/72; 8/24/74; 8/27/74. Comparative Literature: 7/27/72; 9/18/74; 9/23/74.

WILSON, NORMAN L., Department of Parks and Recreation, State of California, Sacramento. Nisenan: 10/2/73; 8/27/74; 10/24/75.

Bibliography

This list includes all references cited in the volume, arranged in alphabetical order according to the names of the authors as they appear in the citations in the text. Multiple works by the same author are arranged chronologically; second and subsequent titles by the same author in the same year are differentiated by letters added to the dates. Where more than one author with the same surname is cited, one has been arbitrarily selected for text citation by surname alone throughout the volume, while the others are always cited with added initials; the combination of surname with date in text citations should avoid confusion. Where a publication date is different from the series date (as in some annual reports and the like), the former is used. Dates, authors, and titles that do not appear on the original works are enclosed by square brackets. For manuscripts, dates refer to time of composition. For publications reprinted or first published many years after original composition, a bracketed date after the title refers to the time of composition or the date of original publication.

ARCIA - Commissioner of Indian Affairs
1849-   Annual Reports to the Secretary of the Interior. Washington: U.S. Government Printing Office. (Reprinted: AMS Press, New York, 1976-1977.)

Abella, Ramon, and Jean Saenz de Lucio
1924   [Reply to the Interrogatorio of 1812, Mission San Francisco.] Pp. 147-153 in San Francisco or Mission Dolores, by Zephyrin Engelhardt. Chicago: Franciscan Herald Press.

Aginsky, Burt W.
1939   Population Control in the Shanel (Pomo) Tribe. American Sociological Review 10(2):209-216.

1943   Culture Element Distributions, XXIV: Central Sierra. University of California Anthropological Records 8(4):393-468. Berkeley.

1958   The Evolution of American Indian Culture: A Method and Theory. Pp. 79-87 in Proceedings of the 32d International Congress of Americanists. Copenhagen, 1956.

1968   The Pomo. P. 210 in Vol. 18 of Encyclopaedia Britannica. 14th ed. Chicago: Encyclopaedia Britannica Company.

Aginsky, Burt W., and Ethel G. Aginsky
1947   A Resultant of Intercultural Relations. Social Forces 26(1):84-87.

1967   Deep Valley. New York: Stein and Day.

Aldrich, Fay G., and Ida McBride
1939   Ancient Legends of the California Indians of the Redwood Empire. Orick, Calif.: Privately Published.

Alexander, Hartley B., ed.
1916   North American [Mythology]. Vol. 10 of The Mythology of All Races. L.H. Gray, ed. 13 vols. Boston: Marshall Jones.

American Friends Service Committee see Friends, Society of

Amorós, Juan
1950   Reply of Mission San Carlos Borromeo to the Questionnaire of the Spanish Government in 1812 Concerning the Native Culture of the California Mission Indians. Maynard Geiger, ed. The Americas: A Quarterly Review of Inter-American Cultural History 6(4):467-486.

Anderson, E.
1956   The Hoopa Valley Indian Reservation in Northwestern California: A Study on its Origins. (Unpublished M.A. Thesis in Anthropology, University of California, Berkeley.)

Anderson, Edgar
1956   Man as a Maker of New Plants and New Plant Communities. Pp. 763-777 in Man's Role in Changing the Face of the Earth. William L. Thomas, Jr., ed. Chicago and London: University of Chicago Press.

Anderson, Eugene N., Jr.
1964   A Bibliography of the Chumash and their Predecessors. University of California Archaeological Survey Reports 61:25-74. Berkeley.

Anderson, Robert A.
1909   Fighting the Mill Creeks: Being a Personal Account of Campaigns against Indians of the Northern Sierras. Chico, Calif.: Record Press.

Andrews, Ralph W.
1960   Indian Primitive. Seattle, Wash.: Superior Publishing Company.

Andrews, Roy C.
1916   Whale Hunting with Gun and Camera: A Naturalist's Account of the Modern Shore-Whaling Industry, of Whales and their Habits and of the Hunting Experiences in Various Parts of the World. New York: D. Appleton.

Angel, J. Lawrence
1966   Early Skeletons from Tranquillity, California. Smithsonian Contributions to Anthropology 2(1). Washington.

Angulo, Jaime de
1926   The Background of the Religious Feeling in a Primitive Tribe. American Anthropologist 28(2):352-360.

1926a   Two Parallel Modes of Conjugation in the Pit River Language. American Anthropologist 28(1):273-274.

1927   Textes en langue Pomo (Californie). Journal de la Société des Américanistes de Paris n.s. 19:129-144.

1928   La Psychologie religieuse des Achumawi. Anthropos 23(1-2):141-166, (3-4):561-589.

1928a   Konomihu Vocabulary, Obtained at Selma, Oregon. (Manuscript No. 30H1c:5 in American Philosophical Society Collection of Materials Relating to the American Indian, Philadelphia.)

[1930]   The Achumawi, a Primitive Tribe of California. (Unpublished Manuscript in Possession of D.L. Olmsted.)

1935   Pomo Creation Myth. Journal of American Folk-Lore 48(189): 203-262.

[1935a]   The Reminiscences of a Pomo Chief: The Autobiography of William Ralganal Benson. (Manuscript No. H5.3 in Boas Collection, American Philosophical Society Library, Philadelphia.)

[1935b]   The Pomo Language, II: Yakaya. (Manuscript No. 5H.1 in Boas Collection, American Philosophical Society Library, Philadelphia.)

Angulo, Jaime de, and Marguerite Béclard d'Harcourt
1931   La Musique des Indiens de la Californie du Nord. Journal de la Société des Américanistes de Paris n.s. 23(1):189-228.

Angulo, Jaime de, and Lucy S. Freeland
1928   Miwok and Pomo Myths. Journal of American Folk-Lore 41(160): 232-252.

1928-1930   The Shasta Language. (Manuscript No. 30H1c:1 in American Philosophical Society Collection of Materials Relating to the American Indian, Philadelphia.)

1931   The Achumawi Language. International Journal of American Linguistics 6(2):77-120.

721

1931a Two Achumawi Tales. *Journal of American Folk-Lore* 44(172):125-136.

1931b Karok Texts. *International Journal of American Linguistics* 6(3-4):194-226.

Anonymous
1851 Sacramento Intelligence. [Article on Reprisal of Maidu Indians at Hock Farm against Colusi Indians.] *The Daily Alta California,* July 30. Alta, Calif.

1852 [Two Letters from "J.N.C." of Colusa, Dated April 5 and April 10 on the Origin of the Name of "Colusa", and Description of a Dance.] *Sacramento Union.* Sacramento, Calif.

1860 Majority and Minority Reports of the Special Joint Committee on the Mendocino War. In Appendix to the Journals of the 11th Session of the Legislature of the State of California. Sacramento.

1882 History of Humboldt County, California. San Francisco: Wallace W. Elliott.

1893 [At Weitchpec.] *Arcata Union,* September 23:2. Arcata, Calif.

1893a [A.H. Hill.] *Arcata Union,* September 9:3. Arcata, Calif.

1923 Mission Indians Open Convention: Red Men Discuss Affairs; Mission Indians at Convention in Riverside Protest Proposed Allotment of Lands. *Los Angeles Times,* May 2, Pt.2:10. Los Angeles.

1959 Yokuts Trail Becomes a Freeway. *Quarterly Bulletin of the Tulare County Historical Society* 39. Los Tulares, Calif.

1968 A Landscape of the Past: The Story of the Royal Presidio Excavations. *Journal of San Diego History* 14(4):5-32.

1968a Treasures of the Lowie Museum: An Exhibition of the Robert H. Lowie Museum of Anthropology..., January 2 - October 17, 1968. Berkeley: University of California Printing Department.

1969 Third Annual Klamath Salmon Festival/New Townsite Dedication, June 29, 1969. Klamath, Calif.: Klamath Chamber of Commerce.

1969a Medicine Woman. *Times-Standard,* January 23:1-2. Eureka, Calif.

1970 Archeological Remains Concern of Area Indians. *Del Norte Triplicate,* June 24:9. Crescent City, Calif.

1971 Kern Canyon Yields Traces of Early Tribe. *Oakland Tribune,* August 8:3-A. Oakland, Calif.

[1972] California Rancheria Task Force Report. (Unpublished Report in Sacramento Area Office, Bureau of Indian Affairs, Sacramento, Calif.)

Anthony, E.M.
1869 Reminiscences in Siskiyou County. (Unpublished Manuscript in Bancroft Library, University of California, Berkeley.)

Anza, Juan Bautista de
1930 Anza's Diary of the Second Anza Expedition, 1775-1776. Pp. 1-200 in Vol. 3 of Anza's California Expeditions. Herbert E. Bolton, ed. 5 vols. Berkeley: University of California Press.

Aoki, Haruo
1963 On Sahaptian-Klamath Linguistic Affiliations. *International Journal of American Linguistics* 29(2):107-112.

Apperson, Eva M.
1971 We Knew Ishi. Red Bluff, Calif.: Walker Lithograph Company.

Applegate, Richard B.
1975 Modes of Reduplication in Ineseño Chumash. In Hokan Studies: Papers from the First Conference on Hokan Languages, 1970. Margaret Langdon and Shirley K. Silver, eds. *Janua Linguarum, Series Practica* 181. The Hague: Mouton.

Arguello, D. Antonio
1821 Diario formado en la expedicion emprendida al diez y siete de Oct (ubre) de 1821, de los acaecimientos occuridos, en ella desde su principio hasta su conclusion. (Manuscript in Bancroft Library, University of California, Berkeley.)

Armstrong, A.N.
1857 Oregon: Comprising a Brief History and Full Description of the Territories of Oregon and Washington; Resources, Climate, Indian Tribes, Interspersed with Incidents of Travel and Adventure. Chicago: Chas. Scott.

Arroyo de la Cuesta, Felipe
1821 Idiomas Californias. (Manuscript in Bancroft Library, University of California, Berkeley.)

1861 Extracto de la grammatica Mutsun, ó de la lengua de los naturales de la Mission San Juan Bautista: Grammar of the Mutsun Language Spoken at the Mission of San Juan Bautista, Alta California. (Shea's Library of American Linguistics 4) New York: Cramoisy Press.

1862 A Vocabulary or Phrase Book of the Mutsun Language of Alta California. (Shea's Library of American Linguistics 8) New York: Cramoisy Press.

Asisara, Lorenzo
1877 Memorias de la historia de California. (Manuscript in Bancroft Library, University of California, Berkeley.)

Azpell, Thomas F.
1877 Klamath. Pp. 463, 465, 467, 469 and 471 in *Contributions to North American Ethnology* 3. Washington: U.S. Geographical and Geological Survey of the Rocky Mountain Region.

Bada, Jeffrey L., Roy A. Schroeder, and George F. Carter
1974 New Evidence for the Antiquity of Man in North America Deduced from Aspartic Acid Racemization. *Science* 184(4138):791-793.

Baker, Bob
1967 Americans in Bondage. Fairfax, Calif.: Friends of the Yurok Indians.

Balbi, Adriano
1826 Atlas ethnographique du globe. 2 vols. Paris: Rey et Gravier.

Baldwin, M.A.
1971 Culture Continuity from Chumash to Salinan Indians in California. (Unpublished M.A. Thesis in Anthropology, San Diego State College, San Diego, Calif.)

Bancroft, Hubert H.
1874-1876 The Native Races of the Pacific States of North America. 5 vols. New York: D. Appleton.

1886 Pioneer Register and Index. (Detached from Vols. 2-5 of Bancroft's History of California.) San Francisco: The History Company.

1886-1888 The History of Oregon. 2 vols. San Francisco: The History Company.

1886-1890 The History of California. 7 vols. San Francisco: The History Company.

1888 California Inter-Pocula. (The Works of Hubert H. Bancroft, Vol. 35.) San Francisco: The History Company.

Barker, M.A.R.
1963 Klamath Dictionary. *University of California Publications in Linguistics* 31. Berkeley.

Barnett, Homer G.
1940 Culture Processes. *American Anthropologist* 42(1):21-48.

1957   Indian Shakers: A Messianic Cult of the Pacific Northwest. Carbondale: Southern Illinois University Press.

Barrett, Samuel A.

1904   The Pomo in the Sacramento Valley of California. *American Anthropologist* n.s. 6(1):189-190.

1906   A Composite Myth of the Pomo Indians. *Journal of American Folk-Lore* 19(72):37-51.

1908   The Ethnogeography of Pomo and Neighboring Indians. *University of California Publications in American Archaeology and Ethnology* 6(1):1-332. Berkeley.

1908a   Pomo Indian Basketry. *University of California Publications in American Archaeology and Ethnology* 7(3):134-308. Berkeley.

1908b   The Geography and Dialects of the Miwok Indians. *University of California Publications in American Archaeology and Ethnology* 6(2):333-368. Berkeley.

1916   Pomo Buildings. Pp. 1-17 in Holmes Anniversary Volume: Anthropological Essays Presented to William Henry Holmes in Honor of his 70th Birthday. Washington: J.W. Bryan Press.

1917   Ceremonies of the Pomo Indians. *University of California Publications in American Archaeology and Ethnology* 12(10): 397-441. Berkeley.

1917a   Pomo Bear Doctors. *University of California Publications in American Archaeology and Ethnology* 12(11):443-465. Berkeley.

1919   Myths of the Southern Sierra Miwok. *University of California Publications in American Archaeology and Ethnology* 16(1): 1-28. Berkeley.

1919a   The Wintun Hesi Ceremony. *University of California Publications in American Archaeology and Ethnology* 14(4):437-448. Berkeley.

1933   Pomo Myths. *Bulletin of the Public Museum of the City of Milwaukee* 15. Milwaukee, Wis.

1952   Material Aspects of Pomo Culture. *Bulletin of the Public Museum of the City of Milwaukee* 20(1-2). Milwaukee, Wis.

1963   The Jump Dance at Hupa, 1962. *Kroeber Anthropological Society Papers* 28:73-85. Berkeley, Calif.

Barrett, Samuel A., and Edward W. Gifford

1933   Miwok Material Culture. *Bulletin of the Public Museum of the City of Milwaukee* 2(4):117-376. Milwaukee, Wis.

Barrows, David P.

1900   The Ethno-botany of the Coahuilla Indians of Southern California. Chicago: University of Chicago Press. (Reprinted: Malki Museum Press, Banning, Calif., 1971.)

Bartlett, John R.

1854   Personal Narrative of Explorations and Incidents in Texas, New Mexico, California, Sonora, and Chihuahua, Connected with the United States and Mexican Boundary Commission, during the Years 1850, '51, and '53. 2 vols. New York: Appleton.

Baumhoff, Martin A.

1955   Excavations of Site Teh-1 (Kingsley Cave). *University of California Archaeological Survey Reports* 33:40-72. Berkeley.

1958   California Athabascan Groups. *University of California Anthropological Records* 16(5):157-238. Berkeley.

1963   Ecological Determinants of Aboriginal California Populations. *University of California Publications in American Archaeology and Ethnology* 49(2):155-236. Berkeley.

Baumhoff, Martin A., and J.S. Byrne

1959   Desert Side-notched Points as a Time Marker in California. *University of California Archaeological Survey Reports* 48:32-65. Berkeley.

Baumhoff, Martin A., and Albert B. Elsasser

1956   Summary of Archaeological Survey and Excavation in California. *University of California Archaeological Survey Reports* 33(1):1-27. Berkeley.

Baumhoff, Martin A., and Robert F. Heizer

1958   Outland Coiled Basketry from the Caves of West Central Nevada. Pp. 49-59 in Current Views on Great Basin Archaeology. *University of California Archaeological Survey Reports* 42. Berkeley.

Baumhoff, Martin A., and David L. Olmsted

1963   Palaihnihan: Radiocarbon Support for Glottochronology. *American Anthropologist* 65(2):278-284.

1964   Notes on Palaihnihan Culture History: Glottochronology and Archaeology. Pp. 1-12 in Studies in Californian Linguistics. William Bright, ed. *University of California Publications in Linguistics* 34. Berkeley.

Baumhoff, Martin A., Robert F. Heizer, and Albert B. Elsasser

1958   The Lagomarsino Petroglyph Group (Site-26-St-1) near Virginia City, Nevada. *University of California Archaeological Survey Reports* 43(2). Berkeley.

Beals, Ralph L.

1933   Ethnology of the Nisenan. *University of California Publications in American Archaeology and Ethnology* 31(6):335-414. Berkeley.

Beals, Ralph L., and Joseph A. Hester, Jr.

1958   A Lacustrine Economy in California. Pp. 211-217 in Miscellanea Paul Rivet Octogenario Dicata, 31st International Congress of Americanists. 2 vols. México, D.F.: Universidad Nacional Autónoma de México.

1960   A New Ecological Typology of the California Indians. Pp. 411-419 in Men and Cultures: Selected Papers of the 5th International Congress of Anthropological and Ethnological Sciences. A.F.C. Wallace, ed. Philadelphia, 1956. Philadelphia: University of Pennsylvania Press. (Reprinted in The California Indians, by R.F. Heizer and M.A. Whipple, University of California Press, Berkeley, 1971.)

Beals, Ralph L., and Harry Hoijer

1965   An Introduction to Anthropology. 3d ed. New York: Macmillan.

Bean, Lowell J.

1960-1971   [Ethnographic Fieldnotes.] (Manuscript in Bean's Possession.)

1962-1972   [Serrano Fieldnotes.] (Manuscript in Bean's Possession.)

1964   Cultural Change in Cahuilla Religious and Political Leadership Patterns. Pp.1-10 in Culture Change and Stability. Ralph L. Beals, ed. Los Angeles: University of California Press.

[1968]   [Fieldnotes on the Southwestern Pomo.] (Manuscript in Bean's Possession.)

1972   Mukat's People: The Cahuilla Indians of Southern California. Berkeley and Los Angeles: University of California Press.

1973   [Ethnographic Fieldnotes on the Cupeño, 1960-1973.] (Manuscript in Bean's Possession.)

1975   Power and its Application in Native California. *Journal of California Anthropology* 2(1):25-33.

1976   California Indian Shamanism and Folk Curing. In American Folk Medicine: A Symposium. Wayland Hand, ed. Berkeley and Los Angeles: University of California Press. In Press.

[1977] Morongo Indian Reservation: A Century of Adaptive Strategies. In American Indian Economic Development. Sam Stanley, ed. The Hague: Mouton. In Press.

Bean, Lowell J., and Thomas F. King, eds.
1974 Antap: California Indian Political and Economic Organization. *Ballena Press Anthropological Papers* 2. Ramona, Calif.

Bean, Lowell J., and Harry W. Lawton
1965 The Cahuilla Indians of Southern California. Banning, Calif.: Malki Museum Press.

————, comps.
1967 A Bibliography of the Cahuilla Indians of California. Banning, Calif.: Malki Museum Press.

1973 Some Explanations for the Rise of Cultural Complexity in Native California with Comments on Proto-Agriculture and Agriculture. Pp.v-xlvii in Patterns of Indian Burning in California: Ecology and Ethno-history, by Henry Lewis. *Ballena Press Anthropological Papers* 1. Ramona, Calif.

Bean, Lowell J., and William M. Mason
1962 Diaries and Accounts of the Romero Expeditions in Arizona and California, 1823-1826. Los Angeles: W. Ritchie Press.

Bean, Lowell J., and Katherine S. Saubel
1972 Temalpakh (from the Earth): Cahuilla Indian Knowledge and Usage of Plants. Banning, Calif.: Malki Museum Press.

Bean, Walton
1973 California: An Interpretive History. 2d ed. New York: McGraw-Hill.

Beardsley, Richard K.
1948 Culture Sequences in Central California Archaeology. *American Antiquity* 14(1):1-28.

1954 Temporal and Areal Relationships in Central California. 2 Pts. *University of California Archaeological Survey Reports* 24-25. Berkeley.

Beattie, George W.
1929 Spanish Plans for an Inland Chain of Missions in California. *Historical Society of Southern California Annual Publication* 14:243-264. Los Angeles.

1930 California's Unbuilt Missions: Spanish Plans for an Inland Chain. Los Angeles: n.p.

Beattie, George W., and Helen P. Beattie
1939 Heritage of the Valley: San Bernardino's First Century. Pasadena, Calif.: San Pasqual Press.

Beechey, Frederick W.
1968 Narrative of a Voyage to the Pacific and Bering's Strait [1831]. New York: Da Capo.

Beeler, Madison S.
1954 Sonoma, Carquinez, Ununhum, Coloma: Some Disputed California Names. *Western Folklore* 13(4):368-377.

1955 Saclan. *International Journal of American Linguistics* 21(3): 201-209.

1959 Saclan once more. *International Journal of American Linguistics* 25(1):67-68.

1961 Northern Costanoan. *International Journal of American Linguistics* 27(3):191-197.

1970 Sibilant Harmony in Chumash. *International Journal of American Linguistics* 36(1):14-17.

1971 Nopṭinṭe Yokuts. Pp. 11-76 in Studies in American Indian Languages. Jesse Sawyer, ed. *University of California Publications in Linguistics* 65. Berkeley.

1972 Interior Chumash. (Paper Read at the Annual Meeting of the Southwestern Anthropological Association, Long Beach, Calif., 1972.)

1975 Barbareño Chumash Grammar: A Farrago. In Hokan Studies: Papers from the First Conference on Hokan Languages, 1970. Margaret Langdon and Shirley K. Silver, eds. *Janua Linguarum, Series Practica* 181. The Hague: Mouton.

Beeler, Madison S., and Kathryn Klar
1974 Interior Chumash. (Manuscript in Beeler's Possession.)

Benedict, Ruth (Fulton)
1924 A Brief Sketch of Serrano Culture. *American Anthropologist* 26(3):366-392.

1926 Serrano Tales. *Journal of American Folk-Lore* 39(151):1-17.

Bennyhoff, James A.
1950 Californian Fish Spears and Harpoons. *University of California Anthropological Records* 9(4):295-337. Berkeley.

1950a Patwin and Coast Miwok Ethnogeography. (Manuscript in University of California, Department of Anthropology, Berkeley.)

1953 High Altitude Occupation in the Yosemite Park Region. *University of California Archaeological Survey Reports* 21(App. B):31-32. Berkeley.

1956 An Appraisal of the Archaeological Resources of Yosemite National Park. *University of California Archaeological Survey Reports* 34:1-71. Berkeley.

1961 The Ethnogeography of the Plains Miwok. (Unpublished Ph.D. Dissertation in Anthropology, University of California, Berkeley.)

Bennyhoff, James A., and Albert B. Elsasser
1954 Sonoma Mission: An Historical and Archaeological Study of Primary Constructions, 1823-1913. *University of California Archaeological Survey Reports* 27:1-81. Berkeley.

Bennyhoff, James A., and Robert F. Heizer
1958 Cross-dating Great Basin Sites by Californian Shell Beads. *University of California Archaeological Survey Reports* 42:60-92. Berkeley.

Benson, William R.
1932 The Stone and Kelsey Massacre on the Shores of Clear Lake in 1849. *Quarterly of the California Historical Society* 11(3):266-273. San Francisco.

Berger, Rainer, Reiner Protsch, Richard Reynolds, Charles Rozaire, and James R. Sackett
1971 New Radiocarbon Dates Based on Bone Collagen of California Paleoindians. Pp. 43-49 in The Application of the Physical Sciences to Archaeology. Fred H. Stross, ed. *Contributions of the University of California Archaeological Research Facility* 12. Berkeley.

Beroza, Barbara
[1974] Sources for California Ethnohistory, 1542-1850. Berkeley: University of California Archaeological Research Facility.

Berton, Francis
[1880] Vocabulaire des Indiens de la vallée de Napa et du Clear Lake en Californie, rédigé en 1851. *Ban-Zai-Sau* 5. Geneva, Switzerland.

Bidwell, John
[1906] Echoes of the Past: An Account of the First Emigrant Train to California, Fremont in the Conquest of California, the Discovery of Gold and Early Reminiscences by the Late General John Bidwell. Chico, Calif.: Chico Advertiser.

Biswell, Harold H.
1967 The Use of Fire in Wildlife Management in California. Pp. 71-86 in Natural Resources: Quality and Quantity.

724

S.V. Ciriacy-Wantrup and J.J. Parsons, eds. Berkeley and Los Angeles: University of California Press.

Blackburn, Thomas C.
1962-1963   Ethnohistoric Descriptions of Gabrieliño Material Culture. *Annual Reports of the University of California Archaeological Survey* 5:1-50. Los Angeles.

————
1974   Ceremonial Integration and Social Interaction in Aboriginal California. Pp. 93-110 in Antap: California Indian Political and Economic Organization. Lowell J. Bean and Thomas F. King, eds. *Ballena Press Anthropological Papers* 2. Ramona, Calif.

————, ed.
1975   December's Child: A Book of Chumash Oral Narratives. Berkeley: University of California Press.

Bledsoe, Anthony J.
1881   History of Del Norte County, California. Eureka, Calif.: Wyman. (Reprinted: Wendy's Books, Crescent City, Calif., 1971.)

————
1885   Indian Wars of the Northwest: A California Sketch. San Francisco: Bacon. (Reprinted: Biobooks, Oakland, Calif., 1956.)

Boas, Franz
1896   Anthropometric Observations on the Mission Indians of Southern California. Pp. 261-269 in *Proceedings of the American Association for the Advancement of Science for 1895*. Vol. 44. Salem, Mass.

Bolton, Herbert E., ed.
1925   Spanish Exploration in the Southwest, 1542-1706. New York: Charles Scribner's Sons.

————, ed.
1930   Anza's California Expeditions. 5 vols. Berkeley: University of California Press.

Boscana, Geronimo
1846   Chinigchinich: A Historical Account of the Origin, Customs and Traditions of the Indians at the Missionary Establishment of St. Juan Capistrano, Alta California; Called the Acagchemem Nation. A. Robinson, trans. Pp. 230-341 in Life in California, by Alfred Robinson. New York: Wiley and Putnam.

————
1933   Chinigchinich: A Revised and Annotated Version of Alfred Robinson's Translation of Father Geronimo Boscana's Historical Account of the Belief, Usages, Customs and Extravagencies[!] of the Indians of this Mission of San Juan Capistrano Called the *Acagchemem* Tribe [1846]. P.T. Hanna, ed. Santa Ana, Calif.: Fine Arts Press.

Bourke, John G.
1889   Notes on the Cosmogony and Theogony of the Mojave Indians of the Rio Colorado, Arizona. *Journal of American Folk-Lore* 2(6):169-189.

Bowers, Stephen
1878   Santa Rosa Island. Pp. 316-320 in *Annual Report of the Smithsonian Institution for the Year 1877*. Washington.

————
1897   The Santa Barbara Indians. (Unpublished Manuscript in Southwest Museum, Los Angeles.)

Bowman, J.N.
1958   The Resident Neophytes of the California Missions, 1769-1834. *Quarterly of the Historical Society of Southern California* 40(2):138-148. Los Angeles.

————
1965   The Names of the California Missions. *The Americas: A Quarterly Review of Inter-American Cultural History* 21(4):363-374.

Boyle, Maida B.
1968   San Luís [Rey] Mission Report on the Historical and Archaeological Study of its Primary Construction and Indian Villages Associated with it (1789-1913). (Manu-

script in Robert L. Schuyler's Possession and in San Luís Rey Mission.)

Brabender, I.
1965   Die paläobiologische Rekonstruktion zweier prähistorischer Bevölkerungen aus Kalifornien. (Unpublished Ph.D. Dissertation in Archaeology, University of Mainz, Germany.)

Brand, Donald D.
1935   Prehistoric Trade in the Southwest. *New Mexico Business Review* 4(4):202-209.

————
1938   Aboriginal Trade Routes for Sea Shells in the Southwest. *Yearbook of the Association of Pacific Coast Geographers* 4:3-10. Cheney, Wash.

Brandes, Raymond
1966   First Summary Report on the University of San Diego Project at Mission San Diego de Alcalá, Summer Session 1966. (Mimeographed Report in the Department of History, University of San Diego, San Diego, Calif.)

————
1967   Second, Third, and Fourth Summary Report on the University of San Diego Project at Mission San Diego de Alcalá. (Mimeographed Report in the Department of History, University of San Diego, San Diego, Calif.)

Bremner, Carl St. J.
1932   Geology of Santa Cruz Island, Santa Barbara County, California. *Santa Barbara Museum of Natural History Occasional Papers* 1. Santa Barbara, Calif.

————
1933   Geology of San Miguel Island, Santa Barbara County, California. *Santa Barbara Museum of Natural History Occasional Papers* 2. Santa Barbara, Calif.

Breschini, Gary S.
1972   The Indians of Monterey County. *Quarterly of the Monterey County Archaeological Society* 2:1-48. Carmel, Calif.

Bright, Jane O.
[1962-1963]   [Linguistic Notes, from approximately 6 Months' Fieldwork among the Smith River (Tolowa) Indians, California.] (Manuscripts in Possession of Victor Golla, George Washington University, Washington.)

————
1964   The Phonology of Smith River Athapaskan (Tolowa). *International Journal of American Linguistics* 30(2):101-107.

Bright, Jane O., and William Bright
1965   Semantic Structures in Northwestern California and the Sapir-Whorf Hypothesis. *American Anthropologist* 67(5):249-258.

Bright, William
1954   Some Northern Hokan Relationships: A Preliminary Report. Pp. 63-67 in Papers from the Symposium on American Indian Linguistics Held at Berkeley July 7, 1951. *University of California Publications in Linguistics* 10. Berkeley.

————
1954a   The Travels of Coyote: A Karok Myth. *Kroeber Anthropological Society Papers* 11:1-17. Berkeley, Calif.

————
1957   The Karok Language. *University of California Publications in Linguistics* 13. Berkeley.

————
1958   Karok Names. *Names* 8:172-179.

————
1960   Animals of Acculturation in the California Indian Languages. *University of California Publications in Linguistics* 4(4):215-246. Berkeley.

————, ed.
1964   Studies in Californian Linguistics. *University of California Publications in Linguistics* 34. Berkeley.

————
1965   The History of the Cahuilla Sound System. *International Journal of American Linguistics* 31(3):241-244.

1965a   A Field Guide to Southern California Languages. *Annual Reports of the University of California Archaeological Survey* 7:389-408. Los Angeles.

1968   A Luiseño Dictionary. *University of California Publications in Linguistics* 51. Berkeley.

1975   Two Notes on Takic Classification: Paper Read at the Third Annual Friends of Uto-Aztecan Conference, Flagstaff, June 19-20, 1975. (Copy, Manuscript No. 76-66 in National Anthropological Archives, Smithsonian Institution, Washington.)

1975a   The Alliklik Mystery. *Journal of California Anthropology* 2(2):228-230.

Bright, William, and Elizabeth Bright
1959   Spanish Words in Patwin. *Romance Philology* 13(2):161-164.

Bright, William, and Jane Hill
1967   The Linguistic History of the Cupeño. Pp. 351-371 in Studies in Southwestern Linguistics. Dell Hymes, with William E. Bittle, eds. The Hague and Paris: Mouton.

Bright, William, and David L. Olmsted
1959   A Shasta Vocabulary. *Kroeber Anthropological Society Papers* 20:1-55. Berkeley, Calif.

Broadbent, Sylvia M.
1964   The Southern Sierra Miwok Language. *University of California Publications in Linguistics* 38. Berkeley.

1972   The Rumsen of Monterey: An Ethnography from Historical Sources. Pp. 45-93 in Miscellaneous Papers on Archaeology. *University of California Archaeological Research Facility Contributions* 14. Berkeley.

Broadbent, Sylvia M., and Catherine A. Callaghan
1960   Comparative Miwok: A Preliminary Survey. *International Journal of American Linguistics* 26(4):301-316.

Broadbent, Sylvia M., and Harvey Pitkin
1964   A Comparison of Miwok and Wintun. Pp. 19-45 in Studies in Californian Linguistics. William Bright, ed. *University of California Publications in Linguistics* 34. Berkeley.

Brookings Institution, Washington. Institute for Government Research
1928   The Problem of Indian Administration; Report of a Survey Made at the Request of Hon. Hubert Work, Secretary of the Interior; Survey Staff: Lewis Merriam, Ray A. Brown, Henry R. Cloud, and Edward E. Dale. Baltimore: Johns Hopkins Press.

Brown, Alan K.
1967   The Aboriginal Population of the Santa Barbara Channel. *University of California Archaeological Survey Reports* 69:1-99. Berkeley.

Brown, Vinson, and Douglas Andrews
1969   The Pomo Indians of California and their Neighbors. Albert B. Elsasser, ed. Healdsburg, Calif.: Naturegraph Publishers.

Browne, J. Ross
1944   The Indians of California. San Francisco: Colt Press.

Bruff, Joseph G.
1949   Gold Rush: The Journals, Drawings, and other Papers of J. Goldsborough Bruff, April 2, 1849 to July 20, 1851. Georgia W. Read and Ruth Gaines, eds. New York: Columbia University Press.

Bryant, Edwin
1849   What I Saw in California: Being the Journal of a Tour by the Emigrant Route and South Pass of the Rocky Mountains, across the Continent of North America, the Great Desert Basin, and through California in the Years 1846-1847. 5th ed. New York: D. Appleton.

Buchanan, R.C.
1857   Report. Pp. 23-26 in Indian Affairs on the Pacific: Reports on the Number, Characteristics etc. of the Indians in the Department of the Pacific. U.S. Congress. House. 34th Cong., 3d sess. House Executive Document No. 76. (Serial No. 906) Washington: U.S. Government Printing Office.

Buffum, Edward G.
1850   Six Months in the Gold Mines: From a Journal of Three Years' Residence in Upper and Lower California, in 1847-8-9. London: R. Bentley.

Bunnell, Lafayette H.
1911   The Discovery of the Yosemite and the Indian War of 1851, which Led to that Event [1880]. 4th ed. Los Angeles: G.W. Gerlicher.

Burnett, E.K.
1944   Inlaid Stone and Bone Artifacts from Southern California. *Contributions from the Museum of the American Indian, Heye Foundation* 13. New York.

Burns, L.M.
1901   "Digger" [Shasta] Indian Legends. *Land of Sunshine* 14(2):130-134, (3):223-226, (4):310-314, (5):397-402.

Burrows, Jack
1971   The Vanished Miwoks of California. *Montana: The Magazine of Western History* 21(1):28-39.

Bushnell, John H.
1968   From American Indian to Indian American: The Changing Identity of the Hupa. *American Anthropologist* 70(6):1108-1116.

California. Department of Industrial Relations, Division of Labor Statistics and Research
1965   American Indians in California. San Francisco: Fair Employment Practice Commission, Division of Fair Employment Practices.

California. Legislature. Senate and Assembly
1851   Journal of the Legislature. 2d sess. Sacramento: Eugene Casserly.

California. Legislature. Senate Interim Committee on California Indian Affairs
1955   Progress Report to the Legislature. Sacramento: Senate of the State of California.

1957   Progress Report to the Legislature. Sacramento: Senate Publications.

California State Advisory Commission on Indian Affairs
1966   Progress Report to the Governor and the Legislature on Indians in Rural and Reservation Areas. Sacramento: California Office of State Printing.

1969   Final Report to the Governor and the Legislature. Sacramento: California Office of State Printing.

Callaghan, Catherine A.
[1956-1960]   [Ethnographic and Linguistic Notes, from approximately 9 Months' Fieldwork among the Lake Miwok Indians, California.] (Manuscripts in Callaghan's Possession.)

1958   California Penutian: History and Bibliography. *International Journal of American Linguistics* 24(3):189-194.

1962   Comparative Miwok-Mutsun with Notes on Rumsen. *International Journal of American Linguistics* 28(2):97-107.

1964   Phonemic Borrowing in Lake Miwok. Pp. 46-53 in Studies in Californian Linguistics. William Bright, ed. *University of California Publications in Linguistics* 34. Berkeley.

1965   Lake Miwok Dictionary. *University of California Publications in Linguistics* 39. Berkeley.

1967   Miwok-Costanoan as a Subfamily of Penutian. *International Journal of American Linguistics* 33(3):224-227.

1970   Bodega Miwok Dictionary. *University of California Publications in Linguistics* 60. Berkeley.

1971 Saclan: A Reexamination. *Anthropological Linguistics* 13(9):448-456.

1972 Proto-Miwok Phonology. *General Linguistics* 12(1):1-31.

1975 J.P. Harrington - California's Great Linguist. *Journal of California Anthropology* 2(1):183-187.

Camp, Charles L.
1923 The Chronicles of George C. Yount: California Pioneer of 1826. *Quarterly of the California Historical Society* 2(1):3-66. San Francisco.

Campbell, Elizabeth W.C.
1931 An Archaeological Survey of the Twenty-nine Palms Region. *Southwest Museum Papers* 7. Los Angeles.

Campbell, Elizabeth W.C., and William H. Campbell
1935 The Pinto Basin Site. *Southwest Museum Papers* 9. Los Angeles.

Campbell, Elizabeth W.C., William H. Campbell, Ernst Antevs, Charles A. Amsden, Joseph A. Barbieri, and Francis D. Bode
1937 The Archeology of Pleistocene Lake Mohave: A Symposium. *Southwest Museum Papers* 11. Los Angeles.

Carden, Georgianna C.
[1944] [Correspondence and Papers.] (Manuscript in Bancroft Library, University of California, Berkeley.)

Cardwell, J.A.
1878 Emigrant Company. (Manuscript in Bancroft Library, University of California, Berkeley.)

Carpenter, Aurelius O., and Percy H. Milberry
1914 History of Mendocino and Lake Counties, California with Biographical Sketches of the Leading Men and Women of the Counties. Los Angeles: Historic Record Company.

Carter, E.S.
1896 The Life and Adventures of E.S. Carter, Including a Trip across the Plains and Mountains in 1852, Indian Wars in the Early Days of Oregon in the Years of 1854-5-6. St. Joseph, Mo.: Combe Printing Company.

Carter, William H.
1971 North American Indian Trade Silver. London, Ont.: Engel.

Castillo, Edward D.
1931 Federation Indian Grievance. *San Diego Sun,* September 22. San Diego, Calif.

Catanich, Brenda (Harmon)
1968 Did Ancient Mysteries Rule along the Trail? Pp. 55-57 in Redwood Cavalcade. Andrew M. Genzoli and Wallace E. Martin, eds. Eureka, Calif.: Schooner Features.

Cesar, Julio
1878 Cosas de Indios de California. (Manuscript in Bancroft Library, University of California, Berkeley.)

Chace, Paul G.
1969 The Archaeology of "Cienaga," the Oldest Historic Structure on the Irvine Ranch. *Pacific Coast Archaeological Society Quarterly* (Special Sepulveda Number) 5(3):39-70. Costa Mesa, Calif.

Chagnon, Napoleon A.
1970 Ecological and Adaptive Aspects of California Shell Money. *Annual Reports of the University of California Archaeological Survey* 12:1-25. Los Angeles.

Chapman, Charles E., ed.
1911 Expedition on the Sacramento and San Joaquin Rivers in 1817: Diary of Fray Narciso Duran. *Publications of the Academy of Pacific Coast History* 2(5):329-349. Berkeley, Calif.

1921 A History of California: The Spanish Period. New York: Macmillan.

Chartkoff, Joseph L., Kerry K. Chartkoff, and Laurie J. Kona
1968 The Archaeological Survey of the Proposed Beartooth, Dyer Creek and Mills Hill Reservoirs in Trinity County, California. (Unpublished Manuscript No. 278 in University of California Archaeological Survey Library, Los Angeles.)

Chase, A.W.
1877 Wooden Figure of Victory. Figure 4 (opposite p. 57) in Tribes of California by Stephen Powers. *Contributions to North American Ethnology* 3. Washington: U.S. Geological and Geographical Survey of the Rocky Mountain Region.

Chase, Don M.
1958 He Opened the West, and Led the First White Explorers through Northwest California, May-June 1828. Crescent City, Calif.: Del Norte Triplicate Press.

Chesnut, V.K.
1902 Plants Used by the Indians of Mendocino County, California. *Contributions from the U.S. National Herbarium* 7(3): 295-408. Washington.

Childress, Jeffrey, and Joseph L. Chartkoff
1966 An Archaeological Survey of the English Ridge Reservoir in Lake and Mendocino Counties, California. (Prepared for and on File at the National Park Service, Western Region, San Francisco.)

Choris, Louis *see* Choris, Ludovik

Choris, Ludovik
1822 Voyage pittoresque autour du monde, avec des portraits de sauvages d'Amérique, d'Asie, d'Afrique, et des iles du Grand Océan... Paris: Firmin Didot.

Chuang, Tsan-Iang, and Lincoln Constance
1969 A Systematic Study of Perideridia (Umbelliferae-Apioideae). *University of California Publications in Botany* 55. Berkeley.

Clemmer, John S.
1961 The Archeology of the Neophyte Village at San Juan Bautista State Historical Monument. (Manuscript No. 115, on File at the California State Division of Beaches and Parks, Sacramento.)

1962 Archeological Notes on a Chumash House Floor at Morro Bay. Sacramento: Central California Archaeological Foundation.

Coats, Thomas H., S.A. Merritt, James W. Coffroth, and W.P. Jones
1852 Majority Report of the Special Committee of the California Assembly on Indian Reservations. Pp. 202-205 in *Assembly Journal,* February 16, 1852. Sacramento.

Cody, Bertha (Parker)
1940 California Indian Baby Cradles. *Masterkey* 14(3):89-96.

1940a Pomo Bear Impersonators. *Masterkey* 14(4):132-137.

1941 Yurok Tales: Wohpekumen's Beads; As Told by Jane Van Stralen to Bertha P. Cody. *Masterkey* 15(6):228-231.

1942 Yurok Fish-Dam Dance; As Told by Jane Van Stralen to Bertha P. Cody. *Masterkey* 16(3):81-86.

1942-1943 Some Yurok Customs and Beliefs. *Masterkey* 16(5):157-162, 17(3):81-87.

Collier, Donald, Alfred E. Hudson, and Arlo Ford
1942 Archaeology of the Upper Columbia Region. *University of Washington Publications in Anthropology* 9(1):1-179. Seattle.

Colson, Elizabeth, ed.
1974 Autobiographies of Three Pomo Women. Berkeley: University of California Archaeological Research Facility.

Colton, Harold S.
1941 Prehistoric Trade in the Southwest. *Scientific Monthly* 52(4):308-319.

727

Cook, Sherburne F.
1939   Smallpox in Spanish and Mexican California, 1770-1845. *Bulletin of the History of Medicine* 7(2):153-191.

1940   Population Trends among the California Mission Indians. *Ibero-Americana* 17. Berkeley, Calif.

1941   The Mechanism and Extent of Dietary Adaptation among Certain Groups of California and Nevada Indians. *Ibero-Americana* 18. Berkeley, Calif.

1943   The Conflict between the California Indians and White Civilization, I: The Indian Versus the Spanish Mission. *Ibero-Americana* 21. Berkeley, Calif.

1943a   The Conflict between the California Indian and White Civilization, II: The Physical and Demographic Reaction of the Non-mission Indians in Colonial and Provincial California. *Ibero-Americana* 22. Berkeley, Calif.

1943b   The Conflict between the California Indian and White Civilization,, III: The American Invasion 1848-1870. *Ibero-Americana* 23. Berkeley, Calif.

1943c   The Conflict between the California Indian and White Civilization, IV: Trends in Marriage and Divorce since 1850. *Ibero-Americana* 24. Berkeley, Calif.

1943d   Migration and Urbanization of the Indians in California. *Human Biology* 15(1):33-45.

1943e   Racial Fusion among the California and Nevada Indians. *Human Biology* 15(2):153-165.

1955   The Aboriginal Population of the San Joaquin Valley, California. *University of California Anthropological Records* 16(2):31-80. Berkeley.

1955a   The Epidemic of 1830-1833 in California and Oregon. *University of California Publications in American Archaeology and Ethnology* 43(3):303-326. Berkeley.

1956   The Aboriginal Population of the North Coast of California. *University of California Anthropological Records* 16(3): 81-130. Berkeley.

1957   The Aboriginal Population of Alameda and Contra Costa Counties, California. *University of California Anthropological Records* 16(4):131-156. Berkeley.

1960   Colonial Expeditions to the Interior of California: Central Valley, 1800-1820. *University of California Anthropological Records* 16(6):239-292. Berkeley.

1962   Expeditions to the Interior of California: Central Valley, 1820-1840. *University of California Anthropological Records* 20(5):151-214. Berkeley.

1964   The Aboriginal Population of Upper California. Pp. 397-403 in *Proceedings of the 35th International Congress of Americanists*. 3 vols. Mexico, 1962.

1974   The Esselen: Territory, Villages, and Population. *Quarterly of the Monterey County Archaeological Society* 3(2). Carmel, Calif.

[1974a]   [Essays on Population History and Development of the California Indians.] (Unpublished Manuscript in Cook's Possession.)

Cook, Sherburne F., and Robert F. Heizer
1951   The Physical Analysis of Nine Indian Mounds of the Lower Sacramento Valley. *University of California Publications in American Archaeology and Ethnology* 40(7):281-312. Berkeley.

1965   The Quantitative Approach to the Relation between Population and Settlement Size. *University of California Archaeological Survey Reports* 64:1-97. Berkeley.

1968   Relationships among Houses, Settlement Areas, and Population in Aboriginal California. Pp. 79-116 in Settlement Archaeology. K.C. Chang, ed. Palo Alto, Calif.: National Press Books.

Cook, Sherburne F., and Adan E. Treganza
1947   The Quantitative Investigation of Aboriginal Sites: Comparative Physical and Chemical Analysis of Two California Indian Mounds. *American Antiquity* 13(2):135-141.

Cooper, Adrienne
1969   The Mission Indian Revolt of 1825. (Unpublished Manuscript in University of California Archaeological Survey, Los Angeles.)

Costansó, Miguel
1910   The Narrative of the Portolá Expedition 1769-1770. A. van Hemert-Engert and F.J. Teggart, eds. *Publications of the Academy of Pacific Coast History* 1(4):91-159. Berkeley, Calif.

1911   The Portolá Expedition of 1769-1770: Diary of Miguel Costansó. Frederick J. Teggart, ed. *Publications of the Academy of Pacific Coast History* 2(4):161-327. Berkeley, Calif.

Costo, Rupert
1968   The American Indian Today. *The Indian Historian* 1(5):4-8, 35.

Coues, Elliot, ed.
1900   On the Trail of a Spanish Pioneer: The Diary and Itinerary of Francisco Garcés (Missionary Priest) in his Travels through Sonora, Arizona, and California 1775-1776. 2 vols. New York: Francis P. Harper.

Coulter, Thomas
1835   Notes on Upper California. *Journal of the Royal Geographical Society of London* 5:67.

Couro, Ted, and Christina Hutcheson
1973   Dictionary of the Mesa Grande Diegueño. Banning, Calif.: Malki Museum Press.

Cowan, Robert E.
1933   Alexander S. Taylor, 1817-1876: First Bibliographer of California. *Quarterly of the California Historical Society* 12(1):18-24. San Francisco.

Coy, Owen C.
1929   The Humboldt Bay Region, 1850-1875: A Study in the American Colonization of California. Los Angeles: California State Historical Association.

Coyote Man (Robert Rathbun)
1973   Sun, Moon and Stars. Berkeley, Calif.: Brother William Press.

1973a   The Destruction of the People. Berkeley, Calif.: Brother William Press.

Craig, Steve
1966   Ethnographic Notes on the Construction of Ventureño Chumash Baskets; from the Ethnographic and Linguistic Field Notes of John P. Harrington. *Annual Reports of the University of California Archaeological Survey* 8:197-214. Los Angeles.

Crespí, Juan
1927   Fray Juan Crespí: Missionary Explorer on the Pacific Coast 1769-1774. Herbert E. Bolton, ed. and trans. Berkeley: University of California Press. (Reprinted: AMS Press, New York, 1971.)

Cressman, Luther S.
1956   Klamath Prehistory: The Prehistory of the Culture of the Klamath Lake Area, Oregon. *Transactions of the American Philosophical Society* n.s. 46 (Pt.4):375-513. Philadelphia.

728

1960   Cultural Sequences at the Dalles, Oregon: A Contribution to Pacific Northwest Prehistory. *Transactions of the American Philosophical Society* n.s. 50 (Pt. 10). Philadelphia.

Crook, George
[1887]   [Pencilled Autobiography, Based on Observations between 1854 and 1861.] (Manuscript in George Crook Papers, Military Historical Research Collection, U.S. Army, Carlisle Barracks, Pa.)

1946   General George Crook: His Autobiography. Martin F. Schmitt, ed. Norman: University of Oklahoma Press. (Reprinted in 1960).

Cuero, Delfina
1968   The Autobiography of Delfina Cuero: A Diegueño Indian, as Told to Florence Shipek. Rosalie Pinto, Interpreter. Los Angeles: Dawson's Book Shop. (Reprinted: Malki Museum Press, Banning, Calif., 1970).

Curtice, Clifford G.
1961   Cultural and Physical Evidences of Prehistoric Peoples of Sacramento County. (Unpublished M.A. Thesis, Sacramento State College, Sacramento, Calif.)

[Curtin, Jeremiah]
1885   [Konkow Vocabulary.] (Manuscript in National Anthropological Archives, Smithsonian Institution, Washington.)

1889   [Pulikla Vocabulary, Klamath River, California.] (Manuscript No. 1459, in National Anthropological Archives, Smithsonian Institution, Washington.)

[1889a]   Way of Burying Dead among Lower Klamath. (Manuscript No. 4750 in National Anthropological Archives, Smithsonian Institution, Washington.)

1898   Creation Myths of Primitive America in Relation to the Religious History and Mental Development of Mankind. Boston: Little, Brown. (Reprinted: Benjamin Blom, New York, 1969.)

1909   Achomawi Myths. Roland B. Dixon, ed. *Journal of American Folk-Lore* 22(5):283-287.

Curtin, Leonora S.M.
1957   Some Plants Used by the Yuki Indians of Round Valley, Northern California. *Masterkey* 31(2):40-48.

Curtis, Edward S.
1907-1930   The North American Indian: Being a Series of Volumes Picturing and Describing the Indians of the United States, and Alaska. Frederick W. Hodge, ed. 20 vols. Norwood, Mass.: Plimpton Press. (Reprinted: Johnson Reprint, New York, 1970.)

Cutter, Donald C.
1950   The Spanish Exploration of California's Central Valley. (Unpublished Ph.D. Dissertation in History, University of California, Berkeley.)

Daggett, John
1965   Tales of Klamath Indians [1911]. *Siskiyou Pioneer* 3(8):53-58, 61.

Dale, Edward E.
1949   The Indians of the Southwest: A Century of Development under the United States. Norman: University of Oklahoma Press.

Dalton, O.M.
1897   Notes on an Ethnographical Collection from the West Coast of North America (more especially California, Hawaii and Tahiti), Formed during the Voyage of Captain Vancouver, 1790-1795 and now in the British Museum. *Internationales Archiv für Ethnographie* 10:225-245.

Dangel, Richard
1927   Der Schöpferglaube der Nordcentralcalifornier. *Studi e Materiali di Storia della Religioni* 3:31-54. Bologna, Italy.

1928   Die Schöpfergestalten Nordcentralcaliforniens. Pp. 481-504 in Vol. 2 of *Proceedings of the 22d International Congress of Americanists.* 2 vols. Rome 1926.

1934   Taikomal and Marumda: Zwei californische Schöpfer. *Studi e Materiali di Storia della Religioni* 10:38-63. Bologna, Italy.

Da Silva, Owen Francis *see* Silva, Owen Francis da

Davidson, George
1889   Pacific Coast. Coast Pilot of California, Oregon and Washington. 4th ed. Washington: U.S. Government Printing Office.

Davis, Edward H.
1919   The Diegueño Ceremony of the Death Images. *Contributions from the Museum of the American Indian, Heye Foundation* 5(2):7-33. New York.

1921   Early Cremation Ceremonies of the Luiseño and Diegueño Indians of Southern California. *Museum of the American Indian, Heye Foundation. Indian Notes and Monographs* 7(3):87-110. New York.

Davis, Emma L.
1961   The Mono Craters Petroglyphs, California. *American Antiquity* 27(2):236-239.

Davis, Emma L., and Richard Shutler, Jr.
1969   Recent Discoveries of Fluted Points in California and Nevada. Pp. 155-177 in Miscellaneous Papers on Nevada Archaeology 1-8. *Nevada State Museum Anthropological Papers* 14. Carson City.

Davis, James T.
1959   Further Notes on Clay Human Figurines in the Western United States. (Papers on California Archaeology 71) *University of California Archaeological Survey Reports* 48:16-31. Berkeley.

1960   The Archaeology of the Fernandez Site, a San Francisco Bay Region Shellmound. *University of California Archaeological Survey Reports* 49:11-52. Berkeley.

1961   Trade Routes and Economic Exchange among the Indians of California. *University of California Archaeological Survey Reports* 54. Berkeley. (Reprinted in Aboriginal California: Three Studies in Culture History. Robert F. Heizer, ed. University of California Press, Berkeley, 1963.)

Davis, James T., and Adan E. Treganza
1959   The Patterson Mound: A Comparative Analysis of the Archaeology of Site Ala-328. *University of California Archaeological Survey Reports* 47:1-92. Berkeley.

Dawson, Lawrence E.
1971   [Handwritten Notes on Yana Twined Basketry from Two Caves in the Southern Cascade Foothills.] (Manuscript in Dawson's Possession.)

1972   [Patwin Basketry.] (Manuscript in Dawson's Possession.)

Dawson, Lawrence E., and James Deetz
1965   A Corpus of Chumash Basketry. *Annual Reports of the University of California Archaeological Survey* 7:193-276. Los Angeles.

De Angulo, Jaime *see* Angulo, Jaime de

Deetz, James
1962-1963   Archaeological Investigations at La Purísima Mission. *Annual Reports of the University of California Archaeological Survey* 5:161-244. Los Angeles.

1964   A Datable Chumash Pictograph from Santa Barbara County, California. *American Antiquity* 29(4):504-506.

Delano, Alonzo
1854   Life on the Plains and among the Diggings: Being Scenes and Adventures of an Overland Journey to California. Auburn and Buffalo, N.Y.: Milner, Orton and Mulligan.

Demetracopoulou, Dorothy *see also* Lee, Dorothy (Demetracopoulou)

Demetracopoulou, Dorothy
1933   The Loon Woman Myth: A Study in Synthesis. *Journal of American Folk-Lore* 46(180):101-128.

———
1935   Wintu Songs. *Anthropos* 30:483-494.

———
1940   Wintu War Dance: A Textual Account. Pp. 141-143 in Vol. 4 of *Proceedings of the 6th Pacific Science Congress.* Toronto, 1939. Berkeley and Los Angeles: University of California Press.

Demetracopoulou, Dorothy, and Cora A. Du Bois
1932   A Study of Wintu Mythology. *Journal of American Folk-Lore* 45(178):375-500.

Densmore, Frances
1932   Yuman and Yaqui Music. *Bureau of American Ethnology Bulletin* 110. Washington.

———
1939   Musical Instruments of the Maidu Indians. *American Anthropologist* 41(1):113-118.

———
1958   Music of the Maidu Indians of California. Los Angeles: Southwest Museum.

Derby, George H.
1933   The Topographical Reports of Lieutenant George H. Derby [1849]. Francis F. Farquhar, ed. *California Historical Society Publications* 6. San Francisco.

Devereux, George
1948   Mohave Pregnancy. *Acta Americana* 6(1-2):89-116.

———
1951   Mohave Chieftainship in Action: A Narrative of the First Contacts of the Mohave Indians with the United States. *Plateau* 23(3):33-43.

Dillon, Richard
1973   The Burnt-out Fires: California's Modoc Indian War. Englewood Cliffs, N.J.: Prentice-Hall.

Dixon, Roland B.
1900   Some Coyote Stories from the Maidu Indians of California. *Journal of American Folk-Lore* 13(51):267-270.

———
1902   Maidu Myths. *Bulletin of the American Museum of Natural History* 17(2):33-118. New York.

———
1902a   Basketry Designs of the Indians of Northern California. *Bulletin of the American Museum of Natural History* 17(1):2-14. New York.

———
1903   System and Sequence in Maidu Mythology. *Journal of American Folk-Lore* 16(60):32-36.

———
1905   The Northern Maidu. *Bulletin of the American Museum of Natural History* 17(3):119-346. New York.

———
1905a   The Mythology of the Shasta-Achomawi. *American Anthropologist* n.s. 7(4):607-612.

———
1905b   The Shasta-Achomawi: A New Linguistic Stock, with Four New Dialects. *American Anthropologist* 7(2):213-217.

———
1907   The Shasta. *Bulletin of the American Museum of Natural History* 17(5):381-498. New York.

———
1907a   Linguistic Relationships within the Shasta-Achomawi Stock. Pp. 255-263 in Vol. 2 of *Proceedings of the 15th International Congress of Americanists.* Quebec, 1906.

———
1908   Notes on the Achomawi and Atsugewi Indians of Northern California. *American Anthropologist* n.s. 10(2):208-220.

———
1908-1910 Shasta Texts. (Manuscript Notebooks No. 30H1c.2 in American Philosophical Society Collection of Materials Relating to the American Indian, Philadelphia.)

———
1910   Shasta Myths. *Journal of American Folk-Lore* 23(87):8-37, (89):364-370.

———
1910a   The Chimariko Indians and Language. *University of California Publications in American Archaeology and Ethnology* 5(5): 293-380. Berkeley.

———
1910b   Nishinam. P. 75 in Vol. 2 of Handbook of American Indians North of Mexico. Frederick W. Hodge, ed. 2 vols. *Bureau of American Ethnology Bulletin* 30. Washington.

———
1910c   Shasta. Pp. 527-529 in Vol. 2 of Handbook of American Indians North of Mexico. Frederick W. Hodge, ed. 2 vols. *Bureau of American Ethnology Bulletin* 30. Washington.

———
1911   Maidu. Pp. 679-734 in Vol. 1 of Handbook of American Indian Languages. Franz Boas, ed. 2 vols. *Bureau of American Ethnology Bulletin* 40. Washington.

———
1912   Maidu Texts. *Publications of the American Ethnological Society* 4:1-241. Leyden, The Netherlands.

———
1913   Some Aspects of North American Archeology. *American Anthropologist* 15(4):549-577.

———
1931   Dr. Merriam's "Tló-hom-tah´-hoi." *American Anthropologist* 33(2): 264-267.

Dixon, Roland B., and Alfred L. Kroeber
1907   Numeral Systems of the Languages of California. *American Anthropologist* n.s. 9(4):663-690.

———
1912   Relationship of the Indian Languages of California. *American Anthropologist* 14(4):691-692.

———
1913   New Linguistic Families in California. *American Anthropologist* 15(4):647-655.

———
1919   Linguistic Families of California. *University of California Publications in American Archaeology and Ethnology* 16(3):47-118. Berkeley.

Dobyns, Henry F., Paul H. Ezell, Alden W. Jones, and Greta Ezell
1957   Thematic Changes in Yuman Warfare. Pp.46-71 in Cultural Stability and Cultural Change. *Proceedings of the Annual Spring Meeting of the American Ethnological Society.* Ithaca, N.Y., 1957. Seattle: University of Washington Press.

Dole, W.P.
1865   [Letter Dated October 3, 1864 to Austin Wiley.] Pp. 135-139 in Annual Report of the Commissioner of Indian Affairs for the Year 1864. Washington.

Dorin, May
1922   The Emigrant Trails into California. (Unpublished M.A. Thesis in History, University of California, Berkeley.)

Dougherty, William
1894   Klamath Indians Off Reservations. Pp. 206-207 in Report on Indians Taxed and Indians not Taxed in the United States. U.S. Census Office. 11th Census, 1890. Washington: U.S. Government Printing Office.

Douglas, Frank
1971   Trip up the Klamath. Pp. 28-29a in The Yurok Language, Literature and Culture Textbook. Thomas Parsons, ed. 2d ed. (Mimeographed; on File, Humboldt State College, Center for Community Development, Arcata, Calif.)

Driver, Harold E.
1936   Wappo Ethnography. *University of California Publications in American Archaeology and Ethnology* 36(3):179-220. Berkeley.

———
1937   Culture Element Distributions, VI: Southern Sierra Nevada. *University of California Anthropological Records* 1(2):53-154. Berkeley.

———
1939   Culture Element Distributions, X: Northwest California. *University of California Anthropological Records* 1(6):297-433. Berkeley.

1961   Indians of North America. Chicago: University of Chicago Press.

Driver, Harold E., and William C. Massey
1957   Comparative Studies of North American Indians. *Transactions of the American Philosophical Society* 47(2). Philadelphia.

Drucker, Philip
1937   Culture Element Distributions, V: Southern California. *University of California Anthropological Records* 1(1):1-52. Berkeley.

1937a   The Tolowa and their Southwest Oregon Kin. *University of California Publications in American Archaeology and Ethnology* 36(4):221-300. Berkeley.

1941   Culture Element Distributions, XVII: Yuman-Piman. *University of California Anthropological Records* 6(3):91-230. Berkeley.

1963   Indians of the Northwest Coast. Garden City, N.Y.: Natural History Press.

1965   Cultures of the North Pacific Coast. San Francsico: Chandler.

Du Bois, Constance (Goddard)
1901   The Mythology of the Diegueños. *Journal of American Folk-Lore* 14(54):181-185.

1904   The Story of the Chaup: A Myth of the Diegueños. *Journal of American Folk-Lore* 17(67):217-242.

1904a   Mythology of the Mission Indians. *Journal of American Folk-Lore* 17(66):185-188.

1905   The Mythology of the Diegueños, Mission Indians of San Diego County, California, as Proving their Status to be Higher than is Generally Believed. Pp. 101-106 in *Proceedings of the 13th International Congress of Americanists.* New York, 1902.

1905a   Religious Ceremonies and Myths of the Mission Indians. *American Anthropologist* n.s. 7(4):620-629.

1906   Mythology of the Mission Indians. *Journal of American Folk-Lore* 19(72):52-60.

1907   Diegueño Myths and their Connections with the Mohave. Pp. 129-133 in Vol. 2 of *Proceedings of the 15th International Congress of Americanists.* 2 vols. Quebec, 1906.

1907a   Two Types or Styles of Diegueño Religious Dancing: The Old and the New in Southern California. Pp. 135-138 in Vol. 2 of *Proceedings of the 15th International Congress of Americanists.* 2 vols. Quebec, 1906.

1907b   Diegueño Mortuary Ollas. *American Anthropologist* n.s. 9(3):484-486.

1908   Ceremonies and Traditions of the Diegueño Indians. *Journal of American Folk-Lore* 21(81-82):228-236.

1908a   The Religion of the Luiseño and Diegueño Indians of Southern California. *University of California Publications in American Archaeology and Ethnology* 8(3):69-186. Berkeley.

Du Bois, Cora A.
1932   Tolowa Notes. *American Anthropologist* 34(2):248-262.

1935   Wintu Ethnography. *University of California Publications in American Archaeology and Ethnology* 36(1):1-148. Berkeley.

1936   The Wealth Concept as an Integrative Factor in Tolowa-Tututni Culture. Pp. 49-65 in Essays in Anthropology Presented to A.L . Kroeber in Celebration of his Sixtieth Birthday. Robert H. Lowie, ed. Berkeley: University of California Press.

1939   The 1870 Ghost Dance. *University of California Anthropological Records* 3(1):1-151. Berkeley.

Du Bois, Cora A., and Dorothy Demetracopoulou
1931   Wintu Myths. *University of California Publications in American Archaeology and Ethnology* 28(5):279-403. Berkeley.

Duflot de Mofras, Eugène
1884   Exploration du territoire de l'Oregon, des Californies et de la mer Vermeille, exécutée pendant les années 1840, 1841, et 1842. 2 vols. Paris: A. Bertrand.

Duncan, John W.
1964   Maidu Ethnobotany. (Unpublished M.A. Thesis in Anthropology, California State University, Sacramento.)

Dunn, Jacob P.
1886   Massacres of the Mountains: A History of the Indian Wars of the Far West. New York: Harper and Brothers. (Reprinted: Archer House, New York, 1958.)

Duran, Narciso, and Buenaventura Fortuny
1958   [Reply to the Interrogatorio of 1812, Mission San Jose.] Pp. 268- 276 in The History of Mission San Jose California, 1797-1835. Francis F. McCarthy, ed. Fresno, Calif.: Academy Library Guild.

Eastwood, Alice, ed.
1924   Archibald Menzies' Journal of the Vancouver Expedition; Extracts Covering the Visit to California. *Quarterly of the California Historical Society* 2(4):265-340. San Francisco.

Eberhart, Hal
1970   Published Archaeological Sites and Surveys in Southern California. *Newsletter of the Archaeological Survey Association of Southern California* 17(2):4-21. Los Angeles.

Eberhart, Hal, and Agnes Babcock
1963   An Archaeological Survey of Mutau Flat, Ventura County, California. *University of California, Archaeological Research Associates Contributions to California Archaeology* 5. Los Angeles.

Eccleston, Robert
1957   The Mariposa Indian War, 1850-1851; Diaries of Robert Eccleston: The California Goldrush, Yosemite, and the High Sierra. C. Gregory Crampton, ed. Salt Lake City: University of Utah Press.

Edwards, Philip L.
1890   California in 1837: Themes. Sacramento: A.J. Johnston.

Edwards, Robert L.
[1966]   An Archaeological Survey of the Yuki: Etsel-Franciscan Reservoir Region, Mendocino County, California. (Unpublished Student Paper in Department of Anthropology, San Francisco State College, San Francisco.)

Edwards, T.C., and C.E. Kelsey
1904   Memorial of the Northern California Indian Association, Praying that Land be Allotted to Landless Indians of the Northern Part of California. U.S. Congress. Senate. 58th Cong., 2d sess. Sen. Doc. No. 131. (Serial No. 4589) Washington: U.S. Government Printing Office.

Elliott, T.C., ed.
1909   Journal of Peter Skene Ogden: Snake Expedition, 1825-1826. *Quarterly of the Oregon Historical Society* 10(4):331-365. Portland.

1910   Peter Skene Ogden, Fur Trader. *Quarterly of the Oregon Historical Society* 11(3):229-278. (Reprinted: Ivy Press, Portland, Oreg., 1910.)

Ellison, William H.
1922   The Federal Indian Policy in California, 1846-1860. *Mississippi Valley Historical Review* 9:37-67.

1925   Rejection of California Indian Treaties: A Study in Local Influence on National Policy. *Grizzly Bear* 36(217):4-5, 86, (218):4-5, 7, (219):6-7.

Elmendorf, William W.
1963   Yukian-Siouan Lexical Similarities. *International Journal of American Linguistics* 29(4):300-309.

1964   Item and Set Comparison in Yuchi, Siouan and Yukian. *International Journal of American Linguistics* 30(4):328-340.

1968   Lexical and Cultural Change in Yukian. *Anthropological Linguistics* 10(7):1-41.

Elsasser, Albert B.
1960   The Archaeology of the Sierra Nevada in California and Nevada. *University of California Archaeological Survey Reports* 51:1-93. Berkeley.

1960a   The History of Culture Classification in California. *University of California Archaeological Survey Reports* 49:1-10. Berkeley.

Elsasser, Albert B., and Robert F. Heizer
1963   The Archaeology of Bower's Cave, Los Angeles County, California. *University of California Archaeological Survey Reports* 59:1-59. Berkeley.

1966   Excavation of Two Northwestern California Coastal Sites. *University of California Archaeological Survey Reports* 67:1-149. Berkeley.

Elston, Robert G.
1971   A Contribution to Washo Archeology. *Nevada Archaeological Survey Research Papers* 2:1-144. Reno.

Engelhardt, Zephyrin
1908-1915 The Missions and Missionaries of California. 4 vols. San Francisco: James H. Barry.

1920   The Missions and Missionaries of California. Local History: San Diego Mission. San Francisco: James H. Barry.

1921   San Luis Rey Mission. San Francisco: James H. Barry.

1922   San Juan Capistrano Mission. Los Angeles: Standard Printing Company.

1923   Santa Barbara Mission. San Francisco: James H. Barry.

1927   San Fernando Rey: The Mission of the Valley. Chicago: Franciscan Herald Press.

1927a   San Gabriel Mission and the Beginnings of Los Angeles. San Gabriel, Calif.: Mission San Gabriel.

1929   San Miguel Arcangel: The Mission on the Highway. Santa Barbara, Calif.: Mission Santa Barbara.

1930   San Buenaventura Mission: The Mission by the Sea. Santa Barbara, Calif.: Mission Santa Barbara.

1932   Mission Santa Inés, Virgen e Martyr and its Ecclesiastical Seminary. Santa Barbara, Calif.: Mission Santa Barbara.

1932a   Mission La Concepción Purísima de Maria Santísima. Santa Barbara, Calif.: Mission Santa Barbara.

1933   Mission San Luis Obispo in the Valley of the Bears. Santa Barbara, Calif.: Mission Santa Barbara.

Ericson, Jonathan E., and Rainer Berger
1974   Late Pleistocene American Obsidian Tools. *Nature* 249(5460):824-825.

Erikson, Erik H.
1943   Observations on the Yurok: Childhood and World Image. *University of California Publications in American Archaeology and Ethnology* 35(10):257-302. Berkeley.

Essene, Frank J.
1935   [Unpublished Kato Folkore Material.] (Manuscript in the University Archives, Bancroft Library, University of California, Berkeley.)

1942   Culture Element Distributions, XXI: Round Valley. *University of California Anthropological Records* 8(1):1-97. Berkeley.

Essig, E.O.
1933   The Russian Settlement at Ross. Pp. 191-216 in The Russians in California. *Quarterly of the California Historical Society* 12(3). San Francisco.

Evans, Albert S.
1889   A la California, or Sketches of Life in the Golden State, 1849-1872. Also, an Authentic Account of the Famous Yosemite Valley. San Francisco: G.H. Bancroft.

Evans, William E.
1966   The Garra Uprising: Conflict between the San Diego Indians and Settlers in 1851. *Quarterly of the California Historical Society* 45(4):339-349. San Francisco.

Evans, William S.
1961   ARA Digs at Los Cerritos Ranch House. *Bulletin of the Archaeological Research Associates* 6(1):2-3. Long Beach, Calif.

1964   A Distinctive Wrought Iron Hasp from Rancho Los Cerritos. *Los Fierros, Los Cerritos Docents Quarterly* 1(2):1-3. Long Beach, Calif.

1969   California Indian Pottery: A Native Contribution to the Culture of the Ranchos. *Pacific Coast Archaeological Society Quarterly* 5(3):71-81. Costa Mesa, Calif.

Fages, Pedro
1911   Expedition to San Francisco Bay in 1770: Diary of Pedro Fages. Herbert E. Bolton, ed. *Publications of the Academy of Pacific Coast History* 2(3):141-159. Berkeley, Calif.

1913   The Colorado River Campaign, 1781-1782: Diary of Pedro Fages. Herbert I. Priestley, ed. *Publications of the Academy of Pacific Coast History* 3(2):133-233. Berkeley, Calif.

1937   A Historical, Political, and Natural Description of California, by Pedro Fages, Soldier of Spain [1775]. Herbert I. Priestley, trans. Berkeley: University of California Press. (Reprinted: Ballena Press, Ramona, Calif., 1972.)

Farmer, Malcom F.
1935   The Mojave Trade Route. *Masterkey* 9(5):154-157.

Farquhar, Francis P.
1932   The Topographical Reports of Lieutenant George H. Derby. *Quarterly of the California Historical Society* 11(2):99-123. San Francisco.

Farrand, Livingston, coll.
1915   Shasta and Athapascan Myths from Oregon. Leo J. Frachtenberg, ed. *Journal of American Folk-Lore* 28(109):207-242.

Fay, George E.
1970   Charters, Constitutions and By-Laws of the Indian Tribes of North America. Pt. 7: The Indian Tribes of California. *University of Northern Colorado Museum of Anthropology, Occasional Publications in Anthropology, Ethnology Series* 8. Greeley.

1970a   Charters, Constitutions and By-Laws of the Indian Tribes of North America. Pt. 8: The Indian Tribes of California (Cont'd). *University of Northern Colorado Museum of Anthropology, Occasional Publications in Anthropology, Ethnology Series* 9. Greeley.

Faye, Paul-Louis
1923   Notes of the Southern Maidu. *University of California Publications in American Archaeology and Ethnology* 20(3):35-53. Berkeley.

1928   Christmas Fiestas of the Cupeño. *American Anthropologist* 30(4):651-658.

Fehrenbacher, Don E.
1964   A Basic History of California. Princeton, N. J.: D. Van Nostrand.

Fenenga, Franklin
1947   Preliminary Survey of Archaeological Resources in the Isabella Reservoir, Kern County, California. West Coast Projects, River Basin Surveys, Smithsonian Institution, Washington.

1952   The Archaeology of the Slick Rock Village, Tulare County, California. *American Antiquity* 17(4):339-347.

Finnerty, W. Patrick
1963   A Burial Site on the Carrizo Plain, San Luis Obispo County, California. (Unpublished Manuscript in Campbell Grant's Possession.)

Finnerty, W. Patrick, Dean A. Decker, and N. Nelson Leonard, III.
1970   Community Structure and Trade at Isthmus Cove: A Salvage Excavation on Catalina Island. *Pacific Coast Archaeological Society Occasional Papers* 1. Costa Mesa, Calif.

Fitzwater, Robert J.
1961-1962 Final Report on Two Seasons' Excavations at El Portal, Mariposa County, California. *Annual Reports of the University of California Archaeological Survey* 4:235-305. Los Angeles.

1968   Big Oak Flat: Two Archaeological Sites in Yosemite National Park. *Annual Reports of the University of California Archaeological Survey* 10:275-314. Los Angeles.

1968a   Excavations at Crane Flat, Yosemite National Park. Pp. 276-302 in Big Oak Flat: Two Archaeological Sites in Yosemite National Park. *Annual Reports of the University of California Archaeological Survey* 10. Los Angeles.

Font, Pedro
1930   Font's Complete Diary of the Second Anza Expedition. Pp. 97-112 in Vol. 4 of Anza's California Expeditions. Herbert E. Bolton, ed. Berkeley: University of California Press.

1933   Font's Complete Diary: A Chronicle of the Founding of San Francisco, 1775-1776. Herbert E. Bolton, ed. Berkeley: University of California Press.

Fontana, Bernard L.
1965   On the Meaning of Historic Sites Archaeology. *American Antiquity* 31(1):61-65.

Forbes, A.
1839   California: A History of Upper and Lower California. London: Smith and Elder. (Reprinted: John Henry Nash, San Francisco, 1937.)

Forbes, Jack D.
1961   Pueblo Pottery in the San Fernando Valley. *Masterkey* 35(1):36-38.

1965   Warriors of the Colorado: The Yumas of the Quechan Nation and their Neighbors. Norman: University of Oklahoma Press.

1966   The Tongva of Tujunga to 1801. *Annual Reports of the University of California Archaeological Survey* 8:137-150. Los Angeles.

1969   Native Americans of California and Nevada: A Handbook. Healdsburg, Calif.: Naturegraph Publishers.

Ford, J.A., and Gordon R. Willey
1941   An Interpretation of the Prehistory of the Eastern United States. *American Anthropologist* 43(3):325-363.

Forde, C. Darryl
1931   Ethnography of the Yuma Indians. *University of California Publications in American Archaeology and Ethnology* 28(4):83-278. Berkeley.

Foster, George M.
1944   A Summary of Yuki Culture. *University of California Anthropological Records* 5(3):155-244. Berkeley.

Frank, B.F. and H.W. Chappell, comps.
1881   History and Business Directory of Shasta County Comprising an Accurate Historical Sketch of the County from its Earliest Settlement to the Present Time....1881. Redding, Calif.: Redding Independent Book and Job Printing House.

Franks, A.W.
[1891]   Objects Obtained during Vancouver's Voyages by Mr. Hewett. (Manuscript Notebook, in Department of Ethnography, British Museum, London.)

Frederick, M.C.
1901   Some Indian Paintings. *Land of Sunshine* 15:223-227.

Fredrickson, David A.
1961   The Archaeology of Lak-261: A Stratified Site near Lower Lake. (Manuscript at California State Department of Parks and Recreation, Sacramento.)

1965   Buena Vista Lake: Thirty Years after Wedel. (Manuscript in Fredrickson's Possession.)

1965a   Recent Excavations in the Interior of Contra Costa County, California. Pp. 18-25 in Symposium on Central California Archeology. Freddie Curtis, ed. *Sacramento Anthropological Society Papers* 3. Sacramento.

1968   Archaeological Investigation at CCo-30 near Alamo, Contra Costa County, California. *Center for Archaeological Research at Davis, Publication* 1. Davis.

1973   Early Cultures of the North Coast Ranges, California. (Manuscript in Department of Anthropology, University of California, Davis.)

1974   Cultural Diversity in Early Central California: A View from the North Coast Ranges. *Journal of California Anthropology* 1(1):41-53.

Fredrickson, David A., and Joel Grossman
1966   Radiocarbon Dating of an Early Site at Buena Vista Lake, California. (Unpublished Manuscript in Frederickson's Possession.)

Freeland, Lucy S.
[1923]   Pomo Kuksu Ceremonial System. (Manuscript in Kroeber Papers, Bancroft Library, University of California, Berkeley.)

1927   Shasta Texts; Originally Collected by R.B. Dixon in 1908 and Rechecked with Informants of Jaime de Angulo and Lucy S. Freeland in 1927. (Manuscript 30 H1C:3 in American Philosophical Society Collection of Materials Relating to the American Indian, Philadelphia.)

1931   The Relationship of Mixe to the Penutian Family. *International Journal of American Linguistics* 6(1):28-33.

1947   Western Miwok Texts with Linguistic Sketch. *International Journal of American Linguistics* 13(1):31-46.

1951   Language of the Sierra Miwok. *Indiana University Publications in Anthropology and Linguistics, Memoir* 6. Bloomington.

Freeland, Lucy S., and Sylvia M. Broadbent
1960   Central Sierra Miwok Dictionary with Texts. *University of California Publications in Linguistics* 23:1-71. Berkeley.

Freeman, John F., ed.
1966   A Guide to Manuscripts Relating to the American Indian in the Library of the American Philosophical Society. *Memoirs of the American Philosophical Society* 65. Philadelphia.

Fried, Morton, Marvin Harris, and Robert Murphy, eds.
1968   War: The Anthropology of Armed Conflict and Aggression. Garden City, N.Y.: Natural History Press.

Friends, Society of
[1957]   Indians of California: Past and Present. San Francisco: American Friends Service Committee.

Fröbel, Julius
1859   Seven Years' Travel in Central America, Northern Mexico, and the Far West of the United States. London: R. Bentley.

Gabel, Norman E.
1952   Report on Archaeological Research Project at La Purísima Mission State Monument during June 25 to August 4, 1952. (Manuscript at California State Division of Beaches and Parks, District 5 Office, Goleta.)

Galvan, P. Michael
1968   "People of the West": The Ohlone Story. *The Indian Historian* 1(2):9-13.

Garcés, Francisco T.H.
1965   A Record of Travels in Arizona and California 1775-1776. John Galvin, ed. San Francisco: J. Howell-Books.

Gardner, Louise
1965   The Surviving Chumash. *Annual Reports of the University of California Archaeological Survey* 7:277-302. Los Angeles.

Garth, Thomas R.
1938-1939 [Ethnographic Data from Five Atsuge and Eight Apwaruge Informants.] (Unpublished Manuscript in Garth's Possession.)

———
1944   Kinship Terminology, Marriage Practices and Behavior toward Kin among the Atsugewi. *American Anthropologist* 46(3):348-361.

———
1945   Emphasis on Industriousness among the Atsugewi. *American Anthropologist* 47(4):554-566.

———
1953   Atsugewi Ethnography. *University of California Anthropological Records* 14(2):129-212. Berkeley.

———
1965   The Plateau Whipping Complex and its Relationship to the Plateau-Southwest Contacts. *Ethnohistory* 12(2):141-170.

Gates, Paul W.
1971   The California Land Act of 1851. *Quarterly of the California Historical Society* 50(4). San Francisco.

Gatschet, Albert S.
1877   Indian Languages of the Pacific States and Territories. *Magazine of American History* 1(1):145-171.

———
1877a   Der Yuma-Sprachstamm nach den neuesten handschriftlichen Quellen. *Zeitschrift für Ethnologie* 9:341-350, 365-418.

———
1877b   Sasti-English and English-Sasti Dictionary. (Manuscript No. 706 in National Anthropological Archives, Smithsonian Institution, Washington.)

———
1879   Classification into Seven Linguistic Stocks of Western Indian Dialects Contained in Forty Vocabularies. Pp. 403-485 in Vol. 7 of Report upon the United States Geographical Surveys West of the One Hundredth Meridian in Charge of Lieut. Geo. M. Wheeler. Washington: U.S. Government Printing Office.

———
1883   Specimen of the Chumeto Language. *American Antiquarian* 5(1):71-73.

———
1886   Der Yuma-Sprachstamm nach den neuesten handschriftlichen Quellen. Pt. 3. *Zeitschrift für Ethnologie* 18:97-122.

———
1890   Dictionary of the Klamath Language. *Contributions to North American Ethnology 2*. Pt. 2. Washington: U.S. Geographical and Geological Survey of the Rocky Mountain Region.

Gayton, Anna H.
1929   Yokuts and Western Mono Pottery-making. *University of California Publications in American Archaeology and Ethnology* 24(3):239-251. Berkeley.

———
1930   Yokuts-Mono Chiefs and Shamans. *University of California Publications in American Archaeology and Ethnology* 24(8):361-420. Berkeley.

———
1930a   The Ghost Dance of 1870 in South-Central California. *University of California Publications in American Archaeology and Ethnology* 28(3):57-82. Berkeley.

———
1935   Areal Affiliations of California Folktales. *American Anthropologist* 37(4):582-599.

———
1936   Estudillo among the Yokuts: 1819. Pp. 67-85 in Essays in Anthropology Presented to A.L. Kroeber in Celebration of his Sixtieth Birthday. Robert H. Lowie, ed. Berkeley: University of California Press.

———
1945   Yokuts and Western Mono Social Organization. *American Anthropologist* 47(3):409-426.

———
1946   Culture-Environment Integration: External References in Yokuts Life. *Southwestern Journal of Anthropology* 2(3):252-268.

———
1948   Yokuts and Western Mono-Ethnography. *University of California Anthropological Records* 10(1-2):1-302. Berkeley.

Gayton, Anna H., and Stanley S. Newman
1940   Yokuts and Western Mono-Myths. *University of California Anthropological Records* 5(1):1-110. Berkeley.

Gebhardt, Charles L.
1962   Historic Archaeology at Vallejo's Petaluma Adobe State Historical Monument. (Manuscript No. 193 at California State Division of Beaches and Parks, Sacramento.)

Geiger, Maynard, ed.
1949   Questionnaire of the Spanish Government in 1812 Concerning the Native Culture of the California Mission Indians. *The Americas: A Quarterly Review of Inter-American Cultural History* 5(4):474-481.

———, ed.
1953   Reply of Mission San Antonio to the Questionnaire of the Spanish Government in 1812 Concerning the Native Culture of the California Mission Indians. *The Americas: A Quarterly Review of Inter-American Cultural History* 10(2):211-227.

Genzoli, Andrew M.
1970   Axel Lindgren Remembers Old Tsurai Village. *Times-Standard*, October 18: Cover, 6-7. Eureka, Calif.

Genzoli, Andrew M., and Wallace E. Martin
1961   Redwood Frontier, Wilderness Defiant. Tales Out of the Conquest of America's Great Forest Land: Humboldt, Del Norte, Trinity, Mendocino. Eureka, Calif.: Schooner Features.

———
1965   Redwood West, the Changing Frontier: Memorable, Exciting Stories from the Big Tree Country. Eureka, Calif.: Schooner Features.

Gerow, Bert A., and Roland W. Force
1968   An Analysis of the University Village Complex, with a Reappraisal of Central California Archaeology. Palo Alto, Calif.: Stanford University.

Gibbs, George, comp.
1851   Sketch of the Northwestern Parts of California Accompanying a Journal of the Expedition of Redick McKee.

(Manuscript Map No. 47 in National Archives, Washington.)

[1852]   [Weitspek (Pohlik Klamath) and Hopah Dictionaries and Ethnographic Notes.] (Manuscript Notebook No. 954, in National Anthropological Archives, Smithsonian Institution, Washington.)

1853   Journal of the Expedition of Colonel Redick M'Kee, United States Indian Agent, through North-Western California. Performed in the Summer and Fall of 1851. Pp. 99-177, 634 in Vol. 3 of Historical and Statistical Information Respecting the History, Condition and Prospects of the Indian Tribes of the United States. Henry R. Schoolcraft, ed. Philadelphia: Lippincott, Grambo. (Reprinted: University of California Archaeological Research Facility, Berkeley, 1972.)

[Gibbs, George]
[1853a]   [Sketch Map Showing Western Shasta Villages, Karok and Yurok Villages of Klamath River, Chilula Villages on Redwood Creek.] (Manuscript Map No. 552-a, in National Anthropological Archives, Smithsonian Institution, Washington.)

Gibbs, George
1853b   Vocabularies of Indian Languages in Northwest California. Pp. 428-445 in Vol. 3 of Historical and Statistical Information Respecting the History, Condition and Prospects of the Indian Tribes of the United States. Henry R. Schoolcraft, ed. Philadelphia: Lippincott, Grambo. (Reprinted: University of California Archaeological Research Facility, Berkeley, 1972.)

1853c   Observations on Some Indian Dialects of Northern California. Pp. 421-423 in Vol. 3 of Historical and Statistical Information Respecting the History, Condition and Prospects of the Indian Tribes of the United States. Henry R. Schoolcraft, ed. Philadelphia: Lippincott, Grambo. (Reprinted: University of California Archaeological Research Facility, Berkeley, 1972.)

1863   Uca. *Historical Magazine,* 1st ser., Vol. 7:123. Boston.

1973   Observations on the Indians of the Klamath River and Humboldt Bay. Pp. 1-23 in Two Nineteenth Century Ethnographic Documents on the Wiyot and Yurok of Northwestern Califonia and the Comanches of New Mexico and Texas. Robert F. Heizer, ed. Berkeley: University of California Archeological Research Facility. (Original Manuscript Dated ca. 1854 in National Anthropological Archives, Smithsonian Institution, Washington.)

Gibson, James R.
1975   Russian Sources for the Ethnohistory of the Pacific Coast of North America in the 18th and 19th Centuries. (Paper Read at the Annual Meeting of the American Anthropological Association. San Francisco, 1975.)

Gibson, Robert O., and Clay A. Singer
1970   Ven-195: Treasure House of Prehistoric Art. *Annual Reports of the University of California Archaeological Survey* 12:149-166. Los Angeles.

Gifford, Edward W.
1916   Composition of California Shellmounds. *University of California Publications in American Archaeology and Ethnology* 12(1):1-29. Berkeley.

1916a   Dichotomous Social Organization in South Central California. *University of California Publications in American Archaeology and Ethnology* 11(5):291-296. Berkeley.

1916b   Miwok Moieties. *University of California Publications in American Archaeology and Ethnology* 12(4):139-194. Berkeley.

1917   Miwok Myths. *University of California Publications in American Archaeology and Ethnology* 12(8):283-338. Berkeley.

[1917a]   Northern and Central (Sierra) Miwok Fieldnotes. (Manuscript No. 203 in the University Archives, Bancroft Library, University of California, Berkeley.)

1918   Clans and Moieties in Southern California. *University of California Publications in American Archaeology and Ethnology* 14(2):155-219. Berkeley.

1922   Californian Kinship Terminologies. *University of California Publications in American Archaeology and Ethnology* 18(1):1-285. Berkeley.

1923   Pomo Lands on Clear Lake. *University of California Publications in American Archaeology and Ethnology* 20(5):77-92. Berkeley.

1923a   Western Mono Myths. *Journal of American Folk-Lore* 36(142):301-367.

1926   Californian Anthropometry. *University of California Publications in American Archaeology and Ethnology* 22(2):217-390. Berkeley.

1926a   Miwok Cults. *University of California Publications in American Archaeology and Ethnology* 18(3):391-408. Berkeley.

1926b   Yuma Dreams and Omens. *Journal of American Folk-Lore* 39(151):58-69.

1926c   Clear Lake Pomo Society. *University of California Publications in American Archaeology and Ethnology* 18(2):287-390. Berkeley.

1926d   Miwok Lineages and the Political Unit in Aboriginal California. *American Anthropologist* 28(2):389-401.

1927   Southern Maidu Religious Ceremonies. *American Anthropologist* 29(3):214-257.

1928   The Cultural Position of the Coast Yuki. *American Anthropologist* 30(1):112-115.

1928a   Notes on Central Pomo and Northern Yana Society. *American Anthropologist* 30(4):675-684.

1931   The Kamia of Imperial Valley. *Bureau of American Ethnology Bulletin* 97. Washington.

1932   The Northfork Mono. *University of California Publications in American Archaeology and Ethnology* 31(2):15-65. Berkeley.

1932a   The Southeastern Yavapai. *University of California Publications in American Archaeology and Ethnology* 29(3):177-252. Berkeley.

1933   The Cocopa. *University of California Publications in American Archaeology and Ethnology* 31(5):257-334. Berkeley.

1936   Northeastern and Western Yavapai. *University of California Publications in American Archaeology and Ethnology* 34(4):247-354. Berkeley.

1937   Coast Yuki Myths. *Journal of American Folk-Lore* 50(196):115-172.

1939   Karok Narratives. I: Myths and Tales. II: Formulae. III: Confessions. IV: Games. (Ethnological Document No. 146 in Department and Museum of Anthropology, University of California; Manuscript in University Archives, Bancroft Library, Berkeley.)

1939a   Karok Field Notes. Pt. 1. (Ethnological Document No. 174 in Department and Museum of Anthropology, University of California; Manuscript in University Archives, Bancroft Library, Berkeley.)

1939b   The Coast Yuki. *Anthropos* 34:292-375. (Reprinted: Sacramento Anthropological Society Papers 2, Sacramento State College, 1965.)

1940   Karok Field Notes. Pt. 2. (Ethnological Document No. 179 in Department and Museum of Anthropology, University of California; Manuscript in University Archives, Bancroft Library, Berkeley.)

1940a   Californian Bone Artifacts. *University of California Anthropological Records* 3(2):153-237. Berkeley.

[1940-1942]   [Ethnographic Notes on the Folklore and Ceremonial Life of the Hupa.] (Unpublished Manuscripts in University of California Archives, Bancroft Library, Berkeley.)

1944   Miwok Lineages. *American Anthropologist* 46(3):376-381.

1947   Californian Shell Artifacts. *University of California Anthropological Records* 9(1):1-114. Berkeley.

1949   Early Central Californian and Anasazi Shell Artifact Types. *American Antiquity* 15(2):156-157.

1955   Central Miwok Ceremonies. *University of California Anthropological Records* 14(4):261-318. Berkeley.

1958   Karok Confessions. Pp. 245-255 in Miscellanea Paul Rivet Octogenario Dicata, 31st International Congress of Americanists. 2 vols. Mexico City, D.F.: Universidad Nacional Autónoma de México.

1967   Ethnographic Notes on the Southwestern Pomo. *University of California Anthropological Records* 25:1-47. Berkeley.

Gifford, Edward W., and Gwendoline H. Block , comps.
1930   Californian Indian Nights Entertainments; Stories of the Creation of the World, of Man, of Fire, of the Sun, of Thunder, etc.; of Coyote, the Land of the Dead, the Sky Monsters, Animal People, etc. Glendale, Calif.: Arthur H. Clark.

Gifford, Edward W., and Stanislaus Klimek
1939   Culture Element Distributions, II: Yana. *University of California Publications in American Archaeology and Ethnology* 37(2):71-100. Berkeley.

Gifford, Edward W., and Alfred L. Kroeber
1939   Culture Element Distributions, IV: Pomo. *University of California Publications in American Archaeology and Ethnology* 37(4):117-254. Berkeley.

Gifford, Edward W., and T.D. McCown
1951   Historical Retrospect [of the Department and Museum of Anthropology, University of California, Berkeley]. Pp. 21-29 in *Annual Report of the Museum of Anthropology for the Year Ending June 30, 1951*. Berkeley, Calif.

Gifford, Edward W., and W. Egbert Schenck
1926   Archaeology of the Southern San Joaquin Valley. *University of California Publications in American Archaeology and Ethnology* 23(1):1-122. Berkeley.

Giles, Rosena A.
1949   Shasta County California: A History. Oakland, Calif.: BioBooks.

Gladwin, Winifred, and Harold S. Gladwin
1935   The Eastern Range of the Red-on-Buff Culture. *Gila Pueblo, Medallion Papers* 16. Globe, Ariz.

Glassow, Michael A.
1965   The Conejo Rockshelter: An Inland Chumash Site in Ventura County, California. *Annual Reports of the University of California Archaeological Survey* 7:19-80. Los Angeles.

1971   Fifth Summary Report on Excavations Conducted at the Site of the Spanish Royal Presidio Chapel. Santa Barbara, Calif.: Santa Barbara Trust for Historic Preservation.

Glennan, William S.
1971   Concave-based Lanceolate Fluted Projectile Points from California. *Masterkey* 45(1):27-32.

Goddard, Ives
1963   The Algonquian Independent Indicative. (Unpublished Honors' Thesis in Linguistics and the Classics, Harvard University, Cambridge, Mass.)

Goddard, Pliny E.
1901   Conscious Word-making by the Hupa. *American Anthropologist* n.s. 3(1):208-209.

1901a   Hōn-sĭtch-ă-tĭl-yă: A Hupa Dance. *Bulletin of the Free Museum of Science and Arts, University of Pennsylvania* 3(2):117-122. Philadelphia.

[1902-1911]   [Unpublished Tolowa Fieldnotes (Tales and Texts), with a Partial Index by A.L. Kroeber and a Table of Contents by Dale Valory.] (Manuscript in the Archives of the University of California, Bancroft Library, Berkeley.)

1903   The Kato Pomo not Pomo. *American Anthropologist* 5(2):375-376.

1903-1904   Life and Culture of the Hupa. *University of California Publications in American Archaeology and Ethnology* 1(1):1-88. Berkeley.

1904   Hupa Texts. *University of California Publications in American Archaeology and Ethnology* 1(2):89-368. Berkeley.

1905   Morphology of the Hupa Language. *University of California Publications in American Archaeology and Ethnology* 3:1-344. Berkeley.

1906   Lassik Tales. *Journal of American Folk-Lore* 19(73):133-140.

1907   Kato Texts. *University of California Publications in American Archaeology and Ethnology* 5(3):65-238. Berkeley.

1907a   Kato. P. 665 in Vol. 1 of Handbook of American Indians North of Mexico. Frederick W. Hodge, ed. 2 vols. *Bureau of American Ethnology Bulletin* 30. Washington.

1907b   Mattole. Pp. 822-823 in Vol. 1 of Handbook of American Indians North of Mexico. Frederick W. Hodge, ed. 2 vols. *Bureau of American Ethnology Bulletin* 30. Washington.

1907c   Lassik. P. 761 in Vol. 1 of Handbook of American Indians North of Mexico. Frederick W. Hodge, ed. 2 vols. *Bureau of American Ethnology Bulletin* 30. Washington.

1909   Kato Texts. *University of California Publications in American Archaeology and Ethnology* 5(3):65-238. Berkeley.

1910   Sinkyone. P. 576 in Vol. 2 of Handbook of American Indians North of Mexico. Frederick W. Hodge, ed. 2 vols. *Bureau of American Ethnology Bulletin* 30. Washington.

1910a   Saia. P. 410 in Vol. 2 of Handbook of American Indians North of Mexico. Frederick W. Hodge, ed. 2 vols. *Bureau of American Ethnology Bulletin* 30. Washington.

1910b   Wailaki. P. 893-894 in Vol. 2 of Handbook of American Indians North of Mexico. Frederick W. Hodge, ed. 2 vols. *Bureau of American Ethnology Bulletin* 30. Washington.

1912   Elements of the Kato Language. *University of California Publications in American Archaeology and Ethnology* 11(1):1-176. Berkeley.

1913   Wayside Shrines in Northwestern California. *American Anthropologist* 15(4):702-703.

1914 Notes on the Chilula Indians of Northwestern California. *University of California Publications in American Archaeology and Ethnology* 10(6):265-288. Berkeley.

1914a Chilula Texts. *University of California Publications in American Archaeology and Ethnology* 10(7):289-379. Berkeley.

1921-1923 Wailaki Texts. *International Journal of American Linguistics* 2(3-4):77-135.

1923 The Habitat of the Wailaki. *University of California Publications in American Archaeology and Ethnology* 20(6):95-109. Berkeley.

1924 The Habitat of the Pitch Indians, a Wailaki Division. *University of California Publications in American Archaeology and Ethnology* 17(4):217-225. Berkeley.

Goldschmidt, Walter R.
1948 Social Organization in Native California and the Origin of Clans. *American Anthropologist* 50(3):444-456.

1951 Ethics and the Structure of Society: An Ethnological Contribution to the Sociology of Knowledge. *American Anthropologist* 53(4):506-524.

1951a Nomlaki Ethnography. *University of California Publications in American Archaeology and Ethnology* 42(4):303-443. Berkeley.

1971 Culture, Behavior, and Ethnographic Methods. *Anthropology U.C.L.A.* 3(1):3.

Goldschmidt, Walter R., and Harold E. Driver
1940 The Hupa White Deerskin Dance. *University of California Publications in American Archaeology and Ethnology* 35(8):103-142. Berkeley.

Goldschmidt, Walter R., George Foster, and Frank Essene
1939 War Stories from Two Enemy Tribes. *Journal of American Folk-Lore* 52(204):141-154.

Golla, Victor K.
1964 An Etymological Study of Hupa Noun Stems. *International Journal of American Linguistics* 30(2):108-117.

1970 Hupa Grammar. (Unpublished Ph.D. Dissertation in Linguistics, University of California, Berkeley.)

Gould, Richard A.
1963 Aboriginal California Burial and Cremation Practices. *University of California Archaeological Survey Reports* 30:149-168. Berkeley.

1966 The Wealth Quest among the Tolowa Indians of Northwestern California. *Proceedings of the American Philosophical Society* 110(1):67-89. Philadelphia.

1966a Archaeology of the Point St. George Site and Tolowa Prehistory. *University of California Publications in Anthropology* 4. Berkeley.

1968 Seagoing Canoes among the Indians of Northwestern California. *Ethnohistory* 15(1):11-42.

1975 Ecology and Adaptive Response among the Tolowa Indians of Northwestern California. *Journal of California Anthropology* 2(2):148-170.

Gould, Richard A., and Theodore P. Furukawa
1964 Aspects of Ceremonial Life among the Indian Shakers of Smith River, California. *Kroeber Anthropological Society Papers* 31:51-67. Berkeley, Calif.

Grant, Campbell
1960 Prehistoric Paintings of the Santa Barbara Region. *Santa Barbara Museum of Natural History, Museum Talk* 35(3):29-34. Santa Barbara, Calif.

1964 Chumash Artifacts Collected in Santa Barbara County, California. *University of California Archaeological Survey Reports* 63:1-44. Berkeley.

1964a California's Legacy of Indian Rock Art. *Natural History* 73(6):32-41.

1964-1965 Rock Paintings in California. *Jahrbuch für Prähistorische und Ethnographische Kunst* 21:84-90. Berlin.

1965 The Rock Paintings of the Chumash: A Study of California Indian Culture. Berkeley and Los Angeles: University of California Press.

Grant, Campbell, James W. Baird, and J. Kenneth Pringle
1968 Rock Drawings of the Coso Range, Inyo County, California. *Maturango Museum Publication* 4. China Lake, Calif.

Graves, Charles S.
1929 Lore and Legends of the Klamath River Indians. Yreka, Calif.: Press of the Times.

1934 Before the White Man Came. Yreka, Calif.: The Siskiyou News.

Greene, Augustus P.
1870 Report of August 30, 1870 to the Commissioner of Indian Affairs. Pp. 90-94 in *Annual Report of the Commissioner of Indian Affairs for 1870.* Washington.

Greengo, R., and D. Shutler
1953 Historical Background. Pp. 229-232 in The Archaeology of the Napa Region. Robert F. Heizer, ed. *University of California Anthropological Records* 12(6). Berkeley.

Greenwood, Roberta S.
1969 The Browne Site: Early Milling Stone Horizon in Southern California. *Memoirs of the Society for American Archaeology* 23. Salt Lake City, Utah.

1972 9000 Years of Prehistory at Diablo Canyon, San Luis Obispo County, California. *San Luis Obispo County Archaeological Society Occasional Papers* 2. San Luis Obispo, Calif.

Greenwood, Roberta S., and Robert O. Browne
1966 New Archaeological Discoveries at the San Buenaventura Mission. (Typed Report in Robert L. Schuyler's Possession.)

1968 The Chapel of Santa Gertrudis. *Pacific Coast Archaeological Society Quarterly* 4(4):1-59. Costa Mesa, Calif.

1969 A Coastal Chumash Village: Excavation of Shisholop, Ventura County, California. *Memoirs of the Southern California Academy of Science* 8. Los Angeles.

Greenwood, Roberta S., and Nicholas Gessler
1968 The Mission San Buenaventura Aqueduct with Particular Reference to the Fragments at Weldon Canyon. *Pacific Coast Archaeological Society Quarterly* 4(4):61-86. Costa Mesa, Calif.

Gregory, Winifred, ed.
1937 American Newspapers 1821-1936: A Union List of Files Available in the United States and Canada. New York: H.W. Wilson. (Reprinted: Kraus Reprint, NewYork, 1967.)

Grekoff, George
1967-1968 [Description of Phonology, Morphophonemics, and Tactics of the Chimariko Language.] (Manuscript in Grekoff's Possession. Copy also in Mary R. Haas' Possession, Department of Linguistics, University of California, Berkeley.)

Griffin, Dorothy W.
1963 Prehistory of the Southern Sierra Nevada: A Preliminary Investigation. Pt. 2. *Masterkey* 37(3):105-113.

Grimstead, Patricia (Kennedy)
1972 Archives and Manuscript Repositories in the U.S.S.R.: Moscow and Leningrad. Princeton, N.J.: Princeton University Press.

737

Grinnell, Joseph, and H.S. Swarth
1913   An Account of the Birds and Mammals of the San Jacinto Area of Southern California. *University of California Publications in Zoology* 10(10):197-406. Berkeley.

Grinnell, Joseph, Joseph S. Dixon, and Jean M. Linsdale
1930   Vertebrate Natural History of a Section of Northern California through the Lassen Peak Region. *Universtiy of California Publications in Zoology* 35. Berkeley.

Grosscup, Gordon L.
1960   The Culture History of Lovelock Cave, Nevada. *University of California Archaeological Survey Reports* 52. Berkeley.

Grossman, Joel W.
1968   Early Cultural Remains at Buena Vista Lake, California: Report on the 1965 Season of Field Investigations. (Manuscript at State of California Department of Parks and Recreation, Sacramento.)

Gudde, Edwin G., ed. and trans.
1933   The Memoirs of Theodor Cordua, the Pioneer of New Mecklenberg in the Sacramento Valley. *Quarterly of the California Historical Society* 12(4):279-311. San Francisco.

Gursky, Karl-Heinz
1965   Zur Frage der historischen Stellung der Yuki-Sprachfamilie. *Abhandlungen der Völkerkundlichen Arbeitsgemeinschaft* 8:1-25. Nortorf, Germany.

H.B.D.
1859   Tradition of the California Indians. *Hesperian Magazine* 3:326.

Haas, Mary R.
1954   The Proto-Coahuiltecan Word for "Water." Pp. 57-62 in Papers from the Symposium on American Indian Linguistics Held at Berkeley, July 7, 1951. *University of California Publications in Linguistics* 10. Berkeley.

―――   1958   Algonkian-Ritwan: The End of a Controversy. *International Journal of American Linguistics* 24(3):159-173.

―――   1963   Shasta and Proto-Hokan. *Language* 39(1):40-59.

―――   1964   California Hokan. Pp. 73-87 in Studies in Californian Linguistics. William Bright, ed. *University of California Publications in Linguistics* 34. Berkeley.

―――   1966   Wiyot-Yurok-Algonkian and Problems of Comparative Algonkian. *International Journal of American Linguistics* 32(2):101-107.

―――   1967   Language and Taxonomy in Northwestern California. *American Anthropologist* 69(3-4):358-362.

Haas, Theodore H.
1957   The Legal Aspects of Indian Affairs from 1887 to 1957. Pp. 12-22 in American Indians and American Life. Philadelphia. (Also in *Annals of the American Academy of Political and Social Science* 311(May), 1957. Philadelphia.)

Haenszel, Arda M.
1957   Historic Sites in San Bernardino County: A Preliminary report. *Quarterly of the San Bernardino County Museum Association* 5(2). Bloomington, Calif.

Hale, Horatio
1846   Ethnography and Philology. Vol. 6 of United States Exploring Expedition of 1838-1842, by Charles Wilkes. Philadelphia: C. Sherman.

Hall, Harvey M., and Joseph Grinnell
1919   Life-zone Indicators in California. *Proceedings of the California Academy of Sciences,* 4th ser., Vol. 9(2):37-67. San Francisco.

Halpern, Abraham M.
1936   [Fieldnotes on Southeastern Pomo Ethnography and Language, December 1936.] (7 Notebooks in Ethnological Documents of the Department of Anthropology, Bancroft Library, University of California, Berkeley.)

―――   1939   [Southeastern Pomo Linguistic Fieldnotes.] (Notebooks 7-11 in Archives of the Survey of California Indian Languages, Department of Linguistics, University of California, Berkeley.)

―――   [1939-1940]   [Fieldnotes on all the Pomo Languages.] (966 Notebook Pages and 6600 File Slips in Department of Linguistics, University of California, Berkeley.)

―――   1964   A Report on a Survey of Pomo Languages. Pp. 88-93 in Studies in Californian Linguistics. William Bright, ed. *University of California Publications in Linguistics* 34. Berkeley.

Hammond, George P., and Agapito Rey, eds.
1940   Narratives of the Coronado Expedition, 1540-1542. Albuquerque: University of New Mexico Press.

Hamp, Eric P.
1970   Wiyot and Yurok Correspondences. Pp. 107-110 in Languages and Cultures of Western North America: Essays in Honor of Sven S. Liljeblad. Earl H. Swanson, Jr., ed. Pocatello: Idaho State University Press.

Hamy, E.
1951   The French Scientific Expedition to California, 1877-1879. *University of California Archaeological Survey Reports* 12:6-13. Berkeley.

Handelman, Don
1972   Aspects of the Moral Compact of a Washo Shaman. *Anthropological Quarterly* 45(2):84-101.

Hanke, Lewis
1959   Aristotle and the American Indians: A Study in Race Prejudice in the Modern World. Chicago: Henry Regnery.

Hardy, Robert W.H.
1829   Travels in the Interior of Mexico in 1825, 1826, 1827, and 1828. London: H. Colburn and R. Bentley.

Harner, Michael J.
1957   Potsherds and the Tentative Dating of the San Gorgonio-Big Maria Trail. *University of California Archaeological Survey Reports* 37:35-37. Berkeley.

Harrington, John P.
[1912-1923]   [Notes on Chumash Linguistics and Ethnography.] (Manuscript No. 6017 in National Anthropological Archives, Smithsonian Institution, Washington.)

―――   [1913]   [Notes from Juan José Funtero, Piru, Calif., 17 March.] (Manuscript in National Anthropological Archives, Smithsonian Institution, Washington.)

―――   [1914-1915]   [Unpublished Fieldnotes, mostly from Arroyo Grande, Calif.] (Manuscripts in National Anthropological Archives, Smithsonian Institution, Washington.)

―――   [1915]   [Fieldnotes on Place Names.] (Box 747-17, J.P. Harrington Papers in Department of Linguistics, University of California, Berkeley.)

―――   1916   Inezeno and Purisimeno Chumash Place Names. (Manuscript No. 6017 in National Anthropological Archives, Smithsonian Institution, Washington.)

―――   [1916a]   [Notes from Kitanemuk Speakers at Tejon.] (Manuscript in Department of Linguistics, University of California, Berkeley.)

―――   [1917]   [Kitanemuk Fieldnotes.] (Box 705, J.P. Harrington Papers in Department of Linguistics, University of California, Berkeley.)

[1920-1930] [Gabrielino Fieldnotes.] (Manuscript in National Anthropological Archives, Smithsonian Institution, Washington.)

[1921] [Chochenyo Fieldnotes.] (Manuscript in Survey of California Indian Languages, Department of Linguistics, University of California, Berkeley.)

1921-1928 [Chimariko Fieldnotes.] (Manuscript on Loan from the National Anthropological Archives, Smithsonian Institution to the Survey of California Indian Languages, Department of Linguistics, University of California, Berkeley.)

1921-1938 [Manuscript Materials on Chochenyo, Mutsun and Rumsen.] (Manuscripts on Loan from the National Anthropological Archives, Smithsonian Institution to the Survey of California Indian Languages, Department of Linguistics, University of California, Berkeley.)

1925-1928 [Cupeño Ethnographic and Linguistic Fieldnotes.] (Manuscript in National Anthropological Archives, Smithsonian Institution, Washington.)

[1926] [Karuk Ethnographic and Linguistic Notes.] (Manuscripts Nos. 4553 and 4556 in National Anthropological Archives, Smithsonian Institution, Washington.)

1928 Exploration of the Burton Mound at Santa Barbara, California. Pp. 23-168 in *44th Annual Report of the Bureau of American Ethnology for the Years 1926-1927*. Washington.

1928-1933 [Konomihu and Shasta Fieldnotes.] (Manuscript in Survey of California Indian Languages, Department of Linguistics, University of California, Berkeley.)

[1929-1939] [Hoomontwash Fieldnotes.] (Manuscript in National Anthropological Archives, Smithsonian Institution, Washington.)

1931 Karuk Texts. *International Journal of American Linguistics* 6(2):121-161.

1932 Karuk Indian Myths. *Bureau of American Ethnology Bulletin* 107. Washington.

1932a Tobacco among the Karuk Indians of California. *Bureau of American Ethnology Bulletin* 94. Washington.

1933 [Report of Fieldwork on Indians of Monterey and San Bernardino Counties.] Pp. 2-3 in *49th Annual Report of the Bureau of American Ethnology for the Years 1931-1932*. Washington.

1933a Fieldwork among the Mission Indians of California. Pp. 85-88 in *Explorations and Fieldwork of the Smithsonian Institution in 1932*. Washington.

1933b Annotations of Alfred Robinson's Chinigchinich. Pp. 91-228 in Chinigchinich: A Revised and Annotated Version of Alfred Robinson's Translation of Father Geronimo Boscana's Historical Account of the Belief, Usages, Customs and Extravagencies [!] of the Indians of this Mission of San Juan Capistrano Called the Acagchemem Tribe. P.T. Hanna, ed. Santa Ana, Calif.: Fine Arts Press.

1934 A New Original Version of Boscana's Historical Account of the San Juan Capistrano Indians of Southwest California. *Smithsonian Miscellaneous Collections* 92(4):1-62. Washington.

1934a Rescuing the Early History of the California Indians. Pp. 54-56 in *Explorations and Fieldwork of the Smithsonian Institution in 1933*. Washington.

1935 Fieldwork among the Indians of California. Pp. 81-84 in *Explorations and Fieldwork of the Smithsonian Institution in 1934*. Washington.

1942 Culture Element Distributions, XIX: Central California Coast. *University of California Anthropological Records* 7(1):1-46. Berkeley.

1962 Preface. Pp. vii-viii in California's Gabrielino Indians, by Bernice E. Johnston. Los Angeles: Southwest Museum. (Frederick Webb Hodge Anniversary Publication Fund 8).

1974 Sibilants in Ventureño. *International Journal of American Linguistics* 40(1):1-9.

Harrington, John P., and C. Hart Merriam
1967 Chimariko Notes. Pp. 226-229 in Ethnographic Notes on California Indian Tribes, II: Ethnological Notes on Northern and Southern California Tribes. Robert F. Heizer, ed. *University of California Archaeological Survey Reports* 68. Berkeley.

Harrington, Mark R.
1939 The Supposed Infirmary Building at La Purísima. (Manuscript at La Purísima State Historical Monument Headquarters, Lompoc, Calif.)

1940 Temporary Indian Barracks at Purísima Mission. (Manuscript at La Purísima State Historical Monument Headquarters, Lompoc, Calif.)

1940a A Forgotten Mission Cemetery at La Purísima. (Manuscript at La Purísima State Historical Monument Headquarters, Lompoc, Calif.)

1943 A Glimpse of Pomo Archaeology. *Masterkey* 17(1):9-12.

1948 An Ancient Site at Borax Lake, California. *Southwest Museum Papers* 16. Los Angeles.

1958 Digging up the Past at San Luís Rey. *Masterkey* 32(2):55-57.

Harrison, William M.
1965 Mikiw: A Coastal Chumash Village. *Annual Reports of the University of California Archaeological Survey* 7:91-178. Los Angeles.

Harrison, William M., and Edith S. Harrison
1966 An Archaeological Sequence for the Hunting People of Santa Barbara, California. *Annual Reports of the University of California Archaeological Survey* 8:1-89. Los Angeles.

Harrison, William M., and Patricia Lyon
1960 Final Summary Report of Investigations at La Purísima Mission State Historical Monument. (Manuscript in Department of Anthropology, University of California, Santa Barbara.)

Harvey, Herbert R.
1968 Cahuilla Settlement Patterns and the Time Perspective. (Unpublished Ph.D. Dissertation in Anthropology, Harvard University, Cambridge, Mass.)

Harwood, Harvey R.
1936 Archeological Reports for the Months of August and December, 1936, La Purísima Camp S.P. 29. (Manuscript at La Purísima State Historical Monument Headquarters, Lompoc, Calif.)

1937 Archeological Report, January 1937, La Purísima Camp S.P. 29. (Manuscript at La Purísima State Historical Monument Headquarters, Lompoc, Calif.)

Hatch, James
1958 Tachi Yokuts Music. *Kroeber Anthropological Society Papers* 19:47-66. Berkeley, Calif.

Havard, V.
1895 Food Plants of the North American Indians. *Bulletin of the Torrey Botanical Club* 22(3):98-123. New York.

Hayes, Benjamin
1929 Pioneer Notes from the Diaries of Judge Benjamin Hayes 1849-1875. Marjorie T. Wolcott, ed. Los Angeles: McBride.

Hedges, Ken
1975   Notes on the Kumeyaay: A Problem of Identification. *Journal of California Anthropology* 2(1):71-83.

Hedrick, Helen
1941   The Blood Remembers. New York: Alfred Knopf.

Heidsick, Ralph G.
1966   Music of the Luiseño Indians of Southern California: A Study of Music in Indian Culture with Relation to a Program in Indian Music. (Unpublished Ph.D. Dissertation in Music, University of California, Los Angeles.)

Heintzelman, H.P.
1855   [Report Dated November 17, 1855.] (Manuscript in U.S. National Archives, Office of Indian Affiars, Record Group 75, Enclosure to Document H1100. Washington.)

Heinzelman, Samuel P.
1857   [Report.] Pp. 34-53 in Indian Affairs on the Pacific: Message from the President of the United States Transmitting Report with Regard to Indian Affairs. U.S. Congress. House. 34th Cong., 3d sess. House Executive Doc. No. 76. (Serial No. 906) Washington: U.S. Government Printing Office.

Heizer, Robert F.
1938   The Plank Canoe of the Santa Barbara Region, California. *Ethnological Studies* 7:193-237. Göteborg, Sweden.

1940   Aboriginal Use of Bitumen by the California Indians. *California State Department of Natural Resources, Division of Mines Bulletin* 118:74. Sacramento.

1940a   The Introduction of Monterey Shells to the Indians of the Northwest Coast. *Pacific Northwest Quarterly* 31(4):399-402.

1941   Archeological Evidence of Sebastian Rodriguez Cermeño's California Visit in 1595. *Quarterly of the California Historical Society* 20(4):315-328. San Francisco.

1941a   A California Messianic Movement of 1801 among the Chumash. *American Anthropologist* 43(1):128-129.

1941b   The Direct-Historical Approach in California Archaeology. *American Antiquity* 7(2):98-122.

1941c   Aboriginal Trade between the Southwest and California. *Masterkey* 15(5):185-188.

1941d   Alexander S. Taylor's Map of California Indian Tribes, 1864. *Quarterly of the California Historical Society* 20(2):171-180. San Francisco.

1942   Walla Walla Indian Expeditions to the Sacramento Valley, 1844-1847. *Quarterly of the California Historical Society* 21(1):1-7. San Francisco.

1946   The Occurrence and Significance of Southwestern Grooved Axes in California. *American Antiquity* 11(3):187-193.

1947   Francis Drake and the California Indians, 1579. *University of California Publications in American Archaeology and Ethnology* 42(3):251-302. Berkeley.

1948   A Bibliography of Ancient Man in California. *University of California Archaeological Survey Reports* 2:1-22. Berkeley.

1948a   The California Archaeological Survey: Establishment, Aims, and Methods. *University of California Archaeological Survey Reports* 1:1-8. Berkeley.

1949   The Archaeology of Central California, I: The Early Horizon. *University of California Anthropological Records* 12(1):1-84. Berkeley.

1949a   The California Archaeological Survey. *American Antiquity* 14(3):222-223.

1950   Observations on Historic Sites and Archaeology in California. *University of California Archaeological Survey Reports* 9(6):1-5. Berkeley.

1951   A Prehistoric Yurok Ceremonial Site (Hum-174). Pp. 1-4 in Papers on California Archaeology 10. *University of California Archaeological Survey Reports* 11. Berkeley.

———, ed.
1952   California Indian Linguistic Records: The Mission Indian Vocabularies of Alphonse Pinart. *University of California Anthropological Records* 15(1):1-84. Berkeley.

———, ed.
1953   The Archaeology of the Napa Region. *University of California Anthropological Records* 12(6):225-358. Berkeley.

1953a   Sacred Rain-Rocks of Northern California. *University of California Archaeological Survey Reports* 20:33-38. Berkeley.

1954   Some Anthropological Perspectives on California History. *Quarterly of the California Historical Society* 33(1):85-88. San Francisco.

———, ed.
1955   California Indian Linguistic Records: The Mission Indian Vocabularies of H.W. Henshaw. *University of California Anthropological Records* 15(2):85-202. Berkeley.

[1955a] Analysis of "Tribes" Signing the Eighteen Unratified 1851-1852 California Treaties. Prepared for Use in Dockets 31-37, Indian Claims Commission. (Copy Catalogued as Manuscript No. 443 in University of California Archaeological Research Facility, Berkeley.)

1955b   Two Chumash Legends. *Journal of American Folklore* 68(267):34, 56, 72.

1958   Radiocarbon Dates from California of Archaeological Interest. *University of California Archaeological Survey Reports* 44(1):1-16. Berkeley.

1958a   Aboriginal California and Great Basin Cartography. *Universtiy of California Archaeologica! Survey Reports* 41:1-9. Berkeley.

1960   California Population Densities, 1770 and 1950. Pp. 9-11 in Papers on California Archaeology. *University of California Archaeological Survey Reports* 50. Berkeley.

1962   The California Indians: Archeology, Varieties of Culture, Arts of Life. *Quarterly of the California Historical Society* 41(1):1-28. San Francisco.

1964   The Western Coast of North America. Pp. 117-148 in Prehistoric Man in the New World. J. D. Jennings and E. Norbeck, eds. Chicago: University of Chicago Press.

1964a   California Archaeology: Its Development, Present Status, and Future Needs. *Masterkey* 38(3):84-90.

1966   Languages, Territories and Names of California Indian Tribes. Berkeley and Los Angeles: University of California Press.

1966a   Salvage and Other Archaeology. *Masterkey* 40(2):54-60.

———, ed.
1968   The Indians of Los Angeles County: Hugo Reid's Letters of 1852. *Southwest Museum Papers* 21. Los Angeles.

1968a   One of the Oldest Known California Indian Baskets. *Masterkey* 42(2):70-74.

1970   A Chumash Census of 1928-1930. *University of California Archaeological Research Facility Contributions* 9:23-28. Berkeley.

—————, ed.
1970a   An Anthropological Expedition of 1913, or Get It Through Your Head or Yours for the Revolution. Correspondence between A.L. Kroeber and L.L. Loud, July 12, 1913-October 31,1913. Berkeley: University of California Archaeological Research Facility.

1971   Two Ethnographic Chumash Stone-weighted Digging Sticks. *Masterkey* 45(2):64-68.

1972   The Eighteen Unratified Treaties of 1851-1852 between the California Indians and the United States Government. Berkeley: University of California Archaeological Research Facility.

1972a   California's Oldest Historical Relic? Berkeley, Calif.: Robert H. Lowie Museum of Anthropology.

—————, ed.
1973   Collected Documents on the Causes and Events in the Bloody Island Massacre of 1850. Berkeley: University of California Archaeological Research Facility.

—————, ed.
1973a   Notes on the McCloud River Wintu and Selected Excerpts from Alexander S. Taylor's Indianology of California. Berkeley: University of California Archaeological Research Facility.

—————, ed.
1974   They Were Only Diggers: A Collection of Articles from California Newspapers, 1851-1866, on Indian and White Relations. *Ballena Press Publications in Archaeology, Ethnology and History* 1. Ramona, Calif.

1974a   Elizabethan California: A Brief and Sometimes Critical Review of Opinions on the Location of Francis Drake's Five Weeks' Visit with the Indians of Ships Land in 1579. Ramona, Calif.: Ballena Press.

[1975]   When Was the Ethnographic Present? (Unpublished Manuscript in Heizer's Possession.)

[1975a]   The California Indians as Described by the Franciscan Missionaries in 1812-1814. (Unpublished Manuscript in Heizer's Possession.)

—————, ed.
1975b   Seven Early Accounts of the Pomo Indians and their Culture. Berkeley: University of California Archaeological Research Facility.

Heizer, Robert F., and Alan J. Almquist
1971   The Other Californians: Prejudice and Discrimination under Spain, Mexico, and the United States to 1920. Berkeley and Los Angeles: University of California Press.

Heizer, Robert F., and Martin A. Baumhoff
1962   Prehistoric Rock Art of Nevada and Eastern California. Berkeley: University of California Press.

Heizer, Robert F., and C. William Clewlow, Jr.
1973   Prehistoric Rock Art of California. 2 vols. Ramona, Calif.: Ballena Press.

Heizer, Robert F., and Sherburne F. Cook
1952   Fluorine and Other Chemical Tests of Some North American Human and Fossil Bones. *American Journal of Physical Anthropology* 10(3):289-303.

Heizer, Robert F., and William W. Elmendorf
1942   Francis Drake's California Anchorage in the Light of the Indian Language Spoken There. *Pacific Historical Review* 11(2):213-217.

Heizer, Robert F., and Albert B. Elsasser
1953   Some Archaeological Sites and Cultures of the Central Sierra Nevada. *University of California Archaeological Survey Reports* 21:1-42. Berkeley.

1964   Archaeology of Hum-67: The Gunther Island Site in Humboldt Bay, California. *University of California Archaeological Survey Reports* 62:5-122. Berkeley.

Heizer, Robert F., and Franklin Fenenga
1939   Archaeological Horizons in Central California. *American Anthropologist* 41(3):378-399.

Heizer, Robert F., and Thomas R. Hester
1970   Names and Locations of Some Ethnographic Patwin and Maidu Indian Villages. *University of California Archaeological Research Facility Contributions* 9(5):79-118. Berkeley.

1970a   Some Early Treaties with California Indians; Document 3a, "Treaty between the Americans and the Indians on the 'Sonoma Frontier', 1848." *University of California Archaeological Research Facility Contributions* 9(5):107-111. Berkeley.

1970b   Shasta Villages and Territory. *University of California Archaeological Research Facility Contributions* 9(6):119-158. Berkeley.

Heizer, Robert F., and Harper Kelley
1962   Burins and Bladelets in the Cessac Collection from Santa Cruz Island, California. *Proceedings of the American Philosophical Society* 106(2):94-105. Philadelphia.

Heizer, Robert F., and Alex D. Krieger
1956   The Archaeology of Humboldt Cave, Churchill County, Nevada. *University of California Publications in American Archaeology and Ethnology* 47(1):1-190. Berkeley.

Heizer, Robert F., and William C. Massey
1953   Aboriginal Navigation off the Coasts of Upper and Baja California. *Anthropological Papers 39, Bureau of American Ethnology Bulletin* 151:285-312. Washington.

Heizer, Robert F., and John E. Mills
1952   The Four Ages of Tsurai: A Documentary History of the Indian Village on Trinidad Bay. Berkeley: University of California Press.

Heizer, Robert F., and Karen M. Nissen
1973   The Human Sources of California Ethnography. Berkeley: University of California Archaeological Research Facility.

Heizer, Robert F., and Henry Rapoport
1962   Identification of *Distichlis* Salt Used by California Indians. *Masterkey* 36(4):146-148.

Heizer, Robert F., and R.J. Squier
1953   Excavations at Site Nap-32 in July, 1951. Pp. 318-326 in The Archaeology of the Napa Region. Robert F. Heizer, ed. *University of California Anthropological Records* 12(6). Berkeley.

Heizer, Robert F., and Adan E. Treganza
1972   Mines and Quarries of the Indians of California. Ramona, Calif.: Ballena Press.

Heizer, Robert F., Albert B. Elsasser, and C. William Clewlow, Jr., comps.
1970   A Bibliography of the Archaeology of California. *University of California Archaeological Research Facility Contributions* 6. Berkeley.

Heizer, Robert F., Karen M. Nissen, and Edward D. Castillo
1975   California Indian History: A Classified and Annotated Guide to Source Materials. *Ballena Press Publications in Archaeology, Ethnology and History* 4. Ramona, Calif.

Heizer, Robert F., D. Bailey, Marke Estis, and Karen Nissen
1969   Catalogue of the C. Hart Merriam Collection of Data Concerning California Indian Tribes and Other American Indian Tribes. Berkeley: University of California, Department of Anthropology, Archaeological Research Facility.

Henderson, Junius
1930   Ancient Shell "Trade Routes." *Nautilus* 43(4):109-110.

Henley, Thomas J.
1857   California Indians. Pp. 715-718 in Vol. 6 of Historical and Statistical Information, Respecting the History, Condition and Prospects of the Indian Tribes of the United States. Henry R. Schoolcraft, ed. 6 vols. Philadelphia: Lippincott, Grambo.

Henry, Jeanette
1970   Textbooks and the American Indian. Rupert Costo, ed. San Francisco: Indian Historian Press.

Henshaw, Henry W.
1879   Translation from the Spanish of the Account by the Pilot Ferrel of the Voyage of Cabrillo along the West Coast of North America in 1542. Pp. 293-314 in Reports upon Archaeological and Ethnological Collections from the Vicinity of Santa Barbara. F.W. Putnam, ed. U. S. Geographical Surveys West of the 100th Meridian, Report 8. Washington.

1890   A New Linguistic Family in California. *American Anthropologist* 3(1):45-49.

1907   Diegueños. P. 390 in Vol. 1 of Handbook of American Indians North of Mexico. Frederick W. Hodge, ed. 2 vols. *Bureau of American Ethnology Bulletin* 30. Washington.

1972   The Luiseno Creation Myth. Robert F. Heizer, ed. *Masterkey* 46(3):93-100.

Henshaw, Henry W., and Frederick W. Hodge
1907   Comeya. Pp. 329-330 in Vol. 1 of Handbook of American Indians North of Mexico. Frederick W. Hodge, ed. 2 vols. *Bureau of American Ethnology Bulletin* 30. Washington.

Henshaw, Henry W., and Alfred L. Kroeber
1910   Salinan Family. P. 415 in Vol. 2 of Handbook of American Indians North of Mexico. Frederick W. Hodge, ed. 2 vols. *Bureau of American Ethnology Bulletin* 30. Washington.

Hertzberg, Hazel
1971   The Search for an American Indian Identity: Modern Pan-Indian Movements. Syracuse, N.Y: Syracuse University Press.

Herzog, George
1928   The Yuman Musical Style. *Journal of American Folk-Lore* 41(160):183-231.

Hewes, Gordon W.
1941   Reconnaissance of the Central San Joaquin Valley. *American Antiquity* 7(2):123-133.

1946   Early Man in California and the Tranquillity Site. *American Antiquity* 11(4):209-215.

[Hewett, George G.]
[1792]   [Ethnographic Specimens Acquired during the Explorations of George Vancouver.] (Manuscript in Museum of Mankind, British Museum, London.)

[1793]   [Manuscript Catalogue of the Hewett Collection.] (Manuscript Notebook in Museum of Mankind, British Museum, London.)

Heye, George G.
1919   Certain Aboriginal Pottery from Southern California. *Museum of the American Indian, Heye Foundation. Indian Notes and Monographs* 7(1). New York.

1921   Certain Artifacts from San Miguel Island, California. *Museum of the American Indian, Heye Foundation. Indian Notes and Monographs* 7(4). New York.

Hicks, Frederic
1958   Archaeological Investigations in the Yucaipa Valley. *Quarterly of the San Bernardino County Museum Association 6(1), Scientific Series* 3:1-43. Bloomington, Calif.

1963   Ecological Aspects of Aboriginal Culture in the Western Yuman Area. (Unpublished Ph.D. Dissertation in Anthropology, University of California, Los Angeles.)

Hill, Dorothy J.
1969   Collection of Maidu Indian Folklore of Northern California. Durham, Calif.: Northern California Indian Association.

1970   Indians of Chico Rancheria: An Ethnohistoric Study. (Unpublished M.A. Thesis in Anthropology, California State College, Chico.)

Hill, Jane H.
1969   Volitional and Non-volitional Verbs in Cupeño. Pp. 348-356 in *Papers from the 5th Regional Meeting of the Chicago Linguistic Society*. Robert I. Binnick et al., eds. Chicago, 1969.

1970   A Peeking Rule in Cupeño. *Linguistic Inquiry* 1:534-539.

1972   Cupeño Lexicalization and Language History. *International Journal of American Linguistics* 38(3):161-172.

Hill, Jane H., and Rosinda Nolasquez
1973   Mulu'wetam: The First People; Cupeño Oral History and Language. Banning, Calif.: Malki Museum Press.

Hill, Joseph J.
1927   History of Warner's Ranch and its Environs. Los Angeles: Privately Printed.

Hill, Kenneth C.
1967   A Grammar of the Serrano Language. (Unpublished Ph.D. Dissertation in Linguistics, University of California, Los Angeles.)

1969   Some Implications of Serrano Phonology. Pp. 357-365 in *Papers from the 5th Regional Meeting of the Chicago Linguistic Society*. Robert I. Binnick et al., eds. Chicago, 1969.

Hillebrand, Timothy S.
1967   Tentative Summary of Archaeological Findings at the Presidio Chapel Site. *Noticias: Quarterly Bulletin of the Santa Barbara Historical Society* 13(4):18-23. Santa Barbara, Calif.

Hindes, Margaret G.
1959   A Report on Indian Sites and Trails, Huntington Lake Region, California. *University of California Archaeological Survey Reports* 48:1-15. Berkeley.

Hinton Thomas B., and Roger C. Owen
1957   Some Surviving Yuman Groups in Northern Baja California. *América Indígena* 17(1):87-102.

Hittell, John S.
1861   Mining in the Pacific States of North America. San Francisco: H.H. Bancroft.

Hittell, Theodore H.
1885-1897   History of California. 4 vols. San Francisco: Pacific Press Publishing Company; N.J. Stone.

Hockett, C.F.
1973   Yokuts as Testing-Ground for Linguistic Methods. *International Journal of American Linguistics* 39(2):63-79.

Hodge, Frederick W., ed.
1907-1910   Handbook of American Indians North of Mexico. 2 vols. *Bureau of American Ethnology Bulletin* 30. Washington.

Hodge, Frederick W., and Alfred L. Kroeber
1907   Moquelumnan Family. Pp. 941-942 in Vol. 1 of Handbook of American Indians North of Mexico. Frederick W. Hodge, ed. 2 vols. *Bureau of American Ethnology Bulletin* 30. Washington.

Hoebel, E. Adamson
1966   Anthropology: The Study of Man. 3d ed. New York: McGraw-Hill.

Hoffman, W.J.
1885 Hugo Reid's Account of the Indians of Los Angeles County, California. *Bulletin of the Essex Institute* 17(1-3):1-35. Salem, Mass.

Hoffman, Michael, and Lynda Brunker
1976 Studies in California Paleopathology. *University of California Archaeological Research Facility Contributions* 30. Berkeley.

Hoijer, Harry
1956 The Chronology of the Athapaskan Languages. *International Journal of American Linguistics* 22(4):219-232.

1960 Athapaskan Languages of the Pacific Coast. Pp. 960-976 in Culture in History: Essays in Honor of Paul Radin. Stanley Diamond, ed. New York: Columbia University Press.

Holmes, William H.
1901 Review of the Evidence Relating to Auriferous Gravel Man in California. Pp. 419-472 in *Annual Report of the Smithsonian Institution for 1899.* Washington.

1919 Handbook of Aboriginal American Antiquities. Pt. 1, Introductory: The Lithic Industries. *Bureau of American Ethnology Bulletin* 60. Washington.

Holt, Catharine
1942 The Relations of Shasta Folklore. (Unpublished Ph.D. Dissertation in Anthropology, University of California, Berkeley.)

1946 Shasta Ethnography. *University of California Anthropological Records* 3(4):299-349. Berkeley.

Holterman, Jack
1970 The Revolt of Estanislao. *The Indian Historian* 3(1):43-54.

1970a The Revolt of Yozcolo: Indian Warrior in the Fight for Freedom. *The Indian Historian* 3(2):19-23.

Hooper, Lucile
1920 The Cahuilla Indians. *University of California Publications in American Archaeology and Ethnology* 16(6):316-380. Berkeley.

Hoopes, Alban W.
1932 Indian Affairs and their Administration with Special Reference to the Far West, 1849-1860. Philadelphia: University of Pennsylvania Press.

Hoopes, Chad L.
1966 Lure of Humboldt Bay Region: Early Exploration, Discoveries, and Foundations Establishing the Bay Region. Dubuque, Iowa: William C. Brown.

Hoover, Robert L.
1968 An Unusual Chumash Pictograph. *University of California Archaeological Survey Reports* 71:117-119. Berkeley.

1971 Some Aspects of Santa Barbara Channel Prehistory. (Unpublished Ph.D. Dissertation in Anthropology, University of California, Berkeley.)

Hostler, Patricia, and Byron Hostler
1967 History of the Hoopa Tribe. Hoopa, Calif.: Hoopa Valley Business Council and Hoopa Valley Tribe.

Howard, Donald M.
1970 Archaeology of the Indian Rancheria at Mission San Antonio de Padua, Jolan California. Pp. 15-16 in *Abstracts of the Annual Meeting of the Southwestern Anthropological Association and the Society for California Archaeology.* Asilomar, Calif., March 25-28, 1970.

1970a Archaeological Investigations at Mission Nuestra Senora de la Soledad (Mnt-233). Pp. 16-17 in *Abstracts of the Annual Meeting of the Southwestern Anthropological Association and the Society for California Archaeology.* Asilomar, Calif., March 25-28, 1970.

1972 Excavations at Tes-haya: The Indian Rancheria at Mission San Antonio de Padua (Mnt-100). *Monterey County Archaeological Society Quarterly* 2(1). Monterey, Calif.

Hrdlička, Aleš
1907 Skeletal Remains Suggesting or Attributed to Early Man in North America. *Bureau of American Ethnology Bulletin* 33. Washington.

Hubbard, L.
1861 Notes on the Tututni. P. 38 in The Indianology of California. A.S. Taylor, ed. *The California Farmer,* Installment 38.

Hudson, J.W.
1902 An Indian Myth of the San Joaquin Basin. *Journal of American Folk-Lore* 15(57):104-106.

Hudson, Dee T.
1969 The Archaeological Investigations during 1935 and 1937 at Ora-237, Ora-238, and Ora-239 Santiago Canyon, Orange County, California. *Pacific Coast Archaeological Society Qarterly* 5(1):1-68. Costa Mesa, Calif.

1971 Proto-Gabrielino Patterns of Territorial Organization in South Coastal California. *Pacific Coast Archaeological Society Quarterly* 7(2):49-76. Costa Mesa, Calif.

Humphrey, Richard V.
1965 The La Purísima Mission Cemetery. *Annual Reports of the University of California Archaeological Survey* 7:179-192. Los Angeles.

Hunt, Ann
1960 The Allen and Jones Massacres and the Extermination of the Yana. Pp. 40-52 in The Covered Wagon. Redding, Calif.: Shasta Historical Society.

1966 Indian Trade Items in Shasta County. Pp. 15-21 in The Covered Wagon. Redding, Calif.: Shasta Historical Society.

Hunter, John E.
1967 Inventory of Ethnological Collections in Museums of the United States and Canada. Milwaukee: The Committee on Anthropological Research in Museums of the American Anthropological Association and the Wrenner-Gren Foundation for Anthropological Research.

Hutchinson, C.A..
1965 The Mexican Government and the Mission Indians of Upper California, 1821-1835. *The Americas: A Quarterly Review of Inter-American Cultural History* 21(4):335-362.

Hyde, Villiana
1971 An Introduction to the Luiseño Language. Ronald W. Langacker et al., eds. Banning, Calif.: Malki Museum Press.

Hymes, Dell H.
1957 A Note on Athapaskan Glottochronology. *International Journal of American Linguistics* 23(4):291-297.

1957a Some Penutian Elements and the Penutian Hypothesis. *Southwestern Journal of Anthropology* 13(1):69-87.

1964 Evidence for Penutian in Lexical Sets with Initial *C- and *S-. *International Journal of American Linguistics* 30(3):213-242.

1964a 'Hail' and 'Bead': Two Penutian Etymologies. Pp. 94-98 in Studies in Californian Linguistics. William Bright, ed. *University of California Publications in Linguistics* 34. Berkeley.

Irvine, Leigh H.
1915 History of Humboldt County, California, with Biographical Sketches of the Leading Men and Women of the County. Los Angeles: Historic Record Company.

Ives, Joseph C.
1861 Report upon the Colorado River of the West. U.S. Congress. House. 36th Cong., 1st sess., House Executive Doc.

No. 90 (Serial No. 1058). Washington: U.S. Government Printing Office.

Ives, Ronald
1961 The Quest of the Blue Shells. *Arizoniana: Journal of Arizona History* 2(1):3-7.

Jackson, Helen M. (Hunt)
1881 Century of Dishonor: A Sketch of the United States Government's Dealings with Some of the Indian Tribes. New York: Harper and Brothers.

1884 Ramona: A Story. Boston: Roberts Brothers.

Jackson, Helen M. (Hunt), and Abbot Kinney
1884 Report on the Condition and Needs of the Mission Indians of California to the Commissioner of Indian Affairs. Pp. 7-15 in Message from the President of the United States. 48th Cong. 1st sess. Senate Executive Doc. No. 49 (Serial No. 2162). Washington: U.S. Government Printing Office.

Jacobs, Roderick A.
1974 Syntactic Change: A Cupan (Uto-Aztecan) Case Study. *University of California Publications in Linguistics* 79. Berkeley.

Jacobsen, William H., Jr.
1954-1958 [Linguistic Notes and Tape Recordings on the Salinan Language: Collected June 18-September 14, October 29-30, 1954, and January 30-February 2, 1958.] (Manuscripts in Department of Linguistics, University of California, Berkeley.)

1958 Washo and Karok: An Approach to Comparative Hokan. *International Journal of American Linguistics* 24(3):195-212.

James, George W.
1902 A Saboba Origin-Myth. *Journal of American Folk-Lore* 15(56):36-39.

1903 The Legend of Tauquitch and Algoot. *Journal of American Folk-Lore* 16(62):153-159.

1909 Indian Basketry, and How to Make Indian and Other Baskets. 4th ed. New York: Henry Malkan. (Reprinted: Dover Publications, New York, 1972).

James, Harry C.
1960 The Cahuilla Indians: The Men Called Master. Los Angeles: Westernlore Press. (Reprinted: Malki Museum Press, Banning, Calif., 1969.)

Jayme, Antonio
1929 [Reply to the Interrogatório of 1812, Mission Soledad.] Pp. 24-26 in Mission Nuestra Senora de la Soledad, by Zephyrin Engelhardt. Santa Barbara, Calif.: Mission Santa Barbara.

Jenkins, Olaf P.
1938 Geologic Map of California. *California State Department of Natural Resources, Division of Mines Bulletin* 158. Sacramento.

Jewell, Donald P.
1966 Excavations at Fort Humboldt, August 1966. (Mimeographed Report Issued from and Located at American River Junior College, Sacramento, Calif.)

Jewell, Donald P., and John S. Clemmer
1959 A Report on the Archeological Findings at Fort Humboldt State Monument, California. (Manuscript No. 17, at the California State Division of Beaches and Parks, Sacramento.)

Joel, Judith
1964 Classification of the Yuman Languages. Pp. 99-105 in Studies in Californian Linguistics. William Bright, ed. *University of California Publications in Linguistics* 34. Berkeley.

Johnson, Frederick
1940 The Linguistic Map of Mexico and Central America. Pp. 88-114 in The Maya and their Neighbors. C.L. Hay et al., eds. New York: Appleton-Century.

Johnson, Jerald J.
1967 The Archeology of the Camanche Reservoir Locality, California. *Sacramento Anthropological Society Papers* 6. Sacramento, Calif.

1970 Archaeological Investigations at the Applegate Site (4-Ama-56). *University of California, Center for Archaeological Research Publications* 2:65-144. Davis.

[1972] [The Archaeology of the Southern Cascade Mountains Region.] (Manuscript in Johnson's Possession.)

1973 Archaeological Investigations in Northeastern California (1939-1972) . (Unpublished Ph.D. Dissertation in Anthropology, University of California, Davis.)

Johnson, Keith L.
1966 Site LAN-2: A Late Manifestation of the Topanga Complex in Southern California Prehistory. *Universtiy of California Anthropological Records* 23:1-36. Berkeley.

Johnson, Kenneth M.
1966 K-344; or The Indians of California vs. the United States. Los Angeles: Dawson's Book Shop.

Johnston, Adam
1958 Letter to the Commissioner of Indian Affairs, Sept. 15, 1850. (In Letters Received by the Office of Indian Affairs 1824-1881. Microcopy No. 234, Roll 32: California Superintendency 1849-1852. Washington: The National Archives and Records Service, General Services Administration.)

1958a Letter to the Commissioner of Indian Affairs July 6, 1850. (In Letters Received by the Office of Indian Affairs 1824-1881. Microcopy No. 234, Roll 32: California Superintendency 1849-1852. Washington: The National Archives and Records Service, General Services Administration.)

Johnston, Bernice E.
1962 California's Gabrielino Indians. (Frederick Webb Hodge Anniversary Publication Fund 8) Los Angeles: Southwest Museum.

Johnston, Francis
1967 The Bradshaw Trail (Manuscripts on File, Archaeological Site Survey Committee, Malki Museum, Morongo Indian Reservation, Banning, Calif.)

Johnston, Francis J., and Patricia H. Johnston
1957 An Indian Trail Complex of the Central Colorado Desert: A Preliminary Survey. *University of California Archaeological Survey Reports* 37:22-34. Berkeley.

Jones, Joseph R.
1971 The Land of Remember. Yreka, Calif.: Privately Published.

Jones, Philip M.
[1900] [Preliminary Report to Mrs. Phoebe A. Hearst on Archaeological and Ethnological Materials in California. Pt. 1.] (Manuscript No. 347 in University of California Archaeological Research Facility, Department of Anthropology, Berkeley.)

1922 Mound Excavations near Stockton. *University of California Publications in American Archaeology and Ethnology* 20(7):113-122. Berkeley.

1956 Archaeological Investigations on Santa Rosa Island in 1901. Robert F. Heizer and Albert B. Elsasser, eds. *Universtiy of California Anthropological Records* 17(2):201-280. Berkeley.

1969   San Nicolas Island Archaeology in 1901. *Masterkey* 43(3):84-98.

Josephy, Alvin M., ed.
1961   The American Heritage Book of Indians. New York: American Heritage Publishing Company.

Joughlin, Roberta, and Salvadora G. Valenzuela
1953   Cupeño Genesis. *El Museo* n.s. 1(4):16-23. San Diego, Calif.

Kasch, Charles
1947   The Yokayo Rancheria. *Quarterly of the California Historical Society* 26(3):209-216. San Francisco.

Keane, Augustus H.
1878   Ethnography and Philology of America. Appendix (pp. 443-561) in Central America, the West Indies, and South America. H.W. Bates, ed. (Stanford's Compendium of Geography and Travel.) London: Edward Stanford.

Kelly, Isabel (Truesdell)
1930   The Carver's Art of the Indians of Northwestern California. *University of California Publications in American Archaeology and Ethnology* 24(7):103-119. Berkeley.

1930a   Yuki Basketry. *University of California Publications in American Archaeology and Ethnology* 24(9):421-444. Berkeley.

1931-1932   [Ethnographic Fieldnotes on Coast Miwok, December, 1931 to May, 1932.] (Manuscript in Kelly's Possession.)

Kelsey, C.E.
1906   Report of the Special Agent for California Indians. Carlisle, Pa.: Indian School Print.

————, comp.
1971   Census of Non-reservation California Indians, 1905-1906. Robert F. Heizer, ed. Berkeley: Miscellaneous Publications of the University of California Archaeological Research Facility.

Kemble, Edward C.
1962   A History of California Newspapers 1846-1858. Helen Bretnor, ed. Los Gatos, Calif.: Talisman Press. (Reprinted from the Supplement to the *Sacramento Union*, December 25, 1858.)

Kennedy, Mary J.
1949   Karok Life Stories. (Manuscript in William Bright's Possession.)

1955   Culture Contact and Acculturation of the Southwestern Pomo. (Unpublished Ph.D. Dissertation in Anthropology, Universtiy of California, Berkeley.)

Kenton, Sannie
1972   Selected Bibliography of Maidu Archeology. In Selected Bibliography of Maidu Ethnography and Archeology, by Norman L. Wilson and Arlean Towne. (Unpublished Manuscript on File, National Park Service, San Francisco.)

Kessler, Edith
1908   The Passing of the Old Ceremonial Dances of the Southern California Indians. *Southern Workman* 37(10):527-538.

King, Chester D.
1968   Excavations at Ala-342: A Summary Report. (Manuscript on File, California State Department of Parks and Recreation, Sacramento.)

1969   Approximate 1760 Chumash Village Locations and Populations. (Map.) *Annual Reports of the University of California Archaeological Survey* 11:3. Los Angeles.

1971   Chumash Inter-village Economic Exchange. *The Indian Historian* 4(1):30-43.

King, Chester D., Thomas Blackburn, and Ernest Chandonet
1968   The Archaeological Investigation of Three Sites on the Century Ranch, Western Los Angeles County, California. *Annual Reports of the University of California Archaeological Survey* 10:12-107. Los Angeles.

King, Chester D., Lester Ross, and Linda King
1970   [Fieldnotes and Collection Resulting from the Salvage Excavation of the Pitas Point Site (Ven-27).] (Manuscript in King's Possession.)

King, Chester, Charles Smith, and Thomas F. King
1974   Archaeological Report Related to the Interpretation of Archaeological Resources Present at Vasquez Rocks County Park. (Manuscript on File, Los Angeles County Parks and Recreation Department, Los Angeles.)

King, Linda B.
1969   The Medea Creek Cemetery (LAn-243): An Investigation of Social Organization from Mortuary Practices. *Annual Reports of the University of California Archaeological Survey* 11:23-68. Los Angeles.

King, Thomas F.
1968   The Archaeology of the Schwabacher Site, 4-Mad-117; Archaeology of the Buchanan Reservoir Region, Madera County California. Pt. 2. *San Francisco State College, Anthropology Museum Occasional Papers* 4. San Francisco.

1969   The Archaeology of the Buchanan Reservoir Region, Madera County, California. *San Francisco State College, Anthropology Museum Occasional Papers* 5:1-321. San Francisco.

1972   Nations of Hunters? New Views of California Indian Societies. *The Indian Historian* 5(4):12-17.

King, Thomas F., and Ward Upson
1973   Protohistory on Limantour Sandspit: Archaeological Investigations at 4-Mrn-216 and 4-Mrn-298. Pp. 115-194 in Contributions to the Archaeology of Pt. Reyes National Seashore: A Compendium in Honor of Adan E. Treganza. Robert E. Schenk, ed. San Francisco: A.E. Treganza Museum.

Klimek, Stanislaus
1935   Culture Element Distributions, I: The Structure of California Indian Culture. *University of California Publications in American Archaeology and Ethnology* 37(1):1-70. Berkeley.

Klyver, F.C.
1931   Major Plant Communities in a Transect of the Sierra Mountains of California. *Ecology* 12:1-17.

Kniffen, Fred B.
1928   Achomawi Geography. *University of California Publications in American Archaeology and Ethnology* 23(5):297-332. Berkeley.

1939   Pomo Geography. *University of California Publications in American Archaeology and Ethnology* 36(6):353-400. Berkeley.

Kostromitonov, P.
1839   Bemerkungen über die Indianer in Ober-Kalifornien, und Wörter aus zwei Sprachen Neu-Kaliforniens. Pp. 80-96 and pp. 234-255 in Vol. 1 of Beiträge zur Kenntnis des Russischen Reiches und der angrenzenden Länder Asiens. K.E. von Baer, ed. St. Petersburg.

1974   Notes on the Indians in Upper California. Pp. 7-13 in Ethnographic Observations on the Coast Miwok and Pomo, by Contre-Admiral F.P. von Wrangell and P. Kostromitonov of the Russian Colony Ross [1839]. Berkeley: University of California Archaeological Research Facility.

Kowta, Makoto
1969   The Sayles Complex: A Late Milling Stone Assemblage from Cajon Pass and the Ecological Implications of its Scraper Planes. *University of California Publications in Anthropology* 6. Berkeley and Los Angeles.

Kroeber, Alfred L.

1902 [Information on Eastern Pomo Ceremonies, Obtained from Raymond Brown at Round Valley Reservation, September 1902.] (Kroeber Papers, Bancroft Library, University of California, Berkeley.)

1903 [Information on Eastern Pomo Ceremonies, Obtained from Tom Mitchell, San Francisco, July 1903.] (Kroeber Papers, Bancroft Library, University of California, Berkeley.)

1904 A Ghost Dance in California. *Journal of American Folk-Lore* 17(64):32-35.

1904a The Languages of the Coast of California South of San Francisco. *University of California Publications in American Archaeology and Ethnology* 2(2):29-80. Berkeley.

1904b Types of Indian Culture in California. *University of California Publications in American Archaeology and Ethnology* 2(3):81-103. Berkeley.

1905 A Ghost-Dance in California. *Journal of American Folk-Lore* 17(64):32-35.

1905a Wishosk Myths. *Journal of American Folk-Lore* 18(69):85-107.

1905b Notes. *American Anthropologist* n.s. 7(4):690-695.

1905c Basket Designs of the Indians of Northwestern California. *University of California Publications in American Archaeology and Ethnology* 2(4):105-164. Berkeley.

1906 Two Myths of the Mission Indians of California. *Journal of American Folk-Lore* 19(75):309-321.

1906a Progress in Anthropology at the University of California. *American Anthropologist* n.s. 8(3):483-492.

1907 The Yokuts Language of South Central California. *University of California Publications in American Archaeology and Ethnology* 2(5):165-377. Berkeley.

1907a Indian Myths of South Central California. *University of California Publications in American Archaeology and Ethnology* 4(4):167-250. Berkeley.

1907b Shoshonean Dialects of California. *University of California Publications in American Archaeology and Ethnology* 4(3):65-166. Berkeley.

1907c Chimariko. P. 270 in Vol. 1 of Handbook of American Indians North of Mexico. Frederick W. Hodge, ed. 2 vols. *Bureau of American Ethnology Bulletin* 30. Washington.

1907d The Religion of the Indians of California. *University of California Publications in American Archaeology and Ethnology* 4(6):320-356. Berkeley.

1908 Wiyot Folk-Lore. *Journal of American Folk-Lore* 21(80):37-39.

1908a A Mission Record of the California Indians. *University of California Publications in American Archaeology and Ethnology* 8(1):1-27. Berkeley.

1908b Ethnography of the Cahuilla Indians. *University of California Publications in American Archaeology and Ethnology* 8(2):29-68. Berkeley.

1908c On the Evidences of the Occupation of Certain Regions by the Miwok Indians. *University of California Publications in American Archaeology and Ethnology* 6(3):369-380. Berkeley.

1908d Notes on the Luiseño. Pp. 174-186 in The Religion of the Luiseño Indians of Southern California, by Constance G. Du Bois. *University of California Publications in American Archaeology and Ethnology* 8(3):69-186. Berkeley.

1908e The Anthropology of California. *Science* 27(686):281-290. (Reprinted with Annotations by D.W. Hymes and R.F. Heizer, in *University of California Archaeological Survey Reports* 56:1-18, 1962.)

1909 California Basketry and the Pomo. *American Anthropologist* n.s. 11(2):233-249.

1909a The Archaeology of California. Pp. 1-42 in Putnam Anniversary Volume: Anthropological Essays Presented to Frederick W. Putnam in Honor of his 70th Birthday. New York: G.E. Stechert.

1909b Classificatory Systems of Relationship. *Journal of the Royal Anthropological Institute of Great Britain and Ireland* 39:77-84. London.

1910 Yurok. P. 1013 in Vol. 2 of Handbook of American Indians North of Mexico. Frederick W. Hodge, ed. 2 vols. *Bureau of American Ethnology Bulletin* 30. Washington.

1910a At the Bedrock of History: Recent Remarkable Discovery of Human Remains over Three Hundred Years Old in the San Joaquin Valley of California. *Sunset Magazine* 25(3):255-260. (Reprinted: *University of California Archaeological Survey Reports* 11:5-10, Berkeley, 1951.)

1911 The Languages of the Coast of California North of San Francisco. *University of California Publications in American Archaeology and Ethnology* 9(3):273-435. Berkeley.

1915 Serian, Tequistlatecan and Hokan. *University of California Publications in American Archaeology and Ethnology* 11(4):279-290. Berkeley.

1915a A New Shoshonean Tribe in California. *American Anthropologist* 17(4):773-775.

1917 California Kinship Systems. *University of California Publications in American Archaeology and Ethnology* 12(9):339-396. Berkeley.

1917a The Tribes of the Pacific Coast of North America. Pp. 385-401 in *Proceedings of the 19th International Congress of Americanists.* Washington, 1915.

1919 Sinkyone Tales. *Journal of American Folk-Lore* 32(124):346-351.

1922 Elements of Culture in Native California. *University of California Publications in American Archaeology and Ethnology* 13(8):259-328. Berkeley.

1922a Earth-Tongue, a Mohave. Pp. 189-202 in American Indian Life. Elsie C. Parsons, ed. New York: B.W. Huebsch.

1923 Anthropology. New York: Harcourt, Brace.

1924 Basket Designs of the Mission Indians of California. *Anthropological Papers of the American Museum of Natural History* 20(2):149-183. (Reprinted: Ballena Press, Ramona, Calif., 1973.)

1925 Handbook of the Indians of California. *Bureau of American Ethnology Bulletin* 78. Washington.

1928 A Kato War. Pp. 394-400 in Festschrift Publication d'Hommage offerte au P.W. Schmidt. W. Koppers, ed. Vienna: Mechitharisten-Congregation-Buchdruckerei. (Reprinted in The California Indians, by R. Heizer and M. Whipple. University of California Press, Berkeley and Los Angeles, 1960.)

1928a Law of the Yurok Indians. Pp. 511-516 in *Proceedings of the 22d International Congress of Americanists.* 2 vols. Rome, 1926.

1929 The Valley Nisenan. *University of California Publications in American Archaeology and Ethnology* 24(4):253-290. Berkeley.

1932   Yuki Myths. *Anthropos* 27(5-6):905-939.

1932a   The Patwin and their Neighbors. *University of California Publications in American Archaeology and Ethnology* 29(4):253-423. Berkeley.

1934   Yurok and Neighboring Kin Term Systems. *University of California Publications in American Archaeology and Ethnology* 35(2):15-22. Berkeley.

1935   Preface. Pp. 1-11 in Culture Element Distributions, I: The Structure of California Indian Culture, by S. Klimek. *University of California Publications in American Archaeology and Ethnology* 37(1). Berkeley.

1936   Culture Element Distributions, III: Area and Climax. *University of California Publications in American Archaeology and Ethnology* 37(3):101-116. Berkeley.

1936a   Karok Towns. *University of California Publications in American Archaeology and Ethnology* 35(4):29-38. Berkeley.

1936b   Prospects in California Prehistory. *American Antiquity* 2(2):108-116.

1939   Local Ethnographic and Methodological Inferences. Pp. 425-429 (Appendix1) in Culture Element Distributions, X: Northwest California, by Harold E. Driver. *University of California Anthropological Records* 1(6). Berkeley.

1939a   Cultural and Natural Areas of Native North America. *University of California Publications in American Archaeology and Ethnology* 38:1-242. Berkeley. (Reprinted: University of California Press, Berkeley and Los Angeles, 1963.)

1939b   Culture Element Distributions, XI: Tribes Surveyed. *University of California Anthropological Records* 1(7):435-440. Berkeley.

1941   Some Relations of Linguistics and Ethnology. *Language* 17(4):287-291.

1943   The Classification of the Yuman Languages. *University of California Publications in Linguistics* 1(3):21-40. Berkeley.

1945   A Yurok War Reminiscence: The Use of Autobiographical Evidence. *Southwestern Journal of Anthropology* 1(3):318-332.

1946   The Museum's First Forty-five Years. Pp. 4-11 in *Annual Report of the Museum of Anthropology for the Year Ending June 30, 1946*. Berkeley, Calif.

1955   Nature of the Land-holding Group. *Ethnohistory* 2(4):303-314.

1955a   C. Hart Merriam as Anthropologist. Pp. vii-xiv in Studies of California Indians, by C. Hart Merriam. Berkeley: University of California Press.

1957   Ad hoc Reassurance Dreams. Pp. 205-208 in Ethnographic Interpretations 1-6. *University of California Publications in American Archaeology and Ethnology* 47(2). Berkeley.

1957a   The California Indian Population about 1910. Pp. 218-225 in Ethnographic Interpretations 1-6. *University of California Publications in American Archaeology and Ethnology* 47(2). Berkeley.

1957b   Some New Group Boundaries in Central California. Pp. 215-217 in Ethnographic Interpretations 4. *University of California Publications in American Archaeology and Ethnology* 47(2). Berkeley.

1958   Notes on Upper Eel River Indians. Appendix II. Pp. 227-229 in California Athabascan Groups. Martin A. Baumhoff, ed. *University of California Anthropological Records* 16(5). Berkeley.

1958a   An Atsugewi Word List. *International Journal of American Linguistics* 24(3):213-214.

1959   Ethnographic Interpretations 7-11. *University of California Publications in American Archaeology and Ethnology* 47(3):235-310. Berkeley.

1959a   Northern Yokuts. *Anthropological Linguistics* 1(8):1-19.

1960   The Yurok Culture. Pp. 567-569 in The Structure of Twana Culture, by William W. Elmendorf. *Research Studies: A Quarterly Publication of Washington State University* 28(3), Monographic Supplement 2. Pullman.

1961   Powell and Henshaw: An Episode in the History of Ethnolinguistics. *Anthropological Linguistics* 3(4):1-5.

1962   The Nature of Land-holding Groups in Aboriginal California. Pp. 19-58 in Two Papers on the Aboriginal Ethnography of California. D.H. Hymes and Robert F. Heizer, eds. *University of California Archaeological Survey Reports* 56. Berkeley.

1963   Yokuts Dialect Survey. *University of California Anthropological Records* 11(3):177-251. Berkeley.

1971   The History of Native Culture in California. Pp. 112-128 in The California Indians: A Source Book. Robert F. Heizer and M.A. Whipple, eds. Berkeley and Los Angeles: University of California Press.

1971a   Elements of Culture in Native California. Pp. 3-65 in The California Indians: A Source Book. Robert F. Heizer and M.A. Whipple, eds. Berkeley and Los Angeles: University of California Press.

[1975] Yurok Myths. Berkeley and Los Angeles: University of California Press. In Press.

Kroeber, Alfred L., and Samuel A. Barrett
1960   Fishing among the Indians of Northwestern California. *University of California Anthropological Records* 21(1):1-210. Berkeley.

Kroeber, Alfred L., and Edward W. Gifford
1949   World Renewal: A Cult System of Native Northwest California. *University of California Anthropological Records* 13(1):1-156. Berkeley.

Kroeber, Alfred L., and George W. Grace
1960   The Sparkman Grammar of Luiseño. *University of California Publications in Linguistics* 16. Berkeley.

Kroeber, Alfred L., and Robert F. Heizer
1970   Continuity of Indian Population in California from 1770/1848 to 1955. Pp. 1-22 in Papers on California Ethnography. *University of California Archaeological Research Facility Contribution* 9. Berkeley.

Kroeber, Alfred L., and Talcott Parsons
1958   The Concepts of Culture and of Social System. *American Sociological Review* 23(5):582-583.

Kroeber, Alfred L., and Dale K. Valory
1967   Ethnological Manuscripts in the Robert H. Lowie Museum of Anthropology. *Kroeber Anthropological Society Papers* 37:1-22. Berkeley, Calif.

Kroeber, Henriette (Rothschild)
1908   Wappo Myths. *Journal of American Folk-Lore* 21(82):321-323.

Kroeber, Theodora
1959   The Inland Whale. Bloomington: Indiana University Press.

1961   Ishi in Two Worlds: A Biography of the Last Wild Indian in North America. Berkeley: University of California Press.

Kroeber, Theodora, and Robert F. Heizer
1968   Almost Ancestors: The First Californians. San Francisco: Sierra Club.

Künzel, Heinrich
1848   Obercalifornien: Eine geographische Schilderung für den Zweck deutscher Auswanderung und Ansiedelung...Erster Beitrag. Mit einer Karte des Rio Sacramento und einem Grundriss des Forts New-Helvetien. Darmstadt, Germany: C.W. Leske.

Kunkel, Peter H.
1962   Yokuts and Pomo Political Institutions: A Comparative Study. (Unpublished Ph.D. Dissertation in Anthropology, University of California, Los Angeles.)

_____ 1974   The Pomo Kin Group and the Political Unit in Aboriginal California. *Journal of California Anthropology* 1(1):7-18.

Kuroda, S.Y.
1967   Yawelmani Phonology. (Research Monograph 43) Cambridge, Mass.: M.I.T. Press.

Laird, Carobeth
1975   Encounter with an Angry God: Recollections of my Life with John Peabody Harrington. Banning, Calif.: Malki Museum Press.

Lamb, Sydney M.
1958   Linguistic Prehistory in the Great Basin. *International Journal of American Linguistics* 24(2):95-100.

_____ 1958a   Northfork Mono-Grammar. (Unpublished Ph.D. Dissertation in Linguistics, University of California, Berkeley.)

_____ 1964   The Classification of Uto-Aztecan Languages: A Historical Survey. Pp. 106-125 in Studies in Californian Linguistics. William Bright, ed. *University of California Publications in Linguistics* 34. Berkeley.

Landberg, Leif C.W.
1965   The Chumash Indians of Southern California. *Southwest Museum Papers* 19. Los Angeles.

Langacker, Ronald W.
1970   The Vowels of Proto-Uto-Aztecan. *International Journal of American Linguistics* 36(3):169-180.

Langdon, Margaret
1968   The Proto-Yuman Demonstrative System. *Folio Linguistica* 2(1):61-81.

_____ 1970   A Grammar of Diegueño: The Mesa Grande Dialect. *University of California Publications in Linguistics* 66. Berkeley.

_____ 1971   Sound Symbolism in Yuman Languages. Pp. 149-173 in Studies in American Indian Languages. Jesse Sawyer, ed. *University of California Publications in Linguistics* 65. Berkeley.

_____ 1974   Comparative Hokan-Coahuiltecan Studies: A Survey and Appraisal. *Janua Linguarum, Series Critica* 4. The Hague: Mouton.

_____ 1975   The Proto-Yuman Vowel System. In Hokan Studies: Papers from the First Conference on Hokan Languages, 1970. Margaret Langdon and Shirley K. Silver, eds. *Janua Linguarum, Series Practica* 181. The Hague: Mouton.

_____ 1975a   Kamia and Kumeyaay: A Linguistic Perspective. *Journal of California Anthropology* 2(1):64-70.

Langsdorff, George H. von
1968   Voyages and Travels in Various Parts of the World during the Years 1803, 1804, 1805, 1806, and 1807 [1813-1814]. 2 vols. (Bibliotheca Australiana 41) New York: Da Capo Press.

Lapérouse, Jean François de Galaup
1959   The First French Expedition to California; Lapérouse in 1786 [1797]. Charles N. Rudkin, trans. Los Angeles: Glen Dawson.

Larkey, Joann L., ed.
1969   Davisville '68; The History and Heritage of the City of Davis, Yolo County, California. Davis: The Davis Historical and Landmarks Commission.

Latham, Robert G.
1856   On the Languages of Northern, Western, and Central America. Pp. 57-115 in *Transactions of the Philological Society of London for 1856.* London.

Lathrap, Donald W.
1950   A Distinctive Pictograph from the Carrizo Plains, San Luis Obispo County. *University of California Archaeological Survey Reports* 9(8):20-26. Berkeley.

Lathrap, Donald W., and Dick Shutler, Jr.
1955   An Archaeological Site in the High Sierra of California. *American Antiquity* 20(3):226-240.

Latta, Frank F., ed.
1936   California Indian Folklore, as Told to F.F. Latta by Wah-nom-kot, Wah-hum-chah, Lee-mee [and others]... Shafter, Calif.: Shafter Press.

_____ 1949   Handbook of Yokuts Indians. Bakersfield, Calif.: Kern County Museum.

Lavrova, Nadia
1928   Traditions of California Indian Tribes Being Perpetuated by Club Organization. *San Francisco Examiner,* June 17:8K.

Lawton, Harry W., and Lowell J. Bean
1968   A Preliminary Reconstruction of Aboriginal Agricultural Technology among the Cahuilla. *The Indian Historian* 1(5):18-24, 29.

Leader, Herman A.
1928   The Hudson's Bay Company in California, 1830-1846. (Unpublished Ph.D. Dissertation in History, University of California, Berkeley.)

Lee, Dorothy (Demetracopoulou) *see also* Demetracopoulou, Dorothy

Lee, Dorothy (Demetracopoulou)
1940   A Wintu Girls' Puberty Ceremony. *New Mexico Anthropologist* 4(4):57-60.

_____ 1941   Some Indian Texts Dealing with the Supernatural. *Review of Religion* 5(4):403-411.

_____ 1943   The Linguistic Aspect of Wintu Acculturation. *American Anthropologist* 45(3):435-440.

_____ 1944   Categories of the Generic and the Particular in Wintu. *American Anthropologist* 46(3):362-369.

_____ 1944a   Linguistic Reflection of Wintu Thought. *International Journal of American Linguistics* 10(4):181-187.

_____ 1946   Stylistic Use of the Negative in Wintu. *International Journal of American Linguistics* 12(2):79-81.

_____ 1950   Notes on the Conception of the Self among the Wintu Indians. *Journal of Abnormal Psychology* 45(3):538-543.

Lehmer, Derrik N.
1929   The First People: Miwok Indian Myths. *Overland Monthly* 87(12):378-379.

Leonard, Charles B.
1928   The Federal Indian Policy in the San Joaquin Valley. (Unpublished Ph.D. Dissertation in Anthropology, University of California, Berkeley.)

Leonard, Nelson N., III
1966   Ven-70 and its Place in the Late Period of the Western Santa Monica Mountains. *Annual Reports of the University of California Archaeological Survey* 8:215-242. Los Angeles.

Leonard, Nelson N., III, and James T. Tooney.
1968   Archaeological Reconnaissance of the Proposed Schneiders Bar, Helena and Eltapom Reservoirs on the Trinity River Drainage in Trinity County, Californa. (Manuscripts No. 239 and No. 279 in University of California Archaeological Survey Library, Los Angeles.)

Leonard, Zenas
1839 Narrative of the Adventures of Zenas Leonard, 1831-1836. Clearfield, Pa.: D.W. Moore. (Reprinted: Burrows Brothers, Cleveland, 1904; University of Oklahoma, Norman, 1959.)

Leonhardy, Frank C.
1961 The Cultural Position of the Iron Gate Site. (Unpublished M.A. Thesis in Anthropology, University of Oregon, Eugene.)

_____
1967 The Archaeology of a Late Prehistoric Village in Northwestern California. *University of Oregon, Museum of Natural History Bulletin* 4. Eugene.

Leopold, Aldo S.
1951 Game Birds and Mammals of California: A Laboratory Syllabus. Berkeley: California Book Company.

Lévi-Strauss, Claude
1964 The Raw and the Cooked: Introduction to a Science of Mythology, I. John Weightman and Doreen Weightman, trans. New York and Evanston: Harper and Row.

Levine, Stuart, and Nancy O. Lurie, eds.
1968 The American Indian Today. Deland, Fla.: Everett Edwards. (Reprinted Pelican Books, Baltimore, 1970.)

Levy, Richard S.
1969 Ethnic Status of Converts at Missions San Carlos, Soledad, and Santa Cruz. (Manuscript in Levy's Possession.)

_____
1970 Costanoan Internal Relationships. (Paper Presented to the 9th Conference on American Indian Languages, San Diego, Calif.; Manuscript in Levy's Possession.)

_____
1970a Proto-Costanoan Phonology. (Paper Read at the 69th Annual Meeting of the American Anthropological Association. San Diego, Calif., November 19-21, 1970.)

[1970b] Miwok-Costanoan Lexicostatistics. (Manuscript in Levy's Possession.)

_____
1972 Ethnic Status of Converts at Missions San Francisco, Santa Clara, and San Jose. (Manuscript in Levy's Possession.)

_____
1972a Linguistic Evidence for the Prehistory of Central California. (Manuscript in Levy's Possession.)

_____
1973 [Notes on the Salinan and Esselen: Letter to R.F. Heizer, January 16, 1973.] (Manuscript No. 450, in University of California Archaeological Research Facility, Berkeley.)

Lewis, E.G.
1880 Illustrations of Tehama County, California, with Historical Sketch of the County. San Francisco: Elliot Moore.

Lewis, Albert B.
1910 San Carlos. Pp. 427-428 in Vol. 2 of Handbook of American Indians North of Mexico. Frederick W. Hodge, ed. 2 vols. *Bureau of American Ethnology Bulletin* 30. Washington.

_____
1910a San Miguel. P. 449 in Vol. 2 of Handbook of American Indians North of Mexico. Frederick W. Hodge, ed. 2 vols. *Bureau of American Ethnology Bulletin* 30. Washington.

Lewis, Henry T.
1973 Patterns of Indian Burning in California: Ecology and Ethnohistory. *Ballena Press Anthropological Papers* 1:1-101. Ramona, Calif.

Li, Fang-kuei
1930 Mattole, an Athabaskan Language. *University of Chicago Publications in Anthropology, Linguistic Series.* Chicago.

Lienhard, Heinrich
1941 A Pioneer at Sutter's Fort, 1846-1850. Marguarite Wilbur, ed. Los Angeles: Calafia Society.

Lillard, Jeremiah B., and W.K. Purves
1936 The Archaeology of the Deer Creek-Cosumnes Area, Sacramento County, California. *Sacramento Junior College, Department of Anthropology Bulletin* 1. Sacramento.

Lillard, Jeremiah B., Robert F. Heizer, and Franklin Fenenga
1939 An Introduction to the Archaeology of Central California. *Sacramento Junior College, Department of Anthropology Bulletin* 2. Sacramento.

Littlejohn, Hugh W.
1928 Nisenan Geography. (Manuscript in Bancroft Library, University of California, Berkeley.)

Lloyd, Nancy
1955 The Chumash: A Study of the Assimilation of a California Indian Tribe. (Unpublished M.A. Thesis in Anthropology, University of Arizona, Tucson.)

Lockley, Fred
[1930] Impressions and Observations of the Journal of Man. Mountain View, Calif.: Beddoe Brothers.

Loeb, Edwin M.
1926 Pomo Folkways. *University of California Publications in American Archaeology and Ethnology* 19(2):149-405. Berkeley.

_____
1932 The Western Kuksu Cult. *University of California Publications in American Archaeology and Ethnology* 33(1):1-137. Berkeley.

_____
1933 The Eastern Kuksu Cult. *University of California Publications in American Archaeology and Ethnology* 33(2):139-232. Berkeley.

Loeffelholz, Karl von
1893 Die Zoreisch-Indianer der Trinidad-Bai (Californien). *Mitteilungen der Anthropologischen Gesellschaft in Wien* 23:101-123. (Translated in The Four Ages of Tsurai, by R.F. Heizer and J.E. Mills, University of California Press, Berkeley, 1952.)

Loew, Oscar
1876 Notes upon the Ethnology of Southern California and Adjacent Regions. Pp. 541-547 in *Annual Report of the U.S. War Department, Report of the Chief of Engineers for 1876.* Vol. 23. Appendix J.J., Part H.14. Washington.

Log of the Ship "Alert"
1841 (Manuscript notes in University of California Archeological Survey, Berkeley.)

Longhurst, W.M., A.S. Leopold, and R.F. Dasmann
1952 A Survey of California Deer Herds: Their Ranges and Management Problems. *California State Department of Natural Resources, Division of Fish and Game, Game Bulletin* 6. Sacramento.

Longinos Martínez, José
1961 Journal: Notes and Observations of the Naturalist of the Botanical Expedition in Old and New California and the South Coast, 1791-1792. Lesley B. Simpson, ed. and trans. San Francisco: John Howell.

Loomis, Noel M.
1971 The Garra Uprising of 1851. Pp. 3-26 in Brand Book 2. San Diego, Calif.: Corral of the Westerners.

Lothrop, Marion L.
1932 The Indian Campaigns of General M.G. Vallejo: Defender of the Northern Frontier of California. *Quarterly of the Society of California Pioneers* 9(3):161-205. San Francisco.

Loud, Llewellyn L.
1918 Ethnogeography and Archaeology of the Wiyot Territory. *University of California Publications in American Archaeology and Ethnology* 14(3):221-436. Berkeley.

Lowy, Michael J.
1965-1975 [Notes on the Eastern Pomo from Four Months' Fieldwork at Big Valley Rancheria.] (Manuscript in Lowy's Possession.)

1973 A Review of Clear Lake Pomo Culture. (Manuscript; Copies in National Anthropological Archives, Smithsonian Institution, Washington, and Archaeological Research Facility, University of California, Berkeley.)

1975 The Impact of Assistance Programs on Leadership in a Native American Community. (Manuscript in Lowy's Possession.)

Lummis, Charles F.
1902 The Exiles of Cupa. *Out West* 16(5):465-479, 16(6):602-612.

Luomala, Katharine
1963 Flexibility in Sib Affiliation among the Diegueño. *Ethnology* 2(3):282-301.

Luomala, Katharine, and Gertrude Toffelmier
1934 [Ethnographic Notes from Two Months' Fieldwork with Northern and Southern Diegueño Informants at Campo, California.] (Manuscript in Luomala's Possession.)

1962 [Two Months' Fieldwork with Northern and Southern Diegueño Informants at Campo, California.] (Manuscript in Luomala's Possession.)

McBeth, Frances (Turner)
1950 Lower Klamath Country. Berkeley, Calif.: Anchor Press.

McClellan, C.
1953 Ethnography of the Wappo and Patwin. Pp. 233-241 in The Archaeology of the Napa Region. Robert F. Heizer, ed. *University of California Anthropological Records* 12(6). Berkeley.

McClellan, Rolander G.
1872 The Golden State: A History of the Region West of the Rocky Mountains. Philadelphia: W. Flint; Chicago: Union Publishing Company.

McCown, B.E.
1945 An Archaeological Survey of the San Vicente Lake Bed, San Diego County, California. *American Antiquity* 10(3):255-264.

1955 Temeku: A Page from the History of the Luiseño Indians. *Papers of the Archaeological Survey Association of Southern California* 3. Los Angeles.

McCoy, L.L.
1926 Land Grants and Other History of Tehama County. Red Bluff, Calif.: The River Rambler.

McGowan, Joseph A.
1961 History of the Sacramento Valley. New York: Lewis Historical Publishing Company.

Macgregor, Gordon
[1936] Report of the Pit River Indians of California. Washington: U.S. Office of Indian Affairs. Mimeo.

McHenry, Henry
1968 Transverse Lines in Long Bones of Prehistoric California Indians. *American Journal of Physical Anthropology* 29(1):1-17.

McKee, John
1853 Minutes Kept by John McKee, Secretary, on the Expedition from Sonoma, through Northern California. Pp. 134-180 in U.S. Congress. Senate. 33d Cong. Special Sess., Senate Executive Doc. No. 4. (Serial No. 688) Washington: U.S. Government Printing Office.

McKee, Redick
1851-1857 Indian Population of North-Western California. P. 634 in Vol. 3 of Historical and Statistical Information Respecting the History, Condition, and Prospects of the Indian Tribes of the United States. Henry R. Schoolcraft, ed. 6 vols. Philadelphia: Lippincott, Grambo.

1853 [Letter to Charles E. Mix.] Pp. 192-195 in Report of the Secretary of the Interior Communicating Correspondence between the Department of the Interior and the Indian Agents and Commissioners in California. U.S. Congress. Senate. 33d Cong., Special Sess. Senate Executive Doc. No. 4. (Serial No. 688) Washington: U.S. Government Printing Office.

McKern, W.C.
1922 Functional Families of the Patwin. *University of California Publications in American Archaeology and Ethnology* 13(7):235-258. Berkeley.

1923 Patwin Houses. *University of California Publications in American Archaeology and Ethnology* 20(10):159-171. Berkeley.

McKusick, Marshall B., ed.
1960-1961 Excavations at Goleta, Pt. 1: Methodology. *Annual Reports of the University of California Archaeological Survey* 3:339-348. Los Angeles.

McKusick, Marshall B., and Claude N. Warren
1958-1959 Introduction to San Clemente Island Archaeology. *Annual Reports of the University of California Archaeological Survey* 1:106-185. Los Angeles.

McKusick, Marshall B., and R.N. Watson
1958-1959 Grinding Implements from Vaquero Reservoir, San Luis Obispo and Santa Barbara Counties. *Annual Reports of the University of California Archaeological Survey* 1:13-16. Los Angeles.

McLendon, Sally
[1959] [Fieldnotes on Northeastern Pomo.] (Manuscripts in McLendon's Possession.)

1959-1976 [Eastern Pomo Linguistic and Ethnographic Fieldnotes.] (40 Notebooks in McLendon's Possession.)

1964 Northern Hokan (B) and (C): A Comparison of Eastern Pomo and Yana. Pp. 126-144 in Studies in Californian Linguistics. William Bright, ed. *University of California Publications in Linguistics* 34. Berkeley.

1969 Spanish Words in Eastern Pomo. *Romance Philology* 23(1):39-53.

1973 Proto-Pomo. *University of California Publications in Linguistics* 71. Berkeley.

1975 A Grammar of Eastern Pomo. *University of California Publications in Linguistics* 74. Berkeley.

McMillin, James H.
1963 The Aboriginal Human Ecology of the Mountain Meadows Area in Southwestern Lassen County, California. (Unpublished M.A. Thesis in Anthropology, California State University, Sacramento.)

Mahr, August C.
1932 The Visit of the "Rurik" to San Francisco in 1816. *Stanford University Publications, University Series, History, Economics and Political Science* 2(2):267-460. Stanford, Calif.

Malécot, André
1963-1964 Luiseño, a Structural Analysis, I: Phonology; II: Morpho Syntax; III: Texts and Lexicon; IV: Appendices. *International Journal of American Linguistics* 29(2):89-95, (3):196-210, 30(1):14-31, (3):243-250.

Mallery, Garrick
1886 Pictographs of the North American Indians. Pp. 3-256 in *4th Annual Report of the Bureau of American Ethnology for the Years 1882-1883*. Washington.

1893 Picture-writing of the American Indians. Pp. 1-882 in *10th Annual Report of the Bureau of American Ethnology for the Years 1888-1889*. Washington.

750

BIBLIOGRAPHY

Mannion, Curtis
1969   A Report of Three Archaeological Sites with Historical Components. Pp. 219-264 in The Archaeology of the Buchanan Reservoir Region, Madera County, California. Thomas F. King, ed. *Occasional Papers of the San Francisco State College Anthropology Museum* 5. San Francisco.

Marshack, Alexander
1972   The Roots of Civilization: The Cognitive Beginnings of Man's First Art, Symbol, and Notation. New York: McGraw-Hill.

Martin, Kenneth
1969   An Old-Fashioned Fourth / Hoopa Indian Games. *Times-Standard,* June 29:10-11. Eureka, Calif.

Martin, Pat
1971   The Shasta. Pp. 34-48, 69 in Vol. 4 of Indian Tribes of the Siskiyou. Yreka, Calif.: Siskiyou County Historical Society. (Siskiyou Pioneer.)

Martin, Stewart, and Elizabeth Satow
1971   An Interim Record of 4-SBa-585 and 4-SBa-586. (Manuscript on File, Archaeological Research Inc., Costa Mesa, Calif.)

Mason, J. Alden
1912   The Ethnology of the Salinan Indians. *University of California Publications in American Archaeology and Ethnology* 10(4):97-240. Berkeley.

1916   The Mutsun Dialect of Costanoan Based on the Vocabulary of de la Cuesta. *University of California Publications in American Archaeology and Ethnology* 11(7):399-472. Berkeley.

1918   The Language of the Salinan Indians. *University of California Publications in American Archaeology and Ethnology* 14(1):1-154. Berkeley.

1940   The Native Languages of Middle America. Pp. 52-87 in The Maya and their Neighbors. C.L. Hay et al., eds. New York: Appleton-Century.

Mason, Otis T.
1889   The Ray Collection from the Hupa Reservation. Pp. 205-239 in *Annual Report of the Smithsonian Institution for 1886.* Pt. 1. Washington.

1904   Aboriginal American Basketry: Studies in a Textile Art without Machinery. Pp. 171-548 in *Report of the U.S. National Museum, Smithsonian Institution, for the Year 1902.* Washington.

Mattz, Raymond
[1968]   When the White Man Came. Crescent City, Calif.: Del Norte County Historical Society.

Mauldin, Henry K.
1945-1975   [Unpublished Notes on the History of Lake County.] (Manuscripts Deposited with the Lake County Library, Lakeport, Calif.)

May, Viola P.
1945   "The Site": The Ghosts of Yesterday. Pp. 15-20 in Shasta Dam and its Builders. Los Angeles: Pacific Constructors.

Mayfield, Thomas J.
1929   San Joaquin Primeval, Uncle Jeff's Story: A Tale of a San Joaquin Valley Pioneer and his Life with the Yokuts Indians. Frank F. Latta, ed. Tulare, Calif.: Tulare Times Press.

Meighan, Clement W.
1950   Excavations in Sixteenth Century Shellmounds at Drake's Bay, Marin County. *University of California Archaeological Survey Reports* 9:27-32. Berkeley.

1951   Glass Trade Beads from La Purísima Indian Barracks. (Manuscript in Department of Anthropology, University of California, Los Angeles.)

1954   A Late Complex in Southern California Prehistory. *Southwestern Journal of Anthropology* 10(2):215-227.

1955   Archaeology of the North Coast Ranges, California. *University of California Archaeological Survey Reports* 30:1-39. Berkeley.

1955a   Excavation of Isabella Meadows Cave, Monterey County, California. *University of California Archaeological Survey Reports* 29:1-30. Berkeley.

1958-1959   Archaeological Resources of Borrego Desert State Park. *Annual Reports of the University of California Archaeological Survey* 1:27-40. Los Angeles.

1959   The Little Harbor Site, Catalina Island: An Example of Ecological Interpretation in Archaeology. *American Antiquity* 24(4):383-405.

1959a   Californian Cultures and the Concept of an Archaic Stage. *American Antiquity* 24(3):289-318.

1965   Pacific Coast Archaeology. Pp. 709-719 in The Quaternary of the United States: A Review Volume for the 7th Congress of the International Association for Quaternary Research. H.E. Wright, Jr., and D.G. Frey, eds. Princeton, N.J.: Princeton University Press.

Meighan, Clement W., and Hal Eberhart
1953   Archaeological Resources of San Nicolas Island, California. *American Antiquity* 19(2):109-125.

Meighan, Clement W., and C. Vance Haynes
1968   New Studies on the Age of the Borax Lake Site. *Masterkey* 42(1):4-9.

1970   The Borax Lake Site Revisited: Reanalysis of the Geology and Artifacts Gives Evidence of an Early Man Location in California. *Science* 167(3922):1213-1221.

Meighan, Clement W., and Robert F. Heizer
1953   Archaeological Exploration of 16th Century Indian Mounds at Drake's Bay. Pp. 73-81 in The Plate of Brass: Evidence of the Visit of Francis Drake to California in the Year 1579. *California Historical Society Special Publication* 25. San Francisco.

Meighan, Clement W., and Francis A. Riddell
1972   The Maru Cult of the Pomo Indians: A California Ghost Dance Survival. *Southwest Museum Papers* 23. Los Angeles.

Meighan, Clement W., and Sheldon Rootenberg
1957   A Prehistoric Miner's Camp on Catalina Island. *Masterkey* 31(6):176-184.

Meigs, Peveril, III
1939   The Kiliwa Indians of Lower California. *Ibero-Americana* 15. Berkeley, Calif.

Menefee, Campbell A.
1873   Historical and Descriptive Sketch Book of Napa, Sonoma, Lake and Mendocino [Counties] Comprising Sketches of their Topography, Productions, History, Scenery and Peculiar Attraction. Napa City, Calif.: Reporter Publishing House.

Menzies, Archibald
1924   Menzies' California Journal [1792]. *Quarterly of the California Historical Society* 2:265-340. San Francisco.

Meredith, H.C.
1900   Archaeology of California: Central and Northern California. Pp. 258-294 in Prehistoric Implements: A Reference Book. Warren K. Moorehead, ed. Cincinnati: Robert Clarke

Merriam, C. Hart
[1851-1939]   [Kato Ethnographic Notes: A Miscellaneous Collection of Abstracts with Some Original Cahto Data.] (Unpublished Notes in Department of Anthropology, University of California, Berkeley.)

[1902-1930] Mewuk (Sierra Miwok) and Mewok (Plains Miwok) Tribes and Villages. (Manuscript in C. Hart Merriam Collection, Department of Anthropology, University of California, Berkeley.)

[1902-1932] California Indian Tribal Synonymies. (Manuscript in C. Hart Merriam Collection, Department of Anthropology, University of California, Berkeley.)

[1902/1933-1934] [Unpublished Notes on the Salinan.] (Manuscript in Department of Anthropology, University of California, Berkeley.)

1904 Distribution of Indian Tribes in the Southern Sierra and Adjacent Parts of the San Joaquin Valley, California. *Science* 19(494):912-917.

1905 The Indian Population of California. *American Anthropologist* n.s. 7(4):594-606.

1905-1929 [Field Check Lists, Pacific Coast Region: United States Department of Agriculture, Biological Survey.] (Manuscript in Department of Anthropology, University of California Archaeological Survey, Berkeley.)

1907 Distribution and Classification of the Mewan Stock in California. *American Anthropologist* n.s. 9(2):338-357.

1907a Ethnography of the Northern and Central Yana. (Manuscripts and Notes in Department of Anthropology, University of California, Berkeley.)

[1908] [Ethnogeography of the Patwin.] (Manuscripts and Notes in Department of Anthropology, University of California, Berkeley.)

1909 Ethnological Evidence that the California Cave Skeletons are not Recent. *Science* 29(751):805-806.

1909a Transmigration in California. *Journal of American Folk-Lore* 22(86):433-434.

———, ed.
1910 The Dawn of the World: Myths and Weird Tales Told by the Mewan Indians of California. Cleveland: Arthur H. Clark.

[1910-1929] [Notes on the Ethnogeography of the Yuki, Huchnom, and Coast Yuki.] (Manuscript in C. Hart Merriam Collection, Department of Anthropology, University of California, Berkeley.)

[1910-1938] [Unpublished Tolowa Fieldnotes and Vocabulary, Collected at Smith River and Crescent City, Calif.] (Manuscript in the Archives of the University of California, Berkeley.)

1916 Indian Names in the Tamalpais Region. *California Out-of-Doors,* April:118.

1923 Application of the Athapaskan Term Nung-kahhl. *American Anthropologist* 25(2):276-277.

[1925] [Unpublished Notes in Department of Anthropology, University of California, Berkeley.]

1925a Vocabulary of O-kwahn´-noo´-choo. (Manuscript in Department of Anthropology, University of California, Berkeley.)

1926 The Classification and Distribution of the Pit River Tribes of California. *Smithsonian Miscellaneous Collections* 78(3):1-52. Washington.

1926a Testimony. Pp. 50-63 in Indian Tribes of California. Hearing Before a Subcommittee of the Committee on Indian Affairs on HR 8063 and HR 9497, May 5, 1926. U.S. Congress. House. 69th Cong., 1st sess. Washington: U.S. Government Printing Office.

[1926b] Analysis of Indian "Tribal" Names Appearing in the Eighteen Unratified California Treaties of 1851-1852. (Manuscript Filed under "Indian Welfare" in C. Hart Merriam Collection, Department of Anthropology, University of California, Berkeley.)

1926c Source of the Name Shasta. *Journal of the Washington Academy of Sciences* 16(19):522-525. Washington.

———, ed.
1928 An-nik-a-del, the History of the Universe as Told by the Mo-deś-se [Achumawi] Indians of California. Boston: The Stratford Company.

1929 The Cop-éh of Gibbs. *American Anthropologist* 31(1):136-137.

1930 The Em-tim-bitch, a Shoshonean Tribe. *American Anthropologist* 32(3):496-499.

1930a Little Known Tribes of the Salmon, New, and Trinity Rivers in Northwestern California. *Journal of the Washington Academy of Sciences* 20(8):148-149. Washington.

1930b The New River Indians Tló-hōm-tah´-hoi. *American Anthropologist* 32(2):280-293.

1955 Studies of California Indians. The Staff of the Department of Anthropology of the University of California, eds. Berkeley: University of California Press.

1957 Wintoon Indians. *University of California Archaeological Survey Reports* 38:40-43. Berkeley.

1962 California Mission Baptismal Records. Pp. 188-225 in Studies of California Indians. The Staff of the Department of Anthropology of the University of California, eds. Berkeley: University of California Press.

1966-1967 Ethnographic Notes on California Indian Tribes. Robert F. Heizer, ed. 3 Pts. *University of California Archaeological Survey Reports* 68. Berkeley.

1968 Village Names in Twelve California Mission Records. Robert F. Heizer, ed. *University of California Archaeological Survey Reports* 74. Berkeley.

1970 Indian Rancheria Names in Four Mission Records. *University of California Archaeological Research Facility Contributions* 9(3):29-58. Berkeley.

Merriam, John C.
1906 Recent Cave Explorations in California. *American Anthropologist* n.s. 8(2):221-228.

Merrill, Ruth E.
1923 Plants Used in Basketry by the California Indians. *University of California Publications in American Archaeology and Ethnology* 20(13):215-242. Berkeley.

Metlar, George W.
1856 Northern California, Scott and Klamath Rivers, their Inhabitants and Characteristics, its Historical Features... Yreka, Calif.: Yreka Union Office; J. Tyson.

Meyer, Carl, *of Basel*
1855 Nach dem Sacramento: Reisebilder eines Heimgekehrten. Aarau, Switzerland: Sauerländer's Verlag. (Translated in The Four Ages of Tsurai, by R.F. Heizer and J.E. Mills, University of California Press, Berkeley, 1952.)

Michels, Joseph W.
1963-1964 The Snow Creek Rock Shelter (Riv-210). *Annual Reports of the University of California Archaeological Survey* 6:85-127. Los Angeles.

Michelson, Truman
1914 Two Alleged Algonquian Languages of California. *American Anthropologist* 16(2):361-367.

1915   Rejoinder to Sapir. *American Anthropologist* 17(1):194-198.

Miller, Joaquin
1873   Life amongst the Modocs: Unwritten History. London: R. Bentley and Son.

Miller, Virginia P.
1970   The Yuki: An Ethnohistoric Approach. (Unpublished M.A. Thesis in Anthropology, University of California, Davis.)

Miller, Wick R.
1961   Review of The Sparkman Grammar of Luiseño, by A.L. Kroeber and G.W. Grace. *Language* 37(1):186-189.

Mills, John E.
1950   Recent Developments in the Study of Northwestern California Archeology. *University of California Archaeological Survey Reports* 7:21-25. Berkeley.

Mission Indian Federation
1967   Posterity Demands the Truth. Mimeo. (Copy in Edward D. Castillo's Possession.)

Mitchell, Annie R.
1949   Major James D. Savage and the Tulareños. *Quarterly of the California Historical Society* 28(4):323-341. San Francisco.

Mohr, Albert, and L.L. Sample
1955   The Religious Importance of the Swordfish in the Santa Barbara Channel Area and its Possible Implication. *Masterkey* 29(2):62-68.

1955a   Twined Water Bottles of the Cuyama Area, Southern California. *American Antiquity* 20(4):345-354.

Molohon, Kathryn T.
1969   Round Valley, California: Social Laboratory for the Study of Rural American Culture. (Unpublished Paper Presented at the Meeting of the Southwestern Anthropological Association, Las Vegas, Nev., 1969.)

Mooney, James
1896   The Ghost Dance Religion and the Sioux Outbreak of 1890. Pp. 641-1110 in *14th Annual Report of the Bureau of American Ethnology for the Years 1892-1893*. Pt. 2. Washington.

Moraga, José Joachín
1930   Moraga's Account of the Founding of San Francisco [1776.] Pp. 407-420 in Vol. 3 of Anza's California Expeditions. Herbert E. Bolton, ed. and trans. Berkeley: University of California Press.

Moratto, Michael J.
1970   Archaeology and Cross-Cultural Ethnics in Coastal Northwest California. (Manuscript No. 28 in Robert E. Schenk Archives of California Archaeology, San Francisco State College, Adan E. Treganza Anthropology Museum, San Francisco.)

1970a   Tsahpekw: An Archaeological Record of Nineteenth Century Acculturation among the Yurok (Manuscript No. 7 in Robert E. Schenk Archives of California Archaeology, San Francisco State College, Adan E. Treganza Anthropology Museum, San Francisco.)

1970b   Archaeology of the Buchanan Reservoir Region, Madera County, California. Pt. 8. *San Francisco State College, Treganza Anthropology Museum Papers* 7:1-85. San Francisco.

_____, ed.
1971   A Study of Prehistory in the Tuolumne River Valley, California. *San Francisco State College, Treganza Anthropology Museum Papers* 9:1-177. San Francisco.

Moriarty, James R., III
1967   Transitional Pre-Desert Phase in San Diego County, California. *Science* 155(3762):553-556.

1971   Mission San Diego de Alcalá. Pp. 21-22 in Pacific West Report. Paul J.F. Schumacher, ed. *Newsletter of the Society for Historical Archaeology* 4(3). Ottawa.

Moriarty, James, R., III, and William R. Weyland
1971   Excavations at San Diego Mission. *Masterkey* 45(4):124-137.

Morrison, Lorrin L.
1962   Warner: The Man and the Ranch. Los Angeles: Privately Published.

Moshinsky, Julius B.
1965-1968   [Linguistic Fieldnotes on Southeastern Pomo.] (Manuscript in Moshinsky's Possession.)

1974   A Grammar of Southeastern Pomo. *University of California Publications in Linguistics* 72. Berkeley.

1975   Historical Pomo Phonology. In Hokan Studies: Papers from the First Conference on Hokan Languages, 1970. Margaret Langdon and Shirley K. Silver, eds. *Janua Linguarum, Series Practica* 181. The Hague: Mouton.

Munz, Phillip A., and David D. Keck
1959   A California Flora. Berkeley and Los Angeles: University of California Press. (Reissued with a Supplement in 1973.)

Murdock, Charles A.
1921   A Backward Glance at Eighty: Recollections and Comment. San Francisco: Paul Elder.

Murdock, George P.
1949   Social Structure. New York: Macmillan.

1960   Ethnographic Bibliography of North America. 3d ed. New Haven, Conn.: Human Relations Area Files. (Superseded by Murdock and O'Leary 1975.)

Murdock, George P., and Timothy J. O'Leary
1975   Ethnographic Bibliography of North America. 4th ed. Vol. 3: Far West and Pacific States. New Haven, Conn.: Human Relations Area Files Press.

Murray, George D., ed.
[1943] The Quest for Qual-a-Wa-Loo, Humboldt Bay. San Francisco: Humboldt County Historical Society. (Reprinted: Holmes Book Company, Oakland, 1966.)

Myrkrantz, J.W.
1927   Indian Burial in Southern California. *Museum of the American Indian, Heye Foundation. Indian Notes* 4(2):154-163. New York.

Nance, J.D.
1970   Lithic Analysis: Implications for the Prehistory of Central California. *Annual Reports of the University of California Archaeological Survey* 12:62-103. Los Angeles.

Navarrete, Martín F. de, ed.
1802   Relacion de Viage Hecho por las goletas Sutil y Mexicana en el año de 1792 para reconocer el estrecho de Fuca. Madrid: Imprenta Real.

Neasham, E.A.
1957   Fall River Valley, a History. Fall River Mills, Calif.: n.p.

Nelson, Nels C.
1909   Shellmounds of the San Francisco Bay Region. *University of California Publications in American Archaeology and Ethnology* 7(4):309-356. Berkeley.

1909a   [Unpublished Notes of the Annual Series of Ceremonies Formerly Observed by the Maidu on the Chico and Durham Rancherias; from Informant Jack Frango.] (Copy Available through R.F. Heizer, University of California, Berkeley.)

1910   The Ellis Landing Shellmound. *University of California Publications in American Archaeology and Ethnology* 7(5):357-426. Berkeley.

Nelson, Winnie
1971   The Indian Tribes of the Siskiyou. Vol. 4. Yreka, Calif.: Siskiyou County Historical Society. (The Siskiyou Pioneer.)

Nettl, Bruno
1954   North American Indian Musical Styles. *Memoirs of the American Folklore Society* 45. Philadelphia.

Nevin, Bruce E.
1975   Transformational Analysis of some 'Grammatical Morphemes' in Yana. In Hokan Studies: Papers from the First Conference on Hokan Languages, 1970. Margaret Langdon and Shirley K. Silver, eds. *Janua Linguarum, Series Practica* 181. The Hague: Mouton.

New, Lloyd K.
1971   A New Vitality Rekindles Proud Fires of the Past. *House Beautiful* 113(6):38-39, 132-134, 136.

Newman, Stanley S.
1944   Yokuts Language of California. *Viking Fund Publications in Anthropology* 2. New York.

1946   The Yawelmani Dialect of Yokuts. Pp. 222-248 in Linguistic Structures of Native America. Harry Hoijer et al., eds. *Viking Fund Publications in Anthropology* 6. New York.

1964   Comparison of Zuni and California Penutian. *International Journal of American Linguistics* 30(1):1-13.

Nicholson, Grace
[1935]   [Papers Covering Trips to the Yurok in the 1930's.] (Photographs and Manuscripts in Grace Nicholson Papers, Huntington Library, San Marino, Calif.)

Nixon, Stuart
1966   Redwood Empire. New York: E.P. Dutton.

Nomland, Gladys (Ayer)
1935   Sinkyone Notes. *University of California Publications in American Archaeology and Ethnology* 36(2):149-178. Berkeley.

1938   Bear River Ethnography. *University of California Anthropological Records* 2(2):91-124. Berkeley.

Nomland, Gladys A., and Alfred L. Kroeber
1936   Wiyot Towns. *University of California Publications in American Archaeology and Ethnology* 35(5):39-48. Berkeley.

Nordland, Ole J., ed.
1968   Coachella Valley Golden Years. Indio, Calif.: Little Grant Printers.

North, Arthur W.
1908   The Native Tribes of Lower California. *American Anthropologist* n.s. 10(2):236-250.

Nuttall, Zelia
1924   Two Remarkable California Baskets. *Quarterly of the California Historical Society* 2(4):341-343. San Francisco.

O'Connell, James F.
1967   Elko Eared/Elko Corner Notched Projectile Points as Time Markers in the Great Basin. *University of California Archaeological Survey Reports* 70:129-140. Berkeley.

Olden, Sarah E.
1923   Karoc Indian Stories. San Francisco: Harr Wagner.

Oliphant, Robert L.
1971   The Archaeology of 4-SMa-101. Pp. 21-36 in Contributions to the Archaeology of San Mateo County, California. M. Moratto, ed. *San Francisco State College, Treganza Anthropology Museum Papers* 8. San Francisco.

Olmsted, David L.
1954   Achumawi-Atsugewi Non-reciprocal Intelligibility. *International Journal of American Linguistics* 20(3):181-184.

1956-1959   Palaihnihan and Shasta, I: Labial Stops, II: Apical Stops, III: Dorsal Stops. *Language* 32(1):73-77, 33(2):136-138, 35(4):637-643.

1958   Atsugewi Phonology. *International Journal of American Linguistics* 24(3):215-220.

1961   Atsugewi Morphology, I: Verb Inflection. *International Journal of American Linguistics* 27(2):91-113.

1964   A History of Palaihnihan Phonology. *University of California Publications in Linguistics* 35. Berkeley.

1965   Phonemic Change and Subgrouping: Some Hokan Data. *Language* 41(2):303-307.

1966   Achumawi Dictionary. *University of California Publications in Linguistics* 45. Berkeley.

Olsen, William H.
1961   Archeological Investigations at Sutter's Fort State Historical Monument, 1959. (Manuscript No. 62 at the California State Division of Beaches and Parks, Sacramento.)

Olsen, William H., and Louis A. Payen
1968   Archaeology of the Little Panoche Reservoir, Fresno County, California. *California State Department of Parks and Recreation, Archaeological Resources Section Report* 11. Sacramento.

1969   Archaeology of the Grayson Site Merced County, California. *California State Department of Parks and Recreation, Archaeological Resources Section Report* 12. Sacramento.

Olsen, William H., and Francis A. Riddell
1962   Salvage of the Rio Oso Site, Yuba County, California. *California State Department of Parks and Recreation, Archaeological Resources Section Report* 6. Sacramento.

1963   The Archeology of the Western Pacific Railroad Relocation: Oroville Project, Butte County, California. *California State Department of Parks and Recreation, Archaeological Resources Section Report* 7. Sacramento.

Olsen, William H., and Norman L. Wilson
1964   The Salvage Archeology of the Bear Creek Site (SJo-112): A Terminal Central California Early Horizon Site. *Sacramento Anthropological Society Papers* 1. Sacramento.

Olson, C.
1948   The Sutter-Marshall Lease with the Yalesumney Indians for Monopoly of the Gold-bearing Lands. *Book Club of California, Letters of the Gold Discovery* 2. San Francisco.

Olson, Ronald L.
1927   Adze, Canoe, and House Types of the Northwest Coast. *University of Washington Publications in Anthropology* 2(1):1-38. Seattle.

1930   Chumash Prehistory. *University of California Publications in American Archaeology and Ethnology* 28(1):1-21. Berkeley.

O'Neale, Lila M.
[1930]   [Fieldnotes on the Basketry of Northwestern California (Yurok-Karok-Hupa).] (Hupa Notebooks 3, in University of California Archives, Berkeley.)

1932   Yurok-Karok Basket Weavers. *University of California Publications in American Archaeology and Ethnology* 32(1):1-184. Berkeley.

Ordaz, Blas
1958   La Ultima exploración española en América [1821]. *Revista de Indias* 18(72):227-241.

Orozco y Berra, Manuel
1864   Geografía de las lenguas de México y carta etnográfica de México. Mexico City, D.F.: J.M. Andrade y F. Escalante.

Orr, Phil C.
1943   Archaeology of Mescalitan Island, and Customs of the Canaliño. *Santa Barbara Museum of Natural History Occasional Papers* 5. Santa Barbara, Calif.

1960   Radiocarbon Dates from Santa Rosa Island, II. *Santa Barbara Museum of Natural History, Department of Anthropology Bulletin* 3. Santa Barbara, Calif.

1968   Prehistory of Santa Rosa Island, Santa Barbara, California. Santa Barbara: Santa Barbara Museum of Natural History.

Osgood, Wilfred H.
1947   Biographical Memoir of Clinton Hart Merriam, 1855-1942. Pp. 1-58 in *National Academy of Sciences Biographical Memoir* 24. Washington.

Oswalt, Robert L.
[1957-1975]   [Fieldnotes on Kashaya: 10 Notebooks, 30,000 File Slips.] (Manuscripts in Oswalt's Possession.)

1958   Russian Loan Words in Southwestern Pomo. *International Journal of American Linguistics* 24(3):245-247.

[1958-1968]   [Fieldnotes on Central Pomo, Boya and Yokaya Dialects: 2 Notebooks, 8,000 File Slips.] (Manuscripts in Oswalt's Possession.)

1960   Gualala. *Names* 8(1):57-58.

1961   A Kashaya Grammar (Southwestern Pomo). (Unpublished Ph.D. Dissertation in Linguistics, University of California, Berkeley.)

[1962-1965]   [Notes from about One Month's Fieldwork among the Northern Pomo.] (Manuscript in Oswalt's Possession.)

[1963-1968]   [Fieldnotes on Southern Pomo.] (Manuscript in Oswalt's Possession.)

1964   Kashaya Texts. *University of California Publications in Linguistics* 36. Berkeley.

1964a   The Internal Relationships of the Pomo Family of Languages. Pp. 413-427 in Vol. 2 of *Proceedings of the 35th International Congress of Americanists*. 2 vols. Mexico, 1962.

1964b   A Comparative Study of Two Pomo Languages. Pp. 148-162 in Studies in Californian Linguistics. William Bright, ed. *University of California Publications in Linguistics* 34. Berkeley.

1971   Inanimate Imitatives in Pomo. Pp. 175-190 in Studies in American Indian Languages. Jesse Sawyer, ed. *University of California Publications in Linguistics* 65. Berkeley.

1971a   The Case of the Broken Bottle. [A Study of the Spread of a Russian Loanword through Three Pomo Languages]. *International Journal of American Linguistics* 37(1):48-49.

1975   Comparative Verb Morphology of Pomo. In Hokan Studies: Papers from the First Conference on Hokan Languages, 1970. Margaret Langdon and Shirley K. Silver, eds. *Janua Linguarum, Series Practica* 181. The Hague: Mouton.

1975a   Kashaya Verb Prefixes. (Working Paper No. 13, Kashaya Pomo Languages in Culture Project, Department of Anthropology, California State College, Sonoma.)

1975b   K'ahšáya cahno kalikakh [Kashaya Word Book.] (Kashaya Pomo Language in Culture Project, Department of Anthropology, California State College, Sonoma.)

1976   Baby Talk and the Genesis of Some Basic Pomo Words. *International Journal of American Linguistics* 42(1):1-13.

[1976a]   [Fieldnotes on Northeastern Pomo from Two Days' Fieldwork.] (Manuscript in Oswalt's Possession.)

Outhwaite, Leonard
1913   Map Showing Location of Santa Cruz Island Archaeological Sites. (Manuscript No. 372 in University of California Archaeological Research Facility, Berkeley.)

Owen, Roger C.
1964   Early Milling Stone Horizon (Oak Grove) Santa Barbara County, California: Radiocarbon Dates. *American Antiquity* 30(2):210-213.

Owen, Roger C., Freddie Curtis, and Donald S. Miller
1963-1964   The Glen Annie Canyon Site, SBa-142: An Early Horizon Coastal Site of Santa Barbara County. *Annual Reports of the University of California Archaeological Survey* 6:431-517. Los Angeles.

Palmer, Edward
1878   Plants Used by the Indians of the United States. *American Naturalist* 12(9):593-606.

Palmer, Lyman
1880   History of Mendocino County, California. San Francisco: Alley, Bowen.

[Palmer, Lyman]
1881   History of Napa and Lake Counties, California Comprising their Geography, Geology, Topography, Climatography, Springs and Timber... and Biographical Sketches. San Francisco: Slocum, Bowen.

Palóu, Francisco
1924   [Description of the Indians in the Vicinity of Mission San Francisco, 1776.] Pp. 59-64 in San Francisco or Mission Dolores, by Zephyrin Engelhardt. Chicago: Franciscan Herald Press.

1926   Historical Memoirs of New California. Herbert E. Bolton, ed. 4 vols. Berkeley: University of California Press.

1930   Palou's Diary of the Expedition to San Francisco Bay [1774]. Pp. 393-456 in Vol. 2 of Anza's California Expeditions, by Herbert E. Bolton. Berkeley: University of California Press.

1930a   Palou's Account of the Founding of San Francisco [1776]. Pp. 383-405 in Vol. 3 of Anza's California Expeditions, by Herbert E. Bolton. Berkeley: University of California Press.

Parker, Horace
1971   The Temecula Massacre. Balboa Island, Calif.: Paisano Press.

Parsons, Thomas, ed.
[1971]   The Yurok Language, Literature and Culture Textbook. 2d ed. Arcata, Calif.: Humboldt State College, Center for Community Development. Mimeo.

Patencio, Francisco
1943   Stories and Legends of the Palm Springs Indians. Margaret Boynton, ed. Los Angeles: Times-Mirror.

Payen, Louis A.
1959   Petroglyphs of Sacramento and Adjoining Counties, California. *University of California Archaeological Survey Reports* 48:66-83. Berkeley.

1961   Excavations at Sutter's Fort. (Manuscript No. 87, at the California State Division of Beaches and Parks, Sacramento.)

1961a   The Walltown Nisenan. (Manuscript in Norman L. Wilson's Possession.)

1966   Prehistoric Rock Art in the Northern Sierra Nevada, California. (Unpublished M.A. Thesis in Anthropology, Sacramento State College, Sacramento, Calif.)

1968   A Note on Cupule Sculptures in Exogene Caves from the Sierra Nevada, California. *Caves and Karst* 10(4):33-39.

1970   A Spearthrower (Atlatl) from Potter Creek Cave, Shasta County, California. *University of California, Center for Archaeological Research Publications* 2:155-170. Davis.

Payen, Louis A., and David S. Boloyan
1963   "Tco'se", an Archaeological Study of the Bedrock Mortar-Petroglyph at Ama-14, near Volcano, California. *Cali-*

755

fornia State Division of Beaches and Parks, *Archaeological Reports* 8. Sacramento.

Peck, Stuart L.
1955   An Archaeological Report on the Excavation of a Prehistoric Site at Zuma Creek, Los Angeles County, California. *Archaeological Survey Association of Southern California Papers* 2. Los Angeles.

Pendergast, David W., and Clement W. Meighan
1958-1959   The Greasy Creek Site, Tulare County, California. *Annual Reports of the University of California Archaeological Survey* 1:1-10. Los Angeles.

Perry, W.J.
1917   An Ethnological Study of Warfare. *Memoirs and Proceedings of the Manchester Literary and Philosophical Society* 61(6):1-16. Manchester, England.

Petersen, Edward
1969   Pierson B. Reading: Shasta County Pioneer. Cottonwood, Calif.: Privately Published.

Peterson, Marcus E.
1957   The Career of Solano: Chief of the Suisuns. (Unpublished M.A. Thesis in History, University of California, Berkeley.)

Phillips, George
1971   The Garra Uprising and its Aftermath: A Study in Indian Resistance and Accommodation. (Unpublished Ph.D. Dissertation in History, University of California, Los Angeles.)

Pickering, Charles
1848   ...The Races of Man: And their General Distribution. Vol. 6 of United States Exploring Expedition. Philadelphia: C. Sherman.

Pietroforte, Alfred
1965   Songs of the Yokuts and Paiutes of California and Nevada. Healdsburg, Calif.: Naturegraph Press.

Pilling, Arnold R.
1948   Archaeological Survey of Northern Monterey County. (Manuscript No. 106 in University of California Archaeological Research Facility, Berkeley.)

1950   The Archaeological Implications of an Annual Coastal Visit for Certain Yokuts Groups. *American Anthropologist* 52(3):438-440.

1951   The Surface Archeology of the Pecho Coast, San Luis Obispo County, California. *Masterkey* 25(6):196-200.

1952   California Mission Maiolica. (Manuscript No. 139 in the Universtiy of California Archaeological Research Facility, Lowie Museum, Berkeley.)

1955   Glazed Ceramics-Relationships in California (Farallon Islands). (Manuscript No. 213 in University of California Archaeological Research Facility, Lowie Museum, Berkeley.)

[1967-1969]   [Notes Based on Interviews with Yurok, Tolowa, and Chilula Informants.] (Manuscript in Pilling's Possession.)

1969   Impact of Modern Industrial Society on Tribal Law. Mimeo.

1969a   The Fishing Site and the Bear Paw. (Manuscript in Possession of Dale Valory and Arnold R. Pilling.)

1969b   Vancouver Collection from Trinidad, California, as Described in the Notes of Arnold R. Pilling, December, 1969. (Manuscript in Humboldt County Collection, California State University, Humboldt.)

Pilling, Arnold R., and Patricia L. Pilling
1970   Cloth, Clothes, Hose, and Bows: Nonsedentary Merchants among the Indians of Northwestern California.

Pp. 97-119 in Migration and Anthropology: Proceedings of the Annual Spring Meeting of the American Ethnological Society. Seattle, 1970.

Pilling, Patricia L.
1972   Nicknames [in Yurok and Hupa]. Leslie Dunkling, ed. *VIZ* 22:243.

Pitkin, Harvey
1963   Wintu Grammar. (Unpublished Ph.D. Dissertation in Linguistics, University of California, Berkeley.)

Pitkin, Harvey, and William Shipley
1958   A Comparative Survey of California Penutian. *International Journal of American Linguistics* 24(3):174-188.

Pohorecky, Zenon S.
1964   Archaeology of the South Coast Ranges of California. (Unpublished Ph.D. Dissertation in Anthropology, University of California, Berkeley.)

Pope, Saxton T.
1918   Yahi Archery. *University of California Publications in American Archaeology and Ethnology* 13(3):103-152. Berkeley.

1920   The Medical History of Ishi. *University of California Publications in American Archaeology and Ethnology* 13(5):175-213. Berkeley.

Portolá, Gaspar de
1909   Diary of Gaspar de Portolá during the California Expedition of 1769-1770. Donald E. Smith and Frederick J. Teggart, eds. *Publications of the Academy of Pacific Coast History* 1(3):31-89. Berkeley, Calif.

Posinsky, Sollie H.
1954   Yurok Ritual. (Unpublished Ph.D. Dissertation in Anthropology, Columbia University, New York.)

1957   The Problem of Yurok Anality. *American Imago* 14(1):3-31.

Powell, John Wesley
1877   Linguistics. Pp. 439-613 in Tribes of California, by Stephen Powers. *Contributions to North American Ethnology* 3. Washington: U.S. Geographical and Geological Survey of the Rocky Mountain Region.

1891   Indian Linguistic Families of America North of Mexico. Pp. 7-142 in *7th Annual Report of the Bureau of American Ethnology for the Years 1885-1886*. Washington.

Power, T.W.
[1907]   Deer Skin Dance. (Manuscript in Arnold R. Pilling's Possession.)

Powers, Stephen
1872   The Northern California Indians 3: [The Euroc]. *Overland Monthly* 8:530-539.

1872a   The Northern California Indians 6: [The Pomo and Cahto]. *Overland Monthly* 9:498-507.

1872b   The Northern California Indians 5: [The Yuka]. *Overland Monthly* 9:305-313.

1873   The California Indians 7: [The Meewocs]. *Overland Monthly* 10:322-333.

1874   The California Indians 11: [Various Tribes]. *Overland Monthly* 12:412-424.

1874a   The California Indians 12: [The Wintoons]. *Overland Monthly* 13: 542-550.

1874b   The California Indians 10: [The Neeshenams]. *Overland Monthly* 12: 21-31.

1874c   Aborigines of California. *Atlantic Monthly* 33:313-323.

1875   Aboriginal Botany. Pp. 373-379 in *Proceedings of the California Academy of Sciences for 1873-1874,* 1st ser., Vol. 5. San Francisco.

1875a   Californian Indian Characteristics. *Overland Monthly* 14(4):297-309.

1877   Tribes of California. *Contributions to North American Ethnology* 3. Washington: U.S. Geographical and Geological Survey of the Rocky Mountain Region.

1975   The Northern California Indians. Robert F. Heizer, ed. *University of California Archaeological Research Facility Contributions* 25. Berkeley.

Pratt, Richard H.
1964   Battlefield and Classroom: Four Decades with the American Indian, 1867-1904. New Haven, Conn.: Yale University Press.

Pritchard, William E.
1970   Archeology of the Menjoulet Site Merced County, California. *California State Department of Parks and Recreation, Archaeological Resources Section Report* 13. Sacramento.

Pritchard, William E., D.M. Hill, Sonia R. Purcell, and Roy Purcell
1966   The Porter Rock Shelter Site (But-S177), Butte County, California. *Annual Reports of the University of California Archaeological Survey* 8:278-315. Los Angeles.

Prucha, Francis P., comp.
1973   Americanizing the American Indians: Writings by the "Friends of the Indians" 1800-1900. Cambridge, Mass.: Harvard University Press.

Pullum, G.K.
1973   Yokuts Bibliography: An Addendum. *International Journal of American Linguistics* 39(4):269-271.

Putnam, Frederic W.
1905   The Department of Anthropology of the University of California. Berkeley: University of California Publications; The University Press.

1906   Evidence of the Work of Man on Objects from Quaternary Caves in California. *American Anthropologist* n.s. 8(2):229-235.

Putnam, Frederic W., C.C. Abbott, S.S. Haldeman, H.C. Yarrow, and H.W. Henshaw
1879   Archaeological and Ethnological Collections from Vicinity of Santa Barbara, California and from Ruined Pueblos of Arizona and New Mexico, and Certain Interior Tribes. Report Upon United States Geographical Surveys West of the One Hundredth Meridian, by George M. Wheeler. Vol. VII: Archaeology. Washington: U.S. Government Printing Office.

Quinn, Charles R.
1964   The Story of Mission Santa Ysabel. Downey, Calif.: Elena Quinn.

Quint, California B.
1960   Jedediah Strong Smith. Pp. 14-18 in The Covered Wagon. Redding, Calif.: Shasta Historical Society.

Radin, Paul
1919   The Genetic Relationship of the North American Indian Languages. *University of California Publications in American Archaeology and Ethnology* 14(5):489-502. Berkeley.

1924   Wappo Texts: First Series. *University of California Publications in American Archaeology and Ethnology* 19(1):1-147. Berkeley.

1929   A Grammar of the Wappo Language. *University of California Publications in American Archaeology and Ethnology* 27:1-194. Berkeley.

Ragir, Sonia
1972   The Early Horizon in Central California Prehistory. *University of California Archaeological Research Facility Contributions* 15. Berkeley.

Rasson, Judith
1966   Excavations at Ahwahnee, Yosemite National Park, California. *Annual Reports of the University of California Archaeological Survey* 8:165-184. Los Angeles.

Rathbun, Robert *see* Coyote Man

Raup, Ruth M.
1959   The Indian Health Program, 1800-1955. Washington: U.S. Division of Indian Health, Department of Health, Education and Welfare.

Ray, P. Henry
1886   Manufacture of Bows and Arrows among the Natano (Hupa) and Kenuck (Klamath) Indians. *American Naturalist* 20(9):832-833.

Ray, Verne F.
1963   Primitive Pragmatists: The Modoc Indians of Northern California. Seattle: University of Washington Press.

Read, Charles H.
1892   An Account of a Collection of Ethnographical Specimens Formed during Vancouver's Voyage in the Pacific Ocean 1790-1795. *Journal of the Anthropological Institute* 21:99-108. London.

Reichard, Gladys A.
1925   Wiyot Grammar and Texts. *University of California Publications in American Archaeology and Ethnology* 22(1):1-215. Berkeley.

Reichlen, Henry, and Robert F. Heizer
1963   La Mission de Léon de Cessac en Californie, 1877-1879. *Objets et Mondes* 3(1):17-34. (English Translation in *University of California Archaeological Survey Reports* 61:9-22, 1963.)

Reichlen, Henry, and Paule Reichlen
1971   Le Manuscrit Boscana de la Bibliothèque Nationale de Paris. *Journal de la Société des Américanistes* 60:233-273.

Reinman, Fred M.
1963-1964 Maritime Adaptation on San Nicolas Island, California: A Preliminary and Speculative Evaluation. *Annual Reports of the University of California Archaeological Survey* 6:47-77. Los Angeles.

Revere, Joseph W.
1849   A Tour of Duty in California. Joseph N. Balestier, ed. New York: C.S. Francis.

Reynolds, Charles R., comp.
1971   American Indian Portraits; from the Wanamaker Expedition of 1913. Brattleboro, Vt.: Stephen Greene Press.

Ricard, Robert
1966   The Spiritual Conquest of Mexico. Lesley B. Simpson, trans. Berkeley: University of California Press.

Riddell, Francis A.
1951   The Archaeology of Site Ker-74. *University of California Archaeological Survey Reports* 10:1-28. Berkeley.

1955   Archaeological Excavations on the Farallon Island, California. *University of California Archaeological Survey Reports* 32:1-18. Berkeley.

1960   Honey Lake Paiute Ethnography. *Nevada State Museum Anthropological Papers* 4. Carson City.

[1960-1974] [Ethnogeographic Notes from Intermittent Fieldwork among the Maidu, Konkow and Nisenan.] (Manuscripts in Riddell's Possession.)

1962   A Bibliography of the Indians of Northwestern California. (Ethnographic Report 2) Sacramento: State of California Resources Agency, Department of Parks and Recreation, Division of Beaches and Parks.

1968   Ethnogeography of Two Maidu Groups. *Masterkey* 42(2):45-52.

1972   The Ethnogeography of the Hill Nisenan. (Manuscript in the Arizona Archeological Center, Tucson.)

Riddell, Francis A., and William H. Olsen
1969   An Early Man Site in the San Joaquin Valley, California. *American Antiquity* 34(2):121-130.

Riddell, Francis A., and William E. Pritchard
1971   Archeology of the Rainbow Point Site (4-Plu-S94), Bucks Lake, Plumas County, California. *University of Oregon Anthropological Papers* 1:59-102. Eugene.

Ritter, Eric W.
1968   Culture History of "Tie Wiah" (4-But-84), Oroville Locality, California. (Unpublished M.A. Thesis in Anthropology, University of California, Davis.)

1970   Northern Sierra Foothill Archaeology: Culture History and Culture Process. Pp. 171-184 in Papers on California and Great Basin Prehistory. Eric W. Ritter, Peter D. Schulz, and Robert Kautz, eds. *University of California, Center for Archaeological Research Publications* 2. Davis.

1972   Form Categories, Cluster Analysis and Multidimensional Scaling: A Case Study of Projectile Points. *Southwestern Lore* 37(4):102-116.

Ritter, Eric W., and Peter Schulz, eds.
1972   Papers on Nisenan Environment and Subsistence. *University of California Center for Archaeological Research Publications* 3. Davis.

Robbins, Millie
1967   Heritage of a People. *Chronicle Sunday Punch,* September 10:6. San Francisco.

Roberts, M.V.
1894   [Letter dated "April 18th/94" from "Arcata."] (Manuscript in Arnold R. Pilling's Possession.)

Roberts, Harry K.
[1969]   [Yurok Tales.] (Manuscripts in Roberts' Possession.)

Roberts, Helen H.
1933   Form in Primitive Music: An Analytical and Comparative Study of the Melodic Form of Some Ancient Southern Californian Indian Songs. New York: W.W. Norton.

1936   Musical Areas in Aboriginal North America. *Yale University Publications in Anthropology* 12. New Haven, Conn.

Roberts, Ruth (Kellett)
[1918-1934] [Photographs and Papers of Ruth Kellett Roberts and Harry Kellett Roberts.] (In Humboldt County Collection, California State University, Humboldt.)

1934   "Rekwoi." *Pacific Sportsman,* March: 3-4, 31.

Robins, R.H.
1958   The Yurok Language: Grammar, Texts, Lexicon. *University of California Publications in Linguistics* 15. Berkeley.

Robins, R.H., and Norma MacLeod
1957   A Yurok Song without Words. *Bulletin of the School of Oriental and African Studies of the University of London* 20:501-506. London.

Robinson, W.S.
1951   A Method for Chronologically Ordering in Archaeological Deposits. *American Antiquity* 16(4):293-301.

Robinson, Alfred
1846   Life in California during a Residence of Several Years in that Territory. New York: Wiley and Putnam.

Robinson, Eugene
1942   Plank Canoes of the Chumash. *Masterkey* 16(6):202-209.

1964   A House Floor in Napa County, California. *State of California Division of Beaches and Parks, Interpretive Services Section, Archaeological Report 10.* Pt. 2. Sacramento.

Robinson, William W.
1952   The Indians of Los Angeles: Story of the Liquidation of a People. (Early California Travels Series 8) Los Angeles: Dawson.

Rogers, Barbara T., and Anna H. Gayton
1944   Twenty-seven Chukchansi Yokuts Myths. *Journal of American Folklore* 57(225):190-207.

Rogers, David B.
1929   Prehistoric Man of the Santa Barbara Coast, California. *Santa Barbara Museum of Natural History Special Publications* 1. Santa Barbara, Calif.

1937   A Reconnaissance. (Field Survey by the Santa Barbara Museum of Natural History in the Cuyama Region.) *American Antiquity* 3(2):184-186.

Rogers, Harrison G.
1918   The Second Journal of Harrison G. Rogers. Pp. 237-271 in The Ashley-Smith Explorations and the Discovery of a Central Route to the Pacific, 1822-1828. H.C. Dale, ed. Cleveland: Arthur H. Clark.

Rogers, Justus H.
1891   Colusa County: Its History Traced from a State of Nature through the Early Period of Settlement and Development, to the Present Day. Also Biographical Sketches of Pioneers and Prominent Residents. Orland, Calif.: n.p. (Reprinted: California Traveler, Volcano, 1970.)

Rogers, Malcolm J.
1929   The Stone Art of the San Dieguito Plateau. *American Anthropologist* 31(3):454-467.

1941   Aboriginal Culture Relations between Southern California and the Southwest. *San Diego Museum Bulletins* 5(3):1-6. San Diego, Calif.

Rollin, M.
1959   Physiological and Pathological Monograph on the Americans. Pp. 97-120 in The First French Expedition to California: Lapérouse in 1786 [1797]. Charles N. Rudkin, trans. Los Angeles: Glen Dawson.

Roney, J.G.
1959   Paleopathology of a California Archaeological Site. *Bulletin of the History of Medicine* 33:97-109.

Rosborough, J.B.
1875   Northwest California Indians. (Manuscript Typescript of Letter in Haynes Collection on the Indians of California, Bancroft Library, University of California, Berkeley.)

Rosborough, Alex J.
1947   A.M. Rosborough - Special Indian Agent. *Quarterly of the California Historical Society* 26(3):201-207. San Francisco.

Ross, John E.
1878   Narrative of an Indian Fighter. (Manuscript in Bancroft Library, University of California, Berkeley.)

Rostlund, Erhard
1952   Freshwater Fish and Fishing in Native North America. *University of California Publications in Geography* 9. Berkeley.

Round Valley Cultural Project
1974   News Release of July 30, 1974, Covelo, Calif. (Copy in Possession of Victor Golla, George Washington University, Washington.)

Royce, Charles C., comp.
1899   Indian Land Cessions in the United States. Pp. 521-964 in *18th Annual Report of the Bureau of American Ethnology for the Years 1896-1897.* Washington.

Rozaire, Charles E.
1959 Archeological Investigations at Two Sites on San Nicolas Island, California. *Masterkey* 33(4):129-152

——— 1959a Pictographs at Burro Flats. *Ventura County Historical Society Quarterly* 4(2):2-6. Ventura, Calif.

Rozaire, Charles E., and S. Craig
1968 Analysis of Basketry from Site LAn-227. P. 131 (Appendix III) in The Archaeological Investigations of Three Sites on the Century Ranch, Western Los Angeles County, Calif. *Annual Reports of the University of California Archaeological Survey* 10. Los Angeles.

Ruby, Jay W.
1961-1962 Aboriginal Uses of Mount San Jacinto State Park. *Annual Reports of the University of California Archaeological Survey* 4:1-10. Los Angeles.

——— 1970 Culture Contact between Aboriginal Southern California and the Southwest. (Unpublished Ph.D. Dissertation in Anthropology, University of California, Los Angeles.)

Ruby, Jay W., and Thomas C. Blackburn
1959 Archeological Investigations at Two Sites on San Nicolas Island, California. *Masterkey* 33(4):129-152.

——— 1964 Occurrence of Southwestern Pottery in Los Angeles County, California. *American Antiquity* 30(2):209-210.

Ruiz, Russell A.
1967 The Santa Barbara Presidio. *Noticias: Quarterly Bulletin of the Santa Barbara Historical Society* 13(1):1-11. Santa Barbara, Calif.

——— 1969 Historical Background of the Royal Presidio Chapel. *Noticias: Quarterly Bulletin of the Santa Barbara Historical Society* 15(4):19-24. Santa Barbara, Calif.

Russell, R.J.
1926 Climates of California. *University of California Publications in Geography* 2(4):73-84. Berkeley.

Russell, Edward
1857 [Letter to Lt. Ferdinand Paine, Actg. Asst. Adj. Gen., Fort Reading, Calif., Jan 25, 1853.] U.S. Congress. House. 34th Cong., 3d sess. House Executive Doc. No. 76. Washington.

Russell, Frank
1908 The Pima Indians. Pp. 3-389 in *26th Annual Report of the Bureau of American Ethnology for 1904-1905.* Washington.

Rust, Horatio N.
1906 A Puberty Ceremony of the Mission Indians. *American Anthropologist* n.s. 8(1):28-32.

Ryan, R. Mark
1968 Mammals of Deep Canyon, Colorado Desert, California. Palm Springs Calif.: Palm Springs Desert Museum.

Salem Indian School
1935 The Chief. Chemava, Oreg.: Chemava Press.

Sample, L.L.
1950 Trade and Trails in Aboriginal California. *University of California Archaeological Survey Reports* 8. Berkeley.

Sapir, Edward
1907 Notes on the Takelma Indians of Southwestern Oregon. *American Anthropologist* 9(2):251-275.

——— 1908 Luck-Stones among the Yana. *Journal of American Folk-Lore* 21(80):42.

——— 1909 Characteristic Traits of the Yana Language of California. *American Anthropologist* n.s. 11(1):110.

——— 1910 Yana Texts, together with Yana Myths. Roland B. Dixon, coll. *University of California Publications in American Archaeology and Ethnology* 9(1):1-235. Berkeley.

——— 1913 Wiyot and Yurok, Algonkin Languages of California. *American Anthropologist* 15(4):617-646.

——— 1915 Algonkin Languages of California: A Reply. *American Anthropologist* 17(1):188-194.

——— 1915a Epilogue. *American Anthropologist* 17(1):198.

——— 1916 Terms of Relationship and the Levirate. *American Anthropologist* 18(3):327-337.

——— 1917 The Position of Yana in the Hokan Stock. *University of California Publications in American Archaeology and Ethnology* 13(1):1-34. Berkeley.

——— 1918 Yana Terms of Relationship. *University of California Publications in American Archaeology and Ethnology* 13(4):153-173. Berkeley.

——— 1920 The Hokan and Coahúiltecan Languages. *International Journal of American Linguistics* 1(4):280-290.

——— 1921 Language: An Introduction to the Study of Speech. New York: Harcourt, Brace.

——— 1921a A Supplementary Note on Salinan and Washo. *International Journal of American Linguistics* 2(1-2):68-72.

——— 1921b A Bird's-eye View of American Languages North of Mexico. *Science* 54(1400):408.

——— 1921-1923 A Characteristic Penutian Form of Stem. *International Journal of American Linguistics* 2(1-2):58-67.

——— 1922 The Fundamental Elements of Northern Yana. *University of California Publications in American Archaeology and Ethnology* 13(6):215-234. Berkeley.

——— 1923 Text Analyses of Three Yana Dialects. *University of California Publications in American Archaeology and Ethnology* 20(15):263-294. Berkeley.

——— 1925 The Hokan Affinity of Subtiaba in Nicaragua. *American Anthropologist* 27(3):402-435, (4):491-527.

——— [1927] Hupa Myths, Formulas, and Ethnological Narratives in Text and Translation. (Manuscript in Harry Hoijer's Possession.)

——— 1929 Central and North American Indian Languages. Pp. 138-141 in Vol. 5 of Encyclopaedia Britannica. 14th ed. London and New York: Encyclopaedia Britannica Company. (Reprinted in Selected Writings of Edward Sapir in Language, Culture and Personality. D.G. Mandelbaum, ed. University of California Press, Berkeley, 1949.)

——— 1929a Male and Female Forms of Speech in Yana. Pp. 79-85 in Donum Natalicium Schrijnen. W.J. Teeuwen, ed. Nijmegen-Utrecht, The Netherlands. (Reprinted in Selected Writings of Edward Sapir in Language, Culture and Personality. David G. Mandelbaum, ed. University of California Press, Berkeley, 1949.)

——— 1936 Hupa Tattooing. Pp. 273-277 in Essays in Anthropology Presented to A.L. Kroeber in Celebration of his Sixtieth Birthday, June 11, 1936. Robert H. Lowie, ed. Berkeley and Los Angeles: University of California Press.

Sapir, Edward, and Leslie Spier
1943 Notes on the Culture of the Yana. *University of California Anthropological Records* 3(3):239-298. Berkeley.

Sapir, Edward, and Morris Swadesh
1953 Coos-Takelma-Penutian Comparisons. *International Journal of American Linguistics* 19(2):132-137.

——— 1960 Yana Dictionary. Mary R. Haas, ed. *University of California Publications in Linguistics* 22. Berkeley.

Sapir, Jean
1928 Yurok Tales. *Journal of American Folk-Lore* 41(160):253-261.

759

Satolli, Dino, and Tullio Tentori
1941   Miti e leggende sulla creazione dei primitivi nordamericani. Rome: Arti Grafiche Cossidente.

Sawyer, Jesse O.
1958-1968   [Unpublished Fieldnotes on the Wappo.] (Manuscripts in Sawyer's Possession.)

_____
1964   The Implications of Spanish /r/ and /rr/ in Wappo History. *Romance Philology* 18(2):165-177.

_____
1964a   Wappo Words from Spanish. Pp. 163-169 in Studies in Californian Linguistics. William Bright, ed. *University of California Publications in Linguistics* 34. Berkeley.

_____
1965   English-Wappo Vocabulary. *University of California Publications in Linguistics* 43. Berkeley.

Scammon, Charles M.
1874   The Marine Mammals of the Northwestern Coast of North America, Described and Illustrated: Together with an Account of the American Whale Fishery. San Francisco: John H. Carmany.

Schenck, Sara M., and Edward W. Gifford
1952   Karok Ethnobotany. *University of California Anthropological Records* 13(6):377-392. Berkeley.

Schenck, W. Egbert
1926   Historic Aboriginal Groups of the California Delta Region. *University of California Publications in American Archaeology and Ethnology* 23(2):123-146. Berkeley.

Schenck, W. Egbert, and Elmer J. Dawson
1929   Archaeology of the Northern San Joaquin Valley. *University of California Publications in American Archaeology and Ethnology* 25(4):289-413. Berkeley.

Schmidt, P. Wilhelm
1926-1949   Der Ursprung der Gottesidee. 9 vols. Münster, Germany: Aschendorfsche Verlagsbuchhandlung.

_____
1936   Donner und Regenbogen beim höchsten Wesen der Yuki. Pp. 299-308 in Essays in Anthropology Presented to A.L. Kroeber in Celebration of his Sixtieth Birthday, June 11, 1936. Robert H. Lowie, ed. Berkeley and Los Angeles: University of California Press.

Schoolcraft, Henry R.
1851-1857   Historical and Statistical Information Respecting the History, Condition and Prospects of the Indian Tribes of the United States. 6 vols. Philadelphia: Lippincott, Grambo.

_____
1860   Archives of Aboriginal Knowledge. Containing all the Original Papers Laid before Congress Respecting the History, Antiquities, Language, Ethnology, Pictography, Rites, Superstitions, and Mythology, of the Indian Tribes of the Unites States. 6 vols. Philadelphia: J.B. Lippincott.

Schulz, Paul E.
1954   Indians of Lassen Volcanic National Park and Vicinity. Mineral, Calif.: Loomis Museum Association, Lassen Volcanic National Park.

Schumacher, Paul
1875   Ancient Graves and Shell-Heaps of California. Pp. 335-350 in *Annual Report of the Smithsonian Institution for 1874*. Washington.

_____
1875a   Etwas über Kjökken Möddinge und die Funde in alten Gräbern in Südcalifornien. *Archiv für Anthropologie* 8:217-222.

_____
1877   Researches in the Kjökenmoddings and Graves of a Former Population of the Santa Barbara Channel Islands and the Adjacent Mainland. *Bulletin of the U.S. Geological and Geographical Survey of the Territories* 3:37-56. Washington.

_____
1878   Ancient Olla Manufactory on Santa Catalina Island, California. *American Naturalist* 12(9):629.

_____
1879   The Methods of Manufacturing Pottery and Baskets among the Indians of Southern California. Pp. 521-525 in Vol. 2 of *12th Annual Report of the Peabody Museum of American Archaeology and Ethnology, Harvard University*. 2 vols. Cambridge, Mass.

Schumacher, Paul J.F.
1971   Pacific West Report: California. *Newsletter of the Society for Historical Archaeology* 3(4):16-18, 4(2):20-22, 4(3):21-23, 4(4):13.

_____
1972   Pacific West Report: California. *Newsletter of the Society for Historical Archaeology* 5(1):17-20.

Schuyler, Robert L.
1970   Historical and Historic Sites Archaeology as Anthropology: Basic Definitions and Relationships. *Historical Archaeology* 4:83-89.

Schuyler, Robert L., and Paul G. Sneed
1968   Historic Sites Archaeology in California: A Review and Prediction. *Newsletter of the Southwestern Anthropological Association* 10(3):37.

Seiler, Hansjakob
1957   Die phonetischen Grundlagen der Vokalphoneme des Cahuilla. *Zeitschrift für Phonetik und Allgemeine Sprachwissenschaft* 10:204-223.

_____
1958   Zur Aufstellung der Wortklassen des Cahuilla: Uto-Aztekisch, Süd-Kalifornien. *Münchener Studien zur Sprachwissenschaft* 12:61-79. München, Germany.

_____
1965   Accent and Morphophonemics in Cahuilla and in Uto-Aztecan. *International Journal of American Linguistics* 31(1):50-59.

_____
1967   Structure and Reconstruction in Some Uto-Aztecan Languages. *International Journal of American Linguistics* 33(2):135-147.

_____
1970   Cahuilla Texts with an Introduction. *Indiana University Language Science Monographs* 6. Bloomington.

Seiter, Herbert D., and Harry D. Williams
1959   Prince Lightfoot: Indian from the California Redwoods. [Palo Alto, Calif.]: Troubador Press.

Señán, José Francisco de Paula
1962   The Letters of José Señán O.F.M.: Mission San Buenaventura, 1796-1823. Lesley B. Simpson, ed. San Francisco: John Howell.

Service, Elman R.
1966   The Hunters. Englewood Cliffs, N.J.: Prentice-Hall.

Shafer, Robert
1947   Penutian. *International Journal of American Linguistics* 13(4):205-219.

_____
1952   Notes on Penutian. *International Journal of American Linguistics* 18(4):211-216.

_____
1961   Tones in Wintun. *Anthropological Linguistics* 3(6):17-30.

Shames, Deborah, ed.
1972   Freedom with Reservation: The Menominee Struggle to Save their Land and People. Madison, Wis.: National Committee to Save the Menominee People and Forests.

Shea, John D.G.
1855   History of the Catholic Missions among the Indian Tribes of the United States, 1529-1854. New York: T.W. Strong.

Shelford, Victor E.
1963   The Ecology of North America. Urbana: University of Illinois Press.

Shepard, Eugene
1965   Southern California Weather Cycles. *Pacific Coast Archaeological Society Quarterly* 1(1):17. Costa Mesa, Calif.

Sherman, Edwin A.
1945   Sherman Was There. *Quarterly of the California Histori-cal Society* 24:47-71. San Francisco.

Shipek, Florence (Connolly)
1954-1971   [Diegueño Fieldnotes.] (Manuscript in Shipek's Posses-sion.)

[1954-1973] [Fieldnotes on Research and Applied Anthropology among the Mission Indians of Southern California and Northern Baja Californa.] (Manuscripts in Shipek's Pos-session.)

1968   Diegueño Marriage Patterns. (Paper Presented at the Meeting of the Southwestern Anthropological Associ-ation, San Diego; Manuscript in Shipek's Possession.)

1971   Demographic Patterns among Southern California Indi-ans. (Manuscript in Shipek's Possession.)

1971a   An Analysis of the Community Development Education Program of the University of San Diego for the Indian Reservations of San Diego County 1970-1971: A Report to the State of California Coordinating Council on Higher Education, Sacramento. (Manuscript in Shipek's Posses-sion.)

[1976]   [Southern California Indian Land Tenure, 1769-1973.] (Manuscript in Shipek's Possession.)

Shipley, William F.
1957   Some Yukian-Penutian Lexical Resemblances. *Interna-tional Journal of American Linguistics* 23(4):269-274.

1961   Maidu and Nisenan: A Binary Survey. *International Jour-nal of American Linguistics* 27(1):46-51.

1962   Spanish Elements in the Indigenous Languages of Central California. *Romance Philology* 16(1):1-21.

1963   Maidu Texts and Dictionary. *University of California Publications in Linguistics* 33. Berkeley.

1964   Maidu Grammar. *University of California Publications in Linguistics* 41. Berkeley.

1966   The Relation of Klamath to California Penutian. *Lan-guage* 42(2):489-498.

1969   Proto-Takelman. *International Journal of American Lin-guistics* 35(3):226-230.

1970   Proto-Kalapuyan. Pp. 97-106 in Languages and Cultures of Western North America: Essays in Honor of Sven S. Liljeblad. Earl H. Swanson, Jr., ed. Pocatello: Idaho State University Press.

1973   California. Pp. 1046-1078 in Vol. 10 of Current Trends in Linguistics. Thomas A. Sebeok, ed. The Hague, Paris: Mouton.

Shuck, Oscar T.
1869   The California Scrapbook: A Repository of Useful Infor-mation and Selected Reading. San Francisco and New York: H.H. Bancroft.

Shumway, George, Carl L. Hubbs, and James R. Moriarty
1961   Scripps Estates Site, San Diego, California: A La Jolla Site Dated 5460 to 7370 Years before the Present. *Annals of the New York Academy of Sciences* 93(3):37-132. New York.

Shur, Leonid A., and James R. Gibson
1973   Russian Travel Notes and Journals as Sources for the His-tory of California, 1800-1850. *Quarterly of the California Historical Society* 52(1):37-63. San Francisco.

Silva, Owen Francis da
1941   Mission Music of California. Los Angeles: Warren F. Lewis.

Silver, Shirley K.
[1957-1963] [Shasta Linguistic Material: Fieldnotes, Tapes, and Texts, from approximately 8 Months' Fieldwork among the Shasta.] (Manuscript in Silver's Possession.)

1964   Shasta and Karok: A Binary Comparison. Pp. 170-181 in Studies in Californian Linguistics. William Bright, ed. *University of California Publications in Linguistics* 34. Berkeley.

1966   The Shasta Language. (Unpublished Ph.D. Dissertation in Linguistics, University of California, Berkeley.)

1975   Comparative Hokan and the Northern Hokan Languages. In Hokan Studies: Papers from the First Conference on Hokan Languages, 1970. Margaret Langdon and Shirley K. Silver, eds. *Janua Linguarum, Series Practica* 181. The Hague: Mouton.

Silverstein, Michael
1970   The Diffusion of Vowel Harmony into California Penu-tian. (Paper Read at the 69th Annual Meeting of the American Anthropological Association. San Diego, Calif., November 19-21, 1970.)

1972   Studies in Penutian, I. California, 1: The Structure of an Etymology. (Unpublished Ph.D. Dissertation in Linguis-tics. Harvard University, Cambridge, Mass.)

Simmons, Kathryn
1905   Traditions and Landmarks of Yolo. *Woodland Daily Democrat,* February 16, 1905. Woodland, Calif.

Sinclair, William J.
1904   The Exploration of the Potter Creek Cave. *University of California Publications in American Archaeology and Eth-nology* 2(1):1-28. Berkeley.

1908   Recent Investigations Bearing upon the Question of the Occurrence of Neocene Man in the Auriferous Gravels of the Sierra Nevada. *University of California Publications in American Archaeology and Ethnology* 7(2):107-131. Berke-ley.

Sitjar, Bonaventure
1861   Vocabulario de la lengua de los naturales de la mision de San Antonio, Alta California: Vocabulary of the Lan-guage of San Antonio Mission, California. (Shea's Library of American Linguistics 7) New York: Cramoisy Press.

Sleeper, Jim
1969   The Many Mansions of José Sepulveda. *Pacific Coast Archaeological Society Quarterly* 5(3):1-38. Costa Mesa, Calif.

Smiley Commission
1891   Report to the Commissioner of Indian Affairs. (Manu-script in National Archives, Beel, Calif.)

Smith, Charles R.
[1968-1972] [Ethnographic and Ethnobotanical Notes, from approxi-mately 12 Months' Fieldwork among the Tübatulabal, California.] (Manuscript in Smith's Possession.)

Smith, Esther R.
1953   The History of Del Norte County, California; Including the Story of its Pioneers with Many of their Personal Nar-ratives. Oakland, Calif.: Holmes Book Company.

Smith, Jedediah S.
1828   Transcript Journal of Jedediah Strong Smith, 1822-1828. Transcribed by S. Parkman. (Manuscript in the Bancroft Library, University of California, Berkeley.)

Smith, Richard
1964   Nisenan Grammatical and Lexical Notes. (Manuscript in Possession of William Shipley, University of California, Santa Cruz.)

Smith, Clarence E., and W.D. Weymouth
1952   Archaeology of the Shasta Dam Area, California. *Univer-sity of California Archaeological Survey Reports* 18:1-45. Berkeley.

Smith, Gerald A., and Mike Moseley
1962   Archaeological Investigations of the Mojave River Drain-
        age. Pt. 1. *Quarterly of the San Bernardino County Mu-
        seum Association* 9(3). Bloomington, Calif.

Smith, Gerald A., and Ruth D. Simpson
1964   An Introduction to the Basketry of the Contemporary In-
        dians of San Bernardino County. Bloomington, Calif.:
        San Bernardino County Museum.

Smith, Jack E., and Jacqueline M. LaFave
1960-1961   Excavation of Site SLO-297, Vaquero Reservoir, San Luis
        Obispo County, California. *Annual Reports of the Univer-
        sity of California Archaeological Survey* 3:149-160. Los
        Angeles.

Soto, Anthony
1960   Recent Excavations at San Luís Rey Mission: The Sunken
        Gardens. *Provincial Annals (Franciscan Order of Friars
        Minor, Province of Saint Barbara)* 22(4):205-210, 247-249.

————
1961   Mission San Luís Rey, California: Excavations in the
        Sunken Gardens. *The Kiva* 26(4):34-43.

Southern, May H.
1942   Our Stories [Storied] Landmarks: Shasta County, Califor-
        nia. San Francisco: P. Balakshin Printing Company.

Sparkman, Philip S.
1905   Sketch of the Grammar of the Luiseño Language of Cali-
        fornia. *American Anthropologist* 7(4):656-662.

————
1908   The Culture of the Luiseño Indians. *University of Califor-
        nia Publications in American Archaeology and Ethnology*
        8(4):187-234. Berkeley.

————
1908a   A Luiseño Tale. Pp. 35-36 in Notes on California Folk-
        Lore. *Journal of American Folk-Lore* 21(80).

————
1908b   Notes on California Folk-Lore: A Luiseño Tale. *Journal
        of American Folk-Lore* 21(80):35-36.

Spier, Leslie
1923   Southern Diegueño Customs. *University of California
        Publications in American Archaeology and Ethnology*
        20(16):295-358. Berkeley.

————
1933   Yuman Tribes of the Gila River. Chicago: University of
        Chicago Press.

Spier, Robert F.G.
1954   The Cultural Position of the Chukchansi Yokuts. (Unpub-
        lished Ph.D. Dissertation in Anthropology, Harvard Uni-
        versity, Cambridge, Mass.)

————
1956   Acorn-leaching Basins: A Case of Convergent Develop-
        ment. *Man* 56(80):83-84.

Spott, Robert
1960   We Are California Indians. P. 1 in Indians of California
        Past and Present. San Francisco: American Friends Ser-
        vice Committee. (Reprinted from *Transactions of the
        Commonwealth Club of California* 21(3):133, 1926.)

Spott, Robert, and Alfred L. Kroeber
1942   Yurok Narratives. *University of California Publications in
        American Archaeology and Ethnology* 35(9):143-256.
        Berkeley.

Squier, Robert J.
1953   The Manufacture of Flint Implements by the Indians of
        Northern and Central California. *University of California
        Archaeological Survey Reports* 19(20):15-32. Berkeley.

Stellmon, Peggy
1967   The Long Trail. Fort Bragg, Calif.: Chamber of Com-
        merce.

Steward, Julian H.
1929   Petroglyphs of California and Adjoining States. *University
        of California Publications in American Archaeology and
        Ethnology* 24(2):47-238. Berkeley.

————
1933   Ethnography of the Owens Valley Paiute. *University of
        California Publications in American Archaeology and Eth-
        nology* 33(3):233-350. Berkeley.

————
1938   Basin-Plateau Aboriginal Sociopolitical Groups. *Bureau
        of American Ethnology Bulletin* 120. Washington.

Stewart, George W.
1906   A Yokuts Creation Myth. P. 322 in Notes on California
        Folk-Lore. *Journal of American Folk-Lore* 19(75).

————
1908   Two Yokuts Traditions. Pp. 237-239 in Notes on Califor-
        nia Folk-Lore. *Journal of American Folk-Lore* 21(81-82).

Stewart, Kenneth M.
1947   Mohave Warfare. *Southwestern Journal of Anthropology*
        3(3):257-278.

Stewart, Omer C.
1941   Culture Element Distributions, XIV: Northern Paiute.
        University of California Anthropological Records 41(3):361-
        446. Berkeley.

————
1943   Notes on Pomo Ethnogeography. *University of California
        Publications in American Archaeology and Ethnology*
        40(2):29-62. Berkeley.

Stickel, E. Gary, and Adrienne E. Cooper
1969   The Chumash Revolt of 1824: A Case for an Archae-
        ological Application of Feedback Theory. *Annual Reports
        of the University of California Archaeological Survey* 11:5-
        21. Los Angeles.

Stone, Livingstone
1874   Report of Operations during 1872 at the United States
        Salmon-hatching Establishment on the M'Cloud River
        and on the California Salmonidae Generally; with a List
        of Specimens Collected. Pp. 168-215 in U.S. Commission
        of Fish and Fisheries. Report of the Commissioner for
        1872 and 1873. Pt. 2. Washington: U.S. Government
        Printing Office.

Strong, William D.
1929   Aboriginal Society in Southern California. *University of
        California Publications in American Archaeology and Eth-
        nology* 26(1):1-358. Berkeley.

————
1935   Archeological Exploration in the Country of the Eastern
        Chumash. Pp. 69-72 in *Explorations and Fieldwork of the
        Smithsonian Institution in 1934*. Washington.

Strong, William D., W. Egbert Schenck, and Julian H. Steward
1930   Archaeology of the Dalles - Deschutes Region. *University
        of California Publications in American Archaeology and
        Ethnology* 29(1):1-154. Berkeley.

Sturtevant, William C.
1959   Authorship of the Powell Linguistic Classification. *Inter-
        national Journal of American Linguistics* 25(3):196-199.

Sullivan, Maurice
1934   The Travels of Jedediah Smith: A Documentary Outline
        Including the Journal of the Great American Pathfinder.
        Santa Ana, Calif.: Fine Arts Press.

Sundberg, Joyce
[1927] [Comments.] (Manuscript in Arnold R. Pilling's Posses-
        sion.)

Susia, Margaret (Weide)
1961-1962   The Soule Park Site (Ven-61). *Annual Reports of the Uni-
        versity of California Archaeological Survey* 4:157-234. Los
        Angeles.

Sutter, John A.
1939   New Helvetia Diary: A Record of Events Kept by John
        A. Sutter and his Clerks at New Helvetia, California, from
        September 9, 1845 to May 25, 1848. San Francisco:
        Grabhorn Press.

Sutton, Dorothy, and Jack Sutton
1969   Indian Wars of the Rogue River. Grants Pass, Oreg.:
            Josephine County Historical Society.

Sutton, Imre
1967   Private Property in Land among Reservation Indians in
            Southern California. *Yearbook of the Association of Pa-
            cific Coast Geographers* 29:69-89. Cheney, Wash.

_____
1975   Indian Land Tenure: Bibliographical Essays, and a
            Guide to the Literature. New York and Paris: Clearwater
            Publishing Company.

Swadesh, Morris
1954   Perspectives and Problems of Amerindian Comparative
            Linguistics. *Word* 10(2-3):306-332.

1956   Problems of Long-range Comparison in Penutian. *Lan-
            guage* 32(1):17-41.

1959   Linguistics as an Instrument of Prehistory. *Southwestern
            Journal of Anthropology* 15(1):20-35.

Swanton, John R.
1907   Exchange, Media of. Pp. 446-448 in Vol. 1 of Handbook
            of American Indians North of Mexico. Frederick W.
            Hodge, ed. *Bureau of American Ethnology Bulletin* 30.
            Washington.

_____
1915   Linguistic Position of the Tribes of Southern Texas and
            Northeastern Mexico. *American Anthropologist* 17(1):17-
            40.

_____
1952   The Indian Tribes of North America. *Bureau of American
            Ethnology Bulletin* 145. Washington.

Sweeney, James R.
1956   Responses of Vegetation to Fire. *University of California
            Publications in Botany* 28(4):143-250. Berkeley.

Swezey, S.L.
1975   The Energetics of Subsistence-Assurance Ritual in Native
            California. *University of California Archaeological Re-
            search Facility Contributions* 23:1-46. Berkeley.

Swezey, S.L., and Robert F. Heizer
[1976]   Ritual Regulation of Anadromous Fish Resources in Na-
            tive California. (Manuscript in Robert F. Heizer's Posses-
            sion.)

Taber, Cornelia
1911   California and her Indian Children. San Jose: The North-
            ern California Indian Association.

Tac, Pablo
1930   Conversion de los San Luiseños de Alta California. Pp.
            635-648 in *Proceedings of the 23d International Congress of
            Americanists.* New York, 1928.

_____
1952   Indian Life and Customs at Mission San Luis Rey [1835].
            Minna and Gordon Hewes, eds. *The Americas: A Quar-
            terly Review of Inter-American Cultural History* 9:87-106.

_____
1958   Indian Life and Customs at Mission San Luis Rey: A
            Record of California Mission Life [1835]. Minna Hewes,
            and Gordon Hewes, eds. San Luis Rey, Calif.: Old Mis-
            sion.

Talmy, Leonard A.
1972   Semantic Structures in English and Atsugewi. (Unpub-
            lished Ph.D. Dissertation in Linguistics, University of
            California, Berkeley.)

_____
1975   The Atsugewi Instrumental-prefix System. In Hokan
            Studies: Papers from the First Conference on Hokan
            Languages, 1970. Margaret Langdon and Shirley K. Sil-
            ver, eds. *Janua Linguarum, Series Practica* 181. The
            Hague: Mouton.

Tatum, Lawrie
1970   Our Red Brothers and the Peace Policy of President Ulys-
            ses S. Grant [1899]. Lincoln: University of Nebraska
            Press.

Tax, Sol
1955   Some Problems of Social Organization. Pp. 3-32 in Social
            Anthropology of North American Tribes. Fred Eggan,
            ed. Chicago: University of Chicago Press.

Tax, Sol, and Sam Stanley
1960   The North American Indians: 1950 Distribution of the
            Aboriginal Population of Alaska, Canada and the United
            States. (Map.) Chicago: University of Chicago, Depart-
            ment of Anthropology.

Taylor, Alexander S.
1860-1863   Indianology of California. *The California Farmer and
            Journal of Useful Sciences.* Vols. 13- 20, February 22,
            1860-October 30, 1863.

_____
1862   The Ecclemachs. (The Indianology of California) *The
            California Farmer and Journal of Useful Sciences,* October
            10, 1862.

_____
1862a   Traces of the Old Pueblo Civilization in California. (The
            Indianology of California) *The California Farmer and
            Journal of Useful Sciences,* March 28: 3, 1862.

_____
1862b   Miscellaneous Notes of the Author Connected with the
            California Indianology--No. 2. *The California Farmer and
            Journal of Useful Sciences,* December 5, 1862. (Reprint of
            Article Entitled "The Curiosities of California"in *Wide
            West,* January, 1, 1857. San Francisco.)

_____
1866   Bibliografia Californica, 1510-1865. *Sacramento Union,*
            June 25, 1863 - March 13, 1866.

_____
1869   Historical Summary of Lower California, from its Discov-
            ery in 1532 to 1867. Pp. 1-77 in Resources of the Pacific
            Slope: A Statistical and Descriptive Summary of the
            Mines and Minerals, Climate, Topography, Agriculture,
            Commerce, Manufactures, and Miscellaneous Productions
            of the States and Territories West of the Rocky Moun-
            tains. With A Sketch of the Settlement and Exploration
            of Lower California. John R. Browne, ed. New York:
            Appleton.

Taylor, Edith S.
1947   Hupa Birth Rites. *Proceedings of the Indiana Academy of
            Science* 57:24-28. Indianapolis.

Taylor, Theodore W.
1972   The States and their Indian Citizens. Washington: U.S.
            Department of the Interior, Bureau of Indian Affairs.

Teeter, Karl V.
1964   The Wiyot Language. *University of California Publica-
            tions in Linguistics* 37. Berkeley.

_____
1964a   Wiyot and Yurok: A Preliminary Study. Pp. 192-198 in
            Studies in Californian Linguistics. William Bright, ed.
            University of California Publications in Linguistics 34.
            Berkeley.

_____
1965   The Algonquian Verb: Notes toward a Reconsideration.
            International Journal of American Linguistics 31(3):221-
            225.

Temple, Thomas W., II.
1958   Toypurina the Witch and The Indian Uprising at San Ga-
            briel. *Masterkey* 32(5):136-154.

Theodoratus, Dorothea J.
1971   Identity Crises: Changes in Life Style of the Manchester
            Band of Pomo Indians. (Unpublished Ph.D. Dissertation
            in Anthropology, Syracuse University, Syracuse, N.Y.)

Thomas, Cyrus
1898   Introduction to the Study of American Archaeology. Cin-
            cinnati: Robert Clarke.

Thompson, L.
[1957] [Costanoan Survey, October 1956-September 1957.] (Manuscript in William F. Shipley's Possession.)

Thompson, Lucy
[1916] To the American Indian. Eureka, Calif.: [Cummins Print Shop.]

Thomsen, Harriette H., and Robert F. Heizer
1964   The Archaeological Potential of the Coast Yuki. *University of California Archaeological Survey Reports* 63:45-83. Berkeley.

Thoresen, Timothy H.H.
1975   Paying the Piper and Calling the Tune: The Beginnings of Academic Anthropology in California. *Journal of the History of the Behavioral Sciences* 11(3):257-275.

Tobin, James R.
1858   Report of a Reconnaissance through the Country around Cape Mendocino. Pp. 403-406 in *Annual Report of the Commissioner of Indian Affairs for 1857*. Washington: U.S. Government Printing Office.

Toffelmier, Gertrude, and Katharine Luomala
1936   Dreams and Dream Interpretation of the Diegueño Indians of Southern California. *Psychoanalytic Quarterly* 5(2):195-225.

Towendolly, Grant
1966   "Bag of Bones," by Marcell Masson. Healdsburg, Calif.: Naturegraph. [Review].

Tower, D.B.
1945   The Use of Marine Mollusca and their Value in Reconstructing Prehistoric Trade Routes in the American Southwest. *Papers of the Excavators' Club* 2(3):2-56. Cambridge, Mass.

Treganza, Adan E.
1954   Fort Ross: A Study in Historical Archaeology. *University of California Archaeological Survey Reports* 23:1-26. Berkeley.

———
1954a   Sonoma Mission: An Archaeological Reconstruction of the Mission San Francisco, Solano Quadrangle. (Manuscript No. 7 at the California State Division of Beaches and Parks, Sacramento.)

———
1954b   Salvage Archaeology in Nimbus and Redbank Reservoir Areas, Central California. *University of California Archaeological Survey Reports* 26:1-39. Berkeley.

———
1958   Archeological Investigations at the William B. Ide Adobe, Red Bluff, California. (Manuscript No. 4 at the California State Division of Beaches and Parks, Sacramento.)

———
1958a   Salvage Archaeology in the Trinity Reservoir Area, Northern California. *University of California Archaeological Survey Reports* 43:1-38. Berkeley.

———
1959   Archaeological Investigations of the Vallejo Adobe, Petaluma Adobe State Historical Monument. (Manuscript No. 5 at the California State Division of Beaches and Parks, Sacramento.)

———
1959a   Salvage Archaeology in the Trinity Reservoir Area Northern California: Field Season 1958. *University of California Archaeological Survey Reports* 46:1-32. Berkeley.

Treganza, Adan E., and Agnes Bierman
1958   The Topanga Culture: Final Report on Excavations, 1948. *University of California Anthropological Records* 20(2):45-86. Berkeley.

Treganza, Adan E., and Martin H. Heickson
1960   Salvage Archaeology in the Whiskeytown Reservoir Area and the Wintu Pumping Plant, Shasta County, California. *San Francisco State College, Occasional Papers in Anthropology* 1:1-49. San Francisco.

———
1969   Salvage Archaeology in the Black Butte Reservoir Region. *San Francisco State College, Occasional Papers in Anthropology* 2:1-59. San Francisco.

Treganza, Adan E., C.E. Smith, and W.D. Weymouth
1950   An Archaeological Survey of the Yuki Area. *University of California Anthropological Records* 12(3):113-128. Berkeley.

Treganza, Adan E., Edith S. Taylor, and William J. Wallace
1947   The Hindil, a Pomo Indian Dance in 1946. *Masterkey* 21(4):119-125.

Trippel, Eugene J.
1889   Yuma Indians. *Overland Monthly*, 2d ser., Vols. 13:561-584, 14:1-11.

True, Delbert L.
1954   Pictographs of the San Luis Rey Basin, California. *American Antiquity* 20(1):68-72.

———
1958   An Early Complex in San Diego County, California. *American Antiquity* 23(3):255-263.

———
1966   Archaeological Differentiation of Shoshonean and Yuman Speaking Groups in Southern California. (Unpublished Ph.D. Dissertation in Anthropology, University of California, Los Angeles.)

———
1970   Investigations of a Late Prehistoric Complex in Cuyamaca Rancho State Park, San Diego County, California. Los Angeles: University of California, Archaeological Survey, Department of Anthropology.

Tuohy, Donald R.
1970   Notes on a Collection of Californian Shell Beads from the Humboldt Sink, Nevada. *Nevada Archaeological Survey Reporter* 4(1):4-9. Reno.

Uhle, Max
1907   The Emeryville Shellmound. *University of California Publications in American Archaeology and Ethnology* 7(1):1-106. Berkeley.

Uldall, Hans J.
[1930] Maidu Grammar. (Manuscript No. 2086 in the Library of the American Philosophical Society, Philadelphia.)

———
1935   Sketch of Achumawi Phonetics. *International Journal of American Linguistics* 8(1):73-77.

———
1940   Nisenan Grammatical Processes and Description of the Modal Complexes. (Manuscript in Possession of William Shipley, University of California, Santa Cruz.)

Uldall, Hans J., and William Shipley
1966   Nisenan Texts and Dictionary. *University of California Publications in Linguistics* 46. Berkeley.

Ultan, Russell
1964   Proto-Maidun Phonology. *International Journal of American Linguistics* 30(4):355-370.

U.S. Board of Indian Commissioners
1920   Fifty-First Annual Report of the Board of Indian Commissioners to the Secretary of the Interior for Fiscal 1920. Washington: U.S. Government Printing Office.

———
1922   Fifty-Third Annual Report of the Board of Indian Commissioners to the Secretary of the Interior for Fiscal 1922. Washington: U.S. Government Printing Office.

U.S. Bureau of Indian Affairs
1963   U.S. Indian Population (1962) and Land (1963). Washington: U.S. Department of the Interior.

———
1969   Tribal Information and Directory. Sacramento Area Office, Bureau of Indian Affairs, August 1969. Sacramento, Calif.

U.S. Bureau of Indian Affairs. Southern California Agency
1975   [Cahuilla Reservation Land Statistics.] (Manuscript in Superintendent's Files, Riverside, Calif.)

U.S. Bureau of the Census
1971   Several Population Characteristics: California; United
            States Census, 1970. Washington: U.S. Government
            Printing Office.

U.S. Census Office
1880   Special 1880 Census of Indians in California. Vol. 4. Rec-
            ords of the Bureau of the Census, Record Group 29, Na-
            tional Archives, Washington.

U.S. Congress. House. Committee on Indian Affairs
1921-1922   Indian Tribes of California. Hearings before a Subcom-
            mittee of the Committee on Indian Affairs, March 23,
            1920. 66th Cong., 2d sess.; 67th Cong., 2d sess. 2 vols.
            Washington: U.S. Government Printing Office.

1926   Indian Tribes of California. Hearings before the Subcom-
            mittee on Indian Affairs, on H.R. 8036 and 9497, May 5,
            1926. 69th Cong., 1st sess. Washington: U.S. Govern-
            ment Printing Office.

1928   Claims of the California Indians. Hearings on HR 951
            Authorizing the Attorney General of California to Bring
            Suit in Court of Claims on Behalf of the Indians of
            California, March 8, and 15, 1928. 70th Cong., 1st sess.
            (Serial No. 8836) Washington: U.S. Government Printing
            Office.

U.S. Congress. House. Committee on Interior and Insular Affairs
1953   Report with Respect to the House Resolution Authorizing
            the Committee on Interior and Insular Affairs to Conduct
            an Investigation of the Bureau of Indian Affairs. 82d
            Cong., 2d sess. House Report No. 2503. (Serial No.
            11582) Washington: U.S. Government Printing Office.

U.S. Congress. Senate
1853   Special Report of the Superintendent of Indian Affairs in
            California. 32d Cong., 2d sess. Senate Document No. 57.
            (Serial No. 665) Washington: U.S. Government Printing
            Office.

1860   Report of the Secretary of the Interior. 36th Cong., 1st
            sess. Senate Executive Doc. No. 46. (Serial No. 1033)
            Washington: U.S. Government Printing Office.

U.S. Congress. Senate. Committee on Indian Affairs
1929   Survey of Conditions of the Indians of the United States.
            Hearings before a Subcommittee of the Committee on In-
            dian Affairs.70th Cong., 2d sess. Washington: U.S. Gov-
            ernment Printing Office.

U.S. Congress. Senate. Documents
1853   Correspondence between the Department of the Interior
            and the Indian Agents and Commissioners in California.
            33d Cong., special sess., March 4 - April 11. Senate Ex-
            ecutive Doc. No. 4. (Serial No. 688) Washington: Robert
            Armstrong.

U.S. Congress. Senate. Special Subcommittee on Indian Education
1969   Indian Education: A National Tragedy, a National Chal-
            lenge. 91st Cong., 1st sess. Senate Report No. 501. (Se-
            rial No. 12834-1.) Washington: U.S. Government Print-
            ing Office.

U.S. Department of the Interior
1933   Annual Report of the Secretary of the Interior to the Pres-
            ident for the Year 1932. Washington: U.S. Government
            Printing Office.

1946   Annual Report of the Secretary of the Interior to the Pres-
            ident for the Year 1945. Washington: U.S. Government
            Printing Office.

Valentine, James W., and Jere H. Lipps
1967   Late Cenozoic History of the Southern California Islands.
            Proceedings of the Symposium on the Biology of the Califor-
            nia Islands. Santa Barbara: Santa Barbara Botanic Gar-
            dens.

Vallejo, M.G.
!875   History of California. 5 vols. (Manuscripts in Bancroft
            Library, University of California, Berkeley.)

Valory, Dale K.
1966   The Focus of Indian Shaker Healing. Kroeber Anthropo-
            logical Society Papers 35:67-111. Berkeley, Calif.

1967   The Stolen Girls. Del Norte County Historical Society Bul-
            letin, August 29:2-3. Crescent City, Calif.

1970   Yurok Doctors and Devils: A Study in Identity, Anxiety
            and Deviance. (Unpublished Ph.D. Dissertation in An-
            thropology, University of California, Berkeley.)

_____, comp.
1971   Guide to Ethnological Documents (1-203) of the Depart-
            ment and Museum of Anthropology, University of Cali-
            fornia, Berkeley. (Now in the University Archives.)
            Berkeley: University of California Archaeological Re-
            search Facility.

Vancouver, George
1798   A Voyage of Discovery to the North Pacific Ocean, and
            Round the World: In Which the Coast of North-West
            America has been Carefully Examined and Accurately
            Surveyed...Performed in the Years 1790-1795 in the Dis-
            covery Sloop of War and Armed Tender Chatham, under
            the Command of Captain George Vancouver. 3 vols.
            London: G.G. and J. Robinson.

Vayda, Andrew
1966   Pomo Trade Feasts. Humanités: Cahiers de l'Institut de
            Science Economique Appliquée. (Reprinted: Pp. 494-500 in
            Tribal and Peasant Economies. G. Dalton, ed. Natural
            History Press, Garden City, N.Y., 1967.)

Victor, Frances (Fuller)
1894   The Early Indian Wars of Oregon. Salem, Ore.: F.C.
            Baker.

Vihman, Eero
[1966-1969] [Linguistic Notes from about 5 Months' Fieldwork on
            Northern Pomo.] (Manuscript in Vihman's Possession.)

1975   On Pitch and Accent in Northern Pomo. In Hokan Stud-
            ies: Papers from the First Conference on Hokan Lan-
            guages, 1970. Margaret Langdon and Shirley K. Silver,
            eds. Janua Linguarum, Series Practica 181. The Hague:
            Mouton.

Vizcaíno, Juan
1959   The Sea Diary of Fr. Juan Vizcaíno to Alta California
            1769. Arthur Woodward, trans. Los Angeles: Glenn
            Dawson.

Voegelin, Charles F.
1935   Tübatulabal Grammar. University of California Publica-
            tions in American Archaeology and Ethnology 34(2):55-190.

1935a   Tübatulabal Texts. University of California Publications in
            American Archaeology and Ethnology 34(3):191-246.
            Berkeley.

1946   Notes on Klamath-Modoc and Achumawi Dialects. Inter-
            national Journal of American Linguistics 12(2):96-101.

1958   Working Dictionary of Tübatulabal. International Journal
            of American Linguistics 24(3):221-228.

Voegelin, Erminie (Wheeler)
1938   Tübatulabal Ethnography. University of California An-
            thropological Records 2(1):1-84. Berkeley.

1942   Culture Element Distributions, XX: Northeast Califor-
            nia. University of California Anthropological Records
            7(2):47-252. Berkeley.

1948   Initial and Final Elements in Tübatulabal Myths. South-
            western Journal of Anthropology 4(1):71-75.

1956   The Northern Paiute of Central Oregon: A Chapter in Treaty-making. Pt. 3. *Ethnohistory* 3(1):1-10.

von Loeffelholz, Karl *see* Loeffelholz, Karl von

von Werlhof, Jay C. *see* Werlhof, Jay C., von

von Wrangell, F.P. *see* Wrangell, F.P., von

Wagner, Henry R.
1929   Spanish Voyages to the Northwest Coast of America in the Sixteenth Century. *California Historical Society Special Publications* 4. San Francisco.

1931   The Last Spanish Exploration of the Northwest Coast and the Attempt to Colonize Bodega Bay. *Quarterly of the California Historical Society* 10(4):313-345. San Francisco.

———, ed.
1942   The Discovery of New Spain in 1518, by Juan de Grijalva. Berkeley, Calif.: The Cortes Society.

Walker, Edwin F.
1945   The Dig at Big Tujunga Wash. *Masterkey* 19(6):188-193.

1947   Excavation of a Yokuts Indian Cemetry, Elk Hills, Kern County, California. Bakersfield, Calif.: Kern County Historical Society.

1952   A Stratified Site at Malaga Cove. Pp. 27-69 in Five Prehistoric Archaeological Sites in Los Angeles County, California. *Publications of the Frederick Webb Hodge Anniversary Publication Fund* 6. Los Angeles.

1952a   A Cemetery at the Sheldon Reservoir Site in Pasadena. Pp. 70-79 in Five Prehistoric Archaeological Sites in Los Angeles County, California. *Publications of the Frederick Webb Hodge Anniversay Publication Fund* 6. Los Angeles.

Wallace, Patricia
1971   A Short History of the Chumash from 1834 to 1900. (Unpublished Paper in Possession of Robert F. Heizer, University of California, Berkeley.)

Wallace, William J.
[1945-1949]   [Ethnographic Notes, from approximately 12 Months' Fieldwork among the Hupa.] (Manuscripts in Wallace's Possession.)

1947   Hupa Child-training--A Study in Primitive Education. *Educational Administration and Supervision* 33:13-25.

1947a   Personality Variation in a Primitive Society. *Journal of Personality* 15(4):321-328.

1948   Hupa Narrative Tales. *Journal of American Folklore* 61(242):345-355.

1949   Hupa Warfare. *Southwest Museum Leaflets* 23. Los Angeles.

1951   The Mortuary Caves of Calaveras County, California. *Archaeology* 4(4):199-203.

1954   The Little Sycamore Site and the Early Milling Stone Cultures of Southern California. *American Antiquity* 20(2):112-123.

1955   A Suggested Chronology for Southern California Coastal Archaeology. *Southwestern Journal of Anthropology* 11(3):214-230.

1959   Historical Research Pertaining to the Original Hugo Reid Adobe House. *Lasca Leaves: Quarterly Bulletin of the Los Angeles County Arboretum* 9(1):14-23. Los Angeles.

1962   Prehistoric Cultural Development in the Southern Californian Deserts. *American Antiquity* 28(2):172-180.

1963   The Hupa Indians of Northwestern California. Pp. 232-242 in The Native Americans. Robert F. Spencer et al., eds. New York: Harper and Row.

1970   Seasonal Indian Campsites in the Lake Isabella Area, California. *Masterkey* 44(3):84-95.

Wallace, William J., and Donald W. Lathrap
1952   West Berkeley: A Culturally Stratified Shellmound on San Francisco Bay. (Manuscript in Wallace's Possession.)

Wallace, William J., and Edith S. Taylor
1950   Hupa Sorcery. *Southwestern Journal of Anthropology* 6(2):188-196.

1952   Excavation of Sis-13, a Rock Shelter in Siskiyou County, California. *University of California Archaeological Survey Reports* 15:13-39. Berkeley.

1961   Historic Objects from the Hugo Reid Adobe. *Lasca Leaves: Quarterly Bulletin of the Los Angeles County Arboretum* 11(2):39-49, (3):61-65. Los Angeles.

Wallace, William J., and Edith T. Wallace
1958   Indian Artifacts from the Hugo Reid Adobe. *Lasca Leaves: Quarterly Bulletin of the Los Angeles County Arboretum* 8(4):74-81. Los Angeles.

1959   Archaeological Excavations in the "Patio" of the Hugo Reid Adobe. *Lasca Leaves: Quarterly Bulletin of the Los Angeles County Arboretum* 9(3):55-60. Los Angeles.

Wallace, William J., Roger J. Desautels, and George Kritzman
1958   The House of the Scotch Paisano: Archaeological Investigations at the Hugo Reid Adobe, Arcadia, California. *Lasca Leaves: Quarterly Bulletin of the Los Angeles County Arboretum* 8(1):2-13. Los Angeles.

Wallace, William J., Edith S. Taylor, Roger J. Desautels, H.R. Hammond, Heriberto Gonzales, James Bogart, and John P. Redwine
1956   The Little Sycamore Shellmound, Ventura County. *Archaeological Research Associates Contributions to California Archaeology* 2. Los Angeles.

Warburton, Austen D., and Joseph F. Endert
1966   Indian Lore of the North California Coast. Santa Clara, Calif.: Pacific Pueblo Press.

Wares, Alan C.
1968   A Comparative Study of Yuman Consonantism. *Janua Linguarum, Series Practica* 57. The Hague: Mouton.

Warner, J.J.
1852   Minority Report of the Special Committee to Inquire into the Treaties Made by the United States Indian Commissioners with the Indians of California. Pp. 597-604 in California Senate Journal, 3d sess., 1852. Sacramento.

Warren, Claude N., ed.
1966   The San Dieguito Type Site: M.J. Rogers' 1938 Excavation on the San Dieguito River. *San Diego Museum Paper* 5. San Diego, Calif.

1967   The San Dieguito Complex: A Review and Hypothesis. *American Antiquity* 32(2):168-185.

1968   Cultural Tradition and Ecological Adaptation on the Southern California Coast. *Eastern New Mexico University Contributions in Anthropology* 1(3):1-14. Portales.

1973   California. Pp. 213-249 in The Development of North American Archaeology: Essays in the History of Regional Traditions. James E. Fitting, ed. New York: Doubleday-Anchor Books.

Warren, Claude N. and Delbert L. True
1960-1961   The San Dieguito Complex and its Place in California Prehistory. *Annual Reports of the University of California Archaeological Survey* 3:246-338. Los Angeles.

Washington, F.B.
1906   Customs of the Indians of Western Tehama County. *Journal of American Folk-Lore* 19(73):144.

1909   Notes on the Northern Wintun Indians. *Journal of American Folk-Lore* 22(83):92-95.

Waterman, Thomas T.
1908   Diegueño Identification of Color with the Cardinal Points. *Journal of American Folk-Lore* 21(80):40-42.

1908a   Native Musical Instruments of California and Some Others. *Out West* 28:276-286.

1909   Analysis of the Mission Indian Creation Story. *American Anthropologist* n.s. 11(1):41-55.

1910   The Religious Practices of the Diegueño Indians. *University of California Publications in American Archaeology and Ethnology* 8(6):271-358. Berkeley.

1918   The Yana Indians. *University of California Publications in American Archaeology and Ethnology* 13(2):35-102. Berkeley.

1920   Yurok Geography. *University of California Publications in American Archaeology and Ethnology* 16(5):177-314. Berkeley.

[1921-1922]   [Unpublished Notes on Tolowa Culture and Geography.] (Manuscript in the Archives of the University of California, Berkeley.)

1922   All Is Trouble along the Klamath. Pp. 289-296 in American Indian Life. Elsie Clews Parsons, ed. New York: B.W. Huebsch.

1925   The Village Sites in Tolowa and Neighboring Areas in Northwestern California. *American Anthropologist* 27(4):528-543.

Waterman, Thomas T., and Alfred L. Kroeber
1934   Yurok Marriages. *University of California Publications in American Archaeology and Ethnology* 35(1):1-14. Berkeley.

Watkins, Frances W.
1944   Charles F. Lummis and the Sequoya League. *Quarterly of the Historical Society of Southern California* 26:99-109. Los Angeles.

Weaver, J.R.
1967   An Indian Trail near Needles, California. *University of California Archaeological Survey Reports* 70:151-157. Berkeley.

Weber, Francis J.
1968   The California Missions and their Visitors. *The Americas: A Quarterly Review of Inter-American Cultural History* 24(4):319-336.

Wedel, Waldo R.
1941   Archeological Investigations at Buena Vista Lake, Kern County, California. *Bureau of American Ethnology Bulletin* 130. Washington.

Weitchpec Grammar School
[1907-1909]   General Records: Books 2, 3. (Manuscript Books in Weitchpec Grammar School, Weitchpec, Calif.)

Wells, Harry L.
1881   History of Siskiyou County, California. Oakland, Calif.: D.J. Stewart. (Reprinted: Pacific Press, Oakland, 1971.)

1889   A Popular History of Oregon, from the Discovery of America to the Admission of the State into the Union. Portland, Oreg.: David Steel.

Weltfish, Gene
1930   Prehistoric North American Basketry Techniques and Modern Distributions. *American Anthropologist* 32(3):454-495.

Werlhof, Jay C. von
1961   Aboriginal Trails of the Kaweah Basin. (Manuscript No. 299 in Archaeological Research Facility, Department of Anthropology, University of California, Berkeley.)

1965   Rock Art of Owens Valley, California. *University of California Archaeological Survey Reports* 65. Berkeley.

Wetmore, Charles A.
1875   The Report of Charles A. Wetmore, Special U.S. Commissioner to the Mission Indians of Southern California. Washington: U.S. Government Printing Office.

Weybret, F., et al.
1955   Progress Report to the Legislature by the Senate Interim Committee on California Indian Affairs. Sacramento, Calif.

Wheeler, Benjamin I., and Frederick W. Putnam
1903   Ethnological and Archaeological Survey of California. *American Anthropologist* n.s. 5(4):727-729.

Wheeler-Voegelin, Erminie *see* Voegelin, Erminie (Wheeler)

Whipple, Amiel W.
1851   Journal of an Expedition from San Diego to the Colorado River. Washington: U.S. Government Printing Office.

1941   A Pathfinder in the Southwest: The Itinerary of Lieutenant A.W. Whipple during his Explorations for a Railway Route from Fort Smith to Los Angeles in the Years 1853 and 1854. Grant Foreman, ed. Norman: University of Oklahoma Press.

1961   The Whipple Report: Journal of an Expedition from San Diego, California, to the Rio Colorado, from September 11 to December 11, 1849. With Introduction, Notes, and Bibliography by E.I. Edwards. Los Angeles: Westernlore Press.

Whipple, Amiel W., Thomas Eubank, and William W. Turner
1856   Report on the Indian Tribes. Explorations and Surveys for a Railroad Route from the Mississippi River to the Pacific Ocean. Made in 1853-1854. Vol. 3. Washington: U.S. Department of War.

Whistler, Ken
1976   Classification of Wintun Languages. (Paper Read at the Annual Meeting of the American Anthropological Association. Washington, 1976.)

White, John R.
1970   Historic Sites as Laboratories for the Study of Culture Change. Paper Delivered at the Annual Meeting of the Society for Historical Archaeology. Bethlehem, Pa., January 10,1970. (Manuscript in R.A. Schuyler's Possession.)

White, Raymond C.
1953   Two Surviving Luiseño Indian Ceremonies. *American Anthropologist* 55(4):569-578.

1957   The Luiseño Theory of "Knowledge." *American Anthropologist* 59(1):1-19.

1963   Luiseño Social Organization. *University of California Publications in American Archaeology and Ethnology* 48(2):91-194. Berkeley.

Whitehead, Thomas A., and Robert L. Hoover
1974   Chumash Place Names Geography. (Manuscript in Authors' Possession.)

Wicks, Clara
1971   Stories by Clara Wicks. Pp. 56-63 in The Indian Tribes of the Siskiyou. *The Siskiyou Pioneer*. Vol. 4. Yreka, Calif.: Siskiyou County Historical Society.

Wieslander, A.E., and Herbert A. Jensen
1946   Forest Areas, Timber Volumes and Vegetation Types in California. *California Forest and Range Experiment Station, Forest Survey Releases* 4. Berkeley.

Wiglama, Anna, ed.
1971   Driving Forces: The Spirit and the Hand. Text by Marion Gough. *House Beautiful* 113(6):40-62.

Wilkes, Charles
1845   Narrative of the United States Exploring Expedition during the Years 1838, 1839, 1840, 1841, 1842. 5 vols. Philadelphia: Lea and Blanchard.

1849   Western America, Including California and Oregon with Maps of those Regions and of "the Sacramento Valley." Philadelphia: Lea and Blanchard.

Willey, Gordon R.
1966   An Introduction to American Archaeology. Vol. I: North and Middle America. Englewood Cliffs, N.J.: Prentice Hall.

Williams, E.L.
1890   Narrative of a Mission Indian. Pp. 45-48 in The History of Santa Cruz County, California, by Edward S. Harrison. San Francisco: Pacific Press.

Williams, Helen M., ed.
1969   [Jimmy Jack Hoppell.] *Del Norte County Historical Society Bulletin,* January 28:[4]. Crescent City, Calif.

Willoughby, Nona (Christensen)
1963   Division of Labor among the Indians of California. *University of California Archaeological Survey Reports* 60:7-79. Berkeley.

Wilson, Benjamin D.
1952   The Indians of Southern California in 1852: The B.D. Wilson Report and a Selection of Contemporary Comment. John W. Caughey, ed. San Marino, Calif.: Huntington Library.

Wilson, Birbeck
1968   Ukiah Valley Pomo Religious Life, Supernatural Doctoring, and Beliefs: Observations of 1939-1941. Caroline L. Hills, ed. *University of California Archaeological Survey Reports* 72. Berkeley.

Wilson, Norman L.
1957-1963   [Nisenan Fieldnotes.] (Manuscript in Wilson's Possession.)

1970   Notes on the Foothill Nisenan Food Technology. Eric Ritter, ed. (Publication on File, National Park Service, San Francisco.)

1972   Notes on Traditional Foothill Nisenan Food Technology. *University of California Center for Archaeological Research Publications* 3:32-38. Davis.

Wilson, Norman L., and Arlean Towne
1972   Selected Bibliography of Maidu Ethnography. (Manuscript on File, National Park Service, San Francisco.)

Winder, William A.
1857   Report on Mission San Diego, California, for 1856. Pp. 123-124 in 34th Cong., 3d sess., House Executive Doc. No. 76.(Serial No. 906) Washington: U.S. Government Printing Office.

Wire, Marcia V.V.
1961   Alamo Creek Site, San Luis Obispo County, California. *Annual Reports of the University of California Archaeological Survey* 3:107-148. Los Angeles.

Wissler, Clark
1938   The American Indian: An Introduction to the Anthropology of the New World. 3d ed. New York: Oxford University Press.

Wollesen, Olive
1972   The Aboriginal Salinan Indians. Lockwood, Calif.: Privately Printed.

Woodruff, Charles E.
1892   Dances of the Hupa Indians. *American Anthropologist* 5(1):53-61.

Woodward, Arthur
1934   An Early Account of the Chumash. *Masterkey* 8(4):118-123.

1934a   Notes on the Indians of San Diego County; from the Manuscripts of Judge Benjamin Hayes. *Masterkey* 8(5):140-150.

1953   Irataba-"Chief of the Mohave." *Plateau* 25(3):53-68.

Woodward, John A.
1968   The Anniversary: A Contemporary Diegueño Complex. *Ethnology* 7(1):86-94.

Wool, John E.
1853   Correspondence about Operations on the Pacific Coast. Pp. 1-128 in U.S. Congress. Senate. 32d Cong., 2d. sess., Senate Executive Doc. No. 16. (Serial No. 660) Washington: U.S. Government Printing Office.

Woolsey, David J.
1908   Cahuilla Tales. Pp. 239-240 in Notes on California Folk-Lore. *Journal of American Folk-Lore* 21(81-82).

Work, John
1945   Fur Brigade to the Bonaventura: John Work's California Expedition, 1832-1833, for the Hudson's Bay Company. Alice B. Maloney, ed. San Francisco: California Historical Society.

Worth, Dean S.
1960   Russian Kniga, Southwestern Pomo Kalikak. *International Journal of American Linguistics* 26(1):62-66.

Wrangell, F.P. von
1974   Some Remarks on the Savages on the Northwest Coast of America: The Indians in Upper California. F. Stross, trans. Pp. 1-6 in Ethnographic Observations on the Coast Miwok and Pomo by Contre-Admiral F.P. von Wrangell and P. Kostromitonov of the Russian Colony Ross. Berkeley: University of California Archaeological Research Facility.

Wuertele, E.
1975   Bibliographical History of California Anthropological Research. *University of California Archaeological Research Facility Contributions* 26. Berkeley.

Yanovsky, E., and R.M. Kingsbury
1938   Analyses of some Indian Food Plants. *Journal of the Association of Official Agricultural Chemists* 21(4):649-665.

Yates, Lorenzo G.
1887   Prehistoric Man in California. *Bulletin of the Santa Barbara Society of Natural History* 1:23-30. Santa Barbara, Calif.

1889   Charmstones: Notes on the So-called "Plummets" or Sinkers. Pp. 296-305 in *Annual Report of the Smithsonian Institution for 1886.* Washington.

1900   Archaeology of California: Southern California. Pp. 230-252 in Prehistoric Implements: A Reference Book. Warren K. Moorehead, ed. Cincinnati: Robert Clarke.

Yount, George C.
1966   Indians of the Napa Valley. Pp. 153-164 in George C. Yount and his Chronicles of the West, Comprising Extracts from his "Memoirs" and from the Orange Clark "Narrative." Charles L. Camp, ed. Denver: Old West Publishing Company.

Zigmond, Maurice L.
1938   Kawaiisu Territory. *American Anthropologist* 40(4):634-638.

Index

Italic numbers indicate material in a figure caption; roman numbers, material in the text.

All variant names of groups are indexed, with the occurrences under synonymy *discussing the equivalences. Variants of group names that differ from those cited only in their capitalization, hyphenation, or accentuation have generally been omitted; variants that differ only in the presence or absence of one (noninitial) letter or compound element have been collapsed into a single entry with that letter or element in parentheses.*

Specific reservations and rancherias are at reservations and rancherias.

The entry Indian words *indexes, by language, all words appearing in the standard orthographies and some others.*

A

abalone (*Haliotis*); food: 17, 22, 30, 31, 261, 492, 497, 498, 517, 552. shell items: 31, 32, *33,* 37, 43, 45-47, *48,* 49, 53, 54, 56, 57, 60-61, 63, 72, 74, 207, 292, 452, 498, 516, 517, 522, 526, 532. *See also* gathering; shellfish
Abella, Father; expedition: 351
Abels, Henry: 531
abortion. *See* birth
acában; synonymy: 280
Acagchemen; synonymy: 562
ʔača ʔ šiná· čawal li; synonymy: 279
Achomawi; synonymy: 235
Achumawi: 223, 225-236, 368. Ajumawi: 89, 235. Astariwawi: 89. Atwamsini: 89. ceremonies: 232. clothing: 227-229, *227,* 375. curing: 228-230, 232-234. death: 232, 233. division of labor: 683. environment: 225-230. external relations: 242, 243. games: 234. Hammawi: 89, 235. Hewisedawi: 89, 235. history: 234-235, 249, 705, 707, 709, 710, 716. Ilmawi: 89, 223. Itsatawi: 89. kinship: 231. language: 86, 89, 180, 211, 225, 230, 242. Madesiwi: 89, 224, 235. marriage: 222, 230, 231. music: 228, 232, 234, 644, 646, 647. mythology: 234, *234,* 654, 656. orthography: 225. Pit River: 222. political organization: 230. population: 5, 98. puberty: 232. Qosalektawi: 89. religion: 113, 232-234, 663, 670. settlements: *226.* shamanism: 232-234. social organization: 5, 230-232, 235. structures: 227-229, *227,* 232. subsistence: 19, 225-230, 238. synonymy: 235. technology: 228, 229, *230,* 365, 628, 633. territory: 225, *226,* 372. trade: 230, 331, 363, 380. transport: 227. warfare: *213,* 230-231, 238, 329, 379. *See also* Indian words
acorns: 329, 423. ceremonies: 174, 188, 198, 210, 246, 251, 254, 297, 303, 384, 419, 422,

664, 672, 688. food: *14,* 16, 22, 53, 57, 156, 164, 165, *166,* 179, 182-183, 192, 201, 202, 208, 216, 217, 221, 222, 229, 238, 243, 246, 252, 253, 255, 261, 265, 290, *304,* 310, 314, 338-339, *340,* 347, 352, 355, 357, 365, 374, 388-389, *389, 390, 394, 395,* 402, 404, 405, 409, 415, 416, 428-429, 431, 443, 450, 473, 474, 483, 491, 493, 497, 501, 516, 536, 552, 553, 571, 578, 599, 600, 636-637. gathering: 43, 108, 110, 130, 138, 150, 158, 165, 177, 179, 182, 208, 214, 217, 243, 246, 338, 355, 364-365, 389, 402, 403, 443, 464, 473, 491, 626. site ownership: 128, 145, 146, 214, 276, 347, 355, 388, 473
Acosta v. *County of San Diego:* 123
Act for the Relief of Mission Indians: 558-559, 610, 611
adhesives: 165, 217, 334, 374, 405, 578, 638. *See also* asphaltum
adolescent rites. *See* puberty
adoption: 215, 267, 355, 392
adornment: *59,* 61, 158, 375. body painting: 184, 186, 207, 217, 266, 328, 332, 333, 367, 375-376, 381, 391, 408, 422, 432, 442, 459, 466, 490, 493, 494, 501, 510, 512, 523, 540, 542, 546, 553, 565, 599, *599,* 603, 605, 666. ceremonial: 131, *131,* 159, 184, 186, 207, 266, 292, 311, 314, 332, 333, 375-376, *378,* 408, 422, 432, 442, 457, 478, 490, 510, 512, 542, 546, 573, 599, 603, 605, 666, *667,* 671. cranial deformation: 217, 408, 511. ear piercing: 167, 184, 196, 207, 217, 232, 240, 252, 267, 311, 328, 336, 366, 367, 375, 381, 391, 417, 432, 451, 478, 494, 509, 523, 599. hairstyles: 167, 184, 186, 197, 202, 207, 209, 216, 217, 232, 241, 245, 246, *247,* 251, 260, 267, 268, 311, 315, 328, 329, 357, 358, 367, 375, 381, 391, 393, 407, *407,* 417, 421, 433, 451, *455,* 478-481, 490-491, 493, *494,* 498, 501, 509, 510, 523, 526, 541, 599, 603. nose piercing: *131,* 133, 184, 217, 232, 252, 336, 366, 375, 391, 432, 451, 478, 494, 501, 509, 599, 603. ornaments: *131,* 133, 184, 207, *212,* 217, 221, 246, 267, 292, *293,* 311, 314, 336, 358, 367, 375, *376,* 382, 391, *391,* 408, *410,* 417, 432, 442, 451, 452, *452,* 457, 464, 478, 494, 498, 501, 509, 510, 516, 522, 553, 554, 599, 671. tattooing: 134, 162, *166,* 167, 168, *168,* 184, *185,* 196, *196,* 207, 217, 246, 252, 265, 328, 336, 367, 376, 391, 407, *407,* 417, *418,* 432, 442, 451, 455, *464,* 478, 494, *495,* 501, 540, 553-554, 599, 603
adultery. *See* marriage
Adwanugdji; synonymy: 243
adzes: 51, 183, 202
afterlife. *See* supernatural beings
Agua Caliente; synonymy: 590
ahana ceremony: 411
ʔahkʰaho ʔwa·ni; synonymy: 280
Ah-mah-ko; synonymy: 280
ʔahšaben; synonymy: 280
ahútireʔé·cu; synonymy: 223
aiʔkitca; synonymy: 484
Ajumawi. *See* Achumawi
Aki ceremony: 384, 667
Akwa'ala; synonymy: 608

Al-agnas; synonymy: 153
A-la-hu-la-po; synonymy: 508
Alameda District: 37, *38-39, 42-43,* 43
Alarcón, Hernando de; expedition: 99, 601
Alchone; synonymy: 494
Aldrich, Fay G.: 151
Alemany, José Sadoc: 113
Aleut; history: 75. language: 278
Alexander Valley Pomo. *See* Pomoan peoples
Algic language grouping: 50, 80, 87, 90, 137, 155
Algonquian language grouping: 82, 87. *See also* Algic language grouping
Algonquian-Wiyot-Yurok. *See* Algic language grouping
Algon-Ritwan. *See* Algic language grouping
Al-i-kwa; synonymy: 153
alimatʰinbe; synonymy: 359
Alioquis; synonymy: 153
Aliquois; synonymy: 153
Aliquor; synonymy: 153
ʔaɫkuʔli; synonymy: 537
Allequa; synonymy: 153
Alliklik: 5, 537. synonymy: 537
ʔaɫliḳliḳini; synonymy: 537
All-Mission Indian Housing Authority: 560, 561, 616
Allotment Act. *See* Dawes Severalty Act of 1887
Alth; synonymy: 153
Alwasa-ontilka. *See* Yuki, Coast
Amador, José María: 105
Amákō; synonymy: 280
ʔam·ak·o; synonymy: 280
ʔam·ak·o-hčamay; synonymy: 280
ʔam·aṭ·a yow; synonymy: 280
amatíʔō; synonymy: 280
ʔame·kyá·ra·m: 188, 189
American Folklore Society: 654
American Indian Historical Society: 124, 616, 716
American Indian Movement: 302
Americans. *See* history
Amic (Amish): 146
Amutahwe; synonymy: 223
Anderson, Ethan: 321, 715
Anderson v. *Mathews:* 715
animal skins. *See* technology
Antoniaño. *See* Salinan
anvil: 473, *473*
Anza, Juan Bautista de; expedition: 505, 514, 583
Apache; language: 194
Apaichi; synonymy: 461
Apiachi; synonymy: 461
Apis, Jose: 114
Apis, Pablo: 106, 114
Aplagamne; synonymy: 470
Applegate Creek: 137
Apwaruge. *See* Atsugewi
Apyachi; synonymy: 461. *See also* Yokuts, Southern Valley
ʔára·r; synonymy: 189
archeology: 157, 194, 250, 322, 341, 372,